2025 Edition

County and Municipal Government in North Carolina

Edited by
Christopher B. McLaughlin

UNC School of Government

The School of Government at the University of North Carolina at Chapel Hill works to improve the lives of North Carolinians by engaging in practical scholarship that helps public officials and citizens understand and improve state and local government. Established in 1931 as the Institute of Government, the School provides educational, advisory, and research services for state and local governments. The School of Government is also home to a nationally ranked Master of Public Administration program, the North Carolina Judicial College, and specialized centers focused on community and economic development, information technology, and environmental finance.

As the largest university-based local government training, advisory, and research organization in the United States, the School of Government offers up to 200 courses, webinars, and specialized conferences for more than 12,000 public officials each year. In addition, faculty members annually publish approximately 50 books, manuals, reports, articles, bulletins, and other print and online content related to state and local government. The School also produces the *Daily Bulletin Online* each day the General Assembly is in session, reporting on activities for members of the legislature and others who need to follow the course of legislation.

Operating support for the School of Government's programs and activities comes from many sources, including state appropriations, local government membership dues, private contributions, publication sales, course fees, and service contracts.

Visit sog.unc.edu or call 919.966.5381 for more information on the School's courses, publications, programs, and services.

Printed in the United States of America

29 28 27 26 25   1 2 3 4 5

ISBN 978-1-64238-096-5

Summary Contents

PART 6. PLANNING, DEVELOPMENT REGULATION, COMMUNITY AND ECONOMIC DEVELOPMENT

PART 7. LOCAL GOVERNMENT SERVICES AND ENTERPRISES

PART 8. HUMAN SERVICES AND OTHER COUNTY FUNCTIONS

PART 9. EDUCATION

Contents

PART 2. TRANSPARENCY, COLLABORATION, AND CITIZEN INVOLVEMENT

Chapter 8

Public Records

Chapter 9

Open Meetings and Other Legal Requirements for Local Government Boards

Chapter 10

Citizen Involvement

Chapter 14
The Attorney and the Clerk

Chapter 15
Strategic Investments in Information Technology

Chapter 16
Performance Measurement: A Tool for Accountability and Performance Improvement

PART 4. FINANCE

Chapter 17
Revenues

Chapter 18
An Introduction to Revenue Forecasting

Chapter 32
Animal Services

Chapter 33
Emergency Management

Chapter 34
Public Library Services

Chapter 35
Parks and Recreation

Chapter 36
Alcoholic Beverage Control

Chapter 44

Community Colleges

Preface

North Carolina is home to over 10 million people, more than 550 cities, and exactly 100 counties, all governed by the laws summarized in this book. The tiny town with just a single stoplight and the major metropolis with a million residents both operate under the same legal framework. The goal of this book is to explain that legal framework so that readers understand what our state's counties and cities do and how they do it.

This book is designed primarily to meet the needs of elected and appointed county and city board members, as well as the employees who, on a day-to-day basis, carry out the functions mandated and authorized for North Carolina local governments. We hope that it will also appeal to a broader audience, including citizens, civic leaders, students, state employees, legislators, media members, and any others who need basic information about the legal authority and responsibilities of North Carolina counties and cities.

The law governing county and municipal government changes constantly. New cases are handed down by state and federal courts, and state laws, which define and control local government authority, are always evolving. This edition covers significant changes to North Carolina local government law through the end of 2024.

Subjects included in this book are described in general rather than detailed terms, in keeping with its purpose of providing an overview and basic information. Most of the chapters include references to additional related materials and resources. More detailed treatments of these subjects are available in other School of Government books, which can be purchased at sog.unc.edu. On this website, you can also access our free local government law bulletins. *Coates' Canons* (canons.sog.unc.edu), our local government law blog, offers over 1,300 posts on many of the topics covered in this book.

The first versions of these materials were created for use in courses for newly elected county and city officials in 1969. This year's edition builds on the work of our previous authors, to whom we are indebted for their contributions to this important resource.

I am especially grateful to Frayda Bluestein, the editor of the 2014 edition of this book. Recently retired, Frayda was for decades a vital source of wisdom for local government officials across our state. She was also a tremendous friend and mentor to me and many of my colleagues at the School of Government. Our state and our School will continue to benefit from Frayda's work for years to come.

This publication would not have been possible without the incredible work of the School's publications staff, including Carol Ann Fitzgerald, Jennifer Henderson, Shaun Horton, Kevin Justice, Kit Sweeney, and Melissa Twomey. This book, and the process of creating it, was significantly improved by their expertise, creativity, flexibility, and good cheer.

Chris McLaughlin
Professor of Public Law and Government
UNC School of Government
Spring 2025

PART 1. Local Government Basics

Chapter 1

An Overview of Local Government

David M. Lawrence

David M. Lawrence is a retired School of Government faculty member who specializes in local government law.

This chapter updates and revises the previous versions authored by A. Fleming Bell, II, Joseph S. Ferrell, and Warren Jake Wicker. The author is indebted to all three professors for their work. He also thanks Alex Phipps, the School's senior legal research associate, for his help in updating the most recent version.

Under the American federal system, state governments are primarily responsible for all governmental functions not delegated to the federal government by the U.S. Constitution. Each of the fifty state governments has divided responsibility for all activities under its control between itself and its local units of government: cities and towns, counties, townships, school districts, other special districts, and authorities. The pattern of responsibility differs from state to state depending on that state's traditions, circumstances, and political judgments, but the state and one or more units of local government are collectively responsible for most of the governmental activities that affect citizens directly and often, such as the following:

- Administration of the courts
- Airports
- Conduct of elections
- Fire protection
- Law enforcement
- Mental health
- Parks and recreation
- Prisons and jails
- Public education
- Public health
- Public libraries
- Public water supply and distribution
- Recording of documents
- Regulation of land use and development
- Regulation of individual conduct
- Sewage collection and disposal
- Social services
- Solid waste collection and disposal
- Streets and highways

This list is not comprehensive, but it does indicate the scope of responsibilities that are met by state government and the various kinds of local governments.

The Primacy of State Government

In North Carolina's governmental system some governmental activities are the responsibility of state government alone, such as regulation of insurance or provision of four-year public colleges and universities. Other activities are provided concurrently or collaboratively by state and local government, activities such as social services, public health, election administration, K-12 education, community colleges, and parks and recreation. Still other activities are provided only by local governments, such as water distribution and sewage collection and disposal, fire protection, and zoning and subdivision regulation. Even with this latter group of activities, however, there is frequently some degree of state supervision or coordination.

The decisions that have created the basic framework for local government in North Carolina, for example, what kinds of local governments there are; how those local governments are created, are structured, and may expand; what activities local governments are permitted to engage in, what activities they are required to engage in; and how they may raise the revenues necessary to pay for it all, have all been made at the state level. One source is the North Carolina Constitution. Although this document is mostly concerned with establishing certain rights guaranteed to the state's citizens and creating the basic structure of state government, it also includes a few provisions that directly affect local government, such as that each county will have an elected sheriff and that certain forms of local government borrowing require voter approval. More important to the day-to-day operations of local government, however, are the many decisions made over time by the North Carolina General Assembly, the entity with the primary constitutional power to structure and modify the provision of governmental activities within the state. In the absence of state constitutional or federal constitutional, statutory, or regulatory restriction, the General Assembly is free under North Carolina's governmental system to create, abolish, and govern cities, counties, and other local governments as it sees fit.[1] As the North Carolina Supreme Court stated in a case involving a county, local governments in this state "are subject to almost unlimited legislative control, except when the power is restricted by constitutional provisions."[2]

A corollary to this primacy of the General Assembly in establishing the system of local government in a state like North Carolina is the understanding that local governments are entities with delegated powers only. Unlike some states, North Carolina is not a *home rule* state, which means that only the General Assembly can empower local governments to act. They have no constitutional capacity to empower themselves in the absence of state legislative action. The mere lack of any prohibition on any specific local government action is not sufficient to allow that action; it must be grounded upon some sort of legislative authorization. It should be stressed, though, that the General Assembly has been generous in its authorizations to local government, and as a result there is ample statutory authority for almost any initiative a local government wishes to take.

The necessary legislative authorizations may take either of two forms: *general laws* that apply statewide or *local or special acts* that pertain exclusively to named counties, cities, or other local government entities.[3] Chapter 160A of the North Carolina General Statutes (hereinafter G.S.),

1. *See* N.C. Const. art. VII, § 1: "The General Assembly shall provide for the organization and government and the fixing of boundaries of counties, cities and towns, and other governmental subdivisions, and, except as otherwise prohibited by this Constitution, may give such powers and duties to counties, cities and towns, and other governmental subdivisions as it may deem advisable."

2. Martin v. Comm'rs of Wake Cnty., 208 N.C. 354, 365 (1935) (quoting Jones v. Madison Cnty. Comm'rs, 137 N.C. 423, 428 (1905)).

3. The North Carolina Constitution contains a number of topical limitations on legislative authority to enact local acts. *See, e.g.,* N.C. Const. art. II, § 24; art. V, §§ 2(2) and 2(3); and art. VI, § 3. N.C. Const. art. XIV, § 3, explains some of the constitutional formulations that restrict the enactment of local or special acts.

which governs the structure and operations of city governments, is an example of a general law; the legislative act creating a particular city, which contains its operating "constitution" or charter, is an example of a local act. One use of local acts is to permit local variation and experimentation. This activity was once denounced by students of government but is now seen as a useful device for exploring new ideas and approaches to government problems, although it occasionally is used by legislators to override decision-making by a specific local government. Given this legislative flexibility, any discussion of city or county powers and responsibilities must always be prefaced with a caution that what is being said about cities or counties in general may not hold true for any particular jurisdiction.

The Current System of Local Government

County and City Governments

The dominant forms of local government in North Carolina are counties and cities. In North Carolina there is no legal distinction between a *city*, a *town*, or a *village*. Each is a *municipality*, and in this state a municipality may call itself by whichever designation it chooses, making that choice in its charter. Although *city* usually refers to a large municipality and *town* or *village* to a small one, there is no requirement that a particular municipality follow that general practice. The *Town* of Cary, for example, is now the seventh-largest municipality in the state, while the *City* of High Shoals has a population of less than 700. In this volume, *city* refers to municipalities of all sizes, both large and small.

Both counties and cities are general-purpose local governments, which means

- their governing boards are elected by the qualified voters of the county's or city's geographic area,
- they have the power to levy taxes,
- they may regulate conduct through adoption of *ordinances* (this ability is called the police power and is discussed in Chapter 5, "General Ordinance Authority," and
- they are authorized and, especially with counties, sometimes required to provide a broad range of services to their citizens.

Although some other types of local governments in the state have at least one of the previously listed characteristics (for example, sanitary district boards and boards of education are elected; boards of health may enact regulations related to health and airport authorities may enact rules governing conduct on airport property; and a wide range of entities from water and sewer districts to hospital authorities provide services), no other local governments combine all of these attributes in the way that counties and cities do. (Types of local governments beyond counties and cities are briefly described at the end of this section.)

Counties and cities historically served very different purposes. Originally, counties were established to serve state purposes, that is, to carry out government on behalf of the state. Sheriffs enforced the state's criminal laws and collected its taxes; registers of deeds recorded the state's deeds and other documents; justices of the peace and clerks of court presided over the lowest rung of the state's judicial system, and the justices established and maintained the state's roads. Eventually, counties came to be seen as the local government that provided services needed by all citizens, regardless of where they lived. Therefore, as government began to provide statewide public education, public health services, and welfare services, it was counties that were given the relevant responsibilities. Cities, by contrast, were created to adopt regulations and provide services more

Table 1.1 Chief Services and Functions Authorized for City and County Government in North Carolina

Services and Functions Authorized for Counties Only

1. Agricultural extension
2. Broadband (grants only)
3. Community colleges
4. County home
5. Court system support
6. Elections
7. Forest protection
8. Juvenile detention homes
9. Medical examiner/coroner
10. Property assessment
11. Public health
12. Public schools (mandated funding)
13. Register of deeds
14. Sheriff
15. Social services
16. Soil and water conservation
17. State streets (authorized funding)

Services and Functions Authorized for Both Cities and Counties

1. Aging programs
2. Air pollution control
3. Airports
4. Alcoholic rehabilitation
5. Ambulance services
6. Animal shelters
7. Armories
8. Art galleries and museums
9. Auditoriums and coliseums
10. Beach erosion control and hurricane protection
11. Bus lines and public transportation systems
12. Civil defense and emergency management
13. Community action
14. Community appearance
15. Community development
16. Drug abuse programs
17. Economic development
18. Fire protection
19. Historic preservation
20. Hospitals
21. Human relations
22. Industrial promotion
23. Inspections
24. Jails
25. Law enforcement
26. Libraries
27. Manpower
28. Mental health
29. National Guard
30. Off-street parking
31. Open space
32. Parks
33. Zoning and land use planning
34. Ports and harbors
35. Public housing
36. Railroad revitalization
37. Recreation
38. Regulations
39. Rescue squads
40. Senior citizens' programs
41. Sewage collection and disposal
42. Solid waste collection and disposal
43. Stormwater drainage and management
44. Urban redevelopment
45. Veterans' services
46. Water
47. Watershed improvement

Services and Functions Authorized for Cities Only

1. Cable television and communication services
2. Cemeteries
3. Downtown and urban area development
4. Electric systems
5. Gas systems
6. Public schools (optional funding)
7. Sidewalks
8. Street lighting
9. Streets
10. Traffic engineering

appropriate to built-up or urban areas. Over time, this meant that cities provided water distribution or sewage collection and disposal, solid waste collection, fire protection, recreation, and similar services, and it was cities that first began to regulate land use and development.

Around the middle of the twentieth century, citizens living outside of cities began to request some of the governmental services characteristic of cities but not of counties. They wanted community water or sewer systems, organized fire protection, and recreational spaces or programs. They wanted to be able to dispose of their trash in some way other than dumping or burning. And they wanted the protection of zoning. The General Assembly's response, over time, was to empower counties to engage in these city-like activities. As a result, although counties continue to serve a crucial role in the provision of state government services, they also have been given the opportunity to provide a range of services almost comparable to those provided by cities. The current authorizations for county and city functions and activities appear in Table 1.1.

As general-purpose local governments, counties and cities have many similarities, and as the General Assembly has authorized counties to provide many of the services once provided by cities only, those similarities have grown. But there remain important differences between counties and cities.

Geographic Extent

All the land in North Carolina is within one or another of the one hundred counties, and, therefore, all the citizens of North Carolina live in a county. But not all live in a city. The municipal population of the state, as estimated by North Carolina's Office of State Budget and Management, is only slightly more than 58 percent of the total state population.[4] Therefore, as noted above, if there is a local government service that is needed by all the state's citizens, it will almost certainly be one that is provided—probably exclusively—by county government.

Because the state's entire territory is allocated among the one hundred counties, those local governments have no need for any sort of annexation power. Cities do, however, have the capacity to grow territorially, and, therefore, over the years the General Assembly has given them various sorts of annexation powers. The current annexation laws are summarized in Chapter 2, "Incorporation, Annexation, and City–County Consolidation."[5]

Authorized Activities

Although counties have gained authority in recent years to provide many of the services traditionally provided by cities, there remain a number of city functions for which there is no comparable county authority, as Table 1.1 indicates. That table also shows a number of important county functions that cities are not authorized to provide. As discussed, these generally are activities that the General Assembly has determined should be provided to all citizens of North Carolina and, therefore, should be provided by counties, the one form of general-purpose local government that covers the entire state. County responsibility for these services is a continuing reminder of their historical role as an agency of state government.

Mandated Activities

In turning to counties as the instrumentalities to provide essential services to North Carolinians, the General Assembly recognized that to achieve its goal of administering those services statewide, counties needed to be given specific mandates. These service mandates make up well over half of

4. The Office of State Budget and Management estimated the state's total population as of July 1, 2022, as 10,705,403 and estimated the total municipal population in North Carolina on that date as 6,205,877. These estimates are available at the office's website, www.osbm.nc.gov/facts-figures/population-demographics/state-demographer/municipal-population-estimates/municipal-and-non-municipal-population.

5. Although most cities are located within only one county, there is no legal reason for that to be so. Rather, city boundaries tend to follow development, which often pays no attention to county lines. There are at least fifty-seven different cities in North Carolina that are in two or more counties; one, the city of High Point, is in four counties. The Office of State Budget and Management lists those municipalities here: www.osbm.nc.gov/facts-figures/population-demographics/state-demographer/municipal-population-estimates/land-area-distribution-municipalities-more-one-county.

any county's annual budget, and many of them involve a substantial degree of state government supervision. The following are the most important mandated activities for counties:

- Public education
- Social services
- Public health
- Mental health
- Jails
- Sheriff
- Medical examiner
- Support of the court system
- Emergency management
- Register of deeds
- Elections administration
- Building code enforcement
- Tax listing and assessment
- Emergency medical services

In contrast, the only mandated activity for cities is building code enforcement, and many smaller cities meet this obligation by contracting with the county to take responsibility for the function.[6] (Federal law requires that some larger cities engage in stormwater management.)

Governmental Structure

Counties are highly decentralized organizations. Two department heads, the sheriff and the register of deeds, are elected, and several important functions—including public education, community colleges, social services, public health, and mental health—are controlled by elected or appointed boards other than the board of county commissioners. These other boards appoint their own employees and make policies for the entities or county departments under their control. In addition, some members of some appointed boards are appointed by persons or entities other than the board of county commissioners.

Cities, on the other hand, are centralized organizations, with almost all employees reporting either to the manager or the governing board. A city manager has a great deal more day-to-day control over city-funded operations than does a county manager over county-funded operations.

Partisan versus Nonpartisan

All elected county officials in North Carolina—commissioners, sheriffs, and registers of deeds—are chosen through partisan elections. Almost all city elected officials, on the other hand, are elected in nonpartisan elections.[7] As a result, county elections are held in even-numbered years, at the same time as statewide and national elections, while city elections are held in odd-numbered years.

Other Types of Local Governments

School Administrative Units

Substantially independent school districts in North Carolina were abolished in 1931. In their place the General Assembly created geographically defined school administrative units overseen by locally elected boards of education with no taxing power. These units are funded by counties and by the state and federal governments. (Elementary and secondary education is discussed in detail in Chapter 43, "The Governance and Funding Structure of North Carolina Public Schools.")

6. Cities incorporated after January 1, 1945, but before January 1, 2000, are required to provide at least two services from a statutory list of options, and cities incorporated on or after January 1, 2000, are required to provide at least four services from a statutory list of options to receive certain state-shared revenues per Chapter 136, § 41.2(c) of the North Carolina General Statutes (hereinafter G.S.), but such cities may choose to forego the revenues and a few have.

7. Cities can choose to conduct partisan elections and to use the three nonpartisan options available under G.S. Chapter 163, Article 24.

Special Districts and Authorities

Special purpose governments also exist in North Carolina, but they have never been as widely used here as elsewhere in the nation. Generally, *special districts* are special purpose governments with taxing power, and *authorities* are such governments without taxing power. The two most common special districts in the state are the sanitary district and the rural fire protection district. North Carolina also has several types of authorities, the most common being

- housing authorities, created under G.S. Chapter 157;
- water and sewer authorities, created under G.S. Chapter 162A; and
- airport authorities, usually created by a local act of the General Assembly.

A few authorities are also involved in operating hospitals, public transportation, off-street parking facilities, and a variety of recreational facilities and activities. Many other states make much more extensive use of authorities, especially to operate revenue-producing enterprise activities.

Townships

North Carolina undertook a relatively brief experiment with township government after 1868 in which townships were subdivisions of counties with independent governmental powers and responsibilities. The experiment was mostly abandoned later in the nineteenth century, although townships remained involved in road construction and maintenance through the 1920s. Unlike some other states, townships exist today in North Carolina only as convenient administrative areas within counties, chiefly for tax-listing and sometimes to provide convenient boundary lines in the drawing of census districts and voting precincts. G.S. 153A-19 allows the board of commissioners to establish, abolish, and name townships, as long as specified procedures are followed.

A Brief History of Local Government in North Carolina

We now turn to a discussion of the history of North Carolina counties, cities, and other local governmental units, followed by a summary of the current characteristics of local government in the state.

Colonial Times through the Civil War

Counties

It was accepted from the earliest days of colonial government in North Carolina that governmental administration could not be efficiently centralized in the colonial capital. Therefore, following the English tradition, the colony established county governments for the local administration of many of the functions of government considered essential throughout the colony: administration of the court system, law enforcement, the conduct of elections, care of the poor, and maintenance of roads. Justices of the peace, as a body or court, administered the county's affairs, exercising both judicial and administrative powers. Independence from England brought no wrenching changes to this system. The county justices of the peace were appointed by the governor to serve at the pleasure of the governor, but in making his appointments the governor relied on recommendations from the General Assembly. Thus, as a matter of practical politics, the members of the legislature from a given county had a powerful voice in the selection of its justices of the peace and, therefore, in its government.

At first, the justices appointed the sheriff, the coroner, and the constables; later, these offices were made elective. The sheriff and coroner were from the county at large and the constables from captains' districts (militia-mustering areas). The justices were also responsible for appointing a clerk of court, register of deeds, county attorney, county trustee (treasurer), surveyor, and overseers or wardens of the poor. In sum, it was a system with very little direct control by the county's voters.

Cities

In contrast to the counties, North Carolina's colonial and early 1800s towns, which served several hundred people, had few functions. They organized the town watches, established volunteer fire departments, built public wells, kept the streets in repair, occasionally (as in Fayetteville and Wilmington) built a town market, and passed ordinances to protect the public health and safety. The early towns supported their activities from fees, charges, fines and penalties, and revenue from the sale of lots.

North Carolina towns remained relatively small trading centers and county seats until after 1865. They did not grow with industrialization during the antebellum period, as many northern cities did. Indeed, by 1850 only one North Carolina city, Wilmington, had a population as great as 5,000. As a result, North Carolina cities were delayed by a half-century or more in encountering a demand for such major municipal functions as water systems and paid police departments. Property, poll, and license taxes were introduced around 1800, but tax levies for cities and towns were very small until after the Civil War.

Local Government from 1868 until 1900

The 1868 Reconstruction constitution of North Carolina attempted a fundamental restructuring of county government. The justices of the peace were restricted to judicial functions, with county government administration transferred to newly constituted—and locally elected—boards of county commissioners. As noted previously, the constitution also added township governments, which were run by elected officials with limited responsibilities. When the so-called Conservatives regained political power in the 1870s, these constitutional changes were reversed. Township government was essentially abolished, and the county commissioners were made subservient to the reinstituted justices of the peace.

This arrangement lasted for twenty years. In 1895, the ability of the people to elect commissioners was restored in most counties, and the requirement that the boards' decisions be approved by the justices of the peace was repealed. Popular election of the commissioners was finally restored in all counties in 1905.

The history of city government in this period was more tranquil. Between 1865 and 1900, city water and sewer systems were first introduced, largely through franchised private companies. Public transportation, such as streetcar systems, was introduced under similar franchises, as were electric and telephone systems. Street lighting became common. The large cities began to spend a lot of money on paving streets, and the large counties began to pave the roads that led beyond the cities. With the demand for paved streets and utilities came special assessments and water charges. Public health regulations also received an increased emphasis. Schools came to be operated by school districts, with better and more expensive schools in the cities and the towns. Wilmington reached a population of 10,000 in 1870, followed by Asheville, Charlotte, and Raleigh in 1880.

Cities and Counties in the Twentieth and Early Twenty-First Centuries

From 1900 through World War II

The first three decades of the twentieth century continued the growth of North Carolina local government that had begun in the final decades of the nineteenth. Streets and roads were paved as the automobile became commonplace. Water and sewer systems came under public ownership as private companies found it difficult to maintain high-quality systems and still produce a profit. A number of cities acquired their own electric systems. Full-time city police departments were established, and full-time paid fire brigades began to supplement the efforts of volunteer companies. The first building codes were adopted. Public support for city and county libraries began, largely in response to Carnegie Foundation grants-in-aid for library construction. Public health departments were first established by counties.

In the 1920s, the statewide system of primary highways connecting county seats and other principal cities and towns was established. Zoning was introduced, and the first county and city managers were appointed. The prosperity of the 1920s encouraged a significant growth of local government.

The Great Depression broke the expansion bubble. All services were cut back, and debt service obligations became a heavy burden. With no one to advise or warn them in marketing their securities, many cities and counties had overextended their obligations and saw their credit ratings drop so low that they had to pay crippling rates of interest; eventually, some faced bankruptcy. Defaults on bond obligations led the legislature to establish the County Government Advisory Commission in 1927 and to give it the supervisory powers necessary to correct the situation. This commission effected a reversal in local government financing. Its successor, the Local Government Commission, remains a bulwark of North Carolina government today. In addition, poor property tax collections threatened continued operation of county road systems and public schools. As a result, the state assumed responsibility for non-city roads in 1931 and for a minimum level of public education in 1933. Independent school districts were abolished.

With all of these changes, state and federal financial aid, virtually unknown until the Great Depression, became a significant source of local government revenue. Federal public works programs built many local government improvements, including the first water and sewer systems in many small towns. Federal aid led to uniform county responsibility for public welfare and encouraged the development of health departments.

1945 to the Present

The immediate postwar period was a time of rapid urban growth and a very rapid expansion of local government facilities, first to make up deficiencies left from the Depression and later to meet new demands, and there has been steady growth in the decades since. In most of this growth, counties and cities could rely and build upon their existing powers, but there were a number of major episodes of significant expansion in local government powers in the latter half of the twentieth century.

The 1959 General Assembly enacted a number of important pieces of legislation, some of which remain important today. The leading product of the 1959 legislation was a city annexation procedure that remained in place until 2011, permitting cities to unilaterally annex areas that had become or were in the process of becoming urban in nature. Thoroughfare planning and land use planning statutes were also passed in 1959, and both laws still exist in modified form. The thoroughfare statute places joint responsibility for thoroughfare planning and the adoption of a major thoroughfare plan on city councils and the state's Department of Transportation. The planning legislation significantly expanded the prior powers of cities and counties to plan, zone, and regulate land development, and it provided for increased joint and cooperative activities by city and county governments. Finally, 1959 also saw the beginnings of today's extraterritorial jurisdiction (ETJ) statute that gives cities an ability to regulate development outside their boundaries. Although smaller cities were not originally given ETJ authority, the extraterritorial jurisdiction law applies statewide today.

In 1967, the General Assembly established a Local Government Study Commission. It operated for six years, successfully proposing significant modernization in the constitutional provisions affecting local government finance, revising and modernizing the basic local government statutes, and transferring important decisions from the General Assembly to county commissioners and city councils. It also continued strengthening legal powers delegated to county government, for example, by extending to counties a general ordinance-making power.

The most significant change in city and county revenues in many years also came in 1967, when Mecklenburg County was authorized to "piggyback" a 1 percent local sales and use tax on the state's general sales tax. The success of this tax in Mecklenburg quickly led to its authorization across the state. Since then, the rate has increased several times, and the tax is levied in all one hundred counties under arrangements by which the proceeds in each county are shared by the county government and the cities within its jurisdiction. The sales and use tax revenues have become increasingly important to local governments as the General Assembly significantly narrowed the property tax base in the last forty years.

The council–manager form of city government and the county manager form of county government have continued to spread in North Carolina over the last several decades. Nearly all cities with more than 10,000 citizens and many with lower populations use the council–manager form. About ninety-nine of North Carolina's counties currently have a manager (the number varies slightly from year to year), although the powers of county managers, particularly over hiring and firing, may be restricted by the board of county commissioners in ways that are not possible under a city's manager system. In addition, an elected county commissioner can and sometimes does serve as the county manager. This is forbidden for cities.[8]

Changes have also occurred in local governing bodies and in city and county workforces. Some counties and cities have moved to district elections for council members and commissioners, although the at-large method retains great popularity. There have also been marked increases in the numbers of women and African Americans elected to city and county offices.

The growth of North Carolina's population and economic changes have created an increasing need for city and county governments to cooperate. Hundreds of cooperative arrangements have developed since 1970, varying from one unit contracting with another to the merger of functions. (See Chapter 11, "Interlocal Cooperation, Shared Services, and Regional Councils," for a more detailed discussion.)

North Carolina Local Government in the National Context

There are important distinctions between North Carolina's current pattern of local government and the patterns commonly found elsewhere. At least nine general features can be identified:

1. ***Primary state responsibility for financing education and highways.*** Two functions for which state and local financial outlays are large—education and highways—are both financed primarily at the state level in North Carolina, and from taxes imposed

8. G.S. 160A-147(a). In the council–manager form of government, the city council makes planning and policy decisions, leaving the day-to-day administration of city affairs to a professional manager. In jurisdictions without a manager, all decisions concerning the city are entrusted to the council. The manager in cities operating under the council–manager plan has statutory hiring and firing authority for all city employees except those appointed directly by the council. Arrangements are more complex in counties, even with a manager, both for the reasons noted here and because of the existence of several boards besides the county commissioners with a role in making policy and choosing employees (e.g., the boards of health, mental health, and social services; the board of education; and the board of elections). For more information, see Chapter 3, "County and Municipal Governing Boards"; Chapter 4, "County and City Managers"; and Part 8, "Human Services and Other County Functions."

by the state. All states support these two functions from the state treasury to some extent, but few to the degree that North Carolina does. In most states the local share of financial responsibility is much greater, and in almost all states, but not North Carolina, county (or township) governments bear a major portion of the responsibility for roads outside municipalities. Moreover, in North Carolina the property tax is less important in financing these two functions than in the nation at large, because of the major state government responsibility.

2. ***Primary county responsibility for areawide, or "human," services at the local level.*** A number of major services and functions, especially health, education, and welfare, are needed by people in both rural areas and urban areas. In North Carolina the local responsibility for these services and functions is vested in the county, the one type of unit that covers the entire state, and the county commissioners have limited discretion in whether or how much to fund them. In contrast, in other states these services and functions may be carried out at the state level or vested locally in cities, counties, special districts, or a combination thereof.
3. ***Primary city responsibility for the high levels of some services that are needed in urban areas.*** Fire protection, law enforcement, solid waste collection, water and sewer services, and street maintenance and improvement are all key city responsibilities in North Carolina, much as they are in many states. However, some states are more likely to use local authorities or special districts to provide water and sewer services, fire protection, and so forth.
4. ***County authority to provide urban types of services.*** North Carolina counties have extensive authority to provide water and sewer services, solid waste collection and disposal, fire protection, recreation, and other services needed by citizens. (As noted previously, counties still have no authority to build or maintain streets.) A county government may, if it chooses, provide urban types of services throughout the county's unincorporated areas as necessary. Counties also frequently cooperate with cities in providing some of these services within city limits (see number 6). In some other states, urban functions could be undertaken in unincorporated areas only by forming special districts or authorities.
5. ***Extensive city and county authority to regulate and direct urban development.*** Both cities and counties in North Carolina are broadly authorized to undertake planning programs and to regulate land use through zoning and subdivision control. Most cities have ETJ with respect to these controls. Local governmental units in other states also have such powers, but not all states grant such broad authority.
6. ***Flexibility in city–county and multi-unit arrangements.*** Cities and counties in North Carolina also have broad authority to take joint or parallel action or to contract with one another for performance of functions that both are authorized to undertake. Such agreements may range from the joint financing of a water line to the merging of tax collection or other offices.
7. ***A model system for major thoroughfare planning.*** Under a procedure established in 1959, each municipality and the state's Department of Transportation jointly develop and adopt a major thoroughfare plan for the municipality and its surrounding area. North Carolina's system is a nationally recognized approach that has served as a model for procedures adopted elsewhere.
8. ***A state–local revenue system that relies on four main taxes.*** The major taxes in North Carolina are the property tax, the general sales tax, the individual and

corporate income taxes, and the gasoline tax. The property tax is levied by local governments only, the general sales tax by local and state governments, and the income and gasoline taxes by the state only (although the gasoline tax is shared with cities). Rates for the sales and income taxes are average to high compared to rates for the same types of taxes in some other states, whereas rates for the property tax are low compared with those found in many other places. In terms of responsiveness to the economy, the property tax everywhere tends to lag economic growth more than taxes tied directly to economic activity, such as income and sales taxes. Because the property tax is relatively less important in North Carolina than it is elsewhere, while income and sales taxes have greater significance, North Carolina's total revenue structure tends to be somewhat more sensitive than most states' tax programs to changes, positive or negative, in the economic environment.

9. ***Reliance on general-purpose local governments.*** At the local level in North Carolina, almost all governmental responsibilities have been vested in city and county governments, two general-purpose types of governmental units. The vast majority of expenditures of local governmental units in North Carolina are also made through cities and counties. In many other states, special districts, school districts, and authorities are relatively much more important. The result is that North Carolina's urban areas generally do not have the multitude of overlapping units frequently found elsewhere.

Summary

North Carolina's pattern of local government reflects an arrangement that is flexible and provides for much local control. The pattern has resulted in a relatively simple governmental structure, with few types of local government and limited overlapping jurisdictions and with both state and local financing being important. At least three main roles have been defined for local governments in this state.

The first major function of cities and counties is protection of the individual and the public as a whole. They carry out this responsibility through fire services and law enforcement (police and sheriff's departments), ordinances that protect the safety of individuals and the public at large from the acts of other persons, and ordinances that protect the use and value of property.

Local governments are also providers of many other services. Most cities provide a local street system, and some build and operate essential facilities such as electric and gas distribution systems. Counties support school systems and health, mental health, and social services programs. Both cities and counties operate water and sewer systems; collect solid waste; sometimes build and operate airports and auditoriums; and contribute to their citizens' cultural and leisure-time activities by supporting libraries, parks, and recreation programs.

Finally, local governments are a major factor in the continued economic development of the community. Cities, for example, share responsibility with the state for the street and highway system that is the key to effective transportation. Cities, counties, and some independent districts and authorities build and operate the water and sewer systems without which urban development is impossible. Local governments often directly support economic and industrial development bodies, sometimes alone and sometimes in cooperation with other local governments. Cities, counties, and in some cases special local authorities provide the civic facilities such as parking, auditoriums, and airports that make an area attractive as an economic center. Local governments help to improve housing. Through all of these activities, local governments are involved in creating attractive, convenient, and appealing communities.

Local governments in North Carolina play a major role in providing the services and functions that are needed in an increasingly urbanized state that also contains large rural areas. They are created by the state legislature, and their powers and functions are authorized by that body. Although many North Carolina cities and counties provide similar kinds of services to other jurisdictions of the same type, each city and to a lesser extent each county has considerable flexibility in determining what functions it will undertake and at what level. Within the limitations prescribed by the state legislature and the courts, city councils and boards of county commissioners have discretion to provide the services and functions that will best serve the needs of their communities.

Additional Resources

Adrian, Charles R. "Forms of City Government in American History." In *The Municipal Yearbook 1988*, 3–12. Washington, D.C.: International City Management Association, 1988.

Adrian, Charles R., and Ernest S. Griffith. *A History of American City Government: The Formation of Traditions, 1775–1870.* New York: Praeger Publishers, for the National Municipal League, 1976.

Corbitt, David L. *The Formation of North Carolina Counties, 1663–1943.* Raleigh: North Carolina Department of Archives and History, 1950.

Griffith, Ernest S. *A History of American City Government: The Progressive Years and Their Aftermath, 1900–1920.* New York: Praeger Publishers, for the National Municipal League, 1974.

Liner, Charles D., ed. *State and Local Government Relations in North Carolina: Their Evolution and Current Status.* 2nd ed. Chapel Hill: Institute of Government, 1995.

Chapter 2

Incorporation, Annexation, and City–County Consolidation

James L. Joyce

James L. Joyce is a faculty member at the School of Government whose areas of expertise include land use regulation, annexation, and local government environmental regulation.

This chapter updates and revises the previous chapter authored by Frayda S. Bluestein, which in turn built upon the work of David M. Lawrence. These professors' expertise and contributions to the field and to this publication are gratefully acknowledged.

Article VII of the North Carolina Constitution gives the General Assembly the authority to "provide for the organization and government and the fixing of boundaries of counties, cities and towns, and other governmental subdivisions" and to grant "such powers and duties to counties, cities and towns, and other governmental subdivisions as it may deem advisable."[1]

When it comes to local government authority, it is important to keep in mind this preeminent role of the legislature. With its constitutional power, the General Assembly created most of North Carolina's one hundred counties, defined their boundaries, and continues to modify them from time to time.[2] Likewise, the state's cities[3] were created and expanded through legislation. As this

1. North Carolina Constitution, article VII, section 1.

2. The current one hundred counties are listed in Chapter 153A, Section 10 of the North Carolina General Statutes (hereinafter G.S.). Avery County was the last of North Carolina's 100 counties to be created, just six days after the penultimate county, Hoke. *See* Public Laws of North Carolina 1911, ch. 33 (creation of Avery County on Feb. 23, 1911); N.C. Pub. Laws 1911, ch. 24 (creation of Hoke County on Feb. 17, 1911).

3. Although the General Statutes typically refer to North Carolina municipalities as "cities," such entities go by a variety of titles: for instance, the Village of Pinehurst, the Town of Edenton, or the City of Asheboro. The rules for incorporation, annexation, and consolidation are the same regardless of which title a municipality uses. This chapter will use the term "city" following the convention in the General Statutes, but the laws described herein apply equally to those municipalities that refer to themselves as villages or towns.

chapter shows, the General Assembly has delegated some of its authority to create and modify local governments, but it retains the power to create, modify, or even dissolve local governments by legislative act.

In addition to the General Assembly's constitutional authority, it has created statutory methods by which others can create and modify local governments: Municipalities can be incorporated through a petition process, and cities have the authority to annex territory in several ways, whether initiated by the city itself or by petition from the owners of property in the area to be annexed. The General Assembly has also authorized city–county consolidation, which has been attempted several times but has not been accomplished in North Carolina to date. This chapter provides an overview of the processes for creating, expanding, dissolving, and consolidating counties and cities in North Carolina.

Municipal Incorporation

In North Carolina, a city is created—that is, incorporated—in only one way: by an act of the General Assembly. Such an act establishes the initial borders of the city and enacts its founding charter. Few standards restrict the legislature's discretion in incorporation. It may incorporate an area with very few people or with a largely rural character; it may even incorporate an area in anticipation of development, before any city in fact exists. Over time, North Carolina has experienced cycles of greater and fewer incorporations, with the current trend moving away from new incorporations. From the 1981 session through the 1994 session, the General Assembly enacted incorporation legislation for forty-nine communities. Of these, thirty-nine became active cities, while voters in ten communities voted incorporation down. From 1995 through 2005, the General Assembly enacted incorporation legislation for an additional thirty-eight communities, twenty-nine of which became active cities. From 2005 to 2013, the legislature enacted incorporation bills for nine communities, of which six became active cities. However, no incorporation bills have passed since 2011.[4]

In most cases, incorporation begins with a petition from registered voters in the prospective city to the General Assembly's Joint Legislative Commission on Municipal Incorporations (the "Commission"). The Commission, through its Municipal Incorporations Subcommittee (the "Subcommittee"), reviews the petition and recommends incorporation if all of several statutory criteria are met.[5] Theoretically, a legislator could bypass this procedure by introducing a local bill to incorporate an area without a petition. However, legislative rules frequently require a bill to have a Commission recommendation before being considered in committee or for its second or third readings.[6]

---

4. *See* S.L. 2011-166 (Town of Castle Hayne, subject to referendum), 2011-114 (Town of Rougemont, subject to referendum), and 2011-110 (Fontana Dam).

5. Some of the statutes assign the review and recommendation of incorporation to the Joint Legislative Committee on Local Government while others refer to the Municipal Incorporations Subcommittee. In 2011, the sections referring to the Subcommittee were updated—*see, e.g.*, G.S. 120-163 through -166—but those referring more generally to the Commission—*see, e.g.*, G.S. 120-170 through -174—were not. Since all of the updated statutes refer to the Subcommittee, and since the Subcommittee is a subset of the Committee, one might presume that the recommendation should come directly from the Subcommittee.

6. *See* North Carolina General Assembly Bill Drafting Division, *Summary of Municipal Incorporation Procedure*, webservices.ncleg.gov/ViewDocSiteFile/56137, at I; *see also, e.g.*, N.C. House Resolution 102, Section 1, Rule 35.1; N.C. Senate Resolution 1, Section 1, Rule 42.3.

Petition Process

The North Carolina General Statutes—specifically G.S. Chapter 120, Article 20, Part 2[7]—describe the process for petitioning for incorporation. The petition must be signed by 15 percent of registered voters in the area to be incorporated, with a minimum of 25 registered voters.[8] The petition must also include a number of details regarding the proposed municipality. These include a proposed name, the form and identity of an interim governing board, an initial tax rate, and a list of municipal services to be provided, as well as several other details.[9] Once the petition is assembled, the county board of elections must verify the petition. Submission to the board of elections triggers several rather particular time clocks. The board of elections has in most cases fifteen working days in which to confirm that the signatories are registered to vote in the area proposed for incorporation and to confirm the number of registered voters in that area against the number verified from the petition.[10] Once the petition is verified by the Board of Elections, the petitioners must notify the county board of commissioners, other cities within that county, and other cities within five miles. They must also publish in the newspaper a notice of their intent to submit the verified petition.[11] Finally, once the notice has been provided and the petition is verified, the petitioners must submit their materials to the Subcommittee at least sixty days before the General Assembly convenes its next regular session.[12]

If the petitioners successfully meet these deadlines, the Subcommittee reviews the petition for compliance with the statutory requirements for content and notice described above. If the petition does not meet the requirements, the Subcommittee returns the petition to the petitioners who can then correct the deficiencies. If the petition meets the statutory standards and petitioners have given proper notice, the Subcommittee publishes notice of receiving the petition in the North Carolina Register and investigates the property in greater detail.[13]

This further investigation requires the Subcommittee to compare the area proposed to be annexed with state statutory standards. These include standards related to its proximity to existing cities, size, urban character, and economic resources.[14] Those proposing incorporation must also submit a plan for providing a reasonable level of municipal services, and the Subcommittee may not make a positive recommendation unless it finds that the proposed municipality could provide municipal services at a reasonable tax rate.[15] The basic tax and service provision criteria also must be met in order to qualify for various shared revenues, including local government sales tax proceeds, state street assistance, state beer and wine tax proceeds, state utility tax proceeds, and other state-shared revenues.[16] These requirements were intended to discourage the incorporation of paper towns (cities that did not provide city services) and the incorporation of gated communities.

---

7. G.S. 120-163 through -174.

8. G.S. 120-163(a).

9. G.S. 120-163(c). Note that the statutes also include minimum criteria for property tax and municipal services. Specifically, the petition must propose that the new city levy a property tax of at least five cents and provide at least four of the following eight services: police protection, fire protection, solid waste collection or disposal, water distribution, street maintenance, street construction or right-of-way acquisition, street lighting, and zoning.

10. G.S. 120-163(b).

11. G.S. 120-164.

12. G.S. 120-163(e); *see also* G.S. 120-163(d) (requiring submission of the *verified* petition).

13. G.S. 120-165.

14. *See* G.S. 120-166 through -169.1.

15. G.S. 120-169.1 and -170.

16. This requirement, which mirrors the petition's requirement for a five-cent property tax minimum and provision of the minimum four services, is set out in G.S. 136-41.2(c) for street assistance and is cross-referenced in other statutes for each of the other affected revenues. *See, e.g.,* G.S. 105-113.82(h) (beer and wine tax proceeds) and G.S. 105-472, -486, and -501 (sales and use taxes).

If the area can meet these standards, the Local Government Commission must make a positive recommendation, upon the condition that the petitioners obtain a legal description of the area to be incorporated.[17] On the other hand, if the area fails to meet all the standards, the Subcommittee is required to make a negative recommendation.[18] Even if a negative recommendation is made, however, the General Assembly may still incorporate the community; the Subcommittee's recommendation in no way binds the legislature.

The General Assembly incorporates an area by enacting a local bill consisting of a charter for the new city and a description of the city's initial boundaries. The charter includes the name, initial boundaries, and form of government for the new municipality.[19] The bill may take effect upon ratification, or it may include a requirement for a referendum by the residents of the area to be incorporated. The decision as to whether or not to require residents' approval rests with the General Assembly; local voters have no inherent constitutional right to approve an incorporation.

In most cases, when an incorporation bill comes before the General Assembly, it can be approved like any other local bill. Article VII, Section 1 of the North Carolina Constitution, however, requires a three-fifths vote in each house if the proposed community lies within one mile of the limits of an existing city of 5,000 people or more, within three miles of a city of 10,000 or more, within four miles of a city of 25,000 or more, or within five miles of a city of 50,000 or more. This provision reflects the assumption that cities will expand as areas near their boundaries grow and develop, and it also suggests a policy preference for annexation rather than incorporation as a way for urbanizing areas to gain access to municipal services. However, the supermajority vote requirement is rarely significant. Most incorporation bills that pass do so unanimously, following the General Assembly's practice of deferring to the local delegation on local matters.[20] Because of this tendency to defer to the local delegation, the support of the legislators who represent an area that is proposed for incorporation is an essential element in the process.[21]

Repealing City Charters and Dissolving Counties

Just as only the General Assembly may incorporate a community or create a county, only the General Assembly may unincorporate, suspend, or merge local governments. Historically, the legislature would do this by repealing a city charter or by repealing or amending the local act that created a county. The General Assembly rarely takes such an action, and it does so usually only on the request of the affected community. A 1971 omnibus act repealed the charters of ninety-five inactive towns,[22]

---

17. G.S. 120-171(b) and (c). Because the statutes in G.S. 120-167 through -174 sometimes refer to the Subcommittee and sometimes to the Local Government Commission, it is not clear if action is to be taken by the Subcommittee and then by the Commission, if the two bodies operate in parallel, or if the intent was to refer only to one body. Most likely the intent was to refer only to the Subcommittee.

18. *See* G.S. 120-166 through -170. If the recommendation is to be negative, the members of the interim board may request a public hearing before the Local Government Commission. G.S. 120-171(a).

19. Further guidance regarding municipal charters is available in North Carolina General Assembly Bill Drafting Division, *Summary of Municipal Incorporation Procedure*, webservices.ncleg.gov/ViewDocSiteFile/56137, at 11–12.

20. Each of the last three municipal incorporation bills that have become session laws passed unanimously. *See* votes on S.L. 2011-166 (incorporating Castle Hayne) at www.ncleg.gov/BillLookup/2011/S237, S.L. 2011-114 (incorporating Rougemont) at www.ncleg.gov/BillLookup/2011/H292, and S.L. 2011-110 (incorporating Fontana Dam) at www.ncleg.gov/BillLookup/2011/S431.

21. *See* North Carolina General Assembly Bill Drafting Division, *Summary of Municipal Incorporation Procedure*, www.ncleg.gov/Documents/1/12151 at II, K.3, 4 (recommending petitioners discuss their proposal with their legislative representatives prior to filing the petition).

22. S.L. 1971-740.

but since 1971 the General Assembly has repealed the charters of only three towns.[23] Charter suspensions are also relatively rare—the General Assembly has only suspended the charters of two towns in the last decade.[24] The General Assembly also has merged local governments—for example, by merging one city into another[25] or by incorporating a new city from two existing cities.[26] In 2021, the General Assembly extended authority to the Local Government Commission to dissolve municipalities by resolution.[27] The Local Government Commission has only exercised this authority once, dissolving the Town of East Laurinburg near the end of 2021.[28]

Annexation

North Carolina's annexation laws have been a significant component of the state's policies for providing government services to newly developed areas and tend to favor the expansion of existing cities over other ways of providing those services. Only cities are authorized by law to provide the full range of basic urban services: water supply and distribution, sewage collection and treatment, law enforcement, fire protection, solid waste collection and disposal, and street maintenance and improvement. Counties are not authorized to provide street maintenance and improvement, and no types of special districts are authorized to provide either law enforcement or street maintenance and improvement. Furthermore, as noted previously in the discussion of incorporation, the law favors the expansion of existing cities over the incorporation of new ones.

Prior to 1947, annexation required legislative action by the General Assembly. In 1947, in order to avoid the burden of facing many of these often controversial annexation bills, the legislature delegated to cities the authority to annex by local ordinance.[29] The initial law allowed cities to extend their borders by ordinance as long as certain notice was given to the public and to the property owners in the area proposed to be annexed. However, residents of the area to be annexed could, by petition, force the matter to be put to referendum, and the annexation of areas with fewer than twenty-five voting-eligible residents required the agreement of all property owners in the area.[30]

This law would be modified in subsequent decades,[31] but until 2011, North Carolina's annexation statutes offered municipalities more flexibility in annexing property than those of most other states.[32] During this time, annexations, particularly those initiated by cities, remained contentious.

---

23. S.L. 1995-119 (repealing the charter for the Town of Sandyfield, subject to a referendum); S.L. 1998-54 (repealing the charter for the Town of Sloop Point); S.L. 2017-43 (repealing the charter for the Town of Centerville).

24. *See* S.L. 2016-45 (temporarily suspending the charter of the Town of Spencer Mountain); S.L. 2019-29 (further suspending the charter of the Town of Spencer Mountain and suspending the charter of the Town of Eureka); S.L. 2023-49 (further suspending the charter of the Town of Spencer Mountain).

25. *See, e.g.*, S.L. 2001-16 (merging the Town of Arlington into the Town of Jonesville).

26. S.L. 1999-66 (creating the Town of Oak Island out of the Towns of Yaupon Beach and Long Beach).

27. S.L. 2021-124, § 6. This power to dissolve is currently codified at G.S. 160A-848.

28. *See* N.C. Department of State Treasurer, "Local Government Commission Dissolves Troubled Town of East Laurinburg" (Dec. 8, 2021), www.nctreasurer.com/news/press-releases/2021/12/08/local-government-commission-dissolves-troubled-town-east-laurinburg.

29. S.L. 1947-725. As part of the rationale for its action, the General Assembly noted that "the General Assembly of North Carolina devotes a large portion of its time in consideration of a multitude of local bills seeking the extension of the corporate limits of cities and towns."

30. *Id.*

31. The General Assembly created the Municipal Government Study Commission in 1957, which produced revisions enacted in 1959. See 1957 N.C. J. Res. 51 and S.L. 1959-713, which substantially modified the process of annexation by petition. Additional changes were made through the 1970s and in the late 1980s.

32. *See* Judith Welch Wegner, "North Carolina's Annexation Wars: Whys, Wherefores, and What Next," 91 *N.C. Law Review* 165, 203 (2012).

Affected property owners often challenged city-initiated annexations in court (and referred to them as "involuntary" annexations, a term that has stuck despite the introduction of a referendum requirement for city-initiated annexations).[33] In these cases, courts generally upheld annexations so long as the statutory procedures were substantially met. In some cases, however, cities annexed an area without providing significant services.[34] In others, the owners of property that was annexed on a city's initiative were required to pay fees for the extension of water and sewer services to their homes.[35]

In 2011, frustrated property owners once again brought their concerns to the attention of their legislators in Raleigh. Complaints included not having a voice in the decision to annex as well as the cost of and delay in receiving services, particularly water and sewer services. The legislature considered enacting a moratorium on annexation but ultimately revised the "involuntary" annexation rules to require the provision of water and sewer services without cost to property owners and to allow property owners to file petitions to deny such annexations.[36] The petition to deny process was to be administered by the county board of elections like a referendum and was also applied, in a series of local acts, to particular annexations that had already been completed.[37] Several cities challenged the petition process on constitutional and other grounds, and a superior court judge invalidated the petition process in the local acts as well as in the general law. The legislature responded to the ruling by replacing the petition process with a referendum.[38] Under the current law, if a city initiates annexation of an area, it may not approve the annexation unless a majority of voters in the area to be annexed vote to approve the annexation.[39]

As a consequence of the 2011 and 2012 legislation, which piled a referendum requirement on top of the requirement that the city provide free utility connections and ensured a lengthy process, municipality-initiated annexations are largely a thing of the past. As of this writing, we are aware of only one successful city-initiated annexation since 2011. When compared to the many annexations and even deannexations that occur across the state every year, it would appear that this legislation has effectively—though not entirely—eliminated municipality-initiated annexation.

Overview of Current Annexation Methods

In general, a city may annex any territory qualifying under the various procedures as long as that territory is not part of another, active city.[40] A city may annex territory that is within a sanitary district or another special district[41] or territory that is within another city's extraterritorial jurisdiction

33. *Id.* at 165, 168.

34. For example, in *Nolan v. City of Marvin*, 360 N.C. 256 (2006), the North Carolina Supreme Court invalidated an annexation because the city failed to provide meaningful services to the annexed area.

35. For some examples of these cases, *see* Wegner, "North Carolina's Annexation Wars: Whys, Wherefores, and What Next," at 204–07.

36. S.L. 2011-396.

37. S.L. 2011-173; 2011-177.

38. S.L. 2012-11.

39. G.S. 160A-58.55(i) and 160A-58.64(f).

40. G.S. 160A-58.54(a)(3) makes this prohibition explicit in the context of involuntary annexation. In the context of satellite annexation, such a prohibition can be inferred from the proximity requirement in G.S. 160A-58.1(b)(2). The older statutory language for voluntary annexations of contiguous property does not explicitly prohibit annexing property currently in another city, but case law principles, specifically the prior jurisdiction rule, may have this effect. For an explanation of the prior jurisdiction rule in annexation cases, see *Town of Hazelwood v. Town of Waynesville*, 320 N.C. 89, 90, 91, 357 S.E.2d 686, 687 (1987) (annexation procedure initiated "prior in time is prior in jurisdiction *to the exclusion of those subsequently instituted*.") (emphasis added)).

41. *See* State *ex rel.* E. Lenoir Sanitary Dist. v. City of Lenoir, 249 N.C. 96 (1958) (sanitary district is not municipality and its territory can thus be annexed).

without additional process. In addition, a city may by ordinance annex property owned by the city itself.[42] Finally, county boundaries are not a bar to annexation; over fifty cities lie within two or more counties.[43]

While the statutes do not authorize contractual agreements with landowners and other private parties over annexation, cities are permitted to enter into interlocal agreements with one another to designate certain property that one municipality or the other will not annex.[44]

The legislature retains authority to add to existing cities and does so on occasion.[45] In addition, three methods are delegated to cities and do not require action by the state legislature. These are (1) annexation by petition (hereinafter referred to as voluntary annexation) of areas contiguous to the city, including a modified process for economically distressed areas; (2) voluntary annexation of areas not contiguous to the city but nearby (also called satellite annexation); and (3) annexation at the city's initiative of contiguous areas that are developed for urban purposes (hereinafter referred to as city-initiated annexation).[46] With only very minor exceptions, these methods are available to all the state's cities.[47]

Voluntary Annexation of Contiguous Areas

G.S. 160A-31 authorizes a city to annex any area contiguous to its borders on receipt of a petition signed by all the owners of real property within the area proposed for annexation. Because it requires the signature of all property owners in the area to be annexed, this method is especially suited to annexations of small areas, new subdivisions (before lots have been sold), and tracts with a limited number of property owners.

The procedure is simple. A petition signed by all property owners in the area to be annexed is submitted to the city government. The city clerk reviews the petition and certifies its sufficiency. Once the clerk does so, the council holds a public hearing on whether or not the statutory requirements—contiguity and signatures by all the owners of the subject property—have been met. If the council determines that the requirements have been met, it may adopt an ordinance annexing the property. That ordinance can become effective immediately, on the June 30 following the hearing or on the June 30 of the calendar year following the hearing.[48]

Two points should be made about the signature requirement. First, the petition must contain the signature of *all* the owners of each lot or tract included in the petition. If a married couple owns a property, for example, both must sign. Second, the North Carolina Supreme Court has held that a property owner may withdraw his or her signature at any time before the council has adopted the

42. G.S. 160A-31(g) (contiguous); 160A-58.7 (satellite).

43. *See* North Carolina Office of State Budget and Management, "Land Area Distribution Municipalities More Than One County" (as of July 2022), www.osbm.nc.gov/facts-figures/population-demographics/state-demographer/municipal-population-estimates/land-area-distribution-municipalities-more-one-county. Examples include Town of Cary (Wake and Chatham counties), Davidson (Mecklenburg and Iredell counties), and High Point (mostly Guilford, but partly in Randolph, Davidson, and Forsyth counties).

44. *See* G.S. Chapter 160A, Article 4A, Part 6 (§§ 58.21–.49). *See also Cunningham v. City of Greensboro*, 212 N.C. App. 86, 711 S.E.2d 477 (2011).

45. A few recent examples of legislative annexation are S.L. 2024-20, § 4 (annexation into High Point) and § 8 (Mount Gilead); and S.L. 2024-21, § 5 (Edenton).

46. City-initiated annexation is often referred to as "involuntary" annexation. After the 2011 statutory revisions that require a referendum to approve any city-initiated annexation, these annexations are somewhat less "involuntary" than under some past versions of the legislation.

47. Charter provisions in several small towns contain exceptions to the general annexation laws. In addition, the General Assembly in more recent years has taken action to suspend or limit the annexation authority of individual municipalities. *See, e.g.*, S.L. 2023-100 (imposing a moratorium on annexations by the Town of Leland).

48. G.S. 160A-31(d).

annexation ordinance.[49] If that happens, the council may not simply annex the remaining property listed in the petition. Rather, because the council no longer has before it a petition signed by all the owners of the property listed in the petition, such a withdrawal invalidates that petition.[50] The same is true if ownership of some of the property changes between the time the petition is signed and the time the city seeks to act. Again, the council no longer has before it a petition signed by all the owners of the property listed in the petition and the petition is no longer valid.

In addition, while the process is relatively straightforward, the statute is silent on some details of the process. For instance, the governing board must "cause the clerk of the municipality to investigate the sufficiency" of the petition and to "certify the result of the investigation," after which the governing board "shall fix a date for a public hearing on the question of annexation."[51] However, it does not explain *how* the board must cause the clerk to review the petition, *how* the clerk memorializes his or her certification, or *how* the board sets a date for the public hearing. In the absence of further guiding language, municipalities have some discretion with regard to how the petition gets to the clerk, what the clerk does to certify the petition, and how the board puts the public hearing on its calendar. Some jurisdictions will issue resolutions directing the clerk to review the petition and schedule a public hearing, while others might simply have the clerk review the petition and put a hearing date on the calendar as they would other agenda items. Either method is sufficient as long as the basic procedure is followed—board gets clerk to review, clerk certifies, then petition is put on calendar and notice is sent.

Voluntary Annexation of Economically Distressed Areas

Amendments to the annexation laws enacted in 2011 addressed an unmet need in the voluntary annexation procedures. Some areas outside of cities are developed and need services but are not attractive prospects for annexation because they have low property values. These areas might also have high percentages of renters, even with absentee landlords, such that those who would benefit from city services might not be able to request access to those services through the usual petition process. In some cases, areas might have been intentionally excluded when the adjacent municipality was formed or when it expanded. In response, S.L. 2011-396, § 10 amended the statute to *require* annexation of distressed areas upon petition of the owners of 75 percent of the parcels in the area to be annexed.[52] This relaxes the usual requirement for 100 percent of the property owners to sign the petition. It also removes the discretion of the city to deny the petition, so long as the area and the petition meet the requirements in the statute. The statute defines a *distressed area* as an area in which 51 percent of the households have incomes that are 200 percent of the most recently published U.S. Census Bureau poverty threshold or lower.[53] There are a handful of other criteria that an area must meet to qualify for this provision: the population in the area to be annexed must not exceed 10 percent of the existing city population, and one-eighth of the external boundary of the area to be annexed must be contiguous to the existing city boundary. If these criteria are met, the city follows the usual procedure for a voluntary annexation of contiguous property but lacks its usual authority to reject the petition. The city can only deny a petition from distressed area property owners if the cost of extending water and sewer lines is too high, as determined by a formula set

49. Cunningham v. City of Greensboro, 212 N.C App. 86, 711 S.E.2d 477 (2011).
50. Conover v. Newton, 297 N.C. 506, 519, 256 S.E.2d 216, 224–25 (1979).
51. G.S. 160A-31(c).
52. G.S. 160A-31(b1).
53. G.S. 160A-31(b1) and (j).

out in the statute and confirmed by the Local Government Commission.[54] If a petition is denied on this basis, another request may not be filed within the next thirty-six months, but during that time, the law requires the city to make ongoing efforts to secure funding sufficient to make the extension feasible.[55]

A second provision allows residents (rather than property owners) in distressed areas to petition for voluntary annexation.[56] Under this provision, the city may consider annexation if it receives petitions signed by at least one adult resident of at least two-thirds of the resident households in the area to be annexed. The statute allows the city to require reasonable proof that the petitioner actually resides at the address indicated. The area must be contiguous, but no minimum amount of contiguity is specified. Unlike the provision regarding petitions from 75 percent of property owners, the provision regarding petitions from residents *does not require* the city to annex upon receipt of a valid petition.[57]

Cities annexing under either of these provisions must provide services such as municipal water and sewer (if offered within the city) to the annexed areas at no cost to the annexed property owners.[58]

Voluntary Annexation of Noncontiguous (Satellite) Areas

Urban areas do not only develop within and adjacent to municipal borders. Often the vicissitudes of the market require the urbanization of areas that are near an existing city but separated from it by undeveloped territory. These areas are not subject to annexation by the methods that limit annexation to contiguous areas, but frequently they are in the normal path for city growth, and property owners in the area desire the advantages of city services—water and sewer systems, police and fire protection, solid waste collection, and street maintenance. Also, early annexation of the areas is an advantage to the city because it enables the city to plan for the orderly expansion of basic facilities to serve both these areas and the intervening areas that will develop in time.

North Carolina has responded to this situation by permitting voluntary annexation of such noncontiguous, or satellite, areas. The procedure was first developed and authorized for Raleigh by local act in 1967.[59] Over the next several years, eleven other cities secured similar local act authority from the legislature. Finally, in 1974, in response to the likelihood of further requests for local acts, the General Assembly enacted general enabling authority for satellite annexation (G.S. 160A-58 through -58.8), repealing the various local acts.[60]

The procedure for satellite annexation is similar to that for voluntary annexation of contiguous areas. Once a petition signed by all the owners of the listed property[61] has been received and certified by the city clerk, the city council holds a public hearing on the petition's sufficiency and the annexation's desirability.[62] If the council determines that the petition is adequate; the property to be annexed qualifies under the statutory standards; and the public health, safety, and welfare of inhabitants of the city and of the area to be annexed are best served by the annexation, then it may

54. G.S. 160A-31(d2)(1).
55. *Id.*
56. G.S. 160A-31(j).
57. G.S. 160A-31(j).
58. G.S. 160A-31(d3).
59. S.L. 1967-989.
60. S.L. 1973-1173. Section 3 of the session law lists twelve specific local acts replaced by the statewide satellite annexation authority.
61. G.S. 160A-58.1(a) provides that the petition need not be signed by owners of property exempt from property taxation, by railroad companies, by public utilities, or by electric or telephone membership corporations.
62. G.S. 160A-58.2.

adopt an ordinance annexing the property. The statute sets out the following four standards that the property must meet:

1. The nearest point on the proposed satellite area must be no more than three miles from the city's primary limits.
2. No point within the proposed satellite area may be closer to another city than to the annexing city. (This standard does not apply if the property in question is subject to an annexation agreement between the two cities and is within the exclusive annexing authority of the city that received the petition.)
3. The total satellite area or areas of the city may not exceed 10 percent of the area of the city within its primary limits. (Many cities have obtained local legislation from the General Assembly waiving this standard.)
4. The city must be able to provide the full range of city services to the satellite area.[63]

The fourth standard deserves elaboration. One situation in which satellite annexation is sometimes sought is when the annexing city allows the sale of beer and wine or mixed drinks and the surrounding county does not. Owners of restaurants or grocery or convenience stores then seek annexation of their single lot or tract in order to sell beer and wine or mixed drinks. Sometimes these owners will assure the annexing city that they do not care about receiving city services and indeed will sign a waiver of such services. City officials need to understand that such a waiver might not obviate the statutory responsibility of the city to be able to provide services.[64] Thus, there may come a time when a subsequent owner (or the same owner under new circumstances) may be entitled to request city services. In part to offset the cost of extending such services, G.S. 160A-58.5 allows a city to charge different rates, fees, and charges for water, sewer, and other public enterprises to owners in satellite areas.

Municipality-Initiated ("Involuntary") Annexation

In 1959, the General Assembly updated its initial annexation law to balance the state's interest in expanding city boundaries to include developed and developing urban territory against residents' and property owners' interest in receiving services equitably and choosing whether to live in a municipality or unincorporated county area.[65] The statute permitted a city to annex an area that is developed in an urban manner if the city can demonstrate plans to provide adequate services to the area on the same basis as it provides services within the existing city.[66] As noted earlier, the amendments enacted in 2011 and 2012 added two key requirements—that the city pay for the cost of extending water and sewer services and hold a referendum—while removing distinctions between the process for small cities (fewer than 5,000 people) and the process for larger cities (5,000 people or more).[67]

---

63. GS 160A-58.1.

64. *See* G.S. 160A-31(e) (contiguous areas annexed by petition "shall be entitled to the same privileges and benefits as other parts of such municipality"), G.S.160A-58.3 (similar language for satellite annexations), G.S. 160A-58.55(j) (substantially similar language for city-initiated annexations).

65. S.L. 1959-1009 and 1010.

66. *See* G.S. 160A-58.54.

67. S.L. 2011-396 (repealing Part 2 and Part 3 of G.S. 160A, Article 4A).

A city may only use this process for an area that meets several criteria:[68]

- It must be adjacent to the municipality's boundaries (areas within a county water and sewer district that are not contiguous can still be annexed if the largest area of the district is adjacent to the city boundary).
- At least one-eighth of the area's boundary must be shared with the city.
- It must not be located within another municipality's boundary.
- The area must be "developed for urban purposes" as defined in the statute, connect the city to another developed area, or be surrounded by the city's primary limits.
- Part or all of the area is between the municipal boundary and another area developed for urban purposes or fills a gap in the urbanized area.

Service Requirements to Annexed Areas

The city must be able to provide police protection, fire protection, street maintenance, solid waste collection, water distribution, and sewerage collection and treatment to the annexation area on the same basis as it provides these services to the existing city. These services must be extended into the annexation area immediately when the annexation becomes effective. Note that if the city does not offer one or more of these services elsewhere in the city, the phrase "on the same basis" suggests that they do not have to offer services to the newly annexed area.[69]

If a city provides water and sewer service, its obligation, effective with the passage of the 2011 revisions to the law, is to provide water and sewer service to each individual property at no cost to the property owner for the installation. Under this provision, at an early stage of the annexation procedure—just after the adoption of the resolution of intent to annex—the city must provide notice to the property owners in the annexed area describing their right to have water and sewer lines and connections installed and extended to their property at no cost to them (other than user fees). Property owners have sixty-five days to request service. The city's obligation to extend lines to these properties at no cost applies only if the owners of a majority of parcels in the area to be annexed request service. (If the owners of a majority of parcels opt in, the law requires a second notice to those who didn't, in case they want to opt in as well.) If the obligation to extend service is triggered, the city must complete all of the improvements necessary to provide water and sewer service to each property within three and a half years of the effective date of the ordinance.[70]

If the owners of a majority of parcels do not request service within the initial time frame, the city is not required to extend service. If the city does extend the lines and property owners later request service, the law sets a sliding scale (based on how much later the requests come in) that limits how much the city may charge these customers, expressed as a percentage of the total cost of installation under the policies then in effect. This limitation on the amounts that may be charged applies to requests received within the first five years following annexation. After five years, property owners requesting service may be charged according to the policies in effect at the time of the request, as though they had not been the subject of a city-initiated annexation.[71]

Contracts with Fire Departments

If an area being annexed under the city-initiated procedure is served by a volunteer fire department, the annexing city must make a good-faith effort to negotiate a contract with the fire department

68. G.S. 160A-58.54(a).
69. *See* G.S. 160A-58.53(3) (municipality must plan to extend services on the effective date of annexation).
70. G.S. 160A-58.56.
71. G.S. 160A-58.56(d).

for the latter to continue to provide fire protection in the annexation area for five years. If the fire department officials think the department has not received a good-faith offer, the department may appeal the matter to the state's Local Government Commission. If the Commission agrees with the fire department, the city must delay the annexation until the city makes the necessary offer.[72]

Procedure for Annexation; Referendum Requirement

The annexation procedures start when the city adopts a resolution of consideration identifying the area under consideration for annexation and provides notice of the resolution.[73] At least one year after the resolution of consideration, a city may adopt a resolution of intent, which officially begins the annexation process for the areas specified in the resolution of intent. The resolution of intent may include some or all of the areas identified in the resolution of consideration. The resolution of intent triggers the requirement to schedule the referendum.[74] Effective with the 2012 amendments to the statute, a city must place the question of annexation on the ballot at the next general municipal election. The annexation must be approved by a majority of voters in the area to be annexed. If the annexation fails in the referendum, the city must wait at least thirty-six months before proceeding with city-initiated annexation of the same area.[75]

Following the notice of intent but before the referendum, the process requires notice to owners of property who are eligible to receive water and sewer service. The city then must prepare a report that demonstrates how the area to be annexed meets the urbanization standards and describes the city's plans for extending and financing major services to the area.[76] After notice to the residents and the property owners of the area, the city council holds a public information meeting on the proposal, at which citizens may ask questions about the annexation, and a public hearing, at which the council listens to public comment.[77]

If the statutory standards are met, the city is able to extend and finance the necessary services, the procedures have been followed, and the voters have approved the annexation, the city may adopt an ordinance to annex the property.[78]

Annexation by Legislative Act

The General Assembly always has the authority to enlarge the boundaries of a city by local act. This was the original method used to effect annexations, and before 1947, it was the only method available. Although the legislature has essentially complete discretion in annexing territory to existing cities and no standards guide its decision-making, in practice it almost never does so except at the request of the city involved. Legislative annexation is especially useful for areas that need annexation but for some reason cannot be annexed under any of the other procedures. Annexation of public facilities surrounded by areas of limited development, annexation of areas involving lakes or rivers, and realignment of existing boundaries to match service areas all fall into this class. The General Assembly also has authority to de-annex, as described later in this chapter.

The Effect of Annexation on Existing Public Services

When a city annexes an area, in the absence of a statute protecting private service providers, the city becomes entitled to be the primary provider of municipal services in the annexation area. A case

72. G.S. 160A-58.57.
73. G.S. 160A-58.55.
74. G.S. 160A-58.64. Only residents in the area to be annexed may vote in the referendum.
75. G.S. 160A-58.64(f).
76. G.S. 160A-58.56.
77. G.S. 160A-58.55(d) through (h).
78. G.S. 160A-58.64.

involving a Winston-Salem annexation illustrates this point.[79] Forsyth County had franchised a number of private solid waste collectors to collect residential and commercial solid waste in the area annexed. Upon annexation, and in conformity to its duties under the annexation statutes, Winston-Salem itself began to collect solid waste in the area. Because the city service was financed from taxes, which the residents had to pay in any event, the effect was to put the private haulers out of business in the annexation area. When they sued the city, the North Carolina Supreme Court held that the county franchises expired on annexation and that the city had no duty to cooperate with the private collectors or to compensate them for lost business. In the absence of a statute, the same rules would apply for other privately provided services.

Several statutes modify this basic principle to protect some volunteer fire departments and private solid waste collectors in certain types of annexations, as described below.

Fire Department Debt

If a city has annexed territory under any of the *statutory* procedures and has not contracted with a volunteer fire department, or if it has contracted with a volunteer fire department and the contract has expired, the city may be responsible for a portion of the outstanding indebtedness of the volunteer department.[80] The city's responsibility extends to any fire department debt that existed when the city began the annexation proceeding. The city's share of the debt repayment obligation is determined by the assessed valuation of the area annexed and served by the fire department in relation to the assessed valuation of the total area served by the fire department. Thus, if the city's annexation area represents 5 percent of the valuation of the fire district served by the fire department, the city must pay 5 percent of the department's debt obligation. This requirement does not apply to legislative annexations.

Contracts with Solid Waste Collectors

The result of the Winston-Salem case described earlier—that there is no recompense for solid waste collectors displaced by a new municipal service—has been reversed by statute, but only in legislative annexations and in city-initiated annexations.[81] If a private solid waste collector has been doing a substantial amount of business in an area to be annexed by a city, and has at least fifty customers in the county in which the city is located, the collector is entitled either to have the city contract with it to continue collecting solid waste on the city's behalf for two years or to have the city make good the losses occasioned by the annexation (defined as fifteen times the firm's average monthly revenues in the annexation area). Like fire departments, the private firm enjoys a right to appeal to the state's Local Government Commission if the city does not offer a contract or compensation.[82] This requirement does not apply to any voluntary annexations.

Taxation of Newly Annexed Property

G.S. 160A-58.10 sets out the rules to be followed in extending property taxes to areas annexed under any of the statutory methods. (Annexations effected by legislative act are frequently made subject to G.S. 160A-58.10 as well.) These rules apply to taxes for the fiscal year during which the annexation becomes effective.

Basically, owners of annexed property are liable for city taxes for that fiscal year on a prorated basis. The city determines what each property owner's tax liability would have been had the property

79. Stillings v. City of Winston-Salem, 311 N.C. 689 (1984).
80. *See* G.S. 160A-31.1 (contiguous); 160A-58.2A (satellite); 160A-58.58 (city-initiated).
81. G.S. 160A-58.59 (city-initiated); 160A-324 (legislative).
82. *Id.*

been in the city for the entire fiscal year, then prorates that amount based on the number of full months remaining in the fiscal year on the effective date of annexation. For example, an annexation becomes effective on March 17. At that time, there are three full months remaining in the fiscal year: April, May, and June. Therefore, an owner who would have been liable for $600 of city taxes had his or her property been in the city the entire year will be liable for three-twelfths of an entire year's taxes, or $150. After that first year, property in the annexation area is taxed in the same manner as all other property in the city.

The preceding paragraph sets out the rules for determining the *amount* of tax owed by property owners in the annexation area. There are additional rules about the *date* on which those taxes are due. If the annexation occurs after June 30 and before September 2, the taxes are due on September 1, in the same manner as all other property taxes in the city. But if the annexation occurs on September 1 or later in the fiscal year, the prorated taxes are not due until the next September 1.

Annexation Disputes between Cities

Sometimes more than one city is interested in annexing the same parcel or parcels of property, and sometimes the owners of property in the area much prefer annexation by one city over annexation by another. The courts have looked to the doctrine of *prior jurisdiction* to determine which of two such cities is entitled to carry out the annexation. Under this doctrine, the city that takes the first formal statutory step toward annexation is entitled to complete its procedure without interference by the other. If this results in a valid annexation, the other city no longer has any rights of annexation over the disputed area. What constitutes the first formal step differs depending on the nature of the annexation: for city-initiated annexations, the first formal step is adoption of the resolution of intent; for annexation by petition, the first formal step is when the annexation petitions are presented to the city's governing board.[83]

The statutes also permit cities that would rather avoid annexation fights of this sort to enter into agreements under which each city is granted a zone of territory that it has exclusive authority to annex.[84] These agreements may extend for up to twenty years, and a city must give five years' notice to withdraw from one. If a city attempts to annex territory in violation of such an agreement, any other city party to the agreement may bring an action to enforce it and thereby invalidate the annexation.

Deannexation

There are no statutory procedures under which a city may de-annex territory. Rather, if a city or a property owner wants to subtract some part of the city's existing territory, the only way it may do so is to seek a local act of the General Assembly effecting the deannexation. Such acts were quite rare and were only enacted at the request of the affected city until 2011. The 2011 and 2012 legislative sessions saw a marked increase in deannexations, which accompanied the changes in the statewide annexation laws. The General Assembly is subject to no standards when it decides to de-annex territory, in the same way that no standards condition its ability to incorporate an area or annex territory to an existing city.

83. *See, e.g.,* City of Burlington v. Town of Elon Coll., 310 N.C. 723 (1984).
84. G.S. 160A-58.21 through -58.28.

Table 2.1 Results of City–County Consolidation Referenda in North Carolina

Governmental Units Involved	Date of Referendum	Votes For / Against	Percentage For / Against
Wilmington and New Hanover County	March 28, 1933	1,189 / 4,128	22 / 78
	February 27, 1973	4,040 / 11,722	26 / 74
	October 6, 1987	7,051 / 10,337	41 / 59
	October 10, 1995	11,377 / 15,923	42 / 58
Durham and Durham County	January 28, 1961	4,115 / 14,355	22 / 78
	September 10, 1974	6,198 / 13,124	32 / 68
Charlotte and Mecklenburg County	March 22, 1971	17,313 / 39,464	31 / 69
Asheville and Buncombe County	November 2, 1982	12,642 / 20,883	38 / 62

Source: Official election returns.

City–County Consolidation

City–county consolidation is the merger of a county government with one or more city governments. As a general rule, the city government is abolished and the county government is legally transformed into one that has all the powers and functions previously held by both governments. Authority for counties and cities to create special commissions to study consolidation and other forms of cooperative action, including the drafting of a charter for a consolidated government, is found in Article 20 of G.S. Chapter 153A.

The History of City–County Consolidation

City–county consolidation has a long history in the United States. New Orleans City and Parish were consolidated in 1813; Boston and Suffolk County in 1821; and Philadelphia City and County in 1854.

In North Carolina, interest in city–county consolidation also has a long history, beginning with a 1927 plan (never submitted to the voters) to consolidate the City of Charlotte and Mecklenburg County. Since that time, consolidation plans have been placed before the electorate four times in Wilmington and New Hanover County, twice in Durham and Durham County, and once each in Charlotte and Mecklenburg County and Asheville and Buncombe County. All the plans were rejected, but the margins of defeat have decreased in the places that have had more than one consolidation attempt. The results of the eight referenda on consolidation are shown in Table 2.1.

In every case, voters inside the city proposed for consolidation were more favorable toward the merger than those outside the city but inside the county. However, only in the three most recent votes—Wilmington and New Hanover County in 1987 and 1995, and Asheville and Buncombe County in 1982—have a majority of the voters inside the city involved favored merger.

Other moves toward city–county consolidation in the four counties mentioned earlier have been made in the past sixty years, but they all stopped short of the referendum. There were efforts in Charlotte-Mecklenburg and in Durham in the 1990s that led to proposed charters, but the governing boards decided not to submit those charters to the county's voters. Interest in consolidation, as evidenced by the creation of study groups, has also been present in recent years in a number of other cities and counties, including Brevard and Transylvania County, Fayetteville and Cumberland County, Roxboro and Person County, Sanford and Lee County, and Elizabeth City and Pasquotank County.

Consolidation of specific agencies has occurred, however. Winston-Salem merged its planning department with that of Forsyth County in the 1940s,[85] and the same has occurred with Durham City and County planning.[86]

Advantages and Disadvantages of City–County Consolidation

The people who have supported consolidation have done so on the grounds of efficiency. They note that the county is a single social and economic community and argue that it could be better served by one local government than by two. They see better coordination of all government services and improved management of growth flowing from consolidation. Merger would also result in greater equity in taxation, in their view, because it typically involves the use of service districts in which taxation is tied to service levels. Proponents also argue that a single governing board, serving all citizens for all local government purposes, would be more responsive and responsible. Furthermore, they assert, consolidation would eliminate city–county conflicts and the objections to municipal annexation decisions being made by a governing board not responsive to those being annexed.

The opponents of consolidation, for their part, have put forth a host of objections. Citizens outside the central city fear that merger would, in effect, result in their being "swallowed up" by the "big city." They note that a merged government would be a larger one and argue that this would mean a less responsive and less efficient government. The fear of higher taxes, especially among residents outside the city, has usually been a major objection to consolidation.

Most of the plans for consolidation proposed in North Carolina have called for changes in the manner in which the governing board was elected and for the merger of administrative departments and offices. These proposed changes have caused some citizens to fear a loss of political influence or jobs or both. Members of rural fire departments and employees of sheriffs' offices, for example, have usually opposed consolidation.

Residents of small towns in counties proposed for merger with a central city have usually opposed consolidation, even though their towns would continue to exist after the merger. They have seen the initial consolidation as a first step that might lead eventually to the merger of their towns and a loss of their identity.

The efforts at city–county consolidation have not yet culminated in a merger of any city and county governments in North Carolina. Almost all of them, however, have been a factor in promoting city–county cooperation by the merger of functions or by an increase in the joint use of facilities. For more information about city–county collaboration and interlocal cooperation, see Chapter 11, "Interlocal Cooperation, Shared Services, and Regional Councils."

Additional Resources

Bluestein, Frayda. *City-County Consolidation in North Carolina* (School of Government microsite), www.sog.unc.edu/resources/microsites/city-county-consolidation-north-carolina.

———. "City Obligations for Providing Services to Annexed Areas." *Coates' Canons: NC Local Government Law* blog (January 30, 2020), canons.sog.unc.edu/2020/01/city-obligations-for-providing-services-to-annexed-areas.

85. S.L. 1947-677.

86. *See* "About Durham City–County Planning," Durham City–County Planning Department, www.durhamnc.gov/338/City-County-Planning.

———. "Satellite Area Boundaries Are Corporate Limits, but Not for Purposes of Contiguous Annexation or ETJ." *Coates' Canons: NC Local Government Law* blog (December 14, 2017), canons.sog.unc.edu/2017/12/satellite-area-boundaries-corporate-limits-not-purposes-contiguous-annexation-etj.

———. "Voluntary Annexation: An Overview." *Coates' Canons: NC Local Government Law* blog (October 9, 2013), canons.sog.unc.edu/2013/10/voluntary-annexation-an-overview.

———. "Deannexation." *Coates' Canons: NC Local Government Law* blog (January 9, 2013), canons.sog.unc.edu/2013/01/deannexation.

Joyce, Jim. "What Happens When Property Changes Jurisdiction?" *Coates' Canons: NC Local Government Law* blog (August 9, 2023), canons.sog.unc.edu/2023/08/what-happens-when-property-changes-jurisdiction.

Lawrence, David M. *Incorporation of a North Carolina Town*. 2nd ed. Chapel Hill: Institute of Government, University of North Carolina at Chapel Hill, 1998.

———. *Annexation Law in North Carolina* (3 volumes); Volume 1. *General Topics*. Chapel Hill: Institute of Government, University of North Carolina at Chapel Hill, 2003.

———. *Annexation Law in North Carolina* (3 volumes); Volume 2. *Voluntary Annexation*. Chapel Hill: Institute of Government, University of North Carolina at Chapel Hill, 2004.

———. *Annexation Law in North Carolina* (3 volumes); Volume 3. *Involuntary Annexation*. Chapel Hill: Institute of Government, University of North Carolina at Chapel Hill, 2006.

McLaughlin, Chris. "Property Taxes and Annexations." *Coates' Canons: NC Local Government Law* blog (July 15, 2021), canons.sog.unc.edu/2021/07/property-taxes-and-annexations.

North Carolina Association of Municipal Clerks. *Mechanics of Annexation for All Municipalities* (August 2012), www.ncamc.com/document-library/manuals-guidelines/annexation.

North Carolina General Assembly Bill Drafting Division. *Summary of Municipal Incorporation Procedure in North Carolina*, webservices.ncleg.gov/ViewDocSiteFile/56137.

Chapter 3

County and Municipal Governing Boards

Kimberly L. Nelson

Kimberly Nelson is a faculty member at the School of Government who specializes in local government management and public administration. She is a Fellow with the National Academy of Public Administration and the coeditor of the journal *State and Local Government Review.*

Previous versions of this chapter were authored by School of Government faculty members Vaughn Upshaw, Carl Stenberg, David Lawrence, Joseph S. Ferrell, and Warren Jake Wicker and North Carolina League of Municipalities attorneys Kimberly S. Hibbard, Andrew L. Romanet Jr., Fred P. Baggett, and S. Leigh Wilson, whose contributions to the field and to this publication are gratefully acknowledged.

This chapter describes the governance structures under which North Carolina's municipal and county governing boards organize and conduct their activities. It also discusses legal responsibilities of and common expectations for local government boards and their presiding officers, the board chair or mayor. The chapter concludes with a description of how a county or municipal governing structure may be changed.

Background

In North Carolina, a county's governing body is known as the *board of county commissioners*. Although commonly referred to as a *city council*, a municipal governing board in North Carolina may be alternatively designated the *board of aldermen*, *board of commissioners*, or *village* or *town council*. The name used makes no difference from a statutory standpoint and is not tied to population or authority; it is likely to have been chosen based on custom and local preference. For ease of reference, this chapter uses the term *council* to refer to a city, town, or village's governing board. Cities, towns, and villages are referred to hereafter as *municipalities*. The terms *local governing board* and *governing board member(s)* are used when discussing matters that apply equally to boards of commissioners and city councils.

Introduction

Counties and municipalities are the two categories of general-purpose local governments in North Carolina. A general-purpose government typically provides a broad array of government services. These are distinct from special- or single-purpose governments that provide a limited number of services. North Carolina is more centralized than most states, with a relatively small total number of local governments.[1] The state's General Statutes (hereinafter G.S.) provide counties and municipalities with different options for operation: The local governing body can (1) carry out local government responsibilities itself or (2) hire a professional to administer local government affairs on its behalf.[2] The General Statutes also describe alternatives for the structure of a county commission or municipal council.[3]

Similar to other Southern states, counties in North Carolina serve as an arm of the state government, distributing state-mandated services throughout the state. All of the state's residents live in a county, while slightly more than half of the population lives within a municipality. Unlike counties that were created by the state early in its history, municipalities are typically created through a voter-driven process. North Carolina does not require municipalities to provide services beyond building permitting.

---

1. According to data from the U.S. Census Bureau's 2022 Census of Governments, North Carolina has 965 total local government units: 552 municipalities, 100 counties, and 313 special-purpose governments.

2. *See* G.S. 153A-76 (counties); 160A-146 (municipalities).

3. *See* G.S. 153A-58 (counties); 160A-101 (municipalities).

Units of Government in North Carolina

Counties

North Carolina created county governments in the seventeenth and eighteenth centuries to give people greater access to public services and make it easier for them to conduct official business. Initially, the governor appointed justices of the peace to oversee each county and carry out the mandated policies and services of state government. Following the civil war, North Carolina adopted the Constitution of 1868 that gave citizens more input into electing their local leaders. Under the new constitution, voters in each county elected the sheriff, coroner, register of deeds, clerk of court, surveyor, treasurer, and board of commissioners. The newly created county commissioners replaced the state-appointed justices of the peace and assumed full financial responsibility for the county, including adopting the budget and setting the property tax rate.[4] All North Carolina counties use the same form of government, commission with a professional manager, also called the *county manager* form of government.

Municipalities

Generally

The *mayor–council* form of government (where, as the name implies, local government administration is handled by a mayor, while policy making is the realm of the governing body) is the original form of general-purpose local government, descended from the English borough mayor-and-council system and instituted in the first American colonies. This form of local government is most closely akin to the federal and state arrangements of government, with a separate executive (mayor) and legislature (council). Throughout its long history and in its many variations—such as a bicameral council, a weak versus a strong mayor's office, and an at-large or district system—it has been successfully employed from the smallest colonial town, dependent on ferry tolls for operating expenses, to the modern megalopolis with a multi-billion-dollar budget. Although North Carolina statutes provide for the option of a mayor–council government, the mayor has no executive authority. Therefore, the mayor–council form in North Carolina does not have separation of powers and is not similar to the mayor–council form found in other states.

Early in America's history, as cities grew in wealth, responsibility, and bureaucracy, a patronage system emerged. Cities grew rapidly due to the Industrial Revolution and immigration. This growth put enormous strains on housing, infrastructure, and public health. Consequently, cities at this time were plagued with public safety issues, filth, and unsafe housing. The resulting anxiety among wealthy, native-born residents over these dramatic societal changes exacerbated popular dissatisfaction over the corruption, inefficiency, and political favoritism that had become associated with city governance.[5]

In the early 1900s, progressive reformers sought to address a host of societal problems, including local government reform. Richard S. Childs was one of the leaders in that movement. It was he who promoted a modified version of a new form of government being used in Staunton, Virginia, in 1910 that he called the "council-manager plan."[6] The council–manager form is similar to the structure used by corporate boards. The elected council and mayor select a professional manager

---

4. For more about local government in North Carolina, see Chapter 1, "An Overview of Local Government."

5. Kimberly L. Nelson and Carl W. Stenberg, "U.S. Local Governments in Historical Context," *Managing Local Government: An Essential Guide for Municipal and County Managers* (Thousand Oaks, Calif.: CQ Press, 2018), 20–24.

6. Richard Stillman, "Richard S. Childs and Louis Brownlow: Two 'Saints' of Public Administration Reconsidered," *Midwest Review of Public Administration* 7, no. 1 (January 1973): 6–8.

Table 3.1 Distribution of Forms of Government in North Carolina, by Population

Government	Municipal Population (no. in size category)											
	<1,000 (219)		1,000–5,000 (201)		5,001–10,000 (50)		10,001–50,000 (66)		>50,000 (16)		Total (552)	
	No.	%	No.	%	No.	%	No.	%	No.	%	No.	%
Mayor–Council Municipalities	203	93	78	39	7	14	0	0	0	0	288	52
Council-Manager Municipalities	16	7	123	61	43	86	66	100	16	100	264	48

Source: "Forms of North Carolina City Government," School of Government microsite, accessed December 11, 2023, www.sog.unc.edu/resources/microsites/forms-north-carolina-city-government.

to run the day-to-day operations of local government. Managers are politically neutral and provide policy advice based on their professional experience. There is no separation of the legislative and executive. The council–manager form has steadily increased in popularity since its inception, and it is now the principal form of municipal government in U.S. municipalities with populations over 10,000. The mayor–council form predominates in very small municipalities (populations less than 2,500) and very large ones (populations greater than 500,000).

Means of Organizing

The form of government under which a North Carolina municipality may operate is set forth in its charter. An initial charter results from an act of the state legislature. Changing the form of municipal government requires the adoption of an ordinance or a change to the city's charter. The options for changing the form of government are described in more detail later in this chapter.

Mentioned briefly above and in more detail below, the council–manager form of government is one of two options available to municipalities under the General Statutes (see Chapter 4, "County and City Managers"). As municipalities with the mayor–council form gain population and offer a more complex array of services, municipal leaders may decide that a change is needed. Some municipalities change their form of government and hire a city or town manager (i.e., adopt the council–manager form of government), while others hire a chief administrative officer (CAO) without immediately changing the form of government. These municipalities may later make the full transition to the council–manager form. Under G.S. 160A-148, adoption of the council–manager form requires that the manager be given hiring and firing authority over all employees not otherwise hired by the council. As a result, councils that want to retain this authority but also want the help of a CAO retain the mayor–council form and hire an administrator. No charter amendment is required for a council to hire an administrator, but if a municipality wants to adopt the council–manager form, it may do so only by amending its charter in one of four defined ways.

Organizing North Carolina Cities—By the Numbers

Table 3.1 shows how common the two forms of municipal government are within each population class. The mayor–council form remains the principal form in North Carolina today. In 2023, it was used by 288 (or 52 percent) of the state's 552 municipalities. It predominates among municipalities with populations of less than 2,500 (78 percent). In 2023, only 14 percent (seven of fifty) of North Carolina municipalities with populations between 5,000 and 10,000 used the mayor–council form of government. The council–manager plan has been the exclusive form in municipalities with large populations (25,000+) in North Carolina since the late 1940s, and it is used by most municipalities with populations between 2,500 and 25,000 (83 percent). Over time, there has been a steady increase in the proportion of council–manager municipalities relative to mayor–council municipalities in North Carolina.

County and Municipal Governing Boards in North Carolina

Generally

There is no typical structure for a county board of commissioners or a municipal council in North Carolina. Each county's board structure is set out in local legislation of the General Assembly, while each municipality's board structure is set out in the municipal charter. Both local acts and charters exhibit considerable variety as to governing body size, whether members are elected by district or at-large, and whether terms are for two years or four. All 100 boards of county commissioners in North Carolina are elected in partisan elections, while almost all city council elections are nonpartisan. Despite the absence of a typical board structure, it is useful to examine the patterns found in the various board structures and to look at the trend of structural change in recent years. (Appendixes 3.1A and 3.1B contain summary figures on the structures of the governing boards of North Carolina municipalities. Comparable information on counties is tabulated by the North Carolina Association of County Commissioners and can be found on its website.)[7]

Size of Board

In North Carolina, county boards of commissioners range in size from five members to nine, although only six have more than seven members.[8] By far the most popular size is five (found in sixty counties). Municipal councils range in size from two members to eleven, although only two have more than eight members. As with county boards, five is the most popular size for municipal councils.

Length of Members' Terms

All terms, both for county commissioners and for municipal council members, are for two years or four, with the larger number of governing boards having four-year terms. Most boards with four-year terms stagger elections so that about half the members are elected every two years; of all the changes made to governing boards in recent years, instituting a staggered four-year term has been the most prevalent. This staggering ensures a degree of continuity in county and municipal affairs and a constant level of experience.

---

7. See "County Commissioner Elections," North Carolina Association of County Commissioners, updated January 2024, www.ncacc.org/research-and-publications/research/county-elections/.

8. S.L. 2023-30 increased the Wake County board from seven to nine members. Wake County is included in this total.

Shared Expectations of Board Chairs and Mayors

1. The chair/mayor effectively manages governing board meetings by
   - presiding at the meetings,
   - being a good timekeeper,
   - keeping board members' dialogue on track,
   - focusing on the job at hand,
   - staying on topic,
   - paying attention to the board's feedback on the conduct of meetings, and
   - avoiding introducing and making important decisions at the same meeting.
2. The chair/mayor serves as liaison to the governing board by
   - staying informed of matters coming before the board,
   - overseeing relations with stakeholders,
   - testing the board's preliminary ideas with key stakeholders, and
   - asking external stakeholders to provide input on strategic issues.
3. The chair/mayor facilitates communication by
   - treating everyone in an even-handed and fair manner,
   - managing board members' contributions so that no one member dominates,
   - encouraging board members to express opinions and perspectives,
   - engaging more reticent members in discussion,
   - fostering healthy participation, especially among those with different views, and
   - employing effective group processes, making it safe to explore alternate views.
4. The chair/mayor serves as spokesperson for the governing board by
   - being a strong advocate and credible representative of local government and the board,
   - honoring the "one voice" principle whereby a vote of a majority of members is recognized as the board's final decision,
   - speaking knowledgeably and energetically about the board's accomplishments and opportunities for the community,
   - using the "Five F's" (**F**ast, **F**actual, **F**rank, **F**air, and **F**riendly),
   - thinking before speaking (imagine what statements will sound like on the evening news before speaking—don't say more than necessary),
   - staying on message,
   - not answering questions "off the record,"
   - remembering the role of the media and the part it plays in democratic government, and
   - talking with the press in advance of a big issue to help reporters anticipate important stories.
5. The chair/mayor helps in county/municipal government team-building by
   - gaining the trust and respect of fellow members,
   - building positive and productive relationships with the manager or administrator,
   - acknowledging the contributions of governing board members,
   - developing and maintaining teamwork between board members and professional staff,
   - being aware of and seeking to improve board dynamics,
   - learning to "lead from behind" so that others can share in accomplishments, and
   - creating a positive culture and establishing expectations that the board and management will work as a team.
6. The chair/mayor manages conflict by
   - increasing governing board consciousness of group dynamics;
   - promoting desirable outcomes of matters relating to group norms, value differences, diversity, honesty, questioning, conflict, and dialogue;
   - suspending judgment until all perspectives have been shared;
   - being independent (able to disagree without being disagreeable);
   - modeling good listening and inquiry skills; and
   - managing conflict on the board constructively.

Sidebar continues →

Shared Expectations of Board Chairs and Mayors, *continued*

7. The chair/mayor shapes the governing board's agenda by
    - actively working with board members and the manager or administrator to identify agenda items,
    - working with the manager and others (as locally determined) to establish the board's agenda, and
    - planning meetings to allow enough time for members to discuss and explore issues and viewpoints.
8. The chair/mayor promotes a high-performing governing board by
    - demonstrating an understanding of local government and the environment in which it operates,
    - learning skills in managing group dynamics,
    - using techniques to help the board look at things differently and from alternative points of view,
    - giving the manager and senior staff opportunities to contribute to the board's dialogue,
    - making sure members of the board read materials in advance and ask for necessary information in a timely and efficient manner,
    - being prepared for meetings,
    - offering and inviting constructive feedback,
    - seeking out opportunities to develop the board's effectiveness,
    - supporting the board–manager or board–administrator relationship, and
    - mentoring newer members.

Election At-Large or by District

Slightly more than half of the boards of county commissioners in North Carolina elect at least some of their members from specific districts. The remaining boards are elected from the county at-large, although more than half of these counties require commissioners to reside in their respective districts. In contrast, nearly all municipal councils—more than 86 percent statewide—are elected from the municipality at-large. Only twelve of the 330 municipalities in the state with populations under 2,500 use any sort of electoral district.

Election on a Partisan or Nonpartisan Basis

As noted above, all 100 boards of county commissioners in North Carolina are elected on a partisan basis, with the elections occurring in even-numbered years. On the other hand, nearly all municipal councils are elected on a nonpartisan basis. Most of these, particularly those in smaller municipalities, are elected on a plurality basis, without a primary. Most municipal elections take place in odd-numbered years. Municipalities have been shifting from odd- to even-numbered years due to improved voter turnout. Recent changes in larger cities include Winston-Salem (2011), Asheville (2018), and Raleigh (2021).

Presiding Officers on Governing Boards

The Chair of the Board of Commissioners

In most counties, the board of commissioners itself selects its chair, who presides at all board meetings. In Buncombe, Jackson, and Swain counties, board chairs are popularly elected. In Graham County, the commissioner with the highest number of votes becomes board chair with a four-year term. Unless directly elected by the voters, the chair serves a term of one year. By law, this official has the same right—indeed duty—to vote on all questions before the board unless excused by a standing rule of the body. However, the chair may not vote to break a tie on any vote in which the chair participated.[9] Although as a general rule, chairs have no more legal power than other members of the board, they do have special authority to declare states of emergency under the state laws governing riots and civil disorders, and they have authority to call special meetings of the board on their own initiative.[10] Unlike mayors (who are expressly prohibited under G.S. 160A-151 from assuming the duties of the municipal manager on any basis), chairs of county boards of commissioners are able to perform county manager duties by action of the board in accordance with G.S. 153A-81.

The Mayor

Mayors in North Carolina enjoy very few formal powers. With a limited number of exceptions, their powers consist of presiding at governing board meetings, voting to break ties at those meetings (at no other time can they be tiebreakers), and signing documents on behalf of the municipality. The *mayor–council system with executive mayor* (sometimes called strong mayor) used in many of the nation's large municipalities, under which the mayor is charged with actually running city government, is not found in North Carolina. Under state statutes, the mayor retains the designation of chief executive officer of the municipality. However, the mayor has no executive authority.[11] The only exception is a limited power of veto granted to the mayor of Charlotte. Despite having so few formal powers, many North Carolina mayors do exercise great influence in the operation of their municipalities. It is common, for example, for the council to delegate to the mayor responsibilities such as working with the clerk to create council agendas, representing the city on regional advisory boards, or serving as the primary contact for local media.

Having a lack of formal authority does not mean a mayor is "weak." Most of the powers held by mayors in the state are created by individual municipal charters, by action of the particular mayor's council, or by the mayor's own political stature. G.S. 160A-67 confers on mayors all powers and duties enumerated in the General Statutes, as well as any others conferred on them by the council. This statute recognizes the mayor as the official head of the municipality for purposes of serving civil process, and most federal and state agencies extend this same recognition for purposes of official correspondence or actions such as grant awards or enforcement of federal laws and regulations. G.S. 160A-69 requires the mayor to preside at council meetings, and G.S. 160A-71 gives the mayor the power to call special meetings of the council.

All but a few mayors in North Carolina are elected by the voters of a given municipality. In a few communities, the governing board elects the mayor from its own ranks or the mayor is the highest vote getter in the election for members of council.[12] If elected by the people, the mayor may, by local charter or ordinance, be given the right under G.S. 160A-101 to vote on all matters before the council; alternatively, the mayor may only have the right to vote to break a tie. If selected from the membership of the council, the mayor does not give up the right to vote as a member of the council and may vote on all matters.

While mayors do not have a great deal of autonomy or authority, they are the chief political officer in municipal government. By force of that perception, combined with the strength of their personalities, many mayors effectively lead their governing boards. In small municipalities without a manager, mayors often serve as de facto chief administrator simply because they are willing to work long hours in the town hall. In council–manager municipalities, discussed in more detail later

9. G.S. 153A-39.

10. G.S. 153A-40.

11. G.S. 160A-1.

12. Thirty-one municipalities have mayors selected by the council. Only two municipalities use the highest vote-getter to select the mayor: Alliance and Beech Mountain.

in this chapter, when there is a managerial vacancy, the mayor might seem like a natural choice as a stand-in until another manager can be found. However, G.S. 160A-151 expressly makes the mayor (and any member of the council) ineligible to serve as manager, interim manager (temporarily filling a vacancy), or acting manager (serving in the manager's absence). Under this provision, mayors can resign their office and be appointed manager, but they cannot hold the elected and appointed offices at the same time.

Responsibilities of the Governing Board

A county or municipal governing board holds ultimate authority to act for the local government. It decides what services the local government will provide and at what level. It establishes the county's or municipality's fiscal policy by adopting the annual budget ordinance, and it levies the unit's taxes. It adopts the local government ordinances. In addition to exercising these sorts of broad policy-making responsibilities, a governing board typically decides numerous separate administrative matters. Thus, it may authorize the local government to enter into a contract, buy or sell a parcel of property, award the successful bid on a purchase or a construction project, or accept the dedication of a street or utility easement.

In order to accomplish these and other responsibilities, the county or municipal governing board must act as a collective body. The members may act as the governing board only when properly convened, in a legal meeting. An individual member may not act on the board's behalf without specific authorization from the board. Moreover, a majority of the entire membership may act on the board's behalf only at a meeting of the board called and held pursuant to law. Legal procedures governing board meetings and actions are described in more detail in Chapter 9, "Open Meetings and Other Legal Requirements for Local Government Boards."

County Board of Commissioners

Statutory Duties

Regardless of the form of government, state law gives a county's board of commissioners broad authority to organize county government.[13] The board of commissioners may create, change, abolish, and consolidate offices, positions, departments, boards, commissions, and agencies of the county government; impose ex officio the duties of more than one office on a single officer; change the composition and manner of selection of boards, commissions, and agencies; and generally organize and reorganize county government in order to promote orderly and efficient administration of county affairs, subject to the following limitations:

1. The board of county commissioners may not abolish an office, position, department, board, commission, or agency established or required by law.
2. The board may not combine offices or confer certain duties on the same officer when law specifically forbids this action.
3. The board may not discontinue or assign elsewhere a function or duty assigned by law to a particular office, position, department, board, commission, or agency.
4. The board may not change the composition or manner of selection of local boards of education, boards of health, boards of social services, boards of elections, or boards of alcoholic beverage control. By law (G.S. 153A-77), these boards appoint their agency

13. County boards of commissioners' powers are described in G.S. 153A-76.

directors. A board of commissioners may create a consolidated health and human services board and appoint a director.

This seemingly broad grant of responsibility nonetheless leaves many county functions outside the commissioners' direct control. For example:

- The sheriff[14] and the register of deeds[15] are separately elected constitutional officers.
- On boards of education, members are separately elected and appoint the superintendent.[16]
- The state board of elections appoints the local board and the local board's director.[17]
- In most counties, the directors of health and social services are appointed by their respective boards. County commissioners are authorized by law to appoint the director of a consolidated health and human services agency.[18]

These exceptions notwithstanding, the commissioners still have fairly broad authority to organize the administrative apparatus of county government to carry out the board's policies, including the option of appointing a county manager to oversee the administration of county services. This option is discussed further below.

Organizational Meeting

New boards of commissioners usually take their oaths of office, and the board as a whole selects its chair, at the board's first regular meeting in December, in odd-numbered years, or on the first Monday in December, in even-numbered years.[19] In three counties, the chair is a separate office elected by the people; in a fourth county, the highest vote getter among the commissioners is automatically designated chair.[20] In all counties in North Carolina, the board itself must choose a vice-chair at its organizational meeting to act in the absence or disability of the chair.[21]

Appointment of County Officers, Boards, and Commissions

The law dictates many features of county government organization. For example, the people elect each county's sheriff and register of deeds. Each county has at least one board of education (and such boards are separate from county government) and a board of elections. A board of health, a social services board (or a consolidated human services agency board), and a mental health, developmental disabilities, and substance abuse board serves every county. Many counties have a community

---

14. N.C. Const. art. VII, § 2.

15. *See* G.S. 161-1.

16. *See* G.S. 115C-271.

17. G.S. 163-30.

18. See G.S. 153A-77, which authorizes boards of commissioners to create consolidated human services agencies that may include public health, social services, or both. A consolidated human services agency is governed by a consolidated human services director, who is appointed by the county manager with the advice and consent of a consolidated human services board. If the consolidated agency includes public health or social services, the consolidated director acquires the powers and duties ordinarily exercised by the directors of those individual agencies. G.S. 153A-77 also authorizes boards of commissioners to directly assume the powers and duties of certain boards, potentially including the local board of health, social services board, or consolidated human services board. A board of commissioners that exercises this authority may thus acquire the power to appoint the directors of health or social services or to give advice and consent to the appointment of a consolidated human services director. For more information, see Chapter 37, "Public Health," and Chapter 38, "Social Services."

19. G.S. 153A-39.

20. Voters in three counties—Buncombe, Jackson, and Swain—elect the chair of the board directly. See www.ncacc.org/research-and-publications/research/county-elections/ for more information about county election methods.

21. G.S. 153A-39.

college board and a board of alcoholic beverage control, both separate from county government. The board of county commissioners participates in choosing at least some of the members of all of these boards, except for the board(s) of education (whose members are wholly elected by voters) and the board of elections (whose members are appointed by the state board of elections). Because these excepted boards are established pursuant to the requirements of state law, a board of county commissioners has little or no power to alter their structure or authority, although the county board may exercise control over the budgets of some of them. (The roles of most of these other boards are discussed in later chapters.) A board of county commissioners has authority to organize other local boards, agencies, departments, and offices not mandated by state law in any way it sees fit.

Three principal officials are appointed by and serve the board of county commissioners: the county manager, the county attorney, and the clerk to the board. This power is retained whether the governing board is operating as a board of commissioners or under the county–manager plan. The process for adopting the county–manager plan is described below. (Chapter 4 outlines county- and city-manager statutory powers, duties, and professional responsibilities. The powers and duties of the county attorney and the clerk to the board are discussed in Chapter 14.) Each of these appointed officials serves at the pleasure of the board. The county commissioners also appoint the tax assessor,[22] and county boards (in addition to municipal governing boards) are authorized to appoint a tax collector.[23] In practice, many municipalities contract with the county for tax collection. Each county (and municipality) in North Carolina is required by law to have a finance officer.[24] In many counties (and municipalities), the manager appoints the finance officer.[25] In counties (and municipalities) without a manager, the governing board usually makes the appointment; the finance officer serves at the pleasure of the appointing authority. See Chapter 22, "Accounting, Fiscal Control, and Cash Management."

City, Town, or Village Council

Statutory Duties

Regardless of the form of government, G.S. 160A-67 states that "except as otherwise provided by law, the government and general management of the city shall be vested in the council." The council has authority to confer powers and duties on both the mayor and the manager in addition to the duties conferred on each official by law. Further, under G.S. 160A-146, the council has authority to organize and reorganize city government. The council can, except when expressly prevented by other laws, "create, change, abolish, and consolidate offices, positions, departments, boards, commissions, and agencies . . . to promote orderly and efficient administration of city affairs." Finally, G.S. 160A-147 provides that in a council–manager municipality (discussed more below), the council as a body appoints the city manager to serve at its pleasure. Thus, by statute, the council has the primary responsibility for establishing the general framework under which the government can meet the needs of the community and, as the employer of the manager, the council is the body to which the manager is directly responsible and accountable.

Organizational Meeting

A new council usually takes office at its first regular meeting in December after the results of the municipal elections have been certified. At this time, the members take the oath of office and

22. G.S. 105-294.
23. G.S. 105-349.
24. G.S. 159-24.
25. G.S. 153A-82 (counties); 160A-148 (municipalities).

organize the government so that business may be conducted.[26] The council may appoint a mayor, if the mayor is not popularly elected, and must appoint a mayor pro tempore to preside over it and to fulfill the mayor's other duties when the mayor is absent or incapacitated.[27]

Appointment of Municipal Officers, Employees, Boards, and Commissions

Generally

The municipal charter and state statutes spell out governing board appointments for the manager, the attorney, and the clerk. In some cases, the charter may also provide for the appointment of a deputy clerk. In council–manager municipalities, the manager appoints all other officers and employees, unless the charter contains exceptions. In a number of municipalities with managers, the board appoints the tax collector and the finance officer and, depending upon the municipal charter, the manager or the council appoints the clerk. In a municipality without a manager, the council appoints all department heads and normally delegates to them the appointment and the supervision of other employees, although in a few mayor–council municipalities, the board delegates employee appointment and supervision to an administrator. For more on the options for appointing clerks, see Chapter 14, covering attorneys and clerks. The council and the mayor are also responsible for appointments to the various boards and commissions of municipal government, such as the planning commission, boards of adjustment, the parks and recreation commission, and the civil service board. In most cases the council makes the appointments; the mayor, however, is by statute the appointing official for the housing authority. The number of board or commission members and their terms of office are established by general law authorizing such boards or by ordinance implementing the authority granted by statute. In addition, the council is authorized to create special resident advisory committees, such as a human relations committee, and to appoint their members.

Officers and Employees

A municipality's charter ordinarily states that certain officers and employees will be appointed by the council and specifies their duties. The General Statutes (relevant sections are indicated in parentheses in the discussion below) require that the following officers be appointed and have, in addition to any other duties specified by the council, the general duties described below.

City clerk. The clerk is responsible for giving the proper notices of regular and special meetings of the council, keeping an accurate journal of the council's proceedings, and acting as custodian of city records.[28] A *deputy clerk* may be appointed to perform whatever duties of the clerk the council specifies.[29]

Budget officer. The budget officer receives budget requests and revenue estimates from the various departments, prepares a proposed budget for submission to the council, and complies with other requirements concerning budget preparation and administration prescribed by the General Statutes. Unlike municipalities with a council–manager form of government—where the manager is the budget officer—municipalities with the mayor–council plan may designate any municipal officer or employee (including the mayor) as budget officer.[30]

Finance officer. The finance officer may also be called the *accountant, treasurer,* or *finance director.* The finance officer has general responsibility for keeping the accounts and disbursing the city's

---

26. G.S. 160A-68.
27. G.S. 160A-70.
28. G.S. 160A-171.
29. G.S. 160A-172.
30. G.S. 159-9.

funds in a manner consistent with General Statute provisions pertaining to the finance officer's duties. These duties may be conferred on the budget officer or on another officer or employee who is eligible to perform the duties of budget officer.[31]

City attorney. The council must appoint a city attorney to be its legal advisor. The attorney serves at the council's pleasure and may be in-house or hired through a contract.[32]

Tax collector. The tax collector has the general responsibility for collecting property taxes, privilege license taxes, and all other taxes due the municipality and for fulfilling the other duties imposed by the General Statutes concerning tax collection.[33] Any officer or employee may be appointed tax collector, except a member of the governing body; the finance officer may be appointed to the office only with the Local Government Commission's consent.[34] Many municipalities, both large and small, contract with the county to collect their taxes.

Department Heads and Employees

Under the mayor–council form of government, the council is responsible for (1) establishing the municipal operating departments deemed necessary or desirable (see next paragraph for examples) and (2) appointing, suspending, and removing department heads and all other municipal employees. The council may delegate to an administrative officer or a department head the authority to appoint, suspend, or remove employees assigned to that department.[35] In mayor–council municipalities with populations of less than 5,000, the mayor and the members of the council may serve as department heads or as other municipal employees and may receive reasonable compensation. In mayor–council municipalities with populations of 5,000 or more, and in council–manager municipalities, they may not do so.[36]

Typical municipal departments are police, fire, public works, recreation, planning, and inspections. Municipalities may choose to consolidate multiple functions within a single department, such as streets, utilities, and solid waste being handled by the department of public works. The council may also choose to appoint one person to supervise several departments or to fill duties in more than one department.[37] For example, a public works director may be appointed to supervise both the streets and sanitation departments, or the fire chief may also be assigned the duties of building inspector.

Vacancies on Governing Boards

When there is a vacancy on a board of county commissioners or municipal council (including a vacancy in the office of mayor), state law gives the remaining members of the board or council the authority to fill the vacancy.[38] The statute pertaining to municipalities leaves the process fairly open to the council's discretion for the majority of municipalities that elect members on a nonpartisan basis. The statute for counties creates a role for political parties in recommending or choosing replacements, as described in more detail below.

---

31. G.S. 159-24 to -25.
32. G.S. 160A-173.
33. G.S. 105-349 to -350.
34. G.S. 105-349.
35. G.S. 160A-155.
36. G.S. 160A-158.
37. G.S. 160A-146.
38. G.S. 160A-63 (cities); 153A-27, -27.1 (counties). G.S. 160A-63 authorizes the council to fill a vacancy in any elective office of the municipality.

In both counties and municipalities, if the vacancy occurs in an office carrying a two-year term or in the last two years of an office with a four-year term, the appointment is for the remainder of the unexpired term. If the vacancy takes place in the first two years of an office with a four-year term, the appointment runs only until the next general election, at which the office is filled for the unexpired term.[39] In addition, the statutes for both municipalities and counties set out contingency procedures for situations when the number of vacancies is such that a quorum is not possible.[40]

There are no public records exceptions or open meetings exceptions for the consideration of nominees or applicants for council or board vacancies. Indeed, the open meetings law specifically prohibits the consideration or evaluation of members or potential members of the governing board from being discussed in closed sessions of that board.[41]

Counties

People who are appointed to fill a vacancy on a board of county commissioners must belong to the same political party as the commissioner being replaced if the person being replaced was elected as the nominee of a political party. If the county is divided into electoral districts, the appointee must also reside in the same district as the person being replaced. Per North Carolina statutes, in most counties, "the board of commissioners or the clerk of superior court, as the case may be, shall consult the county executive committee of the appropriate political party before filling a vacancy, but neither the board nor the clerk of the superior court is bound by the committee's recommendation."[42] In many counties, the board is not required to follow any advice given by the executive committee. However, nearly half of the state's counties are governed by a modified version of this procedure, under which the board *must* appoint the executive committee's nominee if the recommendation is made within thirty days after the seat becomes vacant.[43]

Occasionally, a majority of a board of county commissioners is unable to agree on which person to appoint to fill a vacancy. Since nearly all of these boards have an odd number of members, one vacancy means that the remaining members could become equally divided over two candidates so that neither candidate could receive a majority vote. If the board fails to fill a vacancy in its membership within sixty days (due to a tie vote or any other reason), the clerk to the board must report it to the clerk of superior court, who must fill the vacancy within ten days after receiving the report.

Municipalities

In municipalities that hold nonpartisan elections, the council may appoint any person who is eligible to vote in city elections to fill a council vacancy. In municipalities in which councils are elected on

---

39. If the vacancy occurs at the very end of the first two years of an office with a four-year term, so that there is no time to file for the midterm election, the council fills the vacancy for the remainder of the unexpired term. In county government, this period is the sixty days before the general election, while in municipal government, it is the ninety days before the municipal election.

40. *See* G.S. 153A-27, -27.1 (for counties, the chair must appoint enough members to make a quorum, and the board then fills the remaining vacancies; if the office of chair is also vacant, the clerk of superior court may act in the chair's stead on petition of any remaining member of the board or any five registered voters of the county); 160A-63 (for municipalities, the mayor must appoint enough members to make a quorum, and the council then fills the remaining vacancies; if there are not enough members for a quorum and the mayor's office is vacant, the governor may fill the vacancy upon request of any remaining council member or by petition of any five registered voters of the municipality).

41. *See* G.S. 143-318.11(a)(6).

42. G.S. 153A-27(c).

43. See G.S. 153A-27.1, which lists the affected counties.

a partisan basis, a person appointed to fill a vacancy must belong to the same political party as the last person to fill the position, if that person was elected as the nominee of a political party.

In some municipalities, it is common to fill a council vacancy with the unsuccessful candidate in the most recent municipal election with the most votes, but there is no general statutory requirement to follow this practice. Unlike the statute covering counties, the statute for municipalities does not provide for an alternative method of filling the vacancy if the council becomes deadlocked or for any other reason does not fill a vacancy.[44] For municipalities, there is no statutory requirement that a vacancy be filled within a particular time. A council has an obligation, nonetheless, to act in good faith to attempt to fill a vacancy within a reasonable period of time. In a representative government, the people deserve to have a full complement of lawmakers to represent them.

Organizing the Supervision of Officers and Employees in Mayor–Council Municipalities

In organizing, directing, and supervising the various functions or departments of municipal government, the council may use one of several administrative or organizational plans, unless the charter provides otherwise. Whatever type of administrative plan is used, it is important for the council to clearly define the responsibilities of each officer or department; to coordinate, as far as possible, the activities of each; to establish clear lines of authority between the council, the department heads, and employees; and in general, to establish a sound administrative plan that will enable the council to adequately supervise all municipal activities.

Three basic administrative plans are used in municipalities under the mayor–council form of government: (1) the entire council directly supervises all departments of local government, (2) one council member is assigned to supervise each department, and (3) committees of the council supervise one or more functions or departments. The specifics of each plan are discussed below.

1. Direct Supervision of All Departments by the Council as a Whole

Under this organizational plan, the council appoints and removes all department heads and directs and supervises them in carrying out their duties. Each department head or officer reports directly to the council and is responsible to it for the operation of the department. This plan is widely used but can be cumbersome if the particular municipality has many departments. It is probably best suited to small municipalities with not more than three or four departments or functions that require the council's direct supervision.

2. Assignment of Council Members to Departments

Under this administrative arrangement, a designated council member has charge of a specific department and may exercise such administrative control over the operation of the department and its head as the council may direct. The department head or officer is directly responsible to the selected council member rather than to the entire council, although personnel decisions for the department, such as hiring and termination, remain the responsibility of the entire council. The supervising member reports to and recommends measures to the entire council regarding the department's affairs. This system expedites the administration of departmental affairs, but council

44. Depending upon the method used to submit nominees for consideration, the mayor may or may not be able to break a tie. The mayor has authority under G.S. 160A-69 to vote in the case of an equal number of yes and no votes. If a motion is made to nominate a particular person, and the votes are equally divided for and against, the mayor can break the tie as provided in the statute. If, however, multiple names are submitted for consideration and votes are taken using a ballot method, it's possible for two individual candidates to receive equal numbers of votes. Because of the wording of the statute, the mayor cannot break this type of tie vote.

Table 3.2 Alternative Organizational Plans for a City Council with a Mayor and Five Council Members

Three-Committee System

	Finance[a]	Public Safety[b]	Public Works[c]
Plan 1[a]	Mayor Member 2 Member 3	Member 2 Member 3 Member 4	Member 1 Member 4 Member 5
Plan 2	Member 1 Member 2 Member 3	Member 3 Member 4 Member 5	Member 4 Member 5 Member 2
Plan 3	Member 1 Member 2	Member 3 Member 4	Member 4 Member 5

Two-Committee System

	Finance[a] and Public Safety[b]	Public Works[c]
Plan 4	Mayor Member 2 Member 3	Member 1 Member 4 Member 5

Note: Plans 1 and 4 require the mayor to serve on the finance committee; this is often advantageous. Also, Plan 1 requires only three members to serve on two committees. Plan 2 requires four members to serve on two committees. Plan 3 requires that each member serve on only one committee; this is desirable, but a committee composed of only two members is often unworkable.

a. *Finance* refers to budgets, taxation, recreation, and libraries.

b. *Public safety* refers to police, fire, and health and sanitation.

c. *Public works* refers to streets, transportation, water and sewer, electric light and power, stormwater drainage, and solid waste.

members may become more concerned with their respective departments than with the total operation and administration of all departments, which is the council's principal responsibility.

3. Committee System

The council in this organizational approach creates committees of the council to study and make recommendations concerning the operation of the respective municipal departments; in some places these committees are given the authority to supervise departmental operations. When this system is used, the committees are normally assigned general areas of responsibility that may include several departments. For example, supervision of police, fire, and inspection services might be assigned to a public safety committee that is composed of several council members. Governing bodies should be aware that committees of the council are themselves considered public bodies under the open-meetings law and thus must comply with that statute's requirements.

The number of committees and their membership will vary depending on the council's size, the number of departments, and other factors. If the municipal charter is silent regarding requirements for committees, the council itself may establish committees and assign them such duties, consistent with the charter and general laws of the state, as it deems best. Suggested committee structures for a council consisting of a mayor and five council members appear in Table 3.2.

Expectations for County and Municipal Governing Boards

County and municipal governing boards must operate transparently, in a public setting, and are entrusted to carry out their work legally and ethically. Local governing boards have a direct influence on the culture, effectiveness, and efficiency of county and municipal governments and function best when they adopt common expectations for their work, examples of which are provided below.

1. The governing board sets direction by
   - clarifying the local government's mission and purposes and setting goals for the short and long term,
   - adopting policies to accomplish these purposes,
   - employing professional public managers and administrators as needed for administrative functions and service operations,
   - engaging regularly in strategy development (e.g., during an annual retreat), and
   - routinely monitoring and evaluating local government's ability to administer and provide efficient and effective public services.
2. Members of the governing board act as a body by
   - focusing their discussion with clear and consistent rules of procedure, following a planned agenda, and spending time on important topics;
   - understanding their own legal and ethical responsibilities, as well as those of the local government;
   - making sure they all have the same information with which to make decisions;
   - working to master small-group decision-making techniques;
   - respecting one another;
   - abiding by the decisions of the board's majority; and
   - making clear to the public that decision-making power rests with the majority, not with individual board members.
3. The governing board serves the public well by
   - enhancing the local government's public image,
   - providing members of the public opportunities to respectfully comment on public issues,
   - ensuring the success and viability of the community by convening and facilitating public engagement, and
   - making sure that resources are adequate to serve the public and are used for their intended purposes.
4. The board takes responsibility for its members' behaviors by
   - abstaining from seeking political support from staff,
   - submitting questions about board agenda items ahead of the meeting,
   - providing each member an opportunity to influence and respectfully dissent in board meetings,
   - focusing on issues instead of personalities,
   - having members themselves address inappropriate behavior in their ranks rather than delegating this responsibility to the staff, and
   - working as a team to jointly develop and hold itself accountable to a common code of conduct.
5. The board freely gives and seeks feedback by
   - supporting the manager or administrator by providing clear direction and annually reviewing the manager's performance,
   - annually setting expectations for itself and assessing its own performance,
   - inviting constructive feedback to improve its own performance, and
   - regularly reviewing and monitoring the local government's finances, programs, and services.
6. The board works with the manager or administrator to function as a high-performing governing body by
   - looking to the manager or administrator for assistance in
     - clearly defining roles and relationships,
     - thinking to the future and acting strategically on key issues,
     - operating in a culture of values and ethics,
     - regularly evaluating policy implementation,
     - developing and following protocols for board behavior and board–staff relations,
     - allocating time and energy appropriately,

Sidebar continues →

Expectations for County and Municipal Governing Boards, ***continued***

- setting clear rules and procedures for meetings,
- getting regular assessments of public concerns and its own performance,
- recognizing its position in intergovernmental systems and in building productive partnerships, and
- focusing on personal learning and developing as leaders;

- having the board chair and manager or administrator orient new members to the governing board, providing expectations about how to be successful; and
- working with the manager or administrator to promote behavior that encourages public confidence in local government.

Boards with a manager can benefit from establishing two additional expectations:

7. The governing board respects the role of the manager by
   - channeling communications appropriately to the manager or other responsible person;
   - depending upon employees to respond to public concerns and complaints as fully and as expeditiously as practical;
   - expecting staff to make independent and objective recommendations;
   - expecting the manager, administrator, and staff to support and advocate for adopted board policies;
   - respecting the professionals who work in local government and following appropriate protocols for interacting with staff; and
   - refraining from publicly criticizing an individual employee (where criticism is differentiated from questioning the facts or opinions of staff).
8. Board members give the manager a chance to earn their trust by
   - recruiting, selecting, and hiring the manager or administrator;
   - promoting and encouraging a positive relationship between its members and the manager or administrator;
   - treating and respecting the manager or administrator as a professional; and
   - recognizing that the role of a professional manager or administrator is to serve the governing board as a whole.

Professional Management in North Carolina Local Governments

As has been stated, the North Carolina General Statutes give boards of county commissioners and municipal councils the option of operating with or without a professional manager.[45] If the governing board decides to run local government on its own, it is said to use the *board of commissioner* (counties) or the *mayor–council form* (municipalities) of local government. A county or municipality that uses a professional manager is described as operating under the *county–manager* or *council–manager form.* For more information about the role and responsibilities of professional managers, see Chapter 4. All 100 counties in the state have chosen to employ a full-time professional to administer county government. Under this county–manager plan, county commissioners have a choice in whether or not to grant the manager hiring and firing authority. Chairs of county boards of commissioners are able to serve as county managers by action of their respective boards in accordance with G.S. 153A-81. Municipal mayors cannot assume the role of manager under the council–manager form.[46]

Use of an Administrator in Mayor–Council Municipalities

Some municipalities hire a CAO while maintaining the mayor–council form of government.[47] A charter amendment is not required to have such an administrator in charge, although the

45. *See* G.S. 153A-76, -81 (counties); 160A-146, -101 (cities).

46. *See* G.S. 160A-151.

47. For additional information on this topic, see Frayda Bluestein, "About Town Administrators," *Coates' Canons: NC Local Government Law* blog (October 13, 2010), sog.unc.edu/blogs/coates-canons/about-town-administrators.

municipality may wish to adopt an ordinance to create the position and specify its duties. Typically, *administrator* is the term used for this sort of employee, though *manager* is sometimes used, even when a municipality has not changed to the council–manager form of government.

In a council–manager form of government, managers are granted specific powers and responsibilities by statute, including the power to hire and fire. In the mayor–council form with an administrator, the council determines which appointments to delegate to the CAO. When the governing body in a mayor–council municipality is ready to grant the full powers of a manager to its CAO, that may signal the need to change to the council–manager form.

Procedures for Adopting a County–Manager or Council–Manager Plan

As has been noted, counties in North Carolina may operate under different forms of government, including the county–manager form. If a county's board of commissioners does not choose this option, the county operates without a county manager under the authority of G.S. 153A-76 that permits the board to organize county government however it wishes, consistent with the law. Among other things, commissioners are permitted to hire an "administrator," whose duties might not include all of those granted by statute to a county manager but might be prescribed by the commissioners themselves. Unlike councils in small North Carolina municipalities, boards of county commissioners have seldom used this more circumscribed position.

When a governing board transitions to the county–manager or council–manager form of government, the manager's duties are derived from state statutes. Additional information about the legal responsibilities of county and municipal managers appears in Chapter 4.

Adopting the County–Manager Form of Government

When a county's board of commissioners chooses to use the county–manager plan, it proceeds by passing a resolution adopting the plan by authority of G.S. 153A-81. The plan can be carried out in one of three ways:

1. The commissioners may employ a county manager, who holds no other office and who serves at the pleasure of the commissioners. In this alternative, the managers must be appointed solely on the basis of their administrative qualifications.[48]
2. The board of commissioners may confer the duties of county manager upon its chair or some other commissioner, as was done in Jackson County until 2000.[49]
3. The commissioners may confer the duties of county manager upon any other county employee, as Brunswick County commissioners did when they appointed the county attorney to also serve as county manager.[50]

Unlike municipalities, counties are not required to continue to operate with or without the county–manager plan for any minimum period of time after passing a resolution to change from one arrangement to the other.[51]

---

48. *See* G.S. 153A-81(1).

49. See G.S. 153A-81(2), which is consistent with the provisions of G.S. 128-1.1(b), allowing any person holding an elective state or local government office to concurrently hold one other appointive office in either state or local government. This arrangement has been used only in Jackson County, until November 29, 2000, where the board chair was elected while also serving as county manager.

50. *See* G.S. 153A-81(3). This arrangement was used from 1990 until 1993, when the county manager / county attorney left the position, and the commissioners chose not to continue to combine the offices.

51. Under G.S. 160A-107, if a municipality changes its charter to create or eliminate the council–manager plan, it must keep the change in effect for at least two years.

Exercising Caution in Speaking for the Governing Board

Members of local government boards should be careful when talking with the news media, interest groups, and even individuals to make certain that their comments reflect the governing board's views rather than their own personal opinions. Opinions and statements of position expressed by elected board members are frequently taken to be those of the entire body. If a board member misstates the county or municipality's position, assumes a position that has not actually been taken by the full board, or incorrectly predicts a board position or action, the result can be embarrassment, mistrust, and resentment on the part of the listener and other board members, as well as on the part of the public at large.

Members of the public do not always distinguish between the thoughts of an individual board member and those of the body as a whole, nor do they always remember that other members of the board may not share one particular member's opinion. The listener may take what is actually only a personal expression of opinion to be an authoritative pronouncement of official policy. On important or sensitive matters requiring clarity and careful explanation, it may be desirable for the governing board to designate one of its members as spokesperson. In some situations, it may be advisable to have a written statement, agreed on by the whole governing board, that is available for distribution if the need arises.

Adopting the Council–Manager Form of Government

As has been mentioned, the council–manager plan is one form of municipal government operation available by general law and in use in North Carolina. A city's form of government is set forth in its charter. An initial charter is an act of the General Assembly. The Municipal Board of Control, a now-defunct state commission, originally chartered a few municipalities.

The General Assembly can amend a city's charter, but the General Statutes also allow a city to change its form of government by passing a local ordinance that amends the charter.[52] Thus, a city that has the council–manager form of government may adopt the mayor–council form (and vice versa) by following the statutory procedure for amending its charter. This procedure is discussed in more detail below.

Options for Amending a City Charter to Put a Council–Manager Plan in Place

Amendment by Ordinance

A council may alter its governmental form by amending its charter through the passage of an ordinance adopting the council–manager form of government.[53] This is the amendment option most commonly used by municipalities today. To exercise it, a council must adopt a resolution of intent that describes the proposed charter amendment and, at the same time, call a public hearing to be held within forty-five days. The council must publish a notice of this hearing and a summary of the amendment proposal at least ten days before the hearing date. After the hearing, the council may not take action before its next regular meeting, but it may act on the ordinance at that meeting or at any time after that. If the council adopts the ordinance, the council must publish a notice within ten days of such adoption summarizing the substance and effects of its action.

---

52. *See* G.S. 160A-101 to -111.

53. *See* G.S. 160A-102. The School of Government provides a web-based, question-and-answer resource summarizing the options for changing charters by local ordinance and covering related topics. See "Changing Forms of Government," Forms of North Carolina City Government microsite, UNC School of Government, accessed January 16, 2024, www.sog.unc.edu/node/428.

Under this amendment option, a council may simply adopt an ordinance after following the procedure outlined immediately above, without any vote by its citizens on the matter. However, amendment by this method may have to be confirmed by a referendum if enough voters call for it.[54] If a valid referendum petition is filed with the municipal clerk within thirty days after the council publishes notice of its adoption of the ordinance amending the charter, an election must be held on the question between 60 and 120 days following receipt of the petition. To be valid, the petition must include the signatures of 10 percent or 5,000 of the municipality's registered voters, whichever is less. If the election supports the ordinance, the ordinance takes effect; if not, it becomes void.

Amendment by Ordinance Subject to Referendum

A council may on its own initiative make its amendment ordinance subject to a referendum.[55] This might happen because council members, while believing that the council–manager form is in the best interest of the community, may nonetheless want to give the public an opportunity to confirm or deny that judgment. In such cases, the council will follow the same procedures described earlier for the simple passage of an ordinance without a referendum. However, on passage of the ordinance, the council will simultaneously adopt a resolution calling for a referendum election on the issue. The election must be held within ninety days of the ordinance's adoption. If the council takes the initiative to call an election in this manner, then it must publish a notice of the election at least thirty days before voter registration closes; it does not have to publish a separate notice of the ordinance's passage. If a majority of those voting in the election support the ordinance, it is put into effect; if not, it becomes void.

Amendment Following Initiative, Petition, and Referendum

Voters themselves may initiate a referendum to change their municipality's form of government.[56] If a petition that is valid by the same standards described above is initiated by citizens and submitted to the council, the council must call a referendum election on the issue between 60 and 120 days after receiving the petition. The council need not pass any ordinance before this election, but it must publish a notice of the election, including a description of the issue to be voted on, thirty days before voter registration closes. If the election results favor the proposed changes, then the council must pass an ordinance putting them into effect. In this situation, the ordinance is immune to a petition to put it to a vote after the fact, as provided in G.S. 160A-102.

Amendment by Special Act

A council may ask the General Assembly to enact a bill amending its municipality's charter. The special act may or may not require a referendum. This method is seldom used today because of the ease with which a municipality can decide the matter under the general law just described.

Amendments to Municipal Charters Must Remain in Effect for a Minimum of Two Years

A municipality that changes its charter by any one of the first three general-law provisions discussed above must, under G.S. 160A-107, keep such changes in effect for at least two years after they are adopted. The purpose of this provision is to give the new arrangement an opportunity to get through the transition period and prove itself. In the case of a municipality changing to the council–manager form, this mandate gives the council, the mayor, and the manager a chance to

---

54. *See* G.S. 160A-103.
55. *See* G.S. 160A-102.
56. *See* G.S. 160A-104.

develop and test new ways of doing things, clarify roles and responsibilities, and determine how to make their arrangement work well for everyone involved.

The transition to a council–manager plan is seldom easy. Old habits are difficult to break, and the powers and duties assigned to the manager by statute are ones that the council or staff members may have been exercising for a long time, making them difficult to relinquish under the new arrangement. Adjustment to and acceptance of the roles that various elected and appointed officials will play under the new form of government is usually a more complex and difficult undertaking than was the process of effecting the change in the charter.

A Note about Municipal Charters

Given that North Carolina charters can be amended through action of the council or General Assembly, a number of municipalities in the state have provisions in their charters that differ from what is typically found. It is important that elected officials and people who work in local government have a thorough understanding of their charters and how they may depart from the norm.

Advantages and Disadvantages of the Board-of-Commissioner and Mayor–Council Forms of Government

There is an argument for using a nonmanager style of government in North Carolina, either a board of commissioners or a mayor and council. Particularly in small communities, there is appeal to the idea that those who are elected are also directly responsible for running the local government. However, it is important to note that there is no evidence to support the idea that there is greater accountability provided through the electoral process versus council/commission oversight over the manager and general administrative activities of local government.

There are two established weaknesses inherent in the board-of-commissioner and mayor–council plans as they are used in North Carolina. The first is the absence of any real concentration of executive authority and responsibility, as decision-making ultimately rests with the board of commissioners or municipal council as a group. Responsibility for operating the local government is divided among and shared by all members of the governing board, making it administration by committee. If board members have an affinity for a particular service area or policy, they may be unwilling to compromise. Strong, consistent direction depends on maintaining general agreement, which may be difficult at times.

The second weakness in the board-of-commissioner and mayor–council forms of government is the fact that good politicians are not necessarily good administrators. Those who are elected may be popular with the voters but may be amateurs when it comes to running a county or municipality. A local government organization is considerably different from an organization in the private sector or even other levels of government. For example, local governments use fund accounting and are subject to strict government regulations. Even if inept administration by a given board or council later brings rejection at the polls, the result is usually a new set of popular but inexperienced elected administrators because qualifying for local elected office requires no training or expertise in local government management.

The continued use of the mayor–council form of government in many of North Carolina's smaller jurisdictions belies these weaknesses and indicates that it can and does work where conscientious elected officials work together for the welfare of the municipality. Generally, the smaller the community, the lower level of services offered and the fewer staff to supervise, making the presence of a professional administrator less imperative. As a practical matter, many small communities cannot afford to employ an experienced professional manager. The mayor–council form of government is best suited for and most often used by small towns, where municipal functions are fewer and less complex and can be provided by an elected council and relatively few employees.

Procedures for Changing the Governing Board's Structure

County Board

A county governing board's structure (number of board members, terms, election method) may be changed through one of two methods. First, the General Assembly may enact a local act that is applicable to the county. Second, the governing board itself may propose a change of structure by ordinance, subject to approval by the county's voters. Change by the latter method is limited to specific options set out in the applicable statutory provisions, G.S. 153A-58 to -64; as a practical matter, however, this second restructuring method is almost never used.

Municipal Board

A municipality's governing board structure may be changed through one of four methods. First, as with a board of county commissioners, the General Assembly may change the structure of a council by amending the charter, which amounts to a local act of the legislature. Although the General Assembly retains full legal control of the change process, as a practical matter any such amendment would normally be enacted only at the request of the affected board.[57] Second, the governing board itself may change its structure simply by adopting an ordinance as authorized in Part 4 of G.S. Chapter 160A. Such an ordinance is adopted following a public hearing on the proposed change. Third, the governing board may adopt an ordinance on a change of structure, but the municipality's voters may condition the ordinance's effectiveness upon approval. For example, the governing board itself might decide to require voter approval for the change to be effective, or voters might force a referendum on a board ordinance by submitting petitions with a sufficient number of signatures (e.g., 10 percent of the city's registered voters or 5,000 such voters, whichever is less). Last, voters may initiate such a change in structure by submitting petitions that both propose the change and call for a referendum on the proposal. This method also requires the signatures of 10 percent of the city's registered voters or 5,000 registered voters, whichever is less. Each of the methods that may be carried out locally is limited to specific options set out in the applicable statute's subsections, G.S. 160A-101(1)–(9).[58]

57. It is important to note that there has recently been an increasing number of local bills generated in the General Assembly without the knowledge or support of the local governments affected.

58. Additional information on how to change a municipality's charter and the change options can be found at Frayda S. Bluestein and Robert P. Joyce, "Modifying a City's Charter—Summary with Questions and Answers," Forms of North Carolina City Government microsite, UNC School of Government, accessed January 16, 2024, www.sog.unc.edu/resources/faq-collections/modifying-citys-charter-summary-questions-and-answers.

Additional Resources

Adrian, Charles R., and Ernest S. Griffith. *A History of American City Government: The Formation of Traditions, 1775–1870.* New York: Praeger Publishers, for the National Municipal League, 1976.

Allen, Trey. *Suggested Rules of Procedure for the Board of County Commissioners.* 4th ed. Chapel Hill: UNC School of Government, 2017.

———. *Suggested Rules of Procedure for a City Council.* 4th ed. Chapel Hill: UNC School of Government, 2017.

Allen, Trey and A. Fleming Bell III. *Suggested Procedural Rules for Local Appointed Boards.* Chapel Hill: UNC School of Government, 2020.

Griffith, Ernest S. *A History of American City Government: The Progressive Years and Their Aftermath, 1900–1920.* New York: Praeger Publishers, for the National Municipal League, 1974.

Teaford, Jon C. *The Unheralded Triumph: City Government in America, 1870–1900.* Baltimore: Johns Hopkins University Press, 1984.

Appendix 3.1A Summary Figures on the Structures, Forms of Governing Boards of North Carolina Municipalities

	MUNICIPALITY SIZE (Number in Size Class)							
	Under 500 (126)	500–1,000 (93)	1,000–2,500 (111)	2,500–5,000 (90)	5,000–10,000 (50)	10,000–25,000 (48)	Over 25,000 (34)	Total (552)
STYLE OF CORPORATION								
City	0	3	0	7	14	22	24	70
Town	118	86	110	80	34	24	10	462
Village	8	4	1	3	2	2	0	20
STYLE OF GOVERNING BOARD								
Aldermen	14	13	19	9	5	4	3	67
Commissioners	70	54	65	37	12	7	4	249
Council Members	42	26	27	44	33	37	27	236
FORM OF GOVERNMENT								
Council–Manager	9	7	58	65	43	48	34	264
Mayor–Council	117	86	53	25	7	0	0	288
SELECTION OF MAYOR								
By and from Governing Board	9	9	5	5	2	0	1	31
Council Member with the Most Votes	1	1	0	0	0	0	0	2
Elected	116	83	106	85	48	48	33	519
MAYOR'S TERM								
2 Years	82	50	52	42	22	20	16	284
4 Years	39	38	57	47	27	28	18	254
At Pleasure of Board	5	5	2	1	1	0	0	14
NUMBER OF MEMBERS OF GOVERNING BOARD								
11 Members	0	0	0	0	0	0	1	1
9 Members	0	0	0	0	0	0	1	1
8 Members	0	0	0	0	1	6	4	11
7 Members	0	1	0	1	2	6	7	17
6 Members	1	3	9	16	6	10	14	59
5 Members	69	69	73	55	27	18	6	317
4 Members	27	16	27	17	14	8	1	110
3 Members	27	4	2	1	0	0	0	34
2 Members	2	0	0	0	0	0	0	2
TERM OF OFFICE OF GOVERNING BOARD								
2 Years	66	24	22	14	3	10	9	148
4 Years	16	7	7	1	4	0	7	42
4S (4 Years, Staggered)	41	60	82	72	42	36	18	351
4S/2 Years	3	2	0	3	1	2	0	11

Source: Compiled using data from "Forms of Government and Methods of Election in North Carolina Cities" (School of Government web page), sog.unc.edu/forms-of-government-summary.

Appendix 3.1B Summary Figures on the Mode and Type of Election of Governing Boards of North Carolina Cities

	POPULATION (Total Number of Cities)							
	Under 500 (126)	500–1,000 (93)	1,000–2,500 (111)	2,500–5,000 (90)	5,000–10,000 (50)	10,000–25,000 (48)	Over 25,000 (34)	Total (552)
MODE OF ELECTION OF GOVERNING BOARD								
AL	126	92	100	77	38	28	14	475
D	0	0	3	2	2	4	6	17
DAL	0	0	5	6	5	5	2	23
CDA	0	0	2	3	4	8	10	27
CDAL	0	1	1	2	1	3	2	10
TYPE OF ELECTION								
Majority	0	3	1	1	2	3	5	15
Partisan	0	0	0	0	0	2	3	5
Plurality	125	89	108	85	46	38	16	507
Primary	1	1	2	4	2	5	10	25

AL = Elected at large
D = Elected by and from districts
DAL = Elected at large but with requirement of district residence
CDA = Combination of at-large and district members
CDAL = Combination of at-large members and members elected at large by representing districts
Note: Majority, Plurality, and Primary types of elections are nonpartisan.

Chapter 4

County and City Managers

Carl W. Stenberg

Carl W. Stenberg is a School of Government faculty member whose work has included directing the Public Executive Leadership Academy, serving as liaison with the North Carolina City and County Management Association, serving as lead faculty for the Essentials of Municipal Government program, and teaching in and directing the Master of Public Administration Program.

This chapter updates and revises previous chapters authored by former School of Government faculty members Kurt Jenne and Donald Hayman, whose contributions to the field and to this publication are gratefully acknowledged. The author also expresses appreciation to David Leonetti and Ebony Perkins for research assistance on the previous version of this chapter.

In North Carolina, local governments may operate under different forms of government: (1) a county manager or council–manager form; (2) a mayor–council or county commissioner form; or (3) an alternative form that complies with state law. While a county may choose to adopt the county manager model, if the county board of commissioners takes no action in this respect, it then operates without a county manager under the authority of Section 153A-76 of the North Carolina General Statutes (hereinafter G.S.), which permits the board to organize county government however it wishes, consistent with the law. Similar provisions (G.S. 160A-101(9), -146) govern cities in their selection of an organizational form. Under the mayor–council form of government (discussed in detail in Chapter 3, "County and Municipal Governing Boards"), the governing board is not required to employ a professional manager, but it may do so. Any county or city that has not adopted the council–manager/county manager form may hire an "administrator," whose duties might not include all of those granted by statute to the manager but may be prescribed by the governing body.

This chapter focuses on local governments that have adopted the county manager or council–manager forms of government. As used in this chapter, the term *council–manager* includes both forms.

Council–Manager Form of Government under North Carolina Law

North Carolina's laws authorizing the council–manager form of government, like those of most states, drew on the provisions contained in the National Municipal League's (now the National Civic League) *Model City Charter.* The key provisions of the General Statutes relating to county and city managers are discussed in more detail below.

The County Manager

The powers and duties of the county manager specified in G.S. 153A-82 are typical of those found in most state statutes and are consistent with the general elements of the council–manager plan in North Carolina. The introduction and first subsection of the law read as follows:

> **§ 153A-82. Powers and duties of manager.**
>
> (a) The manager is the chief administrator of county government. The manager is responsible to the board of commissioners for the administration of all departments of county government under the board's general control and has the following powers and duties:
>
> (1) He [or she] shall appoint with the approval of the board of commissioners and suspend or remove all county officers, employees, and agents except those who are elected by the people or whose appointment is otherwise provided for by law. The board may by resolution permit the manager to appoint officers, employees, and agents without first securing the board's approval. The manager shall make his [or her] appointments, suspensions, and removals in accordance with any general personnel rules, regulations, policies, or ordinances that the board may adopt. . . .

Hiring, Firing, and Disciplinary Powers

County managers preside over an administrative apparatus that includes officers who are elected by the people or appointed by authorities other than the commissioners as well as board-appointed individuals such as the county clerk, the county attorney, the tax assessor, and the tax collector. Unlike the city manager in North Carolina, however, the county manager does not have automatic statutory authority to hire, fire, and discipline employees who are not appointed by the governing board. The county manager may perform these actions only with the approval of the board of county commissioners, unless the commissioners take affirmative action to grant the county manager the power to do so without their approval.

Administrative Authority

Under G.S. 153A-82(a)(2), the county manager

> ... shall direct and supervise the administration of all county offices, departments, boards, commissions and agencies under the general control of the board of commissioners, subject to the general direction and control of the board.

This provision makes the county manager responsible for supervision of county operations in accordance with laws, regulations, policies, direction, and guidance decided upon by the board of commissioners. The commissioners' control is meant to be general in nature, leaving the manager to exercise professional judgment as to how to carry out the board's intent. This can be a difficult line to draw, and practice varies from county to county, depending on a variety of factors, such as tradition, confidence in the manager, individual personalities and styles, and the issues involved. To be successful, North Carolina county managers have to be facilitative rather than directive in their management styles and more tolerant of ambiguity in their authority than their counterparts in North Carolina cities.

Duties Related to Governing Body Meetings

Under G.S. 153A-82(a)(3), the county manager (or his or her designee)

> ... shall attend all meetings of the board of commissioners and recommend any measures that he [or she] considers expedient.

This provision acknowledges that one of the manager's fundamental responsibilities is to give professional advice, recommendations, and counsel to the commissioners in their deliberations and to ensure that the board has access to and understands the information it needs to make informed choices in the matters coming before it. The expectation is that the commissioners will be able to access the advice of the manager or the manager's designee any time they gather. Most managers will not miss a meeting if they can help it and will be careful to secure the concurrence of the chair or the entire board if they must be absent. They will also make sure that an assistant or other designee chosen to act in their place is fully able and prepared to give the board the support it needs.

Oversight Regarding Proper Execution of Orders, Ordinances, etc.

The fourth subsection of G.S. 153A-82 mandates that the manager

> ... shall see that the orders, ordinances, resolutions, and regulations of the board of commissioners are faithfully executed within the county.

This general supervisory role of the manager is self-explanatory.

Financial Duties

The manager's financial duties are addressed in G.S. 153A-82(a)(5) and (6):

> (5) He [or she] shall prepare and submit the annual budget and capital program to the board of commissioners.

(6) He [or she] shall annually submit to the board of commissioners and make available to the public a complete report on the finances and administrative activities of the county as of the end of the fiscal year.

In a county that adopts the county manager form of government, the manager is also the budget officer (G.S. 159-9) and is required by G.S. 159-11 to prepare a budget for consideration by the commissioners in whatever form and detail the board might specify. This is a *recommended* budget and capital program; the commissioners may modify these items as they wish before adopting the budget ordinance (see Chapter 20, "Budgeting for Operating and Capital Expenditures"). Further, in addition to the statutorily required annual report (see G.S. 153A-82(a)(6), above), the manager commonly makes periodic financial and administrative reports to the commissioners throughout the fiscal year.

Reports and Miscellaneous Duties

The county manager must, under G.S. 153A-82(a)(7),

> . . . make any other reports that the board of commissioners may require concerning the operations of county offices, departments, boards, commissions, and agencies.

The eighth subsection of G.S. 153A-82 is a "catch-all," requiring that the manager

> . . . perform any other duties that may be required or authorized by the board of commissioners.

In 2021, the General Assembly passed a session law (S.L. 2021-124) that added a ninth subsection to G.S. 153A-82 and G.S. 160A-148. It required county and city managers of jurisdictions on the Unit Assistance List (UAL) compiled by the Local Government Commission to complete a minimum of six hours of education including fiscal management and requirements of the Local Government Finance Act (Chapter 159).[1] In October 2022, 12 counties and 138 municipalities were on the UAL for the following reasons: internal control issues; missing or significant deficiency in the most recently completed audits; water/sewer fund financial issues; and General Fund financial issues. The language for G.S. 153A-82(a)(9) and G.S. 160A-148(a)(9) reads as follows:

(9) The manager shall receive a minimum of six clock hours of education upon the occurrence, or within six months of the occurrence, of any of the following:
   a. The Local Government Commission is exercising its authority under Article 10 of Chapter 159 of the General Statutes with respect to the [county/city].
   b. The [county/city] has received a unit letter from the Local Government Commission due to a deficiency in complying with Chapter 159 of the General Statutes.
   c. The [county/city] has an internal control material weakness or significant deficiency in the most recently completed financial audit.
   d. The [county/city] is included on the most recently published Unit Assistance List issued by the Department of State Treasurer.

1. *See* Kara A. Millonzi, "The Local Government Budget and Fiscal Control Act," in Connor H. Crews, ed., *Introduction to Local Government Finance*, 5th ed. (UNC School of Government, 2023), 29–31.

The City Manager

The powers and duties of the city manager are specified in G.S. 160A-148. Unless otherwise noted, they are similar to those of county managers. The introduction and first subsection of the statute read as follows:

> **§ 160A-148. Powers and duties of manager.**
>
> (a) The manager shall be the chief administrator of the city. The manager shall be responsible to the council for administering all municipal affairs placed in the manager's charge by the council, and shall have the following powers and duties:
>
> (1) He [or she] shall appoint and suspend or remove all city officers and employees not elected by the people, and whose appointment or removal is not otherwise provided for by law, except the city attorney, in accordance with such general personnel rules, regulations, policies, or ordinances as the council may adopt.

Hiring and Firing Powers

As indicated in Chapter 3, "County and Municipal Governing Boards," the laws of North Carolina provide that the city council appoints a city attorney. Appointment of a city clerk is also a statutory requirement. Some city charters authorize the council to appoint the clerk, others specify that the manager makes this appointment, and still others are silent on the matter. In all municipalities, the clerk performs duties for the council, but some clerks report to the council and others to the manager.

A few council–manager cities have charters that require the council to appoint the chief of police, a very high-profile and sensitive position. The General Statutes provide for the council to appoint the tax collector, if such a position exists, although some charters authorize the manager to make this appointment. Otherwise, except for these council appointments, the manager is responsible for the hiring, the disciplining, and the removal of all administrative personnel. Managers consider this authority to be of the utmost importance, because if the council is to hold them responsible and accountable for the performance of administrative units, they feel that they must have hiring and firing authority over personnel directly responsible for the units' work. An important qualification to this authority of city managers is that it must be exercised in accordance with whatever personnel rules the council adopts.

Administrative Authority

G.S. 160A-148(a)(2) states that the city manager

> . . . shall direct and supervise the administration of all departments, offices, and agencies of the city, subject to the general direction and control of the council, except as otherwise provided by law.

This language reflects the long-standing prohibition in the *Model City Charter* on "Interference with Administration," which provides that council members should deal with employees through the city manager. To make sure that the non-interference tenet is honored, some managers have insisted that there be no contact between employees and council members without their permission. However, this can prove frustrating for everyone involved: employees may feel as if they are being deprived of their voice and ability to help council members make good decisions, the manager might find that he or she has to devote too much time to managing communications traffic, and council members could come to regard the contact-only-with-permission rule as unduly restrictive of their ability to keep track of the pulse of government or to get basic information. Most managers find it effective to have an understanding that prevents the council from issuing directives to employees but allows council members to freely seek information. Managers also expect that employees will keep them or their supervisors informed of contacts with council members. If a council member's request for information or a research report will disrupt workflow or schedules, the manager will usually bring the request to the attention of the council and seek its approval.

Research conducted in 2005 found that the charters of nine of the twenty-eight largest municipalities in North Carolina contained "work through the manager" language, while the remaining charters were silent on the matter of council–staff relations. In the latter cities, there was either an informal unwritten policy or no policy at all. The majority of managers interviewed in the 2005 survey agreed that the norm applicable to their city could be best described as "direct communication between council members/mayor and city employees is neither strongly discouraged nor prohibited, but city employees are advised to inform a supervisor when contacted by council members/mayor." They also stated that violations of the council member/staff contact policy or norm seldom occurred. More than three-fourths of the managers indicated that their councils were respectful of the manager's role as chief executive officer and that their city's policy on council member/staff contact was "about right." Reflecting the changing times, one manager stated: "Twenty-five years ago managers wanted everything to go through the manager's office, and that's just not practical today."[2]

Miscellaneous Duties

The remaining subsections of G.S. 160A-148, which outline various other city manager responsibilities, are reproduced below.

> (3) [The manager] shall attend all meetings of the council and recommend any measures that he [or she] deems expedient.
>
> (4) [The manager] shall see that all laws of the State, the city charter, and the ordinances, resolutions, and regulations of the council are faithfully executed within the city.
>
> (5) [The manager] shall prepare and submit the annual budget and capital program to the council.
>
> (6) [The manager] shall annually submit to the council and make available to the public a complete report on the finances and administrative activities of the city as of the end of the fiscal year.
>
> (7) [The manager] shall make any other reports that the council may require concerning the operations of city departments, offices, and agencies subject to his [or her] direction and control.
>
> (8) [The manager] shall perform any other duties that may be required or authorized by the council.
>
> (9) This subsection is discussed in "Reports and Miscellaneous Duties," above.

---

2. Parker Wiseman, "Examining Council Contact with Subordinate Staff in Large and Mid-Size North Carolina Municipalities," a paper submitted to the faculty of the University of North Carolina at Chapel Hill in partial fulfillment of the requirements for the degree of Master of Public Administration, March 11, 2005.

Origins and Reasons for the Growth of the Council–Manager Form

History—North Carolina

North Carolina has a long tradition of using professional managers to assist elected leaders in governing their respective communities and generally ensure that local governments operate efficiently, effectively, and more recently, equitably. In 1917, Catawba and Caldwell counties each secured authorization by special acts of the General Assembly to appoint a county manager, although neither did so at the time.[3] In that same year, Buncombe County designated the chair of the board of commissioners as a full-time manager.[4] In 1927, following the success of a general law allowing cities to determine their form of government by local action, the General Assembly passed similar legislation to allow counties to choose their form of government without special legislation.[5] In 1929, Robeson County became the first county in the United States to adopt the county manager form,[6] and in 1930, Durham County became the second.[7]

Although they were ahead of their counterparts in other states, North Carolina counties were more cautious than municipalities in adopting this new form of government: Until 1960, only nine counties had used the general law to appoint county managers, and three other counties elected commissioners to serve in the capacity of county manager.[8] By 1970, thirty-five counties were using the county manager form, and by 1980, eighty-two had adopted it. Today, all of North Carolina's 100 counties employ a full-time professional county manager.

The cities of Hickory and Morganton first adopted the council–manager plan as part of their charters in 1913, just one year after the first charter adoption of the plan in the country by Sumter, South Carolina. Another twenty-three North Carolina municipalities had adopted the plan by 1940, and two or three more adopted it each year from the 1940s through the 1960s. Between 1994 and 2002, twenty-four additional municipalities adopted the council–manager plan, while the number operating under the mayor–council form decreased by three municipalities.

By 2022, all but thirty-two of the 222 North Carolina municipalities with populations exceeding 2,500 had appointed a manager under their charters, including all of the thirty-four largest municipalities in the state. Small communities (with populations of less than 2,500) favor the mayor–council form (see Chapter 3, "County and Municipal Governing Boards").

---

3. N.C. Pub. Laws 1917, ch. 433 (Catawba); N.C. Pub. Laws 1917, ch. 690 (Caldwell). Almost two decades later, at its organizational meeting in 1936, the Catawba Board of County Commissioners, having decided that the county needed an executive to manage county affairs when the board was not in session, voted to hire Nolan J. Sigmon as county accountant with the intention of making him county manager. In March 1937, the commissioners passed a resolution adopting the county manager form, which had by then been authorized by Chapter 91 of the Public Laws of 1929 (now Chapter 153A, Section 81 of the North Carolina General Statutes (hereinafter G.S.), and appointed Sigmon to the post of county manager.

4. This arrangement continued until December 1984, when the offices of county manager and chairman were separated pursuant to special legislation passed by the 1983 session of the General Assembly (S.L. 1983-129). This arrangement continues in effect today.

5. N.C. Pub. Laws 1927, ch. 91, §§ 5–8, modified and recodified in 1973; now G.S. 153A-81 (adoption of county manager plan; appointment or designation of manager) and 153A-82 (powers and duties of manager).

6. Robeson is the only county in the United States to have had the appointed-manager form of government continuously since the late 1920s.

7. The International City/County Management Association (ICMA) lists Durham County as having adopted the form in 1930.

8. In Catawba, Davidson, Durham, Forsyth, Gaston, Hertford, Rockingham, Guilford, and Robeson counties, commissioners appointed a separate county manager. In Buncombe, Haywood, and Mecklenburg counties, the board of commissioners' chair served as county manager.

History—Generally

Exactly when did this growth in professional management begin? The form of government where there is a professional manager who is accountable to elected officials first appeared in the United States over a century ago. It was created as part of a reform effort to eliminate the corruption in American local government that existed at the time. Nineteenth-century Jacksonian democracy—with its aversion to concentrated power in government—had created a system (the so-called long ballot) in which popularly elected officials filled not only the most critical administrative positions in government but many others as well. Few of these officials had the requisite skills or incentives to cooperate with other officials to run an efficient or effective government.

This system created a leadership void that was quickly filled by party machines, whose political bosses controlled and manipulated voting. In return for delivering the vote, political bosses told elected officials how to run local operations, usually in a way that enriched them and their friends. Public affairs were organized and conducted on the basis of personal favors, political deals, and private benefit. Party machine politics resulted in much inefficiency, laid waste to local government treasuries, and became a blatant affront to notions of a broader public good as the guiding principle of government. To remedy this, progressive reformers promoted widespread citizen access to accountable, elected officials through devices such as the short ballot, the strong executive, nonpartisan at-large elections, the initiative, the referendum, and the recall.

Reformers sought to apply to local government business and scientific management principles that were popular at the time. One such vehicle was the council–manager plan for municipalities, originated by reformer Richard Childs in 1910[9] and officially incorporated into the *Model City Charter* of the National Civic League in 1915. The plan sought to bring a balance of democratic political accountability and honest, competent administration to local government. In a move away from the reformers' previous support of a strong, elected executive, the new plan called for a small, accountable elected body with a presiding officer to employ a politically neutral, expert manager to serve at its pleasure. The manager would give objective, rational advice to the elected body and then faithfully execute whatever decisions the elected body made for the welfare of the citizens, using sound business practices to administer efficiently the day-to-day affairs of government. Many of the early managers were civil engineers by training, and much of their time was spent on public works problems.

While these reforms were initially employed in municipalities, the impetus to use measures aimed at increasing the efficiency of local government affected counties as well, as they grew in population and became more urbanized in some parts of the country. In more than 100 years, the main elements of the plan have changed very little.

ICMA Recognition

The International City/County Management Association (ICMA) officially recognizes jurisdictions "... that, by ordinance, charter, or other legal document, have established positions of professional authority. Recognition means the community is identified as one that provides a legal framework conducive to the practice of professional management." Criteria for ICMA recognition as a

---

9. Childs first articulated the plan in a proposal to combine the commission form of government with a professional city manager. (The commission form of government became popular after its successful use in resurrecting Galveston, Texas, from almost complete destruction from a hurricane in 1900.) Childs drafted a bill incorporating the plan and persuaded the Lockport (N.Y.) Board of Trade to sponsor its introduction in the New York State Legislature with the public support of reform organizations. Thus, the earliest version is known as the Lockport Plan. *See* Robert Paul Boynton, "The Council–Manager Plan: An Historical Perspective," *Public Management* (Oct. 1974): 3–5.

jurisdiction having a *council–manager position* (the term applies to both cities and counties) include that the manager

- be appointed by majority vote of the governing body, based on professional experience, administrative qualifications, and education, for a definite or indefinite term;
- serve at the pleasure of the entire governing body (not the chair or mayor alone) and be subject to termination by majority vote at any time;
- have direct responsibility for policy formulation on overall problems, especially developing and analyzing alternatives, and for implementation of policy approved by the governing body;
- have responsibility for budget preparation and presentation and direct responsibility for administration of the approved budget; and
- have full authority to appoint and remove most heads of principal departments and local government functions who are administratively responsible to the manager.[10]

Roles and Responsibilities of the Manager

Basics of the Council–Manager Plan

A few assumptions implicit in the council–manager plan have influenced North Carolina's (and other states') general laws regarding this form of government and affected the way in which elected officials and managers perceive their roles in relation to one another. The plan, for the most part, assumes that the governing body fairly represents the electorate, that competing public values can be reconciled, that a public interest can be discerned to guide most decisions, and that the governing body can, with some degree of consensus, give the manager clear direction for carrying out its policies. Unlike the mayor–council form of government, where executive and legislative functions are separated, a key feature of the council–manager form of government is the unification of executive and legislative authority. This arrangement encourages cooperation and collaboration between the governing body and the administration with the manager serving as a "bridge" between these worlds of political acceptability and administrative sustainability. The plan promotes separation of the governing body's responsibility for political judgments and policy direction from the manager's responsibility for faithful execution and implementation in accordance with the board or council's overall policy guidance and his or her own politically neutral expertise. In these ways, the plan seeks to create an effective balance between objective, honest, expert governmental operation and democratic access and control through the authority and the accountability of the elected body.

Realities of the Council–Manager Plan's Implementation

Unfortunately, the council–manager plan's underlying assumptions have been difficult to implement and are becoming even more problematic in the political and social landscape of contemporary local government. In 1993, ICMA convened a task force of city and county managers from across the country to examine the state of council–manager relations. This panel began its work by identifying the forces of change that were affecting the council–manager form of government. Managers suggested that citizens seemed to be losing respect for both politics and government itself and that

10. International City/County Management Association, "ICMA Local Government Recognition; Criteria for Recognition of a Council–Manager Position" (adopted Oct. 11, 1969, and revised July 22, 1989), icma.org/icma-local-government-recognition.

the public was becoming increasingly fragmented into interest groups with competing narrow agendas, an unwillingness to cooperate, and a tendency to vie for absolute control. As a result, managers saw themselves faced with mixed signals and sometimes irresolvable conflicts of expectations from elected officials and citizens. Managers felt that directly elected mayors often viewed them as competitors in the arena of local leadership and that the business traditions of the profession had evolved into such a state of "thriving on chaos" that managers who played by the old rules might find themselves characterized as impediments to progress.[11]

Also in 1993, an article was published in ICMA's monthly magazine, *Public Management*, presenting research findings on council members' perceptions of the council–manager relationship. It identified the following seven "unspoken" concerns and beliefs often held by governing body members that restrict "the development of trust and meaningful partnerships in governing"[12]: (1) managers "hide" money amidst complex budget accounts, arcane language, and detailed provisions and are reluctant to inform governing bodies how much discretionary money is available; (2) managers have personal agendas that they advance, especially when the governing body is divided; (3) governing bodies will not acknowledge or deal with personality conflicts with their manager; (4) governing body members want to hire their own manager, so many newly elected officials are not committed to the current manager; (5) governing bodies do not take seriously the task of evaluating the manager, in part because they have not set clear goals and objectives for the community; (6) managers should be out in front of issues that are "lose-lose" for elected officials, like tax hikes and service cuts; and (7) elected officials expect the manager to discipline or coach controversial "mavericks" on the governing body.

A little more than ten years later, contributors to the third edition of the ICMA book *The Effective Local Government Manager* noted trends that create tension in the relationships between managers and governing bodies and could even jeopardize the existence of the council–manager plan in some communities.[13] These trends have continued and include:

- an expectation by citizens and interest groups that local government can deliver "more for less" and provide customized services, sometimes without regard for due process, social equity, and other core values of deliberative democracy;
- perpetuation of antigovernment feelings among the public—even though opinion surveys reveal local governments are considered more honest, trustworthy, and efficient than other levels of government—leading to local candidates running against the government itself, including the professional "bureaucrat" in the manager's office;
- a shift from a "trustee" to a "delegate" or "activist" role for local elected officials, exemplified by increases in single-issue candidates who are more concerned about addressing their particular program or advancing the interests of special constituencies than working collaboratively with the governing body to address general needs or common problems;
- the steadily increasing power and visibility of directly elected mayors in areas such as budget-making, vetoes of governing body decisions, appointment of council committee chairs, and annual state of the city addresses, which creates competition with the manager for publicity and leadership;

---

11. The task force's conclusions were summarized in three parts in *ICMA Newsletter* 74, no. 10 (May 17, 1993); no. 11 (May 31, 1993); and no. 13 (June 28, 1993).

12. R. William Mathis, "What Councils Want from Managers … But Do Not Tell Them," *Public Management* 75 (Sept. 1993): 5–10.

13. *See* James H. Svara, "Achieving Effective Community Leadership," *in* Charldean Newell, ed., *The Effective Local Government Manager*, 3rd ed. (Washington, D.C.: International City/County Management Association, 2004), 27–40.

- a growing tendency among elected officials to focus on implementation matters instead of policy, since their reelection hinges on constituent service, leading to micromanagement of administration;
- the emphasis that governing bodies demand managers place on privatization as a way of dealing with the public's desire for "quicker, better, cheaper" services, making it difficult for a manager to introduce other more potentially useful tools; and
- the technology revolution, which, in addition to providing new ways for the community to obtain services and receive information, has empowered people by enabling them to quickly and easily obtain data about local operations, register complaints to elected officials and administrators, monitor the performance of agencies, and put an administration under the spotlight.

More recently, contributors to the fourth editions of two of ICMA's core publications—*Managing Local Government Services: The Challenge of Change* (2021) and *The Effective Local Government Manager* (2022)—noted other challenges to local managers in the wake of a financial recession, global pandemic, climate change, racial tensions, citizen incivility, cyberattacks, and partisan polarization. Their implications were noted in the Foreword of the former publication by executive director Marc Ott:

> This ongoing state of volatility, uncertainty, complexity, and ambiguity requires professional local government managers to be trained and experienced in the basics of local government, while seizing new opportunities for innovation and transformation ... as a local government leader, the future feels more present now than ever before. New opportunities and challenges are coming at us from all directions—whether that is the promise of new technologies enabling more data-driven, insightful decision-making; the transparency and engagement implications of our 24-hour news cycle and influx of social media; or the threat of a fast-moving economic disruption in a globalized world.[14]

These changes require managers and elected officials to seek ways to forge true partnerships in leading their communities, recognizing that governing body members, chairs, mayors, and managers are mutually dependent on one another, share responsibility for most aspects of local government, and need to divide some of those responsibilities in order to make the system work for the benefit of all.

Concept of Governance

The need for this type of awareness on the part of managers and elected officials has grown with the complexity of local government. Most important public problems, to be successfully addressed, require working across jurisdictional and sector boundaries—with other communities, nonprofit organizations, businesses, citizen groups, and volunteers. Since the 1990s, the term *governance* has been used to describe the reality that "governments" are only one of the players in local service delivery, albeit the key player. The need to manage within and work with a diverse array of vertical and horizontal networks of intergovernmental partners, public–private organizations, and regional and community groups has changed the traditional roles and authority of managers and governing bodies. They have come to act more as facilitators, brokers, networkers, and enablers and to operate

14. Kimberly H. Nelson and Carl W. Stenberg, *Managing Local Government Services: The Challenge of Change* (Washington, D.C.: International City/County Management Association, 2021), vii.

less in a hierarchical, command-and-control, "we know best" model. While the responsibilities of managers and governing bodies have grown, their authority has become more shared.[15]

Professor H. George Frederickson observed that this notion of governance creates two fundamental paradoxes: (1) to serve a locality, elected and appointed officials must transcend the boundaries of their respective communities and share power with others; and (2) since local boundaries are meaningful mainly to elected officials for political and electoral purposes, increasingly interjurisdictional relationships, power-sharing arrangements, and other aspects of democratic governance must be handled by professional administrators.[16]

In the fourth edition of *The Effective Local Government Manager*, former ICMA executive director Bob O'Neill and John Nalbandian, an emeritus professor at the University of Kansas, noted three "disruptive forces" that are key drivers of contemporary local government: the influence of national politics on local governing body culture and dynamics, technological changes such as social media and cybersecurity, and social policy issues. These disruptions have widened the gap between politics and administration and call for "bridging" or "reconciliation" strategies.

> Working the gap—bridge building—is part of the job description for the city/county manager. But, as the consequences of contemporary disruptions are encountered, the gap widens, and the capacity of the manager is stretched. Staff who might have viewed their role in terms of an internal departmental focus are now expected to help work the gap as an ally of the manager. In our view, the relatively recent concept of an administrative "leadership team," in addition to the traditional "management team," reflects the need for staff with a "gap" perspective.[17]

Managers are spending more and more time with their governing bodies seeking to build partnerships that can respond to and survive the diverse, divisive, and difficult demands of contemporary governance. But such partnerships must often be formed and sustained in an arena in which personal interests, constituent expectations, and political and philosophical divisions make building consensus and trust quite challenging.

The responsibilities of the manager that come from the law, from the managers' professional code of ethics, from commonly understood roles in policy and administration, and from expectations of behavior can be helpful in understanding how the manager–governing body partnership might work and how it is often challenged in the context of the council–manager form of government.[18]

ICMA Code of Ethics

The professional county or city manager has a specific set of expectations governing his or her behavior: a code of ethics originally developed in 1924 by the International City Managers' Association (the original name of the International City/County Management Association (ICMA)).[19]

---

15. Svara, "Achieving Effective Community Leadership," at 28.

16. H. George Frederickson, "Transcending the Community: Local Leadership in a World of Shared Power," *Public Management* 87 (Nov. 2005): 14. *See also* Eric S. Zeemering, "Governing Interlocal Cooperation: City Council Interests and the Implications for Public Management," *Public Administration Review* 68 (July/Aug. 2008): 731–41.

17. John Nalbandian and Robert O'Neill, Jr., "The Profession of Local Government Manager: Evolution and Leadership Styles," *in* Robert E. (Bob) Lee and Michael Abels, eds., *The Effective Local Government Manager*, 4th ed. (Washington, D.C.: International City/County Management Association, 2022), 12.

18. John Nalbandian and Shannon Portillo, "Council–Manager Relations Through the Years," *Public Management* 88 (July 2006): 6–7; Gary O'Connell, "Council–Manager Relations: Finding Respectable Ground," *Public Management* 89 (Nov. 2007): 20–23.

19. In 1969, ICMA changed the word *Managers* in its name to *Management* in order to recognize the inclusion of members who are deputies, assistants, directors of councils of governments, and local government chief

The ICMA Code of Ethic's tenets and related guidelines have been modified periodically since then; most recently, the membership amended the tenets in April 2023, and the Executive Board revised the guidelines in June 2023. These changes were the result of a review of the Code through a racial equity and social justice lens as part of the Board's action steps "to advance the profession's commitment to diversity, equity, and inclusion."

The ICMA Code of Ethics is a point of pride among professional managers. Any manager admitted to the association is bound by its ethical tenets and subject to censure by or even expulsion from the association for violations of this professional code. The Code seeks to enforce and balance what ICMA believes to be the prerogatives a professional manager must have to do his or her job properly and the obligations a manager must meet in order to honor the authority of the governing body and promote the overall welfare of the community. The twelve tenets of the ICMA Code of Ethics are as follows:[20]

1. We believe professional management is essential to effective, efficient, equitable, and democratic local government.
2. Affirm the dignity and worth of local government services and maintain a deep sense of social responsibility as a trusted public servant.
3. Demonstrate by word and action the highest standards of ethical conduct and integrity in all public, professional, and personal relationships in order that the member may merit the trust and respect of the elected and appointed officials, employees, and the public.
4. Serve the best interests of all community members.
5. Submit policy proposals to elected officials; provide them with facts, and technical and professional advice about policy options; and collaborate with them in setting goals for the community and organization.
6. Recognize that elected representatives are accountable to their community for the decisions they make; members are responsible for implementing those decisions.
7. Refrain from all political activities which undermine public confidence in professional administrators. Refrain from participation in the election of the members of the employing legislative body.
8. Make it a duty continually to improve the member's professional ability and to develop the competence of associates in the use of management techniques.
9. Keep the community informed on local government affairs. Encourage and facilitate active engagement and constructive communication between community members and all local government officials.
10. Resist any encroachment on professional responsibilities, believing the member should be free to carry out official policies without interference, and handle each problem without discrimination on the basis of principle and justice.
11. Manage all personnel matters with fairness and impartiality.
12. Public office is a public trust. A member shall not leverage his or her position for personal gain or benefit.

---

administrative officers who do not have the title or the traditional authority of a manager. In 1991, ICMA added the word *County* to its name, acknowledging the county managers who had by then become a significant proportion of its membership. Its original, widely recognized acronym, ICMA, did not change.

20. The International City/County Management Association's "ICMA Code of Ethics with Guidelines" (2023) can be downloaded at www.icma.org/.

Roles and Relationships in Policy and Administration

Dichotomy–Duality Model

Although both the law and the ICMA Code of Ethics prescribe responsibilities for the manager and the governing body, these responsibilities are very general and do not describe in any detail how these officials should interact with one another to be effective in the division of labor set out in the Code's twelve tenets, above. Decades ago, popular wisdom promoted the notion of a strict dichotomy between policy-making and administration: the elected body should make policy and the administration should carry it out, each without interference from the other as it performed its functions. The dichotomy concept arose originally from a misinterpretation of a highly respected article by Woodrow Wilson in which he advocated the use of appointed officials to relieve legislators of the burden of administrative functions. According to Professor Kimberly Nelson, while arguing for a separation between politics and administration, Wilson also asserted that public administrators should have "large powers and unhampered discretion… Wilson's concern was with the encroachment of partisan politics in the administrative process rather than administrators encroaching on policy."[21]

The fact that the popular interpretation of this dichotomy theory reduced council–manager relations to a simple, easy-to-follow formula probably accounts for its perpetuation. However, matters are not that neat and simple. For example, the manager often has training, analytical skills, experience in other jurisdictions, and in-depth knowledge of the county or municipality and its governmental operations that can be extremely helpful to the governing body in establishing policy. And when constituents complain about the quality of a service or the treatment they receive from local government employees, a member of the board or council is unlikely to feel that it is an administrative matter that does not concern him or her. Nalbandian, who has also served as council member and mayor of Lawrence, Kansas, has observed:

> The practical world of city management often suggests a more complicated view [than the dichotomy theory]. The manager is deeply involved in policy-making as well as implementation, responds to a multitude of community forces as well as to the governing body, and incorporates a variety of competing values into the decision-making process.[22]

A more realistic relationship between elected officials and managers in policy and administration has been depicted by Professor James H. Svara, as shown in Figure 4.1.[23] Svara's depiction

---

21. Woodrow Wilson, "The Study of Administration," *Political Science Quarterly* 2 (June 1887): 197–222. Wilson was arguing for the provision of administrative support to legislative bodies—not prescribing a strict separation of duties between the two—when he wrote that "administration lies outside the proper sphere of *politics*. Administrative questions are not political questions. Although politics sets the tasks for administration, it should not be suffered to manipulate its offices" (p. 210). *See also* Kimberly Nelson, "Returning to the Politics versus Administration Debate," *PM Magazine* (May 2022): 32–34.

22. John Nalbandian, *Professionalism in Local Government* (San Francisco: Jossey-Bass, 1991), xiii. *See also* Tansu Demir and Christopher G. Reddick, "Understanding Shared Roles in Policy and Administration: An Empirical Study of Council–Manager Relations," *Public Administration Review* 72 (July/Aug. 2012): 516–36; Yahong Zhang and Richard C. Feiock, "City Managers' Policy Leadership in Council–Manager Cities," *Journal of Public Administration Research and Theory* 20 (April 2010): 461–76; and Kimberly L. Nelson and James H. Svara, "The Roles of Local Government Managers in Theory and Practice: A Centennial Perspective," Public Administration Review 75 (Jan./Feb. 2015): 49–61.

23. A more thorough discussion of the relationships among the council, the manager, and the mayor over a continuum from mission to management, as depicted in Figure 4.1, can be found in a series of articles by James H. Svara: "Understanding the Mayor's Office in Council–Manager Cities," *Popular Government* 51 (UNC Institute of Government, Fall 1985): 6–11; "Contributions of the City Council to Effective Governance," *Popular Government* 51 (UNC Institute of Government, Spring 1986): 1–8; and "The Responsible Administrator: Contributions of the City Manager

Figure 4.1 Dichotomy–Duality Model: Mission–Management Separation with Shared Responsibility for Policy and Administration

DIMENSIONS OF GOVERNMENT PROCESS

Council's Sphere

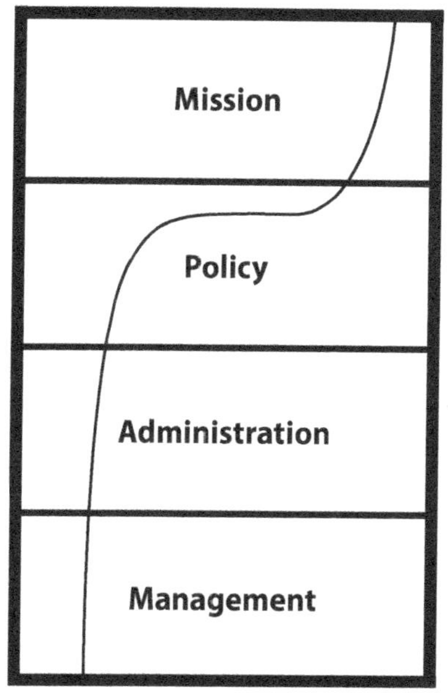

Manager's Sphere

ILLUSTRATIVE TASKS FOR COUNCIL	DIMENSIONS OF GOVERNMENT PROCESS	ILLUSTRATIVE TASKS FOR ADMINISTRATORS
Determine purpose, scope of services, tax level, constitutional issues	Mission	Advise (what city "can" do may influence what it "should" do), analyze conditions and trends
Pass ordinances, approve new projects and programs, ratify budget	Policy	Make recommendations on all decisions, formulate budget, determine service distribution formulae
Make implementing decisions (e.g., site selection), handle complaints, oversee administration	Administration	Establish practices and procedures and make decisions for implementing policy
Suggest management changes to manager, review organizational performance in manager's appraisal	Management	Control the human, material, and informational resources of organization to support policy and administrative functions

The division presented here is intended to approximate a proper degree of separation and sharing. Shifts to either the left or right would indicate improper incursions.

Source: Taken from James H. Svara, "Dichotomy and Duality: Reconceptualizing the Relationship between Policy and Administration in Council–Manager Cities," *Public Administration Review* 45 (Jan./Feb. 1985), 228.

recognizes that there is no strict dichotomy; rather, there is involvement of both elected and administrative officials at all levels of policy and administration. The engagement and the responsibility of each are proportionately different depending on the level at which they occur. At the highest level, the governing body is responsible for setting the overall direction, or *mission*, of local government, including its purpose, scope, and philosophy. Figure 4.1 suggests that although the governing body

to Effective Governance," *Popular Government* 52 (UNC Institute of Government, Fall 1986): 18–27. *See also* James H. Svara, "Mayors in the Unity of Powers Context: Effective Leadership in Council–Manager Governments," *in* H. George Frederickson and John Nalbandian, eds., *The Future of Local Government Administration: The Hansell Symposium* (Washington, D.C.: International City/County Management Association, 2002), 43–54; "Exploring Structures and Institutions in City Government," *Public Administration Review* 65 (July/Aug. 2005): 500–506; "The Myth of the Dichotomy: Complementarity of Politics and Administration in the Past and Future of Public Administration," *Public Administration Review* 61 (Mar./Apr. 2001): 176–83; "Effective Mayoral Leadership in Council–Manager Cities: Reassessing the Facilitative Model," *National Civic Review* 92 (Summer 2003): 57–72; and "Beyond Dichotomy: Dwight Waldo and the Intertwined Politics–Administration Relationship," *Public Administration Review* 68 (Jan./Feb. 2008): 46–52.

has a clearly dominant role in this function, the manager can bring knowledge and experience to the table that enhances the elected official's ability to make informed choices and decisions. The governing body must enact *policy* to achieve the mission that it sets for local government. It does this through functions such as budgeting, capital improvement programming, comprehensive planning, and the making of laws and policies regarding county or municipal quality of life and governmental operations. Although the governing body has final responsibility for adopting budgets, plans, and ordinances, the manager and his or her staff play a major role in developing technical studies and estimates and analyzing the impact of alternative choices. These kinds of policy-making are a shared responsibility in practice.

In government, how something is done is often as important to peoples' satisfaction with the outcome as what is done. Consequently, although the manager and the staff are responsible for implementing the policies adopted by the governing body, elected officials still have a stake in how those policies are carried out—that is, in *administration* and *management*. For example, after making the decision to build a new community center and budgeting funds for it, a governing body will have a continued interest in how the facilities actually look and work. It will be concerned with how well the scheduling of work on a downtown streetscape project minimizes the disruption of business for merchants. It will want to know how increases in public safety spending have affected reported crime rates and citizen perceptions of safety in their neighborhoods. And it will have an interest in how overall employee morale is affected by internal operating policies developed by the administration.

Figure 4.1 describes a partnership at every level of endeavor, with the elected body shouldering most of the responsibility, authority, and initiative at the mission level, the administration shouldering most of it in internal management, and the two sharing it significantly in policy. The line in Figure 4.1 is symbolic; as discussed earlier, multiple factors cause it to vary among jurisdictions and within a particular jurisdiction over time. Some governing bodies want the manager to push aggressively for policies that he or she deems necessary, while others want the manager to stay in the background and respond to the governing body's initiatives. Some elected officials feel the need to be intimately familiar with day-to-day occurrences in service delivery, while others want to concern themselves with administrative matters only when those matters might create public controversy or relate to special interests of constituents.

Other factors influencing where the line is drawn are the manager's experience and tenure and the degree of trust and confidence in his or her relationship with the governing body. Agreement between elected and appointed officials is an essential element of a good working relationship and, because the relationship is dynamic, its contours should be assessed frequently to ensure that everyone involved understands and is comfortable with where the line is drawn.

When it comes to these interrelationships, elected officials have to consider more than their own personal preferences and operating styles, taking into account, for example, how people perceive the relationship between elected and appointed officials. Residents' most important expectation is that quality public services will be provided reliably and efficiently. If the professional staff does not satisfy this expectation, people will expect the governing body to take a more dominant role. If needs are being met routinely, they may be satisfied with elected officials taking a more passive role on a day-to-day basis.

In the dynamic world of local government, it is difficult for both the governing body and the administration to please everyone, difficult for elected officials to achieve consensus on many issues that might have been routine in the past, and therefore difficult for the governing body to continually give the manager clear and consistent direction. As a result, it is difficult for the manager to perform his or her administrative duties in a way that satisfies the entire governing body.

As noted previously, some observers of local government bemoan the nationalization of local governing body deliberations, the growing incivility of constituents, the trend to district representation for governing bodies, and the growing number of single-issue and antigovernment candidates for local elective office as undermining the principles of broad representation of the public good and efficient administration. Others, however, point out that these developments typify the reality of constituent politics and make for more transparent, fairer representation of all the diverse interests in a community, instead of just those of a powerful privileged few or an exclusive majority. Nalbandian has observed the implications of such matters for managers: "In the future the legitimacy of professional administrators in local government will be grounded in the tasks of community-building and enabling democracy—in getting things done collectively, while building a sense of inclusion."[24] Nevertheless, managers may feel it is harder than it used to be to obtain and maintain the kind of clear consensus and direction from the governing body that is one of the fundamental assumptions of the council–manager form of government.

Common Expectations among the Governing Body, the Chair or Mayor, and the Manager

Specific expectations and practices among the governing body, the chair or mayor, and the manager vary greatly from community to community, depending on social and political norms, traditions, and local charters. They can also vary over time in a particular community with changes in the personalities involved as elected offices turn over and managers come and go. However, experience and research have shown that in some critical aspects of these partnerships, there are fairly consistent expectations across jurisdictions and over time. For the most part, these expectations may be regarded as basic and necessary to defining roles and maintaining healthy relationships among the elected members of the governing body, the chair or mayor, and the manager.

Expectation 1: The Manager Is an Organization Capacity-Builder

From the inception of the council–manager form, governing bodies have expected their professional managers to see to it that county and municipal operations run smoothly, services are provided efficiently and effectively, and prudent fiscal practices are followed. This heritage continues as managers seek to advance social equity in their organization and community. In order to meet resident and governing body expectations, the manager must build a modern organization that has both capacity and competence. This entails implementing and updating business practices and processes for personnel administration, finance, purchasing, payroll, contracting, and other basic local management systems. It involves the adept use of tools like strategic planning, performance measurement, benchmarking, community surveys, and program evaluation to ensure continuous improvement of operations. In addition, techniques and technologies like participatory budgeting and websites, social media, and artificial intelligence can be used to increase public outreach, access, and engagement and reduce costs.

A critical component of this organization capacity-building is professional staff. The manager must attract and retain talented and motivated personnel for the systems of government to work well. This involves careful workforce and succession planning and investments in training and professional development. Increasingly, local government workforces are diverse and multigenerational, and strategies need to be put in place to respond to the "changing faces" of the administrative staff, such as bilingual education, job rotation, job sharing, flexible hours, and remote work.

---

24. John Nalbandian, "Facilitating Community, Enabling Democracy: New Roles for Local Government Managers," *Public Administration Review* 59 (May/June 1999): 189.

When the processes and personnel perform as expected, local operations run smoothly and routinely. Their workings might be almost invisible to the public and elected officials. If there is a breakdown in organizational capacity, however, managers and elected officials can be placed under a harsh public spotlight.

Expectation 2: The Manager Is a Valued Advisor to the Governing Body

While both the North Carolina General Statutes and the ICMA Code of Ethics recognize the manager's role and responsibility as valued policy advisor to the governing body, neither deals specifically with some subtle but important aspects of this advise-and-implement process. The General Statutes require the manager to "recommend any measures that he [or she] deems expedient," and the Code of Ethics requires him or her to "submit policy proposals to elected officials" and "provide them with facts, and technical and professional advice about policy options" to help the governing body make policy decisions and set goals. Governing bodies expect the manager to offer balanced and impartial advice—to present alternatives and provide all relevant information that is reasonably available on the different options, assess the advantages and disadvantages of each option, explain the professional reasoning and analysis that leads him or her to a recommendation, and base that reasoning on established professional, technical, ethical, or legal principles and not on personal beliefs, no matter how strongly held, unless the governing body specifically solicits them. Even the appearance or the suspicion that the manager is being selective in the information he or she gives, personally biased in the judgment he or she renders, or manipulative of the governing body's decision in the way he or she presents material can severely damage the manager's credibility and undermine his or her effectiveness.

Most managers will express support (and perhaps advocate) for a course of action they believe in, no matter how unpopular it might be with the public, the board, or the council. This often means that managers must have the courage to make recommendations that might not have very good prospects of being accepted. On such occasions, managers must bear in mind the human propensity for "killing the messenger" who brings bad news. Elected officials or residents who are upset over the facts that are presented by the manager or who disagree with the recommendations made might, at best, attack the validity of the manager's advice or, at worst, attack the competence, motives, or character of the manager himself or herself. One of the most difficult tests for a professional manager acting as policy advisor is to remain cool and non-defensive during heated debate over the information and the recommendations that he or she has brought to the governing body.

Once the governing body has made a decision, the manager must get behind it fully and ensure that the administration does the same. The General Statutes require the manager to see that all actions of the council are "faithfully executed," and the Code of Ethics states that members are "responsible for implementing" all policies adopted and decisions made by elected officials. This sometimes requires the manager to aggressively implement what he or she thinks is a bad idea. If the manager believes that the directive the governing body has given is illegal or deems it professionally or personally repugnant, the manager can try to dissuade the board or council from taking action, and, if that fails, he or she can resign. If the manager chooses to stay, however, he or she is obliged to assist the governing body in carrying out its will.

Sometimes, after arguing strenuously for a course of action that the governing body subsequently rejects, the manager will be put in the awkward position of having to respond when the media asks what he or she thinks of the decision. Unless reasoned debate has changed the manager's mind, to agree completely with the governing body will make the manager look weak. On the other hand, to criticize or denigrate the governing body for its decision will violate the Code of Ethics and invite censure. Most professional managers who find themselves in this situation will acknowledge the different perspectives that were offered in the deliberations and try to explain the reasoning that brought the governing body to its decision. In other words, they will help elected officials explain their decision to the public and help the public understand the governing body's point of view. Carrying out this important responsibility often takes great emotional maturity and keen diplomatic, interpersonal, and communications skills on the part of the manager.

Expectation 3: The Governing Body and the Manager Jointly Strive for Good Service to Citizens

Service to people is the litmus test of local operations, and it is one of the most obvious points where the dichotomy theory, discussed above, fails the test of reality. Regardless of what the governing body accomplishes or the capacity and competence of the administration, if the county or municipality does not satisfactorily deliver basic services, residents will be dissatisfied with the elected officials, and the governing body, in turn, will be dissatisfied with the manager and the administration. Therefore, tirelessly urging his or her staff to provide the very best service possible to the community is one of the key responsibilities of a manager.

Careful planning, budgeting, and management help in ensuring high-quality service delivery, but the manager cannot be everywhere at all times to supervise day-to-day execution. Thus, he or she has to create a culture of responsiveness and performance within the organization, both in providing routine service and in handling special requests and complaints. This usually involves (1) delegating to front-line service providers in the organization the responsibility and authority to make decisions and take action, (2) supporting staff who take initiative, and (3) helping staff learn from mistakes made in good faith. The manager must take personal risks on behalf of employees and fully accept responsibility with the governing body when things go wrong.

The manager should be able to expect that board or council members will give the system he or she has put in place a chance to work and will channel complaints through the manager. The sense of accomplishment an elected official might enjoy as a result of personally wading into a problem and doing something about it is ordinarily short-lived and transitory. More lasting credit usually comes from community recognition that the governing body has created and is maintaining a responsive, customer-service-oriented workforce—an essential ingredient of efficient and effective local government.

Even when an administration excels at responding to needs, people will ask their elected officials for help, usually in good faith. Managers expect governing body members to determine whether a resident seeking assistance has tried administrative remedies and, if not, to steer the person into the system. If the administration has been unresponsive, then the manager expects to be informed of this and to have the opportunity to get the problem fixed. A manager in this situation will give the elected official(s) involved the necessary information to follow up with the resident.

Expectation 4: Elected Officials' Relationships with Employees Are Carefully Managed

Observing a chain of command in answering service needs is desirable, especially from the standpoint of managing resources effectively. The problems that can arise when elected officials intervene directly in service operations include confusing employees with conflicting directives or priorities from supervisors and elected officials, weakening or destroying accountability for work results, wasting staff time and resources, and short-circuiting coordinated plans and schedules developed by the supervisor responsible for day-to-day operations. This does *not* mean that elected officials should not have periodic, or even regular, contact with county or municipal employees. To prohibit such contact would be to ask employees and elected officials to give up some of their basic rights as members of the community, and it would make it harder to build harmony among the critical players in local government operations. It would also be highly inefficient. Funneling all communication through the manager would fill up his or her time with unnecessary traffic and would be awkward and inconvenient for elected officials.

A common arrangement designed to protect planned workflow and still reap the benefits of regular interaction is to encourage direct contact between elected officials and employees for routine inquiries or requests that do not affect administrative workloads and to route more significant requests through the manager. This lets elected officials get the routine information they need quickly and accurately from the persons who are closest to the action and most informed about details; residents should be able to do the same. This arrangement also provides the opportunity for regular informal communication between elected officials and employees, helping each group become more familiar with, more comfortable with, and more trusting of the other over time. Anything an elected official might want from employees that will involve significant and unplanned expenditures of time or money or that will disrupt agreed-upon work schedules is taken up with the manager so as not to put employees on the spot. The manager and the elected official can then make informed choices about whether the official's request should take precedence over existing commitments, whether something could be done that would meet the official's needs but not be disruptive, or whether it should not be done at all, given other commitments. The manager and the elected official who made the request might also agree to submit the question to the entire governing body for a vote by all on whether a change in resource allocation would make sense.

Sometimes managers attempt to cut off direct contact between elected officials and employees in order to counteract council members who meddle with or harass employees or employees who are manipulative and disloyal. Like most treatments of a symptom alone, such an approach usually does little or nothing to solve the problems that underlie these dysfunctional behaviors. Often, it makes matters worse by creating a siege mentality among administrators, anxiety among employees, and distrust and frustration among elected officials.

Expectation 5: The Governing Body Acts as a Body and Is Dealt with as a Body

By law, the governing body takes official action as a body and the majority rules, yet it is made up of two to eleven individual politicians, counting the chair or mayor, with various constituencies, personal interests, public values, political philosophies, and personalities. (Fifty-seven percent of the North Carolina municipalities that operate under the council–manager or mayor–council forms have five-member governing bodies, including the mayor.) This dynamic can sometimes make dealing with the governing body a delicate proposition. Without benefit of consensus or at least formal support of a majority of the board or council, individual elected officials may seek to make their views known and impose their own personal agendas on the administration. Most managers will welcome, discuss, and frequently respond at any time to suggestions from individual members, as long as they do not conflict with the pleasure of the governing body as a whole. However, if a request sets new directions or requires allocation of funds or staff time not anticipated by the governing body, the manager will usually ask the member making the proposal to put it to the entire body for consideration. It is important for the manager to treat all members alike in this respect. Unless he or she is scrupulous in avoiding even the appearance of favoritism, the manager can seriously undermine his or her effectiveness by alienating members who feel slighted or barred from some inner circle, real or imagined. Most managers will keep all members informed of even the most routine transactions with individual members, providing copies of written communications and summaries of conversations to the entire governing body.

One area in which managers must be especially ardent is keeping members up to date on day-to-day events. Elected officials do not like surprises. It is embarrassing for an official to be asked about some newsworthy item of local business and have to admit that he or she does not know much about it. Governing bodies expect their managers to be sensitive, alert, and responsive to their needs for current information, and this expectation includes the manager making occasional extraordinary efforts necessary to ensure that every member has the same level of information and understanding.

Expectation 6: The Manager and Members of the Governing Body Give One Another a Chance to Prove Themselves

One of the implicit foundations of the council–manager form of government is that a professional manager, who is dedicated to serving whatever elected governing body is seated by the people, will provide smooth transitions, institutional stability, and memory and will make changes as different individuals or groups join and leave the governing body. Sometimes members—who sought election because they, too, want to make changes—may find it hard to trust the loyalty of the manager to new members or to have confidence in the ability of the manager to help bring about the changes they (the members) want. Even in communities where the manager routinely makes information available to all candidates about local operations and finances to help guide discussion and debate, this behavior could be viewed as defense of the status quo. In short, the manager is sometimes viewed by members as inextricably tied to the old way of doing things and assumed to be an impediment to progress. It should be noted, though, that managers strive to change the direction of administration in whatever way a majority of the governing body decides (though they can always resign if they feel they cannot serve the new governing body's agenda in good conscience). Therefore, managers are entitled to expect newly elected officials to give them a chance to prove that they can serve new members as well as veterans.

After an election, sometimes the manager must work for one or more board or council members who as candidates criticized the way in which the community was governed and managed. During their campaigns, some of these members may have called for the manager's dismissal. Few elected officials would dispute that, even if they had prior county or municipal involvement on volunteer boards or commissions, the view of government from the inside is very different than the view from the outside. Candidates, upon taking office, usually learn that the simplistic and assured campaign rhetoric seldom stands up to the complexity of governing, leading, or managing. Realizing this, experienced managers will withhold judgment on members whose campaigning seems threatening and will set about to prove that they can serve the new governing body as well as they served the old one. They will hold out hope that, given a chance, they will eventually earn the trust and confidence of new members as those members learn the realities of governing, gain skill as legislators, and observe the manager's performance at close hand.

Expectation 7: The Manager and the Governing Body Freely Give and Seek Feedback

One of the main ingredients for building and maintaining any relationship of trust and confidence is open communication. Managers and elected officials find themselves caught up in a whirlwind of activity on a daily basis. There never seems to be enough time to do everything, let alone do it all just right. So both elected officials and managers make mistakes—they overlook the side effects of actions taken in the heat of urgency and say or do things that convey unintended messages. Any/all of these occurrences can generate dissatisfaction, disappointment, offense, anger, and distrust if not acknowledged and resolved appropriately. The key to dealing effectively with such matters is maintaining clear and open communication between elected officials and the manager.

The nature of both the elected official and manager jobs can make the persons holding them feel very isolated. The manager, accountable to a governing body and responsible for a county or municipal workforce, might feel apart from both constituencies, a part of neither. The elected official, held accountable by voters for oversight of the county or municipality's administration, might feel that he or she has no real direct role to play in making sure things go well. Open communication is one effective cure for these feelings of isolation. Managers must provide all governing body members with accurate, relevant, and timely information, and members must do their homework, be good listeners, take initiative to ask questions, and make their values, positions, interests, and feelings known to the manager.

Most managers appreciate clear signals about how well they are satisfying the elected officials they serve, even when those signals are negative. Being criticized is never pleasant, but it is more comforting than having to infer dissatisfaction from elected officials' behavior (or not to pick up on dissatisfaction at all due to silence). Many people find it easier to give faint compliments or remain silent than to confront others—even subordinates—with criticism. However, dissatisfaction is often hard to conceal for very long—it usually ends up being revealed indirectly by behavior or by rumor. This kind of indirect revelation almost always produces at least some inaccuracy and misinterpretation regarding facts, feelings, and underlying motivations; distracts the manager, who becomes unduly preoccupied with figuring out where he or she stands; and often has the effect of shutting down communication and producing a downward spiral of tension between the manager and the elected official involved. On the other hand, when a governing body member openly directs constructive criticism toward the manager—gets issues out on the table—the manager can ask questions, provide information the member might not have, and respond to his or her concerns. Such dialogue gives members the opportunity to clarify their expectations of the manager by means of concrete examples as they come up, and it gives the manager more certainty about what he or she has to do to satisfy the elected officials and how well he or she is succeeding. Each governing body and its manager must work out how publicly they are willing to give and receive this feedback. They should come to an agreement early in the manager's tenure and confirm or modify it when there is turnover on the governing body.

Many elected officials appreciate the same sort of candor from the manager when they are behaving in a way that frustrates effective management. This attitude is by no means universal, however, and managers must be very careful in determining the comfort zone of a particular body and its individual members regarding the offering of constructive criticism. Nevertheless, the benefits of freely giving and accepting feedback can be as great for elected officials as they are for the manager.

Expectation 8: The Manager and the Governing Body Work Together to Develop a High-Performing Governing Body

The trends discussed earlier have sometimes produced dysfunctional effects on governing bodies. To the extent that elected officials are interested primarily in promoting particular causes or special constituencies, micromanaging administration, and criticizing their colleagues and the manager, prospects for responsible decision-making in the public interest are diminished. Tensions on the governing body are exacerbated in such cases by a knowledge gap that separates a full-time professional staff from a body of part-time elected officials.[25] The usual lack of government expertise on the part of newer members is compounded by the frequency of turnover on boards and councils. In most communities, governing bodies are comprised of "amateurs," in the very best sense of the term, who function as civic-minded citizen-legislators. Although they may be interested in seeking reelection, they are not professional politicians. The vast majority of local elected officials do not derive the bulk of their income from serving on governing bodies. They see themselves individually

25. John Nalbandian, "Professionals and the Conflicting Forces of Administrative Modernization and Civic Engagement," *American Review of Public Administration* 35 (Dec. 2005): 311–26.

and collectively as local government leaders and, as noted earlier, as trustees, delegates, and activists responsible for representing residents and making public policy for their community.

Who is responsible for closing the gap, for giving the board or council the tools it needs to become a high-performing decision-making body and for developing a partnership with the professional staff? While some might say "the chair or mayor" and others might say "the veteran members on the board or council," the manager also has an obligation here. The nature of this obligation is discussed in the sections that follow.

Tips for Ensuring Peak Performance of Governing Bodies

What would a high-performing governing body look like? At least ten common habits have been identified: (1) thinking and acting strategically and with a vision for the community's future; (2) understanding the law and policy processes; (3) demonstrating teamwork; (4) building a positive board culture; (5) honoring the council–staff partnership; (6) allocating governing body time and energy appropriately in four key areas—goal-setting and visioning retreats, work/study sessions, regular public hearings and meetings, and community relations and outreach; (7) having clear rules and procedures for board or council meetings; (8) reviewing feedback and data on community concerns, board and staff performance, and implementation efforts; (9) acting transparently; and (10) being aware of and respecting "shared constituencies" with other governments, nonprofit organizations, and community stakeholders.[26]

There are a number of practical steps a manager can take to help improve the efficiency of governing body deliberations. These include preparing the meeting agenda in a timely manner; scheduling meetings in a way that promotes good time management and the ability to focus on major topics; not overwhelming elected officials with highly detailed, lengthy technical reports; creating an annual policy calendar to identify and address long-range issues; and identifying and costing-out in advance possible alternative courses of action. Managers can also serve as "coaches" for their elected officials and governing bodies to help them develop high-performance habits.

One useful beginning point is for the manager to hold orientation sessions for new members of the governing body. At the same time, the chair or mayor should work with members to improve the conduct of the governing body's business, including encouraging colleagues to do their homework, ask good questions, and not make too many speeches or embarrass the staff with public comments that would be better said in private. The chair or mayor also should let the manager know if elected officials want other professional staff members to be present and contribute to the meeting and whether the agenda and related materials meet the governing body's expectations in terms of the timeliness, priority, quantity, and quality of information. In these respects, both the manager and the chair or mayor can play the important role of "coach" to the governing body.

Becoming a more high-performing board or council can pay important dividends beyond just the efficient and effective conduct of the public's business. Many governing bodies routinely record their public hearings and deliberations, and these meetings are often showcased on social media. An accessible video of members of a deliberative body asking thoughtful questions of one another and the professional staff, listening carefully to the views expressed by residents, treating all who are present at the meeting with courtesy and respect, and making decisions after assessing options, alternatives, and recommendations goes a long way toward maintaining confidence in local government, as well as conveying a sense of genuine partnership between the governing body and manager in the governance process.

---

26. Adapted from Carl H. Neu Jr., "The Manager as Coach: Increasing the Effectiveness of Elected Officials," *ICMA IQ Report* (Oct. 2003), 10. *See also* Chapter 3, "County and Municipal Governing Boards."

There is no set formula for building a high-performing governing body, but the above tips are important steps in that direction. While the lines between policy and administration will always be blurred, the desired outcome is for governing body members to be able and willing to successfully balance a number of competing interests—to focus on the vision and big picture for the community while dealing with concrete projects and programs, to think and act long-term and strategically while dealing with pressing immediate problems and needs, to establish goals and set priorities, and to decide on the community's best interest while satisfying constituent expectations.

Searching for a Manager

Hiring a county or city manager is one of the most important actions a governing body may be called upon to take. It should be evident from the preceding discussion that the working relationship of the manager and the governing body can have a significant influence on the effectiveness of the local government they serve. Whether a governing body is hiring its first manager or replacing one who has resigned or been dismissed, it can take the following basic steps to help ensure that it makes a good choice.

1. *Determine the future needs of the community and the county or municipal government.* It is well worth the governing body's time to discuss what it thinks the future demands on the manager's position will look like. What will be happening in the community? What will be the prominent or controversial issues? What will the workforce be like and how will it change? The answers to questions like these are likely to be different for every community. By thinking about them, the governing body increases the probability of finding somebody for the manager's post who has the right talents and experience to deal with the issues facing its community.
2. *List the critical competencies and skills that are required to deal with those future needs.* More than 13,000 men and women are members of the International City/County Management Association (ICMA) and forty-two affiliated state associations (including the North Carolina City and County Management Association), and there are many capable public administrators working in the public and private sectors who are not members. As of 2023, 1,545 members had successfully completed ICMA's Voluntary Credentialing Program or were candidates for ICMA's Credentialed Manager designation, committed to an additional forty hours of professional development each year. With 167 credentialed managers and candidates, North Carolina was the national leader in 2023, followed by Florida (138) and Texas (138).

   Many applicants for a county or city manager position will have educational credentials and experience that are at least adequate for the job and often are impressive, but no two of them will be exactly the same. Each will have different strengths and weaknesses. The challenge for the governing body is choosing from a large pool of capable applicants the one person who comes closest to having the unique set of skills and abilities needed to deal with local issues and with the board or council's personality. ICMA has identified the following eighteen manager competencies considered essential to effective local government management, and these competencies can guide governing boards in selecting a manager: staff effectiveness; policy facilitation; functional and operational expertise and planning; citizen service; quality assurance; initiative, risk-taking, vision, creativity, and innovation; technological literacy; democratic advocacy and citizen participation; diversity; budgeting; financial analysis; human resources management; strategic planning; advocacy and interpersonal communication; presentation skills; media relations; integrity; and personal development.[27]

3. *Recruit and screen applicants.* This step typically includes setting a salary range within which the governing body is willing to negotiate, advertising the job to attract persons with the attributes the governing body seeks, screening applications, and deciding on and arranging to interview the top candidates. Normally, the governing body needs a staff person or search consultant to assist with this process, and it is important that this be somebody who has the confidence of the entire membership. Care must be taken to preserve the confidentiality of the applications[28] unless and until the applicants release the county or municipality from that obligation. The governing body typically seeks such a release in the interview stage.

   Depending on the candidate pool, screening interviews will be arranged for five to ten semifinalists with a committee of the governing body or with a search consultant who will videotape the interviews, after which three to five finalists will each be invited for an interview with the entire governing body. Alternatively, it might be possible to narrow the field to three to five finalists simply by reviewing and discussing the applications and talking to the candidates' references.
4. *Interview finalists.* The structure of the interview process can vary quite a bit in practice, ranging from (1) simply interviewing each candidate, to (2) having candidates participate in assessment center exercises, taking performance-related tests that touch on key aspects of the manager's job, to (3) conducting highly structured interviews. At the very least, the interviews should be designed to allow governing body members to make reliable judgments about the important attributes they have agreed are needed in a manager and to make valid and consistent comparisons among the candidates. G.S. 143-318.11(a)(6) (a section of the state open meetings law) allows these interviews to be conducted in a closed session.[29] Sometimes candidates are invited to bring their spouses with them to see various aspects of the community and meet key people in and outside of the county or municipal government.
5. *Hire the manager.* After the interviews have been completed, the governing body usually tries to reach consensus on one candidate, with perhaps a backup if the chosen candidate does not accept an offer of employment. Many managers insist on consensus before they will accept an offer, feeling that anything less would make their positions too tenuous to survive the stress and strain that the demands of leadership and management put on the relationship between them and the elected officials. Some

---

27. International City/County Management Association, "Practices for Effective Local Government Management," icma.org/page/practices-effective-local-government-management-and-leadership. For a detailed treatment of the hiring process, see Vaughn Mamlin Upshaw, John A. Rible IV, and Carl W. Stenberg, *Getting the Right Fit: The Governing Board's Role in Hiring a Manager* (UNC School of Government, 2011).

28. Elkin Tribune, Inc. v. Yadkin Cnty. Bd. of Comm'rs, 331 N.C. 735 (1992). The state supreme court held that applications for employment were confidential personnel records under G.S. 153A-98 and that, therefore, their disclosure was prohibited. *See also* Robert Joyce, "Confidentiality of Applicants' Names," *Coates' Canons: NC Local Government Law* blog (UNC School of Government, Oct. 2, 2012), canons.sog.unc.edu/2012/10/confidentiality-of-applicants-names/.

29. The governing body must nevertheless follow all of the other procedural requirements in Article 33C of G.S. Chapter 143. While manager interviews are typically done in closed session, the law does not require it.

managers, however, are willing to start with no more than the tentative security of support from a simple majority.

If the leading finalist is not an inside candidate, sometimes the governing body will choose to send one or more of its members or its search consultant to the candidate's community for confirmation of its impressions. Usually, however, the governing body simply arranges for a final background investigation while it negotiates the terms and conditions of employment with the prospective manager.

When these negotiations are complete, the other candidates are notified, and the governing body takes formal action in open session to hire the successful candidate. The entire recruitment, screening, selection, and hiring process can normally be completed in about six months.

6. *Conclude an employment agreement.* An increasing number of counties and municipalities in North Carolina have formal employment agreements with managers. Sometimes called *contracts,* these documents may set out a variety of conditions specific to the manager's employment. ICMA has a model employment agreement that (1) covers optional and recommended approaches to items such as compensation; health, disability, and life insurance benefits; vacation, sick, and military leave; use of a car for official business; retirement fund contributions; expense accounts; participation in professional activities; moving and relocation expenses; home sale and purchase expenses; and other terms of employment and (2) seeks to establish a clear understanding between the governing body and the manager about the responsibilities, benefits, and privileges of the office. These types of agreements commonly include severance provisions, which, among other things, specify the manager's responsibilities for notifying the governing body in advance of his or her intention to resign and provide for a lump-sum severance payment in the event the manager's employment is involuntarily terminated for reasons other than illegal or improper behavior.[30] These agreements do not and cannot guarantee any tenure to the manager, inasmuch as G.S. 153A-81(1) and 160A-147(a) provide that the board or council shall appoint the manager to serve at its pleasure.

Evaluating the Manager—and the Governing Body

Evaluating the county or city manager is a task that governing bodies often find difficult and uncomfortable. In some cases, when a manager's evaluation is done in the context of a decision about an annual salary increase, the feedback is general or even perfunctory. In other cases, the chair or mayor simply gives the manager informal feedback on how he or she is doing on behalf of the governing body. In still other cases, the fact that the manager continues to hold the job is a clear indication that his or her performance is satisfactory to the majority of the governing body (i.e., it amounts to a positive evaluation). Why, then, should a governing body take valuable time to evaluate the manager more formally, especially if "things are going okay"?

30. *See* International City/County Management Association, "ICMA Model Employment Agreement" (2020), icma.org/documents/icma-model-employment-agreement-editable (this agreement is only accessible to ICMA members).

Clearly Set Expectations

As has been emphasized throughout this chapter, the relationship between a governing body and a manager can greatly enhance or impede the processes of governing, leading, and managing, so it is important that the parties devote time to properly establishing and maintaining it. As soon as possible, they should decide on what they expect of one another beyond the general tenets of statutory and professional responsibilities. No two governing bodies are exactly alike, nor are any two managers. No matter how much previous experience a new manager has had or how many managers a particular community has had, the relationship between a particular board or council and a particular manager is certain to be different in some ways from any other relationship previously experienced by either party. Thus, it is critical for all parties to be clear and in agreement around priorities, performance, and process.

Soon after a new manager is hired, and again if a significant turnover in governing body membership occurs or a new chair or mayor is elected, all parties will find it useful to discuss their specific expectations of one another. Such a discussion allows each party to discover what is needed from him/her and to express what he/she needs from the others to effectively carry out major responsibilities. The chair, mayor, and governing body's expectations of the manager inform their ability to both formally evaluate the manager and give him or her informal feedback about specific behavior and general performance.

Evaluation Process for Managers

Once the governing body and manager have reached agreement on performance expectations in the context of the vision, goals, and objectives for the community, they should agree on the purpose, procedure, and timing of the manager's evaluation. As indicated above, evaluations are often related to the governing body's decisions about adjustments in the manager's compensation.[31] Evaluations also are important tools for giving the manager feedback on specific strengths and weaknesses, which can be useful in improving his or her competencies and approaches. This regular dialogue can go a long way in avoiding surprises on the part of all parties and in building trust between the manager and governing body. The ICMA model employment agreement establishes the following minimum requirements for both the manager and the governing body: (1) an annual written evaluation, (2) a meeting to discuss the evaluation, (3) a written summary, and (4) delivery of the final written evaluation to the manager within thirty days of the evaluation meeting.

There are a variety of evaluation approaches—from "one-on-one" reviews with the chair or mayor to a complete 360-degree assessment of the manager by the governing body, professional staff, and community stakeholders. In accordance with the ICMA model employment agreement, elected officials are asked to complete a written form prior to the evaluation session with the manager, rating the manager on how well he or she exercises general organization management responsibilities, works with the governing body, carries out goals and objectives set by the board or council, develops and executes the budget, provides leadership, relates to the community, deals with the media and external audiences, communicates, delegates and supervises, and performs in other key areas. Usually the manager is also rated on personal characteristics, such as objectivity, integrity, productivity, judgment, initiative and risk-taking, ethics and morals, imagination, drive, self-assurance, stress management, and positive image. The manager normally does a self-assessment, which is shared with governing body members. These materials become the basis for a two-way conversation in closed session about the manager's performance and strengths/weaknesses led by the chair or mayor

31. *See* Vaughn Mamlin Upshaw, *How Are We Doing? Evaluating Manager and Board Performance* (UNC School of Government, 2014).

or, in some cases, by an outside facilitator. In addition to decisions on compensation and continuity, evaluation results are used by managers in their plan for personal and professional development prior to the next evaluation cycle.

More and more governing bodies are using retreats to establish initial expectations for themselves and the manager and to address other issues that contribute to effective governance. This kind of retreat allows the governing body (and other invited parties) to convene at a time and place that is different from its regular meeting time and place[32] in order to deliberate about matters that are difficult to fit into its routine business agendas. Retreats are commonly used by governing bodies for the following purposes: to identify strategic goals, objectives, and priorities to advance the governing body's vision for the community; to identify agreements and differences among members in their beliefs about and goals for the community; to plan how to achieve common goals and accommodate differences; to understand one another's expectations about working together and learn individual leadership styles and behaviors; and to review progress in achieving previously agreed-upon goals.[33] Facilitators from outside the local government are often used to bring neutrality into the retreat proceedings and to enhance listening and communication among the participants. Annual retreats are an effective way to build and sustain a unity of effort that is difficult to develop in the course of a governing body's regular meetings and to help keep elected officials and the manager focused on the "big picture" for the community.

Evaluating the Governing Body

Increasingly, managers are giving feedback regarding the governing body's performance, and boards and councils are evaluating themselves as decision-making bodies and representatives of the citizens. As the previously discussed research by Nalbandian and Svara indicates, the responsibilities of managing, leading, and governing in council–manager communities are shared. Just as the governing body expects the manager to conduct himself or herself in accordance with the General Statutes and the ICMA Code of Ethics, the manager has expectations of the governing body that impact his or her performance. These might include looking to the board or council to take ownership of its decisions, to recognize and uphold its role as policymaker not micromanager, to defend staff members when they are attacked for carrying out board or council policy, to be decisive and consistent, and to show respect and support for professional staff. Elected officials could fill out questionnaires assessing how the governing body as a unit sets goals, makes policy decisions, establishes priorities, understands the budget, engages the public, operates in a businesslike manner, handles information provided by the professional staff, and relates to the manager.[34]

For some governing bodies, annually evaluating the manager might seem like a big step, and evaluating their own effectiveness might seem potentially disruptive. However, just as regular feedback can enhance the manager's performance, introspection by the governing body as to how it conducts its work and relates to professional staff can lead to improvements in its decision-making capacity and ability to represent the community.

---

32. Note: A retreat must still meet all of the requirements set out in the open meetings law (G.S. Chapter 143, Article 33C).

33. For a more thorough discussion of retreats, see Kurt Jenne, "Governing Board Retreats," *Popular Government* 53 (UNC Institute of Government, Winter 1988): 20–26; Amy Cohen Paul, "The Retreat as Management Tool," *ICMA IQ Report* (Jan. 2001); and Robert Porter, "Secrets of a Successful Board Retreat," *Trustee* (May 2000): 26–27.

34. *See* Craig M. Wheeland, "Enhancing the Governing Body's Effectiveness," *in* Charldean Newell, ed., *The Effective Local Government Manager*, 3rd ed. (Washington, D.C.: International City/County Management Association, 2004), 57–69, 79–81.

Conclusion

The council–manager form of government has a long and successful history in the United States and especially in North Carolina. Like any governmental arrangement, it has potential advantages that are not automatically put into practice. However, many of these advantages can be realized if elected officials and managers work together in a good faith effort to observe the tenets on which the council–manager system is based. The General Statutes and the ICMA Code of Ethics constitute a solid foundation for this form of government, but they are only a starting point in a very complex working relationship. Success under the council–manager form depends, ultimately, on the governing body and the manager's ability to establish clear expectations, maintain good communication, build trust, and develop a sense of shared vision and teamwork on behalf of the community.

Additional Resources

Publications

Robert E. (Bob) Lee and Michael Abels, eds. *The Effective Local Government Manager.* 4th ed. Washington, D.C.: International City/County Management Association, 2022.

Kimberly H. Nelson and Carl W. Stenberg. *Managing Local Government Services: The Challenge of Change.* 4th ed. Washington, D.C.: International City/County Management Association, 2021.

Organizations

International City/County Management Association, www.icma.org.
National Association of Counties, www.naco.org.
National League of Cities, www.nlc.org.
North Carolina Association of County Commissioners, www.ncacc.org.
North Carolina City and County Management Association, www.ncmanagers.org.
North Carolina League of Municipalities, www.nclm.org.

Chapter 5

General Ordinance Authority

Rebecca Badgett

Rebecca Badgett is an attorney and School of Government faculty member who specializes in local government finance, internal control, and grants management.

This chapter updates and revises the previous chapter authored by former School of Government faculty member Trey Allen, whose contributions to the field and to this publication are gratefully acknowledged.

The general ordinance authority of local governments in North Carolina is synonymous with their general police power. The term "police power" denotes much more than the enforcement of criminal laws. It is the sovereign power retained by the states under the United States Constitution "to govern men and things within the limits of [their] dominion."[1] Through the police power, states are vested with the authority to enact and enforce laws to protect the health, safety, welfare, and morals of the public. The police power, therefore, is one of the inherent attributes of state sovereignty.

The police power is typically exercised by both the states and their various political subdivisions. How this power is shared varies from state to state, depending on the relevant constitutional and statutory provisions in each jurisdiction. In North Carolina, the General Statutes (hereinafter G.S.) delegate a portion of the police power to counties and cities in the form of their general ordinance authority. Therefore, the terms "police power" and "general ordinance authority" are synonymous and refer to a local government's authority to regulate to promote the common good. The courts understand the police power to encompass anything touching the safety, health, welfare, or morals of the public. While the potential scope of the police power is vast, federal and state constitutional provisions serve to limit its reach. For instance, Article I, Section 19 of the North Carolina

1. Thurlow v. Commonwealth of Mass., 46 U.S. 504, 583 (1847) (footnote omitted).

Constitution and the Fourteenth Amendment to the United States Constitution bar state and local officials from taking an individual's life, liberty, or property without due process of law.[2]

This chapter explores the sources and scope of local governments' general ordinance authority, considers the extent to which local governments may enforce their ordinances, and concludes with a brief description of the legal rules concerning the adoption and filing of ordinances in North Carolina.

Defining the General Ordinance Authority of Counties and Cities in North Carolina

Sources of the General Ordinance Authority

The North Carolina Constitution declares that the General Assembly "shall provide for the organization and government and the fixing of boundaries of counties, cities and towns, and other governmental subdivisions, and, except as otherwise prohibited by th[e] Constitution, may give such powers and duties to counties, cities and towns, and other governmental subdivisions as it may deem advisable."[3] This constitutional language endows the General Assembly with almost unbridled power to create, abolish, or merge counties, cities, and other units of local government and to define and limit their authority.

As creations of the legislature, local governments may act only as permitted by statute. The primary grants of power to local governments are found in G.S. Chapters 153A (counties) and 160A (cities). Strictly speaking, practically all of the statutes in Chapters 153A and 160A concern the police power in some manner. The focus of this chapter is on the general police power delegated to local governments by the statutory provisions located in Article 6 of G.S. Chapter 153A and Article 8 of G.S. Chapter 160A. (To avoid confusion, Articles 6 and 8 will be referred to collectively hereinafter as the "Police Power Statutes.")

The most important of the Police Power Statutes are G.S. 153A-121 and 160A-174. Together, the statutes invest the governing boards of counties and cities with the power to adopt ordinances that define, regulate, prohibit, or abate "acts, omissions, or conditions detrimental to the health, safety, or welfare of [their] citizens" and "the peace and dignity" of their jurisdictions and to "define and abate nuisances."[4] This general ordinance authority is supplemented by other provisions in the Police Power Statutes that expressly authorize local regulation of designated matters, with dangerous animals (G.S. 153A-131, 160A-187) and noise (G.S. 153A-133, 160A-184) being but two examples. A list of many of these supplemental Police Power Statutes is available in Table 5.1, below.

Scope of the General Ordinance Authority

It is not always easy to tell whether a particular matter falls within the general ordinance authority. Grave threats to public health, safety, or welfare are obviously subject to local control unless state or federal law dictates otherwise. The same is true of those matters expressly covered by the Police Power Statutes. Yet reasonable people can disagree over what conditions qualify as "detrimental"

---

2. While the phrase "due process" does not appear in Article I, Section 19, North Carolina's courts have long construed the phrase "law of the land" in Section 19 to encompass many of the requirements of the Fourteenth Amendment's due process clause. *See* John V. Orth & Paul Martin Newby, *The North Carolina State Constitution*, 2nd ed. (Oxford University Press, 2013), 68–72.

3. N.C. Const. art VII, § 1.

4. *See* G.S. 153A-121(a), 160A-174(a).

to the public and, thus, subject to regulation under a local government's police power authority. To a large degree, the reach of the general ordinance authority depends upon how broadly the courts interpret key terms like "detrimental" and "health, safety, or welfare." A brief review of the judiciary's approaches to questions of local government authority reveals that, while the courts have historically narrowly construed statutes granting power to counties and cities, they can be expected to take an expansive view of G.S. 153A-121 and 160A-174 in future cases.

Judicial Approaches to Local Government Power

In 1874, the North Carolina Supreme Court endorsed "Dillon's Rule" for interpreting legislative grants of power to local governments.[5] Named for the Iowa judge who formulated it, Dillon's Rule holds that a local government has only those powers (1) expressly granted to it by the legislature, (2) necessarily or fairly implied in or incident to powers expressly granted, and (3) essential—not simply convenient, but indispensable—to accomplish its declared objects and purposes.[6] Under Dillon's Rule, any reasonable doubt concerning the lawfulness of a challenged action had to be resolved against the local government.

North Carolina's courts applied Dillon's Rule in cases disputing the authority of local governments until the 1970s, often with unpredictable results. Many of the inconsistent outcomes stemmed from judicial attempts to discern whether specific legislative grants of authority "necessarily or fairly implied" certain powers. It is fair to say that the judiciary generally seemed more willing to find implied authority when local governments engaged in historically unremarkable activities than when they embarked upon new, unusual, or controversial endeavors.[7] The courts also tended to disfavor local measures imposing taxes or fees during the Dillon's Rule era.[8]

In 1971, the General Assembly appeared to overrule Dillon's Rule for cities by enacting G.S. 160A-4. This law declares that the provisions of G.S. Chapter 160A "shall be broadly construed and grants of power shall be construed to include any additional and supplemental powers . . . reasonably necessary or expedient to carry them into execution and effect." In 1973, by enacting G.S. 153A-4, the legislature endorsed a substantially identical rule of construction for G.S. Chapter 153A.

Taken at face value, G.S. 153A-4 and 160A-4 direct the judiciary to broadly interpret the county and city statutes. However, for some years after the adoption of 153A-4 and 160A-4, the North Carolina Supreme Court did not uniformly apply this mandate when construing local government authority. In the 1994 case of *Homebuilders Ass'n of Charlotte, Inc. v. City of Charlotte*, the state

---

5. Smith v. City of Newbern, 70 N.C. 14, 70 (1874).

6. David W. Owens, "Local Government Authority to Implement Smart Growth Programs: Dillon's Rule, Legislative Reform, and the Current State of Affairs in North Carolina," 35 Wake Forest L. Rev. 671, 680–81 (2000) (quoting John F. Dillon, *The Law of Municipal Corporations*, 2nd ed. (1873), sec. 55).

7. *Compare City of Newbern*, 70 N.C. at 14 (emphasis in original) (holding that a law granting the city power to "*appoint[] market places* and regulat[e] the same" implied authority to build a public market house) *with* State v. Gulledge, 208 N.C. 204, 208 (1935) (holding that neither the power "to regulate the use of automobiles" conferred by charter nor the authority "to license and regulate all vehicles operated for hire" and "to make . . . regulations for the better government" delegated by statute granted the city express or implied power to require taxicab operators to file proof of liability insurance in designated amounts). One explanation for the different outcomes in *City of Newbern* and *Gulledge* is that public marketplaces go back at least as far as ancient Greece, whereas at the time of *Gulledge* the requirement that taxicab operators have liability insurance was "a public policy hitherto unknown in the general legislation of the State." 208 N.C. at 208.

8. *See* Owens, *supra* note 6, at 683 (noting that the courts "strictly construed" local authority in the area of taxes and fees during the period between 1890 and 1910). In 1893, for instance, the North Carolina Supreme Court invalidated an assessment for sidewalks in Greensboro. *Id.* at 684 (citing City of Greensboro v. McAdoo, 112 N.C. 359, 367–78 (1893)).

supreme court held that a city may charge reasonable fees for regulatory services, such as commercial driveway permit reviews and rezoning reviews, even though no statute expressly authorized the fees in question.[9] In reaching this conclusion, the court opined that G.S. 160A-4 obliged the court to construe the grants of power in G.S. Chapter 160A expansively. Five years later in *Smith Chapel Baptist Church v. City of Durham*, without even considering G.S. 160A-4, the state supreme court struck down a local ordinance on the basis that G.S. 160A-314(a1) prohibited a city from imposing fees in excess of a stormwater and drainage system's cost.[10] The court held that "[w]hen the language of a statute is clear and unambiguous, there is no room for judicial construction, and the courts must give [the statute] its plain and definite meaning." In 2012, the state supreme court again declined to apply G.S. 153A-4 when interpreting the reach of a county zoning ordinance. The court held that the "broad construction" mandate of G.S. 160A-4 and 153A-4 does not apply when the statute at issue is clear and unambiguous.[11] Given the apparent reluctance of the state supreme court to apply G.S. 153A-4 and 160A-4 to broadly construe grants of power, it began to appear that the court was likely to rule against local governments in disputes over the lawfulness of ordinances.

In 2014, the state supreme court was, for the first time, squarely presented with the question of whether the broad construction mandates in G.S. 153A-4 and 160A-4 extend to the general ordinance authority. In *King v. Town of Chapel Hill*,[12] a tow truck operator challenged the legality of towing and mobile phone ordinances adopted by Chapel Hill's town council. The towing ordinance prohibited the removal of automobiles from nonresidential private lots without the vehicle owners' permission unless signs were posted at designated intervals warning that the lots were tow-away zones. It also capped towing and storage fees at amounts set annually by the council and directed towing companies to accept payment by credit card at no extra charge to the owners of involuntarily towed vehicles. The mobile phone ordinance barred individuals 18 years or older from using mobile phones while driving, on pain of a $25 fine but no driver's license points.

The basic issue before the supreme court was whether the general ordinance authority conferred on cities by G.S. 160A-174 could sustain the towing and mobile phone ordinances. To resolve this issue, the court first had to determine whether G.S. 160A-174 would need to be interpreted expansively under G.S. 160A-4. The court explained that it had no choice but to apply G.S. 160A-4 because the police power "is by its very nature ambiguous" and "cannot be fully defined in clear and definite terms."[13] In broadly construing G.S. 160A-174, the court held that cities have the authority to regulate involuntary towing to prevent or mitigate conflicts between the owners of private lots and individuals who park there without permission and between tow truck operators and automobile owners. Turning to the disputed provisions of the towing ordinance, the court found that G.S. 160A-174 was expansive enough to support the ordinance's signage requirements. It further ruled that the town's interest in ensuring that owners have quick and easy access to towed vehicles justified forcing towing companies to take credit cards.

Unlike the signage and form-of-payment provisions, the ordinance's caps on towing and storage fees did not survive judicial scrutiny. The link between the public welfare and the fee caps was too "attenuated" in the court's view for the town to impose the caps without explicit statutory authorization.[14] Additionally, the court expressed concern that the caps would make it impossible for

---

9. Homebuilders Ass'n of Charlotte v. City of Charlotte, 336 N.C. 37, 45–47 (1994).

10. Smith Chapel Baptist Church v. City of Durham, 350 N.C. 805, 815 (1999).

11. Lanvale Props., LLC v. Cnty. of Cabarrus, 366 N.C. 142, 157 (2012).

12. 367 N.C. 400 (2014).

13. *King*, 367 N.C. at 406.

14. *King*, 367 N.C. at 409. As an example of such statutory authorization, the court pointed to G.S. 160A-304, which permits cities to set the rates charged by taxi cabs. *Id.*

towing companies to recover the costs of complying with the ordinance's other mandates. It even suggested that the caps might violate the constitutional right to enjoy the fruits of one's labor.[15] The court also invalidated the ordinance's prohibition against passing credit card fees on to the owners of involuntarily towed vehicles, describing it as tantamount to a fee cap.

The mobile phone ordinance was struck down in its entirety. State law already prohibited individuals of all ages from texting while driving and barred school bus drivers and individuals under the age of 18 from using mobile phones while driving on public streets or highways.[16] The court regarded these laws as evidence that the General Assembly wanted all regulation of drivers' mobile phone usage to occur at the statewide level.

Impact of King v. Town of Chapel Hill *on the General Ordinance Authority*

The most important aspect of *King* is its definitive pronouncement that the provisions of G.S.160A-174, and by implication G.S. 153A-121, must be interpreted broadly. Another valuable attribute of *King* is that it provides lower courts with a framework for analyzing whether an ordinance represents a valid exercise of the general ordinance authority. When facing a claim that a local government has acted outside the bounds of G.S. 153A-121 or 160A-174, a court should begin by first asking whether the contested ordinance targets a problem within the scope of the police power. If the ordinance concerns an activity or condition that threatens the health, safety, or welfare of the public in some way, the answer to this question will probably be yes.[17] If yes, the court should then consider whether the requirements imposed by the ordinance are reasonably calculated to deal with the problem. A finding that such requirements are reasonable will typically warrant a ruling in favor of the local government, even if the requirements are extensive.

Of course, *King* was not a total win for Chapel Hill. The court's rulings against the town highlight a few of the substantial restrictions on the police power of local governments. The court's invocation of the right to the fruits of one's labor is a warning that local governments can violate constitutional rights when they simultaneously increase regulatory burdens on businesses and take steps to limit what the businesses may charge others. Likewise, the invalidation of the mobile phone ordinance reminds local governments that the police power granted by G.S. 153A-121 and 160A-174 is preempted when the General Assembly either expressly or implicitly removes a matter from local control. The principles of preemption and other limitations on the general ordinance authority are discussed in more detail below.

Grants of Specific Authority in the Police Power Statutes

The broad grant of authority contained in G.S. 153A-121 and 160A-174 is supplemented by other provisions in the Police Power Statutes that expressly authorize local governments to adopt ordinances to regulate certain designated matters.

The grants of specific authority listed in Table 5.1 include the power to regulate, restrict, or prohibit amplified noises that tend to annoy, disturb, or frighten citizens (G.S. 153A-133, 160A-184); business activities of itinerant merchants and peddlers (G.S. 153A-125, 160A-178); and begging and

15. *See* N.C. Const. art. I, § 1 (declaring "that all persons are created equal; that they are endowed by their Creator with certain inalienable rights; that among these are life, liberty, the enjoyment of the fruits of their own labor, and the pursuit of happiness").

16. *See* G.S. 20-137.3(b) (forbidding mobile phone use by minor drivers); 20-137.4(b) (outlawing the use of mobile phones by persons operating school buses); 20-137.4A(a) (banning drivers from text messaging while operating automobiles).

17. Minor threats to the public welfare can be enough to bring a matter within the police power's reach. Concerns about odor and noise problems, for example, have been held to justify a city's decision to regulate the number of dogs that could be kept per lot. State v. Maynard, 195 N.C. App. 757 (2009).

Table 5.1 Selected Police Power Statutes for Local Governments

Subject Matter	City Statute (G.S.)	County Statute (G.S.)
Solicitation campaigns, flea markets, itinerant merchants	160A-178	153A-125
Begging/panhandling	160A-179	153A-126
Aircraft overflights	160A-180	—
Places of amusement	160A-181	153A-135
Abuse of animals	160A-182	153A-127
Explosive, corrosive, inflammable, or radioactive substances	160A-183	153A-128
Noise	160A-184	153A-133
Pollutants or contaminants	160A-185	—
Domestic animals	160A-186	—
Possession or harboring of dangerous animals	160A-187	153A-131
Bird sanctuaries	160A-188	—
Firearms	160A-189	153A-129
Pellet guns	160A-190	153A-130
Sunday closings	160A-191	—
Solid wastes	—	153A-136
Public health nuisance	160A-193	153A-140
Stream-clearing programs	160A-193.1	153A-140.1
Regulation/licensing of businesses, trades, etc.	160A-194	153A-134
Curfews	160A-198	153A-142
Removal/disposal of abandoned and junked vehicles	160A-303*	153A-132
Abandonment of junked vehicles	160A-303.2*	153A-132.2
Removal/disposal of trash, garbage, etc.	160A-303.1*	153A-132.1
Registration of mobile homes, house trailers, etc.	—	153A-138

**Denotes a provision found outside of the Police Power Statutes.*

other canvassing of the public for contributions (G.S. 153A-126, 160A-179). Local governments also have express statutory authority to prohibit the abuse of animals (G.S. 153A-127, 160A-182) and to restrict or prohibit the possession of dangerous animals (G.S. 153A-131, 160A-187). The Police Power Statutes invest counties and cities with the power to regulate places of amusement, such as coffeehouses, cocktail lounges, night clubs, and beer halls, so long as their regulations are consistent with any permits or licenses issued by the state's Alcoholic Beverage Control Commission (G.S. 153A-135, 160A-181). Additionally, local governments may restrict or prohibit the discharge of firearms except in defense of persons or property or pursuant to the lawful instructions of law enforcement officials (G.S. 153A-129, 160A-189). Some Police Power Statutes include procedural requirements that must be followed for ordinances dealing with designated subjects to be valid and enforceable. When more than one statute authorizes an action, a local government usually has the choice of proceeding under any or all of them. This principle does not apply, however, when it is clear from the unambiguous text or level of detail in a statute that the General Assembly intended that law to guide local action on a particular matter. A governing board should consult its attorney whenever questions arise about whether to rely on G.S. 153A-121 or 160A-174 or on one of the grants of specific authority in the Police Power Statutes.

As evidenced above, many of the Police Power statutes vest both counties and cities with the authority to regulate in the same areas. However, in a few instances, the statutes have granted regulatory authority over a specific subject to either the county or a city. This does not mean the other is prohibited from regulating in that area. The general ordinance authority extends beyond the individual powers enumerated in the Police Power Statutes, and the existence of specific statutory authority granted only to a city or county could reflect nothing more than a legislative assumption that a problem is more acute in urban or rural areas.

A handful of the Police Power Statutes exclude things from the general ordinance authority of local governments. G.S. 153A-145 and 160A-202 collectively prohibit counties and cities from banning cisterns and rain barrel collection systems used to collect water for irrigation purposes. G.S. 153A-145.2 and 160A-203 prevent local governments from prohibiting the sale of soft drinks above a particular size.

Exercising General Ordinance Authority

Almost every provision in the Police Power Statutes requires a local government to exercise its general police power "by ordinance." The adoption of an ordinance is therefore usually necessary if a county or city wishes to regulate, restrict, or prohibit something. A few statutes permit a county or city to eliminate threats to public health or safety even in the absence of an ordinance. Those statutes are examined briefly in the "Public Nuisance Abatement" section below. When adopting an ordinance pursuant to any of the Police Power Statutes, local governments must ensure compliance with any procedural requirements established within the statute granting the authority to act to ensure the ordinance will be valid and enforceable.

Territorial Limits of General Ordinance Authority

G.S. 153A-122 allows a county to make an ordinance adopted pursuant to any statute in G.S. Chapter 153A, Article 6 applicable to any part of the county that is not within a city. A city's governing board may adopt a resolution allowing a county's police power ordinance to apply inside the city.[18] If the city's governing board later changes its mind, it may by resolution withdraw its consent to enforcement of the county ordinance within its borders. The governing board should promptly inform the county of its withdrawal resolution, as the ordinance will remain in effect inside the city until thirty days after the county receives the notice.

For the most part, a city's police power ordinances apply only within the corporate limits and to any city-owned property or right-of-way outside the city.[19] A city may enforce zoning and other development ordinances inside its corporate limits and within its extraterritorial jurisdiction (ETJ).

18. G.S. 153A-122.
19. G.S. 160A-176.

When a city chooses to enforce development ordinances in its ETJ, the county's development ordinances no longer apply there, but the county's police power ordinances continue in force.[20] Thus, a county's noise ordinance applies within the ETJ, even though its zoning ordinances do not.

Preemption of Local Ordinances

Preemption is a legal concept where a higher level of government has the authority to limit, or even prohibit, a lower level of government from regulating certain areas or subjects. Accordingly, in certain instances, state or federal law may deny local governments the power to regulate matters that would otherwise fall within their general ordinance authority. When this occurs, the local regulation is said to be "preempted."

The six essential rules of preemption for local governments are codified in G.S. 160A-174(b).[21] These rules include:

- Local governments are prohibited from adopting ordinances that violate liberties guaranteed by the state or federal constitution.
- Local governments may not by ordinance prohibit acts, omissions, or conditions expressly made lawful by state or federal law.
- Local governments may not by ordinance make lawful an act, omission, or condition expressly prohibited by state or federal law. For example, because state law criminalizes prostitution, no county or city may legalize prostitution within its borders.
- Local governments have no power to regulate subjects that state or federal law expressly forbids them to regulate.
- Even when no state or federal law expressly deprives counties or cities of the power to regulate a matter, local governments may not regulate subject(s) for which state or federal statutes evidence a legislative intent to provide a complete and integrated regulatory scheme to the exclusion of local regulation. In other words, if federal or state laws regarding a subject are sufficiently comprehensive, the courts will assume that the U.S. Congress or the General Assembly has meant to remove the matter from local control.[22]
- No ordinance may define an offense using the same elements as an offense defined by state or federal law. State law, for instance, already criminalizes various forms of assault, including simple assault, simple assault and battery, and assault inflicting serious bodily injury.[23] Accordingly, counties and cities may not adopt ordinances that prohibit the very same misconduct covered by the assault statutes.

---

20. G.S. 160D-202(b) provides that a city is not allowed to apply a development regulation in the ETJ that it is not also applying within the city.

21. Nothing about preemption appears in the text of G.S. 153A-121, but the North Carolina Supreme Court has repeatedly held that G.S. 160A-174(b) applies to a county's exercise of its general ordinance authority.

22. In *Craig v. Cnty. of Chatham*, 356 N.C. 40 (2002), the North Carolina Supreme Court struck down an ordinance designed to regulate large-scale hog farming operations in Chatham County. The plaintiffs argued that comprehensive state-level swine farm laws preempted the local rules. The supreme court agreed, concluding that "North Carolina's swine farm regulations [and the applicable state statutes] are so comprehensive in scope that the General Assembly must have intended that they comprise a 'complete and integrated regulatory scheme' on a statewide basis, thus leaving no room for further local regulation."

23. G.S. 14-33(a) (making simple assault and simple assault and battery Class 2 misdemeanors); G.S. 14-32.4 (making it a Class F felony to assault and inflict serious injury on another person).

G.S. 160A-174(b) concludes with a reminder that the preemption rules ordinarily do not stop local governments from adopting higher standards of conduct than those demanded by federal or state laws. Many ordinances contain severance clauses, which allow a court to remove or sever the preempted, invalid, or unconstitutional portion of an ordinance, while not affecting the validity of the remaining portions of the ordinance. In *Schroeder v. City of Wilmington*, the court upheld the city's short-term rental regulations that were not "interrelated or mutually dependent" on the invalid [short-term rental] registration requirements.[24]

Ordinance Enforcement

G.S. Chapters 153A and 160A endow counties and municipalities with substantial authority to enforce their ordinances through criminal or civil proceedings. In general, on the criminal side, if the text of an ordinance so provides, a violation of a local ordinance constitutes a Class 3 misdemeanor.[25] On the civil side, an ordinance may provide that a violation shall subject the offender to a civil penalty to be recovered in a civil action and/or an injunction or an abatement order may be pursued to further ensure compliance. The enforcement mechanism will differ depending on the type of ordinance violation. Because an ordinance "may provide, when appropriate, that each day's continuing violation is a separate and distinct offense," an offender risks multiple criminal charges and mounting civil penalties if they refuse to correct a violation.[26]

Criminal Actions

For many years, local ordinances were, by default, criminally enforceable as a misdemeanor or infraction as provided by G.S. 14-4. Therefore, unless an ordinance expressly provided otherwise, local governments had the authority to enforce a local ordinance under G.S. 14-4. As a result, many local governments criminally enforced violations of local ordinances. In 2018, the General Assembly embarked on a project to decriminalize local government ordinances. In 2021, the legislature passed S.L. 2021-138, a law that, in part, modified local governments' authority to enforce ordinances criminally.[27] Specifically, the law amended G.S. 153A-123 and 160A-175 to authorize counties and cities to criminally enforce local ordinances under G.S. 14-4 "only if the [county/city] specifies such in the ordinance." As a result of the amendments, if a local government plans to make the violation of an ordinance a misdemeanor or infraction, it must include a statement in the ordinance to indicate that a violation is a misdemeanor or infraction as established in G.S. 14-4. The ordinance should also specify the maximum fine, term of imprisonment, or infraction penalty that may be imposed for the violation.[28] The amount of money or number of days of imprisonment may not exceed the maximum penalties imposed by G.S. 14-4.[29]

Even when a local government has made an ordinance criminally enforceable, it may not find a person guilty of the ordinance violation if, when tried for that violation, the person satisfied G.S. 14-4(c) by producing proof of compliance with the local ordinance through either of the

---

24. *Schroeder v. City of Wilmington*, 282 N.C. App. 558, 572 (2022).

25. G.S. 14-4(a), 153A-123, 160A-175(b).

26. G.S. 153A-123(g), 160A-175(g).

27. S.L. 2021-138, Part XIII, www.ncleg.gov/Sessions/2021/Bills/Senate/PDF/S300v8.pdf.

28. G.S. 153A-123(b), 160A-175(b).

29. *See* G.S. 14-4(a), which specifies that violators of local ordinances shall be guilty of a Class 3 misdemeanor and shall be fined no more than $500. No fine may exceed $50 unless the ordinance expressly states that the maximum fine is greater. Violations of regulations related to the operation or parking of vehicles are infractions that carry a maximum penalty of $50.

following: (1) no new alleged violations of the local ordinance within 30 days from the date of the initial alleged violation; or (2) that the person has made a good-faith effort to seek assistance to address an underlying factor related to unemployment, homelessness, mental health, or substance abuse that may have affected that person's ability to comply with the local ordinance.[30] G.S. 14-4(c) suggests that criminal enforcement of the local ordinance is disfavored, and it may not be pursued if the violator has taken steps to comply or has made a good-faith effort to seek assistance with underlying issues.

Criminal Enforcement Prohibited

G.S. 153A-123(b1) and 160A-175(b1) set forth a list of types of ordinances that may not be criminally enforced under G.S. 14-4. This list is largely the same for both counties and cities and includes any ordinance adopted under Chapter 160D (except unsafe building regulations) and ordinances that regulate stream-clearing programs; the licensing of businesses or trades; outdoor advertising; solar collectors; cisterns and rain barrels; and tree regulations. In addition, cities are prohibited from criminally enforcing ordinances that regulate taxis, building setback lines, and curb-cut regulations, while counties may not criminally enforce ordinances that regulate mobile homes or house trailers.

Civil Actions

Local governing boards have the option of enforcing their ordinances through a variety of civil measures, including civil penalties and court orders directing offenders to comply with particular ordinances. In most cases, such measures cannot be pursued unless the ordinance at issue contains language identifying them as potential methods of enforcement.[31]

Civil Penalties

To impose a civil penalty for an ordinance violation, the ordinance must specify the amount of the penalty to be charged per violation. Each violation may be charged as a separate offense, and a penalty attaches for the initial violation and each violation thereafter. The local government may pursue payment of the penalty through a civil action against the offender if they fail to pay the penalty within a prescribed time period.[32] There is no statutory cap on the amount of civil penalties, but the Eighth Amendment to the U.S. Constitution prohibits civil penalties that are grossly disproportionate to their corresponding offenses.[33] The courts are unlikely to rule that a civil penalty is too high under the Eighth Amendment, so long as the penalty is not exceptionally large compared with other civil penalties imposed by the county or city.[34]

Local governments may delegate the power to issue civil citations to personnel who are not law enforcement officers. A county or city may have its attorneys pursue civil penalty actions in superior or district court, depending on the amount of penalty at issue. If the penalty amount is small enough, a local government may use non-attorney employees to seek a judgment against the offender in small claims court. A civil penalty action is one "in the nature of debt," which means that a person found responsible for violating an ordinance with a civil penalty provision owes a

---

30. G.S. 14-4(c).

31. Rather than include enforcement language in every ordinance, some jurisdictions have "remedies" sections in their codes of ordinances that cross-reference various ordinances and specify which remedies may be applied for violations of each ordinance.

32. G.S. 153A-123(c), 160A-175(c).

33. David M. Lawrence, "Are There Limits on the Size of Penalties to Enforce Local Government Ordinances?" *Local Government Law Bulletin* No. 128 (UNC School of Government, July 2012).

34. *Id.*

debt to the county or city. Furthermore, the standard of proof in civil penalty cases, as in most civil proceedings, is "by a preponderance of evidence," which is a lower burden of proof for the local government than the criminal "beyond a reasonable doubt" standard. All of these factors (who may issue citations, who may bring the action, the lack of a set dollar maximum on the penalty, and the evidentiary standard) lead some local officials to prefer civil actions to criminal prosecutions for ordinance violations.

The Setoff Debt Collection Act offers local governments an avenue for recovering civil penalties in excess of $50 without having to resort to litigation.[35] As authorized by the Act, the North Carolina Association of County Commissioners and the North Carolina League of Municipalities have set up the Local Government Debt Setoff Clearinghouse. Provided they give debtors the statutorily mandated notice, counties and cities may submit qualifying debts to the Clearinghouse to be recovered from debtors' state tax refunds or lottery winnings. According to its website, the Clearinghouse has collected more than $403 million for local governments since 2002.[36]

Local officials should not assume that incorporating a civil penalty provision into an ordinance will generate significant revenue for county or city coffers. Pursuant to Article IX, Section 7 of the North Carolina Constitution, the "clear proceeds" of moneys collected for most ordinance violations must go to the public school system(s) of the county in which the local government is situated.

Equitable Remedies

The governing board of a county or city may include language in an ordinance providing for its enforcement through an appropriate equitable remedy. An equitable remedy is a legal remedy that is sought in equity and may include such things as injunction, specific performance, and other types of relief. In short, an equitable remedy will allow the county or city to obtain a court order directing an offender to comply with the ordinance. The offender who ignores such an order risks being held in contempt of court.

Public Nuisance Abatement

A public nuisance is "a condition or activity involving real property that amounts to an unreasonable interference with the health, safety, morals, or comfort of the community."[37] The authority of local governments to define and abate such nuisances is usually exercised through ordinances that prohibit certain conditions or uses of real property. One common example is the overgrown vegetation ordinance, which imposes minimum maintenance requirements on residential or commercial lots.

When a nuisance ordinance is violated, the local government may seek a court order directing the defendant to take whatever steps are necessary to comply with the ordinance, including the closure, demolition, or removal of structures; the removal of items such as fixtures or furniture; the cutting of grass or weeds; or the making of improvements or repairs to the property. If the offender fails to obey the order within the time set by the court, the local government can execute the order and automatically obtain a lien on the property for the cost of execution. The offender may be cited for contempt.

It is sometimes lawful for counties and cities to remedy nuisances without going to court. G.S. 153A-140 allows a county "to remove, abate, or remedy everything that is dangerous or

---

35. G.S. 105A-1, -16.

36. North Carolina Local Government Debt Setoff Clearinghouse, www.ncsetoff.org (last visited 1/17/2024).

37. Richard Ducker, "Nuisance Abatement and Local Governments: What a Mess," *Coates' Canons: NC Local Government Law* blog (June 16, 2011), sog.unc.edu/blogs/coates-canons/nuisance-abatement-and-local-governments-what-mess.

prejudicial to the public health or safety," though this authority does not extend to bona fide farms. For a county to exercise its power under G.S. 153A-140, it must provide the property owner with adequate notice, the right to a hearing, and the right to seek judicial review.

G.S. 160A-193 permits a city to "remove, abate, or remedy everything in the city limits, or within one mile thereof, that is dangerous or prejudicial to the public health or public safety." The expense of the removal or abatement of the public health nuisance shall be paid by the person in default. For example, if the city orders the removal of an unsafe swimming pool, the owner of the pool (as the person in default) is responsible for paying for its removal. G.S. 160A-193 declares that the power it confers may be exercised "summarily," that is to say, without affording the property owner notice or a hearing. As interpreted by the North Carolina Court of Appeals, however, G.S. 160A-193 does not authorize a city to demolish a building "without providing notice or a hearing to the owner [unless] the building constitutes an imminent danger to the public health or safety necessitating its immediate demolition."[38]

When a local government eliminates a nuisance pursuant to G.S. 153A-140 or 160A-193, it automatically obtains a lien for the expense of corrective action upon the land or premises where the nuisance occurred. A city also has a lien for the action's cost on any other real property—except a primary residence—owned by the offending property owner inside or within one mile of the city. (The owner can avoid a lien on other property by showing that the nuisance resulted solely from another's conduct.)

Dangerous nuisances do not represent the only situations that can lead to local government action without a court order. In the case of an individual who qualifies as a chronic violator of a public nuisance ordinance, the local government may notify the person that, if his or her property is found to be in violation of the ordinance during the calendar year in which notice is given, the county or city will remedy the violation and the cost of corrective action will be a lien upon the property.[39]

Adoption and Filing of Local Ordinances

Adoption of Ordinances

Consistent with the notion that ordinances regulate important aspects of citizens' lives, special procedural rules govern the adoption of ordinances in most situations.[40] With certain exceptions, the only time a county's governing board may adopt an ordinance at the meeting in which it is introduced is when all board members are present and vote in favor of the ordinance.[41] If the ordinance passes, but does not receive a unanimous vote, the board may adopt the ordinance by majority vote at any time within 100 days of its introduction. For a city's governing board to adopt an ordinance on the date of its introduction, the ordinance must garner an affirmative vote equal to

---

38. Monroe v. City of New Bern, 158 N.C. App. 275, 278 (2003). The court also held that, if a city wishes to destroy a dwelling that does not pose an imminent threat to the public, it must follow the procedures set forth in the Minimum Housing Standards statutes contained in Chapter 160D. *Id.* at 279. Those statutes outline in significant detail the notice and hearing procedures a city has to satisfy prior to the demolition of a dwelling deemed unfit for human habitation.

39. G.S. 153A-140.2, 160A-200.1 (defining a chronic violator as "a person who owns property whereupon, in the previous calendar year, the [local government] gave notice of violation at least three times under any provision of the public nuisance ordinance").

40. These procedural rules also apply to most ordinance amendments.

41. G.S. 153A-45.

at least two-thirds of the board's membership, excluding vacant seats and not counting the mayor unless the mayor has the right to vote on all questions before the board.[42]

A common misconception is that a public hearing must be held any time an ordinance is proposed for adoption. In fact, only a few types of ordinances require a public hearing. The statute granting the authority to take a specific action will specify whether a public hearing is required. If a statute does not include the public hearing requirement, the governing board may, but is not required to, hold a public hearing prior to voting on the ordinance at issue.

Filing of Ordinances

With certain exceptions, every ordinance enacted by the governing board of a county or city must appear in either an *ordinance book* or a *code of ordinances*. It is crucial for a local government to file and index or codify its ordinances as required by law. Pursuant to G.S. 160A-79, any ordinance not filed and indexed or codified is unenforceable. Local governments are under no legal obligation to post ordinances on their websites, though many do so anyway to improve public access to their ordinances.

The primary statutory provisions for ordinance books appear in G.S. 153A-48 and 160A-78, while those for codes reside in G.S. 153A-49 and 160A-77. Some of the county and city rules differ. To avoid confusion, they are considered separately below.

City Ordinance Book

A true copy of each city ordinance must be filed in an appropriately indexed ordinance book. This book is separate from the minutes book and is maintained for public inspection in the city clerk's office. If the city has adopted and issued a code of ordinances, its ordinances need to be filed and indexed in the ordinance book only until they are codified.

City Code of Ordinances

Every city with a population of 5,000 or more must adopt and issue a code of ordinances. A code is a bound or loose-leaf compilation of the local government's ordinances systematically arranged by topic into chapters or articles.

The code must be updated at least annually unless there have been no changes. It may contain separate sections for general ordinances and technical ordinances, or the latter may be issued as separate books or pamphlets. Examples of technical ordinances are those pertaining to the following:

- building construction,
- installation of plumbing and electric wiring,
- installation of cooling and heating equipment,
- zoning,
- subdivision control, or
- the use of public utilities, buildings, or facilities operated by the city.

A city's governing board may omit from the code classes of ordinances that it designates as having limited interest or transitory value—the annual budget ordinance is one example—but the code should clearly describe what has been left out. The council may also codify certain ordinances pertaining to zoning district boundaries and traffic regulations by making appropriate entries upon

42. G.S. 160A-75.

official map books permanently retained in the clerk's office or in another city office generally accessible to the public.

The city is free to choose a code-preparation method that meets its needs. One acceptable method would be for the city to hire a private legal publisher offering ordinance codification services.

County Ordinance Book

The clerk to the board of commissioners must file each county ordinance in an appropriately indexed ordinance book, with the exception of certain kinds of ordinances discussed in the next paragraph. The ordinance book, kept separately from the minutes book, is stored for public inspection in the clerk's office. If the county has adopted and issued a code of ordinances, it must index its ordinances and maintain them in an ordinance book only until it codifies them.

The ordinance book need not include transitory ordinances—like the budget ordinance—and certain technical regulations adopted in ordinances by reference, although the law does require a cross-reference to the minutes book (at least for transitory ordinances). If the board of commissioners adopts technical regulations in an ordinance by reference, the clerk must maintain an official copy of the regulations in his or her office for public inspection.[43]

County Code of Ordinances

Counties may, but are not required to, adopt and issue codes of ordinances. A county that has codified its ordinances should update its code annually unless there have been no changes. Counties may reproduce their codes by any method that yields legible and permanent copies. A county, like a city, is free to select a code-preparation method that suits its needs.

A county may include separate sections in a code for general ordinances and technical ordinances, or it may issue the latter as separate books or pamphlets. The governing board may omit from the code classes of ordinances designated by it as having limited interest or transitory value, but the code should clearly describe the classes of ordinances that have been left out. The board may also codify certain ordinances pertaining to zoning areas or district boundaries by making appropriate entries upon official map books permanently retained in the clerk's office or in some other county office generally accessible to the public.

Records Retention Considerations

Records retention schedules promulgated by the North Carolina Department of Natural and Cultural Resources mandate that local governments keep official copies of their ordinances permanently.[44] To the extent that they have funds available for the purpose, counties and cities likewise have to create preservation duplicates of their ordinances that are durable, accurate, complete and clear. The department's policy is that those duplicates must be maintained in paper form or on microfilm.

---

43. G.S. 153A-47.

44. *See* N.C. Department of Natural and Cultural Resources, Records Retention and Disposition Schedule (Oct. 1, 2021), archives.ncdcr.gov/2021localgeneralstandardspdf/open.

Chapter 6

Civil Liability and Immunity of Local Governments, Public Officials, and Public Employees

Kristi A. Nickodem

Kristi A. Nickodem is a faculty member at the School of Government who specializes in human services law, including the organization and governance of local social services and consolidated human services agencies and the confidentiality of social services information. She also writes and teaches on topics at the intersection of law and technology, including social media, artificial intelligence, and how the First Amendment impacts government regulation of speech.

This chapter updates and revises previous chapters regarding civil liability and immunity authored by Anthony J. Baker, Anita R. Brown-Graham, Michael R. Smith, and Jeffrey Koeze, whose contributions to the field and to this publication are gratefully acknowledged. The author also thanks Justice Trey Allen, whose scholarship on the subject of local government immunity as a School of Government faculty member was an invaluable resource in updating this chapter.

The expense and trouble of lawsuits are unavoidable costs of doing a local government's work. The challenge for local governments is not the impossible task of eliminating all lawsuits; rather, it is providing services while minimizing the cost and disruption that lawsuits bring. The first step in accomplishing that task is learning the basic legal principles that control the liability of local governments and their public servants. This chapter uses the term "public servants" to refer to all the people who do the local government's work, including elected members of the governing board, members of appointed boards, and employees. At times, the chapter differentiates "public employees" from "public officials," which is an important distinction for purposes of public official immunity. The meanings of the terms used should be clear from the context.

This chapter deals with the two most common areas of liability for local governments: tort liability under North Carolina law and liability under Title 42, Section 1983 of the United States Code[1] (Section 1983) for violations of an individual's constitutional rights. The chapter also discusses various types of immunity that may shield local governments and individual public servants from liability in these two areas.

The discussion that follows is a broad introduction to a complex subject. There are many nuances to this area of the law that are not fully described here. Furthermore, there are many state and federal claims that are beyond the scope of this chapter: environmental claims, tax claims, contract claims, and claims involving violations of federal employment statutes, to mention a few.

Civil Litigation Overview

All civil lawsuits begin with a complaint filed by a plaintiff, alleging that the defendant has somehow harmed the plaintiff. Generally, the defendant will respond to the complaint with an answer that admits or denies the plaintiff's allegations while also asserting relevant affirmative defenses and motions to dismiss. A motion to dismiss may be based on a number of different grounds, including an assertion that the plaintiff has not stated a legal claim for which the court could grant relief, even if the court assumes that the plaintiff's allegations are true (a Rule 12(b)(6) motion). If successful, a 12(b)(6) motion will end a lawsuit (or at least dispose of some claims in the lawsuit) very early in the litigation process.

If some (or all) of the claims in the lawsuit survive motions to dismiss, the parties will move on to discovery. The process of discovery allows parties to share and explore the evidence each party may present if the case goes to trial. Common tools of discovery are interrogatories, requests for production of documents, requests for admission, and depositions. The discovery process can be both expensive and time-consuming. Once discovery is completed, either party may file a motion for summary judgment. In this motion, the moving party argues that no significant facts are in dispute and that the court should rule against the opposing party on a claim (or multiple claims) as a matter of law. If a judge grants a motion for summary judgment on a claim, that claim is resolved and does not move forward to trial. If the motion is denied as to one or more claims, those claims proceed to trial before a jury if a jury trial has been requested.

In cases where the local government is a defendant and the local government has lost a motion for summary judgment, the local government sometimes immediately appeals the decision. If the appellate court affirms the trial court's denial of the motion for summary judgment, the case usually proceeds to trial.

---

1. 42 U.S.C. § 1983.

Parties in a civil case are required to engage in mediated settlement efforts prior to trial. A successful mediation allows the parties to retain control of the case rather than relying on a jury to decide it and may save the parties significant amounts of money in attorneys' fees. When a case settles, one party usually pays an agreed-upon amount of money to the other, the parties release claims against each other, and the lawsuit is dismissed.

Tort Liability under North Carolina Law

Tort law serves to protect a person's interest in his or her bodily security, tangible property, financial resources, or reputation. A tort is a wrongful act or omission (other than a criminal act or breach of contract) that causes some form of harm or injury and for which courts will provide a remedy (typically in the form of monetary damages).[2]

Compensation for harm is the primary concern of tort law. This area of law is premised on the idea that individuals who are harmed through no fault of their own should not be required to bear the loss; instead, the person whose wrongful act caused the harm must pay to restore the injured party.

Three types of civil wrongs may be remedied by an award of damages in a civil tort lawsuit: intentional torts, negligence, and nuisances.

Scope of Employment

Generally, a local government is only liable for the torts of its employees if the harm occurs while an employee is acting within the scope of their employment.[3] To be within the scope of employment, an employee must be acting in furtherance of the local government's business and "for the purpose of accomplishing the duties of his employment" at the time of the incident in question.[4] Determining what is inside and outside the scope of employment is sometimes difficult and highly dependent on the facts of the case.

In one case, for example, the Town of Black Mountain was sued when a boy died after falling from a town truck negligently driven by a town golf course employee.[5] The accident occurred while the employee drove the truck on a personal pleasure trip down a public road against the explicit orders of his supervisor. The North Carolina Supreme Court held that the town was not responsible for the employee's negligence because at the time of the accident, he was acting outside the scope of his employment.[6]

Another case took a broader view of the scope of employment. In *Edwards v. Akion*, the plaintiff alleged that a Raleigh sanitation employee assaulted her after an argument arose regarding how he had performed his duties at her residence. The North Carolina Court of Appeals held that the issue of whether the sanitation employee's actions were within the scope of his employment should

---

2. "Tort," *Black's Law Dictionary* (11th ed. 2019).

3. This is based on the doctrine of *respondeat superior*, which holds employers liable for the actions of their employees so long as the actions occur in the employee's scope of employment. A local government would only incur such liability if it has waived governmental immunity, as discussed below.

4. Hendrix v. Town of W. Jefferson, 273 N.C. App. 27, 33 (2020) (citing Troxler v. Charter Mandala Center, 89 N.C. App. 268, 271 (1988)).

5. Rogers v. Town of Black Mountain, 224 N.C. 119 (1944).

6. *See also* Lertz v. Hughes Bros., 208 N.C. 490 (1935), in which the employer was held liable for an automobile accident that occurred when an employee took a joy ride while running an errand for the employer; Munick v. City of Durham, 181 N.C. 188 (1921).

be decided by a jury. Critical to the court's decision was that the argument was apparently about how the sanitation employee performed the duties of his public employment. The court stated that an act could be within the scope of employment "even if it is contrary to the employer's express instructions, when the act is done in the furtherance of the employer's business and in the discharge of the duties of employment."[7]

In *Medlin v. Bass and the Franklin Board of Education*, the North Carolina Supreme Court held that a principal's sexual assault of a student was not within the scope of his employment. The court distinguished between the principal's actions on behalf of his employer and actions taken for personal reasons:

> While [the principal] was exercising authority conferred upon him by defendant Franklin County Board of Education when he summoned the minor plaintiff to his office to discuss her truancy problem, in proceeding to assault her sexually he was advancing a completely personal objective. The assault could advance no conceivable purpose of [the board of education]; [the principal] acted for personal reasons only, and his acts thus were beyond the course and scope of his employment as a matter of law.[8]

In certain situations, a plaintiff may bring a claim against a local government that is based on the tortious acts of the local government itself, rather than the acts of its employees. For example, a plaintiff might bring a claim against a local government for negligently hiring, supervising, or retaining an employee whose actions injured the plaintiff. This is a direct theory of liability, meaning the local government *itself* is alleged to be negligent in selecting an unfit employee or failing to supervise the employee properly.[9]

Intentional Torts

Intentional torts are deliberate wrongful acts that cause personal injury or property damage. These acts give rise to civil liability for damages unless a special privilege or defense applies. To succeed in demonstrating liability, the plaintiff only has to show that the person causing the injury deliberately engaged in the wrongful act. The definition does not require that the defendant intended the consequences of the act. For example, if someone intentionally hits another person, they may be liable for an intentional tort even though they did not intend to cause serious injury.

Intentional torts are "rarely considered to be within the scope of an employee's employment."[10] As the examples below illustrate, however, a local government may sometimes be held liable for the intentional torts of its employees.[11]

---

7. Edwards v. Akion, 52 N.C. App. 688, 693, *aff'd*, 304 N.C. 585 (1981) (per curiam). The court contrasted *Edwards* with *Robinson v. Sears, Roebuck & Co.*, 216 N.C. 322 (1939). In *Robinson*, the North Carolina Supreme Court relieved Sears, Roebuck & Co. of liability where the argument that instigated the assault was based on a personal matter and not related to the work of the Sears employee.

8. Medlin v. Bass, 327 N.C. 587, 594 (1990). See also *Young v. Great American Insurance Co. of New York*, 359 N.C. 58 (2004) (per curiam reversing for the reasons stated in 162 N.C. App. 87 (2004) (Hunter, J., dissenting)), in which the North Carolina Supreme Court adopted the reasoning from the Court of Appeals dissent that a police officer acted outside of the scope of his employment when he sexually assaulted female drivers he had stopped for traffic violations while on duty.

9. *See* Keith v. Health-Pro Home Care Services, Inc., 381 N.C. 442 (2022) (clarifying the elements of a claim for negligent hiring and retention); *see also Medlin, supra* note 8.

10. Brown v. Burlington Indus., Inc., 93 N.C. App. 431, 437 (1989).

11. Borneman v. United States, 213 F.3d 819, 828 (4th Cir. 2000) (cataloging multiple cases in which the question of whether an intentional assault was within an employee's scope of employment was deemed to be a jury question).

Battery

Battery is the intentional touching or striking of another person without that person's consent or a legally recognized authorization.[12] The local government's potential liability will depend, in part, on whether the battery occurred within the scope and course of the employee's duties.

In *Munick v. City of Durham*,[13] a 1921 case, the North Carolina Supreme Court held that Durham was liable when the city's water department manager severely beat the plaintiff for nothing more than paying his $4.50 water bill using three paper bills, a silver dollar, and a wrapped roll of fifty pennies. The court found that the plaintiff could recover damages from the City of Durham because the water department manager was an "officer of the corporation and was acting in the discharge of his duty, and . . . the plaintiff was on the premises at the invitation of the corporation."[14]

Striking another person without that person's consent is not always a battery. For example, a law enforcement officer may use reasonable force to effect a legal arrest.[15] An officer who uses reasonable force and strikes a suspect to prevent an escape does not commit a civil battery. However, if an officer uses force that is excessive under the given circumstances, the officer may be sued in state court for the intentional tort of battery and be required to pay damages.[16]

Assault

An *assault* is the placing of another person in reasonable apprehension of immediate harm or offensive contact.[17] An assault must include an "overt act or an attempt, or the unequivocal appearance of an attempt, with force and violence, to do some immediate physical injury to the person of another."[18] For example, an outraged municipal employee who approaches a customer with clenched fists while shouting angry threats has committed an assault if the customer perceives the threat to be serious and is reasonably fearful of immediate harm.

False Imprisonment

False imprisonment involves restraining the movement of another without that person's permission or without a legally recognized authorization.[19] This claim frequently arises against local governments in the law enforcement context. A subset of the law enforcement cases involves individuals who were detained on suspicion of shoplifting.[20] Chapter 14, Section 72.1(c) of the North Carolina General Statutes (hereinafter G.S.) protects law enforcement officers from civil liability in this situation as long as the search is at or near the store, is conducted "in a reasonable manner for a reasonable length of time," and the officer has probable cause to believe the person committed the offense.[21]

False imprisonment or false arrest claims may arise based on warrantless arrests conducted by law enforcement officers in other circumstances. Per G.S. 15A-401(b)(1), an officer may arrest a

12. Charles E. Daye and Mark W. Morris, *North Carolina Law of Torts*, pt. 1, sec. 3.20 (3rd ed., 2012).
13. 181 N.C 188 (1921).
14. 181 N.C. at 196.
15. Chapter 15A, Section 401(d)(1) of the North Carolina General Statutes (hereinafter G.S.).
16. Bartley v. City of High Point, 381 N.C. 287, 297 (2022); *see also* Houston v. DeHerrodora, 192 N.C. 749 (1926). Use of excessive force may also lead to a claim under 42 U.S.C. § 1983 alleging a Fourth Amendment violation.
17. *North Carolina Law of Torts*, pt. 1, sec. 2.20.
18. Dickens v. Puryear, 302 N.C. 437, 445 (1981).
19. *North Carolina Law of Torts*, pt. 1, sec. 4.20. *See also* Myrick v. Cooley, 91 N.C. App. 209, 212 (1988) (discussing false imprisonment and false arrest under state law).
20. *See, e.g.*, Mullins by Mullins v. Friend, 116 N.C. App. 676 (1994).
21. G.S. 14-72.1(c) also protects shopkeepers and their employees and agents from civil liability under these circumstances.

person without a warrant if the officer has probable cause to believe the person has committed a criminal offense in the officer's presence. There are also statutory grounds for an officer to arrest a person without a warrant when the officer has probable cause to believe the individual has committed a felony (or a misdemeanor, but only under particular circumstances described in the statute) *outside* the officer's presence.[22] An officer has probable cause to make an arrest when the officer "has a reasonable belief, anchored in specific facts and objectively rational inferences, that a particular person has committed a crime."[23]

A less frequently litigated issue regarding false imprisonment involves holding a prisoner beyond the prisoner's scheduled release date. In one case of false imprisonment, an inmate was held on work release for nearly six months following a contempt order issued after the inmate had failed to appear at an equitable distribution hearing in district court. There was apparently some ambiguity in the ordered release date concerning whether it was a time certain or based on when the inmate complied with an order to fulfill his equitable distribution obligation. The inmate brought an action against the Mecklenburg County sheriff, who was found not liable since the court could not find intent to unlawfully imprison the inmate where there was no clear mandate as to the inmate's release.[24]

Non-sworn local government staff could also potentially be held liable for false imprisonment. In one case, a town mayor was found liable for false arrest and imprisonment after ordering a police officer to arrest and detain a man for thirty to forty minutes without legal justification.[25]

Defamation

Defamation is a false written or oral communication made about an individual to a third party that injures the individual's reputation.[26] Defamation in writing is called *libel*; oral defamation is called *slander*.[27] Defamatory remarks might include accusations that a person has committed a crime, statements that impeach someone in his or her trade or profession, or claims that an individual has an infectious disease. For example, a false rumor spread by a city emergency medical services worker that a particular person had a sexually transmitted disease would constitute defamation. In a 1917 case, defamation (as slander) was established against a city employee in a case in which the city manager falsely told a local newspaper that an employee had been dismissed for stealing.[28] However, establishing a defamation claim against a local government via *respondeat superior* (liability of the employer for the acts of its employees) has proven to be much more difficult in light of governmental immunity,[29] and rarely does a local governing body itself collectively make an official comment that might make it directly liable for defamation.[30]

A public servant sued for defamation in his or her individual capacity may have three defenses available. First, the truth of a statement is an absolute defense to liability for damages in a defamation

---

22. G.S. 15A-401(b)(2).

23. State v. Woolard, 385 N.C. 560, 570 (2023) (citing Maryland v. Pringle, 540 U.S. 366, 370 (2003)).

24. Emory v. Pendergraph, 154 N.C. App. 181 (2002).

25. Blackwood v. Cates, 297 N.C. 163 (1979); *see also* Hoffman v. Clinic Hosp., 213 N.C. 669 (1938) (per curiam).

26. Boyce & Isley, PLLC v. Cooper, 153 N.C. App. 25, 29 (2002).

27. *North Carolina Law of Torts*, pt. 1, sec. 28.30.

28. Jones v. Brinkley, 174 N.C. 23 (1917).

29. Houpe v. City of Statesville, 128 N.C. App. 334 (1998); Shuping v. Barber, 89 N.C. App. 242 (1988). The cities' respective liability policies excluded defamation as a covered tort and, thus, the cities retained governmental immunity.

30. Phillips v. Winston-Salem/Forsyth Cnty. Bd. of Educ., 117 N.C. App. 274 (1994). The court held that the board's vice-chairman was not acting as an agent of the board when he made allegedly defamatory comments to a newspaper reporter outside of a board meeting.

lawsuit.[31] Second, a person may avoid liability for a false statement by showing that it was made under circumstances that gave rise to a qualified privilege.[32] A qualified privilege exists when (1) the person who makes a statement has a valid interest in making it or a legal duty to make it and (2) the person makes a statement to someone with a corresponding interest or duty. Public servants protected by a qualified privilege to make a particular statement will not be held liable for defamation unless they act with malice in making it.[33] Even if a plaintiff alleges that a public servant acted with malice in making a statement, the truth of the statement will still defeat a claim for defamation.[34] Finally, if the public servant accused of defamation is a public official, that public official may be protected from liability by public official immunity (described later in this chapter) unless their actions were corrupt, malicious, or outside the scope of their official duties.[35]

Negligence

Negligence involves unintentional torts. To succeed in a negligence lawsuit, a plaintiff must generally demonstrate that the defendant violated a duty of care owed to the plaintiff and that the violation caused harm to the plaintiff or the plaintiff's property. As a general rule, if someone fails to use reasonable care and such conduct causes personal injury or property damage that was a foreseeable result of the carelessness, the person harmed is entitled to compensation. In North Carolina, a party sued for negligence may invoke the defense of *contributory negligence*—a legal rule that bars recovery by any individual whose own negligence, however slight, contributes to his or her injury.

Negligence may occur in an infinite variety of situations, and whether certain conduct is negligent generally cannot be determined in the abstract. Instead, a jury must decide in each specific case whether the defendant acted as a reasonably prudent person would have under the same or similar circumstances. Some examples may help illustrate how negligence claims against local governments arise.

In one case, two local government employees drove a truck that spewed a thick insecticide fog along a road.[36] The fog totally blocked the view of approaching traffic. No warning signs were displayed to give oncoming vehicles notice of the hazard. A man rounded a curve into the fog and slowed his truck, but he was blinded by the fog and sideswiped a car that had pulled off the road to wait for the fog to clear. The North Carolina Supreme Court held that a jury could find that the two employees were negligent in creating a hazardous condition likely to cause injury to the traveling public.

Another case against a local government involved a seven-year-old boy who was riding his bike when he was struck and killed by a drunk driver. The young boy was riding down a steep hill toward a T-intersection and took a right turn. The drunk driver was driving in the wrong lane toward the

---

31. Taube v. Hooper, 270 N.C. App. 604, 612 (2020) (citing Holleman v. Aiken, 193 N.C. App. 484, 496–97 (2008)).

32. *See* Presnell v. Pell, 298 N.C. 715 (1979); Towne v. Cope, 32 N.C. App. 660 (1977). In some instances, state statutes expressly extend this qualified privilege to designated public servants. For example, the General Assembly created a privilege for written communications made by members of nursing home advisory committees in G.S. 131E-128(i).

33. Andrews v. Elliot, 109 N.C. App. 271, 275–76 (1993) (qualified privilege defense does not defeat claim of defamation per se at pleadings stage where complaint alleges actual malice).

34. For example, in *Taube*, 270 N.C. App. 604, a former police sergeant brought a defamation action against the city and police chief, alleging a statement by the police chief in an affidavit of separation was libel. The court found the sergeant's allegations overcame qualified privilege, but the police chief's statement regarding a previous investigation for possible misconduct was true and thus an absolute defense to defamation.

35. Mitchell v. Pruden, 251 N.C. App. 554, 562 (2017); *see also* Shuping v. Barber, 89 N.C. App. 242, 248 (1988) (police officer was not protected by immunity since public official immunity does not apply to malicious acts and allegations gave rise to slander per se, creating the presumption of malice).

36. Moore v. Town of Plymouth, 249 N.C. 423 (1959).

intersection and struck the child as he made the right turn. On the corner of this intersection, in the city's right-of-way, was vegetation that allegedly obscured the drunk driver's ability to see the child coming down the hill and obscured the child's ability to see the drunk driver in the wrong lane. In response to the trial court's denial of the city's motion for summary judgment, the North Carolina Court of Appeals held that multiple issues of fact needed to be decided by a jury, including whether the city knew or should have known that vegetation obstructed the view of those using the streets and whether it was reasonably foreseeable that the vegetation could cause a traffic accident.[37]

In some cases, negligence lawsuits against local governments are dismissed because of a lack of evidence that the local government knew or should have known about a dangerous condition. For example, the City of Charlotte was held not liable for a sewage backflow into a home caused by a baseball-sized rock lodged in the public sewer line where there was no evidence that the city knew or should have known of the blockage.[38] In another case, the City of High Point was held not liable for alleged electrical shock injuries to a cable television installer technician where there was insufficient evidence to show that the city knew or should have known of any break in the electrical wires' insulation.[39]

Nuisance and Inverse Condemnation

A local government that engages in an activity that substantially and unreasonably interferes with the use and enjoyment of someone's land commits a tort called *nuisance.* The local government may be required to pay damages caused by a nuisance even if the damage arises from the performance of a governmental function. For example, in one case a city's sewage treatment plant smelled so bad that the value of the plaintiffs' nearby home was permanently reduced. The state supreme court held that the plaintiffs were entitled to recover damages from the city to compensate them for the reduction in value.[40]

In another sewer-related case, a homeowner's basement flooded with raw sewage from the city-maintained public sewer system during heavy rains. The city's investigation showed that the sewer main in front of the home was at least fifty years old, the elevation of the basement was too low to properly work with the gravity-operated sewer system, and the home required a check valve to prevent sewage from backing into the home. The homeowner claimed that the city's operation of the sewer system, which allowed stormwater to infiltrate the system, was a nuisance. The North Carolina Court of Appeals held that the evidence was sufficient to submit the issue of nuisance to a jury.[41]

A local government may also be liable for lowering someone's land values under constitutional provisions that prevent the government from taking a person's private property without just

---

37. Beckles-Palomares v. Logan, 202 N.C. App. 235, *cert. denied,* 364 N.C. 434 (2010). Governmental immunity was not available as G.S. 160A-296 imposes a duty on cities to maintain streets and keep them free from unnecessary obstruction. That statutory duty has been held to override governmental immunity. Kirkpatrick v. Town of Nags Head, 213 N.C. App. 132 (2011).

38. Ward v. City of Charlotte, 48 N.C. App. 463, *cert. denied,* 301 N.C. 531 (1980). The North Carolina Court of Appeals also rejected the arguments that the City of Charlotte was liable pursuant to breach of contract.

39. Campbell v. City of High Point, 144 N.C. App. 493, *aff'd,* 354 N.C. 566 (2001).

40. Glace v. Town of Pilot Mountain, 265 N.C. 181 (1965). Note that the plaintiff must make some showing of measurable damages to recover. *See* Midgett v. N.C. State Highway Comm'n, 265 N.C. 373, 377–78 (1965) ("One who seeks damages for the taking of property by the sovereign by reason of the alleged creation and maintenance by it of a permanent and continuing nuisance must make a *prima facie* showing of substantial and measurable damages.").

41. Hughes v. City of High Point, 62 N.C. App. 107, *cert. denied,* 309 N.C. 320 (1983).

compensation.[42] If a local government's activities permanently and substantially reduce the value of land, a court may rule that the locality has in effect taken the property and must compensate the property owner.[43] This kind of taking is sometimes called *inverse condemnation* to distinguish it from condemnation or outright appropriation of land for public use. G.S. 40A-51 provides a statutory basis for claims when property is taken by a local government without an official condemnation action.[44] Inverse condemnation under G.S. 40A-51 is the sole remedy for a landowner who is harmed by a government taking without compensation, regardless of whether the government initiated the taking through a condemnation action.[45]

Liability of the Local Government

Governmental Immunity

Governmental immunity is a legal doctrine that bars tort claims against cities, counties, public school districts, and other units of local government when those claims arise from the performance of governmental functions. Governmental immunity is derived from *sovereign immunity,* an English common law doctrine based on the principle that "the king can do no wrong."[46] Sovereign immunity protects the state of North Carolina from liability for torts committed by state employees and officers, except to the extent that the state waives immunity or consents to suit (such as through clear statutory language or by entering into a valid contract).[47] For example, through the State Tort Claims Act, the North Carolina General Assembly has "partially waived [the State's] sovereign immunity by consenting to direct suits brought as a result of negligent acts committed by its employees in the course of their employment."[48]

Governmental immunity for units of local government is more limited in scope than the sovereign immunity enjoyed by the state of North Carolina. The state's sovereign immunity applies to claims arising from both its governmental and proprietary functions, while governmental immunity shields a unit of local government from liability only when claims arise from its governmental functions.[49] The difference between governmental and proprietary functions is explained in more detail later in this section. Even where the local government traditionally performs a specific function,

42. The Law of the Land Clause found in Article I, Section 19 of the North Carolina Constitution is frequently cited to support these claims.

43. *See* Wilkie v. City of Boiling Spring Lakes, 370 N.C. 540, 552 (2018) ("'Inverse condemnation' [is] a term often used to designate 'a cause of action against a governmental defendant to recover the value of property which has been taken in fact by the governmental defendant, even though no formal exercise of the power of eminent domain has been attempted by the taking agency.'")

44. Cases in this area often consider liability under several different theories. For example, in *Wagner v. City of Charlotte*, 269 N.C. App. 656 (2020), a water main pipe burst, temporarily flooding plaintiffs' property. Plaintiffs brought various negligence, private nuisance, inverse condemnation, and trespass claims against the city related to the flooding. The court concluded that the temporary nature of the flooding did not represent inverse condemnation or private nuisance, but let some claims related to the city's negligence in responding to the break go forward.

45. Cnty. of Moore v. Acres, 284 N.C. App. 250, 256, *appeal dismissed, review denied*, 884 S.E.2d 729 (N.C. 2023) (citing McAdoo v. City of Greensboro, 91 N.C. App. 570, 573 (1988)).

46. Est. of Graham v. Lambert, 385 N.C. 644, 651 (2024); Corum v. Univ. of N. Carolina through Bd. of Governors, 330 N.C. 761, 785 (1992); *see also* William Blackstone, *Commentaries on the Laws of England*, 237–39 (1765).

47. Wray v. City of Greensboro, 370 N.C. 41, 47 (2017).

48. Cedarbrook Residential Ctr., Inc. v. N.C. Dep't of Health & Hum. Servs., 383 N.C. 31, 45 (2022) (quoting Teachy v. Coble Dairies, Inc., 306 N.C. 324, 329 (1982)). The State Tort Claims Act is codified in G.S. Chapter 143, Article 31.

49. Evans v. Hous. Auth. of City of Raleigh, 359 N.C. 50, 53 (2004).

the state may legislatively remove the protection afforded by governmental immunity. For example, G.S. 160A-296 imposes a duty on cities to maintain streets. That statutory duty has been held to override governmental immunity.[50]

In addition to protecting cities, counties, and public school districts, governmental immunity also applies to other units of local government and public authorities when they carry out governmental functions.[51] This includes, for example, mental health area authorities, city housing authorities, district health departments, regional public transportation authorities, and regional departments of social services.[52]

As discussed in more depth later in this chapter, cities and counties may waive their governmental immunity by obtaining liability insurance coverage or by funding a reserve expressly in lieu of insurance, but only to the extent of their coverage for claims.[53] Local governments also waive their governmental immunity with respect to breach of contract claims by entering into a valid contract.[54]

Governmental versus Proprietary Activities

A North Carolina local government's liability for the torts of its public servants depends on whether the employee was engaged in a governmental or a proprietary activity on behalf of the local government. If a local government employee harms someone while performing a *governmental* function, the doctrine of governmental immunity protects the local government from tort liability. Conversely, the local government may be held liable if the employee commits a tort while engaged in a *proprietary* function, because governmental immunity does not apply to claims arising from proprietary activities.

The test courts use for determining when an activity is governmental or proprietary has evolved over the years. In 1942, the North Carolina Supreme Court defined governmental activities as "discretionary, political, legislative or public in nature and performed for the public good in behalf of the State," while describing proprietary activities as "commercial or chiefly for the private advantage of the compact community."[55] In 2004, the state supreme court acknowledged that it had used various tests for distinguishing between these two categories but had consistently recognized one key guiding principle: "If the undertaking of the [local government] is one in which only a governmental agency could engage, it is governmental in nature. It is proprietary and 'private' when any corporation, individual, or group of individuals could do the same thing."[56] The distinction between governmental and proprietary activities was often challenging for courts to apply and sometimes resulted in inconsistent characterizations of a local government's activities.

---

50. Kirkpatrick v. Town of Nags Head, 713 S.E.2d 151 (2011).

51. G.S. 153A-435 (counties); G.S. 160A-485 (cities); G.S. 115C-42 (school boards).

52. *See* G.S. 122-152 (area authorities); G.S. 130A-37(k) (district health departments); G.S. 160A-627 (regional public transportation authorities); G.S. 108A15.8(l) (regional departments of social services); *see also Evans*, 359 N.C. at 55–56 (housing authority); Warren v. Guilford Cnty., 129 N.C. App. 836, 838–39 (1998) (area authority).

53. G.S. 153A-435(a) (counties) and G.S. 160A-485(a) (cities). Not all municipal corporations are authorized to waive immunity through the purchase of insurance. Water and sewer districts, for example, are special-purpose municipal corporations that cannot waive immunity in this manner. *See* Thrash v. City of Asheville, 95 N.C. App. 457 (1989), *rev'd on other grounds*, 327 N.C. 251 (1990).

54. *See* Howard v. Cnty. of Durham, 227 N.C. App. 46, 50 (2013); Paquette v. Cnty. of Durham, 155 N.C. App. 415, 420 (2002).

55. Millar v. Town of Wilson, 222 N.C. 340 (1942).

56. *Evans*, 359 N.C. at 54 (quoting Britt v. City of Wilmington, 236 N.C. 446, 451 (1952)).

In 2012, against a backdrop of divergent views in the case law on this issue, the North Carolina Supreme Court adopted a three-step method in *Estate of Williams* ex rel. *Overton v. Pasquotank County Parks & Recreation Department* for analyzing whether a local government's activity was governmental or proprietary in nature.[57]

1. **Has the legislature addressed the issue of whether a function is governmental or proprietary (e.g. in the statute authorizing the activity or in statements of legislative intent)?** If the legislature has clearly and unambiguously addressed this issue, this initial step may be the end of the court's inquiry.[58]
2. **If the legislature has not clearly addressed the issue, the court then considers whether the activity "is one in which only a governmental agency could engage" or provide, in which case the court will treat it as governmental.** This step will rarely help courts determine the issue of whether an activity is governmental or proprietary. As the *Williams* court noted, "[M]any services once thought to be the sole purview of the public sector have been privatized in full or in part. Consequently, it is increasingly difficult to identify services that can only be rendered by a governmental entity."[59]
3. **If neither the first nor the second step of the test are determinative of the issue, then courts will consider several additional relevant factors, including (1) whether the service is traditionally provided by a governmental entity, (2) whether a substantial fee is charged for the service, and (3) whether that fee does more than simply cover the operating costs of the service provider.** Taken on balance, these factors may lead a court to categorize an activity as proprietary if it is intended to produce significant revenue for a unit of local government.[60] However, the *Williams* opinion warns against rigid overreliance on these factors, explaining that "distinctions between proprietary and governmental functions are fluid and courts must be advertent to changes in practice."

Governmental versus Proprietary Classifications since Williams

In the years since *Williams* was decided, North Carolina's appellate courts have held the following activities to be governmental functions:

- a county's maintenance and repair of county-owned property;[61]
- a school board's ownership, maintenance, and repair of a walkway located on a school campus;[62]

---

57. 366 N.C. 195 (2012).

58. Even if the General Assembly has expressly referred to an activity as governmental or proprietary, it may be unclear from the scope of the statutory text whether the legislature intended to cover the precise act or omission that is at issue in a particular lawsuit. This ambiguity may lead a court to consider other factors in the *Williams* test, instead of treating the first step in the analysis as determinative. *See* Trey Allen, *Local Government Immunity to Lawsuits in North Carolina* (UNC School of Government, 2018): 24–27.

59. *Est. of Williams*, 366 N.C. at 202.

60. See Allen, *Local Government Immunity to Lawsuits in North Carolina:* 23, 28.

61. Bynum v. Wilson Cnty., 367 N.C. 355 (2014). In its analysis, the North Carolina Supreme Court looked to G.S. 153A-169, -351, and -352, finding that "the fact that the legislature has designated these responsibilities as governmental is dispositive." *See also* Phifer v. Pasquotank Cnty., 260 N.C. App. 706 (2018) (unpublished).

62. Bellows v. Asheville City Bd. of Educ., 243 N.C. App. 229 (2015) (finding the General Assembly's designation of this responsibility to school boards in G.S. 115C-40 and -521(c) to be determinative of the issue).

- providing a law enforcement presence, regulating traffic and "deciding which roads to keep open for vehicular traffic and which roads should not continue to be open for such travel," approving or denying permits, and providing ambulance services;[63]
- the organization and operation of a fire department;[64]
- ensuring county citizens are provided with emergency medical services and regulating the manner by which those emergency medical services are furnished;[65]
- the operation of a county jail, including the provision of medical services to inmates;[66]
- leasing a historic property to a nonprofit for the purpose or redeveloping and revitalizing the downtown by promoting the arts, where the municipality did not seek to make a profit or charge substantial fees;[67]
- the purchasing and leasing of real estate for the purpose of providing fire protection services;[68] and
- the provision of a federally funded small business loan for purposes of community development.[69]

Applying North Carolina law, the U.S. Court of Appeals for the Fourth Circuit has held that a county was engaged in a governmental function when it entered into a contract that obligated the county "to do things that only a governmental entity can," such as expediting processes for county-required permits and waiving county-imposed permitting, inspection, or development fees.[70] In one case decided since *Williams*, the North Carolina Court of Appeals relied solely on the first step of the *Williams* test—analyzing whether the legislature has designated an activity as governmental or proprietary—to find that stormwater management is a "quintessentially proprietary" municipal function.[71]

These cases may be helpful to local governments trying to understand which of their activities are governmental and which are proprietary for purposes of governmental immunity. The North Carolina Supreme Court has cautioned, however, against assuming that the classification of an activity as governmental or proprietary in prior cases will apply to every future instance of such activity, since "the proper designation of a particular action of a county or municipality is a fact intensive inquiry . . . and may differ from case to case."[72]

---

63. Parker v. Town of Erwin, 243 N.C. App. 84 (2015). *See also* Hinson v. City of Greensboro, 232 N.C. App. 204, 210 (2014) ("Law enforcement is well-established as a governmental function, and includes the training and supervision of officers by a police department.") (quoting Pettiford v. City of Greensboro, 556 F. Supp. 2d 512, 524 (M.D.N.C. 2008)).

64. Pruett v. Bingham, 238 N.C. App. 78, 81 (2014), *aff'd*, 368 N.C. 709 (2016).

65. Fuller v. Wake Cnty., 254 N.C. App. 32 (2017) (finding the authority and responsibilities assigned to counties for the provision of emergency medical services in G.S. 143-517 and 153A-250 to be dispositive of the issue).

66. Butterfield v. Gray, 2021-NCCOA-523, ¶ 16, 279 N.C. App. 549.

67. Meinck v. City of Gastonia, 371 N.C. 497 (2018). The North Carolina Supreme Court warned that this decision "should not be construed as holding that every urban redevelopment activity is a governmental function or even that every lease of historic property to a nonprofit arts group for the purpose of promoting the arts is a governmental function." *Id.* at 517.

68. Providence Volunteer Fire Dep't, Inc. v. Town of Weddington, 2022-NCSC-100, ¶ 28, 382 N.C. 199.

69. Flomeh-Mawutor v. City of Winston-Salem, 906 S.E.2d 1, 5–7 (N.C. Ct. App. 2024). For more analysis of this case, please see Rebecca Fisher-Gabbard, "Governmental Immunity Insights from the Court of Appeals," *Coates' Canons: NC Local Government Law* blog (September 19, 2024), canons.sog.unc.edu/2024/09/governmental-immunity-insights-from-the-court-of-appeals/.

70. S. Power Co. v. Cleveland Cnty., 24 F.4th 258, 268–69 (4th Cir. 2022).

71. Devonwood-Loch Lomond Lake Ass'n, Inc. v. City of Fayetteville, 908 S.E.2d 66, 78 (N.C. Ct. App. 2024) ("Under N.C.G.S. § 160A-311, stormwater management is a quintessentially proprietary municipal function.").

72. *Meinck*, 371 N.C. at 517–18 (quoting *Williams*, 366 N.C. at 203).

*Pre-*Williams *Case Law on Governmental and Proprietary Functions*

Prior to *Williams*, many appellate decisions had determined that particular activities were either governmental or proprietary in nature. However, applying the *Williams* test could lead courts to classify those same activities in different ways in future cases.

In analyzing the factors in the third step of the *Williams* test, courts may look to pre-*Williams* case law regarding whether the government or private corporations typically perform the activity in question.[73] Examples of activities that governments traditionally perform include operating traffic lights,[74] driving a police car,[75] using a police or fire alarm,[76] enforcing zoning regulations or ordinances,[77] furnishing water to firefighters,[78] condemning property,[79] granting franchises,[80] administering sanitation programs,[81] and operating a public hospital,[82] among others.

Likewise, there is a significant body of pre-*Williams* case law reflecting that government operations are more likely to be deemed proprietary if they involve a fee of some sort.[83] Examples of activities held to be proprietary (pre-*Williams*) include charging a fee to maintain a landfill,[84] distributing water for profit,[85] distributing electricity for profit,[86] operation and maintenance of fee-based sewer systems,[87] operating an airport,[88] operating a municipal golf course,[89] operating a public coliseum,[90] and maintaining a public park in which a fee was charged for admission into an amusement area of the park.[91]

Courts may consider whether a local government charges a fee or substantially profits from a particular activity as part of the third step of the *Williams* test, but charging a fee does not automatically render an activity proprietary. Services that are truly governmental in nature are not made

---

73. Activities historically performed by governments but not ordinarily engaged in by private corporations have been held by the courts to be governmental activities. *See* Sides v. Cabarrus Mem'l Hosp., Inc., 287 N.C. 14, 29 (1975). However, the North Carolina Supreme Court has cautioned that "the distinctions between proprietary and governmental functions are fluid and courts must be advertent to changes in practice." *Estate of Williams* ex rel. *Overton v. Pasquotank Cnty. Parks & Recreation Dep't*, 366 N.C. 195, 203 (2012).

74. Hamilton v. Hamlet, 238 N.C. 741 (1953).

75. Lewis v. Hunter, 212 N.C. 504 (1937).

76. Cathey v. City of Charlotte, 197 N.C. 309 (1929).

77. Orange County v. Heath, 14 N.C. App. 44, *aff'd*, 282 N.C. 292 (1972).

78. Howland v. Asheville, 174 N.C. 749 (1917).

79. Dale v. City of Morganton, 270 N.C. 567 (1967).

80. Denning v. Goldsboro Gas Co., 246 N.C. 541 (1957).

81. James v. City of Charlotte, 183 N.C. 630 (1900); Koontz v. City of Winston-Salem, 280 N.C. 513 (1972).

82. Sides v. Cabarrus Mem'l Hosp., Inc., 287 N.C. 14 (1975); *see also* Casey v. Wake Cnty., 45 N.C. App. 522, *discretionary review denied*, 300 N.C. 371 (1980) (holding that provision of birth control in county family planning clinic is governmental function).

83. *Sides*, 287 N.C. 14.

84. Koontz v. City of Winston-Salem, 280 N.C. 513 (1972).

85. Foust v. Durham, 239 N.C. 306 (1954).

86. Rice v. Lumberton, 235 N.C. 227 (1952).

87. Harrison v. City of Sanford, 177 N.C. App. 116, 121 (2006); *see also* Saad v. Town of Surf City, 910 S.E.2d 851, 857 (N.C. Ct. App. 2024).

88. Rhodes v. City of Asheville, 230 N.C. 134 (1949).

89. Lowe v. Gastonia, 211 N.C. 564 (1937).

90. Aaser v. Charlotte, 265 N.C. 494 (1965).

91. Glenn v. Raleigh, 246 N.C. 469 (1957). The plaintiff was injured in a picnic area of the 42-acre park, an area used free of charge. The City of Raleigh charged admission to an amusement area of the same park. The North Carolina Supreme Court determined that the operation of the park was a proprietary function. See *Horne v. Town of Blowing Rock*, 223 N.C. App. 26 (2012) for a discussion of governmental immunity related to maintenance of town park in light of *Glenn* and *Williams*. For more on the topic of governmental immunity for the operation of public parks, see Chapter 6 of Trey Allen, *Local Government Immunity to Lawsuits in North Carolina* (UNC School of Government, 2018).

proprietary merely because a local government charges fees for them.[92] For example, the court of appeals has held that governmental functions include operating a county-owned ambulance service,[93] operating an emergency call center,[94] and providing inspections for building code violations,[95] even though local governments charge fees for these services.

For a more detailed summary and analysis of how North Carolina courts have categorized a wide variety of activities as either governmental or proprietary for immunity purposes, see Chapter 3 of *Local Government Immunity to Lawsuits in North Carolina* by Trey Allen (UNC School of Government, 2018).

Activities with Both Proprietary and Governmental Elements

When an injury results from an activity that includes both governmental and proprietary characteristics, North Carolina courts isolate the particular part of the activity that caused the plaintiff's injury to determine whether governmental immunity applies to that part of the activity. The availability of immunity "turns on whether the *alleged tortious conduct* of the county or municipality arose from an activity that was governmental or proprietary," and accordingly, the court's "analysis should center upon the governmental act or service that was allegedly done in a negligent manner."[96]

For example, it is not uncommon for a county or municipal building to house offices for several different departments, some of which perform governmental functions, while others undertake proprietary functions. The North Carolina Supreme Court has held that the maintenance or repair of such a building is a governmental function, even if part of the building is devoted to proprietary activities. Consequently, governmental immunity may bar the claim of a plaintiff who was injured by a local government's negligent failure to keep the building in proper repair.[97]

Waiver of Governmental Immunity by the Purchase of Insurance

The General Assembly has authorized counties and cities to waive the defense of governmental immunity by purchasing liability insurance.[98] Why might a local government be inclined to waive this defense through the purchase of insurance? First, local governments cannot be certain in advance that governmental immunity will protect them from liability for many activities. Second, by purchasing liability insurance, a local government provides a remedy for citizens who otherwise could not be compensated for injuries caused by the negligence of the local government's employees in performing governmental activities. Third, the defense of governmental immunity is limited to tort claims. It does not extend to other claims against the local government, such as claims for violations of constitutional rights or federal or state statutes.

---

92. *See* Casey v. Wake Cnty., 45 N.C. App. 522, *review denied*, 300 N.C. 371 (1980).

93. McIver v. Smith, 134 N.C. App. 583 (1999). See *Childs v. Johnson*, 155 N.C. App. 381 (2002), in which the court of appeals held that Forsyth County did not have governmental immunity where the director of the Forsyth County EMS services was involved in an automobile accident while driving his assigned county-owned vehicle since the director was on a personal errand at the time of the accident.

94. Wright v. Gaston Cnty., 205 N.C. App. 600 (2010). The fee involved is levied pursuant to G.S. 143B-1403 (previously G.S. 62A-43), which mandates a $0.70 monthly service charge for each active voice communications service connection capable of accessing the 911 system, payable by the subscriber to the provider of the voice communications service.

95. Norton v. SMC Bldg., Inc. and Montgomery Cnty., 156 N.C. App. 564 (2003).

96. *See* Parker v. Town of Erwin, 243 N.C. App. 84, 102, 776 S.E.2d 710, 725 (2015) (quoting Bynum v. Wilson County, 367 N.C. 355, 358–59 (2014).

97. Bynum v. Wilson County, 367 N.C. 355 (2014); *see also* Meinck v. City of Gastonia, 371 N.C. 497 (2018) (holding maintenance of property leased to a nonprofit arts guild for the purpose of downtown revitalization was a governmental function).

98. G.S. 153A-435; G.S. 160A-485.

The statutes that authorize local governments to waive governmental immunity through the purchase of insurance make it clear that the local government's governing body—the board of county commissioners or city council—has full discretion in determining the specific torts to which the insurance policy applies and the officials or employees who will be covered under it. The governing body may decide not to purchase insurance at all.

If the local governing body purchases insurance, an injured person may not recover more than the policy amount on any tort claim for which the local government would have been immune but for the purchase of liability insurance.[99] For example, if the cost of plaintiff's injuries is $57,000, but the policy is limited to $25,000 per occurrence, the plaintiff may recover only $25,000. If a jury returns a verdict in excess of the insurance policy limits on a tort claim for which a city or county would have been immune *without* the purchase of liability insurance, the judge must reduce the award to the maximum limits of the policy before entering the judgment. In other words, governmental immunity is waived only to the extent of a local government's insurance coverage. Similarly, when a local government's insurance policy involves a deductible for which the local government is responsible, the local government retains governmental immunity for damages that fall within the amount of the deductible.[100]

A local government can waive its governmental immunity through insurance coverage in three basic ways. First, the local government may purchase an insurance policy that includes liability coverage. Second, the local government may participate in a local government risk pool, which is considered the equivalent of purchasing insurance. Third, a local government may expressly waive its immunity and set aside funds to cover claims against it.[101]

Local government risk pools are defined in G.S. 58-23-5 as agreements between two or more local governments either to jointly purchase insurance or to pool resources to pay claims for property losses or liability.[102] Risk pools differ from self-insurance, wherein the local government does not pool resources with another entity. A local government may share the costs of administering claims with other government entities without creating a risk pool—and thus retain governmental immunity—to the extent that each government entity is required to reimburse the fund for any claims paid out of it.[103] Courts have also held that a city has not created a risk pool where the city creates, funds, contracts with, and operates a nonprofit corporation to manage claims against the city.[104]

If a local government sets aside a self-insurance reserve, the governing board may adopt a resolution that deems the creation of a funded reserve to be the same as the purchase of insurance under G.S. 160A-485 (for cities) or G.S. 153A-435 (for counties). Adoption of the resolution waives the city's or county's governmental immunity only to the extent specified in the board's resolution, but in no event can a plaintiff recover an amount greater than the funds available in the funded reserve for the payment of claims.[105]

---

99. Jones v. Kearns, 120 N.C. App. 301, *review denied,* 342 N.C. 414 (1995).

100. *See* Wall v. City of Raleigh, 121 N.C. App. 351, 355 (1996).

101. G.S. 160A-485; G.S. 153-435.

102. Only counties, cities, and housing authorities are defined as "local governments" for purposes of joining a local government risk pool. G.S. 58-23-1.

103. Lyles v. City of Charlotte, 344 N.C. 676 (1996); *see also* Schlossberg v. Goins, 141 N.C. App. 436 (2000); Cross v. Residential Support Servs., Inc., 129 N.C. App. 374 (1998). In these cases, courts also focus on the fact that the "funds" or "pools" did not comply with the statutory requirements for the creation of a local government risk pool found in G.S. Chapter 58, Article 23.

104. Blackwelder v. City of Winston-Salem, 332 N.C. 319 (1992).

105. G.S. 160A-485; G.S. 153-435.

The statute authorizing local school boards to waive governmental immunity through insurance coverage differs from the statutes applicable to counties and cities. Unlike cities and counties, a school board does not waive governmental immunity by participating in a risk pool, including the North Carolina School Board Trust.[106] The statute also does not provide that school boards may waive immunity through self-insurance.[107]

A local government may explicitly *preserve* its governmental immunity through the use of a clear, unambiguous exclusionary clause in insurance contracts or policies. In *Patrick v. Wake County Department of Human Services*, the North Carolina Court of Appeals held that a county did not waive its governmental immunity through the purchase of insurance, since the language of the policy stated that it "provides coverage only for occurrences or wrongful acts for which the defense of governmental immunity is clearly not applicable."[108] The court of appeals subsequently acknowledged the "arguably circular nature" of this logic, whereby a "[d]efendant retains immunity because the policy doesn't cover his actions and the policy doesn't cover his actions because he explicitly retains immunity."[109] Nonetheless, the court of appeals has continued to follow this precedent, finding in multiple cases since *Patrick* that explicit exclusionary clauses in liability insurance policies and contracts preserve the defense of governmental immunity.[110] If the language in an exclusionary clause is ambiguous or unclear, however, courts will strictly construe such language in favor of providing coverage to the local government (and therefore waiving governmental immunity).[111]

Waiver of Governmental Immunity by Large Cities

Under G.S. 160A-485.5, any city with a population of 500,000 or more may waive its governmental immunity by adopting a resolution expressing the city's intent to waive its immunity pursuant to the State Tort Claims Act, as modified and limited by various subsections of G.S. 160A-485.5. Adopting such a resolution allows plaintiffs to bring civil tort claims against the city but will cap a plaintiff's potential recovery from the city at $1,000,000 for claims arising out of any one occurrence.[112]

Unlike claims made against the state under the State Tort Claims Act, which must be brought in the Industrial Commission, tort claims against a city that has waived its immunity under G.S. 160A-485.5 must be brought in the superior court of the county where the city is principally located.[113] If a city waives its immunity pursuant to G.S. 160A-485.5, then G.S. 160A-485 (which authorizes cities to waive governmental immunity by purchasing liability insurance as described in the previous section) does not apply to that city.[114] However, G.S. 160A-485.5(c) expressly authorizes such a city to purchase liability insurance or adopt a resolution creating a self-funded reserve in order to pay for tort claims against the city.[115]

---

106. *See* Lail *ex rel.* Jestes v. Cleveland Cnty. Bd. of Educ., 183 N.C. App. 554, 560–61 (2007).

107. For further discussion of issues regarding waiver of immunity by local boards of education, see Trey Allen, *Local Government Immunity to Lawsuits in North Carolina* (UNC School of Government, 2018): 77–78.

108. 188 N.C. App. 592, 596 (2008).

109. Est. of Earley *ex rel.* Earley v. Haywood Cnty. Dep't of Soc. Servs., 204 N.C. App. 338, 343 (2010).

110. *See* Hart v. Brienza, 246 N.C. App. 426 (2016); *Est. of Earley*, 204 N.C. App. 338; White v. Stokes Cnty. Dep't of Soc. Servs., 207 N.C. App. 378 (2010).

111. Meinck v. City of Gastonia, 263 N.C. App. 414, 422 (2019) (citing *Daniel v. City of Morganton*, 125 N.C. App. 47, 53 (1997)).

112. *See* G.S. 143-299.2 (limitation on payments under State Tort Claims Act); G.S. 160A-485.5(b)(3) (State Tort Claims Act limitation on payments applies to claims filed against a city that has waived its immunity pursuant to G.S. 160A-485.5).

113. G.S. 160A-485.5(b)(1).

114. G.S. 160A-485.5(c).

115. *Id.*

Claims Not Covered by Governmental Immunity

Unless waived, governmental immunity bars most tort claims against local governments that arise from the performance of governmental functions. It does not, however, protect a unit of local government from a wide variety of other legal claims. For example, governmental immunity does not shield a local government from the following civil claims:

- **Claims arising under the Constitution of the United States or the North Carolina Constitution.** Claims arising under the Constitution of the United States will be discussed later in this chapter.
- **Claims arising based on allegations of violations of federal or state statutes.**[116] For example, local governments frequently face lawsuits from current or former employees alleging violations of federal employment statutes. Governmental immunity does not apply to such claims.
- **Claims alleging breach of a valid contract.** By entering into a valid contract, local governments consent to be sued for breach of such contract and waive governmental immunity to the extent of the contract.[117]
- **Claims alleging a city's negligent maintenance of its streets or sidewalks.** Despite the fact that road maintenance is recognized as a governmental function, North Carolina courts "have consistently declined to recognize governmental immunity as a defense to negligence claims premised on a city's failure to keep its streets or sidewalks in proper repair."[118]
- **Certain declaratory relief actions.** Governmental immunity does not apply to actions seeking a declaratory judgment that a local government exceeded its statutory authority and "invade[d] or threaten[ed] to invade personal or property rights of a citizen in disregard of the law."[119] Likewise, governmental immunity does not shield local governments from a declaratory relief action "seeking to ascertain the rights and obligations owed under an alleged contract."[120]

The Public Duty Doctrine

For a claim of negligence to be successful, a plaintiff must allege that the defendant owed her a legal duty.[121] The public duty doctrine holds that local governments do not have a duty to protect individual members of the public from crime or from criminal third parties. Although the government

116. Governmental immunity does, however, shield a local government from wrongful death claims, which is a claim created by statute (G.S. 28A-18-2) but also a claim sounding in tort. *See* Wright v. Gaston Cnty., 205 N.C. App. 600 (2010).

117. *See* Wray v. City of Greensboro, 370 N.C. 41 (2017); Data General Corp. v. Cnty. of Durham, 143 N.C. App. 97 (2001). *See also* Bates v. Charlotte–Mecklenburg Historic Landmarks Comm'n, 897 S.E.2d 1, 7–8 (N.C. Ct. App. 2024) (holding governmental immunity was waived with respect to claim for breach of the implied covenant of good faith and fair dealing). For more information about how governmental immunity applies to contract-related claims other than breach of contract, please see Chapter 7 of *Local Government Immunity to Lawsuits in North Carolina*, by Trey Allen (UNC School of Government, 2018).

118. Allen, *Local Government Immunity to Lawsuits in North Carolina*: 132; *see, e.g.,* Sisk v. City of Greensboro, 183 N.C. App. 657, 659 (2007). Governmental immunity does, however, apply to a municipality's decisions regarding which roads to keep open for vehicular traffic. Kirkpatrick v. Town of Nags Head, 213 N.C. App. 132, 142 (2011).

119. T & A Amusements, LLC v. McCrory, 251 N.C. App. 904, 908 (2017) (citing *Charlotte–Mecklenburg Hosp. Auth. v. N.C. Indus. Comm'n,* 336 N.C. 200, 208 (1994)); *see also* Phillips v. Orange Cnty. Health Dep't, 237 N.C. App. 249, 256–57 (2014).

120. Atl. Coast Conf. v. Univ. of Maryland, 230 N.C. App. 429, 442 (2013).

121. Inman v. City of Whiteville, 236 N.C. App. 301, 303 (2014).

may undertake a duty to protect the public at large, individual victims of crime or other harm are generally not entitled to recover damages when law enforcement officers fail to prevent such harm from happening. The public duty doctrine can act to shield a local government from claims of both negligence and gross negligence.[122]

The public duty doctrine has two exceptions.[123] First, a special duty to a specific person can arise in certain circumstances, usually as a result of contact between a unit of local government and the specific person. In most cases, the contact involves a promise to protect a specific individual, the failure to protect that individual, and the individual's reliance on the promise of protection to the individual's detriment.[124] Merely providing public safety controls to a particular area or neighborhood does not create a special duty to people within that area or neighborhood.[125]

The second exception to the public duty doctrine applies when a special relationship exists between the government and the plaintiff. The most often cited example is the relationship between the police and a witness or informant who has aided the police.[126]

In *Lovelace v. City of Shelby*, the North Carolina Supreme Court held that the public duty doctrine, as it applies to local governments, is limited to "law enforcement departments when they are exercising their general duty to protect the public."[127] The plaintiff in *Lovelace* alleged that the City of Shelby emergency operator negligently delayed dispatching fire personnel to her home and that her child died as the result of that delay. On remand to the trial court, the city amended its pleading to clarify that the emergency operator was a sworn police officer and reasserted the public duty doctrine defense under the theory that the doctrine applied where a sworn officer was performing his duties to the general public by dispatching the fire department. The trial court denied the city's motion to dismiss based on the public duty doctrine and that denial was affirmed by the North Carolina Court of Appeals, which clarified that the public duty doctrine did not apply to the 911 operator's dispatch of fire department services, even if the emergency operator was a police officer.[128]

Before the North Carolina Supreme Court's limiting pronouncement in *Lovelace*, the appellate courts had made the public duty doctrine available in cases involving building inspection,[129] safety inspection,[130] planning,[131] taxicab permitting,[132] animal control,[133] and fire protection.[134] These cases are no longer binding in light of *Lovelace*.

Following the state supreme court's limitation of the public duty doctrine in *Lovelace*, North Carolina courts have refused to apply the public duty doctrine in cases involving the following

122. Scott v. City of Charlotte, 203 N.C. App. 460, 464 (2010); Hedrick v. Rains, 121 N.C. App. 466, 471, *aff'd*, 344 N.C. 729 (1996).

123. Braswell v. Braswell, 330 N.C. 363, 371 (1991).

124. *Id.*

125. Prevette v. Forsyth Cnty., 110 N.C. App. 754, 758, *review denied*, 334 N.C. 622 (1993).

126. Stafford v. Baker, 129 N.C. App. 576, 580–81, *review denied*, 348 N.C. 695 (1998).

127. 351 N.C. 458, 461, *reh'g denied*, 352 N.C. 157 (2000); *see also* Thompson v. Waters, 351 N.C. 462, 465 (2000).

128. Lovelace v. City of Shelby, 153 N.C. App. 378 (2002). See also *Jefferson v. County of Vance*, 153 N.C. App. 523 (2002), an unpublished opinion cited below, where the North Carolina Court of Appeals applied the public duty doctrine with regard to an allegation that the county's 911 emergency response system negligently dispatched law enforcement to the scene of a domestic assault.

129. Lynn v. Overlook Development, 98 N.C. App. 75 (1990); Sinning v. Clark, 119 N.C. App. 515 (1995).

130. Stone v. N.C. Dep't of Labor, 347 N.C. 473 (1998); Hunt v. N.C. Dep't of Labor, 348 N.C. 192 (1998).

131. Derwort v. Polk Cnty., 129 N.C. App. 789 (1998).

132. Clark v. Red Bird Cab Co., 114 N.C. App. 400, *review denied*, 336 N.C. 603 (1994).

133. Prevette v. Forsyth Cnty., 110 N.C. App. 754, *review denied*, 334 N.C. 622 (1993).

134. *See, e.g.*, Davis v. Messer, 119 N.C. App. 44 (1995).

parties and scenarios: a school crossing guard,[135] a sewer line excavation,[136] negligent repair of a stop sign,[137] a municipal housing authority,[138] negligent inspection of residential construction,[139] negligent fire suppression,[140] an automobile accident with a police officer in pursuit,[141] an intentional tort committed by a police technician,[142] intentional and negligent torts committed by a school resource officer,[143] a county sheriff's negligent hiring and supervision of a deputy sheriff,[144] and county employees sued solely in their individual capacity.[145]

Since *Lovelace*, the North Carolina Court of Appeals clarified in *Strickland v. University of North Carolina at Wilmington* that the public duty doctrine applies when a plaintiff alleges "negligent control of an external injurious force or of the effects of such a force" but does not apply when the alleged negligence of law enforcement officers was *itself* the "injurious force" that harmed the plaintiff.[146] In *Strickland*, the plaintiff's son was shot and killed by a member of the New Hanover County Emergency Response Team (ERT) after UNC-Wilmington's police department requested assistance in serving an arrest warrant on the son. The plaintiff alleged that UNC-Wilmington's police department negligently provided false information about his son to the ERT in order to get their assistance with executing the warrant, leading the ERT to believe they were dealing with a dangerous gang-affiliated suspect. The court held that the public duty doctrine did not shield UNC-Wilmington from the plaintiff's negligence claim, because the UNC-Wilmington police department's "act of negligently providing misleading and inaccurate information *was itself the injurious force*."[147] The *Strickland* court reasoned that the duty of a law enforcement officer "not to negligently provide false and misleading information during a criminal investigation" does not "resemble the types of duties to the general public for which the public duty doctrine normally precludes liability."[148]

Liability of Individual Public Servants

A local government does its work through the actions of its elected officials, appointed officials, and employees. Just as the local government may sometimes be held responsible for the actions of the public servants, public servants may sometimes be held personally liable for their actions. A public servant may be sued in an *official* capacity—that is, as the representative of the local

135. Isenhour v. Hutto, 350 N.C. 601 (1999).

136. Hargrove v. Billings & Garrett, Inc., 137 N.C. App. 759 (2000).

137. Cucina v. Jacksonville, 138 N.C. App. 99 (2000).

138. Huntley v. Pandya, 139 N.C. App. 624 (2000).

139. Thompson v. Waters, 351 N.C. 462 (2000).

140. Willis v. Town of Beaufort, 143 N.C. App. 106 (2001).

141. Moses v. Young, 149 N.C. App. 613 (2002).

142. Walker v. City of Durham, 158 N.C. App. 747 (2003) (unpublished opinion). The doctrine shielded the city only from negligent behavior of the police technician, not the allegedly intentional behavior.

143. Smith v. Jackson Cnty. Bd. of Educ., 168 N.C. App. 452 (2005). See *Collum v. Charlotte–Mecklenburg Board of Education*, 614 F. Supp. 2d 598 (2008), in which the federal district court judge refused to apply a blanket exception to the public duty doctrine for all school resource officers and distinguished *Smith v. Jackson County Board of Education*.

144. *Smith*, 168 N.C. App. at 465.

145. Murray v. County of Person, 191 N.C. App. 575 (2008).

146. Strickland v. Univ. of N.C. at Wilmington, 213 N.C. App. 506 (2011).

147. *Id.* at 512 (emphasis added).

148. *Id.* at 511–12. *But see* Inman v. City of Whiteville, 236 N.C. App. 301 (2014) (distinguishing *Strickland* and holding that public duty doctrine shielded city from liability for alleged negligence in accident investigation when police officer failed to ascertain the identity of driver who allegedly ran plaintiff off the road).

government—and also in an *individual* (personal) capacity. In some cases, a plaintiff may bring legal claims against a public servant in both their official and individual capacities. The difference between official capacity claims and individual capacity claims is significant. It determines who is potentially liable for damages in the lawsuit and what types of immunity are available to the defendant.

Official Capacity Claims versus Individual Capacity Claims

A legal action brought against a public servant in his or her *official* capacity is, in all respects other than name, an action against the unit of local government for which he or she works.[149] Thus, the same defenses and immunities available to the unit of local government are available to the public servant. Even though a public servant is named as a defendant in such a case, an official capacity lawsuit does not seek to hold the individual public servant *personally* liable. This means that if a monetary judgment is entered in a legal action brought against a public servant in her official capacity, the legal responsibility for paying the judgment lies with the public entity for which she works, and not with the individual public servant.

On the other hand, an action against a public servant in his or her *individual* capacity represents an allegation that the public servant is *personally* liable to the plaintiff. Immunities separate and distinct from those available to the governmental entity often—though not always—insulate public servants from personal liability for acts within the scope of their duties. A local government has authority to defend and settle a claim on behalf of a liable employee who is sued in her individual capacity, pursuant to G.S. 160A-167, thereby providing relief to the claimant without waiving governmental immunity. In the absence of insurance coverage or a local government's decision to pay a judgment on behalf of the employee, however, damages awarded in individual capacity suits must be paid from the public servant's personal assets. More information on a local government's authority to defend employees and pay claims on their behalf is available in the "Defense of Employees, Payment of Judgments, and Settlements" section at the end of this chapter.

To determine the capacity in which the plaintiff seeks to sue the defendant (official, individual, or both), courts look to the caption of the complaint, the allegations set forth in the complaint, and the complaint's prayer for relief.[150] In *White v. Trew*, the North Carolina Supreme Court held that if the plaintiff's "complaint does not specify the capacity in which a public official is being sued for actions taken in the course and scope of his employment, [the court] will presume that the public official is being sued only in his official capacity."[151] If a plaintiff wants to bring an individual capacity claim against a public servant, the complaint's caption, allegations, or prayer for relief must make that intention clear.[152]

Policy Reasons for Immunity for Public Servants

The immunities that may insulate a public servant sued in an *individual* capacity balance the need to protect particular persons involved in certain government functions from liability with the duty to compensate injured plaintiffs and to hold individuals accountable for wrongdoing. Generally speaking, immunities do not protect public servants from criminal liability or civil liability for

149. Dickens v. Thorne, 110 N.C. App. 39 (1993) (citing Whitaker v. Clark, 109 N.C. App. 379, *review denied*, 333 N.C. 795 (1993)).

150. Mullis v. Sechrest, 347 N.C. 548, 554 (1998).

151. 366 N.C. 360, 360–61 (2013).

152. *Id.* at 364 ("Because the indicia of capacity mandated by Mullis are absent from the caption, allegations, and prayer for relief, we must presume that defendant is being sued in only his official capacity.); *see also* Est. of Long by & through Long v. Fowler, 378 N.C. 138, 144–45 (2021).

intentional wrongful acts. For example, public servants are generally liable for damages caused by their intentional torts.[153] No public policy interests support shielding public servants from liability when they intentionally act to harm others.

On the other hand, legitimate policy reasons exist for granting certain public officials immunity from liability for harm caused by their negligence. Public officials whose duties involve the exercise of discretion might be hesitant to take necessary official actions or make challenging decisions if they could be held personally liable for harm caused by simple negligence. The result of this reluctance to act would be a less efficient government. As the North Carolina Supreme Court has opined, "[I]t would be difficult to find those who would accept public office or engage in the administration of public affairs if they were to be held personally liable for acts or omissions involved in the exercise of discretion and sound judgment which they had performed to the best of their ability, and without any malevolent intention toward anyone who might be affected thereby."[154]

Whether or not public servants may be held personally liable for the consequences of their negligent acts depends entirely on the nature of their responsibilities. The three different types of immunity discussed below—legislative immunity, judicial immunity, and public official immunity—only apply depending on the nature of the public servant's role and duties.

Legislative Immunity

Local government officials, including county commissioners and city council members, are entitled to legislative immunity "for all actions taken in the sphere of legitimate legislative activity."[155] Voting on an ordinance, including a budget ordinance, is a legislative activity.[156] Zoning and rezoning have also been expressly recognized by courts as legislative activities.[157] Local government officials may also be individually immune for their *failure* to exercise their legislative powers.[158]

Legislative immunity under state law was not recognized by the North Carolina Court of Appeals until 1996 in *Vereen v. Holden*.[159] Prior to that case, trial courts routinely applied the doctrine of legislative immunity looking to federal decisions for guidance. In 2022, the North Carolina

---

153. *See, e.g.*, McCullers v. Lewis, 265 N.C. App. 216, 222, 828 S.E.2d 524, 531 (2019) (finding that "public official immunity may only insulate public officials from allegations of mere negligence"); Wells v. N. Carolina Dep't of Correction, 152 N.C. App. 307, 320 (2002) (citing Hawkins v. State, 117 N.C. App. 615, 630, *disc. rev. denied*, 342 N.C. 188 (1995)); *see also* Bates v. Charlotte-Mecklenburg Historic Landmarks Comm'n, 897 S.E.2d 1, 8 (N.C. Ct. App. 2024). One exception to this rule concerns the intentional tort of defamation. As discussed earlier, public servants with a qualified privilege to make a particular statement will not be held liable for defamation unless they act with malice.

154. Miller v. Jones, 224 N.C. 783, 787 (1945).

155. Northfield Dev. Co. v. City of Burlington, 136 N.C. App. 272, 281, *aff'd in part, review dismissed in part*, 352 N.C. 671 (2000) (internal quotation marks omitted) (citing Bogan v. Scott-Harris, 523 U.S. 44, 54 (1998)).

156. *Bogan*, 523 U.S. at 55.

157. Walton N. Carolina, LLC v. City of Concord, 257 N.C. App. 227, 234 (2017); *see also* Kerik v. Davidson Cnty., 145 N.C. App. 222, 228 (2001); Northfield Dev. Co. v. City of Burlington, 136 N.C. App. 272, 277, *aff'd in part, review dismissed in part*, 352 N.C. 671 (2000).

158. *See* Moye v. McLawhorn, 208 N.C. 812 (1935) ("The power conferred by statute can be exercised by the defendants only in their corporate capacity, as the board of commissioners of Pitt county. It is a discretionary power. Neither the failure to exercise nor the exercise of the power by the defendants acting in their corporate capacity can impose liability on the defendants as individuals on the facts alleged in the complaint."); see also *Hill v. Board of Aldermen*, 72 N.C. 55 (1875) ("We conceive that nothing can be clearer, than that when a general authority is given to a municipal corporation to be exercised through its proper legislative officers, to make ordinances for the good government, health and safety of the inhabitants and their property, it is thereby left entirely to the discretion of those authorities, to determine what ordinances are proper for those purposes."); *Blackwelder v. Concord*, 205 N.C. 792, 795 (1934) ("The exercise of discretionary or legislative power is a governmental function, and for injury resulting from the negligent exercise of such power a municipality is exempt from liability").

159. Vereen v. Holden, 121 N.C. App. 779 (1996), *review allowed and remanded on other grounds*, 345 N.C. 646 (1997).

Supreme Court recognized legislative immunity as a bar to claims against North Carolina public officials, affirming that it applies if (1) the defendant was acting in a legislative capacity at the time of the alleged incident and (2) the defendant's acts were not illegal.[160] However, the supreme court indicated that this immunity may have limitations, since a public official may still "be held liable in his or her individual capacity if his or her actions were malicious, corrupt or outside the scope of his or her official duties, even if they were legislative in nature."[161]

Judicial Immunity and Quasi-Judicial Immunity

Through the doctrine of judicial immunity, judges, magistrates, clerks of superior court, and prosecutors are protected from civil liability for errors committed in the discharge of their judicial and prosecutorial duties.[162] This immunity is absolute and protects "even conduct which is corrupt, malicious or intended to do injury."[163] However, judicial officials are not entitled to absolute judicial immunity when acting in an administrative, nonjudicial capacity (such as when making personnel decisions) or for "actions taken in the complete absence of all jurisdiction."[164] The North Carolina Supreme Court has held that judicial immunity applies to both official and individual capacity claims.[165]

Members of local boards with quasi-judicial authority, such as the planning board or board of adjustment, also have judicial immunity when acting in their quasi-judicial capacities.[166] Absolute judicial immunity also applies to county commissioners and city council members when carrying out quasi-judicial functions,[167] including, for example, decisions to grant or deny variances or special use permits through quasi-judicial proceedings.[168] As in the case of legislative immunity, state courts often look to federal law for guidance in their determination of whether a public servant is acting in a judicial or quasi-judicial capacity.[169]

Public Official Immunity

Public official immunity protects public servants who are deemed by a court to be *public officers* from individual liability for negligent activity unless they act with malice, for corrupt reasons, or

160. Providence Volunteer Fire Dep't, Inc. v. Town of Weddington, 2022-NCSC-100, 382 N.C. 199, 220 (citing *Vereen*, 121 N.C. App. at 782).

161. *Id.*

162. Fuquay Springs v. Rowland, 239 N.C. 299, 300 (1954) (judges); Sharp v. Gulley, 120 N.C. App. 878, 880 (1995) (court-appointed referee); *Jacobs*, 36 N.C. App. at 64 (citing *Foust*, 21 N.C. App. 268, *review denied*, 285 N.C. 589) (prosecutor); Wynn v. Frederick, 385 N.C. 576, 589 (2023), *reh'g denied*, 896 S.E.2d 254 (N.C. 2024) (magistrates); Bare v. Atwood, 204 N.C. App. 310 (2010) (clerks of court); Greer v. Skyway Broadcasting Co., 256 N.C. 382 (1962) (does not apply to law enforcement officers).

163. State *ex rel.* Jacobs v. Sherard, 36 N.C. App. 60, 64 (1978) (citing Foust v. Hughes, 21 N.C. App. 268, *cert. denied* 285 N.C. 589 (1974)).

164. *See, e.g.*, Savage v. Maryland, 896 F.3d 260, 273 (4th Cir. 2018) (citing Van de Kamp v. Goldstein, 555 U.S. 335, 344 (2009)); Forrester v. White, 484 U.S. 219, 229 (1988); Bare v. Atwood, 204 N.C. App. 310, 314 (2010) (citing Mireles v. Waco, 502 U.S. 9, 11–12 (1991)).

165. Wynn v. Frederick, 385 N.C. 576, 589 (2023), *reh'g denied*, 896 S.E.2d 254 (N.C. 2024).

166. Northfield Dev. Co. v. City of Burlington, 136 N.C. App. 272, 281–82, *aff'd in part, review dismissed in part*, 352 N.C. 671 (2000).

167. *Id.*

168. *Id.* at 282.

169. For example, looking to federal case law, the North Carolina Court of Appeals held that "the act of knowingly making false or misleading statements in an affidavit in the procurement of a search warrant falls outside the protections of quasi-judicial immunity." Crazie Overstock Promotions, LLC v. McVicker, 257 N.C. App. 540 (2018) (citing Butz v. Economou, 438 U.S. 78, 513 (1978)).

outside the scope of their official duties.[170] The North Carolina Supreme Court has stated that the doctrine of public official immunity has two primary goals: "promoting fearless, vigorous, and effective administration of government policies, and dampening trepidation about personal liability that may deter competent people from taking office."[171] Public official immunity is an affirmative defense, which "must be properly asserted by the defendant to receive its protection."[172]

A public official does not qualify for public official immunity if the official's actions were done with malice or for corrupt reasons. North Carolina courts have held that a public official acts with malice if the act at issue is: "(1) done wantonly, (2) contrary to the actor's duty, and (3) intended to be injurious to another."[173] Where physical safety is involved, a court may find constructive intent to cause injury if the public official's conduct was "so reckless or so manifestly indifferent to the consequences . . . as to justify a finding of willfulness and wantonness equivalent in spirit to an actual intent."[174] A public officer acts for corrupt reasons when the act is done with "a wrongful design to acquire some pecuniary profit or other advantage."[175]

Unlike a public officer, a *public employee* is not protected under public official immunity. Therefore, public employees may be held personally liable for injuries caused by their negligence while performing their duties.[176] The distinction between these two categories of public servants is discussed in more detail below.

Public Officers

The significant difference between the exposure of *public officers* and *public employees* to liability means that the distinction between the two categories is an important one. In *Isenhour v. Hutto*, the North Carolina Supreme Court enumerated three key distinctions between public officials and public employees: (1) a public official holds a position created by the constitution or statutes; (2) a public official exercises a portion of the sovereign power; and (3) a public official exercises discretion, while public employees perform ministerial duties.[177] A public servant seeking public official immunity must demonstrate to a court that all three of the *Isenhour* factors are satisfied.[178] The fact that a public servant has taken an oath of office also weighs in favor of finding that individual to be a public official, though it is not a necessary factor.[179]

Even if a public servant's position was not created by statute or the state constitution, courts will find that the first *Isenhour* factor is met if a statute expressly creates the authority to delegate a duty, the duty is in fact delegated to an individual, and that individual performs the duty on behalf

170. Wiggins v. City of Monroe, 73 N.C. App. 44 (1985), *cert. denied*, 320 N.C. 178 (1987)).

171. Est. of Graham v. Lambert, 385 N.C. 644, 654 (2024) (citing Bartley v. City of High Point, 2022-NCSC-63, ¶ 19, 381 N.C. 287, 294) (internal quotation marks omitted).

172. Bartley v. City of High Point, 2022-NCSC-63, ¶ 22, 381 N.C. 287, 295.

173. Hart v. Brienza, 246 N.C. App. 426, 431 (2016) (citing Wilcox v. City of Asheville, 222 N.C. App. 285, 289 (2012)).

174. Hart, 246 N.C. App. at 431 (citing Foster v. Hyman, 197 N.C. 189, 192 (1929)); *see also* R.A. v. Johnson, 36 F.4th 537, 545–46 (4th Cir. 2022) (discussing cases involving constructive intent to injure in the context of the malice exception to public official immunity).

175. Green v. Howell, 274 N.C. App. 158, 167 (2020) (citing State v. Hair, 114 N.C. App. 464, 468 (1994)).

176. Harwood v. Johnson, 92 N.C. App. 306, 309 (1988), *aff'd in part, rev'd in part on other grounds*, 326 N.C. 231 (1990).

177. Isenhour v. Hutto, 350 N.C. 601, 610 (1999); *see also* Meyer v. Walls, 347 N.C. 97, 113–14 (1997); Hare v. Butler, 99 N.C. App. 693, 700, *disc. review denied*, 327 N.C. 634 (1990).

178. McCullers v. Lewis, 265 N.C. App. 216, 222 (2019).

179. *See, e.g.*, Baker v. Smith, 224 N.C. App. 423, 433 (2012); Murray v. County of Person, 191 N.C. App. 575, 579–80 (2008).

of the person or organization in whom the statute vests the delegation authority.[180] Accordingly, public officials who delegate their statutory duties to other government employees should clearly document such delegation in writing.

Based on such factors, North Carolina courts have held the following public servants to be public officers: the county director of social services,[181] certain social workers with a county department of social services,[182] notaries,[183] school trustees and park commissioners,[184] school district superintendents and school principals,[185] coroners,[186] forensic pathologists,[187] the state banking commissioner,[188] the Commissioner of the North Carolina Division of Motor Vehicles,[189] an inspector with the North Carolina Division of Motor Vehicles,[190] the director of the county health department,[191] the chief building inspector,[192] a building inspector,[193] a code enforcement officer,[194] police officers,[195] elected officials,[196] animal control officers,[197] correctional officers,[198] a county emergency

180. McCullers v. Lewis, 265 N.C. App. 216, 223 (2019); *see, e.g.*, Baker v. Smith, 224 N.C. App. 423, 428–30 (2012) (holding that assistant jailers satisfied first *Isenhour* factor where relevant statutes gave the Sheriff the duty to take "care and custody of the jail" and the authority to "appoint a deputy or employ others to assist him in performing his official duties"); Hobbs v. N.C. Dep't of Human Res., 135 N.C. App. 412, 421–22 (1999) (holding that social workers were acting as public officials because G.S. 108A-14 gives the director of social services the authority to "delegate to one or more members of his staff the authority to act as his representative").

181. *Hobbs*, 135 N.C. App. 412.

182. *Id.* (social workers responsible for placing children in foster care pursuant to G.S. 108A-14(a)(12)); Dalenko v. Wake Cnty. Dep't of Human Services, 157 N.C. App. 495 (2003) (social workers responsible for receiving and evaluating reports of abuse, neglect, or exploitation of disabled adults and for taking appropriate action pursuant to G.S. 108A-14(a)(14)); and Hunter v. Transylvania Cnty. Dep't of Social Services, 207 N.C. App. 735 (2010) (social workers responsible for investigating abuse and neglect of children pursuant to G.S. 108A-14(a)(11)). However, see *Meyer v. Walls*, 122 N.C. App. 507, *reversed and remanded on other grounds by* 347 N.C. 97 (1996), in which the North Carolina Court of Appeals held that social workers acting pursuant to G.S. 108A-14(a)(14) regarding disabled adults are not public officials. The North Carolina Supreme Court noted in its reversal in *Meyer* that the issue of whether the social workers were public employees or officials was not appealed and, therefore, the court let stand the earlier ruling of the court of appeals. G.S. 108A-14(b), which allows the director of social services to delegate the authority to act as his or her representative, was enacted on October 1, 1995, and the facts giving rise to the *Meyer* case occurred prior to 1995.

183. McGee v. Eubanks, 77 N.C. App. 369 (1985), *review denied*, 315 N.C. 589 (1986).

184. Smith v. Hefner, 235 N.C. 1 (1952).

185. Petrillo v. Barnes-Jones, 291 N.C. App. 62, 68 (2023); Gunter v. Anders, 114 N.C. App. 61, 67 (1994), *review denied*, 339 N.C. 611 (1995). *See also Jetton v. Caldwell County Board of Education*, 185 N.C. App. 159 (2007), an unpublished opinion in which public official immunity was extended to an assistant principal.

186. Gillikin v. United States Fid. & Guar. Co., 254 N.C. 247 (1961).

187. Cherry v. Harris, 110 N.C. App. 478, *review denied*, 335 N.C. 171 (1993).

188. Sansom v. Johnson, 39 N.C. App. 682 (1979).

189. Thompson Cadillac-Oldsmobile, Inc. v. Silk Hope Automobile, Inc., 87 N.C. App. 467 (1987), *review denied*, 321 N.C. 480 (1988).

190. *Id.*

191. EEE-ZZZ Lay Drain Co. v. N.C. Dep't of Human Res., 108 N.C. App. 24 (1992), *overruled on other grounds by* Meyer v. Walls, 347 N.C. 97 (1997).

192. Pigott v. City of Wilmington, 50 N.C. App. 401, *review denied*, 303 N.C. 181 (1981).

193. McCoy v. Coker, 174 N.C. App. 311 (2005).

194. Al-Nasra v. Cleveland Cnty., 202 N.C. App. 584 (2010).

195. Bartley v. City of High Point, 381 N.C. 287, 295 (2022); *see also* State v. Hord, 264 N.C. 149 (1965). G.S. 20-145 also provides immunity to law enforcement officers with respect to vehicle speed limitations but does not provide immunity for gross negligence. An officer may be held personally liable for injuries caused by an officer's gross negligence when pursuing a suspect. *See* Est. of Graham v. Lambert, 385 N.C. 644, 658 (2024); Higgins v. Mendoza, 910 S.E.2d 920, 923 (N.C. Ct. App. 2025).

196. Town of Old Fort v. Harmon, 219 N.C. 241 (1941).

197. Kitchin v. Halifax Cnty., 192 N.C. App. 559 (2008), *discretionary review denied*, 363 N.C. 127 (2009).

198. Price v. Davis, 132 N.C. App. 556 (1999).

medical services director and emergency medical services medical director,[199] a director of federal programs for a county school system,[200] a state probation officer,[201] a fire chief,[202] a county medical examiner,[203] assistant jailers,[204] and employees of a local housing authority.[205]

Public Employees

Public employees are not protected by public official immunity. Public employee positions are those that do not meet all of the *Isenhour* factors described above. In many public employee positions, the individual acts primarily at the direction of others and has duties that are more administrative than discretionary in nature. Some individuals may be treated by courts as public employees because their positions are not created by the state constitution or statutes, and they do not act pursuant to a delegation of statutory authority from someone whose position was created by the constitution or statutes.

One basis for failing to cover these employees under public official immunity lies in the assumption that they have clearer, simpler responsibilities than policymaking officials and therefore are less likely to be deterred from taking appropriate action by the fear of liability. Another possible justification for the lack of public official immunity for these employees is that they are not expected to exercise a significant amount of discretion in their decision-making or power over the public in their roles.

Courts have held the following positions to be public employee positions that do not qualify for public official immunity: teachers,[206] an environmental health specialist and supervisor,[207] an environmental health administrator,[208] a school crossing guard,[209] an emergency medical technician,[210] staff members of an after-school enrichment program,[211] a parole case analyst,[212] prison physicians,[213] and engineer project managers.[214]

Liability of the Local Government and Its Public Servants under Federal Law

Section 1983 of the Civil Rights Act of 1871 ("Section 1983") authorizes a person to sue and recover damages against a local government or its governing board members, officials, or employees for violating the person's federal constitutional or statutory rights, when the violation is caused by official

---

199. Dempsey v. Halford, 183 N.C. App. 637 (2007). *But see Fraley v. Griffin*, 217 N.C. App. 624 (2011), in which the court of appeals held that a county emergency medical technician is not a public official.

200. Farrell v. Transylvania Cnty. Bd. of Educ., 175 N.C. App. 689 (2006) (the court cited G.S. 115C-287.1(a)(3) in support of the argument that school supervisors are public officials, though the case dealt specifically with the position of federal programs director).

201. Lambert v. Cartwright, 160 N.C. App. 73 (2003).

202. Willis v. Town of Beaufort, 143 N.C. App. 106 (2001).

203. Green v. Kearney, 203 N.C. App. 260, 267–68 (2010).

204. Baker v. Smith, 224 N.C. App. 423, 434 (2012).

205. McCullers v. Lewis, 265 N.C. App. 216 (2019).

206. Daniel v. City of Morganton, 125 N.C. App. 47 (1997).

207. Block v. Person, 141 N.C. App. 273 (2000).

208. Cline v. James Bane Home Bldg., LLC, 2021-NCCOA-266, ¶ 25, 278 N.C. App. 12, 22.

209. Isenhour v. Hutto, 350 N.C. 601 (1999).

210. Fraley v. Griffin, 217 N.C. App. 624 (2011).

211. Schmidt v. Breeden, 134 N.C. App. 248 (1999).

212. Harwood v. Johnson, 326 N.C. 231 (1990).

213. Leonard v. Bell, 254 N.C. App. 694 (2017).

214. Orsbon for Bosworth-Jones v. Milazzo, 910 S.E.2d 706 (N.C. Ct. App. 2024).

conduct.[215] The provision remained dormant until 1961 when the United States Supreme Court held in *Monroe v. Pape*[216] that conduct by local police officers could be the basis of an action under Section 1983. By providing a remedy under federal law for the violation of rights protected by the Constitution of the United States and some federal statutes, Section 1983 creates a framework of liability separate from state tort law. In some cases, an official action may expose a public servant and the local government to liability under both state and federal law. However, Section 1983 does not create a cause of action where there is no violation of federal law or a federal constitutional right.[217]

A person who violates someone's federal rights may be required to compensate the injured party, just as an individual who commits a civil wrong under state law may be required to do. The prevailing party may also recover reasonable attorneys' fees.[218] The following sections discuss types of official conduct that can give rise to liability under Section 1983.

Violation of Constitutional Rights

Section 1983 provides a remedy only for the deprivation of "rights, privileges, or immunities secured by the Constitution and laws" of the United States.[219] In the local government context, several common constitutional violations involve the First Amendment right of free speech, the Fourth Amendment right of freedom from unreasonable searches and seizures, and the Fourteenth Amendment right of due process and equal protection.

First Amendment Rights of Freedom of Speech and Freedom of Association

The Constitution's First Amendment limits how the government may restrict anyone's freedom of speech. First Amendment rights may be implicated in many local government actions, including sign regulations, noise ordinances, prohibitions on solicitation, policing protests, flag restrictions, and more. The First Amendment also protects public employees who speak out on matters of public concern.[220] A local government employee may sue under Section 1983 if, for example, he is fired or disciplined for writing a letter to the newspaper about the misuse of local government funds.[221] First Amendment protections for freedom of association also prohibit firing or otherwise punishing most local government employees because of their political party affiliation.[222]

Fourth Amendment Rights of Freedom from Unreasonable Searches and Seizures

The Fourth Amendment to the Constitution guarantees the right to be free from unreasonable searches and seizures conducted by the government. This right is violated if a law enforcement officer arrests (an arrest being one kind of seizure) someone without probable cause for believing the person committed a crime. An officer may also violate Fourth Amendment rights by searching a person or a person's property without a search warrant or a valid exception to the warrant requirement.

---

215. 42 U.S.C.A. § 1983.
216. 365 U.S. 167 (1961).
217. Clayton v. Branson, 170 N.C. App. 438, 452 (2005) (citing Baker v. McCollan, 443 U.S. 137, 144 n.3 (1979)).
218. 42 U.S.C.A. § 1988.
219. *Clayton*, 170 N.C. App. at 452 (citing Gonzaga Univ. v. Doe, 536 U.S. 273, 283 (2002)).
220. *See, e.g.*, Lane v. Franks, 573 U.S. 228, 235–37 (2014).
221. *See, e.g.*, Pickering v. Bd. of Educ., 391 U.S. 563 (1968).
222. Rutan v. Republican Party, 497 U.S. 62, 75 (1990) ("We therefore determine that promotions, transfers, and recalls after layoffs based on political affiliation or support are an impermissible infringement on the First Amendment rights of public employees.").

Fourteenth Amendment Right of Due Process

The Fourteenth Amendment to the Constitution provides that no person may be deprived of life, liberty, or property without due process of law. Procedural due process is focused on the procedures the government must follow before depriving someone of life, liberty, or property. The complicated rules for criminal trials and for proceedings to terminate parental rights provide examples of procedural due process protections.

In many contexts, the due process clause of the Fourteenth Amendment requires that those who are to be deprived of liberty or property by the government receive prior notice of the reasons for the government's action and an opportunity for a hearing to consider those reasons. *Property* and *liberty* are defined broadly for purposes of this guarantee. For example, under the personnel ordinances of some cities and counties, employees may not be fired without good cause. Such an ordinance creates a "property" right in continued employment,[223] meaning the local government must give the employee procedural due process prior to termination.[224] Local government employees who are subject to the State Human Resources Act (such as employees of non-consolidated county departments of social services and health departments) also have a statutory "property" interest in continued employment.[225]

Due process also protects persons from arbitrary and capricious government actions. For example, a developer was permitted to sue under Section 1983 for violations of due process when a local governing board intervened to prevent the routine issuance of a building permit to which he was entitled under state law.[226] Section 1983 may impose liability when a plaintiff can prove that the local government took away a liberty or property interest created by state or local law through conduct that is arbitrary, capricious, or an abuse of discretion.[227]

Substantive due process protects individuals against "arbitrary legislation" by the government, requiring that the government must have some rational basis for enacting a law.[228] For example, in one North Carolina Court of Appeals case, the plaintiff challenged a town's enactment of an ordinance prohibiting the housing of animals within 200 feet of a lake, arguing that enforcement of the ordinance violated the plaintiff's substantive due process rights.[229] The court held that the question of whether the town's enactment of the ordinance was rationally related to a legitimate government interest in protecting the town's water supply was a question for a jury.

Substantive due process also protects individuals from egregious governmental misconduct, where a government official or employee's executive action is "so egregious, so outrageous, that it

---

223. Bd. of Regents v. Roth, 408 U.S. 564 (1972); *see also* Peace v. Emp. Sec. Comm'n, 349 N.C. 315, 321 (1998); Paschal v. Myers, 129 N.C. App. 23, 29 (1998).

224. Cleveland Bd. of Educ. v. Loudermill, 470 U.S. 532 (1985); Bishop v. Wood, 426 U.S. 341 (1976).

225. *See* G.S. 126-35(a) (just cause protections for a "career State employee"); G.S. 126-5(a)(2)–(3) (categories of local government employees subject to the State Human Resources Act); Brewington v. N.C. Dep't of Pub. Safety, State Bureau of Investigation, 254 N.C. App. 1, 27 (2017) (citing Peace v. Employment Sec. Comm'n of N.C., 349 N.C. 315, 322 (1998)).

226. Scott v. Greenville Cnty., 716 F.2d 1409 (4th Cir. 1983); *but see* Siena Corp. v. Mayor & City Council of Rockville, Maryland, 873 F.3d 456, 463 (4th Cir. 2017) and Gardner v. City of Baltimore Mayor & City Council, 969 F.2d 63, 69 (4th Cir. 1992), standing for the proposition that significant discretion afforded by state law to government officials in zoning or permitting decisions will defeat the claim of a property interest.

227. *Id.* at 1419.

228. Patmore v. Town of Chapel Hill, N.C., 233 N.C. App. 133, 137 (2014) (citing Lowe v. Tarble, 313 N.C. 460, 461 (1985)).

229. Town of Beech Mountain v. Genesis Wildlife Sanctuary, Inc., 247 N.C. App. 444 (2016), *aff'd*, 369 N.C. 722 (2017).

may fairly be said to shock the contemporary conscience."[230] In order to meet this standard, a plaintiff must show that a public servant's behavior lacked "any reasonable justification in the service of a legitimate governmental objective."[231]

Violation of Statutory Rights

Most claims under Section 1983 involve alleged violations of rights under the Constitution. However, Section 1983 also authorizes a person to sue for and recover damages under a limited number of federal statutes. Typically, these are statutes that create rights but do not themselves offer any remedy for the violation of those rights. A plaintiff alleging a violation of a federal statute will only be permitted to sue under Section 1983 if he can demonstrate that the statute "creates an individually enforceable right in the class of beneficiaries to which he belongs."[232] This creates a rebuttable presumption that the right can be enforced under Section 1983, but the defendant may defeat the presumption by showing that Congress did not intend to allow Section 1983 actions as a remedy for the right.[233]

In one case, for example, the U.S. Supreme Court held that an error in billing low-income housing tenants for utilities might violate the Housing Act of 1937 and result in a recovery of damages under Section 1983.[234] Without Section 1983, the tenants would have been left with no potential recourse for the violation, as the Housing Act did not provide for a private right of action to enforce tenants' rights.

Local governments administer a number of federally funded programs, which often have requirements established by federal statutes. If a state fails to comply with federally imposed conditions for receipt of funds under federal spending legislation, "the typical remedy . . . is not a private cause of action for noncompliance but rather action by the Federal Government to terminate funds to the State."[235] For a plaintiff to bring a Section 1983 claim based on a violation of federal spending legislation, a court must find that Congress "unambiguously conferred" individual rights on an identified class of persons.[236]

Liability of the Local Government Under Section 1983

Section 1983 claims against local governments are sometimes called *Monell* claims, in reference to *Monell v. Department of Social Services*,[237] the U.S. Supreme Court case which first established that local governments could be held liable under Section 1983. Under the state tort law principles discussed earlier in this chapter, a local government may be held liable for the negligent actions of its employees performed within the scope of their employment unless governmental immunity applies. In contrast, a local government may only be held liable under Section 1983 if the plaintiff can prove "the existence of an official policy or custom that is fairly attributable to the municipality and that proximately caused the deprivation of their rights."[238]

---

230. Dean *ex rel.* Harkness v. McKinney, 976 F.3d 407, 413–14 (4th Cir. 2020) (citing Terrell v. Larson, 396 F.3d 975, 978 (8th Cir. 2005)).

231. Washington v. Hous. Auth. of the City of Columbia, 58 F.4th 170, 177 (4th Cir. 2023) (quoting Cnty. of Sacramento v. Lewis, 523 U.S. 833, 846 (1998)).

232. City of Rancho Palos Verdes, Cal. v. Abrams, 544 U.S. 113, 120 (2005) (citing Gonzaga Univ. v. Doe, 536 U.S. 273, 283 (2002)).

233. *Id.* (citing Blessing v. Freestone, 520 U.S. 329, 341 (1997)).

234. Wright v. City of Roanoke Redevelopment & Hous. Auth., 479 U.S. 418 (1987).

235. Health & Hosp. Corp. of Marion Cnty. v. Talevski, 599 U.S. 166, 183 (2023) (citing *Gonzaga*, 536 U.S. at 280).

236. *Id.*

237. 436 U.S. 658 (1978).

238. Howard v. City of Durham, 68 F.4th 934, 952 (4th Cir. 2023) (quoting Jordan *ex rel.* Jordan v. Jackson, 15 F.3d 333, 338 (4th Cir. 1994)); *see also* Monell v. Dep't of Social Servs., 436 U.S. 658 (1978).

In other words, the fact that a local government employee violated an individual's constitutional rights is not sufficient *on its own* to hold the local government itself liable for that violation. The plaintiff must go a step further by showing that an official policy or custom of the local government caused the violation. This is a direct theory of liability based on the actions of the local government itself, as a local government cannot be held liable under Section 1983 for the actions of its employees based on a theory of vicarious liability or *respondeat superior*.[239]

How does a plaintiff prove that a local government had an "official policy or custom" that caused a violation of their federal rights? There are four avenues through which a plaintiff can demonstrate such a policy or custom: "(1) through an express policy, such as a written ordinance or regulation; (2) through the decisions of a person with final policymaking authority; (3) through an omission, such as a failure to properly train officers, that manifests deliberate indifference to the rights of citizens; or (4) through a practice that is so persistent and widespread as to constitute a custom or usage with the force of law."[240] Regardless of which avenue a plaintiff uses to prove a "policy or custom," the plaintiff must show that the local government's policy or custom *itself* inflicted the alleged injury in order to hold the local government liable.[241]

In some cases, a local government may violate someone's rights through the explicit implementation of an ordinance, regulation, or other decision officially adopted by the local government's governing board.[242] Some acts less formal than passing an ordinance can also establish "official policy," such as adopting personnel policies or passing formal resolutions supporting particular persons or conduct.[243] In other cases, plaintiffs can prove local government liability by showing that their rights were violated by a public servant who was given final policymaking authority under state or local law in the area involved.[244] For example, the Fourth Circuit held that a town manager's alleged violations of the plaintiffs' First Amendment rights could be imputed to the town because the town expressly delegated "unfettered final policymaking authority with respect to almost all personnel matters" to the manager.[245] A plaintiff can also establish a Section 1983 claim against a local government by showing its policymakers failed "to put a stop to or correct a widespread pattern of unconstitutional conduct."[246]

As discussed in more detail below, individual public servants sued in a Section 1983 lawsuit may be shielded from liability by the doctrine of qualified immunity or absolute legislative immunity. Local governments, however, do *not* receive qualified immunity or legislative immunity from Section 1983 liability.[247] And governmental immunity, which shields local governments from liability in tort claims involving the performance of governmental functions, does not apply to Section 1983 claims.[248]

---

239. *See, e.g.*, Franklin v. City of Charlotte, 64 F.4th 519, 535 (4th Cir. 2023).

240. Lytle v. Doyle, 326 F.3d 463, 471 (4th Cir. 2003) (citing Carter v. Morris, 164 F.3d 215, 218 (4th Cir. 1999) (internal quotation marks omitted).

241. *Monell*, 436 U.S. at 694.

242. *See, e.g.*, Matthias v. Bingley, 906 F.2d 1047, *modified*, 915 F.2d 946 (5th Cir. 1990) (per curiam).

243. *See* Sheldon H. Nahmod, *Civil Rights & Civil Liberties Litigation: The Law of Section 1983* § 6:18 (collecting cases).

244. *See* Nahmod, *Civil Rights & Civil Liberties Litigation: The Law of Section 1983* § 6:32 (collecting cases).

245. Hunter v. Town of Mocksville, N.C., 897 F.3d 538, 561 (4th Cir. 2018).

246. Owens v. Baltimore City State's Att'ys Off., 767 F.3d 379, 402–03 (4th Cir. 2014) (quoting Spell v. McDaniel, 824 F.2d 1380, 1390 (4th Cir. 1987)).

247. Owens v. Baltimore City State's Att'ys Off., 767 F.3d 379, 402 (4th Cir. 2014) ("Unlike public officials, municipalities do not enjoy qualified immunity."); Alexander v. Holden, 66 F.3d 62, 68 (4th Cir. 1995) ("[T]he defense of legislative immunity by a county to a suit under § 1983 is no longer a viable defense in this circuit to alleged constitutional violations based on either the legislative or administrative actions of its legislators.").

248. *See* Owen v. City of Independence, 445 U.S. 622 (1980).

Liability of Public Servants under Section 1983

Public servants may be sued individually in a Section 1983 lawsuit if they violate someone's federal rights. In some cases, however, they may be entitled to the protection of either absolute or qualified immunity from personal liability for damages.

Absolute Immunity for Legislative Functions

Members of local legislative bodies are absolutely immune from personal liability for damages under Section 1983 if the body's legislative acts violate someone's federal rights.[249] Thus, local government governing board members (as well as other local officials engaged in legislative functions) may never be required to personally pay damages for acts taken within the scope of their legislative duties.[250] However, local government board members may be held personally liable for acts taken within the scope of their *administrative* duties, although qualified immunity may sometimes protect them (see the discussion below).[251] For example, the Fourth Circuit Court of Appeals has held that terminating a county employee "is plainly unrelated" to the process of enacting legislation, and thus is not an action that qualifies for absolute legislative immunity.[252] On the other hand, developing and enacting a budget is a legislative activity covered by absolute immunity—even when budgetary changes involve eliminating an employee's position.[253]

The legal distinction between an administrative and a legislative act can be difficult to discern, but the following example may help to illustrate how the lines are drawn.[254] Because passing an ordinance is a legislative action, local government board members are absolutely immune from personal liability if the board enacts a personnel ordinance that lists affiliation with a particular political party by a local government employee as cause for dismissal, even though the ordinance interferes with an employee's First Amendment right to affiliate freely with any political party. However, *enforcing* a personnel ordinance is an administrative action, and board members who vote to dismiss an employee under an unconstitutional ordinance may be held individually liable for that action.[255] How a local government conducts its business makes a difference in the liability exposure of its governing board members.

Notably, public officials and employees do not qualify for legislative immunity for illegal acts, such as bribery.[256]

Absolute Immunity for Judicial and Prosecutorial Functions

Judges and magistrates are absolutely immune from personal liability for damages in Section 1983 claims arising from the performance of judicial acts.[257] Likewise, prosecutors are absolutely immune from personal liability for damages in Section 1983 claims based on prosecutorial actions that are

---

249. Bogan v. Scott-Harris, 523 U.S. 44, 54 (1998) ("Local legislators are entitled to absolute immunity from § 1983 liability for their legislative activities."); Bruce v. Riddle, 631 F.2d 272 (4th Cir. 1980).

250. *See Bogan*, 523 U.S. at 55 (1998) ("[O]fficials outside the legislative branch are entitled to legislative immunity when they perform legislative functions. . .").

251. *See, e.g.*, Scott v. Greenville Cnty., 716 F.2d 1409, 1422–23 (4th Cir. 1983).

252. Roberson v. Mullins, 29 F.3d 132, 135 (4th Cir. 1994).

253. *See* Kensington Volunteer Fire Dep't, Inc. v. Montgomery Cnty., Md., 684 F.3d 462, 470–71 (4th Cir. 2012).

254. On the legislative–administrative distinction, see *Scott*, 716 F.2d at 1422–23.

255. *See, e.g.*, Gross v. Winter, 876 F.2d 165 (D.C. Cir. 1989).

256. *See, e.g.*, Bruce v. Riddle, 631 F.2d 272, 279 (4th Cir. 1980); *Scott*, 716 F.2d at 1422.

257. *See, e.g.*, Stump v. Sparkman, 435 U.S. 349 (1978); Pierson v. Ray, 386 U.S. 547 (1967); King v. Myers, 973 F.2d 354, 356 (4th Cir. 1992).

"intimately associated with the judicial phase of the criminal process."[258] Quasi-judicial immunity also shields court clerks from claims when they are carrying out judicial functions.[259]

Judicial officials are not shielded by absolute immunity if they act "in the clear absence of all jurisdiction over the subject-matter" or when they act in a nonjudicial capacity.[260] For example, the Fourth Circuit Court of Appeals held that a judge was not protected by absolute judicial immunity when she engaged in a search of a private home and the seizure of the homeowner's property. The court found that while the judge may have had the authority to *order* a search (an act that would have been covered by judicial immunity), *conducting* the search operation was a law enforcement function outside of her judicial authority.[261]

Absolute immunity does not protect judicial officials from personal liability when acting in their administrative capacities, such as when making personnel decisions in their capacity as employers.[262]

Qualified Immunity for Public Servants

What if a local government official or employee faces a Section 1983 claim in her individual capacity but does not qualify for absolute legislative or judicial immunity? Public servants who violate someone's federal rights while performing their official duties may be entitled to qualified immunity from personal liability under Section 1983.[263] The qualified immunity defense provides that public servants may not be held personally liable in a Section 1983 lawsuit unless their conduct violates "clearly established statutory or constitutional rights of which a reasonable person would have known."[264] In other words, public servants are shielded from Section 1983 liability if a reasonable person in their situation could have believed their conduct was lawful. Such immunity ensures that public servants are able to make decisions without fear of personal liability for honest mistakes in judgment, by protecting them against liability for "bad guesses in gray areas."[265] In the words of the U.S. Supreme Court, "qualified immunity protects all but the plainly incompetent or those who knowingly violate the law."[266]

Applying the Immunity Doctrines

A single lawsuit involving the actions of local government officials and employees can involve multiple claims, including some claims against the unit of local government and other claims against individual public servants. Likewise, a single lawsuit could involve some tort claims under state law, Section 1983 claims alleging violations of rights under the Constitution of the United States, claims alleging violations of rights under the North Carolina Constitution, and claims under state

---

258. Van de Kamp v. Goldstein, 555 U.S. 335 (2009) (citing Imbler v. Pachtman, 424 U.S. 409, 428, 430 (1976)).

259. *See* McCray v. Maryland, 456 F.2d 1, 5 (4th Cir. 1972); Hamilton v. Murray, 648 F. App'x 344, 345 (4th Cir. 2016) (per curiam) (unpublished); Jarvis v. Chasanow, 448 F. App'x 406, 2011 WL 4564336, at *1 (4th Cir. 2011) (per curiam) (unpublished) (citing Briscoe v. LaHue, 460 U.S. 325, 335 (1983). This immunity does not, however, apply to the clerk's performance of ministerial functions (or failure to perform such functions).

260. Gibson v. Goldston, 85 F.4th 218, 223 (4th Cir. 2023) (citing Bradley v. Fisher, 80 U.S. (13 Wall.) 335, 351 (1872) and *Stump*, 435 U.S. at 360).

261. *Gibson*, 85 F.4th 218.

262. *See* Savage v. Maryland, 896 F.3d 260, 273 (4th Cir. 2018) ("It remains the general rule, of course, that prosecutors will not be entitled to absolute immunity when acting in their administrative capacities as employers.") (citing *Van de Kamp*, 555 U.S. at 344); *see also* Dixon v. Clem, 492 F.3d 665, 674–75 (6th Cir. 2007).

263. Pearson v. Callahan, 555 U.S. 223, 231 (2009).

264. *Pearson*, 555 U.S. at 231.

265. Maciariello v. Sumner, 973 F.2d 295, 298 (4th Cir. 1992).

266. City of Tahlequah, Oklahoma v. Bond, 595 U.S. 9, 12 (2021) (quoting Malley v. Briggs, 475 U.S. 335, 341 (1986)).

Table 6.1 Possible Immunities Available to Different Defendants

DEFENDANT	TYPE OF CLAIM	
	Tort Claim (e.g., Negligence)	**Section 1983 Claim**
Unit of Local Government	Governmental immunity, unless waived by the unit of local government.	None.
Public Official in Individual Capacity	Public official immunity, unless official acted corruptly, with malice, or outside the scope of their official duties. Legislative, judicial, or quasi-judicial immunity may also be available depending on the act at issue.	Qualified immunity, unless the conduct violates clearly established statutory or constitutional rights of which a reasonable person would have known.
Public Employee in Individual Capacity	None, unless a statutory immunity applies.	Qualified immunity, unless the conduct violates clearly established statutory or constitutional rights of which a reasonable person would have known.
Public Official or Employee Engaged in Legislative Activity	Legislative immunity for legislative activity, unless actions were illegal, malicious, corrupt or outside the scope of official duties.	Absolute immunity for legislative activity, but not for illegal acts or acts taken in an administrative or enforcement capacity.
Judicial Official Engaged in Performance of Judicial Acts	Absolute immunity, unless acting in a nonjudicial capacity or acting in the complete absence of all jurisdiction.	Absolute immunity, unless acting in a nonjudicial capacity or acting in the complete absence of all jurisdiction.

or federal statutes. As described in the preceding sections of this chapter, the types of immunity available for each claim will differ based on the nature of the claim, the defendant against whom the claim is brought, and the action alleged to have caused harm to the plaintiff.

Table 6.1 shows examples of how different immunities may be available for tort claims under state law and Section 1983 claims involving violations of federal statutes or constitutional rights, depending on the identity of the defendant.

Insurance against Civil Liability

One prudent way to protect the local government treasury and local public servants from potentially crippling state or federal damage awards is to purchase liability insurance. The General Assembly has authorized counties and cities to purchase insurance to protect themselves and any of their officers, agents, or employees from civil liability for damages.[267] The governing board has absolute discretion in deciding which liabilities and which public servants, if any, will be covered by this insurance. If the governing board so chooses, insurance coverage may extend to claims of both state and federal liability. The coverage may also cover both the entity and its public servants sued in their individual capacities. However, the local government's decision to purchase insurance for certain claims may also waive governmental immunity for those claims up to the extent of coverage (see above, "Waiver of Governmental Immunity by the Purchase of Insurance").

267. G.S. 160A-485.

Defense of Employees, Payment of Judgments, and Settlements

Provision of Defense

Each local government is authorized, but not required, to provide for the defense of any civil or criminal action brought against current or former public servants on account of alleged acts or omissions committed in the scope and course of their employment.[268] A local government may provide such defense through the local government attorney, by contracting with a private attorney, or by purchasing insurance that requires that the insurer defend lawsuits brought against certain public servants. The decision of whether to provide such a defense for a public servant lies with the local government's governing board.

Payment of Judgments

Each local government is also authorized, but not required, to pay all or part of any settlements or judgments in lawsuits against public servants for acts committed in the scope and course of their employment.[269] No statutory limit is placed on the amount a local government may appropriate to pay a settlement or a judgment. However, funds may not be appropriated to pay a public servant's settlement or judgment if the governing board finds that the individual acted or failed to act because of fraud, corruption, or malice.

The local government must meet certain procedural requirements before it may pay a public servant's settlement or judgment.[270] First, the local governing board must have adopted a set of uniform standards under which claims or civil judgments against public servants will be paid. These standards must be made available for public inspection. For school boards, the standards must also state when the board will provide defense for claims.[271] Second, the local government's governing board must have notice of a claim or litigation before a settlement is reached or a judgment is entered.

Settlements

Local governments have broad authority to decide whether to settle particular lawsuits and under what terms. A North Carolina Court of Appeals opinion, *Dobrowolska v. Wall*,[272] raised concerns about consistency among settlement decisions. The plaintiffs in *Dobrowolska* were involved in a car accident with a Greensboro city police officer. The city relied on its governmental immunity defense and refused to settle the case. The plaintiffs alleged that the City of Greensboro violated their equal protection and substantive due process rights under the United States Constitution through an inconsistent practice of refusing to settle some claims based on governmental immunity and paying other claims regardless of governmental immunity. The court of appeals remanded the case for a jury trial, finding that there were genuine issues of material fact as to whether or not the city violated plaintiffs' due process and equal protection rights due to "arbitrary and capricious" settlement practices and whether such practices served a legitimate governmental objective.

In reaction to *Dobrowolska*, many local governments reviewed and revised their settlement policies and practices so that staff discretion in settling claims was defined, clarified, or limited. When later plaintiffs raised similar constitutional claims against other cities based on settlement practices, those cities were able to point to settlement parameters that were more clearly defined than

268. G.S. 160A-167(a); G.S. 153A-97.
269. G.S. 160A-167(b).
270. G.S. 160A-167(c).
271. G.S. 115C-43.
272. 138 N.C. App. 1 (2000).

those challenged in *Dobrowolska*. In later cases, the court of appeals clarified that the *Dobrowolska* decision did not create a new cause of action or strategy for plaintiffs to circumvent the defense of governmental immunity. Rather, *Dobrowolska* stands for the proposition that local governments may not act arbitrarily or capriciously in making settlement decisions and must have a rational basis for differing treatment of similarly situated claimants.[273]

Additional Resources

Allen, Trey. *Local Government Immunity to Lawsuits in North Carolina*. Chapel Hill: UNC School of Government, 2019.

273. *See* Clayton v. Branson, 170 N.C. App. 438 (2005) *and* Jones v. Durham, 183 N.C. App. 57 (2007).

Chapter 7

Ethics and Conflicts of Interest

Crista M. Cuccaro and Kristina M. Wilson

Crista Cuccaro is a School of Government faculty member specializing in government contracting and procurement. Kristina Wilson is a School of Government faculty member specializing in local government law, with a particular focus on transparency, procedure, and board structure and authority.

This chapter updates and revises the previous chapter written by School of Government former faculty members Frayda S. Bluestein and Norma R. Houston, whose contributions to the field and to this publication are gratefully acknowledged.

Ethics in Government: Why It's Important

The conduct of local government officials and public employees affects public perceptions of and trust in government. Citizens expect local officials and public employees to act in the best interest of the public and not to use their office for their personal benefit. North Carolina laws governing the conduct of local officials focus on financial interests in voting and contracting, as well as on other ways in which government decision-makers might personally benefit from the actions they take. Similarly, when federal financial assistance is involved, the Uniform Guidance[1] defines and prohibits certain conflicts of interest and benefits for employees, officers, or agents of a governmental unit. Additionally, constitutional due process requirements focus on the need for fair and unbiased decision-making when certain types of private rights are at stake.

1. The Uniform Administrative Requirements, Cost Principles, and Audit Requirements for Federal Awards (Uniform Guidance) are codified at 2 C.F.R. Part 200.

This chapter describes the state law requirements for elected officials, including when they have a duty to vote and when they are prohibited from voting, and explores statutory prohibitions on receiving benefits related to governmental contracts. It also explains the conflict-of-interest rules that are applicable when governmental units use federal financial assistance.

I. Requirements for Local Elected Officials

Ethics Education Requirement

North Carolina law requires elected and appointed members of the governing boards of cities and counties, unified governments, consolidated city–counties, sanitary districts, and local boards of education to receive at least two clock hours of ethics education within twelve months after each election or reelection (or appointment or reappointment) to office. The education program must cover laws and principles that govern conflicts of interest and ethical standards of conduct at the local government level; it is designed to focus on both the legal requirements and the ethical considerations so that key governmental decision-makers will have the information and insight needed to exercise their authority appropriately and in the public interest. The ethics education requirement is an ongoing obligation triggered by re-election or reappointment to office.[2]

While state law does not require ethics education for local employees and members of local appointed boards (such as boards of adjustment or advisory committees), a local governing board may impose this requirement on these groups under the board's local ethics code or other ordinance or policy.[3]

Local Codes of Ethics

North Carolina law also requires the governing boards subject to the ethics education requirement to adopt ethics resolutions or policies (often referred to as "codes of ethics") to guide board members in performing their duties.[4] The ethics resolution or policy must address all of the following duties:

1. obeying all applicable laws about official actions taken as a board member,
2. upholding the integrity and independence of the office,
3. avoiding impropriety in the exercise of official duties,
4. faithfully performing duties,
5. acting openly and publicly.

The statute does not describe *how* to address these five responsibilities. Furthermore, the statute does not impose or authorize sanctions for failure to comply with ethics codes. Boards have no statutory authority to sanction their members as a means of enforcing the ethics code or for other purposes. However, failure to adopt a code or to comply with its provisions may elicit citizen and media criticism and may itself be considered unethical.

---

2. Chapter 160A, Section 87 and Chapter 153A, Section 53 of the North Carolina General Statutes (hereinafter G.S.).

3. A governing board's local ethics code must be adopted pursuant to G.S. 160A-86(a) and G.S. 153A-53(a). A governing board might also apply its code of ethics to other bodies under its general ordinance power (G.S. 160A-174 for cities; G.S. 153A-121 for counties) or its general authority to organize city or county government. G.S. 160A-146 (organize city government); G.S. 153A-76 (organize county government).

4. G.S. 160A-86; G.S. 153A-53.

As with the ethics education requirement, state law does not require that ethics codes be applied to local employees and members of local appointed boards (such as boards of adjustment or advisory committees), but a local governing board may choose to extend the provisions of its code of ethics to these groups.[5]

Some state government officials and senior employees are subject to the State Government Ethics Act,[6] which establishes ethical standards of conduct for those covered under the act and regulates individuals and entities that seek to influence their actions. The North Carolina State Ethics Commission is responsible for enforcing the act, including investigating alleged violations. Most local government officials and employees are not subject to the State Government Ethics Act by virtue of their local government positions.[7] Consequently, the State Ethics Commission does not have the authority to investigate allegations of unethical conduct by local government officials.

Censuring Board Members

Although state law does not provide specific authority for boards to sanction their members for ethical violations, elected boards do have general authority to pass resolutions or motions. Some boards use a motion or resolution of censure to address ethical or legal transgressions by board members, including violations of the board's code of ethics. This type of censure has no legal effect other than to express the board's disapproval of the actions or behavior of one of its members. There are no specific procedural requirements for such an action. For recommendations on the censuring process, please see the School of Government's model code of ethics.[8]

II. Conflicts of Interest in Voting

Ethical and conflict of interest issues often arise when a board member appears to have some personal interest in a particular matter. In general, a governing board member has a duty to vote. North Carolina law does not explicitly authorize county or city board members to abstain from voting. Instead, the statutes describe limited grounds for which a member may be excused from voting.

The statutes governing voting by county and city board members are slightly different, and especially for cities, there is some ambiguity about the proper procedure for excusing a member. The county statute, Chapter 153A, Section 44 of the North Carolina General Statutes (hereinafter G.S.), provides that the board may excuse a member, whereas the city statute, G.S. 160A-75, simply says that a member "shall be excused" without specifying who does the excusing. Another important difference is that the city statute enforces the duty to vote by providing that if a person is present at

---

5. See the discussion *supra* note 3 on the statutory basis for doing so.

6. G.S. Chapter 138A.

7. Individual officials and employees may be subject to the act if they also serve in a state-level capacity covered under it, such as serving on a covered state board or commission. In addition, voting members of the policy-making boards of Metropolitan Planning Organizations (MPOs) and Rural Transportation Planning Organizations (RPOs) (these boards are often referred to as "transportation advisory committees" or "TACs") are subject to ethics requirements specific to their service on the MPO or RPO TAC (G.S. 136-200.2(g)–(k) for MPOs and G.S. 136-211(f)–(k) for RPOs). For more information about the state ethics and lobbying laws that apply to state officials, see Norma R. Houston, "State Government Ethics and Lobbying Laws: What Does and Does Not Apply to Local Governments," *Local Government Law Bulletin* No. 135 (UNC School of Government, March 2014), www.sog.unc.edu/sites/default/files/reports/lglb135.pdf.

8. A. Fleming Bell, II, *A Model Code of Ethics for North Carolina Local Elected Officials with Guidelines and Appendixes* (UNC School of Government, 2010), sog.unc.edu/publications/books/model-code-ethics-north-carolina-local-elected-officials-guidelines-and-appendixes-print-version.

the meeting, does not vote, and has not been excused, the person is considered to have voted "yes."[9] The county statute does not contain this provision. Both statutes are specific, however, about the reasons for which a person may or must be excused from voting. In addition, four other statutes prohibit board members from voting in situations involving contracting, land use decisions, and quasi-judicial decisions.

The Duty to Vote

Board members have a statutory duty to vote with only a handful of exceptions. They cannot abstain from voting even in situations where voting might appear or feel unethical. The general voting statutes—G.S. 153A-44 (counties) and G.S. 160A-75 (cities)—allow governing board members of cities and counties to be excused from voting *only* on matters

1. involving the consideration of the member's own official conduct or financial interest[10] or
2. on which the member is prohibited from voting under the following statutes (discussed below):
    a. direct benefits from a public contract (G.S. 14-234),
    b. legislative decisions concerning land use and development under G.S. 160D-109(a), and
    c. quasi-judicial decisions under G.S. 160D-109(d).

Additionally, a somewhat recently enacted conflict of interest law, G.S. 14-234.3, also prohibits public officials from voting or otherwise participating in making or administering contracts with certain nonprofits.[11] While G.S. 153A-44 and 160A-75 do not yet include specific exceptions for G.S. 14-234.3, its language is mandatory and violating it results in criminal penalties.[12] As a result, G.S. 14-234.3 likely implicitly trumps the statutory duty to vote.[13]

When there is a question about whether a board member may or must be excused from voting, the first thing to determine is what type of matter is involved. Specific statutes govern the standard to be applied, depending on the nature of the matter before the board. The following is a short list of circumstances that will help identify the appropriate standard to apply:

1. If the matter involves a development regulation in a legislative land use matter, the standard is as follows: a board member *shall not* vote where the outcome of the matter is reasonably likely to have a direct, substantial, and readily identifiable personal financial impact. G.S. 160D-109(a), (b). If the matter involves a zoning amendment, the board member *shall not* vote if the landowner of the property subject to rezoning or the applicant for a text amendment is someone with whom the board member has a close familial, business, or other associational relationship. G.S. 160D-109(a), (b). Close familial relationships are spouses, parents, children, siblings, grandparents, and grandchildren, including step and half relationships under G.S. 160D-109(f).

---

9. G.S. 160A-75 also specifies that if a board member leaves the room without being excused and a vote occurs in the board member's absence, then the absent board member has voted "yes."

10. Board member compensation is not considered financial interest or official conduct under G.S. 160A-75(a) and G.S. 153A-44.

11. Effective Jan. 1, 2022. *See* S.L. 2021-191, § 4.(b).

12. G.S. 14-234.3(a), (b).

13. Kristina M. Wilson, "Conflicts of Interest for Public Officials on Nonprofit Boards: An Analysis for North Carolina G.S. 14-234.3," *Local Government Law Bulletin* No. 142 (UNC School of Government, November 2022), 14.

2. If the matter involves a quasi-judicial function (such as the issuance of a special use permit or an appeal of a personnel decision), the standard is as follows: a board member *shall not participate or vote* if the member has a fixed opinion (not susceptible to change) prior to the hearing; undisclosed ex parte communications; a close familial, business, or other associational relationship with an affected person; or a financial interest in the outcome. G.S. 160D-109(d). Note that this provision applies to any person (not just a governing board member) who serves on a board and exercises quasi-judicial functions.
3. If the matter involves a contract from which the member derives a direct benefit (this comes up only if the contract is allowed under an exception to the statute), the standard is as follows: the board member is *prohibited from participating or voting.* G.S. 14-234(b1).
4. If the matter involves a contract with a nonprofit organization with which a public official is associated, the public official is *prohibited from participating or voting.* G.S. 14-234.3(a).
5. For all other matters that come before the governing board for a vote, the standard is as follows: a county governing board member *may be excused* if the matter involves the member's own financial interest or official conduct. G.S. 153A-44. A city governing board member *must be excused* if the matter involves the member's own financial interest or official conduct. G.S. 160A-75.

Note that each of the statutes above prohibits the member from voting except for G.S. 153A-44. In that statute, it is unclear whether the use of the word "may" is intended to make excusing a county governing board member from voting optional or whether it simply describes the permissible grounds for being excused. G.S. 160A-75 has less ambiguous wording regarding excusal, providing that the board "shall" excuse a member from voting in cases involving the delineated statutory conflicts of interest, financial interest, or official conduct. The use of the word "shall" clarifies that for city governing boards, excusals for financial interest and official conduct are mandatory.[14]

What Constitutes Financial Interest

G.S. 153A-44 (counties) and 160A-75 (cities) offer permissive or mandatory exceptions to a board member's duty to vote in situations that involve the member's "own financial interest."

The statutes do not define the "own financial interest" standard, but case law has suggested certain factors that are instructive in this kind of analysis. For example, in *Kistler v. Randolph County*,[15] board members' ownership of property near the area in which a school site was located was considered insufficient to constitute conflict of interest. In *City of Albemarle v. Security Bank and Trust*,[16] members' direct ties to competing financial institutions did not require them to abstain from voting on a proposed condemnation of a portion of the bank's land. These holdings seem appropriate given the underlying obligation to vote as well as the usual judicial deference given to local government decisions in the absence of a clear abuse of discretion.

The following factors may be useful in determining when a board member may be excused from voting because of personal financial interest.

---

14. City of Albemarle v. Security Bank and Trust Co., 106 N.C. App. 75, 78–79 (N.C. Ct. App. 1992) ("G.S. 160A-75 provides that a member of a city council may not be excused from voting unless the vote concerns matters involving the council member's personal financial interest or official conduct.").

15. 233 N.C. 400 (1951).

16. 106 N.C. App. 75 (1992).

Number of People Affected

The range of potential financial impacts on board members can be thought of as a continuum based on the extent to which the effect is unique to the board member, on one end of the spectrum, or experienced by many or most citizens, on the other end.[17] If the effect on the board member is the same as the effect on a significant number of citizens, then it is fair to allow the individual to vote. The board member is affected as part of a larger group of citizens, and the vote can serve to represent that group. This is perhaps the most important factor. Even a significant financial effect may not be disqualifying if it is one that is universally or widely experienced by citizens in the jurisdiction.

Extent of the Financial Interest (Benefit or Detriment)

The general voting statutes refer to financial *interest*, not financial *benefit*, as some of the other statutes do. This means that a positive or a negative financial impact may be a basis for excusing a member from voting. An insignificant financial interest, however, whether positive or negative, is not enough to sway a person's vote and should not be used to avoid the duty to vote.[18] Obviously, the significance of a financial interest must be considered in relation to the individual's particular situation, though it might be assessed based on what a reasonable person would do in that situation.

Likelihood That the Financial Impact Will Actually Occur

Sometimes several actions in addition to the specific vote in question are needed for an alleged financial interest to materialize. For example, a board member who is a real estate agent votes in favor of a loan to facilitate a project that might eventually become a sales opportunity for the board member's real estate agency. Without more to suggest that this opportunity will actually arise and be available to the board member, however, such a chain of events is probably too speculative to form a basis for being excused from voting.[19]

III. Conflicts of Interest in Contracting

Several North Carolina laws limit the ability of state and local government elected officials and public employees[20] to benefit personally from contracts they make or administer for their governmental units. These laws reflect the public's need to ensure that contracting and other decisions are made in a neutral, objective way based on the public's interest and not in consideration of actual or potential benefit to the decision-maker. However, these laws do not prohibit all activity that the public might consider improper. Instead, they identify particular activities that the legislature has identified as serious enough to constitute a criminal offense. Situations that are not illegal may nonetheless be inappropriate or inadvisable, so public officials should always consider the public perception of their actions in addition to the legal consequences.

---

17. Frayda Bluestein, "Board Member Financial Interest: Mapping the Points on the Continuum," *Coates' Canons: NC Local Government Law* blog (January 25, 2012), canons.sog.unc.edu/2012/01/board-member-financial-interest-mapping-the-points-on-the-continuum/.

18. *Id.*

19. *Id.*

20. While the statutes discussed in this section apply to all state and local government officials and employees, certain senior-level state officials and employees are subject to specific standards of conduct under the State Government Ethics Act, G.S. Chapter 138A. This act does not generally apply to local government officials and employees unless they also serve in a state capacity, such as serving on a state board or commission covered under the act. Similarly, local government officials and employees are generally exempt from G.S. Chapter 120C, which regulates the conduct of those who lobby senior-level state officials and employees.

Contracts for Personal Benefit

The criminal statute G.S. 14-234 prohibits an elected or appointed public officer or a public employee from deriving a direct benefit from any contract in which he or she is involved on behalf of the public agency he or she serves. The statute contains two additional prohibitions. Even if a public official or employee is not involved in making a contract from which he or she will derive a direct benefit, the official or employee is prohibited from influencing or attempting to influence anyone in the agency who is involved in making the contract. In addition, all public officers and employees are prohibited from soliciting or receiving any gift, reward, or promise of reward, including a promise of future employment, in exchange for recommending, influencing, or attempting to influence the award of a contract, even if they do not derive a direct benefit under the contract. Violation of this statute is a Class 1 misdemeanor. Key definitions contained in the statute, along with several important exceptions, are discussed below.

As defined in the statute, a person "derives a direct benefit" from a contract if the person or *his or her spouse* (1) has more than a 10 percent interest in the company that is a party to the contract, (2) derives any income or commission directly from the contract, or (3) acquires property under the contract.[21] Note that while the prohibition includes a direct benefit to a spouse, it does not extend to other family members or friends, or to unmarried partners. If the employee or official or his or her spouse does not derive a direct benefit from it, a contract between a public agency and a family member, friend, or partner of a board member or employee does not violate state law. Another important aspect of the statutory definition is that it does not prohibit contracting with an entity that employs the city or county official as long as the official derives no direct benefit from the contract.

Since the definition of direct benefit includes the acquisition of property, board members and employees who are involved in the disposal of surplus property are prohibited (as are their spouses) from purchasing that surplus property from their unit of government. Elected and appointed officials (but not employees) may be able to do so if the unit falls within the "small jurisdiction exception" described below.

The law also specifies what it means to be involved in "making or administering" a contract, which is a necessary element in the statutory prohibition. Individuals who are *not* involved in making or administering contracts are not legally prohibited from contracting with their unit of government. Activity that triggers the prohibition includes participating in the development of specifications or contract terms, or in the preparation or award of the contract, as well as having the authority to make decisions about or interpret the contract.[22] Performing purely ministerial duties, such as a clerk providing an attestation on a contract, is not considered "making or administering" the contract.[23] The statute also makes clear that a person is involved in making the contract when the board or commission on which he or she serves takes action on the contract, even if the official does not participate. Simply being excused from voting on the contract does not absolve a person with a conflict of interest from potential criminal liability; stated differently, unless an exception applies, there is no means or mechanism that allows a public official with a conflict of interest to contract with the public agency that he or she serves. If an exception applies, as discussed below, the interested party may be excused from voting and may legally contract with the unit.

The broad prohibition in G.S. 14-234 is modified by several exceptions. In any case where an exception applies, a public officer who will derive a direct benefit is prohibited from deliberating

21. G.S. 14-234(a1)(4).
22. G.S. 14-234(a1)(2), (3).
23. G.S. 14-234(a1)(5).

or voting on the contract or from attempting to influence any other person who is involved in making or administering the contract.[24] Contracts with banks, savings and loan associations, and regulated public utilities are exempt from the limitations in the statute,[25] as are contracts for reimbursement for providing direct assistance under state or federal public assistance programs under certain conditions.[26] An officer or employee may, under another exception, convey property to the unit but only through a condemnation proceeding initiated by the unit.[27] An exception in the law also authorizes a county or city to hire as an employee the spouse of a public officer; however, this exception does not apply to public employees.[28]

A final exception, sometimes referred to as the "small jurisdiction exception," applies only in cities with a population of less than 20,000 and in counties with no incorporated municipality with a population of more than 20,000.[29] In these jurisdictions, governing board members as well as certain members of the social services, local health, or area mental health boards, of the board of directors of a public hospital, and of the local school board may lawfully contract with the units of government they serve, subject to several limitations contained in the exception.[30] First, the contract may not exceed $20,000 for medically related services and $60,000 for other goods or services in any twelve-month period. In addition, the exemption does not apply to any contract that is subject to the competitive bidding laws, which includes purchase and construction or repair contracts with an estimated cost of $30,000 or more. Finally, the exception does not extend to real property transactions. Procedurally, contracts made under the small jurisdiction exception must be approved by special resolution of the governing board in open session. The statute imposes additional public notice and reporting requirements for these contracts and prohibits the interested board member from participating in the development of or voting on the contract.[31] A contract entered into under the small jurisdiction exception that does not comply with all the statutory procedural requirements violates the statute.

Contracts entered into in violation of G.S. 14-234 violate public policy and are not enforceable. There is no authority to pay for or otherwise perform a contract that violates the statute unless the contract is required to protect the public health or welfare and limited continuation is approved by the Local Government Commission.[32] Prosecutions under the statute are not common—although some have occurred—but situations in which board members or public officials stand to benefit from contracts involving public funds often make headlines.

---

24. G.S. 14-234(b1).

25. G.S. 14-234(b)(1).

26. G.S. 14-234(b)(4).

27. G.S. 14-234(b)(2). The statute specifically authorizes the conveyance to be undertaken under a consent judgment, that is, without a trial, if approved by the court.

28. G.S. 14-234(b)(3).

29. G.S. 14-234(d1). Population figures must be based on the most recent federal decennial census. The population threshold was increased from 15,000 to 20,000 in 2021 by S.L. 2021-117.

30. Note that the small jurisdiction exception only applies to an elected official or person appointed to fill an elective office; the exception does not extend to public employees.

31. Specifically, a unit shall note the total annual dollar amount of contracts with each official in the unit's audited annual financial statement, and any governing board that contracts with any officials of the unit shall summarize such transactions quarterly for the preceding twelve-month period and post the summary in a conspicuous place in a specified public facility. *See* G.S. 14-234(d1)(3), (4).

32. G.S. 14-234(f).

Contracts with Nonprofits

As discussed previously, state law prohibits public officials from knowingly participating in making or administering contracts with any nonprofits with which they are associated.[33] The statute, G.S. 14-234.3, applies when these three criteria are met: (1) a public official as defined in the statute is involved, (2) a contract is at issue, and (3) the contract at issue is with a covered nonprofit. If all of these elements are present, conflicted public officials must record their recusal with the clerk and cease to have any involvement with the contract at issue.[34] Once conflicted public officials record their recusals, their governmental units can proceed to execute the contract.[35] If a conflicted public official fails to record the recusal in violation of the statute, both the public official and the unit served could face Class 1 misdemeanors.[36] The contract at issue could also be deemed void.[37]

As to the first condition, which individuals are public officials under the statute? A "public official" is "any individual who is elected or appointed to serve on a governing board of a political subdivision of this State, [excluding] employee[s] or independent contractor[s]."[38] Note that unlike the statute prohibiting contracts for personal benefit, this statute does not extend to employees or their spouses or to the spouses of public officials. At a minimum, the statute's definition of "public official" covers city councils, boards of county commissioners, boards of aldermen, and the like.[39] However, the exact scope of the definition is unclear, so if there is any statute or case law indicating that an individual serves on a governing board of a political subdivision, it may be wise for practitioners to assume that the individual is a covered public official for purposes of G.S. 14-234.3.[40]

Second, there must be a contract at issue for G.S. 14-234.3 to apply. G.S. 14-234.3(a) regulates any public official who participates in making and administering a "contract." In particular, it prohibits a public official from "making or administering a contract, *including* the award of money in the form of a grant, loan, or other appropriation" (emphasis added). As the plain language suggests, G.S. 14-234.3(a) is triggered only if a proposed transaction involves a contract. The legislature used the term "including" to illustrate the types of contracts that fall under this statute (i.e., contracts involving "award[s] of money in the form of a grant, loan, or other appropriation"), but if a public entity does not enter into a "contract," G.S. 14-234.3(a) does not apply.[41]

Finally, the contract at issue must be with a covered nonprofit. With the exclusion of boards, entities, or organizations created by the state or its political subdivisions, a covered nonprofit organization is (1) a "nonprofit corporation, or association, incorporated or otherwise, that is organized or operating in North Carolina primarily for educational, charitable, religious, scientific, literary, or public health and safety purposes," and (2) "of which the public official is a director, officer, or governing board member."[42] Using the statutory definition, local governments must first analyze whether the contracting nonprofit entity is organized or operating in the state primarily for educational, religious, literary, scientific, charitable, or public health and safety purposes. Assessing whether a nonprofit operates for one of these enumerated purposes will likely require a case-by-case

33. G.S. 14-234.3.
34. G.S. 14-234.3(a).
35. *Id.*
36. G.S. 14-234.3(b), (c).
37. *Id.*
38. G.S. 14-234.3(d)(3).
39. Kristina M. Wilson, "Conflicts of Interest for Public Officials on Nonprofit Boards: An Analysis for North Carolina G.S. 14-234.3," *Local Government Law Bulletin* No. 142 (UNC School of Government, November 2022), 3.
40. Wilson, "Conflicts of Interest," 4–5.
41. Wilson, "Conflicts of Interest," 7.
42. G.S. 14-234.3(d)(1).

analysis of the specific nonprofit at issue.[43] After determining that the nonprofit is covered, local governments should ask whether it was created by the state or its political subdivisions. If so, G.S. 14-234.3 does not apply. Finally, they should ask whether the involved public official holds a leadership position with the nonprofit. The public official must be a director, executive, officer, or governing board member of the nonprofit for G.S. 14-234.3 to apply. A public official who is merely a volunteer, low-ranking member, or informal participant will not have a conflict under this statute.[44]

Stated differently, there are three ways that a nonprofit may fall outside of G.S. 14-234.3's scope:

- the nonprofit does not operate primarily for the enumerated purposes,
- the state or its political subdivisions created the nonprofit, or
- the involved public official does not hold a leadership position with the nonprofit.

As noted above, if G.S. 14-234.3 applies, the conflicted public official must record their recusal with the clerk.[45] After the clerk records the recusal, the board can legally execute the contract.[46] What does it mean to record a recusal with the clerk? The statute provides no procedural guidance, but its plain language does not require formal board action or approval to excuse a conflicted public official. The public official seemingly can recuse without declaring the conflict or otherwise notifying the rest of the board. However, while the statute apparently permits public officials to recuse themselves, so long as that recusal is recorded with the clerk, this method is not the most transparent procedure. The better approach would be for public officials to declare their conflicts and have boards formally excuse them via majority vote. The vote and the recusal could then be recorded in the meeting minutes. Recording recusals in meeting minutes is likely more efficient than creating a separate recusal document outside of any formal context. Since the statute does not specify any format for the recusal recording, documenting recusals in meeting minutes appears to be a safe harbor approach that increases transparency and clarity.[47]

After recording the recusal with the clerk, conflicted public officials should cease all involvement with the contract at issue. They must not deliberate or vote on the contract, attempt to influence others who are deliberating or voting on the contract, or solicit gifts or favors in exchange for attempting to influence those deliberating or voting on the contract.[48] Given the broad wording of the statute, it is likely wise for conflicted public officials to refrain from discussing the contract or the nonprofit at issue with anyone deliberating or voting on the contract. While the statute does not seem to require conflicted public officials to physically leave the room during deliberations, they may choose to do so, especially if they know that their mere presence may be interpreted as an attempt to influence the deliberations or voting.[49]

Notably, G.S. 14-234.3(b) incorporates several exceptions from its companion statute, G.S. 14-234, including the small jurisdiction exception. As noted above, these exceptions apply to the governmental unit's ability to make or administer a contract, not to the conflicted public official's ability to be involved with it. In other words, these exceptions allow the governmental unit to proceed with a contract even when a public official, employee, or spouse has a conflict with it. The conflicted public official or employee, however, still cannot have any involvement with the contract at issue.

---

43. Wilson, "Conflicts of Interest," 8.
44. *Id.*
45. G.S. 14-234.3(a).
46. *Id.*
47. Wilson, "Conflicts of Interest," 10–11.
48. G.S. 14-234.3(d)(2).
49. Wilson, "Conflicts of Interest," 11.

These exceptions do not appear to have any practical effect in the context of G.S. 14-234.3, which already allows a unit to proceed with a contract once a conflicted public official's recusal is recorded.[50] Thus, the G.S. 14-234 exceptions do not seem to serve any purpose since there is no exception that allows a conflicted public official to participate. Without additional clarification regarding the purpose of these exceptions, local governments should rely primarily on the exception in G.S. 14-234.3(a) that allows a governing board to enter into or administer a contract upon the recording of a conflicted public official's recusal.[51]

At first glance, the statutory restrictions on contracting for personal benefit and contracting with nonprofits may seem very similar. Both can result in criminal penalties and void contracts. Importantly, both statutes prohibit a conflicted individual from having any involvement with the contract at issue, even when an exception might apply. However, there are important differences. The contracting for personal benefit statute, G.S. 14-234, applies to public officials, public employees, and their spouses, while the nonprofit statute, G.S. 14-234.3, applies only to public officials. Additionally, G.S. 14-234 has several exceptions while G.S. 14-234.3 has only one exception in practice. Local governments must pay close attention to the requirements of each distinct contracting statute.

Gifts and Favors

Another statute, G.S. 133-32, is designed to prevent the use of gifts and favors to influence the award and administration of public contracts. The statute applies to any contractors, subcontractors, or suppliers who (1) have a contract with a public agency, (2) have performed under such a contract within the past year, or (3) anticipate bidding on such a contract in the future. For these individuals, giving gifts or favors to public officials and employees who have responsibility for preparing, awarding, or overseeing contracts, or inspecting construction projects, is a Class 1 misdemeanor. The statute also makes it a Class 1 misdemeanor for those officials to receive gifts or favors.

The statute does not define gift or favor. A reasonable interpretation is that the prohibition applies to anything of value acquired or received without fair compensation unless it is covered by a statutory exception. These exceptions include advertising items or souvenirs of nominal value, honoraria for participating in meetings, and meals at banquets. Inexpensive pens, mugs, and calendars bearing the name of the donor firm clearly fall within the exception for advertising items and souvenirs. Gifts of a television set, use of a beach cottage, or tickets to a professional sports event probably are prohibited. Although meals at banquets are allowed, free meals offered by contractors under other circumstances, such as lunch, should be refused. Some local governments have adopted local policies establishing a dollar limit for gifts that may be accepted; however, a gift allowed under a local policy must still be refused if it violates state law.

The statute also allows public officials and employees to accept customary gifts or favors from friends and relatives as long as the existing relationship, rather than the desire to do business with the unit, is the motivation for the gift. Finally, the statute specifically does not prohibit contractors from making donations to professional organizations to defray meeting expenses, nor does it prohibit public officials who are members of those organizations from participating in meetings that are supported by such donations and are open to all members.

It is important to distinguish between gifts to individuals and gifts to the government entity itself. A contractor may legally donate goods and services to the local government for use by the unit. For example, a local business can legally donate products to the unit for its own use or for the

50. G.S. 14-234.3(a). *See also* Wilson, "Conflicts of Interest," 10.

51. Wilson, "Conflicts of Interest," 10.

unit to raffle to employees for an employee appreciation event. Gifts or favors delivered directly to individuals for their personal use should be returned or, in some cases, may be distributed among employees such that each person's benefit is nominal. The latter approach is common for gifts of food brought to a department by a vendor. Public officials should inform contractors and vendors about the existence of the gifts-and-favors statute and about any local rules in effect within the unit addressing this issue.

Misuse of Confidential Information

G.S. 14-234.1 makes it a Class 1 misdemeanor for any state or local government officer or employee to use confidential information for personal gain, to acquire a pecuniary benefit in anticipation of his or her own official action, or to help another person acquire a pecuniary benefit from such actions. Confidential information is any non-public information that the officer or employee has learned in the course of performing his or her official duties.

Other Financial Gain

In 2021, G.S. 14-234.2 was added to the criminal statutes governing conflicts of interest for public officers. The statute makes it a Class H felony for an elected officer of a political subdivision of the state to solicit or receive personal financial gain from the political subdivision for which that elected officer serves by means of intimidation, undue influence, or misuse of the employees of that political subdivision. G.S 14-234.2 does not define "personal financial gain," but this term is used (although not defined) in the State Government Ethics Act, G.S. Chapter 138A. The financial interest analysis earlier in this chapter may be useful when evaluating a scenario under this statute. As a general principle, personal financial gain is not limited to money; it could also include any forbearance, forgiveness of indebtedness, gift, or other thing of value.[52] This statute does not apply if the governing board of the political subdivision approves the financial gain, or if the financial gain is received by the elected official acting in an official capacity.

IV. Conflicts of Interest for Specific Categories of Officials and Public Employees

In addition to the statutes discussed above that apply to all local officials and employees, specific conflict of interest prohibitions apply to certain groups of officials and employees, including those discussed below.

Building Inspectors

Chapter 160D describes several conflicts of interest for members of local government inspection departments. First, no member of an inspection department may have a financial interest or be employed by a business that furnishes labor, materials, or appliances for building construction or repair within the local government's planning and development regulation jurisdiction. Inspection department members also cannot have a financial interest in the making of plans or specifications for any building within the local government's planning and development regulation jurisdiction, unless the member owns the building in question. All inspection department members are prohibited from engaging in any work that is inconsistent with their public duties. In addition to these

52. *See, e.g.*, Colo. Rev. Stat. Ann. § 24-18.5-101.

general prohibitions, the statute requires local governments to find a conflict of interest if the individual, company, or employee of a company contracting to perform building inspections for the local government has a financial or business interest in the project being inspected or has a close relationship with or has previously worked within the past two years for the project's owner, developer, contractor, or manager.[53]

Project Designers

Under North Carolina state law, architects and engineers performing work on public construction projects are prohibited from specifying any materials, equipment, or other items manufactured, sold, or distributed by a company in which the project designer has a financial interest.[54] Project designers are prohibited also from allowing manufacturers to draw specifications for public construction projects.[55] A violation of these restrictions is punishable as a Class 3 misdemeanor; violators lose their licenses for one year and pay a fine of up to five hundred dollars ($500).[56]

Public Hospital Officials and Employees

Boards of directors and employees of public hospitals and hospital authorities and their spouses are prohibited from acquiring a direct or indirect interest in any hospital facility, property planned to be included within a hospital facility, or a contract or proposed contract for materials or services provided to a hospital facility. Limited exceptions to this prohibition apply; a contract entered into in violation of these prohibitions is void and unenforceable.[57]

Local Management Entity (LME) Board Members

Local management entity (LME) board members cannot contract with their LME for the delivery of mental health, developmental disabilities, and substance abuse services while serving on the board (and are not eligible for board service so long as such a contract is in effect).[58] Nor can an individual who is a registered lobbyist serve on an LME board.[59]

Housing Authorities

Commissioners and employees of a housing authority, or of a city or county when acting as a housing authority, are prohibited from having or acquiring any direct or indirect interest in any housing project, property included or planned to be included in any project, or a contract or proposed contract for materials or services to be furnished or used in connection with any housing project.[60]

V. The Uniform Guidance and Conflicts

When governmental units are using federal financial assistance, the Uniform Guidance imposes additional administrative requirements, including rules governing conflicts of interest and gifts in

53. G.S. 160D-1108.
54. G.S. 133-1.
55. G.S. 133-2.
56. G.S. 133-4.
57. G.S. 131E-14.2 (public hospitals) and G.S. 131E-21 (hospital authorities).
58. G.S. 122C-118.1(b).
59. G.S. 122C-118.1(b).
60. G.S. 157-7.

contracting.[61] The Uniform Guidance also obligates federal awarding agencies (e.g., the Environmental Protection Agency) to establish conflict of interest policies for federal awards.[62] Thus, with any federal financial assistance, a governmental unit may need to look to both the Uniform Guidance and the federal granting agency's conflict of interest rules to understand what is permissible.

To complicate matters, the rules about conflicts of interest and gifts found in the Uniform Guidance differ significantly from those found in state law. In order to comply with both state law and federal rules, local governments must have and use "documented procurement procedures, consistent with State, local, and tribal laws and regulations" and the standards found in the Uniform Guidance.[63] In other words, local governments must follow the "most restrictive" requirements of both federal and state law as well as their own local policies.

Maintaining Written Conflict of Interest Standards

Recipients of federal funds are required by 2 C.F.R. § 200.318(c)(1) to maintain "written standards of conduct covering conflicts of interest and governing the actions of its employees engaged in the selection, award and administration of contracts." While the Uniform Guidance does not prescribe any specific form for the written conflict of interest and contracting standards, the written standards must comply with 2 C.F.R. § 200.318 and include disciplinary actions for violations of such standards by officers, employees, or agents of the recipient. The following sections explain the federal rules governing conflicts of interests and contracting that are found in the Uniform Guidance.[64]

Conflicts of Interest Related to the Selection, Award, and Administration of Contracts

Like state law, the Uniform Guidance prohibits an individual from participating in the selection, award, or administration of a contract supported by federal financial assistance if that person has a real or apparent conflict of interest.[65] Unlike state law, though, the applicability of this prohibition is much broader.

First, the individuals prohibited from participating in the contracting process when they have a conflict of interest include not only employees and officers of the recipient, but also agents of the recipient. The Uniform Guidance does not define the term "agent," but the plain meaning of the term suggests that it probably encompasses individuals who are directly under contract with a recipient and who act on behalf of or provide advice to a unit.[66] Arguably, the term could also include individuals who have an ownership interest in a legal entity under contract with a unit.[67] Without specific guidance from a federal granting agency, a recipient may wish to extend this prohibition to the beneficial owners of a legal entity under contract with a unit.[68]

---

61. 2 C.F.R. § 200.

62. *See* 2 C.F.R. § 200.112.

63. 2 C.F.R. § 200.318(a).

64. A sample federal conflict of interest policy (hereinafter "Conflict of Interest Policy"), drafted by former faculty member Connor H. Crews, is available at the School of Government's American Rescue Plan Document Share web page, arpa.sog.unc.edu/document-share (scroll down to the "Uniform Guidance: Procurement and Conflicts of Interest" section).

65. 2 C.F.R. § 200.318(c)(1). The Uniform Guidance does not define an "apparent" conflict of interest. However, some federal agencies have interpreted it as arising when the circumstances are such that a reasonable person with knowledge of the relevant facts would question a public employee, official, or agent's impartiality in the matter. *See* National Institutes of Health, NIH Ethics Program, "Recusals (Disqualifications)," ethics.od.nih.gov/recuse.

66. Crews, "Conflict of Interest Policy," note 5.

67. *Id.*

68. *Id.*

Second, the language of the Uniform Guidance prohibiting "real" conflicts of interest is more expansive than the "direct benefit" language of G.S. 14-234, regarding both the scope of interpersonal relationships and the breadth of what is considered an "interest." The Uniform Guidance instructs that a real conflict of interest arises when the employee, officer, or agent, or any member of his or her immediate family,[69] his or her partner, or an organization that employs or is about to employ any of the aforementioned parties, has a financial or other interest in or a tangible personal benefit from a firm considered for a contract. Hence, when federal financial assistance is involved, recipients must evaluate many more relationships than state law requires. Instead of simply understanding benefits bestowed upon a public official and their spouse as G.S. 14-234 requires, recipients must look at the interests of and benefits to its employees, officials, and agents and their immediate family members, business partners, employers, and future employers. Furthermore, an impermissible interest under the Uniform Guidance is broader than state law; it includes any financial or other interest in or a tangible personal benefit from a firm considered for a contract. While the term "financial interest" is not defined in the Uniform Guidance, federal agencies have interpreted that a financial interest could be considered the potential for gain or loss to any individual or entity covered by 2 C.F.R. § 200.318(c)(1).[70] Likewise, "tangible personal benefit" is not defined in the Uniform Guidance, but federal agencies have opined that it is non-financial in nature and results in a personal benefit for the individual, such as improved employment opportunities, business referrals, or political influence.[71]

Gifts and Favors from Contractors or Parties to Subcontracts

The Uniform Guidance prohibits the officers, employees, and agents of a recipient from soliciting or accepting gifts, favors, or anything of monetary value from contractors or parties to subcontracts.[72] This prohibition applies to *all* officers, employees, and agents of a recipient, not just those individuals involved in the contracting process. In this way, the Uniform Guidance prohibition on gifts and items of value is more far-reaching than state law, which applies only to public employees or officers who prepare plans, award or administer contracts, or inspect or supervise construction.

Recipients are authorized to set standards for situations where a financial interest is not substantial or the gift is an unsolicited item of nominal value. Of course, the Uniform Guidance does not define when a financial interest is "not substantial," and no other guidance from the Office of Management and Budget (OMB) has directly addressed this question. Some federal agencies have robust conflict of interest regulations that distinguish between "significant" and "insignificant" financial interests.[73] Ultimately, unless dictated by a federal granting agency, a recipient has

69. The Uniform Guidance also does not define "immediate family." The lack of clarity in the Uniform Guidance prompted the Council on Governmental Relations to raise concerns related to its inconsistent interpretation and application by various federal agencies. *See* "COGR Submits Letter to OMB on COI Under Uniform Guidance—July 8, 2016," www.cogr.edu/2-cfr-200-uniform-guidance-cogr-comment-letters.

70. Examples of financial interests identified by the Federal Emergency Management Agency (FEMA) that would constitute a real conflict of interest include ownership of certain financial instruments or investments such as stock, bonds, or real estate, or a salary, indebtedness, job offer, or similar interest. *See* FEMA, *Procurement Disaster Assistance Team (PDAT) Field Manual: Procurement Information for FEMA Award Recipients and Subrecipients*, "Chapter 3: General Procurement under Grant Standards," § 1.4.2 (Oct. 2021), fema.gov/sites/default/files/documents/fema_PDAT-field-manual_102021.pdf.

71. *See* U.S. Department of Education, "Questions and Answers Regarding 2 CFR Part 200," www2.ed.gov/policy/fund/guid/uniform-guidance/edfaqs1216.pdf.

72. 2 C.F.R. § 200.318(c)(1).

73. *See, e.g.*, 42 C.F.R. § 50.603 (defining "significant financial interest" in the context of U.S. Department of Health and Human Services grants to include, among other things, any remuneration received or equity interest held in the preceding twelve months valued at $5,000 or more).

discretion to define financial interests that are "not substantial" and gifts of nominal value. In doing so, a recipient may consider consulting federal agency guidance or look to the standards applicable to employees of the executive branch.[74]

Consequences of a Violation

If a federal fund recipient identifies a potential conflict of interest that may violate 2 C.F.R. § 200.318, the recipient must notify the federal granting agency in writing.[75] However, it is unclear whether there is a mechanism to resolve potential conflicts of interest other than avoiding the conflict altogether. The OMB has not addressed whether a prohibited "apparent" conflict of interest can be cured by a governing board member's recusal from action on or administration of a contract with an entity in which the member has a financial interest under 2 C.F.R. § 200.318(c)(1). Some federal agencies allow recipients to disclose potential conflicts of interest to the agency, propose mitigation measures, and receive an agency determination on the effectiveness of those measures.[76] Unless explicit procedures allow for a recipient to proceed when a potential conflict of interest exists, recipients should exercise caution because the consequences for violation can be severe. If a recipient violates the Uniform Guidance or any federal award conditions, the federal awarding agency may impose additional award conditions, such as requiring additional, more detailed financial reports or additional project monitoring.[77] However, if additional conditions cannot remedy noncompliance, federal agencies are authorized to take more substantial action, ranging from withholding payments to the recipient to initiating suspension or debarment proceedings against the recipient or terminating the federal award.[78]

Additional Resources

Bell, A. Fleming, II. *Ethics, Conflicts, and Offices: A Guide for Local Officials*. 2nd ed. Chapel Hill: UNC School of Government, 2010.

———. *A Model Code of Ethics for North Carolina Local Elected Officials*. Chapel Hill: UNC School of Government, 2010.

Bluestein, Frayda S. *A Legal Guide to Purchasing and Contracting for North Carolina Local Governments*. 2nd ed. with supplement. Chapel Hill: UNC School of Government, 2007.

Crews, Connor H. "Conflict of Interest Policy Template" (July 15, 2022). UNC School of Government, American Rescue Plan Document Share, "Uniform Guidance: Procurement and Conflicts of Interest," arpa.sog.unc.edu/document-share/.

"Ethics & Conflicts." *Coates' Canons: NC Local Government Law* blog, canons.sog.unc.edu/category/ethics-and-conflicts/.

Ethics for Local Government Officials (microsite). UNC School of Government, sog.unc.edu/resources/microsites/ethics-local-government-officials.

---

74. Crews, "Conflict of Interest Policy," 6. Federal employees are allowed to accept unsolicited gifts with a fair market value of no more than $20 per occasion with an annual limit of $50 per source. 5 C.F.R. § 2635.204.

75. If the activity violates federal criminal laws, 2 C.F.R. § 200.113 imposes mandatory disclosure of the activity.

76. *See, e.g.*, "EPA's Revised Interim Financial Assistance Conflict of Interest Policy," § 9.0(b) ("[T]he agency will review COI disclosures . . . and measures applicants/recipients propose to resolve the COI and advise applicants/recipients of EPA's determination on the effectiveness of the measures within 30 calendar days of disclosure unless a longer period of time is necessary due to the complexity of the situation.").

77. 2 C.F.R. § 200.208.

78. 2 C.F.R. § 200.339–343.

Houston, Norma R. "State Government Ethics and Lobbying Laws: What Does and Does Not Apply to Local Governments." *Local Government Law Bulletin* No. 135 (UNC School of Government, March 2014), sog.unc.edu/publications/bulletins/state-government-ethics-and-lobbying-laws-what-does-and-does-not-apply-local-government-revised.

Wilson, Kristina. "Conflicts of Interest for Public Officials on Nonprofit Boards: An Analysis for North Carolina G.S. 14-234.3." *Local Government Law Bulletin* No. 142 (UNC School of Government, November 2022), sog.unc.edu/publications/bulletins/conflicts-interest-public-officials-nonprofit-boards-analysis-north-carolina-gs-14-2343.

PART 2. Transparency, Collaboration, and Citizen Involvement

Chapter 8

Public Records

Kristina M. Wilson

Kristina M. Wilson is a School of Government faculty member specializing in local government law.

This chapter updates and revises a previous version authored by Frayda S. Bluestein and David M. Lawrence, whose contributions to the field and to this publication are gratefully acknowledged.

Public Records Law Overview

North Carolina's public records law provides a broad right of access to public agencies' records. The main statutes that define the scope of the law are contained in Chapter 132 of the North Carolina General Statutes (hereinafter G.S.). Exceptions to these access rules, along with other laws that deal with public records, can be found in other statutes. The second edition of former School of Government faculty member David M. Lawrence's publication *Public Records Law for North Carolina Local Governments*, published in 2010, provides a comprehensive guide to these laws and their interpretation by the courts.

As an introduction to this topic, the following list summarizes some of the most important basic concepts in the public records law.

- The law applies to records made or received by government agencies in connection with the transaction of public business.

- The law applies to all types of state and local government agencies and to all types of records, including paper and electronic records, recordings, films, videos, and photographs.
- A record that falls within the scope of the statute is subject to public access unless an exception applies.
- North Carolina courts have been unwilling to recognize exceptions to the law that are not found in existing statutes.
- The statutory exceptions to the right of access fall into one of two categories: (1) confidential records, which a public agency is *prohibited* from releasing except under specified conditions, or (2) nonpublic records, to which there is no right of access but which a public agency *may* release in its discretion.
- A record's content, not its location, determines its status.
- Personal records (not related to the transaction of public business) are not public records, even if they are created using government resources. Records related to the transaction of public business are public, even if they are created using private resources.
- The right of access includes the right to inspect and obtain copies of records, albeit with some limitations.[1]
- Anyone can request access; the right is not limited to residents, citizens, or constituents of the agency from which records are being sought.
- State law limits a public agency's authority to charge for providing access to records. Inspection must be free of charge and, in most cases, agencies can charge only for the actual cost of the paper or other medium, if any, on which copies are provided.
- Public records cannot be removed, altered, or destroyed at will. Instead, requirements for retention of public records are governed by rules promulgated by the State Archives of North Carolina, a division of the Department of Natural and Cultural Resources. These rules apply based on the content, not the form, of a record. For example, there is no general rule for retention of email. Instead, the requirements for email records will vary depending on the content of the email.

Scope of the Public Records Law

What Is a Public Record?

G.S. 132-1 establishes a broad definition of "public record," and G.S. 132-6 entitles any person to examine and obtain a copy of any public record. The state supreme court has concluded that these statutory rights extend to any item that meets the definition of a public record, unless the General Assembly has limited or denied public access to a category of record via statute.[2] As a result, the great bulk of material held by local governments in North Carolina is public record and therefore open to public access. Financial records, leases and contracts, insurance policies, reports, agency minutes, permit applications, emails, and information in computer databases are all examples of records that generally must be made available to the public upon request.

---

1. *See, e.g.*, Chapter 132, Section 1.13 of the North Carolina General Statutes (hereinafter G.S.).
2. News & Observer Publ'g Co. v. Poole, 330 N.C. 465, 474–75 (1992).

The definition of a public record under the statute is expansive and generally not limited by the form of the material in question. The statute's definition has two parts. First, the statute specifies that public records include not only documents and other papers but also "maps, books, photographs, films, sound recordings, magnetic or other tapes, electronic data-processing records, [and] artifacts, . . . regardless of physical form or characteristics." Second, the statute clarifies that records must be "made or received pursuant to law or ordinance in connection with the transaction of public business" to qualify as public. Litigants have sometimes argued that the latter part of the definition—"made or received pursuant to law or ordinance"—is limiting and that only those records whose receipt is specifically required by statute or local ordinance are public records. The North Carolina Court of Appeals rejected such a limiting reading in *News & Observer Publishing Co. v. Wake County Hospital System, Inc.*,[3] holding instead that the term includes any material kept by an agency in carrying out its lawful duties. Given its own public records decisions, the state supreme court has obviously accepted the same broad reading of the statute.[4] In addition, the supreme court has held that the term includes preliminary drafts of documents and that a person need not wait until a record is finalized before examining it or obtaining a copy.[5]

Can privately held government records be considered public? The court of appeals answered this question recently in *Gray Media Group, Inc. v. City of Charlotte*.[6] There, the city contracted with Ernst & Young (EY) to streamline and improve city operations.[7] Under this contract, EY surveyed city councilmembers regarding leadership performance.[8] When a reporter submitted a public records request for the survey and councilmembers' responses to it, the city withheld the records, arguing that those records were not subject to the public records law because they were solely within EY's possession.[9] The court rejected this argument, finding that both the survey and the responses fit the definition of a public record.[10] The survey and responses were made and received by government officials in the course of attempting to improve city operations.[11] Without any applicable statutory exceptions, such documents are subject to public disclosure.[12] Moreover, actual possession is not a requirement under the public records law.[13] The fact that EY—and not the city—possessed the records did not eliminate the city's responsibility to produce the records.[14] The city had "constructive control" over the records because it could request and receive the records from EY.[15] *Gray Media Group* indicates that if a record fits the definition of a public record under G.S. 132-1 and no exceptions apply, government agencies must produce those records, even if not in actual possession of them. The fact that a government record may be held by a private party does not change the public nature of the record. Government agencies therefore must request public records held by private parties when necessary to respond to a public records request.

---

3. 55 N.C. App. 1, 13 (1981).
4. *E.g., Poole*, 330 N.C. 465.
5. *Poole*, 330 N.C. at 484.
6. 290 N.C. App. 384 (2023).
7. 290 N.C. App. at 386.
8. 290 N.C. App. at 386–87.
9. 290 N.C. App. at 388.
10. 290 N.C App. at 393–94.
11. *Id.*
12. 290 N.C. App. at 395–96.
13. 290 N.C. App. at 398.
14. *Id.*
15. *Id.*

To Which Agencies Does the Public Records Law Apply?

G.S. 132-1 extends the public records statute to every agency of state and local government in North Carolina. The statute defines covered agencies to include "every public office, public officer or official (State or local, elected or appointed), institution, board, commission, bureau, council, department, authority or other unit of government of the State or of any county, unit, special district or other political subdivision of government." Thus, at the local level, the law extends to counties; cities; school administrative units; community colleges; special districts, such as sanitary districts and metropolitan sewerage districts; and public authorities, such as water and sewer authorities, housing authorities, and drainage districts. It also extends to joint entities, such as councils of government, district health departments, area mental health authorities, regional libraries, and joint agencies established by contracts between local governments.

At times, even private entities may be subject to the public records law. In *News & Observer Publishing Co. v. Wake County Hospital System, Inc.*, the North Carolina Court of Appeals evaluated whether an incorporated county hospital system was an "agency of North Carolina government" for purposes of the Public Records Act.[16] In considering this question, the court focused on the relationship between the county and the health system, placing particular emphasis on the county's supervisory responsibilities over the health system.[17] Nine facts were found to be important in this analysis: (1) the system would transfer its assets to the county upon the system's dissolution, (2) filling vacancies on the system's board of directors required the county's approval, (3) the system leased county-owned premises for $1 a year, (4) the county approved the system's budget, (5) the county audited the system's finances, (6) the system reported charges and rates to the county, (7) county bond orders financed the system, (8) revenues from the bond orders were county revenues, and (9) the system could not change its corporate existence or amend its bylaws without the county's written consent.[18] Taking all of these factors together, the court ultimately concluded that the county exercised such substantial control over the public health system that the system qualified as an agency of the county subject to the public records law.[19]

The Supreme Court of North Carolina revisited these nine factors in *Southern Environmental Law Center v. North Carolina Railroad Co.* There, the supreme court evaluated whether a private railroad corporation was an agency of North Carolina government subject to the public records law.[20] Instead of systematically applying the nine-factor test from *News & Observer Publishing Co.*, the court applied a "totality of the circumstances approach," analyzing whether the government exercised "such substantial control over the operations of the relevant entity as to render it a governmental agency or subdivision . . . ."[21] The court emphasized that "each new arrangement [must] be examined anew and in its own context."[22] Applying this holistic analysis, the court determined that the railroad company was not a governmental agency subject to the public records law.[23] In support of its conclusion, the court noted that the General Assembly never characterized the railroad company as a governmental agency, despite having many opportunities to do so.[24] Moreover, the railroad maintained a separate corporate identity, had independent decision-making power,

16. 55 N.C. App. 1, 7–8 (1981).
17. 55 N.C. App at 11–12.
18. 55 N.C. App. at 11.
19. 55 N.C. App. at 13.
20. 378 N.C. 202, 203 (2021).
21. 378 N.C. at 215.
22. 378 N.C. at 216.
23. 378 N.C. at 216.
24. 378 N.C. at 216.

adopted its own budget, owned its own property, and retained its own revenues, among other factors.[25] Consequently, the government did not have "a sufficient degree of control over the day-to-day operations of the railroad," removing the corporation from the purview of the public records law.[26]

North Carolina Railroad Co. abolished any rigid test for evaluating whether the public records law applies to a seemingly private entity. Instead, courts apply a totality of the circumstances test, examining each relationship separately in its own context to assess the degree of government control. The degree of government control is the determinative factor in this analysis.

Personal Records Distinguished

Public employees often create records at work and use government resources that do not relate to the transaction of public business. Most commonly, perhaps, these might include email communications with family members, calendar entries reflective of personal activities, and other records of a purely personal nature. Based on the definition of public record under North Carolina's statute, these types of records are not public records since they are not made in connection with the transaction of public business. Under this definition, it is the subject and purpose of the record, rather than its location on a public or private medium, that governs its characterization as a public record. Although North Carolina case law has not addressed this issue to date, courts in other states have held that documents that are personal in nature do not become government records simply because they are found in a government office or on a government computer.

While personal records made on government-owned devices are not subject to general public access, they may be subject to access by the employer (the government agency). Inappropriate or excessive use of email for non-work-related purposes may violate local polices and could therefore become the basis for a personnel action. Policies governing the use of government resources may provide a governmental employer (though not the general public at large) with legal access to material created by local government employees using public resources. Government access to and use of this personal information is limited by constitutionally protected privacy rights, which in turn are affected by the policies and practices in place within each specific jurisdiction.[27]

Records versus Information

The General Assembly's use of the word "records" as opposed to "information" in the public records law somewhat limits the scope of the government's responsibility for responding to public records requests. Government practitioners often receive "public records requests" that are comprised of a list of questions rather than requests for different types of documents or records. Because the public records law applies to *records* rather than information, an agency's obligation in such cases is to produce records that may contain the requested information. The agency is not required, at least under the public records law, to provide responses to the questions themselves.

While the public enjoys a general right to inspect and copy public records, the public typically has no right to demand that a government unit maintain certain records or maintain records in a certain manner. Courts usually express this principle through the statement that the public records law does not require a government agency to create new records, and the General Assembly has affirmed this point in the controlling statute.[28]

---

25. 378 N.C. at 221–22.
26. 378 N.C. at 224.
27. *See* City of Ontario, Cal. v. Quon, 560 U.S. 746 (2010).
28. *See* G.S. 132-6.2(e) ("Nothing in this section shall be construed to require a public agency to respond to a request for a copy of a public record by creating or compiling a record that does not exist.").

There are several important exceptions to this general rule, however. The first occurs when a unit of government, for its own reasons, combines in a single document information that is exempt from public access and information that is not exempt. Simply because the document includes confidential information does not make the entire document exempt from public inspection. Rather, it is the government unit's responsibility to delete (or redact) the confidential information and then make the remaining information public. In a sense this is creating a new record, but the law requires that it be done and that the unit bear the cost of doing it.[29]

The second exception involves access to personnel information. As noted below, most of the information in government employee personnel files is confidential, and local government agencies are prohibited from releasing such information except in limited circumstances. The statutes that govern access to personnel files contain a list of *information* within those files that is open to the public. Because of the specific wording of these statutes, a public agency's obligation is to provide the *information* requested, such as a list of employee salaries or a list of position changes for a particular employee, even if such a list does not exist as a separate record at the time of the request.

The Right of Access

Form of the Request

G.S. 132-6 accords the rights of inspection and copying of public records to "any person," and there is no reason to think that the quoted words are limiting in any way. The rights extend both to natural persons and to corporations and other artificial persons (such as associations, partnerships, and cooperatives). They also extend both to citizens of the government unit holding the record and to noncitizens. Furthermore, as a general rule, a person's intended use of public records is irrelevant to the right of access, and the records custodian may not deny access simply because of the intended use. Indeed, G.S. 132-6(b) *expressly prohibits* custodians from requiring requesters to disclose their purposes or motives for seeking to access or copy records.

There is no specific authority to require that a requester identify himself or herself in order to obtain access to public records. Furthermore, there is no authority to require that requests be in writing (aside from requests for computer databases as described in G.S. 132-6.2(c)). There are legitimate, practical reasons to request and document requests in writing, but it is important for public agencies to recognize their lack of authority to condition access on the requester's completion of such documentation.[30]

Form in Which Records Are Provided

A public agency must provide records in the form in which they are requested, so long as the agency has the capacity to do so. Under G.S. 132-6.2(a), persons requesting copies of public records "may elect to obtain [the records] in any and all media in which the public agency is capable of providing them. No request for copies of public records in a particular medium shall be denied on the grounds that the custodian has made or prefers to make the public records available in another medium." The records may be certified or noncertified, at the option of the person making the request.

---

29. G.S. 132-6(c).

30. For a discussion of what policies and procedures may be implemented for responding to public records requests, see Frayda Bluestein, "Ask, Don't Compel: Local Government Authority to Establish Rules for Public Records Requests," *Coates' Canons: NC Local Government Law* blog (June 15, 2011), canons.sog.unc.edu/2011/06/ask-dont-compel-local-government-authority-to-establish-rules-for-public-records-requests/.

According to UNC School of Government faculty member Frayda Bluestein, the definition of "medium" in this section refers to paper versus electronic records.[31] Therefore, G.S. 132-6.2(a) obligates agencies responding to records requests to provide paper or electronic versions according to the request. The statute does not require responding agencies to put electronic copies in a particular *format*, however.[32] Thus, if a requester asks for electronic copies of a public record in a certain format, such as a PDF or an Excel file, the responding agency is only required to provide an electronic copy in whatever format it typically retains the record.[33] The agency is not required to reformat the electronic copy to the requester's specifications. North Carolina courts have not directly confronted this question, but this interpretation is consistent with a provision in G.S. Chapter 132 expressly stating that responding agencies are not required to create new records.[34] Arguably, an agency converting a record to a format it does not normally use qualifies as creating a new record.[35]

Time for Response

Under North Carolina's public records law, custodians of records must allow public records to be inspected "at reasonable times and under reasonable supervision" and must provide copies of records "as promptly as possible."[36] The law does not set a specific time within which an agency must respond to a records request. What constitutes a reasonable or prompt response will depend on the nature of the request and the availability of personnel and resources at the responding agency. A prompt response to a fairly simple records request can range from immediately, to within a few hours, to within a day or two. As the request becomes more substantial, however, and the burden on the custodian becomes correspondingly greater, it seems reasonable to allow the custodian somewhat more time to locate and deliver the desired records. Among factors that might appropriately delay granting access are the number of records requested, whether they are located in multiple or remote sites, how large the public agency is, and whether any part of the records must be redacted. Unless a request is extraordinary, however, a custodian probably should respond within a couple of weeks. Practically speaking, it is advisable to attempt to build a rapport with the requester and keep them abreast of progress so that they know the agency is diligently working to fulfill their records request.

Electronic Records and Metadata

As previously noted, the public records law applies to electronic records of all kinds, including Word documents, emails, text and voice mail messages, spreadsheets, and other electronically stored data. An emerging—and as yet unclear—aspect of the law deals with the extent to which the right of access extends to information that is embedded in electronic records. The term "metadata" is used to describe this type of information, which can range from email information that is automatically created (such as date and time information) to changes that can be seen in earlier versions of a document, to file name and other embedded data automatically created by computers and

31. Frayda Bluestein, "Form, Format, and Medium: How Must Electronic Records Be Provided?" *Coates' Canons: NC Local Government Law* blog (March 7, 2012) (hereinafter *Form, Format, and Medium*), canons.sog.unc.edu/2012/03/form-format-and-medium-how-must-electronic-records-be-provided/.

32. *Form, Format, and Medium.*

33. *Form, Format, and Medium.*

34. G.S. 132-6.2(e).

35. *Form, Format, and Medium.*

36. G.S. 132-6(a).

applications.[37] Although it's clear that a public agency must provide electronic records if requested, it is not clear how much embedded information in an electronic record is considered part of the record that must be provided. For example, an email from a private citizen to a city official may contain the citizen's email address. Must this information be provided to a person who requests a copy of the email? Neither the statutes nor the courts have addressed this issue to date, but courts in other jurisdictions have begun to develop interpretations of these and other issues related to the status of electronic information in public records.[38]

While the North Carolina statutes do not yet address what metadata is subject to public access, the law is clear about access to programming or other information technology–system data. G.S. 132-6.1(c) specifies that public agencies are *not* required to disclose security features of their computer or telecommunications systems, nor are the agency's computer passwords, system software, or codes subject to public access.

Custodians of Records

The public records law imposes a number of responsibilities on a custodian of public records. This official maintains public records, may bring actions to recover records improperly held by others, and is required to permit public inspection of records and to provide copies of records to those who request them. G.S. 132-2 declares that the official in charge of an office that holds public records is the custodian of those records. Thus, the register of deeds is the custodian of records in the register of deeds' office, the sheriff is the custodian of records held by the sheriff's department, the county assessor is the custodian of records held in the assessor's office, and so on. G.S. 160A-171 provides that the city clerk is the custodian of all city records. This provision should probably be interpreted as applying to general supervision over records management as well as to responsibility for the official records of the unit (such as minutes and ordinances) rather than literally requiring the clerk to be responsible for all records within each department and office of city government.

Although a custodian of records has the legal responsibility to provide access, many records requests necessitate review by an agency attorney and/or other staff prior to their release.

Fees for Providing Copies

G.S. 132-6 and 132-6.2 expressly permit charging fees for *copies* of public records but are silent about fees for the right to *inspect* records. This silence is the common statutory pattern around the country, and courts in other states generally have held that a custodian may not charge fees for mere inspection when the custodian does no more than locate and retrieve a requested record and no copy is provided.

---

37. For more discussion of metadata and emerging case law involving e-discovery and public records, see Kara Millonzi, "Metadata, E-Discovery, and E-Public Records in North Carolina," *Coates' Canons: NC Local Government Law* blog (September 15, 2011), canons.sog.unc.edu/2011/09/metadata-e-discovery-and-e-public-records-in-north-carolina/.

38. *See* O'Neill v. City of Shoreline, 240 P.3d 1149, 1154 (Wash. 2010) (email address is part of record and must be provided if specifically requested); Kara Millonzi, "Is Metadata a Public Record? Case Law Update," *Coates' Canons: NC Local Government Law* blog (October 21, 2010), canons.sog.unc.edu/2010/10/is-metadata-a-public-record-case-law-update/. Note that G.S. 132-1.13 limits access to emails of subscribers to local government email lists, allowing inspection of such lists but not copying.

The statutes do not establish the fees that a custodian may charge for copying a record but, rather, give direction about the proper amount that may be charged. G.S. 132-6.2 directs that the fee be based on the *actual cost* of making the copy. The statute limits a public agency's "actual cost" to "direct, chargeable costs related to the reproduction of a public record . . . [not including] costs that would have been incurred by the public agency if a request to reproduce a public record had not been made." The statute's use of "direct, chargeable costs" seems to rule out the inclusion of indirect costs in determining the fees for a copy of a public record. In addition, because the costs may not include costs that the responding agency would have incurred whether the copy was made or not, in most instances the fee may not include personnel costs; the person making the copy would have been paid whether he or she made the copy or did other work.

In addition to permitting record-copying fees based on the actual costs of copying, G.S. 132-6.2(b) authorizes a "special service charge" in the following circumstances: (1) when a records request requires a responding agency to use extensive information technology (IT) resources or extensive clerical or supervisory assistance or (2) when the medium requested requires a greater use of IT resources "than that established by the [responding] agency for reproduction of the volume of information requested." There are no North Carolina court of appeals or supreme court cases interpreting this provision, so it is unclear when or how it applies. However, the statute's plain language offers several guidelines. First, special service charges are only available for requests for copies of records. The special-service-charge language references the "actual cost of duplication" and is located in the subsection of the statute that addresses charging for copies. Second, for these special charges to apply, a request for copies has to be such that it *requires* extensive IT, clerical, or supervisory assistance. In other words, a responding agency would not be able to respond to the request within the statutory time frame ("as promptly as possible" under G.S. 132-6(a)) without additional IT, clerical, or supervisory assistance. Note that additional assistance in this context does not mean external assistance. The statute specifies that the extensive assistance is rendered by agency personnel, meaning that agencies do not need to contract for outside help in order to take advantage of special service charges. Third, the special service charges must be reasonable based on the actual cost incurred for the extensive assistance. As discussed above, actual cost includes only those expenses that would not have been incurred but for the public records request. Applied in this context, agencies' special service fees should only include IT, clerical, or supervisory fees made necessary by the nature of the request.

For a public agency to qualify to impose a special service charge on a records request under the second circumstance set out above, the IT resources necessary to complete the request must be greater than what the agency typically uses to respond to requests of the same size or type. This "greater use of technology" also has to be related to the medium requested. Therefore, putting the response in the requester's preferred medium has to involve a greater use of technology than is typical at the agency for producing the volume of records requested. In evaluating this type of special service charge, an agency might ask, "Are we using technological resources that we would not normally use to respond to a request of this size? Are we doing that because of the requested medium?" If so, a special service charge seems to be permissible.

Although not binding in North Carolina, some Florida cases provide examples of permissible special service charges.[39] Like G.S. 132-6.2(b), Florida's public records law provides for special

39. Florida courts have upheld local policies imposing special service charges in cases where it takes more than fifteen minutes for agency staff to locate, review, redact, copy, and refile a requested record. *See e.g.*, Bd. of Cnty. Comm'rs of Highlands Cnty. v. Colby, 976 So. 2d 31, 35 (Fla. Dist. Ct. App. 2008); Fla. Institutional Legal Servs. Inc. v. Fla. Dep't of Corrs., 579 So. 2d 267, 268–69 (Fla. Dist. Ct. App. 1991). At least one Florida court has suggested that

service charges when records requests require the extensive use of information technology resources or extensive clerical or supervisory assistance.[40] If North Carolina courts follow the reasoning of courts in Florida, public agencies here may be able to develop their own policies regarding extensive records requests or those requiring greater use of IT resources and impose special service charges under those policies. Courts will likely still evaluate these charges for reasonableness, so agencies must be prepared to justify their charges as directly related to expenses actually incurred. When the appropriateness of a charge is in doubt, G.S. 132-6.2(b) allows a requester to seek mediation from the State Chief Information Officer.

Categories of Records Not Subject to the Right of Access

There are dozens of state statutes that create exceptions to the general right of access to public records. Those that seem most important to local governments are discussed below.

Personnel Records

A number of separate statutes exempt personnel-file information from public access, including most of the records in the personnel files of public employees.[41] As in public records law generally, the content of a personnel record, rather than its location, determines its classification for public records purposes.[42] In other words, a record does not have to physically be inside a personnel file to be considered personnel file information. Under statute, confidential personnel file information is information, in any form, that a public agency collects about an employee relating to some kind of employment action involving the employee.[43] Examples of employment actions include hiring, termination, and suspension.[44] These statutes vary, but most permit a public employee, as well as anyone with supervisory authority over the employee, to have access to almost all types of personnel file information pertaining to the employee. The statutes also permit certain others to access information in the employee's file in very limited circumstances. Each of the personnel file statutes contains a list of information about public employees that is considered public record, including an employee's name; age; current salary and salary history; contract terms; original employment date; current position title and location; history of changes in position classification and disciplinary actions; and, in the case of dismissal for disciplinary reasons, the final notice of dismissal stating

---

agency personnel having to do "extra work" warrants a special service charge. Tampa Television Inc. v. Clay Cnty. Sch. Bd., No. 92-1347-CA, 1993 WL 204090, at *3 (Fla. Cir. Ct., Feb. 11, 1993) (unpublished opinion, which may have limited precedential value, even in Florida). The Florida District Court of Appeal has indicated that the calculation of special service charges can include consideration of both wages and benefits but that the charges still must be reasonable. *Colby*, 976 So. 2d at 35; Carden v. Chief of Police, 696 So. 2d 772, 773 (Fla. Dist. Ct. App. 1996) (remanding a $4,000 special service charge for non-computer research that required an explanation).

40. Fla. Stat. Ann. § 119.07(4)(d).

41. G.S. 153A-98 (county employees); 160A-168 (city employees); 115C-319 through -321 (public school employees); 115D-27 through -30 (community college employees); 130A-42 (district health department employees); 122C-158 (area authority employees); 131E-97.1 (public hospital employees); 162A-6.1 (water and sewer authority employees); and 126-22 through -30 (state employees).

42. G.S. 132-1(a).

43. G.S. 153A-98(a) (county employees); 160A-168(a) (city employees); 115C-319 (public school employees); 115D-27; 130A-42 (district health department employees); 122C-158(a) (area authority employees); 162A-6.1(a) (water and sewer authority employees); 126-22 (state employees).

44. G.S. 153A-98(a) (county employees); 160A-168(a) (city employees); 115C-319 (public school employees); 115D-27; 130A-42 (district health department employees); 122C-158(a) (area authority employees); 162A-6.1(a) (water and sewer authority employees); 126-22(b)(3) (state employees).

the reasons for the employee's dismissal. Other information in a public employee's personnel file is considered confidential, and the agency that employs the employee is prohibited from releasing it except under specific circumstances.

A number of statutes permit local governments to require criminal records checks of prospective employees. G.S. 143B-1209.11 through -1209.45 direct that the records provided as a result of such checks are to be kept confidential.

Criminal Investigation Records

G.S. 132-1.4 establishes special rules for access to records generated while a law enforcement agency is investigating alleged or known violations of the criminal law. In general, the statute denies the public any right of access to these records, with certain exceptions: records involving (1) details of criminal incidents, (2) information about persons arrested or charged, (3) the circumstances of arrests, (4) the contents of 911 telephone calls (these records may be provided with voices altered or may be transcribed to protect callers' identity), (5) radio communications between law enforcement personnel, and (6) information about victims of crime and persons who file complaints or report violations. There is a separate statute for specific types of law enforcement agency recordings like body camera or dashboard camera footage.[45] While this statute, G.S. 132-1.4A, generally provides that these recordings are not public records, it also sets out specific procedures for the disclosure and release of these types of recordings in limited, defined circumstances.

Legal Materials

Two statutes exempt certain legal materials from public access, though one exemption is limited in duration. First, G.S. 132-1.1 exempts written communications to a public body in state or local government when the communications are within the scope of an attorney-client relationship and involve (1) a claim by or against the public body or the government for which it acts or (2) a judicial action or administrative proceeding to which the public body is a party or by which it is affected. This exemption does not expire, meaning covered communications do not become public unless the governmental agency chooses to make them public. Second, G.S. 132-1.9 exempts trial-preparation materials, such as documents showing the mental impressions or legal theories of an attorney or reports from consultants to be used at trial or in support of trial. Once litigation is completed, however, this exemption ends. In addition, G.S. 132-1.3 specifies that settlement documents in any suit or legal proceeding involving a government agency are to be open to the public unless closed by court order.

Trade Secrets

G.S. 132-1.2 prohibits a local government from allowing access to trade secrets that a business has shared with the government, provided the business has designated the material as confidential or as a trade secret at the time it was disclosed to the government.

Local Tax Records

Two statutes prohibit cities or counties from making public any local tax records that contain information about any taxpayer's income or gross receipts.[46] The kinds of local taxes that might generate such records are privilege license taxes, when measured by gross receipts; occupancy taxes; prepared

45. G.S. 132-1.4A.
46. G.S. 153A-148.1 (county tax records); 160A-208.1 (city tax records).

food taxes; and cable-television franchise taxes. In addition, some forms that must be filled out to qualify for property tax classifications—the homestead exemption and use-value taxation—also require taxpayers to reveal their income; that information also is covered by these provisions.

Medical and Patient Records

A variety of statutes exempt from public access records about particular patients held by different sorts of health-related public agencies.[47] These include records held by public hospitals, public health departments, mental health agencies, and emergency medical-services providers.

Closed-Session Minutes and General Accounts

Although the minutes of official meetings of government bodies are public records by default, G.S. 143-318.10(c) permits the sealing of the minutes or the general account of any closed session "so long as public inspection would frustrate the purpose of a closed session." In other words, a government body may withhold its closed-session minutes and general accounts if releasing these items would undermine or defeat the purpose for which the government body held the closed session in the first place. Public bodies can vote to "seal" their closed-session minutes and general accounts. Sealing essentially deems these records non-public and represents a government body's determination that releasing these minutes or accounts would frustrate the underlying closed-session purpose.

Once a closed-session purpose is completely resolved, a government body can no longer withhold related closed-session minutes and general accounts and should release them upon request. Many jurisdictions therefore have a practice of reviewing their sealed closed-session minutes and general accounts periodically to determine if they should remain sealed.

Social Security Numbers and Other Personal Identifying and Personal Financial Information

Two public records statutes restrict or deny public access to information (1) that can be used to steal a person's identity or (2) that reveals certain sorts of financial information about a person. First, G.S. 132-1.10 prohibits government agencies from making public Social Security numbers and other "identifying information" as defined in G.S. 14-113.20. This other information includes drivers' license numbers (except as they appear on law enforcement records), bank account numbers, bank-card account numbers, fingerprints, and a few other types of similar information. Second, G.S. 132-1.1(c) exempts from public access billing information gathered or compiled as part of operating a public enterprise, such as a utility system. The statute defines billing information as "any record or information, in whatever form, compiled or maintained with respect to individual customers."

Records Involving Public Security

Several statutes exempt certain material from public access because of security concerns. G.S. 132-1.7 exempts sensitive public security information, which includes the specific details of public security plans and detailed plans and drawings of public buildings and infrastructure.[48] This provision also

47. G.S. 131E-97 (medical records and financial records of patients at health care facilities); 130A-12 (patient medical records held by local health departments); 122C-52 (patient medical records held by area authorities); 143-518 (medical records held by emergency medical services (EMS) providers).

48. G.S. 132-1.7(a)(1)–(2).

exempts plans to prevent or respond to terrorist activity.[49] G.S. 132-6.1 further exempts from public access the security features of a government's electronic data-processing systems, information technology systems, telecommunications networks, and electronic security systems.[50]

Contract Bid Documents and Construction Diaries

G.S. 143-131 specifies that a government's record of informal construction or purchasing bids it has received is not open to the public until the contract for which the bids have been solicited has been awarded. In addition, G.S. 133-33 permits the state and local governments to adopt rules that make confidential an agency's cost estimates for a construction project and any list of contractors who have obtained proposals for bid purposes.

Economic-Development Records

G.S. 132-6(d) exempts from public access records that relate to the proposed expansion or location of specific business or industrial projects. Once a project has been announced, however, or once a company has communicated a decision not to locate or expand in the state, the exemption ends. The statute expands these protections to include records regarding the evaluation, acquisition, or location of a qualifying site for a potential business or industry expansion. These protections expire once a site has been acquired (or options secured) or deemed unsuitable. After acquiring or rejecting a business or industrial project site, an agency must disclose expansion- or location-related records as soon as practicable within twenty-five days of a request.

Social Services Records

G.S. 108A-80 prohibits any person from obtaining, disclosing, or using a list of names of, or other information about, persons applying for or receiving public assistance or other social services.

Library Records

G.S. 125-19 prohibits a public library from disclosing any record that identifies a person as having requested or obtained specific materials, information, or services from the library.

Telephone Numbers Held by 911 Systems

G.S. 132-1.5 prohibits any local government operating a 911 system from releasing telephone numbers received from any telephone company, if the local government had a prior agreement with the telephone company that such information would be confidential.

Framework for Responding to Public Records Requests

The public records law creates a broad right of access to government records unless an exception applies. The framework in Table 8.1, below, provides a set of questions to be considered when responding to public records requests; each question is followed by a brief explanation of the issues involved in arriving at an answer.

---

49. G.S. 132-1.7(b).

50. See also G.S. 132-1.6, which exempts from public access emergency response plans adopted by a constituent institution of the University of North Carolina, a community college, or a public hospital.

Table 8.1 Framework for Responding to Public Records Requests

Questions	Answers
1. A public records request has been made. Does a record exist that corresponds to the request? *If not, no disclosure is required. If so, continue to Question 2.*	Records can exist in many forms, and there will rarely be an issue about whether a particular record is of a type that is covered by the public records law. The more significant aspect of this first question is whether a record exists that corresponds to the request. Sometimes public agencies receive requests for information that can be found in various records or which is known but not made part of any record. An agency's obligation under the law is to provide access to, or copies of, records that exist; the law specifically says that a public agency is not required to respond to records requests by "creating or compiling a record that does not exist." As noted above, a request for public information from an employee's personnel file is an exception to this legal obligation.
2. Is the record "made or received in the transaction of public business"? *If not, no disclosure is required. If so, continue to Question 3.*	Most of a public agency's records relate to the business of the agency. Records that are personal are *not* related to the work of the agency and are not subject to disclosure under the public records law, even if they are created using government email systems or devices. This category of exempted information can include a great many records, including personal emails and text messages created by public employees or officials.
3. Is there an exception that applies? *If not, the requested access must be provided. If so, continue to Question 4.*	There are numerous exceptions to the public records law. The better part of David M. Lawrence's *Public Records Law for North Carolina Local Governments*, mentioned at the opening of this chapter, explains the various exceptions and is the most complete resource for information on how to interpret them. A careful assessment must be made about whether an exception covers a particular record or category of record since there must be a legal basis for refusing to provide access to records.
4. Does the exception apply to the entire record or only to certain information, and does it prohibit disclosure or deny the right of access? *If a prohibition applies to the entire record, do not disclose. If it applies only to certain information, redact accordingly and disclose. If there is no right of access to some or all of the information but release is not prohibited, determine whether or not to release the entire record or a redacted version.*	Some exceptions are described as exceptions to the right of access, though they do not prohibit the release of the records. The exceptions for criminal investigation information and information related to economic-development projects are examples of these types of exceptions. In these cases, the public agency is not required to provide the records, but it may choose to do so. Other exceptions, like records involving trade secrets or information in a public employee's personnel file, prohibit disclosure. In addition, there are some exceptions that have exceptions within them—that is, some exceptions identify specific information that would fall within the exception but that must nonetheless be made public. Both the personnel file and criminal investigation information exceptions contain these types of provisions. This part of the analysis requires careful attention to the various types of information that may be contained in a single record as well as a determination about whether the public can access all or part of a record. If an exception applies, a public agency may be allowed—or even required—to deny access to an entire requested record. In many cases, however, a particular record may contain a mix of public and nonpublic information. Depending on the wording of a particular exception, a public agency may be required to redact or separate confidential information in a record from other information that is public. Although the public records law applies to records, not information, it provides that a request for access to a record cannot be denied on the grounds that confidential information is commingled with nonconfidential information. Indeed, the law requires a public agency to bear the cost of redacting or separating information in order to comply with a records request. If an exception specifically prohibits the disclosure of an entire record, redaction is not required.

Remedies for Denial of Access

Any individual who has been partially or completely denied access to public records may attempt a mediated settlement under G.S. 7A-38.3E and file an action under G.S. 132-9. An individual who substantially prevails in a claim under the latter statute may be allowed to recover attorneys' fees from the public agency that denied access. A court is prohibited from awarding attorneys' fees, however, if a public agency, in denying access, acted in reasonable reliance on (1) a court judgment or decision applicable to the agency involved, (2) a published opinion or order of any North Carolina court, or (3) a written opinion, decision, or letter of the North Carolina Attorney General.[51] Individual agency employees or officials may be held personally liable for attorneys' fees only if they failed to follow the advice of counsel. A person can also seek injunctive relief, such as a declaratory judgment, under the public records law.[52]

To date, no North Carolina case has addressed whether a delay in producing records violates the public records law. At least one federal court has held that the public records law does not provide a remedy for "mere delay."[53] However, this case is unpublished and deals with a quite minor delay of one week over the Christmas and New Year's holidays.[54] For that reason, while this case suggests that minor delays do not violate the public records law, it does not foreclose the possibility that North Carolina courts would find more substantial delays to be in violation of the public records law.

Records Retention and Disposition

G.S. Chapter 132 and G.S. 121-5 together establish responsibilities for records protection and records management for two kinds of actors: custodians of one or more public records and the state Department of Natural and Cultural Resources. Such custodians and the department together are responsible for maintaining the integrity of public records and for developing a plan for the management of records in every public office or agency in the state.

G.S. 132-3 prohibits any public official from destroying, selling, loaning, or otherwise disposing of any public record except when acting in accordance with G.S. 121-5. The latter provision, in turn, empowers the Department of Natural and Cultural Resources to decide how long particular categories of records are to be kept and whether and when they may be destroyed. In furtherance of that responsibility, the department has adopted a series of Records Retention and Disposition Schedules for almost all forms of records held by local governments. The department maintains current copies of its records schedules on its website.[55]

Once agreed to by the officials of a particular local government, these schedules govern whether various categories of records may be destroyed and when that may occur. For example, the original of all minutes of a city or county governing board must be retained permanently at city or county offices; a microfilmed duplicate set must be maintained by the Department of Natural and Cultural Resources at the State Records Center. Many local government contracts may be destroyed three

---

51. *See* G.S. 132-9(c).

52. G.S. 143-318.16A.

53. Quality Built Homes, Inc. v. Village of Pinehurst, No. 1:06CV1028, 2008 WL 3503149, at *14 (M.D.N.C. Aug. 11, 2008).

54. *Quality Built Homes*, 2008 WL 3503149, at *14.

55. N.C. Department of Natural and Cultural Resources, State Archives of North Carolina, Government Records Section, *Local Government Agencies.*

years after their termination, if there is no outstanding litigation, while records of vehicles owned and maintained by a government unit may be destroyed after one year. Records of "short-term value" need not be retained beyond their usefulness to the custodian of records. As such, most emails may be destroyed by the sender and the recipient as they see fit and need be retained only if the substance of the communication is subject to retention under a specific provision as set out in the applicable schedule.

Additional Resources

Additional information can be found by searching the *Coates' Canons: NC Local Government Law* blog (canons.sog.unc.edu) using the keywords "public records."

For a comprehensive guide to the state's public records laws and their interpretation by the courts, see the second edition of David M. Lawrence's *Public Records Law for North Carolina Local Governments*, published by the School of Government in 2010.

Chapter 9

Open Meetings and Other Legal Requirements for Local Government Boards

Kristina M. Wilson

Kristina M. Wilson is a School of Government faculty member specializing in local government law.

This chapter updates and revises previous chapters authored by Frayda Bluestein, David M. Lawrence, and Joseph S. Ferrell, whose contributions to the field and to this publication are gratefully acknowledged.

The North Carolina open meetings law applies to all public bodies, including local elected and appointed boards, councils, and commissions, and to subcommittees of these bodies. County and city governing boards are subject to additional state statutory requirements regarding meetings and voting. There are numerous locally appointed boards as well. Some are governed by state statutory requirements, such as rules about voting and conflicts of interest for quasi-judicial boards. Other locally appointed boards are created and primarily governed by local ordinance and local rules of procedure.

The first section of this chapter summarizes the open meetings law. The second section deals with procedures that apply only to governing boards of counties and cities. The final section outlines how to determine the procedures that apply to statutorily mandated and locally appointed boards and commissions.

Open Meetings Law Requirements for All Public Bodies

Overview

The North Carolina open meetings law[1] gives the public the right to notice of and attendance at official meetings of public bodies. If public officials conduct an official meeting without complying with statutory notice and access requirements, individuals may seek redress in court, as further outlined below. Failure to comply with the open meetings law often creates negative publicity for the public body and may diminish the public's trust and confidence in their local government representatives.

Official Meetings of Public Bodies

The open meetings law applies only to "official meetings" of "public bodies." The statute defines the term "*public body*" as any elected or appointed board, commission, committee, council, authority, or other body in state or local government that (1) has at least two members and (2) exercises or is authorized to exercise any of these powers: legislative, policy-making, quasi-judicial, administrative, or advisory.[2] This definition—and thus the scope of the statute—is very broad. Public bodies in county or city government include the elected governing board; each committee of that board, whether standing or ad hoc; boards created by statute, such as the board of health and the board of social services; and each body established by action of the governing board, such as a planning board, a zoning board of adjustment, a parks and recreation commission, or a human relations commission. Other local level governing boards include local boards of education, community college boards of trustees, and governing boards of public hospitals. The statute's definition of a public body explicitly excludes groups consisting only of professional staff.[3]

When evaluating whether a group is a public body subject to the open meetings law, practitioners should analyze the group's origin and function. A group must be created by and with proper government authority to be a public body.[4] Unauthorized appointments, even if made by someone with general government authority, are insufficient to create a public body. Additionally, if the group does not serve a public function, the group cannot be a public body.

As defined in the statute, an official meeting occurs whenever a *majority* of the members of a public body gather to take action, hold a hearing, deliberate, or otherwise transact public business.[5] When evaluating whether a gathering is an official meeting, practitioners should focus on 1) the number of public body members present and 2) the action or discussion of the gathered members. A gathering that consists of a minority of a public body cannot be an official meeting. Typically, a majority under the open meetings law means more than half of a body's total membership.[6]

---

1. Chapter 143, Article 33C, Sections 318.9 through 318.18 of the North Carolina General Statutes (hereinafter G.S.).
2. G.S. 143-318.10(b).
3. G.S. 143-318.10(c).
4. DTH Pub. Corp. v. University of North Carolina at Chapel Hill, 128 N.C. App. 534, 539 (N.C. Ct. App. 1998).
5. G.S. 143-318.10(d).
6. *See* Frayda Bluestein, "Calculating Majorities," *Coates' Canons: NC Local Government Law* blog (October 27, 2010), canons.sog.unc.edu/2010/10/calculating-majorities/.

However, there are some special cases where less than a numerical majority still might trigger the open meetings law.[7] Imagine the following situation: A City Council has five members with no vacancies and a nonvoting mayor. A numerical majority would be four; the members plus the mayor is six and more than half of six is four. However, in this scenario, three council members constitute a majority under the open meetings law. If three of the council members meet and form a consensus, that consensus will control the outcome of the board. They will outvote the other two members since the mayor votes only in the case of a tie. Since a meeting of those three council members will direct and control the board's ultimate actions, allowing this meeting without notice and access would violate the spirit of the open meetings law, which is intended to prevent closed-door government action.[8] Consequently, instead of focusing on numerical majorities, local governments should evaluate the *impact* of a certain number of members meeting. Can this number of gathered members control board action? If these members reach a consensus, will that consensus ultimately become the consensus of the board? If so, the gathering is likely a majority for open meetings law purposes.

Notably, the legislature included electronic gatherings in the definition of "official meeting." As a result, a telephone call involving a majority of a public body would violate the open meetings law without public notice and access. Similarly, it is possible that an email or text exchange with rapid back-and-forth messaging among a majority of public body members could constitute an official meeting.[9] Regardless of the form of the gathering, the open meetings law is still only triggered if the majority is discussing, deliberating, debating, voting, or otherwise transacting public business. Thus, even an informal gathering or a social event could trigger open meetings law requirements if a discussion turns to public business. Still, the statute provides that true social gatherings that do not entail any discussion of public business are not official meetings of public bodies.[10]

Notice Requirements

The open meetings law provides the public with two broad categories of rights: notice and access. The statute requires that each public body give public notice of its official meetings, even those that will be conducted in closed session.[11] These requirements apply to meetings of the governing board, to meetings of each appointed board, and to meetings of each committee of any of these boards. The type of notice required depends on the nature of the meeting, as described below. Specific additional types of notice required for county and city *governing boards* are described later in this chapter.

Regular Meetings

Regular meetings are those that occur according to a predetermined, predictable schedule. Boards can set their own schedule of regular meetings, or one may be set by statute.[12] If a public body holds regular meetings, it gives public notice of those meetings by filing its schedule of regular meetings

---

7. *Id.*

8. *Id.*; G.S. 143-318.9.

9. *See e.g.*, N.C. Citizens for Transparent Gov't, Inc. v. Vill. of Pinehurst, 910 S.E.2d 288 (N.C. Ct. App. 2024) and my blog post, "Are E-Mail Conversations Subject to the Open Meetings Law?," *Coates' Canons: NC Local Government Law* blog (December 10, 2024), canons.sog.unc.edu/2024/12/are-e-mail-conversations-subject-to-the-open-meetings-law/.

10. G.S. 143-318.10(d).

11. G.S. 143-318.12.

12. *See e.g.*, G.S. 153A-40(a) (county governing boards may adopt their own schedule but if they do not, the statute provides one); G.S. 160A-71(a) (city governing boards may adopt their own schedule but if they do not, the statute provides one).

in a central location.[13] For public bodies that are part of a county government, that location is the office of the clerk to the board of commissioners unless otherwise specified.[14] For public bodies that are part of a city government, that location is the office of the city clerk unless otherwise specified.[15] For local public bodies that are not part of a county or city, such as a local board of education, that location is the office of its clerk or secretary or of the clerk of the county where the public body normally has its meetings, if it does not have its own clerk.[16] The law also requires the schedule of regular meetings to be posted on the public body's website, if it maintains one.[17] Once this notice is properly filed and posted, no other public notice is required for regular meetings held pursuant to the schedule. Changes in the regular meeting schedule are made by filing and posting a revised schedule at least seven days before the first meeting to occur under the revised schedule.[18]

Special Meetings

Special meetings are official meetings that occur at any time, date, or location different than what is on the regular meeting schedule.[19] Special meeting notices must set out the time, place, and purpose of the meeting and must be provided in three ways.[20] First, notice must be posted on the *principal bulletin board* of the public body (or on the meeting room door if there is no principal bulletin board).[21] Second, it must be mailed, emailed, or delivered to any person who has made a written request for notice of special meetings.[22] Third, it must be posted on the website of the public body, if it has one.[23] The first two forms of notice must occur at least forty-eight hours before the meeting, while the website posting must occur sometime prior to the meeting.[24] A public body may require media requests to be renewed annually.[25] Non-media requesters may be required to renew quarterly and must be charged a fee of $10 per calendar year.[26] No fee may be charged for email notices.[27]

It is important to note that the statute requires the notice to specify the *purpose* of the meeting.[28] Public bodies should be hesitant to discuss or take action on matters not included in the notice.[29]

Emergency Meetings

An emergency meeting is one held to address "generally unexpected circumstances that require immediate consideration by the public body," and only matters related to those circumstances may

---

13. G.S. 143-318.12(a).
14. G.S. 143-318.12(a)(2).
15. G.S. 143-318.12(a)(3).
16. G.S. 143-318.12(a)(4).
17. G.S. 143-318.12(d).
18. G.S. 143-318.12(a).
19. G.S. 143-318.12(b).
20. G.S. 143-318.12(b)(2).
21. *Id.*
22. *Id.*
23. G.S. 143-318.12(e).
24. G.S. 143-318.12(b)(2), (e).
25. G.S. 143-318.12(b)(2).
26. *Id.*
27. *Id.*
28. *Id.*
29. The open meetings law does not specifically address discussing or transacting items that are not listed on the special meeting notice. Courts in other states with similar open meetings laws have found violations when a public body's discussion or action departed from the noticed purposes of the special meeting. For that reason, this is an area to exercise caution. *See* Trey Allen, "Statutory Permission to Take Up Items Not on the Special Meeting Notice," *Coates' Canons: NC Local Government Law* blog (January 26, 2015), canons.sog.unc.edu/2015/01/statutory-permission-to-take-up-items-not-on-the-special-meeting-notice/.

be discussed at the meeting.[30] For emergency meetings, notice must be given to all *local* news media that have requested notice.[31] Notice may be given by telephone or email or by the same method used to notify the members of the public body.[32] As noted later in this chapter, because of a separate notice requirement for city council members, a city council usually must allow at least six hours when scheduling an emergency meeting.[33]

Recessed Meetings

A recessed meeting is when a board continues a meeting at a different time, date, or place, rather than adjourning and starting a new meeting. If a public body is in a properly noticed regular, special, or emergency meeting, it may recess that meeting to a time, date, and place certain through motion and majority vote in favor. Notice of a recessed meeting is provided by announcing the time, date, and place of the recessed meeting in open session at the original meeting.[34] In addition, the statute requires that notice of recessed meetings be posted on the public body's website, if it has one.[35]

Public Right of Access to Open Meetings

The second right afforded under the open meetings law is the right of access. The public's right to attend meetings of public bodies represents a strong policy in favor of transparency in local government decision-making. As part of the right of access, the law allows media broadcast of meetings and permits any person to photograph, film, tape-record or otherwise reproduce any part of an open meeting.[36] The open meetings law does not, however, provide the public the right to speak at public meetings. As noted later in this chapter, a separate statute requires regular public comment periods at certain governing board meetings. Public hearings also provide opportunities for public input and are required for some types of actions.[37] Other than these provisions, however, there is no general right for members of the public to be heard by, or to hear from, members of public bodies. Each board in its discretion may establish additional opportunities for public input, either at meetings or through other channels. For a more complete discussion of citizen involvement in local government, see Chapter 10, "Citizen Involvement."

Closed Sessions

Although the open meetings law favors public access, there are times when public bodies may meet behind closed doors. These meetings are known as closed sessions. The open meetings law authorizes a public body to meet in closed session for any of ten specific purposes listed in the statute.[38] Due to the presumption of transparency in the open meetings law, closed session purposes should be narrowly interpreted and strictly applied.[39] This authority applies to all public bodies

---

30. G.S. 143-318.12(f); G.S. 143-318.12(b)(3).
31. G.S. 143-318.12(b)(3).
32. *Id.*
33. G.S. 160A-71(b)(1).
34. G.S. 143-318.12(b)(1).
35. G.S. 143-318.12 (e).
36. G.S. 143-318.14(a).
37. Public hearings are only required when a statute specifically calls for them or when a board decides to hold a hearing in its own discretion. *See* David Lawrence, "When Are Public Hearings Required," *Coates' Canons: NC Local Government Law* blog (August 21, 2009), canons.sog.unc.edu/2009/08/when-are-public-hearings-required/.
38. G.S. 143-318.11(a)(1)–(10).
39. *See* Garlock v. Wake Cnty. Bd. of Educ., 211 N.C. App. 200, 221 (N.C. Ct. App. 2011) and Boney Publishers, Inc. v. Burlington City Council, 151 N.C. App. 651, 655 (N.C. Ct. App. 2002) (both citing Publ'g Co. v. Bd. of Educ., 29 N.C. App. 37, 47 (N.C. Ct. App. 1976).

(not just governing boards), although many appointed boards rarely have justification to meet in closed session.

Procedures for Closed Sessions

A closed session can be a part of any regular, special, or emergency meeting, and the appropriate notice must be provided, even if the entire meeting will be in closed session.[40] If a public body wishes to hold a closed session, the body must first meet in open session and then vote to hold the closed session.[41] It is not sufficient for the presiding officer simply to announce that a closed session will be held. Rather, there must be a motion to enter closed session, and the motion must identify the permissible purpose from among those authorized in the statute. A specific citation is not necessary as long as it is clear from the motion which provision is being invoked.[42] Once the closed session is complete, the public body must return to the open session to complete its business or to adjourn.[43] There is no authority to adjourn a meeting from within closed session.[44]

A brief overview of the closed session purposes most commonly used by local governments is set out below. For more details, see the School of Government publication *Open Meetings and Local Governments in North Carolina: Some Questions and Answers.*[45]

Confidential Records

A public body may meet in a closed session to prevent the disclosure of privileged or confidential information or information that is not public record.[46] Thus, for example, a board of social services may have a closed session to discuss matters involving recipients of public assistance, because records about recipients are not public.[47] A motion to go into closed session under this provision must state the name or citation of the law that makes the information privileged or confidential.[48]

Attorney Consultations

A public body may meet with its attorney in closed session to preserve attorney–client privilege.[49] Consequently, a closed session held under this exception cannot legally include any person who is not within the scope of the attorney–client privilege.[50] North Carolina courts have yet to define the boundaries of the attorney–client privilege in the local government attorney context, but default guidance from the North Carolina Rules of Professional Conduct is instructive.[51] Under Rule 1.6, attorney–client privilege covers information acquired while representing a client that relates to the

---

40. G.S. 143-318.11(c); G.S. 143-318.12.
41. G.S. 143-318.11(c).
42. *Id.*
43. G.S. 143-318.11(a), (c).
44. *See* 143-318.11.
45. David M. Lawrence and Frayda S. Bluestein, *Open Meetings and Local Governments in North Carolina: Some Questions and Answers*, 8th ed. (UNC School of Government, 2017).
46. G.S. 143-318.11(a)(1).
47. *See* G.S. 108A-80.
48. G.S. 143-318.11(c).
49. G.S. 143-318.11(a)(3).
50. For more detail on the scope of the attorney–client exception, see David M. Lawrence, "Closed Sessions under the Attorney–Client Privilege," *Local Government Law Bulletin* No. 103 (Apr. 2002), www.sog.unc.edu/sites/default/files/reports/lglb103.pdf.
51. *See* Chris McLaughlin, "Ethics and the Role of the Local Government Attorney," *Coates' Canons: NC Local Government Law* blog (October 9, 2014), canons.sog.unc.edu/2014/10/ethics-and-the-role-of-the-local-government-attorney/.

representation of that client.[52] Thus, permissible closed session discussions under this statutory purpose might include evaluations of whether certain proposed actions are legal, explanations of the legal differences between different ordinances, and conversations regarding potential claims or liabilities.[53] In contrast, information that legally must be disclosed to a third party does not fall under the umbrella of attorney–client privilege and is illegal to discuss in closed session using this purpose.[54] For example, an order to terminate a contract must be communicated to the contractor, someone who is outside of the attorney–client relationship.[55] Therefore, final action terminating a contract cannot occur in closed session under this purpose.[56]

This closed session purpose explicitly authorizes public bodies to instruct their attorneys on handling or settling claims, arbitration, litigation, mediation, judicial action, or administrative proceedings.[57] This provision is not limited to specific pending or threatened claims or litigation, but if a board enters closed session under this purpose to discuss an existing lawsuit, the motion must identify the parties to the lawsuit.[58] The phrase "administrative procedures" in this purpose only includes proceedings instituted under the Administrative Procedure Act.[59]

Merely having an attorney in attendance or using the phrases "legal advice" or "attorney–client privilege" in a closed session motion is not enough to justify using this closed session purpose.[60] The board bears the burden of demonstrating that the closed session for attorney–client privilege purposes was warranted using objective evidence.[61] Courts will normally examine the closed session minutes and general account to determine whether there was objective evidence supporting entering closed session under this purpose.[62] This closed session purpose does not authorize discussions of general policy issues, such as general procedure.[63]

Economic Development

A public body may hold a closed session to discuss matters relating to the location or expansion of businesses in the area served by the public body.[64] Using this purpose, a public body may meet in closed session to develop an incentives package to attract a new business or encourage an existing business to expand. Any final action approving the signing of an economic development agreement or commitment or any action authorizing payment of economic development incentives must occur in open session.[65]

---

52. N.C. Rules of Professional Conduct, Rule 1.6, www.ncbar.gov/for-lawyers/ethics/rules-of-professional-conduct/rule-16-confidentiality-of-information/.

53. *See, e.g.*, Multimedia Publ'g of N.C., Inc. v. Henderson Cnty., 136 N.C. App. 567 (N.C. Ct. App. 2000), *rev'd in part, aff'd in part*, 145 N.C. App. 365 (N.C. Ct. App. 2001).

54. H.B.S. Contractors, Inc. v. Cumberland Cnty. Bd. of Educ., 122 N.C. App. 49, 53 (N.C. Ct. App. 1996).

55. *Id.* at 53.

56. *Id.* at 54.

57. G.S. 143-318.11(a)(3).

58. *Multimedia Publ'g* at 577–78, 145 N.C. App. at 374; G.S. 143-318.11(c).

59. *H.B.S. Contractors*, 122 N.C. App. at 54.

60. G.S. 143-318.11(a)(3); *Multimedia Publ'g* at 576, 145 N.C. App. at 374.

61. *Multimedia Publ'g* at 576, 145 N.C. App. at 374.

62. *Id.* at 576, 145 N.C. App. at 374.

63. G.S. 143-318.11(a)(3); Knight v. Higgs, 189 N.C. App. 696, 703 (N.C. Ct. App. 2008).

64. G.S. 143-318.11(a)(4).

65. *Id.*

Purchase of Real Property

A public body may hold a closed session to develop its negotiating position in the acquisition of real property and to give instructions to its bargaining agent in that transaction.[66] Acquisition of real property includes purchase, option, exchange, and lease.[67] A public body may discuss the price and other material terms of a contract or a proposed contract for real property. The North Carolina Court of Appeals has clarified that only negotiable terms can be discussed in closed session.[68] For example, if only one tract of land is being considered for purchase, the location of the land is not subject to negotiation.[69] As a result, discussing the land location in closed session would be inappropriate under this purpose. Instead, the site, as well as its current owners and intended use, would all need to be disclosed in open session upon request.[70] Note that this provision *does not* authorize a public body to meet in closed session when it is *selling* real property.[71]

Employment Contracts

A public body may hold a closed session to develop its negotiating position for employment contracts and instruct its negotiating agent in those transactions, including establishing compensation and other material terms of the employment contract.[72] "Establishing" compensation or other material terms may imply that boards can vote on these matters in closed session. However, final approval of the contract likely should take place in open session, since the statute does not explicitly authorize finally approving the contract in closed session.[73] This provision regarding employment contracts appears in the same subsection as the acquisition of property provision discussed above. That placement may indicate that a court would limit "material terms" in an employment contract to only negotiable items, as discussed above with property acquisition contracts. However, no court has ruled on this issue, so that interpretation is untested.

Public Employees

A public body may hold a closed session to consider the qualifications, competence, performance, character, fitness, and conditions of appointment or employment of a current or prospective public employee or public officer.[74] In addition, a public body may hold a closed session to hear or investigate a complaint, charge, or grievance by or against a public officer or employee.[75] A public body may not use this provision to discuss members of the public body itself or members of other public bodies.[76] This exemption applies only to matters involving specific employees of the unit, not independent contractors or volunteers, and this provision may not be used for general personnel policy discussions.[77] At times, practitioners may struggle to identify what constitutes a prohib-

---

66. G.S. 143-318.11(a)(5).
67. *Id.*
68. Boney Publishers, Inc. v. Burlington City Council, 151 N.C. App. 651, 656 (N.C. Ct. App. 2002).
69. *Id.* at 656.
70. *Id. See also* Frayda Bluestein, "Quick-Reference Guide for Closed Sessions," *Coates' Canons: NC Local Government Law* blog (March 13, 2014), canons.sog.unc.edu/2014/03/quick-reference-guide-for-closed-session-meetings/.
71. Procedures for selling real property are governed by Article 12 of G.S. Chapter 160A and are described in Chapter 23, "Public Contracts, Competitive Bidding Requirements, and Property Disposal," of this publication.
72. G.S. 143-318.11(a)(5).
73. For an analysis of a specific situation involving a city/county manager's contract renewal, see Robert Joyce, "Denying the Manager a New Contract in Closed Session," *Coates' Canons: NC Local Government Law* blog (April 2, 2013), canons.sog.unc.edu/2013/04/denying-the-manager-a-new-contract-in-closed-session/.
74. G.S. 143-318.11(a)(6).
75. *Id.*
76. *Id.*
77. *Id.*

ited general personnel policy discussion. The touchstone in that analysis is whether a discussion pertains to a specific employee or officer. For example, imagine that a public body wants to discuss its organizational hierarchy and whether certain positions should exist. Since these discussions do not involve any particular employee or public officer, the public body should discuss these topics in open session. In contrast, if the public body wanted to discuss whether a certain position should exist *because of* a particular employee's performance in that position, those discussions are appropriate for closed session under this purpose.

Criminal Investigations

A public body may hold a closed session to plan, conduct, or hear reports concerning an investigation of alleged criminal conduct.[78] While there are no cases interpreting this provision, the use of the word "alleged" suggests that no criminal charges need actually be filed before a public body may use this purpose.

Minutes and General Accounts

The open meetings law requires public bodies to prepare "full and accurate minutes" of all official meetings and a "general account" of closed sessions.[79] Separate statutes for county[80] and city[81] governing boards also require each board, through its clerk, to keep full and accurate minutes of its proceedings. Although the statutes do not detail what full and accurate minutes should include, the North Carolina Supreme Court tackled this question in *Maready v. City of Winston-Salem.*[82] According to *Maready*, at a minimum, minutes must include (1) the actions taken by a board, stated specifically enough to be identified and proved; and (2) proof of any conditions necessary to action, such as the presence of a quorum.[83] Additional details about the discussion are often included but are not legally required.

The purpose of the minutes is to provide an official record, or proof, of council action. While not required under statute, public bodies should formally approve the minutes by majority vote as a matter of best parliamentary procedure practices.[84] Approving the minutes establishes them as the official record of a board's meetings and represents the board's agreement to their accuracy.[85] The statutes do not establish a specific time frame within which the minutes must be prepared or approved. Once approved, the minutes may be modified in only two ways: (1) a person may bring a legal action alleging that the minutes are incorrect and seeking a court order to correct them; and (2) much more commonly, a council may itself modify its minutes by majority vote to correct substantial inaccuracies.[86]

---

78. G.S. 143-318.11(a)(7).

79. G.S. 143-318.10(e).

80. G.S. 153A-42.

81. G.S. 160A-72.

82. 342 N.C. 708, 732 (N.C. 1996).

83. *Maready*, 342 N.C. at 733–34.

84. *See* Frayda Bluestein, "Approving Minutes of Meetings You Didn't Attend," *Coates' Canons: NC Local Government Law* blog (February 5, 2014), canons.sog.unc.edu/2014/02/approving-minutes-of-meetings-you-didnt-attend/; Trey Allen, "What Are 'Full and Accurate' Minutes?" *Coates' Canons: NC Local Government Law* blog (January 22, 2019), canons.sog.unc.edu/2019/01/what-are-full-and-accurate-minutes/; and Trey Allen, "'Full and Accurate' Minutes: A Primer," *Local Government Law Bulletin* No. 140 (Jan. 2019): 14, www.sog.unc.edu/sites/www.sog.unc.edu /files/reports/20180867_LGLB-140_Layout_5.pdf.

85. Trey Allen, "'Full and Accurate' Minutes: A Primer," 14, www.sog.unc.edu/sites/www.sog.unc.edu/files/reports /20180867_LGLB-140_Layout_5.pdf.

86. *See generally* Oliver v. Bd. of Comm'rs of Johnston Cnty., 194 N.C. 380 (N.C. 1927) (stating that the board of commissioners had a duty to correct minutes to make them more accurate); Norfolk-Southern R. Co. v. Forbes, 188 N.C. 151 (N.C. 1924) (finding that minutes were properly corrected when there was a substantial inaccuracy).

Since public bodies have limited authority to act in closed sessions, the minutes of closed sessions can be quite skeletal.[87] As a result, the open meetings law requires, in addition to minutes, a general account of closed sessions.[88] General accounts must be detailed enough "so that a person not in attendance would have a reasonable understanding of what transpired."[89] At a minimum, general accounts must include some description of the closed session discussion, unlike the minimum legal standard for minutes.[90] Despite the statute's distinction between minutes and general accounts, it is common for boards to combine the minutes and general account in a single document.

Minutes are public records that must be permanently retained.[91] Closed session minutes, however, may be withheld from public access (sealed) for as long as is necessary to avoid frustrating the purpose of the closed session.[92] Many public bodies initially seal all minutes and general accounts of closed sessions and then delegate to their attorney or other staff the responsibility for periodically reviewing these documents and opening them to public access when appropriate. Like open session minutes, closed session minutes and general accounts should be approved by the public body. To approve closed session minutes, the public body may enter closed session under G.S. 143-318.11(a)(1) if release would still frustrate the purpose of the underlying closed session at the time of approval.[93] Closed session minutes can also be approved in open session if the public body securely circulates the minutes to members before the meeting and uses a vaguely worded motion stating only the date and purpose of the underlying closed session.[94]

Remedies

There are two statutory remedies for violations of the open meetings law. The first is an injunction.[95] Any person may seek an injunction to stop the recurrence of past violations of the law, the continuation of present violations, or the occurrence of threatened future violations. The second is the invalidation of any action taken or considered in violation of the law.[96] Action taken at a meeting held in violation of the open meetings law is not automatically invalid, but a trial judge may enter an order invalidating such action if a lawsuit is filed seeking that remedy. The court may award attorneys' fees to the prevailing party in a lawsuit alleging a violation of the open meetings law, and it may order that they be paid personally by individual members of the public body if those individuals knowingly or intentionally violated the law.[97] Individuals cannot be held liable for costs if they follow the advice of counsel.[98]

---

87. *Maready*, 342 N.C. at 734.
88. G.S. 143-318.10(e).
89. *Id.* A case that sets out an acceptable general account is *Multimedia Publ'g Co. of N.C., Inc. v. Henderson County*, 145 N.C. App. 365 (2001).
90. G.S. 143-318.10(e).
91. *See* North Carolina Department of Natural and Cultural Resources, Division of Archives and Records, Government Records Section, *Records Retention and Disposition Schedule: General Records Schedule, Local Government Agencies* (October 1, 2021): 17, Item 1.54, archives.ncdcr.gov/2021localgeneralstandardspdf/open.
92. G.S. 143-318.10(e).
93. G.S. 143-318.11(a)(1).
94. *See* Frayda Bluestein, "How to Approve Minutes and General Accounts of Closed Sessions," *Coates' Canons: NC Local Government Law* blog (June 5, 2018), canons.sog.unc.edu/2018/06/how-to-approve-minutes-and-general-accounts-of-closed-sessions/.
95. G.S. 143-318.16.
96. G.S. 143-318.16(a).
97. G.S. 143-318.16(b).
98. *Id.*

Additional Meeting Requirements for County and City Governing Boards

Boards of county commissioners and city councils hold ultimate authority to act for the local government. Chapter 3, "County and Municipal Governing Boards," describes the structure and roles of these important bodies. This section describes some other statutory meeting requirements that apply to these governing boards in addition to those in the open meetings law.

Governing Board Meetings

Specific statutes in Chapters 153A (counties) and 160A (cities) of the North Carolina General Statutes (hereinafter G.S.) prescribe procedures for governing board meetings that supplement the requirements of the open meetings law. Governing boards must comply with both sets of requirements.

Organizational Meetings

After each election, the newly elected (or reelected) members must qualify for office by taking and subscribing the oath of office. In addition, the governing board must organize itself. The meeting at which these events take place is known as the *organizational meeting.* If the organizational meeting does not appear on the governing board's previously adopted regular meeting schedule, the governing board should notice the organizational meeting as a special meeting.

Counties

G.S. 153A-26 of the North Carolina General Statutes directs that each commissioner elected or reelected at the November election must take the oath of office on the first Monday in December following the election; at the same time, the board elects its chair and vice-chair for the ensuing year.[99] If a commissioner is unable to take the oath at that time, he or she may take it later.[100]

Cities

Unless a council sets an earlier date,[101] a city council's organizational meeting is held at the board's first regular meeting in December following the election. At the organizational meeting, all newly elected and reelected members, and the mayor, if newly elected or reelected, must take the oath of office. If the city is one in which the board elects the mayor, this is done at the organizational meeting. The board should also elect a mayor pro tempore.[102]

Regular Meetings

Counties

G.S. 153A-40 directs boards of county commissioners to hold at least one meeting each month, although they may meet more often if necessary. The board may select any day of the month and any public place within the county for its regular meetings, but unless it selects some other time or place by formal resolution, the law requires the board to meet on the first Monday of the month at the courthouse.

---

99. G.S. 153A-39.

100. G.S. 153A-26.

101. G.S. 160A-68 permits a board to establish an earlier date, which may be any date within the period beginning on the day that the election results are officially determined and published and ending on the day that the board holds its first regular meeting in December.

102. G.S. 160A-70 specifies that the mayor pro tempore is to serve at the pleasure of the governing board.

Cities

G.S. 160A-71 directs each city's governing board to fix the time and the place of its regular meetings. If the board fails to act, the statute provides that meetings shall be held on the first Monday of each month at 10:00 a.m. Unlike county governing boards, city governing boards are not required to hold a regular meeting every month.

Special Meetings

Although both county commissioners and city councils may hold special meetings, the statutes under which they may do so are somewhat different. Under the county and city statutes governing meeting notice, a *special meeting* is any meeting other than a regular meeting.[103]

In general, a governing board may take any action at a special meeting that it may take at a regular meeting. A few exceptions exist, however, as some statutes require action to be taken at a regular meeting. Examples include adoption of ordinances awarding or amending franchises and action on several procedures for selling property. (Even so, a board may *discuss* these matters at a special meeting; it simply may not act.)[104] Because of these exceptions, before taking any action at a special meeting, a board should consult its attorney to ascertain whether it may properly take the action. As noted earlier, it is also important to limit actions taken at special meetings to those matters identified in the notice of the meeting.

Governing boards must comply with the separate requirements for notice to the public of special and emergency meetings under the open meetings law as well as the procedures for notice to the board members, as described below.

Counties

G.S. 153A-40 permits a special meeting to be called by the chair or by a majority of the other board members. The law sets specific rules for calling special meetings. They must be called by written notice stating the time, place, and subjects to be considered. This notice must be posted on the courthouse bulletin board and delivered to each board member at least forty-eight hours before the meeting. Unless all members attend the meeting or sign a written waiver, only business related to the subjects stated in the notice may be transacted at a special meeting. It is important to remember, however, that expansion of the subjects to be addressed in a special meeting, even if allowed under this statute, may violate the open meetings law.

Cities

G.S. 160A-71 permits special meetings of a city council to be called in either of two ways. First, if a board is convened in a regular meeting or a duly called special meeting, it may schedule a special meeting. Second, the mayor, the mayor pro tempore, or any two members of the board may call such a meeting. They may do so by preparing and signing a written notice of the meeting—setting out the time and place and the subjects to be considered—and delivering this notice to each board member (or to his or her home). The notice must be delivered at least six hours before the meeting, but as noted earlier, the open meetings law requires forty-eight hours' *public* notice of a special meeting.

---

103. G.S. 153A-40(b); G.S. 160A-71(b)(1).

104. G.S. 160A-76(a) (franchises); G.S. 160A-267 (private sale); G.S. 160A-270(b) (public auction of personal property); G.S. 160A-271 (exchange of property).

Emergency Meetings

Counties

G.S. 153A-40 provides that notice to board members is not required for a special meeting that is called to deal with an emergency, but it requires the person or persons calling the meeting to take reasonable actions to inform the other board members and the public of the meeting.

Cities

The city statutes do not specifically address emergency meetings. This means that the six-hour notice for special meetings applies to these types of meetings. Even though there is no minimum time for public notice of emergency meetings under the open meetings law, the six-hour board member notice requirement will usually limit a city's ability to hold a meeting with less than six hours' notice.

Meeting Location

County commissioners' meetings are generally held within the county. G.S. 153A-40 permits out-of-county meetings only in four specific instances:

1. in connection with a joint meeting of two or more public bodies, as long as the meeting is within the boundaries of the political subdivision represented by the members of one of the participating bodies;
2. in connection with a retreat, forum, or similar gathering held solely to provide the county commissioners with information relating to the performance of their public duties (no vote may be taken during this type of meeting);
3. in connection with a meeting between the board and its local legislative delegation while the General Assembly is in session, as long as no votes are taken except concerning matters directly relating to proposed or pending legislation;
4. while the commissioners are attending a convention, association meeting, or similar gathering, if the meeting is held solely to discuss or deliberate on the board's position concerning convention resolutions, association officer elections, and similar issues that are not legally binding.

There are no comparable statutory restrictions for city council meetings.

Rules of Procedure

Each governing board has the power to adopt its own rules of procedure.[105] Enacting rules of procedure can help prevent arguments over *how* boards conduct their meetings. Boards often base their rules on *Robert's Rules of Order* or similar sources. The School of Government, for example, publishes two resources—*Suggested Rules of Procedure for the Board of County Commissioners*[106] and *Suggested Rules of Procedure for a City Council*[107]—that are adaptations of *Robert's Rules* designed specifically for North Carolina county and city governing boards.

---

105. G.S. 160A-71(c) (cities); G.S. 153A-41 (counties).

106. Trey Allen, *Suggested Rules of Procedure for the Board of County Commissioners*, 4th ed. (UNC School of Government, 2017).

107. Trey Allen, *Suggested Rules of Procedure for a City Council*, 4th ed. (UNC School of Government, 2017).

Quorum

As noted earlier, a governing board may take action only when a quorum is present. The rules for determining a quorum, which are slightly different for counties and cities, are described below.

In both counties and cities, once a quorum has been attained and the meeting convened, a member's unexcused departure does not destroy the quorum. G.S. 153A-43, for counties, and G.S. 160A-74, for cities, both provide that if a member withdraws from a meeting without being excused by a majority vote of the remaining members present, he or she is still counted as present for purposes of a quorum. In addition, the city statute provides that a member who departs without being excused is counted as voting "yes" on all matters that come before the board after he or she leaves.[108] There is no comparable provision in the county statute, but many boards of commissioners have adopted the same rule in their local rules of procedure.

Counties

G.S. 153A-43 defines a quorum as a majority of the membership of the board of commissioners, including vacancies. Thus, if a board has six members, its quorum is four, regardless of vacancies.

Cities

G.S. 160A-74 defines a quorum as a majority of the actual membership of the council, including the mayor but excluding vacant seats. Thus, if a city is governed by a five-member board plus the mayor, the actual membership of the group is six, and a quorum is four. If one seat is vacant, however, the membership becomes five, and a quorum is three.

Governing Board Action

Governing boards take action in a variety of forms including ordinances, resolutions, motions, and orders. Textbooks usually define *ordinance* as a permanent rule of conduct or authoritative law or decree imposed by a county or city on its citizens.[109] Thus, ordinances may limit the amount of noise that citizens may make, regulate how they may use their land, or require their businesses to treat sewage before discharging it into the government's system. In North Carolina, local governments also appropriate money and levy taxes by ordinance.[110]

The other sorts of actions are less precise in their meaning. Textbooks often define *resolutions* as expressions of board opinion on administrative matters[111] and *motions* as actions resulting in or expressing a decision.[112] Thus, a board might set out the unit's policy on extension of utilities by resolution while approving specific extensions by motion. In practice, the distinction is not always so carefully drawn; often one board takes actions by motion that another takes by resolution.

Voting Rules

Both county commissions and city councils are subject to complicated rules that determine whether a measure has passed. In both counties and cities, the number of board members who must vote for a measure in order for that measure to pass differs according to a number of factors: whether the measure is an ordinance or some other form of action, when the measure first comes before

---

108. G.S. 160A-75.
109. "Ordinance," *Black's Law Dictionary* (11th ed. 2019).
110. *See, e.g.*, G.S. 159-8; G.S. 160A-208.
111. "Resolution," *Black's Law Dictionary* (11th ed. 2019).
112. "Motion" (parliamentary law), *Black's Law Dictionary* (11th ed. 2019).

the governing board, and whether any members have been excused from voting on the measure. The actual provisions, however, differ between counties and cities.

Counties

The law does not regulate the manner in which boards of commissioners adopt resolutions (beyond the minimum requirement of a valid meeting with a quorum present), but several laws govern the adoption of ordinances.[113] An ordinance may be adopted at the meeting at which it is first introduced only if it receives a unanimous affirmative vote, with all members of the board present and voting. If the ordinance receives less than a unanimous vote, it may be passed by a majority of votes cast (a quorum being present) at any time within one hundred days of its introduction. This rule does not apply to the following ordinances:

- the budget ordinance (which may be passed at any meeting at which a quorum is present);
- any bond order (which always requires a public hearing before passage and in most cases requires approval by the voters as well);
- any ordinance on which the law requires a public hearing before adoption (such as a zoning ordinance);
- a franchise ordinance (which must be passed at two separate regular meetings of the board).[114]

City Ordinances

To be adopted on the day that it is first introduced, a city ordinance must be approved by a vote of at least two-thirds of the actual membership of the council, excluding vacant seats.[115] This rule applies to any city action that has the effect of an ordinance, no matter how it is labeled.[116] In determining actual membership, the mayor is not counted unless he or she has the right to vote on all questions before the board.[117] Thus, if a board has seven members and is presided over by a mayor who votes only to break ties, five members must vote in favor of an ordinance for it to be adopted on the day that it is introduced. If there is a vacant seat, however, the actual membership is then six, and only four votes are required to adopt the ordinance on that first day.

Given this special rule pertaining to the day of introduction, what constitutes introduction? The statute states that the day of introduction is the day on which the board *first votes on the subject matter* of the ordinance.[118] Examples of such a vote might include a vote to hold a hearing on the ordinance, refer it to a committee, or try to pass it.[119]

After the day on which it is introduced, an ordinance may be adopted by an affirmative vote equal to at least a majority of the board membership, including vacancies but excluding members

---

113. G.S. 153A-45 through -47.

114. *Id.* See also G.S. 153A-123(b), which prohibits the adoption of ordinances that carry criminal penalties on the date of their introduction.

115. G.S. 160A-75(c).

116. *Id.* Ordinances on which a public hearing must be held pursuant to G.S. 160D-601 are exempt from this supermajority requirement. Also, under G.S. 160A-175(b), no ordinance carrying a criminal penalty may be adopted on the date of its introduction, even with the requisite supermajority.

117. *Id.*

118. *Id.*

119. *See* Frayda Bluestein, "The Ordinance Voting Statutes and the Meaning of the 'Date of Introduction,'" *Coates' Canons: NC Local Government Law* blog (May 25, 2022), canons.sog.unc.edu/2022/05/the-ordinance-voting-statutes-and-the-meaning-of-the-date-of-introduction/.

who have been properly excused from voting. For example, a six-member board normally requires an affirmative vote of four members to adopt an ordinance. If one member is excused on a particular issue, the board is treated as having only five members on that issue, and only three need vote affirmatively for the measure to pass.

For voting purposes, nonvoting mayors are not counted in determining how many members constitute the board.[120] If there is a tie, however, the mayor's vote is counted in determining whether the requisite majority vote has been attained.[121] Thus, if a six-member board divides three to three on an issue and the mayor votes affirmatively to break the tie, the measure has received the four votes necessary for its adoption.

G.S. 160A-75 requires a majority vote of the board membership on a few other measures besides ordinances: (1) any action having the effect of an ordinance, no matter how it is labeled; (2) any measure that authorizes an expenditure of funds or commits a board to one, other than the budget ordinance or a project ordinance; and (3) any measure that authorizes, makes, or ratifies a contract.

With the exceptions just noted, the general law makes no special provision for the sort of city council vote necessary to adopt resolutions, motions, or measures other than ordinances. (Some charters do require that resolutions or other actions receive the same vote as ordinances.) For these actions the rule is that action may be taken by a majority of those present and voting, as long as a quorum is present. Thus, if a board has eight members, its quorum is five; and if only five members are present, a resolution or a motion may be adopted by a vote of only three of the five.

Excusing Members from Voting

G.S. 153A-44, for counties, and G.S. 160A-75, for cities, permit or mandate the excusal of a board member from voting for two potential conflicts of interest: (1) when the question involves his or her own financial interest, and (2) when it involves his or her official conduct. In addition, these statutes reference two other statutes, G.S. 14-234 and G.S. 160D-109, that *prohibit* a board member from voting in certain circumstances. These statutes are discussed in more detail in Chapter 7, "Ethics and Conflicts of Interest."

For financial interest and official conduct conflicts under G.S. 153A-44, county boards must vote to excuse a member according to the statute. G.S. 160A-75 is silent on city councils' procedure for excusals for these conflicts, but unless the board has adopted a procedural rule authorizing a member to be excused by the mayor or to excuse themselves, excusal should be allowed only by vote of the remaining board members.

Unless a board member is excused, he or she must vote, but the rules for mayors are slightly different than for commissioners or council members. Unless the charter provides otherwise, if a mayor is elected by and from the board, the mayor remains a board member and must vote, but a mayor who may vote only to break a tie has the option of not voting at all.[122] The statute allows, but does not require, the mayor to break a tie.[123] If the mayor refuses to break a tie, the measure is defeated.

Public Hearings and Public Comment

As noted earlier, the open meetings law allows the public to attend meetings but does not provide a right to be heard. The public has opportunities for public comment through hearings and public

120. G.S. 160A-75(c).
121. *Id.*
122. G.S. 160A-69.
123. *Id.*

comment periods. Some hearings are required,[124] such as the hearing on the budget ordinance, a bond ordinance, or a zoning ordinance or amendment. Others are held on the board's own initiative to give interested citizens an opportunity to make their views known to the board on a controversial issue, such as a noise control or towing ordinance.

State statutes also require boards of county commissioners, city councils, and school boards to offer at least one public comment period each month during a regular meeting, at which members of the public may comment on local government affairs more broadly.[125] See Chapter 10 for a more detailed discussion of citizen involvement.

The laws that require public hearings do not specify the manner in which they must be conducted; the laws only require that they be held. Nevertheless, G.S. 153A-52 and -52.1, for counties, and G.S. 160A-81 and -81.1, for cities, allow the governing board to adopt reasonable rules governing the conduct of public hearings and public comment periods. These rules may regulate such matters as allotting time to each speaker, designating who will speak for groups, selecting delegates from groups when the hearing room is too small to hold everyone who wants to attend, and maintaining order as well as decorum. The statutes requiring public hearings and comment periods create constitutionally protected rights of expression for members of the public. Due to First Amendment concerns, governing boards must be careful when regulating conduct to avoid restricting speakers based on the opinion or point of view they are expressing.

Rules for Quasi-Judicial Proceedings

Local government boards sometimes function in a quasi-judicial capacity. Examples include decisions on certain types of land use permits or zoning variances and appeals of personnel actions. In these settings, boards are limited in their process and decision-making by principles of due process, which is required because these actions affect constitutionally protected property rights. The legislature has enacted specific voting rules to avoid conflicts of interest that apply in these situations, including prohibitions on voting and deliberations if a board member has a financial interest in the outcome of the matter, fixed opinion prior to the hearing, undisclosed ex parte communications, or a close familial, business, or other associational relationship with an affected individual.[126] In addition, quasi-judicial hearings must be conducted consistent with the basic rules for a legal proceeding, including swearing in of witnesses and decisions based exclusively on evidence presented in the proceeding.[127] Only those who are qualified as witnesses or who have a stake in the outcome may speak at quasi-judicial hearings.[128]

Remote Participation in Meetings

In response to the COVID-19 pandemic, the General Assembly enacted G.S. 166A-19.24, which specifically authorized remote meetings during a Governor- or General Assembly–declared state of emergency. Outside of these designated states of emergencies, authority for remote meetings remains unclear. As a threshold matter, there is no statute that specifically provides for remote meetings. The open meetings law definition of *official meeting* includes electronic meetings, and G.S. 143-318.13(a) of the open meetings law provides notice and access requirements for electronic

---

124. Public hearings are required only when a statute specifically calls for them. *See* David Lawrence, "When Are Public Hearings Required," *Coates' Canons: NC Local Government Law* blog (August 21, 2009), canons.sog.unc.edu /2009/08/when-are-public-hearings-required/.

125. G.S. 153A-52.1 (counties); G.S. 160A-81.1 (cities); G.S. 115C-51 (schools).

126. G.S. 160D-109(d).

127. *See, e.g.*, G.S. 160D-406(d), (f).

128. G.S. 160D-406(d).

meetings.[129] Arguably, this section provides implicit authority for remote meetings, since it seems unlikely that the General Assembly would provide notice and access procedures for an illegal meeting. Unfortunately, it does not address quorum or voting. In other words, even if remote meetings broadly are permissible, local governments still do not have explicit authority allowing them to count remote participants toward quorum or allowing these participants to vote.

The North Carolina Court of Appeals has provided some clarity on this issue, at least as it pertains to boards of county commissioners. In *State* ex rel. *Cannon v. Anson County*, the court of appeals invalidated the board's actions at a remote meeting, finding that there was no quorum.[130] There, only two commissioners of seven were physically present, while four others participated via remote means.[131] The meeting did not have a quorum because the court of appeals did not count the remote participants toward quorum, and only two commissioners were physically present.[132] This opinion suggests that remote participants do not count toward quorum and consequently cannot vote, although the court did not reach the voting question. Based on the court's reasoning, boards of county commissioners may still allow board members to access meetings remotely, but they should not count remote members toward quorum and should not permit them to vote.

The court focused solely on boards of county commissioners, but its logic can easily be extended to city councils, especially given the city council voting statute's reference to physical presence.[133] City councils also should likely assume that they must have an in-person quorum and that only in-person votes count. Because this case focuses on statutory quorum requirements, appointed boards and commissions who do not have statutory quorum or other meeting requirements may still have the freedom to meet remotely, though this remains an open question. Local governments may authorize remote participation for boards that they create and appoint. Boards that wish to allow remote participation should establish policies governing when it will be allowed.

Meeting Requirements for Appointed Boards

The preceding section of this chapter focused on rules that apply to county and city governing boards. Appointed boards are, of course, subject to the open meetings law but not to many of the more specific rules described above.

For the purposes of understanding meeting requirements for appointed boards, it is helpful to consider them in two categories: those created by statute and those created by local county or city ordinance. Statutory boards include social services, public health, and ABC boards. Statutes establishing these boards include specific procedural and other requirements.[134] Other boards and commissions are created by local ordinance or resolution under the governing boards' general authority to organize the local government[135] or under more specific authority, such as that authorizing the creation of boards of adjustment.[136]

---

129. G.S. 143-318.10(d).

130. State *ex rel.* Cannon v. Anson Cnty., ___N.C. Ct. App. ___, 906 S.E.2d 9, 16–17 (2024).

131. *Id.* at 12.

132. *Id.* at 16–17.

133. G.S. 160A-75(a), (b).

134. G.S. 108A-1 through -11 (social services boards); G.S. 130A-35 (boards of health); G.S. 18B-700 (local ABC boards).

135. G.S. 153A-76 (counties); G.S. 160A-146 (cities).

136. G.S. 160D-302.

Statutes establishing or allowing the creation of specific appointed boards may include membership and procedural requirements that must be met. County and city governing boards establish other local boards by adopting ordinances, which contain the membership, purpose, and procedure under which they are to operate. Two School of Government resources are recommended for the creation and operation of these types of boards: *Suggested Rules of Procedure for Small Local Government Boards*[137] and *Creating and Maintaining Effective Local Government Citizen Advisory Committees*.[138]

Additional Resources

Additional information can be found in the "Open Government: Open Meetings" section of *Coates' Canons: NC Local Government Law* blog (canons.sog.unc.edu/category/open-government/open-meetings-open-government/). Also see the eighth edition of *Open Meetings and Local Governments in North Carolina: Some Questions and Answers* (UNC School of Government, 2017) by David M. Lawrence and Frayda S. Bluestein.

---

137. A. Fleming Bell, II, *Suggested Rules of Procedure for Small Local Government Boards*, 2nd ed. (UNC School of Government, 2012), www.sog.unc.edu/sites/default/files/sropslgbtoc.pdf.

138. Vaughn Mamlin Upshaw, *Creating and Maintaining Effective Local Government Citizen Advisory Committees* (UNC School of Government, 2010), www.sog.unc.edu/sites/default/files/additional_files/creatinglgcactoc.pdf.

Chapter 10

Citizen Involvement

Maureen M. Berner and John B. Stephens

Maureen M. Berner is a School of Government faculty member who specializes in citizen participation and program evaluation. John B. Stephens is a School of Government faculty member who specializes in citizen participation and public policy dispute resolution.

In a democratic republic, government gains its legitimacy exclusively from "the people." The most visible way this occurs is through periodic elections of representatives at all levels of government. Citizen influence can be exercised on a more regular basis, however, by communicating to those representatives—and to others in government—opinions, desires, proposals, criticisms, and even demands about what should be done to create a better community, state, and nation. Citizen involvement is a key element of the First Amendment to the U.S. Constitution—"the right of the people peaceably to assemble, and to petition the government for a redress of grievances."

This chapter presents several aspects of citizen involvement[1] in North Carolina local government. First, the tension between the philosophical and practical value of an involved citizenry for North Carolina cities and counties is examined, including the commonly cited weaknesses and problems of citizen involvement at the local level. Next, North Carolina's statutory requirements for citizen involvement are set out.[2] Third, the chapter describes particular ways government officials invite or create involvement. Primary among these are public hearings and appointed citizen boards.

1. In this chapter "citizen involvement" in local government refers to involvement by any resident of a city or county. Most forms of involvement other than voting are open to any resident of a community, regardless of U.S. citizenship status.

2. Other chapters, primarily Chapter 8, "Public Records," and Chapter 9, "Open Meetings and Other Legal Requirements for Local Government Boards," discuss the law governing public documents, open meetings, and public hearings.

Other means of outreach and response, including citizen surveys and newer avenues created by email and Web-based resources and exchange, are also covered. The chapter also notes the growth of proactive education efforts known as citizen academies and citizen police academies and closes with a description of local government employee responsibility for fostering citizen involvement.

A few passages in the state constitution form the basis of political philosophy about the importance of government's responsiveness to its citizens. Article I, section 2, of the North Carolina Constitution provides, "All political power is vested in and derived from the people; all government of right originates from the people, is founded upon their will only, and is instituted solely for the good of the whole." Later in the same article, Section 3 says, "The people of this State have the inherent, sole, and exclusive right of regulating the internal government and police thereof and of altering or abolishing their Constitution and form of government whenever it may be necessary to their safety and happiness; but every such right shall be exercised in pursuance of law and consistently with the Constitution of the United States." Finally, similar to the U.S. Constitution, Section 12 declares, "The people have a right to assemble together to consult for their common good, to instruct their representatives, and to apply to the General Assembly for redress of grievances. . . ." Such passages serve as a useful reminder that citizen involvement beyond campaigns and elections is a bedrock principle of governance in North Carolina. These very basic rights raise several questions and concerns about how those rights are exercised and about local government's responsibility to provide informal or day-to-day opportunities for citizen involvement.

Lukewarm Interest, Low Voter Turnout, and Other Common Reasons for Lack of Engagement

Does interest in local government translate into citizen involvement? For some citizens, public participation in government occurs primarily through the electoral process. For others, campaigns and elections are just the culmination of an ongoing, interactive relationship between government officials and citizens. If voting in elections is the primary measure of public participation, the data are mixed. In a February 2011 general poll of adults in North Carolina, Elon University found that 89 percent of respondents had some interest (44 percent) or a lot of interest (44.6 percent) in the "actions and activities of state and local governments."[3] Some of this interest translated into seeking out government public documents: 57 percent of respondents tried to obtain some kind of public document, the most common being crime reports, property tax records, and the names and addresses of registered sex offenders.[4]

Since that 2011 statewide survey, the main information relevant to public officials that has been gleaned from polls involves citizens' trust in government and how often they sought government documents. A 2013 Elon poll showed North Carolina residents placing higher trust in local and state government than in the federal government: "Forty-nine percent said they trust their local government to do what is right most of the time or just about always, compared to 26.5% for state government and 14% for the federal government."[5]

3. Elon University Poll, *Poll Methodology* (March 11, 2011), eloncdn.blob.core.windows.net/eu3/sites/819/2019/01/031111_PollMethodology.pdf.

4. Elon University Poll, "N.C. Residents Support State Constitutional Amendment for Open Meeting" (March 11, 2011), www.elon.edu/u/elon-poll/archive/2011-03-11/.

5. Elon University Poll, "Do NC Residents Trust Government?" (Open Government Survey, Nov. 15–18, 2013): 3, eloncdn.blob.core.windows.net/eu3/sites/819/2019/01/120413_ElonPollOpenGovt_ExecSum.pdf.

In general, national polls show that citizens trust local government more than state or federal government. A 2023 national poll showed that 67 percent of the U.S. population trust their local government, but only 59 percent trust their state government. Public trust was 41 percent in the federal executive branch (headed by the President) and 32 percent in Congress.[6] This was mirrored in a 2015 North Carolina statewide poll, conducted by Elon University, which found 53 percent of respondents trusted their local governments "just about always" or "most of the time," compared to 32 percent for state government and 22 percent for federal government.[7]

Unfortunately, public trust levels in government overall have been decreasing over the past few decades. According to Gallup, public trust in local government decreased from 69 to 66 percent from 1997 to 2021. Public trust in state government for the same time period dropped from 68 to 57 percent. Trust in federal government functions decreased much more: from 68 to 39 percent for handling international problems and from 51 to 39 percent for handling domestic problems.[8]

North Carolina voting statistics, when considered alongside the self-reported "interest in politics" discussed above, create an ambiguous picture of citizen engagement with government. According to Carolina Demography, as of September 23, 2023, North Carolina had about 7.9 million voting-eligible adults. Of those, 7.3 million, or over 92 percent, were registered voters.[9]

The percentage of voters voting in elections, however, is usually lower than the percentage of those eligible and registered to vote. National turnout in recent general elections in presidential-election years (2004–2024) ranged from 64 to 69 percent. The 2024 North Carolina voter turnout was 74 percent.[10] For North Carolina "off-year" elections (1994–2022), turnout ranged from 42 to 47 percent in 1994–2014 (with the exception of a 36 percent turnout in 2006), but it increased more recently: to 53 percent in 2018 and 51 percent in 2022.[11] For many local government elections—with votes on bond and tax issues as well as candidate races—the turnout can be very low. For example, in 2023, the North Carolina statewide turnout for municipal elections ranged from 5 to 16 percent.[12]

There is no specific data on why some North Carolina registered voters do not vote, but in general, their reasons for not voting seem to have changed. U.S. Census Bureau surveys from 2000–2016 on why people don't vote show that the "too busy/conflicting schedule" reason has decreased from 22 to 14 percent while the "did not like candidates or campaign issues" reason increased from 8 to 26 percent.[13] Shortly after the 2022 fall elections, a national poll found that voters who didn't vote were "too busy" (48 percent), didn't "like any of the candidates" (52 percent), thought

---

6. Jeffrey M. Jones, "Americans Trust Local Government Most, Congress Least," Gallup (Oct. 13, 2023), news.gallup .com/poll/512651/americans-trust-local-government-congress-least.aspx.

7. Elon University Poll, "Do N.C. Residents Trust Government?" (Open Government Survey, Feb. 16–20, 2015): 3, eloncdn.blob.core.windows.net/eu3/sites/819/2019/01/031115_ElonPoll_ExecSummary.pdf. Elon's extensive poll data archives can be found at www.elon.edu/u/elon-poll/archive/.

8. Megan Brenan, "Americans' Trust in Government Remains Low," Gallup (Sept. 30, 2021), news.gallup.com/poll /355124/americans-trust-government-remains-low.aspx.

9. Nicholas Long, "Who Are North Carolina's 7.3 Million Registered Voters? (2023)," Carolina Demography, University of North Carolina (Sept. 28, 2023), carolinademography.cpc.unc.edu/2023/09/28/who-are-north-carolinas -7-3-million-registered-voters-2023/.

10. North Carolina State Board of Elections, "Voter Turnout," www.ncsbe.gov/results-data/voter-turnout.

11. *Id.*

12. Some turnout data for local elections can be higher or lower if different level contests take place at the same time or if dates are different for municipal-only elections. For 2023 municipal-election-turnout data, see N.C. State Board of Elections, www.ncsbe.gov/results-data/voter-turnout/2023-municipal-election-turnout.

13. Thom File, "Characteristics of Voters in the Presidential Election of 2016: Population Characteristics," U.S. Census Bureau (Sept. 2018), www.census.gov/content/dam/Census/library/publications/2018/demo/P20-582.pdf.

their "vote doesn't matter" (48 percent), and didn't have "transportation to the polls" (41 percent), among other reasons.[14]

Thus, while the vast majority of eligible North Carolina citizens register to vote, only three-quarters or less participate in government through voting in general elections,[15] and the number is much lower than that for local government elections.

What explains this low rate of participation? Low voter turnout in many elections could be due to one or more of four factors: (1) citizens feel disconnected from government, (2) citizens may not have time or access (or face other individual constraints), (3) there is a lack of encouragement or support from the government, and (4) the specific issue at hand seems either too complex or long range.

First, citizens who do not feel a positive connection to government express sentiments of apathy, alienation, or distrust. There are not a lot of polls on voter attitudes toward North Carolina state and local government officials, but two questions in the 2009 Elon poll were about elected state and local officials. Seventy-three percent of the respondents to these questions believed corruption is common among elected officials, and 65 percent believed elected officials in North Carolina are more focused on their own interests than the public interest.[16]

Citizen apathy regarding government may be an important reason for low voter turnout. Some individuals may feel that a single vote does not matter, and others might believe the local, state, or national political situation is simply hopeless. In either case, the perception may exist that voting for one candidate over another will not result in meaningful change. A similar view suggests that candidates are all alike and choosing one rather than another won't make a difference.

A second reason people do not vote may involve personal constraints that go beyond a lack of time. In some cases, citizens cannot get to polling places when they are open. Policies to extend polling place hours, create multiple polling locations and early voting options, and expand electronic voting and voting by mail have all been put in place to address voting accessibility problems. "Lack of time" may also be a variant of voter apathy—if citizens believe voting in an election has little impact, it is no surprise that waiting in line at a polling place would not feel worth their effort.

Third, the public may not feel that government officials are making an obvious and consistent effort to encourage and support citizen participation. Often, when government employees picture an "involved citizen," they imagine an upset citizen. Anecdotes suggest, for example, that if a citizen makes an appointment with a city manager, it is probably not to compliment the local government on a job well done. Local government officials thus tend to anticipate citizen involvement as if it were a problem to solve. Many citizens are aware of this perception. If citizens feel their involvement is unwelcome, it is not surprising that they will be reluctant to participate in the governing process.

Finally, low voter turnout may be due to the issue being considered. Citizens may feel no connection to or may not understand the issue on the ballot, whether it involves a complex matter—such as municipal water and sewer system management, planning, or rate-setting—or a long-range project that seems to have no foreseeable impact. A proposal to build a big-box retail store may elicit a sizable citizen response, positive or negative, because the project's impact is immediate, and the

14. Taylor Orth, "What Reasons Do Americans Give for Not Voting in 2022?," YouGov-USA (2022), today.yougov.com/politics/articles/44434-what-reasons-do-americans-give-not-voting-2022. The top three reasons: I don't like any of the candidates (52 percent); my vote doesn't matter (48 percent); and I was too busy (48 percent). The next three reasons: Didn't have time to research the candidates and proposals (46 percent); didn't have a way to get to the polls (40 percent); and I would have to vote in person and don't want to (39 percent).

15. N.C. State Board of Elections, "General Election Turnout Stats" (1972–2000), www.ncsbe.gov/results-data/voter-turnout#general.

16. Elon University Poll, "N.C. Residents Cynical about Politicians" (Nov. 23, 2009), www.elon.edu/docs/e-web/elonpoll/112309_ElonPollDATA2.pdf.

decision appears clear-cut. On the other hand, a project that updates a community's long-term land use plan may be perceived as overly complex and having too remote of an impact and thus may not generate much citizen interest and input.

These four reasons for low voter turnout concern the citizens themselves. But what about the government's role? Why don't governments seek greater citizen involvement? School of Government training sessions with government employees indicated that some of their reasons mirror the citizens' reasons:

- Encouraging public participation takes significant time and resources but has uncertain payoffs.
- There is a lack of resources with which to provide adequate information and administrative support. Officials mentioned frustration when complex issues are involved; extensive time and effort are required to educate citizens before they can meaningfully participate in decision-making.
- Only a small, vocal, and typically oppositional segment usually participates in the policy process; people who are generally satisfied with government policies and programs do not tend to attend meetings.
- Government officials may fear raising expectations that may not be met.
- Encouraging citizen input may mean giving up or losing some control over the decision-making process.

Thoughts on Effective Citizen Engagement

Citizen involvement in local government has taken on new levels of significance in the wake of close elections, contentious voting processes, and heightened rhetoric. Defining and assessing the costs and benefits of citizen involvement generally and in relation to particular topics is challenging. Beyond staff time, preparation of materials, and other "hard costs" are the important and often amorphous political or civic costs. Informally, officials cite the political and practical dangers in an inadvertent mismatch between citizens' and government officials' priorities. While interest groups may actively participate in the governing process, there are many citizens who do not vote in most

Focus on Citizen Participation in the Local Government Budget Process

The annual local government budget process is a great example of the variety of ways officials can involve citizens. Along with other budget process requirements, local governments must provide an opportunity for citizens to comment on the budget before it is approved. Citizens can be involved through workshops, public hearings, and surveys—there are a wide variety of ways for local governments to seek public input on the annual budget. Some local governments limit citizen involvement and only hear public comments in formal meetings. Other efforts are much more active, such as the participatory budgeting process that Greensboro introduced in 2014, Durham in 2018, Mecklenburg County in 2022, and Raleigh in 2023. Citizen advisory boards (appointed citizen boards) are another common tool to directly engage community members in budget processes.

For more on public participation in the budget process, see Whitney Alfonso, "Citizen Engagement: Active Participation," *Death & Taxes* blog (March 27, 2023), deathandtaxes.sog.unc.edu/citizen-engagement-active-participation/.

elections, let alone attend hearings or other events. This includes those who are satisfied with government services, those unable or unwilling to voice their opinion, and those too discouraged to participate.

For the local governments involved, what are the benefits of participation? First, at a minimum level, participation means sharing information. One of the benefits of public participation cited by local government officials is that citizens will have an increased understanding of problems and thus can offer possible solutions. This interchange lays the foundation for better decisions. For example, active communication with citizens can help government officials decide if a particular policy option is feasible.

Is it acceptable to trade efficiency for effectiveness? After all, efforts to more fully involve the public take time and resources. The resulting decision may be more effective, but the process leading to that decision may be difficult and time-consuming. From a cost-benefit perspective, however, making better and more popular decisions may outweigh the significant costs involved in increasing citizen participation.

Efficiency and effectiveness are only two values underlying a government decision-making process. As discussed above, citizen participation is a fundamental democratic value in North Carolina, and the response to the question of why instigate, continue, or expand efforts to involve the public in local government falls back on assumptions, values, and aspirations that are part of the appropriate relationship between citizens and government in a democratic society.

To foster this appropriate relationship, local governments need more information on practical, efficient, and successful ways of involving citizens in their work.

A recent survey of Oregon local government officials shows a distinction between the methods they see as most effective for sharing information and the methods that are most effective for gaining public input on budget decisions. The respondents considered government websites (70 percent) and social media (60 percent) as very or extremely important for distributing information. Interestingly, traditional methods such as mail/posters (56 percent) and word-of-mouth (52 percent) are still considered very to extremely important by a significant portion of participants. As for collecting public input, Oregon officials considered public hearings (83 percent) and citizen committees (66 percent) to be the most important forums.[17]

A 2011 study on citizen participation examined the perceptions and goals of staff, elected officials, and highly involved citizens in four larger North Carolina cities.[18] When asked what constituted effective participation by citizens, each constituency expressed different expectations. For example,

> . . . elected officials tend to define effective public participation by reflection and a lack of citizen complaints. For staff, [effective participation] means providing information to the public and encouraging them to act as macro-level community advocates[,] . . . thus making informed citizens a valuable resource to get other members in the community to understand tough, controversial, or pressing decisions made by local officials. [Staff members] want citizens to be advocates for the organization out in the community as much as they want to hear from citizens what "the community" thinks.
>
> Citizens view effective participation through a different lens. Overall, [they] believe an effective participation system should include two-way communication (between all

---

17. Frankline Muthomi, "Perceived Values of Public Participation Practices in Budgeting: Insights from Incorporated Local Governments in Oregon," *State and Local Government Review* 56, no. 2 (June 2024): 6.

18. Maureen Berner, Justin Amos, and Ricardo Morse, "What Constitutes Effective Citizen Participation? Views from Stakeholders," *Public Administration Quarterly* 35 (Spring 2011).

> three stakeholder groups), more opportunity to be heard earlier in the process (not in late May at the budget public hearing, for example), and involvement in honest dialogue with staff and elected officials regarding the budget and [the citizens'] role in the process.[19]

There are several organizations and initiatives focusing on civic engagement and supporting local government officials' work for citizen involvement. The National Civic League promotes effective citizen–public official engagement through their annual "All-America City Award" (a competition recognizing communities that leverage civic engagement, collaboration, inclusiveness, and innovation to successfully address local issues[20]) and resources including

- the All-America Conversations Toolkit, a guide for events that bridge divides in the community and engage residents in talking about the community they want to create together,[21] and
- the Promising Practices Database.[22]

The Bloomberg Harvard City Leadership Initiative, in its 2023 *City Leader Guide on Civic Engagement*, states that those wanting to improve citizen involvement in government should leave behind best practice prescriptions and aim for "participatory public problem-solving." In other words, citizens shouldn't be consulted at only prescribed parts of the governing process, such as formal budget hearings, but engaged across the whole effort: from design to implementation to evaluation of budget priorities. "When engagement efforts fail," the *Guide* states, it is often because the engagement itself was not designed to align stakeholder input with desired outcomes."[23]

The Government Finance Officers Association (GFOA) also emphasizes the importance of understanding the purpose of citizen engagement and aligning the implementation of efforts to achieve that purpose. As it notes, "While public participation efforts can be extremely valuable, superficial or poorly designed efforts may simply waste valuable staff time and financial resources, and at worst can increase public cynicism if the public perceives that its input has not been taken seriously."[24]

Given local governments' wish to engage its citizens at some level, of all the options available for reaching citizens, what are some best practices to incorporate citizen input in a meaningful fashion?[25]

In a broad assessment of twenty-first-century public participation, Tina Nabatchi and Matt Leighninger highlight the rise of incivility in public hearings and other settings and identify a mismatch between traditional participation methods and contemporary work and lifestyles. They argue that many parts of our "civic infrastructure" are failing both citizens and government officials. Their

---

19. *Id.* at 158–59.

20. More information about the award can be found on the National Civic League website, www.nationalcivicleague.org/america-city-award/.

21. The free toolkit can be downloaded at www.nationalcivicleague.org/resources/america-conversations-toolkit/.

22. The database, which features successful civic engagement projects in the U.S., can be found at www.nationalcivicleague.org/promising-practices-database/ (note: membership is required for access).

23. *City Leader Guide on Civic Engagement: Designing Pathways for Participatory Problem-Solving* (May 2023): 9, www.cityleadership.harvard.edu/wp-content/uploads/migrate/BHCLI_CivicEngagement_0000CG.pdf?cid=1285.

24. Government Finance Officers Association, "Public Engagement in the Budget Process" (Budgeting and Forecasting Best Practices, 2018), www.gfoa.org/materials/public-engagement-in-the-budget-process.

25. In a 1998–1999 survey, most North Carolina local government officials said that the *least* effective way to involve citizens was public hearings. Surprisingly, most of them also said that the *most* effective way to involve citizens was public hearings.

critique leads to guidance on how to more effectively engage citizens in both short-term individual actions (such as responding to a survey) and working in small groups on community issues.[26]

Legal Requirements

"Participation" is a broad term. By state law, the main requirement relating to participation for local governments is that they provide an opportunity for members of the public to observe the decision-making process in open meetings and to comment on major proposals. The open meetings law, described in Chapter 9, "Open Meetings and Other Legal Requirements for Local Government Boards," covers the responsibilities of government officials to give the public notice of and access to meetings of all public bodies.[27] This law also applies to advisory boards and meetings where no decisions are made.[28] The public records law, discussed in Chapter 8, "Public Records," covers the government's responsibility to make records related to government activities available for public review.[29] Both of these sets of laws focus on the public's access to government information and actions.

On the other hand, what responsibilities does the government have to ascertain the public's view of government decisions? Local governments are required to obtain opinions and feedback from citizens in two ways: (1) in public comment periods held during regular meetings of county commissions or city councils and (2) in public hearings.

Legal Requirements in Relation to Public Comment Periods

In 2005, the North Carolina General Assembly mandated that city councils, boards of county commissioners, and boards of education provide at least one period for public comment per month at a regular board meeting.[30] The history of the act, as well as case law on citizen comment periods as "limited public forums" under the First Amendment, both suggest that the board probably must allow comment on any subject that is within the local government's jurisdiction.[31] A board can, however, adopt reasonable regulations governing the conduct of the public comment period, including but not limited to rules setting time limits for speakers and providing for (1) the designation of spokespersons for groups supporting or opposing the same position, (2) the selection of delegates from groups holding the same position when the meeting hall's capacity is exceeded, and (3) the maintenance of order and decorum in the conduct of the hearing. This authorization of regulations is taken almost verbatim from earlier statutes governing the conduct of public hearings by counties and municipalities, respectively.[32]

---

26. Tina Nabatchi and Matt Leighninger, *Public Participation for 21st Century Democracy* (John Wiley & Sons, 2015).
27. G.S. 143-318.10(a).
28. G.S. 143-318.10(a).
29. G.S. 132-1.
30. G.S. 153A-52.1 (counties) and G.S. 160A-81.1 (cities).
31. For more details, see Kristi Nickodem and Kristina Wilson, "Responding to First Amendment Audits: Examples of Forum Determinations," *Coates' Canons: NC Local Government Law* blog (November 17, 2022), canons.sog.unc.edu/2022/11/responding-to-first-amendment-audits-examples-of-forum-determinations, and Frayda Bluestein, "Public Comment Period Policies: What's Legal?," *Coates' Canons: NC Local Government Law* blog (March 15, 2016), canons.sog.unc.edu/2016/03/public-comment-period-policies-whats-legal/.
32. G.S. 153A-52 (counties) and G.S. 160A-81 (cities). Guidance on the law concerning public comment periods and discretion in their structure and management is available from the School of Government. *See* John Stephens and A. Fleming Bell, II, "Public Comment at Business Meetings of Local Government Boards, Part One: Guidelines for Good Practices," *Popular Government* 62 (Summer 1997): 2–14; A. Fleming Bell, II, John Stephens, and Christopher Bass, "Public Comment at Business Meetings of Local Government Boards, Part Two: Common Practices and

Legal Issues in Relation to Public Hearings

As discussed in more detail below, public hearings are held for many types of activities involving government decision-making. Some of these activities are very common, such as city rezonings and annexations and city or county annual budget adoptions. Sometimes the laws requiring a public hearing are relatively obscure, as in the case of the adoption of an ordinance to franchise ambulance services[33] or regarding changes to the schedule of stormwater charges.[34] Whether a public hearing, or any other type of opportunity for public involvement, is necessary or required depends on the particular issue or action being considered. Local government officials should research the legal requirements for citizen notification and involvement in each case.[35]

Ways to Involve Citizens

Municipal and county government leaders in North Carolina can structure opportunities for citizen input in several ways. Two common and traditional means are public hearings and appointed citizen boards (or citizen advisory boards). Other methods with which governments can solicit citizen participation are also described below. These include community visioning; surveys; electronic communication, including email, websites, and social media; old and new forms of television, radio, and print media; and citizen academies.

Public Hearings and Appointed Citizen Boards

Though voting is an individual and private action (i.e., by secret ballot), taken cumulatively, it is the "voice of the people." Citizens also participate in government on an individual basis through contact with representatives, whether by phone or email or in more informal settings, such as in line at the grocery store or in a restaurant or similar venue. This one-on-one contact with public officials, on the one hand, and voting in elections, on the other, represent two ends of the spectrum of types of citizen involvement with government. In the middle of this spectrum are other types of citizen interaction with government, such as attendance at appointed committee and public hearings, participation in

Example of Notice for a Public Hearing

The Oak Island Town Council will hold a Public Hearing beginning at 6:00 p.m., or as soon thereafter as possible, on Tuesday, May 14, 2024, in Council Chambers at the Oak Island Town Hall, 4601 E. Oak Island Drive. Each speaker will be allotted three minutes. Written comments may be submitted for the record to the town clerk no later than 12 noon the day of the hearing, or during the hearing. The purpose of the Public Hearing is to receive citizens' comments on a Proposed Text Amendment to Article 10 Part IV of the Unified Development Ordinance—Sign Regulations. The proposed amendments would reduce the maximum height of Column/Pole signs to 15 feet. . . .*

*"Town of Oak Island Public Notice," *The State Port Pilot* (May 8, 2024), stateportpilot.com/classifieds/public_notices/pdfdisplayad_61432708-0d42-11ef-bc0a-fb0892663781.html.

Legal Standards," *Popular Government* 63 (Fall 1997): 27–37; Fleming Bell, "Statutorily Required Public Comment Periods: What Are They and How Do They Work?" *Coates Canons: NC Local Government Law* blog (May 20, 2010), canons.sog.unc.edu/2010/05/statutorily-required-public-comment-periods-what-are-they-and-how-do-they-work/.

33. G.S. 153A-250.

34. G.S. 160A-314(a1)(1) (cities) and G.S. 153A-277(a1)(1) (counties).

35. For a summary of the types of local government decision-making activities for which public hearings are required, see David M. Lawrence, "When Are Public Hearings Required," *Coates' Canons: NC Local Government Law* blog (August 21, 2009), canons.sog.unc.edu/2009/08/when-are-public-hearings-required/.

public comment periods, and electronic communications such as blogs and social media. All of these activities are characterized by both government and citizen input to varying degrees. The "Example of Citizen Participation" sidebar illustrates how citizens participate in the common local government process of obtaining and using federal funds through the Community Development Block Grant program.

Public Hearings

Public hearings are a long-standing way that municipal and county elected boards have formally obtained citizen input. As described above, some local government actions can be taken only after a public hearing is held. However, boards of county commissioners (BOCCs) and city councils (CCs) can convene hearings for any matter (other than matters that must be discussed in closed meetings). A hearing can occur as a single agenda item among other matters considered at a governing board's regular business meeting, or it can be held as a separate meeting. In a typical public hearing, citizens are asked to address a topic, question, or proposal being considered by an appointed citizen board or by the principal legislative body (i.e., the BOCC or CC). There may already be a draft ordinance or written policy proposal, and citizens' opinions are solicited on those matters. Alternatively, the issue could be a more general matter of current interest. The board typically regulates the topic and how long and the order in which people speak. Otherwise, there are no legal restrictions on how the hearing is conducted.[36]

Example of Citizen Participation: Requirements for Federal Community Development Block Grant Funding

A grantee must develop and follow a detailed plan which provides for, and encourages, citizen participation and which emphasizes participation by persons of low- or moderate-income, particularly residents of predominantly low- and moderate-income neighborhoods, slum or blighted areas, and areas in which the grantee proposes to use CDBG funds. The plan must:

- Provide citizens with reasonable and timely access to local meetings, information, and records related to the grantee's proposed and actual use of funds.
- Provide for public hearings to obtain citizen views and to respond to proposals and questions at all stages of the community development program, including at least the development of needs, the review of proposed activities, and review of program performance.
- Provide for timely written answers to written complaints and grievances.
- Identify how the needs of non-English speaking residents will be met in the case of public hearings where a significant number of non-English speaking residents can be reasonably expected to participate.

Source: U.S. Department of Housing and Urban Development, CDBG Block Grant Program, www.hud.gov/hud-partners/community-cdbg.

Public hearings vary widely in terms of length, whether people speak for themselves or for a group, whether the hearing is routine with few or no speakers, or whether it draws a large crowd and speakers express strong emotions. As a matter of fairness, equal time (or at least an equal opportunity to speak) is reserved for proponents and opponents of a draft ordinance. Often, proponents and

36. Decisions by boards of adjustment, however, must take place in a quasi-judicial public hearing. See Chapter 25, "Planning, Land Use, and Development," for details about rules for some of these more specialized public hearings.

Formats for Meetings That Satisfy Public Hearing Goals

- Comments and/or questions submitted in writing at the meeting, and responses made by local government staff or elected board.
- Polling the room—seeking views based on particular questions, especially if there is more than one proposal being considered, or there are particular changes sought in a draft ordinance/plan/policy.
- Splitting the audience into small groups for "kitchen-table" style discussion, which can allow more people to speak, in a more informal way, and have give-and-take conversations with local government staff or elected board members.
- Board of county commissioners or city council convenes meetings in different parts of the community—moving away from its regular meeting place—as a way to be more accessible to citizens in certain neighborhoods.

Source: Debra Henzey, John B. Stephens, and Patrick Liedtka, "Listening to Citizens: County Commissioners on the Road," *Popular Government* 64 (Spring 1999): 17–28.

opponents will alternate, with all speakers on behalf of one side speaking, followed by all speakers on the other. Frequently, however, opponents outnumber proponents. As mentioned above, a common complaint about public hearings is that a few individuals who oppose an action attend, and many other citizens who quietly agree with a draft ordinance stay home.

Another common approach is to have people sign up in advance to speak. Usually, a sheet is available in the meeting room, and potential speakers add their names to it shortly before the hearing begins. Again, the structure of hearings varies widely across the state; the formality of a particular hearing often hinges on its size and the prevailing culture in a specific jurisdiction.

Sign-up sheets present both advantages and disadvantages. A benefit of this practice is that the government may be able to identify active potential volunteers for citizen positions on boards or commissions. On the other hand, if individuals must record their names, positions, and/or contact information, they may be inhibited from speaking in the first place. Because there are no strictures on the format for many kinds of public hearings, BOCCs and CCs may employ other approaches for receiving public input during the hearings. For example, local governments may hold public forums or other special outreach or hearing-like events. In this format, the public's questions and comments are the centerpiece of the event.

The "Formats for Meetings That Satisfy Public Hearing Goals" sidebar lists various ways to conduct a hearing. The fundamental objective is to provide citizens a fair and equal opportunity, in a public arena, to express their views and have them heard and recorded by the BOCC, CC, or a body that reports to the local elected governing board. What usually distinguishes hearings from other forms of citizen involvement is that the hearing is structured as part of the board's decision-making process where a particular action is pending.

Appointed Citizen Boards

Another common form of structured citizen involvement is the appointed citizen board (ACB), in which a BOCC or a CC appoints members of the community to a committee, board, or commission. City and county elected boards have full or partial control over ACBs, whose powers and scope of work vary widely. Many are advisory and have little direct influence over resources and modest to moderate influence over policies or personnel. Some, however, have oversight of or policy-making power over departments, agencies, or programs, and some make regulatory decisions.

Appointed Citizen Boards—Powers and Responsibilities

Higher-Level Boards

- Render binding decisions (e.g., board of adjustment)
- Make policies that can be reviewed and changed by elected board (e.g., planning board)
- Review ongoing programs (e.g., social services)
- Hire and fire staff (e.g., social services, mental health)
- Hear appeals

Lower-Level Boards

- Hear complaints
- Serve as a sounding board (representing different viewpoints on the board or providing opportunities for citizens to make presentations)
- Make recommendations to address a particular problem (at the advisory board's initiative or at the direction of the elected board)

Most often, ACBs are formed by and operate at the discretion of a single BOCC or CC. A handful of ACBs must follow state statutory requirements concerning membership and duties; most prominent among these are county social service, health, and county or regional mental health (Mental Health/Developmental Disabilities/Substance Use Services) boards. Occasionally, the federal government can require citizen participation as a condition in order for the local jurisdiction to receive federal funds. For example, the U.S. Department of Housing and Urban Development requires that recipients of its funds, most notably community development block grants, develop and follow a detailed citizen participation plan (see "Example of Citizen Participation" sidebar above).[37]

Common city-appointed citizen boards include parks and recreation boards, planning boards, and zoning boards of adjustment. In larger communities, typical ACBs address greenways and/or open space, alcoholic beverage control, downtown revitalization, and public housing. Many counties also make appointments to a wide variety of boards. Common county ACBs are health, social service, planning, and jury commission boards and county-level or regional boards responsible for mental health, developmental disabilities, and substance abuse services (the technical term for these is "area authority"). Larger jurisdictions may even have policies on how appointments are made, such as Mecklenburg County, where the Appointment Policy includes details on eligibility, the nomination process, voting procedures, terms, attendance requirements, removal of members, and reporting requirements, among others.[38]

A key difference between city and county ACBs is that several county boards are created by statute rather than by an elected board. County human services boards, for example, have statutory obligations, sometimes include elected officials, and may be authorized to enforce laws and create regulations. Thus, some common county boards or committees have distinct powers while at the same time serving in an advisory role on certain matters to the county commission (these types of boards are discussed in other chapters of this publication). Issues or areas addressed by these boards, commissions, and councils may include transportation, airports, adult care homes,

37. 24 C.F.R. § 91.225.

38. Mecklenburg County Board of Commissioners, Appointment Policy, bocc.mecknc.gov/Advisory-Boards/Appointment-Policy.

juvenile crime prevention, nursing homes, volunteer fire departments or fire districts, community colleges, aging, and tourism and conventions.[39]

Some types of boards include appointments from more than one local government jurisdiction. Economic development boards, for example, are commonly made up of members appointed by separate towns and the county. The membership of some ACBs must include appointees with designated skills or training set by law or regulation. For example, state law mandates that county boards of health have eleven members and include a doctor, a dentist, a veterinarian, a registered nurse, an optometrist, a pharmacist, a professional engineer, a county commissioner, and three members of the public. The membership must also "reasonably reflect the population make-up of the jurisdiction."[40]

Several of the more populous counties have dozens of ACBs. For example, at the time of this writing, Guilford County has more than fifty boards and commissions. However, the number of ACBs is not indicative of the importance of citizen involvement to a particular jurisdiction or reflective of the opportunities for citizens to be involved. Beyond legal requirements, factors influencing the establishment of ACBs include (1) BOCC or CC interest in addressing issues in depth, (2) capacity to provide staff and other resources to support ACB operations, and (3) the availability of interested and qualified citizens to serve on ACBs.

> **Example of a Board That Requires Special Skills**
>
> According to the N.C. State Historic Preservation Office, "When a local government decides to provide for the preservation of the historical, cultural, or archaeological resources within its jurisdiction, it can pass an ordinance to create a historic preservation commission. Members of a preservation commission are selected by the local governing board from the general public. A majority of the members must demonstrate a special interest in history, architecture, archaeology, or related fields. . . . [T]he creation of such commissions is a local option authorized and governed by NC GS 160D-940 through 160D-951, 160D-102, 160D-303, 160D-404(c), and 105-278."*
>
> *North Carolina State Historic Preservation Office, "About Historic Preservation Commissions," www.hpo.nc.gov/about-historic-preservation-commissions#Whatpowerdoesacommissionhave-55.

Local jurisdictions that are thinking about forming and managing ACBs should consider the following factors that distinguish the nature and types of boards.

1. ***Substance of the work.*** The subject matter addressed by the board is usually reflected in its name. Common areas addressed are social services, planning and zoning, transportation, environmental protection, neighborhood/community development, senior citizen services, parks and recreation, cemeteries, and juries, among others.
2. ***Geographic reach.*** The city or county jurisdiction of the governing board is typically the geographic area of concern. As noted above, however, some common ACBs address city–county, region, or state government–local government matters.
3. ***Powers and responsibilities.*** The authority and duties of local government ACBs vary significantly. Almost all ACBs serve as a venue in which citizen concerns, complaints, and suggestions may be heard and to which proposals are referred by the governing body for detailed consideration and, possibly, recommendations for action. As the

39. Information regarding prevalent types of boards is drawn from the authors' review of North Carolina city and county government websites and consultations with county and city leaders and employees.

40. For full details on membership of county boards of health, multicounty boards of health, and human services boards, see G.S. 130A-35(b), G.S. 130A-37, and G.S. 153A-77.

Example of a County Board Description

The Perquimans County Economic Development Commission, working in cooperation with its many regional and North Carolina economic development partners, provides a wide range of incentives and assistance to companies that can provide quality jobs for County residents. The Town Council for Hertford appoints two members for two-year terms. One member is a councilor and the other can be a citizen-at-large. Note that a citizen-at-large is not required; at the time of this writing, the members were the Hertford mayor, a councilperson, and the town manager.*

*Town of Hertford, "Boards, Commissions, and Committees," townofhertfordnc.com/boards.

"Appointed Citizen Boards—Powers and Responsibilities" sidebar indicates, however, some boards possess greater rule-making, executive, and even legislative authority (including hiring, firing, and evaluation of high-level staff members[41] and making binding decisions that can only be reviewed by a court).[42]

4. ***Duration and permanence.*** BOCCs and CCs are authorized to appoint temporary task forces, study groups, or committees of which citizen involvement is an important part. These single-topic ACBs are intended to be temporary in nature. They are typically created by passage of a motion specifying the focus of the group and a time limit for completing the work and making a recommendation to the governing body. Other ACBs are long-standing or permanent primarily due to the ongoing nature of the matters they address, such as community planning and economic development, parks and recreation, mental health, social services, and the like. These types of committees are often created by local ordinance. Others are established and regulated by state law such that the BOCC or CC cannot abolish them.
5. ***Membership.*** Most people are eligible to serve on ACBs by simply being an adult resident of the town or county. State law does not, however, restrict appointments to only residents of the jurisdiction, and nonresidents are common on some boards. Membership may be restricted according to other criteria. Youth commissions, for example, are often limited to young adults. Some localities may only appoint people to ACBs who are U.S. citizens or are registered to vote. Others may prohibit individuals with criminal records or a potential conflict of interest; they may also require an oath of office for certain ACBs.[43] Members of BOCCs and CCs (and/or other government employees) often recruit people to fill seats on certain ACBs. Often, current members of ACBs will recommend people to fill vacancies; these recommendations may include citizens who have previously attended meetings or participated in other ACB activities. It is not unusual for local governments to have ACB recruitment materials and applications readily available on their websites.

41. For example, the powers of the board of social services to appoint the director of social services under G.S. 108A-12 and the powers of an area mental health, developmental disabilities, and substance abuse board to employ an area director under G.S. 122C-121.

42. Decisions by a board of adjustment may be appealed to a court for review under G.S. 160D-1401.

43. *See* City of Charlotte, *Handbook for Advisory Board, Commission & Committee Members* (July 2023), www.charlottenc.gov/files/sharedassets/city/v/1/city-government/departments/documents/clerks-office/boards-commissions/boards-handbook-fall-2023.pdf.

Figure 10.1 Levels of Authority

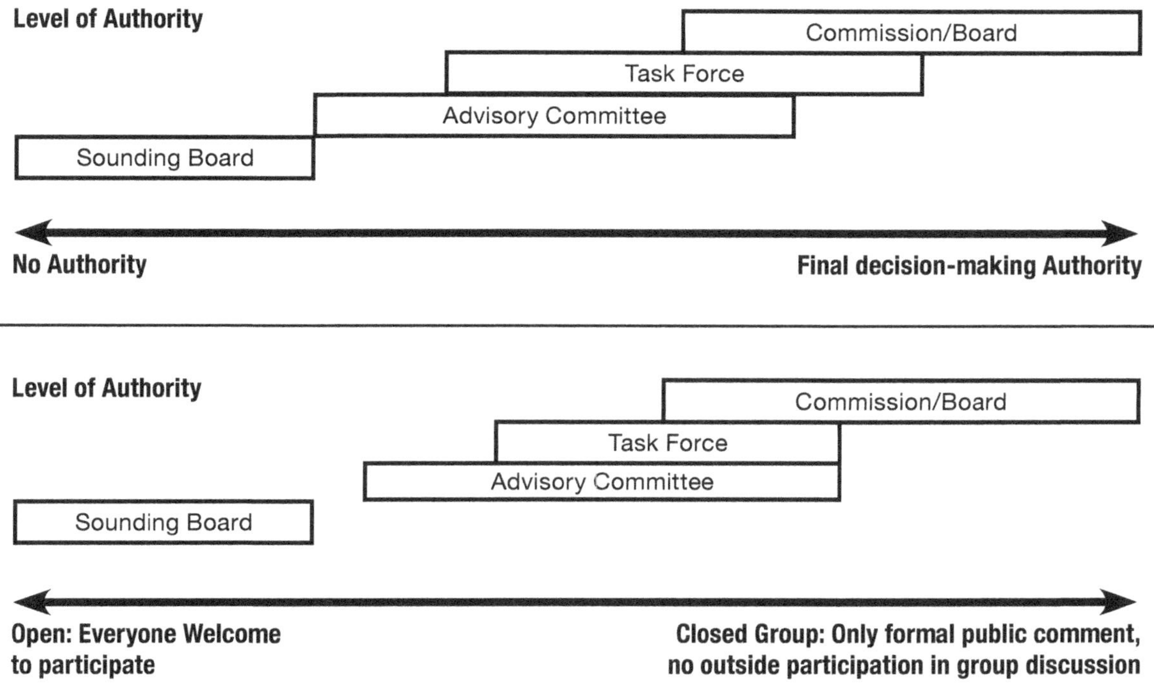

Source: Jeanne Lawson, "Choosing a Format for Public Advisory Groups," *Participation Quarterly* (December 1994).

Figure 10.1 illustrates four basic types of ACBs and their relative levels of formality, authority, and open participation. The first of these, a *sounding board,* solicits views on a topic or proposal. It is not expected to reach consensus or give specific recommendations. Membership is open, less formal, and its duration is normally short to medium term. An *advisory committee,* as its name implies, advises decision-makers on issues, options, and the like, and may serve as a liaison to a neighborhood, constituency, or business group. Members are officially appointed, and its duration can either be medium term or ongoing. A *task force* focuses on an issue-specific recommendation for action or a detailed evaluation of alternatives. Its membership is often officially appointed and is usually smaller than an advisory committee. Its duration can vary greatly. While normally temporary, a task force could operate short, medium, or long term. Finally, *commissions* or *boards* vary the most in purpose, addressing any of a range of topics and sharing various characteristics with the other three types of ACBs. They are of ongoing duration, and members are officially appointed. In North Carolina, they usually have the greatest level of responsibility, some or all of which is spelled out by state law and local ordinance.

Other entities, such as neighborhood councils, a related type of group found in several larger North Carolina cites, often function officially outside of government but still provide a structured opportunity for public input. Homeowner associations or local nonprofit organizations can also serve as a conduit for public views to reach government. These groups and organizations provide grassroots ways for the public to provide feedback from the community to city officials. In some locations, umbrella groups representing multiple participating organizations can represent community views to the local government, in the same vein as chambers of commerce. These can be set

Raleigh's Reinstatement of Citizen Advisory Councils

"Raleigh neighborhoods will once again have a say in city council decisions. On Tuesday, the Raleigh City Council voted unanimously to reinstate Citizen Advisory Councils or CACs. Tuesday's decision reverses a previous council's to disband the grassroots groups that helped decide the fate of development for nearly 50 years. Before the city eliminated the program, there were 18 CACs; half continued to meet even without official recognition from the city. Each CAC represents a different part of Raleigh. . . . The Raleigh City Council created the RCAC 50 years ago in 1974 with the help of Raleigh's first African-American mayor, Clarence Lightner. The RCAC said its purpose is to give a voice to all Raleigh residents. Also, the CACs gave people a voice when developers wanted to rezone land within their neighborhoods. CAC members would vote to recommend or reject projects. . . . The CAC groups will get free access to meet in city facilities and be able to use city-owned technology for their meetings."*

*"Raleigh's Reinstatement of Citizen Advisory Councils Empowers Grassroots Groups," WRAL News (February 6, 2024), https://www.wral.com/story/raleigh-s-reinstatement-of-citizen-advisory-councils-empowers-grassroots-groups/21271060/.

up to provide feedback for particular areas of the local jurisdiction. Examples include the Citizens Advisory Council for the City of High Point[44] and the Citizen Advisory Committee for the Environment for Granville County.[45]

Community Visioning

Community visioning, also known as strategic planning, is an increasingly common method of soliciting citizen involvement and typically addresses long-term goals of a city, county, or region. Often, a task force, such as described above, is formed for six to twelve months' duration and seeks community input and "buy-in" through active citizen participation during the decision process. Participation can involve anything from being an appointed member of the task force and investing many hours in meetings to being interviewed or surveyed for one-time input. City or county governments may initiate community visioning or may participate in an effort launched by a chamber of commerce or some other business, civic, or nonprofit group. A community visioning process can use various approaches to involve stakeholders (see Table 10.1).

Surveys

Surveys are another way for local governments to actively seek public input. In 2017, dozens of local governments in North Carolina conducted citizen surveys and shared them with the School of Government.[46]

Surveys can be very useful for gathering information from the public. They offer (1) the ability to gather direct, and often quantifiable, answers to questions; (2) anonymity and thus the possibility of obtaining more responses and more honest responses; and (3) randomness, or the likelihood of obtaining a true cross-section of views from the public. Surveys can have several disadvantages,

44. City of High Point, Citizens Advisory Council, www.highpointnc.gov/1644/Citizens-Advisory-Council.

45. Granville County, Citizens Advisory Committee for Environmental Affairs, www.granvillecounty.org/339/Citizens-Advisory-Committee-for-Environm. For more details about the benefits and costs of ACBs, including guidance and policies for the establishment and operation of these groups, see Vaughn M. Upshaw, *Creating and Maintaining Effective Local Government Citizen Advisory Committees* (UNC School of Government, 2010).

46. For information about conducting surveys as well as specific examples, see "Citizen Surveys by Local Governments in North Carolina" on the School of Government's Public Participation microsite, www.sog.unc.edu/resources/microsites/public-participation/citizen-surveys-local-governments-north-carolina.

Table 10.1 Example of Different Levels of Involvement in a Community Visioning Process

Telling I tell you what you need to know about my plan.	**"We've got to do this. It's my job to lead. You should be excited about it."** Elected body imposes vision. Stakeholders don't get a voice.
Selling I tell you about my plan and convince you to go along with it.	**"We have the best answer. Let's see if we can get *you* to buy in."** Elected body develops vision and tries to enroll stakeholders in the vision.
Testing I'm thinking about doing it this way. What do you think?	**"What excites *you, the public,* about this work? What doesn't?"** Gauge acceptance, support, and relevance of the elected body's viewpoint. If there is not sufficient community support, officials go back to the drawing board. Success depends on stakeholders' willingness to be truthful and realistic.*
Consulting What do you think we should do, given these criteria and resources?	**"What vision/plan do *other stakeholders (the public)* recommend that we adopt?"** Engage stakeholders in designing the vision and considering the ramifications of various choices;* elected body plays role of judge in accepting/ignoring what stakeholders say. Officials determine the content of the vision and decide how to begin moving in that direction.
Co-Creating What do we want, and how will we get it?	**"Let's create the culture we individually and collectively want."** Every step involves discussion and shared choice involving both leaders and stakeholders.

Source: Adapted by Lydian Altman from *The Fifth Discipline Fieldbook: Strategies and Tools for Building a Learning Organization* by Peter M. Senge, et al. (1994).

*Do various stakeholders know enough about the roles and responsibilities of local government to be able to make these judgments or understand the ramifications of decisions? If not, stakeholders will have to be educated in using this approach.

however. They do not provide an opportunity for citizens to interact directly or expeditiously with government officials. They consist of specific questions and may not offer an opportunity for citizens to provide other relevant input. Finally, due to their expense, surveys may be conducted only infrequently.

The International City/County Management Association partners with the National Citizen Survey to conduct surveys, but other private companies are available to conduct them as well. Costs vary significantly, depending on whether the survey is conducted by mail, by phone, online, or in person. Simply identifying and cleaning the contact information needed to distribute a survey is a significant barrier in and of itself. The type and size of the sample, the survey length, the analysis conducted, and the decision to undertake the related work in-house or to outsource it are other factors that affect cost. Survey costs can run from hundreds of dollars in the case of government employees with a clipboard asking questions of passersby at a summer festival booth to tens of thousands of dollars for a rigorous, representative survey. It is difficult to estimate the costs of conducting surveys due to the wide range of options involved.

A smaller-scale survey, when combined with other efforts to encourage public involvement, can be a more economical method for obtaining citizen feedback. In 2020, the Town of Davidson's Board of Commissioners and town staff developed a strategic plan based on objectives that had been identified by the community.[47] The board prioritized which areas they wanted to focus on for the next two years and settled on these six categories:

- A Well-Planned and Livable Community
- Historic Preservation
- Connecting People and Places
- Operational Excellence
- Equity and Inclusion
- Sustainability and Natural Assets

In 2021, the Town conducted a survey to assess citizen views on the progress of the Town's adopted Strategic Plan. They used a standardized template developed by the National Citizen Survey for a series of general questions, and then added several customized questions. Over 100 citizens responded. They came away with four main conclusions: 1) Davidson residents award exceptional ratings to the town as a place to live and raise children, 2) ratings for government performance are strong and outshine national averages, 3) economy ratings in Davidson are also robust, and 4) mobility ratings have improved since 2019, with some of these changes a likely result of the COVID-19 pandemic.[48]

See the "Additional Resources" section at the end of this chapter for other resources pertaining to local government citizen surveys.

Online Streaming of Meetings

Many cities and counties now use online methods to broadcast their elected board meetings to residents. Common platforms are Facebook Live and YouTube. The online avenues supplement, and in some cases replace, government-access television channels. The streaming of meetings is, in part, the result of significant changes in local and regional media environments during the last twenty years. Many local weekly or daily newspapers have closed or merged. Some radio stations have local call-in programs about community matters, but commentators on national issues have the largest audiences. Still, the North Carolina Press Association membership directory shows that the state has ninety-eight community newspapers, forty daily newspapers, sixteen online newspapers, and six associate newspapers.[49] In short, the distribution of news about local government actions is available through older and newer types of media.

Government Websites and Social Media

As changes in information technology have affected business and home life, so have they affected government and how citizens contact local government officials. Town and county websites are now ubiquitous in North Carolina.[50] On these websites, citizens can find phone numbers (and often email addresses and other communication options) for mayors, commission chairmen, and other elected members of various deliberative bodies.

47. Town of Davidson, *Strategic Plan 2020–2021*, www.townofdavidson.org/DocumentCenter/View/11376/Town-of-Davidson-Strategic-Plan-January-5-2021.

48. The Town's survey can be found at *Davidson, N.C. The National Community Survey*, www.townofdavidson.org/DocumentCenter/View/11370/The-NCS-Report---Davidson-NC-2021.

49. North Carolina Press Association, www.ncpress.com/directory/.

50. The School of Government maintains a clearinghouse for the home pages of North Carolina counties and cities. *See* "Counties in North Carolina," Knapp Library, UNC School of Government, www.sog.unc.edu/resources/microsites/knapp-library/counties-north-carolina, and "Cities in North Carolina," Knapp Library, UNC School of Government, www.sog.unc.edu/resources/microsites/knapp-library/cities-north-carolina.

Online access is uneven, with many citizens having little or no high-speed Internet access. With federal support, broadband internet for every North Carolina community has been a goal of state government. The N.C. Department of Information Technology, Division of Broadband and Digital Opportunity is charged with tracking broadband accessibility and use[51] and works with a variety of organizations to "close the digital divide."[52]

The use of social media for disseminating information and, to a lesser extent, for engaging citizens is growing in North Carolina localities. As with other innovations, larger cities and counties have been early adopters. However, Facebook, YouTube, Instagram, X (formerly Twitter), and other online tools are almost universally used even by smaller communities.[53] An informal survey by the School of Government in May 2024 found that the most common platforms are Facebook, X, YouTube, and Instagram. Some localities have multiple accounts serving agencies or specific facilities (e.g., parks and recreation centers with their own Facebook and/or Instagram accounts[54]). Some cities and counties are not permitted to use TikTok by local policy. LinkedIn is used by five cities or counties. The least cited platforms are Threads, Flickr, and Giphy.

Most of the localities surveyed allow comments on some of their social media platforms but do not promise to respond to those comments. Some do respond when "appropriate" while others send automated messages using, for example, Facebook Messenger.[55] For outreach via online surveys or polls, five localities reported that they use services such as SurveyMonkey, Cognito, ETC Institute, or CivicPlus.[56]

Local governments that use blogs, social media, and other Internet resources should consider accessibility and responsiveness concerns such as:

- How should comments and other postings on government social media sites be monitored? Blogs were initially designed for opinions and responses. How can a local government monitor public input but avoid discriminating among viewpoints expressed in blog comments?[57]
- Although governments are focusing more resources on Web and wireless technology and increasing their reliance on digital and electronic media to disseminate information and interact with citizens, the fact remains many people do not have ready access to those avenues of communication. How can local governments address the different online accessibility and capabilities of its residents?

Elected officials must decide if and how blogs and other electronic interactive tools encourage citizen involvement. In addition, they must consider the legal ramifications of government-owned

---

51. N.C. Department of Information Technology, Division of Broadband and Digital Opportunity, Data and Reports, www.ncbroadband.gov/data-reports.

52. N.C. Department of Information Technology, Division of Broadband and Digital Opportunity, "Closing the Digital Divide," www.ncbroadband.gov/digital-divide/closing-digital-divide.

53. For example, Tyrell County lists Facebook, X, and LinkedIn channels on its website, http://tyrrellcounty.org/en/, and Forest City features YouTube and Facebook links, www.townofforestcity.com/.

54. For example, Greenville, N.C., www.greenvillenc.gov/government/city-manager-s-office/public-information-office/social-media.

55. Linda Clayton, Roxboro City Clerk/Public Information Officer, email correspondence, May 17, 2024.

56. The authors' survey was conducted via the Public Information Officers (NCPIO) listserv May 16–30, 2024. Communication specialists from eight counties and nine cities responded. Their responses were supplemented with an examination of the websites of three counties and three cities. As a convenience sample, its representativeness for all North Carolina cities and counties is undetermined.

57. A sample social media comment policy can be found at the School of Government's Center for Public Technology microsite, www.sog.unc.edu/resources/microsites/center-public-technology/social-media-materials-applications-law-and-policy.

online platforms for providing information and opportunities for interaction as well as other practical issues.[58]

Formal Civic Education about Local Government Operations

An increasing number of communities are employing citizen academies or citizen police academies to educate and inform citizens about government activities and operations. These academies are a relatively new way of fostering civic engagement. The academies combine formal instructional sessions with exposure to the work of either law enforcement or other operational departments of cities and counties. The goals of most citizen academies are to

- inform residents about and orient them to the functions of city or county government,
- increase civic engagement and improve the quality of citizen participation in local government, and
- strengthen communication and relationships between citizens and government officials.

Some academies provide opportunities for more interactive engagement on particular issues, needs, or challenges facing the community. The goal of many programs is to increase citizen participation on advisory boards, interest people in running for local office, or, in the case of police or sheriffs' academies, recruit volunteers to support department operations.

According to a database of citizen academies in North Carolina and other localities, the number of North Carolina counties and cities offering academies has grown from forty-five localities in 2014 to seventy-five or more in 2024.[59] These offerings cover all government services.

Public safety–focused academies typically are sponsored by local law enforcement agencies. Many sheriff and police departments have their own education academies.[60]

The development of citizen and police or sheriff academies reflects a local government's interest in fostering citizen participation and informed involvement through adult education. Typically, the main expense is staff time, as employees may have to work overtime to plan and present a particular program. There is not sufficient data to determine how well academy participants reflect a community's demographics.[61]

Local Government Employee Responsibilities for Citizen Involvement

Interactions with citizens—as property owners, victims or suspects of crime, or community volunteers—are part of the duties of many local government employees. Some jobs involve processing permits for citizens and businesspeople, providing direct services (e.g., libraries, schools), and working on road maintenance or other infrastructure projects. Two types of local government positions in particular, however, have duties that pertain specifically to citizens' views and ideas for county or municipal governments. These are (1) clerks and (2) public information officers. Cities

58. For more information and guidance, see "Citizen Participation: Resources," UNC School of Government, www.sog.unc.edu/node/1509.

59. Rick Morse, email correspondence, May 28, 2024. The Citizens Academies database is available through the "Research" link at www.sog.unc.edu/resources/microsites/citizens-academies.

60. Eddie Caldwell, Executive Vice President of the N.C. Sheriffs' Association, email correspondence, May 24, 2024. Caldwell says that the Association has "numerous" programs, but it does not keep an exact count.

61. For more information about citizen academies in general, see "Citizens Academies," UNC School of Government, www.sog.unc.edu/programs/citizensacademies.

and counties may also employ existing staff and utilize other strategies in efforts to foster civic engagement and improve the quality of interaction between government and the public.

In some jurisdictions, clerks to the board of county commissioners and town clerks may be responsible for monitoring appointed citizen board (ACB) appointments and terms. This responsibility may include informing their respective elected bodies when citizens leave an ACB position or when the term of office in an ACB is about to expire, requiring a new appointment. Clerks' other responsibilities for supporting ACBs may include preparing public notices and managing the minutes of ACBs. Since the ACBs are created for the benefit of elected boards, they typically provide reports to the board. Often, part of the clerk's work is to assemble and distribute material for all board meetings, and this material would necessarily include any ACB reports.

Public information officers (PIOs)[62] are an increasingly important part of the local government staff. Since the 1970s, about forty North Carolina cities and towns have created this position, and approximately twenty counties have similar positions.[63] Recently, a few jurisdictions have created positions such as community participation coordinator or public information and social media specialist that are specifically involved with citizen engagement and public interaction.

While PIOs primarily focus on disseminating information to help further the work and goals of the elected board, town or county manager, or department heads, they also often conduct and design other activities involving citizen interaction and engagement, including hearings, information meetings, surveys, and other means of citizen input. PIOs are usually involved, in conjunction with information technology staff, in creating social media policies and overseeing city- and county-managed postings to Twitter, Facebook, YouTube, and so forth.

Other local government staff members are also involved in activities focused on citizen engagement, especially in the areas of land use and transportation planning, community development, historic preservation, elder services, and health and social services. These employees staff ACBs, arrange for public hearings, solicit input from clients or customers in particular service areas, and have other responsibilities related to increasing citizen interaction and feedback.

A few places have linked their communication strategies with larger community engagement objectives. For example, Raleigh's Office of Community Engagement "works to advance the City's goal of improving and reimagining community engagement efforts. The office helps encourage active participation in decision-making dialogue and public policy."[64] Similarly, Asheville's Communication and Public Engagement Department "is responsible for the city's strategic communications and coordination of public engagement efforts."[65]

62. Other job titles for similar positions include communications manager, communications specialist, and community service or community affairs specialist/manager.

63. The authors' estimates for towns and counties are extrapolated from North Carolina City and County Communicators Association (NC3C) membership data and assume that one-quarter to one-third of towns and counties that are not NC3C members staff a similar position. *See* NC3C, nc3c.com/index.php. The authors directly queried officials from selected mid- and large-sized counties and cities, such as New Hanover County and Winston-Salem.

64. "Community Engagement," City of Raleigh, raleighnc.gov/community-engagement.

65. "Communication and Public Engagement: What We Do," City of Asheville, www.ashevillenc.gov/department/communication-public-engagement/.

Conclusion

While the North Carolina Constitution and general political culture advocate civic engagement and responsive elected officials, local governments face practical challenges when creating and supporting opportunities for citizen involvement. In addition to following the basic requirements mandated by state law, local governments can and do employ a variety of methods to encourage and facilitate citizen involvement in government. As this chapter indicates, many of these methods offer both advantages and disadvantages.

Additional Resources

General Resources

Bobbio, Luigi. "Designing Effective Public Participation." *Policy and Society* 38, no. 1 (March 2019): 41–57, doi.org/10.1080/14494035.2018.1511193.

Creighton, James L. *The Public Participation Handbook: Making Better Decisions through Citizen Involvement.* San Francisco: Jossey-Bass, 2005.

Epstein, Paul D., Paul M. Coates, and Lyle D. Wray (with David Swain). *Results That Matter: Improving Communities by Engaging Citizens, Measuring Performance, and Getting Things Done.* San Francisco: Jossey-Bass, 2005.

International Association for Public Participation (United States), www.iap2usa.org.

International City/County Management Association (ICMA). Citizen and Resident Surveys, icma.org/topics/citizen-resident-surveys.

———. "Citizens' Academies (Town of Lexington)," icma.org/documents/citizens-academy-1.

———. "Citizen Surveys: Give Your Community What They Want," icma.org/blog-posts/citizen-surveys-give-your-community-what-they-want.

Leighninger, Matt, and Bonnie C. Mann. *Planning for Stronger Local Democracy: A Field Guide for Local Officials.* Washington, D.C.: National League of Cities (n.d.), icma.org/sites/default/files/303337_planning-for-stronger-local-democracy.pdf.

Nabatchi, Tina, and Matt Leighninger. *Public Participation for 21st Century Democracy.* Hoboken: John Wiley & Sons, 2015.

The National Coalition for Dialogue and Deliberation, www.ncdd.org.

The National Conference on Citizenship, ncoc.org.

North Carolina Civics Coalition (NC3), www.nccivics.org.

Selected School of Government Publications and Resources

Berner, Maureen, Ashley Bowers, and Laura Heyman. "So You Want to Do a Survey . . ." *Popular Government* 67 (Summer 2002): 23–32, www.sog.unc.edu/publications/articles/so-you-want-do-survey.

Bluestein, Frayda S. "Remote Participation in Local Government Board Meetings." *Local Government Law Bulletin* No. 133 (August 2013), www.sog.unc.edu/publications/bulletins/remote-participation-local-government-board-meetings/.

Community Engagement Learning Exchange (blog), cele.sog.unc.edu.

Death and Taxes (blog), Citizen Engagement, UNC School of Government, deathandtaxes.sog.unc.edu/category/citizen-engagement/.

Stephens, John B. "Creating Effective Citizen Participation in Local Government Budgeting: Practical Tips and Examples for Elected Officials and Budget Administrators." *Public Management Bulletin* No. 6 (June 2011), www.sog.unc.edu/publications/bulletins/creating-effective-citizen-participation-local-government-budgeting-practical-tips-and-examples.

———. *Police Accountability: Civilian Advisory and Review Boards in North Carolina Local Government.* Chapel Hill: UNC School of Government, 2021, www.sog.unc.edu/publications/books/police-accountability-civilian-advisory-and-review-boards-north-carolina-local-government.

Stephens, John, Rick Morse, and Kelley O'Brien. *Public Outreach and Participation.* Chapel Hill: UNC School of Government, 2011, cplg.sog.unc.edu/publication/public-outreach-and-participation/.

UNC School of Government, Public Participation Microsite (citizen participation tools, links, and resources):

- Public Participation (home page), www.sog.unc.edu/resources/microsites/public-participation.
- Citizens Academies, www.sog.unc.edu/resources/microsites/citizens-academies.
- Civic Technology, www.sog.unc.edu/resources/microsites/civictech.
- Citizen Surveys by Local Governments, www.sog.unc.edu/resources/microsites/public-participation/citizen-surveys-local-governments-north-carolina (North Carolina local government surveys through 2017).

Upshaw, Vaughn M. *Creating and Maintaining Effective Local Government Citizen Advisory Committees with Downloadable Model Policy and Tracking Forms.* Chapel Hill: UNC School of Government, October 2010, www.sog.unc.edu/publications/books/creating-and-maintaining-effective-local-government-citizen-advisory-committees-downloadable-model.

Chapter 11

Interlocal Cooperation, Shared Services, and Regional Councils

Ricardo S. Morse

Ricardo S. Morse is a faculty member at the School of Government who specializes in leadership development, collaborative governance, and community engagement.

The author is indebted to Professors David M. Lawrence and the late Warren Jake Wicker, authors of chapters on these topics in earlier editions of this publication. This chapter reflects their contributions. The author also wishes to thank Caitlin Little for her research assistance on Appendix 11.1 and Nathan Ramsey, Anthony Starr, and Lee Worsley for their helpful comments that improved this chapter.

As local governments seek innovative ways to provide public goods and services to their communities, they often find that some facilities and services can be operated more efficiently and/or effectively through cooperative arrangements with other local governments. North Carolina counties and municipalities have entered into a wide variety of agreements establishing such cooperative arrangements. Regional councils have also been established across the state to deliver some services regionally and to provide forums for working on cross-jurisdictional issues. Given the fiscal challenges local governments will continue to face in the foreseeable future, alternative service delivery strategies such as shared services are likely to become even more widespread across the state.

Interlocal Cooperation and Shared Services

Local government cooperation with other governments, as well as with citizens and private and nonprofit organizations, has long been an integral aspect of local governance. As urbanization spills beyond municipal limits, for example, municipal and county governments find it useful to cooperate in the provision of urban services to unincorporated neighborhoods. Many local governments likewise contract out certain functions to private vendors (see Chapter 23, "Public Contracts, Competitive Bidding Requirements, and Property Disposal") and successfully partner with nonprofit organizations to more effectively address public needs (see Chapter 12, "Strengthening Community Ties: Local Government and Nonprofit Organizations in North Carolina"). Citizens also are involved in various aspects of public decision-making and even service delivery (see Chapter 10, "Citizen Involvement").

However, the combination of reduced state and federal aid, pressures to hold steady or to reduce local taxes, and increasing demands for services puts pressure on local governments to innovate and change "the way they do business."[1] In some cases, response to fiscal pressures is in the form of reductions or even elimination of some services. But an alternative approach is to consider cooperative approaches to accomplishing some local government functions. Other chapters in this book (referenced above) address the ways in which local governments work with the private sector, nonprofits, and citizens to deliver services and otherwise address public issues. This chapter provides an overview of *local governments working with other local governments.*[2] The terms most often used when discussing this topic are "interlocal cooperation" and "shared services."

The North Carolina General Assembly, through a series of statutes, has provided ample authority for intergovernmental cooperation among local governments. The critical language, from Chapter 160A, Article 20, Section 461 of the North Carolina General Statutes (hereinafter G.S.), reads as follows:

> *Any* unit of local government in this State and *any* one or more other units of local government in this State or any other state (to the extent permitted by the laws of the other state) may enter into contracts or agreements with each other in order to execute *any undertaking.* The contracts and agreements shall be of reasonable duration, as determined by the participating units, and shall be ratified by resolution of the governing board of each unit spread upon its minutes (emphasis added).

As the statutory language makes clear, the authorization for interlocal cooperation and shared services is as broad as can be. The General Assembly has also set out additional provisions authorizing interlocal cooperation in various service areas. The principal statutes are listed in Appendix 11.1 at the end of this chapter.

"Interlocal cooperation" is a broad term that refers to the myriad ways local governments can work together to accomplish public purposes. Cooperation might take the form of information-sharing or coordinated planning; county contributions to municipal services; municipal provision of services to unincorporated areas through contracts with the county; or jointly financed and operated services. In some cases, municipalities and counties have found advantages in merging (i.e., consolidating) parallel functions in order to have just one agency providing a particular service or activity countywide.[3] While the term "shared services" (or "service-sharing" or "joint public services") is often used interchangeably with interlocal cooperation, it can be thought of as a *specific form of*

---

1. Cheryl Hilvert and David Swindell, "Collaborative Service Delivery: What Every Local Government Manager Should Know," *State and Local Government Review* 45, no. 4 (2013): 240–54.

2. The related topic of municipal–county consolidation is not discussed here. Information on that topic can be found in Chapter 2, "Incorporation, Annexation, and City–County Consolidation," of this publication.

3. Counties also cooperate among themselves in providing services more traditional to county government (e.g., regional health departments).

Cooperation or Collaboration?

The terms interlocal *cooperation* and interlocal *collaboration* are often used interchangeably. Indeed, the first definitions of the verbs *cooperate* (to work or act together, especially for a common purpose or benefit) and *collaborate* (to work together with others to achieve a common goal) are essentially the same.[1] Some academic literature, however, makes a clear distinction between "collaboration" as a true partnership involving shared goals and governance and "cooperation" as a transactional relationship where different entities work together but remain largely independent. While these distinctions are meaningful, this chapter will consistently use the term "cooperation." It's important to note that each instance of interlocal cooperation is unique, with varying degrees of transactional or transformative relationships. Ultimately, the key takeaway is that two or more local governments are *working together* to provide public services or facilities.

1. *The American Heritage Dictionary of the English Language*, 5th Edition (Houghton Mifflin Harcourt Trade, 2011).

cooperation, that is, cooperation for the provision of some public service or public good. Cooperation and shared services offer several potential advantages over sole (in-house) production[4] of a particular public good or service:

1. It may be more efficient and/or less expensive to provide a new service through a cooperative approach. As a county or a small town begins to provide fire inspection services, for example, a contract with an existing municipal inspection department utilizes the services of experienced inspectors available immediately, with no administrative overhead. Many municipalities find it more cost-efficient to contract tax collection with their respective counties for similar reasons.
2. Shared services arrangements may also increase *economies of scale*, which occur when the per-unit cost of service provision *decreases* as a result of *increasing* the size or scale of the operation. A municipal or county recreation program might add additional participants from other jurisdictions with negligible additional administrative costs, for example, resulting in lowering the cost per participant. A water utility with excess capacity might add customers from outside its jurisdiction and significantly lower its average unit cost. The reality of such per-unit cost savings is why there are an increasing number of countywide, and even multicounty, regional libraries. While increasing the scale of a particular public service operation *does not* automatically mean there will be increased economies of scale, there are nevertheless opportunities for achieving greater economies of scale in many municipal and county governments.
3. Cooperation often allows for a more effective response to problems that do not respect jurisdictional boundaries. For example, air and water pollution ignores jurisdictional boundary lines and thus requires a regional problem-solving approach. Multijurisdictional cooperation around emergency dispatch, combined with mutual aid agreements, can lead to shortened response times, as the nearest first responder

4. An important distinction can be made here between local government as service *provider* and local government as service *producer*. A community, through its local government, can decide that a particular service should be provided community-wide. This does not mean, however, that the local government necessarily needs to *produce* that service. Rather, the service can be produced by a private or nonprofit vendor, by another local government, or through a partnership of some kind. The local government remains responsible for service provision, but it may choose between producing the service in-house or through some alternative (often collaborative) means.

may not be in the same jurisdiction as the emergency. In other words, service *effectiveness* can be as compelling a reason to cooperate as efficiency.

4. Interlocal cooperation may increase effectiveness by enhancing communication and coordination of interdependent functions that otherwise are carried out independently. Such coordination may be needed, for instance, to provide water and sewer services in areas just beyond city limits. There, counties often work with municipalities to establish policies on extensions, supplies, costs, and the like.
5. Local governments are able, through cooperation and shared services, to adjust inequitable situations concerning payment for and use of services. For example, municipalities often provide recreational programs that are utilized by people from throughout their respective counties, so many counties contribute funds to these city-sponsored programs.
6. Cooperation is a flexible concept. It may begin with simple actions taken by the governing boards involved in a specific issue, and it may involve various tasks and groups of people. A local government may engage in several cooperative ventures, each differing from the others in scope, administrative structure, and financial support. While a cooperative relationship established for one service may provide a model for another, it in no way establishes a precedent that must be followed.
7. Cooperation can also lead to more cooperation. As the saying goes, success breeds success, and this is often true with shared services and other forms of interlocal and regional cooperation. This kind of cooperation is often required to address complex and interconnected public problems like economic development, pollution control, disaster preparedness, or, in many places, maintaining a sustainable water supply.[5] Thus, local leaders can view efforts around interlocal cooperation and shared services not only as addressing a specific need but also as building capacity for necessary regional cooperation on "big" issues.

Types of Interlocal Cooperation and Shared Services

As mentioned above, interlocal cooperation and shared services are more-or-less interchangeable terms that describe the variety of ways local governments work together to provide public services to a community or support services for an organization, as opposed to producing those services entirely in-house. It should be noted that shared services may include, in addition to local government actors, not-for-profit or even for-profit entities, making the line between private service contracting and shared services arrangements somewhat fuzzy. Shared services arrangements thus may assume a variety of forms; several are discussed below.

Grants or Contributions

Occasionally, a local government will provide a program that benefits the property or citizens of another government without receiving direct financial support from these beneficiaries. In such cases, the government whose citizens are benefitting from the program might contribute funds to the government that is providing it. County financial support for a city recreation program or a municipal contribution to a countywide economic development agency are examples of such contributions.

---

5. See the following publications for excellent overviews of the "whys" of interlocal cooperation and shared services: John Ruggini, "Making Local Government More Workable through Shared Services," *Government Finance Review* 22, no. 1 (2006): 30–35; William A. Holdsworth, "Symbiosis-Symmetry-Synergy: The Case for Interlocal Cooperation," *Government Finance Review* 23, no. 1 (2007): 40–46; Matthew McKinney and Shawn Johnson, *Working Across Boundaries: People, Nature, and Regions* (Lincoln Institute of Land Policy, 2009).

Resource Sharing

Local governments frequently engage in sharing information, personnel, equipment, and other resources. Examples of this practice include two municipalities sharing equipment like street-sweepers or backhoes, or separate local law enforcement agencies sharing personnel in certain situations. Resource sharing is often an informal process based on norms of reciprocity, though it may also be formalized through memoranda of understanding.

Mutual Aid Agreements

Mutual aid agreements are formal agreements between jurisdictions to provide aid to each other, usually with respect to emergency response services (fire, police, EMS) as well as disaster response. These agreements are common and viewed as necessary in responding to emergency situations that cross jurisdictional boundaries or where one jurisdiction's responders are closer to an emergency or where additional resources are needed. The North Carolina Mutual Aid System was established following Hurricane Fran in 1996. A governor's taskforce reviewed the statewide response and recommended a statewide mutual aid agreement and system to promote uniformity in disaster responses across jurisdictions. Managed by the N.C. Division of Emergency Management, the statewide agreement is voluntary, but all 100 counties as well as the Eastern Band of Cherokee Indians and a large majority of the state's municipalities have signed it. A similar statewide mutual aid system, NCWaterWARN (North Carolina Water and Wastewater Agency Response Network), has been established for water and wastewater emergencies. The NCWaterWARN website (www.ncwaterwarn.org) calls its work "similar and complementary to the North Carolina Mutual Aid network as an organized arrangement to facilitate cooperation between local authorities during an emergency."

Cooperative Purchasing

Local governments may find it advantageous to jointly purchase materials and equipment. Often, cost savings can be realized through obtaining volume discounts not available to a smaller, single purchaser. Furthermore, cooperative purchasing may reduce administrative costs and expand purchasing expertise. Cooperative purchasing can be organized in different ways—with a lead agency as purchaser, for example, or through a third-party contracted program or a regional council program. G.S. 143-129(e)(3) provides specific exceptions to competitive bidding statutes, including a "competitive bidding group purchasing program," which is defined as a "formally organized program that offers competitively obtained purchasing services at discount prices to two or more public agencies."

Interlocal Service Contracts

A local government may contract with another local government for the provision of a public service or for administrative support services. Examples include small municipalities contracting with their county sheriff departments for law enforcement and public safety services and (as is very common) municipalities contracting with counties for tax collection. Other common examples include municipalities contracting with counties for fire inspections, animal control, and animal shelter operations. The category of interlocal service contracts includes all agreements in which one government contracts with another to provide a service—either an administrative service to the receiving government itself or a service provided directly to the citizens of that government. In a study of interlocal agreements in Iowa (made possible because Iowa requires all such agreements to be filed with the Secretary of State), service contracts were by far the most common form of interlocal agreement.[6] While this finding was for one Midwestern state, anecdotal evidence suggests that the same is true elsewhere, including North Carolina. Local governments contracting with other local governments for services is very common.

Joint Operations

Sometimes a public service is jointly produced through a partnership between two or more local governments. Examples of such joint operations include recreation programs provided through municipal–county partnerships and jointly operated libraries. The line between joint operations and interlocal service contracts (discussed immediately above) is often a thin one. In theory, a joint operation is different in that it involves two or more government units exercising jointly a power that each could exercise individually. For example, two small towns might jointly employ a manager, or a city and a county might create and operate a joint 911 call center. City–county planning boards fit into this category as well.

Joint Facilities/Assets

Two or more local governments may decide to share a common facility. For example, the Matthews Town Center is a joint venture between the Town of Matthews and Mecklenburg County. It houses both Matthews Town Hall and a branch of the county library. The Towns of Morrisville, Cary, and Apex (in Wake County) came together to build and operate the Western Wake Regional Water Reclamation Facility (WWRWRF) to treat wastewater from all three municipalities. On a smaller scale, organizations can share various types of capital assets. For instance, two or more entities can jointly purchase an expensive piece of equipment (e.g., a backhoe) and then establish agreements on how it will be shared.

Transfer of Functions

Sometimes a county and a municipality, each authorized to perform a particular function, will agree that one of them should assume total responsibility for the activity. Such a transfer of responsibility can be thought of as achieving a functional merger or consolidation of the service involved across two or more jurisdictions. For example, smaller, neighboring municipalities in eastern Wake County have transferred water and wastewater operations to the City of Raleigh Public Utilities Department. Thus, for much of Wake County, water and wastewater is functionally consolidated and operated by the City of Raleigh with agreements in place for the non-Raleigh municipalities being serviced. Such transfers of responsibility occur frequently, with counties assuming responsibility for libraries, hospitals, and solid waste disposal. Less frequently, a municipality might assume countywide responsibility for a particular service or administrative function.

Merged Departments

Local governments may also choose to merge duplicate departments into a single unit that is shared by all partners (though usually administratively located under just one of them). The terms of any such merger are spelled out in formal agreements. For example, several counties in North Carolina have merged separate municipal and county 911 dispatch operations into single, countywide centers. The City of Hickory merged its building inspections with Catawba County's inspections office. The City of Sanford provides water and sewer service to residents of Pittsboro, Chatham County,

6. Jun Li, José Sánchez, Jered B. Carr, and Michael D. Siciliano, "Local Governments and Shared Services: Insights on Institutional Mechanisms, Partners, and Purpose," in *Handbook of Collaborative Public Management,* ed. Jack W. Meek (Edward Elgar Publishing, 2021), 179–95.

Figure 11.1 Continuum of Shared Services

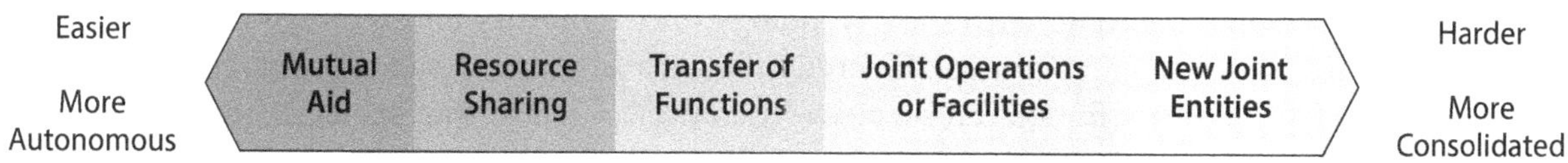

and Siler City under the name "TriRiver Water." TriRiver is a regional water utility operated by one of the partnering entities, the City of Sanford. Durham and Mecklenburg Counties have several merged departments with the cities of Durham and Charlotte, respectively.

New Joint Entities

On occasion, two or more local governments may cooperatively create a new political subdivision or nonprofit organization for the purpose of managing and governing a shared asset and/or service. Oftentimes, the new joint entities are created as public authorities or special purpose local governments. While this form of cooperation is less frequent in North Carolina than in some other states, there are numerous examples, including airport authorities, regional water and sewer authorities, metropolitan water or sewerage districts, regional solid waste management authorities, and regional transportation agencies. Multijurisdictional economic development commissions (EDCs) that are set up as nonprofit organizations, not special purpose local governments (or public authorities) like the examples above, also fit under this category in that they are new entities created jointly by two or more local governments. Most counties in North Carolina have county EDCs that are inclusive of municipalities within their respective counties. There are a variety of different modes of governance for these countywide EDCs (with some functioning more as merged departments, as discussed above), but many operate as nonprofits with representatives of the different partners on the board.

Another new form of joint entity concerns human services. G.S. 130A-36 authorizes two or more counties to merge health departments into new "district" health departments, which function as public authorities, governed by a single board of health. As of 2024, there are six district health departments in North Carolina. In 2019, the General Assembly also authorized counties to similarly join departments of social services together into new regional departments, though no counties (as of 2024) have opted to do so.

It should be noted here that the line between these various forms of interjurisdictional cooperation is often unclear. The labels are not as important as the details of how such arrangements are governed and the extent to which the elected boards involved maintain direct control, or not. Generally speaking, the higher the degree of consolidation (functional or formal) that a particular shared services arrangement has, the harder or more complex it becomes in terms of administration and governance considerations (see Figure 11.1). In other words, sharing "back office" functions or equipment is relatively easy and noncontroversial. Creating a regional water utility or district health department, however, is a whole other matter and will involve much more planning, negotiation, and public scrutiny.

Barriers to Cooperation

It is important to note that there can be barriers to shared services that may be significant enough to stymie interjurisdictional discussions around opportunities for cooperation or prevent discussions from happening in the first place.[7] Some of the more prominent barriers, or potential barriers, to cooperation include the following:

- *"Turf" issues*, having to do with the psychology of community and with natural desires for autonomy and control. Elected officials and managers can be reluctant to explore opportunities for shared services when they perceive that such cooperation may involve a loss of control over the service. Local officials as well as citizens may also feel threatened by the thought of losing something that is viewed as part of their community's identity.
- Lack of, or low levels of, *trust* among potential partners can stem from historical mistrust (rivalries, even) or from differences in community characteristics (e.g., urban versus rural), but such feelings can also simply be the result of not having a history of working together.
- *Transaction costs* include staff time and money involved in developing and monitoring cooperation agreements. If these costs are viewed as outweighing the potential benefits of working together, then this may represent a significant barrier.
- Similarly, it can be difficult to clearly articulate the "business case" for cooperation—why an affirmative decision is warranted based on an analysis of the costs and benefits. On the other hand, even if the benefits of cooperation are clear, *real or perceived inequities* in the distribution of costs and/or benefits can pose a challenge.
- Related to all the issues noted above, *community politics* often play a role in would-be cooperative ventures. Elected officials may be particularly concerned about accountability and control. Staff members may fear change, including the fear of losing jobs held by community members. Community members may fear decreased service quality or customer service. All these concerns can give rise to what might be viewed as "political" barriers to cooperation and shared services.
- Finally, general *lack of awareness* can also be a barrier. Administrative and/or elected officials simply may not realize the wide range of possibilities when it comes to service sharing and interlocal cooperation. Such lack of awareness constrains innovative potential.

The prevalence of these and other barriers to cooperation will vary depending on a variety of factors, including the goods or services in question, financial realities, community history and culture, the nature of interlocal relationships, and the presence of external mandates or incentives.

Overcoming Barriers When Cooperation Is Warranted

Working effectively *within* an organization is difficult enough. Working *across* organizations presents a host of additional challenges, including many potential barriers or stumbling blocks, some of which were summarized above. However, when the advantages of collaboration in the form of shared services or some other kind of interlocal cooperation are compelling, it is incumbent upon public leaders—elected officials and public managers—to try to navigate and overcome those barriers for the greater public good. Leaders can have great impact by:

- cultivating relationships of trust with neighboring jurisdictions (potential partners);
- creating a sense of urgency, communicating clearly the "why now" for a would-be cooperative endeavor; and
- communicating honestly and effectively with stakeholders throughout the process (including early on, before decisions have been made).

7. Robert Agranoff, *Collaborating to Manage: A Primer for the Public Sector* (Georgetown University Press, 2012).

These strategies can help managers and elected officials overcome inertia (or active opposition) and other barriers to cooperation. Public managers in particular can make a difference by ensuring that appropriate groundwork is done, for example, by ordering feasibility studies, examining financial and cost allocations, and generally just making sure that good data is available.

Another effective strategy for overcoming barriers to cooperation involves networking across jurisdictions and participating in and supporting forums for interjurisdictional dialogue.[8] Two practices in particular stand out. First, regional councils (discussed in more detail below) serve as neutral regional forums and can be positive forces for engendering cooperation if member local governments use them as such. Actively participating in regular regional managers' meetings and, in the case of board members, participating in regional council boards, are important capacity-building activities for interlocal cooperation.

Another somewhat common practice, happening mainly at the county level, is for county government officials, along with officials from municipalities within the county, to meet regularly (often quarterly) to encourage relationship-building and discussion of countywide issues. In some cases, the gatherings open with a meal, which is then followed by a business meeting of some sort. These meetings take a wide variety of forms, sometimes including all board members and senior staff from the county, municipalities, and school district, sometimes including just managers and mayors/chairs, and other times something in-between.[9] These opportunities for officials to "break bread" together, or to at least meet and talk to one another, serve an important purpose beyond any specific issue that may be on the agenda. They serve to build relationships and cultivate lines of communication that can serve as a catalyst for identifying opportunities for interlocal cooperation and shared services. County governments and regional councils can play a critical convening role for these kinds of meetings.

Interjurisdictional dialogue also occurs more informally at the staff level. It is common for municipal and county managers within a county to get together for lunch, to network and build relationships. The same can be true for department heads of neighboring departments doing similar work. This kind of networking can be vitally important in building the social infrastructure necessary for cooperation when opportunities arise.

Provisions of Interlocal Agreements

Some forms of interlocal cooperation happen without any kind of explicit agreement. Information sharing, for example, and even some forms of coordination (such as between law enforcement agencies), can occur simply out of courtesy, tradition, or good management practice. However, shared services arrangements usually involve some form of interlocal agreement, though even here the agreement is sometimes informal—a "handshake" agreement, as occurs in many instances with the sharing of equipment or personnel. That said, most shared services agreements do involve formal interlocal agreements. Such a formalized arrangement creates the legal basis for the relationship, outlines a method of financing and cost allocations, spells out governance and administration rules (how decisions are made, disputes settled, etc.), and describes any special procedures or provisions of the partnership.

Some types of cooperative arrangements are quite simple. When one government contributes to an ongoing program of another, the contributing government typically does not concern itself with

8. Kelly LeRoux, Paul W. Brandenburger, and Sanjay K. Pandey, "Interlocal Service Cooperation in U.S. Cities: A Social Network Explanation," *Public Administration Review* 70, no. 2 (2010): 268–78.

9. These standing, multi-jurisdictional bodies are sometimes even formally named, such as the Stokes County League of Governments. It is important to note that these meetings are subject to the requirements of the state open meetings law (see Chapter 9, "Open Meetings and Other Legal Requirements for Local Government Boards").

the administration of the program; it simply includes an appropriation for the program in its budget ordinance. The amount of the appropriation may be negotiated, but the negotiations probably do not extend to other subjects. This same lack of involvement in program administration often exists when program functions are transferred. Once such a transfer is made, the function becomes the sole responsibility of the contributing government. Where there is a compelling interest on the part of the recipient government in how the function is administered, however, such as in the case of one municipality providing water and sewer utilities to neighboring municipalities, it is likely in the recipient government's best interest to have interlocal agreements in place spelling out terms of service, input on infrastructure extensions, and so on.[10]

Other sorts of cooperative arrangements can be quite complex, and negotiations can become difficult. Questions may arise concerning financing, operations, administration, property, and many other matters. This chapter cannot suggest "correct" solutions because the needs, administrative structures, traditions, and services involved can differ depending on the type of collaborative arrangement and the government actors. Nor can it even suggest all the questions that should be asked. But it can point out the most common decisions that negotiating governments might face (see Table 11.1, below).

The General Assembly has provided a framework for interlocal agreements in G.S. 160A-464, which states:

> Any contract or agreement establishing an undertaking shall specify:
> (1) The purpose or purposes of the contract or agreement;
> (2) The duration of the agreement;
> (3) If a joint agency is established, its composition, organization, and nature, together with the powers conferred on it;
> (4) The manner of appointing the personnel necessary to the execution of the undertaking;
> (5) The method of financing the undertaking, including the apportionment of costs and revenues;
> (6) The formula for ownership of real property involved in the undertaking, and procedures for the disposition of such property when the contract or agreement expires or is terminated;
> (7) Methods for amending the contract or agreement;
> (8) Methods for terminating the contract or agreement;
> (9) Any other necessary or proper matter.

Two broad considerations need to be explicitly discussed any time local governments are considering entering into a shared services arrangement. The first is the specific *type* of service-sharing arrangement (discussed above) under consideration. The options can be thought of as falling along a continuum of *more consolidated* or *less consolidated.*

The second consideration that must be factored into the partnership decision is the extent of *shared governance.* Partners could agree that a service should be fully consolidated (into one entity) across the multiple jurisdictions involved, but the parties must still determine the extent to which they will share in the governance of that entity. A high degree of shared governance might involve the creation of a new special purpose government (e.g., a regional water authority), whereas a low degree of shared governance might involve one jurisdiction being the service provider, with the other jurisdictions simply agreeing to a per capita fee for that service.

10. Such is the case for the several municipalities in Eastern Wake County that transferred their water/sewer services over to the city of Raleigh.

Table 11.1 Common Decisions Facing Negotiating Governments

Function	Questions/Decisions
Administrative	Should the units jointly supervise the function, or should one simply contract with the other to supervise it for both units?
Finances	Are user charges to be levied? Should the agreement establish the schedule of charges? Should the agreement establish the basis of charges? How should charges be modified? Should charges be the province of the operating government alone? On what basis are costs to be divided? What should be included as costs attributable to the activity? What will be the timing and the manner of payment between governments? What will be the timing and notification procedures for charges so that partners can incorporate those expenditures into budget preparation? What other budgeting procedures should be established? Are special assessments to be used? If so, on what basis? In capital projects, who will make expenditure decisions?
Operations	What will be the territorial scope of activity? What performance levels will be expected? Can they be modified? If so, how? In capital projects, will the parties mandate specific features? On facilities, what limitations or priorities on use will be necessary?
Personnel	How are personnel to be selected? Whose employees will they be? Should there be special provisions regarding position classification, pay plan, fringe benefits, etc.?
Property	How will decisions to buy real or major personal property be made? How are sites to be selected? How are specifications to be established? How will acquisition be made? Who will own the property? Under what circumstances may the property be disposed of?
Miscellaneous	What reports will be required? What records must be retained? What rights of inspection should be allowed? How will potential liabilities be allocated and paid?
Joint Agencies	How will joint agencies be structured? What will the size of the coordinating body be? What will the terms of members be? Who will appoint them? How often will the body meet? What powers and duties will be conferred on/delegated to the body? What provisions should be made for budgeting? What reports and records will be required?
Duration, Termination, and Renewal	How long will the cooperative activity continue? What should the provisions for renewal, modification, and termination say? How will assets be distributed in the event of termination?

Regional Organizations

The conditions that have given rise to cooperative relationships between local governments have also prompted the creation of regional organizations. The development of road systems, the operation of water and sewer facilities, the protection of air quality, and the regulation of land use are examples of activities that, when undertaken by one jurisdiction, will nevertheless affect people and property in neighboring jurisdictions. Sometimes, as noted above, these common interests may be recognized and managed through cooperative relationships. At other times, however, the administration of some joint interests may be accomplished most effectively by creating a joint, regional agency.

Impetus for Regional Organization

By 1960, an increasing number of federal agencies required some form of regional planning and the creation of multicounty organizations to administer categorical programs under their jurisdictions. State agencies likewise have a long history of dividing the state into local administrative regions. In 1961, the General Assembly authorized the creation of regional planning commissions (G.S. 153A-391, -398) and economic development commissions (G.S. 158-8, -15) by general law. These actions built on the successful experience with regional planning and economic development organizations that had been established in previous years by local legislation. Today's most frequently used form of regional organization, the regional council of government, was authorized by legislation in 1971 (G.S. 160A-470 to -478).

The big push for multicounty regional organizations, however, came from the federal government after Congress enacted the Intergovernmental Cooperation Act of 1968. This act encouraged states to establish a uniform system of area-wide planning and development districts. Regional review of local grant and program proposals, as required by *Circular A-95* of the Office of Management and Budget, became standard procedure. In 1969, the General Assembly directed the Department of Administration to cooperate with "the counties, the cities and towns, the federal government, multi-state commissions and private agencies and organizations, to develop a system of multi-county, regional planning districts to cover the entire State."[11] This charge was part of the department's broader role in undertaking and supporting state and regional planning and development.

Regional Councils in North Carolina

In May 1970, Governor Robert Scott designated seventeen multicounty regions by executive order. Following this designation, many state agencies took action to align their regional administrative organizations with the new regional designations. Cities and counties in the designated regions also moved to create a new regional organization or to reshape an existing one to fit the new pattern. In 1971, the state announced a policy of designating a single organization within each region as the *lead regional organization* (LRO). This organization is open to all cities and counties in the region and is the organization through which many state and federal programs are channeled. While a few LROs are planning and economic development commissions and the balance are councils of governments, all the organizations are today referred to as "regional councils."

It is important to note here that regional designations are not static. Boundaries can be changed by constituent governments via a petition to the governor. In the 1990s, Region H was dissolved and constituent counties were reassigned to other regions. Further, on July 1, 2011, the regional councils

11. G.S. 143-341(6)i.

from regions G and I merged into one (G), called the Piedmont Triad Regional Council. As of 2024, the number of regions (and regional councils) in North Carolina is sixteen.[12]

The governing bodies of the regional councils comprise representatives from member local governments. Most North Carolina counties and municipalities are members. Because the regional councils are not authorized under law to levy taxes, they must depend on membership dues, earnings from technical assistance, and grants from other governments for their financial support. Traditionally, most support has come from federal sources, with state grants, membership dues, and revenues from local projects and miscellaneous revenues accounting for the remainder.

It is notable that regional councils are considered local governments under state law. They are subject to the same laws (such as open meetings, public records, the Budget and Fiscal Control Act) as municipalities and counties. They are also able to directly contract with local governments just like other local governments can with each other. Thus, regional councils have the authority to provide services up to and including regional-level municipal services, such as inspections or fire, if local governments choose to provide their services in that way. In other words, regional councils can be a vehicle for joint operations and merged departments (discussed above).

Programs and activities of regional councils vary. Each engages in economic planning and development, provides intergovernmental review, serves as a data center for the region, and administers programs for the aging in cooperation with state and federal agencies.[13] Most participate in administering community development block grants and the Workforce Innovation and Opportunity Act and provide technical assistance in local solid waste and land use planning, housing, and programs to enhance water quality. For several regional councils, transportation services, regional transportation planning, management consulting, GIS/mapping, and land and water conservation are significant activities. Although these regional organizations focus principally on planning and coordinating activities and technical assistance in the areas within which they work, they are also available to carry out almost any function or activity that their members may require. Some regional councils provide code enforcement, financial administration, resiliency and disaster mitigation planning, broadband Internet infrastructure planning, and local government executive searches for member governments.

Beyond specific programs and services that regional councils provide is their important role as convener of and forum for interlocal and regional discussions on cross-jurisdictional issues in their regions. Regional councils can in this capacity help overcome barriers to cooperation through the provision of time and space for relationship-building and discussion. These organizations also often provide facilitation and technical expertise and thus can be instrumental in fostering interlocal and regional partnerships. Having an organization that can take the lead on cooperative efforts where there is no one in charge is often a key factor in moving projects and partnerships forward.

The broader role of regional councils as catalysts for regional cooperation is evident in the mission and vision of the North Carolina Association of Regional Councils of Governments (NCARCOG). The NCARCOG website states that their vision is to set the standard for providing informed, creative regional answers to intricate challenges facing the state of North Carolina and its local governments. Their mission is to "promote collaboration and partnership at the regional level" and to "find innovative solutions to North Carolina's regional challenges and deliver excellent federal, state, and regional services to our member communities."

---

12. See the North Carolina Association of Regional Councils of Government, ncarcog.org/regional-councils/, for more information on North Carolina's regional councils.

13. All regional councils administer federal and state aging programs in their regions in collaboration with federal agencies and with the North Carolina Division of Aging and Adult Services.

Planning and Implementing Interlocal Cooperation and Shared Services

The following recommendations from a report[14] on shared services in local government published by the IBM Center for the Business of Government are a good starting point for thinking about the main steps in planning for and implementing interlocal cooperation or shared services arrangements.

1. Create a team or task force made up of relevant stakeholders to explore shared services opportunities in a transparent manner.
2. Build on the strengths of participating governments. Local governments should consider the relative strengths of potential partner organizations and be open to service delivery alternatives that leverage the different strengths available.
3. Consider pilot projects that can reduce risk and provide an opportunity for "small wins," ultimately contributing to trusting relationships and creating a track record of success that can lead to more cooperation in the future.
4. Clarify and document roles and responsibilities with partners. Have them clearly articulated in a written agreement and regularly review the agreement to ensure that it is sufficient over time.
5. Be flexible and revise agreements as necessary. Circumstances change, and effective partnerships are able to adapt to changes.

A common best practice for enhancing interlocal cooperation and shared services is to fully leverage one's regional council as a forum for discussing interlocal and regional issues, while also drawing on its areas of expertise and institutional knowledge.

It is important to note that interlocal cooperation and shared services should not be viewed as a panacea to all the problems local governments face. While cost savings may be realized with some shared services arrangements, it is certainly not the case with *all* such arrangements. And cooperation does not guarantee improved service delivery. Thus, opportunities for shared services and interlocal cooperation should be considered as *one of many* potential innovations in service delivery approaches available to local leaders.

At the same time, local government officials in the twenty-first century need to appreciate the highly interconnected nature of the problems their communities face. These complex and interconnected problems point to the increasing relevance of cooperative approaches to local and regional governance to get the public's business done in as efficient, effective, and equitable a way as possible.

14. Eric Zeemering and Daryl Delabbio, *A County Manager's Guide to Shared Services in Local Government* (IBM Center for the Business of Government, 2013).

Appendix 11.1 N.C. General Statutes Authorizing Cities to Cooperate with Other Local Governments

Function	G.S. Citation
General Powers of Cooperation	
Administrative and governmental powers	160A-460 through -464
Revenue and expenditures for joint undertakings	160A-466
Property transactions	160A-274
Buildings	153A-164
Councils of governments	160A-470 through -478
Consolidation study commissions	153A-401 through -405
Elections	
Registration	163-288
Planning and Regulation of Development	
Transfer of territorial jurisdiction	160D-202
Planning contracts	160D-502
Historic preservation commissions	160D-303
Appearance commissions	160D-304
Inspection services	160D-402(c), -1102, -1107
Housing	157-39.5
Community development	160D-1311
Planning Boards	160D-301
Regional planning commissions	153A-391 through -398
Regional economic development commissions	158-8 through -15
Regional redevelopment commissions	160A-507
City–county redevelopment commissions	160A-507.1
Redevelopment project financing	160A-515.1
Annexation agreements	160A-58.23
Environmental Matters	
Air pollution control	143-215.112
Sedimentation control	113A-60
Stormwater runoff programs	143-214.7
Water supply financing	139-49(b)
Public Safety	
Law Enforcement	
Training	160A-289
Auxiliary police	160A-283
General cooperation between agencies	160A-288
Local confinement facilities	153A-219
Fire protection	160A-293
County and municipal emergency management	166A-19.15
Ambulance services	153A-250
Animal shelters	160A-493
Hospitals	131E-7
Social Services	
Human relations programs	160A-492
Manpower programs	160A-492
Community action programs	160A-492

Table continues →

Appendix 11.1 N.C. General Statutes Authorizing Cities to Cooperate with Other Local Governments (*continued*)

Function	G.S. Citation
Social Services (*continued*)	
Senior citizens	160A-497
Library services	153A-270
Recreation, generally	160A-355
Regional sports authorities	160A-479 through -479.17
Regional facility authorities	160A-480.1 through -480.15
Public Enterprises	
Airports	63-56; 153A-278
Water services	153A-278, -274
Sewer services	153A-278, -274
Solid waste services	153A-278, -274
Solid waste collection and disposal facilities	153A-292
Waste reduction and management programs	130A-309.09B
Utility emergencies	160A-318
Water and sewer authorities	162A-1 through -19
Metropolitan water districts	162A-31 through -58
Metropolitan sewerage districts	162A-64 through -81
Regional natural gas districts	160A-660 through -676
Public transportation systems	153A-278, -274
Public transportation authorities	160A-575 through -588
Electric power generation	159B-4 through -49
Regional public transportation authorities	160A-600 through -625
Regional transportation authorities	160A-630 through -651
Regional solid waste management authorities	153A-421 through -432
Research and production service districts	153A-311 through -317.1
Communications services	160A-340 through -340.6
Powers of Cooperation Specific to Counties	
Social Services	
Regional housing authorities	157-35
Regional boards of social services	108A-15.8
Regional social services departments	108A-15.7
Public Education	
Local school administrative units	115C-67 through -68.2
Public Safety	
Fire protection	153A-233

Chapter 12

Strengthening Community Ties: Local Government and Nonprofit Collaborations in North Carolina

Teshanee Williams

Teshanee Williams is a faculty member at the School of Government who specializes in nonprofit management, nonprofit and local government partnerships, community engagement and public management.

The author would like to thank current and former School of Government faculty members James C. Drennan, Margaret Henderson, Kara A. Millonzi, Christopher B. McLaughlin, and Gordon P. Whitaker for their contributions to previous versions of this chapter.

Introduction

North Carolina's nonprofit sector plays a vital role in both economic and social domains. These organizations account for 361,918 jobs, making up 10 percent of private sector employment.[1] They generate $56 billion in revenue, with $19 billion paid out in wages by the state's nonprofit sector.[2]

In terms of size, the majority of nonprofits in North Carolina are small, with 43 percent operating on budgets under $100,000 and 84 percent under $1 million. However, larger nonprofits, particularly in healthcare and education, account for a substantial share of the sector's expenditures. For example, nonprofit hospitals and universities are among the largest employers and generators of revenue in the state.[3]

Geographically, nonprofits are concentrated in urban areas such as the Triangle (Raleigh-Durham-Chapel Hill) and Charlotte, which have over 3,000 and 2,500 nonprofits, respectively. In

1. North Carolina Center for Nonprofits, "Nonprofits' Impact on North Carolina" (September 2022), ncnonprofits.org/resources/nonprofit-starter-kit/nonprofits-impact-north-carolina.
2. *Id.*
3. *Id.*

Figure 12.1 Nonprofits in North Carolina per 10,000 People

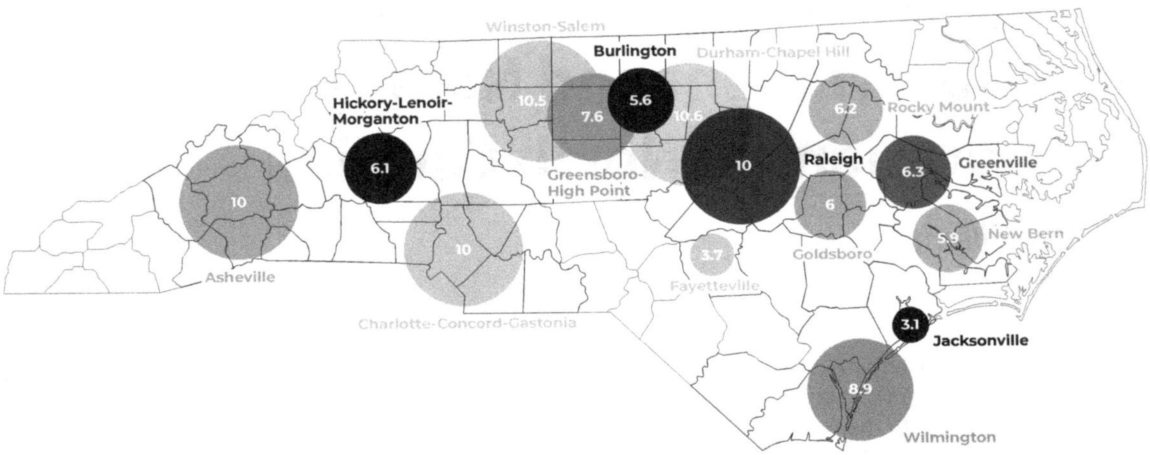

Source: Modified from North Carolina Center for Nonprofits, "Nonprofits' Impact on North Carolina," 2022, ncnonprofits.org/sites/default/files/NCNPSectorImpact_2022_0.pdf.

contrast, northeastern North Carolina has far fewer organizations, with only about 400 nonprofits (see Figure 12.1). Urban areas like Asheville and Winston-Salem also have a higher concentration of nonprofits per capita, while military towns like Fayetteville and Jacksonville have the lowest.[4]

The diversity of North Carolina's nonprofit sector is reflected in the variety of partnerships it forms with local governments to achieve shared goals. These relationships range from service provision agreements to collaborative projects addressing community needs such as healthcare, education, and social services. Local governments often rely on nonprofits to deliver critical services to residents, while nonprofits benefit from public funding and infrastructure support to fulfill their missions. This dynamic partnership is essential in meeting the diverse needs of communities across the state, particularly in regions where the nonprofit presence is more concentrated. This chapter provides local government officials in North Carolina with practical guidance and insights on forming effective collaborations with nonprofit organizations, emphasizing the importance of leveraging partnerships to address community needs, improve service delivery, and maximize impact through shared resources and expertise.

What Are Nonprofit Organizations?

Nonprofit organizations are entities that operate primarily to fulfill community needs and public interests rather than to generate profit. They play a crucial role in providing social goods and services, enhancing community well-being, and influencing public policy. Nonprofit organizations have

4. *Id.*

six common characteristics. They are (1) self-governing, (2) voluntary, (3) private (nongovernmental), (4) for the public benefit, (5) non-distributive of profit,[5] and (6) mission-driven.

1. Nonprofit organizations operate independently under their own governance. This independence is maintained by a board of directors that oversees the organization's activities, ensuring accountability to the board, funders, and stakeholders.[6]
2. Nonprofit organizations are entirely voluntary and not mandated by any entity. These organizations are a manifestation of historical cultural practices aimed at helping those in need or promoting social, cultural, or educational causes.[7]
3. Nonprofit organizations are private and separate from government, although they fulfill some public purposes.
4. The primary purpose of a nonprofit is to serve the public or a specific group of people, rather than to benefit private individuals or shareholders. The nonprofit sector plays a service role by providing essential services; an advocacy role by giving a voice to various causes and interests; an expressive role by offering platforms for diverse perspectives, artistic expression, and cultural preservation; a community-building role by fostering connections and civic engagement; and a value-guardian role by upholding shared values, ethical standards, and morals.[8]
5. Nonprofit organizations are profit-generating, but with a crucial distinction—they are non-profit-distributive. This means that any surplus generated is not distributed to private individuals or shareholders but reinvested in the organization's mission and activities.
6. As mission-driven organizations, nonprofits remain focused on achieving specific social, environmental, cultural, or community-oriented goals, rather than generating profit for owners or shareholders. Unlike businesses, they do not prioritize the bottom line. Instead, they are accountable to their stakeholders (i.e., the communities they serve, volunteers, clients, funders, etc.). Although the general philosophy is "purpose over profit," nonprofit organizations still must make strategic decisions to ensure sustainability.[9]

The Legal Definition of a Nonprofit

The term "nonprofit" is defined based on twenty-nine specific classifications under the Internal Revenue Code. However, the North Carolina General Statutes (hereinafter G.S.) define a nonprofit as an organization "intended to have no income or intended to have income none of which is distributable to its members, directors, or officers."[10] In this context, the members, directors, or officers are volunteers serving on the board of directors. While board members typically serve

5. Benjamin Gidron, Ralph M. Kramer, and Lester M. Salamon, "Government and the Third Sector in Comparative Perspective: Allies or Adversaries," *Government and the Third Sector: Emerging Relationships in Welfare States* 5 (San Francisco: Jossey-Bass, 1992).

6. Elizabeth T. Boris and C. Eugene Steuerle, eds., *Nonprofits and Government: Collaboration and Conflict*, 3rd ed. (Lanham, MD: Rowman & Littlefield Publishers, 2016).

7. C. Eugene Steuerle, Alan Abramson, Ellen Steele, and Virginia Hodgkinson, "Chapter 2: Meeting Social Needs through Charitable and Government Resources," in *Nonprofits and Government Collaboration and Conflict* (Lanham, MD: Rowman & Littlefield Publishers, 2016), 37–64.

8. *Id.*

9. Elizabeth Carnegie and Andreana Drencheva, "Mission-Driven Arts Organisations and Initiatives: Surviving and Thriving Locally in a Time of Rupture," *Arts and the Market* 9, no. 2 (2019): 178–87.

10. G.S. 551-1-40(17).

without pay, they can be compensated for services that go beyond their regular board duties, such as legal, accounting, or consulting work, as long as the compensation is considered "reasonable." Additionally, board members may be reimbursed for reasonable expenses related to their board service, such as travel or meal costs, provided that the process is transparent and properly documented. Although it is generally discouraged for nonprofits to pay board members, as it is often seen as taboo, some states, including North Carolina, allow board members of 501(c)(3) private foundations to receive compensation.

Legal Characteristics

Nonprofit organizations are either corporations, limited liability companies (LLCs), or unincorporated associations. If the nonprofit is a corporation, it is governed by G.S. Chapter 55A. Because the North Carolina laws governing nonprofit corporations are well-established and predictable, and because the corporate form offers additional advantages discussed below, most nonprofits choose to incorporate.

If the nonprofit organization is an LLC, it is governed by G.S. Chapter 57C. Until recently, it was unclear whether an LLC formed under the laws of North Carolina (or any other state) would be granted tax-exempt status by the federal government. While it is now clear that LLCs can be tax-exempt nonprofit organizations, it remains relatively rare for organizations to choose this form.

If the nonprofit is an unincorporated association,[11] it is governed by a combination of G.S. Chapter 59B and North Carolina common law. Until recently, unincorporated associations were governed exclusively by common law, which, because of its diffuse nature, made life unpredictable and inconvenient for nonprofit organizations.[12] Chapter 59B, known as the Uniform Unincorporated Nonprofit Association Act, was designed to provide legal predictability and protection to unincorporated nonprofit organizations; however, because it is new and untested and does not address all legal aspects of a nonprofit organization's existence, most nonprofits continue to choose the corporate form.

Due to the uncertainty associated with nonprofit LLCs and unincorporated associations, governments generally prefer to partner with or fund nonprofit corporations. This chapter focuses on nonprofit corporations and uses the term "nonprofit" throughout the discussion.

Tax-Exempt Organizations

The twenty-nine distinct categories of tax exempt, 501(c) nonprofit organizations, commonly referred to as tax-exempt organizations, can be grouped into four main types, each representing a specific kind of organization with unique purposes and tax-exempt status. These four types include 501(c)(3) charitable nonprofits, 501(c)(4) social welfare organizations, member-serving organizations, and other tax-exempt organizations.[13]

The most well-known category of nonprofit organizations is 501(c)(3) charitable nonprofits. In North Carolina, there are 146,070 nonprofit corporations, with about 40,000 holding the 501(c)(3) designation.[14] These charitable organizations fall into two categories: public charities and private

---

11. For example, many churches are not incorporated but are, rather, unincorporated associations, as are many neighborhood associations or other similar groups.

12. Common law is judge-made law that evolves on a case-by-case basis and is found in the written opinions that accompany the decisions in cases appealed to the North Carolina Supreme Court and the North Carolina Court of Appeals. Because the legal principles of common law are not codified in a single place as statutes are, the legal status of an unincorporated association in a given matter may be more difficult to determine.

13. Steuerle et al., "Chapter 2: Meeting Social Needs through Charitable and Government Resources."

14. North Carolina Center for Nonprofits, "Nonprofits' Impact on North Carolina."

foundations. Public charities receive significant support from the public, government, or foundations. A well-known example is the American Red Cross, which provides disaster relief, blood donation services, and other emergency assistance programs. In contrast, private foundations (non-operating), such as the Bill & Melinda Gates Foundation, typically receive most of their funds from a single individual, family, or corporation. The IRS stipulates that five percent or more of its assets must be distributed to support charitable activities. Operating foundations are a subclass of private foundations that allocate most of their resources to support programs that benefit the public. The Cleveland Clinic Foundation is an example of an operating foundation that funds research and education at the Cleveland Clinic. Though all of these nonprofit categories are generally tax-exempt, private foundations must pay taxes on investment earnings.

Generally, only 501(c)(3) organizations are eligible to receive tax-deductible donations. However, certain other types of 501(c)(3) organizations can also receive tax-deductible contributions if the gifts are exclusively for public purposes or meet specific requirements outlined by the Internal Revenue Code. The tax policy benefits the organization, society, and the government in various ways. For organizations, tax deductions incentivize individuals and corporations to donate, increasing the funds available to further their missions. By addressing critical needs and enhancing community well-being, 501(c)(3) organizations serve the public interest and fill service gaps that the government cannot fully address on its own. The government also benefits by reducing its resource burden while encouraging civic engagement and philanthropy.

The second category of nonprofit organizations is those with the 501(c)(4) designation, also known as social welfare organizations. These organizations focus on promoting community welfare and advocating for public causes, and they are allowed to engage in political and lobbying activities more freely than 501(c)(3) organizations. While 501(c)(4) organizations enjoy tax-exempt status, donations to them are not tax deductible. A well-known example of a 501(c)(4) organization is AARP (formerly known as the American Association of Retired Persons), which advocates for the interests of older Americans, focusing on issues such as health care, retirement planning, and Social Security.

Member-serving organizations represent the third category. These organizations exist to serve the interests of their members, often providing benefits, services, or advocacy on their behalf. Such organizations include labor unions, agricultural organizations, business leagues, and social or recreational clubs.

The fourth category of nonprofit organizations encompasses a wide range of activities, including benevolent life insurance associations, veterans' organizations, and certain state-sponsored health coverage organizations. The third and fourth categories primarily serve their members, customers, or a combination of both. While these organizations are also tax-exempt, they operate under different rules and regulations (see Table 12.1).

Although the IRS has established laws that categorize nonprofits, it is important to understand that some nonprofits have multiple arms. Often, nonprofit organizations create separate entities to help achieve their mission by increasing financial stability or advocating for certain issues beyond allowable limits. For example, the Sierra Club is a 501(c)(4) social welfare organization focused on advocacy and lobbying. However, the Sierra Club Foundation is a 501(c)(3) non-operating foundation that functions as a fiscal sponsor for the Sierra Club.

A common practice for smaller nonprofits is the fee-for-service model. Nonprofit organizations that choose this model can charge fees for services to generate tax-exempt profits, provided these services are related to the organization's mission. For example, a 501(c)(3) children's museum primarily serves to educate and engage children through interactive exhibits and educational programs. The museum charges an entry fee that is exempt because it is "substantially related" to the mission. It also charges fees for birthday parties, allowing patrons to use the space for celebrations.

Table 12.1 IRS Filing Requirements for Nonprofits in North Carolina

Type of Nonprofit	Form Filing Requirements
Nonprofits with annual gross receipts of $50,000 or less	Must file an e-Postcard annually. If your annual budget is less than $5,000 and you've never applied for 501(c)(3) tax-exempt status, you still need to file (you won't be penalized for filing late).
Nonprofits with annual gross receipts of more than $50,000 or with an average of more than $50,000 over the past three years	Must file form 990 or 990-EZ annually, within five and a half months after their fiscal year ends. All supporting or controlling organizations must file Form 990 or 990-EZ.
Nonprofits with annual gross receipts under $200,000 and total assets under $500,000	Can file Form 990-EZ.
Private Foundations	Must file Form 990-PF.
Churches, their integrated auxiliaries, and conventions or associations of churches.	Do not need to file.

Source: How to Start a 501(c)(3) Nonprofit Organization in North Carolina by North Carolina Center for Nonprofits, ncnonprofits.org/sites/default/files/HowToStartA501(c)(3)Nonprofit.pdf.

However, the fees associated with birthday parties are subject to **Unrelated Business Income Tax (UBIT)**. Because the rules for determining what qualifies as "substantially related" are complex, a full discussion of them is beyond the scope of this chapter.[15]

Legal Rules Applicable to Nonprofits

Nonprofits that deal with governments often must answer questions about the extent to which they are subject to laws that regulate the governments themselves. In most cases, a nonprofit's nongovernmental status means it is not subject to rules that apply exclusively to governments. There are exceptions to this general rule, however, and certain laws apply specifically to nonprofits (such as charitable solicitation rules).[16] The general principle is that a nonprofit is not subject to statutes regulating solely governmental activity (typically, "open government" rules), except in unusual circumstances. Furthermore, simply receiving governmental funds through grants or contracts does not subject a nonprofit to government-specific statutes.

Some examples illustrate this. Governments are subject to public records and open meetings laws, but nonprofits, as a rule, are not. Still, there are exceptions. For example, the Nonprofit Corporation Act applies to corporations formed at the request of the state for the sole purpose of financing public projects.[17] In rare instances, a nonprofit may be so closely aligned with a government entity that it must follow the same disclosure rules. This can happen if the nonprofit is (1) organized by

15. Internal Revenue Service, "Substantially Related," accessed September 18, 2024, www.irs.gov/charities-non-profits/substantially-related.

16. *See, e.g.*, G.S. Chapter 131F, Articles 2 and 3 (charitable solicitation rules requiring many nonprofits to obtain licenses from the secretary of state).

17. G.S. 55A-3-07(2).

a governmental unit, (2) operated by a governmental unit, or (3) performing a function so closely associated with the government that it is viewed as part of the government.[18]

There are also transparency requirements for certain entities that receive public funds—namely, nonprofit corporations. Under G.S. 55A-16-24, a nonprofit corporation receiving over $5,000 in public funds (from local, state, or federal governments) in grants, loans, or in-kind contributions during a fiscal year must provide the following information upon written request from any member of the public:

1. The nonprofit's most recent financial statements, including a balance sheet as of the end of the fiscal year, a statement of operations for that year, and "details about the amount of public funds received and how those funds were used."
2. The nonprofit's most recently filed Internal Revenue Service Form 990. This requirement is satisfied if the Form 990 is posted on a website where the public can access it without charge. If the nonprofit does not post this form, it should provide a link to another website (for example, Guidestar.org).

Certain entities are exempt from disclosing this information because they are required to report to the N.C. Medical Care Commission or the Local Government Commission, and some private colleges are exempt because they report to the state.[19]

Apart from these specific situations, nonprofit organizations are not required to open their records to the public. They must, however, provide access to their records for members of the organization,[20] though most Section 501(c)(3) nonprofits do not have members. Federal tax laws require some disclosure of basic informational documents for most nonprofits, other than churches.[21] Additionally, it is common for governments working with nonprofits to specify the kinds of disclosures and access to records required in the legal documents that define their relationship (e.g., contracts or grants).

Charities that solicit funds, unless exempted by law, must comply with the state's rules on charitable solicitations. A comprehensive set of statutes regulates solicitations by many nonprofits.[22] As with other laws, such as civil rights laws, there are no general exemptions specifically for nonprofits, but each law should be analyzed on a case-by-case basis. For example, G.S. 159-40 allows a city or county that appropriates at least $1,000 in any fiscal year to a nonprofit entity to require the nonprofit to "have an audit performed for the fiscal year in which the funds are received" and to file a copy of that audit with the local government. Some entities are exempt from this requirement, including volunteer fire departments, rescue squads, and ambulance squads. However, a local government can still require these entities (and all other private entities and individuals that receive public funds) to provide an accounting of how the funds are spent and comply with other requirements as a condition of receiving the funds. These requirements should be spelled out clearly in any contractual agreement between a local government and a nonprofit.

---

18. For a more extensive discussion of this issue, see Frayda Bluestein, "Privatization: Legal Issues for North Carolina Local Governments," *Popular Government* (Winter 1997): 28–40.

19. *See* Kara Millonzi, "Accountability Requirements for Certain Entities That Receive Appropriations from Local Governments," *Coates' Canons: NC Local Government Law* blog (Sept. 7, 2012), canons.sog.unc.edu/2012/09/accountability-requirements-for-certain-entities-that-receive-appropriations-from-local-governments/.

20. G.S. 55A-16-02.

21. The annual disclosure form is IRS Form 990. Until recently, many small nonprofit organizations were not required to file annual 990s; now, even the smallest nonprofits must file an abbreviated version of the form and can have their exempt status rescinded if they fail to do so. A discussion of the required disclosures is included in Department of the Treasury, Internal Revenue Service, Publication 557, *Tax-Exempt Status for Your Organization* (Oct. 2011), www.irs.gov/pub/irs-pdf/p557.pdf.

22. G.S. Chapter 131F.

Revenue Sources

Nonprofit organizations receive funds from the following revenue sources, listed from largest to smallest: private fees for services, government grants or contracts, individual donations, foundations, bequests, and corporations.[23] While the largest portion of U.S. nonprofit funding comes from private fees for services, in North Carolina, local governments are more likely to interact with smaller nonprofit organizations that rely on government grants or contracts, individual donations, foundations, and corporations.[24]

Previous studies have found that although smaller nonprofit organizations function with leaner budgets, they often demonstrate remarkable effectiveness, efficiency, and adaptability.[25] The size of these nonprofits allows them to be more adaptable and responsive to the unique needs of their local communities. When a community-wide or emergency response need arises that goes beyond standard day-to-day government services, nonprofits step in to fill the gaps, **though often without an adequate level of sustainable capacity.**[26] For example, when schools closed in response to COVID-19, a coalition of nonprofit food assistance organizations, school staff, private food providers, and an army of volunteers stepped in to work with local governments[27] to provide meals to the 900,000+ North Carolina children who typically rely on free and reduced-price breakfast and lunch for almost one-third of their food each week.[28] Nonprofit organizations can mobilize funds and implement actions quickly, thanks to passionate staff, a sizable volunteer base, and fewer bureaucratic hurdles.

While these organizations demonstrate significant adaptability and resiliency, this type of existence perpetuates a starvation cycle. The **nonprofit starvation cycle** (see Figure 12.2) is a self-reinforcing loop where nonprofits are pressured to uphold the long-standing business philosophy of minimizing overhead costs.[29] This practice is largely driven by donor expectations and the need to remain competitive with other nonprofit organizations. As a result, nonprofit organizations

---

23. "Common Problems in Government–Nonprofit Grants and Contracts," National Council of Nonprofits, January 11, 2015, www.councilofnonprofits.org/trends-policy-issues/common-problems-government-nonprofit-grantmaking-and-contracting.

24. Richard C. Feiock and Hee Soun Jang, "Nonprofits as Local Government Service Contractors," *Public Administration Review* 69, no. 4 (2009): 668–80; Sarah Carnochan, Bowen McBeath, Emmeline Chuang, and Michael J. Austin, "Perspectives of Public and Nonprofit Managers on Communications in Human Services Contracting," *Public Performance & Management Review* 42, no. 3 (May 4, 2019): 657–84.

25. Alina Kadyrova and Philip Shapira, "Microfoundations of Dynamic Capabilities for Social Innovations in Small Non-Profit Organizations," *Nonprofit and Voluntary Sector Quarterly* 53, no. 6 (Dec. 2024): 1410–1433; Rong Wang and Hillary Hamilton, "Evaluating the Relationship Between Nonprofit Capacities and Organizational Effectiveness During a Global Pandemic," *Management Communication Quarterly* (April 29, 2024).

26. Fiona Roberts, Frank Archer, and Caroline Spencer, "The Potential Role of Nonprofit Organisations in Building Community Resilience to Disasters in the Context of Victoria, Australia," *International Journal of Disaster Risk Reduction* 65 (November 1, 2021): 102530; Yu Shi, Hee S. Jang, Laura Keyes, and Lisa Dicke, "Nonprofit Service Continuity and Responses in the Pandemic: Disruptions, Ambiguity, Innovation, and Challenges," *Public Administration Review* 80, no. 5 (May 2020): 874–79.

27. Nikolaos Tsoukalis-Chaikalis, Eleftherios Kipoulas, Dimitrios Chaniotis, Vilelmine Carayanni, Athanasia Stamatopoulou, Eleni Stamatopoulou, and Fragkiskos Chaniotis, "The Impact of the COVID-19 Pandemic and School Closures on Children and Young People: A Scoping Review," *Epitheōrīsī Klinikīs Farmakologias Kai Farmakokinītikīs* 37, no. 3 (December 28, 2023): 129–40, doi.org/10.61873/zium1367.

28. "Mobilizing and Delivering Essential Meals to Children and Families Affected by School Closures During COVID-19 and Beyond," *Journal of School Health* 92, no. 7 (April 5, 2022): 646–55, doi.org/10.1111/josh.13188; Lindsay Wagner, "After Two Years, Free School Meals for All Is Over. What Does That Mean for Students and Their Families?," EducationNC, September 20, 2022, www.ednc.org/after-two-years-free-school-meals-for-all-is-over-what-does-that-mean-for-students-and-their-families/.

29. Hal G. Rainey and Barry Bozeman, "Comparing Public and Private Organizations: Empirical Research and the Power of the A Priori," *Journal of Public Administration Research and Theory* 10, no. 2 (2000): 447–70.

Figure 12.2 The Nonprofit Starvation Cycle

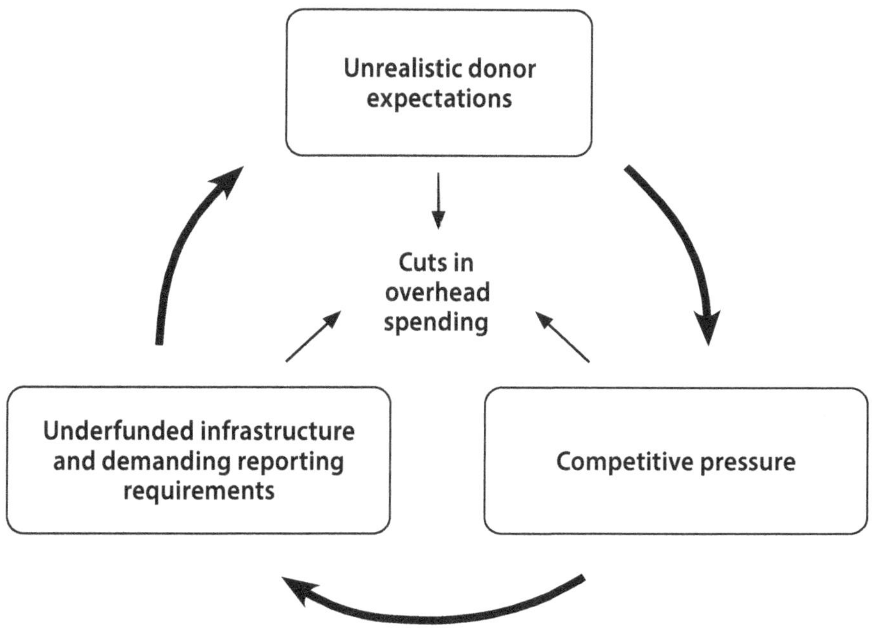

underinvest in innovation and other critical areas, lacking sufficient funds to hire talented individuals. In addition to underinvesting in their organizations, nonprofits often face the administrative burden of completing financial reports that are disproportionate to the size of the grants received. For example, small nonprofit organizations are often required to complete lengthy, complicated financial reports for grants as modest as $500. Underinvestment hinders their effectiveness and long-term sustainability despite continuous efforts to adapt with limited resources. Consequently, the cycle continues as they struggle to fulfill their missions without the necessary support, perpetuating chronic underfunding and operational strain. Understanding the true costs of running a nonprofit can shift expectations around overhead spending.

A different perspective is necessary to align funder expectations with the actual operational needs of nonprofit organizations. Funders often misunderstand overhead expenses, viewing them as unnecessary or signs of inefficiency.[30] This misconception can pressure nonprofits to cut spending on essential operational costs, perpetuating the starvation cycle. By examining a nonprofit organization's *financial allocations, operational needs, and the actual costs of delivering programs,* funders would better understand the need to support not just the direct services but also the infrastructure that makes those services possible.

30. George E. Mitchell and Thad D. Calabrese, "Proverbs of Nonprofit Financial Management," *The American Review of Public Administration* 49, no. 6 (April 30, 2018): 649–61, doi.org/10.1177/0275074018770458.

Table 12.2 Comparison of Characteristics of Nonprofits, Governments, and For-Profit Organizations

	Nonprofit Organizations	Governments	For-Profit Organizations
Focus	Mission	Constituents	Profit
Purpose	Serve a social cause or public benefit	Provide public services and enforce laws	Generate profits for owners/shareholders
Funding Sources	Donations, grants, memberships, fees	Taxes, fees, government bonds	Sales revenue, investments, loans
Accountability	To donors, members, regulatory bodies	To citizens, legislative bodies, oversight agencies	To owners, shareholders, customers
Profit Distribution	Profits reinvested into the organization	N/A (not-for-profit); funds allocated per budget	Profits distributed to owners/shareholders

How Nonprofits and Local Governments Work Together

Local governments are regularly involved with nonprofit organizations. To help meet the challenge of providing more and better services while being constrained by tight fiscal limits, many local governments have engaged nonprofits in service delivery, leveraging these organizations' volunteers, private financial resources, and greater flexibility to act. Some nonprofits have also become skilled advocates for the clients they serve, making persuasive appeals for public funding or otherwise helping to shape government priorities.

Local governments can work effectively with nonprofits to address public needs by contracting with them, providing property, sharing training opportunities, offering expertise, or providing other types of in-kind assistance. They also partner with nonprofits to jointly develop and implement public service programs. Table 12.2 compares the focus, purpose, funding sources, accountability, and profit distribution of nonprofit, government, and for-profit organizations.

Who Are Nonprofits Accountable To?

For both local governments and nonprofits, accountability expectations establish performance responsibilities, limits on responsiveness, and reporting relationships, as well as the authority to evaluate success and adjust plans for the future. Sometimes a government sets these expectations and presents them to a nonprofit as conditions for working together. Other times, mutual negotiations produce accountability expectations. Mutual accountability is particularly important when governments and nonprofits need to learn from each other and from experience in order to better serve the public.

Effective accountability within partnerships is multidirectional and multidimensional. Governments and nonprofits can design new accountability patterns together if they are willing to share decision-making, take time to deliberate and experiment, and respect each other's perspectives. Using a model of mutual accountability, the challenge for community partners is to move beyond the limited principal–agent relationship[31] often found in government–nonprofit contracts and toward real collaboration—ongoing, shared responsibility for improving public services.

31. Fiona Roberts, Frank Archer, and Caroline Spencer, "The Potential Role of Nonprofit Organisations in Building Community Resilience to Disasters in the Context of Victoria, Australia," *International Journal of Disaster Risk*

Sidebar 12.1 Defining Expectations for Mutual Accountability

This exercise offers up a process for defining mutual expectations about future interactions in a local government–nonprofit partnership. Discuss the following four questions as they relate to the mutual accountability dimensions of fairness, performance, financial integrity, relational integrity, and social and environmental responsibility:

Product. Who is expected to carry out which actions and for whose benefit?
Alteration. Who can invoke or alter these expectations?
Information. Who should provide what information to whom about how responsibilities are fulfilled?
Review. Who is expected to use what information to make decisions about the future of the relationship?

The general public often equates accountability with fiscal integrity, focusing on finances instead of fairness and process rather than performance. While financial accountability in relationships with nonprofits is important, limiting a local government's concept of accountability to finances is inadequate when trying to ensure that the services the community wants and needs are provided effectively. A stakeholder-based perspective frames accountability[32] as multidimensional, encompassing five broad categories:

- Fairness: Standards apply to all people, whether they involve hiring practices for staff or eligibility criteria for clients. Fair decisions are made according to impartial standards, not favoritism.
- Performance: Focused on operational effectiveness and the achievement of organizational goals.
- Financial Integrity: Maintaining accurate and transparent financial records, ensuring funds are used appropriately.
- Relational Integrity: Incorporating community and stakeholder engagement into organizational decision-making.
- Social and Environmental Responsibility: Addressing the broader impact on communities and the environment, beyond financial or operational outcomes.

All five categories are important and should be considered in any comprehensive approach to defining and implementing accountability targets. To ensure that all five goals for accountability are addressed, a local government must express them explicitly. That is, key stakeholders must discuss their expectations about fairness, performance, finances, relational integrity, and social and environmental responsibility, and incorporate these expectations into the tools used to manage the relationship. Discussions about mutual expectations—and the contracts, reports, audits, and one-to-one contacts that reflect those expectations—should address all five accountability goals.

Often, the acts of setting accountability expectations and monitoring how well these expectations are met are handled independently by government and nonprofit staffs. Each contingent assesses accountability on its own and decides whether and how to continue the working relationship with

Reduction 65 (November 1, 2021): 102530, doi.org/10.1016/j.ijdrr.2021.102530; Yu Shi, Hee S. Jang, Laura Keyes, Lisa Dicke, "Nonprofit Service Continuity and Responses in the Pandemic: Disruptions, Ambiguity, Innovation, and Challenges," *Public Administration Review* 80, no. 5 (May 2020): 874–79.

32. Ericka Costa and Geiza Goulart da Silva, "Nonprofit Accountability: The Viewpoint of the Primary Stakeholders," *Financial Accountability and Management* 35, no. 1 (February 1, 2019): 37–54.

the other entity. This unilateral approach limits the ability of governments and nonprofits to learn from each other but may save staff time and effort. If the transaction is a one-time purchase and the government has no reason to develop trust in the vendor, then hierarchical accountability may be appropriate. Collaboration is neither sought nor needed.

Frequently, however, governments and their nonprofit partners are interested in exploring ways to address broad public problems together. If both entities want to refine their expectations of each other and develop more effective ways to serve the public, they may choose to work jointly in revising their accountability expectations. Trusting each other helps sustain effective partnerships.

Mutual accountability can improve public service as key stakeholders review a government–nonprofit relationship and decide whether and how to change it. By reviewing their accountability expectations together, the parties can refine and revise those expectations to fit new circumstances or challenges. This process can be time-consuming and difficult, but it will be worth the extra effort if government and nonprofit partners learn how to collaboratively address important public needs that neither party could meet alone. Mutual accountability can shift the focus from surveillance to service.

Nonprofits and Governments: Facing Challenges with Unique Strengths

The primary goal of both nonprofits and governments is to create value for the public.[33] They are key stakeholders in each other's operations to create value. Governments are invested in promoting the well-being of their citizens, while nonprofits aim to address social issues that align with governmental objectives. Although they are different entities facing different challenges, working together enables them to embrace unique opportunities that neither could achieve alone.

Challenges Facing Nonprofits in North Carolina

Nonprofits play a vital role in North Carolina's social safety net. However, they face numerous challenges that hinder their ability to fully serve citizens across the state.

Economic and Demographic Disparities: North Carolina's diverse landscape presents unique challenges. Nonprofits, particularly in rural areas, demonstrate remarkable resilience in the face of limited local funding, greater distances to cover, and fewer volunteers. They address issues like poverty and limited access to resources, showing unwavering dedication to their mission.

Staffing and Volunteer Recruitment: Attracting and retaining qualified staff and dedicated volunteers is a persistent challenge. Nonprofits often cannot offer salaries and benefits that compete with those of the private sector, leading to high turnover rates. Additionally, volunteer engagement may decline due to time constraints or a lack of awareness about available opportunities.

Competition for Resources: With many nonprofits operating in similar sectors, organizations often compete for the same donors, grants, and volunteers. This competition can limit the resources available to any single organization.

Financial Sustainability: Securing consistent and adequate funding remains a primary challenge. Late or delayed payments, particularly from government contracts, significantly contribute to financial instability. These delays can severely impact a nonprofit's cash flow, making it difficult to cover

33. John M. Bryson, Barbara C. Crosby, and Laura Bloomberg, "Public Value Governance: Moving beyond Traditional Public Administration and the New Public Management," *Public Administration Review* 74, no. 4 (July/August 2014): 445–56.

immediate expenses such as salaries, rent, and program costs. Financial strain can hinder program implementation, reduce staff morale, and even jeopardize an organization's credibility with beneficiaries and partners. Late payments often force nonprofits to divert time and resources to manage cash flow issues, sometimes relying on short-term loans or dipping into reserve funds, if available. These stopgap measures are unsustainable and increase financial vulnerability.

Unique Strengths of Nonprofit Organizations

Individual Missions: The mission or purpose of a nonprofit is stated in its organizational charter and forms the basis for its legal status, including its tax classification. The nonprofit's mission also attracts and motivates supporters, including board members, employees, volunteers, and donors, who are dedicated to achieving its goals. Individuals who work or volunteer for a nonprofit often develop considerable knowledge of the organization's goals, along with a strong commitment to fulfilling them.

Connection to Communities Served: Nonprofit board members, staff, and volunteers are frequently members of the community they serve, whether that is defined by geography, shared experiences, common interests, or similar personal characteristics. This shared identity fosters mutual trust and provides valuable insights that external parties might not have.

Less Stringent Procedural Restrictions: Nonprofits can act more quickly and with greater flexibility than local governments when adopting and implementing new programs, hiring and firing employees, and buying and selling property. As private corporations, nonprofits are usually not subject to the requirements for public notice, public hearings, open meetings, or public access to records that apply to local governments. Nonprofits do, however, have to act within the scope of their missions and charters to maintain their tax-exempt status. In addition, nonprofits' personnel actions and property transactions must comply with business regulations, and they are subject to any terms or expectations set forth in their contractual agreements. There are also some special regulations that apply only to nonprofits, including accounting practices and standards that differ from those of businesses and governments.

Dynamics of Nonprofit–Government Relationships

Nonprofit organizations play a vital role in delivering services related to the arts, culture, humanities, education, health and human services, and much more. These services are often provided through a range of relationships with the government. While these relationships are multifaceted and fluid, they can be described through three broad categories that are not mutually exclusive: supplementary, complementary, and adversarial (see Figure 12.3).[34] To better understand these relationships, it is important to consider the driving forces behind them and the outcomes they achieve.

In a **supplementary relationship**, nonprofits fill gaps in services to address social needs that cannot be addressed by the government or the private sector (Derrick-Mills 2015; Weisbrod, 1975). In this role, nonprofits operate independently of the government, providing services such as homeless shelters, food banks, arts and culture, and educational enrichment opportunities without direct

34. Dennis R. Young, "Alternative Models of Government–Nonprofit Sector Relations: Theoretical and International Perspectives," *Nonprofit and Voluntary Sector Quarterly* 29, no. 1 (2000): 149–72; Stefan Toepler, Annette Zimmer, Katja Levy, and Christian Frölich, "Beyond the Partnership Paradigm: Toward an Extended Typology of Government/Nonprofit Relationship Patterns," *Nonprofit and Voluntary Sector Quarterly* 52, no. 1_suppl (April 1, 2023): 160S–186S.

Figure 12.3 Three Modes of Government–Nonprofit Relations

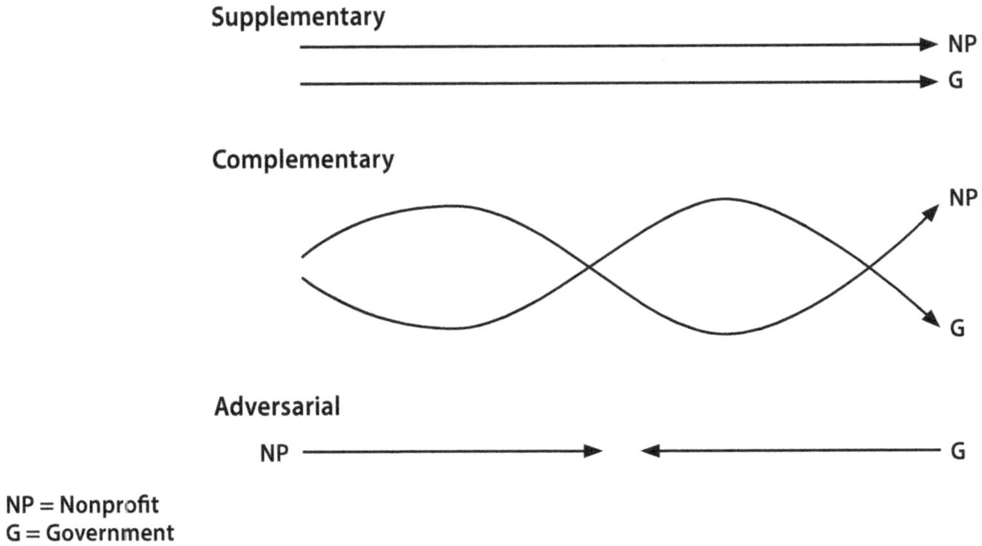

Source: Dennis Young and John Casey, "Supplementary, Complementary or Adversarial? Nonprofit–Government Relations," in *Nonprofits and Government: Collaboration and Conflict* (Rowman & Littlefield, 2016).

coordination. While governments often provide grants to nonprofits to fund these activities today, the situation was different in the late 19th and early 20th centuries. During those periods, nonprofits expanded their supplementary efforts due to technological advancements and economic growth, which led to urbanization that did not benefit everyone.[35] Urban areas began to experience overcrowding, poverty, poor working conditions, inadequate housing, and limited access to education and healthcare, while governments lacked the resources, infrastructure, or political mandate to address these complex societal issues effectively.

To respond to the need for enhanced service delivery, nonprofits and governments engage in **complementary relationships**. Both sectors collaborate, leveraging their respective strengths to achieve shared goals. Examples of complementary activities include public health campaigns conducted in partnership with health departments to increase vaccination rates and improve access to healthcare,[36] or when nonprofits are contracted to administer programs that provide grants, loans, and technical assistance to local entrepreneurs and small businesses.[37] The complementary model became more prominent after World War II when governments sought to address social needs through social welfare programs without expanding bureaucracy. As a result, the adversarial

35. Dennis R. Young and John Casey, "Chapter 1: Supplementary, Complementary or Adversarial? Nonprofit–Government Relations," in *Nonprofits and Government: Collaboration and Conflict* (Lanham, MD: Rowman & Littlefield Publishers, 2016), 1.

36. Shradha S. Parsekar, Lalitha Vadrevu, Monica Jain, Shekhar Menon, and Gunjan Taneja, "Interventions Addressing Routine Childhood Immunization and Its Behavioral and Social Drivers," *Frontiers in Public Health* 12 (June 19, 2024), doi.org/10.3389/fpubh.2024.1364798.

37. Carolina Small Business Development Fund, "CSBDF to Launch 'Vivid Digital Classroom' to Provide Online Technical Assistance to Entrepreneurs," May 6, 2024, www.carolinasmallbusiness.org/post/csbdf-to-launch-vivid-digital-classroom-to-provide-online-technical-assistance-to-entrepreneurs.

model began to take shape, as the relationship between nonprofits and governments became more formalized.

Finally, in an **adversarial relationship**, nonprofits respond to the need for accountability by challenging government actions or inactions, advocating for policy changes, and ensuring that diverse interests are represented. In contrast, governments regulate nonprofits to ensure that they operate ethically, legally, and effectively. Adversarial examples include mobilizing communities to oppose government decisions, such as zoning changes that could impact neighborhoods. From the government's perspective, an example would be developing and enforcing laws to ensure that nonprofits meet legal and financial reporting requirements.

Types of Nonprofit–Government Engagement

The following section explores the various ways government and nonprofit relationships can be structured.

Contracts: Local governments may purchase services from nonprofit organizations in the same way they do from other entities. These purchases can be made through the government's regular processes and may include the same terms and conditions typically applied to other service providers. The conditions of the purchase are managed through contracts. Unlike construction and supplies, the North Carolina General Statutes do not require bidding for the purchase of services. In fact, the process for acquiring these services is left to the discretion of the local government.[38]

Grants: G.S. 160A-20.1 and 153A-449 allow cities and counties to contract with and allocate funds to private nonprofit organizations. A grant is a provision of funds in exchange for a promise by the grantee to perform certain prescribed activities or produce particular results. The process for awarding grants is typically different from the process for purchasing services. Competition is usually structured differently, and grants may describe the required services in less detail than a contract for service purchase.

Other Kinds of Support: Local governments also provide in-kind support to nonprofits by contributing property or personnel assistance to the programs run by those nonprofits. For example, a local government might include nonprofit staff in its training programs or use its purchasing power to purchase goods or services on behalf of the nonprofit for use in programs the local government has authority to fund.[39] Additionally, a local government may provide the expertise of its staff to a nonprofit as a form of in-kind assistance that benefits both parties. In each case, the basic legal limitations on these types of in-kind assistance are the same as those discussed above. If the activity of the nonprofit is something the local government has legal authority to support, the government can provide in-kind assistance in a variety of ways.

---

38. In North Carolina, there are uniform requirements that apply to all governments for two types of public contracts: (1) construction and repair work and (2) the purchase of supplies, equipment, and materials. Generally, contracts for services are exempt from these requirements, but there are specific provisions for architectural, engineering, surveying and construction management services. These requirements are outlined in G.S. Chapter 143, Article 8. For projects valued over $500,000, G.S. 142-129 establishes a formal competitive bidding process. For projects between $30,000 and $500,000, governments may use the informal process in G.S. 143-131. Projects valued under $30,000 are exempt from the competitive bidding requirements of G.S. Chapter 143, Article 8.

39. G.S. 160A-279 and 160A-280 give cities and counties the authority to donate property to nonprofits carrying out a public purpose.

Strengthening Successful Relationships

Nonprofit and local government sectors share fundamental characteristics that make them ideal partners for value creation. While for-profit organizations drive innovation and contribute to the economy, nonprofit organizations and governments both focus on the public good, addressing societal needs, and maintaining transparency and accountability. The challenge lies in defining the relationship.

Despite their shared commitment to the public good, the two sectors have different organizational structures and cultures, which can create tension or obstacles. Local governments are subject to laws and regulations concerning financial management and other issues that do not apply to nonprofits or other private corporations. Local government officials must solicit and consider the viewpoints of many citizens and balance competing interests when making decisions. Many nonprofit organizations rely heavily on volunteers who are deeply committed to their cause. Nonprofits are often attractive to local governments for trying new or pilot programs because they can act quickly. However, this same ability to act quickly can be seen as a liability by local governments, as all necessary viewpoints may not be considered before action is taken.

Close collaboration can help balance nonprofits' focus on specific issues and local governments' need to consider broader community concerns. Collaboration is most effective when:[40]

- an institutionalized champion initiates the collaboration,
- institutionalized champions represent each organization,
- decision-makers' priorities are aligned,
- goals are clearly defined,
- a legal framework supports information sharing,
- stakeholders are involved in the problem-solving process, and
- time and resources are available to support planning.

Developing and maintaining true collaboration over the long term is difficult. Both nonprofits and local governments should explore how closely they want—and can afford—to work together. Both parties can benefit from a joint evaluation of their current relationship and a mutual decision about the desired level of connection and involvement. Furthermore, each entity must identify, evaluate, and set limits on the resources it is willing to expend to work more closely with the other.

There is no single "right" relationship between governments and nonprofit organizations. In a community, the relationship may shift as different issues or events arise. The relationship will also vary from community to community. Each partnership must decide for itself how to achieve the most effective balance of independence and connection. The optimal degree and type of relationship will depend on the specific circumstances of each community. Local governments and nonprofits trying to build effective partnerships face several obstacles, including (1) different perceptions of the same situation; (2) a lack of understanding about each other's work; (3) the varying effects of a community's economic and cultural base on communication styles, information sharing, and decision-making; and (4) power imbalances. Frequent and accurate communication can help overcome these potential roadblocks.

---

40. Tyler C. Doucet, Peter N. Duinker, Melanie Zurba, James W.N. Steenberg, and John D. Charles, "Perspectives of Successes and Challenges in Collaborations between Non-Governmental Organization and Local Government on Urban Forest Management," *Urban Forestry & Urban Greening* 93 (March 1, 2024): 128220, doi.org/10.1016/j.ufug.2024.128220; Russell M. Linden, *Leading across Boundaries: Creating Collaborative Agencies in a Networked World* (John Wiley & Sons, 2010).

Sidebar 12.2 Tips for Strengthening Relationships

What Local Governments Can Do

- Minimize the mistrust, frustration, or misunderstanding that nonprofits experience during budget planning by sharing information about funding, including data about the following:
    - the amount of money available,
    - government priorities,
    - the application and evaluation process,
    - criteria to be used in reviewing applications, and
    - the expectations for reporting and accountability.
- Coordinate nonprofit organizations' funding applications and presentations to the local government or other local private-sector grant makers to minimize duplication of effort and to improve communication among local funders.
- View problems or needs as belonging to the whole community, not just to a nonprofit.
    - Recognize that the clients of nonprofit organizations are community members deserving of resources.
    - Express appreciation for the missions of nonprofit organizations.
- Acknowledge nonprofit organizations as serious businesses.
    - Recognize the value that professional, paid employees can bring to an organization.
    - Support nonprofits in their efforts to strengthen internal professionalism.
    - Consider the impact that the payrolls and programs of nonprofit organizations can have on their local economies.

What Nonprofits Can Do

- Inform local governments about their progress throughout the year, not just during the funding application process.
- Pay attention to the workings of the whole community, not just the target client population.
- Be as financially responsible and accountable as possible, and present evidence of accountability to the public.
- Reinforce their organization's trustworthiness by presenting a reliable, professional image.
- Help the community learn how to deal with issues of concern to the nonprofit organization that are overwhelming, unattractive, or frightening to the general public.

What Nonprofits and Local Governments Can Do Together

- Share information, both during and outside of day-to-day working relationships.
    - Sponsor an annual forum that brings government and nonprofit staff, elected officials, and community volunteers together to focus on shared community concerns.
    - Undertake joint strategic planning efforts, especially around specific issues such as homelessness or juvenile delinquency.
    - Collaborate on community needs assessments.
    - Consider locating varied services that serve the same population at the same site.
    - Hold regular meetings among nonprofit organization directors, county department heads, and program staff of both organizations.
- Share resources.
    - Invite staff of the other type of organization to participate in training opportunities.
    - Offer to share expertise by providing training to or by meeting with staff of the other type of organization.
    - Invite program staff from other organizations to meet in your facility.
    - Make it possible for staff to serve on community boards, committees, and task forces.
- Jointly develop clear, written guidelines about mutual expectations and work to be accomplished together.
- Recognize that each organization can be the other's best support for understanding and handling the stresses associated with working in the public sector. After all, local governments and nonprofits are dealing with similar challenges.

Navigating the tensions between nonprofit organizations and local governments can be challenging. Like any segment of the population, people in the public sector represent a broad diversity of expertise, professional skills, communication styles, and levels of passion for their work. This diversity may be viewed with suspicion or embraced. By using their differences constructively, individuals working in local governments and nonprofits can leverage each other's strengths to compensate for weaknesses. Together, they may be able to serve the public more effectively than either sector could alone.

Conclusion

Nonprofit and local government coordination is critical for public value creation across North Carolina. The robust nonprofit sector makes a significant contribution to employment and economic growth, serving as a cornerstone for addressing a wide range of community needs. By forming strategic partnerships, nonprofits and local governments can enhance their ability to identify innovative solutions to community challenges. These partnerships leverage the unique strengths of both sectors—governments provide essential funding, infrastructure support, and regulatory frameworks, while nonprofits offer flexibility, deep community connections, and specialized expertise.

PART 3. Administration

Chapter 13

Public Employment Law

Diane M. Juffras

Diane M. Juffras is a School of Government faculty member who specializes in public employment law.

(continued on next page)

The employment relationship in North Carolina cities and counties is a function of the North Carolina General Statutes, federal statutes, the United State Constitution, the North Carolina Constitution, decisions of state and federal courts, and the personnel ordinances and human resources policies adopted by cities and counties. Public-sector human resources administration includes classification of positions, recruitment and selection of employees, performance evaluation, pay and benefits administration, and discipline and discharge. The General Assembly has delegated broad authority for human resources management to cities and counties, reflecting the view that providing a framework within which cities and counties may determine their individual employment policies is better than setting out numerous specific requirements. This chapter provides an overview of the law governing the relationship between North Carolina cities and counties and their employees.

The Employment-at-Will Rule

Absent a statute, ordinance, or employment contract that confers some sort of right to continued employment, all employment in North Carolina is *employment at will*. The term "employment at will" is a shorthand way of saying that employment may be ended at the will of either the employer or the employee. An employer can fire an employee for any reason or for no reason at all. An employee can quit for any reason or for no reason at all.[1] The at-will rule also applies to disciplinary actions that fall short of termination. An employer who can fire employees at will may refuse to

1. *See* Value Health Sols., Inc. v. Pharm. Research Assocs., Inc., 385 N.C. 250, 278 (2023), *quoting* Kurtzman v. Applied Analytical Indus., Inc., 347 N.C. 329, 331 (1997) ("In North Carolina, an at-will employment State, 'in the absence of a contractual agreement between an employer and an employee establishing a definite term of employment, the relationship is presumed to be terminable at the will of either party without regard to the quality of performance of either party.'"). *See also* Horne v. Cumberland Cnty. Hosp. Sys., Inc., 228 N.C. App. 142, 146 (2013); McCallum v. N.C. Coop. Extension Serv. of N.C. State Univ., 142 N.C. App. 48, 56–57 (2001); Soles v. City of Raleigh Civil Serv. Comm'n, 345 N.C. 443, 446 (1997).

hire any given applicant, may set the terms of employees' work, may raise and lower their pay, and may demote, suspend, or transfer them, all at will.

The employment-at-will rule is what is called a "common law" rule, that is, law developed in the courts, as opposed to laws found in statutes passed by legislatures or rules issued by agencies. Common law is case law, created by judges as they apply legal principles to various facts. This contrasts with statutory law, which is created by the United State Congress or the North Carolina General Assembly. The employment-at-will rule applies to both public- and private-sector employment in North Carolina and in every other state in the United States except Montana. In the public sector in North Carolina, the at-will status of employees is, in some instances, explicitly stated in the General Statutes. For example, Chapter 160A, Section 147 of the General Statutes (hereinafter G.S.) states that a city manager is appointed by the city council "to serve at its pleasure." Similarly, G.S. 153A-103(2) provides that sheriff's deputies "serve at the pleasure of the appointing officer."[2] But even where the at-will status of a particular position or group of employees is not expressly stated, the presumption is that employment at will applies unless it is stated otherwise.[3]

In the hiring context, the employment-at-will rule means that employers may generally hire whomever they please. There is no legal requirement that the person be the most qualified applicant, that they have relevant experience, or that they even meet the minimum stated qualifications. The decision about whom to hire is completely within the employer's discretion. To put it starkly, where the at-will rule applies, employers may hire whomever they please, even if the person selected is unqualified, a "bozo," or has unspeakable body odor.

The notion that "the decision about whom to hire is completely within the employer's discretion" is, however, qualified by the employment-at-will rule's status as a common law rule. Common law is made by the courts one decision at a time, each decision building on decisions that came before it. At any time, however, a legislature may overrule a rule of common law by passing a statute to the contrary. The employment-at-will rule is thus subject to a number of exceptions that have been created by federal and state statutes. It is therefore more correct to say that under the employment-at-will rule, an employer may hire and fire employees for any reason or no reason at all—just not for a reason made unlawful by federal or state law or local ordinance.

Those sections of the North Carolina General Statutes that set forth who has the authority to hire in North Carolina local government sometimes accord employees at-will status and other times make it lawful only to hire persons with certain credentials or by following certain procedures. These same statutes sometimes allow employers to hire at will but only permit termination of employees for good cause. The next section will discuss hiring and firing authority in cities and counties. The section after that will discuss the major statutory, constitutional, and common law exceptions to the employment-at-will rule.

---

2. *See also* Chapter 153A, Section 81(1) of the North Carolina General Statutes (hereinafter G.S.) (authorizing a board of county commissioners to appoint a county manager to serve at its pleasure); G.S. 160A-173 (the city council appoints the city attorney, who serves at its pleasure); 153A-111 and -114 (both the county clerk and the county attorney are appointed by the board of commissioners and serve at its pleasure).

3. *See* Nantz v. Emp. Sec. Comm'n, 290 N.C. 473, 477 (1976) (holding that a state employee was an employee at will despite her employment contract referring to her position as "a regular, permanent job"). *See also* Cannon v. Town of Long View, No. ST-C-88-88, 1989 WL 132348, at *2 (W.D.N.C. Apr. 19, 1989), *aff'd*, 887 F.2d 1078 (4th Cir. 1989) (holding that the plain language of G.S. 159-24, which provides that "each local government and public authority shall appoint a finance officer to hold office at the pleasure of the appointing board or official," made the plaintiff finance officer an employee at will); Blair v. Randolph Cnty. Bd. of Educ., 212 N.C. App. 419 (2011) (unpublished disposition; same); Roberson v. City of Goldsboro, 564 F. Supp. 2d 526, 530 (E.D.N.C. 2008) (same); Wuchte v. McNeil, 130 N.C. App. 738, 740 (1998) (same); Woods v. City of Wilmington, 125 N.C. App. 226, 229 (1997) (same).

Hiring and Firing Authority in North Carolina Cities and Counties

Municipalities

Mayor–Council Form of Government

G.S. 160A-155 states that the council in mayor–council cities "shall appoint, suspend, and remove the heads of all city departments, and all other city employees." The council may, however, delegate to any administrative official or department head the power to appoint, suspend, and remove city employees assigned to his or her department. *Unless an individual city or town's charter provides otherwise, the mayor has no hiring or firing authority.* For cities with populations of 5,000 or more, neither the mayor nor any member of the council may serve as the head of any city department, even on an acting or interim basis.[4]

Council–Manager Form of Government

Where a municipality has adopted the council–manager form of government, G.S. 160A-147 authorizes a city council to appoint a city manager to serve at its pleasure. Irrespective of the size of a city, neither its mayor nor any member of its council may serve as city manager, on a permanent or a temporary basis.[5] Under the council–manager form of government, the General Statutes delegate the authority to hire employees to the city manager. G.S. 160A-148(1) provides that the manager shall appoint, suspend, and remove all city officers and employees who "are not elected by the people, and whose appointment or removal is not otherwise provided for by law" in accordance with such personnel rules as the council may adopt. Examples of city employees whose appointments are otherwise provided for by law include the city attorney and, in some jurisdictions, the city clerk. The city council appoints the city attorney, who serves at its pleasure.[6] The General Statutes direct cities to appoint a city clerk but fail to specify who is to appoint the clerk.[7] Instead, the hiring and firing authority over the city clerk is usually found in the city charter, with some charters providing that the clerk serves at the pleasure of the city council and others granting hiring and firing authority to the city manager.

Counties

Counties without a Manager

Currently, there are no counties in North Carolina without a manager. Nevertheless, G.S. 153A-87 provides that in counties that do not have a county manager, the board of commissioners shall appoint, suspend, and remove all county officers, employees, and agents, except those who are elected by the people or whose appointment is otherwise provided for by law.

Counties with a Manager

Counties may choose to adopt the manager plan (as they all have), which allows them to hire a county manager to serve at the pleasure of the board of county commissioners—in other words, as

4. *See* G.S. 160A-158.
5. *See* G.S. 160A-151. When a vacancy is created in the office of the city manager, the council is authorized to "designate a qualified person to exercise the powers and perform the duties of manager until the vacancy is filled." *See* G.S. 160A-150.
6. *See* G.S. 160A-173.
7. *See* G.S. 160A-171.

an at-will employee. Although a city council member may not serve as city manager, the General Statutes permit a member of the board of commissioners to serve as county manager.[8]

In counties with a manager, it is the county manager who has hiring authority in most cases. The manager's hiring power is, however, subject to the approval of the board of commissioners—unless the board passes a resolution permitting the manager to act without first securing the board's approval.[9]

Dismissal authority is also vested in the county manager but without the requirement that any dismissal action be ratified by the board of commissioners. There are, however, certain county officers whose appointment and dismissal are required by law to be made by the board. For example, the clerk of the board and the county attorney are appointed by the board and serve at its pleasure.[10] The tax collector is a board appointee who serves for a term determined by the board.[11] The tax collector may be removed only for good cause after written notice and an opportunity for a hearing at a public session, except that no hearing is required if the tax collector is removed for failing to deliver tax receipts properly. The board also appoints deputy tax collectors for specified terms,[12] but the General Statutes do not explicitly state how they are to be removed. Finally, the county assessor is a board appointee who serves a term of not less than two nor more than four years. The assessor may be removed only for good cause after written notice and an opportunity for a hearing at a public session.[13] The county assessor has the authority to hire listers, appraisers, and clerical assistants directly.[14]

Unlike a city council and a city manager, a board of county commissioners and its manager do not have direct authority over all those who work for the county. The General Statutes have established multiple hiring authorities within county government. Some positions are under the control of elected officials; still others are under the control of various county boards and are subject to the North Carolina State Human Resources Act (SHRA).[15] This makes human resources administration at the county level more complex than at the city level.

Counties: Officers Elected by the People

Article VII, Section 2 of the North Carolina Constitution provides that each county shall have a **sheriff** elected by the people for a four-year term, subject to removal for cause as provided by law. G.S. 153A-103(1) states that "[e]ach sheriff . . . has the exclusive right to hire, discharge, and supervise the employees in [the sheriff's] office" (except that the board of county commissioners must approve the appointment of a sheriff's relative or of a person convicted of a crime involving moral turpitude). Each sheriff is entitled to at least two deputies who serve at the pleasure of the sheriff.

The register of deeds is also an elected officer, with a four-year term.[16] As is the case with the sheriff, "[e]ach . . . register of deeds has the exclusive right to hire, discharge, and supervise the employees in [the register of deeds'] office" (except that the board of commissioners must approve the appointment of a relative of the register of deeds or of a person convicted of a crime involving moral turpitude).[17] Each register of deeds is entitled to at least two deputies, provided that the

8. *See* G.S. 153A-81(2).
9. *See* G.S. 153A-82(1).
10. *See* G.S. 153A-111, -114.
11. *See* G.S. 105-349(a).
12. *See* G.S. 105-349(f).
13. *See* G.S. 105-294(a).
14. *See* G.S. 105-296(b).
15. The SHRA is codified at G.S. Chapter 126.
16. *See* G.S. 153A-103(2).
17. *See* G.S. 153A-103(1).

register of deeds justifies to the board the necessity of the second deputy. Deputies serve at the pleasure of the register of deeds.[18]

Employees Whose Appointments Are Made through or Are Subject to Boards

Certain positions are filled either by designated boards or by the county manager in accordance with the requirements established by the board of commissioners. Public library employees, for example, are appointed either directly by the board of commissioners or, where the commissioners have appointed a library board of trustees and delegated hiring authority to it, through the library board. The library board, which may not exceed twelve members, is appointed by the board of commissioners for a term set by the county. Library trustees may be removed only for incapacity, unfitness, misconduct, or neglect of duty.[19] If the county commissioners have granted hiring authority to the library board, the trustees may appoint a chief librarian or a director of library services. The trustees would then appoint other library employees upon the advice of the chief librarian or the director of library services.[20] G.S. 153A-267 states that the employees of a county library system are, for all purposes, employees of the county.

County boards of elections are composed of five members appointed by the State Board of Elections for two-year terms.[21] A board of election's clerk, assistant clerks, and other employees, including precinct transfer assistants, are appointed and dismissed by the county board of elections.[22] The county director of elections is appointed and dismissed by the Executive Director of the State Board of Elections, upon recommendation by the county board of elections.[23]

Employees Subject to the State Human Resources Act (SHRA)

The SHRA governs recruitment, selection, and dismissal in three county departments: health , social services, and emergency management.[24] These departments receive federal funds that require the use of certain recruitment and selection and discipline and discharge procedures as a condition for their receipt. The SHRA incorporates these federal requirements. Rather than requiring each county to adopt a personnel policy consistent with these requirements, the General Assembly has made county health, social services, and emergency management employees subject to the SHRA. Local government employees covered by the SHRA may be dismissed only for "just cause"[25] and have a property interest in their employment that requires certain procedures be followed before an employee may be suspended without pay, demoted, or dismissed. Property interests in employment are discussed later in this chapter.

County health department employees are subject to the SHRA. A county board of health is composed of eleven members appointed by the board of county commissioners to serve three-year terms.[26] In place of a county health department, a district health department that includes more than one county may be formed upon agreement of the boards of commissioners and local boards of health having jurisdiction over each of the counties involved.[27]

18. *See* G.S. 153A-103(2).
19. *See* G.S. 153A-265.
20. *See* G.S. 153A-266(4).
21. *See* G.S. 163-30(a).
22. *See* G.S. 163-33(10).
23. *See* G.S. 163-35(a).
24. *See* G.S. 126-5(a)(2).
25. *See* G.S. 126-35.
26. *See* G.S. 130A-35.
27. *See* G.S. 130A-36.

The local board of health (or boards of health in the case of district health departments) appoints the local health director after consultation with the board (or boards) of commissioners having jurisdiction over the area served by the health department, subject to the final approval of the State Health Director.[28] The local health director may be dismissed only for cause in accordance with the due process requirements of the SHRA. Similarly, health department employees are appointed and dismissed by the local health director in accordance with the statute.[29]

County social services department employees are also covered by the SHRA. The county board of social services is composed of three or five members, appointed for three-year terms.[30] The county director of social services is appointed and dismissed by the board of county commissioners in accordance with the SHRA.[31] Social service employees are appointed and dismissed by the county director of social services, also in accordance with the SHRA.[32]

Emergency management employees are the third category of county employees subject to the SHRA. G.S. 126-5(2)d. defines SHRA coverage as applying to "local emergency management agencies that receive federal grant-in-aid funds," but as most emergency management agencies receive federal funding, county emergency management agencies are likely to be covered by the SHRA. G.S. 166A-19.15(a) and (b) say that the governing body of each county is responsible for emergency management within the county and is authorized to establish and maintain an emergency management agency. The governing body of each county that establishes an emergency management agency is to appoint a coordinator, who will have direct responsibility for the organization, administration, and operation of the county program and will be subject to the direction and the guidance of such governing body.[33] Although there is no General Statutes provision on the dismissal of emergency management coordinators, dismissal must presumably be made in accordance with the SHRA, as it is with local health directors and county social services directors. The General Statutes do not specify who has the appointing authority over emergency management employees. Given the absence of a provision granting hiring authority to any other person or body, the county manager presumably has the hiring authority. Employees of the emergency management agency are appointed and dismissed in accordance with the SHRA[34]—unlike all other county employees over whom the county manager has hiring and firing authority.[35]

"Substantially Equivalent" Personnel Systems

G.S. 126-11 permits the State Human Resources Commission to exempt all SHRA employees in a given county from portions of the State Human Resources System when the commission finds that the county has a substantially equivalent personnel system for all county employees. The commission may approve as "substantially equivalent," for example, portions of a local personnel ordinance that cover the county's position classification plan, selection procedures, salary administration plan,

---

28. *See* G.S. 130A-40.

29. *See* G.S. 130A-41(b); 126-5(a).

30. *See* G.S. 108A-1 through -5.

31. *See* G.S. 108A-9, -12.

32. *See* G.S. 108A-14(2). *See also In re* Brunswick Cnty., 81 N.C. App. 391 (1986) (director has exclusive power to hire and fire department personnel).

33. *See* G.S. 166A-19.15(b)(2).

34. *See* G.S. 126-5(a).

35. The General Statutes also allow a municipality to establish an emergency management agency with the directive that, in doing so, the municipality coordinate with its county emergency management agency. *See* G.S. 166A-19.15(c). The General Statutes also provide for the creation of joint city-county emergency management agencies. *See* G.S. 166A-19.15(d). Employees of both municipal and joint emergency management agencies would be covered by the State Human Resources Act if the agencies receive federal funds.

and grievance and dismissal procedures. A number of counties and area authorities have had all or part of their personnel systems approved as "substantially equivalent."

Consolidated Human Services Agencies

G.S. 153A-77 authorizes each county to consolidate its health and social services agencies into one county department of human services.[36] A consolidated human services agency is managed by a single human services director, who is appointed and supervised by the county manager with the advice and consent of a human services board appointed by the board of county commissioners.[37] The human services director then appoints all human services agency employees subject to the approval of the county manager.[38] When a county consolidates its human services agencies pursuant to G.S. 153A-77, employees of the consolidated agency lose the protections of the SHRA and become subject to county personnel policies. To the extent that federal funds administered by consolidated human services agencies require the use of so-called competitive recruitment and selection procedures, the board of county commissioners will have to adopt such policies for human services employees, if not for all county employees.

Organization of the Human Resources Function in North Carolina Cities and Counties

Cities take the authority to determine their organizational structure and to establish personnel policies from G.S. Chapter 160A, Article 7. Counties take their authority from G.S. Chapter 153A, Article 5. G.S. 160A-162 authorizes a city council to create, change, abolish, and consolidate city offices and departments and to determine the most efficient organization for the city, with only three limitations. G.S. 153A-76 authorizes boards of county commissioners to do the same for county government, again with three limitations. The limitations are first, that neither the council nor the board may abolish any office or agency established and required by law. For example, a council may not abolish the office of city attorney because G.S. 160A-173 requires a city to have one. Similarly, a board may not abolish the office of county attorney, as G.S. 153A-114 requires a county to have one. Second, neither the council nor the board may combine offices when forbidden by law. For example, G.S. 160A-151 provides that neither the mayor nor any member of the council may serve as the city manager, even on a temporary basis. Third, neither the council nor the board may discontinue or assign elsewhere any functions assigned by law to a particular office. For example, G.S. 160A-171 establishes the office of the city clerk and G.S. 153A-111 establishes the office of the county clerk, and certain duties in both cities and counties may be performed only by the clerk or a deputy clerk. In addition, G.S. 153A-76 prohibits the board from changing the composition or manner of selection of a local board of education, board of health, board of social services, board of elections, or board of alcoholic beverage control.

---

36. The statute allows for the consolidation of mental health, developmental disabilities, and substance abuse agencies with a county's health and social services departments. But as a practical matter, the current structure of mental-health service delivery through regional area authorities will preclude the consolidation of mental health services into a single-county consolidated human services agency. *See* G.S. 153A-76(6), -77(c)(1a).

37. *See* G.S. 153A-77(b)(1), (e).

38. *See* G.S. 153A-77(e)(1).

Statutory Responsibility for Human Resources Administration

In mayor–council cities, the council must appoint or designate a "personnel officer" or confer human resources duties on some city administrative officer. This function is usually carried out by the city's human resources director or by the finance director or city clerk. The personnel officer is responsible for administering the city's position classification and pay plan in accordance with general policies and directives adopted by the council.[39] However, in both cities and counties, when there is a manager, he or she is responsible for the personnel or human resources functions unless a human resources director has been appointed.

Position Classification

G.S. 160A-162 and 153A-25, respectively, provide that a city council and board of county commissioners may fix qualifications for any "appointive office." "Appointive offices" are, for the most part, employment positions (although they include appointment to boards like the planning board or the board of adjustment). A governing board's most important use of this authority is to adopt a position-classification plan.

A position-classification plan is one of the basic tools of human resource management. By adopting such a plan, a local unit's governing board determines in advance the duties and responsibilities of each position in the unit and sets the minimum qualifications as to education, training, and experience that will be required of each employee and each applicant for employment. Either the manager, the human resources director and staff, or an outside consultant generally prepares the classification plan for presentation to the board. Plan preparation involves identifying the duties and responsibilities of each position and grouping jobs into classes similar enough in duties and responsibilities that the same job title, the same minimum qualifications, and the same pay range can apply to all positions in that class. An accurate description of duties and responsibilities and minimum qualifications can serve as a basis for or assist in all aspects of city or county administration, including planning; organizing; budgeting; and selecting, training, paying, promoting, transferring, demoting, and discharging employees.

Compensation

Wages

In addition to position management, city councils and boards of county commissioners have the responsibility to make compensation determinations for all city employees and for all county employees. Both city councils and boards of county commissioners control compensation by adopting position-classification plans and pay plans, adopting personnel rules governing the administration of the pay plan, adopting the budget that appropriates funds to the unit's several departments and establishes expense allowances, and reviewing the reports of the manager and the unit's independent auditor.

A pay plan is simply a list of job titles and a schedule of the amount of money to be paid to whomever performs the prescribed duties of each position during a fixed period. The plan establishes pay rates for positions, not persons. Many pay plans are step-based: a salary range is established for each position, and within the minimum and maximum salaries of the range there are specific "steps" pegged to specific salaries or rates. Employees are assigned to a specific step within the range for their position based on some combination of experience, performance, and longevity.

39. *See* G.S. 160A-162(a).

Only city councils and boards of county commissioners have the authority to adopt pay plans. In *Newber v. City of Wilmington*, the North Carolina Court of Appeals interpreted the pay provisions of the statutes to bar the payment of stand-by and on-call time to a police officer when the Wilmington City Council had not previously authorized the payment. Stated the court, "G.S. 160A-148(1) prohibits the city manager from unilateral adoption of a policy establishing the funding for stand-by and on-call duty for any city department. The manager's role is limited to recommending position classification and pay plans to the city council for their ultimate approval."[40]

A mayor and the members of a city council and the members of a board of county commissioners are not considered employees of a local unit except by the Internal Revenue Service for income-tax reporting purposes. The council and the board may fix the compensation and allowances of the chairperson of their respective boards and of other board members (and the council may fix the compensation of the mayor) by including their compensation and allowances in the annual budget ordinance when it is adopted. If the chair of a board of county commissioners or another board member undertakes the duties of county manager full time, his or her salary or allowances may be adjusted during the fiscal year. Otherwise, the compensation of board members may not be changed until the next budget is adopted. The same is true of the expense allowances of board members.[41]

Restrictions on a County Board's Compensation Authority. There are certain restrictions on a board of county commissioners' authority to set salaries. They are as follows:

- Neither a register of deeds' nor a sheriff's compensation may be reduced during a term of office without the officeholder's approval or unless ordered by the Local Government Commission.[42] Commissioners must give notice of intent to reduce the compensation for the next term of either office no later than fourteen days before the last day for filing as a candidate for that office. Further, a register of deeds or sheriff must approve any reductions in the salaries of employees assigned to his or her office, unless the county board has made a general reduction of all county salaries subject to its control. If the board wants to reduce the salaries of one or more employees of the register of deeds or sheriff and the elected officer will not agree, the board may refer the matter to the senior regular resident superior court judge for binding arbitration.
- The salaries paid to county health, social services, and emergency-management agency employees must conform to the pay plan approved for those departments by the State Human Resources Commission.[43]
- Agricultural-extension employee salaries are set jointly by the North Carolina Agricultural Extension Service and boards of county commissioners under a "Memorandum of Understanding"—a contract—entered into by the extension service and a given board.

The policies of the State Human Resources Commission (SHRC) allow counties considerable discretion in developing local salary schedules applicable to health, social services, and emergency-management employees so that they may conform to local ability to pay and local fiscal policy. With the SHRC's approval, counties may add to or reduce the number of salary steps in the state's salary schedule and may vary the percentage change between steps. The pay plan adopted

40. 83 N.C. App. 327, 330 (1986), *app. dismissed by* 319 N.C. 225 (1987).
41. *See* G.S. 160A-64(a); 153A-92.
42. *See* G.S. 153A-92.
43. *See* G.S. 126-9(b).

by a county for these employees is subject to the SHRC's approval, and the SHRC may require a county to provide data and information to justify any deviation from the standard state salary ranges. A county's failure to adhere to the provisions of the State Human Resources Act (SHRA) for compensating county SHRA employees not only makes the county ineligible for certain state and federal funds but also results in an unauthorized expenditure of public money.

Despite these restrictions, a board of county commissioners has an important role in determining the salaries of county SHRA employees. For example, G.S. 108A-13, which authorizes a board of social services to set the social services director's salary, requires that board to obtain the approval of the board of county commissioners for the salary paid. Similarly, a local health department has no authority to raise the salaries of health department employees without the board of commissioners' approval, since all county expenditures must be made in accordance with the provisions of the Local Government Budget and Fiscal Control Act.[44]

Salary Increases. A city council and board of county commissioners may provide for salary increases for all employees or for a class of employees as part of the annual budget. Many local governments in North Carolina have implemented pay systems that have a merit pay component. Others use across-the-board systems that reward all employees equally, regardless of individual performance.

Benefits

The General Statutes set out a nonexclusive list of personnel policies that a city council or board of county commissioners may adopt by rules, regulations, or ordinance.[45] Thus, a council or board may choose to adopt personnel policies governing leave, overtime, training, residency, or any other issue. The important point is that the General Assembly has not mandated that North Carolina cities and counties establish any personnel policies other than classification and pay plans.

Vacation and Sick Leave and Other Time-Off Policies. Most cities and counties provide paid leave to employees. Typically, nine to twelve days a year are designated as paid holidays. In addition, employees usually earn sick leave and vacation leave. Under the General Statutes, the decision to grant employees paid and unpaid leave of various types and amounts rests solely with a city council or board of county commissioners.[46]

Local Governmental Employees' Retirement System. A major benefit available to city and county employees is the Local Governmental Employees' Retirement System (LGERS), established at G.S. Chapter 128, Article 3. G.S. 128-23 authorizes an individual local government to participate in LGERS when a majority of its employees vote to do so. The term *employee* includes all officers and employees in a regular position that requires not less than 1,000 hours of service per year.[47]

An employee enrolled in LGERS may retire at age 60 with five years of creditable service or at any age with thirty years of creditable service. An enrolled firefighter may retire at age 55 with five years of creditable service.[48] Enrolled law enforcement officers may retire at age 50 with fifteen years of creditable service or at age 55 with five years of creditable service.[49]

44. *See* G.S. Ch. 159, Art. 3.
45. *See* G.S. 160A-164; 153A-94.
46. *See* G.S. 160A-164; 153A-94.
47. *See* G.S. 128-21(18a).
48. *See* G.S. 128-27(a)(1).
49. *See* G.S. 128-27(a)(5).

In addition to the regular retirement benefits paid to employees under LGERS, law enforcement officers are entitled to two other retirement benefits. First, cities and counties make a 5 percent contribution to a Section 401(k) retirement plan for each officer they employ.[50] Second, cities and counties must pay a special separation allowance to retiring law enforcement officers.[51]

Exceptions to the Rule of Employment at Will

There are three broad categories of exceptions to the employment-at-will rule: common-law exceptions, constitutional exceptions, and statutory exceptions.

Common Law Exceptions to Employment at Will

In addition to the constitutional exceptions and the statutory exceptions discussed later in this chapter, there are also judicially created exceptions to the rule of employment at will that restrict an employer's right to demote, suspend without pay, or fire an employee. These common-law exceptions include a breach of contract claim and the tort of wrongful discharge. They arise when the court finds either that the parties themselves, through their actions, have created a contractual exception to the employment-at-will rule or that an employer's motive in dismissing an employee violates some principle of public policy.

Employment Contracts

Whenever an individual begins work for an employer, there is a contract. The contract may be oral—in fact, in the work world generally, most people work without written contracts. It may be rudimentary, with the explicit understanding between the employer and the employee covering only pay, hours, location of work, and a general idea of duties, and perhaps not even all of these. In addition to whatever is explicitly understood, the law will add to the agreement the notion of employment at will, unless the parties agree differently.[52] There are two ways the parties might agree differently: by entering an explicit agreement that employment at will does not apply (as by agreeing that the employment is for a particular period of time or that the employee will only be terminated for cause) or by implicitly agreeing that employment at will does not apply.

Employment contracts, to be enforceable, must meet the basic requirements for the formation of contracts. Courts are generally not willing, however, in the case of a breach of contract, to order an employee to fulfill his or her obligations under the contract—known in the law as ordering specific performance. That seems too much like involuntary servitude.

Dismissal of an employee by an employer before the end of a contract term will usually open the possibility of a lawsuit for breach of contract. If the parties agree to employment for a particular period of time, it is a breach of the contract for the employer to dismiss the employee without cause before the term is up.[53]

---

50. In *Abeyounis v. Town of Wrightsville Beach*, 102 N.C. App. 341, 401 S.E.2d 847 (1991), the court held that the employer, not the employee, had to fund the 401(k) plan and that a budget ordinance that gave a 1.5 percent raise to town police and a 3.5 percent raise to all other municipal employees, with the 2.0 percent difference being used to fund the 401(k) plan, violated G.S. 143-166.50(e).

51. *See* G.S. 143-166.42.

52. Unless, of course, the law itself explicitly provides otherwise, as many statutes granting employment protections to public employees do.

53. *See* Smith v. State, 289 N.C. 303 (1976). *See also* Jones v. Carolina Power & Light Co., 206 N.C. 862 (1934) (streetcar operator induced to come to Asheville to operate streetcars on the promise of a job for ten years was entitled

Wrongful Discharge in Violation of Public Policy

Courts in several states, including North Carolina, have recognized an exception to the employment-at-will rule based on the tort of wrongful discharge. In its narrowest form, this theory holds that an employer may not dismiss an employee in violation of a public policy contained in a statute. In its broadest form, the theory holds that an employer may not dismiss an employee for reasons of malice, bad faith, or retaliation because to do so contravenes public policy. In between are many possible formulations.

North Carolina courts have taken a narrow view of wrongful discharge in violation of public policy. The approach that our courts take is typified by the decision of the North Carolina Court of Appeals in the case *Sides v. Duke University*[54]—the case where the court of appeals first recognized the existence of the public policy claim. The plaintiff, a nurse, brought a wrongful discharge action against the hospital, alleging that she had been dismissed in retaliation for her refusal to commit perjury in a medical malpractice trial. The court agreed that such a dismissal would be a wrongful discharge, stating the following:

> [W]hile there may be a right to terminate a contract at will for no reason, or for an arbitrary or irrational reason, there can be no right to terminate such a contract for an unlawful reason or purpose that contravenes public policy. . . . We hold, therefore, that no employer in this State, notwithstanding that an employment is at will, has the right to discharge an employee and deprive him of his livelihood without civil liability because he refuses to testify untruthfully or incompletely in a court case, as plaintiff alleges happened here.[55]

The public policy that the employer in *Sides* violated is that which requires persons under oath in court proceedings to tell the truth.

There is no list of situations that may form the basis of a public policy claim. In subsequent cases, the North Carolina Court of Appeals held that a claim of wrongful discharge in violation of public policy is available where (1) the public policy of North Carolina is clearly expressed within our general statutes or state constitution or (2) potential harm to the public is created by a defendant's unlawful actions.[56] Other circumstances under which the courts have recognized the tort of wrongful discharge in violation of public policy include terminations based on a truck driver's refusal to drive longer than the time allowed under United States Department of Transportation (US DOT) regulations and for refusing to falsify the sleep logs required to be maintained by US DOT,[57] a deputy sheriff's reporting of perjury and falsification of evidence by another deputy,[58] a police chief's refusal to give a town council confidential information about ongoing narcotics cases,[59] employees' complaints that their pay was below the state's minimum wage,[60] truthful testimony at an unemployment compensation hearing,[61] an employee's refusal to give in to the sexual

---

to damages for breach of contract when he was dismissed without cause after five).

54. 74 N.C. App. 331, *review denied,* 314 N.C. 331 (1985).

55. 74 N.C. App. at 342.

56. *See* Woody v. AccuQuest Hearing Ctr., LLC, 284 N.C. App. 540, 544, *appeal withdrawn,* __ N.C. __, 878 S.E.2d 147 (2022); McDonnell v. Guilford Cnty. Tradewind Airlines, Inc., 194 N.C. App. 674, 678 (2009); Considine v. Compass Grp. USA, Inc., 145 N.C. App. 314, 321 (2001).

57. *See* Coman v. Thomas Mfg. Co., 325 N.C. 172 (1989).

58. *See* Hill v. Meford, 357 N.C. 650 (2003).

59. *See* Blakeley v. Town of Taylortown, 233 N.C. App. 441, 452 (2014).

60. *See* Amos v. Oakdale Knitting Co., 331 N.C. 348 (1992).

61. *See* Williams v. Hillhaven Corp., 91 N.C. App. 35 (1988).

advances of their supervisor,[62] an employee's report of possible patient abuse to the State Bureau of Investigation and State Department of Human Resources,[63] and a nurse's refusal to violate state statutes and administrative code provisions regulating the practice of nursing.[64]

Constitutional Exceptions

Public Employers as Part of the Government

When the government becomes an employer, it does not stop being the government. It is constrained in its treatment of its employees in the same ways that it is constrained in its treatment of citizens generally. When citizens become public employees, they do not stop being citizens. They relinquish none of their rights, although the nature of the employment relationship may temper the absolute exercise of those rights. Most significantly for purposes of public human resources administration, no action by a governmental employer with respect to its employees can stand if it violates a provision of the U.S. Constitution or the North Carolina Constitution.

When the government becomes an employer, therefore, it bears burdens that private employers do not bear, related to the First Amendment's guarantee of freedom of speech, the Fourteenth Amendment's guarantee of due process of law in the protection of property and liberty, the Fourteenth Amendment's guarantee of the equal protection of the laws, and the Fourth Amendment's protection against unreasonable searches and seizures. The task for the courts in case after case is to determine the scope of that protection in the context of the workplace.

The First Amendment Right to Freedom of Speech

If a public employee is forced to choose between keeping his or her job and exercising his or her free speech rights, the government has done to the employee indirectly what it may not do directly: denied freedom of speech. It has forced the employee to make such a hard choice that it has deprived them of a constitutionally protected right. The courts, led by the United States Supreme Court, have made it clear that an indirect deprivation of a right is just as unconstitutional as a direct deprivation.[65]

The analysis of whether an employer has violated an employee's First Amendment right to free speech has three parts.

First, was the employee speaking as part of his or her job duties? If so, the speech is simply not protected by the First Amendment. Why is this true? Because the U.S. Supreme Court has said so. In its 2006 decision *Garcetti v. Ceballos,*[66] the Court said that if a government employee is speaking as part of his or her job duties, he or she is speaking as an **employee** doing the work he or she is paid to do, and not as a **citizen** exercising constitutionally protected rights. This restriction makes it much harder for public employees to win free speech cases.

Second, did any of the employee's comments constitute speech on a matter of public concern? If not, they are not protected. The U.S. Supreme Court has made this clear over the years. Comments by a government employee that are of **personal** concern ("my supervisor's husband is a real jerk") and not of interest to the community at large are simply beyond the protection of the First

---

62. *See* Harrison v. Edison Bros. Apparel Stores, 924 F.2d 530 (4th Cir. 1991).

63. *See* Lenzer v. Flaherty, 106 N.C. App. 496 (1992).

64. *See* Deerman v. Beverly Cal. Corp., 135 N.C. App. 1 (1999).

65. *See* Bd. of Regents v. Roth, 408 U.S. 564 (1972); Stroman v. Colleton Cnty. Sch. Dist., 981 F.2d 152 (4th Cir. 1992).

66. 547 U.S. 410 (2006).

Amendment, and a public employer may discipline an employee who makes such comments if it chooses. The initial Supreme Court case establishing this part of the analysis was *Connick v. Myers*.[67]

Third, in weighing the balance of interests, whose interests are more important, the employee's or the employer's? The Supreme Court first articulated this balancing requirement in 1968. The challenge, it said, "is to arrive at a balance of the interests of the [government employee], as a citizen, in commenting upon matters of public concern and the interest of the [government], as an employer, in promoting the efficiency of the public services it provides through its employees."[68]

The Fourth Amendment Right to Freedom from Unreasonable Searches

The Fourth Amendment to the United States Constitution provides, in part, that "[t]he right of the people to be secure in their persons, houses, papers, and effects, against unreasonable searches and seizure, shall not be violated." In the context of public employment, this constitutional protection against unreasonable searches comes up in two contexts: searches of employees' workstations and drug testing.

Workstation Searches

Striking the balance between the interests of the government as employer and the employee as citizen is also at the heart of cases involving searches of employees' workstations. The United States Supreme Court has held that public employees have a reasonable expectation of privacy in desks and file cabinets from which others are routinely excluded.[69] If the employer wishes to go into the desk or file cabinet to look for evidence of job misconduct[70] or personal misconduct,[71] the employer's reasons must outweigh the employee's legitimate expectation of privacy. In that balance, the courts will consider the seriousness of the suspicions against the employee, evidence in support of those suspicions, and the nature of the place searched. If that place contains materials open to anyone other than the individual employee, the protection of the expectation of privacy is greatly reduced.[72]

Drug Testing

The constitutional (and statutory) issues involved in the drug testing of applicants and employees follows from the same principles as those involved in the analysis of workplace searches. In general, however, the Constitution has been interpreted to limit public employers to requiring random drug testing only for safety-sensitive employees. For any other employee, drug testing may only be done if the government employer has reasonable suspicion that the employee is under the influence of drugs while at work.

The Fourteenth Amendment Property Right Exception to Employment at Will

Another exception to the employment-at-will rule found only in public-sector employment is the vesting of a "property right" in employment. For some government employees, their jobs are their property. For a government employer to fire such an employee is to deprive that person of property, which the Fourteenth Amendment to the U.S. Constitution says may not be done without due

---

67. 461 U.S. 138 (1983).
68. *See* Pickering v. Bd. of Educ., 391 U.S. 563 (1968).
69. *See* O'Connor v. Ortega, 480 U.S. 709 (1987).
70. *See O'Connor*, 480 U.S. 709, Diaz Camacho v. Lopez Rivera, 699 F. Supp. 1020 (D.P.R. 1988).
71. *See* Schowengerdt v. Gen. Dynamics Corp., 823 F.2d 1328 (9th Cir. 1987) (pornography stored in employee's locked office, desk, and credenza).
72. *See Diaz Camacho*, 699 F. Supp. 1020.

process of law. So, the termination from employment of a government employee with a property right must be accompanied by due process.[73]

At-will public employees do not have a property right in their employment. So where does an employee of a unit of government in North Carolina acquire "a legitimate claim of entitlement" to his or her job sufficient to move him or her from at-will status to job-protected property interest status?

A property interest arises when a public employee can demonstrate a reasonable expectation of continued employment because the employer has established a *binding* policy that dismissal will occur only for stated reasons. For example, county employees subject to the State Human Resources Act may be fired only for "just cause."[74] These employees have a property right in employment, as do employees of any local government that has adopted a personnel *ordinance* providing that employees may only be fired for "just cause."

The effect of this language that says dismissal is limited to "just cause" or "good cause" is to create a property right in employment that may be taken away from an employee only after the constitutional requirements of substantive and procedural due process have been met. Whether a city's or county's personnel policies confer a property right in employment depends not only on the wording of the policies but also on the form in which those policies were adopted by the city council or board of county commissioners.

Cities and counties may only provide property-status protection of employment for their employees by adopting an actual personnel ordinance.[75] In *Pittman v. Wilson County*, the court held that personnel policies adopted by resolution, not by ordinance, by the Board of County Commissioners of Wilson County were not sufficient to vest county employees with a property right.[76] Instead, the court held that because the restrictions were set forth only in a resolution, not in an ordinance or a statute, they were not binding. The court said:

> [T]he resolution is a part of a manual that describes itself as merely a "Welcome to All Employees of Wilson County." . . . The language simply is not typical of that used in an ordinance or statute having the effect of law. Moreover, the subject matter of the personnel resolution is administrative in nature. It supplies internal guidelines to County officials for the administration of the County's employment positions, including the disciplining and discharge of employees.[77]

Having found no basis for the plaintiff's claim that she was other than an at-will employee, the *Pittman* court concluded that she was not entitled to due process in the termination of her employment.

Similarly, in *Soles v. City of Raleigh Civil Service Commission*,[78] an employee discharged by the City of Raleigh argued that because Raleigh's personnel policies provided that "just cause" had to be shown before an employee could be discharged, he had a constitutionally protected property interest in his continued employment. The North Carolina Supreme Court rejected that claim, finding that the city's personnel policy was not a state statute or city ordinance passed into law, which was required before an employee could claim a property interest in his or her employment. A personnel policy that is not adopted by ordinance, the court said, quoting the policy itself, is

73. *See, e.g.*, Cleveland Bd. of Educ. v. Loudermill, 470 U.S. 532, 541–42 (1985).
74. *See* G.S. 126-35.
75. *See* Howell v. Town of Carolina Beach, 106 N.C. App. 410, 417 (1992).
76. *See* Pittman v. Wilson Cnty., 839 F.2d 225 (4th Cir. 1988).
77. *See Pittman*, 839 F.2d at 229.
78. 345 N.C. 443 (1997).

"designed so as not to restrict operating personnel but to help them solve problems . . . in a fair and equitable manner."[79]

The Components of Due Process

The U.S. Supreme Court has said that due process in the context of a government employee's property interest in employment contains three main elements: notice to the employee of the charges against him or her, an opportunity for the employee to respond, and a final decision made by an impartial decisionmaker.[80]

The initial step in a government employer's meeting these three requirements is a conference with the employee before his or her dismissal (or other adverse employment action, such as suspension without pay or demotion). At that conference, the employee is entitled to "oral or written notice of the charges against him, an explanation of the employer's evidence, and an opportunity to present his side of the story."[81] The conference can be conducted by a city or county manager, assistant manager, department head, or other appropriate supervisor. The employer must take care to ensure that the notice given to the employee is sufficient to permit the employee to understand fully the reasons for the proposed adverse action and to show that the reasons are untrue.[82] The notice should give the employee the full story. Whoever conducts the pre-disciplinary conference must ensure that it is a true opportunity for the employee to be heard. In one North Carolina case, a violation of due process was found where the official conducting the conference had the employee's letter of dismissal already prepared and handed it to the employee at the conclusion of the conference.[83]

After the conference, the decision may be made to go ahead with the adverse action. In that case, due process requires further post-action protections. The employee has the right to appeal the initial decision. The appeal hearing must include the right to confront evidence and witnesses, to present evidence, and to be represented by an attorney.[84]

The government employee's appeal of an adverse action taken against him or her must be heard by an impartial decision-maker. This is the third element of due process. The North Carolina Supreme Court has said clearly that merely having prior knowledge of the facts underlying a decision to dismiss an employee does not cause a decision-maker to be less than impartial.[85] But where a decision-maker has prior knowledge but denies having it, that denial is evidence of bias and

---

79. *Soles*, 345 N.C. at 446–47.

80. *See* Cleveland Bd. of Educ. v. Loudermill, 470 U.S. 532, 542–44 (1985); Crump v. Hickory Bd. of Educ., 326 N.C. 603, 615 (1990).

81. *See Loudermill*, 470 U.S. at 546.

82. *See* Barron v. Eastpointe Human Servs. LME, 246 N.C. App. 364, 383–86 (2016) (an employee was given sufficient notice of the reasons for his dismissal where he received both written and oral notice that a client had accused him of improper conduct, including touching her in an inappropriate manner; that the improper conduct included communicating with the client via text message on his personal cellular telephone; and that a co-worker told the employee of the allegations and he did not report the incident to his supervisor until over a month later); Emp. Sec. Comm'n v. Wells, 50 N.C. App. 389, 393–94 (1991); McMillan v. Cumberland Cnty. Bd. of Educ., 734 F. App'x 836, 841 (4th Cir. 2018), *as amended* (Apr. 4, 2018).

83. *See* Bishop v. Dep't of Hum. Res., 100 N.C. App. 175, *discretionary review allowed*, 327 N.C. 481 (1990), *review denied as improvidently granted*, 328 N.C. 325 (1991).

84. "Determining what process is due in a given setting requires the Court to take into account the individual's stake in the decision at issue as well as the State's interest in a particular procedure for making it." Hortonville Joint Sch. Dist. No. 1. v. Hortonville Educ. Ass'n, 426 U.S. 482 (1976) (citing cases).

85. *See Barron*, 246 N.C. App. at 376 (mere fact that supervisor was familiar with facts and acted as investigator and decisionmaker on matter was not violation of due process).

constitutes a denial of due process. If a decision-maker is a multi-member board, the bias of only one member constitutes sufficient bias, by itself, to constitute the denial of due process.[86]

Another way that public employers may create property interests for employees who would otherwise be at-will employees is by employing those individuals under contracts for a specified term—say, a year or two years. During the term of the contract, that individual would have a property interest in employment. Renewal of the contract, however, would be at the will of the employer.

The Equal Protection Clause of the United States Constitution

What happens when applicants for public employment feel they are being treated unfairly because the employer has a residency requirement? Or when law enforcement officers are fired because they sport tattoos? Can a county prohibit its employees from cohabiting with convicted felons? Government employers have been challenged over policies like these by applicants and employees through lawsuits alleging that the employers' actions violate the Equal Protection Clause of the Fourteenth Amendment to the U.S. Constitution.[87] The Equal Protection Clause provides that no state shall "deny to any person within its jurisdiction the equal protection of the laws." This means that neither the federal government, nor a state or political subdivision of a state, shall intentionally and arbitrarily discriminate against anyone through the terms of a statute or other legislative enactment or through the application of the terms of the statute by an officer or employee of the government.[88]

Most laws do, in fact, differentiate in some way between groups of persons. The Equal Protection Clause does not prohibit this. What the Equal Protection Clause requires is that government not treat any differently persons who are in all relevant respects alike and that it refrain from using invidious classification schemes like those based on race or gender.[89] In the hypotheticals set forth at the beginning of this section, a plaintiff's claims would be that

- the government employer created a classification based on residency that violated the Equal Protection Clause by treating residents of one place as eligible for government employment, while treating residents of other places as ineligible;
- the government employer violated the Equal Protection Clause by treating people with tattoos differently than people without them;
- the government employer burdened its employees' fundamental First Amendment right to free association in violation of the Equal Protection Clause by prohibiting them from residing with convicted felons, while other citizens who do not work for the government employer are free to do so.

The United States Supreme Court has held that it will uphold a law that makes a distinction among citizens so long as it bears a rational relation to some legitimate end, provided that the law making the classification neither burdens a fundamental right, such as voting or marrying, nor targets a protected or "suspect" class such as race or gender.[90] There is no fundamental right to public employment, so applicant and employee equal protection claims must be based on the

86. *See* Crump v. Bd. of Educ., 326 N.C. 603, 616–17 (1990).

87. Public employees are entitled to bring lawsuits alleging that the action of a government employer has violated the Equal Protection Clause. *See* Booth v. Maryland, 327 F.3d 377, 382–83 (4th Cir. 2003); Adams v. Trs. of the Univ. of N.C.-Wilmington, 640 F.3d 550, 566 (4th Cir. 2011). For instances of equal protection challenges similar to the above hypotheticals, see *Lewis v. City of Kinston*, 127 N.C. App. 274 (1997) (residency requirement); *Inturri v. City of Hartford*, 365 F. Supp. 2d 240 (D. Conn. 2005) *aff'd*, 165 F. App' x 66 (2d Cir. 2006) (tattoos); *Via v. Taylor*, 224 F. Supp. 2d 753, 761–62 (D. Del. 2002) (cohabiting with felon).

88. *See* Vill. of Willowbrook v. Olech, 528 U.S. 562, 564 (2000); Yan-Min Wang v. UNC-CH Sch. of Med., 216 N.C. App. 185 (2011) (finding that plaintiff did not identify any classification upon which she was denied equal protection).

89. *See* Romer v. Evans, 517 U.S. 620, 631 (1996); Nordlinger v. Hahn, 505 U.S. 1, 10 (1992).

90. *See* Clark v. Jeter, 486 U.S. 456, 461 (1988).

government employer's burdening of some other right (like the right of free association) or on the employer's classifying applicants/employees by race or gender or in another impermissible manner.[91] This is called the *rational relation test* or *rational basis test*. Under it, courts give great deference "to legislative determinations as to the desirability of particular statutory discriminations."[92] Under rational basis review, is not the court's role to second-guess the government or to determine whether the government's desired goal is served by the challenged statute or regulation. Rather, the court need only determine whether the legislature "rationally might have believed . . . that the desired end might be served."[93]

In contrast to rational basis review, which is referred to as *regular scrutiny*, any classification that does burden a fundamental right or creates a classification along the lines of race or national origin lines (race and national origin being deemed "suspect" classes) will be subject to *strict scrutiny*, passing constitutional muster only if it is narrowly tailored to serve a compelling state interest.[94] Classifications that are created along gender lines are considered "quasi-suspect" and are subject to *intermediate scrutiny* by the courts. To withstand intermediate scrutiny, a statutory classification must be substantially related to an important governmental objective.[95]

Statutory Exceptions to Employment at Will

Statutory exceptions are restrictions on an employer's right to hire and discharge whomever they please that have been enacted either by the U.S. Congress or the North Carolina General Assembly. Federal anti-discrimination laws put the most significant limitations on the way in which North Carolina public employers may hire and fire employees. Five federal statutes prohibit discrimination in public and private employment on nine different bases. Four state statutes prohibit discrimination in public and private employment on those same nine bases.

Federal Anti-Discrimination Statutes

Title VII of the Civil Rights Act of 1964[96] prohibits discrimination on the basis of race, color, gender, religion, and national origin. It provides that

> It shall be an unlawful employment practice for an employer—
> (1) to fail or refuse to hire or to discharge any individual, or otherwise to discriminate against any individual with respect to his compensation, terms, conditions, or privileges of employment, because of such individual's race, color, religion, sex, or national origin.[97]

Title VII applies to all employers with fifteen or more employees.

The categories of race, color, gender, religion, and national origin are referred to as "protected classes." When an employer fails to hire or discharges someone because of their race, for example, employment lawyers say that the employer is discriminating against them because of their membership in a protected class or in the protected class of African-Americans, Caucasians, or Asians, as the case may be.

---

91. *See* United Bldg. & Constr. Trades Council v. Mayor of Camden, 465 U.S. 208, 219 (1984) (holding that there is no fundamental right to government employment for purposes of the Equal Protection Clause); Mass. Bd. of Ret. v. Murgia, 427 U.S. 307, 313 (1976) (holding that governmental employment is not per se a fundamental right requiring strict scrutiny on an equal protection challenge).

92. *See* McCool v. City of Philadelphia, 494 F. Supp. 2d 307, 317 (E.D. Pa. 2007), *quoting* City of New Orleans v. Dukes, 427 U.S. 297, 303 (1976).

93. *See McCool*, 494 F. Supp. 2d at 321.

94. *See* Dunn v. Blumstein, 405 U.S. 330, 335 (1972); *Clark*, 486 U.S. at 461.

95. *See Clark*, 486 U.S. at 461; Miss. Univ. for Women v. Hogan, 458 U.S. 718, 723–24, 724 n.9 (1982).

96. Title 42, Sections 2000e *et seq.* of the United States Code (U.S.C.).

97. 42 U.S.C. § 2000e-2(a)(1).

Passed three years after Title VII and amended several times since, **the Age Discrimination in Employment Act (ADEA)**[98] prohibits employers from refusing to hire, from discharging, and from otherwise discriminating against a person in the terms and conditions of employment on the basis of age. The statute currently protects persons 40 years of age and older.[99] Sometimes, more than one applicant may be over 40, and the ADEA does not prohibit an employer from favoring an older individual over a younger individual, even if the younger individual is 40 or over.[100] The ADEA applies to employers with twenty or more employees.

The Americans with Disabilities Act (the ADA)[101] prohibits employers from discriminating against a qualified individual on the basis of disability with respect to job application procedures; the hiring, advancement, and/or discharge of employees; employee compensation; job training; and other terms, conditions, and privileges of employment. The ADA may be the most complex of the federal anti-discrimination statutes in that it is the only statute that requires employers to take certain actions in addition to abstaining from other actions. For example, the ADA requires employers to provide a reasonable accommodation to any known physical or mental limitations of applicants and employees, unless doing so would impose an undue hardship on the employer's operations. The obligation to make reasonable accommodation is a form of non-discrimination.[102] Each situation is based on an individual assessment of an applicant's or employee's disability with respect to the position in question. The ADA applies to employers with fifteen or more employees.

The Pregnant Workers Fairness Act (PWFA) prohibits workplace discrimination based on pregnancy, childbirth, or related medical conditions.[103] This covers all aspects of employment, including hiring, pay, assignments, promotions, and termination. Mirroring the ADA, the PWFA requires employers to provide reasonable accommodations for known limitations related to pregnancy, childbirth, and associated conditions, unless doing so would impose undue hardship. These accommodations must be determined through an interactive process with the affected worker. Like Title VII and the ADA, the PWFA applies to government employers with fifteen or more employees.

Title II of the **Genetic Information Nondiscrimination Act of 2008 (GINA)**[104] prohibits employers from discriminating on the basis of genetic information and medical history. An employer may never use genetic information to make an employment decision because genetic information is not relevant to an individual's current ability to work. Although the two statutes are related, GINA is distinct from the ADA in that the ADA prohibits discrimination on the basis of manifested conditions that meet the ADA's definition of disability, while GINA prohibits discrimination based on genetic information that may indicate that a condition may manifest itself in the future. GINA applies to employers with fifteen or more employees.

The **Uniformed Services Employment and Reemployment Rights Act of 1994 (USERRA)**[105] was enacted to prohibit employment discrimination against those who serve in the United States armed forces and to make it easier for people to perform non-career service in the armed forces by minimizing the disruption to their civilian careers. USERRA protects any person serving in the

98. 29 U.S.C. §§ 621 *et seq.*

99. *See* 29 U.S.C. §§ 623(a), 631(a).

100. *See* Gen. Dynamics Land Sys., Inc. v. Cline, 540 U.S. 581, 599–600 (2004). *See also* Title 29, Section 1625.2 of the Code of Federal Regulations (C.F.R.).

101. The employment provisions of the ADA are codified at 42 U.S.C. §§ 12111–12213. The ADA regulations of the U.S. Equal Employment Opportunity Commission (EEOC) are located at 29 C.F.R. Part 1630.

102. *See* 29 C.F.R. pt. 1630, app. § 1630.9.

103. The PWFA is codified at 42 U.S.C. §§ 2000gg–2000gg-6. The EEOC's PWFA regulations may be found at 29 C.F.R. Part 1636.

104. GINA is codified at 42 U.S.C. §§ 2000ff–2000ff-11. The EEOC's GINA regulations are located at 29 C.F.R. Part 1635.

105. USERRA is codified at 38 U.S.C. §§ 4301–4333. The U.S. Department of Labor's administrative rules implementing USERRA are located at 20 C.F.R. §§ 1002.1–1002.314.

United States Army, Navy, Air Force, Marine Corps, and Coast Guard and their reserve units, as well as persons serving in the Army National Guard and Air National Guard, the commissioned corps of the Public Health Service, and "any other category of persons designated by the President in time or war or national emergency."[106] USERRA applies to all employers, regardless of the number of employees they may have.

North Carolina Anti-Discrimination Statutes

There are several parallel state statutes that prohibit discrimination in employment. The **North Carolina Equal Employment Practices Act**[107] declares that it is the public policy of the state to "protect and safeguard the right and opportunity of all persons to see, obtain and hold employment without discrimination or abridgement on account of race, religion, color, national origin, age, sex or handicap by employers which regularly employ 15 or more persons."[108]

In 1985, prior to the passage of the federal Americans with Disabilities Act, the North Carolina General Assembly enacted the **North Carolina Persons with Disabilities Protection Act.**[109] The act applies to any employer with fifteen or more full-time employees and makes it a discriminatory practice to "discriminate against a qualified person with a disability on the basis of a disabling condition with respect to compensation or the terms, conditions, or privileges of employment."[110]

Like the federal GINA, a North Carolina law prohibits employers from denying employment to or refusing to hire someone on the basis of genetic information that concerns that person or a member of their family.[111] This law applies to all state agencies and to all local government employers, regardless of size.

Two provisions of the North Carolina General Statutes also prohibit discrimination in employment against military personnel by public entities.[112] Specifically, the statutes enjoin an "officer or employee of the State, or of any county, city and county, municipal corporation, school district, water district, or other district" from discriminating against members of the Armed Forces "with respect to their employment, appointment, position or status" and from denying, disqualifying or discharging them "from their employment or position by virtue of their membership or service in the military forces of this State or of the United States."[113] These provisions do not, however, provide persons serving in the armed forces or reserves any greater rights in employment than does USERRA. Violations of these provisions of the General Statutes constitute Class 2 misdemeanors. A separate state statute prohibits discrimination in employment on the basis that an applicant is a member of the North Carolina National Guard or has performed, applies to perform, or has an obligation to perform service in the National Guard.[114]

While the General Statutes require state agencies and institutions to observe a veteran's preference in employment, they do not require local government employers to do so.[115] Local government employers are free to adopt such a policy.

The North Carolina Retaliatory Employment Discrimination Act (REDA)[116] is probably the most important of North Carolina's employment discrimination statutes. REDA essentially

---

106. *See* 38 U.S.C. §§ 4303(13), (16).
107. G.S. 143-422.1 through -422.3.
108. G.S. 143-422.2(a).
109. G.S.168A-1 through -12.
110. G.S. 168A-5(a)(1).
111. G.S. 95-28.1A.
112. G.S. 127B-12, -14.
113. G.S. 127B- 12.
114. G.S. 127A-202.1.
115. *See* G.S. 126-82, 128-15.
116. G.S. 95-240 through -245.

combines several previously existing statutory provisions in a new article in one place. The act covers all employees, including those of the state, a city, a town, a county, a municipality, a local agency, or another entity of government. It defines retaliatory action broadly to include discharge, suspension, demotion, retaliatory relocation of an employee, or other adverse employment action taken against an employee in the terms, the conditions, the privileges, and the benefits of employment. Thus, an employee need not be fired to assert a cause of action claiming retaliatory discrimination; rather, the employee need show only some action taken that changes some aspect of his or her employment or working conditions. Some of the protections provided by REDA are discussed below.

Workers' compensation claims. Under REDA, it is unlawful for an employer to fire (or to otherwise adversely treat) an employee because the employee files a workers' compensation claim or testifies with respect to the claim of another employee.[117]

Sickle cell. Under REDA, an employee may not be fired (or otherwise adversely treated) because they possess the sickle cell trait or the hemoglobin C trait.[118]

Juvenile order compliance. Under REDA, an employee may not be fired because they attend a court proceeding or take other actions that a court may order in cases where their child is under the jurisdiction of the juvenile court for delinquency.[119]

Domestic violence protection. Under REDA, an employee may not be fired if, with reasonable notice to their employer, they take time off work to obtain, through the judicial system, a domestic violation protection order or civil no-contact order.[120]

Other Exceptions to Employment at Will Found in the General Statutes

How an employee votes. Under G.S. 163-271, if a person works for the government, they may not be fired for how they cast their vote. This provision applies only to units of government.

Serving on election day. As long as an employee gives their employer proper notice that they will be absent from work, the employee may not be fired because they have agreed to serve as a precinct official, appointed by a county board of elections, on election day. This prohibition is not found in REDA but is found instead at G.S. 163-41.2.

Whistleblowing. **The North Carolina Whistleblower's Protection Act**[121] protects employees of the state, of community colleges, and of public schools from being dismissed for reporting violations of law, fraud, misappropriation of resources, specific dangers, and gross mismanagement by their employers. This law does not apply to local government employees or to employees in the private sector.

Law Governing the Hiring Process in North Carolina Cities and Counties

There are no federal or state laws that require employers to use any particular recruiting, interviewing, or decision-making process when it comes to hiring new employees. The decision to advertise positions, to post vacancy announcements, to interview candidates using panels or individual interviews, to use assessment centers or assignments, and to make outreach efforts to improve minority recruitment are all ones that may be freely made by a city or county. Despite that, the hiring process can sometimes feel like a minefield to local government employers. That is because some

117. G.S. 95-241(a)(1)a.
118. G.S. 95-241(a)(1)d.
119. G.S. 95-241(a)(4).
120. G.S. 95-241(a)(5). *See also* G.S. 95-270.
121. G.S. 126-84 through -88.

recruitment and selection practices can run afoul of the anti-discrimination laws—even where the employer has no intention of discriminating.

Before looking at the two major theories of discrimination and considering how they may interact with the hiring process, a definition of a key term is in order. The categories of race, color, religion, gender, and national origin (the bases of discrimination prohibited by Title VII of the Civil Rights Act of 1964[122]) are referred to as "protected classes." When an employer fails to hire or discharges someone because of their race, for example, employment lawyers say that the employer is discriminating against that person because of their membership in a protected class or in the protected class of blacks, whites, or Asians, as the case may be. Similarly, age over 40 is a protected class (under the Age Discrimination in Employment Act[123]), as is being a person with a disability (under the Americans with Disabilities Act (ADA)[124]). Both the *disparate treatment theory* of discrimination and the *disparate impact theory* of discrimination, discussed in more detail below, can apply to discrimination against any protected class.

Disparate Treatment or Intentional Discrimination: The Basic Theory

Imagine that Mike, a department head in Paradise City government, is interviewing candidates for the position of deputy department head. He needs a second in command on whom he can rely. As he shifts through the applications, he decides that his number two should be a man. "It's not that a woman couldn't do the job," he tells himself. "It's that they're always leaving to have a baby or calling in because their kids are sick." Mike doesn't think he is prejudiced against female employees and doesn't think he has committed employment discrimination. "Hey, I think that a woman can do this job as well as a man!" he says later. But Mike has engaged in unlawful discrimination. He has consciously and deliberately decided not to hire any of the female applicants for the deputy department head position ***because*** they are women. The law refers to this as *disparate treatment* discrimination. **Disparate treatment discrimination is the *intentional* decision not to hire (or to fire) a person because of membership in a particular protected class.**

How does an applicant or employee prove that an employer intentionally discriminated against them because of race, color, sex, or any other protected characteristic? These days it is the rare employer who states frankly, "We didn't even bother to read the applications from black candidates." In the absence of direct and indisputable evidence such as this, plaintiffs must prove intent through circumstantial evidence—that is, evidence from which a fact-finder may infer discrimination. In a series of cases, the United States Supreme Court developed a structure of proof for use in disparate treatment cases dependent on circumstantial rather than direct evidence. Take hiring as an example. A plaintiff establishes a *prima facie*, or "first look," case of discrimination in hiring when he or she demonstrates that

(1) he or she belongs to a protected class;
(2) he or she applied and was qualified for a job for which the employer was seeking applicants;
(3) despite his or her qualifications, he or she was rejected; and
(4) after the rejection, the position remained open and the employer continued to seek applicants from persons with similar qualifications.

---

122. 42 U.S.C. §§ 2000e *et seq.*

123. 29 U.S.C. §§ 621 *et seq.*

124. The employment provisions of the ADA are codified at 42 U.S.C. §§ 12111–12213. The U.S. Equal Employment Opportunity Commission's ADA regulations are located at 29 C.F.R. Part 1630.

This structure of proof is usually referred to by the name of the case which gave rise to it, *McDonnell Douglas Corp. v. Green*.[125] A plaintiff who has made this very limited showing is said to have established a *McDonnell Douglas prima facie* case, and the burden of introducing evidence then shifts to the employer.

If an employer does nothing to defend itself in response to a plaintiff's prima facie case, a court will presume intentional discrimination, and a violation of law, on the part of the employer. To avoid such a result, the employer must put forward a legitimate, nondiscriminatory reason why the plaintiff was rejected.[126] Legitimate nondiscriminatory reasons include a failure to meet the minimum qualifications for the position, a lack of experience or required certifications, poor professional and personal references, or a lackluster performance in a personal interview. Sometimes the legitimate, nondiscriminatory reason is simply that the employer preferred the package of experience, qualifications, and self-presentation that another candidate offered. This list is not meant to be exclusive but merely to illustrate the types of reasons that the courts have found legitimate and nondiscriminatory.

Once an employer does offer a legitimate, nondiscriminatory explanation for failing to hire a plaintiff applicant, the case ends unless the plaintiff brings forth evidence that the reasons offered by the employer were not its true reasons but were instead a pretext for discrimination.[127] This evidence is rarely direct; it is almost always circumstantial. Mere evidence of pretext does not require a verdict for a plaintiff applicant. Not only must a judge or jury believe that an employer is not being straightforward or truthful about its reasons for rejecting a plaintiff's application, they must also believe the plaintiff's explanation—that the reason for the employer's lack of forthrightness and for its failure to hire the plaintiff is intentional discrimination on the basis of membership in a protected class.[128] Examples of circumstantial evidence that an employer discriminated include requiring a plaintiff applicant to complete certain application steps not required of other applicants; making, but then withdrawing, a job offer without explanation; and unevenly applying employment criteria to the disadvantage of a plaintiff applicant.[129]

Title VII requires that all complaints of employment discrimination be filed with the United States Equal Employment Opportunity Commission (EEOC) before applicants or employees may bring suit in federal court.[130] The EEOC investigates claims of employment discrimination and issues non-binding findings to the effect that it is reasonably likely that discrimination did— or did not—occur in a given case. Once the EEOC has issued a finding, or where the EEOC has not issued a finding within 180 days of receiving an applicant or employee's complaint, the applicant or employee receives a so-called right-to-sue letter that allows him or her to proceed with a lawsuit in federal court.[131] The EEOC also attempts to mediate disputes between parties where possible.[132] Sometimes the EEOC itself will bring suit against an employer on behalf of the rejected applicant or discharged employee.

---

125. 411 U.S. 792, 802 (1973); Price v. Thompson, 380 F.3d 209, 212 (4th Cir. 2004); Equal Emp. Opportunity Comm'n v. Sears Roebuck & Co., 243 F.3d 846, 851–52 (4th Cir. 2001).

126. *See* Tex. Dep't of Cmty. Affs. v. Burdine, 450 U.S. 248, 254 (1981); *Sears Roebuck*, 243 F.3d at 851–52.

127. *See Burdine*, 450 U.S. at 253; *Sears Roebuck*, 243 F.3d at 851–52.

128. *See* Reeves v. Sanderson Plumbing Prods., Inc., 530 U.S. 133 (2000); St. Mary's Honor Ctr. v. Hicks, 509 U.S. 502, 519 (1993).

129. *See, e.g.*, Raad v. Fairbanks N. Star Borough Sch. Dist., 323 F.3d 1185, 1195 (9th Cir. 2003), *opinion amended on denial of reh'g*, No. 00-35999, 2003 WL 21027351 (9th Cir. May 8, 2003) (different treatment than other candidates.

130. *See* 42 U.S.C. §§ 2000e-4, -5; 29 C.F.R. §§ 1601.6(a), .7(a).

131. 42 U.S.C. § 2000e-5(f)(1); 29 C.F.R. § 1601.28.

132. *See* "Mediation," U.S. Equal Employment Opportunity Commission, eeoc.gov/mediation (last accessed February 1, 2024).

The Bona Fide Occupational Qualification Defense to a Charge of Disparate Treatment or Intentional Discrimination

Employers sometimes require that applicants be male or female, or of a certain religion or national origin to be considered for particular positions. For example, a sheriff might prefer male jailers for positions involving supervision of male prisoners and female jailers for positions involving supervision of female prisoners. A public works director might want to hire men for sanitation and roadwork crews because the director does not think women can lift the weight necessary to do these jobs. A county social services or health department might only want caseworkers or nurses of Latino background to work in outreach programs directed toward Latino immigrants. Restaurants such as Hooters and Playboy clubs are known to prefer an all-female wait staff because those businesses use sexual allure as a theme to attract a majority-male clientele.[133]

With a few exceptions, preferences like those in the examples above are unlawful. For an employer to make hiring decisions based on preferences like these would violate Title VII. But where it is **necessary** for a particular business or organization to hire employees based on *religion, sex, or national origin*, an employer may defend itself against a disparate treatment claim by asserting what is known as the *bona fide occupational qualification*, or *BFOQ*, defense. The BFOQ defense gets its name from the text of the Title VII provision in which it is recognized. Title VII provides that

> it shall not be an unlawful employment practice for an employer to hire and employ employees . . . on the basis of his religion, sex, or national origin in those certain instances where *religion, sex, or national origin is a bona fide occupational qualification* reasonably necessary to the normal operation of that particular business or enterprise . . . .[134]

The BFOQ defense is not available as a defense to charges of race or color discrimination. In practice, the BFOQ defense is rarely used in the context of religious discrimination because those entities that discriminate on the basis of an applicant's religion tend to be religiously-affiliated employers, who are entitled to an independent exemption from Title VII's nondiscrimination mandate as it applies to religion.[135]

An employer bears the burden of proof when it asserts a BFOQ defense. It must prove by a preponderance of the evidence that (1) the job qualification justifying the discrimination is reasonably necessary to the existence of its business and (2) gender or national origin is a legitimate proxy for qualification because either (a) the employer has a substantial basis for believing that all or nearly all members of the protected class lack the qualification or (b) it is impossible or highly impractical for the employer to insure by individual testing that its employees will have the necessary qualification for the job.[136]

Disparate Impact or Unintentional Discrimination in Hiring: The Basic Theory

A Title VII disparate treatment claim requires an applicant to prove that an employer intentionally discriminated on the basis of race, color, gender, religion, or national origin. But employers can unintentionally violate Title VII as well. If an employer adopts a hiring or promotional practice that

133. For Hooters' justification for its hiring policies, see Jacob Shamsian, "The Strange Loophole That Lets Hooters Hire Only Female Servers," *Business Insider*, September 13, 2015.

134. *See* 42 U.S.C. § 2000e-2(e)(1).

135. *See* 42 U.S.C. §§ 2000e-1(a), -2(e)(2).

136. *See* Burwell v. E. Air Lines, Inc., 633 F.2d 361, 369 n.10 (4th Cir. 1980) (gender discrimination); Arritt v. Grisell, 567 F.2d 1267, 1271 (4th Cir. 1977) (in context of age discrimination); Brenier v. Nev. Dep't of Corrs., 610 F.3d 1202, 1210 (9th Cir. 2010) (gender BFOQ in prison context).

causes a disparate impact on members of a protected class, then it has engaged in unintentional discrimination, known as *disparate impact* discrimination. Imagine the following situation:

> *Paradise County, North Carolina, decides that it will consider only county residents for county jobs. The county hopes that it will engender greater employee commitment and loyalty since employees will have a personal stake in the success of county government. The population of Paradise County is and has been historically predominantly white. Because the City of Paradise, where Paradise County government is based, is in the northeast corner of the county, there is a large pool of potential applicants for Paradise County jobs to be found in Heavenly County, which adjoins Paradise County a mere ten miles from the City of Paradise. Heavenly County is predominantly black. By adopting a residency requirement, Paradise County will have a disparate impact on black applicants. They will necessarily be hired disproportionately to the available labor market, which is measured by commuting distance, not by county lines. Without meaning to do so, Paradise County will have violated Title VII.*

Under Title VII, disparate impact cases can be brought on the basis of race, color, gender, religion, and national origin. A 1981 case involving the North Carolina Highway Patrol illustrates how a job requirement that is, like the residency requirement in the hypothetical above, neutral on its face can nevertheless have an adverse impact on a protected class. Prior to 1981, the North Carolina Highway Patrol had had a minimum height requirement of 5'6" for state troopers. In a case brought by the United States Department of Justice, the district court found that this requirement had a substantial adverse impact on women: it automatically eliminated 77.3 percent of women between the ages of 18 and 34 from the pool of women who could apply for a position as a state trooper, while eliminating only 9.4 percent of men. In December 1980, there were 1,131 members of the highway patrol; only one trooper was female. The court further found that the State had never validated the height requirement—that is, had never shown statistically valid evidence that people taller than 5'6" were more likely to perform well in the position of state trooper than shorter people—and that the evidence the highway patrol did produce in support of its claim that the height requirement was job-related lacked factual foundation. Thus, the court concluded that the challenged height requirement discriminated against women in violation of Title VII. The State did not appeal.[137]

Plaintiffs do not have to prove intent in a disparate impact case as they must do in a disparate treatment case. Plaintiffs do, however, have to demonstrate that a particular employment policy or practice that on its fact appears to be neutral has in fact caused a significant statistical disparity in the proportionate numbers of protected class members who are hired when this policy or practice is in effect.[138] A rejected applicant who has identified a practice (such as a residency requirement or a height requirement); has produced evidence of a statistical disparity in the numbers of particular protected class members who have been hired (blacks, for example, or women); **and** can show that the identified policy or practice actually caused the statistical disparity has established a *prima facie* case of disparate impact or unintentional discrimination.

Once a rejected applicant establishes a *prima facie* case, the burden shifts to the employer to show either that the challenged employment policy or practice does not cause a disparate impact or that even though it causes a disparate impact, it is job-related and consistent with business

137. *See* United States v. State of North Carolina, 512 F. Supp. 968 (E.D.N.C. 1981).

138. *See* 42 U.S.C. § 2000e-2(k)(1)(A)(i). *See also* Lewis v. City of Chicago, 560 U.S. 205, 212 (2010); Ricci v. DeStefano, 557 U.S. 557 (2009).

necessity.[139] Employers generally demonstrate job-relatedness and business necessity by showing that the policy or practice in question has been validated, although sometimes job-relatedness and business necessity may be apparent and a formal analysis will not be needed. In the case of a residency requirement, an employer would establish its validity by showing that employees who lived within the employer's jurisdictional boundaries were likely to be better employees than those who lived elsewhere. Without actually doing a validity study, it seems reasonable to assume that persons who live in Buncombe County will make better employees for the city of Asheville than will persons living in Wake County. But it is less easy to see how in the hypothetical above residents of Paradise County will make better employees for Paradise County than residents of Heavenly County. Because the residency requirement there disproportionately screened out blacks from consideration for employment with Paradise County, the county will have to show evidence of the relationship between residency and job performance in county positions. Where the policy or practice in question is a written examination or a physical abilities test, the validity of the test is established by demonstrating that there is a greater probability that high scorers on the test will perform well on the job than will low scorers.

If an employer demonstrates that a policy or practice is required by business necessity, the burden shifts to the plaintiff to prove that an alternative practice exists that (1) does not result in disparate impact and (2) would serve the employer's stated objective equally well. Only if an applicant can establish the existence of such an alternate process will liability for disparate impact discrimination in violation of Title VII have been established.[140]

What kinds of applicant-selection procedures and employment tests have been shown to result in adverse impacts on protected classes? The EEOC's list includes (but is not limited to)

- background checks that provide information on an applicant's arrest and conviction history;
- background checks that provide information on an applicant's credit and financial history;
- English proficiency tests that determine an applicant's English fluency;
- cognitive tests that assess an applicant's reasoning, memory, perceptual speed and accuracy, and skills in arithmetic and reading comprehension;
- tests that assess an applicant's knowledge of a particular function or job; "
- physical ability tests that measure the applicant's physical ability to perform a particular task or the strength of specific muscle groups, as well as strength and stamina in general;
- tests that ask applicants to perform sample job tasks and assess performance and aptitude on particular tasks (for example, an assessment center);
- medical inquiries and physical examinations, including psychological tests, that assess an applicant's physical or mental health.[141]

---

139. *See* 42 U.S.C. § 2000e-2(k)(1)(A)(i). *See also* Griggs v. Duke Power Co., 401 U.S. 424, 431 (1971); Equal Emp. Opportunity Comm'n v. Dial Corp., 469 F.3d 735, 742 (8th Cir. 2006).

140. *See* 42 U.S.C. § 2000e-2(k)(1)(A)(ii). *See also Dial Corp.*, 469 F.3d at 742; Equal Emp. Opportunity Comm'n v. Joe's Stone Crab, Inc., 220 F.3d 1263, 1276 (11th Cir. 2000), Ogletree v. City of Auburn, 619 F. Supp. 2d 1152, 1175 (M.D. Ala. 2009).

141. *See* U.S. Equal Employment Opportunity Commission, "Employment Tests and Selection Procedures," eeoc.gov/laws/guidance/employment-tests-and-selection-procedures (last accessed February 5, 2024).

The Fair Labor Standards Act: Ensuring That Subordinates Are Paid What They Are Owed

The most common distinction made between types of employees is between "exempt" and "non-exempt" employees. These terms mean either exempt from the overtime rules of the Fair Labor Standard Act (FLSA) or not exempt and subject to the FLSA's overtime rules, respectively. The practical difference between an employee's classification as exempt or nonexempt is that an exempt employee may be required to work more than his or her scheduled workweek without receiving any additional compensation beyond their fixed salary. In contrast, nonexempt employees must always be paid overtime at a rate of time-and-one-half their regular rate of pay for every hour they work over forty hours in a given workweek.

Determining Exempt Status

How does an employer determine whether a position is exempt under the Fair Labor Standards Act? A position is *exempt* from the FLSA's overtime rules if it meets three requirements:

1. the position is paid on a salary basis;
2. the position is paid a minimum of $684 per week; and
3. the duties of the position satisfy either the executive duties test, the administrative duties test, or a professional duties test.[142]

An employee paid on a "salary basis" is one who is paid a predetermined amount each pay period without any reductions due to the quality or quantity of the employee's work. "In other words, the employee must receive full salary for any week in which he or she performs *any* work — regardless of the total number of days or hours worked in that week. And that is all that "salary basis" means.[143]

The minimum salary threshold is currently $684 per week—that's $35,568 on an annualized basis—but an employee who does not make at least $684 each and every week cannot be exempt from overtime even if they end up earning $35,568 in a given year.

Each of the duties tests in the third requirement for FLSA exemption is distinct and independent; a position need only satisfy one of them to be considered exempt. The *executive duties test* evaluates whether a given position is a management position with significant authority over other employees. The *administrative duties test* evaluates whether a position is an office position that supports management and has significant decision-making authority in areas other than supervision of employees. The *professional duties test* evaluates whether the position is one that requires an advanced academic degree or other high-level training.

Compensatory Time Off

Some overtime in local units is budgeted, but much is unexpected, the result of temporary understaffing or increased need for services by a city's or county's citizens, especially when there is severe weather and consequent damage to the community. The Fair Labor Standards Act allows government employers an alternative way to compensate nonexempt employees for hours worked in excess of forty hours that it does not allow private-sector employers: use of compensatory time off or, as it is more commonly known, comp time. Comp time allows public employers to provide paid time off in lieu of cash overtime. When a government employer uses compensatory time off instead of cash overtime, the time off must be credited at the rate of one and one-half hours of compensatory

142. *See* 29 C.F.R. §§ 541.100, .200, .204, .300, .400, .602.
143. *See* 29 C.F.R. § 541.602.

time for each hour of overtime work—just as the cash rate for overtime is calculated at the rate of one and one-half times the regular rate of pay. It is a violation of the FLSA for an employer to not compensate a nonexempt employee for overtime hours with hour-for-hour comp time.[144]

The FLSA regulations specify that employers may allow nonexempt employees to accrue up to only 240 hours of comp time, with the exception of employees working "in a public safety activity, an emergency response activity, or a seasonal activity," who may accrue up to 480 hours. Note that employers may only apply the 480-hour limit to employees engaged in public safety and emergency response activities as a regular part of their work. Thus, law enforcement officers, firefighters, emergency medical personnel, as well as 911 dispatchers and telecommunicators may be subject to the higher limit.[145] Employees whose regular work does not involve public safety or emergency response but who undertake such duties during the course of an emergency remain subject to the lower cap of 240 hours. If employees work more than 240 or 480 hours of overtime—as they often do in emergency situations—employers must either begin to pay out overtime hours in cash or send employees home to use their paid time off (although in emergencies, that is not generally an option).

Using Accrued Comp Time

Another condition upon a public employer's use of comp time is the requirement that it allow an employee to use his or her accrued paid time off "within a reasonable period after making the request if the use of the compensatory time does not unduly disrupt the operations of the public agency."[146] Most employers find this easier said than done. One reason that employees accrue comp time in the first place is because there is generally more work to be done or shifts to be covered than there are people or regularly scheduled hours in which to do the work. Allowing employees to take time off may only exacerbate the problem. Nevertheless, an employer must allow an employee who has requested the use of accrued comp time to take time off absent an undue hardship.

One way in which employers can manage accrued comp time is to send employees with accrued comp time home when their departments or sections are experiencing slower work periods. An employee may not object to being sent home since they are not being sent home without pay—comp time is *paid* time off. Employers may also adopt policies that either allow or require employees to use comp time before they use accrued paid sick or vacation leave. Similarly, either employer or employee may require that accrued comp time run concurrently with Family and Medical Leave Act (FMLA) leave, turning unpaid leave into paid leave. Finally, employers can set limits lower than 240 or 480 hours on the amount of comp time employees may accrue. They will necessarily have to pay overtime in cash once the lower limit is reached, but there will be fewer days of time off that require accommodation.[147]

Accrued Comp Time That Remains at Separation

Comp time may only be used in the manner authorized by the FLSA and the U.S. Department of Labor's FLSA regulations. Because neither the statute nor the regulations authorize its use in this way, accrued FLSA comp time may not be made subject to a "lose it or use it" policy. Nor may it be converted to sick or vacation leave. Comp time accrues indefinitely until the statutory maximums of 480 hours for public safety employees and 240 hours for all other nonexempt employees is reached.

---

144. *See* 29 U.S.C. § 207(o); 29 C.F.R. § 553.20.
145. *See* 29 C.F.R. §§ 553.21, .24.
146. 29 U.S.C. § 207(o)(5)(B).
147. *See* 29 U.S.C. § 207(o)(5); 29 C.F.R. §§ 825.207, 553.25.

At that point, the accrued hours remain credited to the employee indefinitely until used, and any additional overtime hours must be paid out in cash.

The statute is clear that upon an employee's separation from service, whether because of retirement, a voluntary departure for a position with another employer, or because the employee has been fired, an employer must pay out any accrued comp time "at a rate of compensation not less than—

(A) The average regular rate received by such employee during the last 3 years of the employee's employment, or
(B) The final regular rate received by such employee, whichever is higher."[148]

The FLSA's Overtime Pay Provisions for Law Enforcement and Firefighting Employees

The Fair Labor Standards Act has an exception from its overtime pay rules for nonexempt law enforcement officers and firefighters who work a different number of hours from week to week. This exception is called the 207(k) exemption because it is found at Title 29, Section 207(k) of the United States Code (it is sometimes called the 7(k) exemption after its location in the original bill). The 207(k) exemption is well-liked by law enforcement agencies and fire departments because it makes calculating the overtime of their employees more efficient and because it reduces overtime costs in a small, but real, way.

The 207(k) exemption allows public employers to figure overtime compensation for law enforcement and fire employees on the basis of work periods longer than the seven-day work period that applies to all other employees. The work period can be as long as twenty-eight days. The employer still maintains whatever payroll schedule it prefers—weekly, bi-weekly or monthly—and law enforcement officers and firefighters still get paid on that schedule. But overtime premium pay for law enforcement officers and firefighters is determined and paid out at the end of the 207(k) work period.[149]

When a law enforcement agency adopts the longest possible work period—twenty-eight consecutive days—officers earn time-and-one-half overtime pay only after they have worked 171 hours within that twenty-eight-day work period. For firefighters on a twenty-eight-day work schedule, overtime is earned only after 212 hours.[150] The FLSA regulations allow law enforcement and fire departments to use the 207(k) exemption for work periods of ***any*** length between seven and twenty-eight days and to prorate accordingly the number of hours that must be worked before overtime kicks in. Most departments use work periods that are multiples of seven. See Table 13.1 for information on hours needed to trigger overtime.

Employees scheduled in accordance with Section 207(k) may be compensated for overtime hours worked with compensatory time off rather than with cash overtime pay, just like employees on a regular one-week work period.[151]

Overtime or Comp Time for Exempt Employees

The Fair Labor Standards Act regulations expressly allow employers to pay exempt employees additional compensation for hours worked beyond what is expected without jeopardizing an employee's exemption. The rules allow such additional compensation to be paid on any basis, including paid time off.[152] North Carolina local government employers typically refer to this additional or bonus

148. *See* 29 U.S.C. § 207(o)(4); 29 C.F.R. § 553.27.
149. *See* 29 C.F.R. § 553.224.
150. *See* 29 C.F.R. § 553.201.
151. *See* 29 C.F.R. § 553.231.
152. *See* 29 C.F.R. § 541.604.

Table 13.1 Hours of Work Needed to Trigger Overtime

Work Period	Law Enforcement	Fire Protection
28 days	171 hrs.	212 hrs.
14 days	86 hrs.	106 hrs.
7 days	43 hrs.	53 hrs.[a]

a. *See* 29 C.F.R. § 553.230.

time off for exempt employees as a form of "comp time," or compensatory time off, although they would be wise to give it another name to avoid confusion. For this reason, this chapter will refer to additional paid time off for exempt employees as "bonus time off."

Although comp time for nonexempt employees must be granted on the basis of one-and-one-half hours off for every hour worked in excess of forty hours in a week, bonus time off for exempt employees may be structured in whatever way a local government employer chooses. Bonus time off may be granted to exempt employees when they have worked more than forty hours in a week, more than their scheduled hours, or more than a certain number of hours per month. The time off may be calculated based on one-and-one-half hours off for each extra hour worked or on an hour-for-hour basis. It may also be calculated based on a half-hour off for each extra hour worked. Because this is a benefit that is not required by law, employers may structure it however they choose.

Unlike comp time for nonexempt employees, which cannot accrue in excess of 240 hours (or 480 hours for public safety employees), bonus time off for exempt employees may accrue without limit. Bonus time off for exempt employees does not have to be cashed out when an employee separates from service. Employers may restrict the carry-over of accrued bonus time off for exempt employees from year to year, in contrast with comp time for nonexempt employees, which remains on the books indefinitely. There is no requirement that bonus time off for exempt employees be paid out to employees when they leave or retire from an employer's service.

Other FLSA Provisions

The Fair Labor Standards Act is a detailed and complex statutory scheme. It has rules for when deductions may be made from the pay of nonexempt and exempt employees (the rules differ); for what counts as time for which a nonexempt employee must be paid (for example, there are rules about on-call time, travel time, and training time); for seasonal employees; and for employees who work a second job for the same employer. These are just a few examples. For a detailed discussion of these issues, see Diane M. Juffras, *A Comprehensive Guide to the Fair Labor Standards Act for Public Employers*, available through the School of Government Publications Division.

Leave under the FMLA: What Managers, Department Heads, and Supervisors Need to Know

Under the Family and Medical Leave Act (FMLA), an employer must grant an eligible employee a total of up to twelve workweeks of job-protected, unpaid leave during any twelve-month period for any of the following reasons:

- the birth of a child;
- the adoption of a child or placement of a child for foster care;
- the employee's own serious health condition where the condition makes the employee unable to perform their job; or
- the serious health condition of the employee's spouse, child, or parent.

Administering leave under the FMLA requires knowledge of a complex set of rules. But there is good news for department heads and supervisors in local government units: your human resources department or personnel officer is usually in charge of figuring out whether an employee should be on FMLA leave, how much leave the employee has left, and a dozen other concerns. Department heads and supervisors can instead concentrate on how an employee's work will get done in their absence. Nevertheless, managers, department heads, and supervisors have an important role to play in ensuring that local government employers administer FMLA leave in compliance with the law.

Below are four things that local government managers, department heads, and supervisors need to do to keep their city, county, or agency from violating the FMLA.

1. Let your unit's human resources department know right away whenever an employee is absent from work for more than three days.
2. ***Immediately*** relay any requests for FMLA leave or sick leave to the human resources department. And, even if the FMLA is not mentioned, immediately let the human resources department know when an employee requests permission to use accrued leave and indicates that they need the leave for medical reasons or to care for a family member.
3. Ensure that the human resources department is up to date on the essential job duties of any employee who may need FMLA leave.
4. Regularly update the human resources department about any positions and job duties for which a fit-for-duty certification should be required when an employee returns from an FMLA leave.

Eligibility for FMLA Leave

To be eligible for FMLA leave, an employee

- must have a total of at least twelve months of service with the employer (although the twelve months need not be consecutive and the employee may have a break in service);
- must have worked at least 1,250 hours during the last consecutive twelve months; and
- must work at a worksite that has at least fifty employees within a seventy-five-mile radius.[153]

That last requirement means that North Carolina local government employers with fewer than fifty employees have no eligible employees and are not required to provide FMLA leave. For FMLA purposes, the number of employees a local government has is determined by counting how many

153. *See* 29 C.F.R. § 825.110.

employees (both full-time and part-time) an employer has on its payroll at any given time. A local government employer with fewer than fifty employees may choose voluntarily to *adopt* a policy extending family and medical leave to its employees under the same terms as provided by the Family and Medical Leave Act.

How Does FMLA Leave Get Started?

United States Department of Labor (US DOL) FMLA regulations require employees who know they will need FMLA leave (because they are expecting a baby, for example, or because they are having elective surgery) to give their employer notice of their need for FMLA leave thirty days in advance.[154] Savvy employees may go straight to their human resources departments, but there is a good chance that some employees will go to their supervisors or department heads instead. Suppose an employee—let's call him Stan—says to his supervisor, "Hey, Mr. Jones. I'm going to be having surgery next month and I'll be out of work for two weeks." What should Mr. Jones do? As Stan's supervisor, Mr. Jones should refer Stan to their unit's human resources department and then immediately contact human resources himself and notify that department that Stan has indicated that he will need FMLA leave. Mr. Jones should take these actions even if FMLA leave was never explicitly mentioned.

It is crucial that supervisors immediately tell their human resources departments that a subordinate has requested FMLA leave or has mentioned a situation that may qualify for FMLA leave, because the law requires employers to respond to a request for FMLA leave within five business days.[155] A department head or supervisor counts as the "employer" in this situation. The five-day clock starts to run the minute the employee tells their supervisor that they are going to need FMLA leave or that they will need leave for a medical reason.

The human resources department must then determine whether the employee is eligible for FMLA leave and, if so, will give the employee a Notice of Eligibility and of Rights and Responsibilities.

What If an Employee Says That They Don't Want FMLA Leave for a Specific Absence?

An employee may wish to "save" their FMLA leave. Maybe they know that they will need FMLA leave in a few months, perhaps for the birth of a child, perhaps for a planned medical procedure. It would not be unreasonable for an employee to want to "save" FMLA leave for that future need and use accrued paid leave or take unpaid leave now instead. But that would be too bad for the employee. In a 2019 Opinion Letter, US DOL made clear that absences that qualify for FMLA leave *must* be designated as FMLA leave that counts against an employee's annual twelve-week entitlement:

> "[A]n employer is prohibited from delaying the designation of FMLA-qualifying leave as FMLA leave. Once an eligible employee communicates a need to take leave for an FMLA-qualifying reason, neither the employee nor the employer may decline FMLA protection for that leave. . . . Accordingly, when an employer determines that leave is for an FMLA-qualifying reason, the qualifying leave is FMLA-protected and counts toward the employee's FMLA leave entitlement. . . . [T]he employer may not delay designating leave as FMLA-qualifying, even if the employee would prefer that the employer delay the designation."[156]

If leave qualifies for FMLA leave, it must be counted as FMLA leave.

---

154. *See* 29 C.F.R. § 825.302.

155. *See* 29 C.F.R. § 825.300.

156. *See* U.S. Department of Labor, Wage and Hour Division, Wage and Hour Opinion Letter 2019-1-A (March 14, 2019).

Is the Leave Really Medically Necessary?

Let's return to the hypothetical featuring Stan and his supervisor Mr. Jones set out above. Maybe Mr. Jones is suspicious about Stan's surgery. Stan seems fine to him. He has never heard Stan complain about his health. He wonders whether Stan really needs to be out of work for two entire weeks. The bad news is that the FMLA prohibits anyone in an employee's supervisory chain of command from seeking out medical information about the employee's condition and need for leave. The good news is that a local government's human resources department, or any one in an administrative position who is not in the supervisory chain of command, may make such inquiries. While the FMLA prohibits human resources departments from sharing that information with department heads and supervisors,[157] supervisors can rest assured that Stan's condition meets the FMLA definition of a "serious health condition" required for FMLA leave if that leave is approved by human resources.

Serious Health Conditions

An employee's medical condition, or the medical condition of an employee's family member, must meet certain criteria to qualify as a "serious health condition" eligible for FMLA protection. The FMLA regulations define a qualifying serious health condition as "an illness, injury or impairment, or physical or mental condition" that involves any period of incapacity

- requiring an absence of more than three calendar days from work that also involves continuing treatment by a health care provider;
- connected with inpatient care;
- due to pregnancy;
- due to a chronic health condition such as asthma, diabetes, or epilepsy;
- that is long-term or permanent due to a condition for which treatment may not be effective (e.g., cancer, AIDS); or
- requiring multiple absences to receive multiple treatments (and to recover from the treatments) for a condition that would likely result in an incapacity for more than three consecutive days if left untreated (e.g., physical therapy, chemotherapy, dialysis).[158]

Most FMLA leaves fall under one of the first three categories of qualifying conditions set out just above. For the FMLA, a "period of incapacity" means an inability to work, attend school, or perform other regular daily activities due to the serious health condition alleged, the treatment for it, or the recovery from it.[159] FMLA leave is not available for colds, stomach viruses, the flu, or similar conditions unless they require inpatient care or continuing treatment by a health care provider.[160]

Medical Certifications of the Need for FMLA Leave

To determine whether an employee's condition qualifies as a "serious health condition," the human resources department of a local government unit may obtain the information it needs to reach a conclusion by asking for a medical certification from the employee's health care provider (or from

157. *See* 29 C.F.R. § 825.500.

158. *See* 29 C.F.R. § 825.113.

159. *See* 29 C.F.R. § 825.113.

160. For more on serious health conditions, see the following blog post: Diane Juffras, "The Difference Between a Serious Health Condition under the FMLA and a Disability under the ADA," *Coates' Canons: NC Local Government Law* blog (February 20, 2020), canons.sog.unc.edu/2024/12/the-difference-between-a-serious-health-condition-under-the-fmla-and-a-disability-under-the-ada/.

the health care provider of the employee's family member, where leave is requested to care for a family member with a serious health condition). The FMLA does not *require* employers to obtain a medical certification. It instead *allows* an employer to request certain information from a health care provider to verify that an employee or family member has a qualifying condition.[161]

Medical certifications may ask for the following information:

1. the approximate date on which the serious health condition commenced and how long it is likely to last;
2. a statement or description of medical facts regarding the health condition that is the reason for the FMLA leave request. The medical facts must be sufficient to support the need for leave and may include information on symptoms, diagnosis, hospitalization, doctor visits, medications prescribed, referrals for evaluation or treatment (physical therapy, for example), or other regimens of continuing treatment;
3. if the employee is the patient, information sufficient to establish that the employee cannot perform the essential functions of their job and how long that inability is likely to last; and
4. if the patient is a covered family member with a serious health condition, information sufficient to establish that the family member needs care and an estimate of the frequency and duration of the leave required to provide that care.[162]

US DOL has developed medical certification forms, one for employee leave[163] and one for leave to care for a family member.[164] Most employers use these forms. Employers must give employees written notice of the need for a medical certification. The employee has fifteen calendar days in which to return the medical certification. If the employee does not return the certification within the fifteen-day window, regulations permit employers to designate the leave as non-FMLA leave, and the employee loses their right to return to employment at the end of the leave.[165] Once the employee returns the medical certification form, the right to return to work is secured, and the employer must designate the leave as job-protected FMLA leave in writing.

The medical certification form allows (but does not require) employers to attach a list of the employee's essential job functions. The employee's health care provider must then explain how the employee's condition makes them unable to perform at least one of those functions. Remember that one of the elements of the definition of a serious health condition is that it makes an employee unable to work for more than three days. Local government department heads and supervisors should do their part in monitoring the use of FMLA leave by making sure that their human resources departments have a good understanding of the current functional requirements and essential job duties of their subordinates. Job responsibilities evolve and change over time.

As noted above, department heads and supervisors cannot see completed medical certification forms. The FMLA prohibits that. As the FMLA regulations instruct, "[s]upervisors and managers may be informed regarding necessary restrictions on the work or duties of an employee and necessary accommodations."[166] In other words, department heads and supervisors are not entitled to

---

161. *See* 29 C.F.R. § 825.305.

162. *See* 29 C.F.R. § 825.306.

163. U.S. Department of Labor, Wage and Hour Division, Certification of Health Care Provider for Employee's Serious Health Condition under the Family and Medical Leave Act, Form WH-380-E (revised June 2020).

164. U.S. Department of Labor, Wage and Hour Division, Certification of Health Care Provider for Employee's Serious Health Condition under the Family and Medical Leave Act.

165. *See* 29 C.F.R. 825.305.

166. *See* 29 C.F.R. § 825.500.

know all the medical facts known to the "employer." They may be informed only of those things they need to know operationally, such as the anticipated length of an employee's leave, if the employee is on intermittent leave or a reduced schedule leave (see below), when they may expect the employee to be present at work, and whether the employee has any work restrictions.

Where FMLA leave is being requested for a planned medical procedure, department heads and supervisors should work with human resources departments to try to make sure that an employee's leave does not fall at a time when it is crucial that they be present at work, on the one hand, and that the employee's surgery is not unduly delayed, on the other.

When an Employee Is Absent without Notice

Not every condition that meets the definition of a serious health condition is predictable or, to use the term preferred by the regulations, "foreseeable." An employee (or the employee's immediate family member) may be in an accident, may suffer a heart attack or stroke, or may collapse due to a yet-undiagnosed condition. A thirty-day advance notice requirement for FMLA leave is unreasonable in these situations. That is why the FMLA requires employees to give notice of the need for FMLA "as soon as practicable" when the need for leave is not foreseeable. The regulations say that "as soon as practicable" will usually be on the same day the condition arises or on the next business day.[167] This means that local government department heads and supervisors should immediately notify their human resources departments if they learn that an employee will be absent due to a serious accident or hospitalization. In the end, the employee may not be out of work for the three days necessary to meet the definition of a serious health condition, but the probability is greater in these situations. This will give a human resources department a head start, as an employer's obligation to respond to a request for, or to a situation calling for, FMLA leave is five days in these circumstances as well.

Fit-for-Duty Certifications When an Employee Returns to Work After FMLA Leave

Any supervisor, but especially those with subordinates working in physically demanding positions, may be concerned about an employee's fitness for work when they return to work from FMLA leave that was based on the employee's own serious health condition. Local government department heads and supervisors should keep in mind that there is *only one opportunity* to request a fit-for-duty certification upon an employee's return to work from FMLA leave. That is on the "designation notice," the form that tells the employee that FMLA leave is approved. If the employer neglects to request a fit-for-duty certification on the designation notice, the employee cannot later be required to return such certification.

Department heads and supervisors must therefore let their human resources departments know the positions for which fit-for-duty examinations should be required after FMLA leave. Some employers require fit-for-duty certifications from all returning employees. In such cases, supervisors may think that they don't need to worry about fit-for-duty certifications. But even when the employer requires all employees to complete these certifications, department heads and supervisors have a role to play. The request for a fit-for-duty examination, just like with a medical certification form, allows an employer to attach a list of job duties and to ask the employee's health care provider to certify that the employee is now fit to perform all their job duties. Department heads and supervisors must work with their human resources departments to keep job descriptions up-to-date so that fit-for-duty certifications accurately reflect current job duties.

167. *See* 29 C.F.R. § 825.302.

Intermittent and Reduced-Schedule FMLA Leave

Intermittent and reduced-schedule FMLA leave is where things get harder for local government department heads and supervisors. FMLA leave need not be for a consecutive twelve-week period. Because some medical conditions are chronic (diabetes, for example) or episodic (epilepsy, for example) and some treatments for certain conditions occur periodically (chemotherapy, for example), leave may be taken on an intermittent basis or on a reduced-leave schedule. Intermittent leave is leave taken in separate blocks of time; a reduced-leave schedule is a temporary reduction in the number of hours that an employee works during the workweek. Employers must grant requests for intermittent or reduced-schedule leave only if that kind of leave is medically necessary.[168]

Department heads and supervisors often find both intermittent and reduced-schedule leave difficult to deal with operationally, although for different reasons. Employees whose serious health conditions (or whose immediate family member's health conditions) are episodic may call out without advance notice, leaving a department short-staffed and without sufficient time to find a replacement. There is not much department heads and supervisors can do about this lack of predictability, as it is the nature of the these types of illnesses, but they can require employees on intermittent leave to comply with the employer's usual requirements for reporting absences and may discipline those who fail to do so. Courts have found that failure of an employee on intermittent FMLA leave to comply with their employer's call-in or reporting policy may be cause for termination.[169] At a minimum, holding employees to call-in requirements will ensure that supervisors have the greatest possible notice under the circumstances.

Occasionally, supervisors notice that an employee's use of intermittent leave seems suspicious. Maybe it regularly falls on Mondays, Fridays, and on days adjacent to holidays, for example. A local government department head or supervisor should not investigate these situations on their own, as tempting as that may be, since, if done improperly, such an investigation could trigger a claim of FMLA interference. Instead, the department head or supervisor should report their suspicions to their human resources department, which can decide, along with the city or county manager or agency director, how an investigation would best be handled under the circumstances.

Reduced-schedule leave presents its own challenges. Although the employer has the benefit of the employee's presence for some part of the workweek, there may or may not be other employees who can take up the work for the other part. It may not be practical to hire a temporary worker when the employee is working part of each day or part of each workweek. The FMLA permits employers to transfer, on a temporary basis, employees taking foreseeable intermittent leave or reduced-schedule leave for their own or a family member's *planned medical treatment* or to recover from their own or a family member's serious health condition. (Note that the regulations explaining the conditions of a permissible temporary transfer do not include intermittent leave for chronic medical conditions). The purpose of the transfer must be to place the employee in a job that can demonstrably better accommodate the employee's FMLA schedule. The job need not have the same duties, but the employee must be qualified for the job and must be compensated at the same rate of pay and with the same benefits as in their regular position. Employees must be returned to their original positions at the conclusion of intermittent or reduced-schedule FMLA leave.[170]

---

168. *See* 29 C.F.R. § 825.202.

169. See Ritenour v. Tenn. Dep't of Hum. Servs., 497 F. App'x 521 (6th Cir. 2012); Bacon v. Hennepin Cnty. Med. Ctr., 550 F.3d 711 (8th Cir. 2008); Lewis v. Holsum of Fort Wayne, Inc., 278 F.3d 706 (7th Cir. 2002).

170. *See* 29 C.F.R. § 825.204.

Return to Work

FMLA leave is job-protected leave. That means two things. First, an employee cannot be fired (or have it held against them at performance-review time) for taking FMLA leave. Second, when FMLA leave concludes, an employee must be returned to the same or an equivalent position. The regulations explain "equivalent position" as follows:

> An equivalent position is one that is virtually identical to the employee's former position in terms of pay, benefits and working conditions, including privileges, perquisites and status. It must involve the same or substantially similar duties and responsibilities, which must entail substantially equivalent skill, effort, responsibility, and authority.[171]

An employee is entitled to reinstatement even if they have been replaced or their position has been restructured to accommodate their absence during FMLA leave.

What a Department Head or Supervisor Should Do When a Subordinate Might Qualify for FMLA Leave

To recap, there are the four things a local government department head or supervisor needs to do to help their city, county, or agency comply with the FMLA:

1. Let the human resources department know right away whenever an employee is absent from work for more than three days. *Why do this? Because department heads and supervisors count as "the employer" for FMLA purposes, and employers must follow up about the possibility that an absence qualifies for FMLA leave* ***within five business days.***
2. Immediately relay any requests for FMLA leave or sick leave to their human resources department and, even if the FMLA is not explicitly mentioned, immediately let human resources know when an employee requests permission to use accrued leave and indicates that they need the leave for medical reasons. *Why do this? Again, because department heads and supervisors count as "the employer," and employers must respond to a request for FMLA leave* ***within five business days.***
3. Ensure that their human resources department is up to date on the essential job duties of any employee who may need FMLA need. *Why do this? Because a description of an employee's job duties may be included in a required medical certification and in a fit-for-duty certification. Those certifications then will help human resources determine that an employee is entitled to FMLA leave in the first place and then, when leave is over, is fit to return to work.*
4. Regularly update their human resources department about any positions and job duties for which a fit-for-duty certification should be required upon an employee's return from an FMLA leave. *Why do this? Because a request for a fit-for-duty certification that addresses job duties can be made only at the beginning of an employee's FMLA leave (on the Designation Notice). The employer cannot ask for a fit-for-duty certification or update the list of job duties after that.*

---

171. *See* 29 C.F.R. § 825.215.

Personnel Records

Introduction

If a record is made or received in connection with the business of the government, it is a public record, open to inspection and copying by anyone who wants to see it. That's what North Carolina's Public Records Law says in G.S. Chapter 132, especially in G.S. 132-1 and -132-6. There are exceptions to this rule, however. Some records created by the government are not open to public inspection, including criminal investigation records; student records; medical records; and other types of records, including most state and local government personnel records.

The personnel privacy statutes for cities and counties are found at G.S. 160A-168 (municipal employees) and 153A-98 (county employees). The two statutes have identical provisions. Note that county social services and health department employees are covered by the county personnel privacy statute, G.S. 153A-98. They are not state employees subject to the state employee personnel privacy statute even if they are covered by the State Human Resources Act.

Ten Things to Know about the Municipal and County Personnel Privacy Statutes

1. A document is part of a public employee's personnel file even if it is not in a manila folder in a file cabinet.

"[A]n employee's personnel file consists of any information in any form gathered by the [employer] with respect to that employee and, by way of illustration but not limitation, relating to his application, selection or nonselection, performance, promotions, demotions, transfers, suspension and other disciplinary actions, evaluation forms, leave, salary, and termination of employment. As used in this section, 'employee' includes former employees of the [employer]."[172]

This language is taken from the city and county personnel privacy statutes. See below for more information on the handling of applicant information.

2. Most of the information in a public employee's personnel file is confidential, in contrast to government records generally.

"Notwithstanding the provisions of G.S. 132-6 or any other general law or local act concerning access to public records, personnel files of employees, former employees, or applicants for employment maintained by a[n employer] are subject to inspection and may be disclosed only as provided by this section."[173]

Again, this is the language used in the city and the county personnel privacy statutes.

3. Some information in a public employee's personnel file is always open to the public, including

a. the employee's name;
b. the employee's age;
c. the employee's date of original employment or appointment to service;
d. the terms of any contract under which the employee is employed, whether written or oral, past and current, to the extent that the employer has the written contract or a record of the oral contract in its possession;
e. the employee's current position;
f. the employee's title;

---

172. G.S. 160A-168(a) (municipal), 153A-98(a) (county).
173. *See* G.S.160A-168(a), 153A-98(a).

g. the employee's current salary;
h. the date and amount of each increase or decrease in salary awarded by the employer;
i. the date and type of each promotion, demotion, transfer, suspension, separation, or other change in position classification that took place while working for the employer.
j. the date and general description of the reasons for each promotion awarded by the employer;
k. (1) the date and type of each dismissal, suspension, or demotion for disciplinary reasons made by the employer; (2) if the disciplinary action was a dismissal, a copy of the written notice of the employer's final decision setting forth the specific acts or omissions that are the basis of the dismissal; and
l. the office to which the employee is currently assigned.[174]

4. A public employee is entitled to see (almost all of) their own personnel file.

"The employee or his duly authorized agent may examine all portions of his personnel file except (i) letters of reference solicited prior to employment, and (ii) information concerning a medical disability, mental or physical, that a prudent physician would not divulge to his patient."[175]

5. Supervisors with active authority over public employees are entitled to see those employees' personnel files.

Supervisors right up to the top of the "chain of command" may have access to employees' personnel files.[176]

6. Other governmental officials may have access to public employees' personnel files where access is "necessary and essential to the pursuance of a proper function" of that official.

A federal, state, or local government official seeking access to an employee's personnel file must have a job-related need to see the material.[177]

7. Files of applicants for public employment are confidential in their totality.

In the early 1990s, a local newspaper wanted the names of every person being considered for the job of county manager in Yadkin County, North Carolina. In the case *Elkin Tribune v. Yadkin County Board of County Commissioners*, the North Carolina Supreme Court held that each candidate's name was part of his or her personnel file because each candidate could be considered an "applicant for employment" and because the personnel records law governing county employees applied to applicants. But the county personnel records statute authorized the public disclosure of information as to name, salary, and so forth only as it pertained to "employees," which the statute defined to include "former employees of the county" but not future employees, i.e., applicants. Because the privacy parts of the statute covered applicants but the disclosure parts did not, the court held that no information at all—not even names—could be released about candidates for the job of manager—or candidates for any other job.[178] Because city and county personnel privacy provisions are identical, the *Elkin Tribune* case's holding that applicant information is confidential in its entirety therefore applies to municipalities as well.

---

174. *See* G.S. 160A-168(b) (municipal), 153A-98(b) (county).
175. *See* G.S. 160A-168(c)(1), 153A-98(c)(1).
176. *See* G.S. 160A-168(c)(3), 153A-98(c)(3).
177. *See* G.S. 160A-168(c)(5) (municipal), 153A-98(c)(5) (county).
178. *See* Elkin Tribune v. Yadkin Cnty. Bd. of Cnty. Comm'rs, 331 N.C. 735 (1992).

8. In special circumstances, confidential personnel information may be disclosed.

"The [city/county] manager, with concurrence of the [council/board] may inform any person of the employment or nonemployment, promotion, demotion, suspension or other disciplinary action, reinstatement, transfer, or termination of an employee and the reasons for that personnel action. Before releasing the information, the [employer] shall determine in writing that the release is essential to maintaining public confidence in the administration of [city/county] services or to maintaining the level and quality of [city/county] services. This written determination shall be retained and is a record available for public inspection and shall become part of the employee's personnel file."[179]

9. Sometimes a city or county must create a written dismissal letter (which would become public under the personnel privacy statutes) when it dismisses an employee for disciplinary reasons.

Whether or not a public employer must create a written dismissal letter depends on the employer and the type of employee being dismissed. The State Human Resources Act (SHRA) requires that employers give SHRA employees a written notice of dismissal setting forth the acts and omissions giving rise to the dismissal. Any county employee covered by the SHRA **must** therefore receive such a letter. Otherwise, a city's or county's personnel policy will state whether non-SHRA employees must receive written letters of dismissal.

The essence of at-will employment, however, is that an employer may dismiss an employee for any reason at any time or for no reason at all. An employer does not have to provide an at-will employee with a reason, much less with a letter setting forth the reason.

10. Sometimes an employer must offer a name-clearing hearing to a dismissed employee when it provides the employee with a letter setting forth the reasons for dismissal since that letter will become a public document.

Disclosure of Reason for Dismissal and Name-Clearing Hearing

The Fourteenth Amendment to the U.S. Constitution provides that the government may not "deprive any person of . . . liberty . . . without due process of law." The word "liberty," like "property" (also protected by the Fourteenth Amendment), has a broad meaning. It means more than just staying out of jail.

Liberty Interest in Engaging in Life's Ordinary Occupations

The term "liberty" incudes the right "to engage in the common occupations of life, unfettered by unreasonable restrictions" imposed by the government.[180] That right is abridged when the government "unfairly imposes some stigma or disability that will itself foreclose the freedom to take advantage of employment opportunities." In one North Carolina case, a veteran dining-room manager alleged that her liberty interest was violated when her supervisor publicly disclosed his belief that the manager was supplying alcohol to painters at the worksite for them to drink on the premises. That public statement by the supervisor, made in connection with the manager's dismissal, would apply a stigma to the manager if left uncontested, making it difficult for her to obtain new employment.

---

179. *See* G.S. § 160A-168(c)(7), 153A-98(c)(7).

180. *See* Presnell v. Pell, 298 N.C. 715, 724 (1979) (internal quotation marks, citations omitted). *See also* Bd. of Regents v. Roth, 408 U.S. 564,73 (1972).

In another case, the North Carolina Supreme Court said that the procedural protections of due process apply when

- the accuracy of the reason for an employee's dismissal is contested,
- there is some public disclosure of the reason, and
- the disclosure is made in connection with termination of employment or other employment actions.[181]

The federal Fourth Circuit Court of Appeals has said that the due process requirement applies when a government unit's statements about one of its employees

- placed a stigma on the employee's reputation,
- were made public by the employer,
- were made in conjunction with the employee's termination or demotion, and
- were false.[182]

Stigma

It is important to keep in mind that only dismissal for reasons that are likely to affect the employee's standing in the community or foreclose the opportunity for future employment implicate an employee's liberty interest. Statements that impugn an employee's ethics, honesty, or morals may, if false, form the basis of a liberty interest claim, but reasons that have to do with an employee's job performance do not. Statements about an employee's incompetence, about an employee not being good at his or her job, or about an employee being inattentive to his or her job duties do not give rise to a protected liberty interest. The mere fact that an employee is being dismissed, that their contract is not being renewed, or that they are not being rehired does not say anything about their reputation, honor, or integrity.[183]

Notice and Hearing

When all the elements for a due process claim set forth by the North Carolina Supreme Court or the Fourth Circuit are present (see the paragraphs and notes above in this subsection), due process requires notice and a hearing. As the state supreme court held, "[W]here [the government] publicly and falsely accuses a discharged employee of dishonesty, immorality, or job-related misconduct, considerations of due process demand that the employee be afforded a hearing in order to have an opportunity to refute the accusation and remove the stigma upon his reputation."[184]

Due Process

The scope of the process that is due to protect an employment liberty interest is more modest and ill-defined than the process due to protect the property interests granted by a statute or ordinance that provides that employees may only be dismissed for good cause. The purpose of the due process hearing, the U.S. Supreme Court has said, is to provide a person who feels that their moral character has been impugned by the government an opportunity to clear his or her name. Once that has happened at the hearing, the employer is free to deny the person future employment. In fact, the

181. *See* Crump v. Bd. of Educ., 326 N.C. 603, 614 (1990).]
182. *See* Sciolino v. City of Newport News, 480 F.3d 642, 646 (4th Cir. 2007).
183. *See Roth*, 408 U.S. at 573.
184. *See Presnell*, 298 N.C. at 724.

hearing may even take place after the termination of employment (or other adverse action), because the focus of the liberty interest is on *future* employment opportunities.[185]

Protection for All Employees

The due process protections of this liberty interest apply equally to all public employees—at-will employees, probationary employees, and employees with property interests in their jobs.

185. *See Presnell*, 298 N.C. at 724.

Chapter 14

The Attorney and the Clerk

Kristina M. Wilson

Kristina M. Wilson is a School of Government faculty member who specializes in local government law. This chapter builds on an earlier version authored by A. Fleming Bell, II, a retired School of Government faculty member who specialized in local government law. His contributions are gratefully acknowledged.

Some of the attorney portions of this chapter were adapted from Grainger R. Barrett, "County Legal Representation: Retained or Full-Time County Attorney?" *Local Government Law Bulletin* No. 20 (October 1980), published by the Institute of Government. Some of the materials on the clerk are based on A. Fleming Bell, II, "City and County Clerks: What They Do and How They Do It," *Popular Government* 61 (Summer 1996): 21–30.

The attorney and the clerk are mainstays of the governing board as it attempts to govern wisely and well. Together, city and county attorneys, city clerks, and clerks to the board of county commissioners help to ensure that local government activities are carried out in a legally correct manner. While governing boards are primarily responsible for ensuring their own compliance with the law, the attorney and clerk play significant supporting roles. The documents created and maintained by the attorney and the clerk provide the written record needed to ensure that the board is accountable to the city's or county's citizens and to other officials. Ideally, the attorney and the clerk work as partners with the manager and the board—the attorney advising on the legal consequences of board actions, the clerk keeping a record of those actions, and both officials ensuring that proper procedures are followed.

The Attorney

Every city council and board of county commissioners in North Carolina must appoint an individual attorney or law firm to be its legal adviser.[1] This section explores practical considerations for obtaining an attorney, as well as the legal framework surrounding city and county attorneys' roles and responsibilities.

Considerations for Obtaining Legal Services

The best way to provide legal services for a particular local government depends on its legal needs. Local governments should be aware of their options for representation as well as key factors in selecting from those options, including cost considerations.

Retained or Full-Time Attorney

General Factors

Whether hiring a full-time attorney is appropriate for a particular city or county depends on the local government's specific legal needs, its governing board, and other relatively subtle issues, such as what *types* of litigation the city or county anticipates and whether a contract or full-time attorney will be more effective with government officials and personnel. Hiring a full-time attorney may offer the most salient advantages since the attorney is able to develop an intimate knowledge of the city's or county's day-to-day affairs and to practice preventive law.

A full-time city or county attorney handles the full range of a local government's legal needs. This might be better service in the sense that a full-time attorney is available for consultation and to provide advice to all governmental departments and offices (such as a purchasing or recreation department), to other local boards and commissions (such as a social services board or a board of adjustment), and, in the case of counties, to other elected county officials (such as the sheriff and the register of deeds). Officials and employees in a city or county with a full-time attorney may also feel that legal consultation is more convenient when the attorney is available full time and has an office close to other local government offices. And, as consultations become more complex or extensive, officials and employees will not feel constrained by the escalating legal fees they would incur if consulting with an independent-contractor attorney. In a jurisdiction with a full-time attorney, the local government's personnel know that they will not be interrupting the attorney while he or she is handling matters for other clients since the attorney's client is the city or county. Similarly, on occasion, retained city or county attorneys may not be readily available because they are entirely occupied with a major matter—perhaps a trial—for another client, or there may be a conflict of interest in a particular situation that involves both the local government and another of the attorney's clients, so that the attorney cannot ethically represent either side. A full-time attorney is more familiar with the local government's business than retained counsel and does not need to be briefed as extensively on most matters. And, of course, because they are full-time salaried employees, no additional charges are associated with legal consultations.

Jurisdictions without continuous, recurring legal needs may not require such an attorney. Some local governments decide to retain an attorney or firm as an independent contractor instead of hiring a full-time, salaried employee. In practice, most city or county attorneys who are retained as independent contractors place an emphasis on advising the council or board of commissioners and the manager, if any, and on attending their meetings. To minimize their retainer fees, some

1. Chapter 153A, Section 114 (counties) and Chapter 160A, Section 173 (cities) of the North Carolina General Statutes (hereinafter G.S.).

attorneys provide routine legal service to only those parties or, in many small towns, attend meetings only when specifically asked to do so. A governing board should consider long-term costs and not just immediate expenses in deciding how much time an attorney needs to devote to local government issues.

Cost Concerns

Whether having a full-time city or county attorney will save the local government money depends on whether it has full-time legal needs. The answer to this question depends on at least two important factors.

First, the amount and the type of litigation in which the city or county is engaged are very important. If the city or county is frequently in court, a full-time attorney may be justified. Court cases tend to raise the cost of a local government's legal services sharply, and the amount of litigation is often unpredictable. Local governments have taxing power, which means that they may be viewed by potential litigants as having deep pockets. This can lead to more frequent threatened or actual lawsuits. A full-time attorney ordinarily can handle much of the jurisdiction's recurring litigation, such as zoning disputes, tax foreclosures, and (for counties) social services child support suits. If the council members or commissioners are contemplating a full-time attorney, they should also keep in mind the nature of the city's or county's litigation as they decide what experience and capabilities that attorney should have.

Also very important to the decision about full-time legal representation are the number and complexity of the transactions in which the city or county is involved on a regular basis. For example, a local government with an active development program in which it has partnerships with private developers may need a great deal of legal work, even without litigation. Similarly, if land development is occurring rapidly in the city or county, local planning and zoning officials will frequently need an attorney's advice.

On the other hand, the city or county may incur significant additional costs if it hires a full-time attorney, costs that are ordinarily covered by the fees charged by a retained attorney. Paralegal and administrative support, subscriptions to legal research services, law books, and computer equipment are among the overhead expense items that a local government must plan to absorb if it has full-time legal representation.

Other matters should also be considered. Will city or county departments and commissions need legal consultation frequently enough to keep an attorney busy throughout the year? A great advantage of in-house attorneys is that they can practice preventive law by counseling the local government's personnel regarding appropriate policies and practices, exploring legal considerations before disputes erupt into lawsuits, advising employees regarding courses of action when problems suddenly arise, and so on. The daily presence of an attorney can have an intangible value in avoiding legal expenses that might otherwise be incurred without timely legal advice.

Does the cost of the local government's litigation fluctuate sharply from year to year? If so, having a salaried attorney can give the city or county a more predictable measure of its annual legal expense, assuming that a full-time attorney is justifiable in other respects. Even if complex or time-consuming litigation is routed to specialized counsel, a full-time attorney may be better able to absorb much of the jurisdiction's unforeseen legal requirements without a large corresponding increase in legal fees. The local government can better anticipate and estimate its budget requirements for legal representation if a full-time city or county attorney can handle most of its routine legal affairs. The attorney's and legal support staff's salaries and benefits, other overhead expenses, and a contingency reserve for outside counsel's representation in extraordinary litigation will be a fair measure of the city's or county's annual budget requirement for legal services.

Typical Arrangements

Regardless of whether a local government chooses to hire a full-time or contract attorney, there is significant variation across cities and counties in how each jurisdiction forms and manages its attorney relationship. Jurisdictions' resources and legal needs will determine their legal services arrangement. The independent contractor relationship can take several forms. In some local governments, all legal work is provided on a fee-for-service basis. In others, the attorney is paid a yearly retainer to provide agreed-on basic services. The retainer may cover such services as

- attending all meetings of the city council or board of commissioners;
- being available for routine consultation with board members and department heads;
- drafting and reviewing ordinances and resolutions;
- preparing and reviewing routine legal documents, such as deeds and simple contracts; and
- preparing and reviewing legal advertisements.

In some cities or counties, the retained attorney's performance of agreed-on retainer services is charged against the retainer on a per-hour basis; the retainer then is a minimum annual fee for legal representation. If the attorney exceeds the number of hours covered by the retainer for the established services or does work not included in the retainer arrangement, he or she is reimbursed on a per-hour or other fee basis. As independent contractors, attorneys are responsible for providing their own insurance, retirement, and other benefits. Their retainer and hourly charges also pay for office and administrative expenses.

As noted earlier, some jurisdictions have at least one full-time salaried attorney, with the larger cities and counties having legal staffs of varying sizes. In addition to the attorneys' salaries, the city or county provides fringe benefits, office space and supplies, and administrative and other assistance.

Some jurisdictions may choose a hybrid arrangement. For example, a city or county may retain an individual attorney as an independent contractor, even though a majority of the attorney's professional time is spent exclusively on the local government's legal matters. This arrangement may be more attractive for attorneys since it allows them the flexibility to hold partnerships at private law firms, while also allowing the city to retain an experienced legal adviser without necessarily providing employment benefits. In another hybrid arrangement, jurisdictions might classify an attorney as an employee even when less than half of that attorney's professional time is devoted to the local government's legal matters. This arrangement is beneficial for the attorney, who gains employment benefits, and for the local government, who pays a salary rather than hourly legal fees or a retainer.

At times, governing boards may need additional, specialized attorneys to work with particular local government officials or departments on a regular basis. For example, counties often have separate attorneys—retained or full-time—for social services work, and both counties and cities frequently have separate attorneys to deal with the unique issues faced by the sheriff's office or the police department. Governing boards may assess these needs on an ongoing basis or may depend on their full-time or retained attorney to alert them to the need for specialized legal counsel. Whether and how specialized legal counsel is retained is within the governing board's discretion unless it specifically delegates this authority to the city or county attorney by majority vote.

Hiring the Attorney

Once a local government settles on its preferred arrangement for legal services, how does the local government actually hire the attorney? Both Chapter 160A, Section 173 (cities) and Chapter 153A,

Section 114 (counties) of the North Carolina General Statutes (hereinafter G.S.) specifically require governing boards to appoint their attorney. This means that governing boards should formally appoint their attorney by majority vote at an open and properly noticed meeting.[2] Are city and county attorneys considered employees, independent contractors, public officials, or all of the above? Whether a city or county attorney is an employee or independent contractor depends on the specific jurisdiction's arrangement. Whether an attorney also qualifies as a public officer depends on several factors, including whether the position is created by state law, whether it has significant governmental power, and whether it has significant discretion in exercising that power.[3] All of these factors weigh in favor of treating city and county attorneys as public officials: the statutes explicitly establish the office of city and county attorney,[4] and the attorney, arguably, has significant governmental authority and discretion in using that authority when acting as the local government's legal representative. Moreover, at least two cases have treated city attorneys as public officials for public records law and tort liability purposes.[5] Still, North Carolina courts have not ruled on whether local government attorneys are public officials outside of the tort and public records law contexts, so their status as public officials remains an open question.

With no clear legal guidance regarding whether to classify local government attorneys as public officials, it is unclear whether the law requires the attorney to take an oath of office. The North Carolina Constitution and city and county statutes (G.S. 160A-61; G.S. 153A-26) require all individuals elected or appointed to public offices to take the constitutional oath in article VI, section 7. Moreover, sections 11-7 and 11-11 require all people elected or appointed to "any office of trust or profit" to take a separate, additional oath.[6] Generally, there is no penalty for taking an oath that is not legally required, but there are significant penalties for failing to take a legally required oath.[7] As a result, it may be in a jurisdiction's best interest to treat its attorney as a public officer for purposes of the oath of office.[8]

Once a local government appoints a city or county attorney, it does not need to reappoint the attorney following an election or a change in board membership, absent any charter or local act provisions to the contrary.[9] If a board wants to *remove* its attorney, it must do so by formal majority vote in open session.[10] For cities, only the governing board has the power to remove its attorney, even in council–manager forms of government.[11] As G.S. 160A-148(a)(1) provides, managers have

---

2. *See* Frayda Bluestein, "Selecting and Appointing a New City or County Attorney: Answers to Frequently Asked Questions," *Coates' Canons: NC Local Government Law* blog (October 6, 2014), canons.sog.unc.edu/2014/10/selecting-and-appointing-a-new-city-or-county-attorney-answers-to-frequently-asked-questions/.

3. *See, e.g.*, Meyer v. Walls, 347 N.C. 97, 113 (N.C. 1997); Cline v. James Bane Home Building, LLC, 278 N.C. App. 12, 22–23 (N.C. Ct. App. 2021); Chastain v. Arndt, 253 N.C. App. 8, 16 (N.C. Ct. App. 2017).

4. G.S. 160A-173; G.S. 153A-114.

5. Womack Newspapers, Inc. v. Town of Kitty Hawk *ex rel.* Kitty Hawk Town Council, 181 N.C. App. 1, 13 (2007); City of Winston-Salem v. Yarbrough, 117 N.C. App. 340, 349 (1994).

6. *See also* Kristina Wilson, "The Most Common Oaths of Office Question," *Coates' Canons: NC Local Government Law* blog (August 4, 2022), canons.sog.unc.edu/2022/08/the-most-common-oaths-of-office-question/.

7. G.S. 14-229.

8. For a consideration of the potential advantages and disadvantages of having public official status for city and county attorneys, see David M. Lawrence, "City and County Attorneys as Public Officers—Possible Downsides," *Coates' Canons: NC Local Government Law* blog (September 18, 2009), canons.sog.unc.edu/2009/09/city-and-county-attorneys-as-public-officers-possible-downsides/ and David M. Lawrence, "City and County Attorneys as Public Officers—a Possible Upside," *Coates' Canons: NC Local Government Law* blog (September 11, 2009), canons.sog.unc.edu/2009/09/city-and-county-attorneys-as-public-officers-a-possible-upside/.

9. *See* Bluestein, *supra* note 2.

10. G.S. 143-318.11(a)(6).

11. G.S. 160A-148(a)(1).

authority to appoint and remove all city officers and employees *excluding* the attorney (and any others whose appointment or removal is provided for by law). As a result, a manager's termination of the city attorney is insufficient to remove the attorney from office. Arguably, the same is true for counties, unless a local act provides otherwise. While the county-manager statute lacks an explicit exception for county attorneys, it does state that the county manager has the power of appointment and removal for all county officers and employees whose appointment and removal is not otherwise provided for by law.[12] The appointment of the county attorney is provided for by law in G.S. 153A-114. Common law principles dictate that the power of appointment necessarily includes the power of removal.[13] The removal of the attorney is therefore provided for by law as incident to the power of appointment in G.S. 153A-114. Though not as clear as G.S. 160A-148, G.S. 153A-82 and common law suggest that county managers do not have the authority to remove county attorneys and that the board of commissioners must act by majority vote to effectively remove a county attorney from office.

Roles and Responsibilities

As the governing board's legal adviser, the attorney's tasks include assisting the board with all legal questions, drafting legal documents, negotiating agreements, and representing the board in any legal proceedings. A city or county attorney should be able to work and communicate effectively with public officials, local government employees, the press, and the public. Governing boards want to rely on the attorney's judgment and his or her ability to articulate ideas clearly when asked an unanticipated question during a public meeting. Also, the attorney must represent the board effectively even when the board members do not agree among themselves. The attorney must be able to understand the job requirements of administrators and department heads and give them accurate and practical legal advice. The county attorney must develop relationships with separately elected county officials such as the sheriff and the register of deeds. The attorney may also represent other local government boards and must be able to deal with them effectively even when they and the governing board do not see eye to eye. The attorney must be both forthright and discreet in dealing with representatives of the news media, who often assume a watchdog role over the affairs of the city or county. The attorney must maintain credibility while not disclosing his or her client's confidences. Finally, the attorney should be able to represent the local government to the public on occasion, even though it is not usually the attorney's role to be a spokesperson for the city or county. All these criteria suggest that an ideal local government attorney should be talented, well-rounded, and experienced.

Among the challenges that governing board attorneys face in carrying out these duties is confusion regarding the attorney–client relationship. In other words, who is the client of a governing board attorney? For city attorneys, the client is the city and for county attorneys, the client is the county, but what exactly does that mean? Rule 1.13(a) of the North Carolina Rules of Professional Conduct states that an organization's attorney "represents the organization acting through its duly authorized constituents." Of course, within the context of a city or county, there might be many different duly authorized agents or constituents. As a result, the attorney must look to the "highest

12. G.S. 153A-82(a)(1).

13. *See, e.g.*, Kinsland v. Mackey, 217 N.C. 508, 8 S.E. 2d 598, 600 (N.C. 1940); Frayda Bluestein, "Removing Members of Appointed Boards," *Coates' Canons: NC Local Government Law* blog (June 3, 2015), canons.sog.unc .edu/2015/06/removing-members-of-appointed-boards/.

authority that can act on behalf of the organization"—the governing board.[14] Note that the attorney's ethical obligation and professional representation extends to the governing board as a whole, not to each individual member.[15] The attorney's client is the board, and the attorney does not necessarily have a professional or ethical obligation to provide individualized legal advice or to advocate for the interests of individual members. That also means that attorney–client privilege may not protect conversations with individual board members.[16] Instead, an attorney may have an obligation to disclose one-on-one conversations with individual board members if the conversation involves elements that may impact the legal interests of the city or county.[17]

The Clerk

The position of clerk is one of the oldest in local government, dating at least to biblical times.[18] Each city and county in North Carolina must have a clerk,[19] and the most important records maintained by the clerk, such as the minutes of governing board meetings, must be kept permanently for the use of future generations.[20] The city council or board of county commissioners may also provide for a *deputy clerk*, who may exercise any of the powers and perform any of the duties of the clerk that the governing board specifies.[21] The clerk is sometimes described as "the hub of the wheel" in local government because of the central role that clerks play in the government's communication network.[22] Clerks provide information daily to governing board members, city or county employees, other government officials, citizens, and the press.

Hiring the Clerk

The city clerk generally works directly for the city council, keeping the city's records, giving notices of meetings, and performing various other functions as the council requires.[23] In mayor–council cities, the clerk is almost always appointed by the council, and the council should make the clerk appointment by majority vote in an open and properly noticed meeting. In council–manager cities, situations vary. Some city charters specifically require the council to appoint the clerk. Without a specific charter provision to this effect, the manager will probably appoint the clerk, although the clerk will still perform duties for the council. G.S. 160A-148(a)(1) specifies that the manager is to appoint and suspend or remove, in accordance with any council-adopted general personnel rules,

---

14. *See* Comment 5 to Rule 1.13 of the North Carolina Rules of Professional Conduct; Chris McLaughlin, "Ethics and the Role of the Local Government Attorney," *Coates' Canons: NC Local Government Law* blog (October 9, 2014), canons.sog.unc.edu/2014/10/ethics-and-the-role-of-the-local-government-attorney.

15. McLaughlin, *supra* note 14.

16. *Id.*

17. *Id.*

18. The book of Acts in the Christian New Testament notes that when a conflict arose between the people of Ephesus and the missionary Paul and his companions, the town clerk quieted the crowd and prevented a riot. Acts 19:23–41.

19. G.S. 153A-111 (clerk to the board of county commissioners); G.S. 160A-171 (city clerk).

20. North Carolina Department of Natural and Cultural Resources, Division of Archives and Records, Government Records Section, *Records Retention and Disposition Schedule—2021 General Records Schedule: Local Government Agencies*, archives.ncdcr.gov/2021localgeneralstandardspdf/open.

21. For cities, see G.S. 160A-172. To create the position of deputy or assistant clerk, boards of county commissioners rely on their general authority under G.S. 153A-76 to create offices and positions of county government.

22. Carolyn Lloyd, "The Hub of the Wheel: Clerks Keep Government Running Smoothly," *Popular Government* 55 (Spring 1990): 36–43.

23. G.S. 160A-171.

regulations, policies, or ordinances, all nonelected city officers and employees "whose appointment or removal is not otherwise provided for by law, except the city attorney." G.S. 160A-171 states, "There shall be a city clerk," but it does not specify how the clerk is to be appointed, so the provision for appointment by the manager probably applies. In contrast, the county statute specifically requires the board of commissioners to appoint the clerk, and they should do so by majority vote in an open and properly noticed meeting.[24]

While no North Carolina court has specifically ruled on this issue, there is a reasonable argument that city and county clerks are public officials who should take an oath of office. Their positions are created by state statute and they exercise significant, discretionary government power over several areas, including notices, minutes, and recordkeeping. Moreover, the clerk is one of the few officials who may administer the oaths of office[25] that are required for elected and appointed city and county officers.[26] Like elected and appointed officials, the clerk should take the constitutional oath in article VI, section 7, as well as the oath in G.S. 11-7, and file both in their office with the other signed copies of oaths administered to city and county officials.[27] There is no similar oath requirement for deputy clerks, but having the deputy clerk take an oath is a helpful practice. Indeed, deputy clerks *must* take an oath to be able to administer oaths to others.[28]

As with attorneys, common law dictates that whoever is empowered to appoint the clerk has the power to remove the clerk.[29] For mayor–council cities and counties, the power of removal likely lies only with the council or board of county commissioners. For manager-council cities, the power of removal lies with the council if the charter specifies that the council is to appoint the clerk. If not, the manager likely has the power of removal under G.S. 160A-148.

Roles and Responsibilities

Under G.S. 160A-171, city clerks are responsible for giving notice and keeping a record of meetings, serving as city-records custodians, and performing any other duties the council or law requires. Similarly, county clerks must perform any duties required by law or the board.[30] As with attorneys, clerks' professional obligations are to the board as a whole. Any tasks assigned to the clerk that are not otherwise covered by statute should be at the behest of or in service to the collective board and should be professional in nature, related to local government operations or public business. Personal errands for individual board members should be discouraged. The clerk's main responsibilities are discussed in more detail below.

Records

Minutes

One of the clerk's most important statutory duties is to prepare and retain the minutes of the governing board.[31] The legal powers of a city and many of the legal powers of a county are exercised

24. G.S. 153A-111.

25. G.S. 11-7.1(a)(7).

26. G.S. 153A-26; G.S. 160A-61.

27. For more on the oaths that incoming public officials are required to take, see Trey Allen, "One Oath or Two? What is THE Oath of Office?" *Coates' Canons: NC Local Government Law* blog (January 27, 2017), www.sog.unc.edu/blogs/coates-canons/one-oath-or-two-what-oath-office.

28. G.S. 11-8.

29. *See* Kinsland v. Mackey, 217 N.C. 508, 8 S.E. 2d 598, 600 (N.C. 1940); Bluestein, *supra* note 13.

30. G.S. 153A-111.

31. *See* G.S. 160A-171 (requiring the city clerk to "keep a journal of the proceedings of the council"); G.S. 160A-72 (requiring the city clerk to keep "full and accurate minutes of the council proceedings"); G.S. 153A-42 (requiring the

by the city council or board of county commissioners, respectively, and the minutes of a board's meetings are the official record of what it does.

The minutes must be "full and accurate,"[32] for they are the legal evidence of what the governing board has said and done. Full and accurate does not generally mean, however, that the clerk must make a verbatim transcript of a meeting's proceedings. Rather, the minutes serve as a record of actions taken.[33] That means that, at a minimum, minutes must record the board's actions, including motions, points of order, votes, and the results of each vote taken by the governing board.[34] Aside from this legal minimum, the board has ultimate discretion over their minutes' level of detail.[35] Some boards may want extremely detailed minutes, while others prefer sparser minutes. Vague and less detailed minutes are permissible so long as the minutes still include a record of actions taken.

Although not required under law, it may be advisable for the clerk to document several other aspects of a meeting. Ideally, minutes should show the existence of any condition that is required before a particular action may validly be taken.[36] For example, if the board awards a formally bid construction contract, the minutes should record the fact that the award standard specified in G.S. 143-129(b) was followed. Additionally, including the full text of each motion, ordinance, or resolution passed by the board may be extremely important in later years to supplement and back up information sources that may be frequently revised, such as ordinance books and codes of ordinances.[37] Other important details include the type of meeting, date and time of convening, members in attendance, members' late arrivals or early departures, and whether those departures were excused.[38] These details help to show compliance with notice requirements and the presence of a quorum at all times. A list of the members who voted each way on a particular question (the "ayes and noes") must be included if any member so requests.[39]

As noted earlier, minutes generally do not need to include a verbatim transcript or even a summary of the discussion that took place at the council or board of commissioners meeting. A verbatim transcript of council or commissioner proceedings may be required when the governing board is sitting as a quasi-judicial body—for example, when it is considering issuance of a special use permit under a zoning ordinance. During quasi-judicial proceedings, the board must act somewhat like a court, and a full transcript of the proceedings must be provided if requested by any court to which the decision is appealed.[40]

Council and commissioner meetings need not be audio or video recorded by the city or county. (Persons attending the meeting may make their own recordings if they desire.)[41] If the clerk or another public official does make a recording for the purpose of minutes preparation, the clerk may

---

clerk to the board of commissioners to "keep full and accurate minutes of the proceedings of the board of commissioners"); and G.S. 143-318.10(e) (part of the open meetings law, requiring public bodies to keep "full and accurate minutes" of their official meetings).

32. G.S. 153A-42; G.S. 160A-72; G.S. 143-318.10(e).

33. Maready v. City of Winston-Salem, 342 N.C. 708, 733–34 (N.C. 1996).

34. *Id.*

35. Trey Allen, "'Full and Accurate' Minutes: A Primer," *Local Government Law Bulletin* No. 140 (Jan. 2019): 2, www.sog.unc.edu/publications/bulletins/full-and-accurate-minutes-primer.

36. *Maready*, 342 N.C. at 733–34.

37. Trey Allen, *Suggested Rules of Procedure for a City Council*, 4th ed. (UNC School of Government, 2017): 13–14; Trey Allen, *Suggested Rules of Procedure for the Board of County Commissioners*, 4th ed. (UNC School of Government, 2017): 12–13.

38. *Id.*; *Maready*, 342 N.C. at 733–34.

39. G.S. 153A-42; G.S. 160A-72.

40. Allen, *supra* note 35, at 4–5.

41. *See* G.S. 143-318.14.

dispose of the recording once the minutes of that meeting are approved.[42] The city's or county's recording of a meeting is a public record available for public inspection and copying for as long as it exists.[43] Recordings of quasi-judicial proceedings are sometimes retained indefinitely in lieu of a transcript, in case they are needed later by a court or one of the parties involved in the case.

Draft copies of council and commissioner minutes are generally sent by the clerk to the board members before the meeting at which they are to be considered for approval. The circulated draft minutes are a public record that must also be made available for public inspection and copying upon request.[44] Council members and commissioners should carefully review the minutes and bring their suggested changes and corrections to the meeting for consideration by the full board. Although the clerk records the draft minutes for the council or the board of commissioners, the governing board itself, acting as a body, must determine what the final, official minutes will include.[45] The minutes do not become the official record of the board's actions until it approves them by majority vote.[46]

The governing board may correct minutes that it has already approved if it later finds that they are inaccurate by majority vote.[47] In such a case, the correction should be noted in the minutes of the meeting at which the correction is made, with an appropriate notation and cross-reference at the place in the minutes book where the provision being corrected appears.[48]

Minutes and General Accounts of Closed Sessions

North Carolina's open meetings law, including the rules for closed sessions, is discussed in detail in Chapter 9. The minutes of these sessions, like other minutes, must be "full and accurate."[49] In particular, the open session minutes must record the motion to go into the session and the purpose of the closed session, while the closed session minutes record any actions taken, the existence of the conditions needed to take particular actions, and the motion to return to open session. In addition to the minutes, G.S. 143-318.10(e) requires a "general account of the closed session so that a person not in attendance would have a reasonable understanding of what transpired." The general account may be either a written narrative or audio or video recordings and must be slightly more detailed than open session minutes. Since only certain actions may be taken in closed session, a description of the substance of closed session discussion likely must be included in a general account. While the open meetings law distinguishes between minutes and general accounts for closed session, it is common practice to combine them into a single document. The minutes and general account "may be withheld from public inspection so long as public inspection would frustrate the purpose of a closed session."[50] If the clerk does not attend the closed session, the clerk should designate someone to record the minutes and general account and should explain to that person the correct procedures for so doing.

---

42. North Carolina Department of Natural and Cultural Resources, Division of Archives and Records, Government Records Section, *Records Retention and Disposition Schedule—2021 General Records Schedule: Local Government Agencies*, Item 1.50, "Public Bodies: Audio and Visual Recordings of Meetings," archives.ncdcr.gov/2021localgeneralstandardspdf/open.

43. G.S. 132-1(a), assuming no exception applies; G.S. 143-318.10(e).

44. G.S. 132-1(a).

45. Allen, *supra* note 35, at 14.

46. *Id.*

47. Allen, *supra* note 35, at 14–15.

48. Allen, *supra* note 35, at 16–17.

49. G.S. 143-318.10(e).

50. *Id.*

Minutes of Meetings of Other Public Bodies

The open meetings law requires that "full and accurate" minutes also be kept of the meetings of the other "public bodies" that are part of city or county government. Included are all boards, committees, and other bodies of the county that perform legislative, policy-making, quasi-judicial, administrative, or advisory functions, including appointed subcommittees of larger bodies, such as the governing board.[51] These public bodies must also keep minutes and general accounts of their closed sessions.[52] The governing board, aided by the clerk, should establish procedures to ensure that the minutes of all public bodies under its direction are properly recorded and maintained, either by the clerk or under the clerk's guidance. The minutes of these various public bodies may be kept either in written form or, at the option of the public body, in the form of sound or video-and-sound recordings.[53] Most minutes of local public bodies are considered permanent public records.[54]

Ordinance Book and Code of Ordinances

Among the other records of the city council's or board of county commissioners' actions maintained by the clerk are the ordinance book[55] and the code of ordinances, if there is one.[56] These books and codes are intended to make the city's or county's laws readily accessible to its citizens. Accordingly, ordinances may not be enforced or admitted into evidence in court unless they are properly filed and indexed or codified.[57] The law presumes, however, that a city or county has followed the proper procedure unless someone proves otherwise.[58] For a description of the ordinance book and code requirements, see Chapter 5.

Other Records

The city clerk is the official custodian of all other city records in addition to minutes and ordinances.[59] Similarly, the clerk to the board of county commissioners and the board itself are the custodians of many other county records.[60] Governing board resolutions, contracts, the correspondence of the governing board and the mayor or chair, signed oaths of office, copies of legal and other notices, financial and personnel records, and a variety of miscellaneous documents (for example, board members' travel records and applications from citizens to be appointed to various local government boards) are all to be maintained in the clerk's office when possible.

The clerk (in the case of cities) or the clerk and the board of commissioners (in the case of counties) are responsible for ensuring that local government records are kept safely, are accessible for use by public and local officials (except as restricted by law), and are disposed of in accordance with

---

51. G.S. 143-318.10(b).
52. G.S. 143-318.10(e).
53. *Id.*
54. G.S. 132-1(a); North Carolina Department of Natural and Cultural Resources, Division of Archives and Records, Government Records Section, *Records Retention and Disposition Schedule—2021 General Records Schedule: Local Government Agencies*, Item 1.54, "Public Bodies: Minutes," archives.ncdcr.gov/2021localgeneralstandardspdf/open.
55. G.S. 153A-48; G.S. 160A-78.
56. G.S. 153A-49; G.S. 160A-77.
57. G.S. 153A-48, -49, -50; G.S. 160A-79(d).
58. G.S. 153A-50; G.S. 160A-79(c), (d).
59. G.S. 160A-171.
60. See G.S. 132-2, which provides that the person in charge of an office having public records is the custodian of those records. *See also* Frayda Bluestein, "Custodians of Public Records," *Coates' Canons: NC Local Government Law* blog (December 19, 2014), www.sog.unc.edu/blogs/coates-canons/custodians-public-records.

the appropriate schedules for records retention and disposition promulgated by the North Carolina Department of Cultural Resources, Division of Archives and Records.[61]

Notice

The clerk is usually responsible for giving notice of governing board meetings and for a variety of other public notices. Giving notice of all meetings of the city council is a statutory responsibility of the city clerk,[62] and it is a common practice for county clerks to give notice of all commissioners' meetings. In addition, both city and county clerks are statutorily responsible for keeping on file up-to-date regular meeting schedules of all public bodies that are part of city or county government, respectively.[63] By making these schedules available for public reference, the clerk gives the main notice of regular meetings that the open meetings law requires.[64] Both city and county clerks often handle the posting and distribution of special meeting notices for other city or county boards as well. The details of these requirements are discussed in Chapter 9. Clerks frequently oversee the legal advertisements required for public hearings, bid solicitations, bond orders, and other matters as well.

Other Duties as Assigned

Research and General Assistance

As noted above, in addition to the responsibilities previously outlined, clerks must perform other duties "that may be required by law or the [governing board]."[65] As a recordkeeper, clerks may have extensive institutional and professional knowledge that can be extremely helpful for newly elected members or officials who are new to government. Individual board members or the board as a whole frequently call on the clerk to find answers to questions. They may ask the clerk to learn how others have solved a particular problem, to find sample ordinances for the attorney, or to search the minutes for information about the actions of a previous board.

The governing board can help the clerk and its other professional staff (the attorney and the manager or administrator) serve it more effectively by remembering the limits of these professionals' roles. For example, the clerk generally performs research and provides information for the benefit of the entire board, just as the attorney serves and provides legal advice for the entire board's benefit. In addition, board members can help their professional staff by remembering the limits of staff members' time and energy when making individual requests.

Agendas and Preparations for Meetings

One of the most important services that the clerk provides to the city council or board of county commissioners is assistance with preparations for meetings. The clerk is usually involved in preparing the tentative agenda for governing board meetings and in compiling background information for the board's agenda packet.[66] Clear procedures for handling these matters can serve both the governing board and the clerk. The board should establish and enforce a realistic schedule for placing items on the agenda that allows adequate time to compile and duplicate background materials, and it should clearly state any preferences concerning the order of items on the agenda. As part of

---

61. Retention schedules for local government agencies are available at the State Archives of North Carolina website, archives.ncdcr.gov/government/local.

62. G.S. 160A-171.

63. G.S. 143-318.12(a).

64. G.S. 143-318.12(a).

65. G.S. 153A-111; G.S. 160A-171.

66. Allen, *Suggested Rules of Procedure for a City Council*, *supra* note 37, at 25–27; Allen, *Suggested Rules of Procedure for the Board of County Commissioners*, *supra* note 37, at 26–27.

his or her meeting-preparation and post-meeting procedures, the clerk is required by law to comply promptly with public and press requests for information about upcoming gatherings and for access to minutes (including draft minutes), tapes, and electronic and other records of prior meetings. (For more information, see the discussion of the laws governing access to public records in Chapter 8, "Public Records.")

Dealing with such a wide variety of information requests requires tact, judgment, empathy, organizational skills, energy, and a good sense of humor. Although clerks work *for the council* or *for the board of county commissioners*, they truly provide *public* service—helping the press understand the meaning of a complicated motion, assisting a citizen in finding the correct person to help with a complaint, keeping department heads advised of governing board actions, and keeping board members informed of administration proposals. As local government becomes larger and more complicated, the clerk's role as a professional, dispassionate provider of information to citizens, government officials, and the media becomes more and more important.

Combination of the Clerk's Position with Other Responsibilities

Many clerks perform still other tasks. City clerks are often tax collectors, and some serve as purchasing agents. A city or county clerk may also be the human resources or finance officer, manager, assistant manager, or assistant to the manager.[67] In North Carolina's smallest towns, the clerk may be the only administrative official and may have to function in every role, from substitute operator of the waste treatment plant to zoning administrator.

Wearing many hats can be both stressful and invigorating for clerks and other public servants. Governing boards can take three important steps to help ensure that their cities and counties continue to attract highly competent clerks and other employees who can perform the varied duties of their offices well or blend their primary positions effectively with other roles. First, they can provide employees with adequate authority as well as responsibility. Second, they can offer sufficient financial rewards to make government service an attractive career choice. Third, they can provide ongoing professional continuing education opportunities for their staff members.

Professionalism and Continuing Education

City and county clerks have the opportunity to participate in two of the most active professional associations of public officials in North Carolina, the North Carolina Association of County Clerks (NCACC) and the North Carolina Association of Municipal Clerks (NCAMC). Both organizations are dedicated to improving the professional competency of clerks through regular regional and statewide educational opportunities.[68] In cooperation with the School of Government and the International Institute of Municipal Clerks (IIMC), the associations help to sponsor a nationally recognized, examination-based certification program that culminates in receipt of the designation of Certified Municipal [or County] Clerk.[69] In addition, the county and municipal associations and the School sponsor state certification programs leading to the designations of North Carolina

---

67. *See, e.g., County Salaries in North Carolina Index*, an annual survey compiled by the MAPS Group for the School of Government, www.sog.unc.edu/resource-series/county-salaries-index-2006-present.

68. The North Carolina Association of County Clerks (NCACC) home page is on the N.C. Association of County Commissioners (also known as NCACC) website at www.ncacc.org/about/affiliate-related-organizations/north-carolina-county-clerks-association/. The North Carolina Association of Municipal Clerks (NCAMC) website is www.ncamc.com.

69. For information about the IIMC Clerks Certification Institute, visit www.sog.unc.edu and navigate to the "Courses" menu.

Certified County Clerk and North Carolina Certified Municipal Clerk, respectively.[70] They also provide opportunities for experienced clerks to obtain the continuing professional education needed to remain state-certified or to earn an advanced Master Clerk designation from the IIMC. Both associations assist clerks in their day-to-day work with mentoring programs for new clerks and resources including reference guides, manuals, and newsletters.[71] Two very active listservs maintained by the School of Government with the cooperation of NCACC and NCAMC allow clerks to exchange ideas and concerns.[72] Some clerks are involved at the state level in potential legislation and other matters of interest while other clerks serve on the Board of Directors or various committees of the North Carolina League of Municipalities and of the North Carolina Association of County Commissioners.

Additional Resources

Clerk Net, UNC School of Government, www.sog.unc.edu/resources/microsites/clerk-net/.

International Institute of Municipal Clerks, www.iimc.com/121/Certification.

N.C. Association of County Attorneys, www.ncacc.org/about/affiliate-related-organizations/north-carolina-association-of-county-attorneys/.

N.C. Association of County Clerks, www.ncacc.org/about/affiliate-related-organizations/north-carolina-county-clerks-association/.

N.C. Association of Municipal Attorneys Membership Application, www.nclm.org/about-us/affiliate-associations/ncama-affiliation/form-join-ncama-assoc/.

N.C. Association of Municipal Clerks, www.ncamc.com/.

70. Details about the certification programs for county and municipal clerks are available at the NCACC website, www.ncacc.org/wp-content/uploads/2021/10/FINAL-2019-Updated-NC-County-Clerk-Certification-Requirements-.pdf, and the NCAMC website, www.ncamc.com/education/certification.

71. *NCAMC Handbook* (2022), *Reference Guide for North Carolina Municipal Clerks* (2008), and *M.O.R.E. Manual (Minutes, Ordinances, Resolutions, Etc.)* are available through the "Document Library" of the NCAMC website, www.ncamc.com/document-library/manuals-guidelines.

72. Local government officials and employees can subscribe to the School of Government's clerks' listservs at "Carolina County Clerks," www.sog.unc.edu/resources/listservs/north-carolina-county-clerks-countyclerks, and "North Carolina City Clerks," www.sog.unc.edu/resources/listservs/north-carolina-city-clerks-clerks. More information about the School's listservs is available at www.sog.unc.edu/resources/microsites/listserv.

Chapter 15

Strategic Investments in Information Technology

Shannon Howle Tufts

Shannon H. Tufts is a professor of public administration and government at the School of Government. She is an expert on the intersection of law and technology in the public sector, cybersecurity, cloud computing, social media, and strategic IT investments, as well as CIO leadership and development.

Introduction

Information technology (IT) has profoundly transformed various facets of daily life, including interactions with government entities. The growing significance of the Internet enables residents to access vital information, purchase goods and services, and engage in virtual communities. Governments have leveraged the Internet revolution to establish new communication channels and participation methods through technology-enabled governance. The substantial impact of IT in the public sector, combined with increasing demands from residents and businesses for information and services, has driven greater government investment in technology-based initiatives. IT infrastructure, hardware, and software investments, once considered luxuries only found in affluent jurisdictions, are now a requirement for government operations. Those investments in IT solutions support every function of a local government. The necessity of robust IT investments was underscored during the COVID-19 pandemic, as governments quickly implemented teleworking options to maintain service continuity while following state or federal mandates. The shift to teleworking also exposed vulnerabilities and increased cybersecurity threats to local governments, which helped drive the recent focus on improving the cybersecurity postures of all government entities.

Several technological advancements have significantly impacted local and state governments. The first major shift is the transition to a digitally converged world. Almost all aspects of communication have merged into single-source platforms, as evidenced by the proliferation of smart devices capable of remotely starting cars, paying bills, and streaming live video. These converged media require robust, secure infrastructures and mobile applications. For instance, local governments can now use basic smartphones to capture video of public meetings and stream the recordings directly to the Internet without sophisticated interfaces or equipment required only a decade or two ago. The COVID-19 pandemic accelerated the adoption of videoconferencing technologies, enabling live, virtual board meetings in jurisdictions of varying sizes and technological sophistication. The rapid advancement and adoption of new technology solutions to address operational needs has led to the massive expansion of IT assets within local and state governments.

Another critical transition involves investment strategies for government entities, as they struggle with supporting older, legacy systems while migrating to more robust technologies. Replacing legacy systems with scalable, future-proof technologies requires substantial financial investments. This necessity has led to an explosion in cloud-based solutions, which often offer subscription-based services with monthly or annual payments instead of large capital outlays. Due to this transition, the role of IT departments has evolved beyond managing internal infrastructure, hardware, and software to negotiating and managing sophisticated vendor contracts and supporting daily technical operations.

Cybersecurity has also grown in importance due to the prevalence of Internet-connected applications and devices supporting every governmental function, from sanitation to financial management. The COVID-19 pandemic further highlighted the importance of cybersecurity as employees worked remotely, increasing the risk of attacks by malicious actors. Technological security, both physical and logical, is crucial for protecting government data and requires intentional investment.

As these examples illustrate, the management of and investment in IT have become more critical than ever. Budgetary pressures and media coverage of large-scale technology failures in the public sector underscore this point. Fortunately, professional IT staff, including chief information officers, coupled with tools and techniques such as IT governance, IT project management, and IT service management, help improve the quality and impact of taxpayer-funded IT investments. Information technology infrastructure, hardware, and software are not merely necessary costs to be controlled in the business operations of government but are vitally important for the daily provision of essential services, from 911 dispatching to sanitation collection. Proper attention to governmental and technological trends can provide a foundation and roadmap to prepare for future technology projects and investments.

Over the past two decades, significant advancements and trends have emerged in IT adoption and implementation within the public sector. This chapter highlights some of the most critical trends, including:

- The role of chief information officers (CIOs) and professional IT staff.
- Cybersecurity for local governments.
- Cloud-based technology services.

These trends have profoundly impacted local government environments on technical, procedural, legal, and management fronts. In previous versions of this book, the role of the CIO has been covered extensively, so only a high-level overview will be provided here. This chapter primarily focuses on cybersecurity, which has drawn significant local government attention and investment in the past five years, and offers a brief overview of cloud computing and contractual considerations related to cloud services.

Trend 1: Chief Information Officers and Professional IT Staff

As discussed in previous editions of this book, the role of CIOs and professional IT staff has continued to gain importance for public organizations. Investments in IT have placed many states, counties, and municipalities on par with leading private sector companies nationwide. IT now plays a vital role in every department and function within governmental jurisdictions. To leverage technology for more efficient and effective services and to maintain a competitive economic development advantage, the role of the CIO has emerged as a crucial link between business units and IT staff.

In high-performing organizations, the CIO has broad authority over all departmental IT project requests to ensure that comprehensive investments are made. To function effectively, the CIO needs full support from senior government leadership to exert authority over technology-related needs and requests and to assess those requests against organization standards, cybersecurity requirements, and other key areas that are easily overlooked when technology is viewed as just a tool that you can "plug and play." Often, efforts for standardization and centralization are circumvented by autonomous departmental decision-making, increasing operational costs and creating security and support challenges. With the CIO's authority and senior management's support, IT departments can deliver more efficient and effective services. When CIOs are included as part of the senior leadership team, providing direction, vision, and support for enterprise IT strategy and investments, then professional IT staff can effectively perform operational and tactical work that creates the best outcomes and impact for the government's IT investments.

The CIO's job is always demanding and often difficult, balancing a need to share critical technology plans with senior executives to garner support while staying abreast of current and emerging cybersecurity threats. Often, they must navigate between business units and the IT department, building bridges between these organizational silos. Essentially, the CIO is charged with securing the government's technology investments and information assets while remaining flexible and focused on achieving business objectives that often increase exposure and risk for the very entity they seek to secure. As one North Carolina local government CIO says, "Security and convenience are mutually exclusive." There is a fine line between systems that are well-secured but may restrict business operations and those that are less secure but easier to use.

Trend 2: Cybersecurity

The digital transformation of local governments has brought about unprecedented efficiency and connectivity, but along with those benefits, it has also introduced a myriad of cybersecurity challenges. Local governments are increasingly reliant on digital technologies, making them attractive targets for cyber threats. The rise of smart city initiatives, digital services, and interconnected systems has expanded the attack surface for malicious actors. Local government entities are entrusted with the provision of essential services, managing critical infrastructure, and protecting sensitive information. As such, they must prioritize cybersecurity to maintain public trust and ensure the continuity of operations. This section delves into the multifaceted aspects of cybersecurity, starting with relevant statutory requirements, followed by an overview of the cybersecurity landscape, and concluding with recommended strategies to protect government assets, sensitive data, and infrastructure.

North Carolina Statutory Requirements

Due to rising cybersecurity attacks and data breaches, coupled with an increased focus on improving local government cybersecurity postures, the State of North Carolina has enacted several statutory requirements related to the reporting and handling of cybersecurity incidents. It has also created a statewide cybersecurity task force designed to quickly respond, at no cost, to public entities experiencing cybersecurity incidents. The following section offers a high-level summary of relevant statutes and associated services related to public sector entities in North Carolina.

Statutory Definitions of Cybersecurity Incidents and Reporting Requirements

Chapter 143B, Section 1320 of the North Carolina General Statutes (hereinafter G.S.) outlines the definitions and scope for requirements for state agencies and local governments in North Carolina to report significant cybersecurity incidents. The statute defines a **cybersecurity incident** as an occurrence that jeopardizes the integrity, confidentiality, or availability of information or an information system, or constitutes a violation or imminent threat of violation of law, security policies, privacy policies, security procedures, or acceptable use policies. A **ransomware attack** is a type of cybersecurity incident where malicious software encrypts data and makes systems unusable, followed by a demand for ransom in exchange for decryption. A **significant cybersecurity incident** is one that is likely to cause harm to the state's security interests, economy, or critical infrastructure, or to residents' public confidence, civil liberties, or public health and safety. It is determined by factors such as incidents involving information that is not public and is restricted according to the North Carolina Department of Information Technology's *Statewide Data Classification and Handling Policy* or incidents involving the exfiltration (theft), modification, or deletion of data; unauthorized access to information or systems, affecting a certain number of records or users; or certain data types with required security controls.

G.S. 143B-1379 outlines the cooperation and reporting requirements for state agencies and local government entities regarding cybersecurity incidents. It mandates that local government entities, as defined in G.S. 143-800(c)(1), are required to report cybersecurity incidents to the N.C. Department of Information Technology (NCDIT) within twenty-four hours of confirmation. Information shared in this process is protected from public disclosure under G.S. 132-6.1(c).

Statutory Requirements Related to Ransomware

G.S. 143-800 of the North Carolina General Statutes stipulates that no state agency or local government entity is allowed to submit payment or otherwise communicate with an entity that has engaged in a cybersecurity incident by encrypting data and then demanding a ransom payment for decryption. If a state agency or local government entity experiences a ransom request due to a cybersecurity incident, they are required to consult with the NCDIT pursuant to G.S. 143B-1379. The statutory definition of "local government entity" is a local political subdivision of the state, which encompasses cities, counties, local school administrative units, or community colleges.

Statutory Requirement for Cybersecurity Assistance and Incident Response

According to G.S. 166A-19.78A, enacted September 22, 2023, any requests for operational support or access to operational cyber resources from units of local government, state agencies, or critical infrastructure partners must be directed to the N.C. Emergency Management 24-Hour Watch for intake and activation. The term "critical infrastructure partners" refers to any entity responsible for managing, overseeing, or otherwise handling critical infrastructure, as defined in 42 U.S.C. § 5195c. All entities in North Carolina requesting operational support during a cyber incident should report to NCEM's 24-Hour Watch by phone, 1-800-858-0368, or email, nceoc@ncdps.gov. This reporting triggers activation of the North Carolina Joint Cybersecurity Task Force for cyber incident response and operational support.

North Carolina Joint Cybersecurity Task Force

The N.C. Joint Cybersecurity Task Force (NC JCTF), as established by the March 2022 Governor's Executive Order 254, is comprised of four core member entities, N.C. Emergency Management, N.C. National Guard Cyber Security Response Force (CSRF), N.C. Department of Information Technology's Enterprise Security and Risk Management Office (ESRMO), and the N.C. Local Government Information Systems Association (NCLGISA) Cybersecurity Strike Team. The NC JCTF works with federal partners, including the Federal Bureau of Investigations, U.S. Secret Service, and Department of Homeland Security. The NC JCTF has been operating under the N.C. Statewide Mutual Aid System since 2019 and has responded to more than 100 significant cybersecurity incidents in North Carolina public sector entities between 2019 and 2024.

The N.C. Joint Cybersecurity Task Force provides incident coordination, resource support and technical assistance to reduce the impact to the affected organization, mitigate vulnerabilities, and offer on-scene response personnel to aid in incident recovery. When supporting the affected organization, the various members of the Joint Cybersecurity Task Force work in tandem to leverage their collective response expertise, apply their knowledge of cyber threats, preserve key evidence, and use their combined authorities and capabilities both to minimize asset vulnerability and bring malicious actors to justice. Specific functions of the no-cost onsite response by NC JCTF members include 1) conducting forensics to identify root-cause; 2) damage assessment and mitigation; and 3) coordination with law enforcement activities as needed. The NC JCTF also works to share anonymized indicators of compromise found during a given incident with the larger public sector body in North Carolina, as well as with federal partners, to reduce similar event occurrence elsewhere. The onsite team also assists in establishing best practice recovery methods, system hardening, restoration of services and infrastructure rebuild, as warranted, alongside impacted local government IT personnel and contractors.

Statutory Requirements Related to Data Breaches

Additional requirements related to data breach notification are also relevant to all government entities, as those requirements apply to any business, governmental agencies, or organization that experiences a data breach involving North Carolina residents' personally identifiable information (PII). The North Carolina Identity Theft Protection Act of 2005 (G.S. Chapter 75, Article 2A) seeks to safeguard personal information and protect consumers from identity theft. It defines PII data elements, protects social security numbers, specifies how consumers can obtain security freezes on their credit, specifies procedures for the destruction of personal information, and mandates government entities to notify consumers in the event of a data breach impacting their personal information. G.S. 132-1.10(c1) applies the requirements of G.S 75-65 to governmental entities, as follows: "If an agency of the State or its political subdivisions, or any agent or employee of a government agency, experiences a security breach, as defined in Article 2A of Chapter 75 of the General Statutes, the agency shall comply with the requirements of G.S. 75-65."

Pursuant to G.S. 14-113.20, G.S. 75-61(10), and G.S. 75-65, personally identifiable information requiring notification under G.S. Chapter 75, Article 2A includes the following:

1. Social security or employer taxpayer identification numbers.
2. Driver's license, state identification card, or passport numbers.
3. Checking account numbers.

4. Savings account numbers.
5. Credit card numbers.
6. Debit card numbers.
7. Personal identification (PIN) code as defined in G.S. 14-113.8(6).
8. Digital signatures.
9. Biometric data.
10. Fingerprints.
11. Any other numbers or information that can be used to access a person's financial resources, such as electronic identification numbers, electronic mail names or addresses, Internet account numbers, or Internet identification names; passwords; or parent's legal surname prior to marriage. These are protected PII only if they can be used to access financial resources.

The following are the required actions that must be undertaken in the event of a qualified PII data breach, pursuant to G.S. 75-65.

1. Notice of breach must be given without reasonable delay, unless warranted due to law enforcement investigation.
2. Notice must be clear and conspicuous with the following items described:
    a. The incident in general terms.
    b. The type of personal information that was subject to unauthorized access and acquisition.
    c. The general acts of the business to protect the personal information from further unauthorized access.
    d. A telephone number that the person may call for further information and assistance, if one exists.
    e. Advice that directs the person to remain vigilant by reviewing account statements and monitoring free credit reports.
3. Allowable Options for Methods of Notice:
    a. Written notice to the impacted person(s).
    b. Electronic notice, for those persons for whom it has a valid e-mail address and who have agreed to receive communications electronically.
    c. Telephonic notice provided contact is made directly with the affected persons or their guardian if minor.
    d. Substitute notice is allowed under one of the following conditions:
        i. The business demonstrates that the cost of providing notice would exceed $250,000.
        ii. The affected class of subject persons to be notified exceeds 500,000 persons.
        iii. The business does not have sufficient contact information or consent to satisfy subdivisions (1), (2), or (3) of this subsection (only for those persons without sufficient contact information or consent).
        iv. If the business is unable to identify specific affected persons (only for those unidentifiable affected persons).
4. If substitute notice is selected, it must consist of all the following:
    a. e-mail notice when business has an electronic mail address for affected persons; and
    b. conspicuous posting of notice on website of business, if one is maintained; and
    c. notification to major statewide media.

5. In addition, the business shall notify the Consumer Protection Division of the Attorney General's Office of:
   a. the nature of the breach;
   b. the number of consumers affected by the breach;
   c. steps taken to investigate the breach;
   d. steps taken to prevent a similar breach in the future; and
   e. information regarding the timing, distribution, and content of the notice.
6. If notice is being provided to more than 1,000 persons at one time pursuant to this section, the business shall notify the Consumer Protection Division of the Attorney General's Office and all consumer reporting agencies that compile and maintain files on consumers on a nationwide basis of the timing, distribution, and content of the notice.

It is important to note that additional reporting requirements to federal agencies, funding entities, and others may apply pursuant to federal law and/or contractual obligations.

Overview of the Cybersecurity Landscape

Cybersecurity is one of the most pressing technological challenges facing local governments today. With the rise in cyberattacks, data breaches, and other incidents across all sectors, governments are increasingly recognizing the need to safeguard their information assets. Governmental entities often have stricter security requirements than private organizations due to the sensitive nature of the data they handle. This impacts all aspects of the IT ecosystem, including teleworking, cloud computing, leadership, policies and procedures, and employee training. However, these entities are often less well-funded than their private sector counterparts, creating additional vulnerabilities for malicious actors.

Cyberattacks on local governments significantly increased from 2020 to 2024. In 2020, local government cyberattacks began to rise, with ransomware being the major threat due to the global pandemic and associated teleworking strategies that governments quickly employed. In 2023, the Center for Internet Security reported that state and local governments experienced 148 percent more malware attacks and 51 percent more ransomware incidents during the first eight months of 2023 compared with the same period in 2022.[1] Even more striking, data breaches and other end-point security compromises rose by 313 percent, with the trend continuing in 2024 due to massive third-party vulnerabilities and exploitations such as the MOVEit Transfer software breach. This upward trend highlights the growing need for robust cybersecurity measures in local governments, as well as an understanding of the timelines associated with an average local government cyber-security incident.

---

1. For more details, see *2022 Nationwide Cybersecurity Review Summary Report*, Department of Homeland Security (DHS) Cybersecurity and Infrastructure Security Agency (CISA) with Multi-State Information Sharing and Analysis Center (MS-ISAC) and Elections Infrastructure Information Sharing and Analysis Center (EI-ISAC), www.cisecurity.org/insights/white-papers/2022-nationwide-cybersecurity-review.

A Day in the Life: A Local Government Experiences a Ransomware Attack

One Friday evening, a local government employee in a 911 call center logs onto her computer and discovers a message that all files have been encrypted and to contact the IT department for assistance. Another employee tries to log on and receives the same message. By this time, the entire network has been compromised, and the IT director has been called to try to rectify the situation. None of the government employees can access their emails, software, or files, and panic is setting in. The IT staff quickly comes onsite and realizes the center is experiencing a ransomware attack. The IT team takes down the entire network, ensuring that all Internet connections are disconnected to prevent any further impact.

The damage is catastrophic, months of recovery efforts are about to begin, and numerous questions abound: "When did the attack begin? How did the threat actor enter the government environment? Was any data stolen by the criminals who attacked the government? What about all the personal data the government holds in its files or databases? When will we be back up and running?"

The following timeline, Figure 15.1, outlines a typical ransomware attack and illustrates the harsh reality that many threat actors are on your network from 30 to 180 days, rifling through your data and stealing or exfiltrating the most valuable datasets before encrypting your files (converting the data into a coded format that renders it unreadable without a decryption key) and installing the ransom note on your computers and servers that alerts you to their malicious presence.

Figure 15.1 Timeline of a Shared Ransomware Attack

November	An employee opens a phishing email and clicks on a link containing ransomware.
December	The ransomware downloads onto the employee's computer and starts executing malicious code.
January	The ransomware creates a connection via the Internet with the threat actor's command and control (C2) server.
February	The ransomware steals/harvests credentials to gain access to more accounts.
March	The ransomware looks for files to encrypt on local computers and servers via the network, moving laterally across the network to compromise multiple accounts. Data exfiltration might also be occurring during this timeframe.
April	The ransomware starts the encryption process, typically attacking domain controllers and backups first. The government is now aware they have been compromised. The threat actor leaves a ransom note demanding payment in exchange for the decryption key.

Recommended Strategies for Improving Local Government Cybersecurity

As local government elected officials, managers, and IT professionals work to secure their organizations from relentless cybersecurity attacks, there are key steps that can help guide their efforts. The list below combines technical and operational tips to help best protect your organization.

1. Proper investment in strong cybersecurity technologies is essential. Firewalls, network monitoring tools, threat detection systems, data loss prevention tools, next generation endpoint protection, and other technical solutions form strong technical layers to protect the organization from unwanted access.
2. Allow IT staff to patch vulnerabilities as soon as possible. Numerous ransomware attacks could have been avoided if a proper patching cadence was permitted in the organizations. Patching does require downtime for some systems, but the minimal impact of that downtime can save months of recovery efforts in the long run.
3. Implement least privileged access (the minimal level of access needed to perform one's work), particularly for third-party vendors. Do not allow vendors to maintain open tunnels into your environment for remote support. Require utilization of secure best practices, such as only allowing access via a jump box system or a remote connection tool, requiring vendors to submit help desk requests for time-limited access and immediately terminating access once their work is completed.
4. Separation of duties is critical. Do not use the same credentials for your domain administrator and local administrator accounts. Many recent breaches have involved compromised domain administrator credentials, often found to be the same as cached local administrator credentials.
5. Invest in immutable backups, stored physically and virtually separate from the network, as they are essential to your recoverability. After attacking the domain controller(s), most current variants go straight to encrypting your backups, which can make data recovery impossible.
6. Local governments should regularly conduct cybersecurity assessments. These assessments can be performed by state or federal agencies, vendors, or even internal IT staff. The goal of the assessment is to determine what and where the organization and its employees store personal, protected, and/or sensitive information. The cybersecurity assessment should include updating information about the network topology and the systems in use (including their versions), as well as ensuring that all antivirus and patches are current. The assessment should also review access controls and permissions to confirm that a most-restrictive model is in place.
7. Data governance and data classification is an emerging requirement due to the large-scale data breaches experienced over the past few years. One of the biggest challenges facing governments during a data breach is determining what data might have been compromised. The easiest remedy is having an updated data map with servers and other resource shares containing clearly identified critical information.
8. Senior management should ensure that written policies and procedures are established and followed in the organization. These policies range from acceptable use policies limiting access to specific Internet sites to employee off-boarding practices, an often-overlooked component of securing organizational systems.
9. Employee training is another key component of a strong cybersecurity posture. Training employees to spot phishing attempts, as well as to avoid social engineering tactics, can prove vital in protecting the organization and its assets. Exposed

credentials and malware downloads are part of the problem and can be limited with proper education.

10. Create a continuity of operations (COOP) plan[2] for your government entity and conduct drills to make sure it works for your team. If you have not experienced a ransomware event, this will be invaluable—nothing generates stress like trying to figure out how to run payroll three days after you get hit.
11. If you see something on your computer or network that looks concerning, contact your IT department immediately. Do not try to stay up and "functional," as it will allow for rapid, catastrophic proliferation across your networks and into any interconnections you might have with neighboring entities.

Trend 3: Cloud Computing in the Public Sector

Local governments have increasingly adopted cloud-based solutions to deliver technology services without having to incur large capital outlay for technology assets. Common cloud solutions, including infrastructure as a service (IaaS), software as a service (SaaS), and platform as a service (PaaS), are found in almost every department of a government agency, from law enforcement record management systems (RMS) to enterprise resource planning (ERP) systems used by human resources and finance departments to cloud-based parks and recreation class registration systems.

Cloud-based services offer several benefits to governments, but there are also significant risks that must be managed. Cloud computing offers scalable, flexible, and agile IT due to the elasticity of resources, but concerns over the reliability and security of these solutions persist. In addition, cloud offerings are not always cheaper, so the projected cost savings from cloud computing need validation to ensure that a move to the cloud is the right solution for an organization.

Given the significant security concerns tied to government data being housed in the cloud without direct control over and physical access to the cloud infrastructure, FedRAMP and StateRAMP programs have been created to provide a standardized approach to security assessment, authorization, and continuous monitoring for cloud products and services, while also ensuring that certified cloud service providers are meeting stringent security standards to best protect government data. By reducing duplicative efforts, FedRAMP and StateRAMP allow governments to work more efficiently by reusing existing security assessments. The standardized security assessments and authorization processes increase transparency and build trust among federal agencies and cloud service providers. The programs also promote the use of secure cloud technologies across the public sector, enabling agencies to leverage modern cloud solutions more quickly.

The widespread shift to cloud-based solutions, where the monthly payments equal a "lease" of a portion of the cloud solution, has given rise to complex, legally ambiguous contracts that often fail to properly protect the government entity. Organizations often sign master service agreements or standard contracts without proper review, negotiation, or modification to meet their organizational needs and legal requirements.

---

2. FEMA defines "continuity of operations," or COOP, as the ability of an organization to continue essential functions, provide essential services, and deliver core capabilities during a disruption to normal operations. A COOP plan might determine, for example, how a jurisdiction will ensure that payroll continues in the event of a ransomware attack that takes down the network and encrypts the servers (and the data contained within), preventing access to time clock and financial systems. For more details, see FEMA's COOP brochure at www.fema.gov/pdf/about/org/ncp/coop_brochure.pdf.

Contract Considerations for Cloud Computing in Local Government

To harness cloud computing's potential while effectively addressing its challenges, it is imperative to spend time developing high-quality cloud computing contracts instead of accepting a solution provider's standard terms and conditions. Some key areas of considerations for cloud-based contracts include:

1. **Data Ownership**: Contracts should state that the government owns all data within the cloud environment, including intellectual property rights.
2. **Access to Data**: The government should have sole discretion to access and retrieve its data, ensuring that no individual employee can prevent access.
3. **Data Retrieval**: Contracts should specify procedures and timelines for data retrieval in emergencies, including validation processes.
4. **Disposition of Data upon Request**: Specify procedures to allow the government to destroy specified records as permitted by law.
5. **Disposition of Data upon Contract Termination**: Document clear instructions for data return or retrieval in standard formats (e.g., plain text, CSV, XML), the costs, if any, that are allowed for the provision of data to a government entity, and data destruction requirements after termination.
6. **Data Breaches**: Specify vendor obligations in the event of data breaches, including reporting requirements, notification timelines to ensure compliance with state and federal laws, breach details, mitigation efforts, and indemnification.
7. **Data Storage Location**: Contracts should include statements about the physical storage location of government data, preferably within the United States.
8. **Legal Data Holds/Public Record Requests**: Seek provisions for litigation holds and public records requests, ensuring data preservation during litigation.

The increased use of cloud computing solutions heightens some risks for government entities and highlights the need for conducting thorough risk assessments of vendors prior to selection, establishing strong contract language that properly protects the government and its information assets, and incorporating processes, policies, and controls. Each government entity must determine its greatest concerns and react accordingly to minimize potential negative impacts.

Conclusion

In an era when technology is reshaping every facet of our lives, its role in government services cannot be overstated. Strategic investments in information technology by local governments have the potential to revolutionize service delivery, making it more efficient, cost-effective, and accessible. As governments strive to become more customer-oriented, the integration of technology becomes indispensable. Simply overlaying technology on flawed systems will not yield the desired improvements in cost savings or service quality, therefore it is crucial to refine the underlying administration, policies, and procedures to fully harness the benefits of technological advancements.

To ensure that technology investments are judicious and impactful, several key steps must be taken. First and foremost, the chief information officer (CIO) must be included in senior leadership discussions. The success of a CIO is largely dependent on the support and involvement of senior management, which amplifies the efforts of the existing IT staff through alignment with organizational goals. Thorough cost-benefit analysis of all projects should be conducted, along with a comprehensive understanding of the total cost of ownership, which includes cybersecurity components, ongoing maintenance and support, as well as proper training for staff. This approach allows for proper financial planning and ensures that projects are adequately funded over their lifespan. Furthermore, it is essential to budget for ongoing IT infrastructure upgrades and maintenance separately from new IT projects.

The wholesale adoption and integration of technology have fundamentally transformed government operations, enhancing service delivery, efficiency, transparency, and accountability. The demand for electronic access to services like building permits, bill payments, and licenses has driven the need for robust IT investments. Moreover, the shift from traditional bureaucratic silos to a more collaborative and customer-focused approach has been facilitated by these technological advancements. Public sector IT investments have also opened new avenues for civic engagement and participation, reflecting the sector's deepening involvement in the information technology revolution. As we look to the future, our reliance on these tools will only grow, underscoring the importance of strategic and well-integrated technology investments in government, with a keen focus on cybersecurity to protect government entities and their information assets from the unending threats of malicious actors.

Additional Resources

DiNapoli, Thomas. "Protecting Sensitive Data and Other Local Government Assets: A Non-Technical Cybersecurity Guide for Local Leaders." New York State Comptroller (June 2016), www.osc.ny.gov/files/local-government/publications/pdf/cyber-security-guide.pdf.

IBM Corp. *The New Voice of the CIO: Insights from the Global Chief Information Officer Study.* Somers, New York: 2009.

Karahanna, Elena, and Richard Watson. "Information Systems Leadership." *IEEE Transactions on Engineering Management* 53, no. 2 (2006): 171–76.

Kerr, Johndavid, and Kwok Teng. "Cloud Computing: Legal and Privacy Issues." Proceedings of the Academy of Business Disciplines Conference (2010).

Kundra, Vivek. *Federal Cloud Computing Strategy.* The White House (February 8, 2011), obamawhitehouse.archives.gov/sites/default/files/omb/assets/egov_docs/federal-cloud-computing-strategy.pdf.

Landsbergen, Jr., David, and George Wolken, Jr. "Realizing the Promise: Government Information Systems and the Fourth Generation of Information Technology." *Public Administration Review* 61, no. 2 (2001): 206–20.

Rosenbloom, David H., and M. Bailey. "What Every Public Personnel Manager Should Know about the Constitution." In eds. Steven W. Hays and Richard C. Kearney, *Public Personnel Administration: Problems and Prospects.* 4th ed. Upper Saddle River, New Jersey: Prentice Hall, 2003: 20–36.

Schelin, Shannon H. "Managing the Human Side of Information Technology: A Public-Private Comparison of Chief Information Officers." Ph.D. diss. North Carolina State University, 2004.

Scruggs, Ron, Thomas Trappler, and Don Philpott. *Contracting for Cloud Services.* Washington, D.C.: Government Training, Inc., 2011.

U.S. Congress. *Public Buildings, Property, and Works.* "Information Technology Management." 40 U.S.C. § 11103 *et seq.*

Wyld, David. "Moving to the Cloud: An Introduction to Cloud Computing in Government." IBM Center for the Business of Government, E-Government Series, 2009.

Chapter 16

Performance Measurement: A Tool for Accountability and Performance Improvement

David N. Ammons

David N. Ammons is the Albert Coates Professor Emeritus of Public Administration and Government at the University of North Carolina at Chapel Hill. During his career at the School of Government, he wrote, taught, and advised local governments and state agencies about performance measurement, benchmarking, and productivity improvement. He served on the National Performance Management Advisory Commission, the North Carolina Governor's Advisory Committee on Performance Management, and the board of directors of the American Society for Public Administration's Center for Accountability and Performance. For more than twenty-five years, Ammons served as a faculty advisor to the North Carolina Benchmarking Project (NCBP). As Professor Emeritus, he serves on the Credentialing Advisory Board of the International City/County Management Association.

Operating in today's environment of limited resources ratchets up the pressure on local government programs to achieve their intended results and to do so efficiently. Citizens depend on county and city services and increasingly are adamant not only that they be produced in sufficient quantity and with adequate timeliness to satisfy public needs but also that they meet reasonable standards of quality.

The local governments that have been most aggressive in their pursuit of service quality and efficiency tend also to be the counties and cities that have been most interested in measuring their performance. For them, performance measurement is a valuable tool that confirms their successes and alerts them to programs needing improvement.

Uses of Performance Measures: Accountability and Performance Improvement

A rudimentary set of performance measures reveals how many units of service have been delivered. A good set of performance measures provides this basic information and much more, revealing how efficiently services are rendered, their quality, and, ideally, the impact the service has on recipients or on the community as a whole.

Good sets of performance measures serve multiple purposes, including:

- Enhancing accountability and communication
- Supporting planning and budgeting efforts
- Acting as a catalyst for improved operations
- Setting performance targets
- Analyzing operations
- Evaluating programs
- Reallocating resources
- Directing operations
- Monitoring the work of contractors
- Benchmarking

Local governments that excel in performance management rarely restrict their measures to a single purpose. Instead, these measures typically support two, three, or even more of the functions noted in the list above. Almost always, one of these uses is accountability.

Citizens like to be reassured that someone in their local government is minding the store. Even if they may not be interested in all the detailed metrics of service delivery, they expect elected and appointed officials to collect and monitor this information, ensuring that quality services are provided at a fair price.

A good set of performance measures is an important tool for building accountability throughout an organization. By compiling key indicators of performance, supervisors can confirm that work crews are meeting expectations and delivering quality services—in short, they can ensure the accountability of front-line employees. Periodic reporting of selected measures allows supervisors to be accountable to department management for their work, department management to be accountable to central administration, and central administration to be accountable to the governing board. In turn, the periodic publication of selected performance measures allows board members to be accountable to the citizenry for local government operations as a whole.

True accountability means more than just assuring the public that revenues are properly collected and reported and that expenditures are made in accordance with prescribed procedures. Accountability includes these important assurances but also entails assurances to the public that government resources are being spent wisely as well as legally and that services of good quality are being produced efficiently. Performance measurement offers a tool for providing such assurances.

The value of performance measurement extends far beyond accountability, important as that purpose is. Good sets of performance measures support a variety of management purposes. The city manager, for instance, might review performance measures with department heads to assess each department's progress on key objectives. The county manager might use performance statistics for parks, recreation, and library services as context for a planning retreat of the board of commissioners focusing on the community's leisure services needs. If a local government plans to make major changes in a particular program, it can use performance measures to establish a baseline before the changes and continue monitoring them after implementation to determine if the new strategies are effective. Some local governments use performance measures within their monitoring systems for contracted services to make sure that contractors are living up to their promises. Some counties and cities compare their own performance to standards or results achieved by other service providers as a step toward improving the quality and efficiency of local services. In each of these examples, performance measurement is an essential tool.

The Importance of Performance Measurement for Management

Good performance measures support a variety of management functions. A good set of measures enables managers and supervisors to identify operating strengths and weaknesses, target areas for improvement, and recognize improvements when they occur. A good set of measures also helps a manager defend good operations against unwarranted criticism.

Some managers and supervisors operate without good sets of performance measures. They rely instead on general observation and the comments of service recipients to form their impressions of operating strengths and weaknesses. Often, such impressions are correct and would be borne out by systematic assessments. More frequently than many managers care to admit, however, occasional observations and anecdotes fail to depict the reality that would be revealed by systematic assessment. Occasionally, programs or departments thought to be strong performers do not look quite so strong when examined in the light of objective evidence, and supposedly weak performers are discovered to be more proficient than previously imagined. With appropriate measurement systems, managers and supervisors can more objectively detect operating deficiencies and target additional attention where it is needed most.

A good measurement system can enhance a talented supervisor's ability to develop the skills of workers, to instruct them in their tasks, to plan and schedule their work, to draw upon the pride and commitment of a work unit, and to motivate greater performance. With the benefit of reliable measures, instructions to subordinates can be more focused, planning more precise, and feedback more objective. In this way, a systematic gauge of program efficiency and effectiveness can augment the value of on-site supervision, with greater value provided not only to upper management but also to the supervisor and the workforce.

Receiving customer or citizen feedback is an important responsibility of managers and supervisors, but listening only to intermittent complaints and compliments can produce an incomplete and sometimes inaccurate picture of service quality and efficiency. With systematic performance measurement and reporting, local government programs are less vulnerable to isolated anecdotes that misrepresent the normal state of affairs in service delivery. With good performance measures, a service complaint can be viewed in the context of the norms for that service rather than isolated from such context. Service units with strong performance can more adequately be defended. Weaker units can be identified with greater confidence and targeted for corrective action.

The Value of Performance Measurement to Governing Boards

Even when the governing board hires a manager to handle matters of day-to-day administration, the board retains responsibility for providing general oversight of the local government as a whole and for establishing program priorities. It also retains responsibility for assessing the performance of the manager in directing local government operations. Good performance measures can be helpful in performing these duties. For instance, the governing board might ask the following questions in performing its oversight role:

- Are services being provided efficiently and equitably?
- Do they meet expectations for quality?
- Could better services be provided at a more reasonable cost by contracting out some functions?
- Have any service deficiencies been identified, and are improvements being made where needed?
- Do service results indicate that programs are being properly managed?

Each of these questions can be answered adequately only if reliable data are available.

In recent years, many management experts have advocated more decentralized decision-making, allowing field unit supervisors and even front-line employees to make more of the service delivery decisions, as long as their decisions are consistent with a vision or culture established and nurtured by central authorities. Much can be said in favor of a strategy that places greater discretion in the hands of those who know the program best and are closest to the problems. However, without a dependable system for guaranteeing accountability, few governing boards will be willing to increase managerial discretion or encourage managers to permit greater discretion at lower levels of the organization. In the absence of a system for compiling and reporting evidence that programs are being run efficiently and effectively, top officials are more likely to believe that their oversight responsibilities require involvement in or approval of a large portion of the individual decisions made on behalf of the government. Upper management and governing boards are more likely to be receptive if greater supervisory discretion and reductions in administrative red tape are accompanied by clear evidence of favorable program results.

The expense of administering a good performance measurement system is not trivial, but neither are the benefits of a good system. Because of its value to board members, appointed administrators, and the general citizenry, performance measurement has been endorsed by a host of professional associations, including the International City/County Management Association, the Government Finance Officers Association, the Governmental Accounting Standards Board, and the National Academy of Public Administration.

Types of Performance Measures

Performance measures may be categorized in various ways, but the following list outlines the most relevant types for tracking and improving performance in local government:

- Output (workload) measures
- Efficiency measures
- Outcome (effectiveness and service quality) measures
- Productivity measures[1]

1. Readers familiar with performance measurement literature will notice that one category of measurement, input measures, has been left off this list. Raw input alone, usually represented by the amount of money or number of personnel allocated to a program or service, does not measure performance. However, when input is incorporated in relation to output, the result is a measure of efficiency, which does reflect performance. Therefore, efficiency measures are included here, while input measures are not.

Output (Workload) Measures

When a department reports the number of applications processed, inspections conducted, or cases handled, it is reflecting its workload or output. These statistics are relatively simple to compile and present. Unfortunately, they offer a limited view of a department's overall performance. They say nothing about the quality or efficiency of the services provided. They simply indicate how many units of service were produced or how much of an activity was undertaken.

Although counting and tabulating workload numbers is the most common form of performance reporting in local government, the value of raw output measures for policy and management purposes is extremely limited. This doesn't mean that tracking output is unimportant. Comparing output from year to year can indicate trends in service demand. More importantly, output numbers are often critical ingredients in the calculation of higher-order measures that hold greater value for managerial and policy decisions. Unfortunately, too many local governments depend almost entirely on raw output or workload measures to report their performance. With workload measures alone, the message conveyed by a department or program cannot be "We are efficient" or "We provide quality services." With raw workload measures alone, the only message is "We are busy!"

Efficiency Measures

Measures of efficiency report the relationship between resources used and services produced. Sometimes this relationship is expressed in terms of unit cost—for example, the cost per application processed or cost per inspection—or as units of service per $1,000. It also may be expressed as the ratio of outputs to staff hours—for example, staff hours needed per license application or curb miles swept per operator hour. When cost accounting systems will not support precise unit cost calculations and the calculation of employee output ratios is impractical, many local governments opt for less precise alternatives by tracking average turnaround time, average daily backlog, or similar operating characteristics.

Outcome (Effectiveness and Service Quality) Measures

Measures of outcome gauge the quality of services and the extent to which a program's objectives are being achieved. Suppose, for instance, that an objective of the solid waste department is to complete at least 95 percent of all refuse collection routes on the scheduled day of collection. If the department compiles statistics showing that 94 percent of the routes were completed as scheduled, this would be an outcome measure, for it measures the extent to which the objective was achieved. Among many other commonly reported types of outcome measures are various measures of responsiveness (for example, average response time to emergencies) and citizen satisfaction (for example, percentage of citizens who are "satisfied" or "very satisfied" with the local recreation program).

Productivity Measures

Productivity measures combine efficiency and effectiveness in a single index. These indices are rare in local government, but their absence is of little concern as long as good measures of efficiency and effectiveness are present to guide program efforts.

Examples of productivity indicators include measures produced by calculating unit costs more restrictively than a government calculates its efficiency measures. Rather than dividing program costs by all cases processed, for instance, a productivity measure might divide total program costs by the number of successful cases (that is, only the cases achieving desired results). In essence, a program is penalized in this ratio for poor-quality outputs or unsuccessful results. The ratio reflects both cost and quality—efficiency and effectiveness.

Developing a Good Set of Performance Measures

Good sets of performance measures include measures that are valid, reliable, understandable, actionable, timely, resistant to undesired behavior, sensitive to data collection costs, and focused on important facets of performance.[2] A good set of performance measures reports not only how much service is provided but also how well and how efficiently. Even more important to local governments intent on truly managing their performance, a good set inspires managerial thinking by providing crucial performance data that cannot be ignored. To truly stimulate managerial thinking, performance data must focus on important dimensions of service and must be compiled in a manner that either reassures operating officials and program staff that services are being provided at suitable levels of quality and efficiency or, if not, prompts them to investigate possible causes of shortcomings and consider options for improvement.[3] A fundamental test for a set of performance measures, then, is whether it provides data of sufficient importance and in a form that can inspire managerial thinking.

Performance measures for traffic safety, presented in the form of a graph, are shown in Figure 16.1. Table 16.1 provides an example of performance measures used to frame performance targets. Tables 16.2 and 16.3 present sets of performance measures for solid waste, recycling services, and public works.

Use of Performance Measures in Budgeting

The budget process provides an opportunity to influence program design and spending priorities across various services. While the budget may be primarily a financial document, it is, in fact, much more than that: It is a document that reflects program planning and service priorities in financial terms and, ideally, in terms of performance expectations.

Some public sector budgets retain a strictly line-item format, listing appropriations for each detailed expenditure category. Many governments, however, have adopted formats more conducive to management and policy deliberations. Program budgets, for example, omit most of the object-of-expenditure details that characterize line-item budgets. Instead, they are organized around programs or types of services and report only broader categories of anticipated expenditures. Program budgets often include several measures of performance that reveal past performance and reflect performance expectations for the future.

Another common budget format is the performance budget. Like program budgets, it omits many line-item details, instead organizing expenditures into broader categories based on departments, activities, or programs. In performance budgeting, measures of performance are central to budget discussions as managers and governing boards review performance successes and disappointments, hammer out plans for performance improvement and resource reallocation, and strive for budgetary decisions that will increase the likelihood of achieving desired performance levels.

---

2. Harry P. Hatry, Donald M. Fisk, John R. Hall Jr., Philip S. Schaenman, and Louise Snyder, *How Effective Are Your Community Services? Procedures for Performance Measurement*, 3rd ed. (Washington, D.C.: International City/County Management Association and The Urban Institute, 2006), 3; Harry P. Hatry, *Performance* Measurement*: Getting Results*, 2nd ed. (Washington, D.C.: The Urban Institute Press, 2006), 62; Theodore H. Poister, Maria P. Aristigueta, and Jeremy L. Hall, *Managing and Measuring Performance in Public and Nonprofit Organizations: An Integrated Approach*, 2nd ed. (San Francisco: Jossey-Bass, 2015), 144–51.

3. David N. Ammons, "Performance Measurement and Managerial Thinking," *Public Performance and Management Review* 25 (June 2002): 344–47.

Figure 16.1 Presenting Performance Measures as a Graph: Traffic Safety

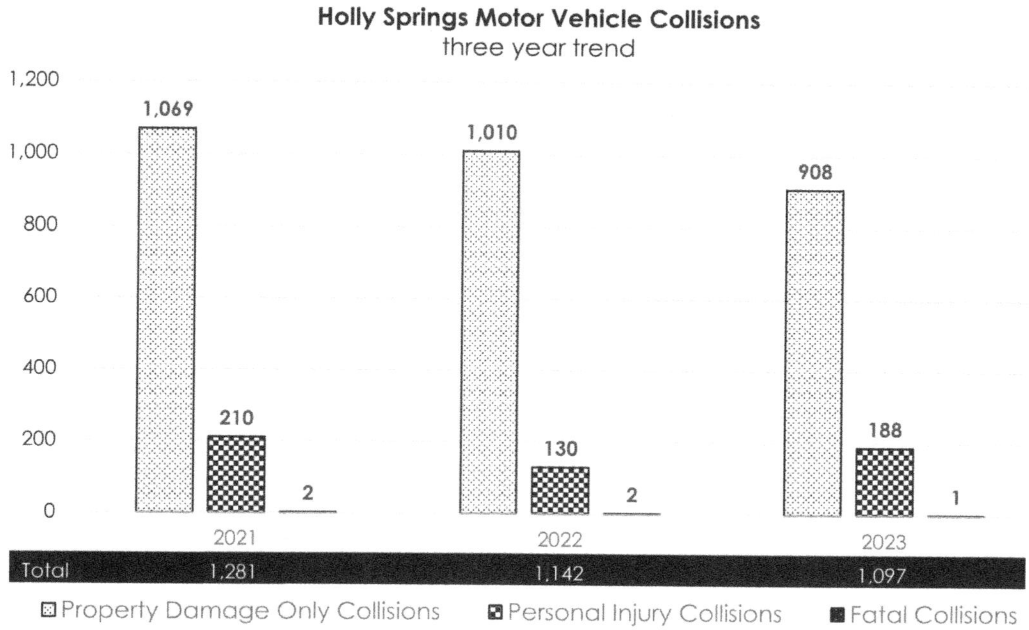

Source: Adapted from Town of Holly Springs, North Carolina, *2023 Annual Report: Town of Holly Springs Police Department*, 17.

Table 16.1 Using Performance Measures to Declare Performance Targets: Utilities and Engineering-Building Services

Performance Measure	Target
Percentage of building inspections scheduled within 2 business days or on the contractor's requested date	99%
Percentage of customer service complaints responded to within 2 business days (inspections)	98%
Customer complaint rate—valid complaints (inspections)	2%
Percentage of plan review customer services complaints responded to within 2 business days	96%
Percentage of commercial building plans reviewed within 10 working days	97%
Percentage of owner/tenant complaints regarding a safety inspection responded to within 2 business days	98%
Percentage of complaints regarding unsafe or hazardous unlawful conditions responded to within 24 hours	99%
Percentage of sediment and erosion control plans reviewed within 10 working days	98%
Customer complaint rate—valid complaints (erosion control)	2%
Percentage of stormwater control plans reviewed within 10 working days	98%
Percentage of code compliance cases closed due to voluntary compliance or within 2 site visits	100%
Customer complaint rate—valid complaints (Permit Center)	1.0%
Percentage of complaints responded to within 2 business days by Permit Center	98%

Source: Excerpted from Catawba County, North Carolina, *Adopted Operating & Capital Budget: Fiscal Year 2024/25*, 193.

Table 16.2 Examples of Performance Measures for Solid Waste and Recycling Services

Performance Measure	Actual 2022–23	Budget 2023–24	Adopted Budget 2024–25	Projected 2025–26
Workload Measures				
Single-family homes served by solid waste services	79,571	n/a	80,071	80,571
Number of multifamily/special collection points	4,723	n/a	4,725	4,725
Residential refuse and bulk tons collected (excluding yard waste)	74,710	n/a	78,446	82,368
Tons of yard waste & leaves collected	29,104	n/a	29,000	30,450
Commercial business subscribers for refuse services	1,198	n/a	1,258	1,321
Efficiency Measures				
Residential refuse tons collected per FTE (including yard waste and bulk collections)	1,505	1,333	1,557	1,635
Residential collection cost per ton				
• Refuse	$1,050	n/a	$1,103	$1,158
• Recycling	$212	n/a	$223	$234
Effectiveness Measures				
Pounds of residential refuse per collection point	2,130	2,071	2,200	2,250
Pounds of residential recycling per collection point	287	338	350	350
Pounds of yard waste and leaves per collection point	732	480	740	750
Recycling recovery rate (household recycling tons as a percentage of total refuse & recycling tons)	13%	16%	18%	18%
Residential recycling contamination rate	26%	23%	22%	20%
Valid complaints per 1,000 residents	1.44	n/a	1.0	1.0

Source: Excerpted from City of Greensboro, North Carolina, *Adopted Budget 2024–2025 and Projected Budget 2025–2026*, 124–25.

A local government's decision to choose a program or performance budget format over a line-item format does not guarantee a change in the focus or nature of budgetary debate. However, it does set the stage for budget deliberations that focus a little less on office supplies, fuel, insurance premiums, and other categories of expenditure, and a lot more on services and program results. Budget formats that incorporate good performance measures—especially efficiency and outcome measures—recognize and advance the planning and managerial opportunities of the budgetary process. They are designed to equip elected and appointed decision makers with the performance facts and figures for a given program, as well as the resource facts and figures, that will help them plan wisely and manage prudently.

Although the Government Finance Officers Association (GFOA) refrains from endorsing any particular budget format over all others, it nevertheless advocates the use of performance measures. Recipients of the GFOA's Distinguished Budget Presentation Award are expected to include in their budgets "objective measures of progress toward accomplishing the government's mission as well as goals and objectives for specific departments and programs."[4] These measures focus on results and accomplishments rather than inputs.

4. Government Finance Officers Association, *GFOA's Distinguished Budget Presentation Award Program*, www.gfoa.org/budget-award-application-information (last accessed Sept. 16, 2024).

Table 16.3 Example of Performance Measures for Public Works

Performance Measure	FY21 Actual	FY22 Actual	FY23 Estimate	FY24 Target
Traffic Signals/Signs				
Percent of emergency traffic signal problems addressed within 2 hours	100%	100%	100%	95%
Percent of emergency requests on critical traffic control signs (e.g., stop sign, yield sign) addressed within 2 hours	n/a	100%	100%	100%
Percent of permits issued within 5 business days for traffic control plans for lanes and street closures	98%	82%	100%	100%
Streets & Parking Lots				
Percent of town-maintained street system rated 81 or better (square yards)	46.5%	n/a	56%	80%
Percent of town-maintained streets (square yards) resurfaced during the year	1.8%	5%	4%	7%
Civil Engineering				
Percent of properly certified and submitted survey plats reviewed and responded to within 5 working days of receipt	100%	100%	98%	100%
Solid Waste Collection				
Tons of residential refuse collected per collection FTE	559	548	535	530
Percent of commercial collection costs recovered via fees	34%	32%	tbd	45%
Percent of community "satisfied" or "very satisfied" with quality of trash/yard waste collection services	88%	87%	87%	88%
Inclement Weather Services				
Percent of priority town roadways pre-treated prior to each significant inclement weather event	100%	100%	No major snow events	100%
Percent of priority streets where initial snow removal is completed within 48 hours	100%	100%	No major snow events	80%
Facilities Management				
Preventive maintenance work orders as a percent of total annual work orders	73%	70%	62%	45%
Percent of customer repair requests completed within 2 business days of receipt	91%	91%	89%	85%
Percent of emergency work orders that personnel respond to within 1 hour	100%	100%	100%	100%

Source: Excerpted from Town of Chapel Hill, North Carolina, *2023–24 Adopted Budget*, 137–38.

The National Advisory Council on State and Local Budgeting lists the four principles of the budget process as the setting of goals, developing approaches and strategies to achieve them, creating a budget that aligns with these goals and strategies, and evaluating performance for any needed adjustments.[5]

> Performance measures, including efficiency and effectiveness measures, should be presented in basic budget materials, including the operating budget document, and should be available to stakeholders. . . . At least some of these measures should document progress toward achievement of previously developed goals and objectives. More formal reviews and documentation of those reviews should be carried out as part of the overall planning, decision-making, and budget process.[6]

Despite all the advantages that performance measurement offers and the numerous endorsements it boasts, the act of incorporating performance measures into the budget process will not render the often-arduous task of making budget decisions suddenly simple. Performance measures will help identify operational strengths and weaknesses and will gauge changes in efficiency and progress toward meeting objectives, but they can neither formulate the perfect budget nor prescribe remedies for operational deficiencies. Governing boards will still struggle to set priorities—and struggle to stretch resources to fund those priorities. Operating officials must still do the challenging work of designing program improvement strategies, but performance measures can provide a baseline and a gauge for assessing the success or failure of those strategies.

Rarely will budget decisions be made solely on the strength of performance measures. Well-intentioned strategies of rewarding good performance with budgetary increases and penalizing poor performance with budget reductions inevitably deteriorate when crucial programs, struggling and seemingly losing ground to intractable problems, might be helped by a budgetary boost. When crime statistics are climbing, should the governing board penalize the police department or sheriff's office with a blanket reduction, or should it reinforce law enforcement efforts with a budgetary increase?

Even if performance measures rarely yield clear budgetary direction, they almost always contribute positively to the process. Difficult decisions are best made with clear evidence of program performance and realistic expectations of future impact. Furthermore, meaningful performance measures can enhance communication between governing boards and managers regarding performance expectations and service priorities.

Where performance measures make their greatest budgetary impact may come much earlier than at the time of final budget deliberations. Months earlier, when managers in various parts of the government spot disappointing performance statistics or a downward performance trend in their department and propose a solution with accompanying facts and figures as part of their budget request, they start the ball rolling toward data-informed decision making. Following thorough vetting during the budget preparation process, the best of the proposed solutions may emerge as part of the recommended budget. This may be when performance measurement has its greatest impact on the budget.

---

5. National Advisory Council on State and Local Budgeting, *Recommended Budget Practices: A Framework for Improved State and Local Government Budgeting* (Chicago: GFOA, 1998), 4–5.

6. National Advisory Council on State and Local Budgeting, *Recommended Budget Practices.* The quoted material is drawn from Practice 11.1, "Monitor, Measure, and Evaluate Program Performance."

Performance Measurement as a Tool for Productivity Improvement

Local government productivity may be defined as "the efficiency with which resources are consumed in the effective delivery of public services."[7] Not only should the quantity of outputs be considered when assessing productivity, but the quality of outputs should be weighed as well. Productivity improvement occurs when the ratio of outputs to inputs is increased, with output evaluated in both quantitative and qualitative terms.

In other words, a department or program may appropriately claim a gain in productivity when, for a given amount of dollars, it can provide services to more citizens without reducing quality, improve service quality without decreasing the number of service recipients, or increase both quantity and quality simultaneously. If efficiency gains for a program are produced by cutting corners and damaging service quality, then gains in one aspect of performance are offset by losses in the other. Furthermore, if gains in quantity or quality are propelled by disproportionately greater amounts of resources (i.e., inputs), the program's productivity—i.e., its ratio of outputs to inputs—is impacted negatively, not positively.

Although productivity improvement strategies do not spring magically from performance measures, it is difficult to imagine effective strategies in the absence of performance measures. A good set of performance measures identifies areas of performance deficiency in which improvement strategies are likely to yield the greatest return. Formal approaches to the design of performance improvements often are guided by benchmarking projects or embedded in larger managing-for-results initiatives—both of which rely on performance measurement. Even less formal approaches, which may depend on someone's hunch that a new approach might work better, can benefit from careful monitoring of the new technique using appropriate performance measures. Such measures will yield feedback that may prompt midcourse corrections in strategies and improve the odds of success. Subsequently, performance measures will help policy makers decide whether a given strategy is working and deserving of additional funding for continuation.

Identifying Strengths and Weaknesses

Local government officials often have a sense of their organization's strengths and weaknesses, based on personal observations and a history of complaints and compliments. In many cases, these notions are correct and can be substantiated by more objective performance measures. In other cases, however, officials' guesses are incorrect. They may be surprised to discover evidence that a favorite program is not as effective as previously thought or that a department once presumed to be wasteful is, in fact, rather efficient.

Serious performance improvement efforts are neither simple nor inexpensive. Done properly, they require considerable time, analysis, and careful implementation. It makes sense, then, to direct these substantial efforts toward opportunities most likely to yield ample returns. Services with the greatest performance deficiencies often offer the greatest opportunity for improvement; however, governments sometimes choose to focus instead on a high-priority service already getting good results that they hope to make even better.

Benchmarking

Benchmarking projects in local government are almost always one of two types:

- Metrics benchmarking
- Best practice benchmarking

7. Nancy S. Hayward, "The Productivity Challenge," *Public Administration Review* 36 (Sept.–Oct. 1976): 544.

The most common type of benchmarking in local government is metrics benchmarking, where government units compare their own performance statistics with established standards or the targets and results of other units.[8] For example, a property appraisal unit in one county government might compare its appraisal accuracy, measured by how closely appraised values match market prices from actual sales, with that of other counties. It could also compare the daily workload of its appraisers with the typical production rates reported by the International Association of Assessing Officers.

Occasionally, major projects of considerable scope are developed using this form of benchmarking. Long-standing examples of metrics benchmarking involving multiple municipalities include the North Carolina Benchmarking Project, coordinated by the University of North Carolina's School of Government; the Florida Benchmarking Consortium; and the Valley Benchmark Communities in Arizona.[9]

Less commonly, some local governments have adopted best practice benchmarking—the second type of benchmarking—as a tool for performance improvement. This type of benchmarking was popularized by corporate giants such as Xerox, Motorola, and IBM when they pioneered efforts to cooperatively analyze and adopt the practices of more successful corporations to improve their own operations. Local governments that follow the best practice benchmarking model focus on a single process in their operation (this might be, for example, the procurement process, the process used for issuance of building permits, or emergency dispatching), identify other organizations that achieve superior results for that process, carefully analyze the process in their own organization alongside that of their benchmarking partners, identify factors that contribute to the superior results of their partners, and figure out how to modify their own process to improve outcomes. Because this approach focuses on processes and identifies performance leaders, it is linked to the search for best practices and carries that label.

In 2006, nine North Carolina cities and towns teamed up on a best practice benchmarking project to find ways to improve their development review processes.[10] They identified three cities as development review exemplars: Henderson, Nevada; San Diego, California; and Tallahassee, Florida. Through information exchanges and site visits to these three cities, the North Carolina municipalities found seventy-eight ideas for improving their processes, many of which were adopted as a result of the project.

Metrics benchmarking differs from best practice benchmarking in two major ways. First, it often focuses broadly on multiple services or operations simultaneously rather than on a single key process. Second, it focuses primarily on results and only secondarily, if at all, on the details of the processes that produce these results.

Local government officials who choose metrics benchmarking over best practice benchmarking accept a trade-off. They exchange the depth of analysis associated with best practice benchmarking for the breadth of coverage that comes with metrics benchmarking's comparison of performance statistics across several government operations. Those who make this trade do not necessarily rule out a more detailed analysis later. In fact, the broad comparison of performance statistics across several departments may help them identify functions that would benefit most from best practice benchmarking, operations analysis, or other performance management strategies.

---

8. For a collection of performance standards and comparative performance measures, see David N. Ammons, *Municipal Benchmarks: Assessing Local Performance and Establishing Community Standards*, 3rd ed. (Armonk, NY: Routledge/M.E. Sharpe, 2012).

9. For current information on the North Carolina Benchmarking Project, see benchmarking.sog.unc.edu. For the Florida Benchmarking Consortium, see www.flbenchmark.org. For the Valley Benchmark Communities, see urbaninnovation.asu.edu/valley-benchmark-communities.

10. For details, see David N. Ammons, Ryan A. Davidson, and Ryan M. Ewalt, *Development Review in Local Government: Benchmarking Best Practices* (UNC School of Government and Alliance for Innovation, 2009).

Managing for Results

Over the past few decades, many governments and government agencies across the nation—local, state, and federal—have been engaged in cost-cutting or performance-enhancing initiatives that are often labeled "managing for results." Various management strategies have been adopted by local government proponents of this approach, including:

- Performance bonuses for achieving targets
- Gainsharing awards, whereby employee efforts that produce savings are rewarded with a share of those savings
- Enterprise management in which selected services charge their customers and raise their own revenues
- Managed competition, whereby local government departments bid against outside competitors for the right to deliver services
- "Bid-to-goal" strategies that simulate market competition without actually seeking outside bids
- Policies that allow departments to carry over a portion of end-of-year savings to the next fiscal year, thereby encouraging savings rather than end-of-year spending sprees
- Giving department heads and supervisors greater purchasing and personnel management flexibility if they achieve targeted results—that is, increasing managerial discretion in exchange for increased accountability[11]

These managing-for-results strategies share one common denominator: each requires a method of gauging results, which means each relies on performance measurement.

Various strategies for productivity improvement are promising but hardly fail-safe. Operational changes often achieve the desired results, but sometimes they do not. Adjustments may be needed. Occasionally, new strategies or techniques fail and should be abandoned. Therefore, it is very important to monitor performance before, during, and after operational changes. Performance measurement provides a tool for doing so.

Keys to the Successful Use of Performance Measures

Many local governments have undertaken performance measurement with the best of intentions. While some have been pleased with the results, others have been disappointed. More often than not, these disappointments can be attributed to falling short on one or more of the following keys to success:

- *Align performance measures with goals and objectives.* Performance measures should focus on important dimensions of service and gauge progress on key objectives.
- *Measure efficiency and effectiveness—not just workload.* Output (workload) measures are the most rudimentary form of performance measurement. Simply counting units of service is akin to "bean counting." Unfortunately, systems that do nothing more than "count beans" have very limited managerial and policy value. In contrast, systems that also report a department's efficiency, service quality, and program effectiveness receive a lot more attention from managers—and they deserve it because they are much more valuable.

11. David Osborne and Peter Hutchinson, *The Price of Government: Getting the Results We Need in an Age of Permanent Fiscal Crisis* (New York: Basic Books, 2004).

- *Link the performance measurement system to important policy processes and other management systems.* High-impact performance measurement systems are linked to important processes and contribute meaningfully to major and minor policy and managerial decisions. Examples include presenting key performance measures as background for policy retreats held by the governing board, reviewing performance measures during managerial or department head performance appraisals, analyzing performance measures in the formulation of operating strategies and budget requests, and using performance measures to diagnose employee training needs.
- *Present performance measures in context.* A performance measure reported out of context is "just a number" to all but the best-informed consumers of that information. For instance, is a five-minute average response time to law enforcement emergencies good? What about a library circulation rate of five items per capita or a citizen satisfaction rate of 87 percent? When information is presented without context, it is difficult to know whether it reflects good performance or not. Last year's numbers offer the simplest context for assessing this year's numbers, but a more informative context might be a comparison either to any recognized standards of service quality and efficiency or to the performance marks of other respected cities or counties. When presented in context, performance statistics become more valuable—and, to a broader audience, even interesting!

Additional Resources

Ammons, David N., *Improving Local Government Performance through Benchmarking.* New York: Routledge, 2025.

———, ed. *Leading Performance Management in Local Government.* Washington, D.C.: International City/County Management Association, 2008.

———. *Municipal Benchmarks: Assessing Local Performance and Establishing Community Standards.* 3rd ed. Armonk, New York: Routledge/M.E. Sharpe, 2012.

———. *Performance Measurement for Managing Local Government: Getting It Right.* Irvine, California: Melvin & Leigh, 2020.

Barrett, Katherine, and Richard Greene. *The Promises and Pitfalls of Performance-Informed Management.* Lanham, Maryland: Rowman & Littlefield, 2020.

Behn, Robert D. *The PerformanceStat Potential: A Leadership Strategy for Producing Results.* Washington, D.C.: Brookings Institution Press, 2014.

Hatry, Harry P. *Performance Measurement: Getting Results.* 2nd ed. Washington, D.C.: The Urban Institute Press, 2006.

Hatry, Harry P., D.M. Fisk, J.R. Hall Jr., P.S. Schaenman, and L. Snyder. *How Effective Are Your Community Services? Procedures for Performance Measurement.* 3rd ed. Washington, D.C.: International City/County Management Association and the Urban Institute, 2006.

International City/County Management Association. *Getting Started: Performance Management for Local Government*, 2nd ed. Washington, D.C.: International City/County Management Association, 2019.

Pasha, Obed, Christopher L. Cole II, Melissa Cordell, Keegan Huynh, Dania Khan, Jenna Kubiak, Caitlin Lancaster, and Reilly Stahl. *North Carolina Benchmarking Project Report 2024: Data and Decisions.* Chapel Hill: UNC School of Government, 2024.

Poister, Theodore H., Maria P. Aristigueta, and Jeremy L. Hall, *Managing and Measuring Performance in Public and Nonprofit Organizations*, 2nd ed. San Francisco: Jossey-Bass, 2015.

PART 4. Finance

Chapter 17

Revenues

Rebecca Badgett

Rebecca Badgett is a School of Government faculty member who focuses on general local government finance.

This chapter updates and revises previous chapters authored by School of Government faculty member Kara Millonzi, whose contributions to the field and to this publication are gratefully acknowledged.

Introduction

Counties and municipalities play a vital role in delivering core public services to the local community. Specifically, in North Carolina, counties are required by state law to fund public schools, social services programs, mental health programs, emergency medical services (EMS), courts, jail facilities, registers of deeds, and building code enforcement. They may also provide many additional services, ranging from zoning and land use planning to water and sewer utilities, to recreation and cultural activities, and economic development. Although state law only mandates that municipalities provide for building code enforcement, with a few exceptions, counties and municipalities may provide, and fund, most of the same discretionary services.

County and municipal elected officials make decisions that directly impact the fiscal stability of the community. One primary objective of a local governing board is ensuring that the unit of government is earning sufficient revenue to fund the state-mandated and discretionary services it provides. Importantly, because local governments are creatures of the state legislature, they may only levy taxes and charge fees when expressly authorized by the General Assembly to do so.

The North Carolina General Statutes define the types of revenue sources available to local governments and outline the legal and procedural requirements for each revenue source. In some cases, only counties are eligible to levy a tax, charge a fee, or receive a distribution of state-shared revenue. In other instances, only municipalities are eligible to do so. This chapter outlines the basic legal authority for the most common county and municipal revenue sources, but it does not describe every legal nuance or procedural requirement that must be complied with to take advantage of a particular revenue source. As such, local government officials must review the applicable constitutional and statutory law to fully understand the legal requirements that attach to the various types of revenue.

Local Taxes

The two most significant sources of revenue for local governments are the property tax and the local sales and use tax. The proceeds from these tax revenues play a vital role in ensuring a unit's fiscal stability and ability to provide services to the community. In addition, local governments collect several other types of locally imposed taxes, some of which are imposed through a local act of the General Assembly. Although the other local taxes do not generate as much revenue as the property and local sales taxes, the revenue does help fund some of the essential local services that contribute to the overall functioning of a local government.

The Property Tax

The property tax, also called the ad valorem tax, is a tax levied on real property, including land, buildings, and improvements to land (e.g., structures or fixtures); personal property (business equipment and automobiles); and on the property of public service companies (electric power companies, telephone companies, railroads, airlines, and certain other companies) that is not otherwise exempt from taxation. The statutory authorizations and related requirements for a county or municipality to levy a property tax are found in Chapter 153A, Section 149 of the North Carolina General Statutes (hereinafter G.S.), G.S. 160A-209, and G.S. Chapter 105, Articles 11 through 30.

A county or municipality is not required to levy a property tax, but it is required to adopt a balanced budget each fiscal year, whereby the sum of estimated net revenues and appropriated fund balance is equal to the appropriations made in each fund. Therefore, if a unit's estimated revenue from sources other than the property tax plus the appropriated fund balance is insufficient to satisfy the appropriations, a property tax must be levied at a sufficient rate to balance the budget.[1]

The property tax is levied each year in the annual budget ordinance, and it is up to the governing board to establish the applicable rate or rates of taxation. A governing board may adopt a single tax rate to meet budgetary needs. It may also adopt multiple, use-specific tax rates that are earmarked to fund certain services—or a combination of both methods may be used. For example, a municipality could adopt one tax rate for general fund revenue and one to fund police and fire services. Importantly, the state constitution requires that property tax rate(s) must be uniformly applied throughout the taxing jurisdiction.[2] A local government is, therefore, prohibited from adopting different tax rates for different property types or by location within the jurisdiction.

Generally, all property is subject to taxation unless specific action has been taken to exempt it or classify it. However, the North Carolina Constitution exempts certain property from taxation, including property owned by county and municipal governments that is used for governmental purposes.[3] The General Assembly has discretion to exempt, classify, or otherwise give a tax preference to a certain type of property, but any such exemptions or classifications must apply on a statewide basis.[4] Importantly, neither counties nor municipalities have the authority to exempt, classify, or otherwise give a tax preference to property within its jurisdiction.

Levying the Property Tax

The "property tax statutes," G.S. 153A-149 (counties) and G.S. 160A-209 (municipalities), describe the rate of taxation and purposes or functions that the property tax revenue may be used to support. The standard property tax rate is $1.50 per $100 of assessed valuation. There are a few purposes for which property taxes may be levied without limitation as to rate or amount. The property tax statutes divide local government functions into three groups for purposes of expending property tax revenue. The functions and the rate of taxation for each group are explained below.

Group 1. For Group 1 functions, the property tax may be levied without voter approval and without restriction on the property tax rate. Only a few functions are included in Group 1. For counties, these functions include many of the state-mandated services they must provide, including courts, schools, deficits, elections, jails, joint undertakings, and social services. The municipal functions in this group are more limited and include debt service on general obligation debt, deficits, and additional staffing to control civil disorders.[5]

Group 2. For Group 2 functions, property taxes may be levied without voter approval but are subject to a combined rate limitation of $1.50 per $100 of assessed valuation. Most county and municipal functions fall within Group 2—the statutes list more than thirty authorized functions subject to the rate limitation, such as airports, arts programs, health, fire, animal protection, libraries, housing, and many others. Because the Group 2 functions include most, if not nearly all, of the functions of a local government, property tax revenue is essentially an unrestricted revenue source—meaning a local government can use the proceeds to support virtually any public purpose. A unit may modify the rate limitation in one of two ways. First, it may conduct a referendum to raise the limitation for all functions listed in Group 2. Second, it may conduct a referendum to modify the tax rate for

---

1. Chapter 159, Section 13(c) of the North Carolina General Statutes (hereinafter G.S.).
2. Article V, section 2(5) of the North Carolina Constitution.
3. *Id.*
4. The property tax is discussed in much greater detail in Chapter 19, "Property Tax Policy and Administration."
5. G.S. 153A-149(b) (counties); 160A-209(b) (municipalities).

a specific function listed within Group 2. Any tax levied pursuant to a referendum is not counted against the Group 2 limit.[6]

Group 3. For Group 3 functions, a unit may hold a vote to levy a property tax on any function it may otherwise lawfully perform that is not already taxed under Group 1 or 2. Group 3 functions may get approvals based on maximum rate, maximum amount, or no restrictions. Therefore, any property tax levied under this option is not necessarily subject to the rate limitation of $1.50 per $100 of assessed valuation.[7]

Tax-Levy Formula

The formula for setting the property tax rate and enacting property taxes is relatively simple. A local government must determine three variables in order to calculate the property tax levy for the next fiscal year. First, it must determine the sum needed to balance the budget. This amount is established by taking the difference between the total estimated appropriations (i.e., expenditures) and the estimated revenues from sources other than the property tax. Second, it must determine the collection percentage for the prior fiscal year, expressed as a decimal point. (Most North Carolina local governments collect 95 to 99 percent of the levy; the estimated collection percentage may not exceed the current year's collection percentage.) Third, it must determine the total value of taxable property in the jurisdiction. Once a unit has these figures, it may calculate the next fiscal year's property tax levy.

To illustrate the process for determining the tax levy and rate, assume that (1) a unit must collect $10,000,000 in property tax revenue to balance the budget; (2) its estimated collection percentage for the previous fiscal year is 95 percent; and (3) its taxable valuation of property is $1.5 billion. The total required levy is determined by dividing $10,000,000 by 0.95, which yields a property tax levy of $10,526,000. This figure is divided by the unit's taxable valuation—$1.5 billion—which yields a tax rate of $0.007017. This figure is multiplied by 100 to produce a tax rate of $0.7017 per $100 valuation. Property taxes are due on September 1, but taxpayers may delay payment until January 5 without incurring a penalty (G.S. 105-360(a)). As a result, local governments generally receive the bulk of property taxes midway through their fiscal year and must rely on fund balances and other revenue sources to finance expenditures during the first part of the fiscal year.

Service Districts

The only exception to the requirement that property tax rates be uniform throughout a jurisdiction is the authority of a county or municipality to designate a certain geographic area as a "service district" and then levy additional property taxes on the taxable properties within that district. The additional tax revenue is used to fund specific services or improvements that will benefit the properties within the service district area to a greater extent than those provided to properties outside the district.

The General Statutes list the purposes for which a county or municipality may create service districts.[8] Counties often establish service districts to help finance the operational and capital expenses of fire and rescue services, but other authorized purposes include trash collection, sewer and water systems, and beach erosion control. Municipalities often create service districts for

---

6. G.S. 153A-149(c); 160A-209(c).
7. G.S. 153A-149(d); 160A-209(e).
8. G.S. 153A-301; 160A-536.

downtown revitalization projects, but other authorized purposes include transit development, drainage, sewage collection and disposal systems, off-street parking facilities, beach erosion control, and more.

A governing board must follow a strict statutory process to establish a service district, but voter approval is not required (nor is a vote authorized).[9] A governing board may define a new service district if it can establish that a proposed district needs one or more of the permissible services, facilities, or functions "to a demonstrably greater extent" than the remainder of the jurisdiction.[10] Before a new service district may be established, a report must be prepared in which the unit defines the boundaries of the proposed service district, justifies the increased need for service, and establishes a plan for the provision of services within the district. The governing board must also hold a public hearing on the matter. Once the procedural requirements are satisfied, a municipality must adopt an ordinance to approve a new service district—and the ordinance must be passed at two council meetings by a majority vote of the voting members present. Counties must pass a resolution to establish a new service district.[11] With a few exceptions, a county or municipality must set the effective date for a new service district at the beginning of a fiscal year—this is because no new ad valorem (property tax) may be levied to support a service district partway through a fiscal year.[12]

A local government that has created a service district may (but is not required to) levy an additional tax upon all taxable properties within the district. When a service-district tax is levied, the district tax rate must be included in each year's annual budget ordinance. The rate of a service-district tax is limited to $1.50 per $100 of the assessed valuation of property subject to taxation and may only be increased if a majority of qualified voters residing within the district vote to increase the rate after a referendum is held on the matter.[13] Counties may place additional tax rate restrictions on fire districts and ambulance and rescue districts.[14] A county or municipality may also allocate any other revenue whose use is not otherwise restricted by law to help fund service district projects or it may issue general obligation bonds.[15] A county or municipality that has defined a new service district is expected to "provide, maintain, or let contracts" for the services for which the residents are being taxed "within a reasonable time, not to exceed one year" after the effective date of the district."[16] Service-district-tax proceeds must be expended to fund the authorized services or projects in the district.

The Local Sales and Use Tax

A second major source of revenue for many counties and municipalities is the local sales and use tax, which is added to the statewide sales and use tax of 4.75 percent. Only counties may levy a local sales and use tax (but municipalities share in the proceeds). The local sales and use taxes include a retail tax on the sale of tangible personal property, certain digital property, and some related services.[17] They also include a complementary "use" tax on tangible personal property purchased, leased, or rented for storage or use in North Carolina; certain digital property purchased for storage

9. G.S. 153A-302; 160A-537.
10. *Id.*
11. *Id.*
12. G.S. 153A-302; 160A-537.
13. G.S. 153A-307; 160A-542.
14. G.S. 153A-309.2; 153A-309.3 (fire districts); 153A-310 (ambulance and rescue districts).
15. G.S. 153A-307, -308; 160A-542, -543.
16. G.S. 153A-305(a); 160A-540(a).
17. G.S. 105-164.4(a).

or use in the state; and services sourced to North Carolina.[18] The General Assembly determines which transactions are subject to the state and local sales and use taxes, and the North Carolina Department of Revenue (NCDOR) is responsible for distributing the tax proceeds according to the distribution requirements established in the statutes.

The authority for counties to levy local sales and use taxes (local sales taxes) is provided in four articles of G.S. Chapter 105, as follows:

- Article 39 (authorizing the levy of a 1-cent sales tax);
- Article 40 (authorizing the levy of a 0.5-cent sales tax);
- Article 42 (authorizing the levy of a 0.5-cent sales tax); and
- Article 46 (subject to voter approval, authorizing the levy of an additional 0.25-cent sales tax).[19]

All North Carolina counties levy Articles 39, 40, and 42 sales taxes. However, only about half of the counties currently levy the Article 46 sales tax, which requires voter approval. Accordingly, the combined state and local sales tax rate is either 6.75 percent or 7 percent (if the 0.25-cent Article 46 tax is levied). Each article sets forth the tax base of items subject to local sales taxes and describes the process used to distribute the tax proceeds. The tax base for the local sales tax is not always identical to the tax base for the statewide sales tax (e.g., sales of groceries are not subject to the statewide sales tax but are taxable under Articles 39, 40, and 42).

Distribution of Sales Tax Proceeds to Counties

Local sales tax revenue is allocated to counties according to the distribution requirements contained in each local sales and use tax article. Article 39 and Article 42 taxes (1.5 percent of the total 2 percent total) are allocated on a point-of-origin basis, meaning that the net proceeds are distributed back to the county in which the purchased goods were delivered.[20] This allocation method benefits counties with higher levels of commercial activity.

Article 40 sales tax proceeds are allocated to counties on a per capita basis, meaning the distribution is based on the total population of a county and its incorporated municipalities, and not upon the taxable transactions that occurred in the county.[21] Each county's distribution of Article 40 taxes is then adjusted. This adjustment is done by taking a county's per capita allocation and multiplying the amount according to an adjustment factor established in G.S. 105-486(b). The adjustment causes counties with larger populations to receive a greater distribution of Article 40 sales tax revenue.

For those counties that levy the Article 46 tax, the proceeds are allocated to the county in which the purchased goods are received or delivered.[22]

Statewide Pool

Beginning in fiscal year 2016–17, the General Assembly created a "statewide pool" under Article 44 of G.S. Chapter 105 as another method by which to distribute local sales taxes. The statewide pool is funded with a portion of diverted Article 39, 40, and 42 local sales tax proceeds. In fiscal year 2016–17, $84,800,000.00 was placed in the pool. In each succeeding fiscal year, the total amount

18. G.S. 105-164.6(a).

19. *See* G.S. 105-471 (Article 39); 105-483 (Article 40); 105-498 (Article 42); 105-538 (Article 46); and 105-537 (requiring voter approval for the Article 46 sales tax).

20. G.S. 105-472(a) (Article 39); 105-501(a) (Article 42).

21. G.S. 105-486.

22. G.S. 105-538.

is adjusted based upon the annual percentage change in Article 39, 40, and 42 collections. The "statewide pool" tax proceeds are distributed to counties based upon each county's "allocation percentage" as established in G.S. 105-524(c). The result is that twenty-one of the more urban counties do not receive a direct allocation of the statewide pool moneys, while seventy-nine of the more rural counties do.[23] Accordingly, the statewide pool system helps to ensure that rural counties receive a fair portion of this sales tax revenue despite not generating as much sales tax revenue as more urban counties. The statewide pool moneys are partially earmarked, with counties being required to spend the revenue to support economic development, public schools, or community colleges. Municipalities that receive a distribution of the statewide pool moneys from counties may spend their allocations on any lawful purpose.[24]

Distributions of Local Sales Tax Proceeds to Municipalities

Although only counties may levy a local sales tax, municipalities are entitled to share in the proceeds. On an annual basis, the governing board of each county must elect one of two methods to calculate how to share the local sales tax revenue. The two distribution methods include the per capita method, which is based on total population, and the ad valorem method, which is based on a percentage share of property taxes. Counties that levy the Article 46 sales tax are neither required nor authorized to share a portion of the Article 46 proceeds with municipalities.

Per Capita Distribution Method

G.S. 105-472(b)(1) sets for the process for distributing the local sales tax proceeds using the per capita method. This method considers the "total population" of the taxing county and the municipalities within the county in calculating a municipality's share of the revenue. If a municipality is in more than one county, only those living in the taxing county will be included as part of the total population of the taxing jurisdiction. To determine the county and each municipality's pro rata share of local sales tax proceeds: (1) add the county population and the population of the incorporated municipalities within the county to determine the total population of the county; (2) divide the amount of sales tax distributed to the county by the total population; and (3) multiply the resulting figure reached in step 2 by the population of the county and each municipality therein. Each respective product will be the amount to be distributed to the taxing county and each municipality.[25] This method does not require counties or municipalities to allocate a portion of the proceeds to any local taxing districts.

Ad Valorem Distribution Method

G.S. 105-472(b)(2) sets for the process for distributing local sales tax proceeds using the ad valorem method. This method distributes the proceeds of the local sales tax revenue to a county and its incorporated municipalities in proportion to the total amount of ad valorem taxes levied by each on property located within the taxing county.[26] The amount of ad valorem taxes levied by the county or municipality on behalf of a special taxing district and collected by the county or municipality is included, and a portion of the local sales tax proceeds is therefore shared with any local taxing district. For example, if a county levies a general property tax, and it levies property taxes for three rural fire protection districts, the total levy includes the general property tax proceeds plus the

23. G.S. 105-524(c).
24. G.S. 105-524(d).
25. G.S. 105-472(b)(1).
26. G.S. 105-472 (boards of county commissioners must select the distribution method each April).

three rural fire district tax proceeds. When the county receives its share of local sales revenue, it must allocate a portion of proceeds to the three rural fire protection districts according to the relative total levies.

Authorized Local Sales Tax Expenditures

A portion of local sales tax revenue is earmarked for specific uses. Counties must reserve 60 percent of Article 42 tax proceeds and 30 percent of Article 40 tax proceeds for public school capital outlay or debt service payments associated with school construction projects.[27] If the amount allocated to a county under Article 40 is higher than the amount allocated to the county under Article 42, the county must also use 60 percent of the difference between the two for public school capital outlay purposes. In addition, the counties must use the distributions from the statewide pool to support economic development, public education, and community colleges.[28] Counties may spend any remaining local sales tax proceeds, including the Article 46 tax proceeds (if levied), to support any public purpose for which a county is authorized to undertake.

Municipalities that receive distributions of Article 39, 40, or 42 tax proceeds, or statewide pool moneys, may expend the revenue to support any lawful public purpose.

Medicaid Hold-Harmless Funds

Prior to 2007, counties paid 15 percent of the non-federal share of Medicaid costs. As part of the "Medicaid Swap" legislation enacted in 2007, the state agreed to cover these costs in exchange for counties forfeiting the authority to levy a local 0.50 percent sales and use tax under G.S. Chapter 105, Article 44.[29] This legislation created two separate local government "hold harmless" payments.

First, because the proceeds of the Article 44 county tax had been shared with municipalities, the legislation required counties to hold municipalities incorporated before October 1, 2008, harmless for lost tax revenue. The municipal hold-harmless payment created under G.S. 105-522 ensures that municipalities receive the equivalent amount of revenue that they would have received if the 0.50 percent tax were still in effect. Half of the former Article 44 revenue was distributed to counties on a point-of-origin basis and half on a per capita basis, and the formula for calculating a municipality's hold-harmless payment reflects that former distribution. A county can calculate a municipality's share of the hold-harmless payment by (1) determining the municipality's share of Article 40 tax proceeds, which is the "base hold-harmless amount"; (2) dividing the "base hold-harmless amount" in half and then subtracting .25 percent of the municipality's share of the Article 39 sales tax proceeds; and (3) adding the base hold-harmless amount determined in step 1 to the sum (positive or negative) reached in step 2. The resulting figure will be the adjusted hold-harmless payment due to the municipality.[30]

Second, the legislation guaranteed that each county would benefit by at least $500,000 as a result of the Medicaid swap. In other words, if a county's gain from not having to pay Medicaid expenses did not exceed its loss from the half-cent sales and use tax by at least $500,000, the state would make a supplemental payment to the county to make up the difference. Over time, the state reduced the guaranteed benefit to $250,000 effective in fiscal year 2015–16 and to $125,000 effective in fiscal year 2016–17. Starting in fiscal year 2017–18, the General Assembly determined that it would only make a supplemental payment if the tax revenue loss exceeded the gain to the county from the

27. G.S. 105-502(a) (Article 42); 105-487(a) (Article 40).
28. G.S. 105-524(d).
29. *See* S.L. 2007-323, § 31; S.L. 2007-345, § 14; S.L. 2008-134, §§ 13–15.
30. G.S. 105-522.

reduction in Medicaid expenses that year.[31] As a result, only those counties that gave up more in lost tax revenue than they would have paid out in Medicaid costs receive a county hold-harmless distribution from the state under G.S. 105-523.

Public Transportation Sales and Use Tax

G.S. Chapter 105, Article 43 authorizes counties and some public transportation authorities to levy an additional local sales tax to fund public transportation systems provided certain conditions are satisfied. A county may only levy this tax if it, or at least one unit of government within the county, operates a public transportation system, and the county has received voter approval to levy the tax.[32]

Mecklenburg, Wake, Durham, and Orange counties, and a regional transportation authority encompassing Forsyth and Guilford counties, have been approved to levy the transportation tax at a rate of 0.50 percent,[33] while all other qualifying counties levying the tax have adopted a tax rate of 0.25 percent.[34] The proceeds of the public transportation sales tax are allocated on a per capita basis to the county and to any unit(s) of local government in the county that operate a public transportation system. Counties or municipalities that do not operate a public transportation system may not receive a share of the proceeds. The public transportation tax revenue must be used to finance, construct, operate, and maintain local public transportation systems.[35]

Other Local Taxes

In addition to the property tax and local sales tax, counties and municipalities have the authority to levy a variety of other local taxes. These taxes include a rental car gross receipts tax, an animal tax, a heavy equipment rental tax, and motor vehicle license taxes.

Rental Car Gross Receipts Tax

Counties (G.S. 153A-156) and municipalities (G.S. 160A-215.1) may, by ordinance, levy a tax of up to 1.5 percent of the gross receipts derived from the short-term lease or rental of vehicles at retail to the public. A short-term lease or rental is a lease or rental of a motor vehicle for a period of less than one year.[36] The taxable transaction occurs at the location where the customer takes delivery of the vehicle. If adopted, the effective date of the ordinance should be no earlier than the first day of the month following its adoption. The county or municipality should identify and notify retail establishments subject to the tax of the obligation to collect the tax and to include a disclosure in each rental or lease agreement that identifies the tax and the applicable rate of taxation.

The retailer must collect the tax and place the proceeds in a segregated account until the funds are remitted to the county or municipality. If the retail establishment is located in a county and in a municipality that levies the tax, it must collect both—the combined rate may not exceed 6 percent. The proceeds of the rental car gross receipts tax may be used to support any lawful public purpose.

Animal Tax

Counties (G.S. 153A-153) and municipalities (G.S. 160A-212) may levy an annual animal tax on the privilege of keeping dogs, cats, or other domestic animals. A local government may decide which

---

31. G.S. 105-523.

32. G.S. 105-507.1 (Mecklenburg); 105-509 (Wake, Durham, and Orange); 105-510 (Forsyth and Guilford); 105-511.2 (all other counties).

33. G.S. Chapter 105, Article 43, Parts 2, 4, and 5.

34. G.S. Chapter 105, Article 43, Part 6.

35. G.S. 105-507.3(b); 105-508.2(b); 105-511.4(b).

36. G.S. 105-187.1.

animals to tax and the tax rate. It is common for the rates to vary based on the type of animal and whether the animal has been spayed or neutered. For example, a unit may charge $10 for fixed dogs and $30 for dogs that have not been spayed or neutered. The revenue generated from the animal tax may be used to support any lawful public purpose.

Short-Term Heavy Equipment Tax

Counties (G.S. 153A-156.1) may, by resolution, impose a tax at a rate of 1.2 percent on the gross receipts from the short-term lease or rental of heavy equipment. A retailer is liable for the tax when the place of business to which the heavy equipment is delivered is located in the county. Municipalities (G.S. 160A-215.2) may, by ordinance, levy a tax at a rate of 0.8 percent on the gross receipts from the short-term lease or rental of heavy equipment if the place of business from which the equipment is delivered is located within the municipality.

Heavy equipment is defined to include any "[e]arthmoving, construction, or industrial equipment that is mobile, weighs at least 1,500 pounds," and is either (1) "a self-propelled vehicle that is not designed to be driven on a highway" or (2) "industrial lift equipment, industrial material handling equipment, industrial electrical generation equipment, or a similar piece of industrial equipment."[37]

When levied, the heavy equipment subject to this tax is exempt from property tax under G.S. 105-275; therefore, a tax on the short-term lease or rental of heavy equipment provides an alternative to a property tax on the equipment. The tax is payable quarterly to the county finance officer or the municipality by the last day of the month following the end of the quarter.[38] The proceeds of the tax revenue may be used to support any lawful public purpose.

County Vehicle Registration Tax

Counties (G.S. 105-570) may levy an annual vehicle registration tax if the county, or any municipality in the county, operates a public transportation system. The maximum annual rate of this tax is $7.00. The levying county must distribute the proceeds of the tax on a per capita basis to the county (if it operates a public transportation system) and to any municipalities within the county that operate a public transportation system. The tax proceeds must be used to operate a public transportation system, including financing, constructing, operating, and maintaining the system. A county or municipality may execute a contract or enter into an interlocal agreement with another entity (a county, municipality, or transportation authority) to allow the entity to operate a public transportation system.[39]

Municipal Vehicle Registration Tax

Municipalities (G.S. 20-97) may levy an annual motor vehicle registration tax upon any vehicle resident in the municipality. The aggregate annual tax levied, including any annual municipal vehicle tax authorized by local legislation, may not exceed thirty dollars ($30.00) per vehicle. A municipality must use the tax proceeds as follows: (1) up to the first $5.00 of the tax may be used for any lawful general purpose; (2) if the municipality operates a public transportation system, up to $5.00 of the proceeds may be used for financing, constructing, operating, and maintaining the public transportation system; and (3) any remaining proceeds must be used for maintaining, repairing, constructing, reconstructing, widening, or improving public streets in the municipality that are

37. G.S. 153A-156.1(a)(1); 160A-215.2(a)(1).
38. G.S. 153A-156.1; 160A-215.2.
39. G.S. 105-570(e).

not part of the state highway system. In addition, municipalities may levy a tax of not more than fifteen dollars ($15.00) per year upon each taxicab in the municipality and may use the proceeds for any lawful public purpose.

Malt Beverage and Wine Retail License Tax

Entities that sell beer and wine at retail must obtain certain permits from the North Carolina Alcoholic Beverage Control (ABC) Commission. These permit holders must also obtain an annual malt beverage or wine license from the county and municipality in which the establishment is located (G.S. 105-113.78; G.S. 105-113.77). The tax rate is set by statute and varies depending on the type(s) of beverage sold and whether consumption will occur on or off-premises.

- **License fees for counties:** $25.00 for the on-premises sale of beer and/or wine; $25.00 for the off-premises sale of wine, or both; and $5.00 for the off-premises sale of only beer (G.S. 105-113.78).
- **License fees for municipalities:** $15.00 for the on-premises sale of beer and/or fortified wine; $10.00 for the off-premises sale of wine, or both; and $5.00 for the off-premises sale of only beer. Entities or persons needing multiple licenses in the same year for different establishments must pay 110 percent of the base license tax, and that increase applies progressively for each additional license (G.S. 105-113.77).
- **Municipal wholesaler license:** Municipalities may require wholesalers of beer and wine located within their jurisdictions to obtain a wholesaler license and pay a corresponding annual tax of up to $37.50 (G.S. 105-113.79).

The proceeds of the taxes related to the issuance of malt beverage and wine licenses may be credited to the general fund and used to support any lawful public purpose.

Taxes Permitted by Local Act

The General Assembly has authorized, by local act, certain counties and municipalities to levy several other local taxes, such as occupancy taxes, prepared food taxes, and real estate transfer taxes. These tax revenues are often earmarked for expenditures specified in the local act.

Occupancy Tax

Counties and municipalities may, by local act of the North Carolina General Assembly, be granted authority to levy an occupancy tax on the gross receipts derived from the overnight rental of an accommodation (e.g., a hotel, motel, inn, tourist camp, short-term rental (e.g., Airbnb), or similar lodging facility).[40] Although a few units have been authorized to levy the occupancy tax at a higher rate, a rate of 3 percent is standard. When a county and a municipality in the county each levy a 3 percent occupancy tax, a total occupancy tax of 6 percent will apply to the rental of the accommodation. The occupancy tax rate is in addition to any state or local sales tax.

Each local act authorizing the levy of local occupancy taxes must include a uniform set of administrative procedures, specified in G.S. 153A-155 (counties) and G.S. 160A-215 (municipalities), that address matters such as collection, administration, and penalties. Units of government that levy these taxes must comply with the statutory requirements and other stipulations included in

---

40. G.S. 105-164.3(1) (defining "accommodation"). For more detail on the types of accommodations to which local occupancy taxes apply, see Rebecca L. Badgett and Christopher B. McLaughlin, *Regulation and Taxation of Short-Term Rentals* (UNC School of Government, 2019), 51–57.

the local act. Some units that levy an occupancy tax establish a Tourism Development Authority (TDA), which is a public authority, to help oversee and administer the tax.

The proceeds of the occupancy tax are generally earmarked for uses that "promote travel and tourism" and for other "tourism-related" expenditures. Expenditures that "promote travel and tourism" are related to advertising or marketing an area or activity, conducting market research, or engaging in similar promotional activities. "Tourism-related" expenditures are designed to help increase the use of lodging facilities, meeting facilities, recreational facilities, and convention facilities as well as "beach nourishment" (replenishing the sand on an eroded shoreline).[41] Occupancy tax proceeds may not be used to develop or construct a hotel or other type of transient lodging facility.[42] A local act will generally stipulate how to divide and expend the tax proceeds. For example, it may provide that at least two-thirds of the proceeds will be spent on projects that "promote travel and tourism," with the remainder allocated to "tourism-related" expenditures.[43]

Prepared Food Tax

A few local governments have been granted authority through local acts to levy a tax on the sale of prepared food and beverages sold at retail for consumption on- or off-premises.[44] "Prepared food" is defined in G.S. 105-164.4L and includes food that is sold in a heated state, food that has been mixed or combined by the retailer for sale as a single item, or food that is sold with utensils provided by the retailer. When authorized, the tax rate is typically limited to 1 percent of the retail sales price of the prepared food. The proceeds of the prepared food tax are generally restricted for the purpose specified in the local act.

Real Estate Transfer Tax

Seven coastal counties have been authorized to levy an excise tax of 1 percent upon the conveyance of real property.[45] The tax is $1 for every $100 of the valued property and is paid in closing costs once a property is sold. The local acts generally impose restrictions upon how the proceeds may be expended.

Local Fees, Charges, and Assessments

There are a handful of fees, charges, and assessment revenues that local governments may charge to help cover costs associated with providing a variety of public services, ensuring regulatory compliance, enforcing ordinances, and constructing and maintaining public infrastructure. The fees and charges discussed in this section fall into one of the following general categories: regulatory fees, general user fees, public enterprise fees, franchise fees, special assessments, and statutory fees.

---

41. See the General Assembly's "Guidelines for Occupancy Tax Legislation," webservices.ncleg.gov/ViewDocSiteFile/52308.

42. G.S. 153A-155(f1); 160A-215(f1).

43. *See, e.g.*, Saluda (S.L. 2017-202).

44. *See, e.g.*, Cumberland (S.L. 1993-413), Dare (S.L. 1991-177), Durham (S.L. 2008-116), Mecklenburg (S.L. 1989-821), and Wake (S.L. 1991-594; S.L. 1995-458) and the municipalities of Charlotte (S.L. 1989-821), Hillsborough (S.L. 1993-449), and Monroe (S.L. 2005-261). For more information, see Connor Crews, "A Lesser-Known Local Government Revenue Source in North Carolina: 'Meals' Taxes," *Coates' Canons: NC Local Government Law* blog (March 27, 2023), canons.sog.unc.edu/2023/03/a-lesser-known-local-government-revenue-source-in-north-carolina-meals-taxes/.

45. These counties include Camden (S.L. 1985-954), Chowan (S.L. 1985-881), Currituck (S.L. 1985-670), Dare (S.L. 1985-525), Pasquotank (S.L. 1989-393), Perquimans (same), and Washington (same).

Regulatory Fees

Regulatory fees are used to fund the oversight and administrative costs associated with performing certain regulatory activities and functions. They include fees for issuing zoning and building permits, inspections, evaluating environmental impacts, reviewing subdivision plats, and enforcing other local ordinances. Counties have broad statutory authority pursuant to G.S. 153A-102 to charge fees in connection with performing regulatory activities and providing services; municipalities do not share this broad authority.

In some cases, a statute that authorizes the performance of a regulatory function will specify the amount of any associated regulatory fee that may be charged in connection with performing the function. For example, G.S. 160A-304 allows municipalities to charge taxi drivers up to $25.00 for a permit to operate a taxicab. In other cases, a statute may authorize a fee but not specify the amount. For example, Chapter 160D, which authorizes units to engage in a range of regulatory activities related to land use planning and zoning, allows units to "fix reasonable fees for support, administration, and implementation of programs authorized by [Chapter 160D], and [to use] such fees . . . for no other purposes."[46]

If a statute authorizes a unit to perform a regulatory activity but does not address whether an associated fee may be charged, a county or municipality may imply the authority to charge a fee. The North Carolina Supreme Court held in *Homebuilders Association of Charlotte, Inc. v. City of Charlotte*[47] that the authority to charge a fee in connection with performing a regulatory activity may be implied from the statutory authority to engage in the regulatory activity. However, the court stipulated that a regulatory fee must be "reasonable." Thus, regulatory fees should not exceed the direct and administrative costs of funding the regulatory activity—and, therefore, regulatory fees may not be used as a general revenue-generating mechanism.

Some statutes earmark the proceeds of regulatory fees for certain uses—usually to support the underlying regulatory activity. For example, G.S. 160A-301 requires municipalities to use the proceeds of parking meters to defray the cost of enforcing and administering traffic and parking regulations. If the statute authorizing the unit to undertake a regulatory activity does not earmark funds, technically the revenue may be used for any public purpose. However, because regulatory fees are charged to support the performance of a specific regulatory activity, the unit may want to separately account for regulatory fees and appropriate the fees in the budget to the corresponding department, function, or activity.

General User Fees

General user fees are charges imposed on individuals who take advantage of a specific government service for which the fee is being charged. The key to general user fees is that only those who take advantage of the service or activity are responsible for paying the fee. General user fees are often charged in connection with recreational activities, community arts programs, cultural events, library fees, on- and off-street parking, and certain public health services. This revenue is usually accounted for in a unit's general fund, and, unless otherwise restricted by state law, it may be used to support any lawful purpose.

Public Enterprise Fees

Counties (G.S. 153A-275) and municipalities (G.S. 160A-312) have broad authority to acquire, construct, establish, maintain, own, operate, and contract for the operation of public enterprises.

---

46. G.S. 160D-402(d).
47. Homebuilders Ass'n of Charlotte v. City of Charlotte, 336 N.C. 37 (1994).

A public enterprise is an activity of a commercial nature that could be provided by the private sector. The most common public enterprise services are water supply and distribution systems, sewage collection and treatment, and solid waste collection and disposal utilities. Both counties and municipalities may also operate public enterprises for airports, public transportation, off-street parking, and stormwater systems.[48] Municipalities have additional authority to operate public enterprises for electric power generation and distribution, gas production and distribution, and cable television.[49]

The authority to regulate the operation of public enterprises includes the authority to establish rates, fees, and penalties for the use of services provided by a public enterprise.[50] These fees include, for example, hookup charges, monthly user fees, and system development fees.[51] State law imposes restrictions on user-fee rates for certain public enterprise services. For stormwater services, the fees assessed may not exceed the cost of administering the stormwater-management program.[52] For solid waste fees (collection fees, disposal and use fees, and availability fees), each fee may not exceed the costs of providing the specific solid waste services for which the fee is authorized.[53] In addition, local governments may not vary rates for individual users unless there is a valid, utility-based reason for doing so. For example, a local unit may not charge lower rates based on a customer's age or ability to pay because these factors do not support a valid, utility-based rationale. Similarly, late fees and penalties generally may not be waived for individual users.

Public enterprises are often self-supporting or largely self-supporting, meaning that the revenue generated through fees and rate charges is sufficient to cover the costs of providing the services. The revenue generated by a public enterprise must first be used to fund the enterprise's operating expenses, capital outlay, and debt service obligations. In some cases, enterprise fee revenue may be transferred to another fund and used to support general government services. Such transfers are only permissible when all the expenses related to the enterprise operation expected to come due during the fiscal year are covered.

Prior to transferring enterprise revenue to another fund to support other general fund services, a local government must determine whether the revenue is earmarked. Certain enterprise fee revenue must be used to support the specific enterprise for which the revenue was generated. For example, availability fees to support solid waste disposal facilities may only be used to cover the costs of operating the facility (G.S. 153A-292; G.S. 160A-314.1). Therefore, if solid waste fee revenue is transferred to the general fund, the revenue must be used to reimburse the general fund for services provided to the solid waste enterprise. The revenue may not be loaned to the general fund to help balance the current year's budget. If solid waste fee revenue is transferred to a debt service fund, the revenue can be used to make debt-service payments related to borrowing for a solid waste project. There is an exception: G.S. 160A-314.1(a) authorizes a municipality that contracts with another local government to collect its solid waste to levy a surcharge on the fee, and the surcharge revenue may be used for any public purpose.

---

48. G.S. 153A-274; 160A-311.

49. *Id.*

50. G.S. 153A-277; 160A-314.

51. *See* G.S. 162A-201 (defining system development fee as a charge or assessment imposed with respect to new development to fund costs of capital improvements necessitated by new development, to recoup costs of existing facilities that serve such new development, to recoup costs incurred by a local government unit to purchase capacity in, or reserve capacity supplied by, capital improvements or facilities owned by another local government unit, or a combination of those costs. It does not include hookup charges, availability charges, or administrative and inspection costs associated with permitting).

52. G.S. 153A-277; 160A-314.

53. G.S. 153A-292; 160A-314.1.

Stormwater fee revenue must be expended to support stormwater management projects; therefore, it may not be transferred to the general fund and used for other purposes (G.S. 160A-314(a1)(2); G.S. 153A-277(a1)(2)). Transfers from electric funds may not exceed the greater of 3 percent of the gross capital assets of the electric system, or 5 percent of the gross annual revenues of the preceding fiscal year (G.S. 159B-39). In some cases, there are additional restrictions imposed on other enterprise revenue by contract, bond covenants, local acts, or grant agreements, which may constrain a local government's ability to transfer money from the enterprise fund. In general, it is a disfavored practice to rely on enterprise fee revenue to fund general government expenditures, and units should use caution and understand the consequences of doing so. Notably, when water or sewer enterprise fund moneys are transferred to the general fund to supplement the general fund revenues, the unit is prohibited from receiving loans or grants for water or wastewater purposes from certain state funding sources, such as the Clean Water State Revolving Fund (G.S. 159G-37(b)). This prohibition applies only to transfers intended to help support the general fund—not legitimate reimbursements for expenses that can be reasonably allocated to the operations of the public enterprise. For more details on the legal authority of counties and municipalities to impose fees and charges for public enterprise activities, see Chapter 30, "Public Enterprises."

Franchise Fees

A county or municipal franchise is a legal agreement or contract granted by the local government to a private company or entity that typically allows the private entity to operate within the unit's jurisdiction to provide certain essential services or utilities to residents. The ability to grant a franchise does not necessarily include the ability to charge a franchise fee—there must be statutory authority to charge a franchise fee. Counties may grant franchises and charge licensing fees for solid waste collection and disposal.[54] Municipalities have broad authority to grant franchises for a range of purposes, including for telephone systems and any of the enterprises listed in G.S. 160A-311, except a cable television system.[55] Municipalities may also grant franchises and charge a fee for taxicab companies.[56]

Special Assessments

Special assessments are a financing tool that counties and municipalities may use to help fund certain capital projects. A special assessment is a charge levied against real property within a defined geographic area to pay for public improvements that benefit that property. Like a user fee, a special assessment is levied in some proportion to the benefit that the assessed property receives. Like a property tax, a special assessment is levied against the property and creates a lien on each parcel of real property assessed, which may be foreclosed in the same manner as a property tax lien.

At present, state law authorizes the levy of two types of special assessments: "traditional" special assessments and "critical infrastructure" special assessments.[57] However, the authority for municipalities and counties to impose critical infrastructure special assessments is set to expire on July 1, 2025, for projects that have not been approved under a final assessment resolution.[58] Under both methods, a governing board must follow a detailed procedural process to impose a special assessment.

---

54. G.S. 153A-136.
55. G.S. 160A-319.
56. G.S. 160A-304; 20-97.
57. G.S. 153A-185; 160A-216.
58. G.S. 160A-239.1; S.L. 2020-58, § 7.2 (municipalities); G.S. 153A-210.1; S.L. 2019-215, § 3 (counties).

Traditional Special Assessments

Counties may levy traditional special assessments to finance the capital costs of water systems, sewage collection and disposal systems, beach erosion control and hurricane protection works, watershed improvement projects, drainage projects, water resources development projects, local costs of N.C. Department of Transportation improvements to subdivision and residential streets located outside of municipalities, and streetlight maintenance. Municipalities may levy traditional special assessments to finance public improvements involving streets, sidewalks, water systems, sewage collection and disposal systems, storm sewer and drainage systems, beach erosion control, and flood and hurricane protection works.[59]

A unit must fund all of a project's costs before it may levy a traditional special assessment to recoup costs from benefited properties—therefore, it is only after a project is complete that a traditional special assessment may be levied. Traditional special assessments may be paid (and often are) in up to ten annual installments along with interest on the amount outstanding. The revenue may be used to support any authorized public purpose.

Critical Infrastructure Special Assessments

Critical infrastructure special assessments may be levied to help cover the capital costs of projects (1) for which project-development-financing debt instruments may be issued under G.S. 159-103 and (2) for the purpose of the installation of distributed-generation renewable energy sources or energy-efficiency improvements that are permanently fixed to residential, commercial, industrial, or other real property.[60] Critical infrastructure special assessments are used to fund a variety of traditional "public" projects ranging from capital costs of airports, parking facilities, sewers, water systems, public transportation facilities, certain park and recreation facilities, and most other capital projects that a county or municipality is authorized to undertake.

Before a county or municipality may impose any critical infrastructure special assessment, it must first receive a petition signed by a majority of the owners of real property to be assessed, whose real property also represents at least 66 percent of the assessed value of all real property to be assessed.[61] Once a signed petition is received, the levying unit generally must follow the same detailed procedural process required to levy a traditional special assessment. Unlike traditional special assessments, the capital project does not need to be completed before a unit may levy a critical-infrastructure assessment. Critical infrastructure special assessments may be paid in annual installments for a period of up to twenty-five years.[62]

For more on special assessments, see Chapter 21, "Financing Capital Projects."[63]

Statutory Fees

The General Statutes establish several statutory fees that counties and municipalities must or may charge in connection with providing certain services. These fees are commonly associated with providing court facilities, certain law enforcement activities, and services provided by registers of deeds.

Court Facility Fees

To offset the expense of maintaining judicial facilities, several statutes impose fees for the use of courtrooms and related judicial facilities. The facility fees are generally remitted to the county in

---

59. G.S. 153A-185; 160A-215; 160A-238.

60. *See* G.S. 153A-210.2(a); 160A-239.2(a).

61. G.S. 153A-210.3; 160A-239.3.

62. G.S.153A-210.5(a); 160A-239.5(a).

63. *See also* Connor Crews, *Introduction to Local Government Finance*, Chapter 7, "Financing Capital Projects" (UNC School of Government, 2023).

which the judgment is rendered, unless judgment is rendered in facilities provided by a municipality, in which case the fee shall be paid to the municipality. The most common facility fees include:

- *Criminal actions*: $12.00 facility fee for cases heard in district court; $30.00 for cases in superior court. Fees are assessed only upon conviction.[64]
- *Civil actions*: $12.00 in cases heard before a magistrate; $16.00 for cases heard in district and superior court.[65]
- *Special proceedings*: $10.00 to be remitted to the county.[66]
- *Administration of estates*: $10.00 to be remitted to the county.[67]
- *Fees on deposits*: A fee of 4 percent of each principal amount deposited by the clerk in an interest-bearing checking account shall be assessed and collected.[68]

The facility fee revenue must be expended to provide, maintain, and construct adequate courtroom and related judicial facilities, including adequate space and furniture for judges, district attorneys, public defenders and other personnel of the Office of Indigent Defense Services, magistrates, juries, and other court-related personnel; office space, furniture and vaults for the clerk; jail and juvenile detention facilities; free parking for jurors; and a law library (including books).[69]

Arrest and Service of Criminal Process Fees

A fee of $5.00 shall be paid to the county for each arrest or personal service of criminal process, including citations and subpoenas. If arrest was made or process was served by a municipality, the fee must be paid to the municipality employing the officer. The fees may be used to support any lawful public purpose.[70]

Service of Civil Process

A fee of $30.00 shall be paid to the county for each item of civil process served, including summons, subpoenas, notices, motions, orders, writs, and pleadings. When civil process is served on two or more persons or organizations, a separate service charge shall be made for each person or organization. The process fee shall be remitted to the county. The civil service fee does not apply to service of summons to jurors. The fee revenue should be appropriated to the account in the general fund (likely law enforcement) and expenditures must be tracked. At least 50 percent of proceeds must be expended to ensure the timely service of process within the county, which may include the hiring of additional law enforcement officers.[71]

Jail Fee

A fee of $10.00 is charged for each twenty-four-hour period of confinement. The fee is not payable if the case or proceeding is dismissed, the defendant is acquitted, probable cause is not found, or the grand jury returns no true bill. Jail fees are not earmarked and may be expended to support any lawful public purpose.[72]

---

64. G.S. 7A-304(a)(2).
65. G.S. 7A-305(a)(1).
66. G.S. 7A-306(a)(1).
67. G.S. 7A-307(a)(1).
68. G.S. 7A-308.1.
69. G.S. 7A-304(a)(2).
70. G.S. 7A-304(a)(1).
71. G.S. 7A-311(a)(1)c.
72. G.S. 7A-313.

Pretrial Release Fee

A fee of $15.00 is payable to the county providing pretrial release services, but only if the defendant was released to the supervision of a county agency providing such services. The pretrial release fee revenue may be expended to support any lawful public purpose.[73]

Register of Deeds

The register of deeds collects fees for performing the official acts set forth in G.S. 161-10. These fees include fees for recording deeds and other instruments that affect land titles, fees for recording security interests under the Uniform Commercial Code, fees for issuing marriage licenses, and several others. Each county must deposit an amount equal to 1.5 percent of fees collected under G.S. 161-10 with the state treasurer every month to help fund a supplemental retirement pension fund for retired registers of deeds.[74] Counties must also remit a portion of the register of deeds fees to various state agencies to support specific programs.[75]

State-Shared Revenue

The General Assembly requires the state of North Carolina to share a portion of certain state tax revenues with counties and municipalities. In general, the North Carolina Department of Revenue (NCDOR) is responsible for collecting taxes and distributing the proceeds. This is beneficial to counties and municipalities as it places the bulk of the administrative burden on the states, not the local units.

In most cases, the state-shared tax revenue is shared with both counties and municipalities. However, there are a few taxes that are shared with either counties or municipalities, but not both. This section discusses the most common sources of state-shared tax revenue and distinguishes which type of jurisdiction(s) are eligible to receive a distribution from the state.

Video Programming Services and Telecommunication Taxes (for Counties and Municipalities)

In 2007, the General Assembly exchanged a local government's authority to collect local cable franchise taxes with the ability to receive a distribution of statewide sales taxes levied upon the sale of telecommunications services, video programming services, and direct-to-home satellite services.[76] The NCDOR distributes the proceeds of the tax revenue on a quarterly basis, with counties and municipalities receiving 7.7 percent of the net proceeds of the telecommunications tax; 23.6 percent of proceeds from the sale of video programming services, and 37.1 percent of proceeds collected from the sale of direct-to-home satellite services.[77]

---

73. G.S. 7A-304(a)(5).

74. G.S. 161-50.2.

75. *See* G.S. 161-11.1 (portion of marriage license fees to be remitted to N.C. Department of Health and Human Services for deposit in Children's Trust Fund), -11.2 (portion of marriage license fees to be forwarded to N.C. Department of Administration for deposit in Domestic Violence Center Fund), -11.3 (portion of fees shall be expended for computer imaging and technology needs for preservation of public records), -11.5 (portion of fees collected shall be remitted to State Treasurer for deposit in Floodplain Mapping Fund, General Fund, or Archives and Records Management Fund of Department of Natural and Cultural Resources).

76. G.S. 105-164.4.

77. G.S. 105-164.44I, -164.44F(a)(1).

The video programming services tax revenue is intended to help local governments support the operation of "qualifying PEG channels." A qualifying PEG channel is a public, educational, or governmental access channel that operates for at least ninety days during a fiscal year and that delivers at least eight hours of scheduled programming a day, with at least six hours and forty-five minutes of the content being non-character-generated programming. Additionally, the programming content may not repeat more than 15 percent of any other PEG channel provided to the same county or municipality.[78]

Distribution Process

Counties and municipalities that operate a qualifying PEG channel are entitled to the first distribution of PEG channel support funds. To receive a distribution, units operating PEG channels must certify by July 15 each year how many PEG channels the unit operates (three is the maximum). The certification is used to determine the amount of each unit's distribution. A unit receiving a share of PEG channel support funds is required to distribute the moneys equally among its qualifying PEG channels.[79]

After the first distribution of PEG channel support funds is made, any remaining net proceeds are distributed to all counties and municipalities based on a unit's "proportionate share."[80] A unit's proportionate share is the ratio of its "base amount" compared to the "base amount" for all other counties and municipalities. For counties and/or municipalities that did not impose a cable franchise tax under either G.S. 153A-154 or 160A-214 before July 1, 2006, the "base amount" is two dollars ($2.00) times the most recent annual population estimate for the jurisdiction. For units that did impose a cable franchise tax before July 1, 2006, the "base amount" is the amount of cable franchise tax and subscriber fee revenue imposed during the first six months of the 2006–07 fiscal year.[81] A unit's proportionate share is adjusted annually to account for its growth or decline in population in the preceding fiscal year.[82]

Use of Proceeds

There are certain restrictions as to how a county or municipality may expend the video programming service tax revenue. Local governments that imposed subscriber fees between July 1, 2006, and December 31, 2006, must use a portion of the funds to support the operation of PEG channels. The amount of funds that must be used for this purpose is the proportionate share of funds that were used for this purpose in the fiscal year 2006–07, which was equal to two times the amount of subscriber fee revenue the county or municipality certified between July 1, 2006, and December 31, 2006.[83] A county or municipality that used part of its franchise tax revenue in fiscal year 2005–06 to support one or more PEG channels, or a publicly owned television station, must expend remaining tax proceeds to continue the same level of support for PEG channels and public stations. Once these requirements are satisfied, a county or municipality may expend the remaining revenue to fund any general government service or activity.[84]

---

78. G.S. 105-164.44J.
79. G.S. 105-164.44J(b).
80. G.S. 105-164.44I(c).
81. *Id.*
82. G.S. 105-164.44I(d).
83. G.S. 105-164.44I(e).
84. *Id.*

Malt Beverage and Wine Taxes (for Counties and Municipalities That Lawfully Sell Alcohol)

Article 2C of G.S. Chapter 105 imposes an excise tax on the sale of malt beverages (i.e., beer), wine, and liquor. The NCDOR distributes annually the following percentages of the net amount of excise taxes collected on the sale of malt beverages and wine during the preceding twelve-month period, ending March 31, to the counties and municipalities in which the retail sale of the beverage(s) is authorized:

1. 20.47 percent of the excise tax on malt beverages,
2. 49.44 percent of the excise tax on unfortified wine, and
3. 18 percent of the excise tax on fortified wine.

The revenue shall be distributed to cities and counties within sixty days after March 31 of each year. The distribution is determined based on population. A county or municipality will only receive a distribution when beer and wine may legally be sold within the jurisdiction. If it is lawful to sell only one type of beverage (beer or wine), the unit may only share in the tax revenue for that beverage. The malt beverage and wine tax proceeds may be expended to support any public purpose or activity (G.S. 105-113.82).

Solid Waste Disposal Tax (for Counties and Municipalities)

Article 5 of G.S. Chapter 105 imposes a $2-per-ton excise tax on the disposal of municipal solid waste and construction and demolition debris in any landfill permitted under the state's solid waste management program and on the transfer of municipal solid waste and construction and demolition debris to a transfer station permitted under the state's solid waste management program for disposal outside the state.[85] The state shares 37.5 percent of the tax proceeds with eligible counties and municipalities on a per capita basis—only units that provide, or contract and pay for, solid waste management programs or services may receive a distribution.[86] The solid waste disposal tax revenue must be expended solely to support solid waste management programs and services.

911 Service Charge (for Counties and Municipalities That Operate PSAPs)

Article 15 of G.S. Chapter 143B establishes the North Carolina 911 Board, which is part of the State Department of Information Technology, and authorizes the Board to develop and oversee the statewide comprehensive system for communicating 911 call information across networks and among local public safety answering points (PSAPs). To support the 911 systems, a monthly 911 service charge is levied on (1) each active voice communication service connection that provides access to the 911 system and on (2) the retail purchase of prepaid wireless telecommunications services.[87]

The 911 Board monitors the 911 Fund (which is where the 911 service charge revenue is deposited) and makes monthly distributions from the 911 Fund to "primary PSAPs"—the entities that serve as the first point of reception for a 911 call.[88] To be eligible for a distribution from the 911 Fund, a local government must (1) operate a primary PSAP, (2) provide "enhanced 911 service," and (3) have received distributions from the 911 Board in the 2008–09 fiscal year.[89] In addition, there

---

85. G.S. 105-187.61. "Municipal solid waste" is defined as any solid waste resulting from the operation of residential, commercial, industrial, governmental, or institutional establishments that would normally be collected, processed, and disposed of through a public or private solid waste management service. *See* G.S. 130A-290(a)(18a).

86. G.S. 105-187.63.

87. G.S. 143B-1403.

88. *See* G.S. 143B-1400(23) (defining "primary PSAP"); 143B-1404(a) (creating the 911 Fund); 143B-1406 (authorizing distributions to primary PSAPs).

89. G.S. 143B-1406(a).

are several ongoing compliance requirements established in G.S. 143B-1406(f) that a PSAP, or its governing body, must satisfy to remain eligible to receive 911 Fund distributions. For example, PSAPs must be included in the local government's annual audit, and the 911 Board must receive a copy of the governing board's budget detailing the revenues and expenditures associated with the operation of the PSAP.

Distribution Process

The 911 Board must make monthly distributions to primary PSAPs from the 911 Fund. A funding formula is used to establish each PSAP's base amount.[90] Each primary PSAP is notified of its estimated distribution amount by December 31 each year and is then informed of its actual allocation by June 1. The 911 service charge revenue is intended to be used to cover eligible costs incurred by each PSAP during the fiscal year. The 911 Board must designate a percentage of any remaining funds (after base distributions are made) to be distributed to primary PSAPs on a per capita basis.[91]

Use of Proceeds

G.S. 143B-1406(d) sets forth how a primary PSAP may use the 911 Fund distributions and requires PSAPs to expend the moneys for the following limited purposes:

4. the lease, purchase, or maintenance of (a) emergency telephone equipment, including necessary computer hardware and software; (b) addressing (the assigning of a street address for enhanced 911 service), (c) telecommunicator furniture; (d) dispatch equipment located exclusively within a building where a PSAP or back-up PSAP is located (but excluding the costs of base-station transmitters, towers, microwave links, and antennae used to dispatch emergency-call information from the PSAP or back-up PSAP); or (e) emergency medical, fire, and law enforcement pre-arrival instruction software;
5. costs incurred by a municipality or county that operates a PSAP to comply with the terms of intergovernmental support agreements if certain conditions are satisfied;
6. expenditures for in-state training expenses of 911 personnel regarding the maintenance and operation of the 911 system; and
7. charges associated with the service supplier's 911 service and other supplier recurring charges.[92]

PSAPs are prohibited from expending revenue on the lease or purchase of real estate, cosmetic remodeling of emergency dispatch centers, hiring or compensating telecommunicators, or the purchase of mobile communications vehicles, ambulances, fire engines, or other emergency vehicles.[93] A PSAP may carry forward distributions for eligible expenditures for capital outlay, capital improvements, or equipment replacement. However, if the amount carried forward exceeds 20 percent of the average yearly amount distributed to a PSAP in the prior two years, the 911 Board may choose to reduce the PSAP's base distribution amount.[94]

---

90. G.S. 143B-1406(a)(3).
91. G.S. 143B-1406(b).
92. G.S. 143B-1406(d).
93. *Id.*
94. G.S. 143B-1406(c).

Real Estate Transfer Taxes (for Counties)

Article 8E of G.S. Chapter 105 imposes an excise tax on each instrument (i.e., deed) that conveys an interest in real property to another person. The tax rate is $1 on each $500 of the value of the interest conveyed (i.e., the sales price).[95] For example, if an acre of land is sold for $100,000.00, the excise tax upon the deed that conveys the property would total $200.00. The tax is paid to the register of deeds of the county in which the real estate is located. If the parcel is in two or more counties, the tax is paid to the register of deeds of the county in which the real estate has the greatest value. The register of deeds must remit the tax revenue to the county finance officer, who then credits one-half of the proceeds to the general fund and remits the other half, less a two-percent allowance for administrative expenses, to the NCDOR on a monthly basis.[96] The county may use the proceeds for any authorized public purpose.

Scrap Tire Disposal Tax (for Counties)

Article 5B of G.S. Chapter 105 imposes an excise tax on each new tire purchased for storage, use, or consumption in North Carolina or for placement on a vehicle offered for sale, lease, or rental in the state. The percentage rate of the tax is based on the bead diameter of the new tire: if it's less than 20 inches, the rate is 2 percent; if it's 20 inches or more, the rate is 1 percent.[97] Each quarter, 70 percent of the tax proceeds are distributed to counties on a per capita basis.[98] Counties must expend the moneys in accordance with earmarks established in G.S. 130A-309.54, which include costs associated with (1) the disposal of scrap tires and (2) the abatement of nuisance tire collection sites. If a county has contracted with another unit of government for the disposal of solid waste, the county is required to transfer the proceeds of the disposal tax to that unit. The transferee is subject to the same restrictions on the use of the funds as the county.[99]

White Goods Disposal Tax (for Counties)

Article 5C of G.S. Chapter 105 imposes a tax of $3.00 on the sale of new white goods.[100] "White goods" are large domestic and commercial appliances such as refrigerators, ranges, water heaters, freezers, unit air conditioners, washing machines, dishwashers, clothes dryers, and similar appliances.[101] Each quarter, 72 percent of the net tax proceeds of the white goods disposal tax are distributed to counties on a per capita basis.[102] The purposes for which the white goods tax proceeds may be expended are set forth in G.S. 130A-309.82 and include expenditures relating to the management and disposal of white goods, such as costs associated with capital improvements for infrastructure to manage discarded white goods; operating costs associated with managing discarded white goods, such as labor, transportation, and freon extraction; and the cleanup of illegal white goods disposal sites.

---

95. G.S. 105-228.30.
96. *Id.*
97. G.S. 105-187.16.
98. G.S. 105-187.19.
99. G.S. 105-187.19.
100. G.S. 105-187.21.
101. G.S. 130A-290(a)(44).
102. G.S. 105-187.24.

Electricity Taxes (for Municipalities)

As of July 1, 2014, Article 5 of G.S. Chapter 105 imposes a statewide sales tax at the combined general rate of 7.0 percent upon the sales of electricity.[103] The state collects the electricity taxes and distributes 44 percent of the net proceeds to municipalities each quarter, less the cost of administering the distribution.[104]

Each municipality's distribution is calculated according to its "franchise tax share" plus its "ad valorem share." Specifically, the first distribution of the electricity tax is based on a municipality's franchise tax share, which is equal to the total amount of franchise taxes on electricity that a municipality received in the same related quarter in fiscal year 2013–14. The remaining tax proceeds are distributed in proportion to a municipality's ad valorem share.[105] A municipality's ad valorem share is its "proportionate share" of the amount remaining for distribution after determining each municipality's quarterly franchise tax share. A municipality's "proportionate share" is the ratio of ad valorem taxes levied in that municipality compared to all property taxes levied by municipalities across the state. When calculating a municipality's ad valorem share, any ad valorem taxes that a municipality collects on behalf of a taxing district are not included.[106] The proceeds of electricity taxes may be used to support any authorized public purpose.

Piped Natural Gas Taxes (for Municipalities)

As with electricity, Article 5 of G.S. Chapter 105 imposes a statewide sales tax at the combined general rate of 7.0 percent on the sales of piped natural gas.[107] The state distributes 20 percent of the net proceeds of the piped natural gas tax to municipalities each quarter, less administrative expenses.[108]

Each municipality's distribution is calculated according to its "excise tax share" plus its "ad valorem share." A municipality's excise tax share is the amount equal to the excise taxes on natural gas that it received for the same quarter in fiscal year 2013–14.[109] A municipality's ad valorem share is its "proportionate share" of the amount remaining for distribution after determining each municipality's quarterly excise tax share. A municipality's proportionate share is the ratio of ad valorem taxes levied in that municipality to all property taxes levied by municipalities across the state.[110] When calculating a municipality's ad valorem share, any ad valorem taxes that a municipality collects on behalf of a taxing district are not included.[111] "Gas cities" that operated a piped natural gas distribution system as of July 1, 1998, receive an additional distribution of the piped gas excise tax.[112] The proceeds of the piped natural gas taxes may be spent to support any authorized public purpose.

---

103. G.S. 105-164.4(a)(9); *see also* S.L. 2013-316, § 4.1, repealing the electric utility franchise tax and adopting a sales tax to the sale of electricity, a portion of which is to be distributed to municipalities. *See* G.S. 105-164.44K (enacted by S.L. 2013-316, § 4.3.(a)).

104. G.S. 105-164.44K.

105. *Id.*

106. G.S. 105-164.44K(c).

107. *See* G.S. 105-164.4(a)(9). Prior to July 1, 2014, the State of North Carolina levied a franchise tax upon electric utilities and shared a portion of the tax proceeds with municipalities. *See* G.S. 105-116, -116.1 (both repealed by S.L. 2013-316, § 4.1.(a)). As part of the repeal, the General Assembly applied a sales tax to the sale of electricity and mandated that the North Carolina Department of Revenue (NCDOR) distribute a portion of the proceeds of the new tax to municipalities. *See* G.S. 105-164.44K (enacted by S.L. 2013-316, § 4.3.(a)).

108. G.S. 104-164.44L.

109. G.S. 105-164.44L(b).

110. G.S. 105-164.44L(c). The amount of ad valorem taxes levied by a city does not include ad valorem taxes levied on behalf of a special taxing district.

111. G.S. 105-164.44K(c).

112. G.S. 105-164.44L(b1). (The municipalities are Bessemer City, Greenville, Kings Mountain, Lexington, Monroe, Rocky Mount, Shelby, and Wilson.)

Telecommunications Tax (for Municipalities)

Article 5 of G.S. Chapter 105 imposes a statewide sales tax at the combined general rate of 7.0 percent on the gross receipts derived from providing telecommunications and ancillary services.[113] The sales tax on telecommunications services was enacted in 2001 to replace a previously levied gross receipts tax on telecommunications services.[114] The state collects this tax and, after subtracting $2,620,948, distributes 18.7 percent of proceeds to municipalities each quarter.[115]

A municipality incorporated before January 1, 2001, receives a distribution based upon its "proportionate share" of the distribution in comparison with other municipalities incorporated before that date. The proportionate share is the percentage share of the telephone gross receipts taxes that the municipality received in the same quarter when the prior sales tax was in effect.[116] A municipality incorporated on or after January 1, 2001, receives a per capita share of the amount to be distributed to all municipalities incorporated on or after this date. The amount is based on the ratio of its population to the population of all municipalities incorporated on or after this date. Municipalities that receive a distribution of the telecommunications tax may use the proceeds to support any authorized public purpose.[117]

Motor Fuels Tax (for Municipalities)

Article 36C of G.S. Chapter 105 imposes an excise tax on the sale of certain types of motor fuel, including gasoline.[118] This motor fuel tax is widely known as the "Powell Bill," and the associated revenue is called "Powell Bill funds." Historically, the statutes automatically appropriated a certain percentage of the motor fuel tax revenues directly to municipalities for maintaining, repairing, and constructing streets. However, as of 2015, there is no automatic appropriation to municipalities; instead, the General Assembly appropriates money on an annual basis to the North Carolina Department of Transportation (NCDOT) as state aid, and the NCDOT distributes the appropriated funds to municipalities twice per year—half on or before October 1 and half on or before January 1.[119]

Each municipality's distribution is determined through a per capita calculation and street-mileage comparison. Specifically, 75 percent of funds appropriated to municipalities shall be distributed among eligible municipalities based on population size, and 25 percent of funds must be distributed based on the number of miles in a municipality of public streets that do not form part of the state highway system compared to the total mileage of public streets in all eligible municipalities that are also not part of the state highway system.[120] The mayor of each municipality must provide information to the Department of Transportation that helps determine a municipality's eligibility to receive funds.

Eligible Recipients

To be eligible to receive Powell Bill funds, a municipality must maintain public streets that do not form a part of the state highway system.[121] In addition, municipalities incorporated after January 1,

113. G.S. 105-164.4(a)(4c).
114. S.L. 2001-430, § 10; G.S. 105-116.1 (repealed July 1, 2014).
115. G.S. 105-164.44F.
116. G.S. 105-164.44F(c).
117. *Id.*
118. G.S. 105-449.80.
119. G.S. 136-41.1.
120. *Id.*
121. G.S. 136-41.2B.

1945, must have (1) held the most recent election required by its charter or the general law, (2) levied a property tax for the current fiscal year of at least $0.05 per $100 valuation and collected at least 50 percent of the total property tax levy for the previous fiscal year, (3) adopted a budget ordinance in substantial compliance with general law requirements, and (4) appropriated funds for at least two of a list of eight possible services. A municipality incorporated after January 1, 2000, must appropriate funds for at least four services.[122] Only a municipality incorporated before January 1, 1945, must demonstrate that it has conducted an election of municipal officers within the preceding four-year period and that it currently imposes a property tax or provides other funds for its general operating expenses.[123]

Use of Funds

Municipalities may only expend Powell Bill funds to support projects authorized in the General Statutes. Powell Bill funds are primarily intended for the resurfacing of municipal streets but may also be used to support a variety of projects related to maintaining, repairing, constructing, reconstructing, or widening any street or public thoroughfare—bridges, drainage improvements, curbs and gutters are included. The funds may also be used for meeting a municipality's proportionate share of assessments levied for such purposes or for the planning, construction, and maintenance of bikeways, greenways, and sidewalks.[124] Additionally, municipalities may match the funds with federal funds administered by NCDOT for independent bicycle and pedestrian improvement projects, or municipalities may elect to have some or all of the allocation reprogrammed for any Transportation Improvement Project currently on their approved project list.[125]

Each municipality receiving funds shall maintain a separate record of accounts indicating in detail all receipts and expenditures of the funds. Any member of the governing board or a municipal employee will be held personally liable for any unauthorized expenditures.[126] NCDOT annually reports to the chairs of the Joint Legislative Transportation Oversight Committee how each municipality used its Powell Bill funds during the preceding fiscal year.[127] Any municipality that accumulates an amount greater than the sum of the past ten allocations (five years' worth) will have an amount equal to such excess deducted from the next allocation. Small municipalities may apply to be allowed to accumulate up to the sum of the past twenty allocations.[128]

Other Local Revenues

There are a handful of other revenue sources that some counties or municipalities take advantage of to generate additional revenue. These revenue sources primarily include Alcoholic Beverage Control (ABC) store profits, investment earnings, grants, fines and penalties, and other miscellaneous revenue sources.

---

122. G.S. 136-41.2.
123. G.S. 136-41.2A.
124. G.S. 136-41.3.
125. G.S. 136-41.4.
126. G.S. 136-41.3(b).
127. G.S. 136-41.3.
128. G.S. 136-41.3(c). A "small municipality"—which NCDOT defines as a municipality with a population of less than 5,000 people—may apply to NCDOT to accumulate up to the sum of the past twenty distributions.

Alcoholic Beverage Control (ABC) Store Profits

Article 7 of G.S. Chapter 18B authorizes counties and municipalities to establish local ABC boards to help administer ABC store revenue and oversee the operation of local stores.[129] After distributing a portion of the gross receipts for expenditures specified by statute, and retaining a portion to use as working capital, an ABC board may distribute profits on a quarterly basis to the county or municipality for which the ABC board was established.[130] A portion of a county distribution must be spent on alcohol or substance abuse research or education programs.[131] The remaining funds may be spent for any authorized public purpose, unless a local act applicable to a particular ABC board requires that all or some of the net profits be spent for a particular purpose.

Investment Earnings

Article 3 of G.S. Chapter 159 authorizes counties and municipalities to deposit at interest or invest all or part of the cash balance of any fund.[132] The finance officer shall manage investments subject to any restrictions the governing board may impose. The types of authorized investment vehicles and associated requirements are set forth in G.S. 159-30. Counties and municipalities most commonly invest in certificates of deposit in banks and savings and loan associations; obligations of the U.S. government (colloquially referred to as "treasuries"); obligations of certain agencies established by federal law (colloquially referred to as "agencies") that mature no later than eighteen months from the date of purchase; or a mutual fund for local government, such as the North Carolina Capital Management Trust or the Capital Management Groups of the Carolinas. Income earned on investments must be credited proportionately to the funds from which the investment moneys were drawn.[133]

Grants

Counties and municipalities have broad authority to make contracts for and to accept grants from the federal and state governments as well as from private sector donors.[134] Expenditures of grant funds are typically restricted to supporting the projects or programs specified in a grant agreement's award terms and conditions. Grant funding can serve as an important source of additional revenue. Local units that are awarded a federal grant, either as a direct recipient or as a subrecipient, must administer the grant in accordance with the federal Uniform Guidance, federal regulations, and any stipulations in the award terms and condition, as well as in compliance with state law and local policy. Because administering a federal award requires compliance with a host of laws and regulations, a local government will want to ensure that qualified personnel are tasked with oversight and financial administration.

Fines and Penalties

Local governments sometimes impose penalties for violations of local ordinances and delinquent payments for government services. Local governments also collect some fines and penalties that are statutorily imposed (such as penalties for a failure to list property taxes or to pay property taxes on time). The primary purpose of these penalties and fines is to punish violators and deter future

---

129. G.S. 18B-600.
130. G.S. 18B-805(e).
131. G.S. 18B-805(h).
132. G.S. 159-30.
133. G.S. 159-30(e).
134. G.S. 160A-17.1(a) (authorizing counties and municipalities "to make contracts for and to accept grants-in-aid . . . from the federal and State governments").

violations. The revenue generated from penalties and fines also may serve to compensate the local government for enforcement or collection costs. There are many instances, however, in which a local government is not allowed to retain the proceeds of locally collected fines and penalties. That is because a constitutional provision directs that the funds be distributed to the public school system.

Article IX, Section 7 of the North Carolina Constitution requires that "the clear proceeds of all penalties and forfeitures and of all fines collected in the several counties for any breach of the penal laws of the state" are to be used for maintaining the public school system. The constitutional provision only applies to penalties and fines (and forfeitures) that are imposed for breaches of the state's penal laws. North Carolina courts, however, have held that certain locally collected penalties and fines are subject to Article IX, Section 7 because they are assessed for either (1) a violation of the state's penal law or (2) a violation of a state statute or state regulatory scheme where the penalty or fine is intended to punish the violator.[135]

For example, a county or municipality may specify in an ordinance that the violation of an ordinance constitutes a criminal offense and results in the imposition of a fine.[136] The "clear proceeds" of any fine attached to the criminal violation of a county or municipal ordinance must be distributed to the public schools. As an alternative to criminalizing the violation of a county or municipal ordinance, a local government may impose a civil penalty for an ordinance violation. In such cases, a county or municipality may generally retain the proceeds of any such civil penalties.

Some statutes include a penalty section that specifies enforcement mechanisms and remedies for noncompliance. When a county or municipality collects a civil penalty (or fine) that is imposed under state statute *and* the penalty is intended to punish the violator, then the clear proceeds of the penalty must be distributed to the local school administrative unit(s) in the county in which the penalty was assessed. Examples of civil penalties that fall within this category are penalties imposed for the late listing of or failure to list property for ad valorem property taxation,[137] penalties imposed for the submission of a worthless check for payment of ad valorem property taxes,[138] penalties imposed for the failure to file or pay occupancy taxes,[139] and penalties imposed for the failure to file or pay motor vehicle and heavy equipment rental gross receipts taxes.[140]

Finally, if the violation of a local ordinance also constitutes a violation of a substantive provision of the state's penal law, the clear proceeds of any civil penalty imposed by the local government for the violation must be distributed to the public schools.[141]

---

135. For more information on this topic, see Kara Millonzi, "Locally-Collected Penalties & Fines: What Monies Belong to the Public Schools?," *Coates' Canons: NC Local Government Law* blog (Nov. 17, 2011), canons.sog.unc.edu/2011/11/locally-collected-penalties-fines-what-monies-belong-to-the-public-schools, and Kara Millonzi, "Locally-Collected Fines & Penalties: Calculating and Distributing Clear Proceeds," *Coates' Canons: NC Local Government Law* blog (Dec. 8, 2011), canons.sog.unc.edu/2011/12/locally-collected-fines-penalties-calculating-and-distributing-clear-proceeds.

136. Effective December 1, 2021, a violation of a county or municipal ordinance is a criminal offense under North Carolina law only if the county or municipality so specifies in the ordinance. *See* G.S. 153A-123(b); 160A-175(b) (enacted by S.L. 2021-138).

137. G.S. 105-312.

138. G.S. 105-357.

139. G.S. 153A-155; 160A-215; 105-236.

140. G.S. 153A-156; 153A-156.1; 160A-215.1; 160A-215.2; 105-236.

141. The General Assembly also may direct local governments to distribute certain revenues to local school administrative units that are not covered by Art. IX, § 7.

Minor Revenue Sources

Local governments receive revenue from numerous minor revenue sources. Minor sources of revenue include payments from other local governments for joint or contractual programs; funds from the management of property, such as the leasing of government-owned building space or land or the sale of surplus equipment; refunds on the state sales taxes that a local government paid; and donations of money or property from individuals or entities to fund one or more services or activities.

Chapter 18

An Introduction to Revenue Forecasting

Whitney B. Afonso

Whitney B. Afonso is a School of Government faculty member whose research focuses on state and local public finance with an emphasis on local sales taxes. Her work has appeared in such publications as the *National Tax Journal*, *Public Budgeting & Finance*, *Public Finance Review*, *Public Administration Review*, and the *Journal of Public Policy*. Whitney won the Burkhead Award for best manuscript published in *Public Budgeting & Finance* in 2015. She also has served on the executive committee of the Association for Budgeting and Financial Management since 2018. Additionally, she is an Academic Fellow at the UNC Tax Center at the Kenan Institute of Private Enterprise.

Introduction

Revenue forecasting is the process of estimating future collections of individual or multiple taxes or fees. As described in the local government finance literature:

> Forecasting attempts to identify the relationship between the factors that drive revenues (tax rates, building permits issued, retail sales) and the revenues government collects (property taxes, user fees, sales taxes) . . . . Revenue forecasts can apply to aggregate total revenue or to single revenue sources such as sales tax revenues or property tax revenues. There is no single method for projecting revenues. Rather, different methods tend to work better depending on the type of revenue. Similarly, there is no standard time-frame over which to attempt a forecast.[1]

1. Thomas A. Garrett and John C. Leatherman, "An Introduction to State and Local Public Finance," *The Web Book of Regional Science* (Morgantown: Regional Research Institute, West Virginia University, 2000), 40, researchrepository.wvu.edu/cgi/viewcontent.cgi?article=1021&context=rri-web-book.

Forecasting revenues is a critical part of quality financial management in both the short and long term. Budgets are built around forecasted revenues, and their reliability can dramatically alter the direction and scope of government services. In fact, it has been said that "without exception, revenue forecasting is the most important task in budget preparation."[2] Although revenue forecasting is critical, no clear, universal rules or guidelines have been established for the process. There is no best forecast method to follow; indeed, each type of forecast method has both merits and weaknesses.

This chapter explains why revenue forecasting is important for local governments and provides information about how to develop an administrative process for forecasting revenues. The different methods used for forecasting—from expert judgment to methods employing advanced statistics—are discussed. Consideration is then given to choosing the *right* method by highlighting issues of concern as well as best practices.

Reasons for Revenue Forecasting

Revenue forecasting is not only considered a best practice, but for local governments in North Carolina, it is required by law. The Local Government Budget and Fiscal Control Act (LGBFCA) provides that "[e]ach local government and public authority shall operate under an annual balanced budget ordinance. . . . A budget ordinance is balanced when the sum of estimated net revenues and appropriated fund balances is equal to appropriations."[3] The estimated net revenues are the revenue forecasts. The law does not dictate how local governments must estimate those revenues, but it clearly requires them to do so. The law also requires that "[e]stimated revenues shall include only those revenues reasonably expected to be realized in the budget year . . ."[4] This suggests that the estimates or forecasts must be reasonable and reliable and should be justifiable.

Beyond legal mandates, there are at least two universally recognized reasons for local governments to perform revenue forecasting. In addition, there are three types of forecasting. The two reasons to engage in revenue forecasting are (1) it improves financial management by reducing uncertainty, and (2) it helps with strategic planning.

Improved Financial Management

The National Advisory Council on State and Local Budgeting provides recommended practices for financial management and a series of guiding principles and corresponding elements.[5] One principle is that a local government should develop a budget consistent with approaches to achieve goals. An element of this principle is development and evaluation of financial options. A recommended practice associated with this element of the broader principle is the preparation of revenue projections.

By estimating future collections of individual or multiple tax instruments or fees, revenue forecasting reduces uncertainty about the future levels of revenue that a local government can expect. Revenue forecasting is also important to bond rating agencies, which look at short- and long-term plans, assumptions, and reserves.

---

2. Robert L. Bland, *A Budgeting Guide for Local Government* (Washington, D.C.: International City/County Management Association, 2007), 35.

3. Chapter 159, Section 8(a) of the North Carolina General Statutes (hereinafter G.S.).

4. G.S. 159-13(b)(7).

5. National Advisory Council on State and Local Budgeting, *Recommended Budget Practices: A Framework for Improved State and Local Government Budgeting* (Chicago: Government Finance Officers Association, 1999), www.gfoa.org/materials/nacslb.

Strategic Thinking

Within a broader framework of financial forecasting, revenue forecasting allows a local government to consider its long-term fiscal health and ability to balance its budget by projecting long-term fiscal outcomes. It also encourages strategic thinking. Creating a financial forecast provides hypotheticals that can be evaluated based on current policies and assumptions. This is a key aspect of forecasting: forecasts provide a set of likely outcomes and costs for different programs to help decision makers better plan for their long-term goals.

Types of Revenue Forecasts

There are three primary types of revenue forecasts: short term, medium term, and long term. Each type serves a different purpose for both managers and elected officials.

Short-term forecasts estimate revenues for the near future, or less than one year. They are most commonly used by managers to make informed operational choices, such as in-year cash flow.[6] They are used more frequently for forecasting expenditures, use, or attendance than for forecasting revenue. One exception is when short-term forecasts are used to update existing forecasts as the year proceeds.

Medium-term forecasts estimate future revenues for a period of one to three years. They are used in developing budgets and programs. Medium-term forecasts provide important budget constraints and decisions and inform more strategic organizational decisions.[7] They balance ongoing trends while incorporating the effects of economic cycles and other short-term considerations. Medium-term forecasts are the focus of this chapter.

Long-term forecasts estimate revenue over a period of longer than three years, most frequently five years. Long-term forecasts are a critical component of long-term strategic planning and can encourage local governments to consider and assess their current path, where it will likely lead in terms of long-term fiscal health, and how changes implemented now may affect that trajectory.

Recommended Process for Revenue Forecasting

There are many ways in which a local government can structure its process for revenue forecasting. Some of these choices depend on capacity, diversity of the revenue portfolio, and the stability of the local economy. There are four basic steps, all consistent with North Carolina law, for creating and implementing a transparent and easily replicated (internally and externally) forecasting process:

1. Create a revenue manual.
2. Compile estimates for major nondepartmental revenue sources.
3. Compile estimates from revenue-generating entities within the local government.
4. Update all estimates.[8]

Each of these steps is discussed in detail below.

---

6. *Cash flow* refers to the money "flowing" in and out of a business, or in this case, a government—revenues and expenditures. *In-year* simply refers to the time frame, here the current fiscal year.

7. See Kenneth A. Kriz, "Long-Term Forecasting," in *Handbook of Local Government Fiscal Health*, ed. Helisse Levine, Jonathan B. Justice, and Eric A. Scorsone (Burlington, Mass.: Jones and Bartlett, 2013), 130.

8. Adapted from Bland, *A Budgeting Guide for Local Government*.

Step 1: Create a Revenue Manual

The first step is to create a revenue manual, which is a complete list of all revenue sources.[9] The list will often include the following information about each revenue source: the statute authorizing the revenue source and any applicable limitations; the current rate, previous rates, and collection rates; the forecast method; what elements in the local economy affect the revenue generated (or the tax base); and the groups that pay the tax or fee. It is also critical to identify who collects the revenue. For example, is it collected by the local government, a public utility, or the state? Ultimately, a revenue manual should contain information on all revenue sources and provide any data that will be helpful in understanding trends (including fluctuations) in revenue generation.

Many local governments perform individual forecasts only for *major* revenue sources and use an additional combined forecast for all other *minor* revenue sources. Even if a local government creates a unique forecast for only three or four revenue sources, it is considered a best practice to create a revenue manual that includes all of the sources from which the local government collects revenue.

Step 2: Estimate Major Revenue Sources

Before beginning work on a proposed budget, the budget office should create and compile estimates of major revenue sources that are not collected directly by departments.[10] The Local Government Budget and Fiscal Control Act (LGBFCA) allows local governments quite a bit of discretion in the ways in which they present budgets and estimate revenues, but it does state that the budget ordinance "shall make appropriations by department, function, or project and show revenues by major source."[11] Local governments should present forecasts of major revenue sources by department or function separately as a best practice and for legal compliance. These estimates or forecasts should constantly be updated as new information surfaces.[12]

It is important to forecast revenue sources separately because they usually have different tax bases and are affected differently by changes in the economy. Two good examples of this principle are the major revenue sources on which North Carolina local governments rely: sales taxes and property taxes. Sales taxes are often estimated based on recent history but also are weighted by recent trends and anticipated fluctuations to the economic base. They are more reactive to these shifts than are property taxes. Also, sales tax revenue grows more quickly with the economy and decreases more quickly than property tax revenue. Therefore, it is unreasonable to expect that sales and property taxes will change at the same rate for forecasting purposes.[13] In fact, a forecaster will likely choose different forecasting methods for each of these revenue sources.

Step 3: Departmental Revenue Forecasts

The third step is for the budget office to request estimates of projected revenues from revenue-generating departments.[14] Examples of such departments include utilities, libraries, and recreation.

---

9. This step is recommended as a best practice by the Government Finance Officers Association (GFOA) in *Recommended Budget Practices*, 49, www.gfoa.org/materials/nacslb.

10. Step 2 and Step 3 happen in parallel but involve different actors and are discussed here separately. The distinction between the two steps is how the revenue is generated and who forecasts it. In Step 2, the revenue forecast is done by the budget office, whereas in Step 3, which is concerned with revenue generated by a department, the forecast is done by the collecting department.

11. G.S. 159-13(a)(4).

12. Bland, *A Budgeting Guide for Local Government*. This type of new information includes relevant economic and political factors as well as current revenue. It is possible that the new information will reinforce or alter the forecast.

13. John L. Mikesell, "Consumption and Income Taxes," chap. 9 in *Management Policies in Local Government Finance*, ed. John R. Bartle, W. Bartley Hildreth, and Justin Marlowe (Washington, D.C.: International City/County Management Association, 2013).

14. Bland, *A Budgeting Guide for Local Government*.

In addition, a budget office may ask the various departments to offer estimates under different scenarios. For example, it may be helpful to have the utilities department provide several estimates based on different levels of expected rainfall. The different examples help elected officials consider options, likely outcomes, and the sensitivity of these estimates to various assumptions.

This process is considered a best practice, but it is also required in North Carolina. The LGBFCA dictates that "before April 30 of each fiscal year (or an earlier date fixed by the budget officer), each department head shall transmit to the budget officer the budget requests and revenue estimates for his department for the budget year. . . . The revenue estimate shall be an estimate of all revenues to be realized by department operations during the budget year."[15]

It is important to keep in mind that Steps 2 and 3 are broadly made up of many substeps.

Step 4: Update Estimates

The quality of the forecasts will improve as more (and more recent) data are collected, so it is critical to update forecasts both before and after the budget is adopted. This includes monitoring actual revenues and comparing those numbers with projections. There are many potential sources of information and data that can aide in this process, including changes in laws and rates, changes to the tax base, changes to the underlying growth factors that drove the forecasts, and actual collection numbers.

This step is especially critical for taxes or fees that generate revenues throughout the year, such as the sales tax, and less critical for taxes or fees that are collected at one time within a specific period, such as the property tax. Actual collections, especially those of a periodic nature, need to be closely monitored and checked against the forecasts. Comparing actual collections to forecasted collections can give budget officers early warning if collections appear to be falling short of budget expectations.[16] This early warning provides time for midyear reductions, if necessary.

A North Carolina local government may amend its budget ordinance any time after the ordinance is adopted.[17] The LGBFCA provides that "[e]xcept as otherwise restricted by law, the governing board may amend the budget ordinance at any time after the ordinance's adoption in any manner, so long as the ordinance, as amended, continues to satisfy the requirements of Sections 159-8 and 159-13 of the North Carolina General Statutes."[18] Although there are more legal restrictions surrounding amendments to the property tax forecasts, the LGBFCA provides for unanticipated events: "If after July 1 the local government receives revenues that are substantially more or less than the amount anticipated, the governing body may, before January 1 following adoption of the budget, amend the budget ordinance to reduce or increase the property tax levy to account for the unanticipated increase or reduction in revenues."[19] Thus, the LGBFCA encourages local governments to carefully monitor their forecasts for accuracy and allows them to make updates throughout the fiscal year.

---

15. G.S. 159-10. This is another reason that revenue manuals are useful. This information should be housed there, adding to the manual's administrative value.

16. Mikesell, "Consumption and Income Taxes."

17. The only exception involves certain aspects of the property tax. "However, except as otherwise provided in this section, no amendment may increase or reduce a property tax levy or in any manner alter a property taxpayer's liability, unless the board is ordered to do so by a court of competent jurisdiction, or by a State agency having the power to compel the levy of taxes by the board." G.S. 159-15.

18. *Id.*

19. *Id.*

Forecasting Methods

There are *many* ways to forecast revenues. This chapter discusses the most common methods used by local governments, but it is by no means an exhaustive list:

> [Forecasting methods] range from relatively informal qualitative techniques to highly sophisticated quantitative techniques. In revenue forecasting, more sophisticated does not necessarily mean more accurate. In fact, an experienced finance officer can often "guess" what is likely to happen with a great deal of accuracy.[20]

The following sections provide an introduction to the concepts and explain why certain methods may be preferable.

In determining what method of forecasting is best for a particular local government, there are two broad categories to choose from: qualitative and quantitative. Qualitative methods rely on expert judgment and do not rely heavily on data. Such methods often do not clearly describe how the final forecasted numbers were estimated and what underlying assumptions drove them. Quantitative methods, in contrast, rely heavily on quantifiable data. Ideally, the assumptions that are used to model and categorize the relationships between variables and historical values are clearly identified. Due to their technical nature, estimates using quantitative methods often include information about their level of certainty and reliability.

Qualitative Methods

Qualitative forecasting relies on the expertise of an individual or a group for forecasting revenue. This may mean that the local government has an internal expert whose judgment is trusted. Often these are budget directors or employees within the agency administering the revenue source (tax or fee). It is also common for the local government to solicit external expertise from academics, economists, business professionals in the community, or other types of consultants. There are two primary types of qualitative forecasting: judgmental and consensus.

Judgmental Forecasting

Judgmental forecasting is the most common form of forecasting used by local governments. Under this method, a single individual estimates likely future conditions. This approach can lead to very good results, especially when the forecaster has experience and the forecaster's expertise, historical trends, the state of the economy, and other factors likely to affect the tax base are considered. According to Garrett and Leatherman, "Judgmental approaches tend to work best when background conditions are changing rapidly. When economic, political or administrative conditions are in flux, quantitative methods may not capture important information about factors that are likely to alter historical patterns."[21]

Consensus Forecasting

Consensus forecasting relies on a panel of experts who provide their input either in a roundtable format or through a survey. Ideally, input should be solicited from experts who understand which factors are important, how those factors have been changing, and how they are likely to change in the future. For a local government, this panel of experts may consist of people who understand the real estate market, economists who study both state and local changes to the relevant sectors

---

20. Garrett and Leatherman, "Introduction to State and Local Public Finance," 41.
21. *Id.*

of the economy, and officials from local financial institutions.[22] One study found that a survey of experts produced a more accurate long-term forecast than did advanced quantitative methods.[23]

Strengths of Qualitative Forecasting

Qualitative forecasting is attractive to local governments and may be the best method to use for several reasons. First, qualitative forecasts are inexpensive and easy to administer. Second, the actual forecasted revenue numbers are easier to understand than data derived from some quantitative methods, which are often complex and so mathematical that they may be intimidating. (This should not be taken to imply, however, that expert judgments may not be guided by numbers and quantitative models.) Third, qualitative forecasting may be a local government's best choice when there is very little data to input into quantitative models.

Weaknesses of Qualitative Forecasting

While there are many benefits to qualitative forecasting, there are also shortcomings. The final forecasted revenue amount is easy to understand, but it may be very unclear where that revenue projection came from and what considerations and assumptions led the expert to that total. This may limit the unit's ability to analyze the sensitivity and reliability of these forecasts. Additional weaknesses include

1. the presence of anchoring events that might cause a current event to unduly shape perceptions of what the future will bring;[24]
2. too much emphasis given to the information that is available to the expert;[25]
3. bad assumptions about the causal mechanisms between certain indicators and fiscal outcomes (what is causing or influencing a particular effect);
4. changing methods or strategies over time producing incomparable and inconsistent results (this is especially problematic when the assumptions and tactics are not laid out or well documented);
5. experts allowing their own worldviews to cloud their judgment or, worse, lead them to ignore conflicting data and information;
6. experts letting the outcomes they prefer guide their assumptions and lead them to inaccurately weigh certain numbers and factors;
7. local governments letting "group think" guide choices instead of independently assessing and evaluating the assumptions; and
8. elected officials allowing political pressures to shape assumptions and estimates.[26]

Despite the potential weaknesses of qualitative forecasting, however, there is consensus that expert judgment should be incorporated into quantitative forecasts as well.

---

22. Garrett and Leatherman, "Introduction to State and Local Public Finance."

23. Reid Dorsey-Palmateer and Gary Smith, "Shrunken Interest Rate Forecasts Are Better Forecasts," *Applied Financial Economics* 17, no. 6 (2007): 425–30.

24. An anchoring event can be many things. Most frequently, it is either something that has happened recently, so that the expectations are built off of it (for example, a stock price is falling, so you expect it to continue to fall), or an event that was dramatic/vivid, that left a strong impression, and that set expectations moving forward.

25. All pertinent or desired information is not always available. It is a risk to make forecasts based exclusively on what is available and exclude any missing data as a factor. For example, imagine that the forecaster had only previous property tax revenue available to make forecasts, even though the municipal government had recently annexed a neighborhood for which it did not yet have property tax values. If the forecast were based exclusively on previous revenues, the estimate would be much lower than an estimate based on updated information.

26. These eight additional weaknesses are laid out in S.A. Guajardo and R.A. Miranda, *An Elected Official's Guide to Revenue Forecasting* (Chicago: Government Finance Officers Association of the United States and Canada, 2000).

Quantitative Methods

There are many quantitative forecasting methods, varying from simple equations and formulas to sophisticated causal models that require technical software and statistical knowledge in addition to high-quality data. Several of these methods are discussed below.

Formula-Based Projections

Formula-based projections are simply mathematical formulas established for estimating future revenues. Once the formulas are created, the forecaster simply plugs in the various values required. If a formula-based projection is used, any additional information about its accuracy, assumptions, and reliability should be included in the revenue manual. The most common formula-based projection for local governments is for property tax forecasts.

Strengths and Weaknesses of Formula-Based Projections

This method works best when the jurisdiction has a great deal of control over the revenue source[27] and it is a stable source, such as property taxes. It is less useful for revenues that fluctuate with the economy, such as sales taxes. Formula-based projections are very transparent and the assumptions are clearly laid out, which makes them easy to understand.

This method's weaknesses include not reflecting changes in assessments, such as when new properties are added or property defaults occur. Fundamentally, formula-based projections are good for property taxes at the local level but not for more dynamic revenues with harder to characterize (and less stable) tax bases.

Trend Analysis

Trend analysis, also referred to as time-series analysis, encompasses a great many methods of forecasting. There are two basic trend analysis models: moving averages and univariate regression.

The moving averages model involves many methods of forecasting. One method is simply to project that revenue will increase or decrease by the average amount it has changed over the past five years, giving no additional weight to recent years. Another method is to forecast the revenue as the average of those years. These methods are often based on the assumption that the revenue source is too volatile for a forecaster reasonably to expect a trend to continue upward or downward.[28]

Univariate regression is a simple way to forecast revenues using a statistical model. *Univariate* simply means that only one independent (or control) variable is used to predict the dependent variable. If modeling property taxes, the independent variable would be year, and the dependent variable would be revenue collections. Regression software captures the relationship between the progression of time and revenue collections. Univariate regression analysis can be performed in many statistical packages, including Microsoft Excel.

Using actual property tax collections, Figure 18.1 presents one year of property tax forecasts using the methods above and the actual collections. In the case of the property tax, the formula-based allocation was much more accurate than moving averages or univariate regression.

27. This method also works best when the jurisdiction controls and has detailed information on the tax base. For property taxes, the local government quantifies the property tax base and sets it via assessments.

28. There are several types of moving averages, which are explained in more detail in Kara A. Millonzi, ed., *Introduction to Local Government Financing*, 2nd ed. (UNC School of Government, 2014), 189–92.

Figure 18.1 Revenue Forecasting Methods

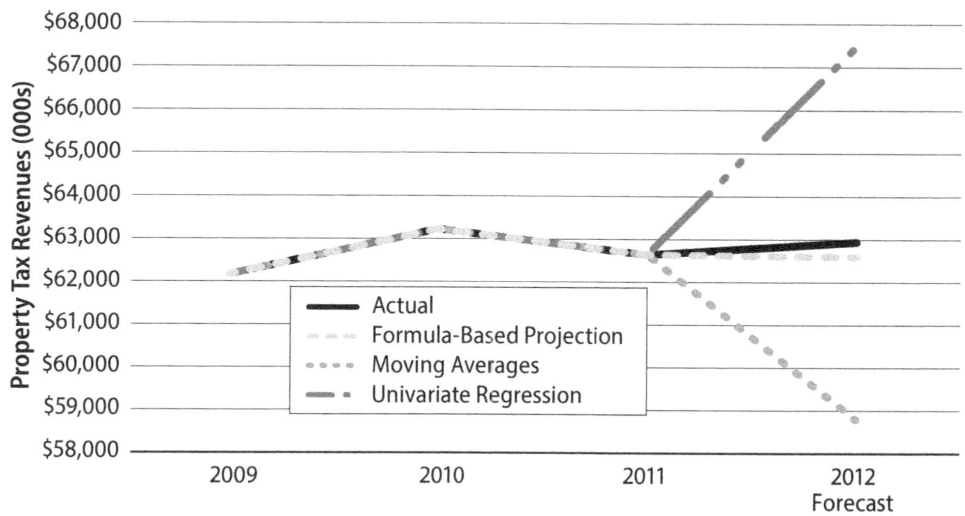

Strengths and Weaknesses of Trend Analysis

Research suggests that trend analysis is most effective when used in combination with expert judgment.[29] Trend analysis is fundamentally based on the idea that the past can be used as a good predictor of the future. However, if a community has experienced large economic shocks or changes, this will not hold true. Not being able to anticipate coming changes or incorporate known changes into the model results in forecasts that lag behind changes to the economy. Nonetheless, trend analysis is largely accurate for more stable revenue sources. It also requires modest data and is relatively straightforward to implement. For that reason, it is heavily used by smaller local governments.[30]

Causal Modeling

Causal modeling, also referred to as econometric modeling or multiple (multivariate) regression, models the relationship between the revenue source and the economic variables that drive the tax base. In other words, this approach looks for the causes behind the amount of revenues collected and creates a model of the relationship.[31] Causal modeling recognizes that demographic and economic changes to a community, such as changes in population, median income, inflation, and industry, will affect tax revenues. It allows the forecaster to take data on an individual local government (and its community) and determine how tax revenue is expected to change when a component of the model changes and how that change is expected to affect a revenue source. Causal modeling becomes more valuable as the size and/or complications of the government, its respective economy, and its revenue portfolio grow.[32]

29. Gloria A. Grizzle and William Earle Klay, "Forecasting State Sales Tax Revenues: Comparing the Accuracy of Different Methods," *State and Local Government Review* 26, no. 3 (1994): 142–52.

30. Trend analysis is also often used by larger local governments, especially for their more minor revenue sources.

31. Mikesell, "Consumption and Income Taxes," 210.

32. Bland, *A Budgeting Guide for Local Government*.

Strengths and Weaknesses of Causal Modeling

Causal models are used less frequently at the local level and can be very complex and challenging to implement. They are also very sensitive to specification and assumptions about the economy, so the forecaster must take particular care in identifying the independent variables to be included.

Forecasters undertake causal modeling because it allows taxes, which are more sensitive to the changing economic environment, to be forecasted based on those changes. This means that causal modeling is more likely to capture shocks and trends. Causal modeling makes it less likely that revenue forecasts will lag behind changes to the tax base in the way they do with trend analysis.

Causal modeling, however, is very difficult to do. Most local governments that use this methodology rely on economists from either a local university or a consulting firm. In addition, data is often incomplete, and "the absence of data on economic and structural variables at the city level" is very restricting.[33] Many of the key variables that are needed, such as personal income and population, are not available annually and potentially are not even collected for a unit of government (some data are collected just for counties and some just for large cities or even Metropolitan Statistical Areas). This makes causal modeling difficult if not impossible to accomplish.

Overall Assessment of Quantitative Methods

In sum, quantitative forecasting methods may more accurately model future revenues than do qualitative methods. When using data, though, it is always important to follow the acronym GIGO: garbage in, garbage out. Reliable data is critical. In addition, evidence suggests that simple, straightforward models perform as well as complicated models. In both the short and medium term, trend analysis models tend to perform better than causal models. Therefore, local governments should not necessarily embark on heroic efforts to perform sophisticated causal models if it is not within their means to do so and if trend analyses have proven reliable for them.

Considerations in Choosing the *Right* Method

There are many factors to consider in determining what method of forecasting is best. This section discusses some of the more universal factors, recognizing, however, that a local government can modify these perspectives in light of its own needs and capacity. Especially with regard to quantitative methods, the capacity of the forecasting staff is a crucial consideration. There is also always the question of the budget and whether or not a local government can afford to hire experts to assist with or conduct qualitative or quantitative analysis. Local governments typically rely heavily on expert judgment (internal and external) and the sophisticated modeling the experts provide.

The forecast method should also be based on the types of revenue sources (taxes, fees, etc.) that are in use within the local government. Typically, a revenue forecast is created for every major revenue source. For the smaller revenue sources, a local government may just look at historical numbers and establish an estimated total for each source. Nonetheless, the same forecast method is most likely not the best choice for all of the revenues to be forecasted.

Another important consideration is looking for trends, patterns, and rates of change and determining how stable each revenue source is; that is, how closely the source follows the trend.[34] For example, sales taxes are more unstable than property taxes, making trend analysis more problematic in light of the cyclical nature of the economy. Therefore, a formula-based forecast or a trend

33. Mikesell, "Consumption and Income Taxes," 211.

34. Guajardo and Miranda, *An Elected Official's Guide to Revenue Forecasting.*

analysis may be best suited for property taxes, and a causal model may be best suited for sales taxes revenue forecasts.

Yet another consideration is economic, political, and social influences on the revenue source. It is important to look beyond the data. Is the revenue instrument, or more accurately its base, likely to be affected by a recession? Is citizen demand for this service growing? Considering these types of relationships and assumptions can help a local government choose the appropriate forecasting method.[35]

Best Practices in Forecasting Revenues

There are many best practices when it comes to forecasting. This section focuses on the most successful practices. This is by no means an exhaustive list, however, and not every method is necessarily right for every local government.

First, local governments should create revenue manuals as described in Step 1 of the recommended process for revenue forecasting, discussed above. All local governments should be able to take this action, which is of universal benefit. If a local government does not have a revenue manual in place, the process of creating one may be a multi-year undertaking. The place to start is at the top, with major revenue sources.

Second, forecasters should consider creating hybrid or conditional models that present alternative forecasts of possible revenues, test assumptions in the model, and provide elected officials options if they are considering changing elements of local government policy. A hybrid model that is transparent, with its assumptions clearly laid out, enables forecasters to adjust their forecasts for other scenarios, such as changes in tax rates and the tax base.[36] For example, in a formula-based allocation, adjusting the tax rate is a straightforward process.[37] In fact, one of the common uses of forecasting, beyond establishing one-year revenue projections for the budget, is guiding tax rate adjustments. This is helpful in trying to establish consistent tax policies so that tax rates do not have to be adjusted every year.[38] It is important to remember, however, that forecasts are projections, not predictions. While a hybrid model may be useful for testing assumptions and providing options, and, in some cases, for advising long-run planning, it is not appropriate or acceptable for annual budget forecasts. Revenue numbers must be decided on and used to balance the budget.

Third, local governments should consider factors beyond the revenue forecasts, such as the local government's fund balance. It is clear that revenue projections or forecasts are not going to be completely accurate, and while it is considered best to err slightly on the conservative side of forecasting, it should nonetheless be apparent that this is one of the many reasons for maintaining a fund balance—not just for downturns, but also for years when estimates are on the high end of the spectrum. This is especially important when a local government is less confident in the forecasts.

---

35. *Id.*

36. "The forecast may even be conditional, in the sense that it is prepared with alternative assumptions (high/low scenarios) for certain economic or developmental factors." Mikesell, "Consumption and Income Taxes," 209.

37. Also, if rates have changed over time, it is critical to adjust the data to reflect that. If the forecaster is engaged in causal modeling, the adjustment may be as straightforward as controlling for rate. However, if a more basic trend analysis is being used, it would be crucial to adjust the data to reflect that the rate, and not a change in the economy or the tax base, is driving the change in collections. This is why it is also advisable for the revenue forecaster to use real dollars (adjusted for inflation) in their analysis, too. It is especially important in periods when inflation is high.

38. William C. Rivenbark, "Financial Forecasting for North Carolina Local Governments," *Popular Government* 73, no. 1 (Fall 2007): 6–13.

For example, if a local government relies heavily on sales taxes and the amount of sales taxes collected has been unpredictable from year to year, the local government may choose to maintain a larger fund balance reserve.[39]

Fourth, local governments should consider creating long-term financial plans. The National Advisory Council on State and Local Budgeting encourages local governments to develop such plans by using a strategic process that gives them greater insights into revenues and expenditures and the information needed to establish policies that will lead to long-term fiscal health.[40]

Forecasting Is Not Perfect

It is important to remember that no forecast is ever completely accurate: the numbers will inevitably be wrong. The goal is to minimize how wrong they are. With that in mind, there are several points to be made about error in forecasting.[41]

The forecaster should always strive to include predicted error with the estimates and should be clear about how confident he or she is that the forecasts are reliable. It should be noted that the farther out in time the forecast extends, the larger the errors are likely to be. As well, forecasts are built on the past, which has two important implications: (1) if the future deviates from the past in a meaningful way, the forecasts will not be accurate; and (2) if key data or trends from the past are ignored, more error will be introduced into the estimates. Finally, forecasting for a period greater than three years will be more reliable if the revenues are more aggregated. While it is useful to forecast individual revenue streams for both the short and medium term, doing so is less valuable for long-term forecasting.

Because errors inevitably do occur, it is advisable to forecast conservatively, but only slightly so. It is not prudent to dramatically underestimate revenues, because budgets do have to be balanced. An unnecessarily conservative forecast could cause the board to make unnecessary cuts to services or to increase taxes unnecessarily. While estimates that are too high can create crises and require expenditure cuts during the execution phase, estimates that are too low can result in needless reductions to programs at the beginning of the fiscal year.[42]

Politics can, unfortunately, hinder the forecasting process. For example, it is often considered a best practice to be slightly conservative and to estimate revenues just below where the forecaster thinks they will be.[43] However, this makes it harder for a local government to balance the budget and may require it to make service cuts or increase taxes, so forecasters sometimes find themselves pressured to be more *optimistic*. It is important for the forecaster to resist these political pressures, however, because "in revenue forecasting, your sins find you out, and they do have a cost."[44]

39. Whitney Afonso, "Diversification toward Stability? The Effect of Local Sales Taxes on Own Source Revenue," *Journal of Public Budgeting, Accounting and Financial Management* 25, no. 4 (2013): 649–74.

40. R. Calia, S. Guajardo, and J. Metzgar, "Putting the NACSLB Recommended Budget Practices into Action: Best Practices in Budgeting," *Government Finance Review* (April 1998).

41. Adapted from Kriz, "Long-Term Forecasting," 125–58.

42. Robert D. Lee, Ronald W. Johnson, and Philip G. Joyce, *Public Budgeting Systems* (Burlington, Mass.: Jones & Bartlett, 2008).

43. "In both larger and smaller counties, the acceptable overestimation range was lower than the acceptable under-estimation range. These findings confirm the conservative behavior among government revenue forecasters in the presence of uncertainty. And, when the county revenue forecasters were asked how conservative they are in forecasting sales taxes, 90% of the counties responded that their estimation was at least somewhat conservative." D. Kong, "Local Government Revenue Forecasting: The California County Experience," *Journal of Public Budgeting, Accounting & Financial Management* 19, no. 2 (2007): 178–99.

44. Bland, *A Budgeting Guide for Local Government*, 37.

The cyclical nature of the economy is also a persistent problem in generating reliable forecasts. Historical data reveal periodic dips in growth, and revenues are cyclical and influenced by the *natural* expansions and shrinkages (recessions) of the economy.[45] As local governments reduce their reliance on property taxes and increase their reliance on user fees and sales taxes, awareness of these cycles will become even more critical. Forecasters must keep this in mind, especially in preparing long-term forecasts.

Conclusion

All local governments perform revenue forecasting. Despite that universality, however, there is a great deal of diversity in the methodologies they employ. Some local governments may simply forecast next year's revenue to equal the previous year's revenue, while others may create sophisticated causal models that attempt to capture the changing nature of the underlying tax base. These potential extremes highlight the need for transparency, both internally and externally. Revenue forecasts should provide not just a number, but also the methodology and assumptions on which a forecast is based. This information should be included in the revenue manual.

In addition, local governments need to be thoughtful when choosing which methods are best for them and should consider employing different methods for different revenue instruments. However, the benefit of having a more advanced forecasting method with *slightly* more accurate forecasts may not outweigh the additional costs of performing it.[46] These costs may be direct, such as paying outside consultants, or indirect, such as staff time and additional training. While expert and trend analyses are the most common methods for forecasting revenues and expenditures in North Carolina, it should not be surprising that there is no standard model or methodology, because each local government develops its own based on its particular needs.[47]

Although revenue forecasting may seem like a challenging undertaking, there are many excellent resources available to local governments in North Carolina.[48] The following organizations provide resources for local government officials and finance officers:

- North Carolina League of Municipalities (NCLM), www.nclm.org
- North Carolina Association of County Commissioners (NCACC), www.ncacc.org
- North Carolina Government Finance Officers Association (NCGFOA), www.ncgfoa.org
- North Carolina Local Government Budget Association (NCLGBA), www.nclgba.org
- UNC School of Government, www.sog.unc.edu

For an in-depth discussion of revenue forecasting, see Whitney B. Afonso's "Chapter 6: Revenue Forecasting" in the fifth edition of *Introduction to Local Government Finance*, edited by Connor Crews (UNC School of Government, 2023).

45. Garrett and Leatherman, "Introduction to State and Local Public Finance."

46. Kong, "Local Government Revenue Forecasting: The California County Experience."

47. Rivenbark, "Financial Forecasting for North Carolina Local Governments."

48. For example, the North Carolina Association of County Commissioners partners with the North Carolina League of Municipalities (NCLM) to prepare quarterly revenue reports and annual revenue projections. While the projections are not specific to individual counties, they can offer insight and direction. Visit NCLM at www.nclm.org/member-services/financial-operational-consulting/research-surveys/ to find annual revenue projections and quarterly revenue updates.

Chapter 19

Property Tax Policy and Administration

Christopher B. McLaughlin

Christopher B. McLaughlin is a School of Government faculty member who specializes in the legal aspects of local taxation.

A slightly different version of this chapter previously appeared in the fifth edition of *Introduction to Local Government Finance*, edited by Connor H. Crews (UNC School of Government, 2023).

Introduction

The goal of this chapter is to educate North Carolina local government officials about the basic structure and operation of our state's property tax system. It should give local officials the information they need to know what local governments must do, what they may do, and, perhaps most importantly, what they cannot do with property taxes. For more details on the topics discussed below, please see Christopher B. McLaughlin, *Fundamentals of Property Tax Collection Law in North Carolina* (UNC School of Government, 2011).

Non-Legal Considerations

This chapter focuses mainly on the legal issues surrounding property taxes. But local governments also face a number of important non-legal decisions concerning property tax policy and practice.

The most basic of these decisions is whether the local government wishes to levy a property tax. Although property taxes are optional, all 100 counties and nearly all the state's 500-plus municipalities levy this type of tax.

Taxpayers may wonder why local governments tax at all in light of the substantial federal and state taxes already affecting their incomes and activities. The simple answer to this question is that without property tax revenues, local governments would be forced to drastically cut services. Property taxes are the *single largest source* of unrestricted revenues for both counties and municipalities in North Carolina. Revenue from these taxes supports the wide variety of services provided by local governments.

The property tax is popular among local governments because it is one of the few sources of revenue under their complete control. Most other taxes are levied at rates set by state statutes or produce revenue that must be shared with the state or with other local governments. Not so for property tax rates and revenues, which are controlled entirely by local governments and subject only to a rather generous statutory maximum rate.

Property tax rates vary across the state from just a few pennies to more than $1 per $100 of property value. The legal parameters concerning the tax rate calculation are discussed in "The Property Tax Rate" section, below. But for the most part, the tax rate decision rests on a policy question beyond the scope of this chapter: What level of services should the local government provide and how should those services be funded?

Other non-legal decisions include how to organize the tax office, whether a municipality should collect its own taxes or contract with the county for such services, what types of enforced collection actions the collector will be authorized to pursue, and when countywide reappraisals of real property should occur. This chapter discusses the relevant statutory constraints and identifies best practices, but it does not attempt to suggest the correct answers to these questions. As with most issues involving local government, there is no one-size-fits-all approach to property taxes.

The Big Picture

As noted above, property taxes represent the single largest source of unrestricted revenue for both counties and municipalities. For fiscal year 2022–2023, property taxes represented 47 percent of county revenues and 23 percent of municipal revenues. Figures 19.1 and 19.2 illustrate the relative importance of property taxes as compared to other revenue sources. Note that both figures exclude debt proceeds, which must be paid back in the future using other revenue sources and therefore are not truly revenue sources.[1]

---

1. Searchable statistics are available on the N.C. Department of State Treasurer's website at www.nctreasurer.com/divisions/state-and-local-government-finance/lgc/data-and-reports.

Figure 19.1 2022–2023 County Revenues: $17.7 Billion Total

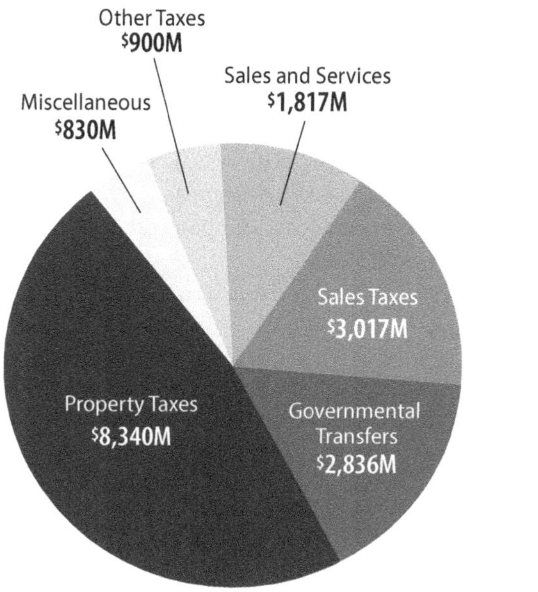

Figure 19.2 2022–2023 City Revenues: $14.6 Billion Total

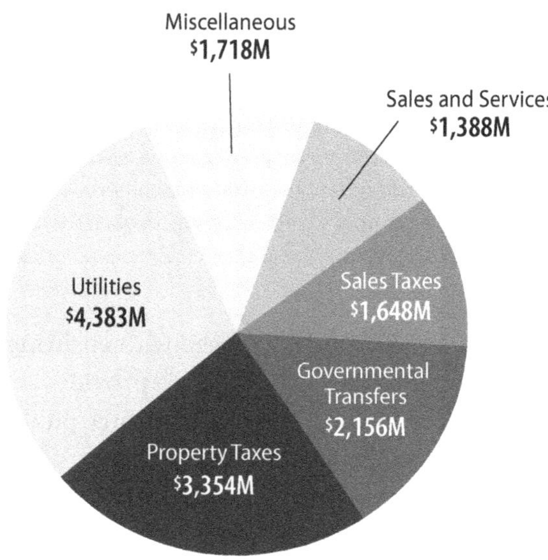

Although utility fees represent a larger percentage of municipal revenues than do property taxes, those funds are not *unrestricted* revenues because generally they must be used to cover the cost of providing those utilities. Were utility fees and charges excluded from the calculation, property taxes would represent more than one-third percent of municipal revenues.

The Governing Law and the Cast of Characters

Article V (finance), Section 2 (state and local taxation) of the North Carolina Constitution sets the basic ground rules for property taxes. Chapter 105, Subchapter II of the North Carolina General Statutes (hereinafter G.S.), commonly known as the Machinery Act, provides the details.

Actors at both the state and local levels play major roles in the property tax process. Table 19.1 identifies the principal characters at both levels of government.

As mentioned above, the property tax process is governed by statutes enacted by the *General Assembly* as part of the Machinery Act. The state *Local Government Division of the N.C. Department*

Table 19.1 Property Tax Cast of Characters

State Level	Local Level
• General Assembly	• Governing Board
• Department of Revenue, Local Government Division	• Assessor (County)
• Property Tax Commission	• Tax Collector
• Court of Appeals	• Board of Equalization and Review (County)
• Supreme Court	

Why Is It Called the "Machinery Act," and Where Can I Find It?

G.S. 105-271 and -272 state that the collection of property tax statutes in Subchapter II of Chapter 105 can be referred to as the Machinery Act because "[t]he purpose of this Subchapter is to provide the *machinery* for the listing, appraisal, and assessment of property and the levy and collection of taxes on property by counties and municipalities" (emphasis added).

The North Carolina Department of Revenue usually produces a hard copy of the Machinery Act every two years to capture the most recent changes to its many sections. However, because the Machinery Act is amended almost every legislative session and the hard copy is produced only every other year, the best source for the most up-to-date Machinery Act provisions is the searchable General Statutes page on the General Assembly's website, www.ncga.state.nc.us/gascripts/statutes/Statutes.asp.

of Revenue (NCDOR) is charged with ensuring that local governments adhere to the Machinery Act's requirements. This division also provides education, training, and guidance to local government tax officials and assesses and allocates public-service-company property to the counties so that it can be subject to local property taxes.

Note that NCDOR's Local Government Division is distinct from the Local Government Commission (LGC), which operates out of the N.C. Department of the State Treasurer. The LGC monitors the fiscal and accounting practices of the state's local governments but does not play a direct role in property tax administration.

County *boards of equalization and review*, the state *Property Tax Commission*, the state *court of appeals*, and the state *supreme court* are all involved with the resolution of appeals concerning property tax values and property tax exemptions and exclusions.

An *assessor* is responsible for listing and assessing all taxable property in a county for property taxes. In other words, he or she must determine the what, the where, the who, and the how much for all property that will be taxed for the coming fiscal year. A *tax collector* must collect the taxes levied on that property, if necessary by use of the enforced collection remedies available under the Machinery Act and other statutes. In many counties, the county commissioners have chosen to appoint a single individual as both assessor and tax collector under the title of "tax administrator."

The role of the *local government governing board* in the property tax process is summarized in Table 19.2. Table 19.3 lists the important dates in the property tax calendar. More details on all these issues are provided in subsequent sections of this chapter.

Real Property versus Personal Property

Collection remedies under the Machinery Act differ depending on whether the property being taxed is real or personal. Real property is essentially land, buildings, and things that are permanently affixed to those buildings—think of light fixtures or kitchen cabinets. Personal property is everything else: vehicles, boats, planes, business equipment, and so forth. With very few exceptions, personal property is taxable only if it is tangible. Intangible personal property—such as cash, stocks, bank deposits, patents, and franchise rights—is not taxable.

Why Cars Are Different

Cars, trucks, vans, motorcycles, and trailers with valid registrations and license plates are called "registered motor vehicles" (RMVs) by the Machinery Act. Although they are considered personal

Table 19.2 Rights and Duties of Local Government Governing Boards

Board of County Commissioners	Town/City Council
• Adopts property tax rate annually • Appoints assessor and tax collector • Reviews performance of assessor and tax collector • Accepts settlement of prior year's taxes from tax collector and charges tax collector with responsibility for current year's taxes • Decides when to conduct countywide reappraisals of real property (at least every eight years) • Appoints Board of Equalization and Review (the county commissioners may serve as this board) • Rules on taxpayer requests for refunds and releases	• Adopts property tax rate annually • Appoints tax collector or contracts with county for tax collection • Reviews performance of tax collector • Accepts settlement of prior year's taxes from tax collector and charges tax collector with responsibility for current year's taxes • Rules on taxpayer requests for refunds and releases

Table 19.3 Important Dates on the Property Tax Calendar

January 1	• Listing date (ownership, situs, value, and taxability determined) • Tax liens attach to real property
July 1	• Fiscal year begins • Deadline for adoption of new budget and tax rate
September 1	• Discounts end (if offered) • Taxes due
January 6 (following year)	• Taxes become delinquent, interest accrues, and enforced collections may begin
June 30 (following year)	• Fiscal year ends, annual collection rate is determined

property under the Machinery Act, RMVs are subject to very different tax rules than those applied to other types of personal property.

In a nutshell, the taxation of RMVs is tied to the registration and renewal process. Registration of most motor vehicles is staggered throughout the year so that different due dates and delinquency dates apply for different RMV taxpayers. Under the "Tag & Tax Together" program that debuted in 2013, owners pay property taxes on their vehicles at the time they obtain their initial registrations or renew their registrations for those vehicles with the N.C. Division of Motor Vehicles (DMV). If the owner refuses to pay the taxes, the DMV will refuse to register the motor vehicle. Under this new system, local governments no longer have any collection authority or responsibility for the property taxes they levy on registered motor vehicles. See the section titled "Registered Motor Vehicles," below, for more details on RMV taxes.

Table 19.4A County and Municipal Property Tax Rates, 2022–2023

	Lowest Rate	Highest Rate	Median Rate
Counties	.320 (Watauga)	.990 (Scotland)	.66
Municipalities	.013 (Wesley Chapel)	.920 (Enfield)	.47

Source: North Carolina Department of Revenue.

Table 19.4B County Tax Bases, 2023

Smallest	$433 Million	Tyrrell County (population 3,400)
Largest	$201 Billion	Mecklenburg County (population 1,164,000)
Median	$17 Billion	
Average	$14 Billion	

Source: North Carolina Department of State Treasurer.

The Property Tax Rate

Although local governments are not required to levy property taxes, nearly all do. The rates at which they levy those taxes vary greatly, as Table 19.4A indicates. Traditionally, the lowest rates were found in counties located along the coast and in the mountains in counties with lots of expensive vacation homes.

Property tax rates for a particular local government are generally capped at $1.50, but that cap is subject to many exceptions. For example, there is no statutory limit on the rate for property taxes used to fund schools or jails. And for uses that are subject to the statutory cap, a local government may obtain voter approval to exceed the $1.50 maximum tax rate.[2]

The $1.50 cap applies to individual taxing jurisdictions, not to individual taxpayers. A taxpayer who lives in a municipality could very well wind up paying a total property tax rate greater than $1.50 because that taxpayer's property is subject to both county and municipal taxes. As a result, a municipality need not worry about the county's property tax when setting its own rate, or vice versa.

The amount of revenue that each county can generate from its property tax depends on that county's tax base, of course. As Table 19.4B demonstrates, county tax bases vary widely. A 1¢ increase in Tyrrell County's property tax would produce an additional

How Do I Use the Tax Rate to Calculate a Tax Bill?

Tax rates are expressed as "$ of tax per $100 dollars of taxable value." For example, if a home is valued for tax purposes at $200,000 and the county tax rate is $0.25, the county property taxes on that home will be $500. First divide the taxable value by 100 ($200,000 / 100 = $2,000), then multiply the result by the tax rate ($2,000 × .25 = $500).

2. G.S. 153A-149 (counties); 160A-209 (municipalities). Note that a handful of municipalities have lower caps on property tax rates in their charters. Clemmons, for example, operates under a charter that caps its property tax rate at $0.15. N.C. Session Law 1985-437.

$43,300 in tax revenue. In Mecklenburg County, that same 1¢ property tax rate increase would generate about $20,000,000.

Tax Rate Uniformity and Tax Districts

Article V, Section 2(2) of the North Carolina Constitution requires that all property within a specific taxing jurisdiction must be subject to the same tax rate. This uniformity requirement prohibits local governments from adopting different tax rates for different property or for different areas of that jurisdiction. For example, a county could not adopt one tax rate for real property and a different tax rate for motor vehicles. Nor could a county choose to adopt one tax rate for its incorporated areas and a different tax rate for its unincorporated areas.

The only exception to the uniformity requirement is the constitutional provision that permits special tax districts. Often called service districts, these tax districts are authorized by Article V, Section 2(4) of the North Carolina Constitution to fund additional services in their geographic areas. Multiple tax districts are permitted in the same local government, so long as each tax district is created for a permissible purpose. The uniformity requirement applies to these special districts in that the additional tax rate levied in a particular district must be uniformly applied to all property sited in that district.

Counties most often use special tax districts to fund fire protection in unincorporated areas, but they can also use them to fund such services as trash collection, sewer and water systems, and beach erosion control. Municipalities can use special tax districts to fund many of those same services, but they more often create districts for downtown revitalization projects. This category is broadly defined to cover a variety of expenditures, including new parking facilities, improved lighting, additional police protection, and tourism promotion within the downtown core.

Another type of special tax district is a special supplemental school district.[3] The supplemental school district tax must be approved by voters before it can be levied and must be used only to fund the public schools in that district. Once adopted, a supplemental school tax applies to all property within that particular school district.

The taxes levied in a special tax district count toward the $1.50 cap on general property tax rates. This means that the total of regular property taxes and special district taxes levied by a local government on a particular piece of property cannot exceed $1.50 for certain uses unless the local government obtains voter approval to exceed that cap.

Use-Specific Taxes

A local government may adopt a single property tax rate to satisfy all its budgetary needs, or it may adopt multiple tax rates with the revenue from each earmarked for a specific use. For example, instead of funding police and fire protection services out of its general property tax revenue, a municipality could choose to adopt two property tax rates: one for general fund revenue and one to fund police and fire services.

There is no limit on the number of different use-specific property tax rates that may be adopted by a local government, so long as each such tax applies uniformly to all taxable property within the jurisdiction. Use-specific taxes may be adopted as part of a local government's annual budget and do not require voter approval.

---

3. G.S. Ch. 115C, Art. 36.

A key difference between use-specific property taxes and special tax district taxes is that use-specific taxes must apply to the entire jurisdiction. Special tax district taxes may be levied on portions of a jurisdiction to fund specific services in that district.

The North Carolina Supreme Court has ruled that spending decisions by local governments are not bound by use-specific property taxes.[4] A local government may change its spending for a particular use regardless of what it promised to spend on that use in its budget through a use-specific tax rate.

For example, assume that a county adopts a $0.50 general tax rate, a $0.12 tax rate for law enforcement, and a $0.02 tax rate for libraries. Based on its budgeted tax base, the $0.12 tax would raise $1,200,000 for county law enforcement and the $0.02 tax would raise $200,000 for county libraries. Despite the adoption of these use-specific taxes, the county could choose to spend more or less than these amounts on law enforcement and libraries in the coming fiscal year. Voters may not take kindly to such variations from the budget, but they are legal.

Setting the Tax Rate

Property taxes are levied on a fiscal year basis despite the fact that many of the important dates on the property tax schedule seem to be configured around the calendar year. A local government that levies property taxes must set its property tax rate(s) in its annual budget, which should be adopted by July 1, the beginning of the fiscal year.[5]

Until a budget is adopted, there can be no property tax levy. Although interim budgets are permitted, they authorize only continued spending by local governments and not the levy of taxes. A delay in the adoption of the budget can delay property tax collections and do serious harm to a local government's revenues.

The property tax rate should be based on the amount of revenue the local government needs to balance its budget after all other revenue sources are accounted for, given the expected tax base for the coming year. Obviously, this amount will be driven by important decisions regarding what services the local government can and should provide.

When balancing the budget with property taxes, a local government must be realistic about how much of its tax levy it will actually collect. While property tax collection percentages are generally very good—99 percent on average—no local government collects every penny of its property taxes.[6] For budget purposes, state law prohibits local governments from assuming a higher collection rate for the coming year than it experienced in the current year.

Changing the Tax Rate

Once the total tax rate is set in the budget, the governing board is generally prohibited from changing it. Absent an order from a judge or from the Local Government Commission, the only justification for adjusting a tax rate after adoption of the budget is when the local government

4. Long v. Comm'rs of Richmond Cnty., 76 N.C. 273, 280 (1877).

5. See the Local Government Budget and Fiscal Control Act, G.S. Chapter 159, Article 3.

6. See, e.g., the following memoranda from the N.C. Department of State Treasurer, State and Local Government Finance Division and the Local Government Commission (LGC): LGC Memo #2022-03, *Management of Cash and Taxes and Fund Balance Available—Counties—for the Fiscal Year Ended June 30, 2020* (Aug. 11, 2021), 2; LGC Memo #2022-04, *Management of Cash and Taxes and Fund Balance Available—Municipalities—for the Fiscal Year Ended June 30, 2020* (Aug. 17, 2021), 2–3.

Calculating the Tax Rate

Assume Carolina County needs to generate $50,000,000 in property tax revenue to balance its budget for the coming fiscal year. The basic property tax calculation is as follows:

(Tax Base / 100) × Tax Rate = Tax Revenue.

First, the county should get from the tax collector the estimated property tax collection percentage for the current fiscal year. This percentage will be an estimate because the current fiscal year will not have ended at the time Carolina County creates the budget for the next fiscal year.

Assume the estimated collection percentage for the current fiscal year is 97 percent. The county should divide the revenue target by this percentage to account for the fact that not every penny of the property tax levy will be collected.

$50,000,000 / .97 = $51,550,000.

The result is the adjusted revenue target for the next fiscal year. In other words, if the county wishes to produce $50,000,000 in property tax revenue next year, it must levy $51,550,000 in property taxes.

Second, the county should get from the assessor the estimated tax base for the next fiscal year. It will be an estimate because subsequent tax appeals, discoveries, and motor vehicle registrations will affect the final figure.

Assume that the estimated tax base is $10,000,000,000. The county should divide the estimated tax base by 100 to reflect the fact that the tax rate is "per $100 in value."

$10,000,000,000 / $100 = $100,000,000.

Finally, the county should divide the adjusted revenue target by the result above to determine the rate.

$51,550,000 / $100,000,000 = $0.516.

Carolina County must levy a property tax of $0.516, or 51.6¢ per $100 of value, to meet its budgetary needs for the coming fiscal year.

When budgeting, many local governments start with a tax rate target rather than a revenue target. Regardless of the approach used, the local government must account for the current year's tax collection percentage when budgeting for next year.

For example, assume that Carolina County wishes to keep its tax rate at $0.51 per $100 of value for the coming year. If next year's tax base is estimated to be $10,000,000,000, a tax rate of $0.51 would produce tax revenue of $51,000,000. However, this estimated revenue must be reduced by this year's collection percentage:

$51,000,000 × .97 = $49,470,000.

As a result, if Carolina County plans to keep its tax rate at $0.51 for the coming year, it should budget for no more than $49,470,000 in property tax revenue.

receives revenues that are substantially different from what was expected. And even then, the change must occur before January 1 following the start of the fiscal year. For example, if a governing board wished to change its 2025–2026 tax rate due to a substantial change in revenues, it would need to act before January 1, 2026.[7]

What type of events could justify a change in the total tax rate under this standard? The relevant statutes do not provide additional details, but presumably changes could occur after a misfortune such as a bankruptcy filing by a large industrial taxpayer that would prevent collection of a

7. G.S. 159-15.

substantial portion of the local government's property tax levy or the elimination of an important revenue source due to new legislation enacted by the General Assembly. Good news—such as the creation of a major new revenue source for the local government—could also justify a mid-year change in the tax rate, but such occurrences are rare.

As mentioned above, local governments may adopt multiple tax rates for different uses. These use-specific rates may be changed during a fiscal year without regard for statutory restrictions so long as the total tax rate levied by the local government does not change.

Consider again the example in which a county adopts a general tax rate of $0.50, a law enforcement tax of $0.12, and a library tax of $0.02, for a total combined rate of $0.64. The county would be free to alter any or all of its three different tax rates so long as the total combined rate still equaled $0.64.

The Revenue-Neutral Tax Rate

To help taxpayers compare tax rates before and after countywide reappraisals of real property, local governments are required to calculate and publish revenue-neutral tax rates (RNTRs) following their reappraisals.[8]

The RNTR would produce the same amount of revenue using the new tax base as was produced in the present year from the existing tax rate and tax base. In other words, if a new tax rate adopted by a governing board is higher than the RNTR, then the local government has increased its total property tax levy, and if the new rate is lower than the RNTR, the local government has decreased its total property tax levy.

In normal economic times, tax bases increase after reappraisals. When the tax base increases, the tax rate can be lowered without decreasing tax revenue. Therefore, the RNTR is normally lower than the existing tax rate. However, when market prices drop, as they have done of late in many areas of the state, a local government's tax base can decrease after a reappraisal. In these circumstances, the government board that wishes to keep revenues constant must raise the tax rate. As a result, the RNTR will be higher than the existing tax rate.

Local governments are not required to adopt the RNTR, but they must publish it as part of their annual budget process. Even if the RNTR is adopted, individual taxpayers may see their tax bills increase or decrease because their individual property appreciated or depreciated more than did the tax base in the aggregate. Much confusion surrounds the RNTR, in large part because, despite its name, it does not guarantee that taxpayers' bills will remain constant.

For example, assume that Carolina County's tax base increased by 10 percent following its 2025 reappraisal. The RNTR is calculated to be $0.50 per $100 of value, a bit lower than the county's 2024–2025 tax rate of $0.55 per $100 of value. The county commissioners decide to adopt the RNTR as the tax rate for 2025–2026 and proudly announce that they have avoided a tax increase. However, when the 2025 tax bills are mailed in August, Tommy TarHeel is furious because his new tax bill is higher than last year's tax bill.

How can this be? The likely answer is that Tommy's real property appreciated more than 10 percent, which was the average increase in value for all real property in the county. Assume that Tommy's real property tax appraisal increased from $100,000 to $150,000 as a result of the 2025 reappraisal. For 2024–2025, Tommy's tax bill was $550 ($100,000/100 × $0.55). For 2025–2026,

8. G.S. 159-11(e).

his tax bill is $750 ($150,000/100 x $0.50). The drop in the tax rate was not enough to offset the increase in Tommy's tax appraisal, meaning that Tommy's tax bill increased by $200 despite the county's adoption of the RNTR.

By adopting the RNTR, a local government may keep its aggregate property tax revenue constant. But individual taxpayers' bills are not guaranteed to remain constant because individual properties are likely to have appreciated or depreciated differently from the countywide tax base.

Listing and Assessing

The process of determining what taxable property exists in a jurisdiction, who owns it, and how much it is worth is known as listing and assessing property for taxation. The county assessor oversees this process, which is closely regulated by the Machinery Act and is intended to be (mostly) uniform from county to county. The only property over which the assessor does not have listing and assessing authority is public-service-company property, described in more detail below.

As a general rule, local government governing boards do not get involved with assigning tax values to individual properties. That process is accomplished by the assessor and his or her staff, ideally free from political pressures.

However, local government governing boards—especially boards of county commissioners—do retain some discretion as to how and when the process unfolds. These discretionary duties include

- appointing the assessor and setting his/her term of office,
- approving the budget for the assessor's office,
- deciding when to hold countywide reappraisals of real property,
- ruling on taxpayer appeals of tax values and tax exemptions while sitting as the board of equalization and review (or appointing a separate board of equalization and review), and
- waiving or refusing to waive discovery bills.

One property tax issue over which local governments have no authority is the creation of property tax exemptions. The North Carolina Constitution grants this authority exclusively to the General Assembly.[9] As a result, property tax exemptions are products of state statutes, not local ordinances. Counties and municipalities may not create their own exemptions from property taxes. Nor may they decide to ignore exemptions mandated by the Machinery Act.

This section briefly describes the listing and assessing process and the appropriate role for governing boards in that process. Readers who seek more details should take a look at *A Guide to the Listing, Assessment, and Taxation of Property in North Carolina*, a comprehensive guide to the process written by my School of Government colleague Shea Riggsbee Denning.

Appointing the Assessor

The assessor, appointed by the board of county commissioners, is responsible for listing and assessing all taxable property in the county. This process includes determining the *situs*—a fancy word for taxable location—of that property, determining who owns that property, deciding whether

9. N.C. Const. art. V, § 2(2).

that property and its owner are eligible for an exemption or exclusion from tax, and, perhaps most controversially, assigning a value for tax purposes to that property.

The Machinery Act creates some minimum qualifications for assessors, but for the most part the board of county commissioners retains great discretion as to who should serve in this role. Candidates must be at least twenty-one years of age, must hold a high school diploma or equivalent, and must be certified by the N.C. Department of Revenue within two years of taking office. Certification involves passing four assessment courses and a comprehensive exam. The assessor must be appointed for a fixed term set by the county commissioners that can vary from two to four years. Once the assessor's term length is set by the commissioners, it cannot be changed until after the term ends or after the assessor is removed from office.[10]

Unlike most employees in most counties, assessors are not at-will employees and cannot be removed from office at the discretion of the commissioners. An assessor may be removed from office before his or her term ends only for "good cause," a term not defined by the Machinery Act. However, similar good cause provisions covering appointed officials elsewhere in the General Statutes suggest that adequate grounds for removal include inefficiency, misconduct in office, and commission of a felony or other crime involving moral turpitude. In other words, the conduct that justifies the removal must either be directly tied to the assessor's job performance or be so serious as to call into question the assessor's fitness for office. For example, the failure to pay property taxes in a timely fashion likely would justify the firing of an assessor, but a conviction for driving under the influence might not.

If the county commissioners wish to remove the assessor from office, they must first provide the assessor with written notice of that intent and the opportunity to be heard at a public session of the board. For obvious reasons, the county attorney should be intimately involved with this process.

The Machinery Act does not create term limits for assessors. A board can repeatedly reappoint a particular assessor for as long as it wishes.

What, Where, Who, and How Much?

The what, where, who, and how much decisions concerning property taxes on *personal* property are made as of the annual listing day, which is the January 1 before the fiscal year begins.[11] For taxes on *real* property, the how much decisions (appraisals) are made as of January 1 of the reappraisal year, but ownership and taxability decisions are made as of January 1 each year, just as they are for personal property. In other words, a snapshot is taken every January 1, and the results of that snapshot control property taxes for the coming fiscal year.

For example, if Tom Taxpayer buys a new boat on February 1, 2025, he will not be required to list that boat for 2025–2026 property taxes because he did not own the boat on January 1. If Tina Taxpayer owns a house in Carolina County on January 1, 2025, that house is taxable by the county for the 2025–2026 fiscal year even if it burns to the ground the very next day. If Tim Taxpayer owns a vacant lot in Carolina County on January 1, 2025, and breaks ground on a new house on that lot on January 2, the new house will not be taxable by the county for 2025–2026 because it did not exist on January 1, the listing day. The house first will be listed and taxed as of January 1, *2026*, meaning it first will be taxed by the county in the 2026–2027 fiscal year. Construction that is partially complete as of January 1 should be assessed a percentage of its estimated value once complete.

10. G.S. 105-294.
11. G.S. 105-285.

Why Are There No Municipal Assessors?

More than five hundred North Carolina municipalities levy property taxes, but not a single one lists and assesses its own property for tax purposes. The Machinery Act requires municipalities to rely on the county assessor to answer the what, where, who, and how much questions related to property taxes, with one exception. Any municipality that sits in more than one county is authorized to appoint its own assessor to list and assess all of its property for taxation. Plenty of municipalities qualify for this exception, but none takes advantage of it. The reasons behind those decisions likely vary from town to town, but the expense involved is almost certainly a driving factor. Why pay for a service that the municipality can get for free from the county? Taxpayer confusion may be another consideration. If a municipality were to appoint its own assessor, taxpayers residing in that jurisdiction could wind up with two different tax values placed on their homes, cars, and other taxable property—one assigned by the county and one assigned by the municipality. More than a few taxpayers would question this result.

Situs

The situs (taxable location) of real property should be easily determined and immutable except when municipalities change their boundaries through annexation or deannexation or, less often, when two counties adjust their borders. But the situs of personal property—cars, boats, and planes especially—can present a major challenge. That movable property is not in a jurisdiction on January 1 does not necessarily mean that the jurisdiction cannot tax that property for the coming year.

With respect to personal property, situs means property that is more or less permanently located in a jurisdiction. For example, if a private jet is flown all over the country throughout the year but always returns to a hangar in Carolina County, Carolina County should be able to tax that plane even if it is not in the county on January 1.

Appraisal of Personal Property

The Machinery Act requires that all property be assessed for tax purposes at its "true value," defined to be the property's market value were it sold in an arm's-length transaction between two willing, able, and informed parties under no compulsion to buy or sell the property.[12]

As mentioned above, all taxable personal property—in other words, all taxable property that is not land or buildings—is appraised annually as of January 1. Generally, tax appraisals for cars, boats, planes, factory equipment, and other personal property decrease from year to year because that property depreciates and loses value over time.

Appraisal of Real Property

The most time-consuming and controversial part of the property tax process is the countywide reappraisal of real property, during which all land and buildings are assigned new tax values. Just as is true for personal property, real property must be valued at its true market value that would be obtained in an arm's-length transaction. Because foreclosure sales are involuntary sales, they are generally not considered when calculating appraisals.

12. G.S. 105-284.

Figure 19.3 Revaluation Cycles across North Carolina

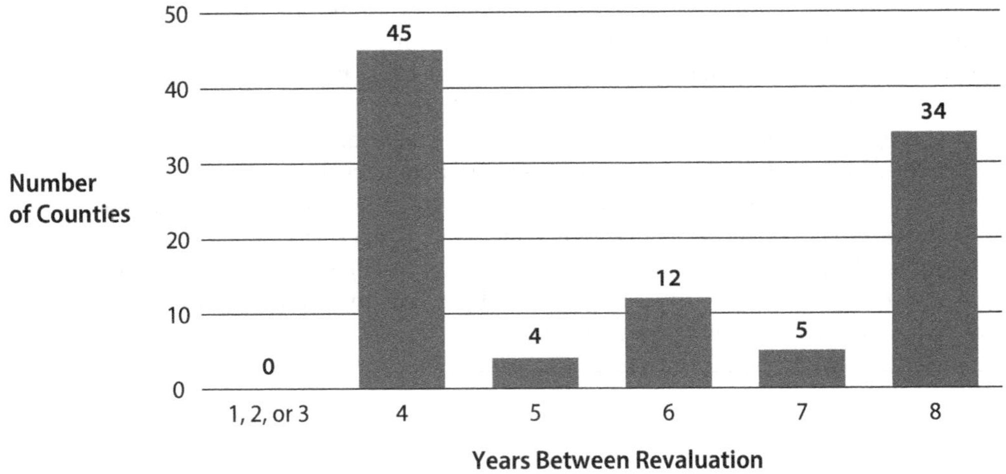

Source: North Carolina Department of Revenue, 2023.

Reappraisals—or "revals" as they commonly are called—must occur at least every eight years. Within this eight-year limitation, a county can choose whatever reappraisal cycle it prefers. A county is also free to change its reappraisal cycle between reappraisals, so long as it stays within the eight-year limitation.[13]

In an ideal world, every county would reappraise all of its real property every year so that its tax values would be pegged to true market value as closely as possible. But annual reappraisal of the many thousands of real estate parcels in each county is simply not practical from either an expense or a workload perspective. As Figure 19.3 demonstrates, just under half of the state's 100 counties are on four-year cycles and about one-third of them are on eight-year cycles. This is a substantial change from a decade ago, when more than two-thirds of the state's counties were on eight-year cycles.

Depending on the size of its assessor's office, a county can either conduct a reappraisal using only in-house staff or hire external consultants to do some or all of the required appraisal work. The process involves what is known as a mass appraisal, meaning not every parcel of real property is inspected by appraisers. Usually a small representative sample of a county's real property will be individually appraised. The rest of the county's real property will be assigned tax values based on an analysis of market prices and physical characteristics at the neighborhood level.

Changes to Real Property Tax Values in Non-Reappraisal Years

Between reappraisals, real property tax values generally should change only due to physical or zoning changes to the property. Changes in general economic conditions or in the local real estate market should not be reflected in tax values until the next reappraisal.[14]

For example, assume that Billy BlueDevil owns Parcel A that was appraised at $300,000 in Carolina County's 2020 reappraisal. The county's next reappraisal is not scheduled until 2028. Billy

13. G.S. 105-286.
14. G.S. 105-287.

sells Parcel A to Tommy TarHeel in late 2025 for $400,000 in an arm's-length, non-foreclosure transaction. Although the true market value of Parcel A may be $400,000 as of January 1, 2026, the tax value of Parcel A should not change until the next reappraisal in 2028. The tax value of Parcel A must remain its true market value as of January 1, 2020. The same would be true if Billy's house sold in 2025 for less than its 2020 tax value.

Now assume that instead of selling Parcel A, Billy increases the size of his house on that lot by 2,000 square feet in 2025. This physical change to Parcel A should be reflected in the 2026 tax value of Parcel A. The tax value of Billy's house would also need to be changed prior to the next reappraisal if it burned down or were rezoned to make it more or less valuable for future development or use.

Public-Service-Company Property

Only one type of property is assessed at the state level: real and personal property owned by electricity providers, gas companies, railroads, telephone service providers, and other public-service companies.[15]

Each year, these companies are required to list their taxable property with the N.C. Department of Revenue (NCDOR), which then assigns a tax value to that property and allocates that value to local governments for taxation. For real property, such as a power plant, the allocation is based on location. For movable personal property, such as buses and trains, the allocation is based on the miles driven in a jurisdiction, the miles of track in a jurisdiction, or a similar formula. If a local government's sales assessment ratio falls below 90 percent in certain years, that local government can lose a percentage of its public-service-company property value.[16] (See the next section for more on sales assessment ratios.)

Once public-service-company property value has been allocated to a local government, it may tax that property just as it taxes all other property in its jurisdiction. Unlike regular property tax appeals, appeals of public-service-company property tax values go directly to the state Property Tax Commission and are not handled at the county level.

Sales Assessment Ratios

Each year, NCDOR studies a sample of real estate sales from each county and compares the sales prices to the property tax appraisals of the sold properties. Foreclosures and other transactions that were not arm's-length transactions are excluded from these studies. A ratio is created for each property by dividing the tax appraisal by the sales price. The median of all of the ratios is that county's sales assessment ratio.

This ratio is a rough measure of how closely the county's tax values reflect actual market values. Ideally, the ratio would be 100 percent, meaning that, on average, tax appraisals are pegged right at market values. If the ratio is below 100 percent, then, on average, tax appraisals are below market values. If the ratio is greater than 100 percent, then, on average, tax appraisals are above market values.

In healthy economic times, sales assessment ratios decrease in the years following appraisals because tax values remain basically constant while market values slowly but steadily increase. When a county conducts its reappraisal, its sales assessment ratio will jump back up close to 100 percent.

15. G.S. Ch. 105, Art. 23.
16. G.S. 105-284.

Only a handful of counties will have ratios over 100 percent, usually those few in which reappraisals have just been conducted and their tax values have been pegged slightly above the market. In weaker economic times, when real property prices are falling or are flat, more counties will have ratios above 100 percent.

The most recent sales assessment ratio from NCDOR reflects the strong real estate market experienced by most of the state in the past few years.[17] Only four counties have sales assessment ratios at or above 100 percent, with the average ratio at 79 percent.[18]

Why the Sales Assessment Ratio Matters

County leaders can use the sales assessment ratio to evaluate the effectiveness of their reappraisals. The ratio can also help predict how the county's tax base will change in the next reappraisal: if a county's sales assessment ratio is well above 100 percent, county leaders should be prepared for a drop in the tax base after the next reappraisal.

There are statutory reasons to pay attention to the sales assessment ratio as well. It is the basis for two Machinery Act provisions intended to promote more frequent appraisals of real property.

The first provision deals with public-service-company property. If a county's sales assessment ratio falls below 90 percent in the fourth or seventh year after a reappraisal, then that county's assessed value of public-service-company property will be reduced. The reduction will roughly equate to the actual sales assessment ratio: if the county's ratio is 85 percent, the county will be allocated and will be able to tax only 85 percent of the full assessed value of the public-service-company property it would otherwise have been allocated.[19]

The second provision involves mandatory reappraisals for counties with populations greater than 75,000. If such a county's sales assessment ratio is below 85 percent or above 115 percent, then the county must conduct a reappraisal within three years.[20] Thanks to the very strong real estate market across the state, in 2022, NCDOR reported that twenty-eight counties triggered mandatory reappraisals because their ratios had fallen below 85 percent.[21] That total is almost twice as many as had done so cumulatively in the previous fifteen years.

Property Tax Exemptions and Exclusions

Only the General Assembly has the authority to create exemptions from local property taxes. Local governments may not carve out their own exemptions, nor may they choose not to administer the exemptions created by the General Assembly. Although the Machinery Act uses two terms—exemption and exclusion—to describe statutes that partially or completely remove property from taxation, for the purposes of this section those terms are interchangeable.

The single largest property tax exclusion category is present-use-value property.[22] This exclusion, which applied to nearly $34 billion of property in 2021–2022, reduces the taxable value of land that is used for agricultural, forestry, or wildlife conservation purposes. Under this program, landowners are allowed to pay taxes on the value of their property at its value for its current use,

---

17. N.C. Department of Revenue, Property Tax Division, *Sales Assessment Ratio Studies as of January 1, 2023*, www.ncdor.gov/2023salesratiobookpdf/open.

18. *Id.*

19. G.S. 105-284(b).

20. G.S. 105-286(a)(2).

21. Email to author from John Simpson, Director, Local Government Division, N.C. Department of Revenue (March 6, 2023).

22. G.S. 105-277.2 through -277.6.

Figure 19.4 Value of Property Covered by the Four Major Exemptions, 2021–2022

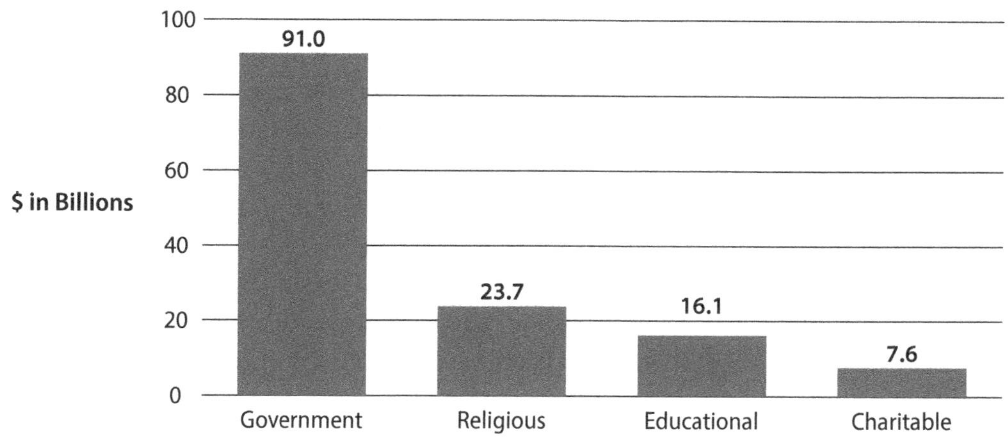

Source: North Carolina Department of Revenue.

as opposed to its actual market value for development or any other use. The taxes on the difference between the land's present-use value and its market value are deferred, with the most recent three years of deferred taxes due and payable when the property is sold or is no longer used for agricultural, forestry, or wildlife conservation purposes. The next most-common exemptions are those for government, religious, charitable, and educational property. As Figure 19.4 illustrates, the largest of these four exemptions is the one for property owned by a government—federal, state, or local.[23] Local governments have no authority to tax property owned by another branch of government, regardless of how that property is being used.

Three property tax exclusions are aimed specifically at elderly and disabled homeowners. The most popular of the three is the homestead exclusion, which reduces the taxable value of a residence by the greater of $25,000 or 50 percent.[24] To be eligible, a homeowner must be 65 or older or totally disabled and must satisfy an income requirement, which was $36,700 or less for 2024.[25] For example, if Tina Taxpayer is eligible for the elderly and disabled exclusion and her home is assessed at $200,000, she will pay taxes only on $100,000 of that value. Roughly $6.7 billion of residential property benefited from this exclusion in 2021–2022.

The other two exclusions are the disabled veterans exclusion (G.S. 105-277.1C), which allows qualified taxpayers to reduce the taxable value of their homes by $45,000, and the circuit-breaker deferred tax program (G.S. 105-277.1B), which permits senior homeowners to cap their current taxes at either 4 or 5 percent of their income. The circuit-breaker program is similar to the present-use value program in that three years of deferred circuit-breaker taxes are due when the taxpayer sells the home or stops using it as his or her primary residence. These two exclusions are much smaller than the homestead exclusion, especially the circuit breaker. In 2020–2021, the disabled veterans exclusion applied to $1.9 billion of property while the circuit breaker applied to less than $1 million.[26]

23. G.S. 105-278.1.
24. G.S. 105-277.1.
25. *See* N.C. Department of Revenue Form AV-9 (2023), Application for Property Tax Relief.
26. Email to author from George Hermane, Local Government Division, N.C. Department of Revenue (Dec. 7, 2022).

Exemption and Exclusion Applications

The default rule is that a property owner must file an annual application to receive any exemption or exclusion.[27]

Many exemptions require only a single application, including those for present-use value, educational, religious, and charitable property.[28] Additional filings by the taxpayer are required only if an exempt taxpayer acquires additional property, makes physical changes to the exempt property, or changes the use of the exempt property.

A handful of exemptions, most importantly the one for government property, apply automatically without the need for an application from the property owner.[29]

Applications for most exemptions and exclusions are due by the end of the listing period, which is January 31 unless the county commissioners decide to extend it. Applications for the three residential property relief programs—the elderly and disabled exclusion, the circuit-breaker exclusion, and the disabled veterans exclusion—are due on June 1.

Despite these deadlines, the Machinery Act permits governing boards to accept applications through December 31 for a "showing of good cause."[30] Because this term is not defined by the Machinery Act, governing boards have a good amount of discretion when deciding which late applications to consider. The only limitation courts have placed on this discretion is that local governments should not base their decisions solely on the amount of property taxes related to a particular application.

An assessor makes the initial determination on all exemption and exclusion applications. North Carolina courts have made clear that all exemptions and exclusions must be strictly construed in favor of taxation.[31] In other words, assessors should begin with a presumption in favor of taxability. The burden of proof is on the taxpayer to prove that an exemption or exclusion is deserved.[32] If the taxpayer disagrees with the assessor's decision concerning an exemption or exclusion, the taxpayer may pursue an appeal to the county board of equalization and review and beyond, as described below.

Taxpayer Appeals

County commissioners play significant roles in resolving taxpayer appeals concerning their tax values and their eligibility for exemptions or exclusions, primarily through the appointment of the county board of equalization and review (BOER). The commissioners themselves may sit as the BOER or, as is most common, they may appoint other individuals to serve in that capacity.

Confusingly, the Machinery Act does not create a fixed deadline for taxpayers to submit appeals to the BOER. Instead, the appeal deadline is tied to the date that the BOER adjourns, which can vary from county to county and from year to year.[33]

In non-reappraisal years, the BOER must adjourn by July 1. In reappraisal years, it must do so by December 1. But in practice, most counties adjourn their BOERs on the same day as or shortly after the BOER's first meeting, which must occur between the first Monday in April and the first

27. G.S. 105-282.1(a).
28. G.S. 105-282.1(a)(2).
29. G.S. 105-282.1(a)(1).
30. G.S. 105-282.1(a1).
31. *In re* R.J. Reynolds Tobacco Co., 52 N.C. App. 299 (1981).
32. *In re* Martin, 286 N.C. 209 (1974).
33. G.S. 105-322(g)(2)(a).

Table 19.5 The Property Tax Appeal Process

1. Informal appeal to the assessor
2. County Board of Equalization and Review
3. State Property Tax Commission (taxpayer only)
4. N.C. Court of Appeals
5. N.C. Supreme Court (maybe)

Monday in May. Once it adjourns, the BOER may still meet to hear appeals that were submitted before adjournment but cannot accept any new appeals.

Table 19.5 lists the five stages of a property tax appeal. Not surprisingly, most appeals occur in reappraisal years when every parcel of real property receives a new tax value. Historically, about 10 percent of real property owners contest their values after a reappraisal. The assessor usually resolves 90 percent of those initial inquiries informally.

Those appeals that are not resolved to the satisfaction of the taxpayer move to the BOER for formal hearings. The BOER's decision is binding on the county, meaning that if the taxpayer prevails, the county has no right of appeal. However, if the county prevails, the taxpayer has the right to appeal to the North Carolina Property Tax Commission, a five-member panel that hears cases in Raleigh. The party that loses before the Property Tax Commission can appeal the case to the North Carolina Court of Appeals, which often is the final stop for property tax appeals. A losing party has the right to continue its appeal to the North Carolina Supreme Court only if at least one judge from the court of appeals voted in its favor. The supreme court may also exercise its discretion to hear the appeal of a unanimous decision from the court of appeals, but that rarely occurs.

Discoveries

A "discovery" occurs when an assessor learns of taxable property that has not been listed for property taxes. The term also applies when the value or volume of property was substantially understated or when a property has received an exemption or exclusion for which it did not qualify.[34]

After a discovery is made, the assessor must correct the listing and assessment of the property and then bill the corrected taxes for the current year plus the five previous years. If the discovery involves personal property or buildings, discovery penalties of 10 percent per listing period apply to the discovery bill. Penalties do not apply to the failure to list land.[35]

For example, assume that Billy BlueDevil builds a house on his vacant lot in 2016 but fails to list the building for taxation with the county. The county finally learns of the house's existence in 2025. Under the discovery provisions, the county is entitled to list, assess, and bill that property for the current year (2025) plus the five previous years (2020–2024). Although the house should have been listed and taxed in 2017, the Machinery Act does not permit the county to extend its discovery bill beyond 2020.

The discovery bill must be based on the assessed value and the tax rate in effect for each year the property was not listed. Table 19.6 shows how Billy BlueDevil's discovery bill would be calculated,

34. See the definition of the term "discover property" in G.S. 105-273(6b).
35. G.S. 105-312.

Table 19.6 Bill for 2025 Discovery of $200,000 House

Year	Assessed Value	Tax Rate	Tax	Penalty	Totals
2025	$200,000	.51	$1,020	$102 (10%)	$1,122
2024	$200,000	.51	$1,020	$204 (20%)	$1,224
2023	$200,000	.50	$1,000	$300 (30%)	$1,300
2022	$200,000	.52	$1,040	$416 (40%)	$1,456
2021	$200,000	.52	$1,040	$520 (50%)	$1,560
2020	$200,000	.50	$1,000	$600 (60%)	$1,600
Totals			**$6,120**	**$2,142**	**$8,262**

assuming that the house would have been assessed at $200,000 as of January 1, 2020, the date of the last county reappraisal. The penalties are calculated at 10 percent per missed listing period for each tax year: for example, the 2020 penalty is 60 percent because Billy missed six listing periods (2020–2025).

Waiving Discovery Bills

Local governing boards possess unusually broad authority over discovery bills. The Machinery Act permits discovery bills to be waived by a governing board at its unfettered discretion.[36] The governing board may agree to waive the entire bill or just a portion of it. It could waive all penalties, the tax and penalties from certain years, or any combination thereof.

In comparison, regular tax bills, penalties, and interest generally cannot be waived by governing boards. See "Refunds and Releases," below, for more details.

While the Machinery Act does not place any specific limits on the authority to waive discovery bills, governing boards are wise to seek consistency in their approaches to this issue. A lack of consistency when making waiver decisions could lead to accusations of favoritism or bias.

When a discovery bill includes municipal property taxes, that municipality's governing board retains the authority to compromise that portion of the bill. The county commissioners may compromise only the portion of the discovery bill that involves county taxes.

Evaluating the Assessor

County commissioners can choose from a variety of metrics to evaluate the performance of their assessors. One major consideration is often the cost and effectiveness of the countywide reappraisal of real property. Reappraisals are usually the most controversial activity undertaken by a county's tax office. To conduct a successful reappraisal, an assessor must possess technical appraisal skills, managerial competence, and perhaps above all, strong public relations capability. Educating taxpayers about the reappraisal and appeal process is a necessity, and the assessor cannot accomplish that key task without the ability to communicate clearly and effectively to different interest groups.

36. G.S. 105-312(k).

From a statistical perspective, the sales assessment ratio discussed earlier in this chapter may be the most useful figure for county commissioners to analyze. Immediately following a reappraisal, a county's sales assessment figure should be very close to 100 percent, meaning that, on average, sales prices equal tax values. If that is not the case, the reappraisal was not very accurate and the assessor should be held accountable.

The assessor should not be held accountable for changes in the tax base due to economic conditions. The fact that tax values have not risen as much as the commissioners might have hoped or have not fallen as much as taxpayers might have expected does not mean that the assessor is incompetent. More often, it means that the observers' expectations were not based on the actual conditions experienced by the county. Pre-reappraisal education is the key to minimizing unrealistic expectations on behalf of both elected officials and taxpayers.

Collection

After an assessor lists and assesses all taxable property in a jurisdiction and the jurisdiction's governing board sets the tax rate, property taxes are handed over to the tax collector for billing and, if necessary, enforced collection efforts, such as bank account attachments, wage garnishments, and real property foreclosures.

As is true of the listing and assessing process, the collection process should normally proceed with minimal involvement by the governing board. The tax collector should apply the same collection procedures to all similarly situated taxpayers, free from political pressures.

The governing board's role in the collection process is limited to

- appointing a tax collector or, for municipalities, choosing to contract with the county for property tax collection;[37]
- deciding whether to offer taxpayers a discount for early payment;[38] and
- reviewing the tax collector's performance throughout the year and after receiving the year-end settlement.[39]

Appointing the Tax Collector

Every local government that levies property taxes must appoint a tax collector who will be authorized to use the Machinery Act collection remedies of attachment and garnishment, levy and sale, and foreclosure. That tax collector can be an employee of the taxing government or an employee of another government with whom the taxing government contracts for tax collection services.

The Machinery Act creates only a few limitations on who can be appointed as tax collector. Members of the governing board are ineligible to serve as tax collector, as are local government finance officers absent special approval from the Local Government Commission. In terms of education and experience, the only requirement is that the appointee be "a person of character and integrity whose experience in business and collection work is satisfactory to the governing body." The appointee's criminal and financial history must not be so bad as to prevent the local government

---

37. G.S. 105-349.
38. G.S. 105-360(c).
39. G.S. 105-373.

from being able to purchase the required bond to cover losses caused by the tax collector's misconduct or neglect. The bottom line is that the governing body has great discretion when deciding whom to appoint as tax collector.[40]

The tax collector must be appointed for a set term determined by the governing board. Most commonly these terms are two or four years in length. Once fixed by the governing board upon the tax collector's appointment, the length of the collector's term may not be changed until the term ends or the collector is removed from office. No term limits exist for collectors, meaning the governing board may reappoint a particular tax collector repeatedly. After appointment, the tax collector can be removed from office only "for cause," the same standard that is applied to the removal of the assessor.

Unlike assessors, tax collectors are not subject to mandatory state certification. However, the North Carolina Tax Collectors' Association (NCTCA) operates a voluntary certification process for tax collectors.[41] Many local governments now expect their collectors to obtain NCTCA certification as part of their required duties.

Tax Bills

Surprisingly, the Machinery Act does not require local governments that levy property taxes to send bills to their taxpayers. For obvious reasons, all do. But because tax bills are not required, a taxpayer cannot rely on failure to receive a tax bill as justification to avoid responsibility for a particular tax. The Machinery Act charges all taxpayers with notice of the fact that taxes are owed on their property even if they never receive actual notice in the form of a tax bill.[42]

Tax bills cannot be created until the tax rate is adopted along with the budget for the new fiscal year. Local governments are expected to finalize their budgets before July 1, the beginning of the fiscal year. But this deadline is far from ironclad, and plenty of local governments delay the final budget decision well into the new fiscal year. Of course, the later the budget is adopted, the later tax bills will go out, and the longer the local government will wait to receive its property tax revenue.

Because the Machinery Act is silent on the issue of tax bills, local governments have flexibility as to the form and content of those bills. Any tax, fee, fine, or other obligation can be included on a property tax bill. But billing an obligation along with property taxes does not automatically empower the local government to use property tax collection remedies to collect that obligation.

For example, some local governments include water, sewer, or stormwater fees on their tax bills. Absent special approval from the state legislature, these fees cannot be collected using property tax collection remedies even though they are included on the same bill with property taxes.

An important exception to this rule concerns solid waste fees. All local governments are authorized to adopt a resolution calling for solid waste fees to be billed with property taxes and collected as property taxes.[43]

---

40. G.S. 105-349.

41. Details of the NCTCA certification process can be found at propertytaxnc.org/page/NCTCACerts.

42. G.S. 105-348.

43. For more on collecting solid waste fees, water bills, and other taxes and charges, please see Christopher B. McLaughlin, "Beyond the Property Tax: Collecting Other Taxes and Fees," *Property Tax Bulletin* No. 174 (UNC School of Government, Jan. 2018).

Should Municipalities Collect Their Own Taxes?

All 100 counties appoint and employ their own tax collectors. So do many municipalities. But a growing number of municipalities have decided not to employ their own tax collectors and instead have appointed the county tax collector as the municipal tax collector through interlocal agreements.

The Machinery Act offers no guidance on the terms of these municipal–county collection agreements, meaning that the compensation provided by the municipality to the county for its tax collection services is up for negotiation between the parties. The compensation typically is set as a percentage of the taxes collected, usually around 1 to 2 percent and sometimes with a bonus if the collection rate exceeds a certain benchmark.

From a financial perspective, relying on the county tax collector makes sense for many municipalities. The county already has the billing infrastructure in place, meaning that the cost it charges to the municipality to bill and collect municipal taxes will likely be less than the cost the municipality would incur to create its own billing system. But some municipalities prefer to retain complete control over the billing and collection process even if that approach costs more in the long run.

Discounts for Early Payment

The Machinery Act permits but does not require local governments to offer taxpayers a discount for paying their property taxes before September 1, the due date for property taxes other than those on registered motor vehicles.[44] Discounts are becoming less and less common. Those jurisdictions that do offer them usually set the discount at 1 or 2 percent. If a jurisdiction wishes to offer a discount, it must set the discount schedule by May and obtain approval from the N.C. Department of Revenue (NCDOR). Once adopted, a discount schedule remains in effect for all subsequent tax years unless and until it is repealed by the governing board.

Interest

Unlike discounts, interest is mandatory. On January 6 following the year in which taxes are levied, unpaid property taxes begin to accrue interest.[45] For example, taxes levied for the 2025–2026 fiscal year will become delinquent and begin to accrue interest on January 6, 2026. (Different rules apply to taxes to motor vehicles—see "Registered Motor Vehicles," below.)

Interest accrues at a rate of 2 percent for the first month and 0.75 percent for every month thereafter.[46] Machinery Act interest is simple interest rather than compound interest, meaning that interest does not accrue on interest. On the first day of each month that a delinquent tax remains unpaid, another 0.75 percent of interest accrues on the principal amount of taxes owed plus any penalties and costs that have been added to that amount. For example, tax collectors are permitted to apply a 10 percent penalty for checks returned by the bank for insufficient funds. That penalty is added to the principal amount of taxes owed and will accrue interest if it remains unpaid past the delinquency date.

Governing boards cannot waive interest charges unless that interest accrued illegally or due to clerical error. These are the same standards that apply to the release and refund of principal taxes. (See "Refunds and Releases," below, for more details.)

44. G.S. 105-360(c).
45. G.S. 105-360(a).
46. *Id.*

Special Rules: Weekends, Holidays, and Postmarks

Two Machinery Act provisions affect when interest accrues in special situations.

The first is the weekend and holiday rule.[47] Whenever the last day to pay a tax without additional interest falls on a weekend or holiday, the deadline is extended to the next business day. For example, January 6, 2025, fell on a Monday, meaning that the last day to pay 2024–2025 property taxes without interest was Sunday, January 5. The weekend and holiday rule extended this deadline to the next business day (Monday, January 6). Interest on unpaid 2024–2025 property taxes began to accrue on Tuesday, January 7.

The second is the postmark rule.[48] The Machinery Act requires that tax offices treat property tax payments made by mail as if the payments were received on their postmark dates. Assume Tommy TarHeel pays his 2024–2025 property taxes in full by mail on January 3, 2025. The tax office does not receive his payment until Wednesday, January 8, one day after interest was to accrue on 2023–2024 property taxes. If Tommy's payment has a U.S. Postal Service postmark date of January 6 or earlier, the tax office must treat the payment as if it were actually received on either date and no interest would accrue on Tommy's property taxes. If the payment has no postmark or only a private postal meter mark, it cannot benefit from the postmark rule and Tommy must be charged interest.

Depending on the size of the locality, it may not be practical for tax office staff to check postmark dates on all payments made on or near an interest deadline. Instead, many tax offices apply a grace period of several days after each interest accrual date. Payments received by mail within the grace period do not accrue interest, without regard to postmark dates. While reasonable, tax offices should be aware that this practice satisfies only the spirit and not the letter of the postmark rule. Tax payments arriving after the grace period that have postmark dates prior to the interest accrual date should not be charged interest.

Deferred Taxes

Ten different Machinery Act provisions provide taxpayers tax relief in the form of deferred taxes. By far the largest of these deferred tax programs is the present-use value program discussed previously. But deferred taxes are also created under the circuit-breaker program as well as under exclusions that cover historic properties, working waterfront property, wildlife conservation land, and future sites for low-income housing.

Program details vary, but the general principle remains the same: some amount of taxes is deferred each year for as long as the property qualifies for the program. Interest accrues on these deferred taxes, but the local government cannot take action to collect them. When the property is sold or otherwise becomes ineligible for the program, several years (usually three) of deferred taxes plus interest become

> ### How Is Interest Calculated?
>
> Assume Tommy TarHeel owes $1,000 in 2024 property taxes to Carolina County that became delinquent on January 7, 2025. He appears in the tax office on May 1, 2025, and asks how much he must pay to satisfy his tax obligation.
>
> The answer is $1,050, consisting of $1,000 in principal taxes and $50 in interest. The interest charge equals 5 percent: 2 percent for January plus 0.75 percent each month for February, March, April, and May.

47. G.S. 105-395.1.
48. G.S. 105-360(d).

Table 19.7 Enforced Collection Remedies

Remedy	Property Targeted
Attachment and garnishment	Wages, bank accounts, rents, or any other money owed to the taxpayer
Levy and sale	Cars, boats, planes, or any other tangible personal property owned by the taxpayer
Foreclosure	Real property subject to a lien for delinquent taxes
Set-off debt collection	State income tax refunds, lottery winnings, or any other money owed to the taxpayer by the state

due and payable. If the deferred taxes are not paid immediately, the local government can proceed with enforced collection remedies.

Enforced Collection Remedies

Once taxes become delinquent on January 6, tax collectors can immediately begin enforced collections. The Machinery Act creates three enforced collection remedies: attachment and garnishment; levy and sale; and, for taxes that are liens on real property, foreclosure. Separate state provisions allow local governments to collect delinquent property taxes through the set-off debt collection process, which targets state income tax refunds and lottery winnings.[49] All four remedies are summarized in Table 19.7.

Local governments can also sue delinquent taxpayers in state court, but few pursue this option because the remedies available to a local government after winning such a lawsuit are essentially the same remedies it already possesses under the Machinery Act.

Unless the governing board directs otherwise, the tax collector normally may use any of these remedies in any order desired. However, once a foreclosure proceeding begins, all other Machinery Act remedies must stop.

Most local governments use all four tax collection remedies. But some refuse to employ collection remedies that taxpayers consider too intrusive, such as wage garnishment or foreclosure. Local governments that ignore any of these remedies suffer reduced collection percentages and lost revenues and do grievous harm to the perceived fairness of the property tax scheme.

Three of these remedies can be initiated without the involvement of the courts. Attachment and garnishment, levy and sale, and set-off debt collection require only notice to the taxpayer and, in the case of attachment and garnishment, notice to the party that holds the property being attached.

A court proceeding is required for foreclosure, which is available only for taxes that are a lien on real property. All taxes on real property automatically become a lien on that real property on the listing date, which is the January 1 prior to the fiscal year for which the taxes are levied. The tax lien on real property also includes the taxes owed on personal property other than registered motor vehicles that is owned by the same taxpayer in the same jurisdiction.

For example, assume that Wanda Wolfpack owns real property Parcel A, a boat, and a registered Honda Civic, all of which are listed for taxes in Carolina County. The taxes on both Parcel A and the boat are a lien on Parcel A. The county could foreclose on Parcel A for Wanda's failure to pay

49. G.S. Ch. 105A.

Table 19.8 Which Owners Can Be Held Personally Responsible for Property Taxes?

Type of Property	Original Owner	Subsequent Owners
Real property	Yes	Yes
Personal property (boats, planes, business property)	Yes	No, unless "going out of business" provision applies
Registered motor vehicles	Yes	No

either the taxes on the real property itself or the taxes on the boat. The taxes on the Honda Civic are *not* a lien on Parcel A, meaning that the tax collector could not foreclose on Parcel A if Wanda failed to pay the taxes on her Civic.

The Machinery Act creates a ten-year statute of limitations for all enforced collections. Foreclosures, attachments and garnishments, and levies must begin within ten years of the delinquent tax's original due date, which for all taxes other than those on registered motor vehicles is September 1 of the year the taxes were levied.

Who Can Be Targeted with Enforced Collection Remedies?

Only property of the responsible taxpayer can be targeted with enforced collection remedies. G.S. 105-365.1 creates different rules for the responsible taxpayer for taxes on personal property as compared to real property. For personal property, the responsible party is the taxpayer that listed the property for taxation, meaning the owner on the previous January 1. In other words, new owners of personal property are not responsible for old taxes on that property. For real property, the responsible parties are the owners as of the date of delinquency (January 6 of the fiscal year) and all subsequent owners. In other words, new owners of real property are responsible for old taxes on that property. Table 19.8 summarizes the rules concerning responsible taxpayers.

Here is how the rules work for real property. Assume that Dave Deacon owns Parcel A, on which taxes from 2024–2025 are delinquent. He sells Parcel A to Susie Seahawk in June of 2025. Normally, Susie (or her attorney) would require that the delinquent taxes be paid at or before the closing. But if those taxes are not paid, Susie would be personally responsible for the old taxes on Parcel A despite the fact that the taxes became delinquent while the property was owned by Dave (on January 7, 2025). Dave would also remain personally responsible. To collect these taxes, the tax collector could foreclose on Parcel A, garnish Dave's or Susie's wages, attach Dave's or Susie's bank account, or seize and sell Dave's or Susie's car or other personal property. If Susie's cash or property is taken to satisfy the taxes, Susie may have a legal action against Dave for reimbursement. But that depends on the terms of the real estate contract between Susie and Dave and has no effect on the taxing unit's right to collect the delinquent taxes using all methods permitted by the Machinery Act.

Now consider a personal property example. Assume that Mike Mountaineer owns a boat on which 2024–2025 property taxes are delinquent. If Mike sells the boat to Wanda Wolfpack, Mike remains the only party personally responsible for the 2024–2025 taxes on the boat because he was the owner of the boat on the listing vote, January 1, 2024. Only Mike's wages, bank accounts, and other property may be targeted with enforced collections. The tax collector cannot seize and sell the boat or target any of Wanda's other property because responsibility for taxes on that boat does not transfer to its new owner.

Although multiple collection actions are permitted for a single delinquent tax, that tax may be collected only once. For example, in the real property example above, the tax collector could simultaneously pursue wage garnishments against both Dave and Susie for the delinquent 2024–2025 taxes on Parcel A. In the personal property example, the tax collector could simultaneously attach Mike's wages and bank account for the delinquent 2024–2025 taxes on the boat. Tax collectors are permitted to proceed with multiple collection actions for delinquent taxes simultaneously. But once the full amount of delinquent taxes plus interest and costs are collected, all collection actions must stop and any excess funds collected must be returned to the targeted taxpayer(s).

Property Taxes and the Register of Deeds

About three-quarters of North Carolina's 100 counties have received authorization from the General Assembly under G.S. 161-31 to prohibit a register of deeds from accepting a deed transferring real property unless the county tax collector first certifies that there are no property tax liens on the property that is the subject of the deed. This certification must cover all property taxes that the tax collector is responsible for collecting, which could include county taxes, municipal taxes, special service-district taxes, rural fire-district taxes, and supplemental school-district taxes. This provision provides great incentive for a closing attorney to ensure that the taxes on property being transferred are paid because, otherwise, the deed cannot be recorded, and the buyer's ownership rights may be jeopardized. Unfortunately, the provision contains a loophole that permits attorneys to record deeds if they promise to pay the delinquent taxes at closing. Too often these promises are broken and the taxes remain unpaid after the deeds are recorded.

G.S. 161-31 lists the counties with the authority to enact this requirement. If a county is not on that list and desires this authority, it should ask its state representatives to introduce legislation adding it to that list. Although the statute covers municipal taxes only if those taxes are collected by the county, at least one municipality that collects its own taxes has obtained a local modification to the law that prohibits the recording of deeds unless municipal taxes are paid along with county taxes.[50]

Advertising Tax Liens

Despite increasing questions about their effectiveness, newspaper advertisements of delinquent real property tax liens are still required every year.[51] The cost of these advertisements can be substantial, with larger counties spending tens of thousands of dollars to buy newspaper space. Tax collectors are permitted to pass these costs along to the delinquent taxpayers, and much of the advertising cost will be recaptured when the delinquent taxes are paid. But because not all of these taxes will be paid, the local government is certain to wind up eating a portion of the advertising cost.

Due to cost and to administrative burden, some local governments have considered eliminating tax lien advertisements. This course of action is not recommended for two reasons.

First, the advertisement is the mandatory initial step for an *in rem* foreclosure, the Machinery Act's expedited foreclosure process that can be accomplished without the need for attorneys. If a

50. *See* S.L. 2010-24 (affecting Duplin County).
51. G.S. 105-369.

tax collector were to move forward with an *in rem* foreclosure without first advertising the tax lien, the taxpayer would have strong grounds for defending or reversing that collection action.

Second, local governments that do not use the *in rem* foreclosure process could place their other collection actions at risk if they intentionally ignore the advertising requirement. While the Machinery Act and state courts are generally tolerant of good faith errors in the tax collection process (see the discussion under "Immaterial Irregularities—Recapturing Lost Taxes," below), they are less likely to be forgiving of willful illegality by a local government.

Evaluating the Tax Collector: The Tax Collection Percentage

The Machinery Act requires tax collectors to make monthly reports to their governing boards about their collection results.[52] These reports, combined with the annual settlement required of tax collectors summing up their efforts and results for the entire fiscal year, give governing boards multiple opportunities to evaluate the performance of their collectors.

Perhaps the most important statistic used in the evaluation process is the tax collection percentage. Thanks to the very effective collection remedies provided by the Machinery Act, county collection percentages are very high, averaging around 99 percent for the past few years. Collections of taxes on registered motor vehicles traditionally lagged behind collections of other property taxes but have increased substantially since the 2013 implementation of the Tag & Tax Together collection system described below.

Two factors that can affect an individual local government's collection percentage are property tax assessment appeals and bankruptcies, both of which prevent a tax collector from pursuing enforced collections against the taxpayer in question.[53] If a jurisdiction experiences either a high number of property tax appeals during a reappraisal year or a bankruptcy filing by a major commercial taxpayer, the tax collector will not be able to collect the taxes involved while the proceedings are pending. As a result, the collection percentage is likely to suffer.

"Settlement" is the term the Machinery Act uses for the required annual accounting that tax collectors must provide to their local governing boards.[54] Presented after the old fiscal year ends and before the tax collector is charged with taxes for the new fiscal year, the settlement accounts for all of the funds received by the tax collector and identifies those taxes that remain unpaid. The settlement must be provided to the board in written form, but most tax collectors also make an oral presentation to the governing board so that they can answer questions in person.

As part of the settlement, the tax collector will usually provide the governing board with tax collection rates, oftentimes broken out by year or property type.

Other Performance Evaluation Measures

Although collection percentage is the most common and usually the most important criterion used to evaluate a tax collector, other aspects of the collector's performance can and should be considered by the local governing board. The collector's ability to communicate with the board and with the public is key to an effective property tax system. Taxpayer complaints and the collector's responsiveness to those complaints are related issues that may provide insight into that official's performance.

52. G.S. 105-350.

53. G.S. 105-378(d) bars any enforcement action for taxes that are under appeal. The automatic stay that applies to all federal bankruptcy cases similarly bars enforcement actions for any taxes owed by a debtor who filed for bankruptcy. 11 U.S.C. § 362.

54. G.S. 105-373.

Consistency and impartiality are vital characteristics for a tax collector. The board needs proof that the collector demonstrates these traits. Does the tax collector treat all similarly situated taxpayers equally? Does he or she employ tax collection remedies in an impartial fashion against all delinquent taxpayers and not play favorites? If not, the local government is likely to face taxpayer dissatisfaction and legal exposure.

Old Taxes

The Machinery Act creates a ten-year statute of limitations that bars enforced collection actions after taxes are more than ten years past due.[55] Most counties rely on this statute of limitations to allow their tax collectors to write off taxes after they hit the ten-year mark. Technically, this approach violates the Machinery Act. The statute of limitations bars enforced collection, but it has no relevance to the tax collector's responsibility for those taxes.

The only technically correct method of writing off taxes and thereby relieving tax collectors of responsibility for them is through the "insolvents list."[56] As part of the settlement process, a tax collector should identify unpaid taxes from the just-ended fiscal year that are not a lien on real property. The governing board can then place those taxes on the insolvents list and, once those taxes are more than five years past due, can write off those taxes by relieving the tax collector of responsibility for them. Taxes on registered motor vehicles that are placed on the insolvents list can be written off after they are more than one year past due.

Note that taxes that are a lien on real property cannot be placed on the insolvents list and, therefore, technically can never be written off by the tax collector. When all other efforts fail, foreclosure remains an option for any tax that is secured by a lien on real property. The problem, however, is that property that makes it through to a foreclosure sale is often worth very little. It may be more effort than it is worth to pursue foreclosure, which is why many counties allow the tax collector to informally write off old taxes on real property despite the Machinery Act's contrary admonition.

Immaterial Irregularities—Recapturing Lost Taxes

From a local government perspective, few Machinery Act provisions are more beneficial than the "immaterial irregularity" provision. Essentially, this provision excuses errors in the listing, assessing, billing, and collecting processes and allows local governments to retroactively correct those errors and levy and collect the taxes in question as if the errors never occurred.[57]

Cities and counties have relied on the immaterial irregularity provision in a variety of situations. They have used it to retroactively bill taxes on property that was listed by the taxpayer but never assessed, to pursue taxes on property that was annexed by a municipality years ago but never taxed by it, and to collect underbillings resulting from computer errors.

About the only type of error that courts have found significant enough not to be excused is the failure to give adequate notice to owners of real property before moving forward with a foreclosure action. Local governments using the foreclosure process should take care to provide timely notice to all parties who may have an interest in the property being foreclosed upon, including lienholders and the heirs of deceased taxpayers.

55. G.S. 105-378.
56. G.S. 105-373(g).
57. G.S. 105-394.

Refunds and Releases

A favorite question from taxpayers, tax collectors, and governing boards across the state is: when can taxes be waived? The short answer is, very rarely. Governing boards cannot waive taxes whenever they choose.

In Machinery Act terminology, waivers are either "refunds" (for taxes that were previously paid) or "releases" (for taxes that have not been paid). Under G.S. 105-381, refunds and releases are permitted in only the following two circumstances:

1. when the tax was levied illegally or
2. when the tax was levied due to clerical error by the tax office.

If a governing board approves a refund or release that does not satisfy one of these two categories, board members can be held personally liable for the lost taxes.

Examples of illegal taxes include

- taxes on property that did not have situs in the jurisdiction,
- double taxation on the same property by the same jurisdiction, and
- taxes that were levied without the required procedural steps.

Examples of taxes levied due to clerical error include

- assessments in which digits were transposed or added (for example, a tax value of $250,000 is mistakenly recorded as $520,000 or a property's square footage is recorded as 25,000 instead of 2,500);
- tax payments applied to the wrong accounts contrary to taxpayer instructions or due to mistakes by the tax office; and
- tax bills calculated on the wrong tax rate.

Two of the most common reasons taxpayers seek refunds and releases *do not* satisfy G.S. 105-381. Governing boards should not approve tax waiver requests based on either

1. value judgments by the assessor's office or
2. clerical errors made by the taxpayer rather than by the tax office.

First, consider value judgments made by the assessor. These judgments must be challenged during the regular appeal process that closes when the county board of equalization and review adjourns. (See "Listing and Assessing," above.) Otherwise, a local government would have great difficulties budgeting each year because its tax base would always be subject to retroactive adjustments due to after-the-fact value appeals. These errors in judgment can be corrected going forward so that future tax bills are accurate, but retroactive changes are not permitted.

The best question to ask when deciding if a mistake by the tax office was a value judgment or a clerical error is: was the resulting assessment the one intended by the assessor? If so, the issue is a value judgment that cannot justify a refund or release. If not, the issue is a clerical error that can justify a refund or release.

For example, consider two houses that were each assessed at $400,000 during Carolina County's last reappraisal in 2024.

House A was intended to be assessed at a square footage of 2,500, but a data entry error resulted in the square footage being recorded at 5,200. As a result, the assessment increased from the intended $300,000 to $400,000.

House B was assessed as if it had a finished basement and third floor, as do all of the other houses in House B's development. The assessor calculated the finished square footage to be 5,200. In fact, House B has neither a finished basement nor third floor, and its actual finished square footage is 2,500. Had the assessor known that the house did not have this extra finished space, the house's assessment would have dropped from $400,000 to $300,000.

Neither owner appealed the tax valuation in 2024. Both learned of the mistakes made by the tax office in 2025 and asked for a refund of the excess taxes they paid in 2024. How should the Carolina County board of county commissioners respond to these requests?

Only the owner of House A is entitled to a refund of 2024 taxes. The mistake involving House A was a true clerical error because the assessor never intended to assess House A as if it had 5,200 square feet. A refund is justified and the assessment reduced for 2025 and future years.

The mistake involving House B did not produce an unintended assessment. Based on the information before the assessor at the time, the assessor intended the assessment for House B to be based on a square footage of 5,200. This was a judgment error, not a clerical error. If the taxpayer disputed this figure, he or she had the obligation to raise the issue during the 2024 appeal process. No refund is justified. The assessor should collect the assessment on House B for 2025 and future years but not retroactively.

Similarly, a taxpayer should not receive a refund based on valuation errors from prior tax years. For example, assume Tommy TarHeel's house is appraised at $500,000 as part of Carolina County's 2024 reappraisal. Tommy does not appeal in 2024. But he does appeal in 2025 and produces evidence that an identical house directly across the street from his house sold in late 2023 for $400,000. The assessor agrees that Tommy's house should have been assessed at $400,000 for 2024. The assessor should change the tax value of Tommy's house to $400,000 for 2025 and subsequent years but should not provide a refund for any taxes paid by Tommy in 2024. This issue was a valuation error, not an illegal tax, and no refund is justified under G.S. 105-381.

Second, consider clerical errors made by the taxpayer. The Machinery Act permits refunds and releases when taxes are "levied due to clerical error." Because only local governments can levy property taxes, the clerical error in question must be one by a local government and not one by a taxpayer.

A common taxpayer error concerns escrow payments. Many taxpayers escrow their property taxes with their mortgage companies and do not pay those taxes directly. If a taxpayer forgets about the escrow fund and mails a tax payment to the tax office, can that taxpayer get a refund of that payment because the mortgage company will be paying those taxes later in the year? The answer is no, because the payment was for a validly levied tax and the taxpayer's mistake cannot justify a refund. The taxpayer should seek a refund from the mortgage company, not from the tax office.

Another common error arises when a mortgage company sends tax payments for multiple parcels and mistakenly instructs the tax office to apply one of those payments to the wrong parcel. When the mortgage company learns of its mistake, is it entitled to have its payment moved to the correct parcel? Again the answer is no because moving that tax payment from one parcel to another

Table 19.9 Time Limits on Refunds and Releases under G.S. 105-381

Releases of unpaid taxes	No time limit
Refunds of paid taxes	The later of: • five years from the original due date *or* • six months from the date the taxes were paid

would constitute a refund of the taxes on the original parcel. Of course, if the tax office made the mistake and applied the payment to the wrong parcel contrary to the mortgage company's instructions, a refund would be justified.

Who Makes the Decision to Authorize a Refund or Release?

The authority to approve refunds and releases lies with the local governing board, not with the tax collector. For small refunds (less than $100), the governing board can delegate the authority to approve refunds and releases to the local government's finance officer, manager, or attorney.

In practice, tax collectors often make routine refunds and seek approval from the board later. For example, if the tax office mistakenly processes a payment for taxes that have already been paid, the tax collector might refund the duplicate payment before seeking permission from the board. Governing boards should discuss this issue with their tax collectors so that all parties are clear on how to proceed before problems arise.

Time Limits on Refunds and Releases

The Machinery Act does not create a time limit for releases of unpaid taxes. But refunds of paid taxes are limited to the later of (1) five years from the date the tax was originally due or (2) six months from the date the taxes were paid (see Table 19.9).

For example, assume that Blue Devil City has been levying taxes on Tommy TarHeel's property for decades under the assumption that Tommy's property is within the municipal limits. Tommy has paid those taxes each year in a timely fashion. In July 2025, Tommy has a new survey done that demonstrates that his property is in fact outside the municipal limits. Tommy immediately asks for a refund of all of the municipal taxes he has paid since purchasing the property in 2000.

Tommy is clearly entitled to a refund because it is illegal for Blue Devil City to tax property not within its borders. But Tommy's refund is limited by the Machinery Act to those taxes that came due within five years of Tommy's refund request. Taxes on real property are due on September 1 each year. The 2020 taxes were due on September 1, 2020, which is within five years of Tommy's request for a refund in July 2025. But the 2019 taxes fall outside of that five-year window because they were due on September 1, 2019. And the six-months-from-payment provision does not apply because Tommy paid those taxes back in 2019, long before submitting his refund request. Taxes from years 2018 and earlier similarly fall outside of the refund limitations. As a result, Tommy is entitled to a refund of municipal taxes only for the years 2020–2024.

Registered Motor Vehicles

The Tag & Tax Together System

The taxation of registered motor vehicles (RMVs) is a world unto itself. The rules and practices described above do not necessarily apply to taxes levied on RMVs.

Under the Tag & Tax Together system that took effect in 2013, the N.C. Division of Motor Vehicles (DMV) collects both registration fees and local government property taxes on registered motor vehicles at the time of registration or renewal. The taxes are passed along to the appropriate local governments minus a small collection fee retained by the state. If the taxes are not paid, the DMV will not permit the motor vehicle to be registered or renewed. Local governments no longer have any collection authority for taxes on RMVs.[58]

Despite the varying collection methods, local governments must levy property taxes on RMVs at the same rate levied on other types of personal property and on real property. The uniformity provisions in the North Carolina Constitution discussed in "The Property Tax Rate," above, prohibit local governments from taxing RMVs at rates different from those applied to other property within their jurisdictions.

Other Local Taxes on Motor Vehicles

In addition to property taxes, both counties and municipalities have the authority to generate other revenues from motor vehicles.

Counties have the authority to levy a registration tax of up to $7 per year if the county or one of the local governments in the county operates a public transportation system.[59] The proceeds from this tax may be used only for the creation or operation of that public transportation system.

All municipalities are authorized to levy taxes on the privilege of operating a motor vehicle within their borders of up to $30 per vehicle.[60] The first $5 of that tax may be used for any legal purpose. An additional $5 of the tax may be used for the creation or operation of a public transit system. Any remaining revenue from the tax must be used for constructing, repairing, or improving public streets. Some municipalities have been exempted from these usage restrictions through local acts of the General Assembly.

The DMV collects these additional local government taxes on RMVs along with property taxes at the time of registration or renewal.

---

58. G.S. Ch. 105, Art. 22A.
59. G.S. Ch. 105, Art. 52.
60. G.S. 20-97.

Chapter 20

Budgeting for Operating and Capital Expenditures

Kara A. Millonzi and William C. Rivenbark

Kara A. Millonzi is a School of Government faculty member who specializes in local government and public school finance law. William C. Rivenbark is a School of Government faculty member who specializes in local government administration.

Introduction

North Carolina counties, municipalities, and public authorities (collectively, local units) are required to budget and spend money in accordance with the Local Government Budget and Fiscal Control Act (LGBFCA), codified as Article 3 of Chapter 159 of the North Carolina General Statutes (hereinafter G.S.). In fact, a local unit may not expend any funds, regardless of their source, unless the money has been properly budgeted through the annual budget ordinance, a project ordinance, or a financial plan adopted by the unit's governing board.[1] On the expenditure side, a local unit may spend public funds only for purposes specifically authorized by the state legislature, through general laws, charter provisions, or other local acts. Revenues and expenditures for the provision of general government services are authorized in the annual budget ordinance.[2] Revenues and expenditures for an internal service fund are authorized in the annual budget ordinance or in a financial plan.[3] Revenues and expenditures for capital projects or for projects financed with grant proceeds are authorized in the annual budget ordinance or in a project ordinance.[4]

This chapter describes the legal requirements for budgeting for operating and capital expenditures. It also presents common budget tools and techniques for both the annual (operating) and capital budgeting processes. The chapter is divided into three sections. The first discusses how to prepare, adopt, and amend a unit's annual budget ordinance and presents various tools available to assist local officials during the budgeting process. The second briefly details the requirements for adopting and implementing a financial plan. Finally, the third section focuses on the adoption of a project ordinance for capital projects and expenditures. It also discusses common strategies for capital planning.

Annual Budget Ordinance

The annual budget ordinance is the legal document that recognizes revenues, authorizes expenditures, and levies taxes for a local unit for a single fiscal year. (Each unit's fiscal year runs from July 1 through June 30.)[5] The budget ordinance must be adopted by the unit's governing board. At its core, it reflects the governing board's policy preferences and provides a roadmap for implementing the board's vision for the unit. The LGBFCA, however, requires the board to include certain items in the budget ordinance and to follow a detailed procedure for adopting it.

---

1. There is an exception to this inclusiveness requirement. The LGBFCA permits the revenues of certain local government trust and custodial funds to be spent or disbursed without being budgeted. G.S. 159-13(a)(3). For example, many counties and municipalities set aside and manage moneys in a pension trust fund to finance special separation allowances for law enforcement officers. The employees and retirees for whom the local government is managing these moneys have ownership rights. Although a county or municipality must budget its initial contributions on behalf of employees into the pension trust fund, once the moneys are in the fund, earnings on the assets, payments to retirees, and other receipts and disbursements of the funds should not be included in the local government's budget. Municipalities sometimes maintain perpetual trust funds for the care and maintenance of individual plots in the unit's cemetery.

Another example is when a county or municipality collects certain revenue for another governmental unit and records this revenue in a custodial fund. Although the moneys are held temporarily by the county or the municipality, they belong to the other unit. The collections, therefore, are not revenues of the county or municipality collecting them and should not be included in its budget.

2. G.S. 159-13.

3. G.S. 159-13.1.

4. G.S. 159-13.2.

5. G.S. 159-8(b). The Local Government Commission may authorize a public authority (as defined in G.S. 159-7) to have a different fiscal year if it facilitates the authority's operations.

Substantive Requirements and Restrictions

The LGBFCA imposes certain substantive requirements and limitations on the budget ordinance.

Balanced Budget

Perhaps the most important statutory requirement is that the budget ordinance be balanced. A budget ordinance is balanced when "the sum of estimated net revenues and appropriated fund balances is equal to appropriations."[6] The law requires an exact balance; it permits neither a deficit nor a surplus. Furthermore, each of the accounting funds that make up the annual budget ordinance (e.g., general fund, enterprise fund) also must be balanced.[7]

Estimated net revenues is the first variable in the balanced-budget equation; it comprises the revenues a unit expects to actually receive during the fiscal year, including amounts to be realized from collections of taxes or fees levied in prior fiscal years. (Typically, debt proceeds are not considered a form of revenue, but for budgetary purposes debt proceeds that are or will become available during the fiscal year are included in estimated net revenues.) The LGBFCA requires that a unit make reasonable estimates of the amount of revenue it expects to receive.[8] A unit should have some demonstrable basis for its estimates, such as historical trends or other comparable data. The law places a specific limitation on property tax estimates. The estimated percentage of property tax collection budgeted for the coming fiscal year cannot exceed the percentage of collection realized in cash as of June 30 during the fiscal year preceding the budget year.[9]

Revenues must be budgeted by "major source."[10] This includes, at a minimum, property, sales, and use taxes; licenses and permits; intergovernmental revenues; charges for services; specific grant programs; and other taxes and revenues. A unit is free to group revenues in more-detailed categories.

The second variable in the balanced-budget equation is *appropriated fund balance*. Appropriated fund balance is best understood as the amount of cash reserves needed to fill the gap between estimated revenues and appropriations. Only a portion of a local unit's fund balance is available for appropriation each year. The LGBFCA defines the fund balance available for appropriation as "the sum of cash and investments minus the sum of liabilities, encumbrances, and deferred revenues arising from cash receipts, as those figures stand at the close of the fiscal year next preceding the budget year."[11] Legally available fund balance is different from fund balance for financial reporting purposes as presented on the balance sheet of a local government's annual financial report. It includes only cash and investments, not receivables or other current assets. Legally available fund balance results when unbudgeted fund balance carries forward from prior years, actual revenues exceed estimated revenues in the current fiscal year, actual expenditures are less than appropriations in the current fiscal year, or actual revenues exceed actual expenditures in the current fiscal year. A portion of this fund balance usually is legally restricted to certain expenditures. A governing board may appropriate restricted fund balance only for those specified purposes.

---

6. G.S. 159-8(a).

7. For a description of the purpose and function of accounting funds, see Chapter 10, "Accounting, Financial Reporting, and the Annual Audit," of *Introduction to Local Government Finance*, edited by Connor H. Crews (UNC School of Government, 2023).

8. G.S. 159-13(b)(7).

9. G.S. 159-13(b)(6). The statute provides for a different calculation when budgeting for property taxes on registered motor vehicles. The percentage of collection is based on the nine-month levy ending March 31 of the fiscal year preceding the budget year, and the collections realized in cash with respect to this levy are based on the twelve-month period ending June 30 of the fiscal year preceding the budget year.

10. G.S. 159-13(a).

11. G.S. 159-13(b)(16).

The calculation for determining the amount of legally available fund balance that may be appropriated to cover new expenditures starts with an estimate of cash and investments at the end of the current year and subtracts from them estimated liabilities, encumbrances, and deferred revenues from cash receipts at the end of the current year. All these figures are estimates because the calculation is being made for budget purposes before the end of the current year. If the estimate of available fund balance is for the general fund, typical liabilities are (1) payroll owed for a payroll period that will carry forward from the current year into the budget year and (2) accounts payable representing unpaid vendor accounts for goods and services provided to the local government toward the end of the current year. Encumbrances arise from purchase orders and other unfulfilled contractual obligations for goods and services that are outstanding at the end of a fiscal year. They reduce legally available fund balance because cash and investments will be needed to pay for the goods and services on order. (Note that the board is required to appropriate in the new budget ordinance this portion of the fund balance to cover the encumbered amounts that will be paid out in the next fiscal year.) Deferred revenue from a cash receipt is revenue that is received in cash in the current year, even though it is not owed to the local government until the coming budget year. Such prepaid revenues are primarily property taxes. They should be included among revenues for the coming year's budget rather than carried forward as available fund balance from the current to the coming year.

A unit's governing board is not required to appropriate all the resulting fund balance, only that which is required, when added to estimated net revenues, to equal the budgeted appropriations for the fiscal year. The remaining moneys serve as cash reserves of the unit, to be used to aid in cash flow during the fiscal year. A unit also may use unappropriated fund balance to save money, which can be used to meet emergency or unforeseen needs or to take advantage of unexpected opportunities. And some units accumulate fund balance as a savings account for anticipated future capital projects, which also helps them maintain or improve their credit ratings.

The third variable in the balanced-budget equation is *appropriations for expenditures*. An appropriation is a legal authorization to make an obligation and expenditure. But it is not an actual obligation or expenditure. An appropriation is a necessary predicate to incurring obligations (through contracts and agreements) and making expenditures. Only a governing board may authorize appropriations. The LGBFCA allows a governing board to make appropriations in the budget ordinance by department, function, or project.[12] For example, a board may appropriate total sums to the finance department, public works department, law enforcement department, planning-and-zoning department, and so on. Each department then has flexibility to fund its operational and capital expenditures from its budget allocation. The term *function* has two possible meanings in budgeting. It allows a local government to group together multiple departments, such as law enforcement and fire, under a broader budgeting category of "public safety." Alternatively, it allows a board to appropriate moneys for major expenditure categories within each department, such as salaries/benefits, utilities, supplies, insurance, capital, and the like. In this case, the budget officer or manager, the department heads, and other staff may not exceed the amounts budgeted for each function category. The same is true if a board appropriates by project. A governing board may not make appropriations by line item or by an individual object of expenditure in the budget ordinance itself. The budget ordinance is a summary document that, for ease of exposition, aggregates expenditures. Many governing boards require submittal of more-detailed line-item budgets by each department to justify the expenditures being requested. A board may require the manager or

12. G.S. 159-13(a).

head of each department to follow the more-detailed budgets ("working budgets") during the fiscal year. The budget ordinance represents the legal appropriations of the unit, though.[13]

A question that often arises is whether a governing board may appropriate money for savings toward projects or programs in future fiscal years. North Carolina law does not allow a local government to appropriate money to fund balance. Fund balance results when either actual revenues exceed budget estimates or actual expenditures are less than budgeted appropriations in any given fiscal year. As detailed below, though, a governing board may appropriate funds to a capital reserve fund to save moneys for future, specific capital projects.

Required Budget-Ordinance Appropriations

In addition to the balanced-budget requirement, the LGBFCA directs a governing board to include certain appropriations in its budget ordinance.[14] These requirements apply to the initial adoption of the budget ordinance as well as to any subsequent amendments.

Debt Service

A governing board must appropriate the full amount estimated by the local government's finance officer to be required for debt service during the fiscal year.[15] During the spring, the Local Government Commission (LGC) notifies each finance officer of that local government's debt-service obligation on existing debt for the coming year. If a county or municipality does not appropriate enough money for the payment of principal and interest on its debt, the LGC may order the unit to make the necessary appropriation; if the unit ignores this order, the LGC may itself levy the local tax for debt-service purposes.[16]

Continuing Contracts

A governing board must make appropriations to cover any obligations that will come due during the fiscal year under a continuing contract, unless the contract terms expressly authorize the board to refuse to do so in any given budget year.[17] Continuing contracts are those that extend for more than one fiscal year.

Fund Deficits

A governing board must make appropriations to cover any deficits within a fund. A deficit occurs if the amount actually encumbered exceeds appropriations within the fund. If a unit follows the provisions on expenditure control in the LGBFCA, a deficit should not occur. However, should a deficit occur, a governing board must appropriate sufficient moneys in the next fiscal year's budget to eliminate that deficit.

---

13. This distinction is significant. For example, the statute governing disbursements of public funds requires that before an obligation may be incurred by a unit, the finance officer or a deputy finance officer must verify that there is an appropriation authorizing that particular expenditure. G.S. 159-28(a). The statute refers to an appropriation in the budget ordinance, not in more-detailed working budgets.

14. Note that the budget-ordinance requirements discussed in this chapter generally are limited to those imposed by the LGBFCA. Units must be mindful that other statutory provisions may place additional requirements or restrictions on the budget ordinance.

15. G.S. 159-13(b)(1).

16. G.S. 159-36. Note that the LGC may not require a unit to make appropriations for repayment of installment-financing debt incurred under G.S. 160A-20 because of the requirement of a nonappropriation clause. The provision also does not apply to contractual obligations undertaken by a local government in a debt instrument issued pursuant to G.S. 159G unless the debt instrument is secured by a pledge of the full faith and credit of the unit.

17. G.S. 159-13(b)(15).

Property Taxes

If a local unit levies property taxes (which it is not required to do), the governing board must do so in the budget ordinance.[18] The levy is stated in terms of rate of cents per $100 of taxable value.[19]

Encumbered Fund Balance

If a local unit incurred obligations in the prior year that have not been paid, it must appropriate sufficient amounts to cover those expenditures in the new fiscal year. Once the fiscal year expires, there is no budget authority to disburse funds under the prior year's budget. The moneys must be included in the new budget ordinance before they can be disbursed. This often occurs when a unit orders goods or enters into service contracts toward the end of the fiscal year.

Limits on Appropriations

Other LGBFCA provisions place upper or lower limits on certain appropriations in the budget ordinance. The statute also specifies the types of funds that may (and sometimes must) be used.

Contingency Appropriations

In each fund, a governing board may include a contingency appropriation, that is, an appropriation that is not designated to a specific department, function, or project. The contingency appropriation may not exceed 5 percent of the total of all other appropriations in the fund, though.[20] The governing board may delegate authority to the unit's budget officer to assign contingency appropriations to specific departments, functions, or projects during the fiscal year.[21]

Tax-Levy Limits

If a unit levies property taxes, the proceeds must be used only for statutorily authorized purposes. A governing board may not include an appropriation of property tax revenue that is not authorized by law. In addition, there is a cap on the aggregate property tax rate per taxing entity of $1.50 per $100 of property valuation.[22] Furthermore, the estimated percentage of collection of property taxes used in the rate calculation may not exceed the percentage of the levy actually realized in cash as of June 30 during the prior fiscal year.[23]

Required Funds

Each unit must maintain funds applicable to it according to generally acceptable accounting principles.[24]

---

18. G.S. 159-13(a).

19. The process of levying property taxes is described in greater detail in Chapter 4, "Revenue Sources," and Chapter 5, "Property Tax Policy and Administration," of *Introduction to Local Government Finance.*

20. G.S. 159-13(b)(3).

21. *See* G.S. 159-15.

22. G.S. 159-13(b)(4). Note that G.S. 160A-209 and 153A-149 authorize a municipality and a county, respectively, to seek voter approval to levy property taxes for purposes not authorized under general law. If a unit receives voter approval to expend property tax proceeds for another purpose, the total of all appropriations for that purpose may not exceed the total of all other unrestricted revenues and property taxes levied for it. G.S. 159-13(b)(5). Voters also vote on levying tax rates for one or more purposes such that the combined total rate exceeds the $1.50-per-$100 valuation cap.

23. For more information on calculating property tax rates, see Chapter 5, "Property Tax Policy and Administration," of *Introduction to Local Government Finance.*

24. G.S. 159-26.

Limits on Interfund Transfers

The annual budget ordinance sometimes includes appropriations to transfer money from one fund to another. The LGBFCA generally permits appropriations for interfund transfers, but it sets some restrictions on them, each designed to maintain the basic integrity of a fund in light of the purposes for which the fund was established. In addition, the LGBFCA prohibits certain interfund transfers of moneys that are earmarked for a specific service.

Each of the limitations on interfund transfers discussed below is subject to the modification that any fund may be charged for general administrative and overhead costs properly allocated to its activities as well as for the costs of levying and collecting its revenues.[25]

Voted Property Taxes

Proceeds from a voted property tax may be used only for the purpose approved by the voters. Such proceeds must be budgeted and accounted for in a special revenue fund[26] and generally may not be transferred to another fund,[27] except to a capital reserve fund[28] (if appropriate).

Custodial Funds for Special Districts

A special district is a unit of local government, other than a county or municipality, "created for the performance of limited governmental functions or for the operation of a particular utility or public service enterprises."[29] Some units collect moneys on behalf of a special district. These moneys must be budgeted and accounted for in a custodial fund and are not part of the local unit's annual budget ordinance.[30]

Enterprise Funds

A governing board may transfer moneys from an enterprise fund to another fund only if other appropriations in the enterprise fund are sufficient to meet operating expenses, capital outlays, and debt service for the enterprise.[31] This limitation reflects the policy that enterprise revenues must first meet the expenses and the obligations related to the enterprise. (Note that other statutory provisions further restrict or prohibit a unit from transferring moneys associated with certain public enterprises.)

Although transferring money from an enterprise fund to another fund is legally allowed, it may have negative consequences. It may, for example, lower a local unit's credit rating or disqualify the unit from certain state loan and grant programs.[32]

---

25. G.S. 159-13(b).

26. G.S. 159-26(b)(2).

27. G.S. 159-13(b)(10).

28. A unit may establish and maintain a capital reserve fund to save moneys over time to fund certain designated capital expenditures. G.S. 159-18. For more information on capital reserve funds, see Chapter 7, "Financing Capital Projects," of *Introduction to Local Government Finance*.

29. G.S. 159-7(b)(13).

30. G.S. 159-14(b).

31. G.S. 159-13(b)(14). Note that "a county may, upon a finding that a fund balance in a utility or public service enterprise fund used for operation of a landfill exceeds the requirements for funding the operation of that fund, including closure and post-closure expenditures, transfer excess funds accruing due to imposition of a surcharge imposed on another local government located within the State for use of the disposal facility, as authorized by G.S. 153A-292(b), to support the other services supported by the county's general fund." *Id.*

32. *See* G.S. 159G-37; *see also* Kara Millonzi, "Transferring Money from an Enterprise Fund: Authority, Limitations, and Consequences," *Coates' Canons: NC Local Government Law* blog (June 5, 2015), canons.sog.unc.edu/2015/06/transferring-money-from-an-enterprise-fund-authority-limitations-and-consequences/.

Reappraisal Reserve Fund

A reappraisal reserve fund is established to accumulate money to finance a county's next real-property revaluation, which must occur at least once every eight years. Appropriations to a reappraisal reserve fund may not be used for any other purpose.[33]

Service-District Funds

A service district is a special taxing district of a county or municipality. Although a service district is not a separate local government unit, both the proceeds of a service-district tax and other revenues appropriated to the district belong to the district. Therefore, no appropriation may be made to transfer moneys from a service-district fund except for the purposes for which the district was established.[34]

Optional Budget-Ordinance Provisions

The annual budget ordinance must contain revenue estimates, appropriations for expenditures, and, if applicable, the property tax levy. The ordinance must show revenues and expenditures by fund and demonstrate a balance in each fund. A governing board, however, is free to include other sections or provisions in the ordinance. For example, it might include instructions on its administration. If a fund contains earmarked revenues and general revenues or supports a function for which property taxes may not be used, the ordinance might specify the use of the earmarked funds or direct which non-property-tax revenues are to support the function in question. The ordinance also may authorize and limit certain transfers among departmental or functional appropriations within the same fund and set rates or fees for public enterprises or other governmental services.

Adoption of Annual Budget Ordinance

In addition to imposing certain substantive requirements related to the annual budget ordinance, the LGBFCA also prescribes a detailed process for adopting the ordinance.

Role of Budget Officer

Before discussing the specifics of the budget process, it is important to understand the role of the budget officer. The governing board of each unit must appoint a budget officer. In a county or municipality having the manager form of government, the manager is the statutory budget officer. Counties that do not have the manager form of government may impose the duties of budget officer on the finance officer or on any other county employee except the sheriff or, in counties with a population greater than 7,500, the register of deeds. Municipalities not having the manager form of government may impose the duties of budget officer on any municipal employee, including the mayor (if the mayor consents). A public authority or special district may impose the duties on the chairperson of its governing board, on any member of that board, or on any other employee.[35]

The LGBFCA assigns to the budget officer the responsibility of preparing and submitting a proposed budget to the governing board each year. Having one official who is responsible for budget preparation focuses responsibility for timely preparation of the budget, permits a technical review of departmental estimates to ensure completeness and accuracy, and allows for administrative analysis of departmental priorities in the context of a local unit's overall priorities. In many units,

---

33. G.S. 159-13(b)(17).

34. G.S. 159-13(b)(18). This restriction also applies to any other revenues that the local unit has appropriated to the service district.

35. G.S. 159-9.

the statutory budget officer often delegates many of the duties associated with budget preparation to another employee, for example, the finance officer or a separate budget director or administrator. This is strictly an administrative arrangement, with the official or employee performing these duties under the direction of the statutory budget officer. Under the law, the budget officer retains full responsibility for budget preparation.

Once the budget ordinance is adopted, the budget officer is charged with overseeing its enactment. As discussed below, the governing board also may authorize the budget officer to make certain limited modifications to the budget ordinance during the fiscal year.

Budgeting Process

Before the budgeting process begins, the budget officer, often with guidance from the governing board, establishes an administrative calendar for budget preparations and prescribes forms and procedures for departments to use in formulating requests. Budget officers often include fiscal or program policies to guide departmental officials in formulating their budget requests. The LGBFCA specifies certain target dates for the key stages in the budgeting process, which should be incorporated into the budget officer's plan.

A budget officer's calendar often includes other steps that, though not statutorily required, are integral to an effective budgeting process. For example, many units kick off the annual budget process with one or more budget retreats or workshops for governing board members, department heads, and others. This allows board members to set policy for the coming year and provide directives to the budget officer and department heads about budget requests at the outset of the budget process.

Sometimes a budget officer will need to include other boards, organizations, or citizens in the budgeting process. Counties must provide funding for several functions that are (or may be) governed by other boards, such as public schools, community colleges, elections, social services, mental health, and public health. These boards have their own processes for formulating proposed budgets and requesting funds from the county. In addition, both counties and municipalities routinely receive requests from nonprofits, other private organizations, or citizens for appropriations to support certain community activities and projects. (A county or municipality generally does not have authority to make grants to private entities (including nonprofits). The county or municipality may, however, enter into a contract with a private entity and pay it to perform a function on behalf of the local government.[36]) The budget officer often serves as the liaison between these other boards, private entities, and citizen groups and the governing board. The budget officer should work with the governing board to establish an organized process for the board to receive and evaluate these various requests.

Budget Calendar

By April 30: Departmental Requests Submitted

The LGBFCA directs that each department head submit the revenue estimates and budget requests for the budget year to the budget officer. Each department, or the unit's finance officer, also must submit information about current-year revenues and expenditures. The budget officer should specify the format for, and detail of, these submissions.[37]

---

36. G.S. 153A-449 (counties); 160A-20.1 (municipalities).
37. G.S. 159-10.

By June 1: Proposed Budget Presented

The budget officer must compile each department head's revenue estimates and budget requests and submit a proposed budget for consideration by the governing board.[38] Generally the proposed budget must comply with all the substantive requirements previously discussed. A governing board, however, may request that the budget officer submit a budget containing recommended appropriations that are greater than estimated revenues.[39] This affords the board a ready opportunity to discuss different expenditure options.

The budget officer must include a budget message when submitting the proposed budget to the governing board.[40] The message should contain a summary explanation of the unit's goals for the budget year. It also should detail important activities funded in the budget and point out any changes from the previous fiscal year in program goals, appropriation levels, and fiscal policy.

If a revaluation of real taxable property in the unit occurs in the year preceding the budget year, the budget officer must include in the proposed budget a statement of the revenue-neutral tax rate, "the rate that is estimated to produce revenue for the next fiscal year equal to the revenue that would have been produced for the next fiscal year by the current tax rate if no reappraisal had occurred."[41] While the LGBFCA is silent on where the revenue-neutral tax rate must be included in the proposed budget, an appropriate place would be the budget message.[42] The rate is calculated as follows:

1. Determine a rate that would produce revenues equal to those produced for the current fiscal year.
2. Increase the rate by a growth factor equal to the average annual percentage increase in the tax base due to improvements since the last general reappraisal.
3. Adjust the rate to account for any annexation, deannexation, merger, or similar events.

After Proposed Budget Presented but before Its Adoption: Notice and Public Hearing

When the budget officer submits the proposed budget to the governing board, a copy must be filed in the office of the clerk to the board, where it remains for public inspection until the governing board adopts the budget ordinance.[43] The clerk must publish a statement that the proposed budget has been submitted to the governing board and is available for public inspection.[44] The LGBFCA does not specify where or when the statement must be published. The clerk should follow the general provisions for legal advertising in Article 50 of G.S. 1. The clerk also must make a copy of the proposed budget available to all news media in the county. It may be helpful for a unit to also post the proposed budget on its website, though it is not legally mandated.

The governing board is required to wait at least ten days after the budget officer submits the proposed budget before adopting the budget ordinance. This is true even if the board makes no changes to the proposed budget.[45] This interim period affords citizens time to review the proposed budget and to voice their opinions or objections to governing board members.

---

38. G.S. 159-11(a).
39. G.S. 159-11(c).
40. G.S. 159-11(b).
41. G.S. 159-11(e).
42. *See* Shea Riggsbee Denning and William C. Rivenbark, "Statement of Revenue-Neutral Tax Rate and Provision for Mid-Year Property Tax Rate Change," *Local Finance Bulletin* No. 32 (November 2004).
43. G.S. 159-12(a).
44. G.S. 159-12(a). The notice also must specify the date and time of the public hearing to be held on the budget.
45. G.S. 159-13. The ten-day period begins to run the day after the notice is published. Weekend days and legal holidays count toward the total number of days. However, the ten-day period may not end on a Saturday, Sunday, or legal holiday. It must instead end on the next weekday that is not a legal holiday. *See* Rules of Civil Procedure, G.S. 1A-1, r. 6.

The governing board also must hold at least one public hearing on the proposed budget before adopting the budget ordinance. During the public hearing, any person who wishes to be heard on the budget must be allowed time to speak. The board should set the time and place for the public hearing when it receives the proposed budget, if not before. This information should be included in the notice published by the clerk. Sometimes a board holds a series of budget-review meetings and briefings on each of the major budget categories. These do not satisfy the statutory requirement. The law requires that at least one public hearing be held on the entire budget. The statute requires no specific minimum number of days between the date on which the notice appears and the date on which the hearing is held; however, the notice should be timely enough to allow for full public participation at the hearing.

By July 1: Adoption of Budget Ordinance

After the governing board receives the proposed budget, it is free to make changes to the budget before adopting the budget ordinance. In fact, based on citizen input, as well as that from other boards and department heads, the governing board often makes adjustments to the proposed budget before finalizing and adopting the ordinance. Questions often arise when a board makes changes to the proposed budget about whether and to what extent it must make the changes known to the public before adopting the ordinance. The statute requires only that the budget officer's proposed budget be made available for public inspection and that one public hearing be held after the proposed budget is submitted to the board. A unit is under no legal obligation to provide notice or solicit public input of modifications to the proposed budget before its adoption.

The LGBFCA allows a budget ordinance to be adopted at any regular or special meeting, at which a quorum is present, by a simple majority of those present and voting.[46] The board must provide sufficient notice of the meeting, according to the provisions in the applicable open meetings law.[47] The budget ordinance is entered in the board's minutes, and within five days of its adoption, copies are to be filed with the budget officer, the finance officer, and the clerk to the board.[48]

Once the board adopts the budget ordinance, it may not repeal it. Any modifications are made pursuant to G.S. 159-15 (discussed below). This is true even if the board adopts the budget ordinance before July 1.[49]

Interim Appropriations

Missing the April 30 or June 1 deadline does not invalidate the budgetary process or budget ordinance. There are some consequences to missing the July 1 deadline, though. After June 30, a unit has no authority to make expenditures (including payment of staff salaries) under the prior year's budget. If a board does not adopt the budget ordinance by July 1 and needs to make expenditures, it must adopt an interim budget, making "interim appropriations for the purpose of paying salaries, debt service payments, and the usual ordinary expenses" of the unit until the budget ordinance is

46. G.S. 159-17. Adoption of the budget ordinance is not subject to the normal ordinance-adoption requirements of G.S. 153A-45, for counties, and 160A-75, for municipalities.

47. *See* G.S. 143-318.12. However, G.S. 159-17 specifies that "no provision of law concerning the call of special meetings applies during [the period beginning with the submission of the proposed budget and ending with the adoption of the budget ordinance] so long as (i) each member of the board has actual notice of each special meeting called for the purpose of considering the budget, and (ii) no business other than consideration of the budget is taken up."

48. G.S. 159-13(d).

49. *See* Kara Millonzi, "Amending a Newly Adopted Budget Ordinance before July 1," *Coates' Canons: NC Local Government Law* blog (June 13, 2011), canons.sog.unc.edu/2011/06/amending-a-newly-adopted-budget-ordinance-before-july-1/.

adopted.[50] This is a stopgap measure. An interim budget should not include appropriations for salary and wage increases, capital items, or program or service expansion. It may not levy property taxes, nor should it change or increase other tax or user fee rates. The purpose of an interim budget is to temporarily keep operations going at current levels. An interim budget need not include revenues to balance the appropriations. All expenditures made under an interim budget are charged against the comparable appropriations in the annual budget ordinance once it is adopted. In other words, the interim expenditures eventually are funded with revenues included in the budget ordinance.

LGC Action for Failure to Adopt a Budget Ordinance

At some point, if a local unit's governing board refuses or is unable to adopt its budget ordinance, the LGC may take action. State law empowers the LGC to "assume full control" of a unit's financial affairs if the unit "persists, after notice and warning from the [LGC], in willfully or negligently failing or refusing to comply with the provisions" of the LGBFCA. If the LGC takes this action, it becomes vested "with all of the powers of the governing board as to the levy of taxes, expenditure of money, adoption of budgets, and all other financial powers conferred upon the governing board by law."[51] LGC takeover will only occur in extreme cases, though. Most of the time, a unit's governing board is left to work out any differences and adopt its budget ordinance.

Budgetary Accounting

The LGBFCA requires local units to maintain an accounting system with applicable funds as defined by generally accepted accounting principles.[52] Local units enter their adopted budgets into their accounting systems at the beginning of the fiscal year; this allows them to accurately track the difference between an appropriation and the accumulated expenditures and encumbrances applied against that appropriation. Budgetary accounting is considered a best practice for several reasons. It provides the foundation for budget-to-actual variance reports, providing critical information to departments for remaining within their budgets and to elected officials who possess the ultimate fiduciary responsibility of the organization. It also provides the information needed for managing budget amendments and for complying with the preaudit requirement.[53] Finally, it provides the needed information for following generally accepted accounting principles when local units issue their annual financial statements.

Amending the Budget Ordinance

The adopted budget ordinance encompasses a unit's legal authority to make all expenditures during the fiscal year. Before a unit may incur an obligation (order goods, enter into service contracts, or otherwise incur obligations of the unit), the finance officer or a deputy finance officer must ensure that there is an appropriation authorizing the expenditure and that sufficient moneys remain in the appropriation to cover the expenditure.[54] Events during a fiscal year may cause greater or less spending than anticipated for some activities, or needs may arise for which there is no appropriation or for which the existing one is exhausted. To address these situations the local unit may need to amend the budget ordinance.

---

50. G.S. 159-16.
51. G.S. 159-181(c).
52. G.S. 159-26.
53. See G.S. 159-15 for budget amendments. See G.S. 159-28 for the preaudit requirement.
54. *See* G.S. 159-28(a).

The budget ordinance may be amended at any time after its adoption.[55] A governing board may modify appropriations for expenditures, recognize additional revenue, and appropriate fund balance to cover new expenditures. As amended, however, the budget ordinance must continue to be balanced and comply with the other substantive requirements previously discussed. Although not legally required to do so, a governing board also may amend the budget ordinance to reflect changes in revenue estimates during the fiscal year.

A budget ordinance may be amended by action of a simple majority of board members so long as a quorum is present. There are no notice or public hearing requirements. Alternatively, a governing board may delegate to the budget officer the authority to make certain changes to the budget. This authority is limited to (1) transfers of moneys from one appropriation to another within the same fund or (2) allocation of contingency appropriations to certain expenditures within the same fund. All other changes to the budget ordinance, including any revenue changes, must be made by the governing board.

Changing the Property Tax Levy

Local government units are limited in their ability to legally change the property tax levy or otherwise alter a property-tax payer's liability once the budget ordinance has been adopted. The property tax levy includes the general property tax rate plus any special taxing-district rates. A board may alter the property tax levy only if (1) it is ordered to do so by a court, (2) it is ordered to do so by the LGC, or (3) the unit receives revenues that are substantially different from the amount anticipated when the budget ordinance was adopted.[56] A board may change the tax levy under the third exception only if it does so between July 1 and December 31.

Common Budgeting Tools and Techniques

Local units may adopt any budgeting process that facilitates effective decision-making for adopting a balanced budget ordinance so long as it complies with the legal requirements of the LGBFCA. Local units, historically, have approached the budget process as a financial exercise, focusing primarily on the financial inputs and outputs of the organization. Today, however, local units often take a broader perspective of the budgeting process and include information derived from their strategic plans and performance-measurement systems to help guide budgetary decision-making. The goal, as articulated by the reinventing-government movement of the early 1990s, is for local units to make decisions that enable them to steer the boat rather than just row it.[57]

Line-Item Budgeting

Line-item budgeting places the focus of decision-making on revenue estimates by each revenue category and on appropriations by each expenditure account. This form of budgeting is often criticized for its incremental approach to decision-making, resulting in an adopted budget for the forthcoming fiscal year that merely reflects the current year's budget with slight adjustments, the assumption being that the group of services contained in the current year's budget should continue for the following fiscal year. While line-item budgeting is often criticized for this reason, it

---

55. G.S. 159-15. Sometimes a board adopts the budget ordinance before July 1. The budget ordinance is not effective until July 1; however, it may be amended at any time after its adoption subject to the limitations set forth in G.S. 159-15.

56. G.S. 159-15. This limitation applies once the budget ordinance is adopted, even if that occurs before July 1.

57. David Osborne and Ted Gaebler, *Reinventing Government: How the Entrepreneurial Spirit Is Transforming the Public Sector* (New York: Addison-Wesley, 1992), 31–34.

nonetheless provides the foundation of budgetary accounting. Local units prepare line-item budgets to accurately appropriate the necessary resources for each expenditure account contained in the categories of personnel, operations, and capital outlay; to record the line-item budgets in the local unit's financial-management system to track budget-to-actual variances over the course of the fiscal year; and ultimately to document budgetary compliance as required by the LGBFCA.[58]

Strategic Budgeting

A management tool that local units often use to embrace long-term decision-making is the creation and adoption of a strategic plan. As previously mentioned, local units often begin their budgetary processes with budget retreats or workshops for elective officials. At these events, officials tend to focus on how the forthcoming budget will help advance the long-term goals contained in their local unit's strategic plan. For example, a local unit may want the annual budget process to focus on infrastructure because economic development is a long-term community goal. Broadening the budget process to include the organization's strategic plan enables the local unit's leadership to shift the focus from individual line-item accounts to long-term strategic goals that influence the direction of the community.

Performance Budgeting

Another common management tool used by local units to track service efficiency and effectiveness is performance measurement, wherein individual programs adopt mission statements, goals, objectives, and performance measures to demonstrate the outputs, efficiencies, and outcomes of service delivery. For example, a major output for public safety is the number of service calls. A major outcome is the timeliness of these service calls as tracked by response time. An advantage of performance budgeting, or the incorporation of performance-measurement information in the budget, is that it enables the local government unit to make resource-allocation decisions based on measures of efficiency and effectiveness.[59] Returning to the public safety example, performance budgeting represents the process of deciding whether to add an additional officer based on the objective of responding to 95 percent of service calls within four minutes rather than solely on the local unit's ability to afford an additional position.

Zero-Based Budgeting

A technique that is commonly cited for its advantage of eliminating or reducing incremental budget decisions is zero-based budgeting. This budgeting technique, in theory, requires that every line item be reviewed and justified from a base budget of zero rather than from the current-year budget. Zero-based budgeting, in practice, requires each department to submit three budget packages for review: its current-year budget, a reduced budget, and an expansion budget.[60] Departments are ranked based on the priorities of the organization and, based on that ranking, assigned one of the three budget packages, thereby reducing the probability that all departmental budgets reflect current-year budgets with slight adjustments. However, reviews on the effectiveness of zero-based budgeting for eliminating or reducing incremental decision-making have been mixed.

---

58. G.S. 159-26(a).

59. Janet M. Kelly and William C. Rivenbark, *Performance Budgeting for State and Local Government*, 2nd ed. (Armonk, N.Y.: M.E. Sharpe, 2011).

60. Robert L. Bland, *A Budgeting Guide for Local Government*, 2nd ed. (Washington, D.C.: International City/County Management Association, 2007).

Balanced Scorecard

The balanced scorecard is designed specifically to help local units translate their visions and missions into tangible objectives and outcomes.[61] Originally designed for the private sector, the balanced scorecard was adopted in the public sector as part of administrative reform and is now used as a management tool that helps local units broaden their budgeting processes during the preparation, implementation, and evaluation stages. The balanced scorecard requires a local unit to track the collection of metrics within the four quadrants of citizens, operations, financial resources, and employees, thereby providing local units with a broader, more balanced context in which to make budgetary decisions.

Financial Plans for Internal Service Funds

An internal service fund may be established to account for a service provided by one department or program to other departments in the same local unit and, in some cases, to other local governments. A service often accounted for in an internal service fund is fleet maintenance. If a local unit uses an internal service fund, the fund's revenues and expenditures may be included either in the annual budget ordinance or in a separate financial plan adopted specifically for the fund.[62]

Adopting a Financial Plan

The governing board must approve any financial plan adopted for an internal service fund, with such approval occurring at the same time the board enacts the annual budget ordinance.[63] The financial plan also must follow the same July 1 to June 30 fiscal year as the budget ordinance. An approved financial plan is entered into the board's minutes, and within five days after its approval, copies of the plan must be filed with the finance officer, the budget officer, and the clerk to the board.

Balanced-Financial-Plan Requirement

A financial plan must be balanced. This is accomplished when estimated expenditures do not exceed estimated revenues of a fund.[64]

Internal-service-fund revenues are principally charges to county, municipality, or authority departments that use the services of an internal service fund. These charges are financed by appropriated expenditures of the using departments in the annual budget ordinance. Internal-service-fund revenues or other resources also may include an appropriated subsidy or transfer unrelated to specific internal services, which would come from the general fund or some other fund to be shown as a transfer in, rather than as revenue for the internal service fund.

Expenditures from an internal service fund are typically for items necessary to provide fund services, including salaries and wages; other operating outlays; lease, rental, or debt-service payments; and depreciation charges on equipment or facilities used by the fund.

In adopting the annual financial plan for an internal service fund, a governing board must decide what to do with any available balance or reserves remaining from any previous year's financial

61. William C. Rivenbark and Eric J. Peterson, "A Balanced Approach to Implementing the Balanced Scorecard," *Popular Government* 74, no. 1 (September 1, 2008): 31–37.

62. G.S. 159-8(a), -13.1.

63. When the budget officer submits the proposed budget to the governing board, the officer must also submit a proposed financial plan for each intragovernmental service fund that will be in operation during the budget year.

64. G.S. 159-13.1.

plan. The law permits fund balance or reserves to be used to help finance fund operations in the next year or, if the balance is substantial, to fund long-term capital needs of the fund. Alternatively, fund balance may be allowed to continue accumulating for the purpose of financing major capital needs of the fund in the future, or it may be transferred to the general fund or another fund in the budget ordinance or to a project or grant ordinance for an appropriate use. A unit should avoid amassing in its financial plans large fund balances that are unrelated to the specific needs of the internal service fund.

Amending a Financial Plan

A financial plan may be modified during the fiscal year, but any change must be approved by the governing board.[65] Any amendments to a financial plan must be reflected in the board's minutes, with copies filed with the finance officer, the budget officer, and the clerk to the board.

Capital Budgeting

In North Carolina, local units may budget revenues and expenditures for the construction or acquisition of capital assets (capital projects), for projects that are financed in whole or in part by federal or state grants (grant projects), or for projects funded by settlement proceeds (settlement projects), either in the annual budget ordinance or in one or more project ordinances. A project ordinance appropriates revenues and expenditures for however long it takes to complete the capital, grant, or settlement project rather than for a single fiscal year.[66]

Capital-Project Ordinance

The Local Government Budget and Fiscal Control Act (LGBFCA) defines a capital project as a project that (1) is financed at least in part by bonds, notes, or debt instruments or (2) involves the construction or acquisition of a capital asset.[67] Although a capital-project ordinance may be used to recognize revenues and appropriate expenditures for any capital project or asset, it typically is used for capital improvements or acquisitions that are large relative to the annual resources of the unit, that take more than one year to build or acquire, or that recur irregularly. Expenditures for capital assets that are not expensive relative to a unit's annual budget or that happen annually usually can be handled effectively in the budget ordinance.

Grant-Project Ordinance

A grant-project ordinance may be used to budget revenues and expenditures for operating or capital purposes in a project financed wholly or partly by a grant or settlement funds included in a grant contract from the federal government, the state government, or a private entity.[68] This budgeting vehicle is most appropriate for multiyear grants, but it can be used even for single-year grants and may provide better documentation for grant compliance than the annual budget ordinance. A grant-project ordinance should not be used to appropriate state-shared taxes provided to a unit on a continuing basis, though. Such revenue or aid, even if earmarked for a specific purpose, should be budgeted in the annual budget ordinance.

---

65. G.S. 159-13.1(d).
66. G.S. 159-13.2.
67. G.S. 159-13.2(a)(1).
68. G.S. 159-13.2(a)(2).

Settlement-Project Ordinance

A settlement project is a project financed in whole or in part by revenues received pursuant to an order of the court or to another binding agreement resolving a legal dispute. A local government may use a settlement ordinance to budget these funds.[69]

As an example, as part of nationwide settlements (and bankruptcy resolutions) with major opioid manufacturers, distributors, and retailers, North Carolina local governments are expected to receive over $1.164 billion in funding over an 18-year period, beginning in FY 2022-2023, to address the ongoing impacts of the opioid epidemic in their communities (collectively "opioid settlement funds"). All 100 counties and the following municipalities will receive the opioid settlement funds: Asheville, Canton, Cary, Charlotte, Concord, Durham, Fayetteville, Gastonia, Greensboro, Greenville, Henderson, Hickory, High Point, Jacksonville, Raleigh, Wilmington, and Winston-Salem. The schedule of payments is available at CORE-NC: Community Opioid Resources Engine for North Carolina.[70] Local governments executed a Memorandum of Agreement (NC MOA) with the State of North Carolina regarding the use of the funds and certain process, compliance, and reporting requirements.[71] Additionally, the LGBFCA (G.S. 159, art. 3) and other related state-law provisions govern the budgeting, contracting, accounting, disbursement, and management of these funds.[72]

Creating a Project Ordinance

A governing board may adopt a project ordinance at any regular or special meeting by a simple majority of board members so long as a quorum is present. This can be done at any time during the year. The ordinance must (1) clearly identify the project and authorize its undertaking, (2) identify the revenues that will finance it, and (3) make the appropriations necessary to complete it.[73]

Each project ordinance must be entered in the board's minutes. Within five days after its adoption, copies of the ordinance must be filed with the finance officer, the budget officer, and the clerk to the board.

The budget officer also must provide certain information about project ordinances in the proposed annual budget submitted to the governing board each year. Specifically, the budget officer must include information on any project ordinances that the unit anticipates adopting during the budget year. The proposed budget also should include details about previously adopted project ordinances that likely will have appropriations available for expenditure during the budget year.[74] This is purely informational. The board need take no action to reauthorize a project ordinance once it is adopted.

Balanced-Project-Ordinance Requirement

The LGBFCA requires a capital- or grant-project ordinance to be balanced for the life of the project. A project ordinance is balanced when "revenues estimated to be available for the project equal appropriations for the project."[75]

---

69. *See* S.L. 2024-1.

70. See "NC Payment Schedule Dashboard," North Carolina Opioid Settlements, updated November 6, 2024, ncopioidsettlement.org/data-dashboards/payment-schedule/.

71. Memorandum of Agreement Between the State of North Carolina and Local Governments on Proceeds Relating to the Settlement of Opioid Litigation (2023), www.morepowerfulnc.org/wp-content/uploads/2023/07/Final-Opioid-MOA-rev-July-2023-re-Ex-E-and-F.pdf.

72. Some local governments will receive opioid-related settlements from other parties. These funds must be budgeted and accounted for separately from the NC MOA funds.

73. A local unit should adopt a separate project ordinance for each capital project or each grant.

74. G.S. 159-13.2(f).

75. G.S. 159-13.2(c).

Estimated revenues for a project ordinance may include bond or other debt proceeds,[76] federal or state grants, revenues from special assessments or user fees, other special revenues, and annually recurring revenues. If property tax revenue is used to finance a project ordinance, it must be levied initially in the annual budget ordinance and then transferred to the project ordinance. Other annually recurring revenues may be budgeted in the annual budget ordinance and transferred to a project ordinance or appropriated directly in a project ordinance.

Appropriations for expenditures in a capital-project ordinance may be general or detailed. A project ordinance may make a single, lump-sum appropriation for the project, or it may make appropriations by line item, function, or other appropriate categories within the project. Appropriations in a grant-project ordinance should be specific enough to align with grant-compliance requirements. For federal grants, that likely requires appropriations to occur at the cost-item level for each project.

The key characteristic of a project ordinance is that it has a project life, which means that the balancing requirement for such an ordinance is not bound by or related to any fiscal year or period. Estimated revenues and appropriations in a project ordinance must be balanced for the life of the project but do not have to be balanced for any fiscal period that the ordinance should happen to span.

Amending a Project Ordinance

A project ordinance may be amended at any time after its adoption but only by the governing board.[77] If expenditures for a project exceed the ordinance's appropriation, in total or for any expenditure category for which an appropriation was made, an amendment to the ordinance is necessary to increase the appropriation and identify additional revenues to keep the project ordinance balanced. A board also may amend a project ordinance to change the nature or scope of the project(s) being funded.

Closing Out a Project Ordinance

Unlike the annual budget ordinance, a project ordinance does not have an end date. It remains in effect until the project is finished or abandoned. There are no formal procedures for closing out a project ordinance when a project is done. Projects sometimes are completed with appropriated revenues remaining unspent. Practically speaking, such excess revenues are equivalent to a project fund balance. The remaining moneys should be transferred to another appropriate project, fund, or purpose at the project's completion. Annual revenues budgeted in a project ordinance that remain after a project is finished may be transferred back to the general fund or to another fund included in the annual budget ordinance. Bond proceeds remaining after a project is finished should be transferred to the appropriate fund for other projects authorized by the bond order or to pay debt service on the bonds. Note that any earmarked revenues in a project ordinance retain the earmark when transferred to another project or fund.

---

76. As with the annual budget ordinance, debt proceeds are treated as revenues for budgeting purposes. A local unit may include debt proceeds that it reasonably expects to receive to fund a project. If a bond issuance requires voter or LGC approval (or both), it likely is not reasonable to include the debt proceeds in the revenue estimate until the local unit has obtained the approval.

77. G.S. 159-13(e).

Justification for Capital Budget

The National Advisory Council on State and Local Government Budgeting encourages the adoption of a comprehensive policy for successfully implementing and managing the various aspects of capital budgeting.[78] A common question in local government is why local officials need to manage two budgeting processes, one for the operating budget and another for the capital budget. There are several reasons for implementing and managing a separate capital budgeting process.[79]

The first reason involves the lasting impact of decisions. For example, a decision to expand bus routes during the current-operating-budget process can be changed during the operating-budget process for the following fiscal year. A decision to expand a police station, however, is more permanent in nature, requiring a level of review beyond incremental adjustments to the operating budget.

A second reason, which builds on the first, is that debt financing is often used to acquire capital assets. The issuing of debt has a long-term impact on a county or municipality because the law requires that debt-service payments be appropriated as part of the budget ordinance.[80] The processes and procedures for capital budgeting can provide a more structured review for a critical decision, such as issuing debt, where additional debt-service payments may affect the organization's financial condition and possibly reduce future operating-budget flexibility.

A third reason for implementing and managing a separate capital-budgeting process can be traced back to state law. The budget ordinance adopted by counties and municipalities in North Carolina covers a single fiscal year, beginning July 1 and ending June 30.[81] The acquisition of major capital assets or the completion of infrastructure projects often extends over multiple fiscal years from approval to completion. State law allows local units to adopt their capital budgets with a capital-project ordinance, which authorizes all appropriations necessary for project completion and prevents project proceeds from having to be readopted in subsequent fiscal years.

A final reason is the variation in assets and costs as compared with the operating budget, wherein decisions are often incremental from one fiscal year to the next. In any given fiscal year during the capital-budgeting process, local officials may be faced with using cash reserves for anything from purchasing a new fire truck for $750,000 to issuing $20 million of debt for infrastructure improvements. Capital budgeting allows for the use of specific techniques for evaluating and prioritizing capital requests in terms of organizational need, capacity for acquisition, and community impact.

Capitalization and Capital-Budget Thresholds

An important policy decision for local units is establishing a capitalization threshold, which dictates how the costs associated with the acquisition of capital assets are reported in the annual financial statements as required by G.S. 159-25(a)(1). The Government Finance Officers Association defines *capital assets* as tangible items (e.g., land, buildings, building improvements, vehicles, equipment, and infrastructure) or intangible items (e.g., easements and technology) with useful lives that extend beyond a single reporting period.[82] The association recommends that local governments adopt a capitalization threshold of no less than $5,000 for any individual item, which means that capital assets costing $5,000 or less are reported as expenditures or expenses in the period in which they

---

78. National Advisory Council on State and Local Government Budgeting, *Recommended Budget Practices* (Chicago: Government Finance Officers Association, 2003).

79. Bland, *A Budgeting Guide.*

80. G.S. 159-13(b)(1).

81. G.S. 159-8(b).

82. "Capitalization Thresholds for Capital Assets," Government Finance Officers Association, February 6, 2006, www.gfoa.org/materials/capitalization-thresholds-capital-assets.

are acquired. Capital assets costing more than $5,000 are reported on the balance sheet and depreciated based on their estimated useful lives.

It is a professional practice for counties and municipalities to establish a financial threshold to determine what capital requests are considered part of the operating-budget process and what capital requests are considered part of the capital budget process—referred to as the *capital budget threshold*. This threshold is often based on the size of the local government. For example, a smaller local government with a population of approximately 20,000 might establish a capital budget threshold of $50,000, meaning that capital assets costing $50,000 or less would be part of the operating-budget process and capital assets costing more than $50,000 would be part of the capital budget process. An additional criterion often used in determining this threshold is the estimated useful life of the capital asset; this is because capital assets with longer estimated useful lives are more appropriate for the capital budget than for the operating budget. A reason for applying this additional criterion is that debt is often used to finance capital assets, and debt payments should never exceed the estimated useful life of the asset.[83]

Common Capital Budgeting Tools and Techniques

As with the annual budgeting process, a local unit may adopt any capital budgeting process that facilitates effective decision-making so long as it complies with the legal requirements of the LGBFCA. An essential component of any well-designed capital budgeting process is planning. Many units have adopted a formalized capital improvement program (CIP) to facilitate the planning process. And, increasingly, units are relying on more sophisticated analysis relating to the financial condition of the unit to make accurate budget forecasts.

Capital Improvement Program

A CIP is a forecast of capital assets and funding sources over a selected period of time. While local officials often refer to the capital budget and CIP as one and the same, they are separate management tools. The capital budget covers one fiscal year and is adopted by ordinance.[84] The CIP, which commonly contains five years of proposed capital assets and funding sources beyond the capital budget, is approved as a long-term plan that local officials update on an annual basis.

There are numerous reasons why local officials prepare and approve a CIP in conjunction with their capital budget. It provides a schedule for the replacement and rehabilitation of existing capital assets, which is fundamental to all CIPs. It allows time for project design and for exploring financing options, both of which are critical to evaluating the merits of a capital asset from a cost-benefit perspective. It also is the primary vehicle for providing the necessary infrastructure to support economic and community development in a coordinated manner, which is fundamental to land-use and master plans. As well, a CIP has the potential to help a local government maintain or improve its credit rating due to the premium that bond-rating agencies place on planning.

Table 20.1 provides an example of a capital budget for a local government. The capital budget of $900,000 is adopted by ordinance for fiscal year 2022, appropriating the necessary financing sources to fund the capital assets aggregated by functional area. The major capital project for fiscal year 2022 is the expansion of the public safety building, which is funded by $100,000 from annual operating revenue and $400,000 from general obligation bonds. The $200,000 of asphalt maintenance (streets

83. Justin Marlow, William C. Rivenbark, and A. John Vogt, *Capital Budgeting and Finance*, 2nd ed. (ICMA Press, 2009).

84. The phrase *capital budget* refers to appropriations for capital outlay in a single fiscal period. A government board may make these appropriations in the annual budget ordinance or in a capital- or grant-project ordinance.

Table 20.1 Capital Budget and Capital Improvement Program (CIP)

	Capital Budget	Capital Improvement Program				
Item	FY 2022	FY 2023	FY 2024	FY 2025	FY 2026	FY 2027
Capital Assets by Function						
Public safety	500,000	50,000	50,000	50,000	50,000	50,000
Environmental services			250,000			250,000
Streets and transportation	200,000			400,000		
Parks and recreation			100,000			
Water and sewer	200,000	50,000			200,000	
Total	**900,000**	**100,000**	**400,000**	**450,000**	**250,000**	**300,000**
Financing Sources						
Operating revenue	100,000	50,000	50,000	50,000	50,000	50,000
Capital reserve fund		50,000	250,000			250,000
Grants			100,000			
General obligation bonds	600,000			400,000		
Revenue bonds	200,000				200,000	
Total	**900,000**	**100,000**	**400,000**	**450,000**	**250,000**	**300,000**

and transportation) is funded from the remaining general obligation bonds, and revenue bonds will be used to fund an expansion of the water and sewer system.

Table 20.1 also provides an example of a five-year CIP for the local government, beginning with fiscal year 2023. While the CIP represents a plan and is updated on an annual basis as new requests are considered, it gives local officials time to prepare for future events. In fiscal year 2024, for example, $100,000 is allocated for a new park, giving local officials the time required to negotiate with multiple landowners to secure the necessary property. And in fiscal year 2025, $400,000 is allocated for general obligation bonds, giving local officials time to prepare for a bond referendum. These two examples highlight another critical reason why local officials prepare CIPs: doing so allows them to anticipate how the funding of capital assets will affect future operating budgets. Once the park is functional, adequate proceeds must be appropriated in the annual operating budget for additional park maintenance. The operating budget also must appropriate the debt-service payments for the issuance of the general obligation bonds as required by G.S. 159-13(b)(1). Preparing CIPs enables departments to consider the impact of proposed capital assets on their operating budgets when evaluating and submitting capital improvement requests.

Financial Condition and Forecasting

The CIP is a management tool that facilitates long-term planning for the acquisition of capital assets in local government. There are two additional management tools that support the capital budgeting process from a financial perspective, financial-condition analysis and financial forecasting. This is critical given the ways in which the acquisition of capital assets can affect an organization's current financial condition and future operating-budget flexibility.

Financial-Condition Analysis

The first of these additional management tools, financial-condition analysis, allows local officials to move beyond reporting on the financial position of the organization with an unmodified audit opinion of its annual financial statements to analyzing and interpreting the financial statements in order to determine and report on the financial condition of the organization. The reason financial-condition analysis is so important to capital budgeting and finance is that acquiring and financing capital assets has the potential to drastically change the financial condition of a county or municipality; therefore, it is imperative to monitor these changes on an annual basis for the financial sustainability of the local government.

Fortunately, local officials have access to two web-based dashboards that provide key financial ratios for analyzing the financial condition of any county or municipality in North Carolina. The LGC benchmarking tool, which is located on the North Carolina Department of State Treasurer's website (www.nctreasurer.com), provides selected financial ratios for a local unit's governmental activities, general fund, water-and-sewer fund, and electric fund. The tool calculates the ratios over a five-year period and benchmarks them against other local governments. The North Carolina Water and Wastewater Rates Dashboard, which is located on the Environmental Finance Center's website at the School of Government (efc.sog.unc.edu), provides financial ratios for selected operations, debt service, and liquidity for water and wastewater activities.

While the details of financial-condition analysis are beyond the scope of this chapter, two financial ratios associated with the general fund and two financial ratios associated with an enterprise fund are discussed below to highlight the critical connection between acquiring financial capital assets and the financial condition of a local government.[85]

General-Fund Financial Ratios

A financial ratio from the general fund's statement of revenues, expenditures, and changes in fund balance is the *debt-service ratio*, which is calculated by dividing principal and interest by total expenditures. This ratio provides feedback on the percentage of annual expenditures being committed to annual debt service, which affects service flexibility. The International City/County Management Association cautions local governments not to exceed 10 percent;[86] however, counties in North Carolina often exceed this percentage because of school financing. This ratio plays an important role when local officials are making the decision to issue additional debt for capital assets. Another financial ratio from the general fund's balance sheet is *fund balance as percentage of expenditures*. This ratio provides feedback on the solvency of the general fund, which is extremely important to monitor because cash reserves often are used to finance capital assets.

Enterprise-Fund Financial Ratios

Two critical ratios calculated from the financial statements of an enterprise fund are the *debt-coverage ratio* and the *capital-assets-condition ratio*. The enterprise fund's debt-coverage-service ratio is calculated by dividing net income of the enterprise by annual debt service—for example, a ratio of 1.25 means that net income exceeded debt service by 25 percent. This ratio is an important indicator of the financial condition of an enterprise fund. It is also important to creditors and bond-rating agencies, particularly when local officials seek to issue revenue bonds. The

85. For more information on financial-condition analysis, see William C. Rivenbark, Dale J. Roenigk, and Gregory S. Allison, "Communicating Financial Condition to Elected Officials in North Carolina," *Popular Government* 75, no. 1 (Fall 2009): 4–13.

86. International City/County Management Association, *Evaluating Financial Condition*, 4th ed. (Washington, D.C.: International City/County Management Association, 2003).

capital-assets-condition ratio provides feedback on the accumulated depreciation of the capital assets assigned to an enterprise fund (the ratio is 1.0 minus (accumulated depreciation divided by capital assets being depreciated)). A high ratio suggests that a county or municipality is investing in its capital assets; a low ratio, that a local unit needs to review its annual investment in capital assets.

Financial Forecasting

Financial-condition analysis provides extremely important information about capital budgeting and finance; however, financial ratios are typically calculated from audited financial statements (historical data). The second management tool, which is more aligned with the CIP, is financial forecasting: a projection of revenues and expenditures (expenses) over a selected period of time to show the future operating results of a fund on the basis of an agreed-upon set of assumptions.[87] Research has shown that a five-year model is standard in local government, which reconciles with the typical CIP.[88] The implementation of a capital budget and CIP, as previously discussed, addresses the operating results of the respective funds based on additional debt-service payments, changes in positions and operating expenses, and additional revenue. Financial forecasting provides local officials with a methodology to estimate how the acquisition of capital assets contained in the CIP will affect the relationship between the inflow and outflow of resources in a fund over the selected forecast period.

Table 20.2 presents an example of a five-year financial forecast for a local government's general fund. The forecast of all revenues and expenditures is based on a 2 percent growth rate, except for property taxes and debt service. The forecast for property taxes is based on a 3 percent growth rate, and the forecast for debt service is based on amortization schedules. The current-fiscal-year balance, as noted, is an estimate based on nine months of annualized data; however, the estimate shows that revenues are expected to exceed expenditures by $5,449 for the current fiscal year, increasing fund balance by that amount. The forecast shows that estimated revenues are expected to exceed estimated expenditures for the following two fiscal years, increasing fund balance to $134,947 at the end of fiscal year 2024. The forecast then shows that estimated expenditures are expected to exceed estimated revenues for the remaining three fiscal years, reducing fund balance to $79,935 at the end of fiscal year 2027. The reason for the reverse in trend is that the local government expects to double its debt-service payment, from $50,000 to $100,000, in fiscal year 2025, once its CIP is implemented.

The five-year financial forecast shown in Table 20.2 gives local officials time to begin discussing how the county or municipality can afford the additional debt-service payment schedule for fiscal year 2025. Changes can be made to operating revenues and expenditures, for example, or to the capital budget and CIP to reduce the impact of taking on more debt. Local officials need information on the different ways in which counties and municipalities in North Carolina can use pay-as-you-go strategies to acquire capital assets and on how they can issue and structure debt to accommodate the needs of the organization and community.

Capital Reserve Fund

A tool available to local units to help them save for future capital projects is the capital reserve fund (CRF). A local unit may establish and maintain a CRF for any capital project it is authorized

87. Larry Schroeder, "Local Government Multiyear Budgetary Forecasting: Some Administrative and Political Issues," *Public Administration Review* 42, no. 2 (1982): 121–27.

88. William C. Rivenbark, "Financial Forecasting for North Carolina Local Governments," *Popular Government* 73, no. 1 (Fall 2007): 6–13.

Table 20.2 Five-Year Financial Forecast for General Fund

	*CFY	Forecast				
Item	**FY 2022**	**FY 2023**	**FY 2024**	**FY 2025**	**FY 2026**	**FY 2027**
Fund balance, beginning	$100,000	$105,449	$117,006	$134,947	$109,551	$91,112
Revenues						
Property taxes	500,140	515,144	530,598	546,516	562,911	579,799
Local option sales taxes	101,985	104,024	106,105	108,227	110,391	112,600
Permits and fees	52,444	53,492	54,562	55,653	56,767	57,902
Intergovernmental	50,000	51,000	52,020	53,060	54,121	55,204
Sanitation fees	74,785	76,280	77,806	79,362	80,949	82,568
Total	779,354	799,940	821,091	842,818	865,139	888,073
Expenditures						
Administration	100,691	102,705	104,759	106,854	108,991	111,171
Public safety	246,123	251,045	256,066	261,188	266,411	271,740
Environmental services	182,654	186,307	190,033	193,834	197,711	201,665
Transportation	98,585	100,557	102,568	104,619	106,712	108,846
Parks and recreation	95,852	97,769	99,724	101,719	103,753	105,828
Debt service	50,000	50,000	50,000	100,000	100,000	100,000
Total	773,905	788,383	803,150	868,214	883,578	899,250
Difference	5,449	11,557	17,941	(25,396)	(18,439)	(11,177)
Fund balance, ending	**$105,449**	**$117,006**	**$134,947**	**$109,551**	**$91,112**	**$79,935**

*Current fiscal year (CFY) balance is an estimate based on nine months of annualized data.

to engage.[89] A CRF is essentially a savings account, but a governing board may only use it to accumulate funds for specified future capital projects. It may not be used for more generalized savings or for an emergency reserve.

To establish a CRF, the governing board must adopt an ordinance or resolution that states the following:

- the fund's purposes, including the nature and scope of each project that moneys are being allocated to;
- the approximate time periods during which moneys will be accumulated for each purpose;
- approximately when moneys will be expended for each project;
- approximately how much will be accumulated for each purpose; and
- the sources of revenue for each purpose (e.g., property taxes, utility fees, sales taxes, use taxes, grants).

89. *See* G.S. 159-18, -48.

Establishing a CRF affords a unit's governing board a more formalized mechanism to save moneys for future capital expenditures. It also provides greater transparency than using fund balance because the board must indicate how it ultimately intends to expend the moneys. It is a less flexible savings option, though. Once moneys are appropriated to a CRF, they must be used for capital expenditures. The moneys may not be used to fund operating expenses, even in an emergency situation.

A governing board, however, may amend its CRF at any time to add new capital projects, delete capital projects, or to change the nature of the capital projects.[90] The board is not required to expend the accumulated moneys for the capital projects initially identified in the CRF.

For example, assume that a city is growing fairly rapidly. The governing board anticipates needing a water-system expansion within the next eight to ten years to accommodate new growth. The board establishes a CRF and allocates moneys to the fund each year for the project. Five years later a major recession hits the city. Growth slows significantly. It now appears that a water-system expansion will not be necessary. The governing board could amend the CRF to delete the expansion project and substitute one or more new projects, such as road improvements, building maintenance, vehicle acquisition, or a new recreation building. The board could not divert the accumulated revenues in the fund to cover operating expenses.

How are moneys expended from a CRF? The governing board must adopt an ordinance or resolution authorizing the withdrawal of moneys from the fund, the transfer of the moneys to another fund (such as the general fund or an enterprise fund) or to a capital-project ordinance, and the expenditure of the moneys for one or more of the capital projects or assets identified in the CRF.

Summary

Local units in North Carolina are required to budget and spend money in accordance with the LGBFCA, which provides a comprehensive legal framework for preparing, adopting, and amending the units' annual budget ordinances, financial plans, and project ordinances. Most of this chapter, as a result, has focused on interpreting the numerous statutes in the LGBFCA, including the definition of a balanced budget ordinance, the limits on appropriations and interfund transfers, the adoption and amending of the budget ordinance, and the use of financial plans and project ordinances. After a brief overview of budgetary accounting, the chapter has presented management tools and processes used by local government to make budgetary decisions within the broader context of the organization.

90. G.S. 159-19.

Chapter 21

Financing Capital Projects

Kara A. Millonzi

Kara A. Millonzi is a School of Government faculty member who specializes in local government and public school finance law.

Introduction

Constructing, acquiring, and maintaining the facilities, equipment, and other capital infrastructure needed to perform public services (collectively, capital projects) are important responsibilities of county and municipal officials. Capital projects also present unique challenges. A capital asset is an asset that is of significant value and has a useful life of more than a single year. This broad definition covers everything from the acquisition of office furniture to the construction of a water treatment facility or a new high school. Thus, in any given year, the capital projects a unit undertakes may vary substantially in number, cost, complexity, and timing. The tools a local government uses to budget and finance capital assets, therefore, are different from those used to budget and finance current assets or operating expenses.

This chapter explores the different tools available to North Carolina local governments to finance capital projects. It focuses on funding public infrastructure—that is, capital outlay used for (or primarily for) governmental purposes. (Chapter 20 "Budgeting for Operating and Capital Expenditures," discusses the capital budgeting process.) The financing mechanisms can be broken into roughly five categories—current revenues, savings, special levies, borrowing money, and grants and partnerships. This chapter discusses most of the specific funding mechanisms, detailing the authority to use each method as well as its procedural requirements and limitations.

Current Revenues

Current revenues are revenues collected by the local unit each fiscal year. The largest source of current revenue in the general fund is property taxes, followed by sales and use taxes. Current revenues in an enterprise fund typically encompass user fees and other specialty charges. Current revenues are used primarily by a local unit to fund government programs and activities and to cover annual operational expenses, including salaries, utilities, and supplies. Most units, however, also use a portion of their current revenues to fund capital projects each year.

Two categories of capital projects are typically funded with current revenues. The first includes capital expenditures that fall below a certain dollar amount. Some units set a capital budget threshold amount in the annual budget ordinance, using current revenues to fund any capital outlay that costs less than that amount. The second category includes capital expenditures that recur on a regular basis, such as maintenance and repair expenditures on existing capital assets. These expenditures may or may not fall below the capital budget threshold but are nevertheless funded in the annual budget ordinance with current revenues.

Savings

Often a unit must save current revenues over a period of time to fund a capital expenditure. North Carolina local governments can do this in two ways. One is to allow money to accumulate in fund balance. The other is to allocate revenue to a capital reserve fund.

Fund Balance

Local governments use fund accounting to track assets and liabilities. An accounting fund is a separate fiscal and accounting entity, with its own set of self-balancing accounts. Thus, a fund has its own assets, liabilities, equity, revenues, and expenses. There are several types of funds, the most common being the general fund, which accounts for the majority of general government revenues and expenditures. The equity associated with a fund is referred to as "fund balance." In the simplest terms, fund balance is an accumulation of revenues minus expenditures.[1]

Fund balance generally serves three purposes. The primary purpose is to provide the unit with cash flow. A local government's fiscal year begins on July 1. Most units, though, do not receive the majority of their operating revenue (in the form of property tax proceeds) until late December or early January. Because of this delay, a local government typically must rely on cash reserves from the prior fiscal year to cover up to several months of expenditures.

The second purpose of fund balance is to provide a unit with an emergency fund, often referred to as a "rainy day" fund. It is difficult for a local government to raise additional money quickly during the fiscal year. Fund balance can provide a unit available cash to cover unexpected operating or capital expenses.

Some units use fund balance for a third purpose—to facilitate saving money over time for anticipated capital expenditures. If a unit knows, for example, that it needs to engage in a capital project in the next several years, it might allow its fund balance to grow each year and then appropriate the accumulated moneys to finance the project.

The Local Government Commission (LGC), a state agency with oversight responsibility for local government financial management practices, encourages counties and municipalities to "develop a fund balance policy to maintain a fund balance that is consistent with their peers that provide similar services."[2] The LGC has also published memoranda that list fund balances available for all counties and municipalities[3] to help local governments determine a unit-specific amount of fund balance to maintain on an annual basis. The LGC recommends that each local government adopt a fund balance policy that can be used to develop operating budgets and provide for corrective action should fund balance drop below the intended level at the close of a fiscal year.[4]

The benefit of using fund balance to save money for future capital projects is that it provides a local governing board a great deal of flexibility. A governing board may use the accumulated moneys to fund either operating or capital expenditures; it is not locked in to spending its unrestricted fund balance on a particular project or asset. (Fund balance, however, often includes some moneys that are restricted to certain purposes.)[5] For example, assume that a county board of commissioners wishes to expand its solid waste disposal facility in approximately five years. The board begins to purposefully accumulate fund balance toward this goal. In year three, a major economic recession hits the county. The county board may divert the accumulated fund balance to pay for operating expenses or more pressing capital expenses. The only exception is if a portion of the fund balance includes earmarked moneys (by grant or state statute) such that they may be used for only the solid waste disposal facility expansion.

To expend fund balance, a governing board must amend its budget ordinance or a project ordinance to appropriate the fund balance and authorize its expenditure for one or more projects.[6]

---

1. For a detailed description of the components of fund balance, see Chapter 22, "Accounting, Fiscal Control, and Cash Management."

2. N.C. Department of State Treasurer, "The Myth of 8% (LGC Staff Guidance on Fund Balance Available)" (July 11, 2022), www.nctreasurer.com/blog/2022/07/11/myth-8-lgc-staff-guidance-fund-balance-available.

3. As used in this book, the term "municipality" is synonymous with "city," "town," and "village."

4. To review the Local Government Commission's (LGC) sample fund balance policy, see N.C. Department of State Treasurer, Local Government Commission, Fund Balance Policy: City of Dogwood (2022), www.nctreasurer.com /documents/files/slgfd/sample-fund-balance-policy-exhibit-e/download.

5. For a detailed description of the components of fund balance, see Chapter 22.

6. *See* Chapter 159, Section 15 of the North Carolina General Statutes (hereinafter G.S.) (budget ordinance amendment); G.S. 159-13.2(e) (project ordinance amendment). For more information on amending budget and project ordinances, see Chapter 20, "Budgeting for Operating and Capital Expenditures."

Using fund balance as a savings account for future capital expenditures is controversial in some units. Citizens may question why a local unit continues to raise revenue (through taxes and fees) when the unit has sufficient reserves to meet its cash flow needs. They may not trust that the governing board ultimately will spend the accumulated fund balance appropriately.

Capital Reserve Funds

Instead of accumulating fund balance, a unit's governing board may establish a capital reserve fund and periodically appropriate money to it. A local government may establish and maintain a capital reserve fund for any purpose for which the unit may issue bonds.[7] And a unit may issue bonds for any capital project in which it is authorized to engage.[8] (The local government does not have to issue bonds to fund a project for the project to qualify for inclusion in a capital reserve fund.) Local government utilities must account for system development fee proceeds in a capital reserve fund, regardless of the type of capital projects the moneys will fund.[9]

To establish a capital reserve fund, a unit's governing board must adopt an ordinance or resolution that states the following:

1. the purposes for which the fund is being created (a board may accumulate moneys for multiple capital projects within a single capital reserve fund, but it must list each project separately);
2. the approximate periods of time during which the moneys will be accumulated and expended for each capital project;
3. the approximate amounts to be accumulated for each capital project; and
4. the sources from which moneys for each purpose will be derived (a board must indicate the revenue sources it intends to allocate to the capital reserve fund to finance each project—for example, property tax proceeds, utility fees, local sales and use tax proceeds, grant proceeds, and so forth).

A unit's governing board may make its appropriations from its annual budget ordinance to the capital reserve fund at any time. Each time it makes an appropriation, the board also must amend the capital reserve fund to account for the additional revenue. The board may not set up an automated appropriation for future fiscal years; it must make the appropriation from each year's budget ordinance.

Establishing a capital reserve fund affords a unit's governing board a more formalized mechanism than fund balance to save moneys for future capital expenditures. Arguably it is more transparent because the governing board must specify the capital projects for which it is accumulating funds. However, appropriating money to a capital reserve fund is a less flexible savings option. Once moneys are appropriated to a capital reserve fund, they must be used for capital expenditures. The moneys may not be used to fund operating expenses, even in an emergency.

---

7. G.S. 159-18.

8. G.S. 159-48.

9. *See* G.S. 162A-211(d) and (e). For a sample capital reserve fund, see Kara Millonzi, "CRFs for SDFs (aka Capital Reserve Funds for System Development Fees)," *Coates' Canons: NC Local Government Law* blog (May 24, 2018), canons.sog.unc.edu/crfs-for-sdfs-aka-capital-reserve-funds-for-system-development-fees/. There is an exception to the CRF requirement if the unit has pledged the SDF revenues as security in a bond financing. G.S. 162A-211(d), (e). In that case, the local government may deposit the proceeds of SDFs in the funds, accounts, or subaccounts in accordance with the relevant bond order, bond resolution, trust agreement, or similar instrument that secures the relevant bonds.

A governing board must list specific capital projects in the capital reserve fund. It may not simply establish the fund to raise money for general capital expenditures. A governing board, however, may amend its capital reserve fund at any time to add new capital projects, delete capital projects, or change the nature of the capital projects.[10]

The board is not required to expend the accumulated moneys for the capital projects initially identified in the reserve fund. For example, assume that a municipality is growing fairly rapidly. The governing board anticipates needing a water system expansion within the next eight to ten years to accommodate new growth. The board establishes a capital reserve fund and allocates moneys to the fund each year for the water system expansion project. Five years later a major recession hits the municipality. Growth slows significantly. It now appears that a water system expansion will not be necessary. The governing board could amend the capital reserve fund to delete the water system expansion project and substitute one or more new capital projects, such as road improvements, building maintenance, vehicle acquisition, or a new recreation building.

How are moneys expended from a capital reserve fund? The governing board must adopt an ordinance or resolution authorizing the withdrawal of moneys from the fund, the transfer of moneys to another fund (such as the general fund or an enterprise fund), and the expenditure of moneys for one or more of the capital projects or assets identified in the capital reserve fund.[11]

Special Levies

Local units derive most of their current revenue and savings from general fund revenue sources. The largest source of general fund revenue for both counties and municipalities is the property tax. And the hallmark of property taxation is that all property owners (except those whose property is statutorily exempt) pay the tax, regardless of whether they directly benefit from the projects or services funded with the tax proceeds. Citizens trust their local elected leaders to expend the proceeds for the general benefit of the community. Local elected leaders, however, often feel pressure to provide and fund an ever-increasing number of projects and services while maintaining or reducing the property tax levy. Thus, units have come to rely on targeted revenue-generation mechanisms, such as user charges, that are paid only by the citizens or property owners who most directly benefit from specific services or projects. For example, in the past many municipalities funded solid waste services, including disposal facilities, convenience centers, and even curbside pickup, with property tax proceeds. Now these units typically assess user charges to cover some or all the costs associated with these services. Other common user charges levied by counties and municipalities are for water and wastewater utilities services, recreational and cultural activities, health and mental health services, ambulance services, parking, public transportation, stormwater, cemeteries, and airports. Units also rely on fee revenue to fund certain regulatory activities, such as inspections and plan reviews. Generally, user charges are feasible for any service that directly benefits individual "users" and can be divided into service units and when the charges can be collected at a reasonable cost.

What about funding capital projects or acquisitions with user charges? Although dividing capital projects or assets into divisible units with defined beneficiaries can be difficult, some units attempt to apportion some of the capital costs associated with a particular service among the users of that service. For example, a unit's water or sewer customer is assessed a monthly or bi-monthly charge for the utility service. The charge typically consists of two components—a usage charge, which

10. G.S. 159-19.
11. G.S. 159-22.

varies based on actual usage, and a fixed overhead charge. The fixed charge covers both operating overhead and at least some capital outlay expenses.

In addition to user fees, the law allows for targeted revenue generation to fund capital projects through four different types of special levies—traditional special assessments, critical infrastructure assessments, special taxing districts, and, to a limited extent, development exactions.

Special Assessments

A special assessment is a charge levied against property to pay for public improvements that benefit that property. It is neither a user fee nor a tax but has characteristics of both. Like a user fee, a special assessment is levied in some proportion to the benefit received by the assessed property. However, like a property tax, it is levied against property rather than persons and is a lien on each parcel of real property assessed. The lien may be foreclosed in the same manner as property tax liens.[12]

Special assessment authority provides local units a potentially important tool for funding capital projects. The ability to recoup some or all the costs of a particular project from those property owners who most directly benefit from the project makes sense both financially and politically, at least in some instances. Levying assessments also allows a local government to collect revenue from property owners who benefit from the capital projects but whose properties are exempt from property taxation.[13] And using special assessments as a part of its revenue mix allows a governing board to direct property tax proceeds and other general fund revenues to services or capital projects that benefit a broader subset of the unit's citizens.

Currently, there are two different statutory methods for levying special assessments in North Carolina—traditional special assessments and critical infrastructure assessments. Under both methods, a governing board defines an area within a unit that includes all properties that will directly benefit from a certain capital project. And under both methods a unit must follow a detailed statutory process to determine and impose the assessments.

Traditional Special Assessment

The traditional special assessment method has not been widely used by North Carolina local governments due to several factors. First, the authority to levy assessments is limited to only a few categories of projects. Counties may levy assessments to fund water systems, sewage collection and disposal, beach erosion control and flood and hurricane protection, watershed improvement, drainage, water resources development projects, local costs of Department of Transportation improvements to subdivision and residential streets outside municipalities, and streetlight maintenance.[14] Municipalities may levy assessments to finance public improvements involving streets, sidewalks, water systems, sewage collection and disposal systems, storm sewer and drainage systems, and beach erosion control and flood and hurricane protection.[15] Second, as detailed below, the process to levy the assessments is fairly onerous. Third, a local unit must front all the costs of the project, which can be high. Only after a project is complete may a unit levy the assessments, and assessments often are paid in installments over a number of years (up to ten). Some local units have set up special assessment revolving funds,

12. For more information on enforcing property tax liens, see Chapter 19, "Property Tax Policy and Administration."

13. A unit may not levy assessments on state or federal government property, however, without the consent of the property owner.

14. G.S. 153A-185.

15. G.S. 160A-216.

using yearly special assessment payments from former projects to fund new projects. Establishing a sufficient revolving fund, however, often takes several years.

For most projects, a unit's governing board may levy assessments within its own discretion. Street and sidewalk projects first require that the unit receive a petition signed by a certain percentage of affected property owners.[16] The amount of each assessment must bear some relationship to the amount of benefit that accrues to the assessed property. The most common basis of assessment is front footage: each property is assessed on a uniform rate per foot of property that abuts the project. Other common bases include the size of the area benefited and the value added to the property because of the improvement. All the permissible bases of assessment mandate that the basis rate be equal across properties. A unit, however, may set up benefit zones—setting different assessment rates in each zone according to the degree of benefit to the properties in the zone. For example, for a beach re-nourishment project, a local unit may assess a higher assessment rate on properties that directly abut the beach than on properties that do not have direct beach access.

To impose the assessments under the traditional method, a unit's governing board must do the following:

- for street and sidewalk assessments only, receive a petition from at least a portion of the affected property owners;[17]
- adopt a preliminary assessment resolution that includes, among other things, a description and estimated cost of the project, the percentage of the cost to be funded through assessments, the basis of assessment, and the terms of payment of the assessments;
- hold a public hearing on the preliminary assessment resolution, after providing proper notice to the affected property owners;
- adopt the final assessment resolution (which locks in project scope);
- begin and complete the project;
- prepare a preliminary assessment roll that describes the lots to be assessed, the amount assessed against each lot, the basis of the assessment, and the terms of payment;
- hold a public hearing on the preliminary assessment roll, after providing proper notice to the affected property owners; and
- confirm the assessment roll.[18]

Once the unit has confirmed the assessment roll, the assessments become a lien on the real properties assessed. The unit may demand full payment of the assessments within thirty days of publication of the confirmed assessment roll. More often, a board will allow assessments to be paid in up to ten yearly installments, with interest.[19]

---

16. Before a county may fund street improvements, it must first receive a petition signed by at least 75 percent of the owners of property to be assessed, who represent at least 75 percent of the lineal feet of frontage of the lands abutting the street or portion of the street to be improved. G.S. 153A-205. Similarly, for street and sidewalk improvements, a municipality must receive a petition signed by a majority of the owners of property to be assessed, who represent at least a majority of all the lineal feet of frontage of the lands abutting the street or portion of the street to be improved. G.S. 160A-217.

17. *See supra* note 16.

18. For more information on the assessment process, see Kara A. Millonzi, "An Overview of Special Assessment Bond Authority in North Carolina," *Local Finance Bulletin* No. 40 (Nov. 2009), www.sog.unc.edu/publications/bulletins/overview-special-assessment-bond-authority-north-carolina.

19. A unit may assess up to 8 percent interest per year on outstanding assessment balances.

Critical Infrastructure Assessment

During the 2008 and 2009 legislative sessions the General Assembly temporarily bestowed the newer special assessment authority—entitled special assessments for critical infrastructure needs—on counties and municipalities to fund a wide range of capital projects.[20] (The legislature has since extended the authority for the newer assessment method several times, most recently to July 2025.)

The purpose of the critical infrastructure assessment authority, modeled on legislation from other states, is to help local units fund public infrastructure projects that benefit new private development. It allows a unit to impose assessments, with payments spread out over a period of years, with the expectation that most assessments will be paid by the eventual property owners (instead of the developer or the local government). As with traditional assessments, the unit can front the costs of the project and recoup its investment over time with the yearly assessment payments. Under the critical infrastructure assessment method, though, the unit can borrow money, pledging the assessment revenue as security, and use the yearly assessment payments to meet its debt service obligations. Alternatively, the unit may contract with the developer to fund and construct the capital project and use the assessment revenue to reimburse the developer over time.[21]

Conceptually, the critical infrastructure assessment authority functions like an impact fee. An impact fee is imposed on new development to pay for infrastructure costs necessitated by the new development. The fees usually are assessed on developers upon the issuance of a building permit. Special assessments also may be used to fund infrastructure projects necessitated by new development. The critical infrastructure assessment method typically imposes fewer costs on the developer than an impact fee. Many, if not most, of the payments are collected once the development is completed (assuming, of course, the development results as expected).

A much broader array of public infrastructure projects may be funded through the critical infrastructure assessment method than through the traditional method. The authorized projects are almost exclusively government infrastructure projects, ranging from constructing and maintaining public roads to building public schools. The list includes most capital projects in which a unit is authorized to engage.[22]

A potential benefit of the critical infrastructure assessment method is that it allows a unit to borrow money to front the costs of a project. The unit pledges the assessment revenue as security for the loan and uses the revenue to make its yearly debt service payments (special assessment–backed revenue bonds). Thus, the unit can avoid committing any of its general fund revenues to the project.

Of course, there is a risk that the unit will not be able to collect all the assessment revenue needed to meet the debt service obligations. The assessments are a lien on the properties assessed, and a unit has the same remedies available to collect delinquent assessments as it does delinquent property taxes. (The bonds likely will include a covenant requiring the unit to use all available collection remedies in the case of nonpayment by a property owner. This may pose some cost to the unit.) Despite the robust collection authority, the debt is relatively risky for investors. And the riskier the debt, the more expensive the borrowing. Thus, special assessment–backed revenue

---

20. *See* G.S. Ch. 153A, Art. 9A (counties); Ch. 160A, Art. 10A (municipalities).

21. These agreements may be subject to LGC approval.

22. *See* G.S. 153A-210.2 (counties); 160A-239.2 (municipalities). For more information on critical infrastructure assessments, *see* Millonzi, *supra* note 18; Kara Millonzi, "Recent Amendments to Special Assessment Authority," *Coates' Canons: NC Local Government Law* blog (Sept. 5, 2013), canons.sog.unc.edu/recent-amendments-to-special-assessment-authority; Kara Millonzi, "Special Assessments for Economic Development Projects," *Coates' Canons: NC Local Government Law* blog (Oct. 31, 2013), canons.sog.unc.edu/2013/10/special-assessments-for-economic-development-projects/.

bonds often carry a very high rate of interest. The interest does not burden the unit's general fund directly, however.

To impose an assessment under the critical infrastructure assessment method to pay for a capital project, a unit must first receive a petition signed by a majority of the owners of property to be assessed, who also represent at least 66 percent of the value of the property to be assessed.[23] In setting this fairly onerous petition requirement, the legislature envisioned that there would be a single owner or, at most, a few owners (developers) of the real property at the time the assessments are imposed. The petition must include a description of the public infrastructure project, its estimated costs, and the percentage of that cost to be assessed. These details, as well as the basis of assessment, the assessment repayment period, and any issues related to borrowing money to pay for the project, typically are negotiated in advance between the developer and the unit.

Once a unit receives a petition, it must follow the same detailed statutory process to impose the assessments as under the traditional method. There are a few differences in the nature of the assessment resolution and project timing. The project need not be completed before the assessment roll is confirmed. Assessments are based on estimated costs. The process takes time but, assuming the developer does not change its mind, is relatively straightforward.

One key difference between critical infrastructure and traditional assessments is that a unit may allow installment payments over a twenty-five-year period. If a unit borrows money to front the costs of the project, the number and amount of installment payments will correspond to the unit's debt service obligations.

Special Taxing Districts

Another targeted revenue-generation mechanism available to a local unit to fund capital projects is to establish one or more special taxing districts. The state constitution requires that a local government's property tax rates be uniform throughout the jurisdiction, but it also authorizes the General Assembly to allow a local government to carve out one or more areas within the unit as special taxing districts. The unit may levy a property tax in each district additional to county- or municipality-wide property taxes and use the proceeds to provide services or fund capital projects in those districts.

Like special assessments, special taxing districts derive from the benefit principle—those who most directly benefit from a government function should pay for it. Special assessments are assessed on a project-by-project basis. Special taxing districts, however, are established to fund a variety of projects and services that benefit properties in the district over time.

County and Municipal Service Districts

The General Assembly has authorized counties and municipalities to establish service districts,[24] which are defined areas within a unit on which additional property tax rates can be imposed to fund certain services and capital projects. All counties are authorized to define a service district for the following functions:[25]

- beach erosion and flood and hurricane protection;
- fire protection;
- recreation;

23. G.S. 160A-239.3 (cities); 153A-210.3 (municipalities).
24. G.S. Ch. 160A, Art. 23 (municipalities); Ch. 153A, Art. 16 (counties).
25. G.S. 153A-301. A few additional purposes are authorized for specified counties.

- sewage collection and disposal;
- solid waste collection and disposal;
- water supply and distribution;
- ambulance and rescue services;
- watershed improvement, drainage, and water resources development; and
- cemeteries.

And all municipalities may establish a municipal service district (MSD) for any of the following functions:[26]

- beach erosion and flood and hurricane protection;
- downtown revitalization projects;
- urban area revitalization projects;
- transit-oriented development projects;
- drainage projects;
- sewage collection and disposal systems;
- off-street parking facilities; and
- watershed improvement, drainage, and water resources development projects.

Counties typically use service districts to fund the operational and capital expenses of fire and rescue services.[27] Municipalities most often use service districts to fund projects and programs in their central downtown areas.[28]

Taxing Authority

A service district is in no way a separate unit of government. It is simply a geographic designation—a defined part of a county or municipality in which the government levies an extra property tax and provides extra services or undertakes capital projects that more directly benefit the properties within that district. Service district taxes are subject to the same exemptions and exclusions as the general property taxes (that is, property that is exempt from property taxes also is exempt from service district taxes).

A unit's governing board sets the service district tax rate each year in its annual budget ordinance. The rate, combined with the unit's general property tax rate, may not exceed $1.50 per $100 assessed valuation of property in the district, unless the unit's voters have approved a higher maximum rate.

All the revenue generated by the service district tax must be used to provide the services or undertake the capital projects in the district. A unit also may supplement the district tax revenue with other unrestricted revenues. The district tax proceeds and any other moneys allocated to the district may not be diverted to other purposes.

---

26. G.S. 160A-536. A few additional purposes are authorized for specified municipalities.

27. For more information on taxing districts for fire services, see Kara A. Millonzi, "County Funding for Fire Services in North Carolina," *Local Finance Bulletin* No. 43 (May 2011), www.sog.unc.edu/sites/www.sog.unc.edu/files/reports/lfb43.pdf.

28. For more information on taxing districts for downtown revitalization, see Kara Millonzi, "A Guide to Business Improvement Districts in North Carolina," *Coates' Canons: NC Local Government Law* blog (Apr. 1, 2010), canons.sog.unc.edu/a-guide-to-business-improvement-districts-in-north-carolina.

Formation

The procedures for establishing a service district vary between counties and municipalities. A county's governing board creates a district by adopting a resolution. A municipality's governing board, however, must create a service district by adopting an ordinance.[29] And the ordinance must be enacted by majority vote at two consecutive board meetings.

Both boards must first follow detailed procedural requirements.[30] Among other things, a municipal board must find that the district needs the proposed functions "to a demonstrably greater extent" than the rest of the municipality.[31] A county board must consider several statutory factors[32] and make the following findings:

1. There is a demonstrable need for providing one or more of the authorized services or projects in the district.
2. It is impossible or impracticable to provide those services or projects on a countywide basis.
3. It is economically feasible to provide the proposed services or projects in the district without unreasonable or burdensome annual tax levies.
4. There is demonstrable demand for the proposed services or projects by residents of the district.[33]

Both counties and municipal boards may initiate the process. No petition from affected property owners is required, though a governing board could establish a policy of defining districts only when it receives such a petition.[34] A voter referendum need not be held within the district to create it. In fact, there is no authority to hold a vote even if the governing board thinks one is desirable.

In practice, most governing boards also factor in the level of support for the services or projects by the affected property owners. With limited exceptions, a county or municipality must set the effective date for a new service district at the beginning of a fiscal year.[35]

Projects and Service Provision

A local government has broad authority to provide services, facilities, functions, or promotional and developmental activities in a service district with its own forces and/or through contracts with external entities. If a unit levies a district tax, the unit must "provide, maintain, or let contracts for" the service or services involved within a reasonable time, not to exceed one year.[36] A municipality

---

29. *See* G.S. 160A-537.

30. The procedural requirements are described in detail at Kara Millonzi, "Municipal and County Service Districts," *Coates' Canons: NC Local Government Law* blog (May 20, 2011), canons.sog.unc.edu/2011/05/municipal-and-county-service-districts/, and Kara Millonzi, "2016 Changes to Municipal Service District (MSD) Authority," *Coates' Canons: NC Local Government Law* blog (June 17, 2016), canons.sog.unc.edu/2016-changes-municipal-service-district-msd-authority.

31. G.S. 160A-537(a).

32. *See* G.S. 153A-302(a).

33. G.S. 153A-302(a1).

34. The MSD statutes provide for an optional property owner petition process. *See* G.S. 160A-537. If a municipal board receives a proper petition, it must consider the request but is not required to establish the district. The MSD statutes also allow a property owner to request that their property be excluded from a proposed district. *Id.*

35. If a local government plans to issue general or special obligation bonds to fund capital projects in a service district, it may specify a different effective date of the district to facilitate the borrowing process. Even in that case, though, it may not levy a district tax until the beginning of the next fiscal year.

36. *See* G.S. 153A-302 (counties); 160A-537 (municipalities).

that contracts with another governmental agency or a private agency must include the following provisions in the contractual agreement:

- Specify the purposes for which municipal funds will be used.
- At the end of the fiscal year (or other appropriate period of time), require an appropriate accounting of the moneys paid out under the contract.
- If the contract is with a private entity, require that the periodic accounting include certain information about any subcontractors, including "the name, location, purpose, and amount paid to any person or persons with whom the private agency contracted to perform or complete any purpose for which city moneys were used for that service district."[37]

Additional contracting requirements and limitations apply when a municipality contracts with a private entity to provide services or projects in certain types of MSDs—those created for downtown or urban area revitalization, including the following:

- Solicit input from the residents and property owners as to the needs of the district.
- Use a bid process to select the private entity that will contract to provide services or undertake projects in the district.
- Hold a public hearing before entering the contract.
- Require the contracting entity to report annually to the municipality.
- Specify in the contract the scope of the service to be provided by the private entity.
- Limit the contract to five years or less.[38]

Funding

Generally, a local unit may borrow money to fund capital projects located in a service district to the same extent, and in the same manner, as it funds similar projects outside a service district. Municipalities, however, have some expanded borrowing authority—they may issue special obligation bonds for any capital projects in an MSD.[39]

Counties and municipalities typically are subject to an additional procedural requirement when issuing general obligations to fund a capital project in a service district. If the general obligation bonds are subject to voter referendum, a majority of the voters registered and voting in the district must approve the bonds, in addition to a majority of the voters within the municipality.[40]

Additional Special Taxing Districts

In addition to the service district authority, counties also are allowed to set up special taxing districts for rural fire protection services,[41] public schools,[42] and water and sewer services.[43] These taxing districts provide counties an additional mechanism to fund both capital and operating

---

37. G.S. 160A-536(d), as amended by S.L. 2016-8. Although not statutorily required to do so, a county should include similar provisions in its contracts with outside entities.

38. *See* G.S. 160A-536(d1). The additional requirements also apply to historic district overlay MSDs, authorized for a few municipalities by G.S. 160A-536(a)(1a). For more information on the requirements and limitations of MSDs, see Millonzi, "2016 Changes to Municipal Service District (MSD) Authority," *supra* note 30.

39. *See* G.S. 159I-30.

40. *See* G.S. 160A-543; 153A-308.

41. G.S. Ch. 69.

42. G.S. Ch. 115C, Art. 36.

43. G.S. Ch. 162A, Art. 6.

expenses associated with the specified functions. A county must hold a successful voter referendum before establishing a special taxing district for the first two purposes.

Development Exactions

Development exactions comprise the final category of special levies for funding public infrastructure projects. Developer exactions can take two forms, either requiring the developer to pay money to the local unit to cover capital expenses incurred by the government to support the new development or requiring the developer to construct certain public infrastructure directly. North Carolina local governments have limited statutory authority to impose development exactions.[44] And constitutionally, development exactions must be rationally related and roughly proportional to the impacts created by the development.[45]

Borrowing Money

The most common method to finance large or costly capital projects is to borrow money. Current revenues, savings, or even special levies are unlikely to generate sufficient revenues to finance a significant construction project or capital acquisition without borrowed funds. Borrowing money allows a local government to leverage future revenue streams—providing the unit cash in the short term that is repaid over time.

When a local unit borrows money, it has a contract with its lenders. The contract typically is referred to as a debt instrument or a debt security. Under that contract, the local unit agrees to pay the principal and the interest on the loan as they come due and to honor any other promises it has made as part of the loan transaction. This contract is enforceable by a lender should the local government breach any obligation.

The traditional debt instrument through which a local government borrows money is the issuance of bonds. A bond is simply evidence of a debt. Local governments are authorized to issue general obligation bonds, revenue bonds, special obligation bonds, project development bonds, and limited obligation bonds. North Carolina local governments also may borrow money through installment finance contracts.

Security

The major distinguishing feature among the different borrowing methods is the nature of the primary security pledged by the unit. The most fundamental promise made when a local unit borrows money is to pay the money back. Closely associated with and reinforcing this promise is the pledge or the designation of one or more forms of security. The security for a debt is defined by reference to the contractual rights of the lender—what the lender can require the borrowing government to do, or give up, should it fail to repay the loan. If the government does not repay its loan, the lender may look to the security to compel repayment or otherwise protect itself.

---

44. For more information on development exactions, see Adam Lovelady, "Exactions and Subdivision Approval," *Coates' Canons: NC Local Government Law* blog (Feb. 1, 2013), canons.sog.unc.edu/exactions-and-subdivision-approval, and Adam Lovelady, "The *Koontz* Decision and Implications for Development Exactions," *Coates' Canons: NC Local Government Law* blog (July 1, 2013), canons.sog.unc.edu/the-koontz-decision-and-implications-for-development-exactions.

45. *See* Nollan v. Cal. Coastal Comm'n, 483 U.S. 825 (1987); Dolan v. City of Tigard, 512 U.S. 374 (1994).

The security for a borrowing affects what form the loan transaction takes, whether voter approval is required, whether LGC approval is required, and how the bond will be marketed and at what cost.

Each of the five authorized borrowing methods involves a distinct primary security pledge. For most of the borrowings, however, state law allows secondary security pledges. Pledging additional security may be necessary to satisfy lenders and make the borrowing feasible, or more affordable, for the unit. The primary securities for each borrowing transaction are discussed in greater detail below.

Entities Involved

When a unit borrows money, it typically requires the assistance of a variety of outside entities, including bond counsel, financial advisers, underwriters, and rating agencies. And most local government borrowings are subject to approval by the LGC. Not all borrowings involve these entities, however; local governments complete many simple, lower-dollar borrowings without any outside guidance or oversight.

Bond Counsel

Bond counsel is a lawyer hired by the local unit to assist in many debt authorization and issuance processes. Bond counsel is one of the key participants involved with issuing debt and usually is selected in the very early stages of the process. The essential role of bond counsel is to issue a legal opinion as to the validity of the bond offering. A typical opinion letter does the following:

1. describes the bond issue in detail,
2. states that in the bond counsel's judgment the bonds are valid and binding obligations of the borrowing unit,
3. describes the nature of the security behind the debt, and
4. indicates the status under the federal tax laws of interest being paid on the debt by the local government and may also indicate other aspects of the taxability of the debt securities or any income derived from holding the securities.

Local units and the purchasers of their bonds typically require this legal opinion as a condition of closing a bond transaction. Prior to issuing its legal opinion, bond counsel guides a local government—in concert with a unit's regular attorney—through the procedural steps required to issue debt under state law. Bond counsel also prepares most of the legal documents required to complete a bond issuance. Through its involvement in this process, bond counsel can provide its approving legal opinion when a transaction is completed.

After an issuance occurs, bond counsel also might advise a local government about how to comply with complex provisions in the federal tax code that regulate how a unit may spend or invest proceeds of "tax-exempt" bonds.[46] Bond counsel also might advise a local government about its obligations under federal securities laws to disclose certain facts affecting bonds issued or the local government's financial condition. The terms of an engagement letter between a unit of local government and a private law firm providing bond counsel services will dictate whether and at what expense these services will be provided.

If a unit of local government is contemplating a bond issuance, it should hire reputable bond counsel with prior experience advising a North Carolina local government in the issuance of debt.[47]

46. For more information about the distinction between "tax-exempt" and "taxable" bonds, see "The Taxability of Interest Paid to Holders of Local Government Debt," below.

47. Although North Carolina law does not require local governments to undertake a competitive process to select bond counsel, many units of local government issue requests for proposals (RFPs) to seek information about prior

In doing so, a unit should seek to understand the specific functions bond counsel will perform during the initial issuance of the bonds and after the debt has been issued.

Financial Adviser

A financial adviser advocates for the borrowing government and provides its officials the information necessary to make informed decisions. A financial adviser often advises the unit on how to structure the financing to get the best interest rate and may coordinate the bond issuance process. A financial adviser that advises a local government in connection with the issuance of its debt—including advice with respect to the structure, timing, and similar matters of debt—must register as a "municipal adviser" with the federal Securities and Exchange Commission (SEC).[48] Municipal advisers have fiduciary duties under federal law to act in the best interests of their clients.[49]

A local government can engage a municipal adviser for a single debt issuance or for a range of services that extend beyond a particular transaction.[50] The staff of the Local Government Commission can assist a local government in considering the structure of its debt or the proper mechanism for financing a project, but unlike a private municipal adviser, these staff may assist in commission decisions to approve or deny a particular debt issuance.

Underwriter

A bond underwriter is a financial institution that purchases a new issue of municipal securities for resale. The underwriter may acquire the bonds either by negotiation with the borrowing unit or by award based on competitive bidding. The underwriter essentially functions as a middleman in the borrowing transaction, bringing together the borrowing government and the investors who ultimately purchase the government's bonds or certificates of participation. General obligation bond sales typically are conducted competitively, with underwriting firms submitting sealed bids to buy the bonds. In a public sale, the underwriter is the formal lender or buyer of the securities; the title to the securities passes to that entity. The underwriter bears the risk of finding enough investors to whom to sell the securities. Other bond sales (revenue bonds, special obligation bonds, project development bonds, limited obligation bonds) and certificates of participation generally are sold by negotiation. The unit selects one or more underwriters at the beginning of the process and negotiates the structure of the financing and the sales price with the underwriters.

Underwriters that purchase and resell a local government's bonds to investors must comply with certain federal securities regulations, including the SEC's "Rule 15c2-12."[51] With some exceptions, these underwriters must (1) obtain disclosure documents from the local government that describe the bonds to be sold and provide certain information about the issuer of the bonds, (2) distribute these disclosure documents to potential investors, and (3) reasonably determine that the issuer

---

experiences of potential bond counsel.

48. *See* U.S. Securities and Exchange Commission, Registration of Municipal Advisors, Final Rule, 78 Fed. Reg. 67,468 (Nov. 12, 2013). Providing such advice while failing to register as a municipal adviser violates federal law. *See* 15 U.S.C. § 78o-4(a)(1)(B).

49. *See* 15 U.S.C. § 78o-4(c)(1).

50. Although North Carolina law does not require local governments to undertake a competitive process to select a municipal adviser, many units of local government issue RFPs to select such a firm. The Government Finance Officers' Association has issued guidance that can assist in creating this type of RFP. *See* Government Finance Officers' Association, *Best Practice: Selecting and Managing Municipal Advisors* (Feb. 28, 2014), www.gfoa.org/materials/selecting-and-managing-municipal-advisors.

51. *See, e.g.,* 17 C.F.R. § 240.15c2-12 (hereinafter Rule 15c2-12).

has agreed to provide continuing disclosure of certain information after the bonds are issued.[52] An underwriter typically hires legal counsel to advise it on the structure of the offering and the underwriter's responsibilities, and a local government typically pays for the cost of such legal counsel at closing out of bond proceeds.

In some cases, a financial institution may not purchase a local government's bond or debt to resell it to other investors. Instead, it may hold this debt on its own balance sheet. A financial institution participating in such a "private placement" may be referred to as a "lender" rather than an "underwriter."

Rating Agencies

When a unit sells bonds publicly, it is subject to disclosure requirements considerably more extensive than those required by a private placement. In addition, as a practical matter, securities that are publicly sold must be rated. Bond ratings play a crucial role in the marketing of bonds.[53] Many investors, particularly individuals, cannot personally investigate the creditworthiness of a government's securities. Bond ratings are an accepted indication of the creditworthiness of a particular issuance. The bond rating often is the single most important factor affecting the interest cost on bonds.

Three national agencies rate local government bonds and certificates of participation for the national market—Moody's Investors Service, Standard & Poor's, and Fitch Ratings. Each agency uses a slightly different formula for determining its ratings. All the agencies assess the following factors—the economy; the particular debt structure; the unit's financial condition; the unit's demographic factors; the management practices of the governing body and administration; and, if applicable, the user charges supporting the issuance and any covenants and other protections offered by the bond documents.

Trustee

A trustee is a corporate entity—typically an arm of a financial institution—that is involved in some, but not all, issuances of local government debt.[54] Subject to the terms of the bond documents under which bonds are issued, a bond trustee usually takes several actions throughout the life of a bond. It might act on behalf of bondholders in the event a local government defaults under the terms of the bond documents, obtain certain disclosures from the local government over the life of the bonds, and, as a "paying agent," collect a local government's payments of principal and interest and ensure their proper application.[55]

---

52. *See* Rule 15c2-12(b)(1) (obligation to obtain official statement); (b)(2) (obligation to distribute certain disclosure documents to investors); (b)(5) (obligation to reasonably determine issuer's commitment to provide continuing disclosure of certain information). The exemptions to Rule 15c2-12 include, among others, primary offerings of municipal securities sold in authorized denominations of $100,000 or more and to no more than thirty-five sophisticated investors meeting certain criteria. *See* Rule 15c2-12(d)(1).

53. The LGC will not approve a public offering of bonds without an "investment grade" rating from a nationally recognized credit rating agency. *See* N.C. Department of State Treasurer, State and Local Government Finance Division, Local Government Commission, *Guidelines on Debt Issuance (Revised)* (March 7, 2023), www.nctreasurer.com/documents/files/slgfdlgc/guidelines-review-and-approval-debt-applications/download?attachment. Investment-grade ratings are those above Baa3 (Moody's) and BBB- (S&P Global Ratings and Fitch).

54. Trustees are most commonly involved in issuances of revenue bonds or special obligation bonds.

55. For helpful general information on the role of a bond trustee, see UMB Financial Corporation, "Defining the Role of a Bond Trustee or Paying Agent," *UMB Blog* (July 29, 2020), blog.umb.com/institutional-banking-guide-defining-the-role-of-a-bond-trustee-or-paying-agent/.

Local Government Commission

The LGC is a nine-member body responsible for fiscal oversight of local governments and public authorities in North Carolina.[56] In addition, the LGC approves most local government borrowings and sells bonds on a unit's behalf. All general obligation bonds, revenue bonds, special obligation bonds, and project development bonds must be approved by the LGC. The same is true of some installment financings, certain leases, and other financial agreements.[57] A unit must determine if LGC approval is mandated by statute for its proposed borrowing transaction because if approval is required and a unit fails to obtain it, the entire borrowing transaction is void.

In reviewing proposed issuances, the LGC must consider statutory criteria, which vary somewhat depending on the type of borrowing. Generally, however, the LGC must determine if the amount being borrowed, when added to the existing debt of the unit and at the rate of interest the unit probably will have to pay, is an amount the unit can afford.

LGC staff members will work with a unit from the outset of the borrowing process to help local officials determine the best borrowing method for the project being funded. The staff also will identify any deficiencies in the unit's financials or management practices that might prevent the unit from receiving commission approval.[58] Thus, local officials should contact LGC staff very early in the unit's internal process—preferably immediately after the scope of the capital project is determined and preliminary engineering studies are completed.

Joint Legislative Committee on Local Government

In 2011, the General Assembly created the Joint Legislative Committee on Local Government as a standing interim legislative study committee.[59] The purpose of the committee, among other things, is to review and monitor local government capital projects that require both approval by the LGC and an issuance of debt exceeding $1 million. The committee's directive does not apply to capital projects related to schools, jails, courthouses, and administrative buildings. It also does not apply to the re-funding of existing debt. Furthermore, the committee's authority is limited to reviewing and monitoring the capital projects and debt issuances within its purview; it is not authorized to approve or reject a capital project or financing.

The committee has promulgated guidelines to carry out its statutory responsibility. A local unit seeking approval from the LGC to borrow money for a capital project subject to the committee's oversight must submit a letter to the committee at least forty-five days prior to the unit's formal presentation before the LGC. The letter must include (1) a description of the project, (2) the debt requirements of the project, (3) the means of financing the project, and (4) the source or sources of repayment for project costs.

The committee may meet at the discretion of its chairs to review a proposed capital project. It may send a letter of objection or support to the LGC for a particular project. It also may ask to speak at an LGC meeting on a particular project. In addition, the committee may make periodic

56. *See* G.S. 159-3.

57. For more information on the types of financial agreements subject to LGC approval, see Kara Millonzi, "Local Government Commission (LGC) Approval of Bonds, Installment Financings, Leases, and Other Contracts Involving Capital Assets (Including Recent Changes Related to Local Governments on the Unit Assistance List)," *Coates' Canons: NC Local Government Law* blog (Oct. 29, 2022), canons.sog.unc.edu/2022/10/local-government-commission-lgc-approval-of-debt-leases-and-other-contracts-involving-capital-assets-including-recent-changes-related-to-local-governments-on-the-unit-assistance-list/.

58. The Department of State Treasurer has issued general guidelines on issuing debt. Revised on March 7, 2023, they are available at www.nctreasurer.com/documents/files/slgfdlgc/guidelines-review-and-approval-debt-applications/download?attachment.

59. S.L. 2011-291.

reports and recommendations to the General Assembly for proposed new legislation related to local government debt authority.

Types of Authorized Debt

The General Assembly may bestow borrowing authority on local units only by general law.[60] The main five debt mechanisms available to local governments are general obligation bonds, revenue bonds, special obligation bonds, project development financings, and installment financings. A municipality has additional borrowing authority under certain circumstances.[61] Some public authorities also have (limited) borrowing authority.[62] Each debt mechanism, including the primary security, the projects which may be funded, and any significant limitations, is described below. (However, a county or municipality is not limited to the above-listed mechanisms when borrowing from the state or federal government.)[63]

General Obligation Bonds

The Local Government Bond Act[64] authorizes the issuance of general obligation (GO) bonds. State law specifies the types of capital projects a county or municipality may fund with GO bonds, which includes most, if not all, capital projects in which a unit is authorized to engage.[65]

Security

GO bonds involve the strongest form of security a county or municipality can pledge for debt—the unit's full faith and credit. All the resources of that government stand behind such a pledge, but specifically, a full-faith-and-credit pledge of a North Carolina county or municipality is a promise to levy whatever amount of property tax is necessary to repay the debt.[66]

Requirements and Limitations

The legal authority to issue GO bonds is very broad. Practically it is much more limited, as the North Carolina Constitution generally requires that a unit hold a successful voter referendum before pledging its full faith and credit.[67] State law also places a limit on the amount of outstanding GO debt a unit may have at any one time, referred to as the net debt limit. Finally, all GO borrowings must be approved by the LGC.

Voter Approval

The voter approval requirement can be a significant hurdle to issuing GO bonds. For example, voters are unlikely to vote for controversial or less popular projects, such as jails or landfills. Even referenda for popular projects, such as schools or parks, sometimes fail. Thus, although issuing GO bonds is a relatively simple form of borrowing, and generally the cheapest, local units often look to

---

60. N.C. Const. art. V, § 3. Any local acts or charter provisions purporting to grant borrowing authority are void.

61. *See, e.g.*, G.S. 160A-512(8); 160A-17.2.

62. *See*, e.g., G.S. 162A-8 (revenue bond authority for water and sewer districts); 162A-90 (revenue and general obligation bond authority for county water and sewer districts); 130A-61 (general obligation bond authority for sanitary districts); 159-210 (lease-backed financings by airport authorities).

63. G.S. 160A-17.1.

64. G.S. Ch. 159, Art. 4.

65. *See* G.S. 159-48.

66. By law, a general obligation pledge is not subject to the $1.50 per $100 valuation property tax rate limitation. G.S. 153A-149(b)(2) (counties); 160A-209(b)(1) (municipalities). Thus, a general obligation pledge is a pledge of the unlimited taxing power.

67. N.C. Const. art. V, § 4(2).

one of the other authorized borrowing mechanisms to avoid the voter-approval requirement. (The state constitution does not require voter approval if any other form of security is used, and therefore voter approval is never necessary for loans secured by the other authorized borrowing methods.)

Voter approval is not always necessary for GO bonds. The constitution carves out a few exceptions, the most significant of which are refunding bonds and two-thirds bonds.[68]

— Refunding Bonds

Refunding bonds are issued to retire, or pay off, an existing debt, replacing it with a new one. They typically are used to refinance existing debt because interest rates have fallen, and the county or municipality wants to reduce its debt service payments. No new debt is being created; rather, a unit merely changes the evidence of an existing debt. Therefore, the constitution excuses refunding bonds from the requirement of voter approval.

Investors typically seek to protect their investment against refunding for as long as possible. GO bonds often include provisions that prohibit the call, or early retirement, of a bond issue for a period of time. A unit may still take advantage of falling interest rates during the prohibited call period. It must utilize a device known as an advanced refunding, wherein the local government issues refunding bonds. Rather than use the proceeds to retire the refunded debt immediately, however, the unit places them in an escrow account (sinking fund) controlled by an independent party. The moneys are invested and used for two purposes—they pay debt service on the original issue until the bonds can be called, and, when allowed, they retire the original debt. Recent changes in federal income tax laws have decreased the usefulness of advance refunding. Prior to January 1, 2018, interest paid to holders of refunding bonds was exempt from federal income tax if the bonds were issued at least ninety days prior to the call date of refunded bonds. In December 2017, Congress repealed that exemption for refunding bonds issued after January 1, 2018—making interest paid on refunding bonds federally taxable.[69] To compensate for the loss of the tax exemption, issuers must pay relatively higher rates of interest to holders of advance refunding bonds issued after January 1, 2018.[70]

— Two-Thirds Bonds

The state constitution also excepts from the voter-approval requirement certain additional debt issuances resulting from principal reductions in outstanding GO issuances. Specifically, article V, section 4(2)(f) specifies that no voter referendum is required when GO bonds are issued

> for purposes authorized by general laws uniformly applicable throughout the State, to the extent of two-thirds of the amount by which the unit's outstanding indebtedness shall have been reduced during the next preceding fiscal year.[71]

In determining the amount of debt reduction during a fiscal year, a local unit counts only principal payments; interest paid is irrelevant. And only the net reduction in principal is counted. If a county

---

68. For a list of all the purposes for which a local government may issue GO bonds without voter approval, see N.C. Const. art. V, § 4(2) and G.S. 159-49.

69. *See* Pub. L. 115-97, § 13532, 131 Stat. 2154 (Dec. 22, 2017).

70. If interest rates are low enough, an issuer still might be able to issue advanced refunding bonds on a taxable basis at a lower rate than existing tax-exempt debt. The LGC has stated that the present value of savings from a refunding should exceed 3 percent of the refunded bonds to receive LGC approval. *See* N.C. Department of State Treasurer, State and Local Government Finance Division, Local Government Commission, *Guidelines on Debt Issuance (Revised)* (Sept. 4, 2019), www.nctreasurer.com/documents/files/slgfd/lgc/localgovdebtmngmt/guidelines-debt-issuances/download.

71. This exception is statutorily authorized by G.S. 159-49.

or municipality borrows during a fiscal year, it may actually have a net increase in outstanding debt and therefore no two-thirds capacity at all.

A local unit must use its two-thirds capacity in the fiscal year immediately following the year in which the debt was reduced. In using its two-thirds capacity, the government generally is not restricted by the purposes for which the retired debt was issued. State law requires, however, that new GO debt incurred for certain purposes always be approved by the voters. These purposes include auditoriums, coliseums, stadiums, convention centers, and similar facilities; art galleries, museums, and historic properties; urban redevelopment; and public transportation.

Once a county or municipal governing board announces its intention to use its two-thirds capacity to issue new GO bonds without voter approval, the unit's citizens can force a referendum by submitting a petition signed by at least 10 percent of the unit's registered voters. The petition must be filed with the county or municipal clerk within thirty days after the date of publication of the bond order as introduced.

Net Debt Limitation

The other restriction on issuing GO bonds is the net debt limitation. A proposed GO borrowing (as well as a proposed installment financing) contract must satisfy this requirement. The limitation recognizes that both GO bonds and installment financings are retired with property tax proceeds, and it therefore restricts the net debt of a unit to 8 percent of the appraised value of property subject to taxation by the unit. Net debt is calculated by taking gross GO and installment financing debt and then deducting the amount of this debt that in most units is repaid from sources other than the property tax. There is a complicated statutory formula for both calculating gross debt and determining the appropriate deductions.[72]

For most local units, the net debt limitation is more of a theoretical than an actual limitation. The net debt of any unit rarely exceeds 2 percent. To retain good credit ratings, many units set a target net debt threshold at an even lower percentage. The finance officer must file a statement of net debt with the clerk to the board and the LGC as part of the debt approval process.

LGC Approval

The LGC must approve all issuances of GO bonds—even those that do not require voter approval.[73] When reviewing a GO bond issuance, the commission considers several factors to help it determine if the unit will be able to repay the debt. Such factors include the unit's outstanding debt, its debt and financial management practices, its tax base and the projected tax rates needed to repay the debt, and the proposed interest rates and total cost of the borrowing.[74]

State law directs the LGC to approve the debt issuance if it determines that:

1. The proposed bond issue is necessary or expedient.
2. The amount proposed is adequate and not excessive for the proposed purpose of the issue.
3. The unit's debt management procedures and policies are good or that reasonable assurances have been given that its debt will henceforth be managed in strict compliance with the law.

72. G.S. 159-55.
73. *See* G.S. 159-51.
74. G.S. 159-52.

4. The increase in taxes, if any, necessary to service the proposed debt will not be excessive.
5. The proposed bonds can be marketed at reasonable rates of interest.[75]

If the commission denies the application, it must notify the unit. At the unit's request, the commission must hold a public hearing on the application. The commission may revisit its decision based on testimony or other information presented at the hearing.[76]

Issuance Process

The process to issue GO bonds that require voter approval is lengthy and requires detailed planning and coordination among a unit's staff, bond counsel, the LGC, and other third parties (for example, financial advisers or ratings agencies).[77] Bond counsel typically assists a unit's staff in the preparation of public notices, required statements a finance officer must prepare or file, and documents to be approved by the governing board and the LGC.

Application for LGC Approval

To initiate the process, a unit must file with the LGC an application for the approval of a GO bonds issuance.[78] The LGC may require the unit's staff to meet with LGC staff prior to the acceptance of the application.[79] Typically, commission staff will meet with unit representatives to aid in structuring the deal and advise the unit on the likelihood of commission approval.

Bond Order

The central document in a GO bond issuance is the bond order. The bond order is adopted by the governing board and serves a double purpose. First, it authorizes issuance of the bonds, stating the purpose for which the proceeds will be spent and the maximum amount of bonds that may be issued. If a unit is proposing bonds for more than one unrelated purpose, it will need a separate bond order for each purpose.[80] Second, the order publicizes the bond issue, not only setting out the purpose and amount but also indicating the security for the bonds. The bond order is "the crucial foundation document which supports and explains" the issue.[81]

The statutory procedure that leads to adoption of a bond order serves two primary purposes: (1) it concludes with the governing board's formal authorization of the bond issue and (2) it provides an opportunity for the public to learn about and comment on the proposed issue and the project(s) it will finance.

Most of the formal steps in the process are largely pro forma. Much of the work to prepare the issuance, obtaining informal approvals from all required parties, typically happens well in advance of the adoption of the bond order. Occasionally testimony at the public hearing will cause a board to modify, delay, or drop its plans, but the real opportunity for citizens to comment on the bond issue is the referendum.

---

75. *Id.*
76. *Id.*
77. Form LGC-107, available from the LGC upon request, lists the major steps necessary for counties and municipalities to authorize the issuance of GO bonds requiring voter approval.
78. *See* G.S. 159-51.
79. *Id.*
80. G.S. 159-48(g).
81. Rider v. Lenoir Cnty., 236 N.C. 620, 631 (1953).

Sworn Statement of Debt

After a unit's governing board has introduced a bond order authorizing the issuance of GO bonds, the unit's finance officer must prepare and file with the clerk to the governing board a sworn statement of debt.[82] This statement reflects the unit's net debt, the assessed value of property subject to taxation by the unit, and the percentage of net debt compared to that assessed value.[83] As discussed previously, that percentage may not exceed 8 percent.

Statement of Disclosures

The finance officer of a unit intending to issue GO bonds also must file a statement of disclosure with the LGC and the clerk to the governing board that contains (1) an estimate of the total interest that will be paid on the bonds over their expected term, if issued, and a summary of the assumptions upon which that estimate is based; (2) an estimate of the increase in property tax rate, if any, necessary to service the proposed debt; and (3) the amount of two-thirds bonds capacity the unit has available for the current fiscal year.[84]

In November 2022, the LGC adopted a "safe harbor policy" to govern its assessment that a unit's finance officer used reasonable assumptions in the statement of disclosure when determining the total interest to be paid over the expected term of the bonds. Under that policy, the LGC will find such assumptions reasonable if they assume that (1) principal will be paid in twenty annual equal principal installments and (2) the interest rate on the bonds will be equal to a Bond Buyer 20 index (BB20) rate published within twenty-five days prior to the introduction of the bond order plus at least 200 basis points (2 percent).[85]

Voter Approval and Issuance

The governing board of a unit of local government must call for a referendum on the bonds to be held within one year after the bond order's passage.[86] In 2023, the legislature amended G.S. 159-61(d), which provides the form of the ballot question to be used for local government general obligation bond referenda.[87] The ballot must include certain information about expected cumulative cost of the bond issuance and whether, and to what extent, a tax rate increase will be required to service the debt. After the bond order is approved by voters, the unit may issue bonds authorized under the order within seven years of the date the bond order takes effect.[88] After the unit adopts

---

82. G.S. 159-55(a).

83. G.S. 159-55(a)(3)–(5).

84. G.S. 159-55.1(a). The statement of disclosure also must be posted online but need not be published in a newspaper. *See* G.S. 159-55.1(c).

85. N.C. Department of State Treasurer, State and Local Finance Division and Local Government Commission, Resolution Adopting Safe Harbor Policy Related to Reasonableness of Estimated Interest Assumptions (Nov. 1, 2022), www.nctreasurer.com/documents/files/slgdaacanddebt/safe-harbor-policy-related-reasonableness-estimated-interest-assumptions/download?attachment. A unit's finance officer may use alternate assumptions, and in that case, the LGC will consider the reasonableness of those assumptions when it reviews the unit's application for approval.

86. *See* G.S. 159-61(b).

87. Section 36.3.(a) of Session Law 2023-134. LGC staff has issued a memorandum to provide guidance to local government units in complying with the modified requirements—specifically, the requirements of both clause (1) and clause (2) of G.S. 159-61(d), as amended. *See* N.C. Department of State Treasurer, State and Local Finance Division and the Local Government Commission, *Guidelines for Compliance with General Obligation Bond Ballot Question Requirements (*G.S. 159-61(d), *as amended*), www.nctreasurer.com/documents/files/slgfdlgc/lgc-guidelines-ballot-question-requirements/open.

88. A unit may obtain a three-year extension, from seven to ten years, with approval from the LGC. *See* G.S. 159-64.

a resolution establishing the details of the bonds to be issued,[89] the LGC sells GO bonds on behalf of the unit, typically on a competitive basis.[90]

Revenue Bonds

The State and Local Government Revenue Bond Act[91] authorizes the issuance of revenue bonds. Revenue bonds are most commonly issued to fund water and sewer utility projects, though legally they may fund a variety of other revenue-generating capital assets, including gas facilities, solid waste facilities, parking, marine facilities, auditoriums, convention centers, economic development projects, electric facilities, public transportation, airports, hospitals, stadiums, recreation facilities, and stormwater drainage.[92]

Security

The primary security for a revenue bond is the revenue generated by the financed asset or the system of which the financed asset becomes a part. By law such a pledge creates a lien on the pledged revenues in favor of the bondholders, and normally the bondholders have the contractual right to demand an increase in the user charges generating the revenues if those revenues prove inadequate to service the debt. If the revenue pledge is the only security, however, the bondholders have no right to demand payment from any other source, or to require an increase in taxes, if facility or system revenues remain inadequate even after charges are increased. As discussed above, a unit also may pledge special assessments levied under the critical infrastructure assessment authority as security for revenue bonds used to finance specially assessed projects.[93]

North Carolina law allows units of local government to pay debt service on revenue bonds only from revenues pledged as security for the bonds.[94] For example, a municipality that issues revenue bonds to finance the construction of a public parking deck may use only revenues generated by operation of that parking deck (for example, parking fees) to pay principal and interest to revenue bondholders. In most cases, holders of revenue bonds have no right to mandate that a local government raise taxes or demand payment from any source other than the revenues of the financed asset or system.[95]

Requirements and Limitations

A vote of the people is not required to issue revenue bonds.[96] However, other requirements effectively limit the types of projects that revenue bonds may be issued to fund. The requirements are reflected in covenants. Revenue bonds also are subject to LGC approval.

Covenants

Because the security for the debt is revenue from the debt-financed asset, or the system of which it is a part, lenders are naturally concerned about the construction, operation, and continued health

89. *See* G.S. 159-65(a).

90. *See* G.S. 159-123(a) (authorizing competitive sale); 159-127 (setting forth procedure for award of sale).

91. G.S. Ch. 159, Art. 5. G.S. 159-61 permits any government authorized to issue revenue bonds to also issue revenue bond anticipation notes.

92. *See* G.S. 159-83.

93. G.S. 153A-210.6; 160A-239.6.

94. G.S. 159-94(a).

95. A local government is authorized to pledge its taxing power as additional security for some types of revenue bond projects. *See* G.S. 159-97. Such pledges are uncommon.

96. If a unit covenants or otherwise agrees to effectively pledge its taxing power as additional security for a revenue bond, the unit must first hold a voter referendum. *See* G.S. 159-97.

of the financed asset or system. The concern is expressed through a series of covenants, or promises, the borrowing government makes to the lenders as part of the loan transaction. The most fundamental of these is the rate covenant, under which the unit promises to set and maintain the rates, fees, and charges of the revenue-producing facility or system so that net revenues will exceed annual debt service requirements by some fixed amount or percentage. For example, a common requirement is that the rate structure generate annual net revenues at some specified level—usually between 120 and 150 percent—of either the current year's debt service requirements or the maximum annual debt service requirements during the life of the loan. This margin of safety required by the rate covenant is referred to as times-coverage of the loan. The times-coverage requirement serves as a practical limitation on the types of projects that may be funded with this loan structure.

Because prospective investors typically will want independent verification that revenues will be adequate to service the bonds, a borrowing government normally is expected to commission a feasibility study by a consulting engineer or other independent professional. The professional will evaluate the demand for the services the financed facility or system will provide, look at likely operating costs, and suggest the net revenue stream likely to result.

Issuers of revenue bonds also typically agree to certain restrictions on their ability to issue additional revenue bonds secured and payable from the same source of revenues as previously issued bonds. Known as an "additional bonds test," this covenant generally permits the issue of additional bonds secured by and payable from the same source of revenues as outstanding revenue bonds only if the issuer can demonstrate that the net revenues have been and will continue to be sufficient to service the additional debt.

Lastly, revenue bond issuers also commonly agree to maintain various funds in connection with the bonds (for example, a revenue fund, a debt-service fund, a construction fund, and a debt-service reserve fund). Each of these funds is restricted by the terms of the bond documents under which the revenue bonds are issued. An issuer will commonly agree that a third-party trustee will maintain the proceeds of the revenue bonds and will disburse the proceeds of those bonds only upon the issuer's submission of proper documentation (for example, relevant evidence of construction pay applications).[97]

State Approval

A unit of local government seeking to issue revenue bonds must submit an application for approval to the LGC.[98] As with GO bonds, the commission will consider the feasibility of the bond issuance and the likely ability of the unit to repay the loan. And, as with GO bonds, the LGC may require the unit's staff to meet with LGC staff prior to the acceptance of the application.[99] Once the LGC accepts the unit's application, it may consider, among other things, whether the probable net revenues of the financed assets will be sufficient to meet the debt service on the proposed revenue bonds.[100] The LGC must approve the borrowing if it determines the following:

1. The proposed revenue bond issue is necessary or expedient.
2. The amount proposed is adequate and not excessive for the purpose of the issue.
3. The proposed project is feasible.

97. G.S. 159-89 provides a full list of covenants to which an issuer of revenue bonds may agree.
98. *See* G.S. 159-85(a).
99. *See* G.S. 159-85(b).
100. *See* G.S. 159-86(a).

4. The unit's debt management procedures and policies are good or reasonable assurances have been given that its debt will henceforth be managed in strict compliance with the law.
5. The proposed revenue bonds can be marketed at a reasonable cost to the unit.[101]

A denial of an application by the LGC is considered a final decision.[102]

Issuance Process

Revenue bonds usually are sold by negotiation rather than by competitive bid, and the borrowing government will select an underwriter or placement agent at the beginning of the process. Each revenue bond financing is unique; the details of the financing and the bond order differ from one financing to another. Typically the details emerge from a series of negotiating sessions attended by representatives of the borrowing government, the bond attorney, one or more underwriters or placement agents and their attorney, and LGC staff members.

Unlike with GO bonds, a unit's governing board may introduce a bond order for revenue bonds at any regular or special meeting and adopt it at the same meeting, as long as the unit has submitted its application for approval to the LGC.[103] To approve a revenue bond issuance, state law does not require the unit to publish notice of a referendum or take any other procedural action other than approving the bond order.

Special Obligation Bonds

North Carolina law authorizes certain units of local government to issue "special obligation" bonds for a limited number of purposes.[104] In particular, counties, municipalities, and regional solid waste management authorities may issue these bonds for solid waste management projects; certain water supply, conservation, and reuse projects; and wastewater collection and treatment projects.[105] Municipalities also may issue special obligation bonds to finance or refinance projects that they may otherwise undertake in an MSD.[106]

Security

A special obligation is secured by a pledge of any revenue source or asset available to the borrowing government, except the unit's taxing power. In a broad sense a revenue bond is a type of special obligation bond. The term "special obligation," as used in North Carolina, however, refers to debts secured by something other than (or in addition to) revenues from the asset or system being financed. For example, a county might pledge proceeds from fees charged for building rentals or from special assessments. A county could not pledge local sales and use tax, animal tax, privilege license tax, or property tax proceeds because these are locally levied taxes. A municipality could pledge local sales and use tax because it is not a unit-levied tax.

Requirements and Limitations

As with revenue bonds, there is no statutory process for issuing SO bonds. Because the debt market perceives the security for special obligation debt as weaker than that for general obligation debt,

---

101. G.S. 159-86.
102. G.S. 159-87.
103. *See* G.S. 159-88(b). It may be adopted by a simple majority of those present and voting if there is a quorum.
104. *See* G.S. Ch. 159, Art. 7A.
105. G.S. 159-146(a) (authorizing issuance of special obligation bonds to finance or refinance a "project"); G.S. 159-146(b)(7) (defining "project").
106. *See* G.S. 159-146(b)(7).

the market normally demands of special obligation debt some of the same safeguards demanded of revenue bonds. And the process for issuing SO bonds is similar to that for issuing revenue bonds.

The LGC must approve all SO bond issuances. The commission may consider the same criteria as it does for a GO bond issuance, a revenue bond issuance, or both.[107] The LGC sells special obligation bonds on behalf of an issuing unit, typically in a privately negotiated sale.[108]

Project Development Financings

As a specialized borrowing structure, North Carolina law authorizes local governments to engage in project development financings.[109] Project development financing is structurally equivalent to a type of borrowing prevalent in other states known as tax increment financing, or TIF.[110] In fact, North Carolina practitioners often refer to this form of borrowing as TIF or TIF bonds.

Project development financing is a method of increasing the overall property value in a currently blighted, depressed, or underdeveloped area within a county or municipality. A unit borrows money to fund public improvements within the designated area (development district) with the goal of attracting private investment. The debt incurred by funding the improvements is secured and repaid by tax increment revenue—the additional property tax proceeds resulting from the district's new development. The Project Development Financing Act[111] permits counties and municipalities to issue project development financing bonds and to use the proceeds for many, but not all, of the purposes for which either taxing unit may issue GO bonds.[112] The act also allows local governments to use the proceeds for any service or facility authorized to be provided in an MSD, though no district actually need be created.[113]

Security

The security for a project development financing bond is the incremental increase in property tax revenue in a defined area. The tax increase results from private development incentivized by the public infrastructure financed with the loan proceeds.

Requirements and Limitations

There are detailed procedure requirements for issuing project development bonds. A unit must define a financing district, adopt a financing plan, and secure various approvals from governmental entities.

Financing District

At the outset of a project development financing project, a county or municipality must establish a development financing district. A county district must consist of property that is

1. blighted, deteriorated, deteriorating, undeveloped, or inappropriately developed from the standpoint of sound community development and growth;

---

107. G.S. 159I-30.

108. *See* G.S. 159-123(b)(3) (authorizing the private sale of special obligation bonds).

109. *See* S.L. 2003-403.

110. For more detailed information on project development financings, see William C. Rivenbark, Shea Riggsbee Denning, and Kara A. Millonzi, "2007 Legislation Expands Scope of Project Development Financing in North Carolina," *Local Finance Bulletin* No. 36 (Nov. 2007), www.sog.unc.edu/sites/default/files/reports/lfb36.pdf.

111. G.S. Ch. 159, Art. 6.

112. G.S. 159-103. For more information on project development financing authority in North Carolina, see UNC Chapel Hill School of Government, *Tax Increment Financing in North Carolina*, "Frequently Asked Questions," www.sog.unc.edu/resources/faq-collections/tax-increment-financing-frequently-asked-questions.

113. *See supra* note 25 and accompanying text for a list of municipal service district purposes.

2. appropriate for rehabilitation or conservation activities; or
3. appropriate for economic development.[114]

A municipal district must consist of property that meets at least one of the conditions set forth for a county district or that meets the criteria of an *urban redevelopment area* as defined by G.S. 160A-503. A municipality's planning commission may designate the following types of property as a redevelopment area:

1. property that is blighted because of dilapidated, deteriorated, aged, or obsolete buildings; inadequate ventilation, light, air, sanitation, or open spaces; high density of population or overcrowding; or unsanitary or unsafe conditions;
2. a nonresidential redevelopment area with dilapidated, deteriorated, aged, or obsolete buildings; inadequate ventilation, light, air, sanitation, or open spaces; defective or inadequate street layout or faulty lot layout; tax or special assessment delinquency exceeding the value of the property; or unsanitary or unsafe conditions;
3. a rehabilitation, conservation, and reconditioning area in present danger of becoming a blighted or nonresidential redevelopment area; or
4. any combination of the above types of areas.[115]

The total land area within a financing district may not exceed 5 percent of the total land area of the taxing unit.[116] Counties also are specifically prohibited from including in a development financing district land located within a municipality at the time the district is created, even though a county and municipality may jointly agree to create such a district.[117] In the absence of such an agreement, any land included in a development financing district established by a municipality that issues debt instruments to be repaid from the incremental valuation does not count against the 5 percent of unincorporated land in that county that may be included in a development financing district.[118] If a county and municipality jointly create a development financing district, with each unit pledging its incremental tax revenue in support thereof, the area included within the district likely counts against the 5 percent limit for both the county and the municipality.

Financing Plan and County Approval

Once it identifies the development financing district, a unit must adopt a financing plan that includes the following:

- a description of the boundaries of the district;
- a description of the proposed development, both public and private;
- the costs of the proposed public activities;
- the sources and amount of funds needed to pay for the proposed public activities;
- the base valuation of the district;
- the projected increase in the assessed valuation of property in the district;

---

114. G.S. 158-7.3(f); 160A-515.1(e).

115. Additional limitations apply to a plan for a development financing district established pursuant to G.S. 158-7.3 and located outside a municipality's central business district. G.S. 158-7.3(a)(1a).

116. G.S. 158-7.3(c); 160A-515.1(b).

117. G.S. 158-7.3(c); 159-107(e).

118. Conversely, land in a county district subsequently annexed by a municipality does not count against the municipality's 5 percent limit unless the county and municipality have entered into an increment agreement; in such an agreement, the municipality agrees that municipal taxes collected on part or all of the incremental valuation in the district will be paid into the reserve increment fund for the district. G.S. 159-107(e).

- the estimated duration of the district (the earlier of thirty years from the effective date of the district or when the bonds are repaid);
- a description of how the proposed public and private development of the district will benefit district residents and business owners in terms of jobs, affordable housing, and services;
- a description of appropriate ameliorative activities if the proposed projects negatively impact district residents or business owners in terms of jobs, affordable housing, services, or displacement;
- a statement that the initial users of any new manufacturing facilities included in the plan will be required to pay certain wages, unless the users are exempted by the secretary of commerce.[119]

The unit must hold a public hearing on the proposed financing plan.[120] After the public hearing, a county board may approve the plan, with or without amendment, unless the plan has been disapproved by the secretary of the North Carolina Department of Environmental Quality (NCDEQ). Municipal boards must also provide notice to the governing board(s) of the county or counties in which the proposed district is located.[121] County governing boards have twenty-eight days to disapprove the plan. If it is not disapproved by the county board(s), the municipal board may proceed to adopt the plan.

State Approval

The plan and district are not effective until the LGC approves the issuance of project development financing bonds for the district. The LGC may consider any matters it deems relevant to whether the bond issuance should be approved, including

1. whether the projects to be financed from the bonds are necessary to secure significant new project development for the district;
2. whether the proposed projects are feasible (taking into account additional security, such as credit enhancement, insurance, or guarantees, as discussed below);
3. the unit's debt management procedures and policies;
4. whether the unit is in default in any debt service obligation;
5. whether the private development forecast in the development financing plan is likely to occur without the public project or projects to be financed by the bonds;
6. whether taxes on the incremental valuation accruing to the development financing district, together with any other revenues available under G.S. 159-110, will be sufficient to service the proposed project development financing debt instruments;
7. whether the LGC can market the proposed project development financing debt instruments at reasonable rates of interest.[122]

Two other state agencies must approve some project development financings. If a development financing plan involves the construction and operation of a new manufacturing facility, the plan must be submitted to the secretary of NCDEQ. The secretary's review will determine whether the facility

119. G.S. 158-7.3(d); 160A-515.1(c).

120. The unit must publish notice of the public hearing in a newspaper of general circulation and mail notice to all affected property owners in the proposed district.

121. G.S. 160A-515.1(e).

122. G.S. 159-105(a); *see also* G.S. 159-105(b) (establishing the criteria used by the LGC to approve proposed project development financing bonds).

will have a materially adverse effect on the environment and whether the company that will operate the facility has previously complied with federal and state environmental laws and regulations.[123]

The plan also must be submitted to the secretary of commerce. The secretary must certify that the average weekly manufacturing wage required by the plan to be paid to the employees of the initial users of the proposed new manufacturing facility is either above the average weekly manufacturing wage in the county in which the district is located or not less than 10 percent above the average weekly manufacturing wage paid in the state.[124] The secretary may exempt a facility if certain criteria are met.

Bond Anticipation Notes

A unit of local government may, in certain cases, issue "bond anticipation notes." As the name suggests, bond anticipation notes are promissory notes a unit issues in anticipation of a future bond issuance.[125] They are secured primarily by the proceeds of future bonds issued[126] and typically mature in less than two years.

A unit might issue bond anticipation notes if it has authorized a bond issue but does not wish to borrow the full sum at one time. It also might issue bond anticipation notes if it intends to use note proceeds for construction financing. A unit must obtain short-term construction financing when it intends to sell an issue of future bonds to the U.S. Department of Agriculture's Rural Development unit (USDA-RD). USDA-RD offers long-term (up to forty-year) financing for the construction or repair of certain types of public infrastructure in rural jurisdictions. To be eligible for such long-term financing, a unit typically must (1) obtain short-term construction financing from a lender other than USDA-RD (for example, a private financial institution) and (2) substantially complete the project to be financed. A unit issues a bond anticipation note to obtain short-term financing, and when the unit issues a long-term bond to USDA-RD, it uses the proceeds of that financing to pay off the initial short-term loan evidenced by the bond anticipation note.

A unit of local government must obtain approval from the LGC to issue bond anticipation notes,[127] and the LGC will sell any notes approved on behalf of the unit.[128]

Installment Financing

The final borrowing method, installment financing, is the borrowing structure most often used by North Carolina local governments. It differs from the other mechanisms in that it often does not involve the issuance of bonds. Both counties and municipalities (along with several other local entities) may borrow money by entering into installment financing agreements.[129] An installment

---

123. G.S. 158-7.3(g); 160A-515.1(f).

124. G.S. 158-7.3; 160A-515.1.

125. Bond anticipation notes may be issued as general obligation bond anticipation notes, revenue bond anticipation notes, special obligation anticipation notes, or project development bond anticipation notes. To issue general obligation bond anticipation notes, a unit must follow the statutory procedures for authorization of a general obligation bond issuance in the Local Government Bond Act. *See* "General Obligation Bonds," above.

126. *See* G.S. 159-162 (security for general obligation bond anticipation notes); 159-163 (security for revenue bond anticipation notes); 159-163.1 (security for project development-financing debt instrument anticipation notes); 159-146(c), (e) (security for special obligation notes).

127. *See* G.S. 159-161.

128. *See* G.S. 159-165.

129. G.S. 160A-20. G.S. 160A-20(h) lists the local entities (including municipalities, counties, water and sewer authorities, sanitary districts, local airport authorities, area mental health authorities, and regional transportation authorities—collectively referred to as "unit of local government") authorized to enter into installment-purchase contracts. In addition, G.S. 115C-528 provides (more limited) authority for local school administrative units to enter into installment purchase agreements for certain purposes.

finance agreement is a loan transaction in which a local government borrows money to finance or refinance the purchase of a capital asset (real or personal property) or the construction or repair of fixtures or improvements on real property owned by the local unit.[130]

Security

The unit of local government must grant a security interest in the asset that is being purchased or in the real property or fixtures and improvements to that real property (or both) being financed with the borrowed funds. A unit of local government may not grant a security interest in real or personal property that is not part of the financing transaction. To illustrate, take a routine construction project of a maintenance garage that will be located on property owned by a county or municipality. The government may borrow money to finance the cost of constructing the maintenance garage and may pledge as security the garage structure itself or the real property on which the garage is built (or both). The unit may not pledge as security any other property it owns, however, such as city hall or the county library.

The authority for this type of borrowing transaction, as well as its procedural requirements and limitations, is found in a single statute—G.S. 160A-20. Thus, installment financings often are referred to as "160A-20s."

A unit of local government can grant a security interest in only real or personal property it owns. Therefore, an installment financing agreement is valid under North Carolina law only if a unit takes legal title to the financed property when the financing term begins. The vendor, bank, or other financier may not take title to the asset at the outset of a transaction and retain title until the loan securing the purchase price is repaid.[131] For example, if a municipality purchases a vehicle and obtains vendor financing with a five-year repayment term, the municipality must acquire a certificate of title to the vehicle when it takes possession of the vehicle—not at the conclusion of the financing term.

North Carolina law does not identify particular sources of revenue a local government must use to repay debt incurred in an installment financing arrangement. Local governments may use any unrestricted funds to repay the debt.

Forms of Installment Financing

Installment financings can take several general forms, each of which is described below.

Vendor Financing

The simplest form of installment financing is commonly referred to as vendor financing. The parties enter a contract under which the vendor conveys the equipment or property to the local government and the local government promises to pay for the equipment or property through a series of installment payments. The contract gives the vendor a lien on the equipment or a deed of trust on

---

130. Specifically, G.S. 160A-20 allows a unit of local government to "purchase, or finance or refinance the purchase of, real or personal property by installment contracts that create in some or all of the property purchased a security interest to secure payment of the purchase price." The statute also allows an authorized entity to "finance or refinance the construction or repair of fixtures or improvements on real property by contracts that create in some or all of the fixtures or improvements, or in all or some portion of the property on which the fixtures or improvements are located, or in both, a security interest to secure repayment of moneys advanced or made available for the construction or repair."

131. This type of transaction is known as a lease-purchase arrangement, a borrowing structure in which North Carolina's local governments are not generally authorized to engage. Even a lease-purchase arrangement that provides a local government an option to purchase an asset at the conclusion of the lease term will not comply with G.S. 160A-20.

the property to secure the government's payment obligations under the contract. If the government defaults under the contract, the vendor may repossess the equipment or foreclose on the property.

Lending Institution Contracts

A more common form of an installment finance contract transaction involves two different contracts—one between the unit of government and the vendor or contractor and one between the unit of local government and a lending institution. The government enters a purchase contract with a vendor or contractor, who is paid in full upon delivery of the asset or completion of the construction project. The government enters into a separate installment finance contract with a financial institution; under this contract, the institution provides the moneys to pay the vendor or the contractor and the local government agrees to repay those moneys in installments with interest. The financial institution takes a security interest in the asset being purchased or constructed (or the land on which it is constructed) to secure the government's payment obligations under the installment finance contract.

Bond Market Financing

Most installment finance contracts are arranged with a single bank or financial institution. If the project is particularly large or if the local government has borrowed a significant amount of money during the current calendar year, however, a single institution usually is unwilling to make the loan and retain it within its loan portfolio. This is because of certain federal tax advantages for a financial institution that loans money to a government that borrows less than $10 million within a calendar year. Governments that fall below this borrowing threshold (and meet certain other criteria) are classified as bank qualified. If a local government is not bank qualified, it typically turns to the bond market—the installment financing is publicly sold. That is, rather than the government borrowing the money from a single bank or vendor, the loan is sold to individual investors through the issuance of limited obligation bonds (LOBs) or certificates of participation (COPs):

— Limited Obligation Bonds

Limited obligation bonds are issued by a local government to either an individual purchaser (for example, a bank) or to one or more underwriters (which resell the bonds to other investors) to (1) purchase real or personal property from a third-party seller or (2) contract to construct or repair fixtures on or make improvements to real property. In an LOB financing, a borrowing government directly enters into a "trust agreement" or "indenture" with a third-party trustee, under which the local government grants a security interest in the financed asset (typically land and any improvements constructed thereon) to the trustee for the benefit of the bondholders. If the borrowing government fails to make scheduled installment financing payments to the trustee, the trustee may foreclose on the property and use the proceeds of any foreclosure to pay bondholders. In this structure, each bond is considered a separate "installment purchase contract."

— Certificates of Participation

A COP is a financing in which a nonprofit corporation makes a "loan" to a local government to finance the unit's (1) purchase of real or personal property from a third-party seller or (2) contract to construct or repair fixtures on or make improvements to real property. In a contract between a unit of local government and a nonprofit corporation, the local government agrees to repay the loan to the corporation and grant the corporation a mortgage on any real property improved, if any. In turn, the nonprofit corporation issues "certificates of participation" in the loan (that is, rights to receive the revenues from the unit of local government) on the public market and assigns its granted rights to a trustee for the benefit of the purchasers of the certificates.

Synthetic Project Development Financings

Because of the risk to investors, project development financing often is the most expensive way for a unit to borrow money to fund public infrastructure. What makes the financing attractive to units, and particularly to governing boards, however, is that a unit does not pledge or obligate any of its current revenues. Instead, it pledges future revenue streams generated by new development.

A synthetic project development financing occurs when a local government determines that the projected increment revenue from proposed new private development in the unit justifies issuing debt to fund a public infrastructure project that will benefit or incentivize the new private development. The unit does not issue project development bonds, however. It uses another form of financing, usually an installment financing—whereby the unit pledges the financed asset as security for the loan—to fund the public improvement. If the private development occurs according to projections, the unit is able to use the new revenue generated to repay the loan. Because local governments in North Carolina can get relatively good bond ratings on installment financing debt, synthetic project development financing is often a cheaper, and thus more attractive, alternative to a formal project development financing.

Requirements and Limitations

A local government must satisfy some constitutional and statutory requirements before entering an installment financing contract. These requirements apply no matter what form the installment finance transaction takes (simple installment financing, COPs, or LOBs).

Non-Appropriation Clause

An installment purchase contract must include a non-appropriation clause. The clause makes all loan repayment obligations subject to yearly appropriation decisions by the unit's governing board. The non-appropriation clause is necessary to avoid an inadvertent pledge of the unit's taxing power. Such a pledge, even a limited pledge, likely would violate the North Carolina Constitution's prohibition against contracting debts secured by a pledge of a unit's faith and credit without obtaining voter approval.[132] G.S. 160A-20 further provides that "no deficiency judgment may be rendered against any unit of local government in any action for breach" of an installment finance contract.

No Nonsubstitution Clause

An installment finance contract may not include a nonsubstitution clause. Specifically, the contract may not "restrict the right of the local government to continue to provide a service or activity" or "replace or provide a substitute for any fixture, improvement, project or property financed, refinanced, or purchased pursuant to the contract."[133]

Public Hearing

A unit of government entering an installment purchase contract that "involves real property" must hold a public hearing on the contract.[134] At a minimum, contracts to finance the acquisition of land or construction of improvements on land would "involve real property." A unit must publish notice

---

132. *See generally* Wayne Cnty. Citizens Ass'n v. Wayne Cnty. Bd. of Comm'rs, 328 N.C. 24 (1991).
133. G.S. 160A-20(d).
134. G.S. 160A-20(g).

of any required public hearing in a newspaper of general circulation in the jurisdiction at least ten days prior to the date on which the hearing will be held.[135]

A unit of local government may, but is not required to, hold a public hearing on an installment financing contract that concerns only the acquisition of personal property.

LGC Approval

Some, but not all, installment financings are subject to LGC approval.[136] And different thresholds apply for local units on the LGC's Unit Assistance List.[137]

If LGC approval is required, the commission considers the same factors as for a GO debt issuance. The commission must approve the financing if it determines the following:

1. The proposed contract is necessary or expedient.
2. The contract, under the circumstances, is preferable to a bond issue for the same purpose.
3. The sums to fall due under the contract are adequate and not excessive for its proposed purpose.
4. The unit's debt management procedures and policies are good or reasonable assurances have been given that its debt will henceforth be managed in strict compliance with the law.
5. The increase in taxes, if any, necessary to meet the sums to fall due under the contract will not be excessive.
6. The unit is not in default in any of its debt service obligations.[138]

The commission need not find all these facts and conclusions, however, if it determines that "(i) the proposed project is necessary and expedient, (ii) the proposed undertaking cannot be economically financed by a bond issue and (iii) the contract will not require an excessive increase in taxes."[139]

If the commission denies the application, it must notify the unit. At the unit's request, the commission must hold a public hearing on the application. The commission may revisit its decision based on testimony or other information presented at the hearing.[140]

The Taxability of Interest Paid to Holders of Local Government Debt

Units of local government in North Carolina can enjoy a substantial advantage in the capital markets when they borrow money. They may, with proper structuring, issue debt on a "tax-exempt" basis, meaning that any interest paid on such debt is not subject to federal income tax.[141] Because

---

135. *Id.*

136. G.S. 160A-20(e); 159-148.

137. For a guide to when LGC approval is required see Kara Millonzi, "Local Government Commission (LGC) Approval of Bonds, Installment Financings, Leases, and Other Contracts Involving Capital Assets (Including Recent Changes Related to Local Governments on the Unit Assistance List)," *Coates' Canons: NC Local Government Law* blog (October 28, 2022), canons.sog.unc.edu/2022/10/local-government-commission-lgc-approval-of-debt-leases-and-other-contracts-involving-capital-assets-including-recent-changes-related-to-local-governments-on-the-unit-assistance-list/, and Kara Millonzi, "Local Government Commission Approval of Certain Public Enterprise Agreements," *Coates' Canons: NC Local Government Law* blog (March 22, 2024), canons.sog.unc.edu/2024/03/local-government-commission-approval-of-certain-public-enterprise-agreements/.

138. G.S. 159-151(b).

139. *Id.*

140. *Id.*

141. *See generally* 26 U.S.C. § 103(a) (noting that, with exceptions, "gross income does not include interest on any State or local bond"); 26 U.S.C. § 103(c)(1) ("The term 'State or local bond' means an obligation of a State or political subdivision thereof."). Interest paid on an obligation of a "political subdivision of [the State], or a commission, an authority, or another agency of [the] State or of a political subdivision of [the State]" is also exempt from North Carolina state income tax. *See* G.S. 105-130.5(b)(1a)a.

such interest is exempt from federal income tax, holders of this debt will accept a lower rate of interest than on comparable taxable debt.

Issuing tax-exempt debt creates administrative costs. To preserve the tax exemption, local governments must comply with complex provisions in the Internal Revenue Code (the Code) and regulations promulgated by the Internal Revenue Service.[142] Among other things, these provisions regulate the following:

1. the allocation and expenditure of the proceeds of tax-exempt debt,
2. the sources of and security for repayment of tax-exempt debt,
3. the investment of the proceeds of tax-exempt debt, and
4. the use and disposition of property financed by the proceeds of tax-exempt debt.[143]

Bond counsel can assist a local government in understanding these provisions, but ultimately the responsibility for compliance falls on local government staff.

Tax Certificates

When a local government issues tax-exempt debt, bond counsel typically prepares a "tax certificate" that the unit's ranking officials execute on the unit's behalf. This potentially lengthy document usually sets forth the following, among other things:

1. how the unit intends to expend tax-exempt bond proceeds,
2. from what sources and with what security it intends to repay and secure the tax-exempt debt,
3. how it intends to invest any proceeds of tax-exempt bonds, and
4. how it intends to operate the financed facility.

In each case, bond counsel drafts the certificate to ensure that, by strictly following its requirements, a local government can preserve the tax-exempt status of interest on its debt.

Taxable Debt

A unit of local government that otherwise has authority to issue debt under state law is not necessarily required to issue tax-exempt debt. In some cases—particularly when interest rates have fallen substantially—a local government may decide that an issuance of taxable debt, in lieu of tax-exempt debt, is worthwhile. Local governments should consult with their financial advisers, the LGC, and bond counsel when seeking to issue taxable debt.

Federal and State Loans

In addition to the borrowing options discussed above, counties and municipalities may borrow money from an agency of the federal government or from the State of North Carolina "for constructing, expanding, maintaining, and operating any project or facility, or performing any function,

142. The relevant provisions of the Internal Revenue Code generally can be found in 26 U.S.C. §§ 103 and 141–150.

143. For a high-level overview of these provisions, see Internal Revenue Service, *Tax Exempt & Government Entities*, "Publication 4079: Tax-Exempt Governmental Bonds" (Sept. 2019), www.irs.gov/pub/irs-pdf/p4079.pdf. For a high-level overview of restrictions on investments of bond proceeds, see Internal Revenue Service, "Publication 5271, Complying with Arbitrage Requirements: A Guide for Issuers of Tax-Exempt Bonds" (Sept. 2019), www.irs.gov/pub/irs-pdf/p5271.pdf.

which such city or county may be authorized by general law or local act to provide or perform."[144] On the state level, counties and municipalities commonly obtain loans from NCDEQ to finance the construction or repair of water or sewer infrastructure. On the federal level, counties and municipalities typically obtain loans from the U.S. Department of Agriculture to finance the construction or repair of a variety of public infrastructure in rural areas.

Grant Funding

North Carolina law authorizes counties and municipalities to accept grants from the federal or state government to construct, expand, maintain, and operate any project or program state law permits the unit to provide or perform.[145] Local governments commonly use these grants to finance—in whole or in part—many types of capital projects, including the acquisition, construction, and equipping of affordable housing, water and sewer facilities, parks or recreation facilities, and other types of public infrastructure. The availability of federal and state grant funding can fluctuate according to the respective willingness of Congress or the General Assembly to appropriate grant funds.

Federal Grants

Federal agencies may award a federal grant to a non-federal entity[146] only when Congress has (1) enacted legislation authorizing an agency to make a grant for a specific purpose and (2) appropriated money to the agency to provide the grant.[147] Once an agency has authority to fund a federal grant, it will announce the availability of the funding opportunity.

In most cases, an agency that awards a federal grant must release a public notice—termed a "notice of funding opportunity" or NOFO. A NOFO includes the following:

- detailed information about the award,
- the types of entities eligible to apply,
- the evaluation criteria for selection,
- required components of an application, and
- how to apply.[148]

NOFOs are accessible at grants.gov, a website maintained by the federal Office of Management and Budget. Local governments can use this website to identify and apply for federal funding opportunities.

---

144. G.S. 160A-17.1(a).

145. *See* G.S. 160A-17.1(a).

146. A non-federal entity includes, among other entities, a local government. *See* 2 C.F.R. § 200.1 (defining *non-federal entity*).

147. *See generally* Robert M. Lloyd, *A Practical Guide to Federal Grants Management—From Solicitation Through Audit*, 3rd ed. (Arlington, Va.: Columbia Books, Inc., 2020), 20 (describing grant-making authority of federal agencies). For a more-detailed treatment of the appropriations process for federal grants, see U.S. Government Accountability Office (GAO), Office of the General Counsel, "Federal Assistance: Grants and Cooperative Agreements," chap. 10 in *Principles of Federal Appropriations Law* vol. 2, 3rd ed. (Washington, D.C.: GAO, 2006).

148. *See* 2 C.F.R. § 200.204 (requiring federal awarding agencies to release notices of funding opportunities for competitive discretionary grants); 2 C.F.R. § 200.1 (defining *notice of funding opportunity*).

Local Government as Recipient

A local government can receive grant funding *directly* from a federal awarding agency as a "recipient" of a federal grant.[149] If a federal agency selects a local government to receive a federal grant as a recipient, the agency typically will issue a notice of award, termed an NOA, and require the local government to execute a grant agreement. A grant agreement is a legal instrument that reflects the terms and conditions upon which a non-federal entity may use awarded funds.[150] Once a local government executes a grant agreement or accepts federal grant funds, it is contractually bound to the awarding agency to abide by the terms and conditions of the award.[151]

Local Government as Subrecipient

A local government also might receive federal grant funding *indirectly* by obtaining a "subaward" of federal funding from another non-federal entity—a "pass-through entity"—that is a recipient of federal grant funds.[152] For example, federal agencies commonly make a variety of grants to state government agencies. In turn, these state agencies commonly act as pass-through entities and subaward federal funds to local governments.[153] A local government acting as a subrecipient will use awarded funds to carry out the objectives of the federal grant program and is obligated to use the funds according to the terms and conditions of a subaward agreement and any other laws and regulations applicable to the awarded funds.[154]

Terms and Conditions

As a recipient or subrecipient of a federal grant, a local government must act as a steward of federal funds. It must administer those funds in accordance with the federal statutes that authorized the grant and other governing laws, regulations, and terms and conditions specified in the grant agreement.

Although the laws and regulations that apply to each federal grant are unique, the federal Office of Management and Budget has recently consolidated and streamlined many of the rules governing the expenditure of federal grants into a single title of the Code of Federal Regulations: 2 C.F.R. Part 200. Entitled the "Uniform Administrative Requirements, Cost Principles, and Audit Requirements" and known popularly as the "Uniform Guidance" or "UG," 2 C.F.R. Part 200 attempts to establish a uniform framework for the administration of federal financial assistance that federal agencies and non-federal entities must follow.

---

149. *See* 2 C.F.R. § 200.1 ("*Recipient* means an entity . . . that receives a Federal award directly from a federal awarding agency.").

150. *See* 31 U.S.C. § 6304.

151. In some cases, a representative of a non-federal entity need not actually sign a grant agreement. Instead, the entity becomes bound to the terms and conditions of a grant agreement by accepting a disbursal of federal funds.

152. *See* 2 C.F.R. § 200.1 ("*Subrecipient* means an entity . . . that receives a subaward from a pass-through entity to carry out part of a Federal award."). A *pass-through entity* is a "non-federal entity that provides a subaward to a subrecipient to carry out part of a Federal program." *Id.*

153. For example, the U.S. Department of Housing and Urban Development awards Community Development Block Grant (CDBG) funds to the North Carolina Department of Commerce (DOC). DOC "passes through" the CDBG grant funds to eligible subrecipients—including county or municipal governments—to enable them to undertake authorized projects with CDBG funds. For more information about the CDBG program, see Chapter 15, "Financing and Public-Private Partnerships for Community Economic Development," of *Introduction to Local Government Finance*, edited by Connor H. Crews (UNC School of Government, 2023).

154. For general requirements that pass-through entities must follow in making subawards, see 2 C.F.R. § 200.332.

The Uniform Guidance

The Uniform Guidance addresses, in significant detail, (1) the obligations of federal agencies prior to awarding federal financial assistance to non-federal entities and (2) how non-federal entities must manage the expenditure of that assistance. In general, recipients and subrecipients of federal grants must adhere to applicable provisions of the Uniform Guidance unless a granting agency has established an exception to those provisions in separate regulations or in a particular grant agreement.

Local governments that receive federal financial assistance, including federal grants, must be familiar with the compliance obligations the Uniform Guidance imposes on their expenditure of federal moneys. Among other things, the Uniform Guidance does the following:

1. dictates and restricts which direct and indirect costs a non-federal entity may charge to a federal award;[155]
2. requires that a non-federal entity adopt and implement internal controls to ensure proper management of federal funds;[156]
3. requires that a non-federal entity, when acquiring property or services with the proceeds of federal financial assistance, adopt and follow documented procurement procedures and a conflict-of-interest policy consistent with state law and procurement standards provided in the Uniform Guidance;[157]
4. mandates that a non-federal entity follow certain standards for the use, maintenance, and disposition of real property, equipment, or supplies acquired using federal financial assistance;[158]
5. requires that a non-federal entity retain records related to an award of federal financial assistance for a minimum of three years;[159] and
6. requires that a non-federal entity undergo a single audit or program-specific audit if it expends $750,000 or more in federal financial assistance during a single fiscal year.[160]

Depending on the grant, other portions of the Uniform Guidance may apply. Prior to accepting a federal award, a local government should confirm all provisions applicable to its expenditure and management of federal funds. Due to the complexity of complying with federal grant conditions in applicable federal laws and regulations, some units of local government that receive these grants have begun to develop and implement comprehensive grants-management compliance programs.

Remedies for Noncompliance

Failure to comply with the terms and conditions of a federal grant or other federal laws or regulations applicable to the expenditure of federal financial assistance can have severe consequences for a local government. Among other things, a federal awarding agency may withhold cash payments from a noncompliant local government, disallow improper costs charged to a federal award, or even partially or completely terminate an award.[161] For more egregious acts of noncompliance, a

155. *See* 2 C.F.R. §§ 200.400–.476 (outlining "cost principles" for federal awards).

156. *See* 2 C.F.R. §§ 200.302–.305. The Uniform Guidance directs non-federal entities to model their internal controls after the Standards for Internal Control in the Federal Government (Green Book) or the Internal Control-Integrated Framework issued by the Committee on Sponsoring Organizations (COSO). *See* 2 C.F.R. § 200.303.

157. *See* 2 C.F.R. §§ 200.317–.327. Non-federal entities may award contracts only to responsible contractors and must ensure that contractors satisfactorily perform under a contract's terms. *See* 2 C.F.R. §§ 200.318(b), (h).

158. *See* 2 C.F.R. §§ 200.310–.316.

159. *See* 2 C.F.R. § 200.334 (requiring maintenance of financial records and supporting documentation pertaining to federal awards for a minimum of three years from the date of the submission of the final expenditure report).

160. *See* 2 C.F.R. §§ 200.500–.521.

161. *See* 2 C.F.R. § 200.339.

federal awarding agency can initiate suspension or debarment proceedings against a unit of local government, which could prohibit the unit—either temporarily or permanently—from receiving federal grant funds.[162]

State Grants

In addition to passing through federal funds to units of local government, the North Carolina General Assembly and various state agencies also regularly make state funds available to local governments for various purposes. The State of North Carolina regularly publicizes a variety of grant opportunities and also has created a database where users can explore available grant programs.[163] When expending state grant moneys for capital projects, local governments may be required to execute a grant agreement with a state agency and follow principles and restrictions contained in the North Carolina Administrative Code similar to those in the Uniform Guidance.[164]

Conclusion

Local governments face unique challenges when funding capital projects. The projects are often very expensive. They also typically last for many years, raising equity issues as to whether current or future citizens should bear the costs. Operating and maintaining capital assets also imposes costs that a unit must anticipate and account for as ongoing operating expenses. Local officials have an array of financing tools available to help fund the initial (and some recurring maintenance) costs of a capital project. A unit must choose the appropriate mix of funding mechanisms based on its community goals, needs, and current and future financial capacity.

---

162. For more information, see 2 C.F.R. Part 180.

163. For a list of grant opportunities and a link to the database, see NC.gov, *Grant Opportunities*, www.nc.gov/your-government/all-nc-state-services/grant-opportunities.

164. *See, e.g.*, Uniform Administration of State Awards of Grants, Title 09, Subchapter 3M, Sections .0101–.0802 of the North Carolina Administrative Code.

Chapter 22

Accounting, Fiscal Control, and Cash Management

Gregory S. Allison and Rebecca Badgett

Gregory S. Allison is a School of Government faculty member who specializes in governmental accounting and financial reporting for state and local governmental entities. Rebecca L. Badgett is a School of Government faculty member who specializes in general local government finance for local government entities.

This chapter updates and revises a previous chapter authored by K. Lee Carter Jr. and A. John Vogt, whose contributions to the field and to this publication are gratefully acknowledged.

Public confidence in government depends on proper stewardship of public moneys. The North Carolina Local Government Budget and Fiscal Control Act (LGBFCA) sets forth requirements for fiscal control that provide a framework for ensuring accountability in a local government's budgetary and financial operations. This chapter focuses on these requirements, which are generally equally applicable both to county governments and city governments. They pertain to the appointment and the role of the finance officer, the accounting system, control of expenditures, cash management and investments, the annual audit, and audits of federal and state financial assistance.

A short discussion of the role of the North Carolina Local Government Commission and its relationship to North Carolina local government entities will facilitate understanding of references that occur throughout this chapter. The Local Government Commission, often referred to as simply the LGC, is briefly mentioned in Chapter 21, "Financing Capital Projects," of this volume.

The LGC, established by Chapter 159, Section 3 of the North Carolina General Statutes (hereinafter G.S.), operates as a division of the Department of State Treasurer. The commission's primary responsibility is to provide fiscal and debt-management oversight to local government entities in North Carolina. The commission's policy directives are carried out on a day-to-day basis by the staff of the LGC, who are employees of the Department of State Treasurer.

The LGC's oversight of the counties and cities in North Carolina is extensive. A local government's financial condition, cash management practices, and audit procurement procedures are all subject to LGC review and approval. As a general rule, counties and cities are not allowed to enter into most types of indebtedness without the express permission of the LGC. Counties and cities in North Carolina have benefited extensively from this level of oversight: their financial condition and reputation in the national debt markets are among the best in the nation.

The Finance Officer

G.S. 159-24 requires that each county and city government have a finance officer who is legally responsible for establishing the accounting system, controlling expenditures, managing cash and other assets, and preparing financial reports. The Local Government Budget and Fiscal Control Act (LGBFCA) does not specify who is to appoint this official, leaving the decision to each jurisdiction. In many counties and cities, the manager appoints the finance officer.[1] In counties and cities that do not have a manager, the governing body typically makes the appointment. According to G.S. 159-24, the finance officer serves at the pleasure of the appointing board or official.

In most counties, the official exercising the statutory duties of finance officer carries that title; in most cities, the official exercising these same duties carries the title of finance director. In some of the larger counties and cities, the title of chief financial officer (CFO) is used. Other titles, such as accountant or treasurer, may be used by some jurisdictions, but this is less common. There are also other derivations in some smaller counties. For example, the county manager may also be the legally designated finance officer, or the finance officer may also serve as an assistant county manager. The LGBFCA permits the duties of the budget officer and finance officer to be conferred on one person. In contrast, G.S. 105-349(e) specifies that the duties of tax collector and those of the "treasurer or chief accounting officer," which should be understood to mean the finance officer, may not be conferred on the same person except with the written permission of the secretary of the North Carolina Local Government Commission (LGC). This limitation recognizes both the hazards to internal control of one person holding the two offices and the fact that some local government entities are too small to make any other arrangement. While it is currently very rare for one person to serve as both the finance officer and the tax collector in a county, the commission has allowed a number of cities to operate under this arrangement. However, these approvals have typically been made with restrictions, such as suggesting that the city contract with the county for property tax billing and collection.

---

1. Chapter 153A, Section 82 (counties) of the North Carolina General Statutes (hereinafter G.S.); G.S. 160A-148 (cities).

The finance officer's duties are summarized in G.S. 159-25(a): establish and maintain the accounting records, disburse moneys, make financial reports, manage the receipt and deposit of moneys, manage the county's or the city's debt service obligations, supervise investments, and perform any other assigned duties.

Official Bonds

A unit's finance officer must give "a true accounting and faithful performance bond" of no less than the greater of the following:

1. $50,000 or
2. an amount equal to 10 percent of the unit's annually budgeted funds, not to exceed $1 million.[2]

The term "annually budgeted funds" has been interpreted by the staff of the Local Government Commission as

1. including expenditures in a unit's or public authority's originally adopted annual budget ordinance in the fiscal year the bond is obtained and
2. excluding expenditures for which a unit or public authority budgeted in a multiyear project ordinance.

The bond must be given on the individual, not the position. The usual public official's bond covers faithful performance as well as true accounting. The bond insures a county or a municipality for losses it suffers as a result of the actions or negligence of its finance officer; it offers no insurance or protection to the officer. The county or the municipality must pay the bond's premium. If a candidate for a finance officer position is unable to obtain a performance bond in accordance with these minimum guidelines, the individual is disqualified from an appointment as a local government finance officer.

G.S. 159-29 also requires that each "officer, employee, or agent . . . who handles or has in his custody more than one hundred dollars . . . at any time, or who handles or has access to the inventories" be bonded for faithful performance. If separate bonds for individuals are purchased, the $100 minimum should be understood to mean that the bonding requirement applies only to those persons who frequently or regularly handle that amount or more. The governing board fixes the amount of each such bond, and the county or city may (and normally does) pay the premium.

In lieu of requiring a separate bond for each employee, a county or city may purchase a "blanket" faithful-performance bond, and nearly all counties and cities do (primarily for cost reasons, as blanket bonds are more economical than the total cost of separate bonds). The blanket bond does not substitute for the separate bond required for the finance officer or other county officials (tax collector, sheriff, and register of deeds) or city officials (tax collector), who must still be bonded individually and separately.

2. G.S. 159-29. *See also* Connor Crews, "Impending Changes to Bonding Requirements for Finance Officers: Prepare Now for January 1, 2023, and Beyond," *Local Finance Bulletin* No. 62 (UNC School of Government, 2022).

The Accounting System

An accounting system exists to supply information. It provides the manager and other officials with the data needed to ascertain financial performance and to plan and budget for future activities with projected resources. The accounting system is also an essential part of internal control procedures.

The governing board depends on accounting information in making its budgetary and program decisions and in determining whether or not they have been carried out. This kind of information is also valuable to outside organizations. The investment community and bond-rating agencies rely on it as they assess a county's or a city's financial condition. Also, in counties and cities where bonds have recently been issued, the local government is often required to provide various types of annual financial information to meet continuing disclosure requirements. State regulatory agencies such as the Local Government Commission (LGC) review data generated by the accounting systems to determine whether counties and cities have complied with the legal requirements regulating accounting and finance. Federal and state grantor agencies use the information to monitor compliance with the requirements of the financial assistance programs they administer. The media and the public depend on the information to evaluate a local government's activities.

County and city accounting practices are formed in response to the general statutory requirements set forth in G.S. 159-26, which are generally accepted accounting principles (GAAP) promulgated nationally by the Governmental Accounting Standards Board (GASB). In North Carolina, the rules and regulations of the LGC as well as the local government's own needs and capabilities directly impact its accounting practices.

Statutory Requirements

G.S. 159-26 requires that each county and city maintain an accounting system, which must do the following:

1. *Show in detail its assets, liabilities, equities, revenues, and expenditures.*
2. *Record budgeted as well as actual expenditures and budgeted or estimated revenues as well as their collection.*
3. *Establish accounting funds as required by G.S. 159-26(b).* A *fund* is a separate fiscal and accounting entity having its own assets, liabilities, equity or fund balance, revenues, and expenditures. Government activities are grouped into funds to isolate information for legal and management purposes. The types of funds set forth in G.S. 159-26(b) for use by counties and cities are discussed later in this chapter.
4. *Use the modified accrual basis of accounting. Basis of accounting* refers to criteria for determining when revenues and expenditures should be recorded in the accounting system.[3] The *modified accrual basis* requires that expenditures be recorded when a liability is incurred (time of receipt) for a good or service provided to the local government. The expenditure should be recorded then, usually before the funds

3. Although the Local Government Budget and Fiscal Control Act (LGBFCA) requires the use of the modified accrual basis of accounting, it also requires that financial reporting conform to generally accepted accounting principles (GAAP). Enterprise, internal service, and certain trust funds primarily follow accrual accounting standards for reporting in accordance with GAAP, similar to the commercial sector. A county's annual financial report must both demonstrate compliance with legal requirements (i.e., the LGBFCA) and report on operations in conformity with GAAP. Therefore, enterprise funds should be reported on both the modified accrual and accrual basis in a county's financial statements, and internal service and certain trust funds should also be reported on the accrual basis in the annual financial report.

are disbursed. This type of accounting also requires that revenues be recorded when the revenues are measurable and available. *Measurable* means that they can be reasonably estimated, and *available* means that they will be received within the current fiscal year or soon enough thereafter to be able to pay liabilities of the current fiscal year. In actual practice, for various reasons some revenues are recorded when they are received in cash. For example, in North Carolina, property tax revenues are generally recorded on the cash basis because taxes receivable are not considered to be collectible soon enough after the year's end to meet the availability criterion. Permits and fees are also recorded on the cash basis because they are not considered to be measurable at the year's end. However, certain revenues collected after the fiscal year end but soon enough thereafter to pay liabilities outstanding as of June 30 would be reflected as revenue for the year ending June 30 because they would be considered measurable and available. For example, the monthly sales tax payments received by counties and cities in July, August, and September are recorded by most local governments as revenue for the year ending June 30 because the payments can be measured; they are directly related to sales that occurred during the previous fiscal year (i.e., the July distribution is related to the previous April's sales, the August distribution is related to the previous May's sales, and the September distribution is related to the previous June's sales), and they are received soon enough after June 30 to be able to pay liabilities at the fiscal year's end.

The modified accrual basis of accounting helps keep financial practices on a prudent footing: expenditures are recorded as soon as the liabilities for them are incurred, and some revenues are not recorded until they have actually been received in cash. In addition, the modified accrual basis enhances the comparability of financial reporting for counties and reduces the opportunity for manipulation of financial information.

5. *Record encumbrances represented by outstanding purchase orders and contractual obligations that are chargeable against budgeted appropriations.* An *encumbrance* is created when a contract that will require a county or a city to pay money is entered into or when a purchase order is issued.

   Although the Local Government Budget and Fiscal Control Act does not explicitly mention any exceptions, in practice, expenditures for salaries and wages, fringe benefits, and utilities are usually not encumbered. Salaries, wages, and fringe benefits are not encumbered because they are generally budgeted at the full amounts expected for all positions, and this significantly reduces the risk of over-expenditure. Utilities expenditures are normally not encumbered because the amounts are generally not known in advance.

   An encumbrance exists as long as the contractor or supplier has not delivered the goods or the services and the contract or purchase order is outstanding. While this is the case, the local government is not yet liable to pay for the goods or the services and has not yet incurred an expenditure for it. G.S. 159-26(d) requires that a county's or a city's accounting system record encumbrances as well as expenditures. This recognizes that the encumbrance is a potential liability, and once the purchase order is filled or the contract fulfilled, liability for payment is created and an expenditure is incurred. Although this requirement applies only to counties with more than 50,000 citizens or cities with more than 10,000 citizens, nearly all counties and cities record encumbrances in their accounting systems.

Generally Accepted Accounting Principles for Governments

Governmental accounting, as a branch of general accounting practice, shares basic concepts and conventions with commercial accounting. However, because of major differences in the governmental environment, a distinct set of national accounting and financial reporting principles has evolved in this field. They are promulgated by the GASB. Established in 1984, the GASB is responsible for the establishment of GAAP for county and city governments as well as state governments. The GASB succeeded the National Council on Governmental Accounting (NCGA), which had formerly established GAAP for government entities. Although the GASB at its creation accepted the existing NCGA pronouncements, it has actively set forth standards in areas of accounting and finance that the NCGA did not formally consider. Likewise, it has updated and modified much of the guidance that it initially accepted.

The LGC plays a key role in defining and interpreting accounting standards and procedures for local governments in North Carolina. It issues rules and regulations that interpret state statutes as well as national professional standards, and it provides advice about requirements and improvements in accounting and financial reporting practices. The commission's staff has focused much attention in recent years on annual financial reports, working closely with local officials and the state's public accounting profession to keep local government accounting systems up to date with the increasingly more rigorous reporting and disclosure standards being promulgated by the GASB.

Counties' and Cities' Own Needs and Capabilities

Counties' and cities' own needs and capabilities also shape their accounting and financial reporting systems. For example, a growing number of counties and cities have improved their annual financial reports to the point that they have earned the Certificate of Achievement for Excellence in Financial Reporting, awarded by the Government Finance Officers Association (GFOA) of the United States and Canada to recognize outstanding achievement in governmental financial reporting. While all North Carolina local governments issue professionally acceptable annual financial reports, those winning the Certificate of Achievement provide full disclosure above and beyond the minimum standards set by GAAP and relate current financial conditions and performance to past financial trends. Approximately five thousand local governments in the United States participate in the Certificate of Achievement program, which offers a tremendous resource to help local governments continually improve their financial reporting.

Nationwide, capital asset accounting and reporting continues to be one of the more significant challenges in state and local government accounting. In recent years, the LGC and the independent public accountants auditing local governments, as well as the aforementioned GFOA, have placed increased emphasis on capital asset records. If they are inadequate, the annual auditor's opinion may be modified, and this may adversely affect a county's or a city's bond rating. Also, a modified audit opinion may affect a county's or a city's ability to obtain approval from the LGC for debt issuance. In addition, an adequate capital asset accounting system can provide significant advantages. It places responsibility for the safekeeping of such assets with management, thereby improving internal control. It also serves as a basis for establishing maintenance and replacement schedules for equipment and for determining the level of fire and hazard insurance that should be carried on buildings and other capital assets.

It should be noted that the capitalization threshold that management establishes for financial reporting purposes should *not* be presumed to be directly correlated to adequate internal control of government property. For years, there has often been the misconception that the lower the capitalization threshold, the less likely it is that the capital asset will be lost, misplaced, or misused. However, low capitalization thresholds simply clutter the internal capital asset records with immaterial items and actually make them less useful. The external financial statements should focus on material items, and there is a significant internal cost to maintaining unusually low capitalization thresholds. For North Carolina governments, it is recommended that capital asset thresholds be no less than $1,000, and thresholds up to $5,000 are preferable. The threshold is only used to determine *where* on the external financial statements capital assets will be reported. The threshold does *not* mitigate the need for management at the departmental level to maintain adequate internal controls and records to safeguard *all* government property. Also, it should be noted that, as a general rule, capitalization thresholds for financial reporting purposes are a management responsibility and there is no required official action by governing boards to establish or modify them.

Obligation and Disbursement of Public Funds

Through the annual budget ordinance and any project ordinances, the governing board authorizes county and city managers and other officials to undertake programs and projects and spend moneys. G.S. 159-8 directs that no county or city "may expend any moneys . . . except in accordance with a budget ordinance or project ordinance." This means that any moneys expended by a unit must be accounted for in the annual budget ordinance or in a project ordinance (e.g., capital project or grant project ordinance). The proper functioning of the budgeting process depends on adherence to the terms of these two types of ordinances. For example, budget and project ordinances are required by law to be balanced.

The principal legal mechanisms for ensuring a local government's spending remains in compliance with budget and project ordinances are the *preaudit* and *disbursement* process requirements prescribed by G.S. 159-28.

Preaudit Requirement

G.S. 159-28(a), (a1), and (a2), collectively referred to as the preaudit requirement, state the following:

> (a) Incurring Obligations.—No obligation may be incurred in a program, function, or activity accounted for in a fund included in the budget ordinance unless the budget ordinance includes an appropriation authorizing the obligation and an unencumbered balance remains in the appropriation sufficient to pay in the current fiscal year the sums obligated by the transaction for the current fiscal year. No obligation may be incurred for a capital project or a grant project authorized by a project ordinance unless that project ordinance includes an appropriation authorizing the obligation and an unencumbered balance remains in the appropriation sufficient to pay the sums obligated by the transaction. Nothing in this section shall require a contract to be reduced to writing.
>
> (a1) Preaudit Requirement.—If an obligation is reduced to a written contract or written agreement requiring the payment of money, or is evidenced by a written purchase order for supplies and materials, the written contract, agreement, or purchase order shall include on its face a certificate stating that the instrument has been preaudited to assure compliance with subsection (a) of this section. The certificate, which shall be

signed by the finance officer, or any deputy finance officer approved for this purpose by the governing board, shall take substantially the following form:

"This instrument has been preaudited in the manner required by the Local Government Budget and Fiscal Control Act.

____

(Signature of finance officer [or duly authorized deputy finance officer])"

(a2) Failure to Preaudit.—An obligation incurred in violation of subsection (a) or (a1) of this section is invalid and may not be enforced. The finance officer shall establish procedures to assure compliance with this section, in accordance with any rules adopted by the Local Government Commission.

Accordingly, G.S. 159-28(a) clarifies that no obligation may be incurred in an activity accounted for in a fund included in the budget ordinance or for a project authorized by a project ordinance unless certain requirements are met. First, the obligation must be authorized; that is, one of the ordinances must contain an appropriation to cover it.[4] Second, the appropriation must not be exhausted; sufficient unspent and unencumbered funds must remain in the appropriation to meet the obligation when it comes due.[5] Finally, G.S. 159-28(a1) requires that, when a contract, purchase order, or agreement to pay moneys is reduced to writing, a preaudit certificate signed by the finance officer (or duly appointed deputy finance officer) must be attached to the face of the written instrument. (The four exceptions to the preaudit certificate requirement are discussed below.)

Preaudit Triggers

A preaudit is necessary whenever a local unit incurs an obligation accounted for in the budget or a project ordinance. An obligation is incurred when a unit commits itself to pay money to another entity—there is no minimum threshold amount to trigger the requirement. If a unit enters into a contract, purchase order, or other agreement that commits the unit to an expenditure of any amount of moneys, an obligation is incurred. The preaudit process must be performed before an obligation is incurred—that is, before the goods are ordered or before the contract is executed. This is because the preaudit process is a statutory internal control mechanism to help ensure budgetary compliance—its purpose is to reduce the chances of a budget violation.

Annual Budget Ordinance Appropriations

If the appropriation authorizing the obligation is accounted for in the annual budget ordinance, and the full amount of the obligation will come due in the current fiscal year, the full amount of the obligation is the sum that will be preaudited. When entering a multiyear contract, the finance officer or deputy finance officer will preaudit only the amount expected to come due in the current fiscal year. The unit is not required to re-preaudit the contract for expenditures made pursuant to the contract in future fiscal years. However, G.S. 159-13 generally requires a governing board to appropriate sufficient moneys each year to cover the amounts due that year under continuing contracts.

---

4. Appropriations are figures that *actually appear* in the annual budget or a project ordinance. For example, if $1 million is appropriated to the parks and recreation department in the budget ordinance, and the ordinance contains no further breakdown of that amount, then $1 million is the maximum the recreation department may spend in that fiscal year, absent a budget amendment.

5. An encumbrance is created when a county or a city enters into a contract that will require it to pay moneys, or when it issues a purchase order. This encumbered portion of an appropriation is unavailable for a proposed expenditure as if the funds had already been expended; once the contract is completed or the purchase order is filled, the encumbrance is replaced by an expenditure.

Occasionally a local government unit will execute a contract or agreement at the end of a fiscal year but will not make payments for that contract or agreement until the next fiscal year. The law is unclear about whether a preaudit is required in these and similar circumstances, although a few appellate court cases suggest that it is not.[6] One option to avoid this situation is to delay executing contracts until the fiscal year in which payments under the contract will be made whenever doing so is possible.

Project Ordinance Appropriations

If an appropriation authorizing an obligation is accounted for in a capital or grant-project ordinance, the preaudit is triggered regardless of whether any amounts are expected to come due in the fiscal year in which the obligation is incurred. Thus, the preaudit will be for the full amount of the obligation. Because project and grant-project ordinances are good for the life of the project or program, the fact that some moneys may be paid in a subsequent fiscal year does not affect the amount of the obligation subject to the preaudit.

Electronic Payments

Electronic payments are payments transacted with charge cards, credit cards, deposit cards, gas cards, procurement cards, or electronic fund transfers. Any payments made by such electronic means are also subject to the preaudit requirements. An obligation is incurred for purposes of the preaudit statute in a credit card transaction when a unit uses the credit card, p-card, or fuel card to pay for goods or services. At that time the unit authorizes the issuing company to pay the vendor or contracting party and thereby commits the unit to pay money (to the issuing company) to cover the costs of the expenditure. As discussed below, local units must comply with rules adopted by the Local Government Commission (LGC) in executing electronic payments.

Compliance

G.S. 159-28(a2) directs a local government's finance officer to "establish procedures to assure compliance" with the preaudit requirements. A local government's preaudit process will differ depending on the unit's size and the various needs of unit departments.

At a minimum, before a local unit incurs an obligation subject to a preaudit, the finance officer (or a deputy finance officer approved by the unit's governing board for this purpose) must ensure the following requirements are satisfied when performing a preaudit:

1. *Verify that there is a budget or a project ordinance appropriation that authorizes the obligation.* This typically is not difficult because the budget and project ordinances are adopted at a very general level of legal control. For example, the annual budget ordinance makes appropriations only by department, function, or project.[7]
2. *Verify that sufficient funds remain in the appropriation to pay the amount expected to come due.* If the obligation is accounted for in the annual budget ordinance, the appropriation must cover only the amount expected to come due in the current

---

6. *See* M Series Rebuild LLC v. Town of Mount Pleasant, 222 N.C. App. 59 (2012) (holding that a preaudit was required when the contract and obligation to pay were both created in the same fiscal year); Davis v. City of Greensboro, 770 F.3d 278 (4th Cir. 2014) (holding that preaudit certificate was not required on law enforcement and firefighter longevity pay contracts, where no payments came due during the fiscal year in which the contracts were entered).

7. A preaudit is not generally performed on line-item appropriations in the unit's "working budget."

fiscal year.[8] However, if the obligation is accounted for in a project ordinance, the appropriation must be for the full amount due under the contract because project ordinances are good for the duration of the project.

3. *If the order, contract, or agreement is in writing, a signed preaudit certificate is affixed to the "writing."* The certificate, which may be printed or stamped, should read substantially as follows: "This instrument has been preaudited in the manner required by the Local Government Budget and Fiscal Control Act." It must be signed by the finance officer or by a deputy finance officer approved for this function by the governing board. If the order, contract, or agreement is not in writing—such as a telephone order or other verbal agreement—a preaudit certificate is not required.[9]

Exemptions from the Preaudit Certificate Requirement

In general, the attachment of a preaudit certificate to any written agreement or purchase order is essential to verify the completion of the preaudit—namely, that the budget includes an appropriation for the obligation and that unspent and unencumbered moneys remain in the appropriation to cover it. However, recognizing some practical difficulties of the preaudit certificate requirement, the legislature has exempted certain transactions from the requirement, even if the order, contract, or agreement is in writing. There are four categories of exemptions. The first two apply automatically. The third applies only if the local government takes the steps required by the LGC. The fourth requires an annual certification of a unit's accounting system. (All of these exemptions apply only to the preaudit *certificate* requirement. A unit still must verify the appropriation and verify that sufficient funds remain to cover the cost of the obligation as required by G.S. 159-28(a) before incurring an obligation.)

Exemption 1: Any obligation or document that has been approved by the LGC. This exemption from the preaudit certificate requirement applies to loan agreements, debt issuances, and other leases and financial transactions subject to LGC approval and so approved. It also likely applies to audit contracts, which must be approved by the LGC pursuant to G.S. 159-34.

Exemption 2: Payroll expenditures, including all benefits for local unit employees.[10] This exemption ensures that salary and benefit changes for current employees, even if in writing, do not need to include a preaudit certificate.

Exemption 3: Electronic payments, defined as payments made by charge card, credit card, debit card, gas card, or procurement card. Electronic payments typically are the most difficult to preaudit because the transaction often occurs off-site or using the vendor's proprietary software. A local unit, therefore, is not easily able to include a signed preaudit certificate. This exemption eliminates

---

8. If a preaudit is required for a multiyear contract for which funds are appropriated in the annual budget ordinance, the finance officer or deputy finance officer will be attesting only that there is a budget appropriation for the amount expected to come due in the current fiscal year. The unit is not required to preaudit the contract in future fiscal years. However, G.S. 159-13 generally requires a governing board to appropriate sufficient moneys each year to cover the amounts due that year under continuing contracts.

9. Other provisions of law may require a particular contract or agreement to be in writing. For example, all contracts entered into by a municipality must be in writing, though the governing board of the municipality may ratify a contract that violates this provision. G.S. 160A-16. All contracts involving the sale of "goods" for $500 or more must be in writing. G.S. 25-2-201. And contracts for purchases and construction or repair subject to formal bidding requirements must be in writing. G.S. 143-129(c).

10. G.S. 159-28(f)(2).

the problem. It only applies, however, if the local unit follows the rules adopted by the LGC for electronic transactions. These rules require the following:

1. The governing board must adopt a resolution authorizing the unit to engage in electronic transactions.
2. The unit must implement an encumbrance system to facilitate tracking expenditures against budget appropriations.
3. The governing board or finance officer must adopt a written policy outlining the unit's procedures for electronic transactions.
4. The local unit must train personnel about the policies and procedures to be followed when engaging in electronic transactions.
5. Staff must prepare and present to the governing board a budget-to-actual statement by fund at least quarterly.[11]

Exemption 4: Automated Preaudit Accounting System. A local government may perform its preaudit process using an automated accounting system.[12] The system, however, must meet all of the functionality requirements of G.S. 159-28(a3), including the following:

1. Embed functionality that determines there is an appropriation to the department, function code, or project in which the transaction appropriately falls.
2. Ensure that unencumbered funds remain in the appropriation to pay out any amounts expected to come due during the budgeting period.
3. Provide real-time visibility to budget compliance, alert threshold notifications, and rules-based compliance measures and enforcement.

If a local unit's accounting system performs these functions, the unit is not required to include a signed preaudit certificate on any contract, agreement, purchase order, or other writing evidencing a transaction subject to the preaudit requirement. Within thirty days of the start of each fiscal year, a local unit's finance officer must certify to the LGC that the unit's accounting system meets all the requirements of G.S. 159-28(a3).[13]

Failure to Comply

Failure to perform the preaudit renders any executed contract, agreement, or purchase order related to a local government transaction invalid and unenforceable—in other words, the contract or agreement is void.[14] The statute also provides that if "an officer or employee [of a local unit] incurs an obligation or pays out or causes to be paid out any funds in violation of [the preaudit statute], he [or she] and the sureties on his [or her] official bond are liable for any sums so committed or disbursed."[15] Thus, if any officer or employee orders goods or enters into a contract or agreement subject to a preaudit before

---

11. *See* Title 20, Chapter 03, Section .0409, of the North Carolina Administrative Code (hereinafter N.C.A.C.). For a detailed explanation of how to comply with the Local Government Commission rules relating to the preaudit certificate exemption for electronic transactions, see also Kara Millonzi, "Preauditing Electronic Transactions Just Got (A Little) Easier," *Coates' Canons: NC Local Government Law* blog (March 23, 2018), canons.sog.unc.edu/2018/03/preauditing-electronic-transactions-just-got-little-easier/.

12. G.S. 159-28(a3).

13. G.S. 159-28(a4). The certification form is available from the N.C. Department of State Treasurer.

14. G.S. 159-28(a2).

15. G.S. 159-28(e). The governing board must "determine, by resolution, if payment from the official bond shall be sought and if the governing board will seek a judgment from the finance officer or duly appointed deputy finance officer for any deficiencies in the amount." *Id.*

the preaudit process is completed, he or she could be held personally liable by the unit's governing board for the amounts obligated, even if the unit never actually incurs the expense.

If the finance officer or deputy finance officer gives a false preaudit certificate, he or she, and the sureties on his or her official bond, may be held personally liable for any sums illegally committed or disbursed.[16] It is also a Class 3 misdemeanor to give a false preaudit certificate, and, if found guilty, the finance officer or deputy finance officer must forfeit their office. They may also incur a fine of up to $1,000 and will be personally liable in a civil action for all damages suffered by the unit or the holders of any of its obligations.[17]

Disbursements

Compliance with the Disbursement Requirement

When an invoice, bill, or other claim against a local government or public authority is presented, the finance officer must either approve or disapprove the disbursement related to the underlying claim for payment. If the amount claimed to be due and owing is accounted for in a fund included in the budget ordinance or a project ordinance, the finance officer, or duly authorized deputy finance officer, must take the following steps before authorizing any payment:

1. *Determine the amount payable.* If the amount claimed is not due and owing because, for example, the goods did not arrive or the services were not performed, then the disbursement may not be authorized.
2. *Verify the appropriation and verify that funds remain to pay the amount due.* The finance officer must verify that the budget ordinance or a project ordinance (still) includes an appropriation authorizing the expenditure and either (1) an encumbrance has been previously created for the transaction or (2) an unencumbered balance remains in the appropriation to pay the amount due. If there is no budget appropriation for the expenditure, or more commonly, if sufficient unencumbered funds do not remain in the appropriation, the finance officer or deputy finance officer may not authorize the disbursement unless or until the board amends the budget (or project/grant) ordinance to make (or increase) the appropriation. (Part of this process requires the officer to verify the preaudit process was properly performed when the obligation was incurred.)[18]
3. *Include a disbursement certificate on the face of the check or draft.* The certificate, which may be printed or stamped on the check, must substantially adhere to the following form: "This disbursement has been approved as required by the Local Government Budget and Fiscal Control Act." The certificate must be signed by the finance officer or a deputy finance officer approved for this function by the governing board.[19] Having a deputy finance officer authorized to sign checks is especially important. The absence of the finance officer could delay their issuance if that officer were the only one authorized to sign certificates.[20] (Certain types of electronic

---

16. G.S. 159-181.

17. *Id.*

18. G.S. 159-181 makes it a Class 3 misdemeanor for any officer or employee to approve a claim or bill knowing it is invalid.

19. G.S. 159-28(d).

20. While not a common practice in cities, in some counties the board of commissioners designates a deputy finance officer in the county finance or another department to regularly sign checks on a limited basis to ensure that specific payments, such as monthly benefit payments to public assistance recipients, are proper and correct. Such delegation of the payment function should occur only with the approval of the county finance officer and only if adequate internal controls are built into the payment procedures used.

payment transactions are exempt from the disbursement certificate requirement if the local government complies with the LGC rules outlined below.)

Exemptions from Disbursement Certificate Requirement

There are three types of transactions exempt from the requirement to affix a disbursement certificate to each draft on the official depository. The first two apply automatically, while the third applies only if the local government follows the rules adopted by the LGC.

1. *Any disbursement related to an obligation approved by the LGC.* This exemption applies to any payments related to loan agreements, debt issuances, and other leases and financial transactions subject to LGC approval and that have been so approved. It also likely applies to audit contract payments.
2. *Any disbursement related to payroll and employee benefits.* This includes payroll expenditures, including all benefits for employees of the local government. New employment contracts must, however, be preaudited.
3. *Any disbursement made by electronic funds transfer, if the unit follows rules adopted by the LGC.* To qualify for an exemption from the disbursement certificate requirement in G.S. 159-28(d1), the local government must (1) adopt a resolution authorizing the unit to engage in electronic payments as defined by G.S. 159-28 and (2) adopt a written policy outlining procedures for disbursing public funds by electronic transaction. The written policy must include internal controls that ensure compliance with the disbursement process.[21]

Governing Board Override

The Local Government Budget and Fiscal Control Act authorizes a governing board to approve by formal resolution a bill, an invoice, or another claim that has been disapproved by the finance officer.[22] The governing board may do this only for a valid claim for which an encumbrance exists or an unencumbered appropriation remains in the budget or a project ordinance. The board must adopt a resolution stating the board's reasons for approving the payment, which must be entered in the board's meeting minutes with the names of members voting in the affirmative. The board's chair, or a designated member, must sign the disbursement certificate. If the board approves payment and it results in a violation of law, each board member voting to allow payment is jointly and severally liable for the full amount of the check or draft. These procedures are rarely, if ever, used.

Form of Payment

G.S. 159-28(d) directs that all bills, invoices, salaries, or other claims be paid by check or draft on an official depository, bank wire transfer from an official depository, electronic payment or electronic funds transfer, or cash. Wire transfers are used, for example, to transmit the money periodically required for debt service on bonds or other debt to a paying agent, who in turn makes the payments to individual bondholders. Local governments use automated clearing house (ACH) transactions to make retirement system contributions to the state, payroll payments, and certain other payments. The state has extended the use of the ACH system to most transfers of moneys between the state and local governments related to grant programs and state-shared revenues. A local unit may pay

---

21. 20 N.C.A.C. 03, § .0410.
22. G.S. 159-28.

for claims with cash only if its governing board has adopted an ordinance authorizing cash as a payment option and specifying when it is allowed.[23]

G.S. 159-25(b) requires each check or draft "be signed by the finance officer or a properly designated deputy finance officer and countersigned by another official . . . designated for this purpose by the governing board." The finance officer's or deputy finance officer's signature attests to completion of review and accompanies the certificate described above. The second signature may be by the chair of the board of commissioners, the mayor of the city, or some other official. (If the governing board does not expressly designate the countersigner, G.S. 159-25(b) directs that for counties it should be the chair or the county's chief executive officer (i.e., the county manager) and for cities it should be the mayor.)

The law intends that the finance officer review the documentation of the claim before signing the certificate and check, and that the second person independently review the documentation before signing and issuing the check. G.S. 159-25(b) permits the governing board to waive the two-signature requirement (thus requiring only the finance officer's signature or a properly designated deputy finance officer's signature on the check) "if the board determines that the internal control procedures of the unit or authority will be satisfactory in the absence of dual signatures." However, waiving this requirement is generally not recommended. The dual signature requirement serves as an internal control mechanism that helps ensure all payments are valid, and it reduces opportunities for fraud.

As an alternative to manual signatures, G.S. 159-28.1 permits the use of signature machines, signature stamps, or similar devices for signing checks or drafts. In practice, these are widely used in counties and cities across North Carolina. The governing board must approve the use of such signature devices through a formal resolution or ordinance, which should designate who is to have custody of the devices. For internal control purposes, this equipment must be properly secured. The finance officer or another official given custody of the facsimile signature device(s) by the governing board is personally liable under the statute for illegal, improper, or unauthorized use of the device(s).

Cash Management

Daily Deposits

Chapter 159, Section 32, of the North Carolina General Statutes (hereinafter G.S.) states that, except as otherwise provided by law, all moneys "collected or received" by an "officer or employee" of a local unit must be deposited daily "with the finance officer or in an official depository" or must be submitted to "a properly licensed and recognized cash collection service. . . ."

Application to Officers and Employees

The daily deposit requirement applies to all local government and public authority officials, even those such as sheriffs and registers of deeds who are independently elected or local board of elections personnel who are independently appointed. If an agency is part of a local unit for purposes of budget adoption and control, it and its officers and employees also are part of the local unit for purposes of the daily deposit requirement.

23. G.S. 159-28(d)(4).

Collected or Received

G.S. 159-32 applies to all moneys "collected or received" by a local unit, including taxes and fees, as well as moneys collected through fundraisers, state or federal appropriations, donations, grants, loans, and gifts. The statute applies, for example, when a sheriff's office receives a check from the federal government pursuant to a federal drug-share program. It applies when a recreation staff member of a municipality collects fees on-site for the local unit's open gym night. It applies when a social services department receives monetary donations around holiday time to support its outreach programs.[24] And it applies if a municipal library holds a used-book-sale fundraiser.[25] Funds that a local unit collects on behalf of other governments or on behalf of private entities or individuals, even though held in a fiduciary or agency capacity, are also subject to the daily deposit requirement because they are "collected or received" by the unit.

Deposited Daily

G.S. 159-32 specifies that moneys must be deposited daily with a local unit's finance officer or in an official depository. Under the latter option, the employee or official depositing the funds must immediately notify the finance officer by means of a "duplicate deposit ticket."[26] Alternatively, moneys may be submitted to a licensed and recognized cash collection service. The finance officer may audit the accounts of any officer or employee collecting or receiving moneys at any time and may prescribe the form and detail of these accounts.[27] The finance officer must audit all such decentralized collections at least once annually. This is an internal audit; the annual independent audit does not satisfy this requirement.

Practically speaking, every dollar collected during a business day cannot be deposited the day it is collected. A reasonable interpretation of this statute is that each department that collects or receives moneys must make at least one deposit each day, either in an official depository or with the unit's finance officer. In many local units, the daily deposit to an official depository is made before the cutoff time (e.g., 2:00 p.m.) set by the depository for crediting interest earnings on deposits made that day. Some funds may therefore be retained overnight (or even over a weekend) in a safe or other secure area within a department.

$500 Threshold

G.S. 159-28 allows a unit's governing board to authorize an individual who collects or receives moneys to make the mandated deposit only when moneys on hand amount to $500 or more, with the exception that a deposit must always be made on the last business day of each month.[28] Only the governing board may approve the use of this exception. The board should adopt a resolution indicating its approval of such a policy and ensure there are sufficient controls to safeguard the amounts outstanding.

---

24. Increasingly, donations to a county's social services department are being made by bank gift card instead of by cash or check. Bank gift cards are not "moneys" for purposes of the daily deposit statute but should be treated as revenue. For budget purposes, if the unit intends to use a gift card to pay for unit expenditures, its governing board must first recognize the amount of the gift card as revenue in the budget ordinance and appropriate it to a specific department, function, or project. The finance officer also should establish appropriate internal controls for accepting and securely storing bank gift cards.

25. As used in this book, the term "municipality" is synonymous with "city," "town," and "village."

26. G.S. 159-32.

27. *Id.*

28. *Id.* Only the governing board may approve the use of this exception. Managers, finance officers, other officers, or advisory boards or commissions may not authorize it.

The $500 threshold applies to all moneys collected or received by the unit as a whole—it does not exempt individual departments from the daily deposit requirement if the department collects less than $500. For example, if a city's parks and recreation department collects only $200 one day, but the city as a whole receives more than $500 that same day, the parks and recreation department must deposit the $200 with the finance officer so that the moneys can be included in the daily deposit.

Exemptions from Daily Deposit Requirement

G.S. 159-32 states that if another law provides for a different method of depositing moneys collected or received, the daily deposit requirement does not apply. For example, G.S. 1-339.70 directs a sheriff to turn over the net proceeds of an execution sale to the clerk of superior court. Similarly, G.S. 15-15 directs a law enforcement officer to disburse the net proceeds of a sale of confiscated, found, or abandoned property to "the treasurer of the county board of education of the county in which such sale is made." Cash seized by law enforcement as evidence of a crime also likely has not been "received" or "collected" by the local unit for purposes of G.S. 159-32. Seized cash should be handled by the law enforcement agency in the same manner as other evidence.

If a unit authorizes a vending company to place vending facilities on the unit's property and to retain the proceeds from those facilities, the moneys are not subject to the daily deposit requirement. Finally, deposits included in sealed bids for construction projects that have yet to be opened by a local unit likely are not moneys that have been "received" or "collected" for purposes of G.S. 159-32 until the sealed bids are open.

Official Depository

All moneys belonging to a county or a city (including those transmitted to a fiscal agent for payment of debt service) must be deposited in an official depository.[29] The governing board designates which banks or financial institutions are to serve as the official depositories. It also decides how many of them there will be. It may designate any bank, savings institution, or trust company in the state, but it may not select a credit union for this purpose. With the permission of the secretary of the Local Government Commission (LGC), the governing board may also designate a nationally chartered bank located in another state to serve as an official depository. For several reasons, the secretary of the LGC will approve the use of out-of-state depositories only in rare circumstances, such as when authorizing a governing board to designate a nationally or state-chartered out-of-state bank as a depository or fiscal agent for payment of debt service.

G.S. 14-234 generally forbids governing board members and other officials involved in the contracting process to make contracts for the local governments in which they have an interest. An exception exists, however, for transacting business with "banks or banking institutions." Therefore, a county or a city may designate as a depository a bank or a savings institution in which a governing board member, for example, is an officer, owner, or stockholder.

Depository accounts may be non-interest-bearing accounts with unlimited check writing privileges; interest-bearing accounts with unlimited check writing privileges (NOW or super-NOW accounts); interest-bearing money market accounts for which check writing privileges are restricted; or certificates of deposit (CDs) that have no check writing privileges. Generally, the use of interest-bearing accounts is recommended.

29. G.S. 159-31(a).

Both counties and cities follow a variety of methods in selecting or designating official depositories. Some name each bank and savings institution with an office located within their jurisdiction as a depository and place an account in each. Others maintain just one account, rotating it among the local financial institutions that are qualified to serve as official depositories and changing it according to a predetermined schedule (commonly every one to three years). Although these methods demonstrate a local government's support of local banks and financial institutions, they can complicate the government's cash-management procedures, hinder its investment program, and cause it to pay more than it would otherwise for banking services. For these reasons, the majority of counties and cities statewide follow a third method—selecting the bank or financial institution to serve as the depository through a request for proposals process. This method awards the business to the institution that offers the most services for the fees charged or the most services for the lowest compensating balance that the county or the city must maintain at the bank or financial institution.

Insurance and Collateralization of Deposits

G.S. 159-31(b) requires that funds on deposit in an official depository (except funds deposited with a fiscal agent for the purpose of making debt service payments to bondholders) be fully secured. This is accomplished through a combination of methods. First, government funds on deposit with a bank or savings institution or invested in a CD issued by such an institution are insured by the Federal Deposit Insurance Corporation (FDIC). If the funds that a county or a city has on deposit or invested in a CD do not exceed the maximum amount of FDIC insurance—currently $250,000 per official custodian for interest-bearing accounts and an additional $250,000 per official custodian for non-interest-bearing accounts—no further security is required. For purposes of FDIC regulation, the finance officer is always the official custodian.

Uninsured county or city funds in a bank or savings institution may be secured through a collateral security arrangement. Under one type of arrangement, the institution places securities with a market value equal to or greater than the local government's uninsured moneys on deposit or invested in CDs into an escrow account with a separate, unrelated third-party institution (usually the trust department of another bank, the Federal Reserve, or the Federal Home Loan Bank). The escrow agreement provides that if the depository bank or savings institution defaults on its obligations to the local government, the county or the city is entitled to the escrowed securities in the amount of the default less the amount of FDIC insurance coverage. Under this method, the local government must execute certain forms and take certain actions to ensure that deposits are adequately collateralized. Responsibility for assuring that the deposits are adequately secured under this method rests with the finance officer, who should closely supervise the collateral-security arrangement.

Alternatively, a bank or savings institution may choose to participate in a pool of bank- and savings institution–owned securities sponsored and regulated by the state treasurer to collateralize state and local government moneys on deposit or invested in CDs with these institutions. A third-party institution, chosen by the various pooling-method banks, holds the securities in the pool. Participating depository banks and savings institutions are responsible for maintaining adequate collateral securities in the pool, although each financial institution's collateral balances are monitored by the state treasurer. In the unlikely event of defaults or similar financial troubles, the state treasurer would be considered the beneficiary of reclaimed deposits and collateral. Certain standards of financial soundness are required by the state treasurer before a financial institution is allowed to participate in this system.

Investments

Local governments cannot afford to let significant amounts of cash lie idle in non-interest-bearing depository accounts. Investment income can amount to the equivalent of several cents or more on the property tax rate. G.S. 159-30 makes the finance officer responsible for managing investments, subject to policy directions and restrictions the governing board may impose. Because of the expanded opportunities and risks associated with the investments that North Carolina counties and cities may legally make, both national investment authorities and the LGC recommend that governing boards establish general investment policies and restrictions for their finance officers to follow.

Such board-adopted policies could, for example, limit the maximum maturities for investments of general fund moneys, require the use of informal competitive bidding for the purchase of securities, authorize the finance officer to invest in the cash and/or term portfolio of the North Carolina Capital Management Trust (discussed below), and make clear that safety and liquidity should take precedence over yield in the county's or the city's investment program. In a growing number of local governmental entities, governing boards are adopting such investment policies.

In conducting their investment programs, finance officers must forecast cash resources and needs, thus determining how much is available for investment and for how long. They must also investigate what types of investment securities are authorized by law and by their own internal investment policies and decide which ones to purchase. If an investment security is to be sold before maturity, the finance officer must make that decision.

Custody of Investment Securities

G.S. 159-30(d) states: "Securities and deposit certificates shall be in the custody of the finance officer who shall be responsible for their safekeeping." Investment securities come in two forms: *certificated* and *noncertificated*. Ownership of certificated investments is represented by an actual physical security. Some CDs and certain other securities are issued in certificated form. To obtain proper custody of certificated securities, the finance officer should hold the securities or the certificates in the county's or the city's vault or its safe deposit box at a local bank or trust company. Alternatively, certificated securities may be delivered to and held by the local government's third-party safekeeping agent, which can be the trust department of a North Carolina bank.

Many investment securities—U.S. Treasury bills, notes, and bonds; federal agency instruments; some commercial paper; and other types of securities—are not certificated. Ownership of them is evidenced by electronic book-entry records maintained by the Federal Reserve System for banks and certain other financial institutions and by the financial institutions themselves. Additionally, for certain other securities, the Depository Trust Company in New York maintains the electronic records of ownership. When a county or a city buys noncertificated securities from a bank or a securities dealer, the record of ownership is transferred electronically from the seller or the seller's bank to the local government's custodial agent. To obtain proper custody of book-entry securities, a local government should have a signed custodial agreement in place with the financial institution that serves as its custodial agent. The financial institution agent should be a member of the Federal Reserve System authorized to conduct trust business in North Carolina. Counties and cities may not use securities brokers and dealers or the *operating divisions* of banks and savings institutions as custodial agents for their investment securities. Generally, the trust department of a bank or financial institution that sells securities to a county or a city may act as the custodial agent for the securities, as long as the trust department itself did not sell the securities to the local government and provided that the institution is licensed to do trust business in North Carolina and is a member of the Federal Reserve. It is essential that a county or a city or its applicable custodial agent obtain custody of all investments. Major losses from investments suffered by local governments in other states have been due to the failure of those governments to obtain proper custody of their investments.

Authorized Investments

Among the securities and instruments in which both counties and cities invest are CDs or other forms of time deposit approved by the LGC offered by banks, savings institutions, and trust companies located in North Carolina.[30] Certificates of deposit issued by banks in the state have traditionally been the most widely used investment instrument, especially by small- and medium-sized local governments. Other investments authorized by G.S. 159-30(c) include the following:

1. *U.S. Treasury obligations (bills, notes, and bonds)—called Treasuries—and U.S. agency obligations that are fully guaranteed by the U.S. government.* Because these obligations are full-faith-and-credit obligations of the United States, they carry the least credit risk—that is, risk of default—of any investment available to either counties or cities. As a result, short-term Treasuries are usually lower yielding than alternative investment securities. Long-term Treasuries and Government National Mortgage Association securities (fully guaranteed by the U.S. government) can experience significant price variations. This is characteristic of long-term securities in general; therefore such securities should be carefully evaluated and should be considered only for investing certain limited funds such as capital reserve moneys that will not be needed for many years.
2. *Direct obligations of certain agencies established and/or sponsored by the U.S. government but whose obligations are not guaranteed by it.* Examples are the Federal Home Loan Bank Board, the Federal National Mortgage Association, and the Federal Farm Credit System. Direct debt issued by these agencies generally carries very low credit risk, although economic conditions adverse to an economic sector the agency finances (e.g., housing) can create some risk for local governments or others who invest in its securities. Some securities of these agencies are not their direct debt and are therefore not eligible investments for either North Carolina counties or cities. Moreover, even though longer-term direct debt of these agencies carries low credit risk, it can experience significant price fluctuations before maturity.
3. *Obligations of the State of North Carolina or bonds and notes of any of its local governments or public authorities, with investments in such obligations subject to restrictions of the secretary of the LGC.* Because the interest paid to investors on these obligations, bonds, and notes is typically exempt from federal and state income taxes, they generally carry lower yields than alternative investment instruments available to counties and cities. However, should the state and local governments in North Carolina begin to issue significant amounts of securities on which the interest paid is subject to federal income taxes, those securities would carry higher interest rates than tax exempt state and local government obligations. This could make the taxable obligations attractive as investment instruments to both counties and cities.
4. *Top-rated U.S. commercial paper issued by domestic U.S. corporations.* Commercial paper is issued by industrial and commercial corporations to finance inventories and other short-term needs. This paper is an unsecured corporate promissory note available in maturities of up to 270 days, although maturities from 30 to 90 days are

30. G.S. 159-30(b), (c)(5).

most common. For any local government to invest in commercial paper, the paper must be rated by at least one national rating organization and earn its top commercial paper rating. If the paper is rated by more than one such organization, it must have the highest rating given by each.

Historically, commercial paper has been relatively high yielding, and many counties and cities have invested heavily in it over the years. In economic recessions, some commercial paper issuers are downgraded. This means that their commercial paper is no longer eligible for investment by North Carolina local governments. Occasionally the downgrade occurs after the investment is purchased but before it matures. In this situation, it is most common for the entity to continue to hold the investment to maturity as the risk of loss is typically low. As long as a commercial paper issuer is top rated and the finance officer closely monitors its ratings, the risk for this type of investment is small. Officials should understand, however, that eligible commercial paper issued by banks is not a deposit and consequently is not covered by insurance and collateralization.

5. *Bankers' acceptances issued by N.C. banks or by any top-rated U.S. bank.* Bankers' acceptances are bills of exchange or time drafts drawn on and guaranteed by banks. They are usually issued to finance international trade or a firm's short-term credit needs and are usually secured by the credit of the issuing firm as well as by the general credit of the accepting bank. Most bankers' acceptances have maturity terms of 30 to 180 days. Both counties and cities may invest in bankers' acceptances issued by any North Carolina bank. Only the largest banks in the state issue them, and they are not as common as they once were. For a local government to invest in bankers' acceptances of non–North Carolina U.S. banks, the institution must have outstanding publicly held obligations that carry the highest long-term credit rating from at least one national rating organization. If the bank's credit obligations are rated by more than one national organization, it must have the highest rating given by each.
6. *Participating shares in the North Carolina Capital Management Trust (NCCMT).* The NCCMT is a money market mutual fund established specifically for investments by North Carolina local governments and public authorities. It is certified and regulated by the LGC, and unlike other state-sponsored investment pools for public entity investments, it is registered with the U.S. Securities and Exchange Commission, which imposes extensive requirements on the fund to ensure the safety of moneys invested. The NCCMT currently manages the Government Portfolio, which was started in 1982 and is intended for the investment of operating cash balances and debt proceeds. The principal value of moneys invested in a share in this portfolio remains fixed at $1. Funds invested in the NCCMT may be withdrawn on the same day of notice; however, portfolio managers do request local governments provide one day's advance notice if large withdrawals will be made. The Government Portfolio may invest only in U.S. Treasury securities and U.S. government agency securities authorized under G.S. 159-30(c). The Government Portfolio maintains "AAA" ratings from Moody's and Standard & Poor's.
7. *Repurchase agreements.* A *repurchase agreement* is a purchase by an investor of a security with the stipulation that the seller will buy it back at the original purchase price plus agreed-upon interest at the maturity date. These agreements were once popular for short-term or overnight investments by North Carolina local governments. Unfortunately, some local governments in other states suffered substantial losses by

buying repurchase agreements from unscrupulous securities dealers. As a result, strict laws and requirements for the safe use of these agreements have been enacted, both in North Carolina and across the country. G.S. 159-30(c) authorizes local governments to invest in repurchase agreements, but only under very limiting conditions.[31] These conditions have greatly reduced the cost-effectiveness of local government investments in repurchase agreements, and such agreements are no longer used to any significant degree by either counties or cities.

8. *Evidence of ownership of, or fractional undivided interests in, future principal and interest payments of stripped or zero-coupon instruments issued directly or guaranteed by the U.S. government.* These instruments were first authorized as a local government investment in 1987. They are sold at discount from face or par value and pay no interest until maturity. At maturity the investor receives the face value, with the difference between that value and the discounted purchase price of the security representing the effective interest earned. Stripped or zero-coupon securities may be a useful investment vehicle for certain limited moneys, such as those held in a Capital Reserve Fund that will not be needed until after the instrument matures. However, because most strips or zero-coupon securities have long maturities, they are subject to considerable price fluctuations before maturity and should not be used for the investment of general county funds. If investments are made in these securities and market interest rates later rise substantially (as they did in 1994), a county that has to cash in the investment before maturity may lose a significant portion of the principal invested in the securities.
9. *Certain mutual funds for moneys held by either a county or a city that are subject to the arbitrage and rebate provisions of the Internal Revenue Code.* The Local Government Budget and Fiscal Control Act authorizes unspent proceeds from bonds or other financings subject to the Internal Revenue Code's arbitrage and rebate provisions to be invested in tax-exempt and taxable mutual funds under strict procedures. Operating moneys and proceeds from financings not subject to the arbitrage and rebate provisions may not be invested in these mutual funds. Because of the complexity of the federal tax code and the wide variety of available mutual funds, a local government entity should consult with its bond counsel before placing moneys in this type of investment.
10. *Derivatives issued directly by one of the federal agencies listed in G.S. 159-30(c)(2) or guaranteed by the U.S. government.* Derivatives are not specifically mentioned in the law, but they may be eligible investments if they are otherwise authorized in G.S. 159-30(c). The term *derivatives* refers to a broad range of investment securities that can vary in market price, yield, and/or cash flow depending on the value of

31. The following restrictions apply to local government investments in repurchase agreements: (1) The underlying security acquired with a repurchase agreement must be a direct obligation of the United States or fully guaranteed by the United States. (2) The repurchase agreement must be sold by a broker or a dealer recognized as a primary dealer by a Federal Reserve Bank or be sold by a commercial bank, a trust company, or a national bank whose deposits are insured by the Federal Deposit Insurance Corporation (FDIC). (3) The security underlying the agreement must be delivered in physical or in electronic book-entry form to the county or its third-party agent. (4) The value of the underlying security must be determined daily and must be maintained, at least, at 100 percent of the repurchase price. (5) The county must have a valid and perfected first security interest in the underlying security. This can be achieved through delivery of the security to the county or its third-party safekeeping agent under a written agreement. (6) The underlying security acquired in the repurchase agreement must be free of a lien or third-party claim.

the underlying securities or assets or changes in one or more interest-rate indices. Derivatives commonly include mortgage pass-through instruments issued by federal agencies, mortgage obligations guaranteed by federal agencies (but not by the U.S. government), callable step-up notes, floaters, inverse floaters, and still other securities that go by even more interesting names. It is beyond the scope of this chapter to explain these different types of derivatives. It shall suffice to say that derivatives are generally complex instruments, and many of them are subject to rapid and major changes in value as market interest rates change. Some local governments in other states have lost vast amounts of moneys by investing in derivatives. The volume of derivatives available to investors has grown dramatically, and investment brokers and dealers often try to sell various types of derivatives to county, city, and other local government finance officers. Many derivatives are not legal investment instruments for North Carolina's local governments. Those that are direct debt (i.e., a balance sheet liability) of the federal agencies listed in G.S. 159-30(c)(2) or guaranteed by the U.S. government are usually legal investments. However, many if not most of these are inappropriate as investment vehicles for counties or cities except in very special circumstances. Even though legal, many of them are subject to extreme price and cash-flow volatility. A finance officer considering investing the county's or the city's moneys in one or more derivatives should do so only pursuant to a governing board investment policy that explicitly authorizes such an investment, only if the finance officer understands the nature of the security and the risks associated with it, and only for a short maturity.

Guidelines for Investing Public Funds

Because of great changes and technological innovation in financial markets, the challenges presented to these markets by international events, and the availability of many new types of investment instruments, the investment and general management of public moneys have become very complex. North Carolina counties and cities can avoid many of the problems that have harmed local governments in other states by adhering to the following guidelines in conducting their investment programs:

1. *The investment program should put safety and liquidity before yield.* A local government should not put its investment funds at risk of loss in the interest of obtaining higher investment earnings. The substantial, highly publicized losses of several local governmental entities across the nation in 1994 and 1995 underscore the potential problems of risky investments. The temptation to sacrifice safety for yield is particularly great when interest rates are falling and local government officials are attempting to maintain investment earnings and revenues. Any local government should always have funds available to meet payment obligations when they come due. This requires maintaining adequate liquidity in an investment portfolio and limiting most investments to securities with short-term maturities.
2. *A local government entity should invest only in securities that the finance officer understands.* Many investment vehicles, including most derivatives, are extremely complex. Before purchasing a security, a finance officer should thoroughly understand all of its components—especially how its value is likely to increase or decrease with changes in market interest rates. Whenever the finance officer is considering investing in a type of security that has not been used before, the finance officer should obtain and study the prospectus or equivalent information for the security and talk to

LGC staff and other informed, disinterested parties about the nature and risks of the security.

3. *The finance officer and other officials involved in investing a local government entity's funds should know the financial institutions, the brokers, and the dealers from which the government buys investment securities.* Investment transactions are made by phone, and investment funds and securities are often electronically transferred in seconds. Funds and securities can be lost or "misplaced" quickly in such an environment. To protect the local government, the officials conducting the investment program must be sure that they deal only with reputable and reliable institutions, brokers, and dealers. In fact, the authoritative literature that establishes generally accepted accounting principles also refers to the importance of knowing one's brokers or dealers. The finance officer should obtain a list of the North Carolina local government clients of any firm or person attempting to sell investment securities and obtain references from officials in these other governments. The finance officer should also obtain and evaluate current financial statements from any institution, broker, or dealer that sells or wishes to sell securities to the local government entity. Local governments in other states have lost invested funds because they placed moneys with firms that later went bankrupt and were unable to return the funds. A county should also enter into an investment trading agreement with any firm or person from which it buys investments. Model investment trading agreements are used by and available from several of North Carolina's large counties.
4. *The finance officer should ensure that the county or the city adequately insures or collateralizes all investments in CDs (as well as other deposits in banks) and that it has proper custody of all investment securities.* Insurance and collateralization must be in accordance with the statutory requirements.
5. *The local government's investment program should be conducted pursuant to the cash management and investment policy approved by the governing board.* Such a policy should be based on G.S. 159-30 and related statutes. It should set forth the governing board's directions and expectations about which investments will be made and how they will be made and should establish general parameters for the receipt, disbursement, and management of moneys.
6. *The finance officer should report periodically to the governing board on the status of the government's investment program.* Such a report should be made at least semiannually and preferably quarterly or monthly and should show the securities in the local government's investment portfolio, the terms or the maturities for investments, and their yields. If possible, average investment maturity and yield should be calculated and also shown in this report.
7. *The local government should understand that the use of investment managers does not relieve the finance officer of the responsibility for the safety of public funds.* A few counties and cities in North Carolina have considered the engagement of outside professional investment managers to administer their routine investment functions. Obviously, there are advantages and disadvantages to this arrangement. The most obvious disadvantage is the inability of the finance officer to have direct control of the investments even though the responsibility for them remains with the finance officer. Also, because of the legal restrictions on the investments that local governments can make, the return that an investment manager can earn once management fees have been deducted may be lower than the return the unit can earn on its own. It should

be noted that local legislation may be required for an entity to engage an outside investment manager. If it is determined that an outside investment manager would be beneficial, a written agreement should be executed outlining permissible investments, safekeeping arrangements, diversification requirements, maturity limitations, the liability to be assumed by both parties, and the fees of the contract.

The Annual Audit

Contents of the Annual Comprehensive Financial Report

G.S. 159-34 requires local governments to have their accounts audited by independent auditors after the close of each fiscal year. The auditor's opinion is set out in an annual financial report, which must include "the [county's/municipality's] financial statements prepared in accordance with generally accepted accounting principles, all disclosures in the public interest required by law, and the auditor's opinion and comments relating to [the] financial statements."

Preparation of the report's financial statements and the accompanying notes is the responsibility of local government management. Some units may not have the internal staff or expertise to prepare the annual financial statements. In those situations, the local government may contract with an independent third party to assist in their preparation. The independent auditor may provide only limited assistance in order to safeguard its independence. Professional standards for auditors have greatly enhanced the requirements for independence in recent years, limiting auditors' ability to provide significant report preparation services.

An increasing number of local governmental entities are preparing an annual comprehensive financial report (ACFR). ACFRs are not required by generally accepted accounting principles (GAAP) or by state statute, but they are very useful to external users of a government's financial statements. These reports significantly exceed the minimum external reporting requirements and provide helpful financial and nonfinancial data about a local government. An ACFR contains three primary sections: introductory, financial, and statistical. A fourth section consisting of the compliance or single-audit reports and schedules may be included but is not required. Table 22.1 summarizes the contents of the ACFR. If a local government does not prepare an ACFR, only the financial section, including financial statements and notes, will be found in that unit's annual financial report.

Introductory Section

The introductory section of an ACFR includes the transmittal letter, which is primarily an overview of the report, a brief introduction to the local government, and the official transmission of the report to external users; an organization chart; and a list of principal elected and nonelected officials. The transmittal letter should provide useful information to members of the public and the business community who may not be aware of all the local government's functions and services.

Financial Section

The financial section of an ACFR contains financial statements, which present information in various formats and levels of detail. The financial section includes the basic financial statements required by GAAP as well as more comprehensive financial presentations that typically exhibit budgetary compliance or provide more detailed analysis.

Table 22.1 Contents of an Annual Comprehensive Financial Report (ACFR)

SECTION	DESCRIPTION
Introductory Section	
Letter of transmittal	Overview of the unit's operations and financial statistics
Organizational chart	Diagram of the unit's organizational structure
List of principal officials	List of elected and appointed officials
Financial Section	
Auditor's opinion	Independent auditor's opinion on the financial statements
Management's discussion and analysis	Overview of the government-wide and fund financial statements and the changes in the financial condition of the local government unit during the reporting year
Government-wide financial statements	Statement of net assets and statement of activities for the unit's governmental activities and its business-type activities
Fund financial statements	Information on a unit's fund activity (e.g., General, Special Revenue, Enterprise), with a focus on the major funds
Notes to the financial statements	Explanations of accounting policies and statutory violations and detailed explanations of financial statement items (e.g., cash and investments, capital assets, receivables, long-term liabilities)
Combining statements	Detailed information supporting columns reported in the fund financial statements that include more than one fund
Individual fund statements	Detailed information about individual funds (e.g., prior year amounts, budgeted amounts, actual amounts)
Required supplementary information	Trend data for funding of pension trust funds
Statistical Section	
Statistical tables	Tables, usually on multiyear basis (e.g., ten years), showing information on financial trends, revenue capacity, debt capacity, demographic and economic information, and operating information of the reporting unit
Compliance Section (optional)	
Single audit reports	Reports from independent auditor on compliance and internal control
Schedule of findings and questioned costs	Listing of grant findings and questioned costs
Schedule of expenditures of federal and state awards	Listing of federal and state financial assistance programs

An independent auditor's opinion is the first item in the financial section of an ACFR. The opinion should be printed on the auditor's letterhead, further emphasizing that it is not a representation made by the unit's management. The next presentation in the financial section is the management's discussion and analysis (MD&A), a written summary and overview of the local government's financial condition and the ways in which it has changed during the year. Governmental entities must prepare an MD&A even if they are not preparing an ACFR.

The basic financial statements are presented after the MD&A. As noted earlier, these statements represent the minimum information required by GAAP for external financial statements. The basic financial statements include two main sections—the government-wide financial statements and the fund financial statements. A single comprehensive set of note disclosures supports each section.

The government-wide financial statements, which include statements of net position and activities, focus on the two broad *activities* of a local government—governmental and business-type. The fund financial statements, however, focus on the *funds* reported by and unique to local governments. The three main categories of funds—governmental, proprietary, and fiduciary—include numerous fund types. The most common fund types in North Carolina counties and municipalities include the general fund, special revenue funds, capital projects funds, enterprise funds (e.g., utility funds), and pension trust funds.

The notes to the financial statements immediately follow the government-wide and fund financial statements and are an integral part of the basic financial statements. The content and form of the notes are prescribed by GAAP. Through written advisory memoranda and illustrative financial statements interpreting GAAP, the Local Government Commission (LGC) provides guidance to local officials and their independent auditors on the content of the note disclosures. These disclosures contain significant information for interpreting the financial statements and understanding a local government entity's finances. While all disclosures are important for a good understanding of the financial statements, the note disclosures related to the definition of the reporting entity, statutory violations (if any), the collateralization of deposits and investments, capital assets, and types and terms of long-term liabilities should be of particular interest.

Statistical Section

The statistical section of an ACFR follows the financial section. It includes multiyear information on a government's financial trends, the government's revenue and debt capacity, relative demographic and economic information, and various operating information. The statistical section is an invaluable tool for bond-rating agencies and potential investors and creditors. Generally the statistical tables in this section include ten years' worth of comparative data.

The Auditor's Opinion

The auditor renders an independent opinion on the accuracy and reliability of the basic financial statements and the related note disclosures as well as their conformity with GAAP. The auditor opines not that the financial statements and disclosures are always exact but that they are reliable enough for a knowledgeable reader to make informed judgments about a local government entity's financial position and operations.

The auditor's opinion typically takes one of two forms. First, it may be *unmodified* (frequently referred to as a "clean" opinion). With an unmodified audit opinion, the auditor opines that the financial statements present fairly the unit of government's financial position at the close of the fiscal year, in conformity with GAAP. Thus, no *modification* is placed on the opinion (i.e., no exceptions are noted). All North Carolina local governments should strive for an unmodified opinion.

A *modified* opinion is the second possibility. If in some way a local government's practices materially vary from GAAP, the auditor's opinion may state that the statements fairly present the local government's financial position except for any such deviation. For example, the most common type of problem that may result in a modified auditor's opinion is inadequate records supporting the valuation of a government's capital assets. An opinion modification also may be due to a *scope limitation*, which occurs when the independent auditor cannot perform certain tests that are an essential part of the audit. For example, a local government's accounting system may fail to provide adequate documentation for some revenue and expenditure transactions, limiting the auditor's ability to test these transactions.

Auditors must present the audited financial statements and overall results of the audit to the unit's governing board in an official open meeting. This presentation should occur no later than forty-five days after the audited financial statements have been submitted to the LGC. The presentation should address, if applicable, any significant deficiencies, material weaknesses, or other findings, including financial indicators of concern as defined by the LGC. The unit's governing board must respond to the LGC, within sixty days of the auditor's presentation, regarding these findings and concerns. The response should include the board's detailed plans of corrective action and be signed by the majority of board members.

In addition, the auditor normally suggests improvements to the local government entity's internal control procedures and operations in a *management letter* that accompanies the audit report. This letter is a public document addressed to the unit's governing board and typically makes various specific suggestions for improving internal control and financial procedures. These suggestions normally arise from the audit but do not meet the threshold of the aforementioned deficiencies or weaknesses. The management letter is delivered at the same time as the audited financial statements. Often the auditor's suggestions have been informally made earlier, and some may already have been addressed at the time of the formal presentation.

In addition to providing the management letter, the independent auditor can often be an excellent source of advice on accounting system design, internal control procedures, and finance in general.

Selection of an Independent Auditor

G.S. 159-34 establishes certain requirements and procedures regarding contracting for a local government's annual audit. First, the auditor must be selected by and report to the unit's governing board. The auditor should not report to the unit's manager, budget officer, or finance officer.

Second, the governing board may choose any North Carolina certified public accountant (CPA) or any accountant certified by the LGC as qualified to audit local government accounts. In practice, no non-CPA accountants have requested certification or met the requirements for certification to perform local government audits in recent years. Governing board members should ascertain that the person or firm selected is familiar with the particular features of government accounting and auditing. Auditors should be engaged early in the fiscal year so they can become familiar with the local government's procedures and complete some of the necessary testing before the fiscal year's end. This also ensures that the auditor can plan the audit engagement and complete the audit in a timely manner.

Many counties and municipalities select the auditor through a request for proposals (RFP) process. Although not required by state statute, using an RFP is recommended by LGC staff to secure the best audit proposal. Also, selecting an independent auditor through a competitive procurement process is often required by federal regulations in many grant agreements where audit costs are chargeable to the grant. Audit agreements procured through an RFP process typically range from three- to five-year terms. The RFP should cover both the technical qualifications of a potential audit firm and the firm's cost proposals. Local officials should give more weight to an auditor's technical skills than to the firm's proposed fees. References from other local government clients should be requested from an auditor. Local government officials should contact these references to obtain information on other local governments' experiences with a potential auditor.

Contrary to popular belief, government entities are not required to rotate auditors periodically. As mentioned earlier, the LGC recommends that governments issue an RFP process at least every three to five years. This does not, however, preclude current auditors from retaining their engagements if they continue to meet an RFP's service and price requirements. Many government entities have retained the same audit firm for years. Some benefits of these established relationships are the auditor's familiarity with the government's environment and the government's avoidance of costs (particularly in staff time) incurred in changing auditors. On the other hand, some governing boards choose to contract with different auditors to provide a fresh look or to allocate the work to other qualified auditors in the region. Both approaches have merit, and the LGC has not encouraged or endorsed either method. It should again be noted that rotation is not statutorily required but is a policy left to the discretion of each entity's governing board.

Finally, a local government's contract with an auditor must be approved by the LGC. Payment may not be made for any auditor services until the commission's secretary has approved the billing, whether interim or final.

Audits of Federal and State Grants

North Carolina law authorizes counties and municipalities to accept grants from the federal or state government to construct, expand, maintain, and operate any project or program that state law permits the unit to provide or perform.[32] As discussed above, all local governments must undergo an annual financial audit pursuant to G.S. 159-34. However, when a local government expends federal or state grant funds, it may trigger additional audit requirements.[33] These additional requirements may include the following:

- *"Yellow Book" audit.* Local governments and public authorities that expend $100,000 or more in combined federal or state financial assistance must undergo a financial audit performed in accordance with the Generally Accepted Government Auditing Standards.[34]
- *State single audit.* Local governments and public authorities that expend $500,000 or more in state financial assistance must undergo a state single audit or program-specific audit performed in accordance with the State Single Audit Act.[35]
- *Federal single audit.* Local governments, as recipients or subrecipients of federal assistance (federal grants), that spend over a certain amount of federal funds during a single fiscal year must undergo a federal single audit for their programs. The Office of Management and Budget (OMB) periodically adjusts the single audit threshold. In 2024, through an update to the Uniform Guidance, the threshold amount was increased from $750,000 to $1 million, effective for federal awards made on or after October 1, 2024.

---

32. G.S. 160A-17.1(a).

33. For additional information on audit requirements, see N.C. Department of State Treasurer, State and Local Government Finance Division and the Local Government Commission, Audit Requirements for Local Governments and Public Authorities in North Carolina, www.nctreasurer.com/documents/files/slgfdaudit/summary-single-audits-north-carolina-2022-35-e-1a/download?attachment (last updated Aug. 2023).

34. Officially known as the Report on Compliance and on Internal Control Over Financial Reporting Based on an Audit of Financial Statements Performed in Accordance with Government Auditing Standards, it is referred to as a "Yellow Book" audit because the book containing the complete set of the Generally Accepted Government Auditing Standards is yellow.

35. *See* 09 N.C.A.C. 03M .0205(b)(4); *see also* N.C. Department of State Treasurer, State and Local Government Finance Division and the Local Government Commission, *supra* note 33.

Federal Single Audit

The federal single audit is performed in accordance with Subpart F of the "Uniform Administrative Requirements, Cost Principles, and Audit Requirements for Federal Awards" (commonly called the "Uniform Guidance").

When a local government is required to undergo a federal single audit, it must procure audit services from an independent auditor in accordance with the requirements of Title 2, Section 200.509, of the Code of Federal Regulations. Single audits are comprised of two main components. The first is a financial statement audit in which the auditor will determine if financial statements are fairly present in all material respects in accordance with the generally accepted accounting principles. The second is a programmatic compliance evaluation in which the auditor must determine if the nonfederal entity has complied with federal statutes, regulations, and the terms and conditions of the federal award(s) that may have a direct and material effect on the entity's major programs.[36] The auditor will also perform procedures to understand and test the effectiveness of internal controls over financial and compliance requirements.

Appendix XI to Title 2, Part 200, of the Uniform Guidance contains the Compliance Supplement, which is updated annually by the OMB and serves as a guide to auditors performing single audits.[37] It identifies the audit objectives for most federal programs and lists the compliance areas to be tested during the audit. Local governments subject to the single audit will find the Compliance Supplement useful in preparing the Schedule of Federal Expenditures (SEFA) and in determining which compliance requirements will be tested. The Compliance Supplement also includes suggested internal control procedures that can be implemented to help effectively administer federal awards. Upon completion of the single audit, the independent auditor will issue compliance and internal control reports to disclose audit findings. The most significant items for local officials in these reports are internal control weaknesses, findings, and questioned costs identified by the auditor. Internal control weaknesses are usually significant deficiencies and should be corrected when possible.

Internal Control in Financial Management

This chapter discusses many of the laws mandated by the Local Government Budget and Fiscal Control Act that relate to depositing, investing, obligating, and disbursing public funds. However, simply becoming familiar with these laws is not sufficient. Local governments must adopt a system of internal control over financial operations to help ensure compliance with these laws. The need for strong internal controls is highlighted by the fact that the Local Government Commission (LGC) has authority pursuant to G.S. 159-25(c) to investigate and require modification of a local government's internal control procedures related to the receipt, deposit, investment, transfer, and disbursement of money. If the LGC consistently finds that a local government has weak internal controls over its financial operations, it may take additional action, such as placing the unit on the Unit Assistance List until it can improve the effectiveness of its internal controls.

---

36. *See* 2 C.F.R. § 200.514.

37. Office of Management and Budget, Compliance Supplement, 2 C.F.R. Part 200, Appendix XI, www.fac.gov/assets/compliance/2023-Compliance-Supplement.pdf.

Responsibility for Internal Control

Internal controls are the procedures and techniques that, when effectively implemented, provide reasonable assurance that the organization's goals and objectives will be met. These objectives include fostering smooth business operations, reliable financial reporting, and compliance with applicable laws and local policy. In short, internal controls help units achieve their goals and prevent fraud, mistakes, and other risks of loss.

The primary responsibility for internal control rests with management and the governing body. Management includes the manager, finance officer, department heads, and others with upper-level responsibilities. The management team must design and implement controls and communicate internal control responsibilities to lower-level staff. The governing board provides oversight of the internal control system and is responsible for ensuring that the controls established by management are effective. Accordingly, the governing board should occasionally meet with management to determine whether the internal controls over financial processes are satisfactorily meeting the unit's needs.

Identification of Risks in Financial Processes

Before implementing internal controls, management should perform a risk assessment to identify and evaluate areas of risk. The risk assessment involves a review of major financial functions and processes, including cash management, preaudits, disbursements, accounts payable, accounts receivable, financial reporting, investments, and similar functions and procedures. To begin the risk assessment process, management, and particularly the finance officer, must identify objectives for each financial function or process. For example, an objective of the accounts payable process could be to ensure transactions are properly recorded in the accounting system as to account, amount, and period. Whether there are risks to this objective being achieved may depend on the answer to questions such as: Is the accounts payable clerk properly trained in the accounting software? Are duties appropriately segregated to ensure the accounts payable clerk does not also reconcile the accounting records? How might an unauthorized payment be made? By asking questions like these for each financial function or process, the local government can begin to identify the risks that, if they occur, may lead to inaccurate financial reporting or result in noncompliance with governing laws.

Implementation of Controls

Control activities form the backbone of any internal control system and include the policies, processes, and techniques utilized to promote reliable financial reporting and compliance with governing laws. Preventive controls are designed to deter the occurrence of an undesirable event, while detective controls help identify when an undesirable event has occurred. Although there are many types of control activities, some controls are generally incorporated into any internal control system. These include the following:

- *Written financial policies and procedures.* Policies and procedures should describe the process for performing all major financial functions within the unit's finance department (e.g., cash management, fund balance, procurement, preaudit, disbursements, accounts payable, accounts receivable, investments, and so forth). The policies must be updated regularly to reflect existing business processes.
- *Segregation of incompatible duties.* An incompatible duty allows a single employee to be in a position to commit an irregularity and then conceal it. Ideally, the authorization, custody, recording, and reconciliation functions related to any

transaction should be segregated. Complete segregation of duties can be a challenge for small units due to limited staffing. At a minimum, one employee should not control more than two functions, and the recording function (entering financial information into the accounting system) and the reconciliation function must always be performed by different employees. Small units may need to adopt compensating controls, such as periodic rotation of duties or having a governing board member spot-check bank reconciliations.

- *Proper authorization and approval processes.* The establishment of clear authorization and approval processes facilitates smooth workflow. Authorization involves the right to perform a specific task or responsibility. Approval is an oversight responsibility—the approver generally will be responsible for verifying the occurrence of a process or transaction.
- *Adequate documentation and record keeping.* Local governments must adopt documentation and record-retention policies and procedures to create and systematically store documentation. Units must anticipate staff turnover and ensure that important documents remain accessible regardless of staff changes.
- *Account reconciliation.* The reconciliation process is a detective control that can identify errors and potential acts of fraud as early as possible. At a minimum, each month the finance officer should reconcile the general ledger balance with the bank statement balance. The unreconciled amount should be zero. Any discrepancies must be investigated.

Once a local government has adopted a system of internal control, it must continue to monitor the effectiveness of those controls. Local governments that make the effort to develop and maintain a strong system of internal control are truly meeting their duty to be good stewards of public funds.

Additional Resources

Crews, Connor H. *Introduction to Local Government Finance.* 5th ed. Chapel Hill: UNC School of Government, 2023.

Government Finance Officers Association (GFOA). *Governmental Accounting, Auditing and Financial Reporting.* 2024 ed. Chicago: GFOA, 2024.

Governmental Accounting Standards Board (GASB). *Codification of Governmental Accounting and Financial Reporting Standards* (available at www.gasb.org).

Larson, Corinne, ed. *A Public Investor's Guide to Money Market Instruments.* Chicago: GFOA, 1998.

PART 5. Contracting and Property Transactions

Chapter 23

Public Contracts, Competitive Bidding Requirements, and Property Disposal

Crista M. Cuccaro

Crista M. Cuccaro is a faculty member at the School of Government who teaches and advises on procurement, contracting, property disposal, and ethics and conflicts of interest related to contracting.

This chapter updates and revises previous chapters authored by Norma R. Houston, Frayda S. Bluestein, David M. Lawrence, and the late Warren Jake Wicker, whose contributions to the field and to this publication are gratefully acknowledged.

Obtaining the goods and services for the operation of counties and cities is a major administrative responsibility. In a legal sense, this responsibility involves questions of proper authority, adequate authorization for the expenditure of funds, and the making of contracts in accordance with statutory requirements. Administratively, the organizational arrangements should be both efficient and legally sufficient. Contracting procedures must also be designed to avoid violation of state and federal conflict-of-interest laws, promote fairness and objectivity, and avoid the appearance of impropriety in contracting decisions.

Similar legal and administrative considerations apply when disposing of surplus property, which must be done according to statutory requirements intended to recoup taxpayer dollars expended to purchase the property.

This chapter outlines the state law requirements applicable to procurement, contracting, and property disposal. It also explains the Uniform Guidance requirements, which are applicable to federal award recipients, including local governments. The Uniform Guidance is codified in the Code of Federal Regulations (C.F.R.) and dictates federal grants administration from pre-award to audit.[1] Local governments must have and use written procurement policies and procedures that comply with state law, local policies, and the Uniform Guidance.[2] This means that local governments must follow the "most restrictive" requirements of federal, state, and local regulations.[3]

I. General Public Contract Requirements

Contracting Authority and Authorized Purposes

The North Carolina statutes that delegate to counties and cities the broad corporate powers necessary to govern and to conduct basic activities include a delegation of authority to contract.[4] Other statutes authorize counties and cities to perform particular functions and contain specific contracting powers.[5] These specific authorizations do not limit the general authority to contract. Indeed, parallel statutes for counties and cities authorize each form of local government to contract with a private entity to perform any activity in which the county or city has authority to engage.[6]

An important legal requirement for local government contracts is that the person or persons who make the contract must have authority to contract on behalf of the entity that will be bound by the contract. A local government is not bound by a contract entered into by an individual who does not have authority to contract on its behalf. North Carolina law provides that the governing board of a county or city is the body that has authority to act for the local government, and this

1. For the Uniform Administrative Requirements, Cost Principles, and Audit Requirements for Federal Awards (Uniform Guidance), see 2 C.F.R. Part 200. The Uniform Guidance is divided into six subparts, including definitions, general provisions, and audit requirements. Subpart D, entitled "Post Federal Award Requirements," includes many of the administrative requirements related to procurement, though, notably, these procurement standards differ from North Carolina law. This chapter explains all of these standards except for those covering conflicts of interest under the Uniform Guidance, which are detailed in Chapter 7, "Ethics and Conflicts of Interest."

2. *See* 2 C.F.R. § 200.318(a).

3. *See* "'Most Restrictive Rule' Procurement Requirements under the Federal Uniform Guidance for North Carolina Local Governments" (UNC School of Government, June 2018), www.sog.unc.edu/resources/microsites/local-government-purchasing-and-contracting/federal-procurement-requirements (click on "Most Restrictive Rule Summary").

4. Chapter 153A, Section 11 (counties) and Chapter 160A, Section 11 (cities) of the North Carolina General Statutes (hereinafter G.S.).

5. For example, G.S. 153A-275 and 160A-312 authorize counties and cities, respectively, to contract for the operation of public enterprises.

6. G.S. 153A-449 (counties); 160A-20.1 (cities).

includes the authority to contract.[7] The governing board may delegate its authority to others within the organization, unless a statute specifically requires action to be taken by the governing board or by another named official. For example, the state competitive bidding laws require the governing board to award construction or repair contracts that are subject to formal bidding requirements[8] and to approve a contract under certain exceptions to the bidding requirements,[9] so the board is not permitted to delegate authority to award these contracts. Similarly, most methods of surplus property disposal require governing board action.[10] For contracts that are not subject to these types of limitations, however, the county or city governing board has discretion to delegate its contracting authority under state law. As a general matter, the Uniform Guidance does not require governing board approval for any specific procurement or property disposal actions.

A delegation of authority to contract may be either explicit or implicit. An example of explicit delegation might be found in a city charter, a local act of the General Assembly, or a county or city policy adopted by a unit's governing board delegating its manager or some other official the authority to enter into contracts on behalf of the local government. A governing board might also adopt a resolution explicitly delegating authority for awarding purchase contracts, as permitted under the formal bidding statute, or in other circumstances, including the awarding of informal contracts where the statutes do not require the governing board to award contracts. In addition, a job description or personnel policy could constitute an explicit delegation of contracting authority if it has been approved by the governing board. Thus, a purchasing agent or department head may have authority to contract if doing so is part of his or her job responsibilities as defined by the board. Implicit authority might be found in cases where employees regularly make contracts with the knowledge and tacit approval of the board but without a formalized policy. Many local government contracts are made by local employees with implicit authority based on historical patterns of activity and consistent with assigned job responsibilities.

The extent to which contracting is delegated within a county or city is a function of local policy, management philosophy, and administrative organization. Responsibility for contracting should be allocated in a manner that best balances the need for efficiency and flexibility with the need to comply with legal contracting and fiscal internal control requirements. Centralization of contracting for items that require bidding or that involve commonly used items helps to ensure compliance with legal requirements and can provide better value through economies of scale and consistency in administration.

Multiyear Contracts

Counties and cities have specific authority to enter into contracts that extend beyond the current fiscal year.[11] The statutes allow a unit to enter into continuing contracts and require the unit's board to appropriate the amount due in each subsequent year for the duration of the contract.

Contracts generally continue to bind the unit despite changes in board membership or philosophy. Courts have held that this rule does not apply, however, to any contract that limits essential governmental discretion, such as a contract that promises not to annex property or a contract in

---

7. G.S. 153A-12 (counties); 160A-12 (cities).

8. G.S. 143-129(b). G.S. 143-129(a) authorizes the board to delegate the authority to award purchase contracts in the formal range.

9. G.S. 143-129(e)(6) (sole sources); 143-129(g) (previously bid contracts/"piggybacking").

10. See part IV in this chapter for a discussion of property disposal procedural requirements.

11. G.S. 153A-13 (counties); 160A-17 (cities).

which the unit promises not to raise taxes.[12] Most county and city contracts, however, involve basic commercial transactions and, assuming all other requirements for a valid contract are met, will be enforceable against the unit for the duration of the contract.

Because a multiyear contract imposes an ongoing fiscal obligation on a unit for the duration of the contract, the unit may include a non-appropriation clause that makes continuation of the contract in subsequent years contingent on the governing board's appropriation of funds for that contract. A non-appropriation clause is required for all installment financings.[13] It also may be required on any other contract, agreement, or lease that could be construed as a borrowing by the unit. Whether a non-appropriation clause should be included in a contract is a matter of policy and is subject to negotiation with, and agreement by, the contractor or vendor concerned.

Expenditures Supported by Appropriations/Preaudit Certifications

State laws governing local government finance require counties and cities to establish internal procedures designed to ensure that sufficient appropriated funds are available to pay contractual obligations. Contracts involving the expenditure of funds that are included in a unit's budget ordinance must be "preaudited" to ensure that they are being spent in accordance with a budget appropriation and that sufficient funds remain available in the appropriation to pay the obligation created by the contract. All written contracts must contain a certification by the finance officer, as specified in Chapter 159, Section 28(a1) of the North Carolina General Statutes (hereinafter G.S.), stating that the instrument has been "preaudited in the manner required by the Local Government Budget and Fiscal Control Act." Under that statute, a person who incurs an obligation or pays out funds in violation of the statute is personally liable for the funds committed or disbursed.[14] Obligations incurred in violation of this requirement are void and are not enforceable against the unit.[15]

Most local governments use computerized financial systems that automatically conduct the preaudit procedure. These programs keep track of appropriated funds by category or account and encumber obligations as they are created by removing them from the pool of available funds. In 2021, the preaudit statute was amended to explicitly allow local governments to use an automated system for the preaudit process if the system meets certain statutory requirements.[16] Additionally, in order to use the automated preaudit system, a local government, through its finance officer(s), must also file an annual certification with the secretary of the Local Government Commission.

Contract Execution

As noted above, counties and cities have broad authority in allocating responsibility for contract approval. It is very important to distinguish, however, between the authority to approve a contract and the authority to execute (sign) a contract. Execution of the contract is a formality that is used to prove assent. Contracts are sometimes executed at the same time that they are approved. In other cases, the contract is executed after approval, such as when a unit's governing board approves a

12. *See* David M. Lawrence, "Contracts that Bind the Discretion of Governing Boards," *Popular Government* 56 (Summer 1990): 38–42.

13. *See* Wayne Cnty. Citizens Ass'n v. Wayne Cnty. Bd. of Comm'rs, 328 N.C. 24 (1991).

14. G.S. 159-28(e).

15. G.S. 159-28(a); *see also* L & S Leasing, Inc. v. City of Winston-Salem, 122 N.C. App. 619 (1996).

16. G.S. 159-28(a3) specifies that the system must have all of the following: (1) embedded functionality that determines that there is an appropriation to the department, function code, or project in which the transaction appropriately falls; (2) functionality ensuring that unencumbered funds remain in the appropriation to pay out any amounts that are expected to come due during the budgeted period; and (3) real-time visibility to budget compliance, alert threshold notifications, and rules-based compliance measures and enforcement.

contract that is later executed by the unit's manager. Even if a contract is properly executed, it is not enforceable against the unit if it was not approved or authorized by someone with authority to contract on behalf of the unit. The fact that someone has authority to execute a contract does not necessarily mean that he or she also has authority to approve a contract, although it may constitute evidence of implicit authority if there is no explicit delegation. Except for the preaudit certification by the finance officer of a unit, state laws do not dictate who must sign county and city contracts, so this is left to local discretion. As with the authority to award, the authority to execute is best delegated through a written policy or resolution approved by the governing board. Ensuring compliance with legal requirements, however, does not end once a contract is executed. Local governments must monitor performance pursuant to the contract, and, in fact, the Uniform Guidance states that entities "must maintain oversight to ensure that contractors perform in accordance with the terms, conditions, and specifications of their contracts or purchase orders."[17]

Form of Contracts and Electronic Contracts

In addition to the specific rules that apply to public contracts, all contracts must be enforceable under general common law and state statutory requirements. Most importantly, contracts must be supported by adequate consideration,[18] and there must be evidence to support any claim that the county or city, as a party to a contract, actually agreed to be bound by the terms of an alleged contractual commitment.

Whether a contract must be in writing depends on the type of contract and the unit of government entering into that contract. A state statute requires that all contracts made by or on behalf of municipalities must be in writing.[19] A municipal contract that is not in writing is void, but the governing board of the municipality can cure this defect by expressly ratifying the written contract. The North Carolina Supreme Court has held that the board's actions as recorded in its minutes do not satisfy the statutory requirement that a contract be in writing.[20] There is no parallel statute that requires county contracts to be in writing. The formal bidding statute, G.S. 143-129, however, requires all local government contracts that are within its scope to be in writing. (See Appendix 23.1, "Dollar Thresholds in North Carolina Public Contracting Statutes," for information on which contracts are subject to formal bidding.)

Another important writing requirement is contained in the Uniform Commercial Code (UCC). The UCC was developed to modernize and standardize the law governing commercial transactions, eliminating variations from state to state and removing many of the technicalities in the common law of contracts. In North Carolina, the UCC has been adopted as G.S. Chapter 25. The provisions governing contracts for the sale of goods are contained in Article 2, beginning at G.S. 25-2-101. Article 2 requires that all contracts (not just local government contracts) for the sale of goods exceeding $500 must be in writing.[21] In addition, while the common law requires that a contract specify all of the essential terms of the agreement, the UCC modifies common law contract requirements relating to the contents of a writing and the formalities for a valid signature.[22]

---

17. 2 C.F.R. § 200.318(b).
18. That is, by something of value on each side of the contract.
19. G.S. 160A-16.
20. Wade v. City of New Bern, 77 N.C. 460 (1877). In addition, board minutes would not satisfy the preaudit certificate requirement under G.S. 159-28(a).
21. G.S. 25-2-201(1).
22. G.S. 25-1-201(b)(37) (a contract can be signed "using any symbol executed or adopted with present intention to adopt or accept a writing.").

Other writing requirements are found in G.S. Chapter 22. Of greatest significance to local governments is the requirement of a writing for any contract or deed evidencing the sale of land or for any interest in land, including an easement; for any sale or lease of mining rights; and for any other lease of more than three years in length.[23]

Even when it is not required by statute or when the agreement at issue does not involve procurement with public funds (such as a lease of government property for a term of less than three years), a writing serves important purposes—the most significant being the clear expression of the agreement between the parties. In addition, for local governments, the written document incorporates the fiscal and departmental approvals required by statute and by local policy, and it provides documentation for the annual audit.

State and federal laws address the acceptability of electronic contracts, providing broad authority for the use of electronic transactions in general and in governmental contracting.[24] These laws generally provide that a contract may not be denied legal effect or enforceability solely because it has been created as an electronic document or has been affixed with an electronic signature. It is up to the county or city to determine whether it wishes to use or accept electronic contracts and to develop systems for assuring their authenticity and enforceability.

II. General Competitive Bidding Requirements

Contracts Covered by Bidding Laws

State and federal laws require local governments to obtain competitive bids before awarding certain types of contracts. The competitive bidding process is designed to prevent collusion and favoritism in the award of contracts and to generate favorable pricing to conserve public funds. As discussed below, the law does not always require that contracts be awarded to the lowest bidder, and the bidding requirements are best viewed as requiring prudent investment of public dollars. This means that quality and value can be as important as initial price in evaluating products and contractors in competitively bid contracts.

Under state law, the two key bidding statutes, G.S. 143-129 (formal bidding) and 143-131 (informal bidding), apply to two categories of contracts: (1) contracts for the purchase or lease-purchase of "apparatus, supplies, materials, or equipment" (hereinafter purchase contracts) and (2) contracts for construction or repair work. As discussed in the next section, many contracts do not fall within either of these categories and thus are not subject to any mandatory competitive bidding requirements. Bidding requirements are triggered when expenditures of public funds for the two specified categories of contracts occur at the dollar thresholds specified in the statutes. These dollar amounts correspond to the cost of the contract itself as opposed to the cost of individual items under the contract or the budgeted amount available for the expenditure. The current dollar thresholds are set forth in Appendix 23.1.

The Uniform Guidance classifies procurements differently than state law and divides procurements into the following three methods: informal procurement, formal procurement, and

23. G.S. 22-2.

24. At the federal level, see the Electronic Signatures in Global and National Commerce Act (E-SIGN), 15 U.S.C. § 7001; at the state level, see the Uniform Electronic Transactions Act (UETA), G.S. Chapter 66, Article 40 (G.S. 66-311 through -330), and the Electronic Commerce in Government Act, G.S. Chapter 66, Article 11A (G.S. 66-58.1 through -58.12).

noncompetitive procurement.[25] Within these three categories, competitive procurement processes are required for what the Uniform Guidance considers simplified acquisitions,[26] sealed bids, and proposals.

Simplified acquisition procedures are used for the acquisition of property or services when the aggregate dollar amount is higher than the micro-purchase threshold but lower than the simplified acquisition threshold.[27] As of the publication date of this edition, the micro-purchase threshold is $10,000. However, through an annual self-certification process, governmental units can increase the micro-purchase threshold up to $50,000 depending on state law thresholds.[28] Sealed bids and competitive proposals are used when the value of property or services being procured exceeds either the simplified acquisition threshold or a lower threshold established by a recipient. Note that where state law imposes competitive requirements at a lower threshold than the simplified acquisition threshold, a recipient must apply the Uniform Guidance requirements—along with state law requirements—at that lower threshold.[29] Under the Uniform Guidance, sealed bids are intended to be used for firm fixed-price contracts and are the preferred method for procuring construction services. Competitive proposals are intended for use when conditions are not appropriate for a sealed bid.

North Carolina competitive bidding requirements apply to counties, cities, local school units, and other local government agencies. With respect to purchase contracts, state agencies, including universities and community colleges, are governed by Article 3 of G.S. Chapter 143 and by the rules and policies of the State Department of Administration, Division of Purchase and Contract. With respect to contracts for construction or repair work, state agencies, including universities and community colleges, are governed by the statutes described here, along with rules and policies of the State Construction Office.

Private entities, whether nonprofit or for-profit, that contract with counties or cities are generally not required to comply with North Carolina bidding statutes, even when they are spending funds they have obtained from counties or cities. The funds are no longer considered public once they are received by the private entity under a contract or grant of local funds from a public agency. A local government contracting with a private entity may, however, require compliance with bidding requirements. On the other hand, federal or state agencies administering grant programs often require as a condition of a grant that private subrecipients use competitive bidding procedures when expending grant funds. Determining whether a private party needs to comply with the competitive bidding procedures in the Uniform Guidance requires evaluating whether the private party is a subrecipient or contractor.[30] In most cases, subrecipients must follow the procurement standards

25. 2 C.F.R. § 200.320.

26. In 2024, the Office of Management and Budget changed the term "small purchases" to "simplified acquisitions," effective October 1, 2024.

27. 2 C.F.R. § 200.320(a)(2). These thresholds are defined in 2 C.F.R. § 200.1. At the time of this book's publication, the micro-purchase threshold was $10,000 and the simplified acquisition threshold was $250,000.

28. For an explanation of the annual self-certification allowed under the Uniform Guidance, see Connor H. Crews, "Raising the Federal Micro-Purchase Threshold: Self-Certification for Units of Local Government in North Carolina," *Coates' Canons: NC Local Government Law* blog (April 23, 2021), canons.sog.unc.edu/2021/04/raising-the-federal-micro-purchase-threshold-self-certification-for-units-of-local-government-in-north-carolina/.

29. For example, North Carolina competitive bidding laws impose formal bidding requirements for purchases of goods starting at $90,000, which is a lower threshold than the current simplified acquisition threshold of $250,000. Thus, if federal financial assistance is being used for the purchase of goods valued at $90,000 or more, a recipient must apply the most restrictive rules of the Uniform Guidance and state law to that purchase, thereby requiring sealed bids for the purchase according to state law.

30. 2 C.F.R. § 200.331 provides guidance for distinguishing subrecipients from contractors.

of the Uniform Guidance. Contractors are not required to comply with the Uniform Guidance; instead, the recipient applies the procurement standards when selecting them.

Contracts Not Covered by Bidding Requirements/Optional Procedures

Under North Carolina law, contracts for many services, such as janitorial, grounds maintenance, and solid waste collection, fall outside the scope of the competitive bidding statutes. When the cost exceeds the micro-purchase threshold, however, contracts for services are subject to the competitive procurement requirements of the Uniform Guidance. As discussed later, special rules apply to contracts for architectural, engineering, and land surveying services (sometimes referred to as "professional services") and alternative construction delivery services.

Contracts for the purchase of real property and contracts for the lease (rental) of real or personal property also fall outside the scope of North Carolina laws that require competitive bidding. However, contracts for the lease-purchase of personal property, the installment-purchase of personal property, or the lease with option to purchase of personal property are subject to competitive bidding under North Carolina law.[31] The Uniform Guidance stipulates that rental costs of real property and equipment are not subject to competitive procurement, but the costs must be reasonable and are subject to other limitations, such as those addressing allowable amounts and specific conflicts of interest.

Finally, under North Carolina law, purchase contracts and contracts for construction or repair work that fall below the informal bidding threshold are not subject to competitive bidding, though many local policies require bidding even at these lower levels. Likewise, purchase and service contracts that fall below the micro-purchase threshold set forth in the Uniform Guidance are not subject to competitive bidding.

It is common for counties and cities to seek competitive bids on contracts even when laws do not require it, such as by issuing a request for proposals (RFP) for solid waste services. This is a good practice whenever there is competition for a particular service or product. Counties and cities often use the statutory procedures when seeking competition voluntarily, but this is not required. It is important for a unit to specify what procedures and standards it will use for awarding contracts in solicitations that are not subject to state statutes, especially if the procedures will be different from those set forth in the statutes. A unit is legally bound to adhere to the procedures it opts to use when bidding is not required by statute, or it may terminate the procedure and contract using some other procedure if it deems this to be in its best interest. The decision to competitively bid a contract when it is not statutorily required does not obligate the unit to use bidding in the future for that contract or for that type of contract.

Exceptions to Bidding Requirements

State and federal bidding laws contain a number of exceptions. County and city officials should be cautious when contracting without bidding to make sure that the contract falls within an exception. Courts have recognized the importance of the public policy underlying the bidding requirements and have strictly scrutinized local government justifications for claiming an exemption from bidding. The exceptions to the competitive bidding requirements pursuant to state law are listed below.[32] Unless noted otherwise, no specific procedures apply to contracts made under

31. G.S. 160A-19.

32. See *Exceptions to State Competitive Bidding Requirements for North Carolina Local Governments*, a chart published by the School of Government that summarizes competitive bidding exceptions under state law.

these exceptions. The "exceptions" to noncompetitive procurement under the Uniform Guidance are discussed later in this section.

- Purchases from other governments: G.S. 143-129(e)(1). Local governments may purchase directly from any other unit of government or from a government agency (federal, state, or local) and may purchase at government surplus sales.
- Emergencies: G.S. 143-129(e)(2). This exception to the formal bidding statute applies in "cases of special emergency involving the health and safety of the people or their property." The only North Carolina case interpreting the emergency exception indicates that it is very limited, applicable only when the emergency is immediate, unforeseeable, and cannot be resolved within the minimum time required to comply with the bidding procedures.[33] In 2023, the General Assembly expanded the definition of the Emergency Management Act, G.S. 166A-19.3, to include supply chain disruption that "creates a significant threat to a local government's ability to acquire products or services required to provide essential services such as electricity and water . . . or required to restore such essential services." This new statutory language exempts from competitive bidding any contracts for goods or construction or repair work requiring goods that are (1) listed in an emergency declaration arising from a supply chain disruption or (2) listed in an order or regulation issued by the federal government under the Defense Production Act.
- Competitive group purchasing programs: G.S. 143-129(e)(3). A group purchasing program is sometimes created by a separate organization on behalf of public agencies, or by a group of public agencies, in order to take advantage of economies of scale for commonly purchased items. Local governments may purchase without bidding items available under contracts that have been established using a competitive process undertaken as part of a group purchasing program.[34] In 2023, the General Assembly modified this exception to specify that "repair work" is limited to heating and cooling equipment obtained through the group purchasing program.[35] Otherwise, construction or repair work related to goods purchased under this exception must be procured according to state law.
- Change order work: G.S. 143-129(e)(4). For construction or repair work, competitive bidding is not required for work undertaken "during the progress" of a construction or repair project initially begun pursuant to the formal bidding statute. Change order work that is not within the scope of the original project could be challenged as an unlawful evasion of the bidding requirements.
- Gasoline, fuel, or oil: G.S. 143-129(e)(5). Purchases of gasoline, diesel fuel, alcohol fuel, motor oil, fuel oil, or natural gas are exempt from the formal bidding procedures but must be carried out using the informal procedures under G.S. 143-131.

---

33. *See* Raynor v. Comm'rs of Louisburg, 220 N.C. 348 (1941).

34. A common question is whether the Uniform Guidance allows for purchases from group purchasing programs. Although 2 C.F.R. § 200.318(e) encourages shared procurement processes among public entities and entities receiving federal funds, this language does not contemplate the group purchasing arrangement allowed by North Carolina state law. Therefore, local governments should consult with their attorneys and proceed with extreme caution when purchasing from a cooperative purchasing program using federal funds.

35. There are additional limitations on repair work related to the purchase of heating and cooling equipment through a group purchasing program: the installation costs cannot exceed $2,000,000, and the equipment must be procured using a group purchasing program that is qualified to sell to the federal government.

- Sole source: G.S. 143-129(e)(6). This exception applies to purchase contracts only, when performance or price competition is not available, when a needed product is available from only one source of supply, or when standardization or compatibility is the overriding consideration. Note that this exception applies when there is only one source for the item; simply being available from one manufacturer does not necessarily qualify the purchase under this exception, as that item may be available from more than one vendor or retailer. The governing board must approve each contract entered into under this exception, even if the board has delegated authority to award purchase contracts under G.S. 143-129(a).
- State and federal contract purchases: G.S. 143-129(e)(9), (e)(9a). Local governments may purchase items from contracts awarded by any North Carolina state agency or federal agency if the contractor is willing to extend to the local unit the same or more favorable prices, terms, and conditions as established in the state or federal contract. This includes purchases of information technology from contracts established by the N.C. Department of Information Technology Services (G.S. 143-129(e)(7)).
- Used apparatus, supplies, materials, or equipment: G.S. 143-129(e)(10). Competitive bidding is not required for the purchase of used items. The exception does not define what constitutes a used item, but it specifically excludes items that are remanufactured, refabricated, or "demo" items.
- Previously bid contracts ("piggybacking"): G.S. 143-129(g). Local governments may purchase from a contractor who has entered into a competitively bid contract with any other unit of government or with a government agency (federal, state, or local), anywhere in the country, within the past twelve months. The contractor must be willing to extend to the local government the same or more favorable prices and terms as are contained in the previously bid contract. This exception applies to purchase contracts in the formal bidding range only. A local government's governing board must approve each contract entered into under this exception at a regular board meeting on ten days' public notice, even if the board has delegated authority to award purchase contracts under G.S. 143-129(a).
- Force account work: G.S. 143-135. For construction or repair work, bidding is not required for projects to be completed using the local government unit's own employees. This exception actually operates as a limitation on the amount of work that may be done by local government employees. The exception limits such work to projects estimated to cost no more than $500,000 including the cost of labor and materials, or to projects on which the cost of labor does not exceed $200,000. The competitive bidding statutes still apply to materials to be used on such force account projects. Some have argued that the exception to the bidding requirements does not limit the use of the unit's own forces as long as the local unit itself submits a bid. There does not appear to be any authority in the statutes for a local government to submit a bid to itself as a way of complying with bidding requirements and avoiding application of the force account limits.
- School food services and publications: G.S. 115C-264 (food services); G.S. 115C-522(a) (publications). Local boards of education may purchase without competitive bidding supplies and food for school food services programs and published books, manuscripts, pamphlets, and periodicals used by public schools.

- Food and food service supplies for detention facilities: G.S. 143-131.1. All counties, through their sheriff's office, may make purchases of food and food service supplies without following competitive bidding law.
- Voting systems: G.S. 163-165.8. Counties may purchase without competitive bidding voting systems that have been approved by the State Board of Elections.
- Information technology requests for proposals: G.S. 143-129.8. A more flexible "request for proposals" (RFP) procedure is authorized for contracts for information technology goods and services, including computer software, hardware, and related services.

Unlike state law, which allows for exceptions to competitive bidding procedures based largely on the subject matter of the contract or the place from which an item is purchased, the Uniform Guidance permits noncompetitive procurement in only five instances: (1) the procurement is under the micro-purchase threshold, (2) the item is only available from a single source (which is synonymous with sole source), (3) a public emergency will not permit a delay, (4) it has been expressly permitted by the federal awarding agency or pass-through entity, or (5) the competition is deemed inadequate after solicitation of a number of sources.[36] Micro-purchases may be awarded without soliciting any competitive quotations if a recipient considers the costs to be reasonable, but these purchases must be distributed equitably among qualified suppliers, to the extent practicable.[37] The Uniform Guidance does not elaborate on the definitions or processes for the remainder of the noncompetitive procurements, and recipients should look to the federal awarding agency for further guidance.

Specifications

While competitive specifications are an essential element of a bidding process, there are no statutory procedures governing the preparation of specifications for purchases. Local officials may develop specifications that are most appropriate for their respective units. Specifications cannot, however, intentionally or unjustifiably eliminate competition by using overly restrictive specifications.[38] The Uniform Guidance requires that solicitations include a clear description of the technical requirements for the material, product, or service to be procured; the requirements that proposers must fulfill; and the factors used in evaluating proposals.[39] Federal rules further explain and prohibit situations that are considered restrictive of competition, such as requiring unnecessary experience and excessive bonding or noncompetitive contracts to consultants that are on retainer contract.[40]

Under state law, if only one brand of product is suitable, the specification can be limited to that brand; however, specifications for materials included in construction projects must be described in terms of performance characteristics, and brands can be specified only when performance specification is not possible. In such cases, at least three brands must be specified unless it is impossible to do so, in which case the specifications must include as many brands as possible. A unit must specifically approve in advance of the bid opening preferred products that are to be listed as alternates in specifications for construction projects. A brand-specific specification is not necessarily a sole-source purchase since there may be more than one supplier of a particular brand. Similarly, the Uniform Guidance characterizes specifying brand names as restrictive of competition and

36. *See* 2 C.F.R. § 200.320(c).
37. 2 C.F.R. § 200.320(a)(1).
38. *See* 2 C.F.R. § 319(b).
39. 2 C.F.R. § 200.319(d)(2).
40. For the list of situations identified in the Uniform Guidance as restrictive of competition, see 2 C.F.R. § 200.319(b). Note that the list is not comprehensive, and federal agencies could interpret other actions as restrictive of competition.

prompts recipients to allow for an equal product to be offered and to describe the performance or other relevant requirements of the procurement.[41] However, the Uniform Guidance notes that if describing the technical requirements of a product is impractical or uneconomical, a "brand name or equivalent" description may be used.[42]

In order to promote full and open competition, some individuals are prohibited from participating in the procurement process. Under North Carolina law, architects and engineers providing design services on public projects are prohibited from specifying any materials, equipment, or other items in which the designer has a financial interest.[43] Similarly, manufacturers cannot be involved in drawing plans or specifications for public construction projects.[44] The Uniform Guidance prohibits contractors that develop or draft specifications, requirements, statements of work, or invitations for bids or requests for proposals from competing for such procurements.[45]

Contracts for the construction or repair of buildings are subject to additional state law requirements for specifications. Depending on the cost, some project specifications must be drawn by a licensed architect or engineer.[46] If the building project is estimated to cost $300,000 or more, separate specifications must be prepared for heating, plumbing, and electrical work as well as general construction work.[47]

Trade-Ins

G.S. 143-129.7 authorizes local governments to include in bid specifications for a purchase an allowance for the trade-in of surplus property and to consider the price offered, including the trade-in allowance, when awarding a contract for the purchase. This statute effects an exemption from otherwise applicable procedures for disposing of surplus property. See part IV of this chapter for a full description of procedures for disposing of property.

III. Summary of Bidding Procedures

Informal Bidding

For North Carolina local governments, informal bidding under G.S. 143-131 is required for contracts for construction or repair work and for the purchase of apparatus, supplies, materials, or equipment costing between the minimum informal bid threshold and the formal bidding limit (see Appendix 23.1 for current threshold amounts). No advertisement is required, and the statute does not specify a minimum number of bids that must be received. Informal bids can take the form of telephone quotes, faxed bids, or other electronic or written bids. The statute requires that the county or city maintain a record of informal bids received and specifies that such records are subject to public inspection after the contract is awarded. This prevents bidders from having access to bids already submitted when preparing their bids, a situation not present in formal bidding because bids are sealed until the bid opening. The standard for awarding contracts in the informal range is the

41. *See* 2 C.F.R. § 319(b).
42. *See* 2 C.F.R. § 319(d)(1).
43. G.S. 133-1.
44. G.S. 133-2.
45. 2 C.F.R. § 319(b).
46. G.S. 133-1.1(a).
47. G.S. 143-128(a).

same as the standard for formal bids—the lowest responsive responsible bidder—and is discussed later in this chapter.

As noted below, for building construction or repair contracts in the informal range, the informal bidding statute requires counties and cities to solicit bids from minority firms and to report to the state Department of Administration on bids solicited and obtained for contracts in this dollar range.

Under the Uniform Guidance, informal bidding procedures apply to "simplified acquisitions," which involve the acquisition of property or services when the aggregate dollar amount is higher than the micro-purchase threshold but lower than the simplified acquisition threshold. At its upper limits and due to the interplay with state law, simplified acquisition procedures currently apply when federal funds are used for procuring goods up to $90,000, construction or repair up to $250,000, and services up to $250,000. Procurement of professional services, which are procured using qualifications-based selection, is covered later in this chapter. Procedurally, the Uniform Guidance requires that a recipient obtain price or rate quotations from an adequate number of qualified sources. This language gives a recipient discretion to determine the "adequate" number of qualified sources but implies that the number must be greater than one. Moreover, the methods of obtaining the price or rate quotations are left up to the recipient. The quote could be obtained in writing, orally, from a vendor price list on a website, or generated via an online search engine, but these quotes and the basis for the contractor selection and contract price must be documented.[48] Somewhat similar to state law, the Uniform Guidance also suggests that federal fund recipients consider contracting with small and minority businesses, women's business enterprises, veteran-owned businesses,[49] and labor-surplus-area firms; these considerations are discussed later in this chapter.[50]

Formal Bidding

The requirements for formal bidding are more rigorous than informal bidding procedures. When local governments are spending public funds at the formal bidding thresholds established by state and federal law, the formal bidding procedures are designed to ensure fairness and transparency in the expenditure of public funds and make available opportunities for contractors. This section describes the elements of state and federal formal bidding processes, including advertisement, the format of the bid, and bonding requirements.

Under state law, formal bidding is synonymous with sealed bidding. The Uniform Guidance, however, classifies two types of procurement methods as formal procurement methods: sealed bids and proposals, referred to in this chapter as "competitive proposals." Sealed bids must be used for solicitations that exceed the simplified acquisition threshold and are the preferred method for procuring construction. Due to the interplay with state law, when federal funds are being used, sealed bids are required for purchases of goods starting at $90,000 and for construction or repair starting at $250,000. Competitive proposals can be used at a dollar amount deemed appropriate by a recipient. This means that soliciting for services could be accomplished by a competitive proposal starting at $250,000, although a recipient could opt for a lower threshold. Additionally, when federal funds are being used, soliciting for architectural or engineering services by competitive proposal must also comply with the North Carolina Mini-Brooks Act, which is discussed later in this chapter.

---

48. *See* 2 C.F.R. § 200.318(i).

49. Veteran-owned businesses were added by final rule, effective October 1, 2024.

50. *See* 2 C.F.R. § 200.321.

Advertisement

The North Carolina formal bidding statute, G.S. 143-129, requires counties and cities to advertise opportunities to bid on contracts for construction or repair, or for the purchase of apparatus, supplies, materials, and equipment, within the formal bid thresholds as described in Appendix 23.1. The minimum time period for advertisement under the statute requires that a full seven days pass between the day of the advertisement and the day of the bid opening. It is common practice to place the advertisement more than once or for a longer period of time prior to the bid opening in order to provide sufficient opportunity for response. The advertisement must list the date, time, and location of the bid opening, identify where specifications may be obtained, and contain a statement that the unit's governing board reserves the right to reject any or all bids. For construction projects, the advertisement may also contain information about contractor licensing requirements that apply to the project.

The formal bidding statute requires the advertisement to be published in a newspaper of general circulation within the given county or city. The statute also authorizes the governing board to approve the use of electronic advertisement of bidding opportunities instead of published notice. The unit's governing board may authorize electronic advertisement of bids for particular contracts or for contracts in general.[51] A sealed bid procurement under the Uniform Guidance, however, only requires "public advertising" that provides a "sufficient response time." Likewise, the Uniform Guidance only requires that competitive proposals be "publicized."

Sealed Bids

Bids must be sealed and submitted prior to the time of the bid opening. Both state law and federal rules require local government to open sealed bids in public. State law allows sealed bids to be opened before the advertised time with the permission of the bidder. Under the "dual-bidding" method of construction contracting authorized under state law (discussed later), separate-prime bids must be received (but not opened) one hour before single-prime bids. Unit staff generally conduct bid openings, but contracts must be awarded by the governing board, except for purchase contracts in jurisdictions where the board has delegated the authority to award these contracts as authorized in G.S. 143-129(a).

Once formal bids are opened, they become public records and are subject to public inspection under North Carolina's public records laws. The only exception to this rule is contained in G.S. 132-1.2, which allows a bidder to identify trade secrets that are contained in a bid and protects that information from public disclosure.[52]

Competitive Proposals

The Uniform Guidance identifies competitive proposals as an additional formal procurement method, generally used when conditions are not appropriate for the use of sealed bids. The Uniform Guidance does not elaborate on circumstances where sealed bids are not appropriate, but a competitive proposal is beneficial where price is not the primary factor for selecting a bidder. There are two ways in which competitive proposals can be used. First, a competitive proposal can be designed as

---

51. The governing board may authorize electronic advertisement of bids for particular contracts or for contracts in general. Action to approve electronic notice of bidding must be taken by the county or municipal governing board at a regular meeting. No specific action is required to provide electronic notice in addition to published notice.

52. A "trade secret" is defined under G.S. 66-152(3). For further discussion of when bid documents become open to public inspection, see Eileen Youens, "When Are Bids and Proposals Subject to Public Inspection?" *Local Government Law Bulletin* No. 119 (Feb. 2009), www.sog.unc.edu/publications/bulletins/when-are-bids-and-proposals-subject-public-inspection.

a Request for Proposals (RFP), whereby proposers are evaluated based on specific factors including price, and an award is made to the most advantageous proposal. Second, competitive proposals can be used for procuring architectural and engineering services, whereby price is not used as a selection factor and the award is made to the "most qualified offeror." This second option is similar to the qualifications-based selection required for procuring architectural, engineering, and land surveying services under North Carolina's Mini-Brooks Act. When a recipient is using an RFP, the Uniform Guidance imposes a few additional requirements. The RFP must identify all of the factors that will be used for evaluation and their relative importance.[53] Additionally, a recipient must have a written method for conducting its evaluations of proposals. Finally, proposals must be solicited from an adequate number of qualified offerors.

Electronic Bids

Counties and cities have several alternatives to receiving sealed paper bids for purchase contracts in the formal bidding range. These options are not available for contracts for construction or repair in the formal range. Under G.S. 143-129.9, formal bids for purchase contracts may be received electronically[54] or through the use of a "reverse-auction" process.[55] Under a reverse-auction procedure, bidders compete to provide goods at the lowest selling price in an open and interactive electronic auction process. An electronic bid or reverse-auction process can be conducted by the unit itself or by a third party under contract with the unit. The statute does not allow the use of reverse auctions for the purchase of construction aggregates, including crushed stone, sand, and gravel, nor does it authorize the use of electronic bids or reverse auctions for construction contracts in the formal bidding range.

Number of Bids

According to G.S. 143-132, three bids are required for construction or repair contracts that are subject to the formal bidding procedures. If three bids are not received after the first advertisement, the project must be readvertised for at least the minimum time period listed under the formal bidding statute (seven days, not including the day of advertisement and the day of the bid opening) before the next bid opening. Following the second advertisement, a contract can be awarded even if fewer than three bids are received.

Note that the statute only applies to contracts for construction or repair work in the formal bidding range. This means that three bids are not required for purchase contracts in the formal range or for any contracts in the informal range. Some counties or cities may have local policies that require three bids for all contracts, but this is not required by state law.

In comparison, the Uniform Guidance requires that at least two bids be received for sealed bids, but it does not impose a minimum number of proposals for competitive proposals. Determining the required number of bids is an instance where local governments may need to apply the "most restrictive rule." For example, if only two bids are received for a federally funded construction project that is above the North Carolina threshold for formal bidding, the procurement process cannot proceed because the three-bid minimum under state law has not been met, even though two bids are sufficient under the Uniform Guidance.

---

53. 2 C.F.R. § 200.320(b)(2)(i).
54. G.S. 143-129.9(a)(1).
55. G.S.143-129.9(a)(2).

Bid, Performance, and Payment Bonds

Bonds or statutorily authorized bond substitutes are required for construction or repair contracts in the formal bid range. A bid for construction or repair work submitted in response to a formal bidding procurement—whether under state law or federal rules—must be accompanied by a bid deposit or bid bond of at least 5 percent of the bid amount. The bid bond or deposit guarantees that the bidder to whom a contract is awarded will execute the contract and provide performance and payment bonds when they are required. North Carolina law specifies the forms in which the bid security may be submitted: a bid bond, a bid deposit in cash, a cashier's check, or a certified check. No other form of security, such as a letter of credit, is authorized under state law. The Uniform Guidance contemplates the bid security in the form of a bid bond or cashier's check but also allows for other negotiable instruments.

Specific procedures are set forth in G.S. 143-129.1 for the withdrawal of a bid. A bid may be withdrawn under those procedures without forfeiting the bid bond only if the bidder can demonstrate that he or she has made an unintentional and substantial error, as opposed to an error in judgment. The law does not allow a bidder to correct a mistake, only to withdraw a bid if proof of an unintentional error is shown. If the bidder can demonstrate that the error was substantial and unintentional, the bid may be withdrawn without the bid bond being forfeited so long as the request for withdrawal is made within seventy-two hours of the bid opening.[56]

State law also requires that counties and cities obtain performance and payment bonds from the successful bidder on major construction or repair projects for projects costing more than $300,000,[57] and the Uniform Guidance requires the same for construction or facility improvements contracts above the simplified acquisition threshold. A performance bond guarantees performance of the contract and provides the county or city with security in the event that the contractor defaults and cannot complete the contract. The payment bond is obtained for the benefit of subcontractors who supply labor or materials to the project and provides a source of payment to those contractors in the event that they are not paid by the general contractor. North Carolina law authorizes counties and cities to accept deposits of cash, certified checks, or government securities in lieu of bonds.[58]

Evaluation of Bids and Responsiveness

Once received, bids must be evaluated to determine whether they meet the specifications and are eligible for award—that is, whether they are responsive bids. The bid evaluation process is important to maintaining the integrity of the bidding process. If a county or city accepts bids that contain significant deviations from the specifications, other bidders may object. Indeed, courts have recognized that a governmental unit receiving bids does not have unlimited discretion in waiving deviations from specifications. North Carolina courts have held that a unit must reject a bid that contains a "material variance" from specifications, defined as a variance that gives the bidder "an advantage or benefit which is not enjoyed by other bidders."[59] Even though specifications may reserve

---

56. *See* G.S. 143-129.1; the statute allows local governments to establish a longer period for bid withdrawal so long as the period was specified in the instructions to bidders. *See also* Ralph Hodge Constr. Co. v. Brunswick Reg'l Water & Sewer H2GO, 284 N.C. App. 419, 421 (2022).

57. For projects costing more than $300,000, performance and payments bonds must be received from each contractor with a contract costing over $50,000. Note that the $300,000 amount is less than the $500,000 threshold for projects in the formal bidding range.

58. The performance and payment bonds required under the formal bidding statute are governed by Article 3 of G.S. Chapter 44A.

59. Prof'l Food Servs. Mgmt. v. N.C. Dep't of Admin., 109 N.C. App. 265, 269 (1993) (internal quotation marks, citation omitted). *See also* Frayda Bluestein, "Understanding the Responsiveness Requirement in Competitive Bidding," *Local*

a unit's ability to "waive minor irregularities," the unit's assessment of what constitutes a minor irregularity must be based upon the legal standard established by the courts. Thus, if the low bid omits a required feature that the unit feels it can live without, the unit must reject the defective bid. Similarly, if waiving the irregularity would give that bidder an unfair competitive advantage over other bidders (such as saving that bidder time or money in compiling the bid proposal), the unit must reject the bid. When the low bid is rejected, the unit then has the option of accepting the next-lowest responsible, responsive bid or rejecting all the bids, revising or clarifying the specifications, if necessary, and rebidding the contract.

A bid must also be rejected as nonresponsive if it fails to satisfy a statutory requirement applicable to the particular contract. For example, a bid in the formal range that is submitted after the advertised bid deadline, or a formal bid for a construction project that is submitted without the required bid bond, must be rejected. While a unit has the discretion to waive minor irregularities, it does not have the authority to waive statutory requirements.

Cost and Price Analysis

When using federal funds, a recipient of federal funds must perform a cost or price analysis before awarding a contract for every procurement action exceeding the simplified acquisition threshold.[60] The independent cost estimate serves as a tool for evaluating the reasonableness of a contractor's proposed costs or prices. Price analysis is essentially price comparison. It is the evaluation of a proposed price without analyzing any of the separate cost elements. Conversely, cost analysis is the evaluation of the separate elements (e.g., materials) that make up a contractor's total cost proposal to determine if the costs are reasonable. A cost analysis is used when price competition does not exist—for example, when negotiating a sole-source contract or when, after soliciting competitive bids, only one bid is received. The method and degree of analysis required for each procurement situation varies, and federal agencies usually issue specific guidance on conducting the appropriate analysis.

Standard for Awarding Contracts

Under state law, both the formal and informal bid statutes require that contracts be awarded to the "lowest responsible, responsive bidder, taking into consideration quality, performance, and the time specified in the bids for the performance of the contract."[61] Similarly, the Uniform Guidance dictates that recipients award contracts only to "responsible contractors possessing the ability to perform successfully under the terms and conditions of a proposed procurement" and that recipients consider matters such as contractor integrity, public policy, past performance, and financial and technical resources.[62] Pursuant to federal rules, small purchases can be awarded to a contractor so long as the price is fair and reasonable.

Although the "lowest responsible, responsive bidder" standard probably creates a presumption in favor of the bidder who submits the lowest dollar bid, it clearly does not require an award to the lowest bidder in all cases. The North Carolina Court of Appeals has held that the formal bid statute authorizes a local government to request information from bidders about their experience

---

Government Law Bulletin No. 102 (May 2002), www.sog.unc.edu/publications/bulletins/understanding-responsiveness-requirement-competitive-bidding.

60. 2 C.F.R. § 200.324. Note that some federal granting agencies, such as the Federal Transit Administration, may also require an Independent Cost Estimate (ICE) to establish a reasonable price for goods or services prior to a procurement action, and recipients should always consult agency guidance to determine if additional requirements apply.

61. *See* G.S. 143-131(a).

62. 2 C.F.R. § 200.318(h).

and financial strength and to consider this information in determining whether the low bidder is responsible.[63] The court found that the term "responsibility" refers to the bidder's capacity to perform the contract and that the statute authorizes the board to evaluate the bidder's experience, training and quality of personnel, financial strength, and any other factors that bear on the bidder's ability to perform the work.

A local government must carefully document the factual basis for any award to a bidder who did not submit the lowest bid and be diligent in investigating the facts to make sure that the information it relies upon is accurate and reliable. The county or city does not necessarily have to demonstrate that a contractor is not responsible generally, only that the contractor does not have the skills, experience, or financial capacity for the contract in question.

Additionally, under state law, construction or repair contracts that are subject to the formal bidding requirements must be awarded by a unit's governing body. For purchase contracts in the formal range, G.S. 143-129(a) authorizes the board to delegate to the unit's manager or chief purchasing official the authority to award contracts or to reject bids and readvertise the contract and opportunity to bid. The informal bidding statute does not dictate who must award contracts. This responsibility is usually delegated to the purchasing agent or to other employees responsible for handling informal contracts.

Local governments also have broad authority under state law to reject any or all bids for any reason that is not inconsistent with the purposes of the bidding laws.[64] Likewise, the Uniform Guidance states that any or all sealed bids may be rejected if there is a "sound documented reason."[65]

Local Preferences

Local governments in North Carolina do not have specific statutory authority to establish preferences in awarding contracts, such as preferences for local or minority contractors.[66] A local preference would conflict with the legal requirement in both the formal and informal bidding range that contracts be awarded to the lowest responsible bidder. Although some may think it economically or politically desirable, it is not legal to assume that a local contractor is more responsible than others under this standard for awarding contracts.[67] Until 2024, the Uniform Guidance explicitly prohibited the use of geographical preferences unless federal statutes mandated or encouraged the preference.[68] However, pursuant to rules that became effective October 1, 2024, the Uniform Guidance now allows recipients to incorporate scoring that rewards bidders who "commit to specific numbers and types of U.S. jobs, minimum compensation, benefits, on-the-job-training for employees making work products or providing services on a contract, and other worker protections."[69] However, any such scoring must comport with the United States Constitution and federal

63. Kinsey Contracting Co., Inc. v. City of Fayetteville, 106 N.C. App. 383, 386 (1992).

64. G.S. 143-129(a).

65. 2 C.F.R. § 200.320(b)(1)(ii)(E).

66. However, several jurisdictions in North Carolina have received authorizing legislation through local bills for small business enterprise programs, which allow those local governments to consider compliance with the programs when selecting a bidder under G.S. 143-129 or -131.

67. Unlike other local governments, local school boards are authorized to adopt policies authorizing an in-state percentage-price preference in competitive bidding for the purchase of food grown or produced in North Carolina pursuant to G.S. 115C-264.4.

68. 2 C.F.R. § 200.319(c). As an example, Section 25019(a) of the *Infrastructure Investment and Jobs Act* (Pub. L. No. 117–58, 135 Stat. 429 (November 15, 2021)) allows recipients to utilize local or other geographic and economic hiring preferences on their federally funded highway projects, subject to state and local laws, policies, and procedures.

69. Guidance for Federal Financial Assistance, 89 Fed. Reg. 30046 (revising 2 C.F.R. § 200.319(f)), www.federalregister.gov/documents/2024/04/22/2024-07496/guidance-for-federal-financial-assistance.

laws. Under state law, preferences or targeted contracting efforts may be permissible, however, for contracts that are not subject to the competitive bidding requirements, such as service contracts or contracts below the minimum bid threshold (see Appendix 23.1). Counties and municipalities can also establish procedures to identify local and minority contractors and notify them of contracting opportunities.

Special Rules for Building Contracts

Bidding and Construction Methods

In addition to the bidding requirements for contracts involving construction or repair work described above, there are several special requirements under state law for construction and repair contracts involving buildings. First, state law limits the bidding and construction methods counties and cities may use for major building construction. For building construction projects that are above the dollar threshold contained in G.S. 143-128 (see Appendix 23.1), local governments may use any of the following contracting methods: separate prime,[70] single prime,[71] construction management at risk,[72] design-build,[73] design-build bridging,[74] or public–private partnership.[75]

Under traditional construction delivery methods, the prime contract is the contract directly between the owner (the unit of government) and the contractor. These contracts are customarily arranged as either single-prime or separate-prime contracts. In a single-prime contract, the general contractor has the prime contract with the owner and all other contracts are subcontracts with the general contractor. Under the separate-prime (also called multiple-prime) system, contractors in the major trades[76] submit separate bids to and contract directly with the owner. Bids may also be received on a "dual-bidding" basis, under which both separate-prime and single-prime bids are solicited. Under dual bidding, the unit may consider cost of construction oversight, time for completion, and other factors it deems appropriate in determining whether to award a contract on a single-prime or separate-prime basis, and it may award to the lowest responsible, responsive bidder under either category.

The procurement process for alternative construction delivery methods—construction management at risk, design-build, design-build bridging, and public–private partnership—is substantially different from that for traditional construction delivery methods. Generally, contracts for alternative construction delivery methods are procured pursuant to state law using the qualification-based process of the Mini-Brooks Act and may be used only after the local government has determined that using an alternative construction delivery method over a traditional delivery method is in the best interest of the project.

The alternative construction delivery methods vary in the applicable procurement and contracting processes.[77] The construction manager at risk contracts to oversee and manage construction and to deliver the completed project at a negotiated guaranteed minimum price. The construction manager is required to solicit bids and award contracts for all of the actual construction work

70. G.S. 143-128(b).
71. G.S. 143-128(d).
72. G.S. 143-128.1.
73. G.S. 143-128.1A.
74. G.S. 143-128.1B.
75. G.S. 143-128.1C.
76. These trades are general contracting, plumbing, electrical, and heating, ventilating, and air-conditioning (HVAC).
77. Other construction methods not specifically authorized by statute may be used only for projects below the threshold set out in the statute or with special approval from the State Building Commission or by authority of local legislation enacted by the General Assembly.

(including general contracting work) to prequalified subcontractors. Under the design-build method, the unit enters into one contract with a team comprised of design professionals and contractors (design-build team) to both design and build the project. The design-build bridging method involves a two-contract process under which the unit first contracts with a design professional to design 35 percent of the project and then contracts with a design-build team to complete the design and perform the construction. While the contract with the design professional is procured using the qualification-based selection method, the contract with the design-build team is awarded under the lowest responsible, responsive bidder standard. A public–private partnership contract involves one contract between the unit and a private developer in which the developer finances at least 50 percent of the project and where the roles and responsibilities of the unit and the developer are delineated in a negotiated development contract.

The use of alternative construction delivery methods in compliance with the Uniform Guidance is challenging, at best, because a conflict exists between selection processes under North Carolina law and the federal procurement standards. In selecting a construction manager at risk or design-builder, a unit must employ a qualifications-based selection process in compliance with the North Carolina Mini-Brooks Act. However, the federal procurement standards contained in the Uniform Guidance specifically limit a recipient's use of qualifications-based selection to the procurement of "architectural/engineering (A/E) professional services" and qualifications-based selection "cannot be used to purchase *other types of services through A/E firms* that are a potential source to perform the proposed effort."[78] Because units must abide by this Uniform Guidance provision when using federal funds, this restriction likely prohibits a unit of local government from employing the state-mandated qualifications-based selection process required to choose a construction manager at risk or design-builder.[79]

Historically Underutilized Business (HUB) and Minority and Women-Owned Business Enterprise (MWBE) Participation

Public agencies, including counties and cities, are required under G.S. 143-128.2 to establish a percentage goal for participation by HUB contractors in major building construction or repair projects, to make efforts to include these contractors in these projects, and to require prime contractors to either meet or make good-faith efforts to attain the established HUB participation goal.[80] The law does not establish or authorize a set-aside of particular contracts for HUB contractors or a preference for HUB contractors in awarding contracts. The statute specifically states, however, that contracts must be awarded to the lowest responsible, responsive bidder without consideration of race, sex, religion, national origin, or handicapping condition. That said, a bidder's failure to make

78. 2 C.F.R. § 200.320(b)(2)(iv) (emphasis added).

79. Note that the North Carolina General Assembly enacted temporary legislation, S.L. 2021-189, which authorizes local governments to consider "price" when issuing a request for qualifications for design-build services when federal funds are being used. The temporary authorization is scheduled to expire on December 31, 2025. You can read an analysis of Section 1.6 of the Session Law in School of Government faculty member Connor Crews's blog post, "Design-Build Contracting in North Carolina Using Coronavirus State and Local Fiscal Recovery Funds," *Coates' Canons: NC Local Government Law* blog (April 14, 2022), canons.sog.unc.edu/2022/04/design-build-contracting-in-north-carolina-using-coronavirus-state-and-local-fiscal-recovery-funds/.

80. G.S. 143-128.2(a), (b). *See also* Norma R. Houston and Jessica Jansepar Ross, "HUB Participation in Building Construction Contracting by N.C. Local Governments: Statutory Requirements and Constitutional Limitations," *Local Government Law Bulletin* No. 131 (Feb. 2013), www.sog.unc.edu/publications/bulletins/hub-participation-building-construction-contracting-nc-local-governments-statutory-requirements-and.

the statutorily mandated minimum good-faith efforts is grounds for rejection of a bid.[81] Counties and cities are required to establish a minority business participation outreach plan and to report data regarding minority outreach and participation on specific projects to the State Department of Administration.

The Uniform Guidance suggests that recipients consider minority businesses, women's business enterprises, veteran-owned businesses, and labor-surplus-area firms contracting opportunities.[82] Methods for considering these businesses can be found in 2 C.F.R. § 200.321 and are similar to the good-faith efforts required of local governments under North Carolina state law. Generally speaking, recipients are not required to meet any federal MWBE goals when using federal funds.

Requirements for Design and Related Services

State law specifies when plans and specifications for public building projects must be prepared by a registered or licensed architect or engineer.[83] The statutory thresholds, set forth in Appendix 23.1, apply based on whether the project involves new construction or renovation that calls for foundation or structural work or that affects life safety systems. This requirement applies even if the work is to be done by the unit's own forces, subject to the force account limits discussed earlier.

When selecting architects, engineers, surveyors, and alternative construction delivery methods (construction manager at risk, design-build, design-build bridging, and public–private partnership), G.S. 143-64.31 requires public agencies to do so based on qualifications instead of bid prices. The statute prohibits public agencies from asking for pricing information, other than unit prices (understood to mean hourly rates), until after the best-qualified person or firm is identified. Fees are then negotiated to develop a final contract. Local government units that do not wish to use the qualification-based process required under the statute have the ability under G.S. 143-64.32 to approve an exemption for any particular project where the fee is less than $50,000. While approval of the exemption by a unit's governing board is not required, the statute does require the unit to exempt itself in writing. Once exempt, the unit can either negotiate a contract or conduct a competitive bidding or other process under which it solicits fee pricing to select the design professional for services in these categories.

Similarly, under the Uniform Guidance, a recipient may use competitive proposal procedures for qualifications-based procurement of architectural/engineering (A/E) professional services. Using this method, an offeror's qualifications are evaluated and the most-qualified offeror is selected, subject to the negotiation of fair and reasonable compensation. Price is not a selection factor.[84]

Protests and Legal Challenges

Unlike the laws governing state contracting, North Carolina laws governing local government contracting do not establish bid protest procedures. North Carolina courts have held that if a contract is subject to the statutory competitive bidding procedures and those procedures are not followed, the contract is void.[85] If a bidder is dissatisfied with a decision of the county or city—for example, to award a contract to the second-lowest bidder or to accept a bid that does not meet specifications—the bidder can discuss his or her complaint with the local official responsible for the contract or take

81. G.S. 143-128.2(c).

82. 2 C.F.R. § 200.321. Prior to 2024, this section of the Uniform Guidance required recipients to take "necessary affirmative steps."

83. G.S. 133-1.1(a).

84. 2 C.F.R. § 200.320(b)(2)(iv).

85. Raynor v. Comm'rs of Louisburg, 220 N.C. 348, 353 (1941).

it directly to the governing board. As a practical matter, it is best for the unit to attempt to resolve the matter, but there is no legal requirement for a hearing or other formal disposition of the complaint. If the matter is not resolved administratively, the only legal option is for the aggrieved party to sue the unit of government, typically for an injunction to prevent the unit from going forward with an illegal contract.[86] It is not unusual for protests to be lodged with local government officials or with governing boards, although legal challenges are rare.

If an issue arises under a contract supported with federal funds, the Uniform Guidance places the sole burden on the recipient to manage the issue.[87] Moreover, because recipients must have written procedures regarding procurement transactions that address all applicable law, recipients necessarily must have written procedures to address procurement and contracting disputes, such as source evaluation, protests, and claims. However, the Uniform Guidance does not require any specific procedures for the resolution of procurement or contracting issues, and the federal government will not substitute its judgment unless the matter is primarily a federal concern.

IV. Property Disposal

Under state law, county and city governments generally dispose of both real and personal property in accordance with the procedures set forth in G.S. Chapter 160A, Article 12, although there are a few other disposition procedures set out in other statutes, applicable to special situations.[88] This section discusses state law property-disposal methods and includes a separate section that briefly examines the disposition of property acquired with federal funds. However, before examining property-disposal methods and rules, it is useful to discuss one introductory matter: the need for consideration when disposing of local government property.

Consideration

Under the North Carolina Constitution, it is generally unconstitutional for a local government to dispose of property for less than its fair market value.[89] A gift of property or a sale at well below market value constitutes the granting of an "exclusive privilege or emolument" to the person receiving the property, which is prohibited by article 1, section 32, of the state constitution. Most of the procedures by which a local government is permitted to sell or otherwise dispose of property are competitive, and the North Carolina Supreme Court has indicated that the price resulting from an open and competitive procedure will be accepted as the market value.[90] If a sale is privately negotiated, the price will normally be considered appropriate unless strong evidence indicates that it is so significantly below market value as to show an abuse of discretion.[91]

It is not always constitutionally necessary that a local government receive monetary consideration when it conveys property. If the party receiving the property agrees to put it to some public

---

86. *See* Frayda S. Bluestein, "Disappointed Bidder Claims Against North Carolina Local Governments," *Local Government Law Bulletin* No. 98 (May 2001), www.sog.unc.edu/publications/bulletins/disappointed-bidder-claims-against-north-carolina-local-governments.

87. 2 C.F.R. § 200.318(k).

88. G.S. 153A-176 requires counties to comply with the procedures for property disposal in Article 12 of G.S. Chapter 160A.

89. Redevelopment Comm'n v. Security Nat'l Bank, 252 N.C. 595 (1960).

90. *Id.*

91. Painter v. Wake Cnty. Bd. of Educ., 288 N.C. 165 (1975).

use, that promise constitutes sufficient consideration for the conveyance.[92] (The recipient in this case is often, but not always, another government unit.) The General Statutes expressly permit the following such conveyances: those made to the state and to local governments within North Carolina (G.S. 160A-274); those made to volunteer fire departments and rescue squads (G.S. 160A-277); conveyances to nonprofit preservation or conservation organizations (G.S. 160A-266(b)); to nonprofit agencies to which the county or city is authorized to appropriate money (G.S. 160A-279); and to governmental units within the United States, nonprofits, North Carolina charter schools, and sister cities (G.S. 160A-280).

Disposal Methods under North Carolina Law

G.S. Chapter 160A, Article 12, sets out three competitive methods of sale, each of which is appropriate in any circumstance for disposing of both real and personal property: sealed bid, negotiated offer and upset bid, and public auction. Article 12 also permits privately negotiated exchanges of property in any circumstance (so long as equal value changes hands) and privately negotiated sales or other dispositions of property in a number of limited circumstances. In addition, a few other statutes permit privately negotiated sales or other dispositions of property, again in limited circumstances. These various methods of disposition are summarized in the following sections. In undertaking any of them, a local government must remember that the statutory procedure must be exactly followed or the transaction may be invalidated by a court.[93]

Sealed Bids

A local government may sell any real or personal property by sealed bid (G.S. 160A-268). The procedure is based on that set forth in G.S. 143-129 for entering into purchase contracts in the formal bidding range, with one modification for real property. An advertisement for sealed bids must be published in a newspaper that has general circulation in the county (for a county government) or in the county in which the city is located (for a municipal government). Publication must occur seven full days (not counting the day of publication or the day of bid opening) before the bids are opened if personal property is being sold and thirty days before the bids are opened if real property is being sold. The advertisement should generally describe the property; tell where it can be examined and when and where the bids will be opened; state whether a bid deposit is required and, if so, how much it is and the circumstances under which it will be retained; and reserve the governing board's right to reject any and all bids. Bids must be opened in public, and the award is made to the highest responsible bidder.

The sealed bid procedure appears to be designed to obtain wide competition by providing public notice and good opportunity for bidders to examine the property being sold. Invitations to bid may be mailed to prospective buyers, just as they are typically sent to prospective bidders in the formal purchasing procedures for personal property.

Negotiated Offer and Upset Bids

A local government may sell any real or personal property by negotiated offer and upset bid (G.S. 160A-269). The procedure begins when the local government receives and proposes to accept

92. Brumley v. Baxter, 225 N.C. 691 (1945). However, see *infra* note 96 regarding the limitation on disposal of local school property.

93. Bagwell v. Town of Brevard, 267 N.C. 604 (1966). Some government boards routinely declare as surplus any property that is to be sold. No statute requires such a declaration, however, and it does not appear to be necessary. A city or county evidences its conclusion that property is surplus by selling it.

an offer to purchase specified government property. The offer may be either solicited by the local government or made directly by a prospective buyer on his or her own initiative. The governing board then requires the offeror to deposit a 5 percent bid deposit with its clerk and causes a notice of the offer to be published. The notice must describe the property; specify the amount and terms of the offer; and give notice that the bid may be raised by not less than 10 percent of the first $1,000 originally bid, plus 5 percent of any amount above $1,000 of the original bid. Upset bids must also be accompanied by a 5 percent bid deposit. Prospective bidders have ten days from the date on which the notice is published to offer an upset bid. This procedure is repeated until ten days have elapsed without the local government receiving a qualifying upset bid. After that time, the board may sell the property to the final offeror. At any time in the process, it may reject any and all offers and decide not to sell the property.

Public Auctions

A local government may sell any real or personal property by public auction under G.S. 160A-270. The statute sets out separate procedures for the auctioning of real and personal property and authorizes electronic auctions. For real property, the unit's governing board must adopt a resolution that authorizes the sale; describes the property; specifies the date, time, place, and terms of the sale; and states that the board must accept and confirm the successful bid. The board may require a bid deposit. A notice containing the information set out in the resolution must be published at least once and not less than thirty days before the auction. The highest bid is reported to the governing board, which then has thirty days to accept or reject it.

For personal property, the same procedure is followed except that (1) the governing board may in the resolution authorize an appropriate official to complete the sale at the auction and (2) the notice must be published not less than ten days before the auction.

G.S. 160A-270(c) permits a local government to sell either real or personal property electronically. The governing board must follow the same procedures as set out above, but in addition the notice must specify the electronic address where information about the property to be sold can be found and the electronic address at which electronic bids may be posted. In recent years, electronic auctions through sites such as GovDeals[94] have largely replaced public auctions and have become the most common method of competitive sale disposal for personal property.

Exchange of Property

Under state law, a local government may exchange any real or personal property for other real or personal property if it receives full and fair consideration for the property.[95] After the terms of the exchange agreement are developed by private negotiations, the governing board will authorize the exchange at a regular meeting. A notice of intent to make the exchange must be published at least ten days before it occurs. The notice must describe the properties involved; give the value of each, as well as the value of other consideration changing hands; and cite the date of the regular meeting at which the board proposes to confirm the exchange.

---

94. Government, educational, and related entities use the site, www.govdeals.com, for the sale of surplus assets to the public.

95. G.S. 160A-271. For a more detailed discussion of exchanging property, see David M. Lawrence, *Local Government Property Transactions in North Carolina*, 2nd ed. (UNC Institute of Government, 2000).

Trade-In

A local government may convey surplus property as a "trade-in" as part of a purchase contract (G.S. 143-129.7). The local government must include a description of the surplus property in its bid specifications, and the amount offered by bidders for the surplus property is taken into account when evaluating bids. The unit awards one contract to the winning bidder for both the sale of the surplus property and the purchase of the new property. While the purchase contract must comply with the applicable competitive bidding requirements, the transaction need not comply with the exchange of property procedures in G.S. 160A-271.

Private Negotiation and Sale: Personal Property

A local government may use private negotiation and sale to dispose of personal property valued at less than $30,000 for any one item or any group of similar items (G.S. 160A-266, -267). Note that this procedure may not be used to dispose of real property. Under G.S. 160A-266(b) and -267, the governing board, by resolution adopted at a regular meeting, may authorize an appropriate official to dispose of identified property by private sale. The board may set a minimum price but is not required to do so. The resolution must be published at least ten days before the sale.

Alternatively, G.S. 160A-266(c) authorizes a governing board to establish procedures under which county or city officials may dispose of personal property valued at less than $30,000 for any one item or any group of similar items without further board action and without published notice. The procedures must be designed to secure fair market value for the property disposed of and to accomplish the disposal efficiently and economically. The procedures may permit one or more officials to declare qualifying property to be surplus, to set its market value, and to sell it by public or private sale. The board may require the official to use one of the statutory methods, including an electronic auction, or may permit other sorts of procedures, such as a consignment agent or a surplus property warehouse. The statute requires the selling official to maintain a record of property sold under any such procedures.

Private Negotiation and Conveyance to Other Governments

G.S. 160A-274 authorizes any governmental unit in the state, on terms and conditions it "deems wise," to sell to, purchase from, exchange with, lease to, or lease from any other governmental unit in North Carolina any interest in real or personal property that one or the other unit may own. "Governmental unit" is defined to include cities, counties, the state, school units, and other state and local agencies. The only limitations on this broad authority are that before a local board of education may lease real property that it owns, it must determine that the property is unnecessary or undesirable for school purposes, and it may not lease the property for less than $1 per year.[96] While governing board approval is required, bids or published notices are not. Thus, when reaching agreements on property with another governmental unit, a unit's governing board has full discretion concerning procedure.

---

96. Although in general local governments may transfer property among themselves without monetary consideration, the North Carolina Supreme Court has held that a local school board must receive fair consideration whenever it conveys property for some non-school use, including some other governmental use. Boney v. Bd. of Trs., 229 N.C. 136 (1948). The $1 requirement for leases of school property presumably is a legislative determination that this amount is adequate consideration when title to the property remains with the school administrative unit.

Other Negotiated Conveyances: Real and Personal Property

A city or county may, in limited circumstances, convey real and personal property by private negotiation and sale, and sometimes without monetary consideration.

Economic Development

G.S. 158-7.1(d) permits a county or city (but no other form of local government) to convey interests in property suitable for economic development by private sale. Before making such a conveyance, the governing board must hold a public hearing with at least ten days' published notice of the hearing. The notice must describe the interest to be conveyed; the value of the interest; the proposed consideration the government will receive; and the board's intention to approve the conveyance. In addition, before making the conveyance the board must determine the probable average wage that will be paid to workers at the business to be located on the property.

The statute requires the governing board to determine the fair market value of the property and prohibits the board from conveying the property for less than that value. The county or city, in arriving at the amount of consideration it will receive, may count prospective tax revenues for the next ten years from improvements added to the property after the conveyance; prospective sales tax revenues generated by the business located on the property during that period; and any other income coming to the government during the ten years as a result of the conveyance.

Community Development

G.S. 160D-1312 permits a city (but not a county or any other sort of local government) to convey interests in property by private sale when such property is within a community development project area. The property must be sold subject to covenants that restrict its eventual use to those consistent with the community development plan for the project area. The statute requires that the property be appraised before it is sold and prohibits the city from selling it for less than the appraised value.

Once a city has reached agreement on a conveyance pursuant to this statute, it must publish notice of a public hearing on the transaction for the two weeks running up to the hearing. The notice should describe the property, disclose the terms of the transaction, and give notice of the city's intention to convey the property. At the hearing itself, the city must disclose the appraised value of the property.

Nonprofit Agencies

G.S. 160A-279 permits a county or city to convey real or personal property to any nonprofit agency to which it is authorized by law to appropriate funds, although property acquired through condemnation may not be so conveyed. The same procedures must be followed as are required by G.S. 160A-267 for other private sales. In making a conveyance under this statute, a county or city may accept as consideration the nonprofit agency's promise to put the property to some public use. G.S. 160A-280 authorizes conveyances of personal property to nonprofits and governmental entities outside of the state.

Property for Affordable Housing

Both counties and cities may convey property by private sale in order to provide affordable housing (i.e., housing for persons of low or moderate income) pursuant to G.S. 160D-1316. This statute allows local government to make two sorts of conveyances. First, a local government may convey residential property directly to persons of low or moderate income; if it does so, it must follow the same procedures as are required by G.S. 160A-267 for other private sales. Second, a local government may convey property to a public or private entity that provides affordable housing for others, so long as the local government imposes conditions or covenants to ensure that the property will be used as affordable housing.

A complicated series of statutes permits cities to convey property specifically to nonprofit entities that will construct affordable housing. First, G.S. 160D-1311 permits a city council to exercise any power granted by law to a housing authority. Second, G.S. 157-9 authorizes a housing authority to provide "housing projects," a term defined in G.S. 157-3 to include programs that assist developers and owners of affordable housing. Third, G.S. 160A-20.1 permits a city to appropriate money to a private organization to do anything a city is authorized to do, including providing affordable housing. And fourth, G.S. 160A-279, summarized above, authorizes a city to convey property to any nonprofit agency to which it may appropriate money.

Fire or Rescue Services

G.S. 160A-277 permits counties and cities to lease or convey to volunteer fire departments or rescue squads serving their jurisdictions land to be used for constructing or expanding fire or rescue facilities. The governing board must approve the transaction by adoption of a resolution at a regular meeting after ten days' published notice. The notice should describe the property, state its value, set out the proposed monetary consideration or the lack thereof, and declare the board's intention to approve the transaction. (Almost all fire or rescue organizations are nonprofit in nature, so a local government may also use G.S. 160A-279 to convey property to them, including personal property; G.S. 160A-280 also provides authority for donating personal property to these nonprofit organizations.)

Architectural and Cultural Property

G.S. 160A-266(b) permits a county or city to convey, after private negotiation, real or personal property that is significant for its archaeological, architectural, artistic, cultural, or historic associations; for its association with such property; or for its natural, scenic, or open condition. The conveyance must be to a nonprofit corporation or trust whose purposes include the preservation or the conservation of such property, and the deed must include covenants and other restrictions securing and promoting the property's protection.[97] A local government making a conveyance under this provision must follow the same procedures as noted earlier for the private sale of real or personal property under G.S. 160A-267.

Open Space

G.S. 160D-1303 permits a local government to conserve open space by acquiring title to property, then conveying it to the original owner or to a new owner, in each case subject to covenants that require the property to be maintained as open space. If the conveyance is back to the original owner, the statute permits it to be made by private sale. If the conveyance is to an appropriate entity, it may be made by private sale pursuant to G.S. 160A-266(b), discussed earlier. Otherwise, however, the government must use one of the competitive sale methods.

97. These deed restrictions must be in the form of a preservation agreement or conservation agreement as defined in G.S. 121-35.

Other Private Conveyances

A number of other statutes permit private sales of property in narrow circumstances; only one of these statutes includes any required procedures.

1. G.S. 160A-321 permits the private sale of any entire city enterprise. Unless the enterprise is conveyed to another government, however, the statute requires the city's voters to approve the conveyance for the following kinds of enterprises: electric power distribution; natural gas distribution; public transportation; cable television; and stormwater management.
2. G.S. 105-376(c) permits a government that has acquired property through a tax foreclosure to convey the property back to the original owner or to any other person or entity that had an interest in the property (such as a deed of trust).
3. G.S. 153A-163 permits a government that has acquired property through a loan foreclosure to sell the property by private sale, so long as it receives at least as much as it paid for the property.
4. G.S. 153A-177 permits a government that has been given property for a specified purpose to give the property back to the donor if it will not use the property for the specified purpose.
5. G.S. 40A-70 permits a government that has acquired property through eminent domain which it no longer needs to convey the property back to the condemnee, so long as the government receives in return its original purchase price, the cost of any improvements, and interest.
6. G.S. 160A-342 permits a city that operates a cemetery to convey it to a private operator of cemeteries upon the condition that the property will continue to be used as a cemetery.
7. G.S. 17F-20 permits a unit's governing board to convey a law enforcement officer's badge and service side arm to a retiring law enforcement officer or to the family of an officer killed in the line of duty.
8. G.S. 17F-21 authorizes government agencies to convey a retiring law enforcement service animal to the animal's handler or to an organization that provides services for retired service animals at a price and under terms and conditions set by the local government.

Lease of Property

A county or city may lease any real or personal property it owns that its governing board finds will not be needed during the term of the lease—in essence, the county or city is permitted to make a temporary disposal of the property since the lease agreement gives exclusive use of the property to the lessee (G.S. 160A-272). The procedure to be followed depends on the length of the lease. The board may, by resolution at any meeting, make leases for one year or less. It may also authorize the unit's manager or some other administrative officer to take similar action concerning government property for the same period.

The governing board may lease government-owned property for periods longer than one year and for up to ten years by a resolution adopted at a regular meeting after ten days' published notice of its intention to do so. The notice must also specify the annual lease payment and give the date of the meeting at which the board proposes to approve the action.

A lease for longer than ten years, including renewal periods, must be treated, for procedural purposes, as if it were a sale of property. It may be executed by following any procedure authorized for selling real property.[98]

Grant of Easements

A county or city may grant easements over, through, under, or across any of its property (G.S. 160A-273). The authorization should be by resolution of the governing board at a regular meeting. No special published notice is required, nor is the grant subject to competition.

Sale of Stocks, Bonds, and Other Securities

A county or city that owns stocks, bonds, or other securities that are traded on the national stock exchanges or over the counter by brokers and securities dealers may sell them in the same way and under the same conditions as a private owner would (G.S. 160A-276).

Property Disposal under the Uniform Guidance

Disposition of federally funded property by a recipient must follow the rules found in the Property Standards section within Subpart D of the Uniform Guidance. The Property Standards classify four major categories of property: real property, equipment, supplies, and intangible property.[99] If federal funds have been used to purchase property, title to the property typically vests in the recipient. However, the Uniform Guidance establishes a "property trust relationship" for real property, equipment, and intangible property acquired or improved using federal funds. This means that for those specific property types, the property is held in trust by the recipient as trustee for the beneficiaries of the program under which the property was acquired or improved.[100] This section focuses on the disposition rules for real property and equipment and supplies. In any instance, disposition of federally funded property must also comply with disposition rules in North Carolina state law, meaning, for example, that even if a federal awarding agency allows a recipient to sell real property, a unit of local government must still follow the procedures required for the sale of real property under Article 12 of G.S. Chapter 160A that were discussed earlier.

Real Property

When real property is no longer needed by a recipient for its original federally funded purpose, the Uniform Guidance provides recipients with three disposition options: paying the federal awarding agency and retaining title to the property, selling the property and compensating the federal awarding agency, or transferring title of the property to the federal awarding agency.[101] The formula for

98. Leases of government property for siting and operation of renewable energy facilities, communications towers, and components of wired or wireless networks in limited circumstances may be for a term of up to twenty-five years without having to be treated as a sale of property.

99. There is an additional category of "exempt property" in the Uniform Guidance. Exempt property is property acquired under a federal award where the federal awarding agency has chosen to vest title to the property to the recipient without further responsibility to the federal government. 2 C.F.R. § 200.312.

100. 2 C.F.R. § 200.316. The U.S. Department of Commerce has further explained that the federal awarding agency retains an undivided equitable reversionary interest in the property and that an agency may assert its equitable reversionary interest in the project if a recipient is failing to meet its obligation of using the property to serve the purpose of the federal program. *See* U.S. Department of Commerce, *Grants and Cooperative Agreements Manual* (2021), www.commerce.gov/oam/files/grants-and-cooperative-agreements-grants-manual-april-20-2021.

101. 2 C.F.R. § 200.311. The Uniform Guidance defines real property as land, including land improvements, structures, and appurtenances but excluding movable machinery and equipment. 2 C.F.R. § 200.1.

calculating the actual amount to be paid to the federal awarding agency varies depending on the option but generally involves paying the awarding agency an amount proportional to the agency's contribution toward the property acquisition or improvement.

Equipment and Supplies

Disposition of federally funded equipment is required when it is no longer needed for the original project or for activities funded by the federal award.[102] A recipient will need to request disposition instructions from the federal awarding agency, unless such instructions are identified in the federal award's terms and conditions. If the federal awarding agency fails to provide disposition instructions within 120 days of the request, or if the items of equipment have a current per-unit fair market value of $5,000 or more, a recipient may either retain or sell the federally funded equipment.[103] Proper sales procedures must be established to ensure the highest possible return. The federal awarding agency is entitled to an amount calculated by multiplying the current market value or proceeds from the sale by the federal percentage of participation in the cost of the original purchase.[104] Items of equipment with a current per-unit fair market value of $5,000 or less may be retained, sold, or otherwise disposed of with no further obligation to the federal awarding agency, but a recipient must still request disposition instructions from that agency.[105]

Once supplies that were purchased with federal funds are no longer needed for any federal award and the aggregate value of the unused supplies exceeds $5,000, a recipient must retain or sell the supplies and must compensate the federal awarding agency for its share.[106] The compensation due to the awarding agency is calculated in the same manner as equipment under 2 C.F.R. § 200.313(e)(2).

Additional Resources

Bluestein, Frayda S. *A Legal Guide to Purchasing and Contracting for North Carolina Local Governments.* 2nd ed. Chapel Hill: UNC Institute of Government, 2004.

Houston, Norma R. *A Legal Guide to Construction Contracting with North Carolina Local Governments.* 5th ed. Chapel Hill: UNC School of Government, 2015.

———. *North Carolina Local Government Contracting: Quick Reference and Related Statutes.* Chapel Hill: UNC School of Government, 2014.

Lawrence, David M. *Local Government Property Transactions in North Carolina.* 2nd ed. Chapel Hill: UNC Institute of Government, 2000.

School of Government materials on purchasing and construction contracting, available at www.sog.unc.edu/resources/microsites/local-government-purchasing-and-contracting.

---

102. 2 C.F.R. § 200.313(e). The Uniform Guidance defines equipment as tangible personal property (including information technology systems) having a useful life of more than one year and a per-unit acquisition cost which equals or exceeds $5,000. 2 C.F.R. § 200.1.

103. 2 C.F.R. § 200.313(e)(2).

104. 2 C.F.R. § 200.313(e)(2). The federal awarding agency may permit the recipient to deduct and retain from the federal share $500 or 10 percent of the proceeds, whichever is less, for its selling and handling expenses. The Uniform Guidance does not explain how a recipient can accomplish this deduction, but presumably a recipient should ask for this deduction in its request for disposition instructions.

105. 2 C.F.R. § 200.313(e)(1).

106. 2 C.F.R. § 314. Supplies means all tangible personal property other than property described in the definition of *equipment.*

Appendix 23.1 Dollar Thresholds in North Carolina Public Contracting Statutes

Dollar limits and statutory authority current as of January 1, 2025

Requirement	Threshold	Statute
Formal bidding	***(estimated cost of contract)***	
Construction or repair contracts	$500,000 *and above*	G.S. 143-129
Purchase of apparatus, supplies, materials, and equipment	$90,000 *and above*	G.S. 143-129
Informal bidding	***(actual cost of contract)***	
Construction or repair contracts	$30,000 to formal limit	G.S. 143-131
Purchase of apparatus, supplies, materials, and equipment	$30,000 to formal limit	G.S. 143-131
Construction methods required for building projects	***(estimated cost of project)***	**G.S. 143-128(a1)**
Separate-Prime	*Over* $300,000	
Single-Prime	*Over* $300,000	
Dual Bidding	*Over* $300,000	
Construction Management at Risk	*Over* $300,000	G.S. 143-128.1
Design-Build	*Over* $300,000	G.S. 143-128.1A
Design-Build Bridging	*Over* $300,000	G.S. 143-128.1B
Public-Private Partnership (P3)	*Over* $300,000	G.S. 143-128.1C
Historically Underutilized Business (HUB) requirements		
Building construction or repair projects		
— Projects with state funding *(verifiable 10% goal required)*	$100,000 *or more*	G.S. 143-128.2(a)
— Locally funded projects *(formal HUB requirements)*	$300,000 *or more*	G.S. 143-128.2(j)
— Projects in informal bidding range *(informal HUB requirements)*	$30,000 to $500,000*	G.S. 143-131(b)
**Note: Formal HUB requirements should be used for informally bid projects costing between $300,000 and $500,000*		
Limit on use of own forces (force account work)	***(not to exceed)***	**G.S. 143-135**
Construction or repair projects	$500,000 *(total project cost)* or $200,000 *(labor-only cost)**	
**Note: Thresholds differ for State agencies and the University of North Carolina and its constituent institutions.*		
Bid bond or deposit		
Construction or repair contracts *(at least 5% of bid amount)*	Formal bids *($500,000 and above)*	G.S. 143-129(b)
Purchase contracts	Not required	
Performance/Payment bonds		
Construction or repair contracts *(100% of contract amount)*	Each contract *over* $50,000 of project costing *over* $300,000	G.S. 143-129(c); G.S 44A-26
Purchase contracts	Not required	
General contractor's license required	**$40,000 *and above***	**G.S. 87-1**
Exemption	Force account work *(see above)*	
Owner-builder affidavit required	Force account work *(see above)*	G.S. 87-14(a)(1)
Use of licensed architect or engineer required		
Nonstructural work	$300,000 *and above*	G.S. 133-1.1(a)
Structural repair, additions, or new construction	$135,000 *and above*	
Repair work affecting life safety systems	$100,000 *and above*	
Selection of architect, engineer, surveyor, construction manager at risk, or design-build contractor		
"Qualification-Based Selection" procedure (QBS)	All contracts unless exempted	G.S. 143-64.31
Exemption authorized	Only specific projects where estimated fee is *less than* $50,000	G.S. 143-64.32

Adapted from *A Legal Guide to Purchasing and Contracting for North Carolina Local Governments*, 2nd ed., by Frayda S. Bluestein,

Chapter 24

Eminent Domain

Charles Szypszak

Charles Szypszak is a School of Government faculty member who specializes in real estate matters.

The United States Constitution forbids government from taking private property "for public use without just compensation" or "without due process of law."[1] The North Carolina Constitution guarantees that no person may be deprived of property "but by the law of the land."[2] The North Carolina Constitution does not expressly give government bodies a right to take private property, but the state's courts have deemed such a power of eminent domain to be inherent in the power to govern and to be essential to the government's ability to provide for the public welfare.

Whenever counties and cities exercise their powers of eminent domain, they must abide by the constitutional requirements of taking property only for public uses and benefits and paying the owners just compensation for the property taken. No power of eminent domain exists unless the legislature has invoked the authority by legislation. The authority of counties and cities to take private property by eminent domain is expressed in Chapter 40A of the North Carolina General Statutes (hereinafter G.S.), which identifies the allowed public purposes for a taking and the procedure for exercising it.[3] Other statutes describe additional public purposes and benefits for which certain districts, authorities, and organizations may take private property.

Compliance with the statutory requirements is important to avoid objections and complications, so any county or city that is taking property by eminent domain should review the current version of the statutes to confirm the existence of authority for the action and to ensure compliance with procedural requirements.

1. U.S. Const. amend. V.
2. N.C. Const. art. I, § 19.
3. Chapter 40A, Article 1 of the North Carolina General Statutes (hereinafter G.S.).

Public and Private Condemnors

The governing body of a county or city is a "public condemnor," as are certain other authorities such as sanitary district boards, hospital and housing authorities, community college boards of trustees, and regional transportation authorities, among others.[4] "Private condemnors" that have a statutory power of eminent domain include railroads, utilities, private educational institutions for water supply purposes, and union bus station companies.[5]

Authorized Public Uses and Benefits

The condemnation statute identifies a number of purposes for which public condemnors may use the power of eminent domain, including

- roads, streets, alleys, and sidewalks;
- systems for water supply and distribution, wastewater, septic, solid waste, and stormwater management;
- airports;
- parking;
- public transportation;
- electric and gas power generation, transmission, and distribution under defined circumstances (cities only);
- parks, playgrounds, and other recreational facilities;
- storm sewer and drainage systems;
- hospital facilities, cemeteries, and libraries;
- city halls, fire stations, office buildings, jails, and other buildings for use by any department, board, commission, or agency;
- drainage programs and programs to prevent obstruction to the natural flow of streams or to improve drainage facilities;
- acquisition of designated historical properties;
- public wharves;
- beach erosion control and flood and hurricane protection; and
- access to public trust beaches and related parking areas (in certain coastal counties and cities).[6]

Local government condemnation authority extends to land outside the local government's boundaries for these authorized purposes.[7] The statutes require most, but not all, local governments and authorities seeking to use eminent domain to acquire land in another county to obtain the consent of the other county's board of commissioners.[8] Other recognized public purposes are identified in statutes creating public bodies or establishing public programs: for example, G.S. 160A-515 allows urban redevelopment commissions to take blighted parcels of property, while G.S. 115C-517 allows local boards of education to acquire suitable sites for schoolhouses or other school facilities.

---

4. G.S. 40A-3(b), (c).
5. G.S. 40A-3(a).
6. G.S. 40A-3(b).
7. *Id.*
8. G.S. 153A-15.

Counties and cities may not condemn property owned by the State of North Carolina unless the state consents to the taking. The state's consent is given by the Council of State or by the Secretary of Administration if the council delegates that authority to the secretary. When state property is taken, the only issue is the compensation to be paid.[9] Except as otherwise provided by statute, public condemnors may take private condemnors' property if the property is not in actual public use or is not necessary to the operation of the owner's business. A public condemnor may condemn another public condemnor's property if the property is not being used or held for future use for any governmental or proprietary purpose.[10]

Just Compensation

The owner is entitled to be paid "just compensation" for the property taken, which must reflect the property's fair market value as of the date immediately before the county or city files a complaint.[11] Fair market value is based on the highest and best uses available for the property, not just the actual uses to which the property has been put. The analysis assumes a ready and able buyer who is willing but not compelled to buy.[12] The usual approach is market comparison based on recent sales data for properties similarly configured, with adjustments for material differences. If only part of a tract is taken, the measure of compensation is the greater of two calculations. The first is diminution in value, which is the amount by which the fair market value of the entire tract immediately before the taking exceeded the fair market value of the remainder immediately after the taking. The second is the fair market value of the part of the property that was taken.[13] In the case of an easement, the assessment of diminution in value, if any, will include consideration of the impact on the value of the property outside the easement area. The compensation will not include changes in value before the date of valuation that were caused by the proposed improvement or project for which the property is taken.[14] Possible future loss of profits for a business operating on the property affected by the taking is not an element of compensable loss, although the anticipated income stream for income-producing property is sometimes an appropriate element of appraisal of the real estate value.

The condemnor may allow the owner to remove timber, buildings, fixtures, and improvements that are not needed for the intended condemnation use. If the compensation award deducted the value of these materials and the owner does not remove them within a reasonable time, the removal and storage cost is chargeable to the owner and secured by a lien on any remaining part of the owner's property.[15]

Condemnation Procedure

In many cases, the condemning authority and the property owner will be able to reach an agreement on the taking and the amount of compensation for it, usually based on appraisal reports. When

9. G.S. 40A-5.
10. G.S. 40A-5(b).
11. G.S. 40A-63.
12. Barnes v. N.C. State Highway Comm'n, 250 N.C. 378, 387–88, 109 S.E.2d 219, 220–21 (1959).
13. G.S. 40A-64.
14. G.S. 40A-65.
15. G.S. 40A-9.

such an agreement cannot be reached, any dispute about the legitimacy of the public purpose for which the property is being taken will be determined by a superior court, and disagreements about the amount of compensation will be determined by the court or by commissioners appointed by the superior court clerk.

Negotiations and Right of Entry

The public condemnor may negotiate with an owner about acquiring the property without impairing its power to take the property by eminent domain. The statute provides that the power to acquire property by condemnation does not depend on any prior effort to acquire the same property by gift or purchase, nor is the power to negotiate for the gift or the purchase of property impaired by initiation of a condemnation proceeding.[16] A condemnor who seeks to acquire property by purchase or gift must give the owner a written notice of the owner's right to reimbursement of taxes allocable to the period before the taking.[17]

With thirty days' advance notice to the landowner, a condemnor may enter on private land, but not structures, to make surveys, borings, examinations, or appraisals without filing a complaint, making a deposit, or taking any other formal action. The condemnor must reimburse the owner for any damages resulting from these activities.[18]

Notice

At least thirty days before filing a complaint for condemnation, the condemnor must give written notice to the owner of the condemnor's intent to institute such an action.[19] This notice must contain information prescribed by G.S. 40A-40, including a description of the property to be taken and the condemnor's estimate of the just compensation, the purpose for which the property is being taken, and the date the condemnor intends to file a complaint.[20] Additional notice requirements apply to condemnation actions in which title will vest upon the filing of the complaint and deposit—the so-called quick take procedure, described below.[21]

Complaint, Registry Memorandum, and Deposit

A public condemnor institutes an eminent domain action by filing a complaint in the superior court of the county in which the land is located, with a declaration of taking. The complaint must include a statement of the authority under which the taking is occurring, a description of the property, the purpose of the condemnation, information about the owner's identity, the estimated just compensation, a statement about whether any improvements may be removed by the owner, a description of any known liens, and a request for a determination of just compensation.[22] The condemnor must deposit the amount of estimated compensation with the court when the complaint is filed.[23] This means that condemning authorities must already have the funds for the estimated compensation at the time the eminent domain procedure is begun. At the same time, the condemnor also must

16. G.S. 40A-4.
17. G.S. 40A-4, -6.
18. G.S. 40A-11.
19. G.S. 40A-40.
20. G.S. 40A-40(a).
21. G.S. 40A-40(b).
22. G.S. 40A-41.
23. *Id.*

give third parties constructive notice of the pending condemnation by recording a memorandum of action with the register of deeds in any county where involved land is located.[24]

The summons, together with a copy of the complaint and a notice of the deposit, is served on the named parties.[25]

Disbursement of Deposit

When there is no dispute about title, the persons named in the complaint may apply to the court for disbursement of all or part of the deposit, without prejudice to the owner's challenge to the sufficiency of the compensation. The condemnor is not entitled to notice of a hearing on the owner's request for disbursement of the deposit.[26]

Transfer of Title

The point at which the condemnor becomes owner of the property depends on the condemnation's purpose. When a county or city condemns property for certain listed purposes, the title to the property and the right to immediate possession vest when the complaint is filed and the deposit is made. This is known as the "quick take" procedure. It applies to such uses as roads, water and wastewater systems, solid waste collection and disposal, and city systems for electricity, gas, cable, and storm sewer and drainage. It also applies to certain beachfront communities for beach erosion control and flood and hurricane protection and for public trust beaches and related parking areas. The quick take procedure does not apply to property to be taken for public transportation systems, off-street parking facilities, airports, and certain other purposes.[27]

When the title does not transfer upon the filing of the complaint, the timing of the transfer depends on the course of the condemnation proceeding. If the owner does not dispute the taking but only the amount of compensation, the title vests when the owner files the answer stating this to be so. If the owner fails to file an answer within 120 days, the title vests when the deadline passes. The title also vests upon disbursement of the deposit at the owner's request. The owner may seek an injunction to prevent the title from vesting.[28]

Answer and Reply

The owner has 120 days to file an answer admitting or denying the allegations of the complaint and stating any affirmative defenses. No answer is filed to the declaration of taking and notice of deposit. The condemnor may file a reply within thirty days of receipt of the answer.[29] If an owner does not file an answer as required, the owner is deemed to have admitted that the amount deposited is just compensation. In such a case, the judge enters final judgment and orders disbursement of the deposited money.[30]

Within ninety days after receipt of the answer, but no sooner than six months after filing the complaint, the condemnor must file a plat of the property taken and of such other areas as are necessary for a determination of the compensation, and this plat is mailed to the parties or counsel.[31]

24. G.S. 40A-43.
25. G.S. 40A-41.
26. G.S. 40A-44.
27. G.S. 40A-42(a).
28. G.S. 40A-42.
29. G.S. 40A-45, -46.
30. G.S. 40A-46.
31. G.S. 40A-45(c).

The court will appoint an attorney to represent any party in interest who is unknown or cannot be found, as may occur when the current holder of an interest in property cannot be determined based on the available public records. In addition, the court will appoint a guardian ad litem to represent those who do not have the legal capacity to defend themselves, such as children or those under a legal disability.[32]

Challenge to Taking

Challenges to the sufficiency of the public purpose for the taking, the condemnor's authority, the area taken, the presence of necessary parties, or any other matters besides the amount of just compensation will be heard and decided by a judge. Either party may raise these issues by motion to the court with ten days' notice.[33]

Appointment and Duties of Commissioners

If the owner disputes the condemnor's just compensation amount, either the owner or the condemnor may, within sixty days after the answer has been filed, request the clerk of superior court to appoint commissioners. The clerk then appoints three competent, disinterested persons who reside in the county to serve as commissioners. The commissioners have the power to inspect the property, hold hearings, swear witnesses, and take evidence as they deem necessary. When they have completed these tasks, they must file with the court a report on a statutorily prescribed form reciting the formalities of the process and stating the amount of compensation. The clerk mails a copy to the parties or their counsel.[34]

If no request is made for commissioners, the case is placed on the court's civil docket for trial to determine the amount of compensation.[35]

Challenge to the Commissioners' Determination

Either party has thirty days after the commissioners' report is mailed to challenge the commissioners' determination and demand a trial on the issue of compensation. The trial will be by jury unless both parties waive the right. The issue of compensation is newly determined by the jury or court based on evidence presented at the trial; the amount of the deposit and the commissioners' determination are not considered. If no exception is filed, the judge still reviews the commissioners' award to determine if it is just, and if it is so determined, the award is entered as a final judgment. If the judge decides the award is not just, the amount is set aside and the matter is set for a trial.[36]

Costs and Interest

An owner is entitled to interest on the award at the rate of 6 percent from the date of taking to the date of judgment, but not on the deposit amount for the period after it was made.[37] The court has the power to order a condemnor to pay an owner's court costs.[38] The court has discretion to order the condemnor to pay the owner's costs of appraisers, engineers, and plats used as evidence in the procedure,[39] and courts typically do order such reimbursement in eminent domain cases. If the

32. G.S. 40A-50.
33. G.S. 40A-47.
34. G.S. 40A-48.
35. G.S. 40A-49.
36. G.S. 40A-48(d).
37. G.S. 40A-53.
38. G.S. 40A-13.
39. G.S. 40A-8(a).

condemnor abandons the condemnation after filing a complaint or is determined not to have had authority for the taking, the court may award the owner compensation for costs, disbursements, expenses, and loss suffered as a result of not being able to transfer title during the proceeding.[40] Owners are also entitled to such compensation if they were forced to bring an action to recover compensation for a taking not instituted by the condemnor.[41]

Inverse Condemnation

A government's occupation or use of property without having followed the eminent domain procedure is referred to as "inverse condemnation," a term that reflects the reversal of the parties' usual roles in the exchange of property rights for compensation. When this happens, a landowner may file an action to compel the government to pay for what it already took without following an authorized eminent domain proceeding. This may occur, for example, if a local government widens a public road beyond the area in which public rights already exist or installs a public utility line across private property without following the eminent domain procedure and paying the landowners the value of what was taken.

The North Carolina Supreme Court described the circumstances under which a taking occurs as follows: "'Taking' under the power of eminent domain may be defined generally as entering upon private property for more than a momentary period and, under the warrant or color of legal authority, devoting it to a public use, or otherwise informally appropriating or injuriously affecting it in such a way as substantially to oust the owner and deprive him of all beneficial enjoyment thereof.'"[42] No claim to inverse condemnation is implicated by normal land use regulations or permitting requirements. The courts deem government to have a "police power" to restrict property use to protect public health and safety. Consequently, owners' rights are subject to changes in regulations governing the nature and extent of permissible property uses. A claim to compensation would only be implicated if the restrictions were not reasonably necessary for public health and safety or the interference was deemed entirely unreasonable.[43]

By statute, an owner may begin an inverse condemnation action for compensation within twenty-four months of the date of the taking or the completion of the public project, whichever occurs later.[44] The procedure in such cases is similar to that in cases in which the action is begun by the condemnor. If the public project has discrete subparts, the statute of limitations is measured from the date when the effects of the subparts become apparent rather than from when the overall project commences.

---

40. G.S. 40A-8(b).
41. G.S. 40A-8(c).
42. Ledford v. N.C. State Highway Comm'n, 279 N.C. 188, 190–91, 181 S.E.2d 466, 468 (1971).
43. Responsible Citizens in Opposition to the Flood Plain Ordinance v. City of Asheville, 308 N.C. 255, 261–62, 302 S.E.2d 204, 208 (1983).
44. G.S. 40A-51(a).

PART 6. Planning, Development Regulation, Community and Economic Development

Chapter 25

Planning, Land Use, and Development

James L. Joyce

James L. Joyce is a faculty member at the School of Government whose areas of expertise include land use regulation, annexation, and local government environmental regulation.

This chapter updates and revises the previous chapter authored by Richard Ducker. Professor Ducker's expertise and contributions to the field and to this publication are gratefully acknowledged.

As far as most North Carolina communities are concerned, growth, development, and change are desirable and probably essential. For many North Carolina communities some form of growth, development, and change is inevitable, while for others growth must be encouraged if it is to happen. Will these changes be haphazard and unpredictable or organized and purposeful? The effectiveness of a community's local planning program will determine the answer. Community planning is based on the premise that the community as a whole has a substantial stake in determining how, when, and where it should grow or develop. It is concerned about capturing the benefits of change and avoiding its pitfalls. North Carolina local governments have a number of tools to use in influencing development. However these tools are used, effective planning also means cooperating intelligently with the inevitable.

At the core of most city or county planning is *land use and development planning.* Land use and development planning involves the application of the planning process to all public and private activities that affect the physical use and development of land, which in turn affect the growth and the character of a community. Some jurisdictions view land use planning as simply an aspect of *community development*, emphasizing that the economic and social development of the community is closely related to its physical development. Many cities and some counties consider growth management to be an especially important aspect of community planning. For others, the task is simply one of managing to grow. No matter the terminology used, influencing the use and development of land is a crucial function of local government.

One feature of land use planning that distinguishes it from many other types of public planning is its concern with private sector activities as well as those of the public sector. Some local governments view their function in this regard as simply accommodating or responding to the growth that private development generates and providing public services wherever and whenever they are needed. It is also undeniable, however, that the location of a new highway, the extension of utilities, or the standards of a zoning regulation may strongly influence the location, type, and timing of private development. This interplay between public and private activities creates the need for community planning.

A city or county may influence development by (1) establishing clear plans and policies providing direction to citizens, businesses, the development community, and other units of government in matters of growth and development; (2) constructing and maintaining public facilities (streets, utilities, parks, schools, and so forth) and providing services in connection with them; (3) regulating the use, development, and maintenance of private and public property (for example, through zoning and subdivision regulations, a minimum housing code, and so forth); and (4) extending subsidies, loans, and financial incentives to induce private parties to act consistently with municipal objectives.

Since community planning involves so much coordination and facilitation, these approaches are often combined. For example, in a community development block grant area, a local government may install drainage facilities and make street improvements while offering subsidized housing rehabilitation loans to property owners in the affected area. Planners concerned about revitalizing a central business district may suggest landscaping plans or building facade designs for downtown merchants who wish to upgrade the area. At the same time, the zoning regulation may establish sign standards and height limits in the same area.

Much of the de facto planning a local government carries out does not primarily involve local staff planners. Street design standards are established in public works departments, and community public reinvestment programs are handled by community development. Utility extension planning may implicate a joint utility provider, and the North Carolina Department of Transportation makes critical road network decisions. Working together to achieve community policy can be both conceptually and practically difficult, but it also illustrates the need for all local government staff and officials to be mindful of its importance.

An Update Long in the Making

North Carolina is a state in which local government authority comes exclusively from legislative grant.[1] For decades, the statutes granting land use regulatory authority to cities and counties were split between Chapter 153A, Article 18 (for counties) and Chapter 160A, Article 19 (for cities) of the North Carolina General Statutes (hereinafter G.S.). Over the years, these statutes had accumulated a number of quirks, inconsistencies, and bits of archaic language. In 2019, a yearslong effort to reorganize and update the planning and development regulation statutes culminated in the adoption of a new Chapter 160D, which consolidated and replaced the separate city and county statutes for development regulation.[2] Chapter 160D also pulled in other statutory provisions related to land use regulation, such as rules for adult businesses, family care homes, and airports, that had been scattered across the General Statutes. While Chapter 160D reorganized the development regulation statutes in a more coherent format, it retained the general scope of authority granted to local governments in prior law, save for a few minor clarifying amendments and consensus reforms.[3]

Land Use and Comprehensive Planning

The centerpiece of a local planning program is a *land use plan* or *comprehensive plan*. A land use plan or comprehensive plan provides a community with an overview of its current physical development and serves as a guide for its future development policy. A land use plan traditionally includes an analysis of current conditions, projections of population growth, and a discussion of current and future land development patterns. It also recommends areas best suited for different kinds of development, such as rural preservation, residential use, high-traffic commerce, and industrial areas. A comprehensive plan includes a land use element but often also includes other elements such as transportation, recreational and open space areas, economic development, and housing.

One of the consensus reforms introduced along with Chapter 160D was a provision that, in order to adopt and enforce zoning regulations, a local government must adopt and reasonably maintain a land use plan or a comprehensive plan.[4] As of 2022, eleven other states required local governments to prepare and adopt comprehensive plans.[5] Those North Carolina counties subject to the Coastal Area Management Act (CAMA) have for decades had to prepare land use plans under that law,[6] but no North Carolina law required the adoption of a plan as a condition of applying zoning regulation. The new statute does not mandate the contents of the plan, though it includes a list of elements that it *may* address.[7]

Plans in North Carolina communities vary widely, from a simple straightforward land use plan to a comprehensive plan that earns national recognition.[8] Typically, the plan includes a sketch of the

---

1. *See* Craig v. County of Chatham, 356 N.C. 40, 44 (2002) ("Counties are creatures of the General Assembly and have no inherent legislative powers.").

2. For more on Chapter 160D and the process that produced it, see David W. Owens and Adam S. Lovelady, *Chapter 160D: A New Land Use Law for North Carolina* (UNC School of Government, 2020).

3. *See* S.L. 2019-111, § 3.2 (stating that the law "clarifies and restates the intent of existing law").

4. *See* Chapter 160D, Section 501 of the North Carolina General Statutes (hereinafter G.S.).

5. *See* American Planning Association, *2022 Survey of State Planning Laws: Land Use, Hazard Mitigation, and Climate Action* (Sept. 26, 2022), storymaps.arcgis.com/stories/142eec1ae7fe42be915b6767ac811e40.

6. G.S. 113A-110; Title 15A, Chapter 7B of the North Carolina Administrative Code (hereinafter N.C.A.C.).

7. *See* G.S. 160D-501(b).

8. On one hand, the School of Government's *PlanNC Guidebook* describes what a streamlined planning process to produce a basic plan might look like. On the other hand is the national-award-winning "Charlotte Future 2040 Comprehensive Plan" adopted by the City of Charlotte, available at cltfuture2040.com/.

city's or county's historical development and statistical information about the community; discusses urban development issues and problems; and presents a series of maps, charts, illustrations, and photos displaying both current information and future projections. However, the primary function of the plan document is to outline in writing the policy the community intends to pursue with respect to growth and development and to help determine the steps necessary to put this policy into effect. For this reason, the process by which the community establishes its development goals and objectives and the extent to which it develops a consensus about the proper role local government can play in influencing development are critical. The comprehensive plan as a document can be only as effective as the process that has shaped it.

The process for developing a comprehensive plan is an important one. Certain parties with interests that will be affected by the plan (land developers and realtors, business owners, chambers of commerce and merchant associations, economic development proponents, members of the farming community, housing and environmental organizations, utility providers, neighborhood groups, and other local governments and state agencies) are typically involved. Still, it is often difficult for local governments to generate enthusiasm about plan-making among citizens at large. In addition, there are some groups, such as traditionally marginalized or geographically marginalized populations, that can be difficult to reach. The Internet, by allowing easy access to comment boxes, illustrative graphics, surveys, and even meetings, can certainly facilitate some of these communications. However, lower-resourced and geographically isolated households may also have limited Internet access, so it is important to engage members of the public where they are.[9] As the COVID-19 pandemic indicated, there are many ways to reach people but there is no complete substitute for face-to-face interactions. Local governments can share proposals in neighborhood community meetings. Planners can test new ideas in small focus groups in ways that can be difficult to communicate otherwise. Some local governments have experimented with charrettes. A *charrette* is an intense design exercise in which decision-makers, supported by a cadre of information, staff resources, and drafting supplies, literally sketch out a proposal for the future of a downtown, a street corridor, a neighborhood, or some other small area. Such an exercise certainly encourages participants to buy into the ideas the charrette generates and reduces planning abstractions to practical applications.

Cities and counties are increasingly preparing and adopting small-area development plans. Such plans may apply to downtowns, older inner-city neighborhoods, major growth corridors, or areas whose development may have implications for other jurisdictions. Small-area plans are typically prepared primarily to assist local governments in determining appropriate development policies for these key areas. In addition, various state and federal aid programs require local government applicants to prepare a plan (often with land use and development implications) to qualify for financial assistance.

The Comprehensive Plan and Zoning Amendments

A comprehensive or land use plan is generally intended to provide guidance to local governments when they make important development-related decisions, including the approval of zoning amendments. It is perhaps no surprise that in 2005 the General Assembly amended the zoning statutes to require consideration of land use plans when making zoning decisions. The revised statutes required that a planning board's report to the governing board on a zoning proposal include comments

9. Other School of Government faculty teach and have published extensively on topics related to citizen engagement. *See, e.g.*, Ricardo S. Morse, Sabrina M. Willard, and Michelle Y. Holder, *The Citizens Academy Handbook: Building Capacity for Local Civic Engagement* (UNC School of Government, 2017); John B. Stephens, Ricardo S. Morse, and Kelley T. O'Brien, *Public Outreach and Participation* (UNC School of Government, 2011).

on "whether the proposed amendment is consistent with any comprehensive plan that has been adopted and any other officially adopted plan," and that the governing board adopt a statement "describing whether its action is consistent with an adopted comprehensive plan and explaining why the board considers the action taken to be reasonable and in the public interest."[10]

The required statements were updated with the reorganization of planning and development statutes in Chapter 160D. The current rules still require a planning board to "advise and comment on whether" a proposed zoning action "is consistent with any comprehensive or land-use plan . . . and any other officially adopted plan that is applicable."[11] When the matter comes before the governing board, that board must "approve a brief statement describing whether its action is consistent or inconsistent with an adopted comprehensive or land-use plan" and, in zoning map amendment cases (rezonings) the board must also approve "a statement analyzing the reasonableness of the proposed rezoning."[12]

There are three important points to make with regard to these statements: First, the statements must *describe*, not just state, the decision's consistency and (where required) reasonableness. While a court may not review the substance of the consistency statement, courts have rejected prior zoning decisions that stated rather than described plan consistency.[13] Second, the current version of the law in Chapter 160D allows consistency review to be inferred from the record of a board meeting.[14] Third, while state law only requires these statements when a governing board makes a decision on a proposed zoning regulation amendment, local ordinances might also require a review of consistency with the comprehensive plan or officially adopted plans in certain other land development permitting decisions.[15]

Strategic Planning

A model that serves as an alternative to comprehensive planning is *strategic planning*. Strategic planning focuses on a few critical issues important to the community's future rather than trying to deal with everything at once. It involves looking outward at trends that may affect a community's destiny but that are beyond the community's control. Strategic planning is designed to be action-oriented, setting out the steps that must be taken to achieve goals, who must take them, how much the planned changes will cost, and who will pay. It is well adapted to the resolution of economic development and housing issues involving a number of players (government units, businesses, private individuals, and nonprofit organizations) when a distribution of responsibility is necessary and the ability to respond to opportunities is important. Strategic planning is particularly useful for making spending decisions. Also, its focus on setting achievable goals and timetables for action make it valuable in resolving regulatory issues. Although comprehensive planning is still the primary model used in land use and development planning, it has been substantially influenced by the principles of strategic planning.

---

10. S.L. 2005-426, § 7.
11. G.S. 160D-604(d).
12. G.S. 160D-605(a) and (b).
13. *See* Atkinson v. City of Charlotte, 235 N.C. App. 1 (2014) (referencing prior version of statute in Chapter 160A of the General Statutes, which applied to cities).
14. G.S. 160D-605(a).
15. Although not required by state law, a local government may bind itself in its zoning regulation to grant a special use permit or to rezone property only if the proposal is consistent with the unit's own land development plan. In addition, a subdivision ordinance may require that the dedication of land and the construction of improvements be consistent with the public facilities element of a comprehensive plan.

Organization for City or County Planning

Planning and zoning decisions involve a number of functions, departments, and local boards. The organizational arrangements often differ from one jurisdiction to another, but there are several key bodies that are part of every local government's zoning apparatus. The duties of some of these entities may be combined as described below, but each is essential to the process of planning and development regulation.

Governing Board

The key to the success of any local land use and development planning program is the governing board. The council or board of county commissioners exercises a number of powers affecting a land use planning program. It approves the budget and the financing for capital projects to be undertaken in the current fiscal year. (It may also approve a five- or six-year capital improvement program as an advisory measure.) The board allocates funds for boards, agencies, and departments that carry out planning-related responsibilities. It approves the location and design of public buildings and other public facilities. In its legislative capacity, the board adopts and amends various land use and development-related regulations. It may retain for itself authority to assume any responsibility of the zoning board of adjustment (for example, granting special use permits for certain land uses outlined in the zoning regulation)[16] and to approve subdivision plats. The governing board also affects the planning program by the quality of the appointments it makes to the planning board, the zoning board of adjustment, and other planning-related commissions and agencies. Finally, it has ultimate authority to enforce local regulations, and it approves any judicial action taken against violators of the various land use and development-related regulations.

Planning Board

One of the primary citizen boards critical to a local planning program is the *planning board*, sometimes called the *planning commission* or the *planning and zoning board* (the function of the board is similar regardless of the name chosen for the board). Most North Carolina cities and counties have established a planning board made up of lay members appointed by the governing board. Many of the planning board's duties and responsibilities are advisory. The planning board is generally responsible for supervising the development of the comprehensive plan. It may arrange for and supervise the preparation of special studies, land use plans and policies, and drafts of ordinances. It may adopt plans and policies, advise the governing board on them, and recommend ordinance amendments and methods of carrying out plans. In addition, the planning board generally has specific duties related to the zoning regulation. As described above, the planning board must provide a written recommendation to the governing board concerning whether a proposed zoning amendment is consistent with the comprehensive plan or any other officially adopted plan and any other matters deemed appropriate by the planning board. City and county planning boards must be granted a thirty-day opportunity in which to make a recommendation concerning any proposed amendment before the governing board may adopt the proposal.[17]

In addition to having advisory responsibilities, a planning board may be delegated the authority to review certain development proposals. In particular, the planning board may be delegated the authority to approve subdivision plats.[18] The planning board's potential versatility is indicated by

---

16. G.S. 160D-302.
17. G.S. 160D-604(b).
18. G.S. 160D-803(c).

the fact that it can take on the duties of certain other agencies if the governing board so desires. For example, the governing board may assign to a planning board any or all of the duties of the zoning board of adjustment (such as approval of zoning variances, issuance of special use permits, and hearing of appeals from decisions of the zoning official).[19] In addition, if at least three planning board members have demonstrated special interest, experience, or education in history or architecture, the planning board may be designated the historic preservation commission.[20]

North Carolina local governments may also establish a joint planning board representing two or more local units of government. The Winston-Salem/Forsyth County City–County Planning Board, the Charlotte–Mecklenburg Planning Commission, and the Durham City–County Planning Commission are some of the better-known examples of such joint agencies.

Board of Adjustment

A *board of adjustment* is an appointed board that makes some or all of the quasi-judicial decisions for a local government (for more about quasi-judicial decision-making, see "Quasi-Judicial Role" in the "Government Roles in Zoning" section, below). Typically, these include appeals of administrative decisions and interpretations, petitions for variance from the zoning regulation, and special use permit applications. The functions of the board of adjustment also may be delegated to the planning board or to the governing board.[21] In fact, many smaller municipalities have chosen to merge their planning boards and boards of adjustment.

Most board of adjustment decisions, such as whether to grant a special use permit or whether to reverse a decision of the zoning enforcement officer, must be made with the concurring vote of a majority of its members. However, the law still requires that a zoning variance may be granted only with the concurring vote of four-fifths of the board's membership.[22] Appeals of board of adjustment decisions may not be appealed to another local board; rather, judicial review of such decisions may be pursued in county superior court through a writ of certiorari.[23]

Other Boards and Commissions

Each local government's charter and ordinances will set the structure of government and identify what parts of the local government take on which roles in the development review process. Although the individuals and groups above appear in all local government planning and zoning structures in the state, other boards are optional and thus do not appear in every jurisdiction. These bodies include, but are not limited to, historic preservation commissions, appearance commissions, and housing appeals boards.[24]

Planning Staff

A local government land use planning program requires some staff to allow it to function. G.S. 160D-402(b) identifies no less than ten duties of planning staff, from determining whether applications are complete to conducting inspections and issuing or denying certain approvals. However, the size and shape of this staffing varies greatly from one community to the next. The largest communities may have entire departments with multiple planners and zoning officials of different

19. G.S. 160D-302.
20. G.S. 160D-303(b).
21. G.S. 160D-302.
22. *See* G.S. 160D-705.
23. G.S. 160D-1402.
24. *See* G.S. 160D-303 (authority for historic preservation commission), -304 (authority for appearance commission), -305 (authority for housing appeals board), and -306 (authority for other advisory boards).

levels of authority and experience. The smallest may delegate these duties to a local government manager or clerk and retain no full-time planning staff. Aside from retaining one or more full-time planners, North Carolina local governments have several options with regard to how they staff planning matters: a local government can agree with another local government to create a joint staff; designate staff from another city or county to serve as its staff; or contract with an individual, council of governments, or other regional planning agency.[25]

It should be noted here that planning department staff are not the only officials involved in implementing a land use plan. For example, in small cities or counties, a manager may make recommendations on matters affecting the city's development, enforce planning-related regulations, and supervise plan preparation. In large cities that have a staff planner, the manager may be less directly involved in planning affairs. Still, he or she may coordinate the capital improvement program; administer the housing, community development, transportation, parks and recreation, and inspection programs; make recommendations on annexation and utility-extension plans, downtown revitalization plans, and economic development proposals; and coordinate the interdepartmental staff review of major development proposals that come before the council. Enforcement and inspection are other planning- and zoning-related duties that may be performed by another local government official. In small cities and in many counties, a building inspector, a city manager or clerk, or a police chief may perform inspection and enforcement duties in addition to their work with other local regulations.

Inspection Department

The inspection department is the primary enforcement agency for a variety of development-related regulations and codes. It typically enforces the North Carolina State Building Code and sometimes also the minimum housing code. In many cities, both large and small, it also enforces the zoning regulation. For the inspection department, as with the planning department, a local government can create its own, form a joint department with other local governments, contract with another local government to provide the services, or arrange for a county inspection department to serve this function within a city.[26] Regardless of how it is constructed, an inspections department is responsible for enforcing laws related to the construction and maintenance of buildings and other structures, as well as some other related duties outlined in the statutes.[27]

Extraterritorial Jurisdiction for Land Use Planning

In North Carolina, as in many other states, a city may exercise jurisdiction in some planning-related matters over areas located outside its boundaries.[28] Extraterritorial jurisdiction is justified on several grounds. It is in a city's interest to ensure that areas that may ultimately be annexed into the city are developed in a manner consistent with the city's development standards and land use planning objectives. Otherwise, unplanned growth and substandard development may thwart whatever

25. G.S. 160D-402(c).

26. G.S. 160D-1102 describes the general scope of code administration and the different methods for performing this function.

27. G.S. 160D-1104 describes these duties.

28. G.S. 160D-202. *See also* David W. Owens, *Land Use Law in North Carolina*, 4th ed. (UNC School of Government, 2023), at 48–59; David W. Owens, "Extraterritorial Jurisdiction for Planning and Development Regulation" (March 2023), www.sog.unc.edu/resources/legal-summaries/extraterritorial-jurisdiction-planning-and-development-regulation.

municipal annexation may occur. Even when a city has no annexation ambitions, unplanned growth and substandard development on the urban fringe may have detrimental effects on nearby city areas and resources.

In general, a city of any size may establish planning jurisdiction for one mile outside its boundaries. However, North Carolina law permits a city to exercise such extraterritorial jurisdiction unilaterally only if the county with jurisdiction over the target area is not already enforcing zoning and subdivision regulations there.[29] Where local governments work cooperatively, other jurisdictional arrangements are also possible. With the approval of the board of county commissioners, a city with a population of 10,000 to 25,000 may extend its jurisdiction up to two miles outside city limits, and a city with a population of over 25,000, up to three miles.[30] Alternatively, at the city council's request, the county may exercise any of the various land use regulatory powers within the city's extraterritorial jurisdiction or even within the city limits.[31]

When a municipality extends extraterritorial jurisdiction, it gains exclusive jurisdiction to exercise all of the powers authorized by Chapter 160D.[32] These powers include planning, zoning, subdivision regulation, enforcement of the State Building Code, minimum housing code regulation, historic district and landmark regulation, and stormwater control. No city may exercise in its extraterritorial area any power it does not exercise within its city limits.[33]

If a city intends to enforce zoning or subdivision regulations in its extraterritorial area, it must provide some means by which residents of the extraterritorial area may influence the decision-making of both the planning agency and the zoning board of adjustment. A city is directed to ask the county commissioners to appoint residents of the extraterritorial area. The number of such appointees and their voting power are determined by the city, but the number of extraterritorial appointees on each board relative to the number of appointees who are municipal residents must reflect the population of the extraterritorial area relative to the municipality's population. If the board of county commissioners does not make these appointments within ninety days after it receives the request, the city council may make them instead.[34]

Subdivision Regulation

The word "subdivision" usually calls to mind a relatively large residential development of single-family homes, perhaps with a whimsical name on a sign at the turn-off from the main road. For regulatory purposes, however, *subdivision* is the division of a tract of land into smaller parcels or building sites for the purpose of sale or development (whether that sale or development is currently planned or not). It also includes all divisions of land that involve dedication of a new street or a change in existing streets.[35]

Most subdivision regulations are based on the premise that the division of land generally signals that the land will soon be developed and used more intensively than it was before subdivision, which in turn will increase demand on community infrastructure, facilities, and services. The platting and recording of a subdivision map offer a local government the opportunity not only to review the

29. G.S. 160D-202(c).
30. G.S. 160D-202(a).
31. G.S. 160D-202(f).
32. G.S. 160D-201(a).
33. G.S. 160D-202(b).
34. G.S. 160D-307.
35. G.S. 160D-802(a).

design of the resulting lots but to ensure that adequate streets, utilities, and other public improvements are installed to serve the needs of those who acquire the subdivided land.

Subdivision Review Process

North Carolina state law outlines separate approval procedures for three main types of subdivision: "exempt" plat approvals, final-plat-only approvals, and a two-step approval that is the most common. While the last step in each process involves recording a plat with the county register of deeds, each process gets there in a different manner.[36]

Exempt Plat Review

The General Statutes exempt certain categories of subdivisions from the definition of "subdivision" to which the subdivision regulation may apply.[37] However, even an "exempt" subdivision requires some review before it can be recorded: the surveyor drafting an exempt plat must certify that the plat is exempt from the definition of subdivision before it can be recorded.[38] In addition, local regulations can mandate review and certification by a plat review officer before the plat can be recorded.[39] In such a case, the extent of the plat officer's review is to confirm that the plat is indeed exempt and to certify it as such. Once the plat is confirmed as exempt and is recorded, the subdivision takes effect.

Expedited and Final Plat Only Review

In addition to exempt plats, two other classes of subdivision receive expedited review. The first class of subdivision is defined in local regulations. Specifically, G.S. 160D-802(b) gives local governments authority to expedite certain classes of subdivisions. How to define these classes of subdivision, as well as the way in which the approval might be expedited, is left to the local government to define in its subdivision regulation. Some regulations refer to these as "minor" subdivisions, though the distinction between which plats are "minor" and which are "major" (or even whether these terms are used at all) is not uniform. Also, the requirements for "minor" or "major" subdivisions can vary. For instance, one jurisdiction's "minor" subdivision plats might require final-plat-only approval while "major" subdivisions require preliminary plat approval. Another jurisdiction's "minor" subdivision plats might require only administrative approval of preliminary plats while "major" subdivision preliminary plats go through a quasi-judicial process. This is one area of land regulation where a close reading of the regulatory language is particularly important.

The second class of subdivision that receives expedited review is set by statute. Since 2017, the North Carolina General Statutes mandate only a final plat review for certain smaller subdivisions of property held by a single owner.[40] Thus, while a local government has broad discretion to set the review of some subdivision approvals as minor or expedited, the state statute *requires* an expedited process for those subdivisions that fall under the final-plat-only statute. Instead of the usual

---

36. For a thorough discussion of subdivision regulation, see Adam Lovelady, *Land Subdivision Regulation in North Carolina* (UNC School of Government, 2016).

37. G.S. 160D-802(a).

38. G.S. 47-30(f)(11)d requires a surveyor to certify that the plat is a "recombination of existing parcels, a court-ordered survey, or other exemption or exception to the definition of subdivision."

39. *See* G.S. 47-30(f)(11) ("the plat shall have, in addition to said surveyor's certificate, a certification of approval, or no approval required, as may be required by local ordinance from the appropriate government authority and the county review officer . . . before the plat is presented for recordation.").

40. *See* S.L. 2017-10 (the affected statutes are now codified at G.S. 160D-802(c)); *see also* Adam Lovelady, "Subdivision Legislation: An Old Exemption and a New Expedited Review," *Coates' Canons: NC Local Government Law* blog (June 13, 2017), canons.sog.unc.edu/2017/06/subdivision-legislation-old-exemption-new-expedited-review/.

two-step process described below, these subdivision plats receive one round of review by staff. If approved, the plat can be recorded and the subdivision takes effect.

The Two-Step Process

The third method—and the most common in larger-scale developments—involves the approval of a "preliminary" plat, which allows the applicant to move forward with certain ground-clearing and infrastructure installation activities prior to the final plat review. This method is discussed in more detail below. When a preliminary plat is required, the local government can by regulation designate the preliminary plat to be approved administratively or through a quasi-judicial process. Final decision-making authority for preliminary plats can also go to the governing board, the governing board on the recommendation of some other body, or a designated person or board (such as a technical review committee or a staff member).[41]

Pre-Application Procedures

Many local governments encourage (or even require) applicants for preliminary plats and other development approvals to submit a sketch plan or design plan to the planning staff or the plat approval agency before submitting their formal application for preliminary plat approval. The purpose of these plans is to bring representatives of the local government and the subdivider together so that the local unit can learn what the subdivider has planned and the subdivider can better understand the unit's requirements for approving the subdivision.

Review and Approval of the Preliminary Plat

The next important step in the review process—except for exempt and final-plat-only approvals—is the submission and approval of a preliminary plat. To call a subdivision map submitted at this stage "preliminary" is rather misleading: the division of lots is not complete until the final plat is recorded, but the "preliminary" plat will, in large measure, fix the nature, design, and scope of the development to follow. By organizing lots and providing plans for the installation of whatever infrastructure or facilities the developer is to provide, the preliminary plat gives a concrete plan for what the development will look like, probably for decades to come. Some regulations or developments may require preliminary plat submissions that include a number of separate plans, such as grading, landscaping, lighting, and utility installation.

This phase also may include additional review by various city and county departments as well as agencies outside of local government before the development work can proceed. Some local governments form a technical review committee of staff members from various departments such as fire, sanitation, water and sewer, transportation, or others that may have an interest in the technical details of how a subdivision is laid out and developed. A technical review committee or staff member might also approve a set of "construction drawings" that provide minute details of the construction of everything from curbs and gutters to individual fire hydrants and water meters. Once a preliminary plat and any required construction drawings are approved, the applicant has a vested right to undertake site development work such as clearing, grading, and installation of infrastructure.

---

41. *See* G.S. 160D-803.

Review and Approval of the Final Plat

The preliminary plat sets the stage for site development work—clearing and grading, installation of stormwater and linear utilities, clearing and paving of roads, and so on. When that body of work is completed, it is time to submit the final plat. An approved final plat is the operative document for any subdivision—this is the document that creates the new lot lines. After a preliminary plat has been submitted and development action has occurred, the review of the final plat is largely a matter of ensuring that the installed infrastructure matches the preliminary plat and the final plat matches what has actually happened on the ground. As with the preliminary plat, the final plat may be subject to review and comment from other agencies in the local government. A final plat may not be recorded prior to its approval by the reviewing body, which must be shown on the face of the plat.[42]

Once the final plat is approved, the plat must be recorded in the county register of deeds' office before lots may be sold. Recording the plat also often includes the local government accepting dedication of any infrastructure, such as streets or water and sewer lines. Lastly, for any of a number of reasons, there may be some improvements that have not yet been completed when the final plat is to be recorded. This is where bonds and other guarantees play an important role.

Guarantee of Developer Performance

In general, a developer may not begin to construct subdivision improvements until the preliminary plat is approved. Once that approval is granted, the developer is obliged to arrange for certain dedications to be made and improvements to be installed or constructed before the final plat may be approved. One way to ensure that streets are properly constructed, and utilities or drainage facilities properly installed, is to withhold final plat approval until these improvements are completed, inspected, and, if appropriate, accepted by the city or another government unit. Another common practice is to allow final plat approval if the subdivider has provided adequate financial assurance to the local government that improvements will be completed after the final plat is approved. If these performance guarantees are required, the regulation must provide a range of options from which a developer may choose. Common forms of guarantees include letters of credit, bonds, and securities held in escrow.[43]

Exactions and the Financing of Subdivision Improvements

The typical development of a new subdivision involves the installation of a great deal of infrastructure, such as utility lines, streets, and other amenities like storm drains and greenways. Someone has to finance, build, and maintain all of this infrastructure. Consequently, the questions of who will finance subdivision improvements and community facilities and how they will be maintained are fundamental to subdivision regulation. Many local governments now expect subdividers to provide certain public improvements at their own expense. These expectations, along with any property the government requires to be given up as a condition of development approval, are called *exactions*. Exactions may also take the form of construction requirements or the installation of infrastructure improvements, dedication of land, payment of fees in lieu of dedication, or payment of impact fees.[44] Because they require property owners to give up something of value, exactions are subject to significant statutory and constitutional constraints.

---

42. G.S. 160D-803(d).

43. The regulations for these performance guarantees, including the allowable amount, duration, and legal responsibilities, are outlined in more detail in G.S. 160D-804.1.

44. For a discussion of development exactions generally, see Richard Ducker, "Development Exactions: An Introduction" (prepared for the North Carolina Legislative Research Commission Study Committee on Property Owner

Forms of Exactions

Virtually all subdivision regulations require the subdivider to construct or install certain subdivision improvements. The subdivision enabling statutes allow cities and counties to require dedication of rights-of-way, the construction of streets, the dedication or reservation of recreation areas, and the "construction of community service facilities in accordance with local government plans, policies, and standards."[45] *Community service facilities* defies exact definition, but the most commonly required subdivision improvements include streets, curbs and gutters, drainage swales or storm sewers, sidewalks, and water or sewer lines or both.

For improvements that are to be available for public use or for connection to a public system, the city or county will require the dedication of the improved land and will accept the dedication only after the improvement has been completed and inspected. For purposes of development approval, then, a *dedication* is a form of exaction requiring that the developer donate to the public some interest in land for certain public uses. North Carolina law allows both cities and counties, as a condition of subdivision plat approval, to require the dedication of sites and easements for streets, utilities, and recreation areas.[46]

Local governments often seek the construction and dedication of streets, utility lines, or stormwater drainage improvements designed not only for a particular subdivision but also for future development. If a sewer line is extended from the end of a sewerage network to a tract being subdivided, the owners of land along the line may wish to connect to it at some future time. A six-inch water line might adequately serve the subdivision currently under construction, yet it might be wise to lay a twelve-inch main that could eventually serve expected development on the far side of the subdivision. If a city or county requires a subdivider to provide capacity exceeding that necessary to serve the subdivision, then the local unit may pay for the extra capacity from its general funds on the theory that the oversized facilities will benefit the community generally.[47]

An alternative to compulsory dedication and improvement is to require or allow a subdivider to pay a fee that represents the value of the site or improvement that would otherwise have been dedicated or provided. These *fees in lieu* represent an attractive option when it is not practical for the developer to provide the contribution in kind or on a time frame that allows the development to proceed successfully. Both city and county regulations may provide for fees in lieu of the dedication of recreation areas and for fees in lieu of road improvements.[48] Because of the administrative burdens of accounting for these funds, relatively few North Carolina jurisdictions allow fees in lieu.

Impact fees, similar to fees in lieu, are charged to new developments for the purpose of offsetting impacts from that new development. The manner in which they are applied and calculated is a bit different, however. They are not "in lieu" of some other contribution but are instead a set fee that attempts to allocate the costs of a wide range of community facilities to new development. Where a fee in lieu might be made to substitute for dedicating park property or installing new sewer infrastructure, an impact fee for similar public facilities would go into a local government fund to be

---

Protection and Rights, North Carolina General Assembly, March 3, 2014), webservices.ncleg.gov/ViewDocSiteFile/33866. Another concise description is at Adam Lovelady, "Exactions and Subdivision Approval," *Coates' Canons: NC Local Government Law* blog (Feb. 1, 2013), canons.sog.unc.edu/2013/02/exactions-and-subdivision-approval/; and a discussion of the constitutional constraints on exactions can be found at Adam Lovelady, "Constitutional Limits on Land Use Exactions in North Carolina," *Coates' Canons: NC Local Government Law* blog (July 17, 2024), canons.sog.unc.edu /2024/07/constitutional-limits-on-land-use-exactions-in-north-carolina/.

45. G.S. 160D-804.

46. *Id.*

47. For more on reimbursement agreements generally, see Adam Lovelady, "Reimbursement Agreements," *Coates' Canons: NC Local Government Law* blog (Jan. 19, 2016), canons.sog.unc.edu/2016/01/reimbursement-agreements/.

48. G.S. 160D-804(c)(3) (transportation) and -804(d) (recreation areas and open space).

used for future park or sewer capital improvement projects. In either case, the fee must be related to the impacts or needs created by that development.[49] They are generally collected when building permits are issued, usually just before the development creating the need for new services actually begins, rather than at the time of plat approval.

The legal status of impact fees is somewhat more tenuous than that of other exactions. The North Carolina General Statutes do not expressly authorize the use of most impact fees, but local acts allow some local governments to charge them. In addition, 2017 legislation allows local governments to assess "system development fees" to recover the cost of capital improvements to serve new development.[50] System development fees are subject to a number of specific requirements, such as calculation of costs and explication of needs, which are detailed in the legislation.

It is not clear what other impacts might legally be addressed with impact fees, but there is one purpose for which North Carolina courts have made clear that impact fees are not allowed: impact fees for school improvement and construction are not legal. In *Durham Land Owners Association v. County of Durham*,[51] the North Carolina Court of Appeals ruled that the general statutes did not provide counties with express or implied enabling authority to adopt impact fees for public school construction. As discussed in the following section, later cases have applied these limitations to adequate public facilities ordinances that act like impact fees.

Adequate Public Facilities Ordinances

Adequate public facility ordinances (APFOs) are based on the principle of concurrency—that is, development approval should not be granted unless and until the public facilities necessary to serve that development are available for use when the development is occupied.[52] Under some programs, if area streets, parks, or schools are already at or near capacity, a developer may be expected to postpone development plans, scale back plans to better fit facility capacity, or "mitigate" the capacity deficiency. Mitigation has sometimes been equated with the dedication of property or the payment of fees to help finance the improvement.

While public facilities ordinances are not clearly allowed or not allowed, some developers have challenged particular APFOs that looked and acted like impact fees. In 2006, Durham County's school impact fee ordinance was invalidated by the North Carolina Court of Appeals on grounds that the county lacked enabling authority to adopt such an ordinance. In 2009, Union County's APFO program was invalidated by the court of appeals in *Union Land Owners Association v. County of Union*.[53] There, developers alleged that, because most APFO-related issues were resolved by mitigation with a fee in lieu, the ordinance effectively worked as an illegal impact fee. The court agreed, holding that neither the county's land subdivision plat approval authority, its zoning authority, nor its general police power authority provided an adequate legislative basis. According to the court, the county's land subdivision control authority was inadequate in spite of language in the statutes allowing ordinances to provide "for the distribution of population and traffic in a manner that will

---

49. Adam Lovelady, "Constitutional Limits on Land Use Exactions in North Carolina," *Coates' Canons: NC Local Government Law* blog (July 17, 2024), canons.sog.unc.edu/2024/07/constitutional-limits-on-land-use-exactions-in-north-carolina/ discusses these constitutional issues in somewhat greater detail.

50. *See* Public Water and Sewer System Development Fee Act, S.L. 2017-138 (amending G.S. 153A-277(a) and 160A-314(a)).

51. 177 N.C. App. 629, *cert. denied*, 360 N.C. 532 (2006).

52. *See* Richard Ducker, "Are Adequate-Public-Facility Ordinances Adequate?" *Coates' Canons: NC Local Government Law* blog (Dec. 16, 2009), canons.sog.unc.edu/2009/12/are-adequate-public-facility-ordinances-adequate/; David Owens, "School Impact Fees and Development Regulations: Another Round," *Coates' Canons: NC Local Government Law* blog (Oct. 16, 2012), canons.sog.unc.edu/2012/10/school-impact-fees-and-development-regulations-another-round/.

53. 201 N.C. App. 374 (2009).

avoid congestion and overcrowding and will create conditions that substantially promote public health, safety, and the general welfare." More recently the North Carolina Supreme Court in *Lanvale Properties v. County of Cabarrus*[54] invalidated similar APFO provisions adopted by Cabarrus County because of inadequate legislative authority. In the *Lanvale Properties* case, developers challenged a county's adequate public facility ordinance, which effectively conditioned approval of new residential construction projects on developers paying fees to subsidize new school construction. The North Carolina Supreme Court held that the statutory parameters set forth did not provide the county with sufficient implied zoning authority to adopt and enforce such requirements. Thus, local governments must look very carefully and narrowly at their enabling authority before drafting APFOs or imposing impact fees.

Exactions and the Constitution

Exactions must be properly and fairly related to the need for the new public facilities generated by a new development. Otherwise, they could amount to an unconstitutional taking of private property for public use without just compensation. Several decisions by the United States Supreme Court provide guidance on this point. In 1987, the Court held in *Nollan v. California Coastal Commission*[55] that if a government unit conditions approval of a development permit on a dedication of property, the condition must have an "essential nexus" to an allowable purpose of the regulation. Seven years later, in *Dolan v. City of Tigard*,[56] the Court also ruled that the U.S. Constitution requires "rough proportionality" between the impact of the development and the nature and extent of the exaction. Although precise mathematical calculation is not required, some sort of individualized determination must be made to justify an exaction requirement as it is applied in a particular case. The Court also held that a local government bears the burden of proving that an exaction is constitutional.

Before the U.S. Supreme Court's decision in *Dolan*, the North Carolina Court of Appeals established a similar test for evaluating the constitutionality of exactions. In *Batch v. Town of Chapel Hill*,[57] the court adopted a "rational nexus" test for determining when an exaction becomes a taking.[58] Later decisions have confirmed that the *Batch* "rational nexus" test is similar to the federal "essential nexus" and "rough proportionality" tests set out in *Nollan* and *Dolan*.[59]

The concept of constitutional and unconstitutional exactions under the U.S. Constitution was extended to monetary exactions by *Koontz v. St. Johns River Water Management District*.[60] In that case, the U.S. Supreme Court held that the *Nollan* and *Dolan* standards apply as well to exactions of funds as they do to exactions of property.[61] The North Carolina Supreme Court in *Anderson Creek Partners v. Harnett County*[62] likewise affirmed that North Carolina courts should view exactions and certain fees through the *Batch* or *Nollan/Dolan* lens. Though the *Harnett County* decision took pains to describe some fees, such as application fees, that are not subject to the *Nollan/Dolan* analysis, it did not delineate which other fees are subject to the rational nexus and proportionality review and which are not.

---

54. 366 N.C. 142 (2012).
55. 483 U.S. 825 (1987).
56. 512 U.S. 374 (1994).
57. 92 N.C. App. 601 (1989); *rev'd on other grounds*, 326 N.C. 1 (1990).
58. *Id.* at 621.
59. *See* Anderson Creek Partners v. Harnett County, 382 N.C. 1 (2022); Franklin Road Properties v. City of Raleigh, 94 N.C. App. 731 (1989).
60. 133 S. Ct. 2586 (2013).
61. *See* Adam Lovelady, "The Koontz Decision and Implications for Development Exactions," *Coates' Canons: NC Local Government Law* blog (July 1, 2013), canons.sog.unc.edu/2013/07/the-koontz-decision-and-implications-for-development-exactions/.
62. 382 N.C. 1.

Zoning

Of all the programs, tools, and techniques associated with land use planning, zoning is perhaps the best known. It may be used to achieve a variety of purposes. First, it can ensure that a community's land uses are properly situated in relation to one another so that one use does not become a nuisance for its neighbors. Second, zoning can ensure that adequate land and space are available for various types of development. Third, it can ensure that the location and density of development are consistent with a government's ability to provide an area with streets, utilities, fire protection, and recreation services.

Zoning involves the exercise of the state's power to regulate private property in order to promote the public health, the public safety, and the general welfare.[63] The zoning-enabling statute, G.S. 160D-701, allows zoning regulations to address at least the following purposes:

> to provide adequate light and air; to prevent the overcrowding of land; to avoid undue concentration of population; to lessen congestion in the streets; to secure safety from fire, panic, and dangers; to facilitate the efficient and adequate provision of transportation, water, sewerage, schools, parks, and other public requirements; and to promote the health, safety, morals, or general welfare of the community.

This statute requires zoning regulations to consider the character of the areas they regulate, the suitability of those areas for particular uses, and the value of buildings while encouraging the most appropriate use of land throughout a local government's planning and zoning jurisdiction. Within this relatively broad general grant of power, zoning can serve a number of public purposes, such as fostering economic development and expansion. However, it can also be unduly restrictive, limiting competition among commercial activities by confining them to certain areas or excluding and marginalizing certain populations, directly or indirectly, by driving up the size of lots and the price of construction.

Because zoning is concerned with the use of property and not its ownership, the identity of owners is irrelevant from a legal perspective. Zoning permits, approvals, and requirements "run with the land" and apply to future owners as well as present ones. Similarly, zoning distinctions based on whether property is owner- or renter-occupied are unenforceable.[64] Although zoning may legitimately be used to protect property values, requirements that new developments meet minimum-floor-area standards or cost a certain amount are probably not legally defensible. The obligation of North Carolina local governments to accommodate low- and moderate-income housing through zoning remains unclear; nonetheless, zoning may not be used to discriminate on the basis of race or national origin. And though zoning is primarily a tool for influencing the use of private property, in North Carolina it is also applicable to the construction and use of buildings by the state and its political subdivisions.[65]

Zoning is prospective in nature: only land uses begun after the regulation's effective date must comply with all the regulations. However, existing buildings and lots with characteristics that do not comply with the regulations are said to be *nonconforming* (see the "Nonconformities and Amortization" section, below), and a special section of the ordinance usually deals with them.

Zoning regulations are distinct from most other types of land use regulations because they differ from district to district rather than being uniform throughout a local government's jurisdiction.

---

63. *See* G.S. 160D-701.

64. *See* Gregory v. County of Harnett, 128 N.C. App. 161, 493 S.E.2d 786 (1997); Graham Court Assocs. v. Town Council of Chapel Hill, 53 N.C. App. 543, 281 S.E.2d 418 (1981).

65. G.S. 160D-913.

This feature permits the tailoring of zoning to address development problems but also means that local governing bodies may be tempted to abuse the power by treating property owners in arbitrary or discriminatory ways.

Basic Elements

A *zoning regulation* consists of two parts: a text and a map (or series of maps). The text includes the substantive standards applicable to each district on the map and the procedures that govern proposals for changes in both the text and the map. The map divides the land within a city's jurisdiction into a number of zoning districts. The land in each district is governed by several types of regulations that vary from district to district: use regulations; dimensional requirements, including setback and density standards; and a range of other requirements dealing with matters such as off-street parking, landscaping and screening, property access, required public improvements, and signs. Dimensional and most other standards are relatively straightforward. Use limitations, however, are somewhat more complex and require additional explanation.

The zoning regulation typically outlines which uses are allowed in which districts in a *table of uses*. For each district, each use of land is designated as permitted by right, permitted with conditions, permitted with a special use permit, or not permitted at all. If a use is *permitted by right*, the zoning standards for that use are typically spelled out in specific terms, and the zoning enforcement official grants the applicant routine permission to proceed if those standards are met. Some uses in some districts might require a few additional conditions that can be approved administratively. These uses are said to be *permitted with conditions*. These conditions should be objective and straightforward (such as increased setbacks or a standard screening yard) or the use may need to go into the "special use" category. There may also be some cases in which an applicant for a zoning permit must hire a design professional (for example, an engineer, a landscape architect, or an architect) to prepare a site plan for a use authorized by right. Such a site plan may have to be reviewed by various departments, outside agencies, or a technical review committee made up of representatives of those departments or agencies. In some cities, the city council or the planning board approves such a *site plan*. As a general rule, however, these site plans must be approved as submitted if they meet local standards.

Some land uses, whether in particular zoning districts or in general, do not fit easily into the previous categories. They may merit closer examination because of their scale and effect or their potential for creating a nuisance. Some examples include small-scale electric substations and day-care centers or large-scale shopping malls and group housing developments. These "special" uses are permitted in a particular district as long as certain facts and conditions exist, and the standards that apply to them often require careful, site-specific scrutiny. This scrutiny is performed by the board of adjustment (or whichever board has been assigned board of adjustment duties), and if the standards are met, the special use receives a *special use permit* (previously called a *special exception* or a *conditional use permit* in some regulations). The zoning regulation must explicitly list the requirements the applicant must meet and the findings the issuing body must make in order for the permit to be issued. Regardless of which body issues the permit, the decision to grant or deny it must be based on evidence supplied at a *quasi-judicial* hearing. These hearings are much more strict than legislative hearings: board members must avoid communications about the substance of the case outside of the hearing and must base their decision solely on competent, material, and substantial evidence in the record.[66] An applicant must present competent, material, and substantial

---

66. *See* Jim Joyce, "Making Quasi-Judicial Decisions," *Coates' Canons: NC Local Government Law* blog (April 4, 2023), canons.sog.unc.edu/2023/04/making-quasi-judicial-decisions/.

evidence to support a finding that each of the special use requirements or standards are met. If they do so, the burden shifts to any opponents to produce competent, material, and substantial evidence to suggest that the standards are not met. If an applicant meets their burden of proof and there is no competent, material, and substantial evidence to the contrary, the board may not refuse to issue the permit.[67] However, in granting a special use permit the board may impose additional conditions and requirements. Such conditions may include specifications on the particular use to be made of the property; sign, parking, or landscaping requirements; requirements that the property owner dedicate land for and construct certain public improvements such as streets, utilities, and parks; and specifications dealing with the timing of development. All conditions must be "reasonable and appropriate," meaning that they should relate in type and scale to the impacts caused by the proposed use.[68] Permission to develop or use land in accordance with a special use permit runs with the land and applies with equal force to future owners of the property.

Types of Zoning Districts

Most zoning regulations include three basic types of zoning districts—residential, commercial, and industrial—and a variety of more specialized zones—office and institutional, flood hazard, mobile home park, agricultural, and perhaps mixed-use districts. In addition, there may be a number of residential districts, each based on different permissible dwelling types and required lot sizes (or densities); a number of commercial districts, based on the kinds of commercial uses allowed (e.g., retail, office, etc.); and several industrial districts based on the intensity of the industrial activity.

Zoning districts may also be classified as *general use districts* or *conditional districts*. All zoning regulations include at least some general use districts. Every general use district area is the same—if two properties on opposite sides of a town are in a Highway Business general use zoning district, the rules that apply to them are the same. In contrast, each conditional district is unique. Though typically based on a general use district, a conditional district incorporates a series of conditions, stipulations, and requirements agreed to by both the property owner and the local government.[69] Rezoning to a conditional district can be a longer and more involved process than a general use rezoning, but it allows a zoning district to be tailored to a specific project.

A third type of district is an *overlay district*. These districts literally provide another layer of zoning in addition to a base zoning district. Where base zoning districts are used to identify areas that are best for particular kinds of use across the jurisdiction, overlay districts are generally related to key or sensitive areas of a jurisdiction, such as the watershed for a drinking water source, the area around an airport, or an essential highway corridor into a community. An overlay district might protect or support any of these features regardless of what base district also applies to the property.

Form-Based Codes

In recent years, an increasing number of towns and cities have adopted zoning and other development regulations that differ from traditional zoning. One of the more prominent alternative forms of zoning involves form-based codes. Form-based codes emphasize physical form rather than the separation of uses as the organizing principle for the code. They also focus on the relationship between buildings and the "public realm," the form and mass of structures, and the scale and

67. *See* PHG Asheville v. City of Asheville, 374 N.C. 133 (2020) (applicants who met their burden of proof, where no contrary competent, material, and substantial evidence was presented, were entitled to permit issued through quasi-judicial process).

68. *See* G.S. 160D-705(c).

69. *See* G.S. 160D-703(b).

types of streets and blocks. At the heart of form-based codes is a plan that classifies sites according to street, block, and district characteristics and includes illustrations of build-to lines, projected building footprints, location of public spaces, and allowable building types for each site. Building envelope standards are intended to ensure that new development fits the desired character of the zone by regulating building height, placement, and orientation.

Form-based codes can apply to specific areas of a community with common characteristics, or they can be used as an alternative to conventional zoning regulations for specific areas. They can also be combined with conventional zoning to form a hybrid in which form-based coding regulates physical form and conventional regulations apply to land use. For example, while the City of Raleigh's Unified Development Ordinance includes many standard use regulations, it also describes a variety of building types that may be used or may be restricted in certain areas.[70] When an ordinance includes form-based elements, it often includes a less granular regulation of uses.

Government Roles in Zoning

In most cities and counties, zoning involves the governing board, a planning board, the zoning board of adjustment, and planning and zoning staff. Collectively, these groups carry out the legislative, quasi-judicial, advisory, and administrative functions of a local zoning program. The legislative and quasi-judicial roles of citizen boards in local zoning can be a source of some confusion, particularly when one board serves multiple functions that require it to act in varying roles.

Legislative Role

The board of county commissioners or city council acts in its legislative role when it adopts or amends the zoning regulation. When it makes the law, such a board has substantial discretion to make decisions as it sees fit. It need not explain its decision or make written findings of fact, but it must hold a legislative public hearing,[71] adopt a regulation effectuating the change, and adopt one or more statements regarding its action. For both zoning map and zoning text amendments, whether the board approves or denies the proposed change, it must adopt a statement describing whether a proposed zoning amendment is consistent with any relevant adopted plans.[72] A plan does not have the force of law, so the board does not have to make a decision that is consistent with adopted plans; it is enough to have considered how the decision relates to the appropriate plan or plans. Similarly, for zoning map amendments (but not text amendments), whether it approves or denies the proposal, the board must also adopt a statement describing how the action taken is reasonable and in the public interest.[73] The hearing required for legislative action is relatively free of formality. Speakers need not make sworn statements or restrict their statements to standards or topics set forth in the regulation. City council members or county commissioners may be subject to lobbying efforts before or after the hearing.

---

70. *See, e.g.*, *Raleigh Unified Development Ordinance*, Article 1.4 (describing building types and which building type is allowed in which zoning district), user-2081353526.cld.bz/UnifiedDevelopmentOrdinance.

71. G.S. 160D-601(a).

72. G.S. 160D-605(a).

73. G.S. 160D-605(b). This statute includes several factors a board might use to analyze the reasonableness of its decision. These factors are drawn directly from *Chrismon v. Guilford County*, 322 N.C. 611 (1988), in which the North Carolina Supreme Court held that so-called "spot" zoning, or zoning one parcel differently than others around it, is legal if it is reasonable. The *Chrismon* court applied several factors for determining reasonableness that are copied in G.S. 160D-605. Thus, the statute effectively requires a local government to explain how its rezoning decision—which in some cases might be considered spot zoning—is a legal one and provides some protection against illegal spot zoning and liability therefor.

Quasi-Judicial Role

Some other important zoning actions require a *quasi-judicial* (or court-like) process. These actions include the following: (1) issuance of variances, (2) issuance of special use permits, and (3) appeal of administrative zoning decisions (such as notices of violation or interpretations of the regulation).[74] Quasi-judicial *evidentiary hearings* differ from legislative hearings in several key respects. The decision must be based on the criteria in the regulation, witnesses must be sworn and offer testimony according to certain rules of evidence, board members may not discuss the case with any of the parties outside the hearing, and the board must justify its decision. Thus, quasi-judicial hearings are more formal than legislative hearings and more demanding on those who participate in them. These actions are often heard by the zoning board of adjustment. However, the duties of the board of adjustment may be assigned to the planning board or governing board instead.[75] Regardless of which board is assigned to a quasi-judicial case, that board must follow quasi-judicial procedures when it hears the case. When the board decides a quasi-judicial case, it must adopt a written decision that is then delivered to the parties and anyone who requests a copy of it before it is filed.[76]

Variances

Because a zoning regulation cannot anticipate every land use or development situation that will arise, state law includes a procedure for varying or waiving a zoning regulation provision when an unnecessary hardship would result from its strict enforcement. The permission granted by this procedure is known as a *variance*. Because every zoning regulation creates some burden on an individual property owner (and to preserve the integrity of the zoning regulation), the board of adjustment's authority to grant variances is limited. The board of adjustment lacks the wide legislative discretion the governing board has, and it may grant an exception only when the specific situation demands it.

In order to grant a variance, state law requires the board to find each of the following: [77]

1. Strictly applying the regulation as written will result in an unnecessary hardship.
2. The hardship affecting the property derives from conditions peculiar to the property.[78]
3. The hardship does not result from the applicant's own actions (purchasing a site with knowledge that development plans may necessitate a variance does not qualify as a "self-imposed" hardship).
4. The requested variance is consistent with the spirit, purpose, and intent of the regulation, such that public safety is secured and substantial justice is achieved.

Note that use variances, which purport to authorize land uses not otherwise authorized in the district, are prohibited by statute.[79] Also, where a common challenge is shared by many property owners, that challenge is more appropriately addressed by the planning board and the governing board through a proposal to amend the zoning regulations.

74. G.S. 160D-705.
75. G.S. 160D-302(b).
76. G.S. 160D-406(j).
77. *See* G.S. 160D-705(d).
78. Certain conditions, such as hardships that are common to the neighborhood or general public, conditions related to the property owner's circumstances, or the existence of private restrictive covenants, may not be the basis for granting a variance. *See* G.S. 160D-705(d).
79. G.S. 160D-705(d).

Special Treatment of Certain Activities

Zoning applies to virtually all uses of property. However, one major exemption is important for both counties and municipalities: bona fide farms and agricultural activity. Many other activities are noteworthy because special state legislation affects how zoning requirements apply.

Bona Fide Farms

Bona fide farms are exempt from zoning in areas of county jurisdiction and municipal extraterritorial jurisdiction.[80] Bona fide farms involve activities relating to the production of crops, fruits, vegetables, ornamental and flowering plants, dairy, poultry, and livestock. The general bona fide farm exemption also includes timber harvesting, the care and training of livestock, aquaculture, agritourism, and various packing, storage, treating, and processing functions, including the storage of grain in elevators.[81] In addition, if a property is located in a voluntary agricultural district and is subject to a conservation agreement, up to 25 percent of the receipts generated by the property may come from the sale of nonfarm products without the farmer losing the bona fide farm exemption.[82] Large-scale swine farms, though, are not exempt from zoning as long as they are not excluded entirely from the jurisdiction.

Manufactured Housing

Manufactured home is the term used in state and federal law for what used to be called a *mobile home*. These units must be built to special construction standards adopted by the United States Department of Housing and Urban Development. The zoning of manufactured homes is subject to legislation adopted by the General Assembly in 1987 designed both to counter the exclusionary tendencies of many local zoning regulations and to clarify that some special treatment of such units is permitted.[83] That legislation, now found at G.S. 160D-910, prohibits cities and counties from adopting zoning regulations that have the effect of excluding manufactured homes from all city and county zoning jurisdictions. However, cities and counties are expressly authorized to adopt special requirements affecting the appearance and dimensions of manufactured homes that do not also apply to site-built homes.

Establishments Selling Alcohol

The sale and consumption of alcohol are activities beyond the scope of zoning. The sale, consumption, and transportation of alcohol are subject to a uniform system of state regulation administered by the North Carolina Alcoholic Beverage Control (ABC) Commission, which controls the issuance of permits for these activities and preempts local zoning. State law provides that the ABC Commission "shall consider" local zoning requirements in determining whether a permit should be issued for an establishment at a particular location.[84] However, a local government may not use zoning requirements to prohibit the sale or consumption of alcohol at a particular establishment if the ABC Commission has issued a permit for that activity. In addition, relatively new "social district" legislation allows local governments to designate an area where alcoholic beverages may be served and carried outside. While the social district must be in a defined area, there are no zoning-related requirements related to social districts.[85]

---

80. G.S. 160D-903.

81. The agricultural activities set forth in G.S. 106-581.1 are incorporated into the exemption by reference.

82. G.S. 106-743.4(a).

83. This legislation does not affect modular homes. Modular homes are built in a factory but meet the construction standards of the State Building Code. For zoning purposes they are typically treated the same as site-built residences.

84. G.S. 18B-901(c).

85. *See* G.S. 18B-300.1.

Historic Districts and Landmarks

In its zoning text and on its zoning map, a city or a county may establish a historic district. Before doing so, it must establish a historic preservation commission; undertake an investigation; and create a report describing the buildings, sites, and features that give the proposed district historical, prehistoric, architectural, or cultural significance.[86] Once a district is established, no exterior portion of a building or a structure may be erected, altered, relocated, or demolished unless the historic preservation commission issues a certificate of appropriateness for the change based on the design guidelines and the regulation criteria adopted for the district.[87] The decision of whether to issue a certificate of appropriateness follows the quasi-judicial procedure. The commission is also authorized to delay the effective date of a certificate of appropriateness for the demolition of a building in a historic district for up to one year after its approval.[88] During this period, the commission and those interested in historic preservation may try to negotiate with the owner to save the building.

The historic preservation commission may also regulate the alteration and demolition of individual buildings or sites designated as historic landmarks. These landmarks may or may not be located within a historic district. Their demolition or relocation may be delayed for up to one year as well.[89]

Outdoor Advertising

The erection and display of billboards (referred to in the statutes as "outdoor advertising" displays) have long been subject to local government zoning. Certain commercial off-premise signs located along particular major federal highways are also subject to requirements imposed by the North Carolina Outdoor Advertising Control Act, which is administered by the North Carolina Department of Transportation.[90] Where both sets of regulations apply, local sign standards for newly erected signs are typically more restrictive and demanding than those adopted by the state and take precedence. However, as described in the "Nonconformities and Amortization" section, below, local governments are prohibited from amortizing nonconforming signs subject to the Outdoor Advertising Control Act without paying "just compensation."[91]

Constitutional Limits on Sign Regulations

In recent years, the U.S. Supreme Court has considered two notable cases related to the scope of sign regulations. In *Reed v. Town of Gilbert, Arizona*,[92] an Arizona town's sign regulations had different size and time limits on "ideological signs," "political signs," and "temporary directional signs." The Supreme Court held that by restricting specific types of subject matter, the ordinance was a content-based restriction on free speech. This meant that it had to meet the strictest constitutional test, which it failed. While this decision answered some questions about the constitutional limits of sign regulations, it left others unresolved.[93] One significant question that was not resolved in *Reed* was whether a sign ordinance could treat on-premise commercial signs differently from off-premise signs. That question was resolved seven years later in *City of Austin, Texas v. Reagan*

---

86. G.S. 160D-941 through -944.
87. G.S. 160D-947.
88. G.S. 160D-949.
89. *See* G.S. 160D-945, -946, and -949.
90. *See* G.S. Chapter 136, Article 11.
91. G.S. 136-131.1.
92. 576 U.S. 155 (2015).
93. For more on this case, see Adam Lovelady, "Sign Litigation: A Brief Analysis of Reed v. Town of Gilbert," *Coates' Canons: NC Local Government Law* blog (July 21, 2015), canons.sog.unc.edu/2015/07/sign-litigation-a-brief-analysis-of-reed-v-town-of-gilbert/.

National Advertising of Austin, LLC,[94] which involved a billboard owner's attempt to digitize their signs. In that case, the ordinance distinguished between signs based on their location (on-premise versus off-premise), which the Court held was not a content-based regulation. This meant that the city's ordinance was subject only to the same constitutional scrutiny as other content-neutral regulations.[95] Together, the *Reed* and *Austin* cases make clear that sign regulations should generally avoid any rule that differentiates between signs based on their content. On the other hand, distinctions such as those between commercial and noncommercial signs or between on-premise and off-premise signs are considered *content-neutral* rather than content-based. As a limit on speech, these still have to meet intermediate scrutiny, but most sign regulations will be able to meet this test because they further important governmental goals such as protecting public safety.

Watershed Protection and Stormwater Runoff Standards

North Carolina's watershed protection legislation, initially adopted in 1989, has important implications for cities and counties whose planning and zoning jurisdictions include land within the watershed of a public drinking water supply. Other water-quality regulations tend to focus on individual "point" sources of pollution such as factories, power plants, and wastewater treatment facilities. Watershed protection rules are designed to protect water supplies from *non-point-source* pollution that does not come from a particular source, such as fertilizer and pesticide runoff from lawns or the stormwater runoff from roads and other land within a watershed. The North Carolina Environmental Management Commission assigned classifications to more than two hundred such watersheds based on their use[96] and established statewide minimum watershed protection requirements that apply to the use and development of land in both the *critical area* of such watersheds and the remainder of the watershed.[97] State law requires affected local governments to incorporate the appropriate land development standards into local zoning, land subdivision, and special purpose watershed protection ordinances.[98]

Solar Energy Facilities

The rise of alternative energy has led local governments to reassess how they treat energy facilities. Solar collectors and systems gather solar radiation as a substitute for traditional energy sources for water heating, active space heating and cooling, passive heating, or generating electricity. Solar energy systems are becoming increasingly common in North Carolina.[99] They can serve as accessory uses (and structures) by primarily producing power for the benefit of a principal use. They can be roof-mounted or ground-mounted. A development regulation cannot prohibit collectors used for detached single-family residences, but it may include certain siting standards.[100]

---

94. 142 S. Ct. 1464 (2022).

95. For more on this case, see Adam Lovelady, "On-Premises and Off-Premises Signs: An Update from the U.S. Supreme Court," *Coates' Canons: NC Local Government Law* blog (Sept. 1, 2022), canons.sog.unc.edu/2022/09/on-premises-and-off-premises-signs-an-update-from-the-u-s-supreme-court/.

96. State rules regarding assignment of classifications and standards can be found at 15A N.C.A.C. 2B, §§ .0100 and .0200. An interactive map showing the various water supply watersheds in the state is available from the North Carolina Department of Environmental Quality (NC DEQ) at nconemap.gov/datasets/fb32d3871a5640a986b72087c4121125/explore.

97. *See* 15A N.C.A.C. 2B, § .0200.

98. 15A N.C.A.C. 2B, § .0623.

99. *See* Adam Lovelady, *Planning and Zoning for Solar in North Carolina* (UNC School of Government, 2014), www.sog.unc.edu/publications/reports/planning-and-zoning-solar-north-carolina.

100. G.S. 160D-914.

Solar generation of electricity for sale serves as the principal use for utility-scale solar farms. Common siting issues, which tend to be aesthetic in nature, concern the height and site location of the equipment, appropriate screening and fencing, and the difficult problem of potential glare. Many local governments require special use permits and decommissioning plans for utility-scale solar farms. Recent legislation now requires the Department of Environmental Quality to review solar farm decommissioning plans.[101] It is not yet clear whether the state requirement will preempt local decommissioning requirements or if some utility-scale projects will need duplicative authorizations.

Amendment of the Zoning Regulation

Zoning Amendment Process

Unlike many local government ordinances, local zoning regulations are amended fairly often. Most zoning regulation amendments are map amendments that change the zoning district classification of particular properties and are known as *rezonings*. However, important alterations may also be made in the regulation text.

When a local governing board amends zoning regulations—either the map portion or the text portion—it acts in its legislative capacity. Proposals to amend zoning regulations may typically be submitted by anyone—a planning board member, a governing board member, a local government agency or commission, or a person in the community whether or not he or she is a property owner. State law stipulates that before the governing board may consider a proposed amendment, the planning board must have an opportunity to review the proposal and make a recommendation regarding the proposal, including whether the proposed amendment is consistent with any applicable adopted plans.[102] In addition, state law requires the governing board to hold a public hearing before it adopts any zoning regulation amendment. Notice of this hearing must be published at least twice in a local newspaper. In addition, in rezoning cases notice must be posted on the property involved and additional notice must be made to neighbors.[103]

As referenced earlier, when the governing board makes a decision on a proposed zoning text or map amendment—whether it approves or denies the proposal—it must also approve a statement regarding whether the decision taken is consistent with applicable adopted plans.[104] The board's decision does not have to be consistent with the plan; the law only requires that the board consider its plans when making zoning decisions, not that it follow those plans. In addition, when adopting or rejecting a rezoning proposal, the governing board must adopt a statement "analyzing the reasonableness of the proposed rezoning."[105] This requirement comes from the concept of *spot zoning*, which is when a relatively small tract is classified differently from those around it.[106] Spot zoning decisions can be legal, *if* there is a reasonable basis for treating the property differently from adjoining properties. In *Chrismon v. Guilford County*,[107] the North Carolina Supreme Court provided a list of several factors upon which the reasonableness of an alleged spot zoning might depend. Those factors, including among others the attributes of the area, the benefits and detriments to the property owner and surrounding community, and the relationship between the proposed use and the uses of adjacent land, have substantially been reproduced in the statutory requirement for the reasonableness statement.[108] In effect, the statute requires a governing board to establish that its

101. G.S. 130A-309.240 (added by S.L. 2023-58).
102. G.S. 160D-604.
103. G.S. 160D-601. The additional rules for zoning map amendments are at G.S. 160D-602.
104. G.S. 160D-605(a).
105. G.S. 160D-605(b).
106. Blades v. City of Raleigh, 280 N.C. 531, 549 (1972).
107. 322 N.C. 611, 628 (1988).
108. *Compare Chrismon*, 322 N.C. at 628, *with* G.S. 160D-605(b)(i)–(v).

rezoning decision is reasonable whether or not it is a spot zoning but also provides support for the legality of any spot zoning that might occur.

Substantive Limitations on Zoning Map Amendments

Rezoning is easily one of the most controversial aspects of zoning. Rezoning procedures do not always conform to the expectations that property owners and neighbors have about how zoning should work. Part of the problem is that property owners, neighbors, and local government board members are interested in discussing the nature of the particular use that will be made of the land proposed for rezoning. However, a change from one conventional zoning district to another involves changing the entire suite of district-specific regulations. As a result, the local government must consider the full range of permissible uses and use restrictions; consideration may not be given to specific plans for any one project. That is, of course, unless the request is for a conditional district. Several important legal principles have been established by North Carolina state courts with regard to rezoning:

1. To be rezoned to a general use district, the land must meet the *general suitability* criterion, which requires that the property be suitable for any use permitted in that district. Any rezoning to a general use district that cannot be justified in terms of all the possible uses permitted in the new district is arbitrary and capricious and may be invalidated. Just how demanding this principle can be is illustrated when a petitioner suggests to the governing board that if the land is rezoned, it will be developed in a particular way. A series of North Carolina court rulings demonstrate that a petitioning developer does so at its peril.[109]
2. *Ad hoc* conditions may not be attached to a zoning amendment involving a general use district. Under North Carolina case law, special requirements not spelled out in the regulation that are added as conditions to a general use rezoning are invalid and hence unenforceable.[110] The rezoning itself is not necessarily invalid, but the city or county does not gain the control that it expected over the land of the petitioning property owner.
3. A local government may not engage in *contract zoning*. Contract zoning involves a transaction in which both the landowner who seeks a rezoning and the governing board itself undertake reciprocal obligations in the form of a bilateral contract.[111] For example, a landowner might agree to subject his property to deed restrictions or make certain road improvements to enhance access to the land if the city council would agree to rezone the land after the landowner takes these steps. Contract zoning of this type is illegal because by agreeing to exercise its legislative power in a particular way at a future date, a city abandons its duty to exercise independent judgment in making future legislative zoning decisions.[112]

---

109. Allred v. City of Raleigh, 277 N.C. 530 (1971); *Blades*, 280 N.C. at 550; Hall v. City of Durham, 323 N.C. 293, *reh'g denied*, 323 N.C. 629 (1988).

110. In *Decker v. Coleman*, 6 N.C. App. 102 (1969), the city council rezoned a property bordering a residential area to permit a shopping center but made the rezoning subject to a proviso that the developer leave a buffer strip around the development and not cut any access road through this strip into residential neighborhoods. The regulations for the particular commercial zoning district made no mention of such requirements. When the developer ignored these conditions, affected neighbors sought compliance in court. The court held that the conditions were unenforceable because they applied only to this property and not to other land with the same zoning district designation.

111. *Chrismon*, 322 N.C. at 635.

112. North Carolina courts have not had the occasion to rule on the validity of such a contract. However, *Chrismon* strongly implies that such contracts are void and unenforceable. *Id.* at 635.

Nonconformities and Amortization

When land is zoned or rezoned, certain legally existing uses and structures may not conform to the new set of zoning regulations. These nonconformities may take a variety of forms: nonconforming uses (uses not allowed in the current zoning district), nonconforming buildings (as to height, setback, and so forth), and nonconforming lots (as to width, frontage, or area). In addition, a property could be nonconforming with respect to any number of other standards, including off-street parking, its landscaping and buffering, or the position or size of advertising signs on it.

It is widely assumed that the policy of zoning is to discourage the perpetuation of nonconformities. However, a close look at many regulations reveals that most communities take a rather passive approach to the elimination of nonconformities. Most regulation provisions allow nonconforming uses or structures to continue. There are, of course, restrictions on their expansion or extension. Nonconforming structures may generally not be structurally altered or replaced. Nonconforming uses generally may not be converted to other nonconforming uses, and uses once abandoned may not be reopened. Nonetheless, nonconformities have been very resistant to attempts to get rid of them.[113]

A quite different method of treating nonconforming situations involves *amortization*. Amortization is based on the assumption that the owner of a nonconforming property may be required to come into full compliance with new development standards if the regulation provides a time period within which the owner may recover the investment made while relying on the former rules. Amortization may require either the removal or the upgrading of a nonconforming use or structure. Amortization provisions are most often applied to nonconforming signs and certain outdoor land uses (such as junkyards), which can be moved to other locations without undue difficulty. These regulations have been upheld both in principle and application by the North Carolina courts, overcoming challenges that they violate the landowner's due process rights or amount to an unconstitutional taking of private property without just compensation.[114]

Nonconforming outdoor advertising signs, whether on-premise or off-premise, have their own special protections. For many years, the amortization of outdoor advertising signs along interstates and certain federal- and state-numbered highways has been effectively prohibited by a statutory requirement providing that if a sign owner is forced to remove such a sign, some governmental unit must pay the owner "just compensation."[115] The amortization of off-premise outdoor advertising signs is also prohibited with respect to signs located anywhere in a city or county.[116] The legislation provides for certain exceptions, however, if the sign owner and local government agree to relocate the nonconforming sign. In 2024, the General Assembly added new protections for "on-premises advertising signs." If a sign is visible from a local or state road or highway, and if that sign advertises either activities on the property or the sale or lease of the property, it is an "on-premises advertising sign" and is protected from any requirements to remove it. The property owner can relocate or reconstruct a lawfully erected on-premises advertising sign, and a local government that requires removal of a lawfully erected advertising sign must compensate the sign owner and be responsible for removing the sign.[117]

---

113. *See* David Owens, "Rick's Cafe Experiences Growing Pains," *Coates' Canons: NC Local Government Law* blog (May 16, 2013), canons.sog.unc.edu/2013/05/ricks-cafe-experiences-growing-pains/.

114. *See, e.g.,* State v. Joyner, 286 N.C. 366, *appeal dismissed*, 422 U.S. 1002 (1975) (validating the amortization of salvage yards and junkyards over three years); Naegele Outdoor Advertising v. City of Durham, 803 F. Supp. 1068 (M.D.N.C. 1992), *aff'd*, 19 F.3d 11 (1994) (validating the amortization of commercial off-premise signs over five and one-half years).

115. G.S. 136-131.1.

116. G.S. 160D-912.

117. G.S. 160D-912.1.

Permitting, Permit Choice, and Vested Rights

Most of the land use and development regulations promulgated by cities and counties are enforced through permits and approvals designed to ensure compliance. These take the form of building permits, zoning permits, preliminary subdivision plat and final plat approvals, grading permits, flood hazard permits, and so on. For each of these approvals, months can pass between issuance of the permit and completion of the work. A major issue in zoning law involves whether rule changes should apply to projects already permitted and underway when the rule change becomes effective. For instance, there is often enough time between the issuance of a preliminary subdivision plat approval and completion of the permitted work for a local government to introduce, consider, and enact a change to subdivision standards. Should the old standards or the new standards apply?

On the one hand, the local government has an interest in rules going into effect uniformly at the time they become effective. But by the time a development proposal gets to the stage at which it is ready for the developer to seek local government approvals, it has already involved much deliberation and expense. Significant amounts of time and money have been committed and investments have been made based on the expectation that a particular project would be completed as designed and approved. If the rules were to change in the middle of the project, the entire enterprise could be thrown into jeopardy, making land development an even riskier project than it already is. To protect the expectations on which significant investments are made, owners and developers are granted *vested rights* to complete a project once a valid permit is issued.

A similar challenge can arise when the applicable regulations change between the time an application is submitted and the time it is approved. Imagine a scenario in which, during the review and hearing for a special use permit, a zoning text amendment goes into effect prohibiting that particular special use in the zoning district. As would be the case in a vested rights scenario, the property owner has likely made a significant investment based on the regulations in place at the time he or she submitted the application. To protect reasonable investment-backed expectations and assumptions at this stage, if a rule or regulation changes after an application is submitted and before it has been approved or denied, the statutes allow the applicant to select which version of the rule or regulation will apply.[118] This concept is aptly referred to as *permit choice*. While permit choice is relatively straightforward in nature, vested rights are a somewhat more complicated subject.

Types of Vested Rights

There are two varieties of vested rights: common law vested rights and statutory vested rights. A *common law vested right* is established if an owner has made substantial expenditures to carry out a project in good faith reliance on a valid project approval. Actual on-site construction is not required; expenditures of money and binding contracts to purchase land, construction materials, inventory, and equipment qualify. So do expenditures of time, labor, and energy. However, proceeding in good faith requires that the owner not work at an extraordinary pace to beat a potential rezoning. In addition, the expenditures must be made in reliance on a valid project approval. A valid zoning or building permit will normally suffice.[119]

Statutory vested rights are similar in form and function, but they derive from statute and have some important differences from common law vested rights. G.S. 160D-108(c) provides that amendments to development regulations are not applicable to buildings, uses, or subdivisions for which a development permit has been approved or issued. For more involved development projects,

118. *See* G.S. 160D-108(b) and 143-755(a).

119. *See* David W. Owens, *Land Use Law in North Carolina*, 4th ed. (UNC School of Government, 2023), at 343–61.

particularly those that proceed in multiple phases or require an array of site-specific approvals, there are a couple of twists on the standard statutory vested right.

First, where a development is to proceed in multiple phases, vested rights apply to the entire project at the time that the initial phase of the project obtains a development approval.[120] This avoids a situation in which a major multiphase development might otherwise obtain vested rights for particular portions of the project but end up with a hodge-podge of applicable rules by the time the development is complete. Instead, the entire development vests at once. A similar protection exists with regard to permit choice rights: when the first permit is submitted for a project that will require multiple permits, the applicant can choose which version of each of the relevant land development regulations will apply to the whole project.[121]

The law also allows development regulations to identify certain *site-specific vesting plans* for which the permit holder has the right to undertake and complete the development and use of the property under the terms of the vesting plan. Approval of such a plan protects against zoning amendments affecting the type and intensity of property use, with certain exceptions. The provisions for site-specific vesting plans contain slightly different vested rights provisions that apply specifically to those plans identified as site-specific vesting plans.[122]

Finally, as described below, a developer may negotiate the right to complete a project under preexisting development standards as part of a development agreement between the developer and the local government.

Development Agreements

Over the last few decades, North Carolina has seen development projects far larger in scope and built over longer periods of time than ever before. Local governments have recognized that the off-site impacts and public facility implications of such projects outstrip the capacity of their regulatory tools to manage them. Developers have major concerns of their own, particularly in regard to the risk involved in committing substantial funds to projects without adequate assurance that local development standards will not become more demanding or that infrastructure capacity will not be used elsewhere as the full extent of the project takes form. Legislation allowing local governments to enter into so-called development agreements provides a way to address these issues.[123]

Through a development agreement, the developer and one or more local governments can agree on construction and dedication schedules, applicable regulations, and other binding commitments that give each party more predictability in a project with a long lifespan. There are a number of conditions and standards that apply to development agreements. First, it is worth noting that development agreements previously could only be entered into for projects that were over 25 acres in size; now, however, local governments can enter into development agreements for projects of any size.[124] The agreement must include a number of details related to the property, its owners, the duration of the agreement, the uses permitted, public facilities that will serve the development and how they will be provided, any reservations or dedications of land, any environmental protections that exceed existing legal requirements, any additional terms and requirements for the protection of public

120. G.S. 160D-108(f). The statute defines a "multi-phased development" as one that contains 25 acres or more, is submitted for approval to occur in more than one phase, and is subject to a master development plan that commits to a certain type and intensity of use in each phase. G.S. 160D-108(j).

121. G.S. 160D-108(c).

122. *See* G.S. 160D-108.1.

123. *See* G.S. 160D-1001 through -1012. This legislation was enacted in 2005 as G.S. 160A-400.20–.32 (for cities) and G.S. 153A-379.1–.13 (for counties).

124. G.S. 160D-1004.

health and safety, and any provisions for historic structures.[125] The agreement may not impose a tax or a fee not otherwise allowed by law, and unless otherwise noted the regulations are those in force at the time of execution. For projects that straddle two or more different local governments, there can be multiple local government parties to the agreement. To be valid, the agreements must be adopted by the governing board of each local government that is party to the agreement, using the same process as a zoning text amendment.[126] Once executed by both parties, the agreement must be recorded, and it binds subsequent owners of the affected land as well as the current owner.[127]

Moratoria

Despite their best efforts to plan, local governments must often react quickly to new development issues or projects that are large, unusual, or impact the community in ways the current land development regulations do not address. This fast pace of change sometimes motivates a local government to want to halt certain kinds of development while it makes plans, formulates development strategies, and revises regulations to meet new challenges. These pauses, called *moratoria* (the singular is *moratorium*), limit certain development approvals for a fixed period of time until a more permanent solution to a particular problem can be devised.

Temporary moratoria may be placed on zoning permits, plat approvals, building permits, or any other development approval required by local regulation. However, as blanket limitations on development approval, moratoria are subject to strict limitations and standards outlined in statute. For instance, a local government may not adopt a moratorium for the purpose of developing and adopting plans or regulations related to residential uses. Further, the moratorium should be no longer than is necessary to resolve the condition that led to it.[128]

Unless there is an imminent and substantial threat to health and safety, the governing board must hold a public hearing before adopting the moratorium.[129] At the time it adopts a moratorium, a local government must approve a detailed statement regarding the problems leading to the moratorium and the necessity of both the moratorium and its scope and length.[130] This necessarily means that a local government must give considerable thought to the need for any moratorium and seek out alternatives before suspending issuance of development approvals.

Development projects on which certain types of progress have been made may not be subject to a moratorium. In the absence of an imminent threat to public health or safety, moratoria do not apply to projects with legally established vested rights—that is, projects for which a valid outstanding building permit has been issued, a site-specific or phased development plan has been approved, or substantial expenditures have been made in good faith reliance on prior administrative or quasi-judicial permission. The law also provides a special benefit to property owners and developers by providing that moratoria do not apply to projects for which a special use permit application or a preliminary or final plat approval application has been accepted by the city or county before the call for the public hearing to adopt the moratorium.[131] All of these measures are designed to prevent moratoria that focus on a particular project proposal, do not have a defined objective, or are broader than is truly necessary.

---

125. G.S. 160D-1006.

126. *See* G.S. 160D-1003 and -1005.

127. G.S. 160D-1011.

128. G.S. 160D-107(a).

129. G.S. 160D-107(b). The notice required for this hearing varies depending on whether the moratorium is to last more than 60 days. *See id.*

130. The detailed requirements for this statement are at G.S. 160D-107(d).

131. G.S. 160D-107(c).

Code Enforcement

Building Code Enforcement

The North Carolina State Building Code, adopted by the North Carolina Building Code Council, applies throughout the state. However, each city and county is responsible for enforcing the code within its jurisdiction. The code generally applies to new construction, but it includes a fire code volume that applies to the use of existing buildings and other provisions governing existing buildings and their rehabilitation, as well as emergency access to new developments.

The North Carolina State Building Code is based on a model international building code that has been adapted with amendments exclusive to North Carolina. The code applies to all types of new buildings, structures, and systems except farm buildings outside municipal code enforcement jurisdiction and several other minor classes of property. Generally, a city or county may not modify or amend the code as it applies locally. However, proposed local amendments to the fire prevention volume of the code found to be more stringent than the state code must be approved by the North Carolina Building Code Council.[132]

Every local government must provide for the inspection and enforcement of building code and other matters the governing board might specify.[133] To arrange for local code enforcement services, a city may (1) create its own inspection department; (2) form a joint inspection department with another local unit; (3) hire an inspector from another unit on a part-time basis, with the approval of the other unit's governing board; (4) contract with another unit that will provide inspection services; (5) request the county of which it is a part to provide inspection services throughout the city's jurisdiction without any contract between the two; or (6) contract with a certified code enforcement official who is not a local government employee. A county may make similar arrangements.

Since 1979, no person may enforce the State Building Code without a certificate from the North Carolina Code Officials Qualification Board. Each inspector must hold a certificate for one of several levels of competency.[134] All inspectors must complete certain training and continuing education courses to obtain and retain their respective certifications. In addition to supervising State Building Code official training and certification, the Code Officials Qualification Board may revoke an inspector's certificate for various reasons, including gross negligence.

Minimum Housing Code Enforcement

A local government is authorized to adopt its own minimum housing ordinance establishing the standards any dwelling unit must meet to be fit for human habitation.[135] The standards may deal with structural dilapidation and defects, disrepair, light and sanitary facilities, fire hazards, ventilation, general cleanliness, and other conditions that may render dwellings unsafe and unsanitary. Most units try to use this authority to encourage the rehabilitation of substandard housing. If a housing inspector finds after a formal hearing that a dwelling is unfit for human habitation but can be rehabilitated, the inspector may issue an order requiring the building to be repaired, improved, or vacated and closed. If the dwelling cannot be rehabilitated, the inspector may issue an order requiring it to be removed or demolished. If the property owner fails to comply with such an order after having every reasonable opportunity to do so, the inspector may carry out the order directly. No demolition order may be executed unless the governing board (typically the city council) enacts an ordinance to that effect for each property to be demolished.[136]

132. G.S. 143-138(e).
133. G.S. 160D-1102(a) and -1104(a) and (b).
134. G.S. 143-151.13.
135. G.S. 160D-1203.
136. *Id.*

Additional Resources

Ducker, Richard. "Are Adequate-Public-Facility Ordinances Adequate?" *Coates' Canons: NC Local Government Law* blog (December 16, 2009), canons.sog.unc.edu/2009/12/are-adequate-public-facility-ordinances-adequate/.

———. "Demolition and Code Enforcement Involving Historic Districts and Landmarks." *Coates' Canons: NC Local Government Law* blog (November 14, 2013), canons.sog.unc.edu/2013/11/demolition-and-code-enforcement-involving-historic-districts-and-landmarks/.

———. "What You Need to Know About Driveway Permits and Road Access: Part I." *Coates' Canons: NC Local Government Law* blog (January 16, 2014), canons.sog.unc.edu/2014/01/what-you-need-to-know-about-driveway-permits-and-road-access-part-i/.

Joyce, Jim. "Making Quasi-Judicial Decisions." *Coates' Canons: NC Local Government Law* blog (April 4, 2023), canons.sog.unc.edu/2023/04/making-quasi-judicial-decisions/.

———. "What Happens When Property Changes Jurisdiction?" *Coates' Canons: NC Local Government Law* blog (August 9, 2023), canons.sog.unc.edu/2023/08/what-happens-when-property-changes-jurisdiction/.

———. "What the Heck Is 'Agritourism'? Defining a Non-Farming Agricultural Use." *Coates' Canons: NC Local Government Law* blog (July 7, 2022), canons.sog.unc.edu/2022/07/what-the-heck-is-agritourism/.

Lovelady, Adam. "Comprehensive Plans and Land Use Plans Required for Zoning." *Coates' Canons: NC Local Government Law* blog (August 19, 2021), canons.sog.unc.edu/2021/08/comprehensive-plans-and-land-use-plans-required-for-zoning/.

———. "Hit the Pause Button: Temporary Development Moratoria in North Carolina." *Coates' Canons: NC Local Government Law* blog (February 23, 2023), canons.sog.unc.edu/2023/02/hit-the-pause-button-temporary-development-moratoria-in-north-carolina/.

———. "The Koontz Decision and Implications for Development Exactions." *Coates' Canons: NC Local Government Law* blog (July 1, 2013), canons.sog.unc.edu/2013/07/the-koontz-decision-and-implications-for-development-exactions/.

———. *Land Subdivision Regulation in North Carolina.* Chapel Hill: UNC School of Government, 2016.

———. "Making Sense of Subdivision." *Coates' Canons: NC Local Government Law* blog (April 27, 2016), canons.sog.unc.edu/2016/04/making-sense-subdivisions/.

———. "Permit Choice Rule for Development Regulations." *Coates' Canons: NC Local Government Law* blog (December 6, 2021), canons.sog.unc.edu/2021/12/permit-choice-rule-for-development-regulations/.

———. *Planning and Zoning for Solar in North Carolina.* Chapel Hill: UNC School of Government, 2014.

———. "Procedures for Legislative Development Decisions." *Coates' Canons: NC Local Government Law* blog (October 1, 2021), canons.sog.unc.edu/2021/10/procedures-for-legislative-development-decisions/.

———. "Reimbursement Agreements." *Coates' Canons: NC Local Government Law* blog (January 19, 2016), canons.sog.unc.edu/2016/01/reimbursement-agreements/.

———. *Reshaping Suburban Spaces: Lessons from North Carolina Cities.* Chapel Hill: UNC School of Government, 2016.

———. "Types of Development Decisions." *Coates' Canons: NC Local Government Law* blog (August 24, 2021), canons.sog.unc.edu/2021/08/types-of-development-decisions/.

Lovelady, Adam, and David W. Owens. *Chapter 160D: A New Land Use Law for North Carolina*. Chapel Hill: UNC School of Government, 2020.

Lovelady, Adam, James Joyce, and Ben Hitchings. *PlanNC Guidebook: A Practitioner's Guide to Preparing Streamlined Community Plans*. Chapel Hill: UNC School of Government, 2021.

Owens, David. "Can Offensive Content on Signs Be Prohibited?" *Coates' Canons: NC Local Government Law* blog (September 6, 2022), canons.sog.unc.edu/2022/09/can-offensive-content-on-signs-be-prohibited/.

———. "Does Zoning Have to Provide a Place for Everything?" *Coates' Canons: NC Local Government Law* blog (May 10, 2010), canons.sog.unc.edu/2010/05/does-zoning-have-to-provide-a-place-for-everything/.

———. *Introduction to Zoning and Development Regulation*. 4th ed. Chapel Hill: UNC School of Government, 2013.

———. *Land Use Law in North Carolina*. 4th ed. Chapel Hill: UNC School of Government, 2023.

———. "Regulating Land Uses Not Specifically Mentioned in a Zoning Ordinance." *Coates' Canons: NC Local Government Law* blog (last revised June 27, 2022), canons.sog.unc.edu/2015/11/dealing-with-land-uses-not-specifically-addressed-in-a-zoning-ordinance-the-saga-continues/.

———. "What Conditions Can Be Included in Conditional Zoning?" *Coates' Canons: NC Local Government Law* blog (November 11, 2021), canons.sog.unc.edu/2021/11/what-conditions-can-be-included-in-conditional-zoning/.

———. "What Does the Farm Exemption from Zoning Regulation Include?" *Coates' Canons: NC Local Government Law* blog (last revised April 30, 2022), canons.sog.unc.edu/2016/02/what-does-the-farm-exemption-from-zoning-regulation-include/.

Chapter 26

Community Development, Revitalization, and Affordable Housing

C. Tyler Mulligan

C. Tyler Mulligan is a faculty member at the School of Government who focuses on community economic development, affordable housing, public-private partnerships for development, and revitalization.

This chapter updates and revises chapters authored by Anita R. Brown-Graham, Kurt Jenne, and David M. Lawrence, whose contributions to the field and to this publication are gratefully acknowledged. The author also expresses appreciation to Caitlin Little, the School's legal research associate, for her help in updating this chapter.

Community development refers to an expansive set of activities designed to address the plight of economically distressed communities. Community development programs undertaken by North Carolina local governments include efforts such as revitalizing neglected neighborhoods or commercial areas, constructing housing that is affordable to low-income wage workers, providing financial counseling and services, fostering local leadership, strengthening civic organizations, conducting visioning and community planning exercises, and alleviating problems associated with unemployment and underemployment.[1] Community development programs are typically instituted under the direction of or in partnership with residents in the affected community. The goal of such programs is to enhance the built, financial, environmental, and social conditions of disadvantaged communities in a way that benefits all members of that community.

This chapter begins by explaining the community capitals framework, an asset-based approach to community development.[2] It focuses particularly on built capital, which often receives the most resources and attention from local governments. The chapter discusses the processes and activities necessary to develop built capital, along with the statutory authority that supports these efforts. Since this authority was established at different times and for various purposes, the chapter organizes its review of legal authority according to these distinct purposes. Additionally, it examines how local governments structure their community development programs. Finally, the chapter concludes with an overview of key federal funding sources for community development initiatives.

Asset-Based Approach to Community Development

The approach to community development that has attracted the most attention from scholars and practitioners is described as asset-based development. This approach starts by identifying the assets available in a particular community—the gifts, skills, and capacities of its residents, associations, and institutions—rather than focusing on what is absent, or what is problematic, or what the community needs.[3] The next step, sometimes referred to as building community capacity, seeks to use or leverage existing community assets to create new ones or enhance what is already there.[4] Outside help may be sought, but in recognition of the scarcity of resources available to assist distressed communities, the focus is more internal than external.

The major categories of community capital are the following:

- Financial assets
- Human assets
- Social and civic assets
- Built assets and affordable housing

Each type of community capital will be addressed in turn. The built assets category, which has traditionally been a major focus of local government authority and resources—particularly around the issue of affordable housing—serves as a springboard for the remainder of the chapter.

---

1. *See, e.g.*, 24 C.F.R. § 570.201 (basic eligible activities for Community Development Block Grants).

2. Gary Paul Green and Anna Haines, *Asset Building and Community Development*, 2nd ed. (Thousand Oaks, Calif.: Sage, 2008).

3. John P. Kretzmann and John L. McKnight, *Building Communities from the Inside Out: A Path toward Finding and Mobilizing a Community's Assets* (Evanston, Ill.: Institute for Policy Research, Northwestern University, 1993), 1–11.

4. C. Tyler Mulligan and Lisa F. Stifler, *Building Assets for the Rural Future: A Guide to Promising Asset-Building Programs for Communities and Individuals on the Economic Margin* (an online guide featuring asset-building approaches for distressed rural communities according to the asset being leveraged or developed), www.sog.unc.edu /resources/microsites/building-assets-rural-future/.

Financial Assets

Affordable credit, basic financial services, and investment of capital are critical to the health of communities. Unfortunately, private capital markets and traditional financial services often do not adequately meet the needs of low-income people, minorities, and small firms in distressed urban and rural areas. As a responsive strategy, community development focuses on creating access to capital to purchase homes, start businesses, obtain schooling, and provide community amenities in economically distressed places. There are two basic approaches to increasing access to capital. The first encourages the existing private market to make financial capital available in these communities. The second creates alternatives to the private market to serve the specific needs of community residents.

An example of the first approach is the federal Housing and Community Reinvestment Act (CRA). The CRA was enacted in 1977 to prevent banks from engaging in the practice of redlining; that is, refusing to make loans in low-income and/or minority areas.[5] Local governments have no direct oversight of CRA activity, but they can seek to partner with banks that hope to make loans in low-income areas in order to comply with CRA mandates.

Most public sector activity in the creation of financial capital involves tools that either provide incentives for private financing or create new sources of capital outside the private market. These mechanisms include special tax credits, the creation of community development financial institutions (CDFIs), microloan programs, financial literacy, and individual development accounts (IDAs). Local governments either engage directly in these strategies or partner with organizations that do.

An example of a financial capital tool that was designed specifically to encourage investment in low-income areas is the New Markets Tax Credit (NMTC), which was enacted as part of the federal Community Renewal Tax Relief Act of 2000.[6] Designed to stimulate new investment in low-income areas, the NMTC allows taxpayers to receive a credit against their federal income taxes for investing in commercial and economic activities that will benefit low-income communities. There are other federal tax credit programs that are used in community development efforts, such as the Low-Income Housing Tax Credit and the Historic Rehabilitation Tax Credit. Federal Opportunity Zones provide capital gains tax relief for taxpayers who make long-term investments in designated low-income census tracts. In addition, North Carolina has developed tax credits at the state level that aim to stimulate private investment in distressed places. For example, the state offers its own tax credit for investments in historic rehabilitation projects. Local governments cannot create their own tax relief programs so they must work within the ones established by the General Assembly. Local governments often help identify areas and projects in their communities that qualify for these tax relief programs.

Human Assets

Beyond access to financial capital, community developers recognize that their work must include linking residents to jobs. This focus is often called "workforce development." Education and formal training, on-the-job training, and family and nonfamily mentoring are all sources of workforce development that must be made available to community residents if they are to be competitive applicants for jobs in the new economy.

The State of North Carolina periodically updates its workforce development plan in accordance with federal plan requirements from the U.S. Department of Labor under the federal Workforce

5. *See* Pub. L. No. 95-128, 91 Stat. 1111 (1977).
6. *See* Pub. L. No. 106-554, 114 Stat. 2763 (2000).

Innovation and Opportunity Act (WIOA) of 2014.[7] Multiple state agencies collaborate in the effort, including the N.C. Department of Commerce, North Carolina Community College System, N.C. Department of Public Instruction, and N.C. Department of Health and Human Services. A network of workforce development boards throughout the state brings together private employers and public agencies to create workforce development programs for local areas.

Social and Civic Assets

In order to harness a community's capacity and focus its efforts toward a common goal, two interrelated community assets must be present. The first consists of the community's social networks and connectedness—the bonds that tie talented residents to each other, to the community, and to resources outside of the community.[8] The second is its civic organizations—those organizations that actively participate in the community, provide examples of leadership, and are capable of organizing talented individuals to accomplish community goals.[9] Local governments are often at the core of each of these assets, but private organizations, such as fraternal, religious, and charitable groups, are just as important to the social and civic health of a community.

Community development corporations (CDCs) are private institutions seeking to build the social and civic fabric of communities while enhancing other community assets. Incorporated as private nonprofit corporations, they typically have broad community betterment missions and engage in a wide variety of activities. They are often formed by neighborhood residents and usually have residents on their boards and in their membership. As such, they are considered to be credible voices for and accountable to the communities they serve. Local governments have worked closely with CDCs, within the limits of local government authority, to accomplish shared community development goals such as affordable housing development and provision of social services.[10]

As described later in this chapter, a certain percentage of funds allocated through the federal HOME Investment Partnerships Program (HOME) must be reserved for Community Housing Development Organizations (CHDOs).[11] CDCs often serve as CHDOs for the purpose of constructing housing through the HOME program.

Built Assets and Affordable Housing

In the context of community development, the built environment refers to buildings (houses, retail stores, factories) and infrastructure (roads, water and sewer, telecommunications). These built assets are essential to attracting private investment to a community, and the implications of absent or inadequate built assets can be far-reaching. Water and sewer infrastructure is almost always a

7. *See* Pub. L. No. 113-128, 128 Stat. 1425 (2014).

8. Cornelia Butler Flora and Jan L. Flora, "Social Capital," in *Challenges for Rural America in the Twenty-First Century*, ed. David L. Brown and Louis E. Swanson (University Park, Penn.: Pennsylvania State University Press, 2003), 214, 222; Robert D. Putnam, *Bowling Alone: The Collapse and Revival of American Community* (New York: Simon & Schuster, 2000), 19.

9. Green and Haines, *Asset Building and Community Development*, *supra* note 2, "Political Capital: Organizing for Power" (Chapter 10), at 197–210.

10. Tyler Mulligan, "Conveying Property to Housing Organization for Low- and Moderate-Income Homeownership," *Coates' Canons: NC Local Government Law* blog (Apr. 24, 2024), canons.sog.unc.edu/2024/04/conveying-property-to-housing-organization-for-low-and-moderate-income-homeownership/. Kristi Nickodem, "County Legal Authority to Fund Non-Mandated Social Services Programs," *Community and Economic Development in North Carolina and Beyond* blog (Oct. 12, 2023), ced.sog.unc.edu/2023/10/county-legal-authority-to-fund-non-mandated-social-services-programs/.

11. 24 C.F.R. § 92.300.

prerequisite for affordable housing and economic development.[12] Access to broadband contributes to both economic development and access to education and health care.[13] A well-maintained historic downtown—even in a rural area—confers benefits on the wider community.[14] In addition, there is evidence of a link between the built environment in a community and public health outcomes, because residents who live in a "walkable" neighborhood or have convenient access to full-service grocers are more likely to engage in greater physical activity and consume a healthier diet.[15] By contrast, a built environment permeated by liquor stores and fast food restaurants with few venues for exercise and recreation tends to facilitate negative and unhealthy lifestyles.

Low-Income Housing

One particular category of built assets, housing for low-income households, merits special attention because it is a primary focus for community development practitioners. For a host of reasons, private housing developers have struggled to produce adequate numbers of housing units that are affordable to low-income workers. In addition, community development is most needed in neighborhoods that have been largely ignored by homebuilders, realtors, and lending institutions, leading to deterioration of existing housing stock. The lack of safe and decent housing at lower price points routinely attracts the attention of local government officials, who then seek to address the need for "affordable housing."

The term *affordable housing* is often a source of confusion in public debate. Affordable housing refers to decent housing for those who, without some special intervention by a government or other provider of housing, could not afford to pay the prevailing rent or mortgage that ordinarily would be available in the private marketplace. The term involves judgments about the proportion of income that a family should pay for housing. "Affordable" units are those for which a family would pay no more than 30 percent of their income.[16] When a family pays more than this percentage, they are considered "cost burdened" by housing. This standard for affordability has changed over time. In 1969, the federal government set the housing affordability standard at 25 percent of income. It raised the standard to 30 percent in 1981. In the 1960s and 1970s, the federal housing affordability

---

12. Faqir S. Bagi, "Economic Impact of Water/Sewer Facilities on Rural and Urban Communities," *Rural America* 17, no. 4 (Winter 2002): 44, 45–46.

13. Peter Stenberg and Sarah Low, eds., *Rural Broadband at a Glance, 2009 Edition*, Economic Information Bulletin No. 47 (Washington, D.C.: Economic Research Service, U.S. Department of Agriculture, Feb. 2009), www.ers.usda.gov/publications/pub-details/?pubid=44324; Peter Stenberg, Mitchell Morehart, Stephen Vogel, John Cromartie, Vince Breneman, and Dennis Brown, *Broadband Internet's Value for Rural America*, Economic Research Report No. 78 (Washington, D.C.: Economic Research Service, U.S. Department of Agriculture, Aug. 2009), www.ers.usda.gov/publications/pub-details/?pubid=46215. North Carolina's efforts are led by the Division of Broadband and Digital Opportunity in the N.C. Department of Information Technology, www.ncbroadband.gov.

14. Dagney Faulk, "The Process and Practice of Downtown Revitalization," *Review of Policy Research* 23, no. 2 (March 2006): 625, 629.

15. The Prevention Institute has profiled eleven examples of predominantly low-income communities that have been transformed by changes in the built environment, particularly in terms of health outcomes. *See* Manal J. Aboelata, *The Built Environment and Health: Eleven Profiles of Neighborhood Transformation* (Oakland, Calif: Prevention Institute, July 2004), www.preventioninstitute.org/profiles/built-environment-and-health-11-profiles-neighborhood-transformation.

16. According to the U.S. Department of Housing and Urban Development (HUD), housing is affordable when all housing costs (combined rent and utilities for renters, and combined mortgage, utilities, homeowners association dues, insurance, and property tax for buyers) do not exceed 30 percent of total household income. This standard applies to any person or household regardless of the source or level of income. Drew DeSilver, "A Look at the State of Affordable Housing in the U.S.," www.pewresearch.org/short-reads/2024/10/25/a-look-at-the-state-of-affordable-housing-in-the-us/; Housing Cost and Housing Quality Fact Sheet, www.census.gov/topics/housing/guidance/cost-quality-fact-sheet.html. *See also* 24 C.F.R. § 91.5 (defining "cost burden").

standard was 25 percent of income. Starting in the 1980s, the standard moved to 30 percent.[17] The federal government considers households paying more than 50 percent of their incomes for housing costs to be severely cost burdened.[18] More recently, advocates have argued that commuting costs should also be considered when assessing the affordability of housing units.

Even higher-income persons may struggle to afford the housing they desire.[19] However, as used in this chapter, affordable housing programs are those that are targeted to low- and moderate-income households. Low-income households are defined by the U.S. Department of Housing and Urban Development (HUD) as those with incomes that are less than 80 percent of the local area median income (AMI).[20] The North Carolina Housing Authorities Law, by contrast, defines low-income households as those earning 60 percent of the "local area median family income" (AMI) as defined by the "most recent figures published by the U.S. Department of Housing and Urban Development."[21] In defining moderate income, the Housing Authorities Law lists several factors to be considered, such as total income, family size, cost of housing, and eligibility for "federal housing assistance of any type."[22] Federal housing assistance typically serves households at or below 60 percent AMI, but some federal housing assistance programs allow a small portion to be used for those earning as much as 80 percent AMI, so an argument can be made for moderate income to be defined under state law as high as 80 percent AMI—but certainly no higher.[23] Local governments possess no constitutional or statutory authority to aid those earning more than 80 percent AMI.[24]

Many of North Carolina's local governments are actively engaged in creating housing opportunities for low-income families facing affordable housing challenges. These families live in diverse circumstances that require a variety of solutions. In some fast-growing communities, teachers, firefighters, and young families may lack the income or savings to buy, or sometimes even to rent, a

---

17. Christopher Herbert et al., *Measuring Housing Affordability: Assessing the 30 Percent of Income Standard*, www.jchs.harvard.edu/research-areas/working-papers/measuring-housing-affordability-assessing-30-percent-income-standard.

18. 24 C.F.R. § 91.5 (defining "severe cost burden"). Cost burden data for each county in North Carolina can be reviewed through the CHAS (Comprehensive Housing Affordability Strategy) data query tool developed by the U.S. Department of Housing and Urban Development's Office of Policy Development and Research, available at www.huduser.gov/portal/datasets/cp.html. The North Carolina Housing Finance Agency (NCHFA) also makes housing data available online. *See* NCHFA, *NC Housing Snapshot* (interactive map with recent data), www.nchfa.com/about-us/policy-research/nc-housing-snapshot.

19. *See* Charles G. Field, "Building Consensus for Affordable Housing," *Housing Policy Debate* 8, no. 4 (1997): 801, 802–807.

20. 42 U.S.C. § 1437a (defining "low-income families").

21. Chapter 157, Section 3(15a) of the North Carolina General Statutes (hereinafter G.S.).

22. G.S. 157-3(15b).

23. The National Housing Trust serves those earning 30 percent AMI, and the federal HOME Investment Partnerships Program (HOME) requires almost all funding to be used for households earning no more than 60 percent AMI. However, a small amount (no more than 10 percent) of HOME funding may be used for those earning up to 80 percent AMI, so an argument can be made that *moderate income* can be defined under the Housing Authorities Law to be as high as 80 percent AMI. Other factors may be considered "without limitation," in order to better define the beneficiaries of a housing program, but other factors won't increase the income threshold set by today's federal housing programs. G.S. 157-3(15b).

24. Moderate-income households may be aided only when necessary and as an extension of a program designed for low-income persons. Housing aid for low-income persons has long been authorized. In 1982, the North Carolina Supreme Court addressed whether it was permissible to aid moderate-income persons alongside low-income persons. The court approved low-interest loans (with an interest rate of 14.5 percent) not only for low-income persons, but also for moderate-income persons, because the General Assembly was "acting with the same public purpose in mind" as when assisting persons of low income, with the goal "to make available decent, safe and sanitary housing" to another group "who cannot otherwise obtain such housing accommodations." *In re* Denial of Approval to Issue $30,000,000.00 of Single Family Hous. Bonds & $30,000,000.00 of Multi-Family Hous. Bonds for Persons of Moderate Income, 307 N.C. 52, 60 (1982) (citation omitted).

home. These families often need only one-time or short-term housing subsidies. Other lower-income households require longer-term subsidy assistance to supplement their inadequate incomes. In some localities, families might need a broad range of housing choices, including manufactured housing. Older adults may require more accessible housing to enable them to age in place.

Cost is only one dimension of the housing problem. In 2022, hundreds of thousands of households in North Carolina were suffering from some kind of housing problem, whether physical inadequacy, overcrowding, accessibility, or cost burdens.[25] Local governments have therefore attempted to address all of these dimensions. Each dimension is discussed below.

Physical Inadequacy

As defined by the U.S. Census Bureau, a housing unit has a complete kitchen facility when it includes all of the following: (1) a sink with piped water, (2) a range or cook top and an oven, and (3) a refrigerator.[26] Estimates in the Bureau's 2022 American Community Survey indicate that almost twenty-three thousand units of *occupied* housing in North Carolina do not contain a complete kitchen facility. To be counted as having complete plumbing facilities, a housing unit must have (1) hot and cold piped water, (2) a flush toilet, and (3) a bathtub or shower.[27] More than thirteen thousand *occupied* housing units in North Carolina failed to meet this standard in 2022.

In addition to inadequate kitchen and plumbing facilities, other conditions might make a home unfit, such as exposed electrical wiring or inadequate heating equipment. Local governments can respond to physical inadequacy by requiring owners to comply with minimum housing codes and then directly repairing the housing when owners fail to make the ordered repairs in a timely manner.[28] Severely dilapidated housing may require demolition, and separate statutory authority is provided for that.[29] Local governments possess statutory authority to seek the appointment of a receiver to manage the repair, demolition, and sale of vacant buildings when the owner fails to comply with code enforcement orders.[30]

In recent years, energy efficiency has become an important component of affordable housing. This is especially true for manufactured housing units (or mobile homes), which make up the lion's share of the state's privately owned affordable housing stock. Some community organizations have offered programs for the removal and replacement of old manufactured housing units with new, energy-efficient units at essentially the same monthly cost to the occupant.[31]

---

25. 2022 American Community Survey, available from the U.S. Census Bureau website at www.census.gov/acs. *See also* HUD CHAS data and the NCHFA housing snapshot as described above in footnote 18.

26. American Community Survey and Puerto Rico Community Survey 2022 Subject Definitions, "Kitchen Facilities" at 24–25, available from the U.S. Census Bureau website at www2.census.gov/programs-surveys/acs/tech_docs/subject_definitions/2022_ACSSubjectDefinitions.pdf.

27. *Id.* at 30, "Plumbing Facilities."

28. G.S. Chapter 160D, Article 12. C. Tyler Mulligan and Jennifer L. Ma, *Housing Codes for Repair and Maintenance: Using the General Police Power and Minimum Housing Statutes to Prevent Dwelling Deterioration* (UNC School of Government, 2011).

29. G.S. 160D-1119 through -1127.

30. G.S. 160D-1130.

31. Mulligan and Stifler, *Building Assets for the Rural Future*, *supra* note 4, § 5.b ("Increase the Asset-Building Potential of Manufactured Housing"), www.sog.unc.edu/resources/microsites/building-assets-rural-future/increase-asset-building-potential-manufactured-housing.

Overcrowding

An overcrowded unit can be thought of as one that contains more than one person per room. According to HUD's more technical definition, overcrowding occurs in a unit that has more than 1.01 persons per room, whereas severe overcrowding occurs when more than 1.51 persons per room reside in a unit.[32] In 1980, 4.5 percent of all occupied housing units in the state were overcrowded. By 1990, this figure had dropped to 2.9 percent. By 2022, an estimated 2.2 percent of households in North Carolina were overcrowded.[33] Local governments respond directly to overcrowding issues by establishing occupancy standards that limit the number of people who can live in a unit. Recognizing that overcrowding is often symptomatic of a tight affordable housing market, local governments may also seek to respond to the issue by finding ways to increase the supply of affordable housing.

Accessibility

As used in this chapter, accessibility refers to the access that individuals have to the full range of available housing choices. The term covers (1) efforts to make housing physically accessible to older adults and the disabled; (2) activities to eradicate illegal discrimination in the housing markets based on race, national origin, religion, gender, familial status, and disability; and (3) efforts to affirmatively expand housing opportunities for groups that have traditionally been discriminated against. The best statewide source of information on barriers to housing access is the North Carolina Human Relations Commission (NCHRC), which was created in 1963 to promote civil rights and equal opportunities for the residents of North Carolina. In addition to other functions, the NCHRC enforces the State Fair Housing Act by receiving and investigating housing discrimination complaints.

In addition to complaints addressed at the state level by NCHRC, a number of complaints are handled locally by human relations commissions established by local governments. These local commissions, in cities such as Charlotte and Winston-Salem, handle all complaints within their respective jurisdictions independently of NCHRC. A local commission is entitled to investigate and adjudicate fair housing complaints locally, provided it possesses all of the same powers and authority of NCHRC.[34]

At the national level, HUD also handles fair housing complaints. HUD is permitted to refer complaints to a local agency only when the agency's procedures and powers are certified to be "substantially equivalent" to HUD's.[35] NCHRC has been certified by HUD for this purpose.

Cost Burdens for Renters

The affordable housing squeeze has led to a significant increase in housing costs for many renters. Periodic shocks to the real estate market, such as the recession that began in 2008 and the pandemic that began in 2020, reduce housing production and exacerbate the problem. Rising housing costs have forced many renters to spend a large percentage of their income on housing. Over 40 percent of all North Carolina renters—over 560,000 households—spent at least 30 percent of their income on rent and utilities in 2020. The statistics are starker when one considers just those renters that HUD defines as low income. It is estimated that some 61 percent of these poorer renters in North

---

32. Comprehensive Housing Affordability Strategy: Background, available from the Housing and Urban Development website at www.huduser.gov/portal/datasets/cp/CHAS/bg_chas.html.

33. Consolidated Planning/CHAS Data available from the Housing and Urban Development website at www.huduser.gov/portal/datasets/cp.html.

34. G.S. 41A-7.

35. 42 U.S.C. § 3610.

Carolina—or more than 535,000 households—spent at least 30 percent of their income on housing.[36] Local governments have sought to ease the burdens on renters by employing either or both of two broad strategies: demand-side strategies and supply-side strategies. Demand-side strategies typically consist of rent subsidies for low-income persons, with funds for these subsidies coming from federal or local sources. Supply-side strategies undertaken by local governments involve increasing the supply of rental housing for low- and moderate-income households. These strategies range from owning and operating rental housing units through a public housing authority to establishing zoning requirements that encourage private developers to build affordable rental units.[37]

Cost Burdens for Homeowners

Homeownership has long been a cherished part of the American dream. Additionally, owning a home has been shown to confer benefits on household members. Compared to renting, homeownership is linked to greater life satisfaction, expanded social networks, greater neighborhood satisfaction, and greater participation in voluntary organizations.[38] Ownership by low-income persons has been shown to lead to greater household wealth, improved health of household members, greater workforce participation, and higher educational attainment by children.[39] In North Carolina in 2023, 65.9 percent of all occupied housing units were owned by their residents. This is slightly higher than the national rate of 65.8 percent but lower than North Carolina's ownership rate in 2000 of 71.1 percent and the 2010 rate of 69.5 percent.[40]

Even when potential homeowners can afford the monthly mortgage payment, the down payment and other financing requirements to secure a loan nonetheless pose insurmountable barriers to home ownership for low-income households. Local governments have used both federal and local funds to help overcome these barriers. Some jurisdictions offer down payment assistance or specialized loan products to low-income, first-time homebuyers. For low-income persons who already own a home, local governments have provided direct assistance to enable them to weatherize and rehabilitate their homes, including manufactured housing.[41]

One innovative model for placing home ownership within reach of low-income persons is a hybrid form of home ownership known as a community land trust (CLT).[42] Under the typical CLT model, a nonprofit land trust purchases land and constructs housing on that land. The land trust retains ownership of the land and sells only the built improvements to a qualified low-income buyer. By selling only the improvements, the cost of land is essentially removed from the sale price, in

36. Consolidated Planning/CHAS Data available from the Housing and Urban Development website at www.huduser .gov/portal/datasets/cp.html.

37. C. Tyler Mulligan and James L. Joyce, *Inclusionary Zoning: A Guide to Ordinances and the Law* (UNC School of Government, 2010).

38. William M. Rohe, Roberto G. Quercia, and Shannon Van Zandt, "The Social-Psychological Effects of Affordable Homeownership," in *Chasing the American Dream: New Perspectives on Affordable Homeownership*, ed. William M. Rohe and Harry L. Watson (Ithaca, N.Y.: Cornell University Press, 2007), 215–232.

39. Michal Grinstein-Weiss, Jung-Sook Lee, Johanna K. P. Greeson, Chang-Keun Han, Yeong H. Yeo, and Kate Irish, "Fostering Low-Income Homeownership through Individual Development Accounts: A Longitudinal, Randomized Experiment," *Housing Policy Debate* 19, no. 4 (2006): 711, 712 (reviewing benefits of homeownership).

40. U.S. Census Bureau, Housing Vacancies and Homeownership (CPS/HVS), "Table 15. Homeownership Rates by State," www.census.gov/housing/hvs/data/prevann.html.

41. The North Carolina Weatherization Assistance Program is administered through the N.C. Department of Environmental Quality. See the Department of Environmental Quality's website, specifically the Weatherization Assistance Program page, www.deq.nc.gov/energy-climate/state-energy-office/weatherization-assistance-program.

42. Variations of the community land trust model are located in Durham and Orange County. *See* Durham Community Land Trustees, dclt.org; Community Home Trust, communityhometrust.org. More information on the community land trust model is available from the Grounded Solutions Network, groundedsolutions.org.

theory making it affordable to a low-income person. The improvements are sold subject to a ground lease that dictates the terms of any future sale, usually requiring that the improvements be sold only to another qualified low-income buyer at a price that is affordable to that buyer at the time of sale. The sale price restriction is typically designed to permit the seller to make a small return on the sale, but the price is capped so that it remains affordable to the next low-income buyer. This arrangement is designed to ensure that the community's initial investment in affordable housing in the CLT is not lost—the housing ideally remains affordable over the long term over the course of many transfers of ownership. In 2009, the General Assembly enacted legislation to clarify that CLT property is to be assessed for property tax purposes based on the restricted sale price, not on the (presumably higher) prevailing market price of similar housing in the community.[43]

Local Government Authority for Community Development and Revitalization of Built Assets

Community development and revitalization involves making investments in built assets to preserve or revitalize distressed areas. A common strategy employed by local governments is acquiring and redeveloping strategically important properties through a process known as "land banking."[44] The term "land banking" usually refers to efforts to address vacant and abandoned *housing*, but the land banking process can be applied to any type of structure and provides a helpful framework for this section.

An initial step in land banking is to establish appropriate zoning and code enforcement in the jurisdiction. After setting up zoning[45] and code enforcement[46] (which are topics beyond the scope of this chapter), the next steps in land banking are as follows:

1. Acquire strategically important properties.
2. Hold and stabilize the acquired properties.
3. Develop the properties or convey them to a developer.
4. Provide financing for development if it is necessary and authorized by law.

Some states, such as Michigan and Georgia, have enacted state legislation to create one or more public authorities to serve as "land banks." In North Carolina, there is no overarching state legislation of

43. S.L. 2009-481 (H.B. 1586, community land trust property taxation), codified at G.S. 105-277.17.

44. Frank S. Alexander, *Land Banks and Land Banking*, 2nd ed. (Flint, Mich.: Center for Community Progress, 2015), communityprogress.org/publications/land-banks-and-land-banking-2nd-edition/. *See also* Tyler Mulligan, "How a North Carolina Local Government Can Operate a Land Bank for Redevelopment," *Community and Economic Development in North Carolina and Beyond* blog (Mar. 18, 2014), ced.sog.unc.edu/2014/03/how-a-north-carolina-local-government-can-operate-a-land-bank-for-redevelopment/.

45. Zoning and land use law is covered in Chapter 25, "Planning, Land Use, and Development." Several local governments in North Carolina have established zoning requirements to encourage developers to produce affordable housing as part of larger market-rate residential developments. These requirements are sometimes referred to as inclusionary zoning or inclusionary housing programs. A detailed examination of inclusionary housing programs and associated regulatory policies is provided in C. Tyler Mulligan and James L. Joyce, *Inclusionary Zoning: A Guide to Ordinances and the Law* (UNC School of Government, 2010).

46. Code enforcement involves conducting inspections and then issuing orders to repair to owners who are found in violation of codes. For an overview of housing codes, see Mulligan and Ma, *Housing Codes for Repair and Maintenance*. This related blog post compares nonresidential maintenance codes to minimum housing codes: Tyler Mulligan, "Maintenance of Vacant or Neglected Commercial Buildings: Options for NC Local Governments," *Community and Economic Development in North Carolina and Beyond* blog (Mar. 20, 2018), ced.sog.unc.edu/2018/03/maintenance-of-vacant-or-neglected-commercial-buildings-options-for-nc-local-governments/.

that sort, but local governments can perform many of the basic functions of a land bank by relying on existing statutory authority.

It should be noted at the outset that North Carolina local governments possess no inherent powers to engage in community development and revitalization. Whatever powers they possess must be granted to them by statute, even when all of the funds to support an activity come from the federal or state government.[47] Any action taken without authority is considered to be *ultra vires*, that is, outside the scope of the powers delegated by the state.

Thus, in order to proceed through the steps of the land banking process, a local government must identify statutory authority for each step it takes. Because the relevant statutes were enacted at different times and in response to different programmatic needs, the statutory authority is not laid out neatly in a single section of the statutes. For purposes of this chapter, the statutes are categorized into the following broad purposes, roughly in the order they were enacted:

1. Low-income housing.
2. Urban redevelopment.
3. Community development.
4. Downtown revitalization.
5. Economic development (the subject of Chapter 27).

Each successive statutory category and its associated constitutional case law builds upon earlier statutory schemes. For example, the Urban Redevelopment Law was enacted to cover activities that were not authorized by the earlier Housing Authorities Law. Each category's statutes grant different authorities and impose different requirements from the other categories, so a local government's authority to engage in an activity depends upon which category is implicated. The powers granted under the first four categories (low-income housing, urban redevelopment, community development, and downtown revitalization) are covered in this chapter. The final category, economic development, evolved more recently and therefore merits separate treatment; it is described in the next chapter.

Development and Rehabilitation of Low- and Moderate-Income Housing

Background on Legal Authority

The General Assembly enacted the Housing Authorities Law in 1935 to enable communities to take advantage of federal grants for public housing. This law, as amended over the decades since its original passage, appears as Chapter 157, Article 1 of the North Carolina General Statutes (hereinafter G.S.). Without this grant of state authority, local governments could not have participated in a string of federally funded housing programs that started with the National Industrial Recovery Act of 1933.[48]

---

47. G.S. 160A-17.1 authorizes local governments to accept state or federal funds to perform activities they are "authorized by *general law* or *local act* to provide or perform"; thus, the funding source or grant agreement—even when the source is the State of North Carolina—does not provide independent authority for an activity. G.S. 160A-17.1 (emphasis added).

48. The National Industrial Recovery Act of 1933 (Pub. L. No. 73-67, Sec. 202; 48 Stat. 195, 201) authorized federal funds to be used to finance "low-cost housing and slum clearance"; the National Housing Act of 1934 (Pub. L. No. 73-479, Sec. 207; 48 Stat. 1246, 1252) created two federal agencies, the Federal Housing Administration (FHA) and the Federal Savings and Loan Insurance Corporation (FSLIC), to insure mortgages to municipal corporations "formed for the purpose of providing housing for persons of low income"; and the United States Housing Act of 1937 (Pub. L. No. 75-412, Sec. 2; 50 Stat. 888, 888), established a permanent public housing program to create "low-rent housing" for "the lowest income group." The Housing Act of 1949 (Pub. L. No. 81-171, Sec. 2; 63 Stat. 413, 413) established the

Most of the public purpose case law on low-income housing pertains to the sweeping Housing Authorities Law, which authorized the provision of "dwelling accommodations for persons of low income," and which defines "low income" as 60 percent of local area median income (AMI) or below.[49] The North Carolina Supreme Court concluded that the Housing Authorities Law serves a constitutional public purpose by addressing the shortage of housing for families of lower income due to private enterprise being unable to meet the need.[50] Indeed, the state constitution declares that it is "one of the first duties of a civilized and a Christian state" to aid "the poor, the unfortunate, and the orphan."[51]

As for households earning "moderate income" (reasonably defined under state law as no higher than 80 percent AMI[52]), the North Carolina Supreme Court approved a state program of low-interest loans not only for low-income persons, but also for moderate-income persons, because the General Assembly was "acting with the same public purpose in mind" as when assisting persons of low income, with the goal "to make available decent, safe and sanitary housing" to another group "who cannot otherwise obtain such housing accommodations."[53] Thus, so long as local governments limit their activities to supporting households earning 80 percent AMI or below, and private enterprise is unable to meet the housing need, then a constitutional public purpose is served when government provides (1) housing and housing aid for low income persons and (2) low-interest loans for housing for low- and moderate-income (LMI) persons.

Can local governments offer support for moderate-income households beyond the low-interest loans that were approved in case law? Probably yes, so long as moderate-income households (earning as high as 80 percent AMI) are integrated into a low-income program, "with the same public purpose in mind" as assisting low-income persons (earning 60 percent AMI or below).[54] A program targeted exclusively for moderate-income households, to the exclusion of low-income households, would not align with constitutional case law.

Government action in the housing arena must be necessary and cannot supplant private activity. Housing activities serve a public purpose "only when the planning, construction, and financing of residential housing is not otherwise available" to "'persons and families of low income'" due to "the inability of private enterprise and investment, without assistance, to meet that need."[55] The

---

national housing policy of "a decent home and a suitable living environment for every American family." A fuller treatment of the evolution of federal housing policy is provided in Nathaniel S. Cushman, "Affordable Housing: An Intimate History" (Chapter 1), in *The Legal Guide to Affordable Housing Development*, ed. Iglesias et al. (3rd. ed., American Bar Association, 2022), 3–24.

49. G.S. 157-9, -3(15a).

50. *See, e.g.*, Wells v. Hous. Auth. of City of Wilmington, 213 N.C. 744 (1938) (holding that the Housing Authorities Law serves a constitutional public purpose "where community initiative has failed and authority alone can prevail"); Mallard v. E. Carolina Reg'l Hous. Auth., 221 N.C. 334 (1942) (holding that the Housing Authorities Law serves a public purpose in rural as well as urban areas); *In re* Hous. Auth. of City of Charlotte, 233 N.C. 649, 660 (1951) (holding that eminent domain may be exercised for the purpose of constructing "low-rent dwellings" despite the fact that the area to be condemned may not be a "slum area"); Martin v. N.C. Hous. Corp., 277 N.C. 29, 49, 50 (1970) (accepting the premise of the legislature that there is "a serious shortage of decent, safe and sanitary residential housing available at low prices or rentals to persons and families of lower income" and "'that private enterprise and investment have not been able to produce, without assistance,' the needed residential housing.")

51. N.C. Const. art. XI, sec. 4.

52. See notes 22–24 and accompanying text above.

53. *In re Denial of Approval to Issue $30,000,000.00 of Single Family Hous. Bonds & $30,000,000.00 of Multi-Family Hous. Bonds for Persons of Moderate Income*, 307 N.C. at 60 (citation omitted).

54. *Id.* Under current law, it is not a constitutional public purpose for local governments to provide housing or housing aid for households earning more than 80 percent AMI. Housing for these higher-income households must be financed, constructed, and operated exclusively within the realm of the private sector.

55. Martin v. N.C. Hous. Corp., 277 N.C. 29, 49, 50 (1970).

failure of private enterprise to meet the need can be demonstrated; as explained earlier, federal data reveals that hundreds of thousands of households in North Carolina are reported to suffer from some kind of housing problem, ranging from physical inadequacy to overcrowding to cost burden. Local governments, relying on localized data for their specific jurisdiction, point to it as evidence that private enterprise is unable to meet their jurisdiction's need for housing for low- and moderate-income households.

The original Housing Authorities Law enabled local governments to establish public housing authorities, and those authorities (not cities and counties) were empowered to use federal funding to develop housing projects. A housing project is a "single plan or undertaking"[56] under common ownership in which the land banking powers described earlier are employed for the purpose of rehabilitating or providing housing for LMI persons.

The area of operation for a housing authority created by a city is anywhere in the city and the area within ten miles from the territorial boundaries of the city, but it cannot undertake a housing project in another city without permission; likewise, the area of operation for a housing authority created by a county is anywhere in the county, but it may not undertake a housing project in a city without the permission of that city.[57]

Counties and cities were granted authority to exercise directly the powers of a housing authority starting in 1975.[58] To employ housing authority powers, a governing board must first designate itself to exercise the powers of a housing authority,[59] and then it must follow the same statutory requirements as if it were a housing authority.[60]

To ensure that federal funds were the primary source of funding for these activities, the General Assembly originally required both cities and counties to conduct a public referendum whenever state or local taxes were used for housing projects and community development.[61] No referendum was required so long as federal funds were used. In 1983, cities were authorized to use sales tax revenues without holding a referendum,[62] and then cities were relieved of the referendum requirement entirely two years later.[63] The original referendum requirement remains in effect for counties, though partial relief was enacted in 1999 when counties were authorized to use state and local tax revenues to construct county-owned housing projects and to convey property without subsidy.[64]

---

56. G.S. 157-3(12). A housing project must be a "single plan or undertaking" with common ownership, management, and financing. The definition of a housing project in state law (in North Carolina and other states) is taken from federal law and the term "single plan or undertaking" has been in the law since its original enactment in 1935. To understand its meaning, see 24 C.F.R. § 92.2, where "Project" is defined as a "site or sites together with any building (including a manufactured housing unit) or buildings located on the site(s) that are under *common ownership, management, and financing* and are to be assisted with [federal] funds as a *single undertaking* under this part" (emphasis added).

57. G.S. 157-39.1.

58. S.L. 1975-435 (enacting G.S. 153A-376, 160A-456); *see* G.S. 160D-1311 (successor to G.S. 153A-376 and 160A-456).

59. The process for a governing board to designate itself to exercise housing authority powers is set forth in G.S. 157-4.1 (cities) and G.S. 157-33 (counties).

60. The N.C. Attorney General opined that local governments were required to follow the procedures applicable to redevelopment commissions when exercising the powers of a redevelopment commission. Letter to Tommy W. Jarrett, 45 Op. N.C. Att'y Gen. 44 (1975). The exercise of housing authority powers is analogous to the exercise of redevelopment commission powers; indeed, the authority to exercise both of those powers is found in the same sentence of G.S. 160D-1311(b) (codifying substance of G.S. 153A-376 and G.S. 160A-456 as enacted by S.L. 1975-435).

61. S.L. 1975-435; S.L. 1975-689 (amending G.S. 153A-367 and G.S. 160A-456, respectively).

62. S.L. 1983-908 (amending G.S. 160A-456(e)).

63. S.L. 1985-665 (repealing G.S. 160A-456(e)).

64. S.L. 1999-366 (enacting G.S. 153A-378 and amending G.S. 159-48). The concept of entering into housing-related transactions without subsidy was not a new concept; S.L. 1979-690, which amended various provisions

Figure 26.1 Flowchart to Determine Statutory Authority for Engaging in Housing Projects

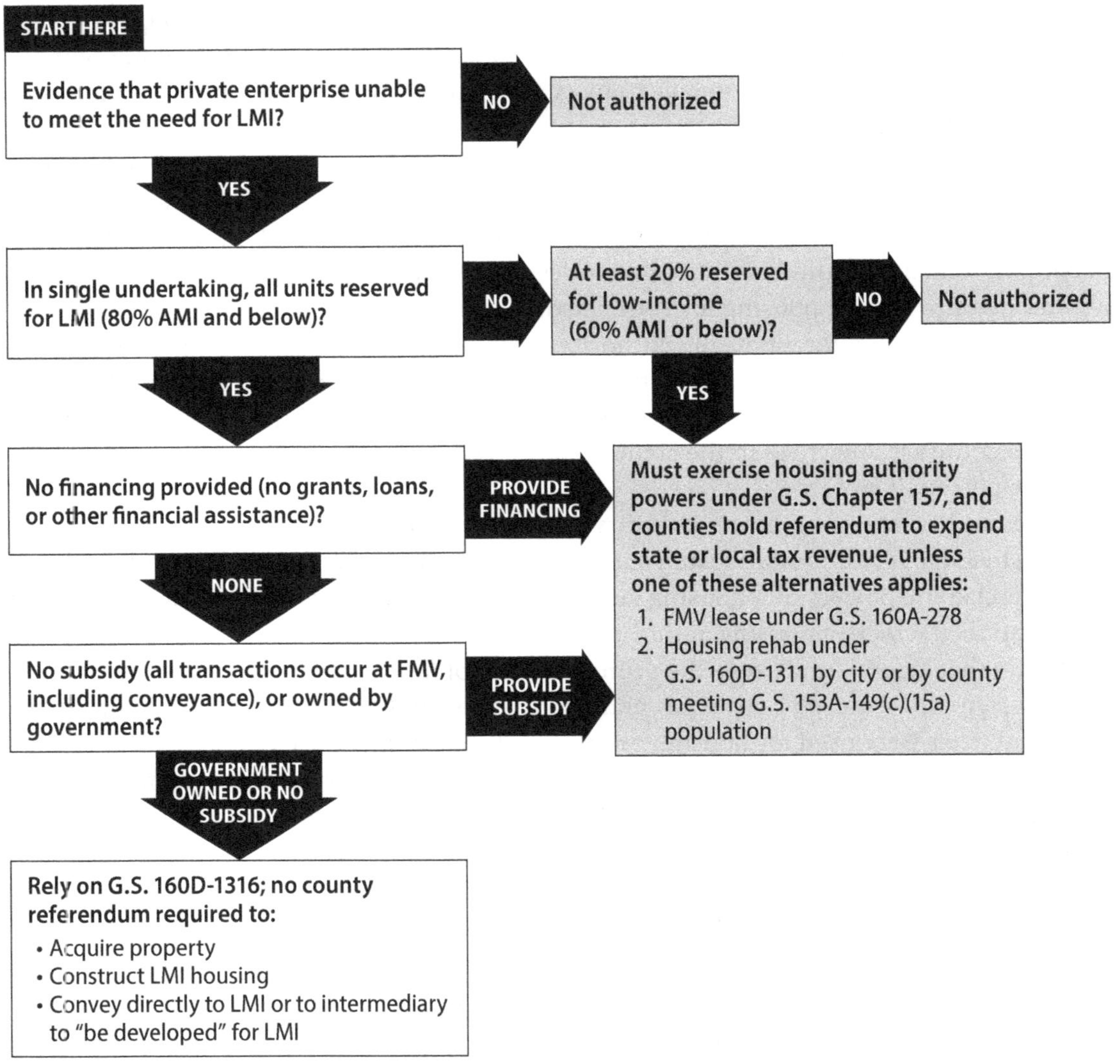

The specific statutory authority for undertaking a housing project and whether a city or county should designate itself as a housing authority is influenced by several factors: who is served by the housing project based on income eligibility restrictions; whether financing (loan) or subsidy (low-interest loan, grant, or financial assistance, including below-market property conveyance) is provided to a private housing project; and, for counties, whether a referendum is held. Figure 26.1 is a flowchart to assist local governments in determining which statutory authority applies depending on the factors at play.

Generally speaking, cities and counties may complete housing projects in their own capacity pursuant to G.S. 160D-1316, without designating themselves to exercise housing authority powers, so long as no financing or subsidy is provided to a private housing project and all units are restricted

of G.S. Chapter 157, was entitled, "An Act to Allow Housing Authorities to Give Mortgages without Government Subsidy."

to LMI households. Activities falling into this category include construction of government-owned housing and conveyance of property at fair market value (FMV) to LMI households directly or to private partners to "be developed"[65] into LMI housing. Counties relying on G.S. 160D-1316 are not required to conduct a referendum even if state or local revenues are expended.[66]

In the case of projects requiring financing or subsidy such as "grants, loans, interest supplements, and other programs of financial assistance," a local government must designate itself as a housing authority under G.S. Chapter 157 to support the project.[67] Any public subsidy must flow to the eligible LMI households, not to the owner or developer of the housing, nor to those earning more than 80 percent AMI.[68] Counties must approve a referendum in order to expend state or local tax revenues to provide financing or subsidy to a housing project.[69] An exception to the county referendum requirement was created for LMI housing rehabilitation programs in populous counties.[70]

Occasionally, a local government will seek to support a "mixed income" housing project that contains some unrestricted market-rate units alongside income-restricted units. When one or more units of a housing project will be occupied by households earning more than 80 percent AMI, the statutes require at least 20 percent of the units to be reserved for the "exclusive use" of low-income households earning 60 percent AMI or below.[71]

The legal authority for local governments to engage in housing projects is described in broad terms above. However, engaging in housing projects requires a local government to complete the land banking activities that were described earlier—i.e., acquiring property, holding and stabilizing properties so acquired, developing those properties or conveying the property to a developer, and providing financing for development if necessary and authorized by law—and each activity involves additional nuance. Each activity, as used by local governments to produce LMI housing, is therefore reviewed below.

---

65. G.S. 160D-1316(3).

66. The reasoning for this conclusion is that G.S. 160D-1311 exempts counties from the referendum requirement when they use state or local tax revenues for an activity explicitly authorized by G.S. 153A-149. G.S. 153A-149(c)(15b) explicitly authorizes housing programs for low- and moderate-income persons as provided in G.S. 160D-1316. Turning to G.S. 160D-1316, local governments are authorized to engage in housing projects where (1) all units are restricted to low- and moderate-income households and (2) no loans, grants, or other forms of financial assistance are provided to a private housing project. Authority to provide "grants, loans, interest supplements and other programs of financial assistance" (including subsidized conveyances) for private owners and developers is found only in the Housing Authorities Law. G.S. 157-3(12)d., e.

67. Provision of "grants, loans, interest supplements and other programs of financial assistance" (including implied grants when property is conveyed for less than fair market value) is a power unique to housing authorities pursuant to G.S. 157-3(12) and G.S. 157-9(a). Cities and counties may exercise the powers of a housing authority pursuant to G.S. 160D-1311(b).

68. The exclusive emoluments clause in the state constitution prohibits gifts to private entities. N.C. Const. art. I, sec. 32. *See also* Frayda Bluestein, "Donating Property: Beware of Constitutional Constraints, *Coates' Canons: NC Local Government Law* blog (Apr. 13, 2015), canons.sog.unc.edu/2015/04/donating-property-beware-of-constitutional-constraints/. Furthermore, "[n]o housing authority may construct or operate its housing projects so as to provide revenues for other activities of the city [or, by extension, developers or other entities]." G.S. 157-29(a). A local government therefore must exercise oversight of the budgets for construction and operation of the housing project to ensure that any public subsidy is going to low- and moderate-income persons and not toward other activities of the third-party owner or developer. A simple approach is to ensure that financial support for a housing project does not exceed the total rent subsidy or down payment assistance provided to low-income residents over the life of the project. Most federal housing programs impose a similar requirement and require financial underwriting. *See, e.g.*, 24 C.F.R. § 92.250.

69. S.L. 1999-366.

70. G.S. 160D-1311, 153A-149(c)(15a) (limited to counties with a population of 400,000 or more).

71. G.S. 157-3(12); 160A-278.

Acquire Property

Any city or county may designate itself to exercise the powers of a housing authority and rely on housing authority powers to acquire property for a housing project.[72] A county must first hold a referendum if state or local funds are expended.[73] Property may even be acquired by eminent domain.[74] A county or city may, without designating itself to exercise housing authority powers, rely on G.S. 160D-1316 to acquire property "by voluntary purchase" to "be developed by" the county or city or "be used by" the city or county to provide housing to LMI households—and under these constraints no county referendum is required.[75]

Hold, Stabilize, and Develop Acquired Property

Local governments possess general authority to hold and improve property they own.[76] In addition, local governments may, in their own capacity under G.S. 160D-1316 without relying on housing authority powers, "expend funds for residential housing construction, new or rehabilitated" under government ownership to create housing "for sale or rental to persons and families of low and moderate income," and "may contract with any person, association, or corporation" for that purpose.[77] State and local funds may be expended by counties for government-owned units without holding a referendum.[78]

Convey Property to a Private Owner or Developer

As a general rule, local governments are always required, unless an exception applies, to convey real property by following competitive bidding procedures: sealed bid, upset bid, or public auction.[79] The price reached through competitive bidding is presumed by the courts to be the fair market value of the property.[80] However, a drawback of competitive sale procedures is that they do not permit the local government to impose restrictions on the use of the property or to select the buyer for reasons other than the bid amount.[81]

In the context of LMI housing projects, however, it is necessary for a local government to choose a buyer (through a privately negotiated sale or private sale) that is capable of constructing and managing a housing project, and to impose conditions and requirements on that buyer. The General Assembly contemplated this necessity. Housing authorities are entirely exempt from typical property conveyance procedures, and so are local governments when they exercise housing authority

72. G.S. 160D-1311, 157-9.

73. G.S. 160D-1311.

74. G.S. 157-11; 40A-3(c)(5). *See also In re Hous. Auth. of City of Charlotte*, 233 N.C. at 660 (holding that eminent domain may be exercised for the purpose of constructing "low-rent dwellings" despite the fact that the area to be condemned may not be a "slum area").

75. G.S. 160D-1316(2).

76. G.S. 160A-11 (cities); 153A-11 (counties).

77. G.S. 160D-1316(1). The statute enables a local government to construct housing under government ownership; this statute does not authorize loans, grants, or financial assistance for a privately owned housing project. Provision of "grants, loans, interest supplements and other programs of financial assistance" for private owners and developers is authorized only when a local government acts as a housing authority. G.S. 157-3(12)d., e.

78. G.S. 160D-1311; 153A-149(c)(15b); 160D-1316(1).

79. G.S. 160A-266, -268, -269, -270 (cities); 153A-176 (counties). *See also* Chapter 23, "Public Contracts, Competitive Bidding Requirements, and Property Disposal."

80. Redevelopment Comm'n of Greensboro v. Sec. Nat'l Bank of Greensboro, 252 N.C. 595, 612 (1960).

81. Puett v. Gaston Cnty., 19 N.C. App. 231, 235 (1973).

Table 26.1 Private Sale/Lease of Real Property *at or above* Fair Market Value (FMV)

Household (HH) income eligibility restrictions imposed	Lease in capacity as city or county	Sale in capacity as city or county	Exercising powers of housing authority per G.S. 160D-1311(b)*
All units for LMI only (no HH over 80% AMI served)	G.S. 160A-278	G.S. 160D-1316(3)	G.S. 157-3(12), 157-9
HHs above 80% AMI served. **At least 20% of units reserved** for 60% AMI or below	G.S. 160A-278	No statutory authority	G.S. 157-3(12), 157-9
HHs above 80% AMI served. **Less than 20% of units set aside** for 60% AMI or below	No statutory authority or supporting constitutional case law		
Compliance period (unless sold to eligible HH)	Entire lease term	Perpetual & reverter	Perpetual & reverter

*Gray highlighting indicates referendum required for counties if property acquired with state or local tax revenues.

powers.[82] As a practical matter, local governments exercising housing authority powers simply follow the private sale procedures of G.S. 160A-267 in order to provide some structure for the conveyance.

Should a city or county wish to convey property without relying on housing authority powers, then there is limited authority under G.S. 160D-1316 to convey property at private sale with perpetual "covenants or conditions that assure the property will be developed . . . for sale or lease to persons of low or moderate income."[83] It should be noted that these conveyance powers do not mean that property can be sold for less than its fair value; the exclusive emoluments clause of the North Carolina Constitution prohibits gifts to private entities.[84] However, an appraiser may consider any binding covenants placed on the property when determining the fair market value of property to be conveyed.[85]

82. G.S. 157-9(a) provides: "No provisions with respect to the acquisition, operation or disposition of property by other public bodies shall be applicable to an authority unless the legislature shall specifically so state." G.S. 160D-1311(b).

83. G.S. 160D-1316(3). Covenants may be released (but are not required to be released) after property is sold directly to a LMI household with all subsidy being passed along to the LMI household.

84. N.C. Const. art. I, sec. 32. The North Carolina Supreme Court expounded on the exclusive emoluments clause in the context of property conveyance in *Brumley v. Baxter*, 225 N.C. 691 (1945), with two important conclusions. First, if a jurisdiction's conveyance of property occurs without full monetary consideration (meaning, payment is less than fair market value), then there must be consideration in the form of an enforceable promise to provide public services for the jurisdiction. Second, if the consideration is in the form of public services, the conveyance must be conditioned on the property's continued use for that purpose by the recipient, and the property must revert back to the local government in the event the recipient ceases to use it for that purpose. This rule applies even if statutes fail to impose an explicit requirement regarding sale price, such as "appraised value." *See also* Frayda Bluestein, "Donating Property: Beware of Constitutional Constraints," *Coates' Canons: NC Local Government Law* blog (Apr. 13, 2015), canons.sog.unc.edu/2015/04/donating-property-beware-of-constitutional-constraints/. Most federal programs impose a similar requirement under 2 C.F.R. § 200.311. For additional background and detail on conveyances for affordable housing, particularly when an intermediary developer is involved, see Tyler Mulligan, "Conveying Property to Housing Organization for Low- and Moderate-Income Homeownership," *Community and Economic Development in North Carolina and Beyond* blog (Apr. 24, 2024), ced.sog.unc.edu/2024/04/conveying-property-to-housing-organization-for-low-and-moderate-income-homeownership.

85. Note that a property's value might be affected by the "covenants or conditions that assure the property will be developed . . . for sale or lease to persons of low or moderate income." G.S. 160D-1316(3). In other words, a requirement for property to be used for LMI housing may reduce the revenue potential of the property and thereby lower

Table 26.2 Private Sale/Lease *below* FMV (Subsidy Flows to Eligible HHs)

Household (HH) income eligibility restrictions imposed	Acting in capacity as city or county	Exercising powers of housing authority per G.S. 160D-1311(b)*
All units for LMI only (no HH over 80% AMI served)	No statutory authority	G.S. 157-3(12), 157-9
HHs above 80% AMI served. **At least 20% of units reserved** for 60% AMI or below	No statutory authority	G.S. 157-3(12), 157-9
HHs above 80% AMI served. **Less than 20% of units set aside** for 60% AMI or below	No statutory authority or supporting constitutional case law	
Compliance period (unless sold to eligible HH)	Not permitted	Perpetual & reverter. PLUS, if rental, 20% of units set aside for 60% AMI for 15 years. G.S. 157-9.4

*Gray highlighting indicates referendum required for counties.

The statutory authority for conveyance of property to a third party for a housing project depends on several factors: whether the conveyance is by lease or sale; who is served by the housing project based on income eligibility restrictions; whether the buyer receives a subsidized conveyance or is required to pay fair market value; and, for counties, whether a referendum is held.

Table 26.1 describes the statutory authority when no subsidy is provided; that is, the property is conveyed at fair market value after accounting for restrictions placed on the property.

Table 26.2 describes the statutory authority when a conveyance of property is accompanied by a subsidy or made at a price below the fair market value. As discussed previously, local governments are not permitted to make gifts or donations to private owners and developers. When property is conveyed for nonmonetary consideration (that is, for less than fair market value in exchange for a promise to use the property for a public purpose), the property must be subject to a reverter and return to the government when no longer used for that purpose, or be sold to an eligible LMI household.[86]

Provide Financing for Development if It Is Necessary and Authorized by Law

Providing financial assistance for housing projects once again implicates the constitutional rule that prohibits local governments from making gifts or donations to private entities. The prohibition against donations even extends to charitable nonprofit entities.[87] Every payment to a private entity, charitable or otherwise, must not only serve a constitutional public purpose, but also must secure the performance of an equivalently valued public service.

Any financial assistance to a housing project, whether in the form of a grant or a loan, should be documented by an agreement in which the housing provider agrees to supply housing units for

---

the fair market value somewhat. So long as the LMI restrictions are binding on the property, the restrictions can be fairly considered by an appraiser when determining the fair market value of the property. If an appraiser finds that the property's value is lower as a result of LMI restrictions, the determination is valid. This lower fair market value is not a subsidy to the buyer—it is a reflection of the market value of the property after accounting for the lawfully imposed restrictions on the use of the property. As a reminder, appraising the fair market value of property is a licensed activity in North Carolina (e.g., G.S. Chapter 93E).

86. See note 84 above.

87. Conveying property at a discount—that is, below fair market value—is analogous to making a grant. The legal analysis regarding donations described in note 84 above applies equally to grants, low-interest (subsidized) loans, and other financial assistance.

Table 26.3 Financial Assistance (Subsidy Must Flow to Eligible HHs)

Household (HH) income eligibility restrictions imposed	Acting in capacity as city or county	Exercising powers of housing authority per G.S. 160D-1311(b)*
All units for LMI only (no HH over 80% AMI served)	No statutory authority	G.S. 157-3(12), 157-9
HHs above 80% AMI served. **At least 20% of units reserved** for 60% AMI or below	No statutory authority	G.S. 157-3(12), 157-9
HHs above 80% AMI served. **Less than 20% of units set aside** for 60% AMI or below	No statutory authority or supporting constitutional case law	
Compliance period (unless sold to eligible HH)	Not permitted	Rental: 20% of units set aside for exclusive use of 60% AMI for 15 years. G.S. 157-9.4

*Gray highlighting indicates referendum required for counties.

eligible households in exchange for the government assistance. The government must satisfy itself that all subsidy flows to eligible LMI households, not to the owner or developer.[88] Grants, loans, and financial assistance provided directly to LMI persons, such as down payment assistance, is constitutionally permissible.[89] The statutory authority for providing financing or financial assistance for housing projects is described in Table 26.3.

When a local government supports a housing project, must rent levels be "affordable" to eligible households? In North Carolina law, there is no requirement to ensure that units reserved for LMI households are actually *affordable* to those tenants. However, when a housing authority (or a local government acting as a housing authority) is involved with a rental-housing project, the rentals must be "within the financial reach" of low-income renters.[90] The "financial reach" requirement does not extend to moderate-income renters. There is no definition of "within the financial reach." Recall that the federal guideline for affordability is that housing costs—defined as combined rent and utilities for renters, and defined as combined mortgage, utilities, homeowners association dues, insurance, and property tax for buyers—do not exceed 30 percent of household income.[91] It is reasonable to assume that meeting the federal standard also meets the "within the financial reach" requirement under state law.

The affordability and eligibility requirements appearing in the statutes are the floor—the minimum required. The statutes impose no ceiling. Local governments in North Carolina routinely demand more from projects. Examples include requiring a project to reserve more low-income units than required by statute; reserving units for extremely low-income households (e.g., 30 percent AMI); and requiring owners to accept federal housing vouchers from tenants.

Urban Redevelopment

Background on Legal Authority

Over time, the federal government expanded its funding beyond housing projects. Starting in the late 1940s, federal funding became available for blight eradication and redevelopment. In 1951,

88. See note 68 above.
89. See notes 50–53 and accompanying text above.
90. G.S. 157-29(b)(2).
91. See note 16 and accompanying text above.

responding to these broader purposes found in the federal Housing Act of 1949, the General Assembly enacted the Urban Redevelopment Law, which, as amended, appears as G.S. Chapter 160A, Article 22.[92]

The Urban Redevelopment Law grants authority to both municipalities and counties[93] to engage in programs of blight eradication and redevelopment through the acquisition, clearance, rehabilitation, or rebuilding of areas for residential, commercial, or other purposes. A redevelopment commission is the primary vehicle for exercising the powers granted by this law.[94] The governing board of a local government must create the redevelopment commission by ordinance or resolution after finding that blighted areas exist within the jurisdiction and that redevelopment of those areas is necessary.[95]

A governing board is authorized to aid a redevelopment commission by appropriating funds[96] and by furnishing property, public facilities, infrastructure, and administrative services.[97] Local governments are authorized to levy taxes and issue and sell bonds for this purpose.[98] Once a redevelopment commission is established, the commission itself may issue bonds of various types and borrow money from any public or private source.[99]

A governing board may designate itself to serve as the commission, but it must nevertheless make the required findings described above and adopt a resolution for designation.[100] A governing board may exercise the powers of a redevelopment commission directly whether or not a redevelopment commission already exists in the jurisdiction.[101] Regardless, whenever a governing board seeks to exercise the powers of a redevelopment commission, it must follow the same procedures as if it were a redevelopment commission.[102]

The resolution creating a commission is just the beginning of the process. After its establishment, the commission's first task is to request for the jurisdiction's planning commission to designate redevelopment areas.[103] The planning commission must certify areas as being one of three types of redevelopment areas (or any combination of them) as defined by statute:

(1) a blighted area;
(2) a nonresidential redevelopment area; or

---

92. Pub. L. No. 81-171, 63 Stat. 413 (1949); S.L. 1951-1095. For an explanation of how redevelopment powers can be used to support and attract private investment, see Tyler Mulligan, "Using a Redevelopment Area to Attract Private Investment," *Community and Economic Development in North Carolina and Beyond* blog (Nov. 20, 2012), ced.sog.unc.edu/2012/11/using-a-redevelopment-area-to-attract-private-investment/.

93. G.S. 160A-503(9) (defining "municipality" to include counties for purposes of Urban Redevelopment Law) and -506 (county redevelopment commission). *See also* G.S. 160A-507 (regional redevelopment commission) and -507.1 (joint county–city redevelopment commission).

94. G.S. 160A-504 through -507.1.

95. G.S. 160A-504.

96. G.S. 160A-520.

97. G.S. 160A-519.

98. G.S. 160A-520. A local government may utilize project development financing, also known as tax increment financing or TIF, pursuant to G.S. 160A-515.1, and may cooperate with a redevelopment commission to that end.

99. G.S. 160A-512(8) and -517. Bonds and obligations of the commission shall not be obligations of the municipality and "shall so state on their face." G.S. 160A-516(b). A commission is a "public authority" governed by the Local Government Budget and Fiscal Control Act, G.S. Chapter 159, unless the governing board assumes responsibility for commission finances under G.S. 160A-505.1.

100. G.S. 160A-505.

101. G.S. 160D-1311(b).

102. G.S. 160A-504 and -505. As discussed previously at note 60, the N.C. Attorney General opined that local governments are required to follow the procedures applicable to redevelopment commissions when exercising the powers of a redevelopment commission. Letter to Tommy W. Jarrett, 45 Op. N.C. Att'y Gen. 44 (1975).

103. G.S. 160A-512(1).

(3) a rehabilitation, conservation, and reconditioning area.[104]

Once an area is certified as a redevelopment area, the redevelopment commission "shall prepare a redevelopment plan" for each area and then seek approval of the plan by following statutory procedures.[105] Ultimately, the redevelopment plan must be approved by the governing board. Until the redevelopment plan is approved, the commission cannot exercise most of its substantial development powers.[106]

Upon approval of a redevelopment plan, the redevelopment commission may exercise extensive powers—essentially all of the land banking powers described earlier—within its area of operation.[107] Each of the land banking powers will be addressed in more detail below.

Acquire Property

A redevelopment commission, or a local government exercising commission powers, may acquire property within its area of operation so long as the acquisition is "necessary or incidental to the proper clearance, development, or redevelopment of such areas or to the prevention of the spread or recurrence of conditions of blight."[108] A commission may acquire property prior to final approval of a redevelopment plan only when the governing board "finds that advance acquisition . . . is in the public interest and specifically approves such action."[109]

Additionally, a redevelopment commission may exercise the power of eminent domain to acquire a "blighted parcel."[110] Only the planning commission can certify an individual parcel as being a "blighted parcel."[111]

Hold, Stabilize, and Develop Acquired Property

A redevelopment commission, or a local government exercising commission powers, is empowered to hold, improve, clear, or prepare property for redevelopment.[112] The commission may enter into contracts to accomplish the work. Compliance with the bidding requirements of Article 8 of G.S. Chapter 143 is required for construction, demolition, moving structures, or repair work, as well as for purchases of materials or equipment.[113]

Convey Property to a Private Owner or Developer

A redevelopment commission may convey property it owns in a designated redevelopment area to a private developer; indeed, this is the primary purpose of the law. Conveyance is permitted only for purposes that accord with the approved redevelopment plan, and the governing board must approve any sale.[114] Whenever a commission sells property to multiple developers, it must find that "the

---

104. G.S. 160A-503(16) (defining "redevelopment area"). *See* G.S. 160A-503(2) defining "blighted area"; (10) defining "nonresidential redevelopment area"; and (21) defining "rehabilitation, conservation, and reconditioning area."

105. G.S. 160A-513.

106. G.S. 160A-513(c), (j).

107. G.S. 160A-512(6) and -513(j). G.S. 160A-503(1) defines "area of operation" as "[t]he area within the territorial boundaries of the city or county for which a particular commission is created."

108. G.S. 160A-503(19) and -512(6).

109. G.S. 160A-513(c).

110. G.S. 160A-515; 40A-3(c)(7).

111. G.S. 160A-503(2a).

112. G.S. 160A-503(19) and -512(6).

113. G.S. 160A-514(b).

114. G.S. 160A-512(6) and -514.

sale . . . will not be prejudicial to the sale of other parts of the redevelopment area, nor in any other way prejudicial to the realization of the redevelopment plan approved by the governing body."[115]

Importantly, a redevelopment commission, or a local government exercising commission powers, enjoys a unique and useful procedure for property conveyance. Competitive bidding procedures must be employed,[116] but unlike other competitive sale statutes, G.S. 160A-514 authorizes the sale to be subject to covenants and conditions to ensure that any redevelopment complies with the redevelopment plan. Typically, a competitive bidding process may not be encumbered by such restrictions on the buyer.[117] The Urban Redevelopment Law, however, uniquely combines competitive bidding procedures with the ability to place restrictions on the buyer.[118] So long as a restriction "accords with the redevelopment plan,"[119] it can include requirements related to design, timing of financial closing and construction, and even housing affordability requirements. Redevelopment commissions will therefore include such timing and particular development requirements in the redevelopment plan; otherwise, such conditions would be unenforceable.

The highest bid received through a properly conducted competitive sale process *is the fair market value of the property.*[120] The practical effect of this conveyance power should be appreciated. A redevelopment commission, or a local government exercising its powers, is authorized to invest in the stabilization of property and prepare it for redevelopment, even when such preparation is extremely costly, such as clearing contaminated property or engaging in extensive demolition and grading. Upon sale, at the conclusion of a competitive sale process, the highest bid might not be sufficient to recoup the commission's original investment in preparing the property, but the sale would still be valid. In this scenario, the commission has invested in the property and made it attractive to private developers, but importantly the commission has not unconstitutionally favored any particular developer nor has the commission conferred an unconstitutional gift on the developer. The developer must pay full fair market value—as determined *by the bid process*—and must develop the property according to the redevelopment plan.

Even a sale to a charitable entity must obtain full fair market value. The commission may choose to sell property to a charitable entity rather than holding a competitive sale process, but the sale price must be no less than the "fair value of the property agreed upon by a committee of three professional real estate appraisers."[121] The commission must impose restrictive covenants to ensure that the property is used perpetually for the intended charitable purpose.[122]

A commission is also authorized to convey property pursuant to G.S. 160A-279, which authorizes conveyances to nonprofit entities carrying out a public purpose.[123] Under this authority, a commission may accept nonmonetary consideration (namely, the promise to use the property for the allowable purpose), but the "city or county [or commission] shall attach to any such conveyance covenants or conditions which assure that the property will be put to a public use *by the recipient entity.*"[124] This codifies the requirement in case law: the conveyance must be conditioned on the

115. G.S. 160A-512(6).

116. Specifically, G.S. 160A-514(c) authorizes the bidding procedures set forth in G.S. 160A-268, -269, and -270.

117. *Puett*, 19 N.C. App. at 235.

118. Only a housing authority, which is entirely exempt from typical conveyance procedures as described previously, can dispose of property in a similar manner.

119. G.S. 160A-514(c).

120. *Redevelopment Comm'n of Greensboro*, 252 N.C. at 612.

121. G.S. 160A-514(e)(4).

122. G.S. 160A-514(e)(4).

123. G.S. 160A-514(c).

124. G.S. 160A-279 (emphasis added).

continued use for that purpose by the recipient, and the property must revert back to the local government in the event the recipient entity ceases to use it for that purpose.[125]

A commission can convey by private sale under G.S. 160A-514 in other limited circumstances. For example, it may enter into property exchanges pursuant to G.S. 160A-271.[126] It may also convey property to local governments, without consideration, for streets, schools, parks, facilities, and other public purposes.[127] A commission is not empowered to enter into leases, but it may *temporarily* lease, operate, and maintain property, even if not in conformity with the redevelopment plan, pending final disposition by sale that does accord with the plan.[128]

Provide Financing for Redevelopment if It Is Necessary and Authorized by Law

The exercise of statutory powers within a formally designated redevelopment area by a redevelopment commission has been upheld by the North Carolina Supreme Court as serving a public purpose.[129] A redevelopment commission is empowered to engage in programs of assistance and financing, "including the making of loans," for the rehabilitation or construction of residential and commercial buildings in a designated redevelopment area.[130] This does not mean that government funds or property may be gifted to a private enterprise. To the contrary, as noted above,[131] even the sale of property to charitable nonprofit entities requires payment of full fair market value. Loans should be offered at higher interest rates and on terms that do not compete with commercial lenders.

Loan programs may complement a commission's power to "carry out plans for a program of voluntary or compulsory repair."[132] A redevelopment commission could therefore engage in area-focused code enforcement and then provide loans to owners who lack the financial capacity to complete the ordered repairs.

Community Development and Redevelopment

Background on Legal Authority

Federal support for community development and revitalization evolved further with the passage of the Housing and Community Development Act of 1974, which established the Community Development Block Grant (CDBG) program to eliminate blight, address the deterioration of neighborhood facilities, preserve the nation's housing stock, and engage in other activities that "benefit persons of low and moderate income."[133] At that time, many of the activities funded by CDBG could be undertaken by housing authorities and redevelopment commissions, but not by cities and counties directly.[134]

---

125. *Brumley v. Baxter*, 225 N.C. 691, discussed in note 85 above.
126. G.S. 160A-514(c).
127. G.S. 160A-514(e).
128. G.S. 160A-514(g).
129. *Redevelopment Comm'n of Greensboro*, 252 N.C. 595.
130. G.S. 160A-503(19)(e).
131. See note 84 above.
132. G.S. 160A-503(19)(d); 160A-512(10).
133. 42 U.S.C. § 5301(c). The "primary objective" of the CDBG program "is the development of viable urban communities, by providing decent housing and a suitable living environment and expanding economic opportunities, principally for persons of low and moderate income." 42 U.S.C. § 5301(c). CDBG is discussed at the end of this chapter.
134. *Community Development Block Grants: Authority under North Carolina Law*, County Finance Bulletin No. 19/Municipal Finance Bulletin no. 12, 2 (UNC Institute of Government, October 1974).

The General Assembly addressed this concern in 1975 by enacting G.S. 160D-1311.[135] This enabling statute authorized counties and cities, for the first time, to exercise directly the powers of housing authorities and redevelopment commissions described earlier.[136] In addition, the statute supplemented those powers with additional authority to engage in activities for which CDBG was eligible.[137] As part of a community development program for the benefit of low- and moderate-income persons, a local government is empowered to engage in programs of rehabilitation and preservation of buildings and neighborhoods, and programs concerned with "employment, economic development, crime prevention, child care, health, drug abuse, education, and welfare needs of persons of low and moderate income."[138]

As noted previously in the affordable housing section, the General Assembly originally required both cities and counties to conduct a public referendum whenever state or local taxes were used for activities authorized by G.S. 160D-1311—namely, housing projects and community development.[139] No referendum was required so long as federal funds were used. In 1985, cities were relieved of the referendum requirement entirely, but the referendum requirement remains in place for counties, except for partial relief granted to counties in 1999 for a limited set of housing programs.[140] Accordingly, counties may need to hold a public referendum prior to expending state or local tax revenues for certain community development activities.

Although the statutory authority was enacted to enable local governments to participate in the CDBG program, the statute is written broadly enough that a local government can use the authority to undertake community development activities outside of the CDBG program that would otherwise meet CDBG requirements. Namely, the enumerated activities in the statute must be undertaken "principally for the benefit of low- and moderate-income persons."[141]

The authority provided by G.S. 160D-1311 includes exercising the powers of a redevelopment commission, but the property acquisition and disposition procedures of a commission were deemed too cumbersome for the short time-frame for project completion imposed by federal community development programs.[142] Therefore, the General Assembly enacted G.S. 160D-1312 to create sep-

---

135. S.L. 1975-435 (enacting G.S. 153A-376 (counties) and G.S. 160A-456 (cities)). G.S. 160D-1311 is the successor to G.S. 153A-376 and G.S. 160A-456.

136. G.S. 160D-1311(b). *North Carolina Legislation 1975*, ed. Joan G. Brannon (UNC Institute of Government, 1975), 51–52 (explaining that the predecessor to G.S. 160D-1311 was enacted in 1975 to address "uncertainty" about the authority of cities and counties to participate in the CDBG program authorized by the Housing and Community Development Act of 1974).

137. Federal law mandates that "not less than 70 percent" of CDBG funds "shall be used for the support of activities that benefit persons of low and moderate income." 42 U.S.C. 5301(c). This has also been referred to as the 70 percent (70%) test, LMI benefit test, or overall benefit requirement. 24 C.F.R. § 570.200(a)(3). Expenditures that count toward the benefit test include amenities that meet the "area benefit activity" test. An area benefit activity is an activity which is available to benefit all the residents of an area which is primarily residential, where at least 51 percent of the residents are LMI persons. 24 C.F.R. § 570.208. Examples of "area benefit activities" include acquisition of land to be used as a neighborhood park, construction of a health clinic, improvements to public infrastructure like the installation of gutters and sidewalks, and development of a community center.

138. G.S. 160D-1311(a). The CDBG program does not authorize "income payments" to individuals. 24 C.F.R. § 570.207(b)(4). For an analysis of county social service programs, including this statute, see Kristi Nickodem, "County Legal Authority to Fund Non-Mandated Social Services Programs," *Coates' Canons: NC Local Government Law* blog (June 6, 2023), canons.sog.unc.edu/2023/06/county-legal-authority-to-fund-non-mandated-social-services-programs/.

139. S.L. 1975-435 and S.L. 1975-689. See notes 58, 61 and accompanying text above.

140. G.S. 160D-1311; 153A-149(c)(15a), (15b); 160D-1316. See notes 66–83 and accompanying text above.

141. G.S. 160D-1311(a). See note 137 above.

142. *North Carolina Legislation 1977*, ed. Joan G. Brannon (UNC Institute of Government, 1977), 237.

arate acquisition and disposition powers for redevelopment.[143] With the addition of these powers, local governments can engage in all land banking activities for community development and redevelopment projects. Each activity is described in more detail below.

Acquire Property

G.S. 160D-1311 contains no authority for property acquisition, outside of the powers granted to housing authorities and redevelopment commissions, but G.S. 160D-1312 enables local governments to acquire property "by voluntary purchase" that is "blighted, deteriorated, deteriorating, undeveloped, or inappropriately developed from the standpoint of sound community development and growth," or that is appropriate for rehabilitation, preservation, housing construction, or for "the guidance of urban development."[144] No special acquisition procedures must be followed. However, the referendum requirements discussed previously still pertain when using state or local revenues for activities covered by G.S. 160D-1311.[145]

Hold, Stabilize, and Develop Acquired Property

A local government is empowered by G.S. 160D-1312 to "clear, demolish, remove, or rehabilitate buildings and improvements on land so acquired" under the statute.[146] New construction is not authorized, though a local government could undertake new construction by exercising the powers of a housing authority or redevelopment commission as described earlier.[147]

Convey Property to a Private Owner or Developer

Property so acquired "shall be [disposed of] in accordance with the procedures of Article 12" of G.S. Chapter 160A.[148] In other words, competitive bidding must be employed and no conditions may be placed on the buyer, except as Article 12 explicitly allows.[149]

An exception to this general rule is provided for property "in a community development project area."[150] Such property may be conveyed "to any redeveloper at private sale" for the appraised value "in accordance with the community development plan."[151] The reference to a community development plan signifies that the activity should be undertaken primarily for the benefit of low- and moderate-income persons and otherwise meet CDBG requirements (described later in this chapter). Examples of a "community development project area" include a Neighborhood

143. S.L. 1977-660 established G.S. 153A-376.1 (counties) and G.S. 160A-456.1 (cities), ultimately codified as G.S. 153A-377 and G.S. 160A-457 and succeeded by G.S. 160D-1312(1)–(3). S.L. 1983-797 enacted G.S. 160A-457(4), succeeded by G.S. 160D-1312(4).

144. G.S. 160D-1312(1).

145. G.S. 160D-1311; 153A-149(c)(15a), (15b); 160D-1316. No separate tax or appropriation power is granted for G.S. 160D-1312 activities (as they are not specifically authorized by G.S. 153A-149), so referendum requirements arguably apply.

146. G.S. 160D-1312(2).

147. Additionally, there is specific authority to engage in construction or rehabilitation of commercial buildings under G.S. 158-7.1 as discussed in the next chapter.

148. G.S. 160D-1312(3). Disposition is also permitted pursuant to the procedures of G.S. 160A-514.

149. For example, conditions may be placed on a lessee low-income housing provider under G.S. 160A-278 and on a nonprofit corporation performing a contracted service for a local government under G.S. 160A-279.

150. G.S. 160D-1312(3), (4). For a brief discussion of the history and evolution of G.S. 160D-1312 (successor to G.S. 160A-457), see *C. Tyler Mulligan, "Conveyance of Property in a Public-Private Partnership for a 'Downtown Development Project,'" Community and Economic Development in North Carolina and Beyond* blog (June 22, 2017), ced.sog.unc.edu/2017/06/conveyance-of-property-in-a-public-private-partnership-for-a-downtown-development-project/.

151. G.S. 160D-1312(4).

Revitalization Strategy Area, which is an area designated by an entitlement community for targeted CDBG programs,[152] and Community Revitalization Strategies created through the CDBG Small Cities Program.[153] In such cases, the sale may be "subject to such covenants, conditions, and restrictions as may be deemed to be in the public interest."[154] These community development sales must be preceded by a properly noticed legislative hearing.[155]

Financing

G.S. 160D-1311 authorizes local governments to engage in programs of assistance and financing for community development purposes, including making loans and grants. These financing activities are intended to be undertaken "principally for the benefit of low- and moderate-income persons" and do not override constitutional prohibitions against aid to private enterprise; indeed, as noted earlier, the conveyance powers mandate that the consideration for property conveyances must be no less than "appraised value."[156]

The same general principle applies equally to financing. Payments to a private enterprise should be made only as part of a contract for public services or goods of equivalent value. Loans should be offered at higher interest rates and on terms that do not compete with commercial lenders. Should any subsidy be provided through a loan or a grant, underwriting should ensure that the subsidy flows to eligible LMI households, not landlords or developers.[157]

A separate but related statutory article authorizes local governments to provide assistance to LMI households who are temporarily or permanently displaced as a result of community development activities undertaken by the government, such as rehabilitation or demolition. G.S. 133-5 through -18, originally enacted in 1971 to accompany the federal Uniform Relocation Assistance and Real Property Acquisition Act, allows local governments to help relocated residents with moving expenses, temporary or permanent rental payments, a down payment on the purchase of a house, or a lump sum to buy another house if a family is permanently displaced.[158] The law also contains procedural requirements that offer some protection to a person or family displaced by a government program. Federal community development programs require relocation assistance to be provided when residents are displaced.[159] State law authorizes local governments to provide relocation assistance in other circumstances beyond federal program mandates, but offering such assistance is optional.[160]

Downtown Development and Revitalization

In addition to the previously discussed authorities for housing, urban redevelopment, and community development, supplemental authority has been granted to local governments to deal with the unique challenges of business districts in downtowns and certain urban areas outside of downtown. The powers include forming a tax district known as a municipal service district (MSD) and entering

152. For an explanation of Neighborhood Revitalization Strategy Areas, see U.S. Department of Housing and Urban Development, HUD Exchange, Notice CPD-96-01 (Jan. 16, 1996).

153. Community Revitalization Strategy areas through the Small Cities Program are described in U.S. Department of Housing and Urban Development, HUD Exchange, Notice CPD-97-1 (Feb. 4, 1997).

154. G.S. 160D-1312(4).

155. G.S. 160D-1312(4). The "legislative hearing" in this statute was formerly known as a public hearing. *See* S.L. 2020-25, § 43.

156. G.S. 160D-1311(a), -1312(4).

157. See note 68 above for a full discussion of the exclusive emoluments clause, N.C. CONST. art. I, sec. 32.

158. S.L. 1971-1107, enacting Article 2, G.S. Chapter 133 (G.S. 133-5 through -18).

159. *See* 24 C.F.R. § 570.606.

160. G.S. 133-18.

into special procurement and conveyance agreements for downtown revitalization projects. Each is discussed below.

Municipal Service District for Downtown Revitalization

Municipalities (but not counties) may create a municipal service district—also known as a business improvement district or BID—in which additional property taxes are levied on property in the district for the purpose of engaging in "downtown revitalization projects" or "urban area revitalization."[161] In addition to the service-district levy, a municipality may allocate other revenues to the service district.[162] The procedures for designating a district and procuring goods and services are complex and beyond the scope of this chapter, but the requirements should be studied by any local government that is discerning whether to form a district.[163]

Once an area is properly designated as a municipal service district for downtown or urban area revitalization, permissible revitalization activities in the area include making infrastructure improvements, marketing the area, sponsoring festivals, and providing supplemental cleaning and security services, among others.[164] In particular, the proceeds from the additional tax levy may be expended for "promotions and developmental activities," such as "promoting business investment" in the district.[165] Notably, no special acquisition or conveyance powers are granted in a MSD for downtown or urban area revitalization—a local government would need to rely on other statutory authority to acquire or convey property.

Downtown Development Projects

A special construction method is available for "downtown development projects"—as the name suggests, only in a designated central business district (CBD)—pursuant to G.S. 160D-1315. Within a CBD, local governments are authorized to engage in joint developments with private developers in which *public* capital facilities are constructed simultaneously alongside a *private* development project. To get a sense of the scale envisioned by the General Assembly, the example described in the statute is a "publicly owned parking structure and publicly owned convention center" being constructed alongside a "privately owned hotel or office building."[166]

Most of the land banking powers described previously are available to a local government. If the governing board finds that it is likely to have a significant effect on the revitalization of the jurisdiction, the local government may acquire, construct, own, and operate (or participate in the acquisition, construction, ownership, and operation of) a joint development project with a private development partner. The local government may finance the publicly owned components of the project, but no authority is provided to offer financing for the private facilities.

The practical benefit of the statute is that it authorizes a local government to procure construction services for publicly owned capital facilities from a private developer who is constructing an adjacent private project. A joint project benefits both the public and private partners by achieving greater scale and coordination of construction than would be possible for the parties acting separately. Additionally, the construction bidding and other procurement requirements of Article 8

---

161. G.S. 160A-536(a). *See* G.S. 160A-536(b), (c) (defining "downtown revitalization" and "urban area revitalization").

162. G.S. 160A-542(a).

163. See Chapter 21, "Financing Capital Projects," for a discussion of the designation and procurement requirements in MSDs.

164. G.S. 160A-536(b), (c).

165. G.S. 160A-536(b).

166. G.S. 160D-1315(a).

of G.S. Chapter 143 do not apply, so long as local government funds constitute no more than fifty percent of the total costs of the joint development project.[167]

A unique conveyance power is available under the statute. The property interests of a local government and a private developer may simply be determined by agreement. The statutes do not override the state constitution's prohibition on making gifts to private developers; any property contributed by the local government should be valued at fair market value, and any development costs paid by the local government for public facilities must be reasonable.[168]

Organizing Local Governments for Delivery of Community Development Programs

Whether a local community development program consists of only federally funded and directed activities or a broad range of federal, local, and private activities, it requires effective coordination and management. Meeting legal requirements as well as community needs and expectations to conduct an effective program necessitates widespread community involvement, on the one hand, and concentrated executive control of a complex set of activities on the other. Neither the federal government nor the General Statutes mandates any specific form of organization to carry out a community development strategy. Each local government, then, must use the options available in the General Statutes to accomplish its community development objectives in a way that satisfactorily balances community involvement and executive control and that best suits its local program and circumstances.

Board of County Commissioners/City or Town Council

The organizational starting point for community development must be the board of county commissioners and the city or town council. Each has the authority either to undertake directly or to appoint an appropriate body to undertake on its behalf all of the community development activities discussed earlier.

Public Housing Authorities

In North Carolina, the General Assembly set out the requirements by which cities with populations greater than five hundred and counties may create traditional housing authorities.[169] Under G.S. 157-4 and 157-33, any twenty-five residents of a county or twenty-five residents of a city (or its environs within ten miles) may file a petition with the clerk to the governing board declaring that there is a need for a housing authority. The clerk will then give notice of the time, place, and purposes of a public hearing at which the governing board will determine the need for the authority. At the hearing, the governing board must determine whether people in the jurisdiction are living in unsanitary or unsafe homes or whether there is a lack of safe or sanitary dwellings in the community.[170] If the board determines that either is true, a housing authority may be duly organized. Thereafter, the mayor will appoint the members of the board for a city's housing authority, and

167. G.S. 160D-1315(e).

168. G.S. 160D-1315(d).

169. *See* G.S. 157-3(3) (defining "city") and -4 (creation of authority).

170. In making these determinations, the governing board must take into consideration the physical age and condition of the buildings, the degree of overcrowding, the percentage of land coverage, the light and air available to the inhabitants, the size and arrangement of rooms in these dwellings, the sanitary conditions, and the extent to

the board of county commissioners will appoint the members of the board for a county's housing authority. A regional housing authority can be created under G.S. 157-35 by two or more contiguous counties with an aggregate population of more than sixty thousand.

G.S. 157-4.1 and 157-4.2 offer several alternative organizational arrangements to the traditional independent housing authority. Under G.S. 157-4.2, a local government may retain a separate housing authority but integrate that authority's budgeting and financial administration activities into its own. Under this arrangement, the housing authority remains a separate organization with personnel and operating responsibilities under the control of the appointed housing authority board, and it is treated like a local government department only for purposes of budgeting, accounting, and expenditure control.

Two organizational alternatives eliminate the housing authority altogether: the governing board may assign the powers, duties, and responsibilities of a housing authority to a redevelopment commission, or it may itself exercise those powers, duties, and responsibilities.[171] Any designation of the governing board as the housing authority should be done by passing a resolution adopted in accordance with the procedures set out in G.S. 157-4 or 157-33 as appropriate. In the event that an action of the housing authority requires recommendation or approval by both the housing authority and the governing board, then under the new arrangement, action by the governing board will be deemed sufficient.[172]

Redevelopment Commissions

A city or county is authorized to create a redevelopment commission by resolution when the governing board finds that blighted areas exist in the jurisdiction and that the redevelopment of such areas is necessary for its residents.[173] Alternatives to the standard redevelopment commission are available. G.S. 160A-505 allows a governing board to eliminate the redevelopment commission and designate itself or a housing authority as a redevelopment commission. G.S. 160A-505.1 allows a jurisdiction to retain a separate redevelopment commission but integrate the commission's budgeting and financial administration activities into its own, similar to the arrangement described above for housing authorities. G.S. 160A-507 and 160A-507.1 permit the creation of a regional commission or a joint county–city commission.

Professional Staff: Coordinators, Departments, and Task Forces

Local governments with professional community development staff have organized themselves using one of three major approaches: a coordinator, a department, or a task force.

Communities that retain only a few specialized staff may use a coordinator. This one person is responsible for initiating, negotiating, monitoring, and evaluating the planning and execution of development activities by several departments—usually planning, public works, and inspection departments and sometimes the rehabilitation staff of a redevelopment authority.

A city or county can form a community development department with status equal to that of the more traditional departments that might have a part in the program: public works, inspection, recreation, and so on. Such an arrangement may originate in a community's decision to abolish its separate redevelopment authority or housing authority and to bring the staff into its administration.

---

which conditions in the dwellings pose a threat to life or property by fire or other causes. G.S. 157-4 (cities) and -33 (counties).

171. G.S. 157-4.1 and -33.

172. *See* G.S. 157-4.1(a).

173. See notes 92–95 and accompanying text above.

The multifunctional department might be formed from an existing planning department and from existing building inspection staff, housing inspection staff, engineering staff, housing and redevelopment staffs, economic development staff, or various combinations of all of these.

A community that takes the broadest possible view of community development—as an endeavor involving many local agencies as well as, from time to time, private sector organizations—might adopt a task force approach to planning and managing its programs. Often, primary responsibility for the program goes to a deputy or assistant manager who, by his or her position, clearly and often acts with the full authority of the manager. This person organizes and supervises department and agency heads who will be responsible for various aspects of program planning and implementation and serves as a critical link to organizations outside the government. The composition of task forces might change over time as the community development program goes through different stages or changes its character.

Citizen Boards, Commissions, and Committees

Although the governing board holds most of the ultimate authority for community development and revitalization activities, it can make efficient use of citizen interest and expertise by appointing a variety of citizen boards, commissions, and committees for advice or for implementation of program mandates.[174] In fact, to help in planning and administering activity funded by the federal Community Development Block Grant program, the board is required to have a citizen advisory body through which to channel public opinion.[175]

Many local governments find these bodies to be helpful. First, such a body can focus its full attention on the community development strategy, whereas the board has many other responsibilities. Second, the board can effectively delegate to the advisory group the time-consuming task of gaining widespread citizen participation in planning. Third, the professional staff can secure from this body a fairly continuous flow of informal comment and information during planning. Fourth, consultants and councils of governments working with the local government will look to this body to provide a meaningful frame of reference on the community to be served. Finally, the advisory body can supplement professional staff advice with a lay point of view when a program is recommended to the governing board.

Other agencies also may play a role. For example, the local government's planning board and its housing authority, if the latter exists, are usually prepared to offer advice on community development activities, so the governing board should consider what role (if any) it expects these agencies to play in planning and executing community development programs. It can be effective to integrate community development programs with the planning board's work on comprehensive planning and capital improvement planning. The governing board should also consider whether to seek advice from other boards and commissions, such as parks and recreation, streets, and public works.

Contracting with Others

The state constitution contains a general authorization for governments to contract with private entities.[176] In addition, parallel statutes for cities and counties authorize them to contract with any private entity to carry out any public purpose in which they have statutory authority to engage. For

174. *See* G.S. 160D-1311(c) (authorizing local governments to create advisory committees to advise and make recommendations regarding community development programs and activities).

175. *See* 24 C.F.R. § 570.486 (requiring, among other requirements, local governments to provide for and encourage citizen participation in slum or blighted areas and areas in which CDBG funds are proposed to be used).

176. N.C. Const. art. V, sec. 2(7).

North Carolina local governments, the authority to contract is directly related to the basic authority to spend money. A local government may contract for any purpose for which it may spend money if the expenditure is for a public purpose, the activity to be supported is one in which the local government has statutory authority to engage, and the expenditure is not inconsistent with the laws of the state or federal government.[177]

Councils of Governments

Regional councils of governments often assist local governments in the preparation and administration of federal or state grants when there is no local government staff to carry out these functions. For more information about regional councils of government, see Chapter 11, "Interlocal Cooperation, Shared Services, and Regional Councils."

Consultants

Many local governments delegate responsibility to private, for-profit consultants for completing applications for and administering federal and state grants. A consultant typically works closely with a member of the local government (usually the manager, mayor, or clerk to the board) and the citizen advisory body to develop and implement the project. The board should be kept informed of important policy decisions, such as program amendments, because it retains ultimate responsibility for the grant.

A primary advantage of using consultants is that the community does not have to maintain staff between grants. A disadvantage may be that consultants are less familiar with local government staff and aspects of the community that may bear on a project.

Nonprofits

Nonprofit organizations have long worked with governments to respond to community needs. At their best, the resulting partnerships combine the flexibility and service-delivery capabilities of the nonprofit sector with the financial and direction-setting capabilities of the for-profit sector. A local government seeking to partner with a nonprofit corporation should understand the legal limitations under which the partnership must operate.

As a threshold matter, the state constitution does not permit state or local governments to make donations to any private entity, whether for-profit or not-for-profit.[178] The fact that a corporation has organized itself as a tax-exempt charity under section 501(c)(3) of the Internal Revenue Code makes no difference. A local government can enter into a contract with a private entity and pay that entity a reasonable price for a valuable public service (such as paying a business to repair the roof of a public building or paying a nonprofit to provide homelessness prevention services), but the government cannot make a gift or donation to a private entity.

A local government may only enter into a contract with a nonprofit for activities that the government is authorized to do on its own. A nonprofit cannot use government funds to do something that the appropriating government is not permitted to do. Public funds remain subject to constitutional requirements even when appropriated to another entity.[179]

Local governments should also keep in mind that *charitable partners are subject to similar requirements as local governments*. Nonprofits are not permitted to make donations to private businesses because a business is not an appropriate charitable object under the Internal Revenue

---

177. G.S. 160A-20.1 (cities); 153A-449 (counties).

178. N.C. Const. art. I, sec. 32. *See also* note 68 above.

179. Briggs v. City of Raleigh, 195 N.C. 223 (1928); Dennis v. City of Raleigh, 253 N.C. 400 (1960).

Code. Federal tax law follows a similar distinction as North Carolina law: aiding needy individuals is permissible, whereas aiding businesses generally is not. Another example relates to affordable housing. The safe harbor for a charity to aid housing developers and retain their charitable status, as described by Revenue Procedure 96-32, requires at least 75 percent of the housing units to be reserved for those earning 80 percent AMI or less, and the units must be affordable to the income-eligible residents.

In the case of conveyances to entities carrying out a public purpose, a local government may accept nonmonetary consideration (meaning the government accepts less than fair market value), but the "city or county shall attach to any such conveyance covenants or conditions which assure that the property will be put to a public use *by the recipient entity*."[180] Thus, the conveyance must be conditioned on the continued use for that purpose by the recipient, and the property must revert back to the local government in the event that the recipient ceases to use it for that purpose.[181]

Local governments may support nonprofit community development efforts in other ways.[182] For example, a local unit might include nonprofit staff in its training programs or use its purchasing power to purchase goods or services on behalf of the nonprofit for use in programs that the local government has authority to fund. Further, a local government may make the expertise of its staff available to a nonprofit as a form of in-kind assistance that can save money for both the local government and the nonprofit. In each case, subject to constitutional requirements and statutory authority, local governments may enter into agreements to provide in-kind support of whatever nature they choose in order to accomplish an authorized activity.

Faith-Based Organizations

Faith-based nonprofit organizations have been involved in community development on behalf of lower-income persons since the eighteenth century, and local government agencies have long funded religiously affiliated organizations, such as Catholic Charities, Lutheran Family Services, the Salvation Army, and others. Recent laws and federal policies go beyond this, however, mandating that local governments must make their federally funded programs available to religious organizations, including even those programs with a primary purpose of providing religious instruction and spiritual support to their members rather than social services to clients.[183] Such laws and policies (including HUD policies) make clear that faith-based organizations are eligible for federal funding on an equal basis with other organizations; they also retain authority over their internal governance, may retain religious terms in their names, and may select board members and employees on a religious basis.

Federal Funding for Housing and Community Development

The primary sources of direct funding for community development activities in North Carolina are the Community Development Block Grant (CDBG) program, the HOME Investment Partnerships (HOME) program, and federal tax credit programs.

---

180. G.S. 160A-279 (emphasis added).

181. *Brumley v. Baxter*, 225 N.C. 691, discussed in note 84 above.

182. For more information, see Chapter 12, "Strengthening Community Ties: Local Government and Nonprofit Organizations in North Carolina."

183. 24 C.F.R. § 5.109; 24 C.F.R. § 570.200.

Community Development Block Grants

The Community Development Block Grant (CDBG) program is the largest and most flexible source of federal community development funds. Created in 1974 as an offshoot of several different existing community development programs, the CDBG program operates in furtherance of three objectives: (1) to benefit low- and moderate-income persons,[184] (2) to prevent or eliminate slums or blight, and (3) to meet urgent needs.[185] The amount of CDBG funds distributed annually to states and populous jurisdictions is determined by a formula that comprises several measures of community need, including population, housing overcrowding, age of housing, population growth lag in relationship to other metropolitan areas, and the extent of poverty.[186]

The CDBG program is divided into two parts: the Entitlement Program (for large municipalities and urban counties) and the Small Cities Program (for the remainder of the state's municipalities and counties). Communities that are eligible for Entitlement Program CDBG funds are generally municipalities that have fifty thousand or more residents and urban counties. These communities receive a direct block-grant allocation from the federal government each year. In North Carolina, four counties and twenty-four municipalities participate in the CDBG Entitlement Program.[187] One county and several cities have been added to the ranks of these entitlement communities since 2010. Together, all North Carolina entitlement communities received a total of approximately $31 million in fiscal year 2023[188] (excluding separate special allocations for disaster recovery), and that total is up from more than $28 million in fiscal year 2010, due in part to the addition of several entitlement communities since then.

The Small Cities Program provides North Carolina (and other states) with annual block grants, which the state in turn awards to local governments that are not part of the Entitlement Program. Each state develops its own method of distributing its received funds to eligible local governments. To maximize the impact of Small Cities Program funds, most states (including North Carolina) create programs with relatively large awards and then hold annual competitions for the available funds. States may reflect statewide priorities by earmarking funds for specific activities (e.g., housing rehabilitation or economic development). States also may keep a small percentage to cover administrative costs and to provide technical assistance to local governments and nonprofit organizations. North Carolina received approximately $46 million in CDBG funds for the Small Cities Program in fiscal year 2023,[189] down from almost $49 million in fiscal year 2010. The North Carolina Department of Commerce administers the portion of the state's CDBG funds designated by the General Assembly for economic development and revitalization projects, and the Department of Environmental Quality administers the portion designated for water and wastewater infrastructure.

North Carolina communities have devoted CDBG funds to a wide range of activities, including the preservation of affordable housing, improvements in public infrastructure, and the enhancement of community facilities and services. The program's funds may be used to support a wide range

---

184. "Low- and moderate-income person" means a member of a household having an income equal to or less than the Section 8 low-income limit established by the U.S. Department of Housing and Urban Development (HUD), which is 80 percent of the area median income. "Definitions," 24 C.F.R. § 570.3.

185. 24 C.F.R. § 570.208.

186. 42 U.S.C. § 5306(b); 24 C.F.R. § 570.4.

187. The entitlement counties are Cumberland, Mecklenburg, Union, and Wake; the entitlement cities are Asheville, Burlington, Cary, Chapel Hill, Charlotte, Concord, Durham, Fayetteville, Gastonia, Goldsboro, Greensboro, Greenville, Hickory, High Point, Jacksonville, Kannapolis, Lenoir, Morganton, New Bern, Raleigh, Rocky Mount, Salisbury, Wilmington, and Winston-Salem.

188. *See* HUD, Community Planning and Development Formula Program Allocations for FY 2023 (on file with the author).

189. *Id.*

of activities, but Congress and the U.S. Department of Housing and Urban Development (HUD) have mandated that, at a minimum, no less than 70 percent of all CDBG funds must be used for activities that directly benefit low- and moderate-income persons.[190] When CDBG funds are used to provide financing for a *private* development project, a local government must conduct underwriting to determine (1) that private contributions in equity and debt are appropriate, (2) that federal funds are necessary to make the project go forward, and (3) that the project, which was infeasible without the federal financing, will attain long-term feasibility and achieve the approved public purpose after the financing is provided.[191]

Even when federal funding has been received by a local government, state law must still be followed. The funding source or grant agreement does not provide independent authority for an activity. G.S. 160A-17.1 authorizes local governments to accept federal or state funds to perform activities they are "authorized by *general law* or *local act* to provide or perform" (emphasis added). Thus, when federal CDBG regulations differ from state law, public officials are required to compare federal and state requirements and follow the most restrictive rule.

The HOME Investment Partnerships Program

HOME is a federal program administered by HUD that is designed to increase the supply of housing for low-income persons. HOME provides funds to states and local governments to implement local housing strategies, which may include tenant-based rental assistance, assistance to homebuyers, property acquisition, new construction, rehabilitation, site improvements, demolition, relocation, and administrative costs.[192]

After certain mandated set-asides, the balance of HOME funds is allocated by formula between qualified municipalities, urban counties, consortia (contiguous units of local government), and states.[193] In North Carolina, the state portion is then reallocated to the remaining jurisdictions by the North Carolina Housing Finance Agency (NCHFA). In fiscal year 2023, the federal government allocated approximately $23 million in HOME funds directly to qualified local jurisdictions[194] (up from $20 million in fiscal year 2010). Approximately $19 million went to NCHFA for use statewide (down from $21 million in fiscal year 2010). The statewide funds are allocated based on each region's housing needs and are available through both competitive and noncompetitive funding programs. Federal regulations require HOME participating jurisdictions (also known as "PJs") to set aside at least 15 percent of HOME funds received for investments in housing to be developed, sponsored, or owned by a designated Community Housing Development Organization (CHDO).[195] In order to qualify for designation as a CHDO, the organization must meet certain requirements pertaining to their capacity and experience, legal status, organizational structure, and accountability to low-income community residents through governing board membership.[196]

---

190. 24 C.F.R. § 570.200(a)(3); 24 C.F.R. § 570.484.

191. "Guidelines and Objectives for Evaluating Project Costs and Financial Requirements," 24 C.F.R. pt. 570, app. A (CDBG underwriting guidelines to ensure public aid is necessary).

192. 24 C.F.R. § 92.1.

193. *See* "Formula allocation," 24 C.F.R. § 92.50.

194. *See* HUD, Community Planning and Development Formula Program Allocations for FY 2023 (on file with the author).

195. 24 C.F.R. § 92.300.

196. 24 C.F.R. § 92.2 (defining "community housing development organization").

Federal Tax Credits

Three federal tax credit programs are designed to induce private investment in community development projects: the New Markets Tax Credit, the Low-Income Housing Tax Credit, and the Historic Rehabilitation Tax Credit. The New Markets Tax Credit (NMTC) was designed to stimulate billions of dollars of new investment in distressed areas by allowing taxpayers to receive a credit against their federal income taxes for investing in commercial and economic activities in low-income communities. The Low-Income Housing Tax Credit provides tax credits to private investors who develop housing with set-asides for persons earning 60 percent or less of the area median income.[197] The Historic Rehabilitation Tax Credit provides tax credits to those who invest in the rehabilitation of historic structures. North Carolina has intermittently offered complementary state tax credits for investments in historic rehabilitation projects, and when combined with federal tax credits, eligible projects are even more attractive to private investors.

Most real estate developers cannot use all of those tax credits themselves, so they sell investment interests in their projects (through a tax credit intermediary or "syndicator") to persons or companies with large tax liabilities. When those entities with large tax liabilities invest in a project in order to receive tax credits—in other words, when they buy tax credits—the investment provides an infusion of capital (or equity) into the project. The amount of equity a project can receive for selling its tax credits may depend on the demand for such tax credits. When tax credits are valuable, a developer can attract more equity for a project, making the project more financially feasible. When tax credits are less valuable, which typically occurs when federal tax rates go down and therefore companies have less tax liability, developers cannot obtain as much equity for a project, thereby making it more difficult to finance a project with tax credits.

Local governments do not typically get involved with tax credit syndication, but the types of projects that take advantage of federal or state tax credits are often those that local governments wish to support. Thus, local governments should seek to understand how tax credits work in order to leverage them effectively. Furthermore, local governments must account for the value of tax credit investments when evaluating the feasibility of a private project that is eligible for tax credits, especially when a public–private partnership is contemplated.[198] Due to the fact that tax credits sometimes help make private development projects possible, local governments are usually active partners in seeking to have projects and qualified areas of their communities designated for special tax treatment.[199]

---

197. Federal Low-Income Housing Tax Credits (LIHTC) are awarded to affordable-housing developers in North Carolina through a competitive process administered by NCHFA. Each year, NCHFA promulgates the Qualified Allocation Plan, which explains how projects will be selected to receive an award of tax credits. A 2018 change in federal law allows for "income averaging" within LIHTC properties; that is, properties may accept residents with higher average median incomes as long as the overall average of tenants in the project does not exceed 60 percent of the area median income.

198. A determination of necessity for public aid to private enterprise is legally significant. *See* C. Tyler Mulligan, "Economic Development Incentives Must Be 'Necessary': A Framework for Evaluating the Constitutionality of Public Aid for Private Development Projects," 11 Harvard Law & Policy Review (2017): S13, journals.law.harvard.edu/lpr/wp-content/uploads/sites/89/2013/11/Mulligan-HLPR-Essay-2017.pdf. *See also* Tyler Mulligan, "Legal and Business Reasons Why Downtown Development Programs Should Involve Secured Loan—Not Grants," *Coates' Canons: NC Local Government Law* blog (Sept. 19, 2017), canons.sog.unc.edu/2017/09/9935-2/.

199. An example of government-designated areas receiving special tax treatment is the federal Opportunity Zones program. *See* Tyler Mulligan, "Federal Opportunity Zones: What Local Governments Need to Know," *Community and Economic Development in North Carolina and Beyond* blog (Sept. 21, 2018), ced.sog.unc.edu/2018/09/federal-opportunity-zones-what-local-governments-need-to-know/.

Chapter 27

Economic Development

Jonathan Q. Morgan and C. Tyler Mulligan

Jonathan Q. Morgan is a School of Government faculty member who specializes in economic development. C. Tyler Mulligan is a School of Government faculty member whose interests include economic development law and development finance.

The authors gratefully acknowledge the contributions of David Lawrence to the field and to earlier versions of this chapter.

Economic development is the process through which municipalities and counties attempt to support and influence private investment decisions in an effort to increase employment, expand the tax base, and raise the standard of living. As North Carolina confronts the challenges of globalization, industrial restructuring, technological innovation, disaster recovery, and fiscal pressures, local officials recognize the importance of being strategic in their approach to economic development. They also recognize that local governments are not the only entities involved in economic development. Various agencies at the federal, state, regional, and local levels spanning the public, private, and nonprofit sectors work to promote economic development. Thus, it is helpful to understand how local government programs relate to the activities of this broader array of organizational players.

This chapter begins by describing four fundamental approaches to economic development and how their use in North Carolina has evolved over time in response to a changing economy. Next, it highlights the key factors that businesses consider when deciding where to make new investments and identifies those factors for which local governments have some responsibility. The chapter then reviews relevant federal, state, and regional programs prior to discussing the specific legal authority allowing local governments to engage in various economic development activities and the organizational options available to them in doing so. The chapter concludes with a set of critical challenges that local governments face in the pursuit of economic development.

Basic Approaches to Economic Development

To understand the role of local government in the development process, it is useful to review four basic approaches to economic development and consider what cities and counties typically do with respect to other organizations. The four broad approaches to economic development are

- business attraction,
- business retention and expansion,
- business creation and entrepreneurship, and
- placemaking.

Historically, industrial recruitment was the primary focus of economic development programs. For years, North Carolina enjoyed a degree of success in attracting large branch plant manufacturing facilities by marketing and promoting the state's relatively cheap labor, lower cost of living, and good quality of life. Over time, incentives became an important, albeit controversial, recruitment tool at both the state and local levels. The upside of the industrial recruitment approach is that it created large numbers of low- to mid-skill jobs for people with limited education. The downside is that these jobs were mostly concentrated in labor-intensive industries that proved to be extremely vulnerable to global competition. The recruitment of branch plant manufacturing worked well for North Carolina until it became cheaper to produce certain goods—such as furniture, textiles, and apparel—outside the U.S. in countries like China, India, and Mexico. At the same time, manufacturing industries increasingly utilized automation and technology, allowing them to produce more with fewer workers. As a result, the state has lost thousands of jobs in traditional manufacturing sectors.

The strategy of recruiting large manufacturing facilities has not benefited communities evenly across the state. Some communities and regions are better suited for traditional industrial recruitment because of their location, workforce, and other advantages. In addition, while the number of large industrial recruitment projects has declined over time, the use of incentives to attract them has increased. It is estimated that, in a given year, around 15,000 communities vie for roughly 1,500 major industrial development projects available nationally.[1] This creates a highly competitive and often costly environment in which the odds of success are low. Moreover, some research suggests that incentives sway only 25 percent or fewer business location decisions.[2] North Carolina now adopts a more targeted approach to business attraction by focusing on specific types of economic

1. Timothy J. Bartik, "Economic Development," in *Management Policies in Local Government Finance*, 5th ed., ed. J. Richard Aronson and Eli Schwartz (Washington, D.C.: International City/County Management Association, 2004), 364; Ted Levine, "Six Revolutions in Economic Development Marketing," *Economic Development Journal* 1, no. 1 (2002): 5–12.

2. Timothy J. Bartik, "Making Sense of Incentives: Taming Business Incentives to Promote Prosperity" (W.E. Upjohn Institute for Employment Research), research.upjohn.org/cgi/viewcontent.cgi?article=1277&context=up_press.

activity and providing inducements to spur investment in certain areas within the state. Two classic examples of major business attraction projects are Dell Computers' location in Winston-Salem in 2005 and Google's decision to build a data center in Caldwell County, which opened in 2008.[3] Some of the state's more recent (2022) sizeable business location projects include:

- Wolfspeed: $5 billion capital investment, 1,800 jobs in Chatham County
- Vinfast: $4 billion capital investment, 7,500 jobs in Chatham County
- Toyota Battery Plant: $2.5 billion capital investment in Randolph County

Although industrial attraction remains central to state and local economic development efforts, strategies focused on business retention and expansion, as well as entrepreneurship development, have gained traction in North Carolina. This is not surprising given the limitations and uncertainties of the recruitment/attraction approach. In addition, some studies suggest that 60 to 80 percent of new jobs come from expansions of existing smaller growth-oriented firms and start-ups.[4] Retaining companies already in a jurisdiction and helping them grow is considered a less risky and more cost-effective approach to economic development because it (1) builds the local economy from within and (2) strengthens a company's ties to the local community. A typical business retention and expansion program aims to build relationships with local companies to identify critical needs and facilitate access to resources and assistance that will help firms become more competitive.

Similarly, small business development and entrepreneurship programs provide support to smaller firms and encourage the start-up of new enterprises in order to stimulate economic development. Local governments usually defer to other entities, such as state agencies, community colleges, universities, chambers of commerce, and local nonprofits, to take the lead on small business development. However, several North Carolina counties and municipalities help fund and facilitate certain activities, including business incubators and revolving loan funds for small firms.

Many communities support placemaking strategies designed to create aesthetically appealing, vibrant, and functional spaces that often link to and amplify distinctive local attributes and amenities. These strategies often go hand-in-hand with downtown revitalization, tourism, and resident attraction, and they can complement efforts in business attraction, retention and expansion, and entrepreneurship. Placemaking focuses on improving the physical built environment and leveraging natural features, cultural heritage, and unique qualities of a place to encourage private investment and economic activity.[5] (These efforts largely rely on the legal authority and activities discussed in Chapter 26, "Community Development, Revitalization, and Affordable Housing.") For example, after losing thousands of jobs when its textile mills were shuttered, the City of Kannapolis pursued an aggressive place-based strategy for its downtown, beginning with the purchase of its entire downtown for $8.75 million in 2015. The City then invested more than $100 million to construct a minor-league baseball stadium and improve downtown streetscapes and core infrastructure. Over

---

3. The Dell facility in Winston-Salem ceased operations and officially closed in November 2010. This highlights the importance of local governments incorporating repayment provisions in incentive contracts in case those companies fail to meet performance targets or shut down. For a detailed discussion of the Dell and Google deals, see Jonathan Q. Morgan, "Using Economic Development Incentives: For Better or for Worse," *Popular Government* 74 (Winter 2009): 16–29, www.sog.unc.edu/publications/articles/using-economic-development-incentives-better-or-worse.

4. *See* David Birch, *Job Creation in America* (New York: Free Press, 1987).

5. *See* William Lambe and C. Tyler Mulligan, introduction to "Local Innovation in Community and Economic Development: Stories from Asheville, Edenton, Kannapolis, Wilson and Winston-Salem," *Carolina Planning* 34 (2009): 17–38.

the next few years, those public investments were matched by more than $200 million in private investment, with more on the way.[6]

Placemaking is not limited to urban areas, as some small towns and rural communities are finding that such strategies can be promising ways to build on local assets for economic development. For example, downtown revitalization efforts, such as streetscape improvements, festivals, and facade improvement programs to encourage storefront renovations, can spark investment in smaller downtowns.[7] The idea is to make downtown spaces more appealing and inviting for residents and visitors, resulting in more foot traffic and economic activity. The small mountain Town of Bakersville has managed to stabilize its tax base through placemaking efforts centered on unique local natural, creative, and cultural assets. The town built a creek walk that features catch-and-release trout fishing and a rhododendron craft fair in an effort to boost retail activity in the downtown vicinity and draw more tourist dollars. Bakersville's placemaking strategy cultivates the creative talent embedded in local arts and crafts activities while leveraging a natural attribute as part of its built environment—Cane Creek. The Rhododendron Festival attracts over 3,000 visitors each year, and new art galleries and shops have opened downtown in recent years.[8]

Some economic development projects represent a combination of approaches. The luring of the NASCAR Hall of Fame to Charlotte in 2006 is an example of how a major recruitment effort involving substantial state and local incentives can be tied to placemaking. Public officials who supported the incentives hoped that the Hall of Fame would become a major tourist attraction because it plays on the region's historical connection to stock car racing and motorsports. Moreover, its location in downtown Charlotte was expected to provide a boost to downtown revitalization efforts. Many small towns pursue development in ways that link entrepreneurship and placemaking strategies to generate greater economic activity from the unique experiences and creative talent embodied in local arts and crafts traditions, musical and cultural venues, and outdoor recreation and sporting activities.[9]

The Process of Economic Development

A primary purpose of economic development is to influence private investment decisions about where to locate, expand, or start a business enterprise. If new private investment is what triggers the job creation, tax base expansion, and income growth that local officials desire for their jurisdictions, then it is important to understand what factors influence the investment decision. Most often, private investment decisions are driven by issues related to the inputs in the production process: land, labor, and capital.

---

6. Collin Huguley, "Kannapolis Gears up for Next Phase of Former Mill Town's Downtown Remake," *Charlotte Business Journal* (August 15, 2022), www.bizjournals.com/triangle/news/2022/08/15/kannapolis-downtown-development-mill-town-ncrc.html. *See also* "A Long-Term, Large-Scale Vision (Kannapolis, NC)," Development Finance Initiative Front Page Stories, dfi.sog.unc.edu/2018/12/a-long-term-large-scale-vision-kannapolis-nc/.

7. Various approaches to facade improvement are described in Tyler Mulligan, "Downtown Facade Improvement Programs," *Community and Economic Development in North Carolina and Beyond* blog (Jan. 16, 2020), ced.sog.unc.edu/2020/01/downtown-facade-improvement-programs/.

8. Information about Bakersville's efforts is available at Homegrown Tools for Economic Development, homegrowntools.unc.edu/index.php/studies/bakersville-and-hayesville/.

9. *See* Nancy Pardue, "The Power of Partnership: How LGFCU and DFI Are Helping N.C. Towns Plan for Bright Futures," *AIM* (Fall 2019): 4–9, www.lgfcu.org/sites/default/files/aim/Aim-Magazine-Fall-2019-Secured-Web.pdf.

Recent surveys indicate that the following are among the most important factors that companies consider when choosing a location for a new facility or an expansion of an existing facility:[10]

- labor costs,
- availability of skilled workers,
- highway accessibility,
- state and local incentives,
- energy availability and costs,
- corporate tax rates,
- high-speed Internet access,
- construction and occupancy costs,
- quality of life.

This list is not exhaustive, and numerous other factors, including some that are beyond the control of individual counties, cities, and towns can shape private investment decisions. Labor and workforce concerns are paramount for most types of companies. Firms in knowledge-based, technology industries, in particular, rely on highly educated and skilled employees in order to compete and grow. County governments play a crucial role in workforce development through their funding of public schools and support for community colleges. Another area that is increasingly important to knowledge-based technology companies is quality of life. Local governments are perhaps most directly responsible for ensuring that their communities are good places to live, work, and play.

The level of local government involvement in economic development varies considerably from place to place, and there are differing viewpoints regarding the extent to which localities should intervene. Some argue that the most effective role for local government is to help create an overall business climate that is conducive to economic growth by maintaining competitive local tax and utility rates and streamlining regulations. From this perspective, counties and municipalities can best support economic development by operating efficiently, providing quality services, and making long-term public investments in infrastructure, education, and local amenities. Others argue that local government should more actively stimulate private investment by providing incentives and other types of direct assistance to businesses, such as those discussed later in this chapter. Counties and municipalities enjoy broad statutory and constitutional authority to engage in economic development activities and can organize these activities in a number of ways. Before describing local government authority and organizational options, however, it is useful to set the context by summarizing federal, state, and regional programs in economic development.

Federal Programs

The federal government offers multiple programs to support state and local economic development efforts. This section describes federal grant and tax credit programs that are commonly used to finance economic development projects.

Community Development Block Grants

As described in Chapter 26, the Community Development Block Grant (CDBG) program is the largest and most flexible source of federal funds to support investments that benefit low- and

10. *See* Area Development's annual corporate survey at www.areadevelopment.com/Corporate-Consultants-Survey-Results/.

moderate-income persons.[11] The amount of CDBG funds distributed annually to states and populous jurisdictions is determined by a formula that includes several measures of community need, such as population, housing overcrowding, age of housing, population growth lag relative to other metropolitan areas, and the extent of poverty.[12]

The CDBG program is divided into two parts: the Entitlement Program (for large municipalities and urban counties) and the Small Cities Program (for the remainder of the state's municipalities and counties). Communities that are eligible for Entitlement Program CDBG funds are generally municipalities with fifty thousand or more residents and urban counties. These communities receive a direct block-grant allocation from the federal government each year. In North Carolina, four counties and twenty-four municipalities participate in the CDBG Entitlement Program.[13]

The remainder of North Carolina's total CDBG allocation goes to the state for the Small Cities Program, which the state then awards to local governments that are not part of the Entitlement Program.

Together, all North Carolina entitlement communities received a total of approximately $31 million in fiscal year 2023, while the balance for the Small Cities program was approximately $46 million. Each state develops its own method of distributing funds in the Small Cities Program. The North Carolina Department of Commerce administers the portion of the state's CDBG funds designated by the General Assembly for economic development and revitalization projects, while the Department of Environmental Quality administers the portion designated for water and wastewater infrastructure.

When CDBG funds are used for economic development purposes, it typically involves the construction of *public* infrastructure to meet the needs of businesses that serve or employ persons of low and moderate income (earning no more than 80 percent of the local area median income). When CDBG funds are used to provide financing for a *private* development project, a local government must conduct underwriting to determine (1) that private contributions in equity and debt are appropriate, (2) that federal funds are necessary to make the project go forward, and (3) that the project, which was infeasible without the federal financing, will attain long-term feasibility and achieve the approved public purpose after the financing is provided.[14]

Other Federal Grant Programs

The U.S. Economic Development Administration (EDA) provides funding for local governments to engage in economic development planning and to implement projects. EDA targets its funding to economically distressed communities and regions through grants for public works (infrastructure), technical assistance, economic and trade adjustment assistance, and planning.[15] EDA also plays a

11. "Low- and moderate-income persons" refers to members of households with incomes equal to or less than the Section 8 low-income limit set by the U.S. Department of Housing and Urban Development (HUD), which is 80% of the area median income. "Definitions," 24 C.F.R. § 570.3.

12. *See* 42 U.S.C. § 5306(b); 24 C.F.R. § 570.4.

13. The entitlement counties are Cumberland, Mecklenburg, Union, and Wake; the entitlement cities are Asheville, Burlington, Cary, Chapel Hill, Charlotte, Concord, Durham, Fayetteville, Gastonia, Goldsboro, Greensboro, Greenville, Hickory, High Point, Jacksonville, Kannapolis, Lenoir, Morganton, New Bern, Raleigh, Rocky Mount, Salisbury, Wilmington, and Winston-Salem.

14. "Guidelines and Objectives for Evaluating Project Costs and Financial Requirements," 24 C.F.R. pt. 570, app. A (Community Development Block Grant underwriting guidelines to ensure public aid is necessary), www.ecfr.gov/current/title-24/subtitle-B/chapter-V/subchapter-C/part-570/appendix-Appendix%20A%20to%20Part%20570.

15. Jonathan Morgan, "U.S. Economic Development Administration (EDA) Reauthorized," *Community and Economic Development in North Carolina and Beyond* blog (March 4, 2025), ced.sog.unc.edu/2025/03/u-s-economic-development-administration-eda-reauthorized/.

vital role in administering supplemental congressional appropriations for disaster recovery. Other federal agencies administer and fund various types of loan guarantees for private lenders, support revolving loan programs, and provide funding for community facilities. These agencies include the Small Business Administration, the U.S. Department of Agriculture, and the U.S. Treasury Department.

Even when federal funding is received by a local government, state law must still be followed. The funding source or grant agreement—even when it is from the State of North Carolina—does not provide independent authority for an activity. G.S. 160A-17.1 authorizes local governments to accept state or federal funds to perform activities they are "authorized by *general law* or *local act* to provide or perform." Thus, when federal CDBG regulations differ from state law, public officials are required to compare federal and state requirements and follow the most restrictive rule.

Federal Tax Credit Programs

Federal grants are awarded to local governments to provide funding for *public* activities. Federal tax credit programs were created to induce *private* investment in projects related to economic development. Two federal tax credit programs designed for economic development are the New Markets Tax Credit and the Historic Rehabilitation Tax Credit. The New Markets Tax Credit (NMTC) was enacted as part of the federal Community Renewal Tax Relief Act of 2000. Designed to stimulate billions of dollars in new investment in distressed areas, the NMTC allows taxpayers to receive a credit against their federal income taxes for investing in commercial and economic activities in low-income communities. The Historic Rehabilitation Tax Credit provides tax credits to those who invest in the rehabilitation of income-producing historic structures. North Carolina has intermittently offered complementary state tax credits for investments in historic rehabilitation projects, such as historic mill rehabilitation. When combined with federal tax credits, eligible projects become even more appealing to private investors.

Most real estate developers cannot use all the available tax credits themselves, so they sell investment interests in their projects (through a tax credit intermediary or "syndicator") to individuals or companies with large tax liabilities. When those entities invest in a project in order to receive tax credits—in other words, when they buy tax credits—the investment provides an infusion of capital (or equity) into the project. The amount of equity a project can receive for selling its tax credits may depend on the demand for those tax credits. When tax credits are valuable, a developer can attract more equity for a project, enhancing its financial feasibility. When tax credits are less valuable, which typically occurs when federal tax rates decrease and companies have less tax liabilities, developers cannot obtain as much equity for a project, making it harder to finance a project with tax credits.

Local governments do not typically get involved with tax credit syndication, but the types of projects that take advantage of federal or state tax credits are often those that local governments wish to support. Thus, local governments must understand how tax credits work to evaluate the necessity of their participation in private projects that use tax credits.[16] In addition, because tax

16. A determination of necessity for public aid to private enterprise is legally significant. *See* C. Tyler Mulligan, "Economic Development Incentives Must Be 'Necessary': A Framework for Evaluating the Constitutionality of Public Aid for Private Development Projects," Harvard Law & Policy Review 11 (2017): S13–34, journals.law.harvard.edu/lpr/wp-content/uploads/sites/89/2013/11/Mulligan-HLPR-Essay-2017.pdf. *See also* Mulligan, "Legal and Business Reasons Why Downtown Development Programs Should Involve Secured Loans—Not Grants," *Community and Economic Development in North Carolina and Beyond* blog (Feb. 2, 2016), ced.sog.unc.edu/2017/09/legal-and-business-reasons-why-downtown-development-programs-should-involve-secured-loans-not-grants/.

credits help make private development projects possible, local governments are usually active partners in seeking to have projects and qualified areas of their communities designated for special tax treatment.[17]

State Programs

North Carolina has embraced a public–private partnership model for implementing economic development at the state level. The N.C. Department of Commerce contracts with the Economic Development Partnership of North Carolina (EDPNC) to handle the state's marketing, business attraction, existing industry support, international trade, tourism, and sports promotion activities. The EDPNC leads national and global marketing and outreach efforts, and its programs and resources are designed to encourage corporate decision-makers to consider North Carolina for business locations and expansions. For large-scale projects in particular, EDPNC staff members are often the first point of contact for prospective businesses considering a location in the state. They help match community assets (sites, buildings, workforce availability, skills, etc.) with the specific site selection criteria.[18]

The N.C. Department of Commerce Rural Economic Development Division (REDD) administers several grant programs that support local efforts to promote private investment, job creation, and community revitalization. State funding is available to local governments for public infrastructure, building demolition, building reuse, downtown development, and disaster recovery. In addition to grant funding, REDD helps build the local capacity of designated communities through its NC Main Street program, which facilitates placemaking strategies by directly assisting communities with strategic planning, downtown revitalization, small business development, and historic property rehabilitation.

Approval for Industrial Revenue Bonds

Industrial Revenue Bonds (IRBs) are a potential source of financing that businesses can use for land, building, and equipment purchases, as well as for facility construction. The interest paid to bondholders is exempt from federal and state income taxes, allowing businesses to access debt at below-market rates. These bonds finance the construction of factories and other industrial facilities, with the debt service paid by the companies using the facilities. The bonds are secured only by the credit of the benefiting company. Counties are authorized to create financing authorities to issue the bonds after obtaining approval from the board of county commissioners, the secretary of the North Carolina Department of Commerce, and the Local Government Commission. The local government, through the financing authority, acts merely as a conduit for the bond issuance and carries no obligation for payment.

---

17. An example of government-designated areas receiving special tax treatment is the federal Opportunity Zones program. *See* Tyler Mulligan, "Federal Opportunity Zones: What Local Governments Need to Know," *Community and Economic Development in North Carolina and Beyond* blog (Sept. 21, 2018), ced.sog.unc.edu/2018/09/federal-opportunity-zones-what-local-governments-need-to-know/.

18. Jonathan Q. Morgan and Crystal Morphis, *Economic Development Handbook*, 5th ed. (UNC School of Government, 2024), www.sog.unc.edu/sites/default/files/full_text_books/Economic-Development-Handbook_5ed.pdf.

Tax Credits and Exemptions

North Carolina has, at various times, supported tax credits and exemptions for companies that create jobs and invest in facilities and equipment within the state. Benefits and credit amounts under state programs are often based on the relative distress of the county where the project is located, as indicated by a county tier designation assigned by the Department of Commerce. For example, the tier designation system employed in 2024 assigned the forty most-distressed counties as tier one, the next forty as tier two, and the twenty least-distressed counties as tier three. The most generous benefits and tax credits are reserved for projects in tier one counties, with lower benefit amounts offered in higher tiers. An example is the state's tax credit for the rehabilitation of income-producing historic structures.[19] The value of the credit is determined in part by the economic development tier of the county in which the historic structure is located.[20]

At the state level, North Carolina's business incentives have shifted away from statutory corporate income tax credits in favor of discretionary grants. This policy shift stems, in part, from skepticism about the ability of tax credits to directly influence business investment decisions, given the time lag in claiming the credits on tax returns. Some companies may not generate enough profit early on to incur sufficient tax liability to claim credits. In addition, there is evidence suggesting that corporate decision-makers may not even realize their company received a tax credit.[21] Furthermore, it can be difficult for the state to accurately estimate how much revenue it will forego due to tax credits in any given fiscal year. For these reasons, discretionary grants now are the foundation of North Carolina's incentives.[22]

Discretionary Incentive Grants for Competitive Industrial Projects

At the state level, the two primary discretionary grant programs are the Job Development Investment Grant (JDIG) and the One North Carolina Fund. The JDIG program provides discretionary grants directly to new and expanding companies to encourage them to increase employment in North Carolina rather than in another state. The grant amount is based on a percentage of withholding taxes paid for each eligible job created over a period of time, with higher amounts awarded for greater levels of capital investment and job creation.[23] The terms of the grant are specified in an agreement that requires the recipient company to comply with certain standards regarding employee health insurance, workplace safety, and wages paid. The grant agreement must include a clawback provision to recapture funds if the company relocates or ceases operations before a specified period.

The One North Carolina Fund awards grants to local governments to secure commitments from private companies to locate or expand within the local government's jurisdiction rather than in another state. The grants must be used to install or purchase new equipment; make structural repairs, improvements, or renovations to existing buildings to expand operations; construct or improve existing water, sewer, gas, or electric utility distribution lines; or equip buildings.[24] Applications for the grants are submitted according to guidelines established by the state Department

19. Articles 3D (Historic Rehabilitation Tax Credits) and 3H (Mill Rehabilitation Tax Credit) of Chapter 105 of the North Carolina General Statutes (hereinafter G.S.).

20. *See, e.g.*, G.S. 105-129.71.

21. G.J. Jolley, M.F. Lancaster, and J. Gao, "Tax Incentives and Business Climate: Executive Perceptions from Incented and Nonincented Firms," *Economic Development Quarterly* 29, no. 2 (2015): 180–86, doi.org/10.1177/0891242415571127.

22. Morgan and Morphis, *Economic Development Handbook*.

23. G.S. 143B-437.52.

24. G.S. 143B-437.71.

of Commerce, with grants awarded based on the strategic importance of the industry, the quality of jobs created, and the specific project. A local government is typically expected to provide some form of matching funds for state incentive awards to businesses within its jurisdiction.

Industrial Development Fund Utility Account for Infrastructure

The Industrial Development Fund Utility Account (commonly known as the Utility Account) provides funds to local governments in the most economically distressed counties for infrastructure projects that are expected to result in job creation.[25] Eligible public infrastructure projects include the construction or improvement of water, sewer, gas, telecommunications, high-speed broadband, electrical utility facilities, and transportation infrastructure.

Workforce Development, Small Business Services, Industrial Extension, and Transportation

In a dynamic economy transformed by technological innovation, it is imperative that North Carolina prioritizes workforce and talent development to meet employers' labor needs. This is a critical component of the state's ability to attract and retain businesses. The N.C. Department of Commerce houses the Division of Workforce Solutions, which assists job seekers, including veterans, youth, and those facing employment barriers, through a network of eighty career centers across the state. The Workforce Solutions Division also supports the NCWorks Commission, which guides the statewide implementation of the federal Workforce Innovation and Opportunity Act and sets standards for service delivery among the local and regional career centers. The N.C. Community College System contributes to economic development by providing customized training for employees of new and expanding industries.[26] The community college system also coordinates a network of small business centers on its campuses that assist new and existing small firms.[27] North Carolina State University administers the state's Industrial Extension Service through regional field offices, providing training and technical assistance to businesses and industries to help them remain competitive. Finally, the Department of Transportation makes road and highway improvements that encourage both industrial and commercial development.

Regional Economic Development Programs

Various organizations work to support and implement regional approaches to economic development within North Carolina. One regional framework consists of eight designated geographic regions that function as "prosperity zones" for economic development purposes. The Economic Development Partnership of North Carolina (EDPNC) has economic developers based in each prosperity zone region who focus primarily on business retention and expansion.[28]

Other regional economic development groups coordinate national and international marketing and related activities on behalf of the multicounty regions they serve. These include the Charlotte Regional Business Alliance, NC East Alliance (based in Greenville), North Carolina's Southeast (based in Elizabethtown), and the Research Triangle Regional Partnership (based in Raleigh). The Greensboro-based Piedmont Triad Partnership is a private leadership organization that advances high-priority transformational economic development projects and promotes the Carolina Core brand, focused on central North Carolina along US 421. These regional economic development

25. G.S. 143B-437.01.
26. See the NCEdge training program at www.nccommunitycolleges.edu/businesses/ncedge/.
27. More information is available from the N.C. Small Business Center Network (SBCN), www.sbcn.nc.gov.
28. Morgan and Morphis, *Economic Development Handbook.*

organizations market the unique assets of their respective regions and work closely with state and local developers to address regional economic issues. Their programs vary and can include generating leads, managing prospect inquiries, promoting product development, providing research assistance, talent attraction, and publicizing improvements in transportation, infrastructure, and the labor force. These entities are funded mainly through membership dues and private investors.[29]

Another regional framework supporting economic development in North Carolina is that of the Councils of Governments (COGs). Sixteen COGs or regional councils serve multicounty regions by assisting local governments with planning and development. COGs provide technical assistance to local governments and help coordinate access to state and federal resources. Several North Carolina COGs administer EDA economic development districts and facilitate regional comprehensive economic development strategies. Some COGs are more directly involved in economic development activities than others. For example, the Upper Coastal Plain COG, located in Wilson, has administered a revolving loan fund and launched a regional business incubator. The Centralina COG in the Charlotte region has a Community Economic Development Department that administers a nonprofit organization called the Centralina Economic Development District.

A third regional framework in North Carolina pertinent to economic development consists of the workforce development boards. There are twenty Workforce Development Boards in the state that oversee and coordinate federal workforce and job training programs at the local level. Some boards serve single counties, but most serve multicounty regions and are based within COGs. Local elected officials appoint board members, a majority of whom must be business representatives.[30]

Local Government Legal Authority for Economic Development Activities

Any discussion of legal authority must begin with the state constitution. Section 32 of Article I of the North Carolina Constitution prohibits local governments from providing "exclusive emoluments"—in other words, gifts of public property—to private entities.[31] This same constitutional rule, sometimes called a gift clause, appears in state constitutions across the nation.[32] Exclusive emoluments are permitted only "in consideration of public services." This means the public must receive something in return—known as "consideration" in contract law—for a payment to a private entity. North Carolina local governments are not even allowed to make donations to charitable not-for-profit entities.[33] Every government payment or transfer of property to a private enterprise must be made in exchange for adequate consideration.[34] For example, a grant may be paid to a

29. *Id.*

30. Morgan and Morphis, *Economic Development Handbook*.

31. The exclusive emoluments clause of the North Carolina Constitution, which prohibits government gifts to private entities, is consistent with gift clauses found in most state constitutions across the nation. *See* Mulligan, "*Economic Development Incentives Must Be 'Necessary*,'" note 16 above.

32. David E. Pinsky, "State Constitutional Limitations on Public Industrial Financing: An Historical and Economic Approach," 111 *University of Pennsylvania Law Review* (1963): 265, 280 ("At the turn of the century, some form of public aid limitation had been incorporated in the constitutions of a large majority of the states."). Most states have similar constitutional rules. In a recent example of gift clause enforcement, the Arizona Supreme Court, en banc in 2010, held that benefits provided to the developer of a mixed-use development were an unconstitutional gift because tax revenues alone were not valid consideration under that state's gift clause. Turken v. Gordon, 224 P.3d 158 (Ariz. 2010).

33. Frayda Bluestein, "Donating Property: Beware of Constitutional Constraints," *Coates' Canons: NC Local Government Law* blog (April 13, 2015) (describing the North Carolina Supreme Court's holding in *Brumley v. Baxter*, 251 N.C. 691 (1945)), canons.sog.unc.edu/2015/04/donating-property-beware-of-constitutional-constraints/.

34. Osborne M. Reynolds, Jr., *Local Government Law*, 4th ed. (St. Paul, Minn.: West Academic Publishing, 2015), 515 ("*Gifts* of property by local governments—at least to private individuals—are generally banned by statute or as a

nonprofit economic development agency, but not as a donation; rather, the grant could be made only in exchange for the agency's contractual agreement to provide services of equivalent value, such as managing the jurisdiction's economic development functions.

A separate set of constitutional provisions requires that expenditures by local governments (including contractual payments to private entities) must serve a public purpose (Section 2 of Article V of the North Carolina Constitution). As long as a payment or expenditure serves a valid public purpose, it satisfies not only the constitutional provisions regarding public purpose but also the exclusive emoluments provision. The courts alone—not the legislature or statutes—decide what constitutes a valid public purpose under the constitution.

Together, these constitutional rules indicate that direct government participation in private development is disfavored under North Carolina law, requiring caution when local governments seek to partner with private entities. North Carolina courts have stated in multiple decisions that "direct state aid to a private enterprise, with only limited benefit accruing to the public, contravenes fundamental constitutional precepts."[35] In addition, government is not permitted to engage in private business.[36]

These rules should be axiomatic for local government officials. If it were permissible for governments to engage in business or make grants or donations to private enterprises without requiring services in return, the legal requirements discussed in other chapters of this publication would become irrelevant. Laws governing property conveyance at fair market value could be circumvented. Grants could undermine uniformity of taxation, as classes of grant recipients could receive the equivalent of tax refunds. Utility law requirements regarding the fair treatment of similarly situated customers could easily be avoided. Procurement rules and the outcomes of bidding processes could be nudged up or down by offering grants to preferred vendors. State law, rooted in longstanding constitutional principles, contains a carefully constructed web of requirements and prohibitions designed to prevent direct government aid to private enterprises.

An additional constitutional requirement is that North Carolina local governments are authorized to make expenditures only as specifically permitted by statute.[37] Statutes do not supersede the constitutional rules regarding exclusive emoluments and public purpose described above. All statutes must be interpreted to be consistent with the state constitution.[38] Indeed, statutes may contain broad language with the presumption that constitutional rules control. This is precisely the

---

matter of common law; any transfer of municipal property must be supported by some reasonable compensation or benefit in return."); John Martinez, 3 *Local Government Law*, 2nd ed. (Eagan, Minn.: Thomson Reuters, 2017), § 21:7, at 21–25 ("Local government property cannot be conveyed to a private party without adequate consideration, for to do so would constitute an improper gift of public property or the granting of a subsidy contrary to state constitutional constraints."). *See, e.g.*, Schires v. Carlat, 480 P.3d 639, 646 (Ariz. 2021) (holding that incentive payment violated state's gift clause because consideration was not proportional to fair market value of consideration received and fiscal impact from tax revenue calculated by expert was irrelevant).

35. Maready v. City of Winston-Salem, 342 N.C. 708, 718 (1996).

36. *See* Mitchell v. N.C. Indus. Dev. Fin. Auth., 273 N.C. 137, 156 (1968) (stating that "it is not the function of government to engage in private business"); Nash v. Town of Tarboro, 227 N.C. 283 (1947) (holding that it is not a public purpose for a town to own and operate a hotel).

37. N.C. Const. art. VII, § 1 ("The General Assembly . . . may give such powers and duties to counties, cities and towns, and other governmental subdivisions as it may deem advisable.").

38. Comm'r of Ins. v. N.C. Fire Ins. Rating Bureau, 291 N.C. 55, 70 (1976) (citation, internal quotation marks omitted) ("When reasonably possible, a statute . . . should be construed so as to avoid serious doubt as to its constitutionality."); *In re* Arcadia Dairy Farms, Inc., 289 N.C. 456, 465 (1976) ("The cardinal principle of statutory construction is to save and not to destroy. We have repeatedly held that as between two possible interpretations of a statute, by one of which it would be unconstitutional and by the other valid, our plain duty is to adopt that which will save the act. Even to avoid a serious doubt the rule is the same.").

case with the primary source of local government legal authority for economic development: the Local Development Act of 1925, codified at Article 1 of G.S. Chapter 158. The Local Development Act provides broad authority to appropriate funds for local development, subject to procedural requirements. Importantly, activities authorized by the statute have been struck down when they conflict with the state constitution.[39]

As noted, even when a project is funded entirely by federal or state grants, it remains subject to constitutional and statutory requirements. G.S. 160A-17.1 authorizes local governments to accept state or federal funds to perform activities that are "authorized by *general law* or *local act* to provide or perform" (emphasis added). The grant programs described earlier in this chapter do not provide independent authority for local government activities—they merely provide funding. Any action taken without statutory authority is considered *ultra vires*—that is, outside the scope of the powers delegated by the state—and can be voided by a court. Thus, when a local government receives funding from the federal government or the state, it cannot expend those funds unless it first identifies separate statutory authority to do so.

With this constitutional and statutory background, the legal authority for three categories of local government activities will be discussed: traditional economic development activities, direct development of industrial and commercial facilities, and business location inducements.

Legal Authority for Traditional Economic Development Activities

Local governments promote economic development by engaging in various traditional activities about which there is little philosophical dispute. These activities include hiring agents to negotiate with and assist companies interested in locating or expanding in the community, conducting surveys to identify community strengths and weaknesses, developing strategic plans for economic development, and advertising the community in industrial development publications. Counties and cities also provide public services and facilities to attract new development and stimulate economic growth by extending public utility lines, expanding public water supply and sewage treatment facilities, and improving roads. Unless a more specific statute applies,[40] the general statutory authority for these activities is outlined in G.S. 158-7.1(a), provided that proper notice and a hearing occur before appropriating funds, and that any recipients account for all expenditures of local government funds as required by North Carolina Supreme Court case law and G.S. 158-7.2.[41]

---

39. For example, the broad language of the Local Development Act of 1925, codified at G.S. Chapter 158, was enacted more than seventy years prior to the seminal economic development case, *Maready v. City of Winston-Salem*, cited in full at note 35 above. In the decades prior to *Maready*, there was no suggestion that the permissive language of G.S. 158-7.1(a) could be used to provide aid to private entities. Horner v. Chamber of Com. of City of Burlington, 235 N.C. 77, 81 (1952) (requiring the return of funds to a municipal treasury that had been appropriated to a Chamber of Commerce ostensibly for "publicity" about the municipality, pursuant to G.S. 158-7.1's predecessor statute, G.S. 158-1, because the expenditures were controlled by the chamber rather than the city). Later, the courts would strike down *loans* to businesses despite clear statutory authority. Mitchell v. N.C. Indus. Dev. Fin. Auth., cited in full at note 36 above (industrial development bonds not a public purpose), and Stanley v. Dep't of Conservation & Dev., 284 N.C. 15 (1973) (financing for pollution control not a public purpose). *Mitchell* and *Stanley* have never been overruled by a court decision; eventually, the constitution was amended to provide clear constitutional authority for industrial development bonds.

40. Trustees of Rowan Tech. Coll. v. J. Hyatt Hammond Associates, Inc., 313 N.C. 230, 238 (1985) ("When two statutes apparently overlap, it is well established that the statute special and particular shall control over the statute general in nature, even if the general statute is more recent, unless it clearly appears that the legislature intended the general statute to control." (citations omitted)).

41. Dennis v. City of Raleigh, 253 N.C. 400, 405 (1960) (explaining that contracting with the Chamber of Commerce to advertise the advantages of the City was different from the situation in *Horner*, discussed above, because the

Legal Authority for Product Development: Industrial Sites and Shell Buildings

Some local governments engage in "product development," which includes preparing industrial sites and constructing shell buildings for eventual sale or lease to job-creating private businesses at fair market value. The Local Development Act of 1925, and particularly G.S. 158-7.1, was enacted specifically for this purpose. The development activities required for product development, as authorized by G.S. 158-7.1, can be organized using the same land banking framework described in Chapter 26: acquire property, hold and develop the property or prepare it for development, convey property to a third party, and provide financing for development as necessary and authorized by law.

Acquire Property for Industrial or Commercial Use

G.S. 158-7.1 authorizes local governments to acquire land for an industrial park or for resale for industrial or commercial use. Counties or cities may also acquire buildings suitable for such purposes. Alternatively, a local government may acquire an *option* to purchase property for industrial or commercial use, with the intent of assigning the option to a job-creating private business later. Specific notice and hearing requirements must be followed before making an appropriation related to property acquisition.

Eminent domain authority has not been granted to local governments for economic development projects. However, see Chapter 26 for a description of how urban redevelopment law allows a redevelopment commission (or a governing board exercising its powers) to condemn blighted parcels for redevelopment.

Hold and Develop Acquired Property

Once property is acquired, G.S. 158-7.1 authorizes it to be held for resale for industrial or commercial use. While the property is under local government ownership, it may be developed by demolishing or rehabilitating existing structures, constructing new buildings suitable for industrial or commercial use (such as industrial shell buildings), installing public infrastructure such as utilities and streets, and otherwise preparing the site for industrial or commercial uses. These improvements generally increase the value of the property.

Convey Property to Third Party at Fair Market Value (No Subsidy) for Industrial or Commercial Use

As a general rule, local governments are required, unless an exception applies, to convey real property through competitive bidding procedures: sealed bid, upset bid, or public auction.[42] The price reached through competitive bidding is presumed by courts to be the fair market value of the property.[43] However, a drawback of competitive sale procedures is that no restrictions or conditions can be imposed on the sale.[44]

In the context of economic development, however, the General Assembly recognized local governments may sometimes need to select their buyer (through a privately negotiated sale or private sale) and impose conditions on the buyer to ensure the property is used for appropriate industrial or commercial purposes. G.S. 158-7.1(d) allows for this. Before property can be conveyed in this manner, a local government must issue notice and hold a public hearing. The governing body must

---

Chamber could not expend the funds "unless and until specific advertising and the cost thereof is first submitted to and approved by the Raleigh City Council").

42. G.S. 160A-268, -269, -270. *See also* Chapter 23, "Public Contracts, Competitive Bidding Requirements, and Property Disposal."

43. Redevelopment Comm'n of Greensboro v. Sec. Nat'l Bank of Greensboro, 252 N.C. 595, 612 (1960).

44. Puett v. Gaston Cnty., 19 N.C. App. 231, 235 (1973). A local government could first record a restrictive covenant running with the land as part of its site preparation, and then afterward hold a proper competitive sale process without imposing any restrictions or conditions through the sale process itself.

determine the average hourly wage proposed for workers at the site and the fair market value of the property (accounting for any conditions or restrictions that could reduce its value). The sale price "may not be less" than the "fair market value," protecting the public in these "private" sales by ensuring the price reflects the objective fair market value, as determined by licensed professionals in North Carolina.[45]

Financing without Subsidy

G.S. 158-7.1(b) provides a non-exclusive list of activities that local governments may engage in to support economic development, including making "grants or loans for the rehabilitation of commercial or noncommercial historic structures, whether the structure is publicly or privately owned." The explicit mention of historic structures does not exclude grants and loans for other types of structures;[46] indeed, the "specific activities listed in subsection (b) of [G.S. 158-7.1] are not intended to limit the grant of authority provided by [G.S. 158-7.1]," especially subsection (a) which authorizes "economic development appropriations" more generally. Thus, in the absence of more specific statutory authorization (such as the community development, revitalization, and housing statutes described in Chapter 26), G.S. 158-7.1 provides ample authority for financing sites and buildings for "industrial" or "commercial" use.

This statutory authorization does not override constitutional prohibitions against aid to private enterprise. As already noted, the consideration for the sale of local government property to a business "may not be less" than the "fair market value."[47] The same principle applies to financing: grant payments to a private enterprise should be made only as part of a contract for public services or goods of equivalent value, and loans should carry higher interest rates and terms that do not compete with commercial lenders.[48]

This legal principle is relevant when local governments seek to finance industrial sites and shell buildings developed by private enterprises, such as nonprofit economic development organizations and for-profit construction firms. This activity is permissible as long as no subsidy is provided; any grant made by a local government should secure an equivalent property interest in the financed project, and any loan should be properly secured and charge an appropriate interest rate that reflects the loan's risk so as not to compete with private capital providers.[49] A low-interest loan in this situation would constitute an unconstitutional subsidy. Subsidies to private enterprises are not authorized except in the very specific incentives scenario described in the next section.

---

45. *See* Article 1 of G.S. Chapter 93A (licensing of real estate brokers) and Article 1 of G.S. Chapter 93E (licensing of real estate appraisers).

46. *See* Tyler Mulligan, "Local Government Economic Development Powers 'Clarified,'" *Coates' Canons: NC Local Government Law* blog (October 26, 2015), canons.sog.unc.edu/2015/10/local-government-economic-development-powers-clarified/.

47. G.S. 158-7.1(d).

48. The constitutional prohibitions on gifts to private enterprise and on local governments acting as or competing with businesses is described above in notes 31 through 36 and the accompanying text. *See also* Tyler Mulligan, "Legal and Business Reasons Why Downtown Development Programs Should Involve Secured Loans—Not Grants," *Coates' Canons: NC Local Government Law* blog (September 19, 2017), canons.sog.unc.edu/2017/09/9935-2/.

49. Tyler Mulligan, "Conveyance of Local Government Property to Nonprofit EDC for Industrial Park," *Coates' Canons: NC Local Government Law* blog (March 17, 2015), canons.sog.unc.edu/2015/03/conveyance-of-local-government-property-to-nonprofit-edc-for-industrial-park/.

Legal Authority for Business Location Inducements: Incentives and Subsidies for Private Enterprises

For most of the past century, North Carolina local governments were not allowed to make incentive payments to private entities. Even loans to private enterprises were prohibited.[50] It wasn't until 1996, following the loss of economic development projects to other states, that the North Carolina Supreme Court ruled in the seminal case *Maready v. City of Winston-Salem*[51] that economic development incentives serve a constitutionally permitted public purpose—*under certain conditions.*[52] Those conditions were reinforced in subsequent cases decided by the North Carolina Court of Appeals, warranting separate treatment here.[53]

In *Maready* and subsequent cases, courts examined numerous economic development incentives provided by local governments to private companies under G.S. 158-7.1. In *Maready*, the court stated that economic development incentives authorized by G.S. 158-7.1 are constitutional "so long as they primarily benefit the public and not a private party."[54] The necessary "net public benefit," according to the court, is achieved by creating jobs, increasing the tax base, and diversifying the economy. A key factor behind the *Maready* decision was the belief that, without incentives, job-creating facilities would be "lost to other states."[55] The court expressed concerns about "the actions of other states" and the "inducements . . . offered . . . in other jurisdictions."[56] Thus, there was an underlying assumption that all the incentives in *Maready* involved interstate competition.[57]

In subsequent cases before the North Carolina Court of Appeals, the court has refused to strike down incentives that are "parallel" to those approved in *Maready*.[58] Determining whether an incentive is "parallel" to *Maready* cannot be reduced to a simple formula, but there are generally two key components to consider.

First, the consideration (or value) that the local government receives in exchange for an incentive must result in a net public benefit, primarily from job creation and capital investment, that "might otherwise be lost to other states."[59] Every incentive approved by *Maready* involved both substantial job creation and new tax revenue that could be lost to other states, and all incentives were recouped by new tax revenue "within three to seven years."[60]

Second, the *Maready* court praised the procedures employed by local governments in approving the incentives before the court.[61] The court essentially treated *cash* incentives as equivalent to the local government *conveying property* to the business for less than fair market value under the statutory section created specifically for that purpose, subsection (d2) of G.S. 158-7.1. The court

50. *See* Mitchell v. N.C. Indus. Dev. Fin. Auth., cited in full at note 36 above, and Stanley v. Dep't of Conservation & Dev., cited in full at note 39 above.

51. 342 N.C. 708 (1996).

52. The section summarizes the framework for analyzing business location incentives discussed in C. Tyler Mulligan, "Economic Development Incentives and North Carolina Local Governments: A Framework for Analysis," *North Carolina Law Review* 91, no. 6 (Sept. 2013): 2021–2116.

53. Haugh v. Cnty. of Durham, 208 N.C. App. 304 (2010); Blinson v. State, 186 N.C. App. 328 (2007).

54. *Maready*, 342 N.C. at 724.

55. *Maready*, 342 N.C. at 726.

56. *Maready*, 342 N.C. at 725, 727.

57. *Haugh*, 208 N.C. App. at 317.

58. *Haugh*, 208 N.C. App. at 319.

59. *Maready*, 342 N.C. at 726. *See also* Mulligan, note 52 above.

60. *Maready*, 342 N.C. at 713.

61. *Maready*, 342 N.C. at 713.

therefore applied all the statutory requirements of that subsection to every incentive, even if no real property was conveyed. In addition, the court described some procedures not explicitly outlined in the statutes. The collective procedures are as follows:

- An initial "but for" or necessity determination is made, typically in a competitive situation, confirming that the incentive is required in order for a project to proceed in the community.
- A written guideline or policy is applied to determine the maximum amount of incentive that can be given to the receiving company.
- Expenditures take the form of reimbursements, rather than unrestricted cash payments.
- Final approval is made at a public meeting with proper notice.
- A written agreement governs implementation.

The court imbued these procedures with constitutional significance, declaring that these "strict procedural requirements" should "prevent abuse" of incentives.[62] Thus, local governments aiming to make their incentive approval process "parallel" to *Maready* should adhere to these procedures.

Some additional statutory requirements should be noted. When a North Carolina local government turns funds over to a private entity for expenditure (such as through an incentive payment), the local government must give prior approval to how the funds will be used, and "all such expenditures shall be accounted for" at the end of the fiscal year.[63] Furthermore, the funds must be subject to recapture in an incentive agreement, where the private entity promises to create a certain number of jobs, exceed a minimum level of capital investment, and maintain operations throughout a defined compliance period.[64]

The criteria and procedural requirements for business location incentives, described above, are not difficult to achieve in a competitive incentive scenario in which a local government is competing with other states to attract a sizable facility with a significant number of permanent jobs. However, not all commercial projects provide the requisite job creation or meet the other criteria listed above. Retail businesses, such as grocery stores and restaurants, along with other real estate developments like office spaces and hotels cannot "be lost to other states" because they are financed on the basis of *local* market demand—and therefore such projects *cannot be considered parallel to* Maready. In addition, local government aid to retail businesses and real estate development inevitably competes with other local property owners, potentially infringing on their constitutional rights and inviting lawsuits.[65] Local governments may support such retail businesses and real estate development only through unsubsidized (or fair market value) transactions, as described in the previous section.

---

62. *Maready*, 342 N.C. at 724.

63. G.S. 158-7.2. *See also* Kara Millonzi, "Local Government Appropriations/Grants to Private Entities," *Coates' Canons: NC Local Government Law* blog (June 17, 2010; updated Aug. 2013), canons.sog.unc.edu/2010/06/local-government-grants-to-private-entities/.

64. G.S. 158-7.1(h). All three recapture provisions are required. *See* S. Power Co. v. Cleveland Cnty., 24 F.4th 258, 267 (4th Cir. 2022) ("The state legislature has said these provisions must be in every development agreement.").

65. King v. Town of Chapel Hill, 367 N.C. 400, 408–09 (2014) ("This Court's duty to protect fundamental rights includes preventing arbitrary government actions that interfere with the right to the fruits of one's own labor.") (citing N.C. Const. art. I, § 1 and Roller v. Allen, 245 N.C. 516, 525 (1957)).

Form of Incentive: Illegal Tax Abatements and Lawful Cash Payments

The previous section described the legal authority for offering subsidies and inducements to private enterprises that are "parallel to *Maready*." Even when such subsidies are authorized, constitutional limitations dictate the form those incentives may take. In several other states, local governments can offer subsidies in the form of special property tax breaks or tax abatements. These tax abatements do not violate those states' constitutional gift clauses because they are available statewide and involve a reduction in taxes owed, rather than an expenditure of public funds.[66]

In North Carolina, local governments have almost no authority to offer such tax abatements. Under Article V, Section 2, of the state constitution, property tax exemptions and classifications can only be made by the General Assembly and must be available on a statewide basis. In other words, a local government cannot constitutionally offer a special property tax classification to a property owner unless it is available statewide.

Some property tax exclusions have been enacted by the General Assembly and made available statewide. For example, a development project on a contaminated site and subject to a brownfield agreement with the State of North Carolina is entitled to a brownfield tax exclusion of 90 percent in the first year, decreasing to 75 percent, 50 percent, 30 percent, and 10 percent in years two through five.[67] A property designated as a historic landmark and properly maintained is entitled to a 50 percent exclusion in perpetuity.[68] North Carolina local governments cannot create their own tax exemption or abatement programs, but they can inform private businesses about various lawful exemptions that are available.[69]

The legislature has not enacted special property tax classifications for new industrial or commercial development, meaning local economic development officials cannot offer property tax abatements. Recently, however, several counties and cities have implemented cash grant incentive policies that resemble tax abatements. These policies typically involve the local government providing annual cash grants over several years (usually five) to industrial or commercial businesses that are parallel to *Maready*. The grant payments reimburse businesses for qualifying investments, and the amount is directly tied to the property taxes paid. For example, a company that invests at least $5 million might be eligible for a cash grant in an amount up to 50 percent of the property taxes on the resulting facility; larger investments could yield grants representing a higher percentage of taxes paid. While these policies are similar to tax abatements, two key differences exist: the company must first pay its property taxes in full, and grant payments depend not only on tax payment but also on performance aligned with *Maready*. It's important to note that no court has yet determined whether these tax-calculated grants constitute an unconstitutional attempt to enact a tax abatement or are permissible cash grants under the law.[70]

---

66. Reynolds, note 34 above, at 129 ("Although taxes may not be levied for private (as opposed to public) benefit, *exemptions* from property taxes may validly be authorized by state law except as such exemptions are prohibited by state constitutions.").

67. G.S. 105-277.13.

68. G.S. 105-278.

69. For a fuller listing of available property tax exemptions related to economic development, see Christopher McLaughlin, "Property Tax Exemptions for Community and Economic Development," *Community and Economic Development in North Carolina and Beyond* blog (Apr. 10, 2024), ced.sog.unc.edu/2024/04/property-tax-exemptions-for-community-economic-development/.

70. *See* Blinson v. State, 186 N.C. App. 328, 335 (2007) (dismissing the plaintiff's claim for lack of standing on the constitutional issue of uniformity of taxation).

Open Meetings and Public Records

Both the open meetings and public records laws allow a degree of confidentiality while a local government negotiates incentives with a company. The open meetings law permits a public body to hold closed sessions to "discuss matters relating to the location or expansion of industries or other businesses in the area served by the public body, including agreement on a tentative list of economic development incentives that may be offered by the public body" (G.S. 143-318.11(a)(4)). The statute requires, however, that any action approving the signing of an incentives contract or authorizing payment of an incentive be taken in open session. Note also that G.S. 158-7.1(c) requires a public hearing before incentives can be approved.

G.S. 132-6(d) permits denying public access to otherwise public records "relating to the proposed expansion or location of specific business or industrial projects . . . so long as their inspection, examination or copying would frustrate the purpose for which such public records were created." However, once the company has committed to locate or expand in the community, or has decided not to locate or expand, the statute requires that the records be made public.

Occasionally, a local government will rely on elaborate economic modeling and impact analysis to assess the value of a company's decision to locate in the jurisdiction. These analyses typically attempt to estimate the fiscal and economic impacts in a community of promised capital investment, jobs, and operations.[71] Whenever a public agency performs such analysis, G.S. 132-1.11 requires that the agency "describe in detail the assumptions and methodologies used in completing the analysis or assessment." This description becomes a public record and must be included in the release of all public records pertaining to a company's location decision.

The open meetings and public records statutes are discussed at length in Chapter 8, "Public Records," and Chapter 9, "Open Meetings and Other Legal Requirements for Local Government Boards."

Public Finance for Economic Development

Land acquisition and public improvements undertaken for economic development purposes may be financed by federal funds or local tax revenues without special voter approval. General obligation bonds may be used to finance any improvement authorized by G.S. 159-48, but generally only with voter approval before issuance. Revenue bonds can be used to finance public service enterprise improvements, such as sewer or water facilities built in conjunction with an economic development project. No vote is required for these bonds, but the facility must generate adequate revenue from operations to retire the debt. Additionally, certain capital projects beneficial for economic development may be financed by project development (or tax increment) bonds, which primarily rely on tax proceeds from new private development generated by the public investment.

In some cases, local governments proactively use the financing mechanisms described above to construct public infrastructure on a speculative basis, such as building water and sewer facilities to facilitate future industrial or commercial development. In other cases, a local government may respond reactively to requests from developers to provide publicly owned infrastructure to support a specific development. Local governments could, using their subdivision and zoning powers, require a new real estate development project to construct the necessary public infrastructure at no cost to the government, which would then be dedicated to the government upon completion.

Occasionally, a local government considers a proposal for infrastructure to be built at government expense to support a specific real estate development project. Such projects cannot be parallel

---

71. Jonathan Q. Morgan, "Analyzing the Benefits and Costs of Economic Development Projects," *Community and Economic Development Bulletin* No. 7 (Apr. 2010).

to Maready and are therefore not eligible for business location inducements. However, providing publicly owned infrastructure does not constitute unconstitutional "direct state aid to a private enterprise."[72] Although a local government has ample authority to construct publicly owned infrastructure on its own initiative, it must evaluate the trade-off between the infrastructure cost and the proposed project's fiscal impact on the government's budget.

To demonstrate to the public that the local government has conducted this evaluation and found the project to yield a net positive fiscal impact, local governments occasionally described these activities using terminology associated with tax increment financing, such as "Synthetic Tax Increment Financing" (Synthetic TIF) or "Tax Increment Grant" (TIG).[73] The idea is that the local government will not spend more on public infrastructure than a certain percentage of the tax revenue generated by the proposed private development. The arrangement typically involves the local government agreeing to pay the developer a specified amount to construct and deliver the needed public infrastructure, capped by a predetermined percentage of tax revenue. Developers often prefer to build the publicly owned infrastructure themselves, as they can control the timing and integrate the construction into the overall development plan.

There is no statute that explicitly uses the terms TIG or Synthetic TIF. Instead, these activities rely on long-standing statutory authority for procuring public infrastructure through a reimbursement agreement under G.S. 153A-451 (counties) and 160A-499 (municipalities).

In a reimbursement agreement, the local government pays for the infrastructure upon its delivery by the developer. If the local government wishes to spread its reimbursement payments over time, such as over the course of years in order to match the timing and amount of property taxes paid by the project, then such an arrangement would amount to a financing of the infrastructure. Capital financing of this sort is governed by other statutes and may require approval from the Local Government Commission. For statutory authority and requirements related to public financing and Local Government Commission approval, see Chapter 21, "Financing Capital Projects."

Interlocal Cooperation on Economic Development

Smaller, rural jurisdictions often find it challenging to develop large-scale projects like industrial parks alone. When municipalities and counties collaborate on such ventures, they can benefit from economies of scale and pursue projects that might otherwise be unfeasible. The General Assembly enacted G.S. 158-7.4 to facilitate interlocal cooperation on economic development. This statute authorizes two or more units of local government to enter into a contract or agreement to share financing, expenditures, and revenues related to joint development projects. It specifically allows for the sharing of property tax revenues generated from a joint industrial/commercial park or site.

An example illustrates how cities and counties might utilize this provision. The Triangle North network of business and industrial parks is a joint effort among Franklin, Granville, Vance, and Warren counties.[74] Officials from each participating county signed an interlocal agreement to share the costs of developing four distinct business and industrial parks—one in each county—that will benefit all four. The interlocal agreement provides for equal representation on the board of the Kerr-Tar Regional Economic Development Corporation, the nonprofit created to develop and

---

72. Maready v. City of Winston-Salem, 342 N.C. 708, 718 (1996).

73. Kara Millonzi, "What Is a Synthetic Project Development Financing (aka Synthetic TIF)?" *Coates' Canons: NC Local Government Law* blog (April 5, 2013), canons.sog.unc.edu/2013/04/what-is-a-synthetic-project-development-financing-aka-synthetic-tif/.

74. *See* Crystal Morphis and Ernest Pearson, "Creating Economic Opportunity: Multi-Jurisdictional Parks as a Product Development Tool," *IEDC Economic Development Journal* 10 (Spring 2011): 28–35.

manage the network of business parks. Additionally, the agreement stipulates how the counties will share costs and allocate revenues generated by the four industrial parks. The Kerr-Tar Regional Council of Government played a central role in facilitating this collaborative effort. Similarly, three municipalities in North Mecklenburg County—Cornelius, Davidson, and Huntersville—established a multi-jurisdictional industrial park called Commerce Station.

Organization for Economic Development

A local economic development program requires coordination and management. Building and implementing an effective program necessitates broad-based community involvement on one hand and concentrated executive control of a complex set of activities on the other. There is no single administrative structure commonly used; rather counties and cities employ a variety of structures, either individually or collectively. Various types of organizations participate in local economic development activities across the spectrum from public to nonprofit to private. A School of Government survey found that about two-thirds of responding local governments reported that a public agency had primary responsibility for economic development, while a third indicated that either a public–private partnership (24 percent) or a private organization (9.2 percent) took the lead. Although local governments tend to play a leading role, they often contract with nonprofits and private groups to carry out certain development functions. Formalized public–private partnership structures can be particularly useful for projects involving specialized real estate development, such as downtown revitalization, housing, and mixed-use developments, etc.

The starting point for organizing economic development activities is the unit's governing board, which has the authority to undertake activities directly or to appoint appropriate bodies to carry out the various functions discussed in this chapter. Some larger jurisdictions have economic development units and staff within the manager's office. G.S. Chapter 158, Article 2, allows the governing board to appoint an economic development commission. Such a commission is a public agency, but once created and with members appointed, it may act with some independence from the government that established it. Advantages of such a commission include ensuring that local business leaders have an active role through their membership and the possibility of cooperating with other jurisdictions to coordinate efforts in one body. One disadvantage is that an economic development commission does not have the authority to own real property, limiting its ability to undertake some development activities authorized for cities and counties by G.S. 158-7.1(b).

Some counties and cities delegate their economic development activities to chambers of commerce or other private nonprofit corporations, limiting the public body's role primarily to providing funding and, in some cases, appointing members to the nonprofit's board of directors. For example, the Alamance County Area Chamber of Commerce is the lead agency responsible for economic development in that county. Similarly, Durham County contracts with the Greater Durham Chamber of Commerce to implement economic development initiatives for the county. The Greater Raleigh Chamber of Commerce administers the Wake County Economic Development program on behalf of twelve municipalities in the county. Onslow County, the City of Jacksonville, and the local Committee of 100 provide funding and support to Jacksonville-Onslow Economic Development, Inc. to carry out development activities for both the city and county. The Catawba County Economic Development Corporation is chartered as a nonprofit, 501(c)(3) organization that receives local government funding while also generating substantial revenue from private sources, including the local Committee of 100. Lastly, the City of High Point relies on the High Point Economic Development Corporation, a public–private partnership, to run its economic development program.

Private groups and hybrid public–private partnership structures share the benefits of an economic development commission by involving the local business community and facilitating cooperation among several local governments. They also offer two advantages not characteristic of economic development commissions. First, there are no restrictions on their ability to own real property, enabling them to act directly as developers of industrial parks or shell buildings or to hold industrial sites for transfer to new companies.[75] Second, as private organizations, they can raise private funds within the community and spend those funds without concern for the constitutional or statutory limitations on public funds, though they must remain mindful of restrictions related to their tax-exempt status, if applicable. (Any public funds appropriated to these organizations retain their public character and remain subject to such limitations.) A potential disadvantage of using these private organizations, depending on how their governing boards are selected, is their considerable independence from local government, which may lead them to pursue goals and strategies inconsistent with the wishes of local government officials. Some local governments may therefore seek to appoint elected officials to the boards of these private organizations, but potential conflicts of interest should be carefully evaluated. Any elected official appointed to a board of a private organization should also review state law regarding recusal when local government appropriations involve the private organization.[76]

Over time, some counties and cities may adopt different structural arrangements for implementing economic development activities to better coordinate resources and promote greater efficiency and effectiveness (see Table 27.1). For example, Wayne County decided in 2006 to replace its Economic Development Commission, which had been in existence since 1966, with a new, nonprofit, public–private organization to conduct economic development for the entire county. This entity, called the Wayne County Development Alliance, represents a formal partnership between the county, municipalities (Goldsboro and Mt. Olive), and multiple private sector investors and stakeholders. A second example is the Carolinas Gateway Partnership, which was formed in 1995 to merge the economic development activities of Edgecombe and Nash counties into one nonprofit organization.

Conclusion: Challenges for Local Government

Economic development is a long-term process that involves numerous organizational players and a variety of tools and strategies. Much of what occurs in a rapidly changing global economy may seem beyond the control of individual local governments. Yet local officials do what they can to help their communities adapt, respond, and prosper in an environment of economic transition and uncertainty. Counties and cities face several challenges as they seek to stimulate private investment, promote job creation, and expand the tax base in their jurisdictions:

1. *Strategy, governance, and organizational structure.* Jurisdictions increasingly recognize the need to be proactive and deliberate in their choice of strategies and tools for economic development. There are no quick fixes or silver bullets in this field. An effective approach includes a mix of strategies and tools that align

---

75. *See* Tyler Mulligan, "Conveyance of Local Government Property to Nonprofit EDC for Industrial Park," *Coates' Canons: NC Local Government Law* blog (March 17, 2015), canons.sog.unc.edu/2015/03/conveyance-of-local-government-property-to-nonprofit-edc-for-industrial-park/.

76. *See* Kristina Wilson, "S.B. 473: Frequently Asked Questions," *Coates' Canons: NC Local Government Law* blog (December 21, 2021) (describing the requirements of Session Law 2021-191, codified at G.S. 14-234.3), canons.sog.unc.edu/2021/12/s-b-473-frequently-asked-questions/.

Table 27.1 Characteristics of Organizational Structures for Economic Development

Characteristics	Line Department	Economic Development Commission	Dependent Nonprofit	Independent Nonprofit
Powers (for industrial or commercial use)				
Acquire and own property	Yes	No	Yes	Yes
Develop property	Yes	No	Yes	Yes
Construct shell building	Yes	No	Yes	Yes
Convey property by private sale	Yes	No	Yes	Yes
Borrow money	Yes	No	Yes	Yes
Make loans	Yes	w/grant funds	Yes	Yes
Guarantee private loans	No	No	No	Yes
Not Available under G.S. Ch. 158				
Zoning	See, e.g., Sanitary District Board (G.S. 130A-55)			
Targeted code enforcement	See, e.g., Urban Redevelopment Commission (G.S. 160A-512(10))			
Finance and Taxation				
Subject to Budget/Fiscal Control Act	Yes	Yes	No	No
Income tax status	Exempt	Exempt	Exempt	Exempt
Contributions deductible	Yes	Yes	If 501(c)(3)	If 501(c)(3)
Property tax status	Exempt	Exempt	Presume taxed	Presume taxed
Not Available under G.S. Ch. 158				
Levy separate property tax	See, e.g., Sanitary District Board (G.S. 130A-55)			
Make special assessments	See, e.g., Sanitary District Board (G.S. 130A-55)			
Procedural Considerations				
Subject to open meetings/public records laws	Yes	Yes	Yes	No, unless contract requirement
Public hearing prior to all expenditures	Yes	N/A	Prior to contract	Prior to contract
Governing board approves all expenditures by third party	Yes	N/A	If using local government funds	If using local government funds
Public-origin property returns to local government when not used	Yes	N/A	Yes	Yes
Public-origin property returns to local government prior to sale	Yes	N/A	Yes	Yes
Follow local government procurement procedures with government funds*	Yes	Yes	Not clear, use contract requirement	Not clear, use contract requirement
Policy Coordination/Control				
Policy coordination	High	Medium	Medium	Low
Financial control	Appropriation	Appropriation	Contract	Contract
Employee benefits	Public	Public	Private	Private
Private sector involvement	Low	Medium	Medium	High

*Construction funded by local government should be owned by local government and follow construction procurement. Not required for loans for construction of private improvements.

Source: Adapted from David M. Lawrence, *Economic Development Law for North Carolina Local Governments* (UNC School of Government, 2000).

with a community's long-term vision and goals. Finding the optimal governance and organizational structure for program implementation and service delivery is essential.[77]

2. *Using incentives as a public investment.* Though widely used, incentives are often viewed as a necessary evil to compete for investment and jobs. Few jurisdictions are willing to risk losing a potential project by not offering a competitive incentive package. The challenge for counties and cities that choose to use incentives is to structure them as investments of public dollars for the greater good rather than mere subsidies for private business activities. To achieve this, some local governments target incentives toward industries expected to yield higher returns on public investment and tie incentives to specific job creation and investment levels. Additional mechanisms to protect public investment include payback guidelines, performance agreements, clawback provisions, and cost-benefit analyses of incentive projects.
3. *Balancing the tax base.* Several counties and cities in North Carolina have experienced rapid population growth and a corresponding increase in residential development, leading to the emergence of many "bedroom" communities across the state. Local governments must figure out how to fund the additional public services that this growth necessitates. However, residential development does not tend to generate sufficient tax revenue to cover expanded public services. In contrast, industrial and commercial development typically more than pays for itself in terms of the ratio of tax revenues to the cost of public services. Therefore, as communities grow, they should pay attention to the diversification, or lack thereof, in their tax base.
4. *Ensuring that the benefits of economic development are widely shared.* Using public funds for economic development assumes that doing so serves a larger public interest. Local governments face the challenge of ensuring that public economic development activities benefit the community as a whole, rather than just narrow private interests. Some local governments specifically attempt to direct growth and development to disadvantaged areas and residents. Indeed, providing jobs for dislocated workers was highlighted in the *Maready* decision as one of the public benefits that justified offering direct incentives to private companies.
5. *Measuring and evaluating success.* Much of what is done in economic development occurs without a clear understanding of its impact on communities. A comprehensive approach to gauging success will focus on a broad set of performance measures. Systematic evaluation of economic development programs can reveal what is working and where resources should be focused.

Additional Resources

Digital Learning Module

Mulligan, Tyler C., and Jonathan Q. Morgan. Economic Development Tools and Strategies (a 60-minute online video module, 2021), www.sog.unc.edu/courses/online-modules/economic-development-tools-and-strategies.

---

77. *See* C. Tyler Mulligan and Jonathan Q. Morgan, *Economic Development Tools and Strategies* (a 60-minute online video module, 2021), www.sog.unc.edu/courses/online-modules/economic-development-tools-and-strategies.

Publications

Lawrence, David M. *Economic Development Law for North Carolina Local Governments*. Chapel Hill: UNC Institute of Government, 2000.

Leigh, Nancy Green, and Edward J. Blakely. *Planning Local Economic Development: Theory and Practice*. 6th ed. Thousand Oaks, Calif.: Sage Publications, Inc., 2016.

Malizia, Emil, Edward Feser, Henry Renski, and Joshua Drucker. *Understanding Local Economic Development*. 2nd ed. New York: Routledge, 2021.

McLaughlin, Christopher. "Property Tax Exemptions and Community Economic Development." *Community and Economic Development in North Carolina and Beyond* blog, ced.sog.unc.edu/2024/04/property-tax-exemptions-for-community-economic-development/.

Morgan, Jonathan Q. "Clusters and Competitive Advantage: Finding a Niche in the New Economy." *Popular Government* 69 (Fall 2004): 43–54.

———. *The Role of Local Government in Economic Development: Survey Findings from North Carolina*. Chapel Hill: UNC School of Government, 2009.

———. "Using Economic Development Incentives: For Better or for Worse." *Popular Government* 74 (Winter 2009): 16–29.

———. "Analyzing the Benefits and Costs of Economic Development Projects." *Community and Economic Development Bulletin* No. 7 (Apr. 2010).

———. (2010). "Governance, Policy Innovation, and Local Economic Development in North Carolina." *Policy Studies Journal* 38, no. 4 (Oct. 2010): 679–702.

———. "Community and Economic Development." In Kimberly L. Nelson and Carl W. Stenberg, eds. *Managing Local Government Services: The Challenge of Change*. 4th ed. Washington, D.C.: ICMA Press, 2021.

Morgan, Jonathan Q., and Jamie R. McCall. "COVID-19 and North Carolina's Economic Development Organizations: Perspectives on Response, Recovery, and Shifting Priorities." *Community and Economic Development Bulletin* No. 10 (UNC School of Government, 2022), www.sog.unc.edu/sites/default/files/reports/2022-08-15 20220125 CEDB_10_Morgan.pdf.

Morgan, Jonathan Q., Michele Hoyman, and Jamie McCall. "Everything but the Kitchen Sink: Factors Associated with Local Economic Development Strategy Use." *Economic Development Quarterly* 33, no. 4 (Nov. 2019): 267–78, doi.org/10.1177/0891242419857152.

Mulligan, C. Tyler. "Economic Development Incentives and North Carolina Local Governments: A Framework for Analysis." *North Carolina Law Review* 91, no. 6 (Sept. 2013): 2021–2116.

———. "Using a Redevelopment Area to Attract Private Investment." *Community and Economic Development in North Carolina and Beyond* blog, ced.sog.unc.edu/2012/11/using-a-redevelopment-area-to-attract-private-investment/.

———. "When May NC Local Governments Pay an Economic Development Incentive?" *Community and Economic Development in North Carolina and Beyond* blog, ced.sog.unc.edu/2013/12/when-may-nc-local-governments-pay-an-economic-development-incentive/.

———. "How a North Carolina Local Government Can Operate a Land Bank for Redevelopment." *Community and Economic Development in North Carolina and Beyond* blog, ced.sog.unc.edu/2014/03/how-a-north-carolina-local-government-can-operate-a-land-bank-for-redevelopment/.

———. "Acquiring Real Property for Redevelopment—Can Local Governments Keep It Confidential?" *Community and Economic Development in North Carolina and Beyond* blog, ced.sog.unc.edu/2014/06/acquiring-real-property-for-redevelopment-can-local-governments-keep-it-confidential/.

———. "Sale of Historic Structures by NC Local Governments for Redevelopment." *Community and Economic Development in North Carolina and Beyond* blog, ced.sog.unc.edu/2014/12/sale-of-historic-structures-by-nc-local-governments-for-redevelopment/.

———. "Conveyance of Local Government Property to Nonprofit EDC for Industrial Park." *Community and Economic Development in North Carolina and Beyond* blog, ced.sog.unc.edu/2015/03/conveyance-of-local-government-property-to-nonprofit-edc-for-industrial-park/.

———. "Follow Procedures Prior to Acquiring Property for Redevelopment." *Community and Economic Development in North Carolina and Beyond* blog, ced.sog.unc.edu/2016/03/follow-procedures-prior-to-acquiring-property-for-redevelopment/.

———. "Conveyance of Property in a Public-Private Partnership for a 'Downtown Development Project.'" *Community and Economic Development in North Carolina and Beyond* blog, ced.sog.unc.edu/2017/06/conveyance-of-property-in-a-public-private-partnership-for-a-downtown-development-project/.

———. "Reasons Why Downtown Development Programs Should Involve Secured Loans—Not Grants." *Community and Economic Development in North Carolina and Beyond* blog, ced.sog.unc.edu/2017/09/legal-and-business-reasons-why-downtown-development-programs-should-involve-secured-loans-not-grants/.

———. "Notice and Hearing Requirements for Economic Development Appropriations." *Community and Economic Development in North Carolina and Beyond* blog, ced.sog.unc.edu/2019/11/notice-and-hearing-requirements-for-economic-development-appropriations-2/.

———. "Downtown Facade Improvement Programs." *Community and Economic Development in North Carolina and Beyond* blog, canons.sog.unc.edu/2020/01/downtown-facade-improvement-programs/.

Organizations (listed in order of relevance)

State-Level

North Carolina Department of Commerce, Commerce Finance Center: www.commerce.nc.gov/about-us/divisions-programs/commerce-finance-center.

North Carolina Community College System: www.nccommunitycolleges.edu.

North Carolina Commission on Workforce Development: www.commerce.nc.gov/business/workforce-development.

N.C. Regional Councils (N.C. Association of Regional Councils of Government): ncarcog.org/regional-councils/.

N.C. Economic Developers Association: www.nceda.org.

N.C. Industrial Extension Service: www.ies.ncsu.edu.

Federal/National

U.S. Economic Development Administration (U.S. Department of Commerce): www.eda.gov.

U.S. Small Business Administration: www.sba.gov.

International Economic Development Council: www.iedconline.org.

PART 7. Local Government Services and Enterprises

Chapter 28

County and Municipal Law Enforcement

Jeffrey B. Welty

Jeffrey B. Welty is a School of Government faculty member specializing in criminal law and procedure. His research interests include the law of policing, search and seizure, digital evidence, and criminal pleadings.

This chapter provides a short overview of the county and municipal law enforcement agencies that exist in North Carolina, including how such agencies are organized, the scope of their work, and the extent to which they are subject to oversight by other public bodies. It also briefly addresses the civil liability risks that come along with the law enforcement function.

County and Municipal Law Enforcement Agencies in North Carolina

Most residents of North Carolina likely think that counties have sheriffs and cities have police departments. That's not far from the mark, but the complete picture is slightly more complex.

County Agencies

The state constitution requires each county to have a sheriff.[1] Sheriffs are elected to four-year terms.[2] A person who has been convicted of a felony cannot serve as sheriff, and a sheriff must be over 21 and a "qualified voter" in the county he or she serves.[3] There are few other formal requirements for the job. Notably, the sheriff does not need to be a sworn law enforcement officer.

1. N.C. Const. art. VII, § 2.
2. N.C. Const. art. VII, § 2.
3. N.C. Const. art. VII, § 2; Chapter 162, Section 2 of the North Carolina General Statutes (hereinafter G.S.).

Sheriffs may resign,[4] be removed for cause,[5] or die during their terms of office. When that happens, the board of county commissioners selects a replacement to serve the unexpired portion of the sheriff's term.[6] In certain counties, the former sheriff's political party effectively controls the selection of a successor.[7]

Chapter 162 of the North Carolina General Statutes (hereinafter G.S.) sets out some of the duties of the sheriff. Most of the listed duties relate to the sheriff's role in serving civil process such as summonses and subpoenas. Other provisions relate to the bond that the sheriff must post, essentially to guarantee "the faithful execution of his [or her] office."[8]

Neither the constitution nor the General Statutes define the sheriff's law enforcement responsibilities in any detail, but appellate case law makes clear that "[t]he sheriff is the chief law enforcement officer of the county."[9] Deputy sheriffs, who work for the sheriff, have the authority to arrest and other law enforcement powers.[10] The sheriff is also in charge of the jail in each county.[11] The duties of the sheriff and his or her deputies are discussed further below.

Although every county must have a sheriff, counties are not necessarily precluded from having other agencies that exercise law enforcement functions. A county may establish a county police department if authorized by an act of the North Carolina General Assembly. In the 1910s and 1920s, a number of counties were granted the authority to create some sort of county police. These bodies often were designated as "rural police." They sometimes focused specifically on alcohol-related offenses and had varying degrees of independence from the sheriff.[12] More recently, Mecklenburg County had a county police department[13] until it merged in 1993 with the Charlotte Police Department to create the Charlotte-Mecklenburg Police Department.[14]

Today, Gaston County is the only county in the state with its own police department.[15] That agency assumes some of the general responsibility for enforcing criminal law traditionally associated with the sheriff's office.[16] The sheriff's office provides law enforcement services as well. The sheriff's office also retains its statutory responsibility for executing court-issued civil process.

---

4. G.S. 162-3.

5. N.C. Const. art. VII, § 2; G.S. 128-16 (explaining that the sheriff may be removed by a superior court judge upon a finding that the sheriff has acted corruptly, has "refus[ed] to perform the duties of his [or her] office," or on certain other grounds listed in the statute).

6. G.S. 162-5.

7. G.S. 162-5.1.

8. G.S. 162-8.

9. S. Ry. Co. v. Mecklenburg Cnty., 231 N.C. 148 (1949).

10. G.S. 15A-401, -402.

11. G.S. 162-22.

12. *See, e.g.*, S.L. 1913-92 (authorizing Richmond County rural police); S.L. 1913-114 (authorizing Scotland County rural police); S.L. 1913-418 (authorizing Robeson County rural police); S.L. 1915-68 (authorizing New Hanover County rural police). *See also S. Ry. Co.*, 231 N.C. at 151–52 (discussing the creation and duties of the rural police force for Mecklenburg County).

13. S.L. 1917-664 authorized Mecklenburg County to employ rural police. The Mecklenburg County Police Department grew from that. Meanwhile, S.L. 1969-1170 gave the Charlotte Police Department countywide jurisdiction, effectively allowing the merger of the two departments into one countywide force. The two departments officially merged in 1993. Charlotte-Mecklenburg Police Department (CMPD), *CMPD Celebrates 30-Years of Combined Excellence* (Sept. 26, 2023).

14. Angela Wright, "One Force: Merger's Visible Signs Still Months, Years Away," *Charlotte Observer*, September 30, 1993, at 1C.

15. Amy Rainey, "Unique in N.C.: For 50 Years, a Force in the County," *Charlotte Observer*, July 8, 2007, at 1L.

16. In S.L. 1957-16, § 11, the General Assembly described the department's responsibility as "the proper enforcement of the laws of the State of North Carolina in the rural sections of Gaston County."

Municipal Agencies

Most North Carolina municipalities have police departments. However, it is not mandatory to have a police department and many small municipalities do not have one.[17] Some small municipalities simply rely on the sheriff's office for law enforcement services, while others enter into contracts with the sheriff to provide certain guaranteed levels of service.

Duties and Jurisdiction of Law Enforcement Officers

Law enforcement officers investigate crimes and apprehend offenders, but their duties also encompass much more. As the North Carolina Court of Appeals has noted, "law enforcement personnel are expected to engage in activities and interact with citizens in a number of ways beyond the investigation of criminal conduct," including "a general safety and welfare role" and "helping citizens who may be in peril or who may otherwise be in need of some form of assistance."[18]

There is no single court case, statute, or other source of law that details all the things that law enforcement officers can or should do. Officers today provide a wide range of services, including directing traffic, conducting welfare checks, searching for missing persons, executing involuntary commitment orders for the mentally ill, responding to natural disasters, providing security in schools and at public events, and handling the incredible variety of calls that come in through the 911 system.

The duties officers perform may vary from locality to locality. For example, in some localities, law enforcement officers write parking tickets, while in others, parking enforcement is a separate function. Similarly, in some localities, the animal control function falls within a law enforcement agency, while in others, animal control is performed by non-sworn civilian personnel. Finally, in many jurisdictions, investigating and documenting motor vehicle collisions is a law enforcement function, but in 2023, the General Assembly authorized cities to use civilian personnel to investigate and document non-injury accidents.[19]

Despite their broad authority and varied duties, the power of law enforcement officers has limits. Those limits are generally defined in two ways. Territorial jurisdiction refers to *where* an officer may take law enforcement action. Subject matter jurisdiction refers to the *types of laws* an officer may enforce.

County officers—for the most part, deputy sheriffs—have territorial jurisdiction throughout their counties. As a matter of law, their jurisdiction includes incorporated areas within the county. However, as a matter of professional courtesy and efficient resource allocation, deputies normally do not take law enforcement action inside the city limits of municipalities that maintain police departments. A deputy may arrest a suspect outside the deputy's county if the deputy is in hot pursuit of the suspect and the pursuit began in the deputy's county. Finally, a deputy may make an arrest outside his or her county if the arrest is for a felony offense committed in the deputy's county.[20]

---

17. Jeff Welty, "Should Small Towns Have Police Departments?" *N.C. Criminal Law: A UNC School of Government Blog* (August 29, 2022), nccriminallaw.sog.unc.edu/should-small-towns-have-police-departments/.

18. State v. Smathers, 232 N.C. App. 120 (2014) (quoting Ullom v. Miller, 705 S.E.2d 111 (W. Va. 2010)).

19. G.S. 160A-499.6. Some cities already had this authority by virtue of local acts, but the new statute allows cities across the state to use civilian traffic investigators. They are not law enforcement officers and do not have the power of arrest, and they must go through a training program designed by the North Carolina Justice Academy. *Id.*

20. G.S. 15A-402.

Municipal officers generally have territorial jurisdiction within their cities and up to one mile outside city limits.[21] They also may arrest a suspect outside their city if the arrest results from a hot pursuit of the suspect that began within the city or less than a mile outside it.[22]

An officer's territorial jurisdiction may be increased through the use of mutual aid processes. Under G.S. 160A-288, "the head of any law enforcement agency may temporarily provide assistance to another agency if so requested in writing by the head of the requesting agency." These requests are commonly used when one agency provides an officer to work undercover in another jurisdiction or when a large event in a jurisdiction requires more law enforcement presence than the resident agency is able to provide on its own.

As to subject matter jurisdiction, some law enforcement officers, such as State Highway Patrol officers,[23] may make arrests only for certain kinds of offenses. However, city law enforcement officers may make arrests for any criminal offense.[24] Sheriffs, deputy sheriffs, and county police officers also may make arrests for any criminal offense.[25]

Management and Oversight of Law Enforcement Agencies

Administrative Authority

As independently elected officials, sheriffs administer their offices as they see fit. They generally are not subject to supervision or control by their county boards. For at least some purposes, employees of the sheriff's office are not even considered county employees.[26] However, as discussed further below, the county board has budgetary authority over the sheriff's office.

By contrast, municipal police departments are departments of city government, generally subject to oversight by the city manager (where there is one) and by the city's elected board. Police officers are city employees. Occasionally, disputes arise over whether the manager or the board can direct certain aspects of police operations—for example, by requiring the police to prioritize certain types of investigations or by prohibiting the police from using certain tactics. When these disagreements arise, police may contend that officers have been granted statutory authority that cannot be limited by municipal authorities.[27] Whether this is indeed the case, and if so, the extent of officers' independent authority, remains unclear.

---

21. For a longer discussion of the one-mile rule and related issues, see Jeff Welty, "Police Jurisdiction in Satellite and Related Areas," *N.C. Criminal Law: A UNC School of Government Blog* (November 3, 2014), nccriminallaw.sog.unc.edu/police-jurisdiction-in-satellite-and-related-areas/.

22. G.S. 15A-402.

23. G.S. 20-188 (authorizing officers of the Highway Patrol to arrest those "engaged in the violation of any of the laws of the State regulating travel and the use of vehicles upon the highways").

24. G.S. 15A-401, 160A-285.

25. The arrest authority of sheriffs and their deputies is not expressly set forth in the General Statutes but, rather, descends from the common law. *See* State v. Hill, 25 N.C. 398 (1843) (noting that "[b]oth the sheriff and constable have authority to arrest"). Further, G.S. 15A-401 gives broad arrest authority to "officers" generally, a category that certainly includes sheriffs and their deputies. *See* State v. Crawford, 125 N.C. App. 279 (1997) (upholding the arrest authority of a deputy by referring to G.S. 15A-401).

26. McLaughlin v. Bailey, 240 N.C. App. 159 (2015) (holding that employees of sheriff's office are not county employees for purposes of statute protecting county employees' political activity); *see also* Young v. Bailey, 368 N.C. 665, 669–70 (2016) ("In light of the distinct demarcation between county government and the office of the sheriff, we conclude that a sheriff's office is not a program or department of a county and . . . a deputy sheriff or employee of a sheriff's office is not a county employee.").

27. Statutes sometimes cited in support of this idea include G.S. 15A-221 (allowing officers to conduct consent searches), 15A-401 (giving officers arrest authority), and 160A-285 (granting officers "all of the powers invested in law-enforcement officers by statute or common law").

Budgetary Authority

Sheriffs' offices are funded primarily by their counties, and police departments are funded primarily by their cities. Both types of agencies may receive some funds from other sources, including grants and forfeitures. Because county boards do not have direct administrative control over sheriffs' offices, it is not uncommon for these boards to attempt to use the power of the purse to incentivize sheriffs to behave in ways desired by the boards. Similar dynamics occasionally arise in cities but, given cities' more direct administrative control over police departments, it is less common.

Citizen Oversight Boards

Beyond the administrative and budgetary oversight described above, law enforcement agencies in some localities are subject to oversight by citizen boards of various kinds. These boards go by different names and have different powers: "Sometimes referred to as citizen oversight, civilian review, external review and citizen review boards, this form of police accountability is often focused on allowing non-police actors to provide input into the police department's operations."[28]

In North Carolina, a few dozen such boards exist. Most are connected to municipal police departments with only a few being connected to sheriffs' offices. Many were created by a local act of the General Assembly,[29] which is necessary if a citizen board will be handling confidential personnel information. Some of the boards are focused on reviewing agencies' handling of citizen complaints and officer discipline, while others are designed to provide community input into agency policies and take no part in personnel matters. Readers interested in learning more about citizen review or oversight boards in North Carolina may wish to consult School of Government faculty member John P. Stephens' 2021 book, *Police Accountability: Civilian Advisory and Review Boards in North Carolina Local Government.*[30]

Internal Affairs and the State Bureau of Investigation

Most law enforcement agencies have processes in place for investigating allegations of wrongdoing by their officers. This function may be called internal affairs, professional standards, or something different.

When allegations of wrongdoing are sufficiently pervasive or serious, the State Bureau of Investigation may be called upon to conduct an investigation. The Bureau is a law enforcement agency with statewide jurisdiction. It is authorized to "give assistance to sheriffs, police officers, district attorneys, and judges when called upon by them and so directed,"[31] and it frequently conducts investigations into allegations of wrongdoing by public officials. The Bureau may also be asked to investigate officer-involved shootings or other high-profile incidents even when there is no specific claim of wrongdoing; the Bureau's involvement may provide the public with assurance that a neutral entity has reviewed the matter.

---

28. Joseph De Angelis et al., *Civilian Oversight of Law Enforcement: Assessing the Evidence* (National Organization for Civilian Oversight of Law Enforcement, 2017).

29. *See, e.g.*, S.L. 1997-305 (Charlotte); S.L. 1998-142 (Durham); S.L. 2001-20 (Greensboro); S.L. 2003-238 (Wilmington).

30. Professor Stephens also maintains a website, *Citizen Advisory and Review Board for Police Accountability*, with resources, profiles, and updates on the North Carolina advisory and review boards: civilianboards.sog.unc.edu.

31. G.S. 143B-917.

Officer Certification and Decertification

Law enforcement officers in North Carolina must be certified by one of the state's law enforcement commissions. The North Carolina Criminal Justice Education and Training Standards Commission certifies municipal police officers, along with correctional officers and probation officers. The Commission is authorized by G.S. Chapter 17C. It has promulgated a large number of administrative rules that set minimum standards for an officer's age (at least 20 years), education (at least a high school diploma or the equivalent), training (must complete the Basic Law Enforcement Training course and pass a comprehensive examination), prior criminal record, and other qualifications.[32] It has also promulgated rules concerning officers' continuing education and conduct. A candidate who does not meet the minimum standards set by the Commission cannot be certified, and an officer who runs afoul of the Commission's rules risks decertification. Individual agencies may set higher standards than those required by the Commission.

The North Carolina Sheriffs' Education and Training Standards Commission certifies deputy sheriffs and certain other personnel, such as detention officers who work in the county jail. The Commission is authorized by G.S. Chapter 17E. It functions in a manner that is similar to the Criminal Justice Education and Training Standards Commission. In other words, it too has promulgated a variety of administrative rules governing who may be certified as a deputy sheriff and under what circumstances they may be decertified.[33] Individual sheriffs may, of course, set higher standards than the minimums set by the Commission.

Law Enforcement and Public Records

North Carolina law makes many documents and other records created by public employees available to members of the public upon request.[34] City and county law enforcement officers are public employees. However, many records created by law enforcement officers are exempt from the general public records laws.

Under G.S. 132-1.4, records of "criminal investigations" and "criminal intelligence information" are not public records. Therefore, while an agency may release these records if desired, the public is not entitled to access them as a matter of right. A court could order the release of such records for sufficient reason. Furthermore, the statute designates certain categories of information as being public, including "[t]he time, date, location, and nature of a violation or apparent violation of the law reported to a public law enforcement agency," and the contents of 911 calls.[35] Debates sometimes arise over which records—or which portions of a specific record—fall in these categories. Interested readers may wish to consult the second edition of former School of Government faculty member David Lawrence's book, *Public Records Law for North Carolina Local Governments*, published in 2010.

32. The relevant rules may be found at Title 12, Chapter 09B, Sections .0101 through .0701 of the North Carolina Administrative Code (hereinafter N.C.A.C).

33. The Commission's rules may be found at 12 N.C.A.C. 10B, §§ .0101 through .2201.

34. G.S. 132-1(b) ("The public records and public information compiled by the agencies of North Carolina government or its subdivisions are the property of the people. Therefore, it is the policy of this State that the people may obtain copies of their public records and public information free or at minimal cost unless otherwise specifically provided by law.").

35. G.S. 132-1.4(c).

A separate statute, G.S. 132-1.4A, governs the release or disclosure of audio and video recordings in the custody of law enforcement agencies, such as footage from body-worn cameras. The statute is complex, but in general, it gives law enforcement agencies limited authority under certain circumstances to "disclose" recordings upon the request of an interested party by playing the recording for the party. Otherwise, a court order is required to allow disclosure, and a court order is almost always required before a recording may be "released" by providing a copy of the recording.[36]

Records related to specific officers and their job performance may be personnel records protected by the relevant statutes, a discussion of which is beyond the scope of this chapter.[37]

Civil Liability Arising from Law Enforcement Activities

Local governments are often concerned about the potential for civil liability arising from law enforcement activities. That is a complex subject, and Chapter 6 of this book attempts to provide an overview of governmental liability issues. Below are a few brief comments on liability as it concerns law enforcement activities.

First, the concern is a legitimate one. Citizens sometimes sue law enforcement officers and the local governments for which they work based on allegations of discriminatory policing, excessive use of force, or a failure to respect constitutional rights. Entities that operate jail facilities—generally, counties through their sheriffs' offices—may also face litigation alleging substandard jail conditions or misconduct by jail personnel. These lawsuits may be filed in state or federal court and under a host of different legal theories. Larger jurisdictions and their insurers pay millions of dollars each year as a result of litigation.

Second, the courts recognize that law enforcement is a difficult undertaking and that even under the best of circumstances, it is likely to leave some people unhappy. For that reason, courts have created doctrines called "immunities" that shield officers and their employers from liability under many circumstances. These doctrines provide substantial protections but generally have exceptions for conduct that is far beyond the pale.[38] Conduct that is found to be malicious or to violate clearly established law is not likely to be protected by any type of immunity.

Third, while it is impossible to eliminate all risk of liability, there are steps agencies may consider taking to reduce the risk. Among the precautions agencies may wish to evaluate are the following:

- Conducting careful background checks on individuals who apply to be law enforcement officers, especially those who were unsuccessful at other agencies. Many agencies today are short-staffed and want to expedite hiring, but in the long run, performing due diligence is worthwhile.
- Providing quality training to officers, especially in high-liability areas such as the use of force to arrest. The North Carolina Justice Academy provides training at low or no cost to officers across the state.
- Keeping agency policies up to date and in conformity with the law and with best practices in the profession. Agency policies provide guidance to officers, aid

36. For more detail, see Shea Denning, "May a Police Department Release its Own Body Worn Camera Footage to the Public?" *N.C. Criminal Law: A UNC School of Government Blog* (May 11, 2023), nccriminallaw.sog.unc.edu/may-a-police-department-release-its-own-body-worn-camera-footage-to-the-public/.

37. *See generally* G.S. 153A-98, 160A-168.

38. *See, e.g.,* Dean ex rel. Harkness v. McKinney, 976 F.3d 407 (4th Cir. 2020) (finding no qualified immunity for a sheriff's deputy who operated his vehicle at 80 mph without lights or siren and collided with another vehicle).

supervisors in overseeing subordinates, and standardize agency procedures. They may also be a statement of an agency's values and priorities. Seeking agency accreditation is one way of ensuring that policies are reviewed periodically.

- Using technology to monitor officer performance. Available tools include software-based early warning systems that may identify potentially problematic officers before an adverse interaction with a member of the public, and body-worn cameras that may be used to confirm officers' compliance with agency policies.
- Maintaining a robust internal affairs or professional standards group that thoroughly and proactively investigates allegations of wrongdoing by officers. Holding an officer accountable for his or her misconduct sends a message not only to that officer, but to others.
- Having access to legal counsel, whether in-house, through the office of the city or county attorney, or by contract with a law firm.
- Purchasing liability insurance. Most North Carolina municipalities are insured through the insurance pools administered by the North Carolina League of Municipalities. Most of the counties in the state are covered by the North Carolina Association of County Commissioners County Risk Group. Some local governments, most often larger cities and counties with the ability to pay smaller claims themselves, choose to purchase insurance on the private market.

Chapter 29

Fire Services

Kara A. Millonzi

Kara A. Millonzi is a School of Government faculty member who specializes in local government and public finance law.

Introduction

Local governments are not required to furnish (or fund) fire protection services for their citizens, but many provide, or contract for the provision of, these services within their units. In fact, fire protection has been considered a core municipal service since the nineteenth century, when a few of the larger cities in the state boasted firefighting companies with hand- and horse-drawn steam-powered fire pumpers. Fire protection was important in cities, where compact development with largely wooden buildings posed a constant danger of community-wide conflagration. Until the mid-1900s, fire protection in rural, unincorporated areas was regarded as a matter of concern for individual property owners. Yet, as urban development spread to formerly rural areas and citizen expectation for fire protection in such areas increased, county governments and, to a limited extent, sanitary districts, also assumed a greater role in providing these services. Most areas in the state today are afforded some level of fire protection. And, typically, that fire protection extends beyond basic fire prevention and suppression services to include, among other things, emergency dispatch services, medical and other response services, and state building fire code enforcement. In recent years, the costs of providing fire and rescue services have risen considerably. Volunteer firefighters are increasingly being replaced with paid staff, and the capital costs of acquiring and maintaining fire suppression equipment are significant.

The types and level of fire services that cities, counties, and sanitary districts (collectively, local units) provide and fund often vary across territorial boundaries. There is no duty of equal service to all properties or citizens within a unit. A local governing board may choose to provide fire services in some areas within its jurisdiction and not in others, or it may choose to provide a higher level of fire services in some areas than in others. Because of the unique nature of fire protection services, units need flexibility in both service provision and funding. This chapter discusses the options available to local units in North Carolina. It begins by identifying the various legal structures available to local units for providing fire services. It then analyzes the local revenue options available to these entities for this purpose. Finally, it describes fire insurance districts and the insurance rating system and discusses the relationship between fire insurance districts and fire tax districts.

Fire Services Provided by Local Governments

There are three local governmental entities—cities, counties, and sanitary districts—that are authorized under general law to provide fire protection services. Each local unit may establish a fire department to provide fire protection and rescue services. Alternatively, each unit also is authorized to contract with external entities—municipal fire departments or corporate fire departments—to carry out these duties. Some units use a combination of these structures. The most common arrangements are described below.

Municipal, County, or Sanitary District Fire Department

One option available to a local unit is to establish and maintain its own fire department. Many local units have a fire department, but the size and scope of its duties varies widely across jurisdictions. Some departmental fire departments provide full-fledged fire protection and rescue services. Other departments provide a more limited array of services, relying on contracts with other governmental or private entities to fulfill most fire suppression and rescue duties.

Municipal Fire Department

A city is authorized to "establish, organize, equip, and maintain a fire department."[1] Many cities provide fire protection services through a municipal fire department, which typically encompasses multiple fire stations. Under this structure, a city's governing board sets all policies related to the fire services. The fire department's assets, including fire stations, fire trucks, and all related equipment,

1. Chapter 160A, Section 291 of the North Carolina General Statutes (hereinafter G.S.).

are titled to the city. Fire personnel are city employees. (A city has the option to staff its department with volunteer or paid firefighters and other staff members.)[2]

The primary function of most municipal fire departments is to provide fire suppression services. Many fire departments also support rescue squads, ambulances, and other emergency management services. In addition to these response activities, a municipal fire department often undertakes fire prevention activities, such as community outreach programs and fire safety demonstrations, to inform and educate the public about preventing and extinguishing fires. Fire departments commonly sponsor installation and battery-replacement programs for residential smoke alarms and carbon monoxide detectors. This is just one example of the myriad of community programs and services typically provided by a municipal fire department. Another function that most municipal fire departments serve is to perform inspections to enforce the state fire code. Since 1991, a fire prevention code has been included in the North Carolina State Building Code (hereinafter State Building Code). Counties and cities are responsible for enforcing the State Building Code within their jurisdictions.[3]

May a municipal fire department provide services outside the municipality? The answer is yes. A municipal fire department may contract with other units of government to provide services. A municipal fire department also may enter into mutual aid agreements with other fire departments and may send "firemen and apparatus beyond the territorial limits which it normally serves."[4] The most common arrangements are described below.

The city's general fund is the primary source of funds for capital expenditures, equipment, and salaries. Thus, the city council's ability and willingness to appropriate funds to the fire department largely controls the level and breadth of service it is able to provide. Courts have ruled that failure to provide adequate facilities or to control a fire does not constitute a liability against a city. Nevertheless, people expect the fire department to be reasonably competent in controlling fire—taking into consideration, of course, the adequacy of equipment, personnel, and water supply; the nature of the fire; and its headway when discovered.

Fire Chiefs

Regardless of whether a city establishes a municipal fire department or contracts with one or more private or municipal fire departments to provide fire services, a city may appoint a fire chief. Fire chiefs are charged with directing firefighting and training activities, maintaining equipment, correcting fire hazards, and, where appropriate, making annual reports to the city council concerning department activities.[5] A fire chief also often is charged with conducting inspections to enforce the fire prevention sections of the State Building Code.[6]

County Fire Department

A county may "establish, organize, equip, support, and maintain a fire department; may prescribe the duties of the fire department. . . ."[7] A county fire department is authorized to provide the same fire suppression and prevention services as a municipal fire department, both within and outside

---

2. If a unit employs five or more full-time paid firefighters and other full-time paid staff, special rules apply to calculating overtime pay and trade time. *See* G.S. 160A, Article 14A.

3. The fire prevention chapters of the 2018 North Carolina State Building Code (hereinafter State Building Code) are available at www.ncosfm.gov/codes/codes-current-and-past (last visited July 25, 2024). For more information on the State Building Code, see Chapter 25, "Planning, Land Use, and Development."

4. G.S. 58-83-1.

5. G.S. 160A-291.

6. *Id.* The fire chief must be certified in accordance with G.S. 143-151.13.

7. G.S. 153A-233.

the county's territorial jurisdiction. It also may support rescue squads, ambulances, and other emergency management services. And, like a city, a county is responsible for enforcing the fire prevention provisions in the State Building Code. Many counties do not maintain full-fledged fire departments. Serving geographically disparate and often rural areas generally proves cost prohibitive. Instead, counties typically contract with incorporated fire departments or municipal fire departments to provide fire protection and rescue services within their unincorporated territories. To delineate the different service areas, a county's governing board may divide its unincorporated territory into multiple fire response zones, each of which is served by one or more fire departments. The response zones often correspond to fire insurance districts.

Fire Marshal

Most counties, even those that do not maintain a county fire department, appoint a fire marshal or assign the duties of a fire marshal to another employee or official. By statute, a fire marshal is charged with the following:

1. Advising the board on improvements in the firefighting or fire prevention activities under the county's supervision or control.
2. Coordinating firefighting and training activities under the county's supervision or control.
3. Coordinating fire prevention activities under the county's supervision or control.
4. Assisting incorporated volunteer fire departments in developing and improving their firefighting or fire prevention capabilities.
5. Making fire prevention inspections, including the periodic inspections and reports of school buildings required by Chapter 115C of the North Carolina General Statutes (hereinafter G.S.) and the inspections of child care facilities required by G.S. Chapter 110, Article 7.[8]

A county board may prescribe other duties to the fire marshal as warranted. For counties that contract with multiple incorporated fire departments or municipal fire departments, the fire marshal performs an important coordination role, often serving as a liaison between the county and the various fire departments. The fire marshal advises the county board about budgetary requests from fire departments, monitors contract compliance, oversees training of firefighting personnel, conducts public outreach programs and services, and aids the county in drawing and amending fire service areas and fire tax districts.

Sanitary District Fire Department

A sanitary district is a regional unit of local government that is created by the Commission for Public Health.[9] The primary function of a sanitary district is to provide water and sewer services within its territorial boundaries. The boundaries of a sanitary district often include territory in two or more cities or even two or more counties. In addition to water and sewer services, a sanitary district is authorized to provide fire protection services. Specifically, G.S. 130A-55(13) allows a sanitary district to "provide or contract for rescue service, ambulance service, rescue squad or other emergency medical services for use in the district." These services must be provided within the territorial boundaries of the district.

---

8. G.S. 153A-234.

9. G.S. Chapter 130A, Article 2, Part 2. The process is initiated by a petition of 51 percent of the freeholders in the proposed district. G.S. 130A-48. No municipal territory may be included in a sanitary district unless approved by the municipality's governing board. G.S. 130A-47.

A sanitary district that maintains its own department performs many of the same duties as a municipal or county fire department, with the exception of State Building Code inspections. A sanitary district will rely on the counties and/or cities in which it is located to enforce the building code.

Contracting with Incorporated Fire Departments or Other Governmental Fire Departments

As an alternative to (or in addition to) maintaining a fire department, a local unit may contract with one or more municipal fire departments or, more commonly, with one or more private incorporated fire departments to deliver fire protection and rescue services. Additionally, some municipalities allow the county or counties in which they are located to contract for and fund the fire services within the municipal territory.

There is broad authority for local units to enter into contractual arrangements whereby the unit appropriates revenues to a corporate or municipal fire department to pay for both the capital and operating costs associated with fire suppression and prevention throughout all or a portion of the unit.[10] Cities and counties have equally broad authority to contract with and appropriate funds to "rescue squads or teams to enable them to purchase and maintain rescue equipment and to finance the operation of the rescue squad either within or outside the boundaries of the city or county."[11]

Contracting with Municipal Fire Departments

Some counties, sanitary districts, and even other cities contract with municipal fire departments to provide fire protection services. The structure of these contractual arrangements varies significantly. Some units rely entirely on the municipal fire department to procure the necessary equipment, supplies, and personnel and to provide the necessary training to carry out the contracted fire protection services. A municipal fire department is authorized to install and maintain water mains and hydrants, as well as buildings and equipment, outside its territorial limits.[12] In addition, personnel and equipment may be dispatched to protect unincorporated areas pursuant to an agreement between a city and another government entity or between a city and the owner of property to be protected.

Other units purchase some or all of the needed real property or equipment and donate or lease it to the municipal fire departments that serve the unit. A county, sanitary district, or city has authority to lease, sell, or convey land, with or without consideration, and to donate personal property, to a municipal fire department.[13]

Neither a city nor its employees may be held liable for failure to answer or delay in answering a fire call outside the corporate limits.[14] Moreover, cities (but not individual firefighters) are immune from civil suit for acts committed in rendering fire protection outside their city limits.[15] Employees of city fire departments, while performing services outside the city on the orders of the fire chief or the city council, have the same jurisdiction, authority, rights, privileges, and immunities as they enjoy within the city.[16] One important privilege conferred by this provision is coverage under the North Carolina Workers' Compensation Act.

---

10. *See* G.S. 160A-20.1 and -461 (cities); and -233; 160A-461 (counties); 130A-55 (sanitary districts).
11. G.S. 160A-487.
12. G.S. 160A-293.
13. G.S. 160A-274; 160A-280.
14. G.S. 160A-293(b).
15. *Id.*
16. G.S. 160A-293(c).

Contracting with Incorporated Fire Departments

An incorporated fire department is a nonprofit corporation, established in accordance with G.S. Chapter 55A. Corporate status allows the fire department to raise funds, purchase equipment and real property, set up bank accounts, conduct fundraisers, receive grants, qualify for special state and federal tax breaks, and negotiate contractual agreements. An incorporated fire department is not a government entity, even if it receives most or all of its revenue from a local unit. Incorporated fire departments are often referred to as nonprofit fire departments. Incorporated fire departments that are composed entirely or mainly of volunteer personnel are volunteer fire departments (VFDs). And incorporated fire departments that serve rural areas typically are called rural fire departments.

A local unit may contract with one or more incorporated fire departments to provide the full range of fire protection and rescue services. Similar to contracts with municipal fire departments, these contractual arrangements are structured in a variety of ways. Some units enter into yearly contracts with the incorporated fire department that commit the unit to paying the department a certain sum of money in exchange for the department providing a certain level of service within a defined area and maintaining a certain fire insurance rating.[17] Other local units enter into multiyear service contracts and set a fixed appropriation each year. Still others enter into multiyear contracts but renegotiate the budgeted amounts annually.

With respect to capital outlay, a local unit may appropriate money to the fire department to cover the costs of purchasing or leasing real and personal property. Alternatively, a unit may choose to purchase real property or equipment and sell, lease, or otherwise convey it to the fire department. State law allows a local unit to "lease, sell, or convey to a volunteer fire department or to a volunteer rescue squad any land or interest in land, for the purpose of constructing or expanding fire department or rescue squad facilities, if the volunteer fire department or volunteer rescue squad provides fire protection or rescue services to the [unit]."[18] The statute does not define "volunteer fire department." It likely includes incorporated fire departments that are staffed exclusively or at least primarily with volunteers. A city or county (but not a sanitary district) also may convey real or personal property to an incorporated fire department by private sale as long as the property is used for a public purpose.[19]

In addition to providing capital resources to a corporate fire department, a local unit sometimes employs some or all of the department's firefighters or other staff members. Being classified as employees of the local unit may afford the staff members additional benefits, such as retirement plans and health insurance.

County Contracts for Service in Municipality

Another common arrangement for providing fire services is for counties to contract for, and pay for, the provision of fire protection services in one or more of their municipalities (with the permission of the affected municipal boards). This arrangement derives from the fact that counties have authority to set up special taxing districts to fund fire services and to include municipal territories within these districts.[20] Counties typically contract with one or more incorporated fire departments to provide the fire protection services in the municipal territory.

---

17. For more information on fire insurance ratings, see note 108 and accompanying text.

18. G.S. 160A-277.

19. G.S. 160A-279. For more information on disposal of property procedures, see Chapter 23, "Public Contracts, Competitive Bidding Requirements, and Property Disposal."

20. For more information on special tax districts for fire services, see notes 31–96 and accompanying text.

Funding Fire Services

Local units have broad authority to levy property taxes to fund fire services.[21] Counties may fund these services with general property tax proceeds or may establish special taxing districts, or a combination of both. Sanitary districts also have authority to assess fire fees.

Property Taxation

Authority to Levy Property Taxes

The property tax is levied against real and personal property within the local unit and ultimately is an obligation of the property, not just its owner(s). The property tax base consists of real property (land, buildings, and other improvements to land); personal property (business equipment, automobiles, and so forth); and the property of public service companies. Not all property is subject to taxation, though. Government-owned property is exempt under article V, sections 2(2) and (3) of the North Carolina Constitution. In addition, the General Assembly may exempt property from taxation or classify property to exclude it from the tax base, give it a reduced valuation, or subject it to a reduced tax rate. It must do so, however, only on a statewide basis.[22] A local government itself may not exempt, classify, or otherwise give a tax preference to property within its jurisdiction.[23]

A unit's governing board determines whether or not to levy property taxes each year and at what rate or rates. The board may adopt a single tax rate, the revenue generated from which is used to fund a variety of authorized local government services. As an example, a city may adopt a general property tax rate of $0.63 per $100 in assessed valuation of taxable property in the unit to fund its general administration, public safety, fire services, recreation services, zoning services, and solid waste services. In its annual budget ordinance, the city's governing board may divvy up the revenue generated by the general property tax rate to fund these services in any manner it chooses. And, with few exceptions, the board may, at any time after the budget is adopted, amend the budget ordinance to change its appropriations.[24]

Alternatively, a board may adopt a series of property tax rates, the proceeds from which are earmarked for specific services. For example, it may adopt a $0.15 per $100 valuation for general administration, a $0.06 per $100 valuation for recreation services, a $0.20 per $100 valuation for law enforcement, a $0.13 per $100 valuation for fire services, and so forth. If a governing board adopts its property tax rates in this manner, it provides greater transparency as to how particular services and activities are funded. However, even if a governing board adopts separate property tax rates for each service or activity, it retains discretionary authority to amend the budget ordinance in order to divert the property tax revenue for different purposes during the fiscal year.[25]

---

21. G.S. 160A-209 (cities); (counties); 130A-55(3) (sanitary districts).
22. G.S. 105-275 through -278.9.
23. The administration of the property tax, including statutory exclusions and exemptions is discussed in much greater detail in Chapter 19, "Property Tax Policy and Administration."
24. *See* G.S. 159-15.
25. *See* Long v. Comm'rs of Richmond Cnty., 76 N.C. 273, 280 (1877) ("We know of no statute nor any rule of law or of public policy which prevents County Commissioners from applying a tax raised professedly for one purpose, to any other legitimate purpose."); *see also* Parker v. Comm'rs of Johnston Cnty., 178 N.C. 92 (1919). Note that a city's or county's governing board may hold a referendum to get voter approval to expend property tax dollars on any expenditure item that is specifically authorized by the property tax statute. G.S. 153A-149 (county); 160A-209 (city). A unit also may seek voter approval to fund with property tax proceeds an item that is not listed in the property tax statutes but is an activity that the local government otherwise has statutory authority to undertake. If the voters specifically approve a tax levy for a specific purpose, the governing board likely is prohibited from using the tax proceeds for a different purpose.

Finally, a governing board may take a hybrid approach, adopting a general property tax rate to cover most general fund activities and adopting one or more additional property tax rates (listed separately in the budget ordinance), the proceeds of which are earmarked for particular purposes, such as to fund fire protection services. At least a few local governments have taken this approach because it allows governing boards to justify a property tax increase if it is to support what is deemed by the public to be an essential (or at least very important) service. Again, however, the governing board retains discretionary authority to amend the budget ordinance to divert the property tax revenue for different purposes during the fiscal year.[26]

Legal Restrictions on Amount of General Property Tax Rates

For cities and counties, the total of all property tax rates may not exceed $1.50 per $100 assessed valuation of property in the unit.[27] A governing board may hold a referendum to increase the $1.50 limit or to specifically approve a dedicated property tax rate for a particular purpose, such that it does not count against the $1.50 limit. For example, a city's governing board could put to the unit's voters the question of whether or not to levy a dedicated property tax, at a specific rate, to fund fire services.[28] There is no statutory limit on a sanitary district's tax rate.

Use of General Property Tax Revenue to Fund Fire Services

If a local unit uses its general property tax revenue to fund fire services, the governing board determines how much to allocate yearly to providing these services as well as what specific programs or activities are to be funded. The board may use the money to fund a fire chief or marshal and to fund inspection, training, and education programs that are furnished unit-wide. The revenue also may be used to fund fire prevention or suppression services in specific areas within the unit. Services may be provided by the unit's personnel or through contracts with one or more private incorporated or municipal fire departments. The benefit of funding fire services in this manner is that the property tax provides a relatively stable stream of revenue, and a local unit's governing board has a good deal of flexibility in allocating this revenue to provide different types and levels of services in different response areas.

Limitations of the General Property Tax

The difficulty with this funding mechanism is that the tax is levied on all (nonexempted or nonexcluded) properties within the unit. A fundamental tenet of property taxation in North Carolina is that a local government's property tax rate(s) must be applied uniformly to all taxable properties within a unit's jurisdiction.[29] That means that, unlike some local taxes and fees, property taxes generally may not be assessed only on property owners that directly benefit from particular services provided by the local government. Fire services are not required to be provided equally across a

---

26. See note 25.

27. *See* G.S. 153A-149(c) (counties) and 160A-209(d) (municipalities). There are a few purposes for which property taxes may be levied without limitation on the rate or amount. For municipalities, the most important of these purposes is to fund debt service on general obligation debt. For counties, the purposes include debt service on general obligation debt as well as the most significant state-mandated services: schools and social services. On the flip side, there are some (very limited) services or activities that a local government is not authorized to fund with property tax dollars without specific approval through a voter referendum.

28. If the voters approve a dedicated property tax, at a specific rate, for a particular purpose, the governing board may not divert the proceeds to a different purpose.

29. This limitation stems from article V, section 2 of the North Carolina Constitution, which provides that "[n]o class of property shall be taxed except by uniform rule, and every classification shall be made by general law uniformly applicable in every county, city and town, and other unit of local government."

unit's territorial boundaries, though. In fact, differences in topography and development densities throughout a county often necessitate different types of service and equipment. The result is that some taxpayers pay for fire services they do not receive.[30]

County Special Taxing Districts

The North Carolina Constitution carves out an exception to the general rule of uniform taxation allowing the General Assembly to "enact general laws authorizing the governing body of any county, city, or town to define territorial areas and to levy taxes within those areas, in addition to those levied throughout the county, city, or town, in order to finance, provide, or maintain services, facilities, and functions in addition to or to a greater extent than those financed, provided, or maintained for the entire county, city, or town."[31] Recognizing the disparate needs for fire protection throughout a county, in particular, fire services are among the handful of purposes for which the General Assembly has authorized counties to establish special tax districts to fund.[32] Thus, instead of appropriating its general property tax revenue to fund its fire services, a county may establish one or more special tax districts to fund different types and levels of fire services in different parts of the county. This exception only applies to counties. Cities and sanitary districts are not authorized to establish special taxing districts for this purpose.

There are actually two different types of tax districts—rural fire protection districts and fire service tax districts. The major difference between the two is how the districts are formed and how they can be altered or abolished, but there are a few other distinctions. Each type of taxing district will be discussed in turn.[33] For many years, counties have been phasing out rural fire protection districts in favor of county service districts because the latter structure is more flexible.

Rural Fire Protection Districts

One of the methods that a county may employ to raise revenue only from those citizens who directly benefit (or most directly benefit) from fire services provided by the county is to establish one or more rural fire protection districts and levy an additional ad valorem tax on all taxable real and personal properties within each of the districts, the revenue from which is earmarked specifically to fund the fire services provided within the districts. The General Assembly bestowed this authority on counties in the early 1950s in recognition of the fact that rural areas were increasingly becoming subject to urban-type development, resulting in pressure on county governments to provide and fund fire protection services in these areas.

Establishing a Rural Fire Protection District

A county's governing board may not simply establish a rural fire protection district. It first must receive a petition signed by at least 35 percent of the resident freeholders living within the proposed district. The proposed district must encompass only territory outside the corporate limits of

---

30. For example, a county's general property tax is levied on all (nonexempted or nonexcluded) properties located in incorporated municipalities. Counties typically do not provide any fire services within municipal territory, though.

31. N.C. Const. art. V, § 2(4).

32. Under general law, neither municipalities nor sanitary districts are authorized to establish special tax districts to fund fire services.

33. For a more detailed explanation of how to establish, maintain, modify, and abolish a special tax district for fire services, see Kara A. Millonzi, "County Funding for Fire Services in North Carolina," *Local Finance Bulletin* No. 43 (May 2011), www.sog.unc.edu/publications/bulletins/county-funding-fire-services-north-carolina.

any municipality,[34] but it may include territory that lies in more than one county. (If the proposed district falls within more than one county, the petition must be submitted to the boards of county commissioners of all the counties in which the area lies.) The county tax office must verify the freeholder status and confirm the location of the property owned by the petitioners.

Once a county board of commissioners receives a valid petition, it must call an election within the proposed district on the question of whether or not the county may levy a special property tax to fund fire services within the district.[35] The statute sets the maximum tax rate at $0.15 per $100 assessed valuation of taxable property. A county is not required to accept a petition that calls for a different maximum rate limit, even if it is lower than $0.15 per $100 valuation.[36] In fact, the statutorily prescribed ballot language allows citizens to vote only to approve or not approve the levy by the county commissioners of the statutory maximum rate of $0.15 per $100 valuation.[37] It does not authorize the county to hold an election on any tax rate that differs from the statutory maximum rate. Thus, for example, a county board of commissioners may not propose a maximum rate of $0.12 per $100 valuation on the ballot, even if it receives a petition signed by at least 35 percent of the resident freeholders in the proposed district requesting the $0.12 maximum tax rate.[38]

All qualified voters in the proposed district may vote in the election.[39] The county board of commissioners, after consulting with the county board of elections, must adopt a resolution setting the date for the election.[40] The election is conducted by the county board of elections, with the cost borne by the county.[41] If a district ultimately is established, the county may recoup the costs of the election from tax revenue generated by the district tax. (If the proposed district lies within multiple counties, each board of county commissioners must call for an election and the election must be conducted jointly by the counties' boards of elections, with the cost shared equally by all counties.)[42]

If a majority of the voters voting in the election approve the ballot issue to allow the county to impose a special property tax to fund fire services within the district (rural district tax), the county board(s) of commissioners must establish the district.[43] The district is a municipal corporation, a separate legal entity from the county or counties in which it lies. As a municipal corporation, a rural fire protection district's governing board is authorized to enter into contractual agreements to purchase property or procure fire protection services.

---

34. As discussed below, municipal territory may be added to an existing rural fire protection district after the district is established. G.S. 69-25.11(5).

35. G.S. 69-25.1.

36. *Id.*; *see* Op. N.C. Att'y Gen. July 8, 1969 (on file with author).

37. G.S. 69-25.3.

38. A more difficult issue is whether a county may call for a referendum if it receives a petition that specifies a tax rate that differs from the statutory rate of $0.15 per $100 valuation. The safest approach is for a county board to reject the petition and not call an election unless and until a proper petition is presented. If the board chooses to proceed with the referendum despite receiving a petition that specifies a different maximum tax rate, the referendum may not specify a maximum tax rate that is different from that provided in the statute. Thus, for example, even if the petition calls for a maximum tax rate of $0.12 per $100 valuation, if the county holds a referendum on establishing the rural fire protection district and the referendum is successful, the maximum authorized tax rate is $0.15 per $100 valuation. It is possible, however, that the levy of the rural district tax subsequently could be challenged as invalid because the petition calling for the referendum did not satisfy the statutory requirements. As of this writing, there is no case law addressing this issue.

39. *See* G.S. Chapter 163, Article 6, for voter qualification requirements.

40. G.S. 69-25.2. Note that the board of county commissioners likely may not proceed to call for an election if, before the board takes action, one or more resident freeholders withdraws his or her signature from the petition, thereby keeping the 35 percent threshold from being met. *Cf.* Idol v. Hanes, 219 N.C. 723 (1941).

41. The county board of elections must advertise and conduct the election in accordance with the applicable provisions in G.S. Chapter 163.

42. G.S. 69-25.9.

43. If the ballot issue fails, the issue may not be put to the voters again for at least two years. G.S. 69-25.1.

Governing a Rural Fire Protection District

If the district lies within a single county, the county's board of commissioners serves as the district's governing board. If the district lies in more than one county, the boards of commissioners of those counties jointly govern the district. And whether the district lies in a single county or in multiple counties, the board or boards of county commissioners may appoint a three-member fire protection district commission (fire commission) that serves "at the discretion of and under the supervision of the board[s] of county commissioners."[44] Members of the fire commission must be qualified voters who reside in the district. The fire commission legally functions as an advisory board to the county board(s) of commissioners. The fire commission may make recommendations to the board(s) of county commissioners related to budgeting, setting the tax rate, and administering all aspects of the district. The board(s) of county commissioners must make all final decisions related to the district.[45] The county commissioners also are statutorily responsible for determining the methods of providing fire services in the district (discussed below), though this function likely may be delegated to the fire commission.[46] In fact, the fire commission typically enters into the actual contractual agreements with the volunteer or municipal fire department(s) on behalf of the district.

Levying the Rural Fire Protection District Tax

The county commissioners levy the rural district tax each fiscal year at a rate not to exceed $0.15 per $100 valuation. (If the district was formed before June 9, 1959, the maximum tax rate is $0.10 per $100 valuation, unless the district's voters have approved an increase to $0.15 per $100 valuation.)[47] With one exception, the rural district tax applies to all real and personal property subject to the county's ad valorem property tax.[48] Property owners in the district may not opt out of paying the rural district tax even if the property owners procure their own fire protection. Commissioners are not required to levy the tax—instead, the board is instructed to "levy and collect [the district tax] *in such amount as it may deem necessary.*"[49] Commissioners determine whether or not to levy the district tax, and at what rate, each year during budget time. The tax is adopted in the county's budget ordinance.[50]

If the district lies in more than one county, each county board of commissioners may adopt a yearly rural district tax rate for the portion of the district that lies within its county.[51] The tax rate adopted in each county need not be the same as that adopted in the other counties that comprise the district, though the boards of county commissioners may agree in any given year to adopt the same rate. No county may adopt a tax rate that exceeds the maximum rate approved by the voters.[52]

---

44. G.S. 69-25.7.

45. *See* G.S. 69-25.4. The fire protection district commission may advise the county commissioners as to whether or not to levy a district tax each year and at what rate, but the county commissioners likely must retain the discretionary authority to determine the tax rate each year. *See* Plant Food Co. v. City of Charlotte, 214 N.C. 518 (1938). *See generally* David M. Lawrence, "Contracts That Bind the Discretion of Governing Boards," *Popular Government* 56 (Summer 1990): 38–42.

46. *See* G.S. 69-25.5.

47. G.S. 69-25.1.

48. If the rural fire protection district was established after May 1, 1971, the district tax does not apply to any electric generating plant that provides electricity to the public.

49. G.S. 69-25.4 (emphasis added).

50. Once the tax is adopted, it may not be altered during the fiscal year unless it satisfies one of the criteria set forth in G.S. 159-15.

51. G.S. 69-25.9.

52. Although the statutes specifically allow for the formation of a rural fire protection district that crosses county boundary lines, for purposes of adopting the district tax rate, each county controls the revenue generation for the portion of the district that lies within its territory.

Also, the rate adopted in each county must apply uniformly to all taxable properties that lie within that county's portion of the rural fire protection district.[53]

Providing Services within a Rural Fire Protection District

In administering the fund, the district's governing board may expend district tax proceeds to finance any fire suppression or prevention programs or activities in the district.[54] Additionally, district tax revenue may be used for "furnishing emergency medical, rescue, and ambulance services to protect persons within the district from injury or death."[55] Service provision does not need to be provided uniformly throughout the district.

A rural district's board has much discretion in allocating funds in any manner it chooses—splitting the funds among multiple fire and rescue departments or even appropriating a portion of the funds to support the county's fire marshal—to procure the desired fire services in the district.[56] That said, many district boards contract with a single incorporated fire department or municipal fire department to serve an entire rural fire protection district. There often is confusion as to who controls the district—the district's advisory board, the county board(s) of commissioners, or the fire department serving the district. The practical answer is that all three have some degree of control. The county board(s) of commissioners must set the tax rate and determine how services will be provided in the district. The district's governing board (which is also the county board(s) of commissioners) enters into contractual agreements with the fire department to procure services for the district. The fire department is a contracting agent of the district. As such, its degree of control over service provision is dictated by the contract's terms.

A district governing board may enter into multiyear contractual arrangements with fire departments to procure fire services. These contracts can take many different forms. They may provide for specified types and levels of services in exchange for specified reimbursement each year.[57] Alternatively, they may set forth a general agreement that a fire department will serve a particular area but leave the specific service and pay provisions to be negotiated each year. If a district has valid contractual agreements with one or more fire departments, it must abide by the provisions in those contracts or face liability for breach of the agreements.[58] However, subject to any existing contractual agreements, a district's governing board may change service providers or the nature of the services that are being provided at any time.[59] An incorporated or municipal fire department does not have a statutory right to continue to serve a particular district, even if the fire department has incurred significant expense (or even borrowed money) to fund operating or capital expenses to serve the district.[60]

---

53. *See* N.C. Const. art. 5, § 2(2).

54. A rural district's governing board may not expend the tax proceeds to procure services or finance projects outside the district's boundaries.

55. G.S. 69-25.4(b). A rural fire protection district that provides ambulance services is subject to the provisions in G.S. 153A-250.

56. Thus, although rural district tax revenue must be used to fund services in the district, there is no requirement that the funds be used to support a single fire department.

57. Note that a county board of commissioners likely may not contract away its legal authority to determine the rural district tax rate each year.

58. *See, e.g.*, Knotville Volunteer Fire Dep't, Inc. v. Wilkes Cnty., 85 N.C. App. 598 (1987), *other proceeding*, 94 N.C. App. 377 (1989).

59. *See Knotville*, 85 N.C. App. 598.

60. With the exception of some limited protections when a municipal annexation occurs (see G.S. 160A-58.57), a rural volunteer fire department's only legal protection is pursuant to the contractual arrangements it enters into with the district.

Funding Capital Projects in a Rural Fire Protection District

In addition to being used for the provision of services in the district, district tax proceeds may be used to fund capital projects. A question sometimes arises as to which entity owns the real or personal property funded with the rural district tax revenue. The answer to this question depends, at least in part, on which entity purchased the capital assets or engaged in the construction project. If a municipal or volunteer fire department that serves a rural district purchases land, vehicles, or other equipment or constructs or makes capital improvements to a fire station or substation, it is the fire department (not the district or the county) that owns the property. This is true even if the district's governing board appropriated district tax moneys to fund all or a portion of the capital outlay. On the other hand, if the district's governing board purchases the capital assets or engages in the construction project itself, the real or personal property belongs to the district. The district may convey the property to a fire department, though. Or it may otherwise allow a fire department to use the property as part of a service contract. A county also has the option to fund capital projects related to the provision of fire services in a rural district with general fund moneys.

What if the fire department, district, or county needs to borrow money to fund the capital projects? A rural fire protection district has no authority to borrow money. The fire department that serves a rural district may borrow money to fund capital equipment or projects necessary to furnish the appropriate level of fire protection services. If an incorporated or municipal fire department borrows the money, neither the district nor the county (or counties) in which the district lies legally is responsible for the debt service payments. As a practical matter, the fire department likely will use some of the moneys it receives from the district pursuant to its service contract to repay the loan.

The county or counties in which a rural district lies also may borrow money to fund certain capital expenses related to the provision of fire services within the district. According to G.S. 159-48(b)(6), a county may issue general obligation debt to provide "facilities for fire fighting and prevention, including without limitation headquarters buildings, station buildings, training facilities, hydrants, alarm systems, and communications systems." By issuing general obligation debt, the county pledges its general taxing power as security for the debt. That means that if the county failed to meet its debt service payments, the bondholders could force the county to raise its general property tax rate (not its district tax rate) to a sufficient amount to cover the payments. A county also could finance the purchase of real or personal property (or improvements made to real property) by borrowing funds and pledging the property as security for repayment of the loan.[61] If the county borrows money to fund a capital project related to the provision of fire service in a rural district, it may use rural district tax revenue to meet its debt service obligations.

Altering a Rural Fire Protection District

From time to time a county, or citizens residing in a county, may wish to alter an existing rural fire protection district to, for example, increase the maximum tax rate, add territory, or remove territory. Changes are also necessitated when property included in a rural fire protection district becomes part of an incorporated municipality (through incorporation or annexation). Each of these actions requires fairly detailed, statutorily prescribed processes.[62]

---

61. *See* G.S. 160A-20.

62. For detailed explanations of the required processes to alter a rural district, see Kara A. Millonzi, "County Funding for Fire Services in North Carolina," *Local Finance Bulletin* No. 43 (May 2011), www.sog.unc.edu/publications/bulletins/county-funding-fire-services-north-carolina. Note that district boundaries also may be altered or districts may be abolished by local act of the General Assembly.

It is important to note that although it may be difficult to officially alter a rural fire protection tax district's boundaries or increase its maximum allowable tax rate, a county has much discretion to change the nature of the fire services provided within a district and to change who provides those services. Rural fire protection districts are simply taxing districts. Counties are in no way impeded from establishing fire protection response areas or insurance districts that cut across one or more rural fire protection districts. Thus, in many instances a county board of commissioners may make the desired changes to its fire protection services without resorting to officially altering rural fire protection district boundaries.

Abolishing a Rural Fire Protection District

In order to abolish a rural fire protection district altogether, a board of county commissioners (or the joint boards of county commissioners if the district lies in more than one county) must receive a petition with the signatures of at least 15 percent of the resident freeholders within the district requesting that it be abolished.[63] Upon receiving a valid petition, the board(s) of county commissioners must call for an election on the issue in the district, to be conducted by the county board of elections.[64] If a majority of voters voting in the election approve of abolishing the district, then the board(s) of county commissioners must cease collecting the rural district tax. County commissioners are not required to cease providing fire services to properties or citizens located in the district, though. As discussed above, counties are free to provide and fund fire protection services with general property tax proceeds or other unrestricted general fund revenues. Any unused district tax funds that remain after the district is abolished revert to the county's (or counties') general fund(s) to be used for any public purpose.[65] And any district property may be used or disposed of by the board(s) of county commissioners.[66]

Instead of abolishing the district, which requires both a petition and a voter referendum, could the commissioners allow the district to remain but treat it as if it had been abolished by not levying a rural district tax? The answer is yes. County commissioners have full discretion to choose whether or not to levy a district tax in any given year. If the commissioners wish to cease providing fire services within the district, or to fund the fire services in a different manner,[67] they may simply cease levying the district tax. Unless the district is officially abolished, though, any unused district tax proceeds must be used to provide fire protection services within the district.

County Fire and Rescue Service Districts

The second type of special tax district that a county may establish to fund fire protection and rescue services is a county service district.[68] A county is authorized to define one or more areas within the county to establish a service district to "finance, provide, or maintain" one or more of a specific list of authorized services, facilities or functions "in addition to or to a greater extent than those financed, provided or maintained for the entire county."[69] This authority stems from an effort by

---

63. G.S. 69-25.10.

64. The election must be conducted according to the procedures prescribed by G.S. 69-25.2.

65. G.S. 69-25.10.

66. *Id.*

67. As discussed below, county commissioners effectively may convert a rural fire protection district to a county fire service district (authorized by G.S. Chapter 153A, Article 16) without actually abolishing the rural fire protection district by ceasing to levy a rural fire protection district tax and establishing a county fire service district and imposing a county fire service district tax instead.

68. County service districts are governed by G.S. Chapter 153A, Article 16.

69. G.S. 153A-301.

the General Assembly in the mid-1970s to make municipal-type services more widely available to county residents. Among the authorized services for which service districts may be created are "fire protection" and "ambulance and rescue" services.[70] Unlike a rural fire protection district, a county service district is not a municipal corporation and has no independent authority. It is established and maintained by the county and is under the control of the county board of commissioners as a county revenue source.

Establishing a Fire or Rescue Service District

It is much easier to establish a fire or rescue service district than to create a rural fire protection district. A county board of commissioners may create one or more fire service districts or one or more rescue service districts (collectively, service districts) without receiving a petition from affected property owners and without holding a voter referendum. (There is no provision for multiple counties to establish fire or rescue service districts that cross county borders.) The board simply must find that

1. there is a demonstrable need for providing one or more of the services in the district,
2. it is impossible or impracticable to provide the services on a countywide basis,
3. it is economically feasible to provide the proposed services in the district without unreasonable or burdensome annual tax levies, and
4. there is a demonstrable demand for the proposed services by persons residing in the proposed district.[71]

In making its determination, the board must consider a number of factors, including the resident or seasonal population and population density in the proposed district, the appraised value of property subject to taxation in the proposed district, the present tax rates of the county and any municipalities or other special districts in which the proposed district is located, and the ability of the proposed district to sustain the additional taxes necessary to support the proposed district.[72] Although a county board does not need to solicit formal citizen approval to create a district because it must establish "demonstrable demand" for the services that will be provided in the district, it likely may not create a county service district if there is strong opposition to the county providing the fire protection services in the proposed district by the current residents.

Once the board makes the appropriate findings, it must hold a public hearing on the proposed creation of the service district. At least four weeks before the public hearing, the board (or staff) must prepare and make available for public inspection in the office of the clerk to the board a report that contains a map of the proposed district, a statement that the proposed district meets the required standards, and a plan for providing the fire or rescue services (or both) to the district.[73] After it holds the public hearing, the county board may adopt a resolution establishing the district. The district must take effect at the beginning of a fiscal year.[74]

70. G.S. 153A-301(a)(2) and (7).

71. G.S. 153A-302(a1).

72. G.S. 153A-302(a)(1)–(4).

73. G.S. 153A-302(b) and (c). Notice of the public hearing must state "the date, hour, and place of the hearing and its subject, and [must] include a map of the proposed district and a statement that the report . . . is available for public inspection in the office of the clerk to the board." G.S. 153A-302(c). The notice must be published at least one week before the date of the hearing and mailed at least four weeks before the date of the hearing to the owners of all property located within the proposed district. *Id.*

74. G.S. 153A-302(d).

A county may include municipal territory in a newly established district, but only if the municipality's governing board adopts a resolution agreeing to the inclusion.[75] If municipal property becomes part of a county fire service or rescue district, the county board of commissioners controls the tax levy and service provision (to the extent funded by the service district tax) in the municipality. The municipality's governing board has no authority to determine the amount of the service district tax or how its proceeds are expended. A municipality is free to supplement the fire services provided to municipal property in the district with municipal revenue.

Levying a Fire or Rescue Service District Tax

Once a service district is created, the county board of commissioners may levy an annual property tax within the service district in addition to the property tax or taxes it levies throughout the county (service district tax), but it is not required to do so. The service district tax applies to all real and personal property that is subject to the county's ad valorem property tax(es). As with rural fire protection districts, property owners in a county service district may not opt out of paying the tax, even if they procure their own fire protection. The board typically adopts the service district tax rate in its annual budget ordinance. Once the rate is adopted, the board generally may not alter it during the fiscal year.[76] County commissioners may adopt a new tax rate each year to reflect the estimated costs of servicing the district. Unlike rural fire protection districts, service districts generally have no specific maximum tax rate. Such taxes are subject to the general aggregate property tax limit of $1.50 on each $100 valuation. That means that the district tax rate, when combined with the county's general ad valorem property tax rate(s), may not exceed $1.50, unless the portion of the rate in excess of the limitation is submitted to and approved by a majority of the qualified voters in the district.[77]

Under certain circumstances, a county board of commissioners is restricted to a lower maximum allowable service district tax rate. With respect to a fire protection service district, if within ninety days before holding the public hearing on the proposed district (and before the first publication of notice of the public hearing) the board of commissioners adopts a resolution that states that property taxes within the fire protection service district may not exceed $0.15 per $100 valuation, then the yearly service district tax may not exceed this maximum rate.[78]

Similarly, with respect to an ambulance and rescue district, if within ninety days before holding the public hearing on the proposed district (and before the first publication of notice of the public hearing) the board of commissioners adopts a resolution stating that property taxes within the ambulance and rescue service district may not exceed $0.05 per $100 valuation, then the yearly service district tax may not exceed this maximum rate.[79]

---

75. G.S. 153A-302(a1). Similarly, if territory to be included in the proposed district lies within a sanitary district, the sanitary district's governing board must consent to its inclusion. *Id.*

76. *See* G.S. 159-15.

77. G.S. 153A-307.

78. G.S. 153A-309.2. The notice requirements for the public hearing are different if the county commissioners adopt a resolution restricting the maximum tax rate for the district. Notice must be published at least twice, with one publication not less than two weeks before the hearing and the other publication on a different day that is also not less than two weeks before the hearing. *Id.*

Note that there also are special rate limitations for industrial facility property that meets certain requirements and that is removed from an existing fire protection service district and simultaneously placed within a new fire protection service district. *See* G.S. 153A-309.3.

79. G.S. 153A-310. The notice requirements for the public hearing are different if the county commissioners adopt a resolution restricting the maximum tax rate for the district. Notice must be published at least twice, with one

Revenue generated from the service district tax is specifically earmarked to finance the fire or rescue services to be provided in the district.[80] Service district tax proceeds may not be diverted to any other purpose, even if a service district is abolished. In addition to the service district tax revenue, a county may allocate to a service district any other unrestricted revenues.[81] Once these revenues are allocated to the service district they also are specifically earmarked to be used only to fund the fire or rescue services provided within the district.

Providing Services within a Fire or Rescue Service District

The service district tax revenue must be used to furnish fire or rescue services "in addition to or to a greater extent than those financed, provided or maintained for the entire county."[82] That means that a county may create a service district to provide fire or rescue services that it is not providing at all in other areas of the county or that it is not providing at the same level in other areas of the county. Service provision need not be uniform throughout the district. A county also may establish multiple service districts to provide fire or rescue services in different areas of the county. Each district may have the same tax rate and support the same level of services, or each may have different rates to fund different types or amounts of services. In addition, multiple authorized services may be provided within the same district. For example, fire protection services and ambulance and rescue services may be provided within the same district.[83] Alternatively, a county may establish co-extensive service districts to provide different services. For example, a county may establish a fire service district and an ambulance and rescue service district with the exact same boundaries.

A county must "provide, maintain, or let contracts for the services for which the residents of the district are being taxed within a reasonable time, not to exceed one year, after the effective date of the definition of the district."[84] The statutes are silent, though, as to how services may be provided within the district. Counties generally are authorized to contract with any private entity to "carry out any public purpose that the county is authorized by law to engage in."[85] So, as with rural fire protection districts, a county is free to establish and maintain a county fire, ambulance, or rescue department to provide the services within its service districts, or it may contract with one or more municipal or volunteer fire departments to furnish these services. (Many adopt some combination of both.) The county has a good deal of flexibility in how it allocates the service district tax revenue to procure services for the district.

As with rural fire protection districts, the relationship between counties and municipal or volunteer fire departments is of a contractual nature. The county board of commissioners retains legal control over setting the service district tax rate each year, and the county board of commissioners determines what fire services are provided within the district and by whom. That means that, subject to any existing contractual agreements, a board of county commissioners may change service

---

publication not less than two weeks before the hearing and the other publication on a different day that is also not less than two weeks before the hearing. *Id.*

80. G.S. 153A-307.

81. *Id.*

82. *Id.*

83. Generally, in order to provide multiple services within a single district, the services need to have been identified in the report generated on the proposed district and adopted in the governing board's resolution establishing the district. G.S. 153A-309 provides an exception to this process. If a service district initially was established for fire protection purposes only, the board of county commissioners may adopt a resolution to permit the service district to provide emergency medical, rescue, and ambulance services and to use service district tax proceeds to fund these services. The resolution must take effect at the beginning of a fiscal year.

84. G.S. 153A-305.

85. G.S. 153A-449.

providers or the nature of the services that are being provided at any time. A volunteer or municipal fire department does not have a statutory right to continue to serve a particular district, even if the fire department has incurred significant expense (or even borrowed money) to fund operating or capital expenses to serve the district.

Single County Fire or Rescue Service District

In recent years several counties have explored ways to increase their flexibility in allocating resources among the various fire or rescue service areas. One option that is gaining popularity is to create a single county fire or rescue service district that encompasses the entire unincorporated area of the county. Under this approach, a county levies a single tax rate across the entire service district and allocates the proceeds among the various fire and rescue departments that service each response zone according to their individual budgetary needs. This approach provides a county board with the same flexibility as using its general property tax proceeds, with the added advantage that the tax is not levied in municipal territories. And creating a single county fire or service district that comprises the county's unincorporated area satisfies the statutory requirements for creating a service district: the district tax proceeds are used to provide services "in addition to or to a greater extent than those financed, provided or maintained for the entire county"[86] because services are not being provided in the incorporated areas.

Funding Capital Projects in a County Fire or Rescue Service District

District tax proceeds also may be used to fund capital projects. As with rural fire protection districts, a question sometimes arises as to which entity owns the real or personal property funded with the rural district tax revenue. The answer is the same as for rural districts: it depends, at least in part, on which entity purchased the capital assets or engaged in the construction project. If a municipal or volunteer fire department that serves a fire or rescue service district purchases land, vehicles, or other equipment or constructs or makes capital improvements to a fire station or substation, it is the fire department (not the county) that owns the property. This is true even if the county effectively funded the capital with moneys provided to the fire department pursuant to the service agreement. On the other hand, if the county's governing board purchases the capital assets or engages in the construction project itself, the real or personal property belongs to the county. A county may use district tax proceeds or county general fund revenue to fund the capital project. And the county may convey the property to a fire department, or it may otherwise allow a fire department to use the property as part of a service contract.

What if the fire department or county needs to borrow money to fund the capital projects? A county fire or rescue service district is not an independent legal entity and has no authority to borrow money. The fire department that serves a service district may borrow money to fund capital equipment or projects necessary to furnish the appropriate level of fire protection services. If an incorporated or municipal fire department borrows the money, the county is not legally responsible for the debt service payments. As a practical matter, the fire department likely will use some of the appropriated district tax moneys to repay the loan, though.

The county in which a service district lies also may borrow money to fund certain capital expenses related to the provision of fire services within the district. According to G.S. 159-48(b)(6), a county may issue general obligation debt to provide "facilities for fire fighting and prevention, including without limitation headquarters buildings, station buildings, training facilities, hydrants,

86. G.S. 153A-307.

alarm systems, and communications systems." By issuing general obligation debt, the county pledges its general taxing power as security for the debt. That means that if the county failed to meet its debt service payments, the bondholders could force the county to raise its general property tax rate (not its district tax rate) to a sufficient amount to cover the payments. A county may also finance the purchase of real or personal property (or improvements made to real property) by borrowing funds and pledging the property as security for repayment of the loan.[87] If the county borrows money to fund a capital project related to the provision of fire service in a rural district, it may use rural district tax revenue to meet its debt service obligations.

Note that before a county may issue general obligation debt, it must first receive specific voter approval through a referendum process. And G.S. 153A-308 stipulates that if general obligation bond proceeds will be used to fund a capital project within a county service district and will be repaid with district tax proceeds, "the proposed bond issue must be approved concurrently by a majority of those voting throughout the entire county and by a majority of the total of those voting in all of the affected or to-be-affected service districts."[88] There is no statutory counterpart to this provision applicable to rural fire protection districts.

Altering a Fire or Rescue Service District

Once a county establishes a service district, it may alter it by adding additional territory to the district, consolidating it with one or more other service districts, relocating the boundaries with an adjoining service district, or (under certain circumstances) removing territory from the service district. It also may abolish the district. A county board of commissioners must follow the appropriate statutory procedures for accomplishing each of these actions.

As with rural fire protection districts, it is important to note that a county has much discretion to change the nature of the fire services provided within a district and to change who provides those services without actually altering the district's boundaries. County fire or rescue service districts are simply taxing districts. Counties are in no way impeded from establishing fire protection response areas or insurance districts that cut across one or more service districts. Thus, in many instances a county board of commissioners may make the desired changes to its fire protection services without resorting to officially altering service district boundaries.

Abolishing a Fire or Rescue Service District

If the board of county commissioners determines that a fire or rescue service district tax is no longer needed to fund the fire or rescue services provided in the district, it has two options. The first option is to adopt a resolution abolishing the district.[89] The board may not abolish a district, however, if the county has any "outstanding bonds or notes issued to finance projects in the district."[90] That means that if the county issued general obligation debt to purchase capital equipment or fund infrastructure projects associated with fire or rescue protection, it may not abolish the district until the debt is repaid.[91] The board must hold a public hearing before abolishing a district, and the abolition must

---

87. *See* G.S. 160A-20.

88. This requirement is imposed because district tax proceeds likely will be used to make debt service payments.

89. G.S. 153A-306.

90. *Id.*

91. The restriction does not apply if a volunteer fire department or municipal fire department that serves the district borrows money to fund capital purchases or projects. The restriction also technically may not apply if the county has entered into installment purchase contracts, pursuant to G.S. 160A-20, to fund the projects in the district. Although installment financing is a form of borrowing, a county does not always issue bonds or notes when it enters into such financing agreements.

take effect at the end of a fiscal year.[92] Any service district tax funds remaining after a district is abolished must continue to be used to provide fire services to properties that were in the district. The moneys may not be diverted for a different purpose.

The second option is to keep the district but simply not levy a service district tax.[93] The county board could levy the district tax again in future fiscal years without having to re-establish the district. Even if the county does not levy the service district tax, it may continue to provide fire and rescue services in the district, funded through alternative means.

Relationship between Rural Fire Protection Districts and County Fire or Rescue Service Districts

It is not uncommon for a county to have a mix of rural fire protection districts and county fire and rescue service districts within its territorial boundaries. As described above, there are various procedural processes (some more onerous than others) to modify the boundary lines of the two different types of districts. But what if a county wishes to replace one type of district with another or modify boundary lines between the two different types of districts? Both types of districts serve largely the same purpose—namely, they both provide a mechanism to target a county's taxing power on those property owners who most directly benefit from the expenditure of the tax proceeds. Despite this, there is not an easy process to convert one type of taxing district into another type of taxing district or to modify the boundary lines between the different types of taxing districts.

Converting a Rural Fire Protection District to a County Fire Service District

Most often, counties wish to convert a rural fire protection district to a county fire service district (or transfer property from a rural fire protection district to a county fire service district) because the latter has fewer statutory restrictions. Territory in a rural fire protection district may not be transferred directly into a county fire service district. There are two methods, however, to accomplish this result indirectly. The first is to abolish the rural fire protection district according to the relevant statutory procedures and then establish one or more county fire service districts, again according to the relevant statutory procedures. The second is to overlay one or more county fire service districts over a rural fire protection district.

Under the latter option, a county's board of commissioners could continue to levy the rural fire protection district tax and also levy the county service district tax on real and personal properties located in both districts.[94] Alternatively, the governing board could cease levying the rural fire protection district tax and rely only on the service district tax to fund fire services in the area that is encompassed by both districts. Several counties have taken advantage of this second option in recent years. They have stopped levying taxes in some or all of their existing rural fire protection districts (without actually abolishing the districts) and they have established one or more county fire or rescue service districts in their place. The county service districts often have the same boundaries as the rural fire protection districts, but the new service district boundaries need not be co-extensive with the existing rural district boundaries.[95] Even if a county service district has the same boundaries as an existing rural fire protection district, the county establishes, maintains, and modifies the county service district according to the provisions set forth in G.S. Chapter 153A,

---

92. G.S. 153A-306. Notice of the public hearing must state the "date, hour and place of the hearing, and its subject." It must be published at least one week before the hearing. *Id.*

93. G.S. 153A-307 allows a county's governing board to determine whether or not to levy the service district tax, and at what rate, each fiscal year.

94. Note that a county service district may not contain territory in more than one county.

95. As discussed above, at least a few counties have created a single county fire service district that encompasses the entire unincorporated territory in the county.

Article 16 (not the provisions in G.S. Chapter 69, Article 3A). The county board, for example, is not limited to the statutory maximum tax rate (of $0.15 or $0.10 per $100 valuation) imposed on rural fire protection districts.

Converting a County Fire Service District to a Rural Fire Protection District

A county may overlay a county service district over an existing rural fire protection district, but it may not overlay a rural fire protection district over an existing county service district. G.S. 153A-304.2 provides that all or any portion of a fire service district that is annexed by a rural fire protection district immediately ceases to be a county fire service district or a part of a county fire service district. Although the statute is not entirely clear, it likely applies if an existing rural fire protection district annexes territory in a county fire service district according to the provisions in G.S. 69-25.11 and if a new rural fire protection district is created pursuant to G.S. 69-25.1 that encompasses territory in a county fire service district. Once the territory becomes part of a rural fire protection district, the county no longer has authority to levy a service district tax on the properties within the annexed territory. The properties in the annexed territory are subject instead to the rural fire district tax.[96]

Fees and Charges

Under general law, cities and counties do not have authority to impose fees on citizens or property owners to fund most fire protection services. Local units also do not have authority to assess fees on motor vehicle owners, drivers, or insurance companies to recoup the costs of responding to, and cleaning up after, accidents or other incidents. There are some limited exceptions, though. For example, local units have authority to charge fees to recoup costs associated with responding to and mitigating a hazardous materials emergency.[97] Cities and counties also have authority to impose reasonable fees and charges to fund their fire code inspection services. The North Carolina Supreme Court has held that local governments have inherent authority to recoup the costs of performing a regulatory function as long as the amounts collected are reasonable and do not exceed the aggregate (direct and indirect) expenses of performing the regulatory activity.[98] Counties are authorized to franchise ambulance operators and adopt a schedule of rates, fees, and charges to be imposed by those ambulance operators for emergency rescue services.[99]

Sanitary districts, on the other hand, have explicit authority to "apply service charges and rates based upon the exact benefits derived."[100] A sanitary district board may charge fees for responding to fires or providing other fire protection or rescue services. A district also may charge fees for some services and use property tax revenue to cover other fire protection costs.

---

96. The transfer of territory from a county fire service district to a rural fire protection district does not present much difficulty if it occurs at the beginning of a fiscal year. If the annexation occurs at a time other than the beginning of a fiscal year, however, the property owners in the affected territory likely will end up paying both the county fire district tax and the rural fire protection district tax for the fiscal year in which the annexation occurs. That is because, according to G.S. 153A-304.2(b), once the county board of commissioners levies the fire service district tax, property owners within the fire service district are responsible for paying the tax even if the property is subsequently annexed into a rural fire protection district. And, pursuant to G.S. 69-25.12, property owners whose properties are annexed into a rural fire protection district are responsible for paying the rural fire protection district tax as if the properties had been part of the district at the time the tax was levied.

97. *See* G.S. 166A-27.

98. *See* Homebuilders Ass'n of Charlotte v. City of Charlotte, 336 N.C. 37 (1994).

99. *See* G.S. 153A-250.

100. G.S. 130A-64.

Grant Funding

Although fire departments typically receive the majority of their funding from the local units where they provide services, most departments engage in additional fundraising efforts. They also routinely seek out grants to support projects, programs, and services. The state provides aid to volunteer fire departments and volunteer rescue and emergency medical services (EMS) units.

State Grant Programs

Volunteer Fire Department Fund

The General Assembly created the Volunteer Fire Department Fund, which authorizes the state's fire marshal to make grants to eligible fire departments.[101] To be eligible for a grant, a fire department must have no more than eight full-time paid members and be certified as serving a rated fire district by the North Carolina Office of the State Fire Marshal. A department may receive up to one $40,000 grant per fiscal year and requires a match for certain departments. Grants are awarded in May each year.

Volunteer Rescue/EMS Fund

The General Assembly also has established the Volunteer Rescue/EMS Fund, authorizing the state's fire marshal to make grants to eligible rescue or rescue/EMS units.[102] There are two types of grants—a matching grant of up to $25,000[103] and a nonmatching grant of up to $3,000. The grants may be used only for equipment purchases or other capital expenditures. To be eligible, a unit must have no more than ten full-time paid positions, must be recognized by the Office of the State Fire Marshal as a unit that provides rescue or EMS (or both) services in a particular district, and must be recognized by the Office of the State Fire Marshal having met the requirements of the North Carolina Association of Rescue Squads and EMS, Inc. Grants are awarded in December each year.

State Fire Protection Grant Fund

The purpose of the State Fire Protection Grant Fund is to compensate local fire departments for providing local fire protection to state-owned buildings and other state-owned property. The fund is administered by the DOI.[104]

Other Aid to Fire Departments

The state supplies targeted aid to fire and rescue personnel.[105] There are also numerous federal government and private grant opportunities for incorporated fire departments, particularly those that are staffed entirely or mainly with volunteers.[106]

---

101. *See* G.S. 58-87-1.

102. *See* G.S. 58-87-5.

103. If an applicant has $1,000 or less in liquid assets, it is not required to provide matching funds.

104. G.S. Chapter 58, Article 85A.

105. *See, e.g.*, G.S. Chapter 58, Article 84 (Local Firefighters' Relief Funds), Article 86 (North Carolina Firefighters' and Rescue Squad Workers' Pension Fund), Article 88 (Rescue Squad Workers' Relief Fund), Article 87 (Volunteer Safety Workers Assistance), and G.S. 58-87-10 (Workers' Compensation Fund for the benefit of certain safety workers).

106. The U.S. Fire Administration provides a list of grant opportunities at www.usfa.fema.gov/a-z/grants/(last visited March 28, 2024).

Insurance Districts and Ratings

Generally, there are two types of fire protection that are available to a property owner. The first is private fire protection, such as automatic sprinklers, automatic fire detection systems, and automatic extinguishing systems like those found in commercial property and other particularly hazardous areas. The second is normally referred to as public fire protection, which consists of a publicly supported fire department, a public water system, and a building inspection function. The availability of both private and public fire protection services to a real property parcel affects the ability of the property owner to procure property insurance and the cost of that insurance.

Counties are authorized to establish fire insurance districts within their unincorporated territories, with the approval of the Office of the State Fire Marshal of the North Carolina Department of Insurance.[107] The primary purpose of insurance districts, as their name suggests, is to delineate the fire protection coverage afforded to particular properties for purposes of determining whether those properties may be covered by fire insurance and at what cost.

The North Carolina commissioner of insurance and the state fire marshal are responsible for rating departments that serve areas with populations of 100,000 or less.[108] A private corporation, the Insurance Services Office, Inc. (ISO), rates departments that serve more populous areas. Insurance ratings are based on the staffing levels and apparatus of the fire department itself as well as on the applicable emergency response communication system and available water supply. A fire department that serves the properties within an insurance district is rated on a scale of 1 to 10, with 10 effectively constituting no fire protection for purposes of setting insurance rates. Thus, the minimum insurance grade for departments rated by the commissioner of insurance is 9S.

A secondary (and related) purpose of fire insurance districts is to delineate fire response areas for particular fire departments. Fire insurance district boundaries often are co-extensive with fire tax district boundaries. This allows for ease of administration by identifying a particular funding source for a particular set of services provided in a particular area by a particular service provider. Fire insurance districts are legally distinct from fire tax districts, though, and they do not have to have the same boundaries. There may be times when a county alters its insurance districts to account for new growth and development or new service providers, but it is not practical for it to change its existing tax districts. As a result of the change, an insurance district may cut across two or more tax districts. If properties in the insurance district are served by a single fire department, the county's (or rural district's) governing board may appropriate moneys from each of the tax districts to the fire department to provide services across the insurance district. A change in insurance district boundaries also may result in a tax district that comprises properties in two or more insurance districts. In this case, the county's (or rural district's) governing board may divvy up the district's tax proceeds and allocate them among the various fire departments that serve the tax district.

As described above, in recent years a handful of counties have officially (or unofficially) abolished their rural fire protection tax districts and established a single county fire service tax district that encompasses all the unincorporated territory in the county. These counties maintained their insurance districts, and they contract with multiple fire departments to serve the different insurance

107. G.S. 153A-233. The statute authorizes a county to "designate fire districts or parts of existing districts and prescribe the boundaries thereof for insurance grading purposes." There is no mention of approval by the state fire marshal. However, the North Carolina Department of Insurance requires that proposed insurance boundaries be submitted to the state fire marshal for approval. *See North Carolina Fire Service Reference Manual* (2017), ncsfa.com/wp-content/uploads/2020/01/Fire-Service-Reference-Manual-Update-2017.pdf (last visited March 28, 2024).

108. *See* G.S. 58-36-10(3) and -40-25(4).

districts. The counties' governing boards appropriate the service district tax revenue among the various fire departments according to their yearly budgetary needs.

Conclusion

Although no local unit is required to provide fire services to its citizens, fire protection has become one of the core local government services. Local governments in North Carolina have a variety of options for providing the array of fire protection and rescue services within their units. Most of the services are paid for with property tax proceeds—derived either from the general property tax or, increasingly, from special taxing districts.

Chapter 30

Public Enterprises

Kara A. Millonzi

Kara A. Millonzi is a School of Government faculty member who specializes in local government and public finance law.

Introduction

North Carolina counties and municipalities (collectively, local units) are authorized to engage in certain public enterprise activities.[1] A *public enterprise* is an activity of a commercial nature. When a local unit owns or operates a public enterprise, it acts in a proprietary capacity and has more flexibility to treat the enterprise like a private business venture than a traditional government function. Many public enterprises are funded with user charges and are self-supporting (or predominantly

This chapter reflects the law as of June 1, 2024.

1. As used in this book, the term "municipality" is synonymous with "city," "town," and "village." Note that, as discussed below, in addition to counties and municipalities, a handful of special-purpose local government entities also are authorized to provide certain public enterprise services.

self-supporting). That means that each year the local government generates enough income from the user charges to support the operating and capital expenses of the enterprise.

A local unit is not required to provide any public enterprise services. Further, if a local government chooses to provide one or more of the authorized public enterprises, it need not make them available to all citizens or property owners within the unit.[2] Generally, as long as it is not unlawfully discriminating, a local government can choose where, and under what circumstances, it will provide the services. If, however, a municipality involuntarily annexes property into its jurisdiction, the annexation triggers special statutory requirements regarding the provision of water and sewer services. Under certain circumstances, a municipality may be required to provide these services to newly annexed properties.[3]

Authorized Types of Public Enterprise Services

The most common types of public enterprises are water, sewer, and solid waste utility services, but the North Carolina General Statutes (hereinafter G.S.) authorize both counties and municipalities to operate public enterprises for all of the following purposes:

- water supply and distribution,
- sewage collection and treatment,
- solid waste collection and disposal,
- airports,
- public transportation,
- off-street parking, and
- stormwater-management programs and structural and natural stormwater and drainage systems.[4]

Municipalities are authorized also to operate enterprises for the following purposes:

- cable television (and broadband),[5]
- electric power generation and distribution, and
- gas production and distribution.[6]

Scope of Authority

Local government authority to operate public enterprises is broad—the statutes allow a county or municipality to "acquire, lease as lessor or lessee, construct, establish, enlarge, improve, extend,

2. *See* Ramsey v. Rollins, 246 N.C. 647 (1957).

3. *See* Frayda Bluestein, "Water and Sewer Extensions 'At No Cost'—Analyzing the New Annexation Law," *Coates' Canons: NC Local Government Law* blog (Aug. 2, 2011), canons.sog.unc.edu/2011/08/water-and-sewer-extensions-at-no-cost-analyzing-the-new-annexation-law/.

4. *See* Chapter 153A, Section 274 (counties) and Chapter 160A, Section 311 (municipalities) of the North Carolina General Statutes (hereinafter G.S.). Note that counties are authorized also to establish county water and sewer districts to provide water supply and distribution and sewage collection and treatment services. G.S. Chapter 162A, Article 6.

5. In *BellSouth Telecommunications, Inc. v. City of Laurinburg*, 168 N.C. App. 75 (2005), the North Carolina Court of Appeals held that the authority to provide cable television services included the authority to provide broadband services. Under G.S. 153A-459, counties have limited authority to provide grants to certain unaffiliated or nonprofit Internet providers to expand service in unserved areas.

6. *See* G.S. 160A-311.

maintain, own, operate, and contract for the operation of" the above-listed functions.[7] Subject to some limitations, a county and municipality may provide the enterprise services both inside and outside its territorial boundaries. A county may provide the services in its unincorporated and incorporated areas.[8]

The authority is not absolute, though. State law often imposes limitations on enterprise activities. For example, a unit of local government may not "displace" a private company that is providing collection services for solid waste or recycled materials without providing appropriate notice and waiting at least fifteen months or providing due compensation to the displaced company.[9] Displacement of a private provider occurs when a local government either (1) takes any formal action to prohibit a private company from providing all or a portion of the collection services that the company is providing in the affected area or (2) uses availability fee or tax revenue to fund competing collection services. Similarly, the General Assembly has significantly limited the authority of municipalities to provide cable television and broadband services in competition with the private sector.[10] And, as detailed below, state law limits the authority of local units to charge certain fees for enterprise activities.

Governments also must be careful not to exceed the scope of an authorized enterprise function. In *Smith Chapel Baptist Church v. City of Durham*,[11] the City of Durham had established a stormwater enterprise and assessed a fee on all properties within the unit. The fee revenue funded, among other things, educational programs and other outreach efforts associated with the city's comprehensive stormwater-management program. The city established the program to satisfy state and federal regulatory requirements. The North Carolina Supreme Court held that the city had exceeded its public enterprise authority when it used revenue generated from the stormwater fee to fund the stormwater-quality management program because the relevant statute at the time specified that a unit could establish a public enterprise only for structural and natural stormwater and drainage systems. Note that the General Assembly subsequently amended the statute to allow a unit to establish an enterprise to fund a comprehensive stormwater-quality management program.[12]

Interlocal Cooperation to Provide Enterprise Services

Counties and municipalities have largely coextensive authority to provide most public enterprise services. And, as discussed below, there are a handful of other local government entities authorized to provide certain public enterprise services, often on a regional basis. Two or more of these local governments may enter into interlocal agreements authorizing one unit to provide services to citizens in the other unit or authorizing the units to jointly engage in the provision of services.[13] An interlocal agreement is a contract that sets forth the terms or conditions of service and payment and, as long as it does not conflict with state or federal law, governs the parties' relationship. State

7. *See* G.S. 153A-275(a) (counties); 160A-312(a) (municipalities).

8. Note that a county does not need a municipality's governing board's permission to construct utility lines or other infrastructure within the municipal boundaries. The county may negotiate with private property owners to obtain the necessary easements and other property rights. A municipality, however, may use its franchise authority to limit a county's ability to provide utility services within the municipality or to prohibit it altogether. *See* G.S. 160A-319.

9. *See* G.S. 160A-327.

10. *See* G.S. Chapter 160A, Article 16A.

11. 350 N.C. 805 (1999).

12. *See* G.S. 160A-311 (municipalities); 153A-274 (counties); *see also* G.S. 160A-459; 153A-454.

13. *See* G.S. Chapter 160A, Article 20.

law limits a municipality to a forty-year contract for the supply of water and a thirty-year contract for the supply of other public enterprise services.[14] A county is not subject to the same term limits. Use of interlocal agreements to contract for water and sewer services between and among local governments is common practice. The Environmental Finance Center at the University of North Carolina has documented numerous interlocal agreements related to the provision of water and wastewater across the state.[15] The agreements represent a variety of interlocal structures, including joint provision of services, bulk water purchases, reserved capacity, and backup resources for emergency purposes only.

The authority to enter into interlocal agreements, however, applies only to the services that all parties to an agreement are allowed to provide. For example, a county could execute an interlocal agreement to provide solid waste services to one or more other counties or municipalities, but it could not contract with a municipality through an interlocal agreement related to the provision of cable television services, because only a municipality has authority to provide these services.

Franchise Agreements

In addition to interlocal agreement authority, a municipality also may enter into one or more franchise agreements with another government entity or a private entity[16] to provide any of the authorized public enterprise services (except cable television and broadband).[17] A county may enter into franchise agreements only for solid waste collection and disposal.[18] The franchise authority includes the ability to prohibit any government or private provider from furnishing a public enterprise service within a unit's territorial boundaries without a franchise. A municipal or county governing board may use a franchise agreement to impose reasonable terms of service on a provider, and except for solid waste, an agreement may authorize the operation of the franchised activity for up to sixty years.[19] (A solid waste franchise agreement may not exceed thirty years.)[20] As discussed below, the state's Local Government Commission (LGC) must approve certain franchise agreements that transfer or cede control of a public enterprise to a nongovernmental entity.[21]

Other Local Government Public Enterprise Service Providers

Counties and municipalities are not the only authorized government providers of public enterprises. There are a number of limited-purpose government entities that can provide one or more of the authorized public enterprise services. These other government entities often are created to serve regional populations that cut across municipal or county boundaries. For example, there are several

14. G.S. 160A-322.

15. *See* Environmental Finance Center, *Interactive Map of Community Water System Interconnections in North Carolina* (July 2015).

16. A privately owned public utility corporation may petition the state's Public Utilities Commission to provide services in a designated area. *See* G.S. Chapter 62, Article 6.

17. G.S. 160A-319.

18. G.S. 153A-136.

19. Note that if a municipality is providing the services to another municipality under a franchise agreement, it is subject to G.S. 160A-322, which limits the time periods for contracts for the provision of water services to forty years and the provision of other public enterprise utility services to thirty years.

20. G.S. 160A-319; 153A-136.

21. The requirements come from Part IV of S.L. 2023-138 and are codified in G.S. 159-154.

government entities that are authorized to provide water and sewer services: (1) counties or two or more political subdivisions (such as municipalities or sanitary districts) can organize water and sewer authorities;[22] (2) a county may establish a county water and sewer district;[23] (3) any two or more political subdivisions in a county can petition the board of commissioners to create a metropolitan water, sewer, or water and sewerage district;[24] and (4) the Commission for Health Services can create a sanitary district to operate sewage collection, treatment, and disposal systems and water supply systems for the purpose of preserving and promoting public health and welfare, without regard for county or municipal boundary lines.[25] (Sanitary districts also may provide solid waste collection, fire protection, recreation, and rescue services.) There also are parking authorities,[26] public transportation authorities,[27] regional natural gas districts,[28] regional solid waste management authorities,[29] and various airport authorities and commissions.[30] The authorities, districts, and commissions may serve customers within a county or municipality directly or may contract with the unit of local government to furnish the utilities.

Regulating Public Enterprises

Local Government Regulatory Authority

When public enterprise services are provided by counties and municipalities, or by the other local government entities listed above, they are *not* subject to regulation by the state's Public Utilities Commission. The Public Utilities Commission has jurisdiction only over privately owned utility companies (which, confusingly, are referred to as public utilities). The General Assembly has accorded a county or municipal board "full authority to protect and regulate any public enterprise system belonging to or operated by it by adequate and reasonable rules."[31] The rules must be adopted by ordinance and must apply throughout the area in which the public enterprise service is provided. (The limited-purpose government entities discussed in the section immediately above have similar authority with respect to the public enterprise service(s) they are authorized to provide.)

A local governing board may impose reasonable restrictions on who may connect to its public enterprise systems and how those connections are made. Furthermore, a unit may specify terms of continued service and may discontinue service to any customer if those conditions are not met. All regulations must be adopted by ordinance, and because most public enterprise services are provided under contract with a customer, regulations, restrictions, and other terms of service should be memorialized in a written contract as well. In fact, the more detailed the provisions in an enterprise service contract, the more protection afforded to a local government to deal with a customer who fails to live up to the terms of service.

---

22. *See* G.S. Chapter 162A, Article 1.
23. *See* G.S. Chapter 162A, Article 6.
24. *See* G.S. Chapter 162A, Articles 4, 5, and 5A.
25. *See* G.S. Chapter 130A, Article 2, Part 2.
26. *See* G.S. Chapter 160A, Article 24.
27. *See* G.S. Chapter 160A, Articles 25, 26, and 27.
28. *See* G.S. Chapter 160A, Article 28.
29. *See* G.S. Chapter 153A, Article 22.
30. *See* G.S. 63-4.
31. G.S. 160A-312(b); *see also* G.S. 153A-275(b).

Local Government Commission Oversight

The legislature has bestowed on the state's Local Government Commission (LGC) some oversight authority over the financial management of a county's, municipality's, or other local entity's water or sewer system. The LGC is a nine-member state body within the Department of State Treasurer that approves most local government borrowing transactions and issues bonds on behalf of local units.[32] The LGC monitors the fiscal health of local units in the state. It is empowered to "issue rules and regulations having the force of law governing procedures for the receipt, deposit, investment, transfer, and disbursement of money and other assets by units of local government. . . ."[33] The LGC also "may inquire into and investigate [a local unit's] internal control procedures" and issue warnings to units of any internal control deficiencies or violations of the Local Government Budget and Fiscal Control Act.[34]

Under certain circumstances, the LGC is empowered to take more drastic action, including assuming "full control of [a local unit's] financial affairs. . . ."[35] The LGC becomes "vested with all of the powers of the governing board as to the levy of taxes, expenditure of money, adoption of budgets, and all other financial powers conferred upon the governing board by law."[36]

The LGC may assume full control of a unit's water or sewer system and assume all powers of the governing board as to the operation of the public enterprise if the system, for three consecutive fiscal years, experiences negative working capital, has a quick ratio of less than 1.0, or experiences a net loss of revenue.[37] Working capital is defined as "current assets, such as cash, inventory, and accounts receivable, less current liabilities. . . ."[38] A quick ratio of less than 1.0 "means that the ratio of liquid assets, cash and receivables, to current liabilities is less than 1.0."[39] Before the LGC assumes full control of a local unit's public enterprise system, it must find that the financial stability of the unit is threatened and that the unit has failed to make corrective changes in its operation after having received notice and warning from the LGC.[40]

In October 2023, the legislature made certain public enterprise agreements subject to LGC approval.[41] The law compels LGC approval of any agreement in which a local government or public authority concedes or transfers control of a public enterprise that the local government owns or operates to a nongovernmental entity.[42] It also mandates that the local unit's governing board hold a public hearing on the agreement and make certain findings before proceeding.

32. G.S. Chapter 159, Article 2.
33. G.S. 159-25(c).
34. G.S. 159-25(c).
35. G.S. 159-181(c).
36. G.S. 159-181(c).
37. S.L. 2013-150.
38. S.L. 2013-150.
39. S.L. 2013-150.
40. S.L. 2013-150.
41. G.S. 159-154.
42. For public authorities, this law only applies to public enterprises authorized by G.S. Chapter 162A. These are water, wastewater, and stormwater services as provided by Article 1 (water and sewer authorities); Article 6 (county water and sewer districts); Article 4 (metropolitan water districts); Article 5 (metropolitan sewerage districts); and Article 5A (metropolitan water and sewerage districts). The law does not apply to other water and sewer providers, such as sanitary districts or those created by local act of the General Assembly, nor does it apply to public authorities carrying out other enterprise activities that are not listed in G.S. Chapter 162A.

LGC approval is not required of all public enterprise agreements, only those in which the local government or public authority *concedes or transfers control of all or a material portion of a public enterprise to a nongovernmental entity.* Let's take a closer look at what these terms mean:

Nongovernmental Entity. A nongovernmental entity includes any entity other than the State (or state agency), local government, public authority, or joint municipal power agency (formed pursuant to G.S. Chapter 159B).

Concede or Transfer. The new law does not define these terms. "Concede" likely means "to grant as a right or privilege"[43] the control of a public enterprise's operations and related decision-making. It may be a reference to concession agreements, whereby a private entity is given the right to operate a local government enterprise for a period of time and under specified conditions. "Transfer" likely refers to a local government giving up ownership or possession (or both) of public enterprise assets.

Control. The term "control" is defined in the law. It means that the private entity assumes any of the following as part of the agreement:

- The authority to expend or otherwise manage during any fiscal year more than 50 percent of a public enterprise's adjusted revenues. Adjusted revenues are gross revenues minus the cost of commodity purchases and wholesale electricity purchases, if applicable, for the public enterprise.
- Responsibility for provision to the public of the services previously provided by the public enterprise.
- Responsibility for operation and maintenance of a material portion of the assets and facilities of the public enterprise.
- The authority to manage a material portion of the staff responsible for operation and maintenance of the assets and facilities of the public enterprise.

Material Portion. Unfortunately, the new law does not define "material portion." And there is no universal or even analogous definition. The phrase is sometimes used in real property contracts, but it is defined specifically (and uniquely) by the parties to those contracts. Analyzing the new law as a whole, it seems reasonable to assume that a material portion would be represented by (1) an agreement to transfer more than 50 percent ownership of a public enterprise's assets/system, (2) a concession of more than 50 percent operational and maintenance responsibility for the public enterprise assets/services, or (3) a concession of the management of more than 50 percent of the public enterprise's staff. But what about an arrangement that involves less than 50 percent? It is hard to know. Factors a court might consider include the degree to which the private entity has decision-making authority over the operations and services provided by the public enterprise and/or how reliant the public enterprise is on the nongovernmental entity to be able to provide the enterprise services. A local unit must work with its attorney to make this determination.

Statutory Exemptions

The new law applies to a variety of public enterprise agreements—some involving partial or full sales of public enterprises to private entities and others involving operating agreements. But some public enterprise contracts that might otherwise fall under its purview are explicitly exempted from it—namely those that solely involve the maintenance of a public enterprise by a nongovernmental entity, regardless of the fee structure for the maintenance agreement. The sale of a public enterprise to a public utility regulated by the North Carolina Utilities Commission is also exempted, but other transactions involving transferring or conceding control (short of a full sale) to a regulated utility

43. "Concede," *Merriam-Webster* (2024).

are not. What about granting an operational franchise to a private entity? If the nature of the franchise agreement meets the definition of transferring or conceding control of the local unit's public enterprise, as discussed above, that agreement is subject to this law.

Requirements for Public Enterprise Arrangements

Before a local government or public authority executes a public enterprise agreement that transfers or concedes control to a nongovernmental entity, it must (1) hold a public hearing, (2) make certain findings, and (3) get LGC approval.

Public Hearing

The local unit's governing board must hold a public hearing on the proposed arrangement. Notice of the hearing, describing the agreement in general terms, must be published in a newspaper of general circulation in the county or counties in which the local unit is located at least ten days before the public hearing. The purpose of the hearing is to assist the governing board in determining whether the proposed arrangement is in the public interest.

Governing Board Findings and Approval

After the public hearing, the local unit's governing board may proceed only after adopting a resolution declaring that the proposed arrangement is in the public interest. In making this determination, the board must consider *all* of the following:

1. The physical condition of the public enterprise.
2. The capital replacements, additions, expansions, and repairs needed for the public enterprise to provide reliable service and meet all applicable federal standards.
3. The availability of federal and state grants and loans for system upgrades and repairs of the public enterprise.
4. The willingness and the ability of the nongovernmental entity to make system upgrades and repairs and provide high-quality and cost-effective service.
5. The reasonableness of the amount to be paid to the unit of local government to enter the arrangement.
6. The reasonableness of any amounts to be paid by the unit of local government to exit the arrangement.
7. The service quality guarantees provided by the arrangement and the consequences of any failure to satisfy the guarantees.
8. The most recent income and expense statement and asset and liabilities balance sheet of the nongovernmental entity and any consolidated nongovernmental entity.
9. The projected rates to customers of the public enterprise during the term of the arrangement and the affordability of the services of the public enterprise resulting from such projected rates.
10. The experience of the nongovernmental entity (and, if applicable, its affiliates within the consolidated nongovernmental entity) in the operation of utility systems similar to the public enterprise that is the subject of the arrangement.
11. The alternatives to entering the arrangement and the potential impact on utility customers if the arrangement is not entered.

Local units should record the governing board's findings addressing all these considerations as part of the written resolution or supporting documentation.

LGC Approval

Once the governing board adopts its resolution, the LGC may consider the proposed arrangement for approval. Like a bond issuance, the local government will apply to the LGC for approval and work with Department of State Treasurer staff to prepare the appropriate documentation and address any concerns. If a local unit is considering a public enterprise arrangement that requires LGC approval, it should contact staff as soon as possible to map out required steps and prepare and submit appropriate documents. For example, the LGC may require that the local unit engage a qualified independent expert to prepare projections or other analysis related to the proposed arrangement.

The LGC may only approve the proposed arrangement if it "finds and determines that the customers of the public enterprise will enjoy reasonable and material short-term and long-term savings and other net benefits from the arrangement during the term of the arrangement without the imposition of any material cost or charge on the [local government or public authority] or its customers upon termination of the arrangement."[44]

The LGC may consider any of the following in making its determination (this is a non-exclusive list):

1. The projected financial feasibility of the proposed arrangement in the short-term and long-term, its effect on rates to be charged to the customers of the public enterprise under the arrangements being proposed, and its effect on the quality of services to be provided by the public enterprise under the arrangement.
2. The projected rates to customers of the public enterprise during the term of the arrangement, the basis for the establishment of such rates and the reasonableness of the basis, and the affordability of the services of the public enterprise resulting from such projected rates.
3. If the unit of local government will receive an initial payment for participating in the arrangement, a summary of the unit of local government's proposed plans for the use of the initial payment.
4. If there is any indebtedness of the unit of local government associated with the public enterprise, the plans for the retirement or defeasance of such indebtedness.
5. The financial condition of the nongovernmental entity and its affiliates within the consolidated nongovernmental entity and its ability to carry out the undertakings required of the nongovernmental entity in the arrangement.
6. The experience of the nongovernmental entity and its affiliates within the consolidated nongovernmental entity in the operation of utility systems similar to the public enterprise that is the subject of the arrangement.
7. The nongovernmental entity's plans to finance its initial participation in the arrangement and future improvements to the public enterprise and the expected participation of the unit of local government in any financing.
8. The obligations of the nongovernmental entity set forth in the agreement for the maintenance of the public enterprise and the installation of improvements to the public enterprise during the term of the arrangement and the requirements of the agreement that adequate reserves be maintained during the term of the arrangement for such maintenance and improvements.
9. The plans set forth in the agreements for the arrangement for maintaining the quality of the components of the public enterprise to be returned to the control of the unit of local government at the end of the term of the agreement.

44. G.S. 159-154(e).

10. Any ongoing financial and other commitments of the unit of local government under the arrangement during its term.
11. Any financial payments the unit of local government is expected to be required to pay to the nongovernmental entity or any other person or entity at the end of the arrangement.
12. The effect, if any, of the arrangement on the tax status of interest on debt obligations issued by the unit of local government or by any other units of local government on account of contractual arrangements it may have with the unit of local government proposing the agreement under consideration.

The LGC must then issue an order approving or denying the application.

LGC Approval of Amendments to or Termination of an Approved Arrangement

A local government unit must also get LGC approval (following a similar process) of any material amendments to the originally approved arrangement or of a proposed termination of the arrangement prior to its stated end period, unless the termination is for breach of contract.

Mandating Participation in Public Enterprise Services

Water and Sewer Enterprises

Under certain circumstances, a county or municipal governing board may mandate that a property owner connect his or her property to the local unit's water and/or sewer system and may fix the charges for the connections.

County-Mandated Water Connections

A county may require the owner of any property that is developed with one or more residential or commercial units, and that is located within a reasonable distance of the unit's water lines, to connect, unless the property has a valid well permit.[45]

County-Mandated Sewer Connections

A county may require the owner of any property that is developed with one or more residential or commercial units, and that is located within a reasonable distance of the unit's sewer lines, to connect, as long as the county has adequate capacity to transport and treat proposed new wastewater from those premises at the time of connection.[46]

Municipality-Mandated Water Connections

A municipality may require the owner of any property to connect to its water system only if *all* of the following criteria are met:

- The property is within municipal limits.
- The property is developed with one or more residential or commercial units.
- The property is located within a reasonable distance of a water line owned, leased, or operated by the municipality or on behalf of the municipality.

---

45. G.S. 153A-284. "In accordance with G.S. 87-97.1, when developed property is located so as to be served by a county water line and the property owner has connected to that water line, the property owner may continue to use any private water well located on the property for nonpotable purposes as long as the water well is not interconnected to the county water line and the county shall not require the owner of any such water well to abandon, cap, or otherwise compromise the integrity of the water well." *Id.*

46. *Id.*

- Adequate water pressure can be achieved using the same piping size as the meter provides to the owner's premises. Adequate water pressure means the average water pressure delivered to all connected customers within a quarter-mile radius in either direction of the owner's point of connection. To establish adequacy or inadequacy, the property owner shall submit to the city a determination prepared by a professional engineer, licensed in accordance with the provisions of G.S. Chapter 89C.[47]

Municipality-Mandated Sewer Connections

A municipality may require the owner of any property to connect to its sewer system only if all of the following criteria are met:

- The property is within municipal limits.
- The property is developed with one or more residential or commercial units.
- The property is located within a reasonable distance of a sewer line owned, leased, or operated by or on behalf of the municipality.
- The municipality has adequate capacity to transport and treat proposed new wastewater from the premises at the time of connection.
- The costs of connection (including underground piping and connections to unit) do not exceed the costs of installing an on-site sewer system. Comparative costs must be performed by: (1) a licensed soil scientist, as defined in G.S. 89F-3, (2) an on-site wastewater contractor certified under Article 5 of G.S. Chapter 90A, or (3) a plumbing contractor licensed under Article 2 of G.S. Chapter 87. (It is unclear whether the municipality or property owner pays for the cost comparison.)

Sanitary districts and some water and sewer authorities also have similar authority.[48]

Well Permits

A local government unit *must* issue a permit for a drinking water well if

1. the property is undeveloped or unimproved, even if the property could be served by a government water system or[49]
2. the property is developed or improved **and** (a) a government water system has not yet installed water lines that are directly available to the property **or** (b) the government water system cannot provide water service to the property at the time the property owner desires service.[50]

As noted above, if a property owner has a permitted, functioning drinking water well, a local unit may not mandate connection to the unit's water system.[51]

---

47. G.S. 160A-317. Note that when developed property is located so as to be served by a municipal water line and the property owner has connected to that water line, "the property owner may continue to use any private water well located on the property for nonpotable purposes as long as the water well is not interconnected to the city water line and the city shall not require the owner of any such water well to abandon, cap, or otherwise compromise the integrity of the water well." *Id.*

48. G.S. 130A-55(16) (sanitary districts); G.S. 162A-6(a)(14d) (authority to mandate connections applies only to water and sewer authorities whose membership includes all or part of a county with a population of at least 40,000).

49. G.S. 87-97.2(a).

50. G.S. 87-97.2(b).

51. *See* G.S. 87-97.2(c). The same limitations apply to water systems owned or operated by water and sewer authorities and sanitary districts.

However, even if a property owner has a permit for a drinking water well, there are a few situations in which a local unit may mandate connection to the unit's water system.[52] Under G.S. 87-97.2, a government utility may still require a property for which a permit has been issued to connect to its water system if one or more of the following apply:

1. "The private drinking water well serving the property has failed and cannot be repaired." The statute does not specify who determines whether or not the well can be repaired. It is up to the government utility to establish a process for verifying the functionality of each private drinking well.
2. "The property is located in an area where the drinking water removed by the private drinking water well is contaminated or likely to become contaminated due to nearby contamination." This determination is made or confirmed by the local health department.
3. Operation of the government utility "is being assisted by" the LGC. The statute does not define the circumstances under which the LGC would be deemed to be assisting the government utility. Arguably, all local governments and public authorities are assisted to some extent by the LGC, inasmuch as the LGC monitors the fiscal health of each unit by reviewing its annual audit. But to read "assisted by" this broadly would cause the exception to swallow the rule. It is likely, therefore, that the legislature intended the phrase to mean something more.

It is possible that for purposes of this statute, "assisted by" means that the LGC has issued debt on behalf of the government utility. When a local government or public authority borrows money through general obligation bonds, revenue bonds, special obligation bonds, or project-development bonds, it is the LGC that actually issues the bonds. Even this interpretation of "assisted by," however, seems broader than what the legislature likely intended.

In an extreme case, the LGC has the authority to impound the books and records associated with a government utility, assume full control of all its affairs, or take any other actions deemed necessary by the LGC to deal with a government utility that is in financial trouble.[53] Thus, "assisted by" could refer only to situations in which the LGC takes action under this statute or when it compels a government utility to make its debt-service payments pursuant to G.S. 159-36. That seems too restrictive of an interpretation, though. If the legislature intended this result, it could simply have stated that the exception applies only when the LGC takes action under G.S. 159-181 or 159-36. Instead, by using the phrase "assisted by," it appears that the legislature intended for the exception to apply to a broader set of circumstances.

In fact, viewing the exception in the context of the whole statute, it is likely that the legislature intended it to apply when a government utility is in financial trouble, or on the verge of financial trouble, such that prohibiting the utility from mandating connections might affect the utility's continued viability. Thus, I think the most likely interpretation of "assisted by" is that the LGC has placed the unit on its Unit Assistance List.[54]

---

52. *See* G.S. 87-97.2(e).

53. *See* G.S. 159-181(c).

54. The Unit Assistance List (UAL) is developed by LGC staff to assist in prioritizing the allocation of staff resources, developing guidance and resources for units, and engaging in enhanced fiscal monitoring. The list is published periodically throughout the year based on audited financial statements and associated data submitted to the LGC as required under G.S. 159-34(a). It identifies units (1) with concerns related to units' general fund, water/sewer quick ratio, income, cash flow, and internal controls or (2) that have not yet submitted their audited financial statements (due four months following the end of the fiscal year).

Solid Waste Enterprise

A municipality also has authority to compel certain property owners to participate in the municipality's solid waste collection service. If a property owner has not contracted for solid waste collection services with a private hauler or another government hauler, a municipality may require that the property owner use the municipality's hauler. (A municipality may collect the solid waste itself or contract with one or more private or government haulers to act on its behalf.) A county does not have analogous authority. And neither a municipality nor a county may require that a property owner participate in the local unit's collection of recyclables.[55]

Using Public Enterprise Authority to Enforce Other Laws and Regulations

Questions often arise about whether a local unit may use its relationship with public enterprise customers to enforce other state or local rules or requirements. For example, if a unit provides water services to a customer who has not paid his or her property taxes, may the local government discontinue the water services until the property taxes are satisfied? Or may a unit refuse to provide sewer services to a business that is operating without a required privilege license or to one that is not in compliance with the fire code? The answer to all these questions is "no." That is because when a local government owns, operates, or contracts for the provision of public enterprise services, it is acting in a proprietary capacity (as opposed to a governmental capacity).[56] The North Carolina Supreme Court has distinguished between the two functions as follows:

> Any activity . . . which is discretionary, political, legislative or public in nature and performed for the public good in behalf of the State, rather than to itself, comes within the class of governmental functions. When, however, the activity is commercial or chiefly for the private advantage of the compact community, it is private or proprietary.[57]

The North Carolina Supreme Court has held that a local government must not comingle its proprietary and governmental functions. Specifically, in *Dale v. City of Morganton*,[58] the court specified that the municipality's right to refuse a service it renders in its capacity as a public enterprise utility provider must be determined separately from the functions it performs in its role as a unit of local government. In that case, the municipality had supplied electricity and water to a certain house in a newly annexed area but later inspected the dwelling and found it unfit for human habitation. It subsequently cut off the electrical supply to the house and refused to reconnect the service. In its review of a challenge to the municipality's actions, the court concluded that a municipality could

---

55. *See* G.S. 153A-136(a)(6) (counties); 160A-317(b)(3) (municipalities). Recyclables are defined in G.S. 130A-290(a)(24). Note that a municipality and a county may prohibit a property owner from placing recyclables within solid waste that is disposed of in the local unit's disposal facilities. *See* G.S. 153A-136; 160A-317.

56. This distinction has two significant consequences. The first is that it allows a government more flexibility to operate a public enterprise like a private business entity. A local government must continue to operate within the confines of statutory authority, but often that authority is much broader in the public enterprise context, affording a unit much discretion in setting service terms. The second is that it may raise liability issues. When a local unit acts in a governmental capacity, it generally is immune from civil liability for torts arising out of the negligence of the unit's employees when acting within the scope of their employment. The state does not grant governmental immunity to a local government when it acts in a proprietary capacity.

57. Millar v. Town of Wilson, 222 N.C. 340 (1942).

58. 270 N.C. 567 (1967).

not deprive an inhabitant "otherwise entitled thereto, of light, water or other utility service as a means of compelling obedience to its police regulations, however valid and otherwise enforceable those regulations may be."[59]

There is an apparent exception to this general principle, and that is when a municipality uses its public enterprise authority to compel voluntary annexation. Municipalities generally are authorized to provide utility services outside their territorial boundaries. They are under no obligation to do so, though. A municipality is free to negotiate with utility customers outside municipal borders and to define by contract the conditions under which services will be provided and the terms of those services. Some municipalities agree to provide utility services to "outside" properties only if the property owners contractually agree to voluntarily petition for annexation into the municipality when future criteria are met. The North Carolina Court of Appeals has held that a municipality had authority to cease providing wastewater services to a customer located outside the municipality's territorial boundaries because the property owner refused to honor its contractual commitment to voluntarily annex the property into the city limits.[60]

Funding Public Enterprises

User Fee Authority

As stated above, public enterprises tend to be funded primarily by the collection of user fees. Both counties and municipalities, as well as most of the other local government utilities, have the same authority to impose "schedules of rents, rates, fees, charges, and penalties for the use of or the services furnished or to be furnished, by a public enterprise."[61] This authority is very broad. And the fees may be assessed on all users of the enterprise services, regardless of their property status. Unlike with property taxes, there are no statutory exemptions from paying user fees for government property or property used for educational, charitable, or religious purposes.[62] The authority is not limitless, though. State law imposes restrictions on the types of upfront charges that may be assessed on new development.[63]

Units almost always assess periodic (monthly or bimonthly) user charges on public enterprise service customers to fund operational elements of an enterprise system. The periodic charges usually

---

59. 270 N.C. at 573.

60. U.S. Cold Storage, Inc. v. Town of Warsaw, 246 N.C. App. 781, 788 (2016) (Hunter, J., dissenting). In a dissenting opinion, Judge Robert Hunter Jr. argued that *Dale v. City of Morganton* prohibited the town from discontinuing wastewater service "on the basis of a collateral dispute" not related to the provision of utility service.

61. *See, e.g.*, G.S. 153A-277 (counties); 160A-314 (municipalities).

62. Note that a local government may have difficulty collecting stormwater fees from certain state entities. That is because unlike other enterprises, a unit need not have a contractual agreement with a "customer" before imposing a stormwater fee. The fee may be imposed on all real properties within the unit. Several state agencies have argued that they are shielded from paying the stormwater fee under the doctrine of sovereign immunity in the absence of a written contractual agreement with the local government.

63. *See* S.L. 2017-138. For more information on these limitations, see the following blog posts by the author (Kara A. Millonzi): "System Development Fees Are the New Impact Fees," *Coates' Canons: NC Local Government Law* blog (Aug. 15, 2017), canons.sog.unc.edu/2017/08/system-development-fees-new-impact-fees/; "2018 System Development Fee Law Changes," *Coates' Canons: NC Local Government Law* blog (June 26, 2018), canons.sog.unc.edu/2018/06/2018-system-development-fee-law-changes/; "Assessing System Development Fees (SDFs): It's All About the Timing," *Coates' Canons: NC Local Government Law* blog (Apr. 12, 2021), canons.sog.unc.edu/2021/04/assessing-and-collecting-system-development-fees-sdfs-its-all-about-the-timing/; "2023 Updates to System Development Fee Law," *Coates' Canons: NC Local Government Law* blog (Oct. 25, 2023), canons.sog.unc.edu/2023/10/2023-updates-to-system-development-fee-law/.

constitute a variable component based on actual usage as well as a fixed component to cover operating and capital overhead costs. Many local governments also have implemented various block-rate fee structures—either charging increased (increasing-block) or decreased (decreasing-block) rates based on additional units of usage of an enterprise service. In addition, local units have targeted revenue-generating options for certain public enterprise capital projects, such as special assessments,[64] critical-infrastructure assessments,[65] special taxing districts, and system-development fees.[66] Finally, most local governments have categorized consumers into various classes for purposes of setting rate schedules that closely track the costs of providing the enterprise services.

User fee schedules are influenced by the policy prerogatives of a local government's governing board. Consequently, the numbers and types of classifications vary greatly among North Carolina's counties and municipalities. A local government that wishes to promote conservation may impose a different rate structure from that of a local unit hoping to foster commercial or industrial development. Municipalities also may configure rates so as to encourage or discourage annexation of extraterritorial property.

User-Fee Rate Classifications

A unit may establish service classifications for purposes of charging different rates to different customer groups.[67] These classifications are subject to the common law of utilities, though.[68] Under the common law, different rate classifications may reflect differences in the costs of providing services to certain customer groups. In addition, rate classifications may be "based upon such factors as . . . the purpose for which the service or the product is received, the quantity or the amount received, the different character of the service furnished, the time of its use or any other matter which presents a substantial ground of distinction."[69] In other words, courts have upheld classifications for purposes of assessing different utility rates when there is a utility-based reason for the differentiation. However, classifications based on the type—or status—of the customer, or customer group, that do not relate to one of the above-listed purposes are not valid. For example, a local unit may assess a different rate for water used for irrigation purposes than for household or other commercial purposes (classification based on the purpose for which the water is used), but it cannot charge a different rate to all farmers (classification based on status). A unit may vary its sewer rates based on the size of a house or the number of bathrooms (proxies for different costs or capacity demands), but it may not charge a different rate based on customer income levels (classification based on status). A unit may charge all its commercial customers a solid waste collection fee rate that is different from the rate it charges residential customers (proxy for different capacity demands), but it may not charge a different rate to all churches or all nonprofit organizations (classification based on status). And a unit may assess a different rate to customers who request service after a certain date (again, proxies for different costs or capacity demands), but it may not set rates based on the age of its customers (classification based on status).

---

64. *See* G.S. Chapter 153A, Article 9 (counties); Chapter 160A, Article 10 (municipalities).

65. *See* G.S. Chapter 153A, Article 9A (counties); Chapter 160A, Article 10A (municipalities).

66. *See* G.S. Chapter 153A, Article 16 (counties); Chapter 160A, Article 23 (municipalities); Chapter 162A, Article 8 (all government utilities).

67. G.S. 160A-314 (municipalities); 153A-277 (counties).

68. For more information on utility ratemaking, see the following bulletins by the author (Kara A. Millonzi): "Lawful Discrimination in Utility Ratemaking, Part 2: Classifying Extraterritorial Customers," *Local Finance Bulletin* No. 34 (Oct. 1, 2006); "Lawful Discrimination in Utility Ratemaking, Part 1: Classifying Customers within Territorial Boundaries," *Local Finance Bulletin* No. 33 (Oct. 1, 2006).

69. *See* Wall v. City of Durham, 41 N.C. App. 649 (1979).

One further statutorily sanctioned rate differentiation is between customers located within a unit's territorial boundaries and customers residing outside these boundaries. This authority applies to all public enterprise activities, though it is used primarily for water and sewer services. Counties and municipalities typically assess higher fees on extraterritorial customers. For municipalities, the rate differential often serves as an incentive for voluntary incorporation by customers in surrounding unincorporated communities.

Special Limitations on User-Fee Rates

The law imposes a few additional limitations on user-fee rates for certain public enterprise services. For stormwater services, the fees assessed by a local government unit may not exceed the costs of the unit's stormwater-management program. Fee schedules must apply throughout the unit and may vary only

> according to whether the property served is residential, commercial, or industrial property, the property's use, the size of the property, the area of impervious surfaces on the property, the quantity and quality of the runoff from the property . . . the characteristics of the watershed into which stormwater from the property drains, and other factors that affect the stormwater drainage system.[70]

Both counties and municipalities have authority to impose three different types of solid waste fees—collection fees, disposal use fees, and availability fees.[71] Each fee may be charged only under certain circumstances. And the aggregate revenue from each fee may not exceed the costs of providing the specific solid waste services for which the fee is authorized.[72]

Process for Adopting Public Enterprise User Fees

Generally, the process for adopting public enterprise fees is simple. The governing board of a local unit sets the fees in its annual budget ordinance or in a separate ordinance. With a few exceptions, there are no notice, public hearing, or other formal public comment requirements. The governing board also is free to change the fees at any time during the fiscal year.

There are additional procedural requirements for adopting a stormwater fee. The governing board must hold a public hearing and provide sufficient notice of that hearing.[73] There also are added procedural requirements for water and sewer charges that apply to new subdivision development. Unless the applicable fees are adopted in the unit's annual budget ordinance, the unit must give notice of the fees and provide an opportunity for public comment.[74] Finally, a separate set of procedural requirements applies to the adoption of water and wastewater system-development fees.[75]

General Fund Subsidies for Certain Utility Customers

Note that there are methods by which a local government may accomplish a purpose similar to discounting public enterprise rates, at least for certain customer groups. First, counties and municipalities are to "undertake programs for the assistance and care of [their] senior citizens" (defined

70. G.S. 153A-277; 160A-314.

71. *See* G.S. 153A-292; 160A-314.1.

72. For more information on solid waste fees, see Kara Millonzi, "Funding Solid Waste Services," *Coates' Canons: NC Local Government Law* blog (Oct. 7, 2010; updated 2013), canons.sog.unc.edu/2010/10/funding-solid-waste-services/.

73. G.S. 160A-314; 153A-277.

74. G.S. 160A-4.1; 153A-102.1.

75. *See* G.S. Chapter 162A, Article 8.

as citizens who are at least sixty years of age).[76] Under this authority, a county or municipality may establish a utility rate subsidy program for its senior citizens. The program must be established in the unit's general fund (not its enterprise fund) but can be structured in a number of different ways. For example, the program may authorize a unit to transfer moneys from the general fund to the enterprise fund to pay all or a portion of a qualifying senior citizen's utility bill. It also may set up a reimbursement system for utility customers from the general fund. In addition, a county or municipality may apply a rate subsidy program to all its senior citizens, or it may limit the program to senior citizens at or below a certain income level or senior citizens who are disabled.

Second, counties and municipalities may undertake community-development programs "concerned with . . . welfare needs of persons of low and moderate income."[77] Under this authority, a local unit likely may establish a utility rate subsidy program similar to the one described above but for low- or moderate-income citizens. Again, the unit must use general fund moneys, not enterprise fund proceeds, to fund the subsidy program. Although the authorizing statute does not expressly define "low or moderate income," it does reference the Housing Authorities Law (G.S. Chapter 157, Article 1) and, by extension, local officials can reasonably employ the definitions of "persons of low income" and "persons of moderate income" found in that law (G.S. 157-3) when interpreting the statute's scope. Local officials might also consult the Section 8 income limits established by the federal Department of Housing and Urban Development for guidance in determining qualifying income limits.

Third, G.S. 158-7.1 provides broad authority for counties and municipalities "to make appropriations for economic development purposes." Under this authority, as part of a properly structured economic-development incentive, a local government may provide a cash grant to a prospective commercial or industrial entity that reimburses the entity for all, or for a portion, of its utility fees over a period of time.[78] A unit also may fund the extension of utility lines or facilities to serve the entity. Again, appropriations for such incentive programs should derive from the general fund, not an enterprise fund.

Additional Financing Sources

In addition to imposing user fees, a local government is authorized to finance the cost of any public enterprise "by levying taxes, borrowing money, and appropriating any other revenues therefor, and by accepting and administering gifts and grants from any source on behalf thereof."[79] For accounting purposes, enterprise services often are budgeted and accounted for in an enterprise fund, whereas general government activities and revenues are accounted for in the general fund.[80] Local governments are free to transfer any property tax proceeds or unrestricted revenues from the general fund to an enterprise fund to finance the capital or operating costs of an enterprise activity.

---

76. G.S. 160A-497.

77. G.S. 160D-1311(a)(2) (formerly contained within G.S. 153A-376 and 160A-456).

78. For more information on legal economic-development incentive options, see the following blog posts by UNC School of Government faculty member Tyler Mulligan: "Local Government Economic Development Powers 'Clarified,'" *Coates' Canons: NC Local Government Law* blog (Oct. 26, 2015), canons.sog.unc.edu/2015/10/local-government-economic-development-powers-clarified/; "When May NC Local Governments Pay an Economic Development Incentive?," *Coates' Canons: NC Local Government Law* blog (Dec. 17, 2013), canons.sog.unc.edu/2013/12/when-may-nc-local-governments-pay-an-economic-development-incentive/.

79. G.S. 160A-313; *see also* G.S. 153A-276.

80. *See* G.S. 159-26. If a local unit funds an enterprise service exclusively with property tax proceeds, or with other general fund revenues, it may budget for the services in the general fund.

Transferring Moneys from an Enterprise Fund to the General Fund

What about transferring moneys the other way? May a unit transfer funds from an enterprise fund to the general fund? The answer is a little more complicated. There are two types of transfers. The first is a transfer of funds from the enterprise fund to the general fund to reimburse the general fund for administrative overhead expenses to support a public enterprise activity, such as covering a portion of the unit's manager's and finance officer's salaries (which are paid out of the general fund). A reimbursement is allowed to the extent that it represents actual expenses incurred (or reasonable approximations thereof) on behalf of the public enterprise. (Note that for accounting and financial reporting purposes a local unit should refer to these appropriations as "reimbursements," not "transfers.")

The second type of transfer involves using revenue generated by a public enterprise activity to support other general government programs and functions. As to this type of transfer, G.S. 159-13 specifies that

> [n]o appropriation may be made from a utility or public service enterprise fund to any other fund than the appropriate debt service fund unless the total of all other appropriations in the fund equal or exceed the amount that will be required during the fiscal year, as shown by the budget ordinance, to meet operating expenses, capital outlay, and debt service on outstanding utility or enterprise bonds or notes.[81]

Although the statute is written as a prohibition, it actually allows a local government to transfer moneys from an enterprise fund to the general fund to support general government functions as long as all of the enterprise activity expenses that will come due during the fiscal year are covered. In essence, it allows a unit to transfer profits generated by the enterprise activity to the general fund to supplement other general fund revenue sources.

There are some limits to the authority to transfer money from an enterprise fund. The authority to transfer must be read in conjunction with the authority to set rates for the particular enterprise service. There are a few enterprise activities for which the ratemaking authority of a local unit's governing board is much more constrained. And those constraints affect the unit's ability to appropriate or loan money from an enterprise fund. For example, solid waste fees must be used only to fund solid waste activities.[82] In *Manning v. County of Halifax*,[83] the North Carolina Court of Appeals held that the county's practice of setting solid waste availability fees such that the aggregate revenue generated exceeded the aggregate costs of operating the county's disposal facilities was unlawful. And the reason the court knew that the fee revenue exceeded the costs of the solid waste program was that the county had transferred the "profit" from the solid waste fund to the general fund and used the money to support general government activities.

In determining whether or not a transfer from an enterprise fund is lawful, a unit must first examine any earmarks on the money being transferred. If the money itself may be spent only to support the enterprise activity, it may not be appropriated or loaned to another fund to pay for an unrelated expenditure. Thus revenue from solid waste fees may be transferred to the general fund or to the debt-service fund to make debt-service payments on a borrowing incurred for a solid waste project. It may be moved to the general fund to cover legitimate reimbursements for services provided to the solid waste enterprise but financed in the general fund. The revenue, however, may not be appropriated to the transportation fund to purchase a new bus. It may not be appropriated

---

81. G.S. 159-13(b)(14).
82. *See* G.S. 160A-314.1, -317 (municipalities); 153A-292 (counties).
83. 166 N.C. App. 279 (2004).

to the general fund to pay for community park improvements. And it may not be loaned to the general fund to help balance the current year's budget.[84]

In addition to the statutory earmark on solid waste fees, state law requires stormwater-fee revenue to be used only to support stormwater management.[85] And transfers from the electric system funds of certain municipalities may not exceed the greater of (1) 3 percent of the gross capital assets of the electric system or (2) 5 percent of the gross annual revenues of the preceding fiscal year.[86] There may also be restrictions imposed on other enterprise revenue by contract, bond covenants, local acts, or grant agreements. None of these restrictions prohibits a local unit from using the enterprise revenue to compensate the general fund for any reasonable overhead expenses allocated to the enterprise activity. But they do constrain a unit's ability to transfer money from the enterprise fund.

Even if legally allowed, a local unit should carefully consider whether a transfer from an enterprise fund (by means of an appropriation or loan) is appropriate. Transfers that occur frequently, or that involve a large amount of money, might be masking a problem with the unit's financial condition. Relying on enterprise ratepayers to fund general government expenditures also may raise issues of equity, fairness, and accountability. This argument resonates particularly in jurisdictions where ratepayers compose only a subset of taxpayers of the unit or where ratepayers come from outside the unit's territorial boundaries. Moreover, this practice could have negative financial implications for the unit, particularly related to issuing debt. Credit-rating agencies are likely to look unfavorably upon any effort that destabilizes an enterprise fund.

In recent years, the General Assembly has indicated that it strongly disfavors transfers from an enterprise fund. In 2014, it enacted G.S. 159G-37(b), which prohibits a local government from receiving loans or grants for water or wastewater purposes from the Clean Water State Revolving Fund (CWSRF), Wastewater Reserve, Drinking Water State Revolving Fund (DWSRF), or Drinking Water Reserve if the unit has transferred money from its water or sewer enterprise fund to the general fund to supplement the resources of the general fund. The prohibition applies only to transfers. It does not apply to legitimate reimbursements of the general fund for "expenses paid from that fund that are reasonably allocable to the regular and ongoing operations of the utility, including, but not limited to, rent and shared facility costs, engineering and design work, plan review, and shared personnel costs."[87]

The statutory language, however, does not contain a specific time period limitation on transfers. The Department of Environmental Quality requires that a local unit certify that it has not transferred funds from an enterprise fund since the law's effective date, July 1, 2014.[88]

---

84. A municipality that has a fund balance in its solid waste fund that exceeds the costs of funding a landfill, including closure and post-closure costs, may transfer excess funds accruing due to the imposition of a surcharge imposed on another local government in the state to the municipality's general fund to support other services. *See* G.S. 160A-314(a2) (municipalities).

85. *See* G.S. 160A-314(a1)(2) (municipalities); 153A-277(a1)(2) (counties).

86. G.S. 159B-39.

87. G.S. 159G-37(b).

88. *See* N.C. Department of Environmental Quality, Division of Water Infrastructure, Fund Transfer Certification form (rev. June 2019).

Collection Methods for Public Enterprise Revenues

Because most public enterprise services are voluntary, they often are governed by an express or implied contract between the government and each enterprise customer. And it is the contracting party that the government must look to for payment for enterprise services. Sometimes payment is collected before services are rendered. In many cases, however, and particularly for utility services, customers are billed after the services are received. What happens when a customer fails to pay? The following collection remedies are at a local unit's disposal.

Disconnecting Services

A local unit generally may disconnect public enterprise services at the property or premises where the delinquency occurred.[89] A county- or municipal-owned or -operated enterprise must wait ten days from the date the account becomes delinquent to suspend service. If a government operates more than one public enterprise and includes the fees for multiple public enterprises on the same bill, its governing board may adopt an ordinance ordering partial payments. That means that if a customer does not satisfy the bill in full for all enterprise services, the governing board determines which fees are paid first, and a unit may disconnect any services that remain unpaid (after the ten-day waiting period). Typically, a unit organizes payments such that water service is paid for last because it is more essential than other public enterprise services.

Civil Suit

A local unit may institute a civil suit against the contracting party to recover the amounts owed. The statute of limitations for collecting delinquent water, electric, and natural gas payments is four years.[90] The statute of limitations for collecting delinquent sewer, cable television, stormwater, and solid waste payments is three years.[91] The statute of limitations is the time period during which the unit must institute suit in order to collect on the debt.

Debt Set-Off

Another option for a local unit seeking to collect on a delinquent public enterprise service account is to submit the claim to the state's debt set-off program for recovery against the contracting party's state income tax return or state lottery winnings, if any.[92] The amount owed must exceed $50 to be eligible for debt set-off, and the unit must follow the detailed statutory procedural requirements to participate in the program.

Prohibited Collection Methods

A local utility provider is legally prohibited from taking some collection actions. A local government may not place a lien on the property where enterprise services are provided. It also may not hold

---

89. G.S. 153A-277(b); 160A-314(b). A water and sewer authority must wait thirty days. G.S. 162A-9. Note that if a customer has filed for bankruptcy, a utility provider may not disconnect service, at least for a period of time. *See* 11 U.S.C. § 366.

90. *See* G.S. 25-2-725.

91. *See* G.S. 1-52. State law allows solid waste fees to be billed on the property tax bill. *See* G.S. 153A-293; 160A-314.1. If a unit chooses this billing method, the unit may use the same collection remedies available to collect delinquent property taxes, and the statute of limitations for civil suits is ten years.

92. *See* G.S. Chapter 105A. For more information on the state's debt set-off program, see Chris McLaughlin, "Suped-Up Set-Off Debt Collection," *Coates' Canons: NC Local Government Law* blog (July 29, 2010), canons.sog.unc.edu/2010/07/suped-up-set-off-debt-collection/.

anyone other than the contracting party liable for the enterprise debts.[93] If, for example, a tenant establishes an account for water service with the local government, the tenant is the contracting party. That means that if the tenant defaults on his or her water payments, the local government may enforce collection only against the tenant. It may not proceed against the property owner. The unit also may not refuse service to a new tenant at the property where the delinquency occurred. This action would be akin to holding the new tenant liable for the former occupant's debt.

Finally, a local government generally may not refuse service to a delinquent former customer at a new property or premises. Although there is very little case law addressing this issue, a unit may be able to refuse future service if it has adopted a detailed written policy stating that the public enterprise service is conditioned on satisfaction of all previously owed (and still legally collectible) debts to the government.

Discontinuing a Public Enterprise Service Altogether

As stated above, a local government is not required to provide any public enterprise services. If, however, a municipality chooses to furnish one or more of these services, it is restricted from discontinuing the services altogether. State law prohibits a municipality from selling, leasing, or discontinuing an electric power generation, transmission, or distribution system; a gas production, storage, transmission, or distribution system; or a public transportation system, unless the proposed transaction is first approved in a voter referendum.[94] A municipality may, but is not required, to hold a referendum on a sale, lease, or discontinuance of a water treatment or distribution system or a wastewater collection or treatment system.[95] A voter referendum is not required (or authorized) before the sale, lease, or discontinuation of airports, off-street parking systems, solid waste collection or disposal systems, or cable television services.[96] A county is free to sell, lease, or discontinue any of its public enterprise functions without voter approval.[97]

---

93. Under very limited circumstances, a local government may add the amount owed by the delinquent former customer to the bill for services provided at a new property (and disconnect services at the new property for nonpayment) if the former customer resides at the new property receiving the services, even if the former customer is not the contracting party for services at the new property. *See* G.S. 160A-314; 153A-277.

94. G.S. 160A-321(a).

95. G.S. 160A-321(b).

96. *See* G.S. 160A-321; 160A-340.1(b).

97. *Cf.* G.S. 153A-283 ("In no case may a county be held liable for damages for failure to furnish water or sewer services.").

Chapter 31

Streets

Charles Szypszak

Charles Szypszak is a School of Government faculty member who specializes in real estate matters.

Jurisdiction over Streets

North Carolina's highways and streets are an interconnected system of federal, state, and municipal rights-of-way. The Federal Highway Administration maintains the interstate highways and other federal highways. The North Carolina Department of Transportation (NCDOT) maintains state highways and streets outside of municipalities. Inside municipalities, the state maintains major highways and some other roads, and municipalities maintain the other non-federal public roads within their boundaries. The states and its municipalities work together to determine whether a particular public road is to be state or municipally maintained. Within this network, private development occurs, resulting in new connectors that merge into the municipal street system and beyond.

Metropolitan planning organizations (MPOs) develop comprehensive transportation plans to serve present and anticipated travel demand in and around urban areas.[1] These comprehensive plans are multimodal in nature and include not only a highway or thoroughfare element but also transit and bicycle or pedestrian elements. Once completed, a plan must be adopted by the relevant MPO and NCDOT so that it can serve as the basis for future improvements within the MPO. The plan also serves as the basis for determining which roads and streets will be part of the state highway system and which streets will be part of municipal street systems. Once an MPO plan is adopted, any municipality within the MPO yields its transportation planning and programming interests to the MPO. In other words, the MPO represents the interests of its municipalities to the NCDOT. In addition, each municipality that is not a part of an MPO is also directed by statute to develop a comprehensive transportation plan using similar procedures.[2]

1. Chapter 136, Section 202 of the North Carolina General Statutes (hereinafter G.S.).
2. G.S. 136-66.2.

There are some identifiable differences within the local, state, and federal road systems. North Carolina municipalities name their own roads. Counties in the state do not maintain roads. North Carolina state highways include primary highways numbered under 1,000. State highways numbered higher than 1,000 are considered secondary. Federal highways are marked according to a national numbering system. Interstate routes are designated with an "I" on a red, white, and blue sign, and other federal highways with a "U.S." on a white shield. Generally, north-south interstate highways have odd numbers and east-west interstate highways have even numbers. Usually, a highway has only two digits (such as I-40 or I-95); three digits are used when a highway splits around cities, with the last two digits being the same (such as I-280 and I-480). Despite these differences in naming conventions, a typical driver may not be aware of the transition from municipal to state or federal roads.

Most of the legal issues that arise concerning rights-of-way concern the source of public rights to roads that cross what used to be private land. Disputes also arise about the interrelationship of the public's use of a street, the government's maintenance of it, and abutters' rights.

Measures for Financing Street Improvements

North Carolina's municipalities use a variety of sources of funds in the construction and maintenance of streets and for improvements within street rights-of-way.

General Local Taxes

All municipalities may levy taxes to finance street and sidewalk improvements.[3] The property tax is the chief local tax used for this purpose, although receipts from other taxes may also be used, as may revenues received from other government sources, including community-development grants and shared taxes, such as sales, franchise, and beer and wine taxes.

State Funds

Ever since 1951 the state has shared part of its gasoline tax receipts with municipalities for use on streets.[4] These moneys are sometimes called "Powell Bill funds" and are named after the sponsor of the bill in the General Assembly that established the revenue-sharing program.

Powell Bill funds are available for a wide range of purposes related to the construction, repair, and maintenance of municipal streets. However, the funds may also be used for a variety of improvements, including the construction and maintenance of bridges, drainage systems, curbs and gutters, bikeways, greenways, and sidewalks.

Special Assessments

Special assessments allow the assignment of at least some of the costs of public street improvements to the owners of property that stand to benefit from the work. Because they can be procedurally a bit complex to administer, assessments are more popular among large municipalities than mid-sized and smaller ones.

Chapter 160A, Section 217 of the North Carolina General Statutes (hereinafter G.S.) allows a municipality to levy an assessment for the costs of street or sidewalk improvements if the municipality receives a petition signed by the owners of a majority of the lineal feet of frontage of the lands abutting the street. Unless the petition provides otherwise, no more than 50 percent of the costs may be assessed. However, a number of municipal charters (perhaps over fifty) include provisions that allow municipalities to use special assessments in the absence of property-owner petitions and

3. G.S. Ch. 160A, Art. 9.
4. G.S. 136-41.1.

to assess more than 50 percent of the cost of improvements. Special assessments may be apportioned against benefited property in proportion to front footage, land area, or value added by the improvement; on a per-lot basis; or on a combination of these bases. Assessments may be paid as soon as their amount is known or in installments over a period of up to ten years, as the municipal council determines.

Counties also may play a role in upgrading NCDOT secondary roads through the use of special assessments. G.S. 153A-205 allows a county to finance the local share of the cost of improving residential subdivision streets in unincorporated areas that are already on the NCDOT secondary system. That local share is then assessed against benefitting property. The remainder of the cost is paid by NCDOT, if funds are available. The same approach may also be used to bring streets that have been offered for dedication but not (yet) accepted up to NCDOT's current design and construction standards so they may be accepted. The entire cost of these latter projects is assigned to the affected property owners. Counties also have the authority to use special assessments to pay for street lighting to serve residential subdivisions in unincorporated areas.[5]

Developer Exactions

Municipalities commonly require a developer to set aside land for new streets and construct streets to municipal standards pursuant to the municipality's statutory local planning and development authority.[6] The developer will then offer the streets to the municipality for its acceptance. In other instances, when a street is on the perimeter of a development, a developer may be expected to dedicate additional street rights-of-way but make no improvements. Occasionally a developer will be required to construct an acceleration or deceleration lane on an existing street if the land being developed adjacent to the street is, for example, a shopping center or other major commercial development. The extent to which a local government may require a developer to provide right-of-way or traffic improvements as a condition of development approval must be related to the traffic generated by the development project itself, if the requirement is to avoid being an unconstitutional taking of land.

In some instances, it may make more practical sense for a municipality to accept funds from a developer rather than insisting upon in-kind contributions. G.S. 160D-804(c)(2) allows a municipality to accept fees in lieu of street construction as a condition of subdivision plat approval. Fees such as these can be pooled for a later, more comprehensive road construction or right-of-way purchase. A municipality may use such funds for land acquisition, design, and construction of streets and roads that serve more than one subdivision or development.

Creation of Streets

A city may acquire control of a street in one of four ways: conveyance, dedication, prescription, or condemnation through eminent domain.

Conveyance

The most straightforward way for a municipality to acquire necessary rights in land for a public street or utility line is the same way by which most individuals become owners of real estate: with a voluntary conveyance in writing using the customary form of deed. Such a transaction does not involve legal vagaries that can arise with rights-of-way acquired through offers of dedication, which are more common than conveyances, nor does this type of arrangement involve the potential for dispute and litigation costs involved with acquiring property through an eminent domain

5. G.S. 153A-206.
6. G.S. 160D-804(c).

proceeding. Municipalities may be able to widen or extend streets through the same method: by purchasing the needed land in exchange for compensation equal to its market value.

Offer of Dedication and Acceptance

Acquisition by offer of dedication and acceptance consists of an offer by an owner of property to dedicate that property to a public use, and the acceptance of that offer by the public. By far the most common procedure for offering a dedication is through subdivision plat approval. Most local subdivision ordinances require developers to offer to dedicate streets, utility easements, and other public spaces to the public. The recorded plat for a regulated subdivision typically expressly states the required offer on its face. In areas of the state not subject to local subdivision regulation, the common law reaches a comparable result. Under common law, the preparation of a subdivision plat showing rights-of-way for streets (and other public uses) and the subsequent sale of at least one lot by reference to that plat constitutes an offer of dedication.

Inclusion of an express dedication on the face of a subdivision plat, or, in a common law context, the sale of a lot by reference to the plat, constitutes an offer of dedication, but neither constitutes acceptance of the dedication by the public. For that, the acceptance by proper authorities is necessary.[7] One method of public acceptance is formal action by a public body, such as a municipal council or the State Board of Transportation, or by its delegate, such as a municipality's manager or public works director. This formal method is preferable to others because it indicates an official decision by the appropriate government to accept the dedication and provides a record, such as through the minutes of the public body, of the acceptance.

A municipality may also, however, indicate acceptance of a dedication simply by beginning to maintain the subject street.[8] Because the municipality has no responsibility for maintenance until it accepts the offer of dedication, its undertaking to maintain the street has been held to imply the necessary acceptance.

An owner of property who has made an offer of dedication may withdraw the offer before the public has accepted it. Under G.S. 136-96, if the public does not open a dedicated street within fifteen years after the offer is made, the dedicator may file a notice of withdrawal in the office of the register of deeds. Until that notice is filed, however, the public retains the right to accept the offer and open the street, even if more than fifteen years have passed since the offer was made.

A question that often arises with subdivisions and apparent dedications is who is responsible for a roadway within a subdivision in a municipality when there is no record that the municipality accepted it as a public street. Municipal acceptance of an offer to dedicate a right-of-way for street purposes gives the local government control to ensure that the street will be kept up to its standards. Most subdivision lot owners want a municipality to take over the subdivision's roads, and many of the cases involving implied dedication and acceptance were brought by such owners. In circumstances in which a municipality has not taken control over a road, the case law recognizes that lot owners nonetheless may have a right to keep a subdivision road open when they have relied on a developer's express or implied promise of such use. Although in such cases lot owners will not have the benefit of municipal maintenance, what they are seeking is a protected means of travel, and they may be able to organize an association for private maintenance. The North Carolina Supreme Court said that "where lots are sold and conveyed by reference to a map or plat which represents a division of a tract of land into subdivisions, streets and lots, such streets become dedicated to the public use, and the purchaser of a lot or lots acquires the right to have all and each of the streets

7. Owens v. Elliott, 258 N.C. 314 (1962).

8. Foster v. Atwater, 226 N.C. 472 (1946).

kept open, and it makes no difference whether the streets be in fact open or accepted by the governing board of the towns or cities if they lie within municipal corporations."[9] The nature of such a lot owner's access rights is an easement, and it is only for the benefit of owners of lots who were part of the subdivision and who relied on the easement's inclusion when purchasing their lots. Lot owners who have a legal right to use subdivision roads may still face challenges in matters of control and maintenance, as often the developer is no longer present or willing to accept any responsibility for the right-of-way. Such subdivisions may choose to have the roads conveyed to a homeowner's association, with member lot owners responsible for costs.

Prescription

Although not often used anymore, another method of acquiring control of streets is by prescription. Prescription differs from dedication (discussed immediately above) in that the owner of the property does not intend to offer it for public use. Rather, the public simply uses the property as a street over an extended period—at least twenty years—in a way that is adverse to the interests of the owner, but also known to him or her. The use must be of a specific, definite right-of-way, which must be maintained by the public. If all these elements are met, then acquisition by prescription is possible. In practice, this method is rarely used except to confirm title to old streets for which the original title documents are lost.

Condemnation through Eminent Domain

American law has always sustained the power of federal, state, and local governments to use eminent domain to take property for use as a public road provided just compensation is paid to the owner for what is taken. North Carolina state statutes authorize municipalities to use eminent domain to acquire property for roads and utilities, and they prescribe the procedure for accomplishing the acquisition and paying the required just compensation.[10] G.S. Chapter 40A describes the basics of eminent domain and eminent domain procedure.

Closing of Public Streets

Once a municipality has acquired the right-of-way to a street, it may eventually want to close that street. The street may never have been opened, and closing may be necessary to clear neighboring titles. The municipality also may wish to relocate the street. Whatever the reason, the municipality may close a street under the procedure set out in G.S. 160A-299. Similarly, counties enjoy authority to close streets under procedures set out in G.S. 153A-241. In practice, counties most often use this authority to close formerly state-maintained roads that have been abandoned by NCDOT. The two statutes create very similar procedures.

The statutes require the governing board of a municipality or a county to hold a public hearing on a proposed street closure after it has published notice, mailed notice to owners of abutting property, and posted notice on the street itself. After the hearing, the board must find that the closing is not contrary to the public interest and would not deprive any person of "reasonable means of ingress and egress to his [or her] property." The North Carolina courts have held that although owners are entitled to access to a particular street from their property, they have no right to have traffic pass directly by their property. Thus, cutting off access to a street at one end, making that end in effect a cul-de-sac, does not deny reasonable means of ingress or egress to a property owner along the

9. Hughes v. Clark, 134 N.C. 457, 462 (1904).
10. G.S. 40A-51.

street.[11] When a street is closed in this fashion, the legal effect is that title to the land involved is divided along the middle of the street, among owners of the abutting land.

Other Uses of a Street Right-of-Way

G.S. 160A-273 permits a municipality to grant easements "over, through, under, or across . . . the right-of-way of any public street or alley that is not a part of the State highway system" as long as the easement will not "substantially impair or hinder the use of the street or alley as a way of passage." Thus, a municipality is authorized to permit a utility company to lay pipes or erect poles and string wires in the right-of-way of a street or to permit the owners of property that abuts a street to join their properties by a bridge across the street. If the municipality's title to the street is itself but an easement for street purposes (rather than full title in fee simple), however, the municipality's authority to permit other uses of the right-of-way, such as for laying pipes or erecting wires, is subject to the continuing property rights of the owner of the underlying title. The North Carolina Supreme Court has held that utility pipes or poles constitute an additional burden on a street right-of-way and that the owner of the underlying title is entitled to additional compensation, however small that may be. Payment of that compensation, though, is the responsibility of whoever lays the pipes or erects the poles, not the municipality.[12]

Street Maintenance

A municipality's power over its streets is a matter of legislatively delegated statutory authority.[13] Included within the provisions of G.S. 160A-296, which addresses municipal control of streets, are two specific duties: "to keep the public streets, sidewalks, alleys, and bridges open for travel and free from unnecessary obstructions" and "to keep the public streets, sidewalks, alleys, and bridges in proper repair."[14] These duties are grounded in common law. As the North Carolina Court of Appeals summarized, "municipalities have the positive duty to maintain their streets and sidewalks in a safe condition and keep them free of unnecessary obstructions and are civilly liable for negligently failing to discharge that duty."[15]

A municipality has the power to regulate points of access as long as an affected lot is left with the reasonable possibility of legal use of the public street. A municipality may limit the number of points of vehicular access to a street and regulate their location[16] and may also require that an existing point of access be relocated.[17] Installation of traffic medians,[18] removal of sidewalks,[19] and designation of one-way streets have become well-settled, permissible regulations.[20]

Street Names and Numbers

Inherent in a municipality's "general authority and control" over municipal streets is the authority to name streets and establish a system for numbering houses and other buildings along streets. Counties, by contrast, enjoy authority to name and number streets in unincorporated areas under

11. Wofford v. N.C. State Highway Comm'n, 263 N.C. 677 (1965).
12. Van Leuven v. Akers Motor Lines, 261 N.C. 539 (1964).
13. Town of Emerald Isle v. State, 320 N.C. 640, 656 (1987).
14. G.S. 160A-296(a)(1)–(2).
15. McDonald v. Vill. of Pinehurst, 91 N.C. App. 633, 635 (1988).
16. Abdalla v. State Highway Comm'n, 261 N.C. 114, 118–20 (1964).
17. Haymore v. N.C. State Highway Comm'n, 14 N.C. App. 691, 694–96 (1972).
18. Gene's, Inc. v. City of Charlotte, 259 N.C. 118, 121 (1963).
19. Crotts v. City of Winston-Salem, 170 N.C. 24, 27–28 (1915).
20. Barnes v. N.C. State Highway Comm'n, 257 N.C. 507, 517–18 (1962).

a specific statute, G.S. 153A-239.1. Most current naming of streets goes on in new subdivisions, and the typical subdivision ordinance addresses street names within the subdivision. This ordinance often requires that any new street that is a clear continuation of an existing street bear the same name as that street, and it prohibits new names that duplicate or sound very much like the names of existing streets. If these conditions are met, the names of the new streets are left to the subdivider. The power to name streets is legislative in nature, however, and, therefore, the municipality or county may change the name of a street at any time.

As noted, municipalities and counties also have statutory authority to establish a system of house numbering for municipal or rural streets. In a municipality, such a system usually begins with reference streets that divide the municipality into quarters: north, south, east, and west. The house numbers then proceed from the reference streets to the municipality's outer boundaries. Any ordinance that sets up a numbering system must establish frontage intervals so that a new number is given at each succeeding interval. Intervals are commonly in the range of 20 to 30 feet, although shorter intervals may be necessary in downtown areas. In addition, the ordinance should also maintain even numbers on one side of the street and odd numbers on the other in a manner that is consistent throughout the municipality. (The preferred practice is for the even numbers to be on the right side—low to high—and the odd numbers on the left side, going away from the reference streets.) It is also very desirable to establish the numbers so that the building numbers on parallel streets are comparable. Counties number lots or tracts under similar principles, although the lower population densities usual in unincorporated areas often lead to larger numbering intervals than are found in municipalities.

When municipalities exercise their power to name or number streets, there is no statutory procedure they must follow. A county's power to do so, however, is conditioned upon the board of commissioners first holding a public hearing on the matter after both publishing and posting notice of the hearing.

Additional Resources

Szypszak, Charles. *The Law of Municipal Streets and Utility Easements in North Carolina.* Chapel Hill: School of Government, University of North Carolina at Chapel Hill, 2019.

Chapter 32

Animal Services

Aimee N. Wall and Christopher Tyner

Aimee N. Wall is the dean of the School of Government. Christopher Tyner is a research attorney with the School. They are the coauthors of *North Carolina Guide to Animal Services Law.*

In North Carolina, local governments take the lead in managing traditional animal services activities. Much of their work is discretionary as state law only requires them to provide services in the areas of rabies control and the management of dangerous dogs. Because the state-mandated duties are so limited, many local governments have elected to offer more comprehensive animal services programs. As a result, a patchwork of local ordinances and customs largely govern the state's animal services activities. This chapter provides a general overview of the administrative and legal framework that applies to these services, with a particular focus on the role of local government.[1]

Administrative Responsibility

Because of the flexibility provided to local governments under state law, there is not a standard approach to animal services administration throughout North Carolina but, rather, a relatively fragmented set of local government programs, agencies, and staff. In some areas, the county is responsible for many or all functions while in others, the municipalities develop independent programs that run parallel to or complement the county program. Elected boards in some municipalities have, for example, adopted resolutions agreeing to have some or all of the county animal services ordinance apply within the municipality. Some local governments have entered into interlocal agreements related to staffing and service provision within the different jurisdictions.

Various local government agencies, offices, and departments assume responsibility for animal services activities. County animal services programs are often housed in county health departments

1. For more detailed information about all topics addressed in this chapter, see Aimee Wall and Christopher Tyner, *North Carolina Guide to Animal Services Law* (UNC School of Government, 2018).

because health directors have several statutorily mandated duties related to rabies control. Some local governments have elected to make animal services a function of law enforcement or public safety. Having law enforcement officers available to enforce laws concerning animals can be advantageous when it becomes necessary to conduct a search or to make an arrest. Other local governments place animal services responsibilities directly in the manager's office or within a separate department. Finally, some contract with private nonprofit agencies to manage animal services functions.

Primary responsibility for enforcing animal services laws and running related programs often rests with local government employees, whose primary duties concern animal services and programs. However, as mentioned above, in some jurisdictions law enforcement officers are responsible for animal-related issues. The state's rabies control law defines the position of "animal control officer" as:

> A city or county employee whose responsibility includes animal control. The term "Animal Control Officer" also includes agents of a private organization that is operating an animal shelter under contract with a city or county whenever those agents are performing animal control functions at the shelter.[2]

As discussed in more detail below, the state's rabies control law implicitly contemplates that every county will have at least one animal control officer responsible for certain duties required by statute,[3] but determining whether the officer is a county employee, a city employee, an agent of a private organization, or an employee or agent of another county or city operating under an interlocal agreement is left up to each jurisdiction. A local government employee may be an animal control officer[4] under state law even if he or she is primarily employed for another purpose.

Because there are so many different administrative homes for animal services programs, the local government personnel who are involved in animal issues across the state have very different training and backgrounds. The same may even be true within a single jurisdiction, depending on the animal services structure chosen by the county and its municipalities. State law imposes training and certification requirements in only two areas—rabies vaccinators and euthanasia technicians. In all other areas, local governments have leeway to develop their own training programs or to seek out opportunities available from national organizations, community colleges, and other potential partners.

---

2. Chapter 130A, Section 184(1) of the North Carolina General Statutes (hereinafter G.S.). *See also* G.S. 67-30 (authorizing counties to appoint animal control officers). At one time, many counties relied on "dog wardens," officials who were authorized to enforce laws related to dogs. G.S. 67-31. Some counties have entertained the idea of appointing dog wardens because G.S. 67-31 grants wardens the power of arrest. The statute is misleading, though, because wardens would be able to exercise the power of arrest only if they were also sworn law enforcement officers. G.S. 17C-11 (prohibiting persons from making arrests if they fail to satisfy the standards and requirements established by the North Carolina Criminal Justice Education and Training Standards Commission).

3. G.S. 130A-192 generally directs that "[t]he Animal Control Officer shall canvass the county" to determine whether any animals required to wear a rabies tag are not wearing a tag and to maintain a record of any animals impounded because they are not wearing a tag and their owner is unknown.

4. This chapter uses the statutory term "animal control officer" only when referring to a local government employee or agent responsible for the rabies control activities required by Article 6, Part 6 of G.S. Chapter 130A, which are discussed in more detail below. When referring to a local government employee who has responsibility for animal issues but is not necessarily an animal control officer under the statutory definition, this chapter uses the more general term "animal services official."

Local Government and Rule- and Ordinance-Making Authority

As discussed earlier, state law imposes relatively few requirements upon local governments to provide animal services but many jurisdictions choose to go beyond the statewide minimum requirements. The primary way that local governments accomplish this is by enacting local ordinances that regulate the treatment, keeping, and behavior of animals. A violation of a local ordinance often is punishable as a misdemeanor criminal offense, though some jurisdictions elect to use civil law remedies such as monetary fines, injunctions, or other equitable relief as alternative mechanisms for addressing such violations.

State law provides local governments with broad authority to enact ordinances regulating the treatment and keeping of animals; a local government may even enact an ordinance that addresses activity that already is the subject of state or federal law. However, a local ordinance must not duplicate or undermine state or federal law but instead must impose higher standards or expectations within the jurisdiction. Though local governments commonly choose to enact ordinances regulating animal issues, the nature and scope of these ordinances vary greatly among jurisdictions.

In some counties, animal services programs are administered in whole or in part by local health departments, and each of those departments is governed by a local board of health. Local boards of health have the authority to adopt local laws called "rules," which generally must pertain to issues affecting human health.[5]

Services

Local government animal services vary among jurisdictions. The key areas of service include rabies control, management of dangerous dogs, prohibiting animal cruelty, preventing stray and nuisance animals, and shelter management. This chapter focuses on the state laws governing each of these primary functions. It also briefly discusses how some local governments choose to address issues that go beyond these primary functions, such as exotic animal regulation and animal licensing programs. Note that some significant animal-related topics are largely outside the scope of this chapter. Hunting, fishing, and other activities involving wildlife fall under the jurisdiction of the state Wildlife Resources Commission, and, for the most part, its officers enforce statewide laws. Farm and other animals raised to be commercially processed as food fall under the jurisdiction of the North Carolina Department of Agriculture and Consumer Services. Some of the limited areas of overlap between the animal services programs provided by local governments and the work of the Wildlife Resources Commission and the Department of Agriculture and Consumer Services are discussed below.

Rabies Control

Rabies is a viral infection that may be transmitted to humans, most often through the bite of infected animals such as raccoons, bats, and dogs. If left untreated, the disease is almost always fatal for humans; therefore, the public health system has a significant interest in ensuring that the disease, whenever present, does not spread. North Carolina, like most other states, has adopted a series of state laws governing the control of rabies. The statutes can be found in the public health chapter of the North Carolina General Statutes (hereinafter G.S.), Chapter 130A, Article 6, Part 6. These statewide laws require the vaccination of cats, dogs, and ferrets and also provide a detailed

---

5. For more details about the rulemaking authority of local boards of health, see Chapter 37, "Public Health."

framework for responding to animal bites and other potential exposures to the rabies virus. Some jurisdictions supplement state law with local ordinances or rules. Public health, animal services, and wildlife management officials work together to enforce state and local laws designed to minimize the spread of rabies and the risk of human exposure.

The cornerstone requirement of the rabies control laws relates to pet vaccination. Every owner of a dog, cat, or ferret over four months of age is required to have the animal vaccinated against rabies (G.S. 130A-185). At the time of vaccination, the owner is given a copy of a vaccination certificate (G.S. 130A-189) and a rabies tag (G.S. 130A-190). State law requires that dogs wear their rabies tags at all times; cats and ferrets must wear their rabies tags at all times, unless exempted from the tag requirement by a local ordinance (G.S. 130A-190). While state law does not currently require other types of animals to be vaccinated, a local government could adopt such a requirement as a local ordinance or rule.

Vaccinations may be administered by a licensed veterinarian, a registered veterinary technician (under the supervision of a veterinarian), or a person who has been designated as a certified rabies vaccinator (G.S. 130A-185). Certified rabies vaccinators are persons appointed by a local health director and trained and certified by the state public health veterinarian (G.S. 130A-186). Pet owners may take their animals to a private veterinarian to be vaccinated. Alternatively, they may be able to take their pets to a public rabies clinic. Local health departments are required to organize (or assist other county departments in organizing) at least one public vaccination clinic per year (G.S. 130A-187). Boards of county commissioners are required to establish their clinics' vaccination fee, which is limited by statute to the actual cost of the vaccine, the certificate, and the tag plus an administrative fee not to exceed ten dollars. Often, the county coordinates these public clinics with private veterinarians in the area. The county's role may be to organize and advertise the clinic with the veterinarians participating at selected locations or, at times, in their own offices.

Local government animal control officers are required to canvass their jurisdictions to find animals not wearing the required rabies tags (G.S. 130A-192). If an officer finds an animal without a required tag, the officer has the authority to take action, which may include impounding the animal. If the officer knows who owns the animal, he or she must notify the owner in writing about the vaccination requirements. The owner must produce a copy of the animal's vaccination certificate within three days of receiving the notification. If the owner fails to do so, he or she may be charged with a Class 1 misdemeanor. In lieu of criminal prosecution, a local government could consider seeking an injunction against the owner.

If an officer does not know who owns an animal, he or she may impound it. Note that the officer is not *required* to impound the animal; state law provides local governments with the authority to seize animals found without the required rabies tags but does not require it. If the officer does seize an animal, the officer is required to make a reasonable effort to locate its owner, which may include scanning the animal to determine if it has a microchip. The local government is required to hold the animal for a time period established by the board of county commissioners, which must be at least seventy-two hours. Many cities and counties hold animals for longer periods.

If an impounded animal is not claimed by its owner within the established time period, the local government may return the animal to the owner, allow another person to adopt the animal, or euthanize the animal using a procedure approved by rules adopted by the North Carolina Department of Agriculture and Consumer Services.[6]

---

6. The Animal Welfare Section of the Veterinary Division of the Department of Agriculture and Consumer Services maintains a website that provides information about euthanasia regulations and training classes, www.ncagr.gov/divisions/veterinary/aws/euthanasia.

In addition to their important role in ensuring that animals are vaccinated, local governments also become involved in situations where an animal bites a person, has rabies, or is suspected of having rabies. If a person is bitten by a dog, cat, or ferret—regardless of whether the animal has or is suspected of having rabies—both the victim (or the victim's parent, guardian, or caretaker) and the animal's owner (or person possessing or in control of the animal) are required to immediately notify the local health director. This law applies to all dogs, cats, and ferrets regardless of their vaccination status—not just those suspected of having rabies. The offending animal then must be confined for ten days in a place designated by the local health director, which may be the owner's property. If an owner fails to confine the animal as directed, he or she may be charged with a Class 2 misdemeanor. Additionally, if an owner refuses to confine the animal, the local health director may order seizure and confinement of the animal for the ten-day period at the owner's expense. Physicians treating persons bitten by an animal known to be a potential carrier of rabies also must notify the local health director (G.S. 130A-196).

If a dog, cat, or ferret has been bitten or otherwise exposed to rabies by a rabid animal or an animal reasonably suspected of having rabies, state law requires that certain control measures be taken with respect to the exposed animal. Local health directors play an important role in deciding what control measures are appropriate, a decision that depends on the vaccination status of the exposed animal in accordance with national and state public health recommendations and guidelines (G.S. 130A-197).[7]

If an animal is suspected of having rabies, the owner (or person who possesses the animal) must notify the local health director or animal control officer and securely confine the animal for ten days at a place designated by the health director (G.S. 130A-198). The state public health veterinarian has discretion to order that other animals suspected of having rabies be destroyed.

If an animal is diagnosed as having rabies, it must be destroyed and its head must be sent to the State Laboratory of Public Health (G.S. 130A-199). The head of an animal that dies during a required rabies confinement period also must be sent to the state laboratory. The county typically assumes responsibility for the shipping of animal heads to the state laboratory.

If a local government or the state finds that a geographical area has a particularly high number of rabies cases, the local health director may declare a quarantine of dogs, cats, and ferrets in the area (G.S. 130A-194; 130A-195). While quarantined, the animals must stay on their owners' premises, in a veterinary hospital, or on a leash (or otherwise under the owners' control). The local health director also may petition the state health director to declare a rabies emergency in the jurisdiction if rabies is found in a wild animal other than a bat (G.S. 130A-201). If a rabies emergency is declared, the state health director petitions the Wildlife Resources Commission to develop a plan to minimize the threat of rabies exposure to humans and domestic animals from foxes, raccoons, skunks, or bobcats. Such a plan could, for example, suspend or liberalize hunting restrictions for those animals until the emergency has passed.

While state law governing rabies control is fairly comprehensive, many local governments choose to adopt local ordinances or board of health rules addressing rabies. Local governments do not have specific authority to regulate in this area but can rely on their general ordinance-making power or board of health rulemaking authority. As discussed above, any ordinance that is adopted should supplement rather than duplicate or contradict state law.

---

7. For a detailed discussion of rabies exposure management, see *North Carolina Guide to Animal Services Law.*

Dangerous Dogs

Every local government has probably faced the issue of a dog that is threatening or dangerous to citizens or to other animals. State law provides a ready framework for handling dangerous dog situations by defining the term "dangerous dog" and imposing certain criminally enforceable restrictions and obligations on the owners of such dogs (G.S. Chapter 67, Article 1A). Local governments often choose to supplement state law by adopting local ordinances defining their own programs for handling dangerous dogs.[8] Many local ordinances impose additional procedural requirements on dangerous dog determinations, restrictions on dogs deemed dangerous, and penalties for violations of the restrictions.

Under state law, the owner of a dangerous dog must comply with a series of restrictions on the freedom of that dog. For example, the dog must be muzzled and securely restrained when it is off its owner's property. Also, if the owner of the dog transfers its ownership or possession to another person, he or she must notify the new owner of the animal's status as a dangerous dog.

State law defines a "dangerous dog" as one that

- has, without provocation, killed or inflicted severe injury on a person;
- is owned or harbored primarily or in part for the purpose of dog fighting;
- is trained for dog fighting; or
- is determined by a local government to be "potentially dangerous."

A local government has the responsibility under state law to appoint a person or create a board responsible for designating dogs as potentially dangerous according to a specific statutory definition (or an alternative definition if one is provided by local ordinance). In addition, the local government must appoint a separate board charged with hearing appeals from citizens whose dogs have been declared potentially dangerous. There are no requirements or limitations regarding the size or membership of either the designation or the appeals board. For example, some local governments have elected to give an animal control officer or other animal services employee the responsibility for initially determining whether a dog is potentially dangerous while authorizing an existing board (such as the board of health or the board of county commissioners) or a subset of an existing board to hear appeals on that initial determination. An owner has the right to appeal the decision of the appeals board to superior court.[9]

An owner who violates the restrictions and obligations established in state law for dangerous dogs may be subject to criminal penalties. In addition, an owner may be strictly liable for any injuries or property damage inflicted by his or her dog. Strict liability means that if a property owner or individual files a civil lawsuit against a dog owner for money damages, the court will not require proof that the dog owner was negligent in caring for or restraining the animal.

In addition to the statewide dangerous dog laws and any applicable local ordinance, two other options are available to local governments in addressing problems related to dangerous animals of any kind, including dogs. Local governments have the general authority to regulate, restrict, or prohibit the possession or harboring of animals that are dangerous to persons or property

---

8. State law explicitly states that the dangerous dog statutes must not be "construed to prevent a city or county from adopting or enforcing its own program for control of dangerous dogs." G.S. 67-4.5. This language arguably affords local governments leeway to craft dangerous dog programs that differ from state law to a greater extent than typically is the case when a local government exercises its ordinance-making authority to address an issue that already is the subject of state law.

9. Caswell Cnty. v. Hanks, 120 N.C. App. 489 (1995) (upholding the constitutionality of the dangerous dog law and recognizing that the appeal to superior court must be held de novo).

(G.S. 153A-131; 160A-187).[10] In addition, local health directors have the authority to declare an animal vicious and a menace to the public's health and to require the owner to confine the animal to his or her property (G.S. 130A-200). This vicious animal authority may be exercised if an animal has attacked a person without provocation, causing bodily harm.

In rare cases, the misdeeds of a dog can result in serious criminal charges. In *State v. Powell*,[11] the owner of two Rottweilers was convicted of involuntary manslaughter after his unattended dogs attacked and killed a jogger. In another case, a man was convicted of assault with a deadly weapon on a government official after he directed a dog to attack a police officer and the dog obeyed.[12]

Animal Cruelty

Local government animal services officials or law enforcement officers are usually the first people called when someone discovers a starving animal or suspects that a person is abusing an animal. At the state level, North Carolina law includes both civil and criminal remedies for addressing animal cruelty. Many local governments choose to adopt ordinances that supplement these remedies.

State law establishes a civil process that allows a court to impose restrictions it deems necessary to protect an animal that is being treated cruelly. Under this law, any citizen, including an animal services official, an animal control officer, or a law enforcement officer, is empowered to seek an injunction in civil court allowing the removal of an animal from the defendant and termination of his or her right of ownership or possession of the animal (G.S. Chapter 19A, Article 1). The remedy also may be pursued by a political or corporate body, including a local government or an animal welfare organization. This type of civil action is relatively unique compared to other civil actions because it does not require the plaintiff to have "standing" to bring the case. It is an important complement to the state's criminal laws prohibiting animal cruelty because it permits any person to quickly seek injunctive relief from a district court judge, regardless of the status of any criminal prosecution. In addition to its expediency, the civil remedy provides an avenue for addressing situations in which criminal prosecution is not the most appropriate solution for a person's inability to properly care for an animal.

Apart from the civil remedy, North Carolina law defines misdemeanor and felony criminal offenses for animal cruelty (G.S. Chapter 14, Article 47). The misdemeanor offense applies to situations in which a person intentionally treats an animal cruelly while the felony offense applies to situations in which a person does so maliciously; there also are differences between the offenses based on the manner in which the animal is harmed. Instigating or promoting animal cruelty also is punishable as a criminal offense. Animal fighting, which includes being a spectator at an animal fight, is subject to criminal penalties that vary depending on the type of animal and activity involved. In addition to these offenses, North Carolina's criminal laws address the poisoning of animals as well as the killing, harming, or taunting of law enforcement, assistance, or search and rescue animals.[13]

North Carolina law permits counties to appoint private citizens on a volunteer basis to serve as "animal cruelty investigators" (G.S. Chapter 19A, Article 4). Animal cruelty investigators are appointed by the board of county commissioners for one-year terms and serve without compensation

---

10. As noted above, primary jurisdiction with respect to wildlife is vested in the North Carolina Wildlife Resources Commission, and for the most part, its officers enforce statewide laws.

11. 336 N.C. 762 (1994).

12. State v. Cook, 164 N.C. App. 139, *aff'd per curiam*, 359 N.C. 185 (2004).

13. See *North Carolina Guide to Animal Services Law* for a detailed account of criminal laws related to animal cruelty issues, including various misdemeanor and federal offenses not discussed in this chapter.

or benefits (though they can be reimbursed for expenses). These individuals must take at least six hours of training related to investigating animal abuse, and they also must take an oath of office and wear a badge that identifies them as animal cruelty investigators. Typically, an animal cruelty investigator is a concerned citizen or an animal welfare advocate, not a county employee. He or she does not have criminal law enforcement authority and relies on the civil remedy described above (i.e., injunction) to resolve cruelty cases. Animal cruelty investigators also have the unique authority to obtain a magistrate's order authorizing them to seize an animal *prior* to filing a civil complaint in district court. Absent exigent circumstances, other individuals or corporate bodies that pursue a civil animal cruelty remedy do not have the authority to seize animals until a court has so ordered.

In addition to the state laws governing cruelty described above, local governments have specific authority to adopt their own ordinances related to animal abuse (G.S. 153A-127; 160A-182). The term "abuse" is not defined in the law but probably is comparable to the terms "cruelty" or "cruel treatment," which are defined broadly in the context of the state's civil remedy to include "every act, omission, or neglect whereby unjustifiable physical pain, suffering, or death is caused or permitted" (G.S. 19A-1).[14] A similar definition is used in the criminal cruelty laws (G.S. 14-360). Given the broad scope of the state's animal cruelty laws, local government officials drafting ordinances pertaining to animal abuse should be sure that the ordinances supplement rather than undermine or conflict with state law. Some local governments, for example, appropriately have relied on their ordinance-making authority to outlaw specific types of abuse or cruelty that are not explicitly identified in state law, such as leaving an animal inside an unattended vehicle. Others have adopted procedural requirements related to the role of animal services officials when responding to complaints. Note that legislation enacted in 2015 prohibits local ordinances that regulate standards of care for certain farm animals.[15]

Stray and Nuisance Animals

Local animal services officials often spend a great deal of time dealing with citizen complaints about nuisance animals and animals found wandering at large. Although a handful of state laws address at-large animals, they are quite limited in scope. The statutes prohibit dogs from running at large at night, female dogs from running at large while in heat, and unmuzzled dogs from running at large in wildlife management areas (G.S. 67-12; 67-2; 67-14.1). It is a criminal offense to permit a dog to "go at liberty" when that dog has killed a domestic animal or a person and evidence of that behavior has been presented to a district court judge (G.S. 67-3). It also is a criminal offense to permit livestock to run at large (G.S. 68-16).

While North Carolina does not have a statewide leash law, animal control officers are authorized to impound unidentified animals that are not wearing rabies tags, as discussed above (G.S. 130A-192). Local governments regularly rely on this authority in the rabies law to impound stray animals, but some have found that a local leash law is necessary as well. Cities have specific authority to adopt ordinances regulating animals that run at large (G.S. 160A-186). Under this statute, cities may adopt ordinances providing that animals allowed to run at large may be seized and, after reasonable efforts to notify their owners, either sold (which likely includes adoption) or destroyed. Counties do not have specific authority related to at-large animals but may enact

14. *See also* William A. Reppy Jr., "Citizen Standing to Enforce Anti-Cruelty Laws by Obtaining Injunctions: The North Carolina Experience," 11 Animal L. 39, 46–49 (2005) (arguing that the term "cruelty" as used in the state's civil remedies laws should also include mental suffering and that the term "unjustifiable" inappropriately limits the scope of the definition).

15. For a discussion of this legislation, see Chapter 2 of *North Carolina Guide to Animal Services Law.*

ordinances on the issue by relying on their general ordinance-making power to define, regulate, prohibit, or abate acts, omissions, or conditions detrimental to the health, safety, or welfare of their citizens as well as to define and abate nuisances (G.S. 153A-121). There is no statewide law pertaining to nuisance animals, but local governments commonly address the issue by ordinance. Apart from a local government's ability to deal with nuisance and at-large animals, it is conceivable that in some situations an individual may decide to pursue a civil action against the owner of a nuisance or at-large animal under the common law torts of nuisance, trespass by animal, or negligence.

Shelter Management

Though they are not required to do so, local governments are allowed to establish, equip, operate, and maintain an animal shelter or contribute to the support of an animal shelter established and operated by another entity (G.S. 153A-442; 160A-493). Local governments across the state have taken a variety of different approaches to animal sheltering. Many have chosen to establish public shelters within their jurisdictions while others have elected to pool resources with other localities to operate a regional shelter. Quite a few local governments have entered into agreements with humane societies or other nonprofit organizations that allow them to house animals at private shelters or, in the case of large animals such as horses, on private farms or in local boarding facilities.

Providing room and board as well as veterinary care to impounded animals can be expensive. In some situations, the shelter may be able to recover some of its costs, such as when a stray animal is retrieved by its owner or an animal is adopted. Also, a shelter that houses an animal seized in the course of a civil or criminal cruelty case, an animal fighting case, or a dangerous dog case may ask the court to order the defendant to pay for the care of the animal or to make other arrangements for the animal's care until the case is resolved (G.S. 19A-70). In most cases, however, the local government and its nonprofit partners absorb the costs of sheltering and caring for impounded animals.

Shelters must comply with the state's Animal Welfare Act, which is enforced by the Animal Welfare Section of the Veterinary Division of the Department of Agriculture and Consumer Services (G.S. Chapter 19A, Article 3). The law addresses the physical condition of shelters, minimum holding periods for animals, public inspection of animals, animal care, euthanasia practices, and training of euthanasia technicians.

In 2015, the General Assembly established a new fund that provides grants to local governments for certain animal shelter–related expenses that are incurred due to (1) the denial, suspension, or revocation of a shelter's registration or its compliance with applicable requirements of the Animal Welfare Act or rules adopted by the Board of Agriculture or (2) an unforeseen catastrophic disaster at a shelter (G.S. Chapter 19A, Article 5A).[16] Board of Agriculture rules govern eligible expenses and grant application guidelines. Grants are limited to $50,000 per grantee in any fiscal year.[17]

---

16. The Animal Shelter Support Fund statutes were modified by S.L. 2021-180, § 105B, subsequent to the publication of *North Carolina Guide to Animal Services Law*, which includes a discussion of the program under previous law.

17. The Animal Welfare Section of the Veterinary Division of the Department of Agriculture and Consumer Services maintains a website that provides information about the Animal Shelter Support Fund, www.ncagr.gov/divisions/veterinary/aws/ShelterSupportFund.

Licensing

Local governments have the authority to require pet owners to pay an annual license tax (G.S. 153A-153; 160A-212). Some local governments have generated significant income streams from these taxes. The licensing and taxing authority not only generates revenue but also can serve two other purposes. First, it can provide local governments with an additional mechanism for dealing with stray animals. A local ordinance, for example, could authorize animal services officials to impound any animal found without a license. Second, a jurisdiction that adopts a program of differential licensing (i.e., higher license taxes for animals that have not been spayed or neutered) can help reduce the population of stray and unwanted animals. Some jurisdictions have concluded, however, that the administrative burden of collecting such a tax outweighs its potential benefits.

Service Animals

Some individuals with disabilities work with service animals to help them carry out daily activities. An animal may be trained, for example, to guide a person with a visual impairment, open doors for a person with a physical disability, or remind a person to take his or her medication, as well as to perform many other important support functions. State and federal law provide various legal protections to individuals who rely on service animals (G.S. Chapters 168, 168A).[18] Members of the public often rely on local government animal services officials to help them interpret and apply these laws.

Of particular importance to local governments is the general rule under state and federal law requiring them to make reasonable modifications of their policies, practices, and procedures so that a person with a disability can be accompanied by a service animal wherever members of the public, invitees, or program participants are allowed to go. Generally speaking, a local government may refuse to permit a service animal to accompany a disabled individual only in the rare circumstance where allowing the animal would require the fundamental alteration of the nature of a service, program, or activity provided to the public, or when the animal is out of control or not housebroken. An individual with a disability may register a service animal with the state and receive a special tag that identifies it as a registered service animal, though it is not necessary to register a service animal or have such a tag. By law, a local government may not *require* individuals to register their service animals or to otherwise verify that an animal is a service animal. It may, however, create a *voluntary* registry of service animals. A local government's improper refusal to allow an individual with a service animal to access facilities, programs, or services can have a range of serious consequences, including the possibility of becoming subject to civil litigation, federal investigation, or the withholding of federal funds.

Spay/Neuter Assistance Program

The state operates a program that allocates funding to local governments to reimburse them for the direct costs of spay/neuter surgeries for cats and dogs owned by low-income individuals (G.S. Chapter 19A, Article 5). The Animal Welfare Section of the Veterinary Division of the Department of

---

18. See *North Carolina Guide to Animal Services Law* for a more detailed overview of the state and federal law relevant to service animals, including prohibitions on types of discrimination not discussed here. The Americans with Disabilities Act of 1990 and its implementing regulations are the primary sources of relevant federal law.

Agriculture and Consumer Services is responsible for administration of the program. In 2023, the state reimbursed thirty-two local governments more than $300,000 for almost 6,000 surgeries.[19] The program is funded in part by a $20 surcharge on every specialized "I Care" Animal Lovers license plate purchased in the state.

Exotic Animals

North Carolina does not have a general statewide law regulating the ownership or possession of exotic animals. The Wildlife Resources Commission exercises jurisdiction over native North Carolina wildlife, but it does not have authority to regulate nonnative animals, such as tigers and elephants. The General Assembly has considered establishing a more comprehensive statewide law on the subject but has yet to do so.

In the absence of a statewide law, many local governments have adopted local exotic animal ordinances. Local governments can rely on their specific authority under state law to regulate any animals that are deemed dangerous to persons or property (G.S. 153A-131; 160A-187). This specific authority is clearly applicable to animals that may injure a person (e.g., tigers, venomous reptiles) and could also be interpreted more broadly to extend to, for example, the regulation of animals that could transmit diseases to persons or domestic animals. Local governments also can rely on their general ordinance-making authority to protect citizens' health, safety, and welfare as an additional basis for regulating exotic animals. In the absence of a local ordinance, a county health director may place restrictions on any "vicious" animal that has attacked a person without being provoked (G.S. 130A-200).

19. More information about the spay/neuter program, including quarterly and yearly reports on reimbursements to local governments, is available from the Veterinary Division of the North Carolina Department of Agriculture and Consumer Services, www.ncagr.gov/divisions/veterinary/aws/fix.

Chapter 33

Emergency Management

Norma R. Houston

Norma R. Houston is a former School of Government faculty member whose areas of interest include emergency management law.

The author thanks the following officials for their help in preparing the original draft of this chapter: Holly Hollingsworth, FEMA; David Humphrey, NCDEM; and Sandy Sanderson, Dare County Emergency Management.

Earlier versions of this chapter were developed with assistance from Samantha Surles, David Goldberg, and Timothy Reavis. Alex Phipps, the School's senior legal research associate, updated the chapter for this edition.

Cities and counties are vested with both the authority and the responsibility to prepare for, respond to, recover from, and mitigate the impact of natural and man-made disasters. These functions are carried out through local emergency-management agencies. Growing out of World War II–era civil defense organizations, today's emergency-management agencies are expected to prepare for and to respond to a wide array of disasters ranging from floods, tornadoes, and hurricanes to terrorist attacks and pandemic disease outbreaks. As a result, the skills, training, and resources necessary to respond effectively to these threats have become increasingly specialized and complex. In today's post-9/11 world, there is greater public concern about threats both natural and man-made. In today's post-Katrina world, there is also increased public scrutiny of the government's responsiveness to these threats. Regardless of their magnitude or scope, all disasters are, at their core, local events, requiring local governments to act as first responders in protecting public health, safety, and welfare.

What Is Emergency Management?

Protecting the public health, safety, and welfare is a basic function of government at all levels. When a disaster strikes, this function is carried out under what is generally referred to as "emergency management," which is collectively "those measures taken by the populace and government at federal, state, and local levels to minimize the adverse effect of any type [of] emergency."[1] Examples of such measures include evacuation, sheltering, search and rescue, emergency medical care, and debris removal.

Emergency management is, however, more encompassing than the obvious and necessary activities that occur during and immediately after a disaster event. It is a "never-ending preparedness cycle of prevention, response, recovery, mitigation, warning, movement, shelter, emergency assistance, and recovery."[2] Emergency managers typically refer to the following activities as the four phases of emergency management: preparedness, response, recovery, and mitigation. Under federal law, local governments are encouraged to develop comprehensive disaster-preparedness and -assistance plans, threat analyses, and community risk assessments, as well as hazard-mitigation measures to reduce losses from disasters (including developing land use and construction regulations).[3] Under state law, each county is required to coordinate all emergency-management efforts within the county, including any municipalities inside the county.[4] Ideally, each county will develop emergency-management plans that address not only initial post-disaster first response and subsequent recovery activities, but also prevention and mitigation measures, all of which, when taken together, result in effective and efficient management of disasters in which injury and loss of life and property are minimized.

Sources of Authority

Emergency-management programs and authorities are governed by both state and federal law. North Carolina law also authorizes the adoption of local emergency-management ordinances that are required for local governments to exercise certain emergency powers.

At the federal level, emergency-management activities are governed by statutes, regulations, policies, and guidance documents. The Robert T. Stafford Disaster Relief and Emergency Assistance Act (commonly referred to as "the Stafford Act")[5] is the statute enacted by Congress empowering the federal government to support a state's response in times of crisis. It authorizes the president to issue disaster declarations and establishes the programs and processes the federal government uses to provide emergency and major disaster assistance to states, local governments, and other eligible recipients of federal disaster aid, including individual citizens. Various parts of Title 44 of the Code of Federal Regulations (Emergency Management and Assistance) further define this assistance. Administrative policies and guidance documents adopted by various federal agencies (including the U.S. Department of Homeland Security and the Federal Emergency Management Agency) provide detailed instructions for administering federal disaster-assistance programs.

In North Carolina, the legal authority for emergency-management activities by state and local governments is found in Chapter 166A of the North Carolina General Statutes (hereinafter G.S.)

---

1. Chapter 166A, Section 19.3(8) of the North Carolina General Statutes (hereinafter G.S.).
2. G.S. 166A-19.3(8). *See also* Ward v. Long Beach Volunteer Rescue Squad, 151 N.C. App. 717 (2002).
3. 42 U.S.C. § 5121(b); 44 C.F.R. § 206.3(b).
4. G.S. 166A-19.15(a).
5. Pub. L. No. 93-288, 88 Stat. 143 (1974), *codified as amended at* 42 U.S.C. §§ 5121–5206. Enacted by Congress in 1988, the Stafford Act, Pub. L. 100-707, 102 Stat. 4689 (1988), amended the Disaster Relief Act of 1974.

(the North Carolina Emergency Management Act of 1977).[6] Article 1A of Chapter 166A outlines the powers of and the relationships between state and local governments for disaster planning and response activities and authorizes both state and local governments to issue disaster declarations. Article 36A of G.S. Chapter 14 (Riots, Civil Disorders, and Emergencies) imposes criminal penalties for certain activities undertaken during riots and emergency situations.

Disaster declarations at the federal, state, and local levels trigger a wide array of governmental powers as well as disaster-relief assistance. These declarations, and their significance, are discussed more fully in this chapter.

What Is the Difference Between a "Disaster" and an "Emergency"?

In North Carolina, the word "disaster" often conjures up images of major hurricanes, such as Hugo, Fran, Floyd, and Helene, or of severe ice storms accompanied by prolonged power outages. In recent years, tornadoes have struck a number of North Carolina communities with devastating effects. While these examples are certainly disasters in every sense of the word, the meaning of the word "disaster" in North Carolina law refers only to the declaration issued by the governor based on the impact of an "emergency."

State law defines an "emergency" as "[a]n occurrence or imminent threat of widespread or severe damage, injury, or loss of life or property resulting from any natural or man-made accidental, military, paramilitary, terrorism, weather related, public health, explosion-related, riot-related cause, or technological failure or accident, including, but not limited to, a cyber incident, an explosion, a transportation accident, a radiological accident, or a chemical or other hazardous material incident."[7] Federal law, through the Stafford Act, defines a "major disaster" as "any natural catastrophe (including any hurricane, tornado, storm, high water, winddriven water, tidal wave, tsunami, earthquake, volcanic eruption, landslide, mudslide, snowstorm, or drought) or, regardless of cause, any fire, flood, or explosion in any part of the United States, which in the determination of the President causes damage of sufficient severity and magnitude to warrant major disaster assistance under this [Act] to supplement the efforts and available resources of states, local governments, and disaster relief organizations in alleviating the damage, loss, hardship, or suffering caused thereby."[8] The Stafford Act defines an "emergency" as "any occasion or instance for which, in the determination of the President, Federal Assistance is needed to supplement state and local efforts and capabilities to save lives and to protect property and public health and safety, or to lessen or avert the threat of a catastrophe in any part of the United States."[9]

Two points regarding these definitions are worth noting. First, North Carolina's definition of emergency and the federal definition of disaster both include natural and man-made occurrences. Thus, local governments should plan for a broad array of potential threats (not just hurricanes or ice storms). Second, under the Stafford Act, federal assistance is supplemental to the resources of state and local governments, which bear responsibility for the initial disaster response. Indeed, the primary responder in any disaster is, first and foremost, the local government in whose jurisdiction the emergency has occurred.

6. Enacted in 1977, G.S. Chapter 166A is a rewrite of the former G.S. Chapter 166, the Civil Defense Preparedness Act. Article 1 of Chapter 166A was repealed and recodified as Chapter 1A in 2012. The chapter was further updated and amended after the COVID-19 pandemic and as part of the Hurricane Helene response in 2024.

7. G.S. 166A-19.3(6).

8. 42 U.S.C. § 5122(2); *see also* 44 C.F.R. § 206.2(a)(17).

9. 42 U.S.C. § 5122(1); *see also* 44 C.F.R. § 206.2(a)(9).

Roles and Responsibilities—Federal and State

Federal Government

Emergency-management operations in any major disaster necessarily involve coordination and cooperation between a myriad of federal, state, and local government agencies and personnel, as well as private disaster-relief organizations such as the Red Cross and the Salvation Army. This coordinated effort is led at the federal level by the Federal Emergency Management Agency (hereinafter FEMA).

FEMA was formally authorized in 1979 in an executive order issued by President Jimmy Carter.[10] Its mission is to lead the national effort to prepare for all hazards and to effectively manage federal response and recovery efforts following any national incident. FEMA also initiates proactive mitigation activities, trains first responders and other emergency-management personnel, and manages the National Flood Insurance Program. FEMA operated for more than twenty years as an independent federal agency, with its director appointed by and reporting directly to the president. In March 2003, however, FEMA joined twenty-two other federal agencies, programs, and offices to form the U.S. Department of Homeland Security. Now the director of FEMA serves under the Secretary of Homeland Security, though he or she still retains responsibility for the agency's core mission. Functionally, FEMA is not a *direct* response agency (i.e., FEMA officials are not first responders), but it is a *support* agency, coordinating federal resources and assets to supplement those of state and local governments. In major disasters, this effort can involve numerous federal, state, and local agencies and private disaster-relief organizations from across the country.

To better facilitate communication and coordination between multiple governmental agencies across multi-jurisdictional lines in domestic disaster-response situations, President George W. Bush directed the Department of Homeland Security to develop and administer a National Incident Management System (NIMS).[11] Under NIMS, federal, state, and local governments are expected to utilize standardized terminology and organizational structures, interoperable (technically compatible) communications, consolidated action plans, unified command structures, and other similar measures designed to facilitate consistent, efficient, and effective incident management.[12] These unified efforts are to be employed in all disaster situations whether natural or man-made (the "all-hazards" approach). By proclamation, Governor Mike Easley established NIMS as the standard for incident management in North Carolina in May 2005 and directed all counties to adopt and apply NIMS for management of all incidents. Similarly, federal directives also require local governments to adopt and utilize NIMS and to train local personnel "directly involved" in emergency-management operations on NIMS procedures and protocols.[13] Local governments were required to meet this compliance requirement by October 1, 2006 (corresponding with the beginning of federal fiscal year 2006), in order to be eligible for federal preparedness-assistance funds (which include first-responder grants, emergency-management planning grants, and hazardous-materials program grants). Federal disaster-relief funds administered

---

10. Federal emergency-response efforts had actually existed since the early 1800s but had been handled in a fragmented manner by multiple and sometimes overlapping agencies without overall coordination at the federal level.

11. U.S. Department of Homeland Security, Homeland Security Presidential Directive/HSPD-5—Management of Domestic Incidents (Feb. 28, 2003) (hereinafter HSPD-5).

12. A key component of NIMS is the Incident Command System (ICS) used by major firefighting agencies for almost thirty years. ICS is a standardized on-scene system used by all emergency responders that allows for coordinated use of equipment and personnel with standardized processes for response to all sizes and types of incidents. ICS is used at the local, state, and federal levels and by private sectors involved in emergency-management activities. Information about ICS, including available training courses, is available at the ICS Resource Center, which is located on the Emergency Management Institute's webpage on the FEMA website at training.fema.gov/emiweb/is/icsresource/trainingmaterials (last accessed March 12, 2025).

13. HSPD-5 § 20.

under the Stafford Act are not considered "preparedness funds," so local governments not in compliance with NIMS are still eligible for federal aid in a federally declared disaster.

In early 2025, President Donald Trump signed Executive Order 14180, creating the Federal Emergency Management Agency Review Council. This executive order directs the council to prepare a report assessing FEMA's response to disasters, recommending improvements to FEMA's structure and considering the role of state and local governments in disaster response. Although it is unclear whether this will result in the elimination or modification of FEMA's responsibilities or the statutes and regulations governing federal disaster response, local governments should ensure they consult up-to-date federal guidance when preparing for or requesting assistance after a disaster. This includes guidance from entities such as the Office of Management and Budget, Centers for Medicare & Medicaid Services, and other federal entities outside the traditional disaster-response framework that may be revising guidance under the Trump administration.

State Government

In North Carolina, the governor has general direction and control of the state's emergency-management program and is vested with broad powers to act when necessary in a disaster situation.[14] Under the governor, the Secretary of the Department of Public Safety oversees state emergency-management activities. Within the public safety department, the Division of Emergency Management (NCDEM) has direct responsibility for day-to-day operations and primary responsibility in coordinating the state's disaster-response efforts. To fulfill this responsibility, NCDEM oversees the State Emergency Response Team (SERT), a group of state agency personnel designated to carry out emergency-management support functions and to coordinate "the activities of all State agencies for emergency management within the State, including planning, organizing, staffing, equipping, training, testing, and activating and managing the State Emergency Response Team and emergency management programs."[15] NCDEM also administers the state's hazard-mitigation program and flood-plain mapping program and is authorized to promulgate standards for local emergency-management plans and programs and to provide technical assistance to local governments.[16] Other responsibilities of NCDEM include maintaining the State Emergency Operations Center, planning for emergencies at nuclear power plants, and managing mutual aid.

In responding to disasters, the state coordinates with local emergency-management agencies. During disaster response and recovery operations, local governments communicate damage assessments and requests for assistance to the state, and deployment of assets and resources are coordinated at the state level. Similarly, in a major disaster involving federal agencies, local needs not met at the state level are communicated by NCDEM to FEMA. NCDEM also delivers training programs and planning assistance for local emergency-management agencies.[17]

On September 27, 2024, Hurricane Helene struck North Carolina, causing major damage and loss of life across the western counties of the state. In response, the General Assembly passed several bills, collectively known as "The Disaster Recovery Act of 2024," to provide funding and reform the state's disaster response.[18] A major priority of the 2025 legislative session, as well as of newly elected Governor Josh Stein, is passing additional relief packages likely to contain reforms to North

---

14. G.S. 166A-19.10(b).
15. G.S. 166A-19.12(1).
16. G.S. 166A-19.12(5).
17. *See* N.C. Department of Public Safety (website), "Emergency Management," ncdps.gov/our-organization/emergency-management (last accessed June 7, 2024); *see also* N.C. Department of Public Safety, *2020 North Carolina Disaster Recovery Framework*, January 2020.
18. S.L. 2024-51 ("The Disaster Recovery Act of 2024"); S.L. 2024-53 ("The Disaster Recovery Act of 2024—Part II"); and S.L. 2024-57 ("The Disaster Recovery Act of 2024—Part III").

Carolina's emergency management laws. Local governments should consult NCDEM and other responsible agencies for up-to-date guidance.

Roles and Responsibilities—Local Government

Emergency-management response activities are initiated at the local level, augmented by state resources where local resources are insufficient, and, in major emergencies, augmented by federal resources at the request of the state. Local governments clearly play a critical role in the "never-ending preparedness cycle" of emergency management operations.[19]

Legal Authority

Under the North Carolina Emergency Management Act, the governing body of each county is specifically charged with the responsibility for coordinating all emergency-management efforts at the local level, including those of *cities within the county*.[20] To accomplish these functions, counties are authorized to

- establish local emergency-management agencies;
- appoint an emergency-management coordinator;
- appropriate and expend local funds;
- make contracts;
- obtain and distribute equipment, materials, and supplies;
- develop emergency-management plans;
- establish voluntary registries of functionally and medically fragile persons; and
- provide for the health and safety of persons and property.

Counties are also authorized to adopt ordinances imposing restrictions and prohibitions during a declared state of emergency.[21] While cities are similarly authorized,[22] their agencies and activities are still subject to coordination by the counties in which they are located.[23]

Organizational Structure

Each county is required to designate an emergency-management coordinator (or director; the terms are used interchangeably herein), and many cities have similarly designated personnel. Roughly, only a quarter of the counties in the state employ full-time emergency-management coordinators; the majority designate an employee or department head who performs other duties generally related to emergency management and first responder activities (such as EMS director, fire marshal, or 911 supervisor). The emergency-management coordinator maintains and implements the jurisdiction's emergency-management plan and oversees other administrative and operational functions. His or her duties include coordinating the activities of other local departments involved in disaster response and recovery operations, such as public information, public works, EMS, fire and rescue, law enforcement, finance, social services, and public health, as well as coordinating local efforts with those of state and federal agencies and private relief organizations. The number of additional staff assigned to local emergency-management agencies varies from jurisdiction to jurisdiction and

19. G.S. 166A-19.3(8).
20. G.S. 166A-19.15(a).
21. G.S. 166A-19.22.
22. G.S. 166A-19.31.
23. G.S. 166A-19.15(c).

traditionally has been small. Employees of local emergency-management agencies receiving federal grant-in-aid funds are covered under the State Personnel Act[24] and are subject to certain statutory requirements as conditions of employment.[25]

As with federal and state emergency-management agencies, local agencies serve a coordinating role in emergency events; they are not ordinance-enforcing agencies. Some emergencies, by their nature, require other agencies to take certain actions and even assume lead roles, such as public health agencies in pandemic flu outbreaks or law enforcement agencies in terrorism events. Whatever the specific nature of the emergency, however, the local emergency-management director is still responsible for coordinating response and recovery efforts and for communicating the local government's needs to state and federal agencies. An effective emergency-management director is not only well-prepared and well-trained, but he or she also fully understands the state and federal emergency-management systems and has developed within the state the contacts necessary to effectively and efficiently secure the resources his or her local government and community need in times of crisis.

Planning

One of the most important ongoing responsibilities of the local emergency-management director is developing and maintaining the local government's emergency-management plan. Local plans must be consistent with federal NIMS requirements and are subject to state and federal approval. The county or local emergency-operation plan (EOP) may be a single or a multi-jurisdictional (watershed) plan.[26] Taking the federal "all-hazards" approach to incident management, local plans should identify all potential risks and hazards to the community and outline procedures for responding to and recovering from those threats. Plans delineate the roles and responsibilities of agencies and resources at the local level (including volunteer organizations) and set out the chain of command through which decisions are made and communicated. Plans must be updated every five years to be eligible for FEMA hazard-mitigation grant funding.[27] Ideally, local jurisdictions conduct exercises and drills of their plans and operations to maintain readiness. Some jurisdictions containing certain high-risk facilities, such as nuclear power plants, have additional planning and exercise requirements mandated by both state and federal law. If properly developed, exercised, and implemented, a local plan can effectively guide a jurisdiction's response and recovery operations in a disaster event and can also serve as the basis for determining whether local resources are sufficient to meet community needs. If not, local jurisdictions can seek emergency aid and assistance from other units of government.

State and local governments must also adopt hazard-mitigation plans in which mitigation strategies are identified for hazards that threaten the particular jurisdiction.[28] FEMA's Local Mitigation Plan Review Tool may be used to assist local departments and elected officials involved in

---

24. G.S. 126-5(a)(2)d. For more information about the State Personnel Act and its application to local government employees, see Chapter 13, "Public Employment Law."

25. G.S. 166A-19.75.

26. 44 C.F.R. § 201.6(a)(4). Multi-jurisdictional hazard-mitigation plans are prepared jointly by more than one jurisdiction and may include counties, municipalities, cities, towns, townships, school districts or other special districts, councils of government or other regional organizations, or unincorporated areas. These plans may contemplate cost-saving measures through sharing resources and personnel in large-scale events. For more information about multi-jurisdictional mitigation planning, see FEMA, *Local Mitigation Planning Policy Guide, FP 206-21-0002*, effective April 19, 2023 (hereinafter *Planning Policy Guide*).

27. 44 C.F.R. § 201.6(d)(3).

28. The requirements and procedures for state, tribal, and local mitigation plans are set out in 44 C.F.R. Part 201. *See generally* FEMA (website), "Regulations and Guidance," fema.gov/emergency-managers/risk-management/hazard-mitigation-planning/regulations-guidance (last accessed March 12, 2025).

implementing a local mitigation plan.[29] Regulations require documentation that all stakeholders, including "neighboring communities, local and regional agencies involved in hazard mitigation activities, agencies that have the authority to regulate development, as well as businesses, academia and other private and nonprofit interests," had an opportunity to be involved in plan development.[30] Local emergency managers are encouraged to solicit public participation in maintaining their emergency-management plans through presentations to elected officials and community groups.[31]

Intergovernmental Cooperation

Disasters rarely impact an area conveniently located within just one government's jurisdiction and can exceed the response capabilities of local and even state governments. Recognizing the need for coordinated responses and emergency assistance across jurisdictional lines, North Carolina law authorizes three main forms of interlocal cooperation with other units of government. First, for cooperation with other jurisdictions *outside North Carolina*, the General Assembly enacted the Emergency Management Assistance Compact (EMAC), under which North Carolina and other EMAC member states provide reciprocal emergency assistance when a state of emergency has been declared in an affected state.[32] The governor is authorized to enter into mutual aid agreements with other states and with the federal government for disaster assistance and relief, and local governments in North Carolina are authorized to enter into mutual aid agreements with units of local government in other states (subject to the governor's approval).[33] Operating under mutual aid agreements allows for effective and efficient cooperation among units of government, addresses liability and insurance issues (personnel operating under a mutual aid agreement enjoy the same liability protections as employees of the unit of government to whom the assistance is rendered), and can expedite federal reimbursement in a federally declared disaster. North Carolina personnel providing disaster assistance to out-of-state jurisdictions are advised to do so either under the direction of the state through EMAC or through a mutual aid agreement entered into directly with the jurisdiction they are assisting.

Second, for cooperation between local jurisdictions *within North Carolina*, local governments are authorized to enter into mutual aid agreements with one another for reciprocal emergency-management aid and assistance.[34] This assistance includes furnishing or exchanging supplies, equipment, personnel, and services on a temporary basis during an emergency event. A common example of mutual aid is law enforcement personnel from other cities and counties deploying to the affected jurisdiction to assist in enforcing curfews, traffic control, and re-entry checkpoints.

Third, to facilitate coordination *between North Carolina counties and the cities within those counties*, state law authorizes counties and cities within those counties to form joint local emergency-management agencies.[35] Typically, each unit of local government participating in the joint agency assigns a representative to serve on that unit's behalf in the command structure of the joint agency, and all units agree to coordinate emergency-management functions under a unified set of standard operating procedures. Local governments may also enter into interlocal agreements under Article 20 of G.S. Chapter 160A to cooperatively undertake any function they are authorized to carry

29. FEMA, *Planning Policy Guide*, Appendix A.
30. 44 C.F.R. § 201.6(b)(2).
31. 44 C.F.R. § 201.6(c)(4)(iii); see also FEMA, *Planning Policy Guide*, 17.
32. G.S. Ch. 166A, Art. 4.
33. G.S. 166A-19.72.
34. G.S. 166A-19.72(c).
35. G.S. 166A-19.15(d).

out. Under such interlocal agreements, units of local government may agree to perform specific services or functions (such as debris removal) jointly or on behalf of one another instead of forming a joint agency.

Disaster and Emergency Declarations—Federal and State

Federal Declarations

A declaration of a state of disaster (or, in the case of state and local governments, a state of emergency) is issued when the declaring authority has determined that a disaster (or emergency) or the threat thereof exists. At the federal level, a disaster declaration is issued by the president, upon request of the governor of an affected state (after a state declaration has been issued), when the president finds that the disaster is of such severity and magnitude that effective response is beyond the capabilities of the state and the affected local governments and that federal assistance is necessary.[36] The severity and magnitude of a disaster is initially evaluated through preliminary damage assessments that gauge the scope of the damage, estimated repair costs, the combined capabilities of state and local governments to respond, and unmet needs for which supplemental federal assistance is required.[37] In evaluating a state's request and preliminary damage-assessment reports, consideration is given to such factors as

- the amount and type of damage;
- the impact of that damage on state and local governments and individual citizens;
- the level of resources available to affected states, local governments, and their citizens;
- the extent and type of insurance in place to cover losses;
- the existence of imminent threats to public health and safety; and
- any other factors relevant to determining whether federal assistance is needed.

If FEMA recommends and the president finds that a situation is of sufficient severity and magnitude to warrant federal assistance, a presidential major disaster declaration is issued identifying the affected geographic areas covered under the declaration and authorizing federal assistance under various individual and public-assistance programs.[38]

State Declarations

At the state level, a state of emergency can be declared by either the governor or the General Assembly upon a finding that an emergency exists.[39] A state of emergency declaration activates the state's emergency operations plan. Once the emergency has passed, the severity and magnitude of the event is determined by preliminary damage assessments. Based on those assessments, the governor is authorized to issue a disaster declaration.[40] Depending on the level of damage and losses, along with additional statutory criteria, one of three types of state disaster declarations can be issued, in ascending order of severity: Type I, Type II, or Type III.[41] A disaster declaration describes the affected geographic area covered under the declaration and authorizes state assistance programs. The length of time that a disaster declaration remains in effect depends on its type, ranging from

---

36. 42 U.S.C. § 5170.
37. 44 C.F.R. § 206.36.
38. 44 C.F.R. §§ 206.37, .38.
39. G.S. 166A-19.20.
40. G.S. 166A-19.21.
41. G.S. 166A-19.21 (describing the three types of declarations in more detail).

sixty days to twenty-four months. A state disaster declaration may be extended by either the governor or the General Assembly, depending on the declaration type. G.S. 166A-19.21(c) specifies the period of time for which each type of declaration may be renewed, the total number of renewals permitted, and the procedures to be followed for renewal.

A state disaster declaration triggers a broad array of gubernatorial powers (some of which require concurrence by the Council of State), including the power to direct or compel evacuations; restrict movement of people and vehicular traffic; deploy resources and assets of the state for relief efforts and to maintain public order and safety; establish a system of economic controls over critical resources (such as rationing or price freezing); and condemn, seize, or otherwise take property.[42] The governor also has the authority to declare the existence of an "abnormal market disruption" to the production, distribution, or sale of goods and services resulting from a natural or man-made disaster in this state as well as in other states where a federal declaration has been issued (an example would be the threat of disruption to fuel supplies in North Carolina following Hurricane Katrina and the resulting spiraling increase in gas prices). If the governor finds and declares that an abnormal market disruption exists, then excessive pricing practices prohibitions are triggered and remain in effect for forty-five days unless extended by the governor.[43]

State of Emergency Declarations—Local

At the local government level, only cities and counties are authorized to issue local state of emergency declarations.[44] Such declarations activate local plans, mutual aid and interlocal agreements and compacts, and local ordinances authorizing certain restrictions, prohibitions, and other measures taken to protect public health, safety, and welfare during the period of an emergency declaration in the affected areas covered by the declaration.

Through a local state of emergency declaration, local officials may put in place temporary restrictions and other measures necessary to preserve public order and protect public safety and welfare during the emergency. When properly authorized by local ordinance, law enforcement personnel (including those from other jurisdictions assisting under mutual aid agreements) can aid in emergency response efforts by fully enforcing locally imposed restrictions and prohibitions. Local declarations are also, in most instances, a prerequisite to receiving financial assistance through state and federal disaster-relief programs. This assistance is critical to a local government's response and recovery efforts; it can also help mitigate the fiscal disaster that can follow a natural or man-made disaster.

Who Can Issue a Declaration?

State law authorizes the governing board of a city or a county to issue a local state of emergency declaration. By local ordinance, a board may delegate its declaration authority to the board chair or to the mayor.[45] State law does not require a governing board to ratify a local official's declaration. The state of emergency remains in effect until terminated by the official or governing body that declared it.

42. G.S. 166A-19.30.

43. G.S. 75-38.

44. G.S. 166A-19.22.

45. G.S. 166A-19.22(a); 166A-19.15(f)(4). In the case of the mayor's or the board chair's absence or disability, the person authorized to act in that official's stead may act. G.S. 166A-19.3(2), (11).

Where Do Local Declarations Apply?

A state of emergency may apply to all or part of a declaring jurisdiction's geographic area. This allows local officials to impose restrictions only on the affected areas of their jurisdictions. If a declaration does not specify a particular geographic area, it applies throughout the entire jurisdiction.[46]

Declarations issued in an individual local jurisdiction are not applicable to neighboring jurisdictions except by consent. Thus, ordinances adopted by a county imposing the kinds of restrictions and prohibitions discussed above do not apply in a city within that county unless consented to by the city's mayor or council. Similarly, a city can only enforce its emergency ordinance within its own corporate jurisdiction. However, the chair of a county board of commissioners may extend to some or all parts of the county emergency restrictions imposed within a city by a mayor if so requested, even if the emergency has not occurred directly within the county itself.[47] Such an extension of city-imposed measures may be necessary to assist the city in responding to an emergency. In a major event, it is common for a state of emergency declaration to be issued jointly or cooperatively by a county and by cities within the county imposing county-wide uniform prohibitions and restrictions.

The authority granted independently to cities and counties to declare emergencies and impose restrictions does not override the management structure set out in G.S. Chapter 166A, where the county is designated as the primary coordinator of emergency management activities at the local level. Cities, while vested with independent authority to declare states of emergency within their jurisdictions,[48] must still coordinate emergency-management plans, activities, and operations with and under the direction of the county in which they are located.[49] While these statutory provisions may at first appear to be in conflict, taken together, they properly distinguish between the legal authority to impose restrictions and take other such measures necessary in times of emergency and the operational planning and implementation of such plans necessary to respond to emergencies in an efficient and coordinated manner.

What Restrictions Can Be Imposed?

Local governments may adopt ordinances that are then triggered by local state of emergency declarations.[50] If authorized in a local ordinance, a local governing board or official (if operating under delegated authority) may impose during a state of emergency the following restrictions and prohibitions, alone or in combination depending on the circumstances and severity of the emergency:

- restrictions/prohibitions on the movement of people in public places, including imposing curfews; directing and compelling the voluntary or mandatory evacuation of all or part of the population from any stricken or threatened area within the governing body's jurisdiction; prescribing routes, modes of transportation, and destinations in connection with evacuation; and controlling ingress and egress of an emergency area and the movement of persons within the area;
- restrictions/prohibitions on the operation of businesses and other places to or from which people may travel or congregate;
- restrictions/prohibitions on the possession, transportation, sale, purchase, and consumption of alcoholic beverages;

---

46. G.S. 166A-19.22(b)(1).
47. G.S. 166A-19.22(b)(3).
48. G.S. 166A-19.22.
49. G.S. 166A-19.15.
50. G.S. 166A-19.31. The constitutionality of these restrictions and prohibitions has been upheld as a proper delegation of the state's police powers to local governments. State v. Dobbins, 277 N.C. 484 (1971); United States v. Chalk, 441 F.2d 1277 (4th Cir.), *cert. denied*, 202 U.S. 943 (1971).

- restrictions/prohibitions on the possession, transportation, sale, purchase, storage, and use of dangerous weapons and substances and gasoline, except that restrictions on dangerous weapons cannot be imposed on lawfully possessed firearms (handguns, shotguns, and rifles) and ammunition; and/or
- restrictions/prohibitions on any other activity or condition the control of which may be reasonably necessary to maintain order and protect lives or property during a state of emergency.

A local government is not *required* to impose these measures when it declares a local state of emergency; it may *elect* to impose only those measures it determines are required to effectively respond to that particular emergency. In order to be legally effective, however, these measures *must* be authorized by local ordinance; measures not authorized cannot be triggered under a state of emergency declaration. Nor can such measures be enforced by law enforcement officials without having been authorized by local ordinance. For example, if a local government restricts or prohibits general public access to a particularly devastated area within its jurisdiction because of public safety concerns (washed-out roads, sinkholes, environmental contamination, unstable and falling buildings, etc.), law enforcement personnel will have difficulty enforcing this restriction, and prosecutors will have difficulty prosecuting violators of it, without proper legal authority for imposing the restriction in the first place. Violations of any such measures or other emergency ordinance provisions are punishable as Class 2 misdemeanors.[51]

Emergency restrictions and prohibitions may remain in effect for the duration of an emergency event, or they may be modified and rescinded as the affected unit progresses through response and recovery after the event. For example, a mayor might impose a curfew city-wide immediately after a tornado strikes, and then lift the curfew in unaffected areas of the city after damage assessments have been completed. Modifications to emergency declarations are issued in the same manner as the original declaration.

Other Restrictions and Prohibitions

In addition to the restrictions that may be imposed through local ordinance during a state of emergency, Article 36A of G.S. Chapter 14 directly prescribes other restrictions on public conduct in times of emergency. Among these are prohibitions against rioting (G.S. 14-288.2), looting, and trespassing during an emergency (G.S. 14-288.6); manufacturing or possessing weapons of mass destruction (G.S. 14-288.8); and assaulting emergency personnel (G.S. 14-288.9). Additionally, law enforcement officers are authorized to frisk persons who are violating an emergency curfew (G.S. 14-288.10) and to inspect vehicles entering or approaching a city in which a state of emergency has been declared (G.S. 14-288.11).

A local state of emergency declaration also triggers protections for consumers against price gouging, which, unfortunately, often follows soon after a major disaster.[52] G.S. 75-38 prohibits excessive pricing practices during a state of emergency by a seller of goods or services (1) consumed or used as a direct result of the emergency or (2) consumed or used to preserve, protect, or sustain life, health, safety, or economic well-being. This prohibition applies not only to the seller, but to all parties in the chain of distribution of the good or services (such as the manufacturer, wholesaler, or distributor). A state disaster declaration also triggers these consumer protection measures.

51. G.S. 14-288.20A.
52. G.S. 166A-19.23.

Paying for Disasters—Who Bears the Costs?

Local Funding

The regular operational costs for most local emergency-management agencies are funded through local General Fund appropriations. All counties receive federal emergency-management-planning grant (EMPG) funds to support local emergency-management operations and are eligible for other federal grant funds for one-time expenses (equipment, training, etc.). Some local governments (typically those in high-risk areas of the state) have established reserve funds to pay for expenses incurred during emergencies. Normal local funding levels are often inadequate to cover the costs of emergency response and recovery operations, however, especially in major disasters. In these instances, federal and state disaster declarations authorize various assistance programs through which eligible local governments can receive supplemental funding.

Federal Assistance Programs

Under a federal disaster declaration, three main categories of assistance can be authorized: *public assistance* (PA), which is assistance to public entities such as cities, counties, school systems, and other units of government; *individual assistance* (IA), which is assistance to private individuals; and *hazard mitigation*, which is available to both public entities and private individuals. Examples of PA include reimbursement for costs incurred for repair to public infrastructure, debris removal, and emergency protective measures. Examples of IA include temporary housing assistance, home-repair funds, unemployment benefits, food coupons, legal services, crisis counseling, and small-business loans. Examples of hazard mitigation include funding for building elevation and flood-control measures.

The guidelines for PA are described in 44 C.F.R. Part 206. PA programs operate primarily on a cost-sharing reimbursement basis—a local government incurs an eligible cost directly associated with a declared disaster and applies to the federal government for reimbursement. Federal reimbursement is provided at a rate of at least 75 percent of eligible costs[53] and may be extended to cover as much as 100 percent of eligible costs in severe disasters. The nonfederal share of these costs is traditionally funded by the state, but local governments could be required to assume some portion of the nonfederal share if that share is not fully covered by state funds.

Local governments can seek cost reimbursement for three main categories of disaster-related work expenses: debris removal, emergency protective measures, and permanent restoration (such as repair of public infrastructure). While there are specific eligibility criteria for each category of work, all work performed and all costs incurred must be as a direct result of a declared emergency and must occur within an area covered under an emergency declaration, and the work must be the legal responsibility of the affected local government. Federal reimbursement is not available for costs that are covered by another source (such as insurance) or for "losses" (as opposed to costs), such as lost tax revenues.

53. 42 U.S.C. § 5170b(b); 44 C.F.R. § 206.65. In extraordinary circumstances, the president may authorize direct federal assistance under which the federal government itself performs the emergency work and bears 100 percent of the costs.

There are seven specific categories of disaster-related work for which local governments may seek PA reimbursement:[54]

1. *Debris removal*—generally limited to the removal of debris from public property; debris that presents an imminent threat to public health or safety or to property; or debris removal necessary for the economic recovery of the community.
2. *Emergency protective measures*—includes activities such as Emergency Operations Center activation; search and rescue; emergency medical care; sheltering; distribution of food, water, and other essential supplies; and security measures.
3. *Roads and bridges*—covers repairs to transportation infrastructure not covered under other federal programs such as the Federal Highway Administration (FHWA).
4. *Water-control facilities*—covers repairs to dams, reservoirs, levees, irrigation facilities, and pumping stations.
5. *Building and equipment*—covers repairs to public buildings and repairs or replacement of damaged contents such as furnishings and equipment.
6. *Utilities*—covers repairs to water-treatment plants, power-generation and -distribution facilities, and sewage systems.
7. *Parks, recreational, and other*—covers repairs to publicly owned recreational facilities such as playgrounds, boat docks and piers, golf courses, and so on.

When a local government requests reimbursement for an eligible cost, that request is reviewed and processed by FEMA in conjunction with state emergency-management personnel and, if granted, funding is awarded. The complexity of this review process depends on the size, scope, and cost of the project. If a reimbursement request is denied, the local government may appeal that decision within FEMA. If a reimbursement request is granted, the local government must manage the federal funds consistent with federal regulations and guidelines governing most federal grant-in-aid programs; individuals who mismanage FEMA PA funds are subject to civil fines and criminal penalties.[55] When all funding requests have been fully processed (including appeals if necessary) and all federal funds have been obligated, the local government's receipt and expenditure of federal PA funds is audited (or reconciled).[56]

IA programs provide assistance directly to eligible individuals and are administered by federal agencies. Local governments might be called upon to help facilitate the delivery of IA assistance to eligible members of their communities through efforts such as publicizing information about the availability of federal assistance or providing temporary office space for federal program counselors.

The Stafford Act also authorizes post-disaster assistance designed to stimulate hazard-mitigation efforts at the state and local levels.[57] Hazard mitigation involves measures that are cost-effective and that substantially reduce the risk of future damage and loss, especially where there is evidence of repetitive loss in past disaster events. A typical example of hazard mitigation is property acquisition and relocation assistance for homeowners in flood-hazard areas who have suffered repeated flood damage. Other examples include structural hazard controls and retrofitting of facilities. The amount of funding made available for hazard-mitigation projects ranges from 7.5 to 20 percent

54. For more information about PA programs and eligibility criteria, see FEMA, *Public Assistance Program and Policy Guide, FP 104-009-2*, effective June 1, 2020; see generally FEMA (website), "Public Assistance Resource Library," fema.gov/assistance/public/library (last accessed March 12, 2025).

55. 44 C.F.R. § 206.14.

56. 42 U.S.C. § 5161(c).

57. 42 U.S.C. § 5170c; 44 C.F.R. Part 206, Subpart N.

(depending on the grant amount and the state's hazard-mitigation plan) of the total PA and IA federal funds awarded following a major disaster. The federal funding available for each individual hazard-mitigation project may be up to 75 percent of the total project cost. Although federally funded, hazard-mitigation programs may be administered at the state level. In order to receive hazard-mitigation funding, both the state and the local government applicant must have adopted federally approved hazard-mitigation plans, and each hazard-mitigation project must be consistent with the jurisdiction's plan.

State Assistance Programs

The state also provides a number of disaster-assistance programs that are triggered by a state disaster declaration issued by the governor.[58] State disaster assistance can be made available in certain circumstances regardless of whether a federal declaration is issued, but it does require that a local state of emergency declaration be issued. Mirroring the structure of federal programs (and intended to supplement federal programs where federal assistance is either not available or not adequate), the scope and number of state programs available depends on the type of disaster declaration issued. For Type I disasters (the least severe in terms of damage), both state IA and PA programs are authorized. State IA programs include assistance for temporary housing and home repair, relocation, replacement of personal property and vehicles, medical and dental expenses, and funeral or burial expenses. State PA programs include assistance to local governments for costs incurred in disaster activities such as debris removal, emergency protective measures, road and bridge repair, crisis counseling, and public transportation needs.

In order to be eligible for Type I PA assistance, a unit of local government must meet four criteria: (1) it must have suffered at least $10,000 in uninsurable losses; (2) those uninsurable losses must equal or exceed 1 percent of the unit's annual operating budget; (3) it must have an approved hazard-mitigation plan; and (4) for flood damage, it must participate in the National Flood Insurance Program. If the local government meets these criteria, it becomes eligible to receive reimbursement for 75 percent of eligible costs; the local government must absorb the remaining 25 percent of the costs. No PA programs are authorized for Type II and Type III disasters, and only a limited number of IA programs are authorized for these two types of disasters (for which, presumably, greater federal assistance is available).

Contracting and Other Requirements for Reimbursement

It should be noted that compliance with all applicable federal regulations and guidelines is a condition of any federal grant award. Where federal guidelines specify conditions or restrictions not found in state law, those conditions or restrictions still must be followed by local government applicants. Local governments should seek the advice of counsel about applicable federal requirements that may not exist within state law and yet could present a barrier to funding awards if not followed. For example, debris-removal contracts are considered service contracts under state law and, as such, are not subject to North Carolina bidding laws. However, federal law requires that certain competitive bidding procedures be followed in the award of service contracts for which federal funds are spent.[59] A local government may, in good faith, award a debris-removal contract without utilizing a competitive bidding process and act entirely consistent with state law yet not be in compliance with federal law. This is also the case with "piggybacking" onto another local

---

58. G.S. 166A-19.41.

59. *See* 2 C.F.R. Part 200 (also referred to as the "Uniform Guidance," 2 C.F.R. Part 200 was revised significantly in 2024 and may be subject to further amendments).

government's existing debris-removal (or other service) contract. While not prohibited under state law, this practice violates federal procurement procedures.

Similarly, North Carolina law allows waivers of competitive bidding requirements "in [c]ases of special emergency involving the health and safety of the people and their property."[60] Again, in a disaster situation, a local government may choose to enter into a service contract without following competitive bidding requirements under this emergency exemption.[61] When seeking federal funding assistance, a local government may engage in noncompetitive procurement methods if "[t]he public exigency or emergency for the requirement will not permit a delay resulting from publicizing a competitive solicitation."[62] When using this exception to federal competitive-solicitation requirements, a local government should consult FEMA guidance to ensure that it properly documents the justification for the exception in the procurement record and observes other applicable federal-funding eligibility requirements.[63]

Another example of a conflict between state/local and federal law that can be a barrier to reimbursement involves personnel costs. Generally, overtime pay for *nonexempt* employees is eligible for federal reimbursement in a federally declared disaster. Some local governments will authorize, by local ordinance or in their personnel policies, the award of overtime compensation for *exempt* employees in disaster situations, and they will leave the decision to award the overtime compensation in any particular disaster to the discretion of their governing board or manager; others will award overtime compensation only if a federal disaster declaration has been issued. Such policies are not prohibited under state law. Under federal regulations, however, compensation for personnel costs is contingent on an affected local government having an established policy that is "consistently applied to both Federal and non-Federal activities."[64] Thus, if the award of overtime pay for exempt employees is not in a written policy and is either discretionary or dependent on a federal disaster declaration, it is not considered "consistently applied to both federal and non-federal activities" and is not eligible for federal reimbursement.

Infrastructure

One of the primary concerns of all local officials is how to expedite the disaster-recovery process as much as possible to reinstate private services and begin economic and budgetary recovery. Building and inspections is one area in which local governments may implement extraordinary procedures, such as modifying local ordinances or employing additional inspectors and personnel to expedite recovery. Several inspections and assessments take place in the days following an event. Local building officials may initially conduct safety and habitability inspections of damaged buildings to assess whether each structure is safe to enter, has limited access, or is condemned. Local floodplain-management and permitting officials may also inspect structures to assess zoning or floodplain

60. G.S. 143-129(e)(2).

61. For more information on North Carolina purchasing and contracting requirements, see Frayda S. Bluestein, *A Legal Guide to Purchasing and Contracting for North Carolina Local Governments*, 2nd ed. (UNC School of Government, 2004).

62. 2 C.F.R. § 200.320(c)(3).

63. For further guidance about the emergency and exigent circumstances exception, see FEMA (website), "An Exception to the Rules During Emergency or Exigent Circumstances" (last updated July 22, 2020), fema.gov/grants/procurement/understand-exception (last accessed March 12, 2025).

64. Office of Management and Budget, *OMB Circular A-87 Revised*, May 2004, Attachment B, "Selected Items of Cost."

status and obtain information on each property owner's rebuilding plan and compliance with state and local regulations. Under state law, every inspector or code-enforcement official must hold a valid certification of qualification issued by the North Carolina Code Officials Qualification Board for building, electrical, mechanical, plumbing, or fire code enforcement.[65] The Board may issue probationary or temporary certificates to any newly employed Code enforcer who lacks prerequisite qualifications for a standard certificate for one to three years, and it may designate specialty levels with special conditions relating to place of employment, supervision, or other matters necessary to protect public health and safety.[66] The Board may also issue standard certificates following a short course to any person licensed under state law as an architect, general contractor, plumbing or heating contractor, electrical contractor, or professional engineer.[67]

Under state law, ambulatory surgical centers[68] and hospitals[69] are required to develop emergency-preparedness programs with input from local emergency-management officials. Such programs must comply with the Emergency Preparedness Requirements for Medicare and Medicaid Participating Providers and Suppliers Final Rule promulgated by the Centers for Medicare and Medicaid Services (CMS).[70] Under Title 10A, Chapter 13, Subchapter B, Section .4110 of the North Carolina Administrative Code, each hospital in the state is required to describe services available during an external disaster, the role of its emergency department in a disaster, procedures for an internal disaster, and connections to public agencies and emergency suppliers such as the Red Cross.[71] All hospital emergency-preparedness programs must also provide for evacuation and transfer of all inpatients in case of internal disaster and for mutual agreements with area providers.[72] If local hospitals are damaged or overwhelmed during a given disaster incident, this may greatly affect the availability of emergency transportation and recovery.

Continuity of Government in the Event of Enemy Attack

In the cold-war era of the late 1950s, the General Assembly enacted not only the Civil Preparedness Act (G.S. Chapter 166, the forerunner to Chapter 166A), but also G.S. Chapter 162B, establishing measures to ensure continuity of local governments in the event of an enemy attack on the state. These statutes, which are triggered only when the governor and Council of State declare the state to be subject to impending or actual hostile attack, authorize local governments to identify alternate sites within and outside of their jurisdictions to serve as emergency locations from which the local governments might operate and at which they might meet to transact public business.[73] A governing body may even waive compliance with "legally prescribed procedural requirements relating to the conduct of meetings and transaction of business" if the situation makes compliance with such requirements impossible.[74] Local governments are also authorized to enact ordinances providing

65. G.S. 143-151.13(a), (b).
66. G.S. 143-151.13(d).
67. G.S. 143-151.13(f).
68. Title 10A, Chapter 13, Subchapter C, Section .1403 of the North Carolina Administrative Code (hereinafter N.C.A.C.).
69. 10A N.C.A.C. 13B, § .6102(b).
70. CMS (website), "Emergency Preparedness Rule," effective Nov. 16, 2016, cms.gov/medicare/health-safety-standards/quality-safety-oversight-emergency-preparedness/emergency-preparedness-rule.
71. 10A N.C.A.C. 13B, § .4110(a).
72. 10A N.C.A.C. 13B, §§ .4110(c)(5), (6).
73. G.S. 162B-1, -2.
74. G.S. 162B-3.

for emergency interim succession to local offices in the event that local officials are unavailable.[75] In cases where a legally empowered official is unavailable, a successor may exercise the powers and discharge the duties of that office until the vacancy is filled according to statute or the official returns.[76] An interim successor may exercise the powers of the office he or she assumes only in the event of an attack on the state,[77] and his or her status as an interim successor may be terminated by the local governing body at any time.[78]

At the federal level, continuity of government and operations is not limited to enemy attack. The FEMA Office of National Continuity Programs has provided guidance on continuity matters for all federal executive branch agencies as well as for state, local, and tribal governments.[79]

Immunity and Liability

Broad immunity is granted for emergency-management functions. G.S. 166A-19.60 exempts from liability the state, any political subdivision of the state, and any emergency-management worker who is, in good faith,[80] complying or attempting to comply with any order, rule, regulation, or ordinance relating to any emergency-management measures. This immunity includes situations resulting in death or injury to persons or in damage to property and applies wherever an emergency-management worker is engaged in emergency-management activities or services, whether inside or outside of the worker's own jurisdiction. Moreover, any professional work or service that would normally require a license under North Carolina law can be performed without a license by an emergency-management worker during a declared state of disaster.

Under this statute, an "emergency management worker" is broadly defined as a full- or part-time paid, volunteer, or auxiliary employee of the federal government, the state, political subdivisions of the state, or any agency or organization performing emergency-management services in any place in the state, so long as he or she is subject to the order or control of, or is working at the request of, state or local government.[81] The definition also includes state medical assistance teams and emergency healthcare workers. While this definition is very broad, it may not extend to private vendors and contractors working for hire under contract with state or local governments in a disaster situation. Even though an affected unit of government itself is granted immunity (and is presumably protected even if its vendors and contractors are not), local governments would be well-served by requiring liability indemnification and hold-harmless clauses in all contracts with private companies, vendors, and individuals for any and all claims arising out of the performance of the contracts.[82]

---

75. G.S. 162B-6.

76. G.S. 162B-9.

77. Attacks may be accomplished by "sabotage or by the use of bombs, missiles, shellfire, or atomic, radiological, chemical, bacteriological, or biological means or other weapons or processes." G.S. 162B-7.

78. G.S. 162B-11.

79. *See* FEMA (website), Continuity Resources (searchable database), fema.gov/emergency-managers/national-preparedness/continuity/documents (last accessed March 12, 2025), and FEMA Office of National Continuity Programs, *Continuity Guidance Circular*, February 2018 (2024 Update), fema.gov/sites/default/files/documents/fema_continuity-guidance-circular_082024.pdf.

80. The immunity under G.S. 166A-19.60 does not extend to cases of willful misconduct, gross negligence, or bad faith.

81. G.S. 166A-19.60(e).

82. The Stafford Act requires indemnification of the federal government in all contracts involving private property debris removal. 42 U.S.C. § 5173(b).

Chapter 34

Public Library Services

Frank Alford, Emily Roscoe, and Alex Hess

Frank Alford is the School of Government's librarian. Emily Roscoe is a former legal research associate for the School of Government.

This chapter is a modified version of the public library services chapter by Alex Hess in the second edition of *County and Municipal Government in North Carolina*. Hess was the School of Government's librarian from 1998 to 2021.

The public library is a community-focused educational institution whose objective is to assist people of all ages and interests in continuing to learn. Its purpose is to help individuals educate themselves, keep better informed about public affairs, and enjoy the pleasure of reading. A public library accomplishes this by acquiring, assembling, organizing, and making freely available the resources in its collection and by providing access to remote information sources. The public library plays an important role in the development of a democratic society by giving individuals access to a wide and varied range of knowledge, ideas, and opinions. Automation of local public library operations, creation of systems of shared resources, and advancements in technology that provide access to global networks of information and expansive digital content have combined to allow a tremendous increase in the speed and breadth of service delivery to library users.[1] The book *Introduction to Public Librarianship* describes the public library as "a community commons, a place for lifelong learning, a place for early childhood, emergent literacy, a creator space, and perhaps most subtly, a statement of community value."[2]

1. See, for example, Christie Koontz and Barbara Gubbin, "The Mission and Purposes of the Public Library," in *IFLA Public Library Service Guidelines*, ed. Koontz and Gubbin, IFLA Publications Series 147 (Berlin/Munich: De Gruyter Saur, 2010), 1–20, perma.cc/ZAJ3-TCFS; Martin Garnar and Trina J. Magi, "Public Libraries" in *Intellectual Freedom Manual*, 10th ed. (Chicago: ALA Editions, 2021), 13–16, 61–66.

2. Kathleen de la Peña McCook, Jenny S. Bossaller, and Felton Thomas Jr., *Introduction to Public Librarianship*, 3rd ed. (Chicago: ALA Neal-Schuman, 2018), 14.

Library Establishment and Operation

Statutory Authority

The public library—whether city, county, or multicounty (regional)—traditionally has been primarily the responsibility of local government. The legislature may grant authority to a local unit of government to establish library services by a general enabling law or by a special local act. Although most public libraries in the state have been established and are supported by local governments under the general law (Chapter 153A, Article 14 of the North Carolina General Statutes (hereinafter G.S.)), some operate under local acts with provisions different from the statewide statutes. The law also authorizes counties and cities to appropriate funds to support libraries that provide free services to all (G.S. 153A-263(6); 153A-264). The local governing body should be familiar with all the laws that created and govern its library.

Library Board of Trustees

The governing body of a city or county (board of county commissioners or city council) may appoint a library board of trustees (G.S. 153A-265). Appointments to the board are made at the discretion of the local governing body, which is authorized to determine the number of trustees (not to exceed twelve), their terms of office, rules for their removal from office, and any compensation they might receive. Powers that may be delegated to a library board by a governing body are listed in G.S. 153A-266. The board is required to make an annual report on library operations to the local governing body and to the Department of Natural and Cultural Resources as required by G.S. 125-5. (If a board of trustees has not been established, the local governing board itself would have to submit the report.)

Library Employees

G.S. 153A-267 requires that the chief administrator of any public library system in North Carolina have a professional librarian certificate issued by the secretary of cultural resources, pursuant to G.S. 125-9 and 125-10 under regulations for certification established by the Public Librarian Certification Commission (G.S. 143B-67; Title 7, Chapter 2J of the North Carolina Administrative Code (hereinafter N.C.A.C.)). All employees of a public library are "for all purposes" bona fide employees of the county or city that supports it (G.S. 153A-267). They are covered by workers' compensation insurance and are eligible for membership in the local retirement system and other fringe benefits. G.S. 160A-463 provides that employees of regional libraries (established under G.S. 153A-270) are entitled to the same rights and privileges as employees of the individual governments that participate in these libraries.

Area Served by the Library

The earliest public libraries in the state were city libraries, serving the immediate community. Local initiative and interest were instrumental in their organization and support. By the mid-1920s, however, the county library had been recognized as a more efficient unit of library service. Primarily for this reason, more libraries that provide countywide rather than citywide service have been established. Also partly accounting for the preponderance of this type is the fact that, until 1979, state aid was given only to libraries that served entire counties.[3]

Both the American Library Association (ALA) and the International Federation of Library Associations (IFLA) have stressed the importance of cooperation and joint action among libraries and

3. In 1979, G.S. 125-7(c) was amended to allow city and regional libraries to share in state-provided library equalization funds.

between libraries and other entities to sustain and enhance services. Public libraries that are bound together formally or informally in systems and those that establish links with other local organizations are better able to provide needed resources, materials, and access to remote networks of information to meet the full needs of their clientele. The trend toward such broader-based library systems has proved practical not only because the per capita cost is less if the library serves a large area but also because the quality and number of services and resources is improved through cooperation.[4]

The position of the North Carolina Library Association has also been to encourage public libraries to share resources and services. In 1987, it stated as follows:

> Since on a per capita basis it takes more to run a small library than a large one, many communities cannot raise sufficient tax funds to support public libraries that will meet . . . minimum standards. Whenever inadequate support makes it impossible to meet these standards, libraries should find an alternative method of providing library service, either by combining [libraries in] small localities into a large library unit or by contracting for local services with an existing, strong library unit. In this way, effective library services can be made available to any community, no matter how small.[5]

Toward this end, the law enables two or more units of local government to operate libraries and other undertakings jointly (G.S. Chapter 160A, Article 20, Part 1; 7 N.C.A.C. 2I, § .0300 (Apr. 2011)) and to acquire or construct public buildings together (G.S. 153A-164). The units may acquire the necessary land for such purposes, or they may use land already belonging to one of the participating governments. In 2023, fifty-nine counties and thirteen cities maintained their own individual units, while forty-one counties had formed twelve regional library systems, making larger book collections and more varied services possible.[6] These systems are defined as "public authorities" and are subject to the Local Government Budget and Fiscal Control Act (LGBFCA).[7]

The examination of local needs in determining the best way to provide library services has now become the standard criteria. In 1980, the Public Library Association (PLA), a division of the ALA, first recommended that national standards for library performance be abandoned in favor of formulating local goals and objectives based on the needs of particular communities. In *A Planning Process for Public Libraries*,[8] a report of the recommendations from a study commissioned by the association, the importance of such differences between communities was explicitly recognized. The report emphasized the needs of individual citizens as the basis for analyzing the area to be served, and it urged libraries to seek active participation from every segment of the locality in conducting a community survey. As currently formulated, excellence in providing library services must be defined locally and results only when services match community needs, interests, and priorities. In

---

4. Standards Committee, Public Library Association (PLA), *Minimum Standards for Public Library Systems, 1966* (Chicago: ALA, 1967), 10–11; Koontz and Gubbin, *IFLA Public Library Service Guidelines*, 52–54, perma.cc /ZAJ3-TCFS.

5. Standards and Measures Committee, Public Libraries Section, N.C. Library Association, *Standards for North Carolina Public Libraries* (Raleigh: State Library of North Carolina, 1987), 7.

6. Correspondence with State Library of North Carolina personnel on Nov. 21, 2023; two regional libraries (Hyconeechee and Gaston–Lincoln) composed of all or part of five counties (Caswell, Orange, Person, Gaston, and Lincoln) were dissolved in 2012.

7. Letter from Harlan Boyles, secretary, N.C. Local Government Commission, to Elaine von Oesen, assistant state librarian, Oct. 2, 1973; *see also* Title 7, Chapter 2I, Section .0306 of the North Carolina Administrative Code (hereinafter N.C.A.C.); G.S. 159-7(b)(10).

8. Vernon E. Palmour, Marcia C. Bellassai, and Nancy V. DeWath, *A Planning Process for Public Libraries* (Chicago: PLA/ALA, 1980), xi–xii.

addition, excellence in the provision of services is considered a moving target, and its maintenance requires constant monitoring and planning.[9]

Following the ALA's recommendation, community analyses were conducted by most of the public library systems in North Carolina, and now, as a requirement for eligibility to receive state aid, each library must be prepared to submit an assessment of a community's library needs if requested by the State Library. Each library also must submit annually a current long-range plan of service (covering at least five years) to the State Library.[10]

Financing the Public Library

Local Financial Support

Since library service to the general public has been considered chiefly a function of local government, financial backing predominately has come from the locality served. Both counties and cities have authority to support libraries from any available source of funds (G.S. 153A-263(6); 153A-268), including, most importantly, the property tax (G.S. 153A-149(c)(19), for counties; 160A-209(c)(20), for cities). Since both types of governments may finance libraries, cities may contribute to the operation of county or regional libraries. Also, counties may make appropriations to city libraries that are used by county residents who live outside the city. In a few places, libraries are legally entitled to share in the profits of the local alcoholic beverage control (ABC) system,[11] and some libraries have their own endowment funds. (See Tables 34.1 and 34.2, below.)

State Aid

History

State financial aid to county and regional public libraries usually takes the form of cash grants and/or services. The state aid fund for public libraries was established in 1941. The first appropriation of $100,000 per annum for "payment to counties" was increased during each successive session of the General Assembly until 1957, when the figure reached $425,000. It remained at that level until an increase was approved in 1965.[12]

In 1964, the Governor's Commission on Library Resources was appointed to study the overall status of libraries in the state and to suggest ways to meet steadily increasing needs for educational and informational materials as well as services. The commission recommended that "continued study be given to the development of a plan for joint local-state-federal responsibility for public library financing."[13]

In 1967, by joint resolution, the General Assembly created the Commission to Study Library Support in the State of North Carolina. Concluding that sources of public revenue for local governments are more limited than other sources of public revenue, this commission recommended that the state gradually assume equal responsibility with local government for public library support. It

9. Sandra Nelson, *The New Planning for Results: A Streamlined Approach* (Chicago: ALA, 2001), 1–2, and *Strategic Planning for Results* (Chicago: ALA, 2008), 4, 7, 35–42.

10. 7 N.C.A.C. 2I, § .0201(10); G.S. 125-7. *See also* G.S. 125-5. The State Library of North Carolina website offers extensive resources for libraries, statelibrary.ncdcr.gov/services-libraries.

11. *See, e.g.*, S.L. 1947-835 for a specific grant of 5 percent of net ABC profits to the Public Library of Charlotte and Mecklenburg County.

12. Financial records on file in the N.C. Department of Natural and Cultural Resources, State Library of North Carolina, Raleigh.

13. North Carolina Governor's Commission on Library Resources, *Resources of North Carolina Libraries*, ed. Robert B. Downs (Raleigh, N.C.: The Commission, 1965), perma.cc/9BCX-2PRL.

proposed that this goal be accomplished over a period of several years, during which time annual increases in state grants to public libraries would amount to approximately twenty cents per capita.[14]

The Present System

State funds are intended to stimulate the improvement and expansion of public library services. They are allocated among qualifying library systems on the basis of the rules and regulations formulated by the secretary of the Department of Cultural Resources in accordance with G.S. 125-7 (7 N.C.A.C. 2I, § .0200).

The present formula for distributing state aid for public libraries was adopted in 1983 after a four-year study of the financial needs of library systems. Under this formula, 50 percent of the state aid appropriation is distributed among qualifying county and regional libraries in equal block grants. Regional libraries receive one overall grant in addition to the ones that are received for each county in the region. The remaining 50 percent of the appropriation is awarded as per capita income equalization grants. Each eligible county, regional, and city library system receives a per capita grant that is inversely proportional to the per capita income of the area served. In the most affluent system the local per capita income is approximately twice that of the least affluent. The per capita equalization grant, therefore, results in the poorest system receiving about twice as much per capita as the richest. The formula thus directs more aid to the counties and cities that are less able to support libraries from local treasuries.[15]

General Assembly appropriations for the state aid fund for public libraries increased rapidly from 1983 to 1987, with the annual total moving from $4.8 million in fiscal year 1982–83 to $11.3 million in fiscal year 1987–88. The annual appropriation declined to below $11 million from 1990 to 1996 but started rising again in the late 1990s to a peak of $16.9 million for fiscal year 1998–99. The appropriation remained in the $14–16 million range through fiscal year 2010–11 (the only exception was the $12.7 million for fiscal year 2001–02). For fiscal years 2011–12 through 2014–15, the appropriation fell to about $13.5 million. Since fiscal year 2015–16, the appropriation has remained above $14 million.[16]

The rules for the allocation of state aid to public libraries, compiled by the Department of Natural and Cultural Resources, specify application procedures for receiving this type of assistance (7 N.C.A.C. 2I, § .0201). State aid is designed to supplement local funds rather than to replace them (7 N.C.A.C. 2I, § .0201(4)). Thus, if an appropriation a library system receives from local government sources is less than that of the previous year, a state grant will not be terminated but instead reduced in proportion to the decrease. (See Tables 34.1 and 34.2, below.)

Federal Aid

The Library Services and Construction Act

Federal aid began when Congress passed the Library Services Act[17] in 1956 to help states improve and extend public library services in rural areas. This act was replaced in 1964 by the Library

---

14. North Carolina Legislative Commission to Study Library Support in the State of North Carolina, *Report*, Aug. 1968.

15. "Keeping Up," *North Carolina Libraries* 41 (Fall 1983), 162, perma.cc/B96V-SVG8; State Library of North Carolina, *State Aid to Public Libraries* (Raleigh: N.C. Department of Natural and Cultural Resources, n.d.); Caroline (Cal) Shepard, *State Aid in North Carolina*, presented to the North Carolina Public Library Directors Association (NCPLDA), Mar. 25, 1999, perma.cc/PA9E-2F7V.

16. State Library of North Carolina, *Public Library Statistics*; *Directory of North Carolina Public Libraries, 1981–1982* through *1999–2000*; *State Aid to Public Libraries, 2000–2001* through *2014–2015* (Raleigh: N.C. Department of Natural and Cultural Resources, n.d.); *Statistical Report of North Carolina Public Libraries, 2015–2016* through *2021–2022* (Raleigh: N.C. Department of Natural and Cultural Resources, n.d.), perma.cc/CWH7-LFSU.

17. Pub. L. No. 84-597, 70 Stat. 293 (1956).

Table 34.1 Sources of Income for Public Library Services (in Dollars)

Year	Municipal Funds	County Funds	State Aid*	Federal Aid**	Other Income***	Total
1942–1943	194,741	201,377	95,380	—	120,168	611,666
1952–1953	612,138	717,319	350,000	—	214,868	1,894,325
1956–1957	822,816	1,019,072	390,000	14,301	266,184	2,512,373
1966–1967	1,649,781	3,041,989	686,250	717,713	550,587	6,646,320
1976–1977	4,454,919	10,859,461	3,514,635	1,262,289	1,969,069	22,060,373
1986–1987	8,026,586	36,347,438	10,789,462	1,335,700	4,911,091	61,410,277
1996–1997	14,828,375	77,065,067	13,910,516	2,534,943	7,783,003	116,121,904
2006–2007	21,790,080	144,971,608	17,226,909	1,157,718	13,709,991	198,856,306
2007–2008	22,899,349	153,593,718	16,920,382	1,419,558	15,058,012	209,891,019
2008–2009	23,140,788	154,772,050	15,844,888	1,635,317	13,827,172	209,220,215
2009–2010	23,152,245	152,400,189	15,776,220	1,633,388	13,883,287	206,845,329
2010–2011	24,624,751	146,453,343	15,876,985	1,436,147	11,182,470	199,573,696
2011–2012	22,911,594	150,739,709	14,174,305	1,420,010	10,876,480	200,122,098
2012–2013	23,433,091	153,773,303	14,040,630	1,675,778	13,237,483	206,160,285
2013–2014	24,246,828	158,928,952	13,851,494	1,606,642	13,967,234	212,601,150
2014–2015	24,337,828	168,150,642	13,596,746	1,669,041	10,548,202	218,302,244
2015–2016	25,469,591	173,529,444	14,673,741	1,811,433	10,272,593	225,756,802
2016–2017	26,185,274	183,328,797	14,796,434	1,607,567	10,344,747	236,262,819
2017–2018	27,323,832	188,437,225	15,011,790	1,416,009	10,621,330	242,810,186
2018–2019	27,483,779	193,936,759	14,571,180	1,729,114	10,182,316	247,903,148
2019–2020	28,652,839	203,024,829	14,415,707	1,570,272	15,082,442	262,746,089
2020–2021	29,267,239	214,722,759	14,451,054	3,230,675	15,479,558	277,151,285
2021–2022	31,008,589	213,181,626	14,572,238	14,572,238	23,629,472	286,043,085

Note: Capital expenditures are not shown in this table.

Sources: Biennial reports of the State Library of North Carolina (1942–1943 through 1966–1967); Library Development Section, State Library of North Carolina, *Public Library Statistics; Directory of North Carolina Public Libraries, 1981–1982* through *1999–2000*, and North Carolina State Library, *Statistical Report of North Carolina Public Libraries, 2006–2007* through *2021–2022* (Raleigh: N.C. Department of Natural and Cultural Resources, n.d.), Table 4: Operating Income.

*Includes Aid to Public Libraries Fund.

**Includes LSCA and LSTA.

***Private donations, etc.

Table 34.2 Percentage Contribution and Per Capita Income for Libraries by Source, 1966–2022

Year	County and Municipal Funds Contribution / Per Capita	State Aid Contribution / Per Capita*	Federal Aid Contribution / Per Capita**	Other Support Contribution / Per Capita***	Population July 1
1966–1967	71% / $0.96	10% / $0.14	11% / $0.15	8% / $0.11	4,896,000
1976–1977	69% / $2.73	16% / $0.63	6% / $0.23	9% / $0.35	5,607,964
1986–1987	72% / $7.02	18% / $1.71	2% / $0.21	8% / $0.78	6,321,578
1996–1997	79% / $12.25	12% / $1.85	2% / $0.34	7% / $1.04	7,500,670
2006–2007	84% / $18.70	9% / $1.93	1% / $0.13	7% / $1.54	8,917,270
2007–2008	84% / $19.37	8% / $1.86	1% / $0.16	7% / $1.65	9,113,037
2010–2011	86% / $17.89	8% / $1.66	1% / $0.15	6% / $1.17	9,561,558
2012–2013	86% / $18.17	7% / $1.44	1% / $0.17	6% / $1.36	9,752,073
2016–2017	89% / $ 20.61	6% / $ 1.46	1% / $ 0.16	4% / $ 1.02	10,161,802
2017–2018	89% / $ 21.00	6% / $ 1.46	1% / $ 0.14	4% / $ 1.03	10,275,758
2020–2021	88% / $ 23.35	5% / $ 1.38	1% / $ 0.31	6% / $ 1.48	10,449,445
2021–2022	85% / $ 23.11	5% / $ 1.38	5% / $ 1.38	8% / $ 2.24	10,565,885

Sources: Biennial reports of the State Library of North Carolina (1966–1967); Library Development Section, State Library of North Carolina, *Public Library Statistics; Directory of North Carolina Public Libraries, 1981–1982* through *1999–2000*, and North Carolina State Library, *Statistical Report of North Carolina Public Libraries, 2006–2007* through *2021–2022* (Raleigh: N.C. Department of Natural and Cultural Resources, n.d.), Table 4: Operating Income; U.S. Census Population Annual Estimates for States.

*Includes Aid to Public Libraries Fund.

**Includes LSCA and LSTA.

***Private donations, etc.

Services and Construction Act (LSCA),[18] which broadened and increased federal assistance to the states for public library services and specified that urban areas could share in those funds on the same basis as rural areas. The 1964 act extended the use of federal allocations to library construction and gave the library agency of each state (the State Library of North Carolina in this state) full authority to plan for the use of LSCA funds.

The act was divided into titles to achieve its objectives. The three main titles to be administered by the State Library of North Carolina were established in the first two years of the LSCA's existence: Title I for Library Services, Title II for construction and improvements, and Title III to encourage interlibrary cooperation.[19] Further titles were added over the next thirty years to extend the use of funding to include development of foreign language materials, literacy programs, services for Indian tribes, library learning centers, evaluation and assessment, and aid for the physically handicapped.[20]

In addition to Title II construction funds, LSCA funding was distributed in the form of direct grants for the enrichment of collections and services, the automation of library services, and the

18. Pub. L. No. 88-269, 78 Stat. 11 (1964). Before its repeal in 1996, the LSCA was codified at 20 U.S.C. § 351 *et seq.*
19. *Id.*; Pub. L. No. 89-511, 80 Stat. 313 (1966).
20. Pub. L. No. 91-600, 84 Stat. 1660 (1970); Pub. L. No. 98-480, 98 Stat. 2236 (1984) (Titles IV, V, VI); Pub. L. No. 101-254, 104 Stat. 107 (1990) (Titles VII, VIII).

establishment of Internet and local area network services.[21] The LSCA was reauthorized and modified several times between 1964 and 1996, and the State Library of North Carolina continued to submit annual plans and reports to the U.S. Department of Education, the federal oversight agency for funds awarded under provisions of the act.

The Library Services and Technology Act

In 1996, Congress enacted the Library Services and Technology Act (LSTA).[22] It continued the LSCA approach of using a state agency (still the North Carolina State Library in our state) as the conduit for federal funds to local libraries but transferred federal oversight from the U.S. Department of Education to the Institute of Museum and Library Services and expanded the definition of which libraries were to be funded. The LSTA serves as a successor to the library programs found in the Higher Education Act (HEA) as well as those of the LSCA and includes appropriations for programs for library education and academic libraries as well as for local public libraries.[23] The act focused on two key priorities: (1) activities using technology for information sharing among libraries and between libraries and other community services and (2) programs that make library services more accessible to urban and rural communities, to low-income people, and to others who have difficulty using traditional library services.[24] Specifically, as reauthorized in 2003 and 2010, the act requires that 96 percent of the funds provided to a state library administrative agency be expended either directly to support statewide initiatives and services or indirectly, through subgrants and cooperative agreements, for the following purposes:

1. expanding services for learning and access to information and educational resources in a variety of formats, in all types of libraries, for individuals of all ages in order to support such individuals' needs for education, lifelong learning, workforce development, and digital literacy skills;
2. establishing or enhancing electronic and other linkages and improved coordination among and between libraries and entities, as described in section 9134(b)(6) of this title, for the purpose of improving the quality of and access to library and information services;
3. (A) providing training and professional development, including continuing education, to enhance the skills of the current library workforce and leadership, and advance the delivery of library and information services; and (B) enhancing efforts to recruit future professionals to the field of library and information science;
4. developing public and private partnerships with other agencies and community-based organizations;
5. targeting library services to individuals of diverse geographic, cultural, and socioeconomic backgrounds, to individuals with disabilities, and to individuals with limited functional literacy or information skills;

---

21. State Library of North Carolina, *North Carolina Public Library Services Grant Awards, 1996–97* (Raleigh: N.C. Department of Natural and Cultural Resources, Nov. 15, 1996) and *LSCA Title I Public Library Services Grants FY 1997–98* (Raleigh: N.C. Department of Natural and Cultural Resources, n.d.).

22. Pub. L. No. 104-208, 110 Stat. 3009 (1996). The LSTA is codified at 20 U.S.C. § 9121 *et seq.*

23. State Library of North Carolina, *Discussion Paper: Implementing the Library Services & Technology Act in North Carolina, June 1997* (Raleigh: N.C. Department of Natural and Cultural Resources).

24. State Library of North Carolina, *Library Services & Technology Act: Plan for Implementation in North Carolina—2003–2007* (Raleigh: N.C. Department of Natural and Cultural Resources, Aug. 2002), perma.cc/TR7W-MFCV.

6. targeting library and information services to persons having difficulty using a library and to underserved urban and rural communities, including children (from birth through age 17) from families with incomes below the poverty line (as defined by the Office of Management and Budget and revised annually in accordance with section 9902(2) of Title 42) applicable to a family of the size involved; and
7. developing library services that provide all users access to information through local, State, regional, national, and international electronic networks;
8. carrying out other activities consistent with the purposes set forth in section 9121 of this title, as described in the State library administrative agency's plan.[25]

The LSTA provided greater flexibility and reduced the administrative burden on the state administering agency. There were no separate titles with individual purposes and no provision for a continuation of the old LSCA Title II construction and facilities funds. Continuity lay instead with the old Title I and III allocations for library services and cooperation, with an emphasis on technological innovation. The LSTA also required the state library agency to file a five-year implementation plan and included strong requirements for increased accountability and evaluation, including an independent evaluation prior to the end of the five-year plan.[26]

The 2003 reauthorization changed the requirement of submitting an initial five-year implementation plan to one requiring a plan to be submitted to the director of the Institute of Museum and Library Services once every five years. The State Library had already prepared an implementation plan in August 2002 that covered the next five-year span (2003–2007). The plan included criteria for eligibility and policies for evaluating proposals in the grant-awarding process established for future fund distribution to public, academic, school, special libraries, state agency libraries, and the State Library of North Carolina. Other eligible entities included library cooperative organizations, library-related organizations, state and local professional library associations, library/media center administrative units, graduate library educational programs, and national or regional library organizations.[27]

In summary, the chief goals were to (1) achieve equity in library service for all North Carolinians, (2) create a climate for innovation and change in response to changing needs, opportunities, and environments, (3) have libraries and librarians lead in support of learning and discovery for children and teens, and (4) enable the State Library to serve as a leader in library and information services.[28]

In 2007, the required evaluation of the plan found that these goals had been accomplished and that without the programs and activities of the State Library, "the overall extent and quality of library and information services in North Carolina would have been diminished."[29] The State Library operated under two further LSTA five-year plans covering 2008–2012 and 2013–2017 that sought to address the needs of a state undergoing rapid economic and demographic change. Eligibility

---

25. 20 U.S.C. § 9141. See also 20 U.S.C. § 9132(a), which allows up to 4 percent of the funds provided to a state library administrative agency to be expended on administrative costs.

26. This description is based on the August 1997 State Library of North Carolina "Library Services and Technology Act: Plan for Implementation in North Carolina," which was revised in February 1999 and January 2000 (Raleigh: N.C. Department of Natural and Cultural Resources, n.d.).

27. State Library of North Carolina, *Library Services & Technology Act Plan for Implementation in North Carolina—2003–2007*, esp. III-3 and III-4, perma.cc/TR7W-MFCV.

28. For the full text and context, see II-3 and II-4 of State Library of North Carolina, *Library Services & Technology Act Plan for Implementation in North Carolina—2003–2007*, perma.cc/TR7W-MFCV.

29. Jeffrey Pomerantz, Carolyn Hank, and Charles R. McClure, *Program Evaluation of the Library Services and Technology Act Plan for Implementation in North Carolina, 2003–2007* (Raleigh: N.C. Department of Natural and Cultural Resources, Division of the State Library, Mar. 2007), ii–iii, perma.cc/26LZ-LGWW.

criteria for aid remained the same, while new goals were developed to meet the state's requirements. Intended to advance excellence and equity in North Carolina's libraries and to encourage creativity and innovation, the plan's goals emphasized (1) partnerships and collaboration, (2) continuing education, (3) literacy and lifelong learning, and (4) access, digitization, and preservation. The five-year plans for 2018–2022 and 2023–2027 centered on (1) strengthening capacity, (2) expanding access, (3) equitable access, (4) community engagement, and (5) responsive organizations.[30]

To achieve these goals, the State Library is awarding several different types of grants. As part of the LSTA planning process, the grants are under constant review and are subject to modification depending on their impact for positive change in meeting the goals of the program. Currently, most competitive grants fall under two general categories: EZ Grants and Project Grants.

EZ Grants have a simplified application process, do not require a letter of intent, and are limited to requests for $5,000 to $50,000. Applications are reviewed and evaluated by State Library staff, and funding decisions are made by State Library senior management (applicants have the opportunity to appeal these decisions, and awards are not final until the appeals process is complete).[31] Details and application packages are available at the LSTA Grants section of the State Library website.

Project Grants are awarded for more complex projects, require submission of a Letter of Intent Application that explains the proposed project, and provide $50,000 to $100,000 in funding. State Library staff, the LSTA Advisory Committee, and, in some cases, peer reviewers review Letters of Intent. The LSTA Advisory Committee recommends which libraries are approved to submit a full application. Full applications are reviewed and evaluated by the staff and outside peer reviewers, after which the LSTA Advisory Committee makes funding recommendations to the state librarian. No appeal is available since the Project Grants have already been reviewed by all the entities that would consider an appeal.[32] As with EZ Grants, further information on Project Grants is available at the LSTA Grants section of the State Library website.

A third category, called Statewide Leadership Grants, makes funds available for initiatives with a broad impact for libraries across the state and is managed directly by the State Library of North Carolina. For examples of this type of grant, see the award pages at the LSTA Grant Information section of the State Library website.[33] Included is funding for the N.C. Cardinal consortium (see the Interlibrary Cooperation section, below). N.C. Cardinal Grants made available for fiscal year 2024–2025 will aid eligible public libraries to join the consortium. For details, see the N.C. Cardinal information page.[34]

Public libraries are also required to comply with the provisions of the Children's Internet Protection Act (CIPA) in order to receive LSTA funds that are to be used in conjunction with Internet access. Required actions include a policy of Internet safety for minors that includes the operation of a technology protection measure with respect to any computers with Internet access. Further

30. State Library of North Carolina, *Library Services and Technology Act Five-Year Plan, 2008–2012* (Raleigh: N.C. Department of Natural and Cultural Resources, Aug. 2007), 3–4; State Library of North Carolina, *Library Services and Technology Act Five-Year Plan, 2013–2017* (Raleigh: N.C. Department of Natural and Cultural Resources, June 2012), 3; State Library of North Carolina, *Library Services and Technology Act Five-Year Plan, 2018–2022* (Raleigh: N.C. Department of Natural and Cultural Resources, June 2017), 6; State Library of North Carolina, *Library Services and Technology Act Five-Year Plan, 2023–2027* (Raleigh: N.C. Department of Natural and Cultural Resources, n.d.), 12.

31. This description of EZ Grants is based on information provided at the Apply for a LSTA Grant section of the State Library website under Grant Types; see the Program Guidelines section for the latest grant cycle.

32. This description of Project Grants is based on information provided at the Apply for a LSTA Grant section of the State Library website under Grant Types; see the Program Guidelines section for the latest grant cycle.

33. The awards are listed by category on the LSTA Grant Information page of the State Library website.

34. Information, resources, and eligibility requirements are available at the N.C. Cardinal section of the State Library website.

measures are required if the library also receives Universal Service (E-rate) discounts for Internet access or internal connections.[35]

Other Federal Aid

Public libraries continue to apply for and receive funding from a variety of federal grant programs, such as those of the National Endowment for the Humanities (NEH) or the Institute of Museum and Library Services (IMLS), in which the funds are distributed directly to the libraries or through state entities, such as the North Carolina Humanities Council or the North Carolina Arts Council. Naturally, the amount varies from year to year, but these funds can have a considerable impact. For the state as a whole, $1,282,100 was received for the 2020–2021 reporting period and $390,107 for 2021–2022—a sizable amount of funding for potential projects. There was an increase in funding during those reporting periods because of the Covid-19 pandemic. Some additional federal funds were administered through IMLS and LSTA. The additional funds were largely sub-granted to local libraries and reported as federal funding.[36]

For several years, the Albemarle Regional Library System has been receiving over $55,000 per year to help pay for Internet access and telecommunications needs from the Schools and Libraries USF Program (commonly referred to as the E-rate program) of the Federal Communications Commission (FCC). The program is paid for through a competitive bidding process with money from the Universal Service Fund administered by the Universal Service Administrative Company (both created by the FCC).[37]

The State Library

General Information

The reorganization of state government enacted by the General Assembly in 1971 brought the State Library of North Carolina under the new Department of Art, Culture, and History (S.L. 1971-864, § 19). The Executive Organization Act of 1973 renamed the latter the Department of Cultural Resources (in 2015, it was renamed the Department of Natural and Cultural Resources) and assigned it to the Division of State Library (S.L. 1973-476, § 31).[38]

G.S. 125-2(8) and 125-2(10) authorize the State Library to give assistance to all libraries in the state as to the best means of administering and managing such libraries, to plan and balance cooperative programs between the various types of libraries within the state of North Carolina, and to coordinate state development with regional and national cooperative library programs. In carrying out this mandate, the State Library develops and promotes strategies and initiatives focusing on support for current and emerging technologies in delivering library services, access to digital

---

35. See the Federal Communications Commission (FCC) website, www.fcc.gov, for the latest CIPA Compliance Information. There is more information on the E-Rate program on the Universal Service Administrative Company (USAC) website, www.usac.org/e-rate/.

36. State Library of North Carolina, *Statistical Report of North Carolina Public Libraries, 2020–2021* and *2021–2022* (Raleigh: N.C. Department of Natural and Cultural Resources, n.d.), Table 4: Operating Income; correspondence with State Library of North Carolina personnel on Nov. 21, 2023.

37. See the E-Rate Search Commitments Tool on the Universal Service Administrative Company (USAC) Open Data website, www.usac.org/e-rate. Correspondence with Albemarle Regional Library System personnel on Nov. 20, 2023.

38. *See* S.L. 2015-241, § 14.30.(a).

collections, effective library partnerships and resource sharing, inspiration and support for literacy and lifelong learning, and the provision of equitable library service for all North Carolinians.[39]

The State Library consults with public libraries on management and intellectual freedom issues, provides training for library trustees and directors, and coordinates statewide programs providing library services for children and teens. Library Development (LD) of the State Library works with library staff in public, academic, and community college libraries across North Carolina. LD provides resources and services to support libraries in implementing best practices and innovative services to meet the information needs of their communities. LD's core services include administering state and federal grants, public librarian certification, professional development training, cooperative resource sharing, and consulting services in the areas of management, evaluation, youth and adult services, and digital literacy. These services are intended to promote high-quality, equitable library service throughout North Carolina.[40]

In addition to administering state and federal grant programs, the State Library provides a program of reference assistance through the Government and Heritage Library, which embraces the range of services traditionally available to users of the State Library's physical and digital collections. It provides information and reference services concerning North Carolina and state government to state employees and the general public. The Government and Heritage Library serves as the State Library's resource for population, housing, business, and government statistics about North Carolina, including data from the U.S. Census Bureau, North Carolina state agencies, and other state and federal sources, and is a coordinating agency of the North Carolina State Data Center. The Government and Heritage Library also provides cataloging support for other state government libraries, including the N.C. Department of Labor Library, N.C. Department of Transportation Library, the Legislative Library, the N.C. Museum of Art Library, the N.C. Historic Sites Library, and more.[41]

The State Library, in promoting better public libraries, has sought to establish standards and guidelines to help them attain their greatest potential in service to their communities. It seeks to serve as the catalyst for exceptional library services and thus ensure that all North Carolinians have access to the information resources they need to achieve their personal, educational, and professional goals. The continued development and implementation of cost-effective services and modern technology for sharing knowledge have become even more essential in the current environment of rapidly changing methods for compiling, sending, and receiving information.[42]

State Documents Depository System and North Carolina State Publications Clearinghouse

In 1987, the General Assembly enacted the Documents Depository Act to improve public access to publications of state agencies and to provide a better system for preserving them (G.S. Chapter 125, Article 1A). The law named the State Library as the official depository of all these publications and created the State Publications Clearinghouse in the Department of Natural and Cultural Resources to receive and distribute publications to depository libraries. Considering regional distribution

39. State Library of North Carolina, "Vision," "Mission," and "Goal" sections, *Strategic Plan 2019–2023* (Raleigh: N.C. Department of Natural and Cultural Resources, n.d.).

40. Correspondence with State Library of North Carolina personnel on Nov. 9, 2023.

41. This description is based on information in the Government and Heritage Library section of the State Library website, statelibrary.ncdcr.gov/about-us/government-and-heritage-library; the North Carolina State Publications Clearinghouse, Guidelines for State Agencies website, perma.cc/T6NN-W36V; and correspondence with State Library of North Carolina personnel on Nov. 9, 2023.

42. State Library of North Carolina, "Vision," "Mission," and "Goal" sections, *Strategic Plan 2019–2023* (Raleigh: N.C. Department of Natural and Cultural Resources, n.d.), perma.cc/U4PA-XBXJ.

patterns and persons served so that the publications will be conveniently accessible to all residents of the state, the State Library may designate at least one library in each congressional district to serve as a depository. The State Library is responsible for formulating standards of operation and rules under which the depository system will be administered.

In addition, the Government and Heritage Library is mandated to serve as the official permanent depository for all state publications. Clearinghouse staff and depository librarians work together to facilitate access to current and historic agency publications by all North Carolinians. In response to shifting publication practices from print to digital publishing, the Clearinghouse is now collecting, cataloging, and adding digital publications to the State Publications Collection within the N.C. Digital Collections (a joint project of the State Library of North Carolina and State Archives of North Carolina) and adding records for these items to WorldCat. The Government and Heritage Library digitizes historical state government publications and manages digital preservation for all "born digital" (originating in digital format) state publications. Through a joint initiative with the State Archives of North Carolina, the Government and Heritage Library also archives state government websites and social media.[43]

Interlibrary Cooperation

Besides formal organizations, such as regional libraries, other cooperative efforts are being made to help libraries meet increasing demands for a variety of services and materials. On a broad scale, G.S. 125-12, the Interstate Library Compact, authorizes local and state library agencies of those states that are parties to the agreement (North Carolina is one) to engage in joint and cooperative library programs and services.

NC LIVE (North Carolina Libraries and Virtual Education) is a statewide electronic information project serving more than two hundred member libraries and dedicated to providing North Carolinians with online library and information resources that support education, enhance statewide economic development, and increase residents' quality of life. Since its inception in 1997, NC LIVE has grown into a vast information gateway and now offers the citizens of North Carolina online access to a diverse collection of electronic resources, including millions of eBooks; full-text journals, magazines, and newspapers; videos; images and maps; and interactive tests and tools. NC LIVE is available free of charge to library patrons, students, and educators of NC LIVE–affiliated libraries in North Carolina—public libraries, community colleges, the state's university system, and independent colleges and universities. Continuous access is available from any Internet connection through the websites of local (public, college, university) libraries or through the NC LIVE website with the patron's library's password.[44]

Another cooperative endeavor is the Triangle Research Libraries Network (TRLN). Consisting of Duke University, the University of North Carolina at Chapel Hill, North Carolina Central University, and North Carolina State University, TRLN seeks to marshal the financial, human,

---

43. This description is based on information in the For Agencies section of the State Library website, statelibrary.ncdcr.gov/research/state-employees-and-government-information/agencies, and correspondence with State Library personnel on Nov. 9, 2023. Some of these services were established by the Digital Information Management Program (DIMP), which laid the groundwork for increasing public access to state government information. For more information about DIMP, see Alex Hess, "Public Library Services," *County and Municipal Government*, 2nd ed. (UNC School of Government, 2014), 602.

44. For more information, see the NC Live website, www.nclive.org, and the "Get to Know NC LIVE Handout," nclive.libguides.com/ld.php?content_id=44776769.

and information resources of their research libraries to create a rich and unparalleled knowledge environment that furthers the universities' teaching, research, learning, and service missions.

TRLN goals include extending the scope of information resources available to users through libraries and campus networks, creating new library and information services, and making information accessible to users in a convenient, timely, and equitable manner. TRLN hopes to develop strategic partnerships that enhance the delivery of information and services, provide a forum for discussing cooperative library and information issues, seek external funding in support of its goals, and maintain a leadership role among universities in the provision of collaborative research library services.[45]

The State Library also coordinates N.C. Cardinal. N.C. Cardinal is a consortium of North Carolina public libraries that share an online catalog, integrated library system (ILS), and information resources with member libraries (including the Government and Heritage Library) by shipping materials between systems. N.C. Cardinal has been operating since July 2010. It is yet another example of the state's innovative efforts to share technology and funding.

Additional Resources

Anderson, Cordelia. *Library Marketing and Communications: Strategies to Increase Relevance and Results.* Chicago: American Library Association, 2020.

Chilton, Galadriel, ed. *Managing Licensed E-Resources: Techniques, Tips, and Practical Advice.* Forest Grove, Oregon: Pacific University Press, 2022.

Greenwell, Stacey, and G. Edward Evans. *Library Programs and Services: The Fundamentals.* 9th ed. New York: Bloomsbury Libraries Unlimited, Bloomsbury Publishing, 2023.

Haines, Claudia, Cen Campbell, and Chip Donohue. *Becoming a Media Mentor: A Guide for Working with Children and Families.* Chicago: American Library Association, 2016.

Hall, Kate, and Kathy Parker. *The Public Library Director's Toolkit.* Chicago: American Library Association, 2019.

Larson, Jeanette. *Children's Services Today: A Practical Guide for Librarians.* Lanham, Maryland: Rowman & Littlefield, 2015.

Leggett, Elizabeth R. 2015. *Integrating the Web into Everyday Library Services: A Practical Guide for Librarians.* Lanham, Maryland: Rowman & Littlefield, 2015.

Marquez, Joe J., and Annie Downey. *Getting Started in Service Design: A How-to-Do-It Manual for Librarians.* Chicago: American Library Association, 2017.

Matthews, Joseph R. *The Evaluation and Measurement of Library Services.* 2nd ed. Santa Barbara, CA: Libraries Unlimited, Bloomsbury Publishing, 2017.

Mon, Lorri. *Social Media and Library Services.* San Rafael, California: Morgan & Claypool, 2015.

VanDuinkerken, Wyoma, and Wendi Arant Kaspar. *Leading Libraries: How to Create a Service Culture.* Chicago: American Library Association, 2015.

---

45. Memorandum of Understanding Regarding the Triangle Research Libraries Network (TRLN) (originally signed Aug. 29, 1989; last modified Oct. 19, 2018), trln.org/wp-content/uploads/2019/07/MOU-Triangle-Research-Libraries-Network-Janaury-16-2019.pdf.

Chapter 35

Parks and Recreation

Candace Goode Vick and Paul H. Armstrong

Candace Goode Vick is a former faculty member of North Carolina State University and former director of Recreation Resources Service. Paul H. "Pete" Armstrong is the former Director of Recreation Resources Service.

This chapter was updated by Alex Phipps, the School of Government's senior legal research associate, whose work is gratefully acknowledged.

Parks and recreation are essential public services that contribute to the economic and environmental well-being of communities, helping to ensure the health of families and individuals and establish and maintain a better quality of life. According to the National Recreation and Park Association, "There are no communities that pride themselves on their quality of life, promote themselves as a desirable location for businesses to relocate, or maintain that they are environmental stewards of their natural resources, without such communities having a robust, active system of parks and recreation programs for public use and enjoyment."[1] The economic value provided by parks and recreation ranges from increased property values for private property adjacent to a park to revenue generated by regional sporting and special events. Recreation programs, greenways, and open spaces provide services and places where children, youth, and adults can get healthy and stay fit. The environmental benefits of parks and open spaces include improved water quality, flood prevention, improved air quality, and wildlife protection.

The North Carolina General Assembly "declares that the public good and the general welfare of the citizens of this State require adequate recreation programs, that the creation, establishment, and operation of parks and recreation programs is a proper governmental function, and that it is the policy of North Carolina to forever encourage, foster, and provide these facilities and programs for all its citizens."[2] The development of public parks and recreation activities as a local government function in the United States stems from the public park and playground movement that began in large cities such as Boston and Chicago in the 1890s. Since the early days of settlement houses,

1. National Recreation and Park Association, *Why Parks and Recreation Are Essential Public Services* (Ashburn, Va.: National Recreation and Park Association, 2011).

2. Recreation Enabling Act of 1945, codified as Chapter 160A, Section 351 of the North Carolina General Statutes (hereinafter G.S.).

the provision of parks and recreation services has generally been regarded as a municipal responsibility. The first municipal parks and recreation department in North Carolina was established in 1925 in Durham.[3] The subsequent growth of parks and recreation services in North Carolina and throughout the nation has been such that even most small towns and cities now provide some measure of financial support for these services. However, parks and recreation did not become an accepted county function in North Carolina until the 1960s, with the establishment of the Person County Parks and Recreation Department in 1961. Acceptance of public parks and recreation as a county function in the state was slow: in the late 1960s, there were only thirteen such departments in North Carolina. By 1974, the number had grown to twenty-seven. Today, there are more than 250 full-time local parks and recreation departments in North Carolina.[4] Many other counties and cities provide financial support of varying degrees but less than the amount required for full-time, year-round operation.

Local parks and recreation services are not uniform in either type of activity or level of service. Some are primarily oriented toward team league sports, while others offer a variety of arts, crafts, music, dance, aquatics, drama, boating, environmental education, adventure, and wellness programs for all ages. Many departments have a system of ball fields, tennis and pickleball courts, golf courses, community centers, greenways, and aquatic facilities. A number of new types of facilities, such as dog parks, disc golf courses, equestrian arenas, and outdoor adventure areas are being built. Others may provide only one or more park sites with limited facilities. Under the Community Schools Act of 1977,[5] some communities have also opened up schools for a variety of recreational uses. Many local parks and recreation departments are expanding their offerings to include nontraditional services such as child daycare, afterschool child care programs, literacy programs, and child care for parents participating in recreation programs. Others have taken over the operation of historic sites, museums, cultural resources, and convention centers, and some departments' services include the maintenance of public buildings, road rights-of-way, and cemeteries. Although each department is unique, all recreation departments share the goal of improving the quality of life for their residents.

Authority to Provide Parks and Recreation Services

The North Carolina Recreation Enabling Act, Chapter 160A, Article 18, of the North Carolina General Statutes (hereinafter G.S.), authorizes local governments to provide parks and recreation services to their citizens. The statute defines *recreation* broadly for purposes of the enabling act: "Recreation" means activities that are diversionary in character and aid in promoting entertainment, pleasure, relaxation, instruction, and other physical, mental, and cultural development and leisure time experiences.[6]

This legislation specifically authorizes local governments to do the following:[7]

1. Establish and conduct a system of supervised recreation.
2. Set apart lands and buildings for parks, playgrounds, recreational centers, and other recreational programs and facilities.

3. Paul L. Gaskill, *Introduction to Leisure Services in North Carolina* (Dubuque, Iowa: Kendall Hunt Publishing Co., 2006).

4. North Carolina State University/College of Natural Resources, Recreation Resources Service, *North Carolina Parks and Recreation Services Study: Focus on Finances* (2021–2022), rrs.cnr.ncsu.edu/wp-content/uploads/sites/284/2022/01/Services-Study-Final-Report-Finances-2021-2022.pdf.

5. G.S. Chapter 115C, Article 13.

6. G.S. 160A-352.

7. G.S. 160A-353.

3. Acquire real property, either within or without the corporate limits of the city or the boundaries of the county, including water and air rights, for parks and recreation programs and facilities by gifts, grant, purchase, lease, and exercise of the power of eminent domain or any other lawful method.
4. Provide, acquire, construct, equip, operate, and maintain parks, playgrounds, recreation centers, and recreation facilities, including all buildings, structures, and equipment necessary or useful in connection therewith.
5. Appropriate funds to carry out the provisions of the Article.
6. Accept any gift, grant, lease, loan, bequest, or devise of real or personal property for parks and recreation programs. Devises, bequests, and gifts may be accepted and held subject to such terms and conditions as may be imposed by the grantor or trustee, except that no county or city may accept or administer any terms that require it to discriminate among its citizens on the basis of race, sex, or religion.

The law provides for local governments to operate a parks and recreation system as a line department or to create a policymaking parks and recreation commission.[8] They may also join with other units of local government to operate a single system of parks and recreation.[9] Cities and counties are permitted to contract with and appropriate money to private entities to provide recreational services as long as they are provided in a nondiscriminatory fashion appropriate for a public activity and the private organization properly accounts to the local government for its expenditures.[10]

Legislation

The funding and operation of parks and recreation departments is being affected more and more by legislation on the state and national level. On the national level, in 1965, Congress authorized the Land and Water Conservation Fund (LWCF) to assist in "preserving, developing, and assuring accessibility to . . . outdoor recreation resources [in order to] strengthen the health and vitality of the citizens of the United States."[11] For a number of years, the LWCF was one of the most important sources of funding for parks and recreation agencies, but suffered from inconsistent appropriation authorizations until Congress approved a permanent authorization in 2019.[12] In 2020, Congress passed the Great American Outdoors Act,[13] which included funding of $900 million annually for the LWCF.[14] This includes the Outdoor Recreation Legacy Partnership (ORLP) program, which provides matching grants for parks projects in underserved communities.[15]

The Americans with Disabilities Act (ADA), which was first authorized in 1990, offered suggested guidelines to follow in accommodating citizens with special needs; these are now legally mandated requirements. Title II of the ADA provides that disabled people cannot be excluded from participating

8. G.S. 160A-354.
9. G.S. 160A-355.
10. G.S. 153A-449 and G.S. 160A-20.1 authorize counties and cities, respectively, to contract with and appropriate money to any person, association, or corporation in order to carry out any public purpose that the county or city is authorized by law to engage in.
11. Land and Water Conservation Fund Act of 1965, Pub. L. No. 88-578. The National Parks Service maintains a website about state and local grant funding through the LWCF at nps.gov/subjects/lwcf/stateside.htm.
12. The John D. Dingell, Jr. Conservation, Management, and Recreation Act, Pub. L. No. 116-9.
13. Pub. L. No. 116-152.
14. The Department of the Interior maintains a website related to LWCF funds and program lists at doi.gov/lwcf/permanent-funding.
15. This program is administered by the National Parks Service, which maintains a website on ORLP at nps.gov/subjects/lwcf/outdoor-recreation-legacy-partnership-grants-program.htm.

in or enjoying the benefits of the services, programs, or activities of a local government due to their disability. The Civil Rights Division of the Department of Justice has issued several rulemakings related to Title II and local government compliance, and 28 C.F.R. Part 35 ("Nondiscrimination on the Basis of Disability in State and Local Government Services") contains the full text of these rules.[16] The "new construction and alterations" rule in 28 C.F.R. § 35.151 requires that any construction commenced on or after March 15, 2012, must comply with the 2010 ADA Standards for Accessible Design. Chapter 10 of the 2010 Standards specifically addresses recreation facilities.[17]

Volunteers in parks and recreation programs are protected by the Volunteer Protection Act (VPA) of 1997.[18] In broad terms, the VPA protects volunteers serving governmental entities and nonprofit organizations from liability for harm caused by negligent acts or omissions during their volunteer service.

On the state level, other legislation permits both counties and cities to finance public parks and recreation and provides ways to acquire land, lease facilities, and fund the development of recreation facilities. For example, the enabling statutes for subdivision regulations permit counties or cities to require that developers reserve or dedicate recreation areas to serve the residents in new subdivisions.[19] The requirement may be imposed only as part of a subdivision ordinance adopted by the city or county to guide and regulate subdivision development. The rationale is that each developed subdivision both increases the demand for recreation and open space and removes open space through land development. The subdivider is thus required to furnish such space for the local government in relation to the need the subdivider creates. The subdivider ordinarily passes the economic cost on to purchasers of subdivision lots. Once the land is dedicated, the cost of maintaining it falls on the city or county. A subdivision ordinance that requires dedication or reservation of land should indicate the amount of land per subdivision that must be dedicated (for example, 5 percent of the total area); the location of the land to be dedicated; and some standard relating to the degree of improvement required. The ordinance should include some provisions to ensure that the land is well suited and properly located for recreation purposes. Local governments also may require developers to provide funds in lieu of land so that additional recreation lands may be acquired to serve the new developments.

The General Statutes contain another authority for local governments to acquire open space: G.S. Chapter 160D, Article 13, Part 1 *Open space* is an area (1) that is characterized by great natural scenic beauty or (2) whose openness, natural condition, and present state of use, if retained, would enhance the present or potential value of abutting or surrounding urban development or would enhance or maintain the conservation of natural or scenic resources.[20] Open space includes undeveloped land in an urban area that has value for (1) parks and recreation purposes, (2) conservation of land or other natural resources, or (3) historic or scenic purposes.[21]

The law authorizes local governments to preserve for public access or enjoyment open areas of significant scenic or aesthetic value that might otherwise be lost because of rapid urban growth and development, and it expressly declares the acquisition and the preservation of open space to be a public purpose of local governments.[22] Cities and counties can acquire open space by purchase, gift, grant, bequest, lease, and through the expenditure of public funds.[23] Local governments may acquire outright

16. The Department of Justice website, ada.gov, provides the full text of relevant laws and regulations, as well as guidance materials.

17. The 2010 Ada Standards for Accessible Design are available at ada.gov.

18. 42 U.S.C. § 14501–05.

19. G.S. 160D-804(d).

20. G.S. 160D-1307(1).

21. G.S. 160D-1307(2).

22. G.S. 160D-1302.

23. G.S. 160D-1303.

ownership of open space or any lesser interest, such as a conservation easement. A local unit may acquire a conservation easement for open space such as farmland, preserving the scenic characteristics of the property for public enjoyment without opening it to public access or granting public access.[24]

Local governments are also authorized to exchange, lease, sell, or purchase property with, to, or from other government units.[25] In general, such arrangements may include whatever terms and conditions the units involved deem wise. This authority has permitted boards of county commissioners and school boards, for example, to work cooperatively to transfer surplus school lands and structures to parks and recreation uses.

The only significant constraint on such transfers is found in Article IX, Section 7, of the North Carolina Constitution, which prevents school systems from giving away school property. As long as the school system receives value in return, however, a transfer to another government unit is permissible. Under G.S. 115C-518(a), the school board must give the board of commissioners the first opportunity to purchase whenever it disposes of real property that is no longer suitable or necessary for public school purposes.

The 1977 Community Schools Act[26] has also benefited recreation programs. It opens schools for a variety of community uses, including recreation. A city or county can agree with a school board to use school gyms, playgrounds, and fields for its recreation programs and thus avoid having to construct or acquire expensive capital facilities in areas where facilities already exist.

In 1994, the North Carolina General Assembly established the Parks and Recreation Trust Fund (PARTF).[27] Other than the Recreation Enabling Act, PARTF has had the most significant impact on parks and recreation agencies in North Carolina. In 2013, the North Carolina Legislature replaced its dedicated funding source (the deed stamp tax proceeds) with annual appropriations.[28] The nine member North Carolina Parks and Recreation Authority allocates 65 percent of the available funds to the state parks system, 30 percent to provide matching grants for local parks and recreation purposes, and 5 percent to the Coastal and Estuarine Water Beach Access Program.[29] Since its beginning, PARTF has funded 993 projects, representing approximately $745 million in total park projects throughout North Carolina.[30] Grants have been awarded in all 100 of North Carolina's counties. Under the PARTF fund, a matching-grant program was established for local parks and recreation purposes.[31] These grants may be used by local governments for:

1. fee-simple acquisition of real property for preservation of natural areas and future recreation development;
2. projects for construction, expansion, and renovation or repair of both outdoor and indoor recreation facilities; and
3. construction of support facilities and improvements that support primary recreation facilities.[32]

---

24. Information about farmland preservation easements is available from the N.C. Department of Agriculture and Consumer Services, www.ncagr.gov/adfp.

25. G.S. 160A-274.

26. G.S. Chapter 115C, Article 13.

27. G.S. 143B-135.56(a).

28. S.L. 2013-360, § 14.4(a), (b) (codified at G.S. 143B-135.56(b)).

29. G.S. 143B-135.56.

30. The North Carolina Division of Parks and Recreation website, ncparks.gov, provides detailed information about the PARTF program as well as annual reports and a Geographic Information Systems (GIS) map showing grants per county.

31. 7 N.C.A.C. 13K, .0107.

32. 7 N.C.A.C. 13K, § .0108. Information about applying for funds is available from Recreation Resources Service, rrs.cnr.ncsu.edu; the N.C. Division of Parks and Recreation, ncparks.gov; and the PARTF website, ncparks.gov/about-us/grants/parks-and-recreation-trust-fund.

In 1995, the North Carolina General Assembly passed the North Carolina Recreational Use Statute limiting the liability of landowners who make their land and water areas available to the public at no cost for educational and recreational purposes.[33] In 2003, the legislature passed the Hazardous Recreation Parks Safety and Liability Act to encourage governmental owners or lessees of property to make land available to a governmental entity for skateboarding, inline skating, or freestyle bicycling.[34]

Financing

Before the 1973 revision of Article V of the North Carolina Constitution, recreation was not considered a necessary expense and could not be financed by property tax revenues without a vote of the people. Under the revised constitution and enabling legislation enacted pursuant to it in 1973, public parks and recreation are among the purposes for which counties and cities may levy property taxes without a vote, subject to an overall limitation of $1.50 on the property tax rate.[35] Local governments also may allocate to parks and recreation any other revenues whose use is not restricted by law.

Although local parks and recreation departments are primarily funded through property tax revenues, they do receive operating and capital improvement moneys from other sources, including user fees and state, federal, and private grants.

Because of limited federal, state, and even local funding for parks and recreation, local departments are exploring innovative alternative sources of funding for facilities and programs. There is an increased reliance on user fees, use of occupancy tax revenues for recreation facilities as part of tourism development programs, publication of gift catalogs to allow donors to give particular needed items to parks and recreation programs, partnerships between local governments and private businesses to build recreation facilities, and establishment of local foundations and trust funds.

Organization

A local government may provide parks and recreation services through one of three alternatives: (1) a line department within local government, (2) a policymaking parks and recreation commission, or (3) a joint agreement with another city or with a county.

A Line Department

The most common organizational method used in North Carolina is to organize parks and recreation as a line department within a city or county. Under this approach, the parks and recreation department is usually administered by an executive who reports to the city/county manager, the city council, or county commissioners. When a department is established, its mission and scope of services determine the title of the department. The most commonly used titles are Parks Department, Recreation Department, or Parks and Recreation Department. There is ongoing discussion regarding making the titles of departments more indicative of the services and benefits they provide (for example, Cary Parks, Recreation, and Cultural Resources Department; Town of Leland

33. G.S. Chapter 38A.
34. G.S. Chapter 99E, Article 3.
35. G.S. 153A-149(c)(25) for counties and 160A-209(c)(24) for cities.

Department of Parks, Recreation, and Environmental Programs; Wake County Parks, Recreation, and Open Space). More departments likely will be working to redefine themselves through their titles. In times of budget cuts and "right-sizing," some park maintenance divisions have been moved from parks and recreation to public works. While on paper this seems a viable alternative, caution should be used when consolidating all maintenance under one department. The public works staff must understand the demands for maintenance created by the scope of recreation services and facilities. Recreation facilities are often open seven days a week and operate beyond the traditional hours of many local government services. Maintenance services must be provided when programs are scheduled and facilities are open. Also, participants' demands for quality facilities often dictate the need for a higher standard of maintenance for recreation facilities in order for these facilities to remain competitive with facilities in surrounding communities.

When the line-departmental approach is used, it is beneficial to establish a parks and recreation advisory committee. Appointed by the local governing body, this committee interprets the needs of citizens, works closely with paid professional staff, and assists in providing direction for the department. The advisory group, ideally made up of seven to nine members, has no policymaking authority but can provide a critical link between citizens, department staff, the city/county manager, and local government. Members of the advisory board should be appointed to staggered three-year terms, with all members limited to two consecutive terms. Ideally, the committee membership will be representative of the population based on race, gender, community interests, and geography. Training for advisory committees is imperative to ensure an effective group and is available from Recreation Resources Service, which operates through a partnership with the Parks, Recreation, and Tourism Management Department at North Carolina State University and the North Carolina Department of Natural and Cultural Resources.

A Policymaking Parks and Recreation Commission

A local government may establish a parks and recreation department and appoint a policymaking parks and recreation commission to oversee departmental operations. This commission then has responsibility for the department's organization, personnel, fiscal matters, areas and facilities, programs, and other functions. The commission members report directly to the local government officials. The commission may be established by an ordinance, which ordinarily spells out the commission's general powers and duties, including its relationships to the local government and its finances. This organizational option is not frequently used in North Carolina.

A Joint Agreement with Another City or with a County

A local government may elect to enter into a joint agreement with another city or with a county to provide parks and recreation services for its residents. This type of arrangement is authorized by G.S. 160A-355. The future is likely to bring more joint agreements between cities and counties due to their common purposes and their desire to provide services as efficiently as possible.

The authority of a local government to enter into joint agreements with other governmental entities or agencies to provide parks and recreation services is an important right. These arrangements are authorized by G.S. 160A-355 and G.S. Chapter 160A, Article 20, Interlocal Cooperation. A city or county that does not wish to hire and maintain its own staff may contract with another city or with the county for the use of certain parks and recreation facilities by its residents or for professional staff support from the other unit, or it may agree to set up a joint parks and recreation agency with the other unit. Contracting for support personnel or services is a satisfactory arrangement when one or two units of government are in effect buying the use of park facilities for their residents or seeking professional staff support from another unit's program and when a second full-time staff person is not feasible or a second policymaking body is not needed. Certain contents of the contract are specified in G.S. Chapter 160A, Article 20. The contract must state its purpose and duration and the arrangement for handling the ownership of real property. It should also provide for its own amendment and termination.

A joint agency with its own staff also may be established under G.S. Chapter 160A, Article 20. This approach can provide services that would be impossible or too expensive for any one local unit to provide with its own resources. It can take advantage of the wider population and tax base of several units. Administrative costs can generally be reduced, making more money available for programs and services. The professional staff can be appointed either by one unit or jointly by all participating units. The agency is funded by appropriations from participating units. Title to real property can be held jointly or can continue to be held by the individual participating units. As when services are provided by contract, the contract establishing the joint agency should specify the agency's purpose, duration, organization, appointment of personnel, financing, and methods for amending and terminating the contract. Examples of this type of arrangement include Elizabeth City/Pasquotank County Parks and Recreation Department, Kinston/Lenoir Parks and Recreation, and Henderson–Vance Parks and Recreation.

A Joint Agreement Involving Several Units

A county or city that chooses not to hire and maintain its own staff may find some advantages in arranging for professional services or for the use of certain parks and recreation facilities through contractual agreements with a town or city in the same county or with another county. These joint arrangements could be for a temporary summer program or a year-round program. Several cities and counties have found that this approach has economic value and is a fair way to provide leisure services for county residents who live in fringe or suburban areas of larger cities and towns. Such a relatively simple contractual arrangement is most likely to prove satisfactory in those situations where one or two units of government are in effect buying the use of parks and recreation facilities and professional staff services from an existing program and when a second full-time staff person is not feasible or a second policymaking body is not needed.

If, instead, a large number of local governments are involved—as might be the case when several counties (including perhaps the smaller towns within each county) band together to provide a regional parks and recreation system or facilities—a more appropriate form of organization may be an independent, jointly financed parks and recreation commission with its own staff. This latter approach is allowed by both the general wording of G.S. 160A-355 and the legislation authorizing interlocal cooperation found in G.S. Chapter 160A, Article 20.

Agency Accreditation

No matter how an agency is organized, consideration should be given to national certification. The National Recreation and Park Association has established the Commission for Accreditation of Park and Recreation Agencies (CAPRA), which provides quality assurance and quality improvement of accredited park and recreation agencies throughout the United States. CAPRA is the only national accreditation for park and recreation agencies, and it is a valuable measure of an agency's overall quality of operation, management, and service to the community. While it is not possible for every agency to achieve this level of certification, the accreditation standards are an excellent model for local governments to follow in establishing their parks and recreation agencies. Topics include staff qualifications, planning, fiscal management, and programs and services management. Currently, seven cities and one joint city–county department are accredited in North Carolina. Additional information is available from the National Recreation and Park Association.

Professional Staff

Professional leadership is probably the most essential ingredient for a successful parks and recreation program. The administrator's major job responsibilities are to organize the department, train and supervise staff, select appropriate program activities, coordinate planning, manage the budget, acquire needed parklands, develop sustainable revenue streams, and construct a variety of recreational facilities. Additionally, the administrator must address safety and liability issues for both staff and participants.

The administrator will also need to hire a number of supervisors, based on the scope of the department's services. Highly competent parks and recreation professionals are available in North Carolina, and county and city officials should hire educated and experienced personnel to administer the department and its programs. Volunteers may provide some supplemental assistance, but experience indicates that they should be used to enrich the program and not as a substitute for paid professional leadership.

Many parks and recreation professionals participate in the National Recreation and Park Association Certification for the Park and Recreation Professional Program. Parks and recreation professionals can voluntarily become credentialed as Certified Park and Recreation Professionals and Certified Park and Recreation Executives, verifying that they have met the minimal requirements to practice as parks and recreation professionals. They can also keep up-to-date by joining the North Carolina Recreation and Park Association and the National Recreation and Park Association. In 1986, the General Assembly enacted G.S. Chapter 90C, the Therapeutic Recreation Personnel Certification Act (now known as the North Carolina Recreational Therapy Licensure Act), to credential therapeutic recreation specialists. Other certifications available to professionals include Certified Playground Safety Inspector and Aquatic Facility Operator.

North Carolina is fortunate to have more than twenty colleges and universities that grant bachelor's degrees in parks and recreation. Four state universities confer master's degrees: North Carolina State University, East Carolina University, the University of North Carolina at Greensboro, and the University of North Carolina at Wilmington. North Carolina State University offers a doctor of philosophy degree in Parks, Recreation, and Tourism Management.

Parks and Recreation Planning

Parks and recreation services and facilities must be carefully planned if they are to operate efficiently and economically and provide an appropriate level of service. A parks and recreation program should be a part of a countywide comprehensive strategic plan.

A parks and recreation department should have a system-wide master plan as well as site-specific plans for its facilities. These plans often are a prerequisite for receiving grants to assist with development and programming, such as those offered by the North Carolina Parks and Recreation Trust Fund. All plans should be developed with active citizen input and updated every five to ten years. The facilities must be built with the users' requirements in mind. Proper location is important, as is acquisition of property before land values have risen to the point that the designation of land for park purposes is no longer feasible. Sites and buildings should be neither too large nor too small for their intended long-term use or for the size of the geographical area to be served. Ideally, parcels of land should be of sufficient size to permit later expansion and the addition of more facilities in an environmentally sensitive manner. The adoption and enforcement of a county zoning ordinance is often required to protect major recreational facilities from possibly adverse uses of nearby property. As noted earlier, subdivision regulations may be helpful in acquiring public parks and recreational areas as large tracts are subdivided for residential purposes.

Whenever possible, planning should occur on a regional basis in order to provide the most efficient and effective recreation opportunities. The Mountains to Sea Trail, the Carolina Thread Trail, and the Overmountain Victory Trail are good examples of regional planning for trails in North Carolina. Planning with local boards of education can also be beneficial: recreation areas can sometimes be jointly financed, constructed, maintained, and operated. As mentioned earlier, the Community Schools Act[36] has encouraged the cooperative planning and use of schools for a multitude of community purposes. Public recreational use of schools has been growing rapidly since the act's passage in 1977.

Parks and recreation planning should include the design of all areas and facilities for use by the disabled and elderly. Local governments must be certain that project designers are aware of and follow pertinent statutes and regulations pertaining to use by the elderly, handicapped access, and safety.

Planning for parks and recreation facilities and services is a cooperative effort. A well-run planning program involves close coordination among the parks and recreation department, its planning department, the local school board(s), user groups, stakeholders, and other interested boards and departments. A number of resources are available to assist agencies with planning, including Recreation Resources Service, regional councils of government, regional resource conservation and development councils, and private consulting agencies.

Since 1945, the state of North Carolina has offered park and recreation technical and advisory services to local governments. Today, Recreation Resources Service continues to be the primary source of assistance for local governments that provide local parks and recreation services or are contemplating the establishment of a parks and recreation department.

Recreation Resources Service provides a wide range of technical assistance to local parks and recreation agencies, including educational workshops on topics such as playground safety, the Americans with Disabilities Act, and athletic field maintenance; training of parks and recreation advisory board members; publication of technical assistance manuals, directories, and a monthly job bulletin; applied research; evaluative studies of parks and recreation agencies; production of park conceptual maps; and provision of individual technical assistance.

The North Carolina League of Municipalities, the North Carolina Association of County Commissioners, and the UNC School of Government can also help with legal, budgetary, and financial aspects of parks and recreation services.

36. G.S. Chapter 115C, Article 13.

Chapter 36

Alcoholic Beverage Control

Michael Crowell and Alex Phipps

Michael Crowell, a former School of Government faculty member with extensive experience in ABC law, originally drafted this chapter. It has been updated by Alex Phipps, the School's senior legal research associate.

North Carolina long has had a conservative approach to the sale of alcohol. The state was dry well before national Prohibition and waited longer than many other states to open up sales after alcohol became legal again. Ever since the end of Prohibition, hard liquor has been available in North Carolina only through government alcoholic beverage control (ABC) stores, and it was not until 1978 that the state became the next to last state to allow the sale of mixed drinks. Today, North Carolina still has fewer outlets for alcohol than most other states, but those sales generate more revenue per capita than in most other jurisdictions.

The basic scheme of alcohol regulation in effect today was established in the 1930s after the repeal of Prohibition. Hard liquor is sold through ABC stores operated by local boards whose members are appointed by counties and cities after approval of stores by the voters.[1] All ABC store

1. North Carolina is one of seventeen states in which liquor sales go through government wholesalers or retailers, often referred to as the "Control" model of liquor sales.

inventory comes through a state warehouse run by the state ABC Commission. Taxes on hard liquor generate hundreds of millions of dollars for the state each year, and local governments reap profits from their ABC stores.

Beer and wine are sold by private retailers—grocery stores, convenience stores, restaurants, bars—in communities where voters have approved such sales. All retailers must have permits from the ABC Commission, which also has authority to suspend or revoke the permission to sell. The ABC Commission will listen to local governments' concerns about permits, but final decisions are made at the state level. Local governments that operate convention centers, ballparks, and theaters may themselves get in the business of selling alcohol. The state and local governments share revenue from beer and wine taxes.

While the basic structure of the ABC system has remained the same for eighty years, there have been changes on the edges. In recent years it has become more common for the General Assembly to allow sales of alcohol, including mixed drinks, in certain specified communities or particular kinds of businesses, without the need for a local election. Local governments now have the authority to create "social districts" that loosen restrictions on pedestrians carrying open alcohol containers away from bars and restaurants where beverages were purchased. Other changes, such as mixed drinks to-go, online ABC store orders, and the option to expand ABC store hours on certain holidays, have also been included in recent legislation.

Kinds of Alcohol

The state ABC laws are found in Chapter 18B of the North Carolina General Statutes (hereinafter G.S.). The law's catchall term for all kinds of alcohol is "alcoholic beverage."[2] The term "spirituous liquor" refers to distilled spirits such as whiskey, rum, vodka, brandy, and gin, all of which typically are around 40 percent (80 proof) alcohol, plus liqueurs. "Hard liquor" is used throughout this chapter to mean the same thing.

"Malt beverages," which include beer, lager, porter, ale, and other fermented beverages, range from half a percent alcohol to about 15 percent, but most are around 5 percent. This chapter uses "beer" as synonymous with malt beverage. The sale of beer with more than 6 percent alcohol was authorized in 2005. Any beer over 6 percent alcohol must have a label showing the alcohol content of the beer.

"Unfortified wine" refers to wine produced by natural fermentation from grapes, fruits, berries, rice, or honey, and it is not more than 16 percent alcohol. When brandy is added to boost the alcohol content, the result is "fortified wine," which ranges from 16 to 24 percent alcohol. Under federal law, any wine over 14 percent alcohol must indicate the alcohol percentage on the label.[3]

As a general rule, spirituous liquor and fortified wine may be possessed and consumed only where state law specifies.[4] Beer and unfortified wine may be possessed and consumed in any location not specifically prohibited by state law or local ordinance.[5] No alcohol may be sold except with a permit from the ABC Commission. Depending on what kinds of sales have been approved for a given community, some permits may allow sale for consumption at a business ("on-premises" permits) and some may allow only take-out sales ("off-premises" permits). The kinds of places that can get permits, and the kinds of permits allowed, are discussed below.

---

2. The definitions of the different kinds of alcohol, along with other relevant definitions for the ABC laws, are found in Chapter 18B, Section 101 of the North Carolina General Statutes (hereinafter G.S.).

3. 27 C.F.R. § 4.36(a).

4. G.S. 18B-102, -301.

5. G.S. 18B-300.

State Administration

The state ABC Commission is made up of three members who are appointed by and serve at the pleasure of the governor.[6] The appointments usually but not always are based on political connections. The chair is paid a full-time salary, while the other two members are paid on a per diem basis. Commission members are subject to the State Government Ethics Act.[7]

The ABC Commission operates the state warehouse and distributes liquor to local ABC boards.[8] It decides what brands of liquor, beer, and wine may be sold in the state and issues all permits to wineries, breweries, distilleries, wholesalers, restaurants, hotels, grocery stores, and so on. The commission also may revoke and suspend permits and levy fines against permit holders for selling to minors, staying open after legal hours, allowing fights on premises, and other violations of the ABC statutes and regulations. To investigate complaints the commission relies on state Alcohol Law Enforcement (ALE) agents and on local ABC officers. Commission lawyers handle hearings on violations of the law by permit holders.

Although the commission does not appoint local ABC board members or employees, it has general supervisory authority over all local ABC systems. It also issues regulations that local boards must follow, conducts mandatory training for local board members, audits local boards' finances and general operations, and in some circumstances may remove local board members and employees. The location of all ABC stores has to be approved by the commission. When a local ABC system is losing money, the commission may step in and close stores or require the system to merge with another to maintain solvency.

Local ABC Systems

ABC stores sell only hard liquor and fortified wine.[9] They are operated by units of local governments, not by private businesses, and provide significant revenue to those governments. When a referendum passes to establish ABC stores, the operation of the ABC system is turned over to a local ABC board. The ABC board operates independently of the given county or city, but the relationship is close and interactive.

Elections

Any county may hold a referendum on whether to establish a local ABC system to operate ABC stores.[10] A city may hold an ABC store election only if it has at least 1,000 registered voters and the county does not already have an ABC system.[11]

A referendum may be called by the board of county commissioners or the city council.[12] If the governing body does not want to call a referendum, the ABC system election may be forced by a petition submitted to the county board of elections by 35 percent of the registered voters in the jurisdiction. Petitioners have ninety days from the time they register the petition with the board of elections to get the required signatures. Elections officials then have thirty days to verify the signatures.

---

6. G.S. 18B-200.
7. The act is codified at G.S. Chapter 138A.
8. The commission's duties and powers are described in Article 2 of G.S. Chapter 18B.
9. G.S. 18B-800.
10. G.S. 18B-600.
11. G.S. 18B-600(d). When a county approves ABC stores after a city has already established its own ABC system, the city continues to operate its separate stores. There may be pressure to merge the two systems, however.
12. G.S. 18B-601.

Whether the election is called by the local government or by petition, the actual date for voting is set by the board of elections. All ABC elections must be held at the same time as the state and county general election in even-numbered years or at the time of the spring primary preceding that election, or at the same time as a city general election in odd-numbered years.[13] The election procedures are the same as for any other election.[14] A county or city may not hold an election on ABC stores within three years of a previous election on the same issue.[15] Other alcohol issues, such as the approval of mixed drinks, may be voted upon at the same time as the referendum on ABC stores.

All elections are conducted by the county board of elections. A city is required to reimburse the county for the cost of a municipal ABC election.[16]

Number of Local ABC Systems

In 2024, there were 171 active local ABC systems in North Carolina, operating more than 430 stores. About half of the counties, mostly in the eastern part of the state, have county ABC systems; municipal systems operate in the other counties. There are no completely "dry" counties in North Carolina where all alcohol sales are prohibited; however, Graham and Madison Counties do not have any ABC stores.[17]

The number of ABC systems in the state proliferated after the enactment of liquor-by-the-drink in the late 1970s. To be eligible to have a mixed drink election, a community had to have its own ABC stores to sell the liquor to permit holders, prompting a number of places to approve ABC stores so that a few local restaurants could serve mixed drinks. As a consequence, the number of small ABC systems grew, and some of them had difficulty making money. It was not unusual for new, small municipal systems to take business from neighboring towns, putting their long-term profitability into question. In 2019, the General Assembly took steps to restrict the creation of new local ABC boards and created a mandatory merger process when a jurisdiction holds an ABC store election and is in a county where an ABC board is already in operation.[18] These changes prevent the creation of new local ABC boards when another local board is already in operation and require a merger when an election to approve ABC stores is successful. The changes also added requirements on cities attempting to hold ABC store elections. The ABC laws currently require that a city may hold an ABC store election if it is located in a county that does not operate ABC stores but contains at least one other city-operated ABC store.[19] If the election is successful, the city must enter into an agreement for a merged local ABC board with an existing board in that county.[20]

Board Size, Members[21]

A county ABC system is governed by an ABC board appointed by the county commissioners; a city ABC board is appointed by the city council. Under state law the board may have either three

13. G.S. 18B-601(f) and G.S. 163-287.

14. For example, just as with any other municipal election, the use of mail-in absentee voting and early voting has to be approved by the city council. G.S. 163-302(a). Once approved, the use of absentee and early voting remains in effect until rescinded by the city.

15. A city could hold an election on off-premises sale of beer one year, for example, and then vote on on-premises sale of beer and wine the next year, but it could not have another referendum on off-premises beer for three years.

16. G.S. 163-284.

17. The ABC Commission provides an online legal sales area and early Sunday sales guide at abc2.nc.gov/Search/PermitLegalSalesArea.

18. G.S. 18B-600(a1), -700(c1).

19. G.S. 18B-600(d).

20. G.S. 18B-700(c1).

21. G.S. 18B-700.

or five members. Members serve staggered, three-year terms. The size of the board is set by the appointing authority—the county commissioners or city council—when the ABC system is established. If an existing board has three members, the appointing authority may increase it to five by adding two new members with three-year terms. If the commissioners or council want to reduce the ABC board from five to three members, they can do so only when terms expire and only with the agreement of the state ABC Commission. The appointing authority designates one ABC board member to be the chair.

State law says that ABC board members should be appointed on the basis of their "interest in public affairs, good judgment, knowledge, ability, and good moral character."[22] Otherwise, there are no specific qualifications for the job, although conviction of a felony or violation of the ABC law may disqualify a person from serving on or being employed by an ABC board for up to three years from the time of conviction.[23] The law does not require that an ABC board member be a resident of the community, but counties and cities usually will not appoint nonresidents.

Occasionally, a board of county commissioners or city council will appoint one or more of its own members to the ABC board, usually in response to troubles in the ABC system. Such appointments are allowed, and the ABC board position does not count as a separate office for purposes of the state dual office-holding law.[24] The commissioners or council might even appoint their manager, attorney, or finance officer. The ABC board is intended to be an independent entity, however, and typically those appointments last only until the ABC board's problems are straightened out.

Duties

The ABC board is responsible for running the local ABC system. The board hires and fires employees and selects one employee to be the manager of the system. The board also designates someone other than this general manager as the system's finance officer, or it may use the finance officer of its county or city appointing authority.[25] The board is required by the state ABC Commission to establish personnel policies and is encouraged to model these after the policies and procedures of the county or city in which the ABC board operates.[26] The ABC board sets employees' salaries but may not pay the general manager more than the salary set by the legislature for the county clerk of court, unless the board of county commissioners or city council that appointed the ABC board agrees to the higher salary.[27] The general manager may not be given any benefits not offered to all other employees, and no other employee may be paid more than the general manager.

The ABC board decides what products to buy for its ABC stores; buys and leases property as necessary to operate the ABC system; decides where to locate ABC stores (with the approval of the ABC Commission); and oversees the finances of the system. Retail prices for products sold in ABC stores are set by distillers using a statutory markup formula[28] that is to be uniform throughout the state. The local ABC board may dispose of surplus property the same as a city council.[29]

---

22. G.S. 18B-700(d).

23. G.S. 18B-202. Note that this penalty must be imposed by a judge after a conviction.

24. *See* G.S. 128-1.2. "Except when the resolution of appointment provides otherwise, whenever the governing body of a county or city appoints one of its own members or officials to another board or commission, the individual so appointed is considered to be serving on the other board or commission as a part of the individual's duties of office and shall not be considered to be serving in a separate office."

25. G.S. 18B-702(j).

26. Title 14B, Chapter 15A, Section .1006, of the North Carolina Administrative Code (hereinafter N.C.A.C.).

27. G.S. 18B-700(g1).

28. G.S. 18B-804; *see also* 14B N.C.A.C. 15A, § .1500.

29. G.S. 18B-701(a)(12). The statutes on disposal of property are found in Article 12 of G.S. Chapter 160A, §§ 160A-265 to -280.

All local ABC board members, general managers, and finance officers are required to complete a training course offered by the state ABC Commission within the first year of being appointed or employed.[30] Board members, the general manager, and the finance officer also are required to be bonded for at least $50,000.[31] The county commissioners or city council may increase the required bond for any member or employee handling ABC board funds.

Compensation

Compensation to local ABC board members is limited to $150 per meeting, unless a different amount is approved by the appointing board of commissioners or city council.[32] Any higher amount has to be reported to the ABC Commission. Travel reimbursement is to be at the same rate as for state government generally, unless the appointing authority has a different policy and the ABC board adopts that policy, with the approval of the board of commissioners or city council.[33] Expenses not covered by the travel policy may be paid only with the written authorization of the county or city's finance officer, and the authorization has to be copied to the ABC Commission.

Ethics

Like other local government officials, local ABC board members are not subject to the financial disclosure laws and other provisions of the State Government Ethics Act,[34] but the ABC statutes regulate the ethical conduct of local board members and subject them to several other important general state laws concerning ethics.[35] The ABC statutes restrict the employment of relatives; require board members to report and refrain from participating in decisions that may benefit certain relatives financially; prohibit board members from using their position to financially benefit themselves or family members; and subject board members to general state law provisions about self-dealing and acceptance of gifts. Board members are obligated to disclose in writing any conflict or potential conflict of interest that might affect their participation in a board action. Each local ABC board is to adopt a code of ethics, which can mirror the model ethics policy prepared by the ABC Commission, and members must complete ethics training within a year of appointment or reappointment.[36]

Removal of Board Members

Local ABC board members serve set terms of three years but may be removed from office sooner under some circumstances. For instance, any board member or employee may be removed from office or discharged from board employment by a judge upon the person's conviction of a felony or any violation of the ABC laws.[37] The board of county commissioners or city council that appointed an ABC board member may remove the member "for cause," but the statute does not specify what "cause" means.[38] A more useful statute allows either the appointing authority or the ABC Commission to remove a local ABC board member or employee for any violation of the ABC laws, for failing to complete any training required by law or by the commission (e.g., ethics training), and for "any conduct constituting moral turpitude or which brings the local board or the ABC system into

30. 14 N.C.A.C. 15A, § .2001.
31. G.S. 18B-700(i).
32. G.S. 18B-700(g).
33. G.S. 18B-700(g2).
34. *See* G.S. Chapter 138A.
35. See, in particular, G.S. 18B-201 and -700(h), (k).
36. G.S. 18B-706.
37. G.S. 18B-202.
38. G.S. 18B-700(f).

disrepute."[39] G.S. 18B-704 sets out a specific procedure for removal, including notice in writing of the grounds for removal and a hearing before the commission. The statute also says that the ABC Commission's decision on removal is final, but it allows an appeal to the North Carolina Court of Appeals.

Open Meetings and Public Records

Local ABC boards are governmental bodies subject to the state open meetings and public records laws.[40] Like all other governmental bodies, ABC boards must give notice of each meeting to be held; may call special meetings only on forty-eight hours' notice, unless there is an emergency; may go into closed session only for one of the reasons listed in the open meetings law; must specify the reason for the closed session; must keep minutes of the closed session; and must make its records available to the public. Local ABC boards that have only three members must remember that any meeting of a majority of the board to discuss board business is a meeting requiring notice and public access. Thus, two members of a three-member board may not talk on the telephone about ABC business without taking all of the steps required of an official board meeting.

Mergers and Dissolution of Local Systems

A board of county commissioners or city council may merge its ABC system with that of any other neighboring county or city, with the approval of the state ABC Commission.[41] The appointing authorities have to agree on a joint ABC board and on the distribution of profits. A negotiation to merge ABC systems is required before a jurisdiction located in a county where an ABC board is already in operation can hold an ABC store election, and the jurisdiction must provide the details of the planned merger to the registered voters before the election.[42]

County commissioners and city councils with ABC systems also may agree to have one of those governmental unit's ABC board operate a store or stores for the other.[43] Again, such an agreement has to be approved by the ABC Commission.

A local ABC system may be shut down if it is not operating profitably. The local ABC board may apply to the state ABC Commission to close the system; the commission may investigate; and if the commission finds that the system cannot be operated profitably, it may order it closed.[44] When that happens, the ABC Commission schedules a phaseout of the system's business and from that point on represents the local board in negotiations with creditors and other interested parties.

Another circumstance in which a local ABC system may be closed or merged is when it fails to meet the performance standards that the ABC Commission sets for all local ABC systems. When this happens, the commission may require the board of commissioners or city council operating the failing system to develop and implement an improvement plan.[45] The plan developed by the commissioners or city council is to set a deadline of not more than twelve months for the specified improvement; the deadline may be extended six months. If at that time the ABC Commission determines that the performance standards cannot be met, the commission may close stores, shut

---

39. G.S. 18B-704(c).
40. *See generally* G.S. Chapter 143, Article 33C and G.S. Chapter 132. The open meetings and public records statutes are discussed at length in Chapter 8, "Public Records," and Chapter 9, "Open Meetings and Other Legal Requirements for Local Government Boards."
41. G.S. 18B-703.
42. G.S. 18B-600(a1).
43. G.S. 18B-703(h).
44. G.S. 18B-801(d).
45. G.S. 18B-705.

down the system, or merge it with another local ABC system. As part of that process, the ABC Commission may seize the assets of the local ABC board and liquidate any assets to satisfy debt.

ABC Finances

Alcohol is taxed heavily by both the federal and state governments. Hard liquor is the source for most of the alcohol revenue that goes to state and local governments. The state receives the excise tax proceeds from the sale of liquor in ABC stores; a markup in the price is designed to cover the operating expenses of the stores; and local governments receive the stores' profits. Beer and wine wholesalers collect and pay to the state the excise taxes on beer and wine, and a portion of those moneys is shared with counties and cities where the beer and wine are sold. The state also receives some revenue from the fees charged for ABC permits, and local governments collect license fees from the permit holders located in their communities.

State Revenue

North Carolina law requires uniform pricing for liquor sold in ABC stores throughout the state. Distillers set the price for their products according to a formula set by state law, with various taxes and markups added to the distiller's base price.[46] The statutory formula includes a 30 percent excise tax to be collected by local ABC boards and paid to the state.[47] In the fiscal year that ended on June 30, 2023, the excise tax was worth nearly $403 million to the state. When added to mixed beverage taxes of $26 million, the tax revenue to the state from hard liquor was nearly $430 million.[48]

There also are state excise taxes of different amounts on beer and wine.[49] Those taxes are collected by the wholesalers who distribute the beer and wine to retail accountholders,[50] and they amount to about $159 million a year. The majority of the beer and wine excise tax proceeds are kept by the state, but a portion is paid to the counties and cities where those products are sold, as explained further below.

The ABC Commission also collects and pays to the state general fund fees for all of the permits it issues; these fees generated more than $22 million in fiscal year 2023. As of early 2024, the fees ranged from $50 for a vendor representative to $1,000 for a mixed drink permit.[51] Most ABC permit fees, including those for the sale of beer and wine and the fees for breweries, wineries, and wholesalers, are one-time fees, but beer and wine permit holders still have to pay an annual registration and inspection fee of $400.[52] A mixed drink permit is only good for one year, and a renewal fee has to be paid annually.

Calculating the Price of Liquor

In addition to the excise tax described above, and the markups for local governments described below, the markup formula for liquor sold in ABC stores includes several other charges that provide

46. G.S. 18B-804; 14 N.C.A.C. 15A, § .1502.
47. G.S. 105-113.80, -113.83(a).
48. For more information, see N.C. Department of Revenue, *Statistical Abstract of North Carolina Taxes 2023*, www.ncdor.gov/documents/reports/statistical-abstract-north-carolina-taxes-2023/open, and the ABC Commission website, www.abc.nc.gov.
49. G.S. 105-113.80.
50. G.S. 105-113.83(b).
51. G.S. 18B-902(d).
52. G.S. 18B-903.

revenue to both the state and local governments. For example, there is a penny charge on each bottle of 50 milliliters or less, and a nickel on each bottle of 50 milliliters or more (for reference, a "fifth" of alcohol is 750 milliliters); a second bottle charge of the same amount; and a $20 charge on each four liters sold to a mixed drink permit holder.[53] The revenue from the first bottle charge goes to the county commissioners to be used for alcoholism programs, while the revenue from the second bottle charge becomes part of the profit to be distributed by the local ABC board to its county or city.[54] Half the revenue from the $20 charge to mixed drink permit holders goes to the state general fund, 5 percent to the state Department of Health and Human Services for alcoholism and substance abuse programs, and the remainder to the county government for the treatment of alcoholism or substance abuse.[55]

Local Revenue

A local ABC system pays its profits to the county or city that appoints its board. In the fiscal year ending June 30, 2023, the profits paid to local governments totaled more than $132 million statewide. The price on liquor sold in ABC stores includes markups that go to the local ABC board. The general markup, set at the discretion of the ABC Commission, becomes part of the ABC board's revenue to be mixed into its gross receipts; a second markup of 3.5 percent is earmarked for the local government that appoints the ABC board[56] (along with other profit as discussed below). Counties and cities where beer and wine are sold also share in the excise tax on those products collected by the state.[57] The amount shared currently is slightly more than 20 percent of the excise tax on beer, nearly 50 percent of the excise tax on unfortified wine, and 18 percent of the fortified wine excise tax. Those tax proceeds are allocated to counties and cities based on population.

Counties and cities also collect and keep modest annual ABC license fees set by state law.[58] The fees apply to beer and wine permit holders operating in the county or city and to wholesalers with business locations in cities. Local governments may not charge fees to ABC permit holders other than those specified in state law.[59] Local school systems receive the fines levied by the ABC Commission on permit holders who have violated ABC laws and regulations.

Allocation of ABC Profits

General state law requires a local ABC board to allocate certain portions of its revenue for specified purposes; the remaining profit typically goes to the county or city for which the ABC system is operated.

By law, 5 percent of gross receipts are to be spent on law enforcement, either for the board's own officers or through contract with local law enforcement agencies or with the Alcohol Law Enforcement division of the state Department of Public Safety.[60] Another 7 percent are for alcoholism programs, unless the ABC board is subject to a local act of the legislature setting a different allocation.[61] After those distributions, the remaining profits are to go to the county or city unless, again, there is a local act setting a different distribution.[62] Such acts are not as common today as they

53. G.S. 18B-804(b).
54. G.S. 18B-805(b)(4), (c)(1).
55. G.S. 18B-805(b)(2), (3).
56. G.S. 18B-804(b)(3), (5), and -805(c)(1).
57. G.S. 105-113.82.
58. G.S. 105-113.77, -113.78, -113.79.
59. G.S. 105-113.70(d).
60. G.S. 18B-805(c)(2).
61. G.S. 18B-805(c)(3).
62. G.S. 18B-805(e).

used to be, but a number of boards still are subject to local acts specifying that a certain percentage of profits must go to schools, parks, or other particular activities. Those local acts for county ABC systems sometimes specify that a certain percentage of profits are to go to each municipality within the county as well as the portion that is to go to the county itself. In those situations, the affected cities and the county may alter the distribution by mutual agreement.[63]

Local Fiscal Control

Although local ABC boards are not subject to the Local Government Budget and Fiscal Control Act,[64] as are boards of county commissioners and city councils, they are subject to statutes with essentially the same provisions.[65] Under the ABC statutes, for example, the local ABC board's general manager serves as the board's budget officer, with responsibility for preparing and presenting a budget to the board in the same manner as a county or city manager does.[66] The budget year is from July 1 to June 30, the same as for other governmental entities in North Carolina, and the budget process is much the same as for counties and cities. The budget officer—i.e., the general manager—is to submit the proposed budget and a budget message to the board by June 1, and there must be a public hearing where anyone wishing to be heard on the budget is permitted to appear. The ABC law specifies the form of the budget and requires a balanced budget.

In addition to the budget officer, the local ABC board must appoint a finance officer. The board may designate one of its employees for that role or may use the finance officer of the county or city in which the ABC system operates, with the approval of that other board. The local board may appoint the general manager as the finance officer only with the approval of the state ABC Commission, and the commission is to allow such an appointment only for good cause. The fact that the local board operates no more than two stores is considered good cause.[67]

The finance officer keeps the board's books, receives and deposits all moneys, disburses funds, maintains debt records, supervises the investment of idle funds, and otherwise sees that the board follows its budget and the rules of the ABC Commission. Payment of any bill generally requires the approval of the finance officer, but the board may override the finance officer and pay a bill itself if there is an appropriation in the budget for that purpose. The override has to be by adoption of a resolution, and the board members approving the payment can be individually liable if the payment turns out to break the law.[68]

The statutes allow a local ABC board to set aside a portion of its profits as working capital to operate the system, subject to the rules of the ABC Commission.[69] The current commission rule provides that working capital is to be not less than two weeks' average gross sales nor more than two to four months' average, the maximum being tiered according to the boards' gross sales.[70] With the approval of its board of county commissioners or city council, the local ABC board also may set aside funds for special capital improvement projects.[71] The local board may deposit its money in savings accounts or certificates of deposit and may invest its cash balances in the same kinds

63. *Id.*
64. *See generally* G.S. Chapter 159, Article 3.
65. *See* G.S. 18B-702.
66. *Id.*
67. G.S. 18B-702(j).
68. G.S. 18B-702(o).
69. G.S. 18B-702(g)(3), -805(d).
70. 14B N.C.A.C. 15A, § .0902.
71. G.S. 18B-805(d).

of funds as allowed for counties and cities or may deposit the moneys with the State Treasurer for investment.[72]

A local ABC board may borrow money only to buy land, buildings, equipment, or stock needed to operate the ABC system.[73] The board may pledge as security its interest in any of its real or personal property other than the alcohol. The county or city appointing the ABC board is not responsible for the board's debts.[74]

Each local ABC board is required to have an annual independent audit following a chart of accounts prescribed by the ABC Commission.[75] The audit report is to be provided to the appointing authority and the ABC Commission, either one of which may require additional audits.

Mixed Drink Elections

Mixed drinks are sold in qualified hotels, restaurants, clubs, and other locations. Whether such sales are allowed in a community usually, but not always, is decided in a local referendum.

Standard Election Provisions

To hold a mixed drink election, a county must either already operate ABC stores or have an ABC store election at the same time;[76] there has to be a store for mixed drink permit holders to get their liquor. Any city with at least 500 registered voters is eligible to have a mixed drink election; if the city does not have ABC stores, the permit holders may buy their liquor from a store located elsewhere that has been approved by the ABC Commission.[77] If the county or city governing body does not want to call a mixed drink election, it can be required to do so by a petition from 35 percent of the registered voters.[78]

As with elections for ABC stores, a mixed drink election is conducted by the county board of elections using the same rules that apply for all other elections.[79] See the discussion above about the conduct of ABC store elections; the same rules apply to mixed drink elections. A county or city may not hold a mixed drink referendum within three years of an earlier referendum on the same issue.[80]

Special Provisions on Elections

In addition to the general provisions on mixed drink elections discussed immediately above, the ABC statutes have a number of carefully written sections that describe other kinds of places that may have mixed drink elections. The reason for these provisions is the state constitution's prohibition on local acts regulating trade.[81] Under the constitution, the General Assembly could not enact a bill allowing mixed drink sales in, say, Caldwell and Iredell Counties because the sale of mixed drinks is the regulation of trade, and the limitation of the act to specifically named counties makes

72. G.S. 18B-702(t).
73. G.S. 18B-702(r).
74. *Id.*
75. G.S. 18B-702(s).
76. G.S. 18B-600(b).
77. G.S. 18B-600(e).
78. G.S. 18B-601(b)(2), (c)(2).
79. For example, just as with any other municipal election, mail-in absentee voting and early voting may not be used in an ABC referendum unless approved by the city council. G.S. 163-302(a). Once the use of absentee and early voting is authorized, it remains in effect until rescinded by the city council.
80. G.S. 18B-604(a).
81. N.C. Const. art. II, § 24(j).

it a local act. One way around that constitutional restriction is to enact a law applicable to a defined category of counties or cities rather than to specific named locations. An example would be an act allowing mixed drink sales in all counties and cities with populations of 200,000 or more.

The use of such classifications to avoid the unconstitutional local act problem has become a staple of the ABC law, especially with respect to mixed drinks. The categories are crafted to sound like something other than local acts while being limited to a very few targeted communities. One provision, for example, allows mixed drink elections in all cities with at least 200 registered voters located in a county with at least one other city that has approved mixed drinks.[82] Another more egregious example allows any kind of alcohol election in a township (a geographical subdivision of a county that serves no other governmental purpose) that meets all of the following requirements: The county in which the township is located has already approved ABC stores; a third of the employment in the county is travel-related; travel spending exceeds $400 million per year; the entirety of two townships consists of a single island; the island has a population of at least 4,000; and one side of the island faces the ocean and the other side faces a sound.[83]

These categories do not really fool anyone, and it is obvious that they are simply another way of limiting a provision to a specific community without saying its name out loud. If challenged in court, they could be found to be invalid local acts, but generally they have not been questioned and have served as a convenient fiction to allow the legislature to extend mixed drink elections to a number of additional localities.

Beer and Wine Elections

Beer and wine are sold both for consumption on-premises and on a take-out basis. Off-premises sales occur in commercial retail outlets like grocery stores and convenience stores, not in ABC stores. On-premises sales take place in restaurants, hotels, bars, movie theaters, cafes, and a host of other places. For the most part, the decision on whether to allow on- or off-premises sale of beer or wine is made in a local referendum.

Beer and Wine Election Choices

Counties and cities may vote on a variety of options for the local sale of beer and wine. They may vote for either on-premises (sale and consumption at the location) or off-premises (carry-out) sales of beer, wine, or both. Once a category of sales is approved, state law dictates the kinds of places that may obtain permits. In an on-premises beer election, for example, the local government can choose to limit sales to Class A hotels, motels, and restaurants only.[84]

Any county may hold a beer or wine election.[85] A city may by law have such an election only if the last county election was against such sales—that is, the kind of sales the city wants to put on the ballot are not already legal in the county—and the city has a population of 400 or more.[86] As discussed above in connection with mixed drink elections, there are various, narrowly drawn provisions of the ABC statutes that allow particular local governments to have ABC elections even

82. G.S. 18B-600(e1) (amended by S.L. 2024-41, § 6.(b)).
83. G.S. 18B-600(f).
84. G.S. 18B-602(a)(4). The ABC Commission refers to these as "modified plan" permits and requires that a restaurant have inside seating for at least thirty-six people to qualify for such a permit. *See* 14 N.C.A.C. 15B, §§ .0101(3), .0105(a).
85. G.S. 18B-600(b).
86. G.S. 18B-600(c) (amended by S.L. 2024-41, § 6.(b)).

though they would not qualify under these general requirements for county and city elections. Those other provisions typically are written to allow mixed drink elections, but some also authorize beer and wine elections. Thus, for example, certain seasonal ski resorts can qualify to conduct beer and wine elections based on the weekly average number of skiers, though they otherwise would not be eligible for an election.[87] The section on mixed drinks, above, explains the reasons for such provisions.

As with ABC store and mixed drink elections, a beer or wine referendum may be called by a board of county commissioners or city council or by a petition submitted by 35 percent of the registered voters in the county or city.[88] The same rules apply as for all other elections, as discussed earlier. Thus, a county or city may not hold a beer or wine election within three years of the same kind of election in the same jurisdiction.

The Fallout Effect of Some Elections

Some elections for particular kinds of alcohol affect the sale of other products. The approval of ABC stores, for example, automatically results in the lawfulness of on- and off-premises wine sales in that jurisdiction, regardless of any separate election on wine.[89] Similarly, if mixed drinks are approved in a referendum, the establishments eligible for permits to serve them automatically qualify also for beer and wine permits, even if those sales have not been separately approved.[90] The reasoning is that once the sale of a more potent form of alcohol has been approved, the community also should have access to products with a lower percentage of alcohol.

Mixed Drink, Beer, and Wine Sales Allowed without an Election

In an increasing number of situations, the legislature has allowed the sale of beer, wine, and mixed drinks in localities without voter approval at an election. Some of these provisions are applicable statewide, authorizing the issuance of permits to particular kinds of establishments regardless of whether alcohol sales have been approved in that community, while other provisions target specific localities using the same kind of thinly disguised local acts described above for mixed drink elections.

Covered by the first category of provisions are, for example, "tourism resorts," which are eligible for all ABC permits even if located in a county or city that has not approved sales.[91] A tourism resort is a restaurant and lodging facility with a golf course and two tennis courts or a restaurant with an equestrian center and two tennis courts.[92] "Sports clubs" receive similar treatment under the ABC laws. A sports club is an equestrian facility that hosts events sanctioned or endorsed by the United States Equestrian Federation or an establishment with an 18-hole golf course, two or more tennis

87. G.S. 18B-600(e2).
88. G.S. 18B-601(b)–(c).
89. G.S. 18B-603(c)(2).
90. G.S. 18B-603(d)(3a).
91. G.S. 18B-603(f)(8).
92. G.S. 18B-101(14b).

courts, or four or more pickleball courts, whether public or private,[93] and it may receive beer, wine, and mixed drink permits regardless of the outcome of any local election on such sales.[94]

Examples falling under the second category of provisions include "historic ABC establishments" and "tourism ABC establishments," each of which qualifies for permits regardless of local elections.[95] A historic ABC establishment, it turns out, is a restaurant or hotel that is on the National Register of Historic Places or within a state historic district; is located on a state highway within 1.5 miles of a designated North Carolina scenic byway and within 15 miles of a national scenic highway; and is in a county in which at least two cities have approved on-premises sale of beer or wine.[96] A tourism ABC establishment has to be within 1.5 miles of an entrance or exit ramp for a national scenic parkway between the North Carolina state line and milepost 460.[97]

Just as with the statutes that authorize elections in certain narrowly defined categories of communities rather than coming right out and naming the city or county, the only purpose of these provisions is to avoid the constitutional prohibition on local acts regulating trade (discussed above). If they were challenged in court, they could be tossed out, but until then they serve as a means for the legislature to extend alcohol sales to certain small pockets within larger communities that may not be favorably disposed to beer, wine, and mixed drinks.

As a consequence of these various local provisions, it is not correct to say that the sale of beer, wine, and mixed drinks is allowed only in areas in which they have been approved in a local referendum. There are numerous exceptions to that rule and one needs a scorecard to figure out where sales really are allowed.

Retail Permits

Once sales of beer, wine, or mixed drinks become lawful in a community, either through an election or a provision of the law allowing sales without voter approval, the kinds of establishments that may receive permits is set by state law. And it is the state ABC Commission in Raleigh that issues all permits. Local governments generally have little influence over the issuance of permits. Statewide, there are more than 18,000 retail outlets with permits to sell some kind of alcohol on or off the premises. Recently, the ability to sell "to-go" mixed drinks and wine by the glass for on-premises permittees was granted by the General Assembly; the to-go provisions were temporarily allowed during the COVID-19 pandemic but were made permanent through amendments passed in 2024.[98]

Establishments Eligible for Permits

Generally speaking, almost any kind of retail business is eligible for a permit to sell beer or unfortified wine on its premises.[99] Such sales are not limited to just breweries and wineries, restaurants, hotels, and convention centers—movie theaters, snack bars, and even shoe stores and hardware

93. G.S. 18B-1000(8) (the definition of "sports club" was amended by S.L. 2024-41, § 33).

94. G.S. 18B-1006(k). This provision contains another exception prohibiting permits "if the sale of mixed beverages is not lawful within a jurisdiction and that locality has voted against the sale of mixed beverages in a referendum conducted on or after September 1, 2001." However, existing permits may be renewed and existing business locations are still eligible for new permits.

95. G.S. 18B-603(f)(7), (9).

96. G.S. 18B-101(7b).

97. G.S. 18B-101(14a).

98. S.L. 2024-41, § 5.(a).

99. G.S. 18B-1001(1), (3).

stores could sell beer or unfortified wine if they wanted to.[100] Most off-premises sales of beer and unfortified wine are in grocery stores and convenience stores, but restaurants and hotels can get such permits as well, as can other kinds of retail businesses.[101]

Fewer places qualify for permits to sell mixed drinks or fortified wine. A restaurant must have seating for at least ten and do at least 30 percent of its business from food and nonalcoholic beverages to be eligible.[102] Hotels, private clubs, bars, breweries and wineries, convention centers, sports and entertainment venues, and community theaters also may get permits, as may some nonprofit and political organizations.[103]

Special Permits

Some places that do not have regular ABC permits may get permits for particular events. For example, a restaurant, hotel, diner, club, or convention center may get a "special occasion permit" that allows the host of a party or reception, with the permission of the owner of the business that holds the permit, to bring alcohol onto the premises to serve—not sell—to guests.[104] A "limited special occasion permit" is a slightly different version of the same type of permit; it is obtained by the host of the event, not the establishment, and allows the host to bring liquor in to serve to guests.[105] A business can also obtain a "mobile bar services permit" to provide bartending services at locations that do not hold ABC permits, and if the alcohol is served by a permittee holding a mobile bar services permit, a special occasion permit is not required.[106] These permits tend to be used for wedding receptions, anniversary parties, and similar events where the host wants to serve guests but is not in the business of selling drinks.

There also are permits that allow businesses that already have wine and beer permits, usually wine shops or grocery stores, to have wine and beer tastings on the premises. A "malt beverage shop" permit allows a store otherwise engaged in selling malt beverages, unfortified wine, and fortified wine for off-premises consumption to hold malt beverage tastings on the premises.[107] Likewise, a distillery may have liquor tastings.[108] These are promotional events in which small samples are given to customers, not sold.

Additionally, there are special permits that allow particular kinds of organizations to sell or serve alcohol at one-time events.[109] A one-time permit may be issued, for example, to a nonprofit organization to sell beer, wine, or mixed drinks at a fundraising event, or to a local government or political organization to serve alcohol at a fundraiser to which patrons must buy tickets.

Local Government Involvement

All ABC permits are issued by the state ABC Commission according to the requirements of state law. The commission also may suspend or revoke permits or fine permit holders for violations of the

---

100. If, however, a county or city beer referendum is being held on the proposition of limiting beer sales to "Class A hotels, motels, and restaurants," permits are limited to that kind of establishment, mainly meaning that a restaurant must seat at least thirty-six to be eligible for a permit. *See* G.S. 18B-602(a) and 14 N.C.A.C. 15B, §§ .0101(3), .0105(a).
101. G.S. 18B-1001(2), (4).
102. G.S. 18B-1000(6).
103. *See* G.S. 18B-1000.
104. G.S. 18B-1001(8).
105. G.S. 18B-1001(9).
106. G.S. 18B-1001(12a). Note that this permit does not allow the retail sale of individual alcoholic beverages to guests.
107. G.S. 18B-1001(16a).
108. G.S. 18B-1001(15) (wine tastings), (18) (beer tastings), (19) (liquor tastings).
109. G.S. 18B-1002.

ABC law and other offenses.[110] Before approving one of the regular on- or off-premises permits, the ABC Commission notifies the city or county where the establishment seeking the permit is located and asks the local government to complete a couple of forms. One is a zoning and compliance form simply to verify that the premises meet local zoning, building, and fire codes. The other form allows the local government to object to the issuance of the permit.[111]

If the establishment is in an area zoned for that type of business—say, a retail business zone that allows restaurants, and is not otherwise disqualified under state law—the ABC Commission will issue the permit even though local officials would prefer not to have restaurants that serve alcohol in that part of town. In other words, local officials may not exclude businesses from an area based solely on the fact that they sell alcohol, if other businesses of the same nature are allowed there.

The statutes list a number of different factors the ABC Commission is to consider in deciding whether to issue a permit, but no one of those factors by itself explicitly disqualifies an application.[112] The factors include the character of the applicant, the number of establishments with ABC permits already in the area, parking and traffic conditions, proximity to churches and schools, and prior problems with ABC permits in the area. The commission tries to be uniform in its application of the permit requirements throughout the state and rarely will deny a permit application that meets the minimum standards of state law. The commission will be more sympathetic and helpful to local governments when problems arise at a permitted location and will suspend or revoke permits if the owner is unable to control the premises properly, but it is not likely to prejudge a location by denying a permit application.

As discussed above in the "Local Revenue" section, state law provides for annual county and city license fees for beer and wine permit holders, but local governments are specifically prohibited from charging any other local license fees.[113]

Brown-Bagging

While "brown-bagging" used to be common in North Carolina, it now is mostly a thing of the past. Brown-bagging is the practice of bringing one's own bottle of alcohol to a club or restaurant, having it stored in a locker, and then consuming it or serving it to one's guests. It does not refer to consuming alcohol outside of a bar or restaurant in social districts, which is discussed below in the "Local Control of Alcohol Rules" section. Brown-bagging once was a popular means of social drinking before mixed drinks became legal. The law still provides for various kinds of establishments to obtain brown-bagging permits so their patrons can bring in their own liquor. Fewer and fewer businesses and clubs are interested in doing so, however. There are no separate elections on whether to allow brown-bagging in a county or city; brown-bagging follows automatically when a community approves ABC stores.[114] If a city or county votes in mixed drinks, brown-bagging may continue for private clubs and veterans organizations but no longer is available for restaurants, hotels, and other businesses that are eligible for mixed drink permits.[115] Brown-bagging permits are issued by the ABC Commission, just like all other ABC permits.

---

110. *See generally* G.S. 18B-203, -901.
111. G.S. 18B-901(b), (c).
112. G.S. 18B-901(c).
113. G.S. 105-113.70(d).
114. G.S. 18B-603(c)(3).
115. G.S. 18B-603(d)(4).

Local Governments as Permit Holders

Local governments may own and operate some of the establishments that are eligible for ABC permits. Convention centers are eligible for beer, wine, and mixed drink permits, for example, and ballparks, snack bars, and other establishments may sell alcohol.[116] If a local government operates a hotel, it would be eligible for ABC permits as well. Additionally, local governments may rent facilities to organizations or individuals who may want special occasion permits to serve alcohol to guests. A local government itself is eligible for a one-time permit to serve alcohol at a ticketed fundraising event at which it will serve beer, wine, or hard liquor.

Under general state law, beer and wine may be possessed and consumed anywhere except where prohibited by law.[117] Accordingly, there is nothing unlawful about having beer and wine, and serving it without charge, in county or city buildings or grounds. It is lawful, therefore, to serve beer and wine at a reception, retirement celebration, or other event at city hall. Only if beer or wine is going to be sold is a permit necessary.

For spirituous liquor, the general rule is just the opposite. Spirituous liquor may be possessed and consumed only in those places specifically authorized by law.[118] Consequently, a permit such as a special occasion permit is required to even serve hard liquor at a local government event.

The ABC statutes specifically prohibit the issuance of a permit to sell alcohol on the property of a public school or college.[119] There are many exceptions, however. In one notable example, permits are allowed at stadiums, athletic facilities, or arenas on public college or university property if the board of trustees for the college or university has voted to allow permits at that facility.[120] There are additional exceptions for locations like restaurants, nonprofit alumni organizations, and golf courses on public college or university property.[121]

Local Control of Alcohol Rules

The ABC statutes give local governments limited control over the possession, consumption, and sale of alcohol. A county or city may adopt an ordinance prohibiting possession of open containers and public consumption of beer and wine on county or city property and also prohibiting possession on streets and parking lots closed for special events.[122] A county or city may by ordinance prohibit Sunday sales of alcohol except in places that have mixed drink or brown-bagging permits.[123] A county or city may also allow permitted locations to sell alcohol beginning at 10:00 a.m. on Sunday by local ordinance.[124]

One notable recent expansion of local control is the authority to create "social districts" where customers may take alcohol they purchase from a bar, restaurant, or other permitted location into another defined area of a city or county where the normal restrictions on open containers do not apply.[125] The social district is not a full-fledged open-container zone, but instead requires

116. *See* G.S. 18B-1001.
117. G.S. 18B-300(a).
118. *See* G.S. 18B-102(a), -301(f).
119. G.S. 18B-1006(a).
120. G.S. 18B-1006(10).
121. G.S. 18B-1006(a)(4)–(6).
122. G.S. 18B-300(c). Local ordinances are not needed to prohibit public possession and consumption of hard liquor because state law makes such conduct unlawful except where specifically authorized by law. *See* G.S. 18B-301.
123. G.S. 18B-1004(d). State law prohibits off-premises alcohol sales before noon on Sunday. The requirement in G.S. 160A-191 that a city have a public hearing before adopting a Sunday closing ordinance does not apply to ordinances to stop Sunday alcohol sales.
124. G.S. 153A-145.7 (counties); 160A-205.3 (cities).
125. G.S. 18B-300.1.

customers to use specific marked containers sold by participating ABC permitted businesses in geographic zones identified by the local government, during times defined in the social district plan.[126] Businesses that are not ABC permittees may also allow customers to bring in alcoholic beverages purchased from ABC permit locations in the social district, subject to restrictions in the law.[127] Other than those local controls, the rules on consumption, possession, and sale of alcohol are governed by state law.

Breweries, Wineries, and Distilleries

North Carolina has a number of breweries, wineries, and distilleries. Almost all the breweries are brewpubs or craft breweries, and almost all the distilleries are small craft operations as well. The requirements for ABC permits are the same, though, regardless of the size of the operation. These kinds of commercial facilities can be located anywhere in the state; they do not depend on local approval at a referendum. In addition to producing their product and selling it to wholesalers for distribution to retail accounts, breweries and wineries also may sell their beer and wine directly to customers at their facilities and at several other locations in the state if they get the regular on-premises permits. They also may hold tastings.[128]

The Three-Tier System of Distribution

Like almost all other states, North Carolina law mandates a three-tier system of distribution of beer and wine.[129] Generally, a brewery or winery, no matter where located, that wants to sell its products in North Carolina may sell only to a wholesaler in the state; the wholesaler may sell only to a retail business like a grocery store or restaurant; a retailer may buy beer or wine only from a wholesaler; and producers and wholesalers may not own retail businesses. This system of regulation was introduced after Prohibition to guard against the abuses of any one entity having too much control over the distribution and sale of alcohol. The three-tier system, for example, prevents a brewery from pressuring a restaurant to carry only its products.[130]

To help enforce the three-tier system and assure that larger commercial businesses cannot exercise undue influence over the smaller fish, the ABC statutes and ABC Commission's rules include detailed instructions on the kinds of goods, favors, and services breweries and wineries and wholesalers can provide to retailers. The rules limit, for instance, the value of neon lights and clocks and other displays a wholesaler may provide to a bar or restaurant with a particular brand name on them.[131]

Smaller breweries and wineries may distribute their products directly to retail accounts without going through a wholesaler. When their production passes a specified level, however, they must use a wholesaler.[132]

---

126. G.S. 18B-300.1(d)–(f).
127. G.S. 18B-300.1(h).
128. *See* G.S. 18B-1001.
129. *See generally* G.S. Chapter 18B, Articles 11, 12, 13.
130. G.S. 18B-1116(a)(1).
131. *See, e.g.,* 14 N.C.A.C. 15C, § .0711.
132. *See, e.g.,* G.S. 18B-1114.3(b).

The rise of the Internet has increased the interest in direct sales of alcohol to customers. State law allows wineries, whether located in North Carolina or elsewhere, to ship a very limited number of cases directly to customers in the state. The winery must obtain a permit from the ABC Commission and is restricted in both the number of cases that may be sent to any one individual and the total number of cases that may be shipped directly to customers in North Carolina.[133] Those limitations mean that this kind of purchase tends to be used only by wine connoisseurs. It does provide the means for a North Carolinian who has enjoyed a particular wine at a California or other out-of-state winery to have a case shipped home. ABC stores may take online orders, but all alcohol must be picked up in person by the individual who placed the order; online gift cards may be delivered digitally.[134]

Law Enforcement

Many violations of the ABC law, such as serving to a minor or to someone who is already intoxicated, are criminal and may be investigated by city police or sheriffs' deputies. Additionally, local ABC boards are required to spend a certain portion of their revenue on law enforcement, either through their own local ABC officers or contracting with other agencies.[135] The ALE division of the Department of Public Safety is also charged with alcohol law enforcement.[136] Unlike regular police, those local and state alcohol officers look for violations of the ABC Commission's rules.

The Law to Be Enforced

Chapter 18B of the General Statutes contains almost all of the state's regulations pertaining to alcohol. Though other parts of the statutes address alcohol taxation, drunken behavior and driving, minimum ages for employees in establishments that sell alcohol, and a variety of ancillary matters, all the essential regulatory provisions—who may get permits, hours of sale, approval of brands, etc.—are in Chapter 18B. Those laws are the principal enforcement priority for local and state alcohol enforcement officers. Some violations are criminal and may be prosecuted in court; many others are regulatory and form the basis for actions by the ABC Commission to deny, suspend, or revoke permits or to assess fines against permit holders.

ALE agents and ABC officers also apply the extensive rules of the ABC Commission. Those rules describe in considerable detail how permit holders may conduct their businesses. There are rules governing advertising, storage of bottles, approval of new labels, promotions, gifts from suppliers, recordkeeping, consumer contests, and a host of other issues for the breweries, wineries, distilleries, importers, wholesalers, hotels, restaurants, grocery stores, convenience stores, theaters, ballparks, and numerous other businesses that hold ABC permits. Local and state alcohol officers have authority regular police do not have, namely, the authority to enter licensed premises to inspect for compliance with the many regulatory provisions found in Chapter 18B.[137] That kind of regulatory enforcement takes up much of the officers' time.

---

133. G.S. 18B-1001.1.
134. G.S. 18B-800(c3).
135. *See* G.S. 18B-501, -805(c)(2).
136. *See* G.S. 18B-500.
137. G.S. 18B-502.

State Alcohol Law Enforcement Section

The ALE division is within the state Department of Public Safety, as is the ABC Commission, but they are separate agencies. While ALE agents' primary mission is enforcement of the ABC laws, they also concentrate on drug, tobacco, and lottery-related offenses.[138] The 100+ agents, operating out of regional offices, have performed background checks for ABC permit applications, conducted educational programs for permit holders, routinely inspected ABC premises, and investigated violations of both the ABC laws and the ABC Commission's rules. Although ALE agents work closely with the ABC Commission and initiate many of their investigations at the request of the commission, they are not employees of nor supervised by the commission.

Local ABC Enforcement

Each local ABC board is required to itself employ one or more law enforcement officers or to contract with a city police department, sheriff's office, or ALE for the enforcement of ABC laws in its jurisdiction.[139] Some counties, including several of the larger ones, still have their own enforcement officers, while most ABC systems contract with the city police or sheriff. A separate statute requires each board to set aside at least 5 percent of its gross receipts for enforcement and says that the local ABC board may contract with ALE for that purpose.[140]

Local ABC officers are authorized to, and often do, assist other law enforcement agencies.[141] Before that can happen, the local ABC board has to adopt a resolution authorizing such assistance and there then has to be a specific written request, acknowledged in the board's minutes.[142] The local board continues to be responsible for any assisting officer's salary, benefits, and workers' compensation while the officer is helping the other agency, unless a different arrangement is agreed upon. Local ABC boards also may work out interlocal agreements with other boards or with cities or counties for mutual assistance in law enforcement. Because of potential liability for actions taken by its enforcement officers while they are working for another agency, a local ABC board needs to review any proposed assistance or mutual aid agreement carefully and consider whether those liability issues should be explicitly addressed in the agreement.

Local ABC officers have the same inspection authority that ALE agents have.[143] That is, they may enter licensed premises at any time to check for compliance with the ABC statutes and the ABC Commission rules. When a local ABC board contracts with city police or the sheriff for ABC law enforcement, the police officers or deputies assigned to that duty acquire the inspection authority of an ABC officer.[144] As regular law enforcement officers they would have no right to enter and look around a restaurant or bar if the owner did not want them there, but as ABC enforcement officers they are authorized to do so. For that reason, city police departments and sheriffs like to contract with their local ABC boards; the inspection authority gives them easier access to troublesome locations than they would otherwise have. To prevent abuse of the inspection authority, the law allows no more than five city police officers or sheriffs' deputies to be designated as having that power.[145]

To ensure that city police officers and sheriffs' deputies are actually performing the ABC enforcement duties for which the local board has contracted, the respective agencies must submit a monthly

138. G.S. 18B-500(b).
139. G.S. 18B-501.
140. G.S. 18B-805(c)(2).
141. G.S. 18B-501(d)–(e).
142. G.S. 18B-501(e).
143. G.S. 18B-502.
144. G.S. 18B-501(f).
145. *Id.*

report to the local board of the number of (1) ABC arrests in locations with permits and elsewhere and (2) ABC educational programs conducted.[146] The board then shares the report with its appointing authority and with the state ABC Commission.

Seizures and Forfeitures

The ABC statutes include detailed provisions on the disposition of alcohol seized due to violations of the law.[147] Generally, in such cases the alcohol is held until trial and then, depending on the outcome of the trial, is returned to the owner or destroyed or sold. Vehicles, boats, and airplanes used to transport illegal alcohol (typically bootleg whiskey) and equipment used to unlawfully manufacture alcohol are subject to forfeiture, and the statutes set out detailed procedures for seizing and holding such property and then disposing of it following the resolution of the criminal charges.[148]

146. G.S. 18B-501(f1).
147. G.S. 18B-503.
148. G.S. 18B-504.

PART 8. Human Services and Other County Functions

Chapter 37

Public Health

Jill D. Moore and Kirsten E. Leloudis

Jill D. Moore and Kirsten E. Leloudis are School of Government faculty members who work in public health law.

In 1988, the Institute of Medicine defined public health as "what we, as a society, do collectively to ensure the conditions in which people can be healthy."[1] The emphasis this definition places on collective action and the conditions that promote good health reflects a distinction between public health and medicine: public health is concerned with the health of populations, not just the health status or condition of particular individuals.

The oldest and most traditional concerns of public health systems—sanitation and disease control—reflect this focus. Practices such as isolation of the ill and proper food handling are described in the Old Testament book of Leviticus, a book that is viewed by some public health

1. Institute of Medicine, *The Future of Public Health* (Washington, D.C.: National Academy Press, 1988), 1. This definition retains its currency in the twenty-first century. *See, e.g., The Future of the Public's Health in the 21st Century* (Washington, D.C.: National Academy Press, 2002); K.B. DeSalvo, Y.C. Wang, A. Harris, J. Auerbach, D. Koo, and P. O'Carroll, "Public Health 3.0: A Call to Action for Public Health to Meet the Challenges of the 21st Century," *Preventing Chronic Disease* 14 (Sept. 7, 2017), dx.doi.org/10.5888/pcd14.170017.

scholars as the first written public health code.[2] The focus on collective action and population-based activities is also the reason public health has long been a function of government.

In North Carolina, state laws addressing public health concerns date back to colonial times, when a maritime quarantine law was adopted to prevent the introduction of contagious diseases into the population.[3] Subsequent laws began to define an infrastructure for public health, beginning with an 1877 statute creating the first State Board of Health and designating county medical societies to serve as boards of health for their respective counties.[4] The first county health departments were formed in the early twentieth century.[5]

Today, every county in the state is served by a local health department. A full chapter of the North Carolina General Statutes (hereinafter G.S.), Chapter 130A, is devoted to the laws that address the authority and roles of the state and local agencies that constitute North Carolina's public health system and prescribe many of the methods and programs through which public health activities are carried out.

The public health system continues to carry out the traditional functions of ensuring sanitation and controlling infectious diseases, but its focus has expanded over the years to include other duties and embrace other roles. Among other things, the public health system today systematically monitors the health status of the state's residents, serves as a provider of health care services, and engages in community-based activities designed to promote health and prevent chronic disease or injury.

Responsibility for Public Health in North Carolina

The General Assembly has declared that the purpose of the state's public health system is "to ensure that all citizens in the State have equal access to essential public health services," and the system's mission is to promote and contribute to the highest level of health possible for the people of North Carolina by

- identifying and preventing or reducing community health risks;
- detecting, investigating, and preventing the spread of disease;
- promoting healthy lifestyles and a safe and healthful environment;
- promoting the accessibility and availability of quality health care services in the private sector; and
- providing health care services when they are not otherwise available.[6]

North Carolina has a decentralized public health system, in which the state and county governments share legal authority to act to protect and promote public health as well as the responsibility for assuring that public health services are available to all the state's residents. However, most public health service delivery occurs at the local level, through various forms of local health departments.[7]

---

2. Philip A. Mackowiak and Paul S. Sehdev, "The Origin of Quarantine," *Clinical Infectious Diseases* 35, no. 9 (November 1, 2002): 1071–72, doi.org/10.1086/344062.

3. Walter Clark, *Colonial and State Records of North Carolina* (Documenting the American South: 1905), 23:956, docsouth.unc.edu/csr/index.php/document/csr23-0054.

4. S.L. 1876-77, ch. 96, ncleg.gov/Files/Library/sessionlaws/1871-1880/pubs_lawsresolutionso187677.pdf.

5. William S. Powell, ed., *Encyclopedia of North Carolina* (University of North Carolina Press, 2006), 920–24.

6. Chapter 130A, § 1.1 of the North Carolina General Statutes (hereinafter G.S.).

7. The term "local health department" encompasses county health departments, district health departments, public health authorities, and the public health components of consolidated human services agencies (CHSAs). *See* G.S. 130A-2(5); 130A-43. The term also includes a hospital authority that provides public health services pursuant to S.L. 1997-502, § 12. Cabarrus county is the only county that provides public health services in this manner.

The State Level

Statewide public health activities and programs in North Carolina are carried out by several officials and agencies. The officials with primary responsibility for public health are the secretary of health and human services and the state health director. The principal agencies are the Commission for Public Health, the North Carolina Department of Health and Human Services Division of Public Health (NCDHHS DPH), and the North Carolina Local Health Department Accreditation Board. Together, these individuals and agencies

- make and enforce statewide rules for public health programs,
- administer statewide public health programs and provide some direct services,
- oversee and provide technical assistance for local public health programs,
- distribute federal and state funds to local public health agencies,
- assure that local public health agencies meet state law requirements for accreditation, and
- coordinate North Carolina's public health activities with other state and federal agencies.

State Officials

The North Carolina Secretary of Health and Human Services is appointed by the governor and oversees all of NCDHHS's activities.[8] A state statute gives the general responsibility for administering and enforcing most of the state's public health laws to the secretary of NCDHHS,[9] but in practice many duties are carried out by the state health director, who is appointed by the secretary.[10] In addition, a few state laws give powers and duties directly to the state health director. For example, the communicable disease laws give the director the power to issue temporary orders requiring health care providers to report certain health conditions,[11] the authority to inspect medical records in an outbreak,[12] and the authority to order isolation or quarantine.[13]

Commission for Public Health

The Commission for Public Health is the primary rulemaking body for public health in North Carolina. State statutes establish the membership of the commission and give it the general authority to

---

8. As of this writing, NCDHHS has seventeen divisions and offices, including early childhood programs; services for the deaf and blind; aging services; health care facilities regulation; public health, social services, mental health, developmental disability, and substance use services; and the state's Medicaid program. *See* NCDHHS, Divisions and Programmatic Offices, perma.cc/8P9F-PGUZ. The department is also responsible for thirteen state facilities, including psychiatric hospitals, substance use treatment centers, and developmental centers for individuals with developmental disabilities. *See* NCDHHS, State Operated Healthcare Facilities, perma.cc/J9JQ-BD38. Some statewide services and programs related to child and maternal health that were previously under the Division of Public Health (DPH) are now housed in the Division of Child and Family Well-Being within NCDHHS, which was formed in 2022. *See* NCDHHS, "NCDHHS Launches New Division of Child and Family Well-Being," perma.cc/UTM8-TA32.

9. G.S. 130A-4(a). The secretary of the Department of Environmental Quality has responsibility for administering public health laws related to solid waste management and the N.C. Drinking Water Act. G.S. 130A-4(c).

10. G.S. 130A-3.

11. G.S. 130A-141.1.

12. G.S. 130A-144(b).

13. G.S. 130A-145. Local health directors have some of the same powers and duties as the state health director. For example, local health directors may exercise comparable communicable disease powers, including the authority to order isolation or quarantine. G.S. 130A-145(a); *see also* G.S. 130A-2 (defining *isolation authority* and *quarantine authority*). But some powers are given to the state health director alone. For example, the public health bioterrorism laws authorize the state health director to close property or order examinations of individuals during a suspected bioterrorism event. G.S. 130A-475(a). Local health directors do not have a similar authority related to bioterrorism.

adopt rules to protect and promote the public health, including rules necessary to implement statewide public health programs.[14] In addition, numerous provisions throughout G.S. Chapter 130A direct the commission to adopt rules regarding specific public health activities or programs, ranging from communicable disease control, to the inspection and grading of restaurants, to the decontamination of properties used for the manufacture of methamphetamine.[15] It also has the authority to create metropolitan water districts, sanitary districts, and mosquito control districts. The commission's rules are codified in the North Carolina Administrative Code.[16]

Division of Public Health

DPH is the state agency with primary responsibility for carrying out the public health system's statutory mission "to promote and contribute to the highest level of health possible for the people of North Carolina."[17] DPH is divided into sections and offices that are responsible for a wide variety of statewide public health services and programs that address chronic disease and injury prevention; environmental health; epidemiology; local and community support; health equity; oral health; women, infant, and community wellness; and the Title V maternal and child health block grant program. DPH also operates the Office of the Chief Medical Examiner and statewide medical examiner system, the State Laboratory for Public Health, the Office of Vital Records, and the State Center for Health Statistics.[18]

DPH also supports local health departments. It monitors local services, performs periodic reviews of local health departments, and assists local health departments by providing training and technical assistance and conducting quality assurance activities. DPH also ensures local compliance with state public health program standards through its distribution of state and federal funds to local agencies. NCDHHS receives federal and state money for public health programs and determines local public health agencies' allocations. To receive certain funds, a local health department must enter into a contract with NCDHHS called the "consolidated agreement." The consolidated agreement requires local public health agencies to comply with all public health statutes and rules and specifies how funds must be managed. This contract has a significant effect on how local public health agencies operate, because noncompliance with its terms can result in loss of state and federal funds. The consolidated agreement is renewed annually.

DPH maintains relationships and coordinates its work with federal public health agencies, including the Centers for Disease Control and Prevention (CDC). It also works with other state agencies that have responsibilities related to public health. For example, the North Carolina Department of

---

14. G.S. 130A-30; 130A-29.

15. *See, e.g.,* G.S. 130A-144 (communicable disease control); 130A-248 (sanitation of food and lodging establishments); 130A-284 (decontamination standards for methamphetamine sites). These are examples only and not a complete list of statutes authorizing the commission to adopt rules. The N.C. Environmental Management Commission also has some rulemaking authority in public health. It makes statewide rules regarding water sources, including rules governing local health departments' inspection and permitting of private drinking water wells. G.S. 87-97; *see also* G.S. 143B-282 (creating the Environmental Management Commission and setting forth its rulemaking authority).

16. The rules for environmental health programs are in Title 15A, Chapter 18 of the North Carolina Administrative Code (hereinafter N.C.A.C.). The rules for all other public health programs are in Title 10A, Chapters 39–48.

17. G.S. 130A-1.1. There are other divisions within NCDHHS relevant to the provision of public health services in North Carolina. These include the Office of Rural Health, which works to increase access to health care in underserved communities; the Division of Health Benefits, which administers the Medicaid program; the Division of Health Service Regulation, which is responsible for licensure and certification of health care facilities; and the Division of Mental Health, Developmental Disabilities, and Substance Use Services. The mental health, developmental disabilities, and substance use services system is described in Chapter 38.

18. As of this writing, DPH is composed of twelve sections and offices. *See* NCDHHS, Division of Public Health, Programs and Services, perma.cc/Z9XZ-SWVQ.

Agriculture & Consumer Services (NCDA&CS) operates the Grade A milk sanitation program and the sleep products sanitation program, and it shares responsibility with public health for the safety of some foods served to the public for pay. NCDA&CS also monitors certain diseases in livestock animals, including some diseases that could spread to humans.[19] The state Department of Environmental Quality is responsible for the sanitation of public water supplies, shellfish sanitation, and recreational water quality.[20] The state Department of Labor is responsible for occupational health and safety investigations and enforcement.[21] The North Carolina Department of Public Safety leads the state's emergency management operations, including responding to natural disasters and other events that affect public health.[22]

North Carolina Local Health Department Accreditation Board

Every agency functioning as a local health department in North Carolina must obtain and maintain accreditation from the North Carolina Local Health Department Accreditation Board.[23] The board is responsible for developing a schedule by which local health departments must apply for accreditation, reviewing each department's application for accreditation, and assigning an accreditation status as follows:

- *Accredited* means that the department has satisfied the standards for accreditation. Accreditation expires after four years, and the department must apply for re-accreditation.
- *Conditionally accredited* means that the department has failed to meet the standards for accreditation but has been granted short-term accreditation status subject to conditions set by the board. This status is good for two years. By the end of that time, the department must have satisfied the board's conditions and met the criteria for accreditation, or it will become unaccredited.
- *Unaccredited* means that the department has continued to fail to meet the standards after a period of conditional accreditation.[24]

The Commission for Public Health adopts rules and standards for the accreditation process that provide for local health department self-assessments, site visits by the accreditation board, and informal review of board decisions.[25] Local public health agencies must be accredited by the North Carolina board to maintain their eligibility to receive state and federal funding from the Division of Public Health.[26]

The accreditation board is composed of seventeen members appointed by the secretary of NCDHHS. The membership includes representatives of boards of county commissioners, local boards of health, local health directors, staff from DPH, and the public.[27]

---

19. *See* N.C. Department of Agriculture & Consumer Services, About NCDA&CS, perma.cc/HBB7-LQXE.
20. *See* N.C. Department of Environmental Quality, NCDEQ Divisions, perma.cc/94RH-HYRD.
21. *See* N.C. Department of Labor, Occupational Health and Safety Division, perma.cc/A88P-VJAA.
22. *See* N.C. Department of Public Safety, Emergency Management, perma.cc/9EH5-GPYT.
23. G.S. 130A-34.1. The statutory definition of *local health department* includes a county health department, a district health department, or a public health authority. G.S. 130A-2(5). Although the definition does not mention consolidated human services agencies that include public health, a separate law states that such agencies "shall have the responsibility to carry out the duties of a local health department." G.S. 130A-43(a). Obtaining and maintaining accreditation is one such duty.
24. G.S. 130A-34.1(d).
25. The rules are codified in 10A N.C.A.C. ch. 48.
26. G.S. 130A-34.4(a)(1).
27. G.S. 130A-34.1(a).

The Regional Level

North Carolina law does not contain a formal regional structure for public health services. However, in practice, there are several regional entities that carry out either state or local public health responsibilities.

DPH hires employees—often called consultants—assigned to serve local health departments in designated regions. Consultants work in different disciplines or service areas. For example, there are administrative consultants, nurse consultants working in areas such as child health or school health, and regional environmental health specialists.

The state is divided into four regions for purposes of public health preparedness and response. Each region has a field office and staff, including planning consultants, training facilitators, industrial hygienists, pharmacists, and program support specialists. Regional staff members are employed by the state and work with local public health officials. Regional public health preparedness and response staff monitor public health conditions in the regions they serve. They are also responsible for several public health preparedness activities, including training the public health workforce and developing public health emergency response plans in collaboration with local and regional entities that work with emergency response or disaster management.[28]

The Local Level

Local Health Departments

Each county in North Carolina is required by law to provide public health services.[29] A county may satisfy this duty by operating a county health department, participating in a multi-county district health department, forming or joining a public health authority, establishing a consolidated human services agency that includes public health, or contracting with the state to provide public health services. Each type of agency is captured in the generic term "local health department."[30] Every local health department has a governing board, which may be called a "board of health," a "public health authority board," or a "consolidated human services board." For purposes of this chapter, the term "board of health" is used to refer to all of those.[31] Boards of health are discussed in further detail later in this chapter.

County Health Departments

A county health department is a single-county agency that provides local public health services. It is created by the board of county commissioners and typically is governed by a board of health appointed by the commissioners.[32] The board of health appoints a local health director after consultation with the county commissioners.[33] The county health director must meet minimum education

28. *See* NCDHHS, Epidemiology, Public Health Preparedness and Response, epi.dph.ncdhhs.gov/phpr/index.html.

29. G.S. 130A-34.

30. G.S. 130A-2(5) (defining *local health department* as "a district health department or a public health authority or a county health department"); 130A-43(a) (giving consolidated human services agencies the responsibility to carry out the duties of a local health department); 153A-77(b) (authorizing boards of county commissioners to create consolidated human services agencies that include public health). Cabarrus County provides public health services pursuant to an uncodified state law that authorizes a hospital authority to provide local public health services. S.L. 1997-502, § 12. The Cabarrus Health Alliance exercises the legal powers and duties of a local health department.

31. G.S. 130A-2(4) (defining *local board of health* as "a district board of health or a public health authority board or a county board of health"); 153A-77(d) (providing that a consolidated human services board acquires the powers and duties of a local board of health).

32. G.S. 130A-35.

33. G.S. 130A-40.

and experience requirements and has a number of legal powers and duties, described in greater detail in the section on local health directors later in this chapter.

District Health Departments

A district health department (sometimes called a regional health department) is a multi-county agency that provides local public health services for all the counties in the district. A district health department may be formed upon agreement of the boards of county commissioners and the boards of health of two or more counties. A county may join an existing district health department upon a similar agreement entered by each affected county.[34] A district health department may have health department offices in each component county, but it is governed by one board of health and administered by one health director.

The governing board is called a "district board of health." Each county in the district appoints one county commissioner to serve on the board, and those commissioners appoint the remaining members.[35] If a county joins or withdraws from an existing district health department, the district board of health is dissolved and a new board is appointed. After consultation with the board of commissioners of each county in the district, the board of health appoints a district health director.[36] The district health director must meet the same minimum education and experience requirements as a county health director and has the same legal powers and duties.

Any county may withdraw from a district health department when a majority of its county commissioners determines that the district is not operating in the best interests of health in that county. The district may be dissolved upon a similar decision by the boards of commissioners of all the counties in the district. Withdrawal or dissolution may take place only after written notice is given to NCDHHS and only at the end of the fiscal year. A certified public accountant or an auditor certified by the Local Government Commission (LGC) distributes surplus funds to the counties according to the percentage each county contributed. When an entire district dissolves or when a county withdraws, any rules adopted by the district board of health remain in effect in the county or counties involved until amended or repealed by the new board or boards governing the affected counties.[37]

Public Health Authorities

A county may meet its obligation to provide public health services by creating a public health authority. A public health authority may be formed by a single county or by two or more counties jointly. To form a single-county public health authority, the board of commissioners and the county board of health must jointly adopt a resolution finding that it is in the interest of the public health and welfare in the county to create a public health authority and provide public health services through it. In the case of a multi-county authority, the resolution must be adopted jointly by the board of commissioners and board of health governing each affected county. A county may join an existing public health authority upon joint resolution of the board of commissioners and board of health of each county involved. Before adopting any such resolution, the boards of county commissioners must give notice to the public and hold a public hearing.[38]

---

34. G.S. 130A-36(a).
35. G.S. 130A-37.
36. G.S. 130A-40.
37. G.S. 130A-38.
38. G.S. 130A-45.02.

After the resolution has been adopted, a public health authority board is appointed. The board of a single-county public health authority is appointed by the county commissioners of the county. For a multi-county public health authority, the chair of the board of commissioners of each participating county appoints one county commissioner (or designee) to the board, and those members appoint the remaining members.[39] The board replaces the prior local board of health and becomes the rulemaking, policy-making, and adjudicatory body for the authority. The public health authority board appoints a public health authority director after consultation with the appropriate county commissioners.[40] The public health authority director must meet the same minimum education and experience requirements as a county health director and has similar legal powers and duties.

Once created, a public health authority operates more independently of the board (or boards) of county commissioners than a traditional county health department. For example, a public health authority is not required to submit its budget to the county commissioners. While it may request funding from county commissioners, the public health authority acts on its own to develop its budget in accordance with state financial management laws. It also may acquire or sell real property without going through the county commissioners.

A board of county commissioners may dissolve a public health authority (or withdraw from a multi-county authority) upon a finding that the authority is not operating in the best health interests of the county. Dissolution may occur only after written notification to NCDHHS and only at the end of a fiscal year. If the authority was a multi-county authority, a certified public accountant or an auditor certified by the LGC distributes surplus funds to the counties according to the percentage each county contributed. All rules adopted by the authority board continue in effect until amended or repealed by the new authority board or local board of health.[41]

Consolidated Human Services Agencies

Some counties provide public health services through a consolidated human services agency (CHSA). G.S. 153A-77(b) authorizes boards of county commissioners to create a CHSA to "carry out the functions of any combination of commissions, boards, or agencies appointed by the board of county commissioners or acting under and pursuant to the authority of the board of county commissioners." It specifies that a CHSA may include public health, but it does not require public health to be included.[42]

A CHSA is typically governed by a consolidated human services board. If the CHSA includes public health, the consolidated human services board acquires the powers and duties of a local board of health, with one exception: the board is not authorized to appoint the consolidated human

---

39. G.S. 130A-45.1.

40. G.S. 130A-45.5.

41. G.S. 130A-45.2.

42. The state law governing CHSAs was changed significantly by legislation enacted in June 2012. S.L. 2012-126 (amending G.S. 153A-77). Under prior law, the only counties that could create CHSAs were those with populations exceeding 425,000. Further, CHSAs were required to include public health services; social services; and mental health, developmental disabilities, and substance use services. The 2012 legislation removed the population threshold and amended the language describing a CHSA, with the result that counties have a great deal of flexibility in determining which services will be provided.

There are some limitations on what may be included in a CHSA. Among other things, G.S. 153A-76 prohibits county commissioners from including a public health authority in a CHSA. However, a separate law permits commissioners to dissolve or withdraw from a public health authority at the end of a fiscal year. A county that is part of a public health authority could therefore create a CHSA including public health, but the commissioners would have to take the additional step of dissolving or withdrawing from the authority first. Similarly, a county that is presently part of a multi-county district health department could not include public health in a CHSA without first withdrawing from the district at the end of a fiscal year.

services director. Instead, the director is appointed by the county manager with the advice and consent of the board. The consolidated board also has powers and duties set forth in the CHSA statute.[43]

If the CHSA includes public health, then the consolidated human services director acquires most of the legal powers and duties of a local health director, with two provisos: (1) the director may serve as the CHSA's executive officer only to the extent and in the manner authorized by the county manager and (2) the director may appoint CHSA staff only with the approval of the county manager.[44] If the consolidated human services director does not meet the education and experience requirements for a local health director set out in G.S. 130A-40(a), the consolidated human services director must appoint someone who does meet those requirements to serve as the local health director.[45]

Governance: Local Boards of Health

Each local public health agency in North Carolina has a governing board that is responsible for public health within its jurisdiction. What the board is called varies by agency: a county health department has a county board of health, a district health department has a district board of health, a public health authority has a public health authority board, and a consolidated human services agency has a consolidated human services board. The generic term "local board of health" embraces all of these types of boards when they are carrying out public health duties.[46] A board of health may be an independent board appointed by the county commissioners, or the commissioners may elect to serve as the board of health themselves by adopting a resolution abolishing the board and conferring its powers and duties upon the board of commissioners.[47] When the board of county commissioners serves as the local board of health, it must appoint an advisory committee on health that meets the membership requirements of a county board of health.[48]

The composition of the different types of boards varies, as illustrated in Table 37.1. In general, board members are county commissioners, professionals with expertise in health care or public health (including physicians, pharmacists, veterinarians, and professional engineers, among others), and the general public. The powers and duties of each type of board also vary somewhat, but each is charged with protecting and promoting the public health and with serving as the policymaking, rulemaking, and adjudicatory body for public health in the county or counties in its jurisdiction. Each board has limited authority to set fees for public health services. Each board also influences the day-to-day administration of the local health department, public health authority, or consolidated human services agency.[49]

---

43. G.S. 153A-77(d).

44. G.S. 130A-43(c).

45. G.S. 153A-77(e)(9). The county manager must approve the appointment. If the CHSA director meets the statutory requirements for a local health director, a separate individual need not be appointed.

46. This is consistent with statutory definitions and usage. G.S. 130A-2(4) defines *local board of health* to mean "a district board of health or a public health authority or a county board of health." G.S. 153A-77(d) gives consolidated human services boards the powers and duties of local boards of health, except when the statutes specifically provide otherwise.

47. G.S. 153A-77(a) authorizes commissioners to directly assume the powers and duties of a county board of health or a consolidated human services board. It requires the board of county commissioners to give thirty days' notice of a public hearing and hold the public hearing before adopting a resolution to abolish the appointed board of health.

48. *Id.* The role of the advisory committee is in the name: it is *advisory*, and generally the committee cannot wield or be delegated the powers and duties statutorily assigned to a board of health.

49. G.S. 130A-35 (county board of health); 130A-37 (district board of health); 130A-45.1 (public health authority board); 153A-77(d) (consolidated human services board).

Table 37.1 Board Membership Requirements by Type of Local Public Health Agency Board*

	County Board of Health	District Board of Health	Single-County Public Health Authority Board	Multi-County Public Health Authority Board	Consolidated Human Services Board
Number of members	11	15 to 18	7 to 9	7 to 11	Up to 25
Members of the public or consumers	3	✔	✔	✔	4 or more[c]
County commissioner	✔	✔[a]	✔	✔[b]	✔
Physician	✔	✔	✔	✔	✔[d]
Psychiatrist					✔
Psychologist					✔
Social worker					✔
Hospital administrator			✔	✔	
Dentist	✔	✔	✔	✔	✔
Optometrist	✔	✔	✔	✔	✔
Veterinarian	✔	✔	✔	✔	✔
Registered nurse	✔	✔	✔	✔	✔
Pharmacist	✔	✔	✔	✔	✔
Engineer	✔	✔	✔	✔	✔
Accountant			✔	✔	

Shaded area: Two professionals representing the following fields must serve on the board: optometry, veterinary science, nursing, pharmacy, engineering, or accounting. In other words, not *all* of these professions will necessarily be represented.

*These requirements do not apply if the county commissioners serve as the board for a county health department or a consolidated human services agency including public health.

a. One commissioner from each county involved.

b. One commissioner from each county involved. The commissioners may designate someone other than a commissioner to serve in this position.

c. At least four members must be consumers of human services.

d. Two licensed physicians must serve on the board, one of whom must be a psychiatrist.

Board Membership Qualifications and Terms

The statutes authorizing county boards of health, district boards of health, and consolidated human services boards all require that board members be residents of the county or district. For county and district boards, if there is no resident available to serve in one of the licensed professional positions, a member of the general public must be appointed instead.[50] There is no similar provision for consolidated human services boards, suggesting that a licensed professional position on such a board would simply remain vacant if there were no resident available to serve. Members of public health authority boards are not required to be residents of the county or multi-county area served by the authority.

County and district board of health members are appointed to three-year terms and may serve a maximum of three consecutive three-year terms. There are a couple of exceptions to this general

50. There is an exception for the member of a county board of health who serves in the licensed optometrist spot. G.S. 130A-35(b). If a licensed optometrist who is a county resident is not available for appointment, the county commissioners may fill the position with either (1) a licensed optometrist who resides in another county or (2) a member of the general public who is a county resident. This provision does not apply to a district board of health.

rule. First, if the member is the only county or district resident who is a member of one of the licensed professions that must be represented on the board, the member may serve more than three consecutive three-year terms.[51] Second, if a member of a district board of health is serving in his or her capacity as a county commissioner, the North Carolina Attorney General has advised that the member may serve for as long as he or she remains a commissioner, even if that time exceeds three consecutive three-year terms.[52] Consolidated human services board members are appointed to four-year terms and may serve a maximum of two consecutive four-year terms. There is no exception for a situation in which a member is the only county resident who is a member of a licensed profession that must be represented on the consolidated human services board.[53] The county commissioner member of the consolidated human services board may serve only as long as he or she remains a county commissioner. Public health authority board members are appointed to three-year terms, and there is no limit on the number of terms they may serve.[54] For county boards of health and consolidated human services boards where the county commissioners are serving as the board of health, a person's service as a board of health member ends when his or her service as a county commissioner ends.

An appointed board of health member may be removed from office if there is cause for removal under state law. The laws for county and district boards of health, consolidated human services boards, and public health authority boards all state that a member may be removed for any of the following reasons:[55]

- commission of a felony or other crime involving moral turpitude;
- violation of a state law governing conflict of interest;
- violation of a written policy adopted by the county commissioners (or all of the applicable boards of commissioners, if it is a multi-county board);
- habitual failure to attend meetings;
- conduct that tends to bring the office into disrepute; and
- failure to maintain qualifications for appointment (for example, professional licensure, residency in the county, and so forth).

District boards of health and public health authority boards may remove their own members for cause.[56] By contrast, only the board of county commissioners may remove members of a county board of health or a consolidated human services board.[57]

Rulemaking

A local board of health has the duty to protect and promote the public health and the authority to adopt rules necessary to those purposes.[58] A board of health rule is valid throughout the county or counties in the board's jurisdiction, including within any municipalities served by the board.[59]

---

51. G.S. 130A-35(c) (county board of health); 130A-37(c) (district board of health).
52. County Commissioner Serving Extended Term on District Board of Health, Op. N.C. Att'y Gen., 1998 WL 856356 (Oct. 8, 1998).
53. G.S. 153A-77(c).
54. G.S. 130A-45.1.
55. G.S. 130A-35(g) (county board of health); 130A-37(h) (district board of health); 153A-77(c) (consolidated human services board); 130A-45.1(j) (public health authority board). If the board of commissioners is serving as the board of health, these sections do not apply.
56. G.S. 130A-37(h) (district board of health); G.S. 130A-45.1(j) (public health authority board).
57. G.S. 130A-35(g) (county board of health); 153A-77(c) (consolidated human services board).
58. G.S. 130A-39.
59. G.S. 130A-39(c) ("The rules of a local board of health shall apply to all municipalities within the local board's jurisdiction.").

There are several limitations to the board's rulemaking authority set out in statutes:

- A board may not adopt rules concerning the issuing of grades and permits to food and lodging facilities or the operation of those facilities.[60]
- A board may issue its own regulations regarding on-site wastewater management only with the approval of NCDHHS, which must find that the proposed rules are at least as stringent as state rules and are necessary and sufficient to safeguard the public health.[61]
- A board of health rule regulating smoking in public places must abide by statutory restrictions on this authority and must be approved by the applicable board(s) of county commissioners.[62]

Additional limitations on the rulemaking authority have been imposed by state courts. The North Carolina Supreme Court has held that a local board of health rule may be preempted by state law if the state has already provided a complete and integrated regulatory scheme in the area addressed by the local rule. However, state law expressly permits a board to adopt a more stringent local rule even in the presence of statewide rules on the same issue if a more stringent rule is required to protect the public health.[63] The supreme court has interpreted this to mean that a board adopting a more stringent rule must provide a rationale for local standards that exceed the statewide standards. To do this, the board likely needs to be able to demonstrate that conditions in the board's jurisdiction are different from the rest of the state in a way that warrants higher standards.[64]

In addition, the North Carolina Court of Appeals has enunciated a five-part test that a local board of health rule must satisfy to be valid. The rule must

1. be related to the promotion or protection of health,
2. be reasonable in light of the health risk addressed,
3. not violate any law or constitutional provision,
4. not be discriminatory, and
5. not make distinctions based upon policy concerns traditionally reserved for legislative bodies.[65]

Before adopting, amending, or repealing any local rule, the board of health must give the public notice of its intent and offer the public an opportunity to inspect its proposed action. Ten days

---

60. G.S. 130A-39(b).

61. G.S. 130A-39(b); 130A-335(c). If a local board of health adopts rules governing wastewater collection, treatment, and disposal, then it must also adopt rules for imposing administrative penalties when the local wastewater rules are violated. G.S. 130A-22(h).

62. G.S. 130A-498.

63. G.S. 130A-39(b).

64. *See* Craig v. Cnty. of Chatham, 356 N.C. 40 (2002). The *Craig* court considered two local actions regulating swine farms: an ordinance adopted by the Chatham County Board of Commissioners and a rule adopted by the Chatham County Board of Health. The court held that both the ordinance and the rule were preempted by state statutes that amounted to a complete and integrated regulatory scheme for swine farms. *Id.* at 50. However, the court acknowledged that local boards of health may regulate an area already subject to a comprehensive statewide regulatory scheme in some circumstances. G.S. 130A-39 specifically authorizes local boards of health to adopt more stringent rules in areas that are already subject to statewide regulation by the Commission for Public Health or the Environmental Management Commission, but only when a more stringent local rule is necessary to protect the public health. The court concluded that this statute does not authorize a local board of health to "superimpose additional regulations without specific reasons clearly applicable to a local health need." *Id.* at 51–52. The court noted that the board of health had not provided "any rationale or basis for making the restrictions in Chatham County more rigorous than those applicable to and followed by the rest of the state," and it invalidated the rule on that basis. *Id.* at 52.

65. City of Roanoke Rapids v. Peedin, 124 N.C. App. 578 (1996).

before the proposed action is to occur, notice of the proposal must be published in a local newspaper with general circulation. The notice must contain a statement of the substance of the proposed rule or a description of the subjects and issues involved, the proposed effective date, and a statement that copies of the proposed rule are available at the local health department. At the same time, the board must make the text of the proposed rule, amendment, or rule to be repealed available for inspection by placing it in the office of each county clerk within the board's jurisdiction.[66]

Fees

A local board of health may impose a fee for many services rendered by the health department.[67] County and district boards of health and consolidated human services boards must base their fees on a plan proposed by the local health director, and any fees adopted by the board must be approved by the county commissioners (in the case of a district health department, all applicable boards of county commissioners). Public health authority boards may establish fee schedules and are not required to obtain commissioner approval.[68]

There are some limitations to a board's fee-setting authority. First, a board may not charge fees for services rendered by a health department employee acting as an agent of the state. This covers most environmental health programs, but there are exceptions: cost-related fees may be charged for services provided under the on-site wastewater treatment program, the public swimming pools program, the tattooing regulation program, and the local program for inspecting and permitting drinking water wells.[69]

Second, while local health departments may charge fees for some of their clinical services, the local board of health has limited discretion in determining the amount of the fee. Fees may reflect Medicaid reimbursement rates established by the state Division of Health Benefits or fees set by a state or federal program that provides funds for a particular service. Also, local health departments are specifically prohibited by state law from charging health department clients for the following services:[70]

- testing and counseling for sickle cell syndrome,[71]
- examination for and treatment of tuberculosis,[72]
- examination for and treatment of certain sexually transmitted diseases,[73] and
- testing and counseling for HIV.[74]

Additionally, immunizations that are required by law and supplied by the state must be provided at no cost to uninsured or underinsured patients with family incomes below 200 percent of the federal poverty level.[75]

---

66. G.S. 130A-39(d).
67. G.S. 130A-39(g); 130A-45.3(a)(5); 153A-77(d)(1).
68. G.S. 130A-39(g); 130A-45.3(a)(5); 153A-77(d)(1).
69. G.S. 130A-39(g).
70. Sometimes a third-party payer such as Medicaid provides reimbursement for one of the listed services. A local health department may bill a third-party payer for the services, but it may not bill the client. Pursuant to 10A N.C.A.C. 41A, § .0209(9), a third-party payer may be billed for HIV testing and counseling services only if the patient provides written consent.
71. G.S. 130A-130.
72. G.S. 130A-144(e).
73. *Id.*
74. 10A N.C.A.C. 41A, § .0202(9).
75. G.S. 130A-153(a).

Sometimes federal laws affect a local health department's ability to set fees or charge clients for services. For example, Title VI of the federal Civil Rights Act of 1964 prohibits recipients of federal financial assistance from charging their limited-English proficient clients for interpretation services.[76] Similarly, the federal Health Insurance Portability and Accountability Act (HIPAA) medical privacy rule limits the fees that may be charged for copies of medical records.[77]

Adjudicating Disputes

In some circumstances, a local board of health acts as an adjudicatory body.[78] When a person is aggrieved by the local health department's interpretation or enforcement of a local board of health rule, or the local imposition of administrative penalties, the person may appeal the department's decision to the board of health. The board hears the case and issues a written decision either upholding or overturning the department's decision. The rules of evidence enforced in courtrooms do not apply at the board hearing, but the board's decision must be supported by adequate evidence. The board must put its decision in writing and state the factual findings upon which it is based. If the person is not satisfied with the board of health's decision, he or she may appeal to district court. The procedures and time frames for actions are set out in G.S. 130A-24(b) through (d).

When a person is aggrieved by the local health department's enforcement of state rules promulgated by the North Carolina Commission for Public Health, such as the food and lodging rules, the local board of health is not authorized to hear the appeal. Those cases go to the state Office of Administrative Hearings.[79]

Local Health Department Administration

The administrative functions within local health departments include managing operations and programs; providing in-service training for staff; preparing the budget; explaining the department's activities to the board of health, local elected officials, and the public; informing the public of health laws and rules as well as enforcing them; suggesting new rules and services; and purchasing equipment and supplies. These duties generally are the local health director's responsibility, but the management of particular functions may differ from county to county.

Local Health Directors

The local health director administers the health department and exercises specific powers and duties prescribed by law. The term "local health director" includes the director of a county health department, a district health department, or a public health authority, as well as the person appointed to serve as local health director in a consolidated human services agency.[80] A director of a county or district health department or a public health authority must meet minimum education and

76. *See* Voluntary Compliance Agreement between the Office for Civil Rights, U.S. Department of Health and Human Services, and N.C. Department of Health and Human Services, perma.cc/H4DA-PCJU.

77. 45 C.F.R. § 164.524(c)(4).

78. G.S. 130A-24.

79. G.S. 130A-24(a).

80. The term *local health director* is defined by statute to mean "the administrative head of a local health department appointed pursuant to this Chapter." The same statute defines *local health department* as "a district health department or a public health authority or a county health department." G.S. 130A-2. Although these definitions do not capture consolidated human services agencies and directors, a separate statute assigns local public health roles to a CHSA by giving the agency "the responsibility to carry out the duties of a local health department" and providing that the consolidated human services board "shall have all the powers and duties of a local board of health" except for appointing the director and transmitting or presenting the budget for local health services. G.S. 130A-43(a), (b). The director of a CHSA that includes public health also acquires most of the powers and duties of a local health director, G.S. 130A-43(c), but if the CHSA director does not satisfy the minimum statutory qualifications under G.S. 130A-40

experience requirements.[81] In general, the director must have a degree in medicine, public health, public administration, or another field related to public health, as well as experience in health programs or health services.[82] A consolidated human services director is not required by statute to meet particular education or experience requirements. However, a consolidated human services director who does not satisfy the statutory qualifications to be a local health director must appoint a person who does, with the approval of the county manager.[83]

The appointment of the local health director varies by type of local public health agency. For a county or district health department, the local health director is appointed by the local board of health after consultation with all applicable boards of county commissioners. Although the board must consult with the commissioners, the commissioners are not required to approve the appointment.[84] The same procedure is followed by a public health authority board when it appoints the public health authority director.[85] A consolidated human services agency director is appointed by the county manager with the advice and consent of the consolidated human services board, and the person who serves as local health director in the agency is appointed by the consolidated human services director with the approval of the county manager.[86] If the county commissioners have abolished the board of health and assumed direct control of the health department pursuant to G.S. 153A-77(a), then the commissioners have all the powers and duties of the local board of health, including the power to appoint the local health director. This is the only circumstance in which the county commissioners may directly appoint the local health director.

All local health directors have powers and duties that come from multiple sources of law.[87] A local health director's powers and duties fall into five general categories:

1. **Administration.** The local health director administers programs under the direction of the board of health. All types of local health directors have the authority to employ and dismiss health department staff, but the employment decisions of a director of a consolidated human services agency must be approved by the county manager. In addition, the director of a county health department, a district health department, or a consolidated human services agency may enter contracts on behalf of the department, but the law that gives local health directors this authority also states that it shall not "be construed to abrogate the authority of the county commissioners."[88] Thus, it is a common practice to have county managers involved in the approval or execution of health department contracts.

---

to be a local health director, the CHSA director must, with the approval of the county manager, appoint a person with those qualifications to serve as the local health director. G.S. 153A-77(e)(9).

81. G.S. 130A-40(a); 130A-45.4.

82. Another law provides for a limited pilot program (one county only) to allow a person with education and experience in public health nursing to serve as a local health director if the appointment is approved by the secretary of NCDHHS. G.S. 130A-40.1.

83. G.S. 153A-77(e).

84. G.S. 130A-40.

85. G.S. 130A-45.4.

86. G.S. 153A-77(e).

87. The main statutes setting forth the powers and duties of local health directors are G.S. 130A-41 (county and district health directors); 153A-77(e) (consolidated human services directors); and 130A-45.5(c) (public health authority directors). However, other powers and duties appear in several other statutes in G.S. Chapter 130A. Except as otherwise noted, the powers and duties discussed in this section of the chapter either originate or are cross-referenced in G.S. 130A-41.

88. G.S. 130A-41(b)(13). A public health authority director does not have the power to enter contracts. Instead, the public health authority board holds that power. The board could, however, delegate contracting authority to the director or another agent or employee. G.S. 130A-45.3(a)(9) (allowing the public health authority board to "delegate to its agents or employees any powers or duties as it may deem appropriate").

2. **Remedies.** The local health director is responsible for enforcing public health laws within his or her jurisdiction and may employ legal remedies when public health laws are violated. The director may
   - initiate civil or criminal proceedings against a public health law violator,[89]
   - abate public health nuisances or imminent hazards,[90]
   - impose administrative penalties (fines) for violations of state or local laws regulating smoking in public places,[91]
   - embargo food or drink in some circumstances,[92] and
   - impose administrative penalties for violations of local on-site wastewater rules, or conditions imposed on permits issued under such rules.[93]

   The local health director may also play a role in actions taken by local public health employees to suspend or revoke permits, such as a permit to operate a restaurant.[94]
3. **Communicable disease control.** The local health director must investigate cases and outbreaks of communicable diseases and ensure that communicable disease control measures are given.[95] The director may order isolation or quarantine if the legal conditions for exercising the isolation or quarantine authority are met.[96] The local health director also has the duty to enforce the North Carolina laws regarding the immunization of children.
4. **Other disease control.** The local health director must examine, investigate, and control rabies in accordance with state public health laws. The director must also investigate the causes of other diseases in the jurisdiction, whether or not they are communicable.
5. **Educate and advise.** The local health director must disseminate public health information, promote the benefits of good health, and advise local officials about public health matters.[97]

This list is not exhaustive. Local health directors are responsible for the overall operation of the local public health agency, which makes the director ultimately accountable for administrative activities associated with the agency's performance of local public health services and functions. A consolidated human services director also has duties that go beyond those of a traditional local health

---

89. G.S. 130A-18 authorizes the local health director to institute an action for injunctive relief in superior court. G.S. 130A-25 makes violation of most state and local public health laws or rules a class 1 misdemeanor (see also G.S. 14-3, providing for the classification of misdemeanors). However, violations of laws and rules pertaining to smoking in public places may not be prosecuted as misdemeanors. G.S. 130A-497(d). Further, in counties in which the county commissioners have assumed the role of the local board of health, the commissioners are authorized to enforce local rules through civil penalties—an option that is not available in counties with other forms of public health governance. G.S. 153A-77(a). However, if the commissioners exercise the option to impose a civil penalty, violation of the local rule subject to the penalty is *not* a misdemeanor unless the rule specifically states that it is.

90. G.S. 130A-19 (public health nuisance); 130A-20 (imminent hazard).

91. G.S. 130A-22(h1).

92. G.S. 130A-21.

93. G.S. 130A-22(h). Most North Carolina counties do not have local on-site wastewater rules. Rather, the state rules apply within the county and different remedies are available.

94. See G.S. 130A-23, authorizing the secretary of NCDHHS to revoke or suspend permits upon finding a violation of state environmental health laws. Although the power to exercise this remedy is given to a state official, in practice violations are discovered and permit actions are taken by local environmental health specialists acting under the supervision of the local health director.

95. G.S. 130A-144.

96. G.S. 130A-145.

97. G.S. 130A-41(6).

director, largely reflecting the consolidated human services director's role as the chief administrator for human services programs other than public health.

Most of the powers and duties of a local health director may be delegated to another person; however, the director's authority to embargo food and drink in some circumstances may not be delegated.[98]

Local Health Department Personnel

In addition to a director, each type of local public health agency must have certain other staff members. A state regulation that addresses minimum staffing requires each local health department to employ a full-time health director who meets the education and experience requirements of G.S. 130A-40, a full-time public health nurse who meets specified licensure and training requirements, a full-time registered environmental health specialist who is authorized as an agent of the state, and a full-time administrative assistant.[99] In general, these staff members must be full-time employees, but there is an exception that allows an agency to share a health director with another agency. The local health department accreditation rules also address staffing both directly and indirectly. One of the accreditation standards requires a local agency to employ or contract with one or more licensed physicians to serve as medical director.[100] Portions of the accreditation rules refer to other categories of staff members or to specific expertise that the agency must possess or have access to, but they do not explicitly require the agency to have staff positions for those categories or expertise.[101]

There are no other requirements in law for specific numbers or types of staff, but local health departments need sufficient personnel to provide public health services and perform all the activities and functions associated with other duties of the health department (such as assuring compliance with state and federal laws). Many departments employ or contract with health care providers and environmental health specialists, as well as health educators, social workers, medical records specialists, epidemiologists or statisticians, and administrative staff.

The employees of county and district health departments ordinarily are subject to the North Carolina State Human Resources Act (SHRA).[102] Public health authorities are exempt from the SHRA and establish their own personnel policies and salary plans.[103] The employees of consolidated human services agencies are subject to county personnel policies or ordinances, unless the board of county commissioners elects to make the CHSA employees subject to the SHRA.[104] When the agency employees are covered by the SHRA, their qualifications and terms of employment are governed by the rules of the State Human Resources Commission.

The hiring authority for local health department employees varies by agency type. The director of a county or district health department is authorized to employ or dismiss department employees in accordance with the SHRA.[105] The director of a public health authority is authorized to employ, discipline, and dismiss employees of the authority.[106] The director of a consolidated human services agency may appoint employees, but the appointments must be approved by the county manager.[107]

---

98. G.S. 130A-6; 130A-21(a).

99. 10A N.C.A.C. 46, § .0301(a).

100. 10A N.C.A.C. 48B, § .0901(b)(3).

101. *See, e.g.,* 10A N.C.A.C. 48B, § .0203 (directing agency to assure staff have expertise in data management); 48B .0301 (requiring access to and consultation with an epidemiologist); 48B, § .0701 (referring to unit directors for communicable disease, nursing, and environmental health).

102. G.S. 126-5(a)(2). Local health department employees may be removed from State Human Resources Act (SHRA) coverage if the State Human Resources Commission determines that the local personnel system is substantially equivalent to the SHRA. G.S. 126-11(a).

103. G.S. 130A-45.12; 130A-45.3(a)(7).

104. G.S. 153A-77(d).

105. G.S. 130A-41(b)(12).

106. G.S. 130A-45.5(c)(12).

107. G.S. 153A-77(e)(1); 130A-43(c)(2).

Financing Local Public Health Services

Public health activities in North Carolina are financed at the state level through federal funds, state funds, private grants, and fees. The precise mix of funds to support local public health services varies by locality.

Federal and State Funds

Local health departments receive federal funds both directly and indirectly. Indirect federal support comes from federal funds paid to the state and then channeled by the state to the local agencies. Federal categorical funds support maternal and child health services, family planning, the WIC (special supplemental nutrition for women, infants, and children) program, and several other services and programs. The major source of direct support is the state Medicaid program, which in fiscal year 2022 was composed of about 75 percent federal funds and 25 percent state funds.[108] Medicaid provides direct reimbursement for services to Medicaid-eligible clients, as well as an annual cost settlement. In 2023, North Carolina expanded eligibility for enrollment in the state's Medicaid program to an estimated 600,000 adults.[109] Some local health departments also receive federal funds in the form of Medicare reimbursement for services such as home health or diabetes care.

The state provides general aid-to-county funds, which are distributed to local public health agencies by NCDHHS. Categorical grants, which may include a combination of federal and state funds, provide additional support. The state also awards other grant or contract funds for special projects. Finally, the state reimburses some services on a fee-for-service basis.

To receive state and federal funds the state distributes, a local health department must sign a contract with NCDHHS called the "consolidated agreement." The consolidated agreement contains general provisions governing how local health departments must use and account for money flowing from the state, as well as special requirements for using certain funds.[110] If a department fails to comply with the terms of the contract, the state may discontinue state funding for the program that is out of compliance by following steps outlined in the consolidated agreement.[111]

Local Sources of Revenue

County Appropriations

Local boards of health have no power to tax, so a board and its department must depend on other sources for funds. Boards of county commissioners are authorized to appropriate funds from property tax levies and to allocate other revenues whose use is not otherwise restricted by law for the local health department's use.[112]

---

108. Kaiser Family Foundation, Federal and State Share of Medicaid Spending, perma.cc/8R8G-QCZC. The match rate varies from state to state and may vary from year to year.

109. S.L. 2023-7. *See also* Jada Raphael and Robin Rudowitz, "An Update on ACA Medicaid Expansion: What to Watch in North Carolina and Beyond," Kaiser Family Foundation, December 18, 2023, www.kff.org/policy-watch/an-update-on-aca-medicaid-expansion-what-to-watch-in-north-carolina-and-beyond.

110. *See, e.g.*, NCDHHS, DPH, FY 2024 Consolidated Agreement, perma.cc/MY92-WTGJ.

111. At the time of this writing, the NCDHHS process to enforce compliance with the consolidated agreement includes the following steps: The state first notifies the department that it has sixty days to comply. If the problem is not corrected to the satisfaction of the state within that period, the state may temporarily suspend funding for the program that is out of compliance. If the deficiency remains uncorrected thirty days after the temporary suspension, program funds may be permanently suspended until the department provides evidence that the deficiency has been corrected. After all other reasonable administrative remedies have been exhausted, the state may cancel, terminate, or suspend the contract in whole or in part and the department may be declared ineligible for further state contracts or agreements.

112. G.S. 153A-149.

For county health departments, county commissioners approve the health department budget as a regular part of their responsibility for county finance. For consolidated human services agencies, the budget for public health is a part of the budget planned by the consolidated human services director, recommended by the consolidated human services board, and approved by the county commissioners. Public health authorities and district health departments prepare and approve their own budgets and need not obtain county commissioners' approval. These agencies seek county appropriations, however, and the county commissioners must approve those expenditures.

Two non-supplantation provisions in the statutes prohibit reductions of county appropriations when state money increases in certain circumstances. G.S. 130A-4.2 requires NCDHHS to ensure that local health departments do not reduce county appropriations for health promotion services because of state appropriations. G.S. 130A-4.1 places the same requirement on maternal and child health services.

Grants

Local health departments may receive grants from government agencies or from private entities, such as foundations. These grants are essentially contracts between the local health department and the granting agency and usually are provided to enable the department to develop a particular project or provide a specific service.

Local Fees

Public health agencies may charge and collect fees, as described earlier in this chapter. Revenues from fees imposed by local boards of health must be used for public health purposes.[113]

Management of Local Funds

All funds received or spent at the local level must be budgeted, disbursed, and accounted for in accordance with the Local Government Budget and Fiscal Control Act (G.S. Ch. 159, Art. 3). The budgeting, disbursing, and accounting for a county health department or consolidated human services agency is done by the county's budget officer and finance officer. District health departments and public health authorities (both single-county and multi-county) are responsible for performing these functions themselves.

Local Public Health Services

Local public health agencies provide services at both the community and individual level. While there is no single law describing the minimum services that a local agency must provide, there are three primary state laws that affect the scope and range of local service provision.

The first of these is a law that describes the public health services that the General Assembly has determined are essential to promoting and contributing to the highest levels of health and that should be available to everyone in the state.[114] This law incorporates the "ten essential public health services," a nationally recognized set of services adopted in 1994 by a national committee charged with providing a framework for effective public health systems,[115] and directs local health

---

113. G.S. 130A-39(g).

114. G.S. 130A-1.1.

115. *See* Centers for Disease Control and Prevention, Public Health Professionals Gateway, "Original Essential Public Health Services Framework," perma.cc/6JY5-P5DH.

departments to ensure that the services are available and accessible to the population served by the department. The ten essential public health services fall into three categories: assessment of community health status and health problems; policy development to educate the community about health, solve community health problems, support individual and community health, and protect health and ensure safety; and assurance of quality public health and public and private health care services within the community. In 2020, the list of the ten essential public health services was revised by an expert taskforce convened by the Public Health National Center for Innovations and the de Beaumont Foundation.[116] Although the North Carolina statute continues to reference the original ten essential public health services, the 2020 revised list is still oriented around the same three-part framework that includes assessment, policy development, and assurance.

Another law requires each local public health agency in the state to be accredited by the North Carolina Local Health Department Accreditation Board (NCLHDAB).[117] To be accredited, a local agency must satisfy accreditation standards that address the agency's capacity to provide the ten essential public health services, as well as several additional duties imposed by state law.[118] The NCLHDAB assesses a local health department's performance of specific activities described in rules promulgated by the Commission for Public Health with input from the NCLHDAB. A health department must satisfactorily perform about 90 percent of the activities to obtain or maintain accreditation.[119]

A third statute authorizes the North Carolina Commission for Public Health to establish standards for the nature and scope of local public health services.[120] The commission has adopted rules, known as the "mandated services rules," which specify some of the public health services local public health agencies must guarantee.[121] The mandated services rules address twelve types of services that fall into one of two categories: (1) services that the local agency must provide under the direction of the local health director and the supervision of the local board of health or (2) services that a county may provide through the local agency, contract with another entity to provide, or not provide at all if the local agency can certify to the state's satisfaction that the services are available in the county from other providers. Each of the mandated services has its own rule that identifies more specifically which services must be provided or assured. Table 37.2 identifies the mandated services.

These laws provide a starting point for understanding local public health services, but they do not paint the complete picture. Local public health agencies also must provide services or perform activities to comply with other laws. For example, to comply with the federal HIPAA medical privacy rule, local health departments must develop and maintain numerous forms, notices, and policies and procedures for keeping health information confidential and secure and honoring individuals' rights regarding their health information.[122]

NCDHHS conducts a biennial survey of services provided by local public health agencies in North Carolina, contributing additional insight into the range of local public health services

116. *See* Centers for Disease Control and Prevention, Public Health Professionals Gateway, "10 Essential Public Health Services," perma.cc/NZ73-QVVB.

117. G.S. 130A-34.1.

118. 10A N.C.A.C. ch. 48.

119. The accreditation rules specify the exact number of activities that must be satisfied in each category for the department to be accredited. 10A N.C.A.C. 48B, § .0103(a).

120. G.S. 130A-9.

121. 10A N.C.A.C. 46, § .0201–.0216.

122. 45 C.F.R. Parts 160, 162, and 164.

Table 37.2 Mandated Public Health Services in North Carolina (10A N.C.A.C. 46, § .0201–.0216)

Local health department must provide	Local health department must provide, contract for, or certify available
• Food, lodging, and institutional sanitation • Individual on-site water supply • Sanitary sewage collection, treatment, and disposal • Communicable disease control • Vital records registration	• Adult health • Home health • Dental public health • Maternal health • Child health • Family planning • Public health laboratory

provided by the state's local agencies. The services typically included in the survey cover a wide range of activities, from epidemic investigations, to school nursing services, to childhood lead poisoning prevention, to chronic disease control, to name just a few.[123]

Other Statewide Public Health Programs with Local Components

The focus of this chapter has been on the state and local system for carrying out the core public health functions reflected in the statute setting forth the mission and purpose of the state's public health system.[124] The bulk of the state's public health laws and structure are focused on those functions and the duties that accompany them. However, the North Carolina public health code also addresses a number of other governmental functions and duties related to the protection of public health. Two statewide programs that have significant local involvement are the medical examiner system and the vital records program.

Medical Examiner System

North Carolina has a centralized, state-administered medical examiner system for postmortem investigations.[125] The system is composed of a chief medical examiner (CME), a central staff of professionals, and a network of county medical examiners. Its purpose is to investigate and determine the cause and manner of deaths that are unattended to ensure that appropriate medico-legal follow-up occurs when a death is suspicious or unnatural.

The chief medical examiner is appointed by the secretary of NCDHHS. By statute, the CME must be a forensic pathologist certified by the American Board of Pathology and licensed to practice medicine.[126] The CME has a staff that includes pathologists, toxicologists, and other professionals

123. For a list of the specific services included in the NCDHHS survey for fiscal year 2017, see NCDHHS, DPH, State Center for Health Statistics, "Local Health Department Staffing and Services Summary: Fiscal Year 2017," perma.cc /SVY3-AT9P. Reports for fiscal years 2019, 2021, and 2023 were not available at the time of publication due to delays in data collection caused by the COVID-19 pandemic.

124. G.S. 130A-1.1.

125. G.S. Ch. 130A, Art. 16; 10A N.C.A.C. ch. 44.

126. G.S. 130A-378.

who assist with autopsies and forensic investigations. Although county medical examiners are responsible for investigating deaths within their jurisdictions, the CME has oversight of all cases and may assume jurisdiction over any case or reassign a case to another local medical examiner. The CME or a member of his or her staff reviews each case investigated by a county medical examiner and is authorized to amend death certificates filed by the local examiners.[127]

For each county, the CME appoints one or more individuals to serve three-year terms as county medical examiners. In making appointments, the CME must give preference to licensed physicians, but he or she may also appoint licensed dentists, physician assistants, nurse practitioners, nurses, emergency medical technician paramedics, or pathologists' assistants who meet certain certification criteria.[128] Deaths within the medical examiner's jurisdiction include those that:

- result from violence, poisoning, accident, suicide, or homicide;
- occur suddenly when the deceased had been in apparent good health or when unattended by a physician;
- occur in a jail, prison, or correctional institution or in police custody;
- occur in state-operated psychiatric hospitals, substance use treatment facilities, and certain other state facilities that provide services to individuals with developmental disabilities;
- are the result of an execution carried out under the state's death penalty laws; or
- occur under any suspicious, unusual, or unnatural circumstance.

Such deaths are typically reported to the county medical examiner by health care providers or law enforcement, but the law requires anyone who suspects that a death may fall in one of the above categories to report it.[129] The county medical examiner's duty to investigate is triggered by the receipt of the report. Each county must provide or contract for a facility for the examination and storage of bodies subject to medical examiner jurisdiction.[130]

To facilitate death investigations, state laws authorize county medical examiners to inspect physical evidence and documents, including confidential medical records. The medical examiner may seek an administrative search warrant or issue subpoenas for information as the case requires.[131] A medical examiner may order an autopsy if he or she determines that it would be "advisable and in the public interest."[132] A district attorney or a superior court judge may also authorize an autopsy in a medical examiner case.[133] If a question about a death arises after the body has been buried, the

127. G.S. 130A-382.

128. *Id.* This statute was amended by S.L. 2023-65, § 6.2 to expand the list of professionals eligible to serve as county medical examiners.

129. G.S. 130A-383. In addition, a person who discovers a deceased body or anatomical material that may be part of a human body must report the discovery to the county medical examiner.

130. G.S. 130A-381.

131. G.S. 130A-385 (authority to inspect physical evidence and records and to seek an administrative search warrant); 130A-386 (authority to issue subpoenas for the appearance of persons or production of documents).

132. G.S. 130A-389.

133. *Id.* There is a fee for each autopsy in an amount that is set in the statute and adjusted periodically. If the deceased was a resident of the county in which the investigation occurred, then the fee is paid partly by the county and partly by the state, with the county's share historically being larger. If the deceased was not a resident of the county in which the investigation occurred, the state pays the entire fee. If the medical examiner determines that an autopsy is not necessary but the deceased's next of kin requests it, the CME or a designated pathologist may perform an autopsy, and the fee is paid by the next of kin.

CME may authorize an investigation of the death. In such a case, the district attorney petitions a superior court judge to order the body exhumed and turned over to the CME for investigation.[134]

Upon completion of an investigation, the county medical examiner must complete a certificate of death that states the cause and manner of death. The cause of death is the illness or injury that resulted in death, while the manner of death refers to the medical examiner's conclusion about whether the cause was natural, an accident, suicide, homicide, or undetermined. The county medical examiner must make a full report of the investigation to the CME.[135] The county medical examiner receives a fee for each completed investigation and report. If the deceased was a resident of the county in which the investigation occurred, the fee is paid by the county; otherwise, the state pays the fee.[136]

A North Carolina county may have a county coroner, an elected official whose duty is to conduct inquests and preliminary hearings into deaths that may have resulted from criminal acts or omissions.[137] In a county with a coroner, the county medical examiner must notify the coroner of deaths within the medical examiner's jurisdiction, and the coroner must hold an inquest and file a report with the district attorney and the county medical examiner. However, the medical examiner retains custody and control of the body. He or she also retains the ultimate duty and authority to conduct the medico-legal examination of deaths and file the reports required by law.[138]

Vital Records Program

The North Carolina Vital Records Program is responsible for registering vital events that occur in North Carolina. The vital events registered through the program are births, deaths, fetal deaths, marriages, and divorces. The state program is administered by NCDHHS, DPH.[139] At the local level, county registers of deeds and local health departments have extensive duties related to vital records, and clerks of court have a role in the system as well. Private individuals and entities also play a significant role in the vital records system. For example, hospitals and other birthing facilities file birth certificates with local registrars, and funeral directors file death certificates.

The secretary of NCDHHS appoints a state registrar to lead the state program.[140] Each county has a local registrar of vital records and a deputy registrar. Some counties also have sub-registrars.[141]

The state registrar's ultimate responsibility is to ensure that records of vital events are completed accurately and registered. To that end, the state registrar's statutory duties include examining vital records received from local registrars to ensure their satisfactory completion, preserving vital records permanently and in a systematic fashion, and enforcing the state's vital records laws and rules.

---

134. G.S. 130A-390. The cost of the exhumation, autopsy, transportation, and disposition of the body is paid by the county if the deceased was a resident of the county in which the death or fatal injury occurred; otherwise, the state pays those costs.

135. G.S. 130A-385 (investigation reports); 130A-389 (autopsy reports).

136. G.S. 130A-387. The amount of the fee is set in the statute and adjusted periodically.

137. G.S. Chapter 152 creates the office of county coroner and prescribes the duties of the office. At the time of writing, only one county—Yadkin—still elects a county coroner.

138. G.S. 130A-394.

139. G.S. 130A-90, 10A N.C.A.C. 41H, § .0101. The statute requires the state to maintain a vital statistics program. Regulatory definitions clarify that the terms *vital statistics* and *vital records* mean the same thing: "'Vital statistics' or 'vital records' means records of birth, death, fetal death, marriage, divorce, and data related thereto." 10A N.C.A.C. 41H, § .0102.

140. G.S. 130A-91.

141. G.S. 130A-94, -96.

The state registrar also supervises local registrars, deputy registrars, and sub-registrars.[142]

By law, the local health director serves as the local registrar for each county within the local health department's jurisdiction.[143] He or she must designate in writing a deputy registrar to assist with the local registrar's duties and to act as local registrar in the event of the health director's absence, illness or disability, or removal from office. The local registrar may also appoint one or more sub-registrars with the approval of the state registrar. Sub-registrars are authorized to receive certificates and issue burial-transit permits and are supervised by the state registrar.[144]

The local registrar's duties include the following:

- registering vital events that occur in the county,
- furnishing certificate forms provided by the state registrar to persons who require them and examining certificates that are submitted to assure their satisfactory completion,
- transmitting a copy of each birth or death certificate to the county register of deeds within seven days of receipt,
- sending original certificates to the state registrar, and
- maintaining records and making reports as required by the state registrar.[145]

The county is responsible for ensuring that the local health department has sufficient staff, funds, and other resources necessary to administer the vital records program.[146] Historically, the statewide vital records system relied heavily on paper copies, but the creation of the North Carolina Database Application for Vital Events (NC DAVE) has enabled the electronic processing of certain vital records since 2022.[147]

County registers of deeds are a significant component of the vital records system and have numerous legal duties associated with it, including the following:

- filing and preserving copies of birth and death certificates furnished by the local registrar,
- making and keeping an index of certificates,
- keeping certificates open to inspection and examination, and
- providing copies or abstracts to persons who request them.[148]

Clerks of court play an important role in the vital records program as well. The clerk of court with jurisdiction must report divorces and annulments of marriages to the state registrar[149] and

142. G.S. 130A-92.

143. G.S. 130A-94.

144. G.S. 130A-96.

145. G.S. 130A-97.

146. G.S. 130A-98.

147. G.S. 130A-115(h). *See also* S.L. 2023-46, § 12.

148. G.S. 130A-99. Under this statute, copies of certificates maintained by registers of deeds must be open to inspection and *uncertified* copies or abstracts of the certificates must be provided to any person on request. However, the provision of *certified* copies of vital records is restricted. G.S. 130A-93(c). For more information about obtaining certified copies of vital records, see NCDHHS, DPH, NC Office of Vital Records, "NC Vital Records: FAQs," vitalrecords.nc.gov/faqs.htm or contact the county register of deeds. While the copies of certificates that are available in the offices of registers of deeds are open to inspection, only the state registrar may have access to original vital records. G.S. 130A-93. In addition, birth certificates filed with a local health department contain additional medical information that is not open to inspection. G.S. 130A-102.

149. G.S. 130A-111.

must notify the state registrar of judgments determining the paternity of a child.[150] The clerk of superior court also has a role in establishing the fact of birth by persons without birth certificates.[151]

The vital records program activity that is most visible to the public is the provision of certificates that prove the occurrence of vital events. Certificates of vital events may be obtained from either the state vital records office[152] or a local official. Locally, county registers of deeds provide certificates of births, deaths, or marriages.[153] (However, birth certificates for an adopted child must be obtained from the state office.) Certificates of divorce may be obtained from the clerk of court in the county where the divorce was filed.

Additional Resources

Websites

School of Government, North Carolina Human Services Hub: humanservices.sog.unc.edu.

School of Government, Interactive Maps—Organization and Governance of NC Human Services Agencies: humanservices.sog.unc.edu/visualization-all.

North Carolina Division of Public Health: www.dph.ncdhhs.gov.

North Carolina Local Health Department Accreditation: nclhdaccreditation.unc.edu.

Online Publications

School of Government, Health Law Bulletin Series: www.sog.unc.edu/publications/bulletin-series/health-law-bulletin.

School of Government, *Coates' Canons: NC Local Government Law* blog: canons.sog.unc.edu/category/human-services/.

---

150. G.S. 130A-119.

151. G.S. 130A-106.

152. *See* NCDHHS, DPH, North Carolina Vital Records, vitalrecords.nc.gov.

153. In Mecklenburg County, certificates of births or deaths that occurred in the county are obtained from the local health department. *See* Office of Vital Records, Mecklenburg County, N.C., health.mecknc.gov/services/office-vital-records.

Chapter 38

Social Services

Kristi A. Nickodem

Kristi A. Nickodem is a faculty member at the School of Government who specializes in human services law, including the organization and governance of local social services and consolidated human services agencies and the confidentiality of social services information. She also writes and teaches on topics at the intersection of law and technology, including social media, artificial intelligence, and how the First Amendment impacts government regulation of speech.

This chapter updates and revises previous chapters authored by Aimee Wall, John Saxon, and Janet Mason, whose contributions to the field and to this publication are gratefully acknowledged.

The term "social services" refers to a diverse mix of programs and services intended to help individuals and families in need. In some cases, social services address personal safety needs by providing protection to a child or adult who has been abused or neglected. In other cases, social services address financial needs, by connecting low-income individuals and families with programs that can help them buy food or pay for heat in the winter. Some of these services and programs are offered by local public agencies, including county departments of social services, consolidated human services agencies, and agencies serving senior citizens, veterans, or survivors of domestic violence. Private organizations, including nonprofits and religious institutions, also offer many social services programs in North Carolina communities. This chapter will focus on the services and programs administered by county departments of social services and consolidated human services agencies (collectively referred to herein as "local social services agencies") in North Carolina.

Table 38.1 Examples of Social Services Programs

Means-Tested	Not Means-Tested
Food and Nutrition Services	Child protective services
Medicaid	Adult protective services
Work First	Public guardianship
Child Care Subsidy	Child support enforcement

Social services programs address a range of economic and social problems that impair the ability of individuals to function and thrive in society. These problems include poverty, hunger and food insecurity, lack of medical care, homelessness, child abuse and neglect, abuse and neglect of vulnerable adults, and unemployment. Such problems affect the general well-being and stability of society as a whole, not just the individuals and families experiencing them directly. When local social services agencies address these problems, they make an investment in the long-term flourishing and stability of the community.

North Carolina counties are mandated by state law to provide certain social services programs within their jurisdiction. Many counties also offer additional (non-mandated) programs tailored to community needs. Each local social services agency administers dozens of social services programs, and each of these programs has its own rules regarding eligibility, assistance, administration, and funding.

The services and programs provided by a local social services agency can be divided into two primary categories: economic services and social work services. Economic services, also referred to as public assistance programs, assist eligible people through monetary payments and other economic supports. This category includes programs such as Food and Nutrition Services, Medicaid, Work First, and Low-Income Energy Assistance. Most economic services programs are *means-tested*, meaning that eligibility is determined based on a person's or family's income and resources.[1] Social work services, on the other hand, are typically provided without regard to income. Social work services provided by a local social services agency include protecting children and vulnerable adults who are at risk of abuse or neglect, acting as a public guardian to individuals adjudicated incompetent by a court, and helping families navigate the licensing process for foster care and adoption. Table 38.1 lists some examples of programs that are means-tested and some that are not.

History of Social Services in North Carolina

North Carolina's first state constitution, adopted in 1776, did not address public care of the poor. Nevertheless, the General Assembly subsequently passed laws calling for locally elected "overseers of

1. The federal poverty guidelines (sometimes called the "federal poverty level") provide one important measure for determining whether an individual or family qualifies for means-tested services. The federal poverty guidelines are established by the U.S. Department of Health and Human Services. They are adjusted each year and attempt to provide a rough measure of the income a family needs to obtain adequate housing, food, and other necessities. In 2024, the federal poverty guideline for a family of three living in North Carolina was $25,820 per year. Various social services programs have different rules regarding whether and how the federal poverty guidelines are used to determine eligibility for services.

the poor," providing for wardens of the poor to be appointed by county courts and authorizing counties to build almshouses or poorhouses to provide employment and housing for the poor.[2] In 1868, the General Assembly transferred responsibility for poor relief from the county courts to boards of county commissioners.[3] Slowly but steadily the use of public tax funds to provide some care for needy citizens became accepted as an important and legitimate function of county government.

The North Carolina Constitution of 1868 established a role for *state* government with respect to social services:

> Beneficent provision for the poor, the unfortunate and orphan[s] being one of the first duties of a civilized and a Christian state, the General Assembly shall, at its first session, appoint and define the duties of a Board of Public Charities, to whom shall be entrusted the supervision of all charitable and penal State institutions, and who shall annually report to the Governor upon their condition, with suggestions for their improvement.[4]

In response to this new mandate, the General Assembly established a five-member state Board of Public Charities in 1869, which ceased functioning only a few years later in 1873 but was later revived in 1889.[5]

Statewide public welfare laws, enacted in 1917 and supplemented in 1919, marked the beginning of North Carolina's system of state supervision and local administration of social services.[6] These laws expanded the authority of the state Board of Charities and Public Welfare, including giving the Board responsibility for some child welfare functions, and provided for a state Commissioner of Public Welfare. The 1917 and 1919 laws also provided for the appointment of three-member county boards of charity and public welfare and county superintendents of public welfare—the precursors to North Carolina's current structure of local boards of social services and directors of social services.[7] While the state's role in social services increased because of these laws, both the funding and administration of social services remained primarily county responsibilities into the 1930s.

Congress's enactment of the Social Security Act of 1935 created a fundamental shift in the government's role in providing and funding social services programs.[8] It included public assistance programs for low-income people in specified categories. In 1937, the North Carolina General Assembly enacted laws requiring all counties to participate in these new federal programs, designating a single state agency to supervise administration of these programs and assigning to counties primary responsibility for the nonfederal share of the programs' costs.[9]

Since 1937, North Carolina's social services system has primarily evolved in response to changes in federal law, including the creation of new federally funded social services programs (including the federal Food Stamp Program, federal funding for child welfare and child support enforcement, Medicaid, and Temporary Assistance for Needy Families, among others). In 1969, the General Assembly

---

2. Roy M. Brown, *Public Poor Relief in North Carolina* (Chapel Hill: The University of North Carolina Press, 1928), 26–33; Acts of the North Carolina General Assembly, 1777, ch. VII; N.C. Pub. Laws 1846, ch. 64.

3. N.C. Pub. Laws 1868, ch. 20, sec. 8.

4. N.C. CONST. of 1868 art. XI, § 7.

5. N.C. Pub. Laws 1868–69, ch. 170; Brown, *Public Poor Relief in North Carolina*, 72, 82.

6. N.C. Pub. Laws 1917, ch. 170; N.C. Pub. Laws 1919, ch. 46.

7. Starting in 1919, the state Board of Charities and Public Welfare was responsible for appointing the members of these county boards of charity and public welfare. The county superintendent of public welfare was jointly appointed by the board of county commissioners and the board of education.

8. Social Security Act, Pub. L. 74-271 (49 Stat. 620), 1935.

9. N.C. Pub. Laws 1937, ch. 288. This law also revised the appointment authority for county welfare boards by requiring the board of county commissioners to appoint one member, the state Board of Charities and Public Welfare to appoint a second member, and those two appointees to appoint a third member.

changed the name of the state Board of Public Welfare to the state Board of Social Services and created a state Department of Social Services.[10] In 1970, the revised North Carolina Constitution recognized the state's responsibility to establish charitable and benevolent institutions "as the needs of humanity and the public good may require."[11] The next year, the General Assembly transferred the powers and duties of the state Board of Social Services, the state Commissioner of Social Services, and the state Department of Social Services to a new Department of Human Resources, with a secretary to be appointed by the governor.[12] The Department of Human Resources was renamed as the North Carolina Department of Health and Human Services (NCDHHS) in 1997.[13]

Though the state has exercised greater control over the supervision of county social services agencies since the 1960s, county governments are still responsible for administering most social services programs at the local level and paying some portion of the cost of these programs from county tax revenues.

Overview of North Carolina's Social Services System

North Carolina has adopted a county-administered, state-supervised social services system under which social services programs are *administered* primarily by county agencies under the *supervision* of various state-level entities. North Carolina is one of only a small number of states in which social services programs are directly administered by counties rather than by the state.[14] In most states, the state directly administers social services programs through a centralized administrative system.[15] This means that in these states, local governments have "little or no role in administering or financing state and federal social services programs."[16] North Carolina's unique model has implications for counties related to funding, governance, liability, staff, and program administration.

As described in the remainder of this chapter, each local social services agency is situated at a complex intersection of federal, state, and county involvement.

The Federal Government's Role

A significant number of programs administered by local social services agencies in North Carolina were created by Congress and are funded, in whole or in part, with federal dollars. Federal law does not require any state to operate particular social services programs. Rather, Congress enacts laws that establish certain programs and appropriates funds available to states that agree to operate the programs in accordance with applicable federal laws and regulations. The level of federal financial

---

10. S.L. 1969-546.

11. N.C. Const. of 1971 art. XI, § 3.

12. S.L. 1971-864, § 15.

13. S.L. 1997-443, § 11A.1.

14. For example, the majority of states have state-administered child welfare programs. Only nine states can be described as county-administered: California, Colorado, Minnesota, New York, North Carolina, North Dakota, Ohio, Pennsylvania, and Virginia. Two "hybrid" states, Nevada and Wisconsin, are partially administered by the state and partially administered by counties. Child Welfare Information Gateway, *State vs. County Administration of Child Welfare Services* (2018), www.childwelfare.gov/pubs/factsheets/services/.

15. North Carolina General Assembly, Program Evaluation Division, *Statutory Changes Will Promote County Flexibility in Social Services Administration*, Rep. No. 2011-03 (May 2011), sites.ncleg.gov/ped/wp-content/uploads/sites/11/2022/07/DSS_Report.pdf.

16. *Id.* at 3.

participation varies from program to program, and within programs, the percentage of federal funds often differs for administrative versus direct benefits costs.

With respect to the costs of programs that involve federal or state financial participation or both—that is, excluding programs funded only by counties—NCDHHS estimated that for state fiscal year 2024–25, federal funds would provide

- over 95 percent of the direct costs of public assistance programs;
- over 62 percent of associated administrative costs for public assistance programs; and
- over 56 percent of the costs of services programs.[17]

Though the federal government does not require states to provide social services programs, the federal government offers significant financial incentives for states to make federally supported social services programs available to their residents.

The federal executive agency with primary responsibility for overseeing most social services programs is the U.S. Department of Health and Human Services. The U.S. Department of Agriculture oversees food and nutrition programs. These agencies promulgate regulations to carry out federal laws, issue policies to the states, and monitor state compliance with federal requirements. They can impose financial sanctions on states for failing to meet these requirements. Federal laws and regulations may dictate many different aspects of program administration, including eligibility, benefit amounts, duration of assistance or services, and confidentiality of program information.

There is no direct relationship between the federal government and counties with respect to federally funded social services programs. The federal government provides funding for these programs to each state and holds the *state* accountable for complying with federal requirements and conditions. However, counties are still required to comply with the federal laws associated with these programs because the federal mandates that are imposed on the state are passed on to counties along with federal funding for social services programs.

The State Government's Role

In North Carolina, most social services programs are administered by counties under the state's supervision. State direction and supervision for locally administered social services programs come from the General Assembly, NCDHHS, and appointed rulemaking commissions.

The General Assembly

Since enacting laws in 1937 to enable North Carolina to participate in federally funded welfare programs, the General Assembly has amended or rewritten those laws many times to establish new programs, conform state law to federal changes, modify program features that federal law leaves to the state to determine, and establish or modify programs based solely on state law. Chapter 108A of the North Carolina General Statutes (hereinafter G.S.) contains most of the state's social services legislation, including specific authority for NCDHHS to accept all grants-in-aid for social services programs that may be available under the Social Security Act, other federal laws or regulations, and nonfederal sources. Chapter 108A addresses confidentiality, appeal rights, and other subjects to ensure the state's compliance with federal requirements. It also reflects state policy regarding

17. North Carolina Department of Health and Human Services (NCDHHS), *County Budget Estimates—State Fiscal Year 2024–2025*, www.ncdhhs.gov/divisions/social-services/county-staff-information/budget-information/dss-budget-estimates (click on "Budget Estimates State Totals" to access PDF).

other social services matters, such as the provision of adult protective services and requirements for the appointment of local boards of social services.

Laws governing some social services programs are found in other chapters of the General Statutes, such as Chapter 7B (child welfare services), Chapter 108D (Medicaid), and Chapter 110 (child support enforcement). Many program details do not appear in the General Statutes. Some are addressed by administrative rules and policies pursuant to authority the General Assembly has delegated to NCDHHS and the state Social Services Commission (described later in the chapter). Others are decided by the legislature when it appropriates funds for public assistance and social services programs.[18]

The General Assembly determines how the state and counties will share responsibility for the nonfederal portion of the cost of federally supported programs. For example, for many years the state and counties shared responsibility for paying for the nonfederal share of the cost of Medicaid services: the state would pay 85 percent and the counties would pay 15 percent.[19] In 2007, the General Assembly enacted legislation that ultimately phased out the counties' share for Medicaid services but still required counties to help pay for the costs of administering the program.[20] Another example is found in G.S. 108A-49.1, which provides that the nonfederal share of foster care and adoption assistance payments will be divided equally between the state and county.[21]

In addition to appropriating state funds to pay the state's share of the cost of certain social services programs, the legislature allocates lump-sum federal funds the state receives under federal block grants for social services programs and approves plans for the expenditure of these funds. The General Assembly also decides issues that federal law leaves to the states' discretion. It determines what other nonfederally based social services programs counties must provide; decides whether to provide state funding for services for which federal funds are not available; and defines counties' responsibilities in relation to administering social services programs.

The North Carolina Department of Health and Human Services

NCDHHS is the state agency that is responsible for supervising the administration of state and federal-state social services programs.[22] This includes issuing policies, program manuals, guidance documents, and forms for use by local social services agencies in interpreting and implementing the various laws and regulations governing social services programs.[23] NCDHHS also handles some administrative functions directly or through contracts with private vendors.

In addition to creating policies and providing technical assistance, NCDHHS also has the authority to take corrective action in the event that a local social services agency is noncompliant with the law.[24] Each local social services agency is required to enter into an annual written *memorandum of*

18. These provisions appear in session laws but are not codified as part of the General Statutes. See, e.g., S.L. 2011-145, § 10.27 (requiring the Division of Medical Assistance to prepare a fiscal analysis before implementing certain changes to medical policy for the N.C. Health Choice program).

19. *See* S.L. 2005-276, § 10.11(b).

20. S.L. 2007-323, § 10.36.(a); *see also* G.S. 108A-54(a). For a detailed discussion of this legislative change, see Kara A. Millonzi and William C. Rivenbark, "Phased Implementation of the 2007 and 2008 Medicaid Funding Reform Legislation in North Carolina," *Local Finance Bulletin* No. 38 (September 2008), www.sog.unc.edu/publications/bulletins/phased-implementation-2007-and-2008-medicaid-funding-reform.

21. Chapter 108A, Section 49.1(d) of the North Carolina General Statutes (hereinafter G.S.) (added by S.L. 2011-145, § 10.51).

22. G.S. 108A-71; G.S. 143B, art. 3.

23. NCDHHS policies, manuals, and forms are available at policies.ncdhhs.gov/divisional. "Dear County Director" letters issued by the NCDHHS Division of Social Services to county directors of social services are available at www.ncdhhs.gov/divisions/social-services/county-staff-information/county-director-letters.

24. G.S. 108A-74 (authorizing NCDHHS to take various remedial measures when a county or a regional social services agency fails to comply with its mandated performance requirements or applicable law, ranging from a corrective

agreement with NCDHHS (sometimes referred to as a memorandum of understanding, or MOU) that sets out specific performance requirements and administrative responsibilities for all mandated social services programs, with the exception of Medicaid.[25] When a local social services agency fails to comply with the terms of the written agreement, the mandated performance measures, or other applicable laws, NCDHHS has the authority to provide technical assistance, create and implement a corrective action plan, divest the county director of social services of service delivery powers, and ultimately control county service delivery directly or through a contract with a public or private agency.[26] If NCDHHS determines that a local social services agency is not providing child protective services, foster care services, or adoption services in accordance with state law and regulations, NCDHHS may act on an emergency basis to temporarily take over the delivery of child welfare services in that county, and it may withhold state and federal funding for child welfare services from the county.[27] As of the writing of this chapter, NCDHHS has exercised this emergency takeover authority with respect to child welfare services in three different county departments of social services.[28]

State Commissions

While a number of rulemaking commissions may have an impact on social services programs, two commissions play a particularly significant role: the Social Services Commission and the State Human Resources Commission. These commissions adopt rules found in the North Carolina Administrative Code, which are regulations that have the force and effect of law.

Social Services Commission

This commission has broad authority to adopt rules that govern most of the state's social services programs.[29] The commission is also authorized to establish standards for inspecting and licensing maternity homes and residential child care facilities, as well as for inspecting and operating jails and local confinement facilities. The commission may authorize investigations of social problems, subpoena witnesses, and compel the production of documents.[30] In counties having an appointed county board of social services, the Social Services Commission appoints either one or two members (depending on whether the county has a three- or five-member board).[31] The governor appoints the commission's fourteen members, one from each congressional district, for four-year terms.[32]

State Human Resources Commission

This commission, in conjunction with the Office of State Human Resources, establishes policies and rules related to many aspects of the State Human Resources Act (SHRA).[33] All employees of a nonconsolidated county department of social services are subject to the SHRA and to the

---

action plan to an NCDHHS takeover of the agency, in which the director of social services is divested of service delivery powers).

25. *Id.* G.S. 108A-74 also sets forth the procedures for NCDHHS intervention, including notice requirements.

26. G.S. 108A, § 74(a)–(c).

27. G.S. 108A-74(h).

28. Pursuant to its authority under G.S. 108A-74, NCDHHS temporarily assumed responsibility for delivery of child welfare services in Cherokee, Bertie, and Nash counties.

29. G.S. 143B, art. 3, pt. 6. The secretary of NCDHHS, rather than the Social Services Commission, has rulemaking authority for the Medicaid program.

30. G.S. 143B-153.

31. G.S. 108A-3.

32. G.S. 143B-154.

33. G.S. 126-4. Prior to 2013, the Office of State Human Resources was named the Office of State Personnel and the commission was named the State Personnel Commission. S.L. 2013-382.

State Human Resources Commission's rules for local government employees.[34] The commission has nine members—four appointed by the General Assembly and five by the governor—that serve for four-year terms.[35]

The County's Role

Under North Carolina's state-supervised and county-administered system, local social services agencies are primarily responsible for administering social services programs, under the supervision of NCDHHS.[36] Under this system, county social services agencies are part of county government, and employees of county social services agencies are county employees. In addition, North Carolina counties must pay part of the administrative costs associated with social services programs and part of the cost of the direct assistance and services provided under many social services programs.

For instance, NCDHHS estimated that for state fiscal year 2024–25, county funds would provide

- 1.85 percent of the direct costs of public assistance programs;
- 37.84 percent of associated administrative costs for public assistance programs; and
- 38.71 percent of the costs of social services programs (such as child protective services, adult protective services, and child support enforcement).[37]

These estimated totals group together many different programs, which may receive highly differing levels of county funding.

North Carolina's unique social services system reflects the state's long history of county responsibility for social services, the strength of county government in the state, and the role of North Carolina's counties as the primary vehicle for the delivery of basic services to citizens. It provides counties with a high level of flexibility and control over the structure, governance, and internal operations of their social services agencies. However, the state-supervised, county-administered nature of North Carolina's social services system continues to generate ongoing debates regarding intercounty collaboration, county funding obligations, information sharing between counties, child welfare reform, and the nature of state supervision over county operations.[38]

As shown in Table 38.2, North Carolina counties have a substantial amount of responsibility for the local administration and funding of social services programs. However, the powers and duties of county commissioners, county social services agencies, directors of social services, and social

---

34. *See* G.S. 126 (State Human Resources Act); Title 25, Subchapter 1I of the North Carolina Administrative Code (hereinafter N.C.A.C.). Even though the director and staff of county social services departments are county employees, their employment is governed by the SHRA unless (1) the county's personnel system, or a portion of it, has been approved by the State Human Resources Commission as being "substantially equivalent" to the SHRA or (2) the county has incorporated the social services department into a consolidated human services agency and elected to remove the agency's employees from the SHRA. *See* G.S. 153A-77(d).

35. G.S. 126-2.

36. *See* G.S. 108A, §§ 1, 14(3), 25.

37. *See* NCDHHS, *County Budget Estimates—State Fiscal Year 2024–2025*, www.ncdhhs.gov/divisions/social-services/county-staff-information/budget-information/dss-budget-estimates (click on "Budget Estimates State Totals" to access PDF).

38. For more information on these issues, see, e.g., Center for the Support of Families, *Social Services Reform Plan* (May 6, 2019), www.osbm.nc.gov/documents/files/socialservicesreform-finalplan/download; Social Services Regional Supervision and Collaboration Working Group, Stage One Final Report (UNC School of Government, March 2018); and Social Services Regional Supervision and Collaboration Working Group, Stage Two Final Report (UNC School of Government, December 2018). Both of the working group's final reports are available at www.sog.unc.edu/resources/microsites/social-services/reports.

Table 38.2 Division of State and County Responsibility for Social Services in North Carolina

State	County
• Accept federal funding for social services programs; transmit federal and state funding to counties • Develop state law and policy • Provide oversight and supervision of county-level administration of social services programs • Provide technical assistance to county agencies	• Allocate county funding to social services agency; pay county's share of nonfederal costs for federally funded programs • Administer programs locally in compliance with federal and state laws and state policy • Hire, train, and supervise local staff to administer and deliver social services programs • Determine local social services agency structure and governance model

services governing boards are defined by and subject to state law and state supervision. In some instances, these powers and duties are also constrained by federal law, including federal confidentiality laws and federal requirements attached to funding for social services programs.

County Organization and Governance

Each board of county commissioners is responsible for establishing an agency to provide social services and choosing a governance structure for that agency.[39] Counties have several different options regarding the type of agency that will provide social services in the county and the type of board that will govern that agency. The agency and governance structure a county chooses will affect the hiring process for the agency director and agency staff, who are all recruited and hired at the local level.

Until 2012, almost all North Carolina counties had a county department of social services that was governed by an appointed county board of social services.[40] Legislation enacted in 2012 authorized boards of county commissioners to adopt different approaches to the organization and governance of county human services functions.[41] For example, this law allowed any board of county commissioners to combine two or more county human services functions—such as social services and public health—into a single consolidated human services agency under the control of a human services director appointed and supervised by the county manager.[42] It also allowed any board of county commissioners to directly assume the powers and duties of a county board of social services or county board of health.[43]

---

39. *See* G.S. 108A-1.

40. Wake and Mecklenburg counties were the exceptions, as both counties operated consolidated human services agencies prior to the enactment of S.L. 2012-126. Prior to S.L. 2012-126, G.S. 153A-77 only allowed a county to establish a consolidated human services agency if its population was greater than 425,000. Wake County's agency is governed by an appointed consolidated human services board and Mecklenburg County's agency is governed by the board of county commissioners.

41. S.L. 2012-126.

42. *See* G.S. 153A-77(b) (limiting this authority to any county with a county manager). These human services functions may include, but are not limited to, social services and public health. Some consolidated human services agencies include other human services functions, such as veterans' services or transportation. The term "human services" is not defined in G.S. 153A-77. See G.S. 153A-76 for some limitations on which county functions may be consolidated into a consolidated human services agency.

43. G.S. 153A-77(a).

Since March 2019, North Carolina counties have had authority to voluntarily join together to create regional (multicounty) departments of social services.[44] However, to date, no counties have elected to establish a regional department of social services. Like a district health department (which is also composed of multiple counties), a regional department of social services is a separate legal entity from the counties involved. Specifically, a regional department of social services is a "public authority."[45] This means that a regional department of social services is a special-purpose local government entity, subject to many of the same laws that apply to county departments (e.g., laws relating to public records, open meetings, and financial management), but it is not a county department or a unit of local government and has no power to levy taxes.[46] A regional department would have its own director, governing board, staff, and budget—all separate from the counties that have formed the regional department. Neither the regional director nor the director's staff would be county employees. A regional department of social services may be formed upon mutual agreement of each of the county boards of commissioners involved.[47]

Agency Organization

Counties have three options available for organizing the agency that delivers social services within the county. They may

- operate a county department of social services,
- establish a consolidated human services agency that includes social services,[48] or
- establish a regional (multicounty) department of social services.[49]

As of January 2025, sixty-six counties still operate a single-county, stand-alone department of social services. Thirty-four counties—including many of North Carolina's most populous counties—have established a consolidated human services agency that includes social services.

Agency Governance

State law requires every county in North Carolina to have a governing board for social services, which may be

- an appointed county board of social services,
- an appointed consolidated human services board,
- a regional board of social services, or
- a board of county commissioners that exercises the powers and duties of a county board of social services or a consolidated human services board.[50]

The governance options available to each county depend in part on the organizational model that the county has chosen for providing social services, as shown in Table 38.3.

For counties with a stand-alone county department of social services or a consolidated human services agency, the board of county commissioners may directly assume the powers and duties of

44. G.S. 108A-15.7. This change in the law was enacted in S.L. 2017-41, § 4.1.

45. G.S. 108A-15.7(g); G.S. 159-7(b)(10).

46. For more information about public authorities, see Kara Millonzi, "Special Purpose Local Governments and Public Authorities," *Coates' Canons: NC Local Government Law* (blog) (Feb. 10, 2015), canons.sog.unc.edu/2015/02/special-purpose-local-governments-and-public-authorities/.

47. G.S. 108A-15.7(a). For more information about regional departments of social services and their governing boards, see Chapter 17 of *Local Social Services Boards in North Carolina* by Kristi A. Nickodem (UNC School of Government, 2023).

48. *See* G.S. 153A-77(b).

49. G.S. 108A-15.7.

50. G.S. 108A-1.

Table 38.3 Local Social Services Organization and Governance Options at a Glance

Organization	Governing Board	Board Members Selected by[a]	Director Appointed by	Employees
County DSS	County board of social services	Appointment (3 or 5)	Board	Subject to SHRA
County DSS	BOCC	Election	BOCC	Subject to SHRA
CHSA	Appointed CHS board	Appointment (up to 25)	County manager, with the advice and consent of the CHS board	SHRA optional
CHSA	BOCC[b]	Election	County manager, with the advice and consent of the BOCC	SHRA optional
Regional DSS	Regional board of social services	Appointment (12–18)	Board	Subject to SHRA

Note: SHRA = State Human Resources Act; BOCC = board of county commissioners; CHS = consolidated human services; CHSA = consolidated human services agency.

[a] Numbers in parentheses represent the number of members on each appointed board.

[b] An advisory committee for public health must be appointed if the CHSA includes public health. The requirement for a health advisory committee applies only to counties that abolish their health boards after January 1, 2012. This amounts to an exception for Mecklenburg County, which abolished its health boards (a county board of health and subsequently a CHS board) before that date.

an appointed county board of social services or consolidated human services board after a public hearing with thirty days' advance notice to the public.[51] By doing so, the board of county commissioners abolishes the appointed board. The county commissioners cannot abolish and assume the powers of a governing board for a regional (multicounty) department of social services.[52]

As of January 2025, of the sixty-six counties that have a single-county (nonconsolidated) department of social services, fifty-four departments are governed by an appointed board of social services and twelve by the board of county commissioners. Of the thirty-four counties with consolidated human services agencies, sixteen agencies are governed by appointed consolidated human services boards and eighteen by the board of county commissioners.

Composition of Appointed Social Services Boards

If the agency delivering social services in the county is a single-county, stand-alone department of social services, the governing board may be either an appointed county board of social services or the board of county commissioners. Appointed boards of social services for single-county, stand-alone departments of social services may have either three or five members (as determined by the board of county commissioners).[53] Most counties have five-member boards. For a five-member board, two members are appointed by the board of county commissioners, two by the state's Social Services Commission, and the final member by a majority of the other board members.[54] Members must be county residents. A county board of commissioners may select one of its members as an

51. G.S. 153A-77(a).

52. G.S. 153A-76.

53. G.S. 108A-2.

54. If a majority do not agree on a fifth member (or if the two appointed members of a three-member board do not agree on a third member), the senior regular resident superior court judge of the county makes the selection. G.S. 108A-3(b).

Table 38.4 Comparison of Key Features of Appointed Social Services Governing Boards

	County Board of Social Services	Consolidated Human Services Board
Size	3 or 5 members	Up to 25 members
Appointments	Board of county commissioners (1 or 2) State Social Services Commission (1 or 2) Majority of other members (1)	Board of county commissioners from nominees presented by the consolidated human services board
Term Length	3 years	4 years
Term Limit	2 consecutive terms	2 consecutive terms
Qualifications	County resident	County resident Board must include: • 4 consumers of human services • 10 professionals: a psychologist, pharmacist, engineer, dentist, optometrist, veterinarian, social worker, registered nurse, psychiatrist, and physician • 1 county commissioner • Others, including members of the general public Members may represent more than one of these categories at the same time
Regular meetings	Monthly	Quarterly
Additional meetings	At the call of the chair	At the call of the chair or three members

appointee to the social services board, and many boards of commissioners do so to enhance communication between the two bodies. Subject to some exceptions, board members may not serve more than two consecutive three-year terms.[55]

If the agency delivering social services in the county is a consolidated human services agency, the governing board may be either an appointed consolidated human services board or the board of county commissioners. Appointed consolidated human services boards may have up to twenty-five members. All members are appointed by the board of county commissioners from a list of nominees presented by the consolidated human services board.[56] The board must include representation from a variety of different professions and groups, as required by statute.[57] Some key differences between county boards of social services and consolidated human services boards are illustrated in Table 38.4.

55. G.S. 108A-4. This limitation does not apply to members who were county commissioners at any time during the first two consecutive terms and are serving in that capacity at the time of reappointment. In addition, if a person is appointed during a term to fill a vacancy, service on the board for the remainder of the former member's term does not count as a term for purposes of determining whether the member has served two consecutive terms.

56. When a consolidated human services agency is first established, the initial members of the board must be appointed based on the recommendation of a nominating committee comprising members of the preconsolidation board of health and social services board. G.S. 153A-77(c).

57. G.S. 153A-77(c).

Table 38.5 Appointment of Local Social Services Board Members

Board Type (No. of Members)	Appointing Authority: BOCC	SSC	Board Members Appointed by BOCC and SSC
County social services (3 or 5)	Appoints 1 member on a 3-member board or 2 members on a 5-member board	Appoints 1 member on a 3-member board or 2 members on a 5-member board	Appoint 1 member
Consolidated human services (CHS) (up to 25)	Appoints all members from a slate of nominees presented by the CHS board[a]		
Regional social services (12–18)	BOCC of each county involved appoints 2 members[b]	Appoints 2 members	Appoint members to fill all remaining vacancies on the board

Note: BOCC = board of county commissioners; SSC = Social Services Commission.

[a] When a CHS board is first formed, the BOCC must create a nominating committee composed of members of the current (preconsolidation) board of health and social services board. The nominating committee recommends members for the new CHS board, and the BOCC must make appointments based upon those recommendations.

[b] If more than eight counties join the regional department, each BOCC appoints only one member.

The governing board for a regional department of social services, known as a regional board of social services, must include at least twelve members but may be increased up to eighteen members by agreement of all boards of county commissioners for counties making up the regional department of social services.[58] The board of commissioners of each county in the region appoints two members;[59] the state Social Services Commission appoints two members; and the seated members of the regional social services board appoint members to fill any remaining vacancies. A member may not serve more than three consecutive three-year terms on a regional board of social services.[60]

Differences in appointment authority for each type of social services board are shown in Table 38.5.

Role of the Governing Board

All of the various types of social services governing boards have several powers and duties in common, as well as some distinct differences in their authority.

The most significant responsibility of an appointed county board of social services or a regional board of social services relates to the agency director. A county board of social services or a regional board of social services has the exclusive authority to recruit and select the department director.[61] Implicit in the board's authority to appoint the director is the authority to discipline or dismiss a director if necessary, in accordance with State Human Resources Commission rules, and a responsibility to evaluate the director's performance.

58. G.S. 108A-15.8(b). This agreement to increase the size of the board must be evidenced by concurrent resolutions adopted by the affected boards of county commissioners.

59. If more than eight counties join the regional social services department, the board of commissioners of each county in the region appoints only one member to the regional board (who may be a county commissioner).

60. G.S. 108A-15.8(d).

61. G.S. 108A, §§ 12, 15.8(a), .10.

In a county with a consolidated human services agency, the county manager is responsible for recruiting, appointing, and supervising the human services agency director, but the manager must seek and obtain the "advice and consent" of the consolidated human services board (which may be an appointed board or the board of commissioners) on the director's appointment and dismissal.[62]

Another responsibility of a social services governing board is advising county and municipal authorities regarding policies and plans to improve a community's social conditions.[63] This broad advisory responsibility indicates that a local social services governing board has some authority that extends beyond the programs and activities of the local department of social services.

Some other key responsibilities of local social services governing boards include the following:

- ***Consulting with the county social services director about problems relating to the director's office.*** A social services board does not have authority to overrule or interfere with the day-to-day operational or personnel decisions of the director of social services, but it does have a responsibility to offer guidance and support regarding problems facing the director or the local social services agency as a whole.
- ***Assisting the director in planning the department's budget.*** The extent to which social services boards are actively involved in planning and presenting the department's budget varies from county to county. County social services directors consult with the county social services board on budget matters, and some directors submit the department's proposed budget to the social services board for a formal vote of approval. Some boards actively help the director develop and advocate for the budget. A consolidated human services board is required to play a more proactive role, as it must "plan and recommend" the agency's budget along with the agency director.
- ***Establishing policies for programs established by G.S. Chapter 108A.*** While the law specifically grants this authority to the governing board, social services programs are so heavily regulated by federal and state policy already that there is little room for county boards to engage in policymaking. However, state law does give county social services boards some authority to make certain decisions regarding public assistance programs, such as the Work First program and programs funded by the Social Services Block Grant.[64]
- ***Contracting to provide services for a fee.*** A social services board may enter into a contract for a social services agency to provide services for a fee.[65] The fees may not exceed the cost of furnishing the services and must be based on a plan recommended by the county social services director and approved by both the social services governing board and the board of commissioners. The board has no authority to charge a fee for a particular service if charging such a fee is specifically prohibited by law, the department of social services is required by law to render the service, or the recipient of the service is required by law to obtain the service from the department of social services.[66]

---

62. G.S. 153A-77(e).
63. G.S. 108A-9(2).
64. For a more comprehensive explanation of a local social services board's role in social services policy and programs, see Chapter 9 of *Local Social Services Boards in North Carolina* by Kristi A. Nickodem (UNC School of Government, 2023).
65. G.S. 108A-10.
66. Social Services, Adoptions, Fees for Services by County Departments of Social Services, 53 Op. N.C. Att'y Gen. 54, 1984 WL 182160 (Jan. 26, 1984).

- ***Inspecting social services records.*** A state statute, G.S. 108A-11, authorizes county social services board members to examine the county social services agency's records regarding applications for and provision of public assistance and social services. However, there are other state and federal confidentiality laws that significantly narrow the board's right of access to records.[67] For example, a 1995 advisory opinion issued by the North Carolina Attorney General's Office concluded that social services board members do not have any right to access child protective services records because these records are subject to provisions of North Carolina's Juvenile Code that do not allow access by governing boards.[68]
- ***Carrying out any other duties and responsibilities the General Assembly, NCDHHS, the state Social Services Commission, or the board of commissioners assigns to the board.***[69] For example, the state Social Services Commission rules give social services boards responsibility for reviewing cases involving suspected public assistance fraud, while a NCDHHS policy authorizes social services boards to review cases of suspected Medicaid beneficiary fraud. A board may exercise this authority directly or may delegate it to the county social services director and staff.[70]

In addition to the social services related powers and duties described in this section, a consolidated human services board has responsibilities related to other human services functions provided by the agency.[71] For example, with respect to a consolidated human services agency that includes public health, the governing board assumes all the powers and duties of a county board of health, which are described in Chapter 37 of this book.

Role of the Board of County Commissioners

A primary role of the board of commissioners in relation to social services is ensuring the adequacy of funds for social services programs in the county budget. That role is discussed in the section "Financing County Social Services Programs," later in this chapter. The commissioners' other powers and responsibilities include the following:

- ***Determining the type of agency that will provide social services in the county.*** As discussed above, the county may have a county department of social services or a consolidated human services agency. Alternatively, it may coordinate with other counties to establish a regional social services department.
- ***Determining the type of governing board for the social services agency.*** Depending upon the type of agency that provides social services in the county, the governing board may be an appointed county board of social services, an appointed consolidated human services board, a regional board of social services, or the board of commissioners.

---

67. For more analysis on this topic, see Aimee Wall, "Access to Confidential Client Records by Social Services Governing Boards," *Coates' Canons: NC Local Government Law* blog (April 26, 2016), canons.sog.unc.edu/2016/04/access-confidential-records-social-services-governing-boards/.

68. North Carolina Department of Justice, Office of the Attorney General, Advisory Opinion: Access to Records by Social Services Boards, Op. N.C. Att'y Gen. (April 20, 1995), ncdoj.gov/opinions/access-to-records-by-social-services-board/. The Juvenile Code is found in Chapter 7B of the North Carolina General Statutes. Provisions in the Juvenile Code that restrict the disclosure of child-protective-services records include G.S. 7B-302(a1) and G.S. 7B-2901.

69. G.S. 108A-9(5).

70. For a more comprehensive explanation of a local social services board's role in reviewing cases of suspected fraud, please see Chapter 9 of *Local Social Services Boards in North Carolina* by Kristi A. Nickodem (UNC School of Government, 2023).

71. *See* G.S. 153A-77(d).

- ***In a county that has an appointed county board of social services, determining whether the county should have a three- or five-member board.*** The board of county commissioners may change the size of the county social services board from three to five members or from five to three members.[72] Most county social services boards consist of five members.
- ***Appointing social services or consolidated human services board members.*** In counties with an appointed social services board, the board of commissioners has authority to appoint one member to a three-member board or two members to a five-member board.[73] The board of commissioners often appoints one of its own members to serve on the board (though it is not required to do so).[74] In counties with an appointed consolidated human services board, the board of commissioners has authority to appoint *all* of the board's members (and is required to appoint a county commissioner to serve on the board).[75]
- ***Establishing per diem rates and policies for subsistence and travel reimbursement for governing board members.***[76] In addition to establishing these rates and policies, the board of commissioners should include funds in the budget to cover these expenses.
- ***In a county with a county department of social services, approving the county social services director's salary.***[77] The county social services board appoints the director and determines the director's salary based on the State Human Resources Commission's pay classification plan, but the salary must be approved by the board of commissioners. Although the two boards should make every effort to reach agreement, the commissioners, having control over the budget, have the final say in accepting or rejecting the social services board's recommendation.
- ***Appointing a special county attorney for social services matters.***[78] State law allows the board of commissioners, with the approval of the county social services board, to appoint an attorney as the "special county attorney for social services" or to designate a county attorney to serve in that role. A county is not *required* to have a special county attorney for social services, but if it does, that attorney's duties include serving as legal adviser to the board of commissioners, the director of social services, and the social services governing board regarding social services matters. The board of commissioners is also responsible for determining the attorney's compensation.
- ***Determining whether financial assistance for certain disabled persons will be provided under the State-County Special Assistance program.***[79] State law requires

---

72. G.S. 108A-2.
73. G.S. 108A-3.
74. When the board of commissioners appoints a commissioner to serve on the county's board of social services or a consolidated human services board, it is an ex officio appointment. This means that a county commissioner is considered to be serving on the social services board as a part of the commissioner's duties as a commissioner and not as a separate public office. The term of a county commissioner who serves ex officio on an appointed county board of social services is the same as other board members and is not tied to or affected by the commissioner's term on the board of commissioners. However, a county commissioner who serves ex officio on an appointed consolidated human services board may only serve on the board for as long as the member is a county commissioner.
75. G.S. 153A-77(c).
76. G.S. 108A-8.
77. G.S. 108A-13.
78. G.S. 108A-16 through -18.
79. G.S. 108A-45.

counties to operate the State-County Special Assistance program, which is designed to assist needy aged or disabled adults in paying for room and board in adult care homes, special-care units, and in-home living arrangements. The board of commissioners has authority to determine whether this program will also provide financial assistance for a different category of "certain disabled persons" who are in private living arrangements but may not otherwise qualify for State-County Special Assistance under the eligibility requirements set forth in state law.[80]
- ***Deciding which non-mandated social services programs the county will fund and provide.*** State law requires counties to participate in a number of social services programs but also authorizes counties to "undertake, sponsor, organize, engage in, and support other social services programs intended to further the health, welfare, education, safety, comfort, and convenience of its citizens."[81] Some counties, for example, provide some form of general assistance to help address emergency needs of people not eligible for other benefits. State law authorizes counties to levy property taxes, subject to a tax rate limitation, to pay the cost of non-mandated public assistance and social services programs.[82]
- ***Approving, along with the county social services board, fees for certain nonmandated services the social services board contracts to provide.***[83] The board of commissioners should receive an annual report from the social services board concerning the receipt of such fees.
- ***Determining which agency or entity will operate the Child Support Enforcement program in the county.***[84] Each county must administer a Child Support Enforcement program. Most county child support enforcement programs are operated by the county department of social services or consolidated human services agency. However, each board of county commissioners has the option of creating an independent county department for child support enforcement, locating the program in another county department or office, or contracting with a private entity or another county to operate the program.
- ***Planning for, or both planning for and administering, the Work First program in the county.*** State law allows each board of commissioners to indicate to NCDHHS whether the county wants to be a "standard" or "electing" county for purposes of the Work First program (which is described later in this chapter).[85] In a standard

80. Per G.S. 108A-42, a "Certain Disabled" person is a person in a private living arrangement who is at least eighteen but younger than sixty-five, "having a physical or mental impairment which substantially precludes him from obtaining gainful employment, which impairment appears reasonably certain to continue without substantial improvement throughout his lifetime." By contrast, eligibility for State-County Special Assistance requires that the recipient meet certain income criteria, along with being (1) sixty-five years of age or older or (2) between the ages of eighteen and sixty-five and permanently and totally disabled or legally blind. G.S. 108A-41. Eligibility requirements for the "Certain Disabled Program" are set forth at Title 10A, Chapter 71P, Section .0805 of the North Carolina Administrative Code (hereinafter N.C.A.C.).

81. G.S. 153A-255. For more information about potential limits on this authority, see Kristi Nickodem, "County Legal Authority to Fund Non-Mandated Social Services Programs," *Coates' Canons: NC Local Government Law* blog (June 6, 2023), canons.sog.unc.edu/2023/06/county-legal-authority-to-fund-non-mandated-social-services-programs/.

82. *See* G.S. 153A-149(c)(30).

83. G.S. 108A-10.

84. G.S. 110-141.

85. G.S. 108A-27(e). When notifying NCDHHS of the county's desire to be designated as electing or standard, the county must submit documentation demonstrating that three-fifths of its county commissioners support the desired designation.

county, NCDHHS is responsible for the development and supervision of the Work First program, which is administered by the county department of social services.[86] In an electing county, the board of commissioners is directly responsible for the development, administration, and implementation of the Work First program.[87] An electing county also has more authority to set eligibility criteria, payment levels, and other program features that the state sets for standard counties.[88] A board's request to be an electing county must be supported by a three-fifths vote by the commissioners. The General Assembly designates each county as either a standard county or an electing county based on recommendations from NCDHHS.[89]

In electing counties, the board of commissioners must appoint a committee of individuals to identify the needs of the population to be served by Work First and to assist in developing the county's Work First plan to respond to those needs.[90] NCDHHS policy also requires standard counties to establish a committee for the biennial Work First planning process.[91]

Role of the Social Services Director

Regardless of the type of organization that administers social services programs in a county, someone must be appointed to serve in the role of director of social services. The director administers social services programs directly and through the local social services agency's staff. In a county with a stand-alone department of social services, the governing board must appoint a social services director for the department. In a county with a consolidated human services agency, the county manager must appoint a consolidated human services director who assumes all the powers and duties of a social services director.[92] The consolidated human services director may delegate some or all of these powers and duties to other people, but the consolidated director retains the ultimate responsibility for ensuring that all obligations and functions involving social services programs and policies are carried out.

The person serving in the role of social services director has overarching administrative responsibilities related to running the agency, many of which are found in G.S. 108A-14. The director also has many program-specific duties set forth in other statutes and regulations. The director is responsible for administering all of the department's public assistance and social services programs, but may do so by delegating many of these responsibilities to department staff.[93] A county director of social services has the exclusive authority to hire, supervise, discipline, and dismiss social services employees, but those duties must be carried out in a manner consistent with applicable

---

86. G.S. 108A-27.8(a).
87. G.S. 108A-27(f).
88. *Compare* G.S. 108A-27.3 (duties of electing counties) *with* G.S. 108A-27.6 (duties of standard counties).
89. G.S. 108A, § 27.2(12)–(14).
90. G.S. 108A-27.3(c).
91. *See* North Carolina Department of Health and Human Services, "The Planning Process for Work First," in *Work First Manual*, Policy § 003 (July 1, 2011), policies.ncdhhs.gov/divisional-n-z/social-services/work-first/wf-policies-manuals/.
92. G.S. 153A-77(e).
93. G.S. 108A-14(a)(3), (b).

federal, state, and local personnel laws and policies.[94] In a consolidated human services agency, the consolidated human services director may only appoint and dismiss employees with the approval of the county manager.[95]

In a county with an appointed board of social services, the director serves as the executive officer of the board and acts as its secretary.[96] The director is not a member of the board, however, and may attend closed sessions of board meetings only at the board's invitation.

Some of the director's more specific, programmatic duties are described below.

- ***Assessing reports of child abuse and neglect and taking appropriate action to protect children who are alleged to be abused, neglected, or dependent.***[97] The state Juvenile Code (G.S. Chapter 7B) requires anyone who suspects that a child is abused, neglected, or dependent, or has died as a result of maltreatment, to make a report to the county director of social services.[98] The law requires the director to make a prompt and thorough assessment of each report, to evaluate the level of risk to the child or to other children in the home, and to take appropriate protective action.
- ***Arranging and supervising children's placements in foster care.***[99] Under the Juvenile Code, a district court judge may place children alleged to be abused, neglected, or dependent in the custody of the county department of social services. Many of these children are placed by the department of social services in state-licensed foster homes.
- ***Investigating adoption cases and supervising adoptive placements.***[100] Under the state adoption law (G.S. Chapter 48), county departments of social services have many responsibilities in relation to the adoption of children. They arrange for and supervise adoptive placements; recruit, screen, and supervise adoptive parents; and evaluate and report to the court on adoption cases.
- ***Receiving and responding to reports of abuse, neglect, or exploitation of disabled adults.***[101] Under G.S. Chapter 108A, Article 6, anyone with reasonable cause to believe that a disabled adult needs protective services must make a report to the county director of social services, who must evaluate each report promptly and thoroughly and respond appropriately. The director is also responsible for receiving and evaluating reports of financial exploitation of disabled and older adults and taking appropriate action to protect those adults from financial exploitation.[102]
- ***Monitoring and investigating adult care homes for aged or disabled persons.***[103] Under G.S. Chapter 131D, adult care homes must be licensed by NCDHHS. The county social services director's responsibilities include monitoring implementation of the Adult Care Home Residents' Bill of Rights (G.S. Chapter 131D, Art. 3) and

---

94. In a county with a department of social services, social services employees are subject to the State Human Resources Act and the State Human Resources Commission Rules for local governments, as well as any supplemental county personnel policies. *See* G.S. 126-5(a)(2); G.S. 108A-14(a)(2).

95. G.S. 153A-77(e)(1). In a county with a consolidated human services agency, the board of commissioners may elect to remove the employees from the State Human Resources Act. G.S. 153A-77(d). If it does so, any applicable county personnel ordinances or policies must comply with federal merit personnel standards, found at 5 C.F.R. Part 900, Subpart F.

96. G.S. 108A-14(a)(1).

97. G.S. 108A-14(a)(11); *see also, e.g.,* G.S. 7B, §§ 300, 302, 307, 320, 500.

98. G.S. 7B-301.

99. G.S. 108A-14(a)(12); *see also, e.g.,* G.S. 7B, §§ 505, 903, 910.

100. G.S. 108A, § 14(a)(6), (13); *see also, e.g.,* G.S. 48, §§ 1-109, 2-501, 3-201, 3-203, 3-303, 3-309, 3-601(3)a.

101. G.S. 108A-14(a)(14); *see also* G.S. 108A, §§ 103–06, 108, 109.

102. G.S. 108A-14(a)(15); *see also* G.S. 108A, §§ 115–17.

103. G.S. 108A-14(a)(8); *see also* G.S. 131B, §§ 2.11(b), 26.

investigating complaints relating to violations of these rights, as well as investigating alleged violations of state law that occur at adult day care programs.[104]

- ***Serving as the guardian for adults found to be incompetent when appointed by the clerk of superior court to do so.***[105] In practice, the social services director is typically appointed as a guardian when there is no family member or other qualified individual available to serve in that role, or when there is significant family conflict such that the appointment of any family member as guardian could have detrimental effects on the ward.[106]

This list of the director's powers and duties is not exhaustive. Other statutes address the county social services director's duties or authority in areas such as arranging for the disposition of unclaimed dead bodies;[107] issuing certificates that authorize the employment of young people under age eighteen in accordance with applicable child-labor laws;[108] working on certain issues related to prisoners,[109] and serving on the county's Juvenile Crime Prevention Council.[110]

Financing County Social Services Programs

Social services financing is complicated by the interplay of federal, state, and county funding. The federal government plays a major role in financing many social services programs. Those programs contribute many federal and state dollars to local economies, but they also require the expenditure of substantial county funds. In some cases, the North Carolina General Assembly assigns responsibility to the counties for a portion of the nonfederal cost of certain federally funded programs. In other cases, county expenditures are required as a condition of receiving other federal and state funds for social services. Additionally, counties may need to spend county funds to provide services and programs for which state and federal funds are either unavailable or insufficient.

Federal Funding for Social Services

All federal funding for social services comes with certain conditions attached, meaning that recipients of these funds must comply with certain legal requirements. Among other things, these legal requirements may specify who is eligible for assistance under a given program, what types of assistance and services may be provided, how much assistance may be provided, how long assistance may be provided, when confidential program information may be disclosed, and how much states (or, in North Carolina, state and local governments) must contribute to the cost of these programs.

Some federally funded public assistance programs, such as Food and Nutrition Services and Medicaid, are known as "entitlement programs," meaning that benefits must be provided to every person who applies and meets the program's eligibility requirements. Regardless of how many people qualify for benefits under an entitlement program, the federal government must provide funds sufficient to pay the federal share of benefits for all eligible individuals.

---

104. G.S. 131D-6; 10A N.C.A.C. 06R, § .0102.

105. G.S. 35A, §§ 1202(4), 1213(d).

106. *See* Meredith Smith, "The Guardian of Last Resort," *On the Civil Side* (blog) (February 3, 2016), www.sog.unc.edu/blogs/civil-side/guardian-last-resort.

107. G.S. 130A-415. *See also* Kristi Nickodem, "The Role of a Director of Social Services in the Disposition of Unclaimed Bodies," *Coates' Canons: NC Local Government Law* blog (September 17, 2021), canons.sog.unc.edu/2021/09/the-role-of-a-director-of-social-services-in-the-disposition-of-unclaimed-bodies/.

108. G.S. 108A-14(a)(7); G.S. 95-25.5; 13 N.C.A.C. 12, § .0402.

109. G.S. 148-4(7); G.S. 148-33.1(f).

110. G.S. 143B-846.

In other programs, such as Work First, the Low Income Energy Assistance Program, and most social service programs, the amount of federal funding is capped. Federal appropriations provide a fixed amount of funding, often called a block grant. To receive these funds, state and local governments must contribute either a specified percentage of "matching" funds or an amount representing a "maintenance of effort" tied to amounts expended or budgeted for the program in a designated prior period. The state must develop comprehensive state plans describing the proposed use of the federal block grant funds and related state and local funds. The General Assembly is responsible for approving the distribution of federal block grant funds to counties.

If the federal funds and the required state and local contributions are insufficient to provide benefits or services to everyone who is eligible for a particular program, the state or local government must either limit the number of people served by the program, limit the amount of benefits or the level of services provided, or provide additional state or local funding for the program. In some cases, the ability to limit eligibility, benefits, or services may be constrained by program requirements associated with federal funds.

State and County Funding for Social Services

The General Assembly has the authority to decide whether and how to divide the nonfederal share of costs for social services programs between the state and counties.[111] North Carolina generally requires counties to pay the bulk of the nonfederal share of administrative costs for public assistance programs, as well as a significant portion of the cost of social services provided to county residents.[112]

Every board of county commissioners is required to levy and collect taxes sufficient to meet its county's share of expenses for state-mandated social services programs.[113] If a county does not pay or arrange for payment of its full share of the costs, the state budget director is authorized to withhold from the county any state appropriations for public assistance and related administrative costs or to direct the secretary of revenue and the state controller to withhold specified tax revenues owed to the county. The state budget director must notify the chair of the board of commissioners of the proposed action prior to withholding any funds.[114]

The board of county commissioners has complete discretion as to how much county money to budget for *nonmandated* social services programs.[115]

In some instances, counties must fill a funding gap with county funds to fulfill a legal mandate that is unfunded or underfunded by state and federal funds. For example, state law requires county departments of social services to provide adult protective services, but there is relatively little state or federal funding available for such services. To fulfill the legal mandate to protect vulnerable adults, county commissioners must appropriate county funds to support a county department of social services' provision of adult protective services. Likewise, federal and state funding are sometimes inadequate to support a sufficient number of social workers and attorneys to handle all the child welfare cases in a given county, in which case the county must "fill the gap" in services for these children with county funds.

---

111. G.S. 108A-87.

112. *See* NCDHHS, *County Budget Estimates—State Fiscal Year 2023–2024*, www.ncdhhs.gov/divisions/social-services/county-staff-information/budget-information/dss-budget-estimates (click on "Budget Estimates State Totals" to access PDF).

113. G.S. 108A-90.

114. G.S. 108A-93.

115. *See* G.S. 153A-255 (giving each county the authority to "undertake, sponsor, organize, engage in, and support . . . social service programs intended to further the health, welfare, education, employment, safety, comfort, and convenience of its citizens").

Before February 15 of each year, NCDHHS is required to notify the county social services director, the director of public health, the county manager, and the board of commissioners of the amount of state and federal funds estimated to be available to the county for public assistance, social services, and public health programs and related administrative costs for the next fiscal year.[116] The notice states the percentage of county financial participation expected to be required for each program. Periodically, the state revises these estimates to reflect new state-budget figures and actions taken by the General Assembly, Congress, and federal agencies. Accordingly, the budgeting process for county social services agencies involves some degree of uncertainty regarding the exact amount of county funds that will be needed to fund a county's share of the cost of mandated programs.

County social services budgets generally estimate expenditures that are higher than the amounts indicated in NCDHHS's estimates. These higher county-level estimates are often due to needing to fill a funding gap. For example, federal and state funds available to the county for child protective services, along with NCDHHS's estimate of the county's match, may be insufficient to hire the number of social workers necessary to carry out the county's legal responsibility to provide protective services to abused and neglected children. In other cases, counties may need to spend additional funds to comply with state mandates that are not accompanied by state funding. Additionally, counties may want to provide nonmandated social services programs to meet unique local needs. Those optional, nonmandated programs and services are not reflected in NCDHHS's budget estimates and must be supported by county funds if other federal and state funding is not available.

Programs and Services

State law requires counties to administer or assist in the administration of a number of social services and economic services programs, including

- Medicaid,[117]
- Work First,[118]
- Food and Nutrition Services,[119]
- Low Income Energy Assistance,[120]
- State-County Special Assistance,[121]
- Foster Care and Adoption Assistance,[122]
- child protective services,[123]
- adult protective services,[124]
- guardianship services,[125] and
- child support enforcement services.[126]

116. G.S. 108A-88.
117. G.S. 108A-25(b).
118. G.S. 108A-27(f), (g).
119. G.S. 108A, §§ 25(a)(3), 51.
120. G.S. 108A-25(a)(5).
121. G.S. 108A, §§ 25(a)(2), 40.
122. G.S. 108A-25(a)(4).
123. G.S. 7B-300.
124. G.S. 108A-103.
125. G.S. 108A-15.
126. G.S. 110-141.

If a county identifies a need in the community that is not addressed by these mandated programs, state law authorizes each county to undertake, sponsor, organize, engage in, and support any other social services program that will further the health, welfare, education, employment, safety, comfort, and convenience of its citizens.[127]

Several of the largest programs provided by county social services agencies are described below. However, this list is by no means exhaustive.

Food and Nutrition Services

State law requires every county to operate the federally funded Supplemental Nutrition Assistance Program (SNAP), known in North Carolina as the Food and Nutrition Services (FNS) program.[128] This was previously referred to as the "food stamp" program. Through this program, counties issue electronic benefit transfer (debit) cards to eligible recipients for the purchase of food products.[129] Eligibility is based on federal income and resource guidelines. The federal government pays the full cost of SNAP benefits. The federal government also pays half of the administrative costs for the program, while in North Carolina, counties pay the other half.[130] In December 2024, the state reported that this program was providing assistance to more than 1.5 million individuals.[131]

Medicaid

Medicaid is a public assistance program that covers most of the cost of medical care and services for several categories of people who cannot afford these costs.[132] Those who may receive Medicaid include low-income aged, disabled, or blind persons; needy children; pregnant women; individuals who receive federal Supplemental Security Income (SSI) benefits; and others with low incomes who meet eligibility requirements. In state fiscal year 2024, the federal government provided 67.9 percent of North Carolina's Medicaid funding, while the state contributed 32.1 percent of the program's total funds.[133] As of December 2024, over 3 million North Carolinians were enrolled in Medicaid.[134]

Work First

The federal Temporary Assistance for Needy Families (TANF) program is called "Work First" in North Carolina.[135] The federal government provides a set amount of TANF funding (a block grant) to each state to implement programs intended to support families who are in need.[136] Work First focuses on providing eligible families with short-term assistance to help them achieve self-sufficiency

---

127. G.S. 153A-255. For examples of some potential limitations on this authority, *see* Kristi Nickodem, "County Legal Authority to Fund Non-Mandated Social Services Programs," *Coates' Canons: NC Local Government Law* blog (June 6, 2023), canons.sog.unc.edu/2023/06/county-legal-authority-to-fund-non-mandated-social-services-programs/.

128. G.S. 108A-51.

129. G.S. 108A, §§ 51–53.

130. See NCDHHS, *County Budget Estimates State Totals—State Fiscal Year 2023–2024*, www.ncdhhs.gov/divisions/social-services/county-staff-information/budget-information/dss-budget-estimates (click on "Budget Estimates State Totals" to access PDF).

131. See NCDHHS, Food and Nutrition Services, *FNS Caseload Statistics Reports*, www.ncdhhs.gov/divisions/social-services/program-statistics-and-reviews/fns-caseload-statistics-reports (click on "FNS Cases and Participants" to download the Excel file).

132. G.S. 108A, §§ 54–70.16.

133. *See* NCDHHS, *State Fiscal Year 2024 Medicaid Annual Report Tables*, medicaid.ncdhhs.gov/reports/annual-reports-and-tables.

134. *See* NCDHHS, *NC Medicaid Enrollment Reports*, medicaid.ncdhhs.gov/reports/nc-medicaid-enrollment-reports#FiscalYear2024EnrollmentReports-2073.

135. G.S. 108A-25(b1).

136. 42 U.S.C. § 601.

through employment.[137] The program provides cash assistance as well as assistance with child care, transportation, job searches, and job training. In December 2024, the state estimated that this program was providing cash assistance to over 11,000 individuals.[138]

Other Public Assistance Programs

Social services agencies are also involved with administering other public assistance programs, such as the Child Care Subsidy Program, the Low Income Energy Assistance Program (LIEAP), the State-County Special Assistance for Adults Program, the Foster Care and Adoption Assistance Programs, and the Refugee Assistance Program (RAP).

Child Support Enforcement Program

The Child Support Enforcement program assists parents in establishing and enforcing child support obligations, including locating absent parents for the purpose of obtaining child support and establishing paternity of dependent children.[139] In most counties, the program is administered by the county department of social services or a consolidated human services agency, but in some counties it is administered by another department of county government or by a contracted provider.[140] Child support agencies must seek support on behalf of dependent children who receive public assistance through certain programs and must also provide services to anyone else who applies and pays a low application fee.[141]

Protective Services for Children

State law requires that cases of suspected child abuse, neglect, dependency, and death from maltreatment be reported to a county social services agency.[142] The North Carolina Juvenile Code, which includes this reporting requirement, is designed to protect children under age 18 from neglect, abuse, or dependency by parents or other caregivers.[143] When a county social services agency receives a report, it must conduct a prompt assessment and take appropriate action to protect the child.[144] Each agency provides a wide range of protective services to children and their families in these cases, often while the children remain in the home, since one purpose of the law is to keep families intact unless the risk of harm to a child requires the child's removal from the home.[145] When necessary, a county social services agency may file a petition in district court seeking either legal custody of a child or some other court order to protect the child.[146]

---

137. G.S. 108A-27.

138. *See* NCDHHS, *Work First Caseload Statistics: Work First Cash Assistance and Participants*, www.ncdhhs.gov/divisions/social-services/program-statistics-and-reviews/work-first-caseload-statistics (click on "Work First Cash Assistance Cases and Participants" to download the Excel file).

139. G.S. 110, art. 9.

140. *See* G.S. 110-141 (requiring all counties to administer a child support enforcement program).

141. *See* G.S. 110-130.1; 42 U.S.C. §§ 608(a)(2), 654(29); 42 C.F.R. §§ 433.145–.148.

142. G.S. 7B-301. For more information about the child protective services system in North Carolina, please see Chapter 1 of *Abuse, Neglect, Dependency, and Termination of Parental Rights Proceedings in North Carolina*, Sara DePasquale (UNC School of Government, 2024).

143. G.S. 7B, subch. I.

144. G.S. 7B-302.

145. G.S. 7B-100.

146. G.S. 7B-302(c), (d).

Permanency Planning Services

Permanency planning services are provided by every county social services agency to children who are separated from their parents or caretakers and are in the custody of the social services agency.[147] The goal of permanency planning services is to provide all children with permanent homes, preferably with their own families of origin, as early as possible.[148] While the emphasis is on preserving or reunifying families, there is a complementary focus on moving children into long-term plans like adoption or guardianship when returning them to their own homes is not possible.

Adoptions

Adoption placement services are designed to find safe and permanent homes for children whose parents have relinquished them for adoption or had their parental rights terminated. In some cases, the children may be abused, neglected, or dependent and have adoption designated as a permanent plan by the court hearing the child protection case. Every county social services agency has an adoption program that includes accepting children for placement, recruiting and screening adoptive parents, and arranging and supervising placements.[149] State adoption law requires that either a county social services agency or a licensed child-placing agency conduct a preplacement assessment of every prospective adoptive home and complete a report to the court on almost every adoptive placement.[150] The NCDHHS Division of Social Services supervises county adoption programs and provides resources for families interested in adoption.

Protective Services for Adults

When a county social services agency receives a report of abuse, neglect, or exploitation of a disabled adult, it must conduct a prompt assessment and take appropriate action to protect the vulnerable adult.[151] In some cases, the agency may need to petition the district court for an order authorizing the provision of protective services to the vulnerable adult.[152]

Services to Aged or Disabled Adults

In addition to adult protective services, county social services agencies provide a number of services to older adults and adults with disabilities that include in-home services, community-based services, and institutional care. Some of these services are mandatory, while others are optional.[153] An example of a mandated service is the agency's duty to conduct regular inspections of adult care homes to ensure their compliance with state licensing requirements and other state laws and regulations concerning the care and treatment of elderly or disabled residents.[154] While some services and programs are provided by a county department of social services or a consolidated human services agency, some jurisdictions have created separate departments of aging and adult services or offer services through another county department.

---

147. North Carolina Division of Social Services, *Permanency Planning Services Policy, Protocol, and Guidance*, in NC Child Welfare Manual (updated November 2023), policies.ncdhhs.gov/wp-content/uploads/permanency-planning_manual-april-2022_-1.pdf; see also G.S. 7B, §§ 906.1, 906.2.

148. G.S. 7B-100.

149. G.S. 108A, § 14(a)(6), (13).

150. G.S. 48-1-109; *see generally* G.S. 48.

151. G.S. 108A, §§ 103–106.

152. G.S. 108A, §§ 104–106.

153. Local governments, both cities and counties, have the authority to "undertake programs for the assistance and care of [their] senior citizens" but are not required to do so. G.S. 160A-497.

154. G.S. 131D-2.11(b); *see also* 10A N.C.A.C. 13F, § .1212.

Conclusion

Unlike many states, North Carolina continues to call on counties to be the primary deliverers of public social services. North Carolina's arrangement of county administration and state supervision, and the intergovernmental cooperation it requires, generates some unique frustrations and problems. But it also results in a social services system that combines state oversight and accountability with some measure of local flexibility and control.

In terms of funding, regulation, and policymaking, the social services system is perhaps the most complex example of federal-state-county interaction in North Carolina. Social services programs in North Carolina will continue to be greatly influenced by changes at the federal level. Even apart from federal influences, however, the state and counties must continue to address serious issues regarding how best to meet the needs of children, families, and disadvantaged adults within the limited resources available.

Additional Resources

Publications

DePasquale, Sara. *Abuse, Neglect, Dependency, and Termination of Parental Rights Proceedings in North Carolina*. Chapel Hill: UNC School of Government, 2024.

Nickodem, Kristi A. *Local Social Services Boards in North Carolina.* Chapel Hill: UNC School of Government, 2023.

Smith, Meredith S. and Wall, Aimee N, *Legal Framework for North Carolina's Elder Protection System*, Chapel Hill: UNC School of Government, 2020.

Websites

The North Carolina Adult Protection Network, protectadults.sog.unc.edu. This School of Government website provides resources and information related to North Carolina's system of protection for vulnerable adults.

The North Carolina Human Services Hub, humanservices.sog.unc.edu. This School of Government website provides up-to-date resources related to North Carolina's social services and consolidated human services agencies and boards.

Chapter 39

The County Jail

James M. Markham

James M. Markham is a School of Government faculty member. His area of interest is criminal law and procedure, with a focus on the law of sentencing, corrections, and the conditions of confinement.

Almost all North Carolina counties have a jail. Jails, also referred to by statute as *detention centers* or *local confinement facilities*, should not be confused with prisons. Jails are local facilities used primarily to incarcerate criminal defendants awaiting trial or serving short sentences of imprisonment, usually for misdemeanors. Prisons, on the other hand, are state-run facilities that house convicted inmates serving longer sentences, usually for felonies.

No specific North Carolina law expressly requires a county to build or operate a jail, but several statutes imply that each county will have access to one. For instance, Chapter 15, Section 6 of the North Carolina General Statutes (hereinafter G.S.) says that "[n]o person . . . shall be imprisoned except in the common jail of the county, unless otherwise provided by law." Another statute, G.S. 162-56, states that "[p]ersons committed to the custody of a sheriff shall be confined in the facilities designated by law for such confinement, and shall not be confined in any other place." Read together, these laws indicate an expectation that a county will have a jail to house the inmates committed to the custody of its sheriff. As a practical matter, not having access to a jail would impede the smooth operation of the criminal justice system.

Shared Responsibility for Jails

Responsibility for a jail is shared between the board of county commissioners and the sheriff. Generally speaking, the county funds the jail and the sheriff manages it. That division of responsibility is reflected in the statutes. G.S. 153A-218 allows the county to "establish, acquire, erect, repair, maintain, and operate" a jail and to appropriate money to do so, while G.S. 162-22 says that the "sheriff shall have the care and custody of the jail in his county; and shall be, or appoint, the keeper thereof."

The state also has responsibilities related to local jails. Principally, the state Department of Health and Human Services (DHHS) is responsible for issuing minimum statewide standards in the construction and operation of jails, and then inspecting the jails for compliance with those standards.[1] The standards are printed in Title 10A, Chapter 14, Subchapter J of the North Carolina Administrative Code (hereinafter N.C.A.C.). The Construction Section of DHHS's Division of Health Service Regulation inspects each jail at least twice per year, as provided in G.S. 153A-222. If the jail does not meet standards and the DHHS secretary finds that the conditions put inmates' safety at risk, the secretary may order corrective action or close the jail.[2]

Finally, the court system has a role related to the jail. Judicial officials control admissions to and releases from the jail by setting conditions of pretrial release for arrested defendants and by sentencing convicted offenders. Additionally, the grand jury is required to inspect the jail under G.S. 15A-628.

Construction of Jails

Given the size and diversity of a state like North Carolina, there is no one-size-fits-all approach to jail construction. To illustrate, Mecklenburg County houses almost 2,000 inmates in multiple jails and annexes, while the Graham County jail has fewer than a dozen beds. Regardless of the size of the facility, jail construction is expensive. A variety of factors impacts the ultimate cost of a jail. For example, single cells are more expensive than dormitory space. A county also must consider whether it wishes to build a jail with sufficient capacity to house federal inmates or inmates from other counties, both of which can be a source of additional income for the county. But even for counties that have such contractual arrangements in place, local tax revenues are the primary source of funds for jail construction.

Jail construction must comply with DHHS standards, which are set out in the state Administrative Code. Under 10A N.C.A.C. 14J, § .1203, counties must obtain DHHS approval before beginning construction of a new jail or altering an existing jail. The standards include specific requirements for visitation, medical, and housing areas, as well as special requirements for electrical and plumbing systems. The standards are detailed. For example, each single occupancy cell must, under the applicable standard, have 50 square feet of floor space, while a multiple occupancy cell must have 50 square feet of floor space for the first inmate and 35 additional square feet for each additional inmate. In general, the standards emphasize security, fire safety, and the health and welfare of inmates and staff.

District (Regional) Jails

Several counties have, over the years, found it advantageous to share a jail facility, which is allowed under G.S. 153A-219. Under that statute, two or more counties may join together to establish a district confinement facility, providing for an administrator to manage it. Several such facilities

1. G.S. 153A-221.
2. G.S. 153A-223.

exist in North Carolina, including the Albemarle District Jail in Elizabeth City, which is operated pursuant to an agreement between Pasquotank, Perquimans, and Camden counties.

The Jail Population

Inmates in the county jail can be divided into different categories depending on the legal basis for their confinement. These categories are listed and briefly discussed below.

Pretrial Detention

By far, the largest category of jail inmates is pretrial detainees—those who have been arrested on a criminal charge and who are unable to satisfy conditions of pretrial release, such as an appearance bond. Well over half of all jail inmates in North Carolina fall into this category.

Sentenced Confinement

Relatively short sentences for misdemeanors are served in the jail. Many years ago, when there was no state prison system, all criminal sentences were served in jails. The state assumed responsibility for some prisoners around the time of the Great Depression, but short sentences were still served in county facilities. Since then, the sentence-length threshold at which responsibility for an inmate shifted from the county to the state has varied, fluctuating between 30 and 180 days.

Today, under G.S. 15A-1352, most misdemeanor sentences of 90 days or less are served in the local jail. Misdemeanants with sentences in excess of 90 days are housed in a jail that has volunteered to provide space for them through the Statewide Misdemeanant Confinement Program, created as part of the Justice Reinvestment Act of 2011.[3] All active sentences for driving while impaired (DWI), regardless of length, are served through the program. The law includes limited exceptions to these rules for times when the local jail is overcrowded (G.S. 148-32.1) or for inmates who are dangerous or in need of special medical attention (G.S. 162-39).

Active sentences for felonies may not be served in the local jail—except to the extent that inmates remain in so-called backlog status at the jail after sentencing to await transfer to the prison system.[4]

Probationary Confinement

Several forms of confinement that may be ordered as part of a probationary sentence can be served in the local jail. First, special probation under G.S. 15A-1351, often referred to as a split sentence, can be served in the jail, either in a single continuous period or in noncontinuous intervals, such as weekends. Second, a probation officer may order a probationer to serve a short, two- or three-day stint in the jail—sometimes referred to as a "quick dip"—in response to a violation of probation. And third, a judge can hold a probationer in contempt for violating a condition of probation.

Contempt of Court

Periods of incarceration for persons held in contempt of court, either civil or criminal, are served in the county jail. Contempt includes things like being disruptive during court proceedings or willfully failing to comply with a court order, such as an order to pay child support.[5]

---

3. S.L. 2011-192.
4. G.S. 148-29.
5. G.S. 5A-11 (criminal contempt); 5A-21 (civil contempt).

Public Intoxication

Under G.S. 122C-303, a law enforcement officer may, in certain circumstances, assist a person found intoxicated in a public place by taking him or her to the jail. That statute envisions the jail as a last resort in such situations, to be used only if the person is not in need of immediate medical care and no other facility is available. The intoxicated person may be detained at the jail only until sober or a maximum of twenty-four hours and may be released to a relative or other individual willing to be responsible for his or her care at any time.

Federal Inmates

Some jails house federal prisoners for the Federal Bureau of Prisons, Immigration and Customs Enforcement (ICE), or the U.S. Marshals service. This is permissible under G.S. 162-34 when adequate space is available. The reimbursement rate for such arrangements is set by agreement between the county and the United States government.

Financing Jail Operations

Paying for operation of the jail is primarily a county responsibility, although the state and, to a certain extent, the inmates themselves make some contribution. Before 2009, the state would reimburse the counties for some inmates serving sentences in the jail of 30 days or more. That provision has been repealed, but some other reimbursements and fees remain. These fees help offset jail expenditures but by no means cover the full cost of housing inmates, which varies by facility.

Jail Backlog

Beginning on the day after the sheriff has notified the prison system that a sentenced offender is ready for transfer to prison, the state must, under G.S. 148-29, reimburse the county for housing the offender at a per diem rate set by the General Assembly, plus certain medical costs. As of 2024, the reimbursement rate is $40 per day.[6]

Statewide Misdemeanant Confinement Fund

Counties that volunteer to house misdemeanor inmates pursuant to the Statewide Misdemeanant Confinement Program are paid a per diem rate for each inmate they house. The current reimbursement rate—set by the North Carolina Sheriffs' Association in the terms and conditions of the program—is $40 per day. Out-of-jail medical expenses are also reimbursed. The money for the program comes from a legislative appropriation.

Jail Fees

Certain inmates must pay a fee for each day they are confined in the jail. There are two types of jail fees under G.S. 7A-313.

The first type of jail fee is for time spent in jail awaiting trial. Defendants who wind up getting convicted are liable to the county in the sum of $10 for each twenty-four hours of pretrial confinement. No fee is assessed if a person is acquitted or the case against him or her is dismissed. The pretrial jail fee is often collected as a condition of the defendant's probation, flowing back to the county through the clerk of court.

6. S.L. 2023-134, § 19A.3.

The second fee, set out in the second paragraph of G.S. 7A-313, is for "[p]ersons who are ordered to pay jail fees pursuant to a probationary sentence." The exact meaning of this portion of the law has never been crystal clear, but it has generally been interpreted to authorize a fee for every day served in jail as part of a sentence to special probation, also known as a split sentence. The amount of the probationary-sentence jail fee is set at the same per diem rate paid by the state to local jails for maintaining a prisoner, as set by the General Assembly in its appropriations acts. Today, the only such per diem rate paid by the state to the jails is the $40 per day backlog fee, and so that is also the probationary confinement fee.

The $10 pretrial confinement fee is mandatory unless the sentencing judge waives it. The $40 probationary-sentence jail fee, by contrast, applies only when ordered by the sentencing judge.

Work Release Earnings

Under G.S. 148-33.1(f), a jail may collect from a jail inmate's work release earnings an amount of money sufficient to pay for the actual costs of the inmate's keep. The sentencing court determines the amount to be collected.

Administering Jail Sentences

The sheriff and jail administrator are responsible for administering sentences to the jail. Proper administration of a sentence requires a careful accounting of the time a person has already served and the incentive credits to which he or she may be entitled.

Jail Credit

The jail administrator must reduce an inmate's sentence by the amount of time he or she already served before being convicted, known as jail credit. For example, if an inmate sentenced to 30 days of imprisonment for a misdemeanor has spent 20 days in pretrial confinement, then he or she is said to have 20 days of jail credit, and thus only 10 days left to serve. Under G.S. 15-196.4, the sentencing judge is responsible for awarding jail credit and telling the custodian (the sheriff or the prison system) how much credit to apply. As a practical matter, however, the court system will often ask the jail for help in determining how long a defendant was in custody before trial—a determination that can sometimes be difficult when a person has multiple pending charges with varying conditions of release.

Sentence Reduction Credits

Most inmates do not serve every day of their imposed sentences. Many receive sentence reduction credits, which reward work or completion of educational programming with a reduction in the amount of time the inmate must serve. Sentence reduction credits incentivize good behavior by inmates, which is a benefit to themselves, their fellow inmates, and the jailer. Under G.S. 148-13(e), the sentence credit policies of the state Department of Adult Correction (DAC) must be distributed to and followed by local jail administrators with respect to sentenced jail prisoners.

For misdemeanor sentences subject to Structured Sentencing (North Carolina's primary sentencing law), the main sentence reduction credit is called *earned time*. State law and DAC regulations allow for up to 4 days of earned time credit per month of incarceration. Thus, an inmate who receives a 90-day sentence could have that sentence reduced by approximately 12 days if he or she were to start a job immediately upon arriving at the jail.

A different rule applies to inmates serving time for impaired driving. They are eligible to receive a sentence reduction credit called *good time*, which is awarded at the rate of 1 day deducted for each day served without an infraction of inmate conduct rules. The practical effect of that day-for-day credit rule is that active DWI sentences are cut in half by good time credit for well-behaved inmates.

Work and Education Programs in the Jail

A sheriff may, under G.S. 162-58, have a program to allow sentenced inmates to work during their time in the jail. The work must be on projects to benefit units of state or local government and must be done pursuant to rules issued by the board of county commissioners and approved by the sheriff. Inmates participating in the work program must be supervised by county employees or sheriff's office personnel. A sheriff or jail administrator may also allow a convicted misdemeanant to participate in an adult high school equivalency diploma program or any other education, rehabilitation, or training program under G.S. 162-59.1 (no board approval is required for these programs). An inmate is entitled to a sentence reduction of 4 days for each 30 days of work performed or each 30 days of classes attended, with the caveat that an inmate's total sentence reduction for earned time and work or education programs may not exceed 4 days per month of incarceration under G.S. 15A-1340.20(d).

The work programs described immediately above should not be confused with work release, which is the temporary release of a sentenced prisoner to work on a paid job in the free community. Authorization to participate in work release comes from an order or recommendation by the sentencing judge, and the jail can recover a portion of a work release inmate's earnings to pay for the cost of housing him or her.

Care and Custody of Inmates

The sheriff is responsible for operating the jail. Most sheriffs appoint a jail administrator to manage day-to-day operations, but the sheriff retains final responsibility under G.S. 162-24. A web of constitutional, statutory, and regulatory provisions informs the proper administration of the jail. The jail must have an operations manual with written policies addressing everything from security to food service (DHHS regulations list the required topics). The operations manual must be reviewed and updated annually.

Security

Under G.S. 153A-224, the jail must have sufficient custodial personnel to provide continuous supervision of its prisoners. Under the Eighth Amendment, the Constitution prohibits detention officers from imposing cruel and unusual punishment, which includes using excessive force against sentenced prisoners to maintain order and security in jails. When evaluating whether officers used excessive force against an inmate, courts will apply a test set out by the Supreme Court of the United States, asking "whether force was applied in a good-faith effort to maintain or restore discipline, or maliciously and sadistically to cause harm."[7] If the inmate is a pretrial detainee, a different test applies as a matter of due process under the Fourteenth Amendment: whether the force was objectively unreasonable.[8] The Eighth Amendment also requires officers to protect inmates from assaults on one another. The jail is not required to guarantee inmates' safety, but officials can be

7. Hudson v. McMillian, 503 U.S. 1, 7 (1992).
8. Kingsley v. Hendrickson, 576 U.S. 389 (2015).

held accountable if they are deliberately indifferent to a known risk of harm.[9] DHHS regulations offer more detailed guidance on day-to-day security requirements. For instance, they require that officers directly observe each inmate at least two times within a sixty-minute time period on an irregular basis, with no more than forty minutes between rounds, or more frequently in the case of inmates who are intoxicated, abusive, or who have previously attempted or threatened suicide.[10]

Medical Care

The jail has a duty to provide medical care for its prisoners—an obligation that can be both challenging and costly. Many who wind up in a jail are not in the best of health to begin with, and being incarcerated can sometimes aggravate preexisting physical and mental health conditions. Nevertheless, the Supreme Court of North Carolina long ago stated that "[i]t is but just that the public be required to care for the prisoner, who cannot, by reason of the deprivation of his liberty, care for himself."[11] Jails satisfy that obligation in different ways—some with in-house medical staff, some through contracts with full-service correctional health-care providers, and some by accessing medical providers and hospitals in the local community. Regardless of the particular method, inmates must be provided an opportunity each day to communicate their health complaints to a health professional or to an officer, and qualified medical personnel must be available to evaluate the medical needs of inmates.[12]

Under G.S. 153A-225, every jail is required to have a medical plan, developed in consultation with local health officials and approved by the local or district health director. When necessary, the jail must provide emergency medical care from a licensed physician according to its jail medical plan. The county must pay for the costs of that care unless the inmate has third-party insurance. For non-emergency care, the jail may set and collect a fee not exceeding $20 per incident. A jail may also establish a fee of not more than $10 for a 30-day supply or less of a prescription drug. If the jail establishes these fees, it also must have a procedure for waiving them for indigent inmates. The jail is not required to address inmates' every elective or preventative health-care issue, but officials must not be deliberately indifferent to inmates' serious medical needs, as that would violate the Eighth Amendment.[13]

Other Conditions of Confinement

Jail inmates do not forfeit all of their constitutional rights when they are incarcerated. Some rights may, however, be limited in the name of security and as part of an inmate's punishment. In general, the jail is justified in limiting a constitutional right when doing so is "reasonably related to legitimate penological interests."[14] For example, to avoid violating an inmate's First Amendment right to practice his or her religion, the jail should be prepared to accommodate special diets necessary for an inmate to practice his or her sincerely held beliefs, but only to the extent that doing so does not create an unreasonable administrative burden or security risk. A similar analysis applies to other limitations, such as limits on inmate mail, access to publications, and visitation.

---

9. Farmer v. Brennan, 511 U.S. 825 (1994).
10. 10A N.C.A.C. 14J, § .0601.
11. Spicer v. Williamson, 191 N.C. 487 (1926).
12. 10A N.C.A.C. 14J, § .1001(c).
13. Estelle v. Gamble, 429 U.S. 97 (1977).
14. Turner v. Safley, 482 U.S. 78, 89 (1987).

Court interpretations of inmate rights evolve over time. For instance, for decades courts routinely held that a blanket policy of strip-searching all arrestees as they were booked into jails violated the Fourth Amendment's prohibition on unreasonable searches and seizures. In 2012, however, the Supreme Court of the United States upheld that practice for inmates entering a jail's general population.[15] That change of course serves as a reminder to jail officials that policies should be reviewed periodically to ensure they are up to date in light of recent cases and legislative amendments. Additionally, federal laws such as the Religious Land Use and Institutionalized Persons Act (RLUIPA)[16] and the Prison Rape Elimination Act (PREA)[17] may grant some inmates additional rights and impose additional requirements on some jails. At a minimum, DHHS regulations require an annual review of a jail's operations manual by the sheriff or jail administrator.

A background right that ensures the protection of other rights is the right to meaningful access to the courts. To protect that right, a jail should give its inmates access to an adequate law library or assistance from persons trained in the law.[18] According to DHHS regulations, the jail must address inmates' access to legal assistance or legal materials in its operations manual.

Managing the Jail Population

Overcrowding can be a problem for some jails—especially on weekends, when inmates serving split sentences typically report to serve the active portion of their time. Though not necessarily a constitutional violation in and of itself, overcrowding can have side effects that lead to liability.

Counties employ different strategies to manage their jail populations. First, when the jail population becomes too high, the sheriff can ask a judge to transfer inmates to another jail or to the prison system under G.S. 148-32.1. Some counties also take a preventative approach, conducting pretrial services programs or providing electronic supervision technology as an alternative to pretrial confinement in the jail. For sentenced inmates, the jail should of course be sure to award all appropriate jail credit and sentence reduction credits to ensure that inmates do not serve more time than required by their sentence.

Jail officials cannot manage or limit the inmate population by themselves. Under G.S. 15-126, the sheriff may not refuse to accept inmates committed to his or her custody by the court system, even when the jail is overcrowded. With that in mind, an interagency approach is often the best strategy for long-term management of the jail population. Some counties have formed planning committees or task forces for this purpose, typically including representatives from the sheriff's office and the board of county commissioners, in addition to local judges, magistrates, prosecutors, defense lawyers, probation officers, the clerk of court, and others. Regular communication between these stakeholders will aid in the efficient administration of justice in the county.

---

15. Florence v. Bd. of Chosen Freeholders, 566 U.S. 318 (2012).

16. Religious Land Use and Institutionalized Persons Act of 2000 (RLUIPA), Pub. L. 106-274, 114 Stat. 803 (codified at 42 U.S.C. §§ 2000cc-1 to -5 (2018)) (stating that no government shall impose a substantial burden on the religious exercise of a person in jail unless doing so serves a compelling governmental interest and does so by the least restrictive means).

17. Prison Rape Elimination Act of 2003, Pub. L. No. 108–79, 117 Stat. 972 (codified at 34 U.S.C. §§ 30301–30309 (2018)).

18. Bounds v. Smith, 430 U.S. 817 (1977).

Chapter 40

The Courts

Shea Riggsbee Denning

Shea Riggsbee Denning is the director of the North Carolina Judicial College. She specializes in judicial administration and judicial education. This chapter borrows heavily from an earlier version written by retired School of Government faculty member James C. Drennan.

The framework of North Carolina's court system is established in Article IV, the judicial article, of the state constitution, which was substantially revised in 1962. Article IV created a unified statewide and state-operated General Court of Justice composed of three divisions: the Appellate Division (which includes the Supreme Court and the Court of Appeals), the Superior Court Division, and the District Court Division.

Virtually all current operating costs of the General Court of Justice are borne by the state, and it employs all judicial system personnel. However, local governments—primarily the counties—must provide appropriate and adequate space as well as furniture for court system functions carried out at the local level. These functions include practically all operations of the system except central administration and the work of the appellate courts. Thus, the court system is a major governmental activity executed largely at the level of the county and housed at its expense.

History of North Carolina's Court System

The current structure of the court system, in its most important organizational principles, dates back to the 1950s and 1960s. Beginning about 1955, a study of the court system was undertaken and a new framework for the state's judiciary was created. This new organizational structure was approved by the voters as part of a series of constitutional amendments and gradually implemented statewide. The transition to the new system concluded in December 1970, fifteen years after the initial studies began.

Several important organizational principles directed and shaped the reform effort.

- The 1950s trial court system was largely a local system, with almost every county having a slightly different structure. The reformed court structure eliminated these local courts and replaced them with a unified system, the General Court of Justice, that is nearly completely state-funded.
- In the 1950s, each local court system had unique jurisdictional rules and charged different costs and fees, and the methods of selection for judges and justices of the peace varied by county. The reformed court structure has uniform jurisdictions, cost structures, and methods of selection for all judicial officials.
- In the 1950s, many court officials were compensated from the fees they collected, and in criminal cases, then as now, only those found guilty were assessed fees. Under the reformed court structure all court officials are state employees, paid only by salaries.
- The 1950s court system had no central administration, since counties and cities provided most of the funding. The reformed court system is administered by a state agency, the Administrative Office of the Courts.

The guiding principle of the system that resulted from this sustained reform effort is that a person who seeks justice from the courts should find that the matter is heard by a judicial official who has the same powers, is selected in the same way, and has no financial stake in the outcome, regardless of where that person may live in North Carolina. In short, the goal is equal justice for all, in small towns and large cities, in the east and in the west, in the mountains and on the coast. The remainder of this chapter describes the organizational structure that is the product of the court reform efforts of the 1950s and 1960s and as it has since been modified.

Appellate Division

The Supreme Court

The supreme court has seven justices (Chapter 7A, Subchapter II of the North Carolina General Statutes (hereinafter G.S.)). One of those justices is the chief justice, who, in addition to serving as jurist, has special authority and responsibilities related to the overall administration of justice. Supreme court justices, like all judges, must be attorneys authorized to practice law in the courts of North Carolina and may not practice law while serving as a judge. They all are elected in statewide partisan elections for eight-year terms. The chief justice is elected to the seat of chief justice.

Meeting as a body in Raleigh, the court hears oral arguments by attorneys representing the various parties in cases appealed from the lower courts. It is also authorized to meet in both Edenton and Morganton. The supreme court does not have a jury, and it makes no determinations of fact; it considers cases on the written record of the trial only, and it decides questions of law. Its opinions (decisions) are printed in bound volumes and become state law to the same extent as enactments of the General Assembly.

The supreme court primarily decides cases involving questions of constitutional law or legal questions of major significance to the state as a whole or murder cases including a sentence of death. These cases may already have been decided in the court of appeals or may come to the supreme court directly from the trial court.

The Court of Appeals

The court of appeals is composed of fifteen judges elected in the same manner and for the same term as the supreme court justices. Court of appeals judges generally sit and render decisions in panels of three. The court is authorized to sit as an entire fifteen-judge court (in other words, en banc), though as of August 2024, it had never elected to do so. The court may preside in Raleigh and at other locations within the state as permitted by the state supreme court. Like the supreme court, this court decides only questions of law, including whether a trial procedure was free of error that would have been prejudicial to the appellant.

The court of appeals was created in 1967 to relieve the supreme court of a portion of its case load, which had become more than it could reasonably handle. Unlike the supreme court (which is required to hear only certain kinds of cases), the court of appeals initially hears and decides all appealed cases, except those that go directly to the supreme court. No matter what the issue, every appellant has a right to be heard by at least one of these appellate courts, except in one instance: a defendant who pleads guilty to a criminal charge in the superior court may have his conviction reviewed only by petitioning the court of appeals for a writ of certiorari. The court of appeals then decides whether to issue the writ and hear the case. Similarly, a person appealing a court-martial proceeding may have the case reviewed only by the court of appeals.

Operation of the Appellate Courts

The supreme court is housed in the Justice Building in Raleigh, across the street from the southeast corner of the North Carolina State Capitol. The Court of Appeals Building is similarly situated, but on the southwest corner. Both courts are supported by the Supreme Court Library, housed primarily in the Justice Building, and each has a clerk, who is that court's administrative officer. The opinions of each court are prepared for publication by an appellate division reporter. Each justice or judge has two research assistants who must be law school graduates.

Vacancies often arise in the supreme court or the court of appeals other than at the end of a judge's term, usually through death or midterm retirement. In this case, the governor may fill the vacancy by an appointment effective until the next general election. At the general election, the incumbent appointee frequently runs for the office. Appellate judges may be removed by impeachment or by the appellate courts (the supreme court in the case of a court of appeals judge and the court of appeals for a supreme court justice) on recommendation of the Judicial Standards Commission, discussed later in this chapter.

Supreme court justices and judges of the court of appeals must retire by age seventy-six, and, of course, they may do so earlier. A judge retiring before age seventy-six can become an "emergency" judge who may be recalled to active service for temporary duty on the court from which he or she retired (a retired supreme court justice can also serve in a similar capacity on the court of appeals). The governor issues commissions to emergency justices and judges that are valid until the holder is seventy-six. After that age, a judge may continue to serve temporarily as a "recalled retired" judge. The compensation and jurisdiction are the same for both kinds of temporary service: $400 per day.

Figure 40.1 North Carolina Superior Court Districts (Effective January 1, 2024)

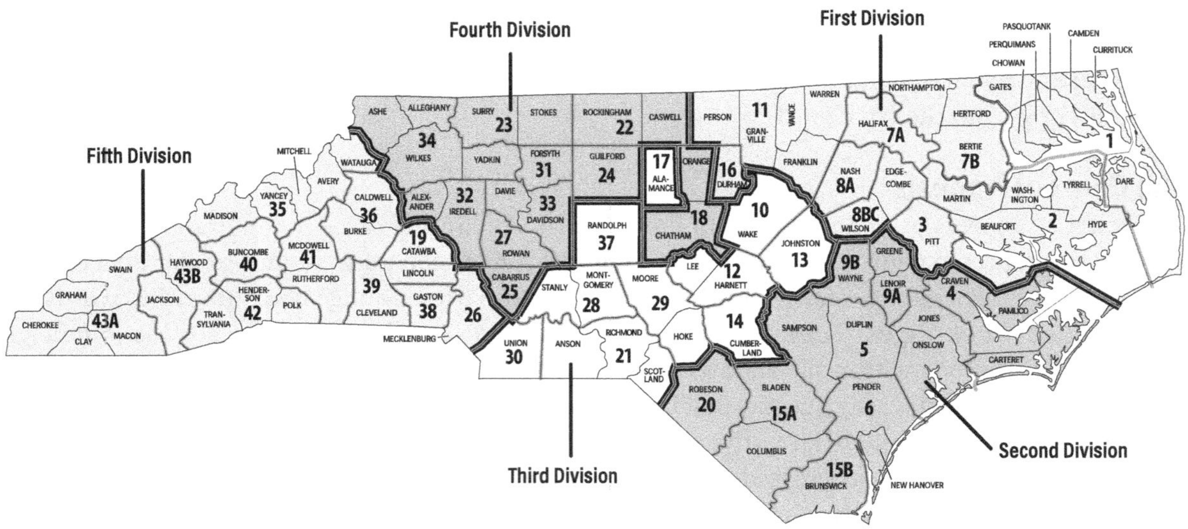

Note: Districts that have more than one letter associated with the district number (i.e. 9A, 9B) are divided into separate districts for electoral purposes. For administrative purposes, they are combined into a single district.

Superior Court Division

Organization

The Superior Court Division consists of the superior court, which is the trial court for most cases involving a jury. At least two sessions of superior court for the trial of cases involving a jury are held each year in each county; in the busiest counties, several judges conduct sessions each week. The state is divided into judicial districts and then into larger judicial divisions (G.S. Chapter 7A, Subchapter III). Superior court judges have statewide jurisdiction but must be assigned by the chief justice to particular districts for terms and sessions of court to have authority to act outside their home district.

In January 2024, there were seventy-three districts, regions that generally were established based on geographical considerations, caseload, and population. A specified number of judges must reside in and be elected from each of those districts (the number ranges from one to three). Some districts are composed of part of one county, others of a single county, others of parts of two counties, and others of several counties. Some of the districts serve only as units for election and are grouped with other districts to form a single administrative entity. Those grouped districts are called "sets of districts." The forty-eight administrative judicial districts are grouped into five divisions (see Figure 40.1).

Judges

In January 2024, there were 101 regular resident superior court judges. These judges are elected in partisan elections by voters in the districts where they live for eight-year terms. In addition, there are twenty special superior court judges. Ten are appointed by the governor and confirmed by the General Assembly. Ten are appointed by the General Assembly; five of these are nominated by the Speaker of the House, with one residing in each of the five judicial divisions, and five are nominated by the President Pro Tempore of the Senate, with one residing in each of the five judicial divisions. Six special superior court judges are designated as business court judges by the chief justice. They preside in the state's business court and are charged with hearing and deciding complex business cases. Special superior court judges, like regular resident superior court judges, serve eight-year terms. Special judges may reside anywhere in the state and may be commissioned to preside over a session of court in any county of any judicial district. In each judicial district, a regular resident judge serves as the senior regular resident superior court judge; this judge has special administrative powers and duties related to the management of the superior courts in that district. In every judicial district other than Districts 10A–F (which consists of Wake County), the judge with the most continuous service as a regular resident superior court judge (or, if two judges are of equal seniority, the older of the two) is the senior regular resident superior court judge. In Districts 10A–F, the chief justice of the supreme court designates a regular resident judge to serve as the senior regular resident superior court judge.

All superior court judges, whether resident or special judges, serve full time and may not practice law while serving as a judge. Vacancies in resident judgeships are filled by appointment of the governor until the next general election.

North Carolina's superior court judges travel more than any other group of judicial officials in the state and, indeed, more than trial judges anywhere else in the country. That is because the state constitution requires that superior court judges rotate through the districts in their divisions (Article IV, Section 11 of the North Carolina Constitution), a practice historically referred to as "riding circuit." The practice of rotation, which sometimes operates in tension with a desire for maximum efficiency, serves to insulate judges from local political pressures and to assure that justice is afforded to those who hail from outside the local community as well as to those within. The chief justice, with the assistance of the assistant director of the Administrative Office of the Courts, assigns judges to terms of court (six-month assignments) and to one-week sessions within those terms through the issuance of a master calendar. G.S. 7A-47.3(c) directs the chief justice in making those assignments to "strive" to assign each regular resident superior court judge to his or her home district for at least half of the calendar year. Special superior court judges are assigned by the chief justice to hold court in any county where needed, without regard to district of residence or rotation requirements.

Retirement rules for superior court judges are similar to those for Appellate Division justices and judges, though the retirement age is different. Superior court judges must retire at age seventy-two. Those who retire before reaching the mandatory retirement age of seventy-two can become "emergency" judges and may be assigned by the chief justice to temporary service on the superior court bench until they are seventy-two. An older judge may continue to serve temporarily as a "recalled retired" judge. The compensation ($400 per day) and jurisdiction are the same for both kinds of temporary service. A retired judge who engages in private legal practice is not eligible for this temporary service. Retired judges may serve as mediators or arbitrators and still serve as temporary judges.

Superior court judges may be removed by impeachment or by the supreme court upon recommendation of the Judicial Standards Commission (see the "Judicial Standards Commission" section, below).

Jurisdiction

Civil

Civil jurisdiction is concurrent between the two trial divisions (superior and district) of the General Court of Justice (G.S. Chapter 7A, Articles 20 and 22). The "proper" division, however, for cases that involve $25,000 or less in controversy is the District Court Division; for cases over that amount, the Superior Court Division. Normally, this $25,000 dividing line is followed, but by consent of the parties and for reasons of speed or convenience, cases may be filed and tried in the "improper" division.

Exceptions to the general rule that the amount in controversy determines the proper forum arise in certain specific subject-matter categories. For example, civil domestic relations matters (divorce and custody and support of children) are properly the business of the district court, while the superior court is the proper forum for constitutional issues, special proceedings, corporate receiverships, and reviews of certain administrative agency rulings. The clerk of superior court (rather than a superior or district court judge) handles probate of wills and appointment of guardians, and in doing so discharges duties performed by probate judges in many other states. Civil cases involving amounts not over $10,000 may, under certain conditions, be assigned to a magistrate for trial.

Criminal

The superior court hears cases involving felonies (serious crimes), misdemeanors (less serious crimes), and occasionally related infractions (noncriminal law violations such as minor traffic offenses). Misdemeanor and infraction cases are normally heard first by the district court. Because there is no jury trial right for criminal cases tried in district court, a defendant may appeal a district court conviction for a misdemeanor (and a related infraction) to superior court, where he or she may demand a jury trial. The superior court has exclusive, original jurisdiction over felonies, and felony trials occur only in the superior court. Defendants are tried by a jury of twelve.

If the charge is a felony, the process usually begins when a grand jury of eighteen members issues an indictment. A defendant may waive the indictment process, except in capital (potential death sentence) cases. A defendant also may waive the right to a jury trial, with the consent of the judge. When that happens, the judge conducts the trial, rules on motions, and renders the verdict. Trial of misdemeanors and infractions appealed from district court is de novo—that is, the case is tried anew, without regard to the original trial court proceedings. Less than 20 percent of the superior court's criminal caseload consists of such appeals from the district court.

District Court Division

Organization

The District Court Division is divided into forty-nine judicial districts (G.S. Chapter 7A, Subchapter IV). Most of these districts are established as units for elections and for court administration, except in three places (Districts 11A–B, Districts 30A–C, and Districts 10A–F). These districts are combined into three sets of districts for administrative purposes (see Figure 40.2). Like the superior court, the district court sits in the county seats. It may also convene in certain other cities and towns specifically authorized by the General Assembly. Most counties have no additional seats of court, but a few have several (a table in G.S. 7A-133 lists the additional seats).

District court judges serve an entire district. Unlike superior court judges, they do not hold court out of their district of residence unless specially assigned by the chief justice of the supreme court for a particular session of court.

Judges

As of January 2024, the General Assembly has authorized 285 district court judges. They are elected in partisan district elections for four-year terms. They must be attorneys authorized to practice law in the state of North Carolina, serve full time, and may not practice law while serving as a

Figure 40.2 North Carolina District Court Districts (Effective January 1, 2024)

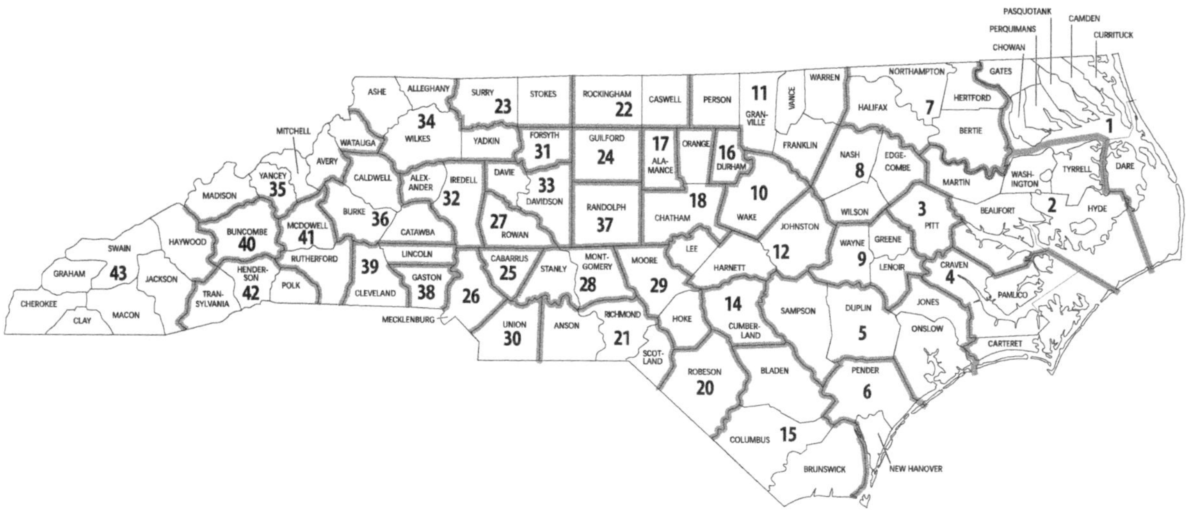

judge. The state constitution requires that judges be residents of the districts from which they are elected. While that requirement has generally been interpreted to allow residents of any county in a district to seek election for any judgeship in the district, in two districts (Districts 12 and 15) the legislature has required candidates for each judgeship to come from specified counties. In District 15, for example, only candidates from Bladen County may run for one of the judgeships assigned to that district, but voters from all three counties in that district may vote for the judgeship.

Each district has from two to twenty-one judges, depending on population and geography. Specialization by subject matter (for example, juvenile or domestic relations cases) is encouraged by law but can be achieved to a significant degree only in districts with several judges; in less populous counties, district court judges must be generalists.

The chief justice appoints one judge in each district as chief district judge. Their responsibilities include assigning themselves and the other judges in their districts to sessions of court, prescribing the times and places at which magistrates will discharge their duties, and assigning civil ("small claims") cases to magistrates for trial. Chief district judges are required to meet at least once a year to discuss mutual problems; make recommendations concerning improvement of the administration of justice; and promulgate a schedule of minor offense for which clerks of court and magistrates may accept written appearances and pleas of guilty or admissions of responsibility. These offenses are the type that a person may resolve by paying costs and a pre-set fine or monetary penalty without appearing in court.

Vacancies in the office of district court judge are filled by the governor; the appointee holds the office until the next general election. The local district bar association provides nominations to the governor, but the governor is not bound to select from that list of nominees. The mandatory retirement age for district court judges, like superior court judges, is seventy-two.

Magistrates

Magistrates for each county are appointed for initial two-year terms by the senior regular resident superior court judge based on nominations of the clerk of superior court (G.S. Chapter 7A, Article 16). Subsequent terms are for four years. Magistrates are officers of the district court. They are supervised by the chief district court judge in nondiscretionary judicial matters and by the clerk in clerical matters. Magistrates serve only in their counties of residence, subject to special temporary duty assignments by the chief district court judge. Magistrates are full- or part-time officials, as determined by the chief district judge and the Administrative Office of the Courts. Magistrate salaries, which are paid by the state, vary based on their length of service and whether they are licensed to practice law. All magistrates appointed after July 1, 1994, must (1) have a four-year degree from an accredited college or university, (2) have a two-year associate degree and four years of experience in a related field, or (3) have at least eight years' experience as a clerk of superior court or a law enforcement officer in North Carolina. During their first two-year term, new magistrates must complete a course of basic training of at least forty hours in the civil and criminal duties of a magistrate. The mandatory retirement age for magistrates is seventy-two.

The minimum number of magistrates allowed for a county is fixed by law. If the minimum quota is inadequate and funds are available, additional magistrates may be authorized by the Administrative Office of the Courts on recommendation of the chief district judge. A vacancy in the office of magistrate is filled for the remaining unexpired term in the same manner as the original appointment was made. A magistrate may be removed from office by a superior court judge following the filing of a formal complaint establishing grounds for removal (the same grounds applicable to judges) and a hearing. A magistrate may appeal an order of removal to the court of appeals.

Jurisdiction

Civil

As noted in the discussion of the superior court's civil jurisdiction, most jurisdiction of this type is held concurrently by the superior and district courts (G.S. Chapter 7A, Articles 20 and 22). Domestic relations cases are an exception, however. They are heard in the district court regardless of the amount of money involved. When large monthly child-support awards are entered or large amounts of marital assets are distributed on divorce, a district court's orders can involve millions of dollars.

Juvenile

The district court also has jurisdiction over juvenile matters. These cases concern children under the age of eighteen who are involved in either (1) the child welfare or (2) the juvenile justice systems.

The child welfare system addresses cases of children under the age of eighteen who are dependent, neglected, or abused. The children in these cases have been, or are threatened with being, harmed, and the court is seeking to protect them. The processes used are designed to promote the safety, permanency, and well-being of each child.

Juvenile justice system cases involve children between the ages of eight and eighteen who have committed acts that, if committed by adults, would be crimes or infractions. These are called juvenile delinquency cases. The most serious crimes committed by youth who are sixteen and seventeen years old either bypass juvenile court entirely and are handled in criminal court or they begin in juvenile court but are ultimately prosecuted as criminal matters. The juvenile justice system also includes cases of children who are beyond parental control, truant from school, or have run away. These are called undisciplined cases. While these are civil cases, the processes used in court include many components similar to those used in criminal cases.

All juvenile court proceedings begin with the filing of a petition (documents similar to warrants or indictments in adult criminal cases and complaints used in other civil cases). The cases are divided into two parts. First, an adjudication hearing is conducted to determine if the allegations in the case are true. If the court finds that they are true, then a less formal dispositional hearing is held to determine the appropriate action to take as a result of the adjudication. Social services staff may be involved in investigating a child welfare matter and the involved child's background before the case is heard in court. This information may be used in court to determine how best to respond to the needs of the child. Juvenile court counselors (whose functions are akin to those of a probation officer in the criminal system) complete assessments on the risks and needs of juveniles involved in the juvenile justice system. They share this information with the court to help develop a dispositional plan. The judge's authority in delinquency cases ranges from placing children on probation to confining them in secure state institutions. In abuse, neglect, and dependency cases, the judge has wide latitude in deciding how to protect children. No juvenile cases are heard by a jury.

Involuntary Commitment

The district court has jurisdiction over the involuntary commitment of mentally ill persons, inebriated individuals, and alcoholics to mental health and alcoholic treatment facilities.

Criminal

The criminal jurisdiction of the district court is limited in felony cases. Since they must be tried or otherwise disposed of in the superior court, the district court has authority only to conduct preliminary hearings to determine whether there is probable cause (that is, a good reason exists for believing the defendant is probably guilty) to bind the defendant over to the superior court for trial. In addition, with the consent of the prosecutor and defendant, a district court judge may accept a guilty plea to the two lowest levels of felonies (Classes H and I) and enter a judgment in the case. In misdemeanor and infraction cases, the district court has exclusive original jurisdiction that, with respect to some very minor offenses, it shares with the magistrate.

Magistrate

The magistrate's jurisdiction is both civil and criminal. This official's authority in criminal matters is limited to the following:

- Accepting admissions of responsibility and entering judgment for infractions for which the maximum punishment is a $50 fine.
- Accepting guilty pleas and entering judgment for certain Class 3 misdemeanors (not including the types of offenses listed immediately below).
- Accepting guilty pleas and imposing a fine fixed by a uniform statewide schedule promulgated by the Conference of Chief District Judges in cases involving minor alcohol offenses, traffic offenses, hunting, fishing, state park and recreation area rule offenses, state forest rule offenses, boating offenses, open burning offenses, and littering offenses.
- Trying worthless-check cases or accepting guilty pleas when the amount of the check is $2,000 or less.

In addition, magistrates have the important duties of issuing arrest and search warrants and setting conditions of pretrial release.

The magistrate is also authorized to try small civil claims that involve up to $10,000, including summary ejectment (landlord's action to evict a tenant) cases, on assignment of the chief district judge. The plaintiff must request that the claim be assigned to a magistrate and at least one defendant must reside in the county in which the action is filed.

The typical small claim is for recovery of personal property, for money for goods sold or services rendered, or for summary ejectment, and the parties frequently are not represented by attorneys.

Often, the claim is uncontested. Simplified trial procedures are followed. The magistrate's judgment has the same effect as that of a judge and is recorded by the clerk of superior court.

The magistrate is also authorized to perform various quasi-judicial or administrative functions. Of these, performance of the marriage ceremony is the most common; magistrates are the only judicial officials in the state who are authorized to officiate at weddings. Other authorized functions include administering oaths, verifying pleadings, and taking acknowledgments of (notarizing) instruments.

Judicial Standards Commission

The historical methods of removing judges—impeachment and joint resolution by the legislature—have not been used in North Carolina since the nineteenth century. These procedures are still authorized by Article IV of the state constitution, but that article was amended in 1973 to require the General Assembly to provide another method for the "removal of a Justice or Judge of the General Court of Justice for mental or physical incapacity interfering with the performance of his duties which is, or is likely to become, permanent" and for the censure and removal of a justice or judge "for wilful misconduct in office, wilful and persistent failure to perform his duties, habitual intemperance, conviction of a crime involving moral turpitude, or conduct prejudicial to the administration of justice that brings the judicial office into disrepute." Legislation accompanying this amendment created a Judicial Standards Commission (G.S. Chapter 7A, Article 30) composed of judges and laypersons (who may or may not also be attorneys) that is charged with investigating complaints and making recommendations to the North Carolina Supreme Court for the censure or removal of a justice or judge. The supreme court is authorized to prescribe standards of judicial conduct for justices and judges. It has adopted by rule the North Carolina Code of Judicial Conduct, consisting of seven canons that address matters including a judge's responsibility to uphold the integrity and independence of the judiciary, the standards for recusal, limitations on a judge's participation in extra-judicial activities, required financial disclosures, and permissible political activity.

The Judicial Standards Commission may issue a private letter of caution to a judge if it determines that the judge engaged in conduct that violated the Code of Judicial Conduct but that does not warrant a recommendation of discipline by the North Carolina Supreme Court. If the commission concludes that disciplinary proceedings should be instituted, or that a judge should be suspended or removed for temporary or permanent physical or mental incapacity, it conducts a confidential hearing after which it may make recommendations to the supreme court. The affirmative vote of at least five members of a commission hearing panel is required to make a recommendation to the supreme court that a judge be publicly reprimanded, censured, suspended, or removed from office. The supreme court acts as a court of original jurisdiction in reviewing such a recommendation from the commission; as such, it is not bound by the commission's findings of fact, conclusions of law, or recommendations regarding the appropriate disciplinary action. Only if the supreme court issues a public reprimand, censure, suspension, or removal do the documents associated with the matter become public.

Court-Related Personnel

District Attorneys

In criminal matters, the district attorney represents the state in the superior and district courts (G.S. Chapter 7A, Article 9). This official is elected in partisan district elections for a four-year term. In each prosecutorial district, full-time assistant district attorneys, paid by the state, serve at the district attorney's pleasure. With one exception (Johnston County), prosecutorial district lines are identical to district court lines.

A district attorney may be suspended or removed from office for misconduct or mental or physical incapacity after a hearing before a superior court judge (G.S. 7A-66).

Clerks of Superior Court

The office of the clerk of superior court is created by the state constitution, which provides that there shall be one clerk in each of North Carolina's 100 counties (Article IV, Section 9(3) of the N.C. Constitution). The clerk is elected in partisan county elections for a four-year term (G.S. Chapter 7A, Article 12). Each elected clerk hires a staff of assistant and deputy clerks and a head bookkeeper, who is paid as an assistant clerk but may be a deputy or an assistant clerk. While a clerk's office may have no fewer than five staff positions plus the elected clerk, there is no statutory maximum on the number of employees. Clerk's offices in the state's more urban counties have more than 100 staff members. Assistant and deputy clerks support the elected clerk in carrying out the duties of the office. They serve at the elected clerk's pleasure. Unlike trial and appellate judges, clerks need not be attorneys. The clerk is responsible for all clerical and recordkeeping functions of the superior and district courts for both civil and criminal cases. Thus, in each county there is only one clerk's office for the two trial courts.

The clerk is also the ex officio judge of probate and is thus the first to hear matters relating to the probate of wills and the administration of decedents' estates. In addition, the clerk has jurisdiction over the guardianship of minors and incompetent adults and is authorized to hear a variety of special proceedings, such as adoptions, foreclosures, condemnation of private lands for public use, and partitions.

A clerk may be suspended or removed from office after a hearing before the senior resident superior court judge in the county of the clerk's residence based on a determination that the clerk has engaged in willful misconduct or lacks mental or physical capacity (G.S. 7A-105).

Court Reporters

Court reporters are appointed for the superior court by the senior regular resident superior court judge in each judicial district. Compensation is set by the appointing judge, within limits fixed by the Administrative Office of the Courts. Reporters are required to record verbatim trial proceedings, including witness testimony and orders, judgments, and jury instructions by the judge. Transcripts of courtroom proceedings are required when an appeal is taken, and reporters receive a per-page fee in addition to their salaries for preparing transcripts for appellants. The reporter's original tapes, notes and other records are state property and are preserved by the clerk of superior court.

If a reporter is not available, the state will furnish electronic recording equipment on request of the senior regular resident superior court judge. The clerk of superior court is responsible for operating such equipment and for preserving the record produced, and the Administrative Office of the Courts is responsible for transcribing the record if that becomes necessary.

All civil and juvenile proceedings in district court are recorded by audio recording equipment. No verbatim records are kept of district court criminal proceedings, since they may be appealed for a new trial in superior court, which does keep these records.

Juvenile Court Counselors

A statewide system of court counselors provides intake, probation, and after-care services to juveniles in the jurisdiction of the district court. Each judicial district is assigned one or more counselors. Juvenile court counselors receive complaints when they are first filed. They complete an intake process and often have the authority to divert or close cases without sending them to court. If they do approve cases for court, they conduct risk and needs assessments of system-involved youth and provide a predisposition report to the court when a juvenile is found responsible for committing an act of delinquency. Court counselors also help the court monitor cases in which children require detention before or after a hearing, and they provide supervision when juveniles are placed on probation.

Office space for court counselors is provided by the county. Court counselors are not court system employees; they are employed by the N.C. Division of Juvenile Justice and Delinquency Prevention, which is part of the N.C. Department of Public Safety.

Probation and Parole Officers

North Carolina has a statewide correctional system, which includes adult probation officers (G.S. Chapter 15, Article 20). These officers, who supervise adult defendants placed on probation, are employees of the state Department of Adult Correction. Their salaries and program-operating costs are paid by the state, but space for local offices must be furnished by the county. The same officers supervise parolees and post-release supervisees upon their release from prison.

Guardians ad Litem

In child abuse, neglect, and dependency cases, parents who cannot afford an attorney are entitled to a court-appointed attorney. The county department of social services represents the state's interest, advocating through its attorney for what it believes is in the best interests of the child. Even with the involvement of these advocates, judges presiding over these cases benefit from having input from an advocate who is focused on the child's best interest and who is independent of the agency responsible for implementing court orders. A statewide guardian ad litem program fills that gap by providing advocates who represent the interests and protect the legal rights of involved children (G.S. Chapter 7B, Article 12). The program applies a team approach. Coordinators recruit volunteers to work with the children and hire attorneys to represent the children in the court case.

The county must provide office space for the coordinator and any other employees of the guardian ad litem program.

Community Service Program Personnel

In some criminal cases, judges require convicted defendants to perform community service for a specified number of hours as a condition of probation. The state Department of Adult Correction administers a community service program that assigns offenders to appropriate local work sites to perform this service. Department personnel assigned to the judicial district report back to the court on the offender's compliance. These personnel are state employees, but their office space must be provided by the county.

Supporting Staff for Court Officials

Court managers assist judges with their administrative responsibilities, providing services ranging from clerical to case management support. Family court or drug court personnel or arbitration or custody mediation staff work in locations where those programs are established; they provide professional, clerical, and case management support for the operation of these court programs. Most of these employees are paid by the state, but in some instances their salaries are paid from grants or by a local government. In 2013, the General Assembly eliminated all state support for drug courts, so any drug courts are now funded from other sources.

Bailiffs and Security Personnel

Courthouse security is primarily the responsibility of the sheriff, whose office is funded by the county (G.S. 17E-1). Bailiffs, employed by the sheriff, provide security inside the courtroom. The sheriff also is responsible for the care and custody of the jail and for transporting incarcerated persons to and from the court.

The county also plays a role beyond simply allocating funds for security-related personnel and equipment to the office of the sheriff. Providing adequate security in and around the courthouse involves facilities planning and maintenance, which is a county responsibility.

Public Defenders and Representation of Indigents

Defendants accused of crimes for which confinement is likely and who are financially unable to employ an attorney to represent them are entitled to such services at state expense (G.S. Chapter 7A, Subchapter IX). Persons in this financial circumstance are referred to as being indigent. The state also must provide an attorney to an indigent person in other statutorily enumerated circumstances including juvenile delinquency proceedings, involuntary commitment and incompetency proceedings, and proceedings to terminate parental rights. The Office of Indigent Defense Services (IDS) is responsible for establishing, supervising, and maintaining a system for providing legal representation to those defendants and others entitled to counsel at state expense. IDS is an independent office administratively housed within the Administrative Office of the Courts. It is administered by the Director of Indigent Defense Services and includes the Commission on Indigent Defense Services (the IDS Commission), a thirteen-member body responsible for determining the way legal services are provided to indigent persons. Representation is most frequently provided through one of the state's twenty-seven public defender districts, which cover sixty of the state's one hundred counties. In those districts, a public defender administers an office staffed with assistant public defenders, investigators, and other staff who serve at his or her pleasure. The public defender is appointed by the senior resident superior court judge of the district to a four-year term. IDS provides office equipment and supplies, and the state pays the salaries. The county must provide office space. For a list of the counties served by these public defenders, see Table 40.1.

In districts without a public defender's office, indigent defendants are represented by private attorneys appointed by the court. Those attorneys generally are paid by the state for that service on a per-case, hourly basis. Private attorneys also may be assigned to represent indigent defendants in public defender districts when the public defender's office has a conflict of interest or an overload of cases.

A statewide appellate defender is charged with representing indigent persons whose convictions are appealed. The IDS Commission appoints the appellate defender to a four-year term.

Table 40.1 North Carolina Public Defender Districts

Public Defender District	Counties
1	Camden, Chowan, Currituck, Dare, Gates, Pasquotank, Perquimans
2	Beaufort, Hyde, Martin, Tyrell, Washington
3	Pitt
4	Carteret, Craven, Pamlico
5	Duplin, Jones, Sampson
6	New Hanover, Pender
7	Bertie, Halifax, Hertford, Northampton
10	Wake
13	Johnston
14	Cumberland
15	Bladen, Brunswick, Columbus
16	Durham
17	Alamance
18	Chatham, Orange
20	Robeson
21	Hoke, Scotland
24	Guilford
26	Mecklenburg
30	Union
31	Forsyth
32	Alexander, Iredell
38	Gaston
39	Cleveland, Lincoln
40	Buncombe
41	McDowell, Rutherford
42	Henderson, Polk, Transylvania
43	Cherokee, Clay, Graham, Haywood, Jackson, Macon, Swain

The appellate defender, in turn, may appoint assistant attorneys and staff as authorized by IDS. IDS funds the operations of the office, including providing space, equipment, and salaries.

A defendant who is provided representation at state expense and who is convicted may be ordered to repay the state for the costs of his or her representation. In every such case, attorney fees for assigned counsel are a civil judgment against the convicted defendant. One way in which such a judgment may be collected is through garnishment of a person's state income tax refund. The entire amount of attorney fees is rarely collected, but the state does recover a small percentage of its costs each year (8 percent in 2021–22).

The IDS Commission manages the budget for indigent defense and promulgates standards related to various aspects of the indigent defense system. Funds for indigent defense are provided by the General Assembly. In 2021–22, the budget to provide these services (public defenders and assigned counsel) was $141 million.

Jury Selection

Each county has a three-member jury commission charged with preparing a master list of potential jurors to be used for grand juries (the bodies that determine whether probable cause supports the issuance of an indictment) as well as for trial (petit) juries (G.S. Chapter 9). That master list, which is drawn from the list of registered voters and persons with driver's license records supplied to the county by the Commissioner of Motor Vehicles, must be prepared at least every two years and may be compiled annually. One member of the jury commission is appointed by the senior regular resident superior court judge, one member by the clerk of superior court, and one member by the board of county commissioners. Jury commissioners serve two-year terms. The board of county commissioners determines their compensation, which, along with the jury commission's operating expenses, is paid from the county's general fund.

To acquire a pool of prospective jurors for a particular session of court, the clerk of superior court or his or her designee prepares a randomized list of names from the master list. Those persons are then summoned by the sheriff for jury duty.

To be qualified to serve as a juror, a person must

- be a citizen of the state and a resident of the county in which the juror serves,
- have not served as a juror during the past two years,
- be at least eighteen years old,
- be physically and mentally competent,
- understand the English language,
- have not been convicted of a felony for which the person's citizenship rights have not yet been restored, and
- not have been adjudged mentally incompetent.

No one is automatically exempt from jury duty though a person may, for compelling personal hardship or for reasons of public welfare, health, or safety, be excused from service. Excuses may be granted by the chief district court judge or his or her designee (another district court judge, the clerk, or judicial support staff).

There is no maximum age for jury service. A prospective juror who is seventy-two years old or older may request to be excused without appearing personally. The excuse is not automatic, and a person over age seventy-two may be required to serve.

A person who is a full-time student at an out-of-state educational institution may request to be excused from jury service. If the session of court for which the full-time student is summoned is scheduled during a period of time when the student is taking classes or exams, the person must be excused upon making a proper request supported by documentation showing his or her enrollment at the out-of-state institution.

Trial jurors usually serve for one trial or one day, whichever is longer. Jurors receive $12 for the first day of service and $20 per day afterwards. A person who serves as a juror for more than five days in any two-year period receives $40 per day for each day of service after the fifth day.

Grand jurors usually serve for one year, and generally are on duty for no more than the first day of a session of superior court for the trial of criminal cases. In districts where criminal sessions occur weekly, the grand jury typically convenes every few weeks. The typical pattern for the selection of grand jurors is for nine new grand jurors to be selected each six months. A grand juror receives $20 per day.

The superior court uses a twelve-person jury in both civil and criminal cases. The district court also uses a twelve-person jury in civil cases only; criminal cases are tried by a district court judge without a jury.

Table 40.2 Basic Civil Court Costs, January 2025 (G.S. 7A-305)

	Civil	Amount*
Magistrates	General Court of Justice Fee	$80.00
	Facilities Fee	$12.00
	Telecommunications and Data Connectivity Fee	$4.00
	Total	**$96.00**
District Court	General Court of Justice Fee	$130.00
	Facilities Fee	$16.00
	Telecommunications and Data Connectivity Fee	$4.00
	Total	**$150.00**
Superior Court	General Court of Justice Fee	$180.00
	Facilities Fee	$16.00
	Telecommunications and Data Connectivity Fee	$4.00
	Total	**$200.00**
There is a $30 service fee for each item of civil process served by the sheriff.		

*Updated civil court costs are available on the North Carolina Judicial Branch website at www.nccourts.gov/documents/publications/current-court-costs.

Administrative Office of the Courts

The Administrative Office of the Courts, with its central office in Raleigh, handles the administration of the statewide court system (G.S. Chapter 7A, Article 29). Its director is appointed by the chief justice. The director is a nonjudicial officer, responsible for a variety of administrative functions including preparing and administering the Judicial Department's budget, fixing the number of employees in the respective clerks of court offices, supervising the statewide guardian ad litem system, prescribing uniform forms, records, and business methods for the clerks' offices, keeping statistics, and representing the courts in the legislature and other forums.

The Judicial Department budget for fiscal year 2022–23 was approximately $713 million (not including funds for IDS).

Costs, Fees, and Fines

The state collects costs and fees in civil and criminal cases, amounts that defray a portion of the expense of operating the courts (G.S. Chapter 7A, Article 28). In civil actions, special proceedings, and administration of estates, there are three cost items: a General Court of Justice fee, which accrues to the state for financing the courts generally; a telecommunications and data connectivity fee, credited to the Court Information Technology Fund; and a facilities fee, which is distributed to counties and municipalities. In criminal actions, there are five items in the uniform bill of costs. In addition to the three fees applicable in civil cases, there is a law enforcement officers' retirement and insurance benefits fee, disbursed to the state treasurer, and a fee for legal representation to indigent defendants, which is disbursed to IDS. The basic costs in each case vary with the nature of the action or proceeding and with the court in which it is tried. Tables 40.2 (civil) and 40.3 (criminal) provide the most recent fee levels.

Table 40.3 Basic Criminal Court Costs, January 2025 (G.S. 7A-304)

	Criminal	Amount*
District Court (including criminal cases before magistrates)	General Court of Justice Fee	$147.50
	Facilities Fee	$12.00
	Telecommunications and Data Connectivity Fee	$4.00
	LEO* Retirement/Insurance	$7.50
	Indigent Defense Fee	$5.00
	Total	**$176.00**
Superior Court	General Court of Justice Fee	$154.50
	Facilities Fee	$30.00
	Telecommunications and Data Connectivity Fee	$4.00
	Law Enforcement Officers (LEO) Retirement/Insurance	$7.50
	Indigent Defense Fee	$5.00
	Total	**$201.00**
There is a $5 service fee for each arrest or service of criminal process.		

*Updated criminal court costs are available on the North Carolina Judicial Branch website at www.nccourts.gov/documents/publications/current-court-costs.

Besides these basic cost items, in any particular case additional expenses—such as a fee for service of process, a fee for failure to appear, a fee for notice of hearing, and fees for laboratory testing and expert testimony—may be incurred. These charges are assessed along with the basic costs against the party liable for them. In criminal cases, costs may be assessed against a defendant only upon his or her conviction. The costs assessed for criminal actions in district court also are applicable to infractions; thus, a person adjudicated responsible for an infraction (typically a minor traffic violation) may be ordered to pay court costs.

The state constitution (Article IX, Section 7) provides that fines, penalties, and forfeitures (which differ from costs) are owed to the public schools in the county involved. A *fine* is the monetary penalty imposed by the sentencing judge as part or all of the punishment when a defendant is convicted of a crime. A *penalty* is the monetary payment ordered for commission of an infraction. A *forfeiture* occurs when a defendant who has been released from confinement pursuant to a secured bond fails to meet the conditions it specifies (usually a court appearance), and the bond is forfeited. Forfeitures also may include the proceeds from vehicles seized and sold when driven by persons convicted of alcohol, impaired driving, or drug offenses. In fiscal year 2022–23, the fines, penalties, and forfeitures collected by the courts throughout the state totaled nearly $36 million.

Allocation of Financial Responsibility for the Court System

Operating expenses of the Judicial Department are borne by the state (G.S. Chapter 7A, Subchapter VI). These include salaries and travel expenses of all judges, district attorneys, clerks and their assistants, magistrates, court reporters, public defenders, and guardians ad litem. Also included are the books, supplies, records, and equipment in all these officials' offices and the fees of all jurors and witnesses for whom the government is responsible. This arrangement is a direct result of the court reform efforts of the 1950s and 1960s. Before then, salaries and other operating expenses for most trial court officials (clerks, lower court judges, justices of the peace, and so forth) were the responsibility of local governments. Correspondingly, most fees collected accrued to local governments or directly to court officials as their compensation. The current arrangement reflects the fundamental policy decisions made during this court reform effort that all court officials should have the same duties and be paid the same salaries. As a result, citizens should receive roughly the same services from the courts wherever they live. This commitment to uniformity, reflected in an original policy of requiring all operational funding to come from the state, has, since the late 1990s, begun to erode somewhat. Acting on the request of local court and local government officials, the legislature has authorized local governments to supplement the operations of the courts serving their counties or cities, and in some instances they have funded temporary positions in the office of the district attorney, the public defender, or the clerk.

In the court reform effort of the 1960s, the primary responsibilities counties (and a few cities) retained for court operations was to provide "adequate" physical facilities for the courts. That duty has not changed since. Courtrooms are the most obvious of such facilities, but this responsibility also extends to the provision of office and storage facilities, parking, and related spaces for judges, the clerk of superior court and the clerk's staff, district attorneys, and magistrates. In addition, most of the ancillary personnel described in this chapter also are entitled to county office space, either by virtue of a specific statute or because they are part of the court system. The obligation to provide facilities includes the responsibility for furniture (but not equipment) and the cleaning and maintenance of the courthouse.

Questions often arise about whether particular expenses should be covered by the county or by the state. The issue usually concerns whether a particular item is an operating expense or part of a facility. Is an audiovisual system for use in courtrooms an operating expense or part of the facility? (It's probably an infrastructure item and thus part of the facility.) What about court security equipment like metal detectors? (Security is the sheriff's responsibility, and if the equipment is permanent, it is part of the infrastructure.) Sometimes the classification is clear—furniture and fixtures are part of the facility, and computers and specialized court equipment are operating expenses. But often the distinction is not clear and is usually resolved through negotiation.

Sometimes the question arises as to whether a facility or the furnishings are "adequate." In such cases, the initial determination is made by the county when it allocates and maintains the space allotted to the courts, pursuant to its general authority to control the use of its property. When court officials or others question the adequacy of the facilities, they almost always do so informally, and usually the issue can be settled informally as well. But if officials or citizens believe the county's allocation or maintenance of facilities is inadequate, the North Carolina Supreme Court determined in In re *Alamance County Court Facilities*, 329 N.C. 84 (1991), that courts have inherent power to direct county commissioners to ameliorate those deficiencies. Even in these circumstances the county retains discretion as to how to fashion that remedy.

When the state assumed the costs of operating the trial courts in the 1960s, a facilities fee was preserved as a local government source of revenue to help offset the continuing costs paid by the county for court operations. This fee (collected as a standard court cost) is distributed to counties with a proportionate share going to municipalities for cases heard in municipally owned district court facilities. The total amount collected from this fee has declined significantly in recent years, dropping from more than $20 million in 2008–09 to less than $12 million in 2022–23. The amounts appropriated to even the largest county, Mecklenburg ($1,027,946), do not cover the entire cost of operating a court facility and would never support the cost of construction of new facilities.

Additional Resources

Commission for the Future of Justice and the Courts in North Carolina. "Without Favor, Denial or Delay: A Court System for the 21st Century" (December 1996), www.sog.unc.edu/sites/www.sog.unc.edu/files/WithoutFavorDenialOrDelayAll.pdf.

Crowell, Michael. "The Significance of a Trial Judge's Commission" (UNC School of Government, June 2012), www.sog.unc.edu/sites/default/files/additional_files/Judge%27s%20comm%27n%20for%20webpage%20June%2012.pdf.

North Carolina Administrative Office of the Courts. 2022–2023 *North Carolina Judicial Branch Annual Report*, www.nccourts.gov/assets/documents/publications/2022-2023-North-Carolina-Judicial-Branch-Annual-Report-web.pdf.

———. *2022–2023 Statistical and Operational Report of Budget Management and Financial Services*, www.nccourts.gov/assets/documents/publications/2022-23-Statistical-Operational-Report-Budget-Financial.pdf.

———. *North Carolina Court Security Guidelines* (September 1998), www.sog.unc.edu/sites/default/files/reports/AOC%20Court%20Security%20Guidelines%201998.pdf.

Turner, Hannah. "North Carolina 2024 Public Defender Expansion." *NC Criminal Law: A UNC School of Government Blog* (April 3, 2024), nccriminallaw.sog.unc.edu/north-carolina-2024-public-defender-expansion/.

Chapter 41

Registers of Deeds

Charles Szypszak

Charles Szypszak is a School of Government faculty member who specializes in real estate matters.

County governments perform the usually inconspicuous but essential function of maintaining public records of real estate ownership. The responsibility for this function is entrusted to registers of deeds. The records for which they are responsible also include marriage records and other vital records.

Register's Office

The county's voters elect a register of deeds every four years. The county commissioners set the register's budget, the hours during which the office is to be open, and the number of employees.[1] Registers have sole authority to select and supervise the office staff.[2] Although much of what registers do is considered to be performance of what the law calls "ministerial" duties that involve following clear rules, registers also exercise discretionary judgment in many ways, such as when they manage their offices and hire and supervise assistants and deputies. They also regularly must make decisions about actions for which the rules are not entirely clear.

The register's permissible fees are set by statute. The prescribed fees are based on the type of record involved with designated amounts and guidelines for certified and uncertified copies.[3] Most receipts are deposited into the county's general fund, while statutorily designated portions must be remitted to or set aside in various state or local accounts, including a nonreverting county "automation enhancement and preservation fund" (AEPF) for computer and imaging technology needs in the register's office.[4] Various venues in the state offer valuable training and education for registers

1. Sections 153A-92, 153A-94(b), and 161-8 of the North Carolina General Statutes (hereinafter G.S.).
2. G.S. 153A-103.
3. G.S. 161-10(a)(11).
4. G.S. 161-11.3.

and their assistants and deputies. The North Carolina Association of Registers of Deeds regularly hosts educational sessions at conferences and regional workshops. The School of Government at the University of North Carolina, Chapel Hill, offers basic and advanced programs for registers of deeds as well as an array of relevant courses for local government officials. State departments, including the North Carolina Secretary of State, State Archives, and Vital Records, offer training opportunities in matters for which a register is responsible. Participation in educational opportunities like these is important not only for handling the job's basic responsibilities but for keeping up with changes in the law, regulations, and technology.

Real Estate Records

The register's most consuming responsibility is recording and maintaining real estate records, including deeds, deeds of trust and mortgages, financing statements for real estate–related property, and maps and plats. No conveyance of real estate, contract to convey, option to convey, or lease of more than three years is valid against third parties unless it is recorded with the register in the county in which the real estate is located.[5] North Carolina has a "race" type of recording statute, in which the first to record prevails in a contest of priorities, with only very narrow exceptions.[6] Thus, the act of recording and accessibility to the records are vital and can have a dispositive legal impact on real estate transactions.

Recording Requirements

Registers are directed to record only after determining "that all statutory and locally adopted prerequisites for recording have been met."[7] Documents submitted for recording must meet statutorily prescribed format requirements relating to size, margins, and legibility.[8] Registers must also review an instrument that requires an acknowledgment or proof to determine if the instrument "appears to have been proved or acknowledged before an officer with the apparent authority to take proofs or acknowledgments, and the proof or acknowledgment includes the officer's signature, commission, expiration date, and official seal, if required."[9] By statute, a "register of deeds is not required to verify or make inquiry concerning any of the following: (1) The legal sufficiency of any proof or acknowledgment. (2) The authority of any officer who took a proof or acknowledgment. (3) The legal sufficiency of any document presented for registration."[10]

Registers may accept electronic documents requiring acknowledgments if they can confirm that the acknowledgments have been completed.[11] Registers can accept electronic documents from two kinds of submitters: the government or a "trusted submitter." Someone could become a "trusted submitter" only by agreeing to the register's requirements in a memorandum of understanding. The submitter is responsible for complying with the originality requirements. The statutes do not require any register to accept electronic submissions nor do they require registers who decide to allow electronic documents to accept them from anyone other than the submitter authorized by the register.

5. G.S. 47-18.
6. *Id.*
7. G.S. 161-14(a).
8. G.S. 161-14(b).
9. G.S. 47-14(a).
10. *Id.*
11. G.S. 47-14(a1), (a2).

Documents submitted by trusted submitters must include the following statement, which will appear on the public record:

> Submitted electronically by _________(submitter's name) in compliance with North Carolina statutes governing recordable documents and the terms of the submitter agreement with the _________(insert county name) County Register of Deeds.

The record will therefore show who was entrusted to comply with the recording requirements for documents submitted electronically by trusted submitters. The statute makes clear that the register may rely on the trusted submitter's representation of compliance with the requirements.[12]

If a document originates in electronic form, submitters are responsible for complying with North Carolina statutes and rules pertaining to electronic recording and notary certifications. They are also responsible for not electronically recording a document that originated on paper unless the paper document would have been recordable in that form. For example, a submitter could not properly scan a copy of a document and submit it electronically if the document is not recordable in its paper form. Also, a submitter could not properly record an altered document that does not conform to the paper document rerecording requirements.

Registers may accept electronically submitted plats only if they are submitted by a governmental unit or instrumentality or a trusted submitter authorized to do so by the county's registers, as is the case for other electronically submitted instruments.[13]

Maps and Plats

Registers also record plats, which must meet size, reproducibility, and other requirements.[14] Registers may accept plats submitted electronically.[15] Required certifications must appear on the digitized image of the document as it will appear on the public record. If the plat is submitted by a trusted submitter, it must include the same statement required for other documents submitted electronically. The plat image must comply with the other applicable laws and rules that prescribe recordation.

With few exceptions, plats and maps must contain prescribed surveyor certificates.[16] County commissioners are required to designate one or more persons to serve as review officers to review maps and plats submitted for recording.[17] Maps and plats must be examined by the review officer unless they are certified to be of existing parcels, streets, structures, or natural features, or they are control surveys, proposed public utility easements, maps of a municipal boundary or annexation, highway right-of-way plans, transportation corridor maps, or certain types of illustrative maps attached to deeds if they meet statutory requirements, including a prescribed legend.[18] Review officers check maps and plats for required information and for subdivision approvals if required; their responsibilities do not supplant the authority of local land use boards.

Financing Statements

Financing statements are used to create security interests in property not classified as real estate under state law. These statements are governed by the Uniform Commercial Code. Since July 1,

---

12. *Id.*
13. G.S. 47-30.
14. *Id.*
15. G.S. 47-30(o).
16. *Id.*
17. G.S. 47-30.2.
18. G.S. 47-30.

2001, registers are custodians only of financing statements pertaining to real property–related collateral, which includes fixture filings (personal property that has become attached to real estate, such as a furnace), as-extracted collateral (oil, gas, minerals), and timber to be cut.[19] Financing statements usually are submitted on standard forms. To be recorded with the register they must identify the debtor, the secured party, and the collateral; indicate that they cover real property–related collateral; provide a description of the real property to which the collateral is related; and, if the debtor is not the real property owner, state the name of the record owner.[20] The grounds on which a register may reject a financing statement submitted for recording are limited to submissions by a method not authorized, such as electronically to a registry not so equipped, failure to pay the required fee, and omission of specifically required information.[21] Registers index financing statements and subsequent related instruments, such as statements continuing or terminating the security interest, in the Consolidated Real Property Index of all the real estate records.

Excise Tax

Registers collect an excise tax on conveyances of real estate interest except conveyances by federal, state, county, and municipal governments and their instrumentalities. The tax rate is $1 on each $500 or fractional part thereof.[22] When a tax is owed, it must be paid when the instrument is presented for recording. Exceptions from the tax include transfers made by operation of law, such as a survivor's acquisition of full ownership after the death of a tenant by the entireties or a joint tenant; transfers by will or intestacy; leases; and any transfer that is for no consideration.[23] This state excise tax applies to transfers when someone assumes another's debt and when property is exchanged because consideration is deemed paid for the transfer. It also applies to a transfer by deed at foreclosure or in lieu of foreclosure, even if the grantee is the secured creditor.[24] The tax also applies to timber deeds.[25] A few counties have an additional excise tax that applies to the same instruments as the state excise tax but not to conveyances to a secured creditor as the result of foreclosure or in lieu of foreclosure.[26]

Recordkeeping and Indexing

Registers maintain records sequentially in order of recording. Records are made available for public use in a variety of formats including electronic and are accessible on the office's website.

All real property records are indexed in the Consolidated Real Property Index.[27] Indexes are arranged alphabetically by the names of the parties to the instrument—one index for grantors, such as sellers, and one for grantees, such as buyers—with references to the book and page where the identified instrument can be viewed. They are subdivided into human and nonhuman names. Registers must comply with the Minimum Standards for Indexing Real Property Instruments, which are regulations approved by the North Carolina Association of Registers of Deeds and the North Carolina Bar Association and adopted by the North Carolina Secretary of State. These rules contain detailed requirements for index components, name formatting, and sort order, among other things.

---

19. G.S. 25-9-501(a).
20. G.S. 25-9-502.
21. G.S. 25-9-516(b).
22. G.S. 105-228.30.
23. G.S. 105-228.29.
24. G.S. 45-45.2.
25. G.S. 105-228.30(a).
26. G.S. 45-45.2.
27. G.S. 147-54.3.

A few counties maintain a parcel identifier number (PIN) index, in which parcels of real property are assigned unique numbers and references are provided to each instrument affecting the parcel. The county may choose to designate the PIN index as its official index.[28]

When registers index real estate instruments, they use the information in the instrument to determine the capacity and names of the parties and other information to be indexed. Unlike public filings received in many other government offices, no forms or cover pages are required to assist registers with indexing, and real estate instruments can be drafted in an infinite variety of formats. To facilitate document indexing and make instruments easier to locate, drafters should

- clearly indicate the names of the parties to the document and their capacities as grantor or grantee;
- include all party names in the forefront of the document (not in the middle or in attachments);
- clearly separate from the name to be indexed any additional information about prior names, affiliates, or underlying documents;
- avoid adopting names for real estate title that include symbols, unusual spacing, or punctuation that will force unfamiliar alphabetizing;
- ensure names appear consistently throughout the document and in signatures;
- use a single document title from the common document types listed in the local rules; and
- provide a clear, brief description of the property for indexing reference.

Redaction and Presentation Refusal

Once registered, a real estate document is part of the permanent public record and a register may not remove it from that record. If a document is registered that causes unlawful harm, a court may issue an order that declares the document void or otherwise addresses its legal effect, and that order when recorded is linked to the original harmful record with the subsequent instrument indexing method. The statutes contain only one authorized basis for removal of information from a registered real estate record: redaction of personal identification numbers from Internet records.[29] Individuals may request redaction of their Social Security, driver's license, state identification, passport, checking account, savings account, credit card, or debit card number or a personal identification code or password contained in the public records that are displayed on the register's Internet website and available to the general public. Redaction applies only to the identified personal information—not the entire record—and only to records on the Internet website. A request should be legibly signed by the person to whom the information belongs or by someone with demonstrated legal authority for such a person, such as someone with an applicable power of attorney, and it may be submitted in person or by mail, facsimile, or electronic transmission. It must specify the relevant document and the nature and location within the document of the information to be redacted. Access to inspection of the requests for redaction is restricted to the register of deeds, the clerk of court, their staff members, or to another party by court order. Registers are authorized but not required to redact such information from the Internet website without a request.[30]

By statute, registers are authorized to reject instruments that seem to be falsely claiming a lien against an owner or beneficial interest holder, and the law requires certain actions if this occurs. The

28. G.S. 161-22.2.
29. G.S. 132-1.10(f).
30. G.S. 132-1.10(f1).

statute provides that "if a register of deeds has a reasonable suspicion that a lien or encumbrance is materially false, the register of deeds may refuse to record the purported lien or encumbrance" and that the register will not "be liable for recording or the refusal to record a purported lien or encumbrance" according to this law.[31] This law is permissive and not mandatory—it does not impose a duty on registers to review documents claiming liens or encumbrances and to judge whether they appear to be valid. If a register refuses to record an instrument based on this law, the presenter may record a "Notice of Denied Lien or Encumbrance Filing" on a form that the N.C. Secretary of State has approved. Any interested person, including the presenter, then has ten business days to file a court action to challenge the rejection.

Marriage Records

The register of deeds issues marriage licenses.[32] Couples may apply for licenses on statutorily prescribed forms supplied to registers by the Vital Records division of the North Carolina Department of Health and Human Services.[33] North Carolina law requires the register to determine whether the applicants are "authorized to be married in accordance with the laws of this State," and the register must make a "reasonable inquiry" into whether the applicants meet the requirements.[34] The form, once completed by the register's office, becomes the marriage license and must be completed and returned with a record of the marriage ceremony.[35]

The register of deeds keeps a record of marriage licenses issued and the returns showing the solemnization.[36] The register indexes the licenses alphabetically by last name of the intended husbands and wives. The index entries must include the spouses' full names, the ceremony dates, and the locations of the original licenses and returns.[37] The register keeps one copy of returned licenses and submits another to North Carolina Vital Records on a monthly basis.[38] These are public records.[39] An uncertified copy may be obtained by anyone who pays the required fee, and a certified copy may be obtained by a subject of the license or the subject's spouse, sibling, direct ancestor or descendant, stepparent or stepchild, a person seeking information for a legal determination of personal or property rights, or an authorized agent, attorney, or legal representative of the aforementioned individuals.[40]

Other Records

Other commonly used records for which the register is custodian include birth and death certificates, military discharges, and records of assumed business names.

31. G.S. 14-118.6.
32. G.S. 51-8.
33. G.S. 51-16.
34. G.S. 51-17.
35. G.S. 51-16.
36. G.S. 51-18.
37. *Id.*
38. G.S. 130A-110(a).
39. G.S. 130A-110(d).
40. G.S. 130A-93(c); G.S. 130A-110(c).

Birth and Death Certificates

The register files and preserves copies of birth and death certificates furnished by the local health director.[41] County birth and death certificates are public records, and copies must be provided to anyone upon request. The statutes prohibit registers from providing a copy of a vital record to someone seeking his or her own record but who is known to be deceased, in which case attempted fraud is obvious.[42] Certified copies may be obtained by the subject and the subject's spouse, sibling, direct ancestor or descendant, or stepparent or stepchild; an authorized agent, attorney, or legal representative of any of these individuals; and someone "seeking information for a legal determination of personal or property rights."[43] A funeral director or funeral service licensee may also obtain a copy of a death certificate.[44] The State Registrar handles new birth certificates in the case of adoption and may direct that the county remove an adopted child's prior certificate.[45]

Registers assist individuals who seek to make corrections to the state's official Vital Records office in Raleigh. Registers do not make these changes. They collect and forward the required documentation to N.C. Vital Records for its review and implementation through the state's electronic system. To fulfill their role, registers must adhere to the state office's current regulations and guidelines.

Military Discharges

Registers are required to keep a separate, permanent book for official discharges from the armed forces.[46] Public access to copies of or information on the discharges is restricted to discharges received since January 1, 2004, and to discharges kept in separate books prior to that date and that have been on file for less than eighty years.[47] Restricted access is limited to the veteran; the veteran's widow or widower; and the veteran's agents and representatives authorized in writing by the veteran, the veteran's widow or widower, someone appointed by a court to represent the veteran, or the deceased veteran's executor. Additionally, access to such restricted records is permitted to authorized agents of the N.C. Department of Military and Veterans Affairs, the U.S. Department of Veterans Affairs, the Department of Defense, a court official with an interest in assisting a veteran or a deceased veteran's beneficiaries, and representatives of the North Carolina State Archives.[48] Registers may refuse to accept a discharge if it is submitted by someone other than the aforementioned persons and authorities or if it is not an original, a carbon copy, or a photocopy issued or certified by a state or federal agency.[49] No fees may be charged for filing the documents or for providing certified copies of discharge records to authorized parties. The register may charge standard fees for uncertified copies.[50]

Assumed Business Names

Any person or partnership that uses an assumed name in North Carolina and any limited partnership, limited liability company, corporation, or other business entity that uses a name other than

41. G.S. 130A-97; G.S. 130A-99.
42. G.S. 130A-93(g).
43. G.S. 130A-93(c), (c1).
44. *Id.*
45. G.S. 48-9-107; G.S. 130A-93(d).
46. G.S. 47-109.
47. G.S. 47-113.2.
48. G.S. 47-113.2(b)(1).
49. G.S. 47-113.2(d).
50. G.S. 47-113.2(n), (o).

the organizational name filed with the Secretary of State must also file a certificate of assumed business name with a register of deeds before engaging in business in the state using that name.[51] The filing can be made in one county in which business is done even if business is conducted in multiple or all counties in the state. Initial filings for assumed business names, and amendments and withdrawals of them, are presented at a register of deeds office, which transmits the data and images to a central database that the North Carolina Secretary of State maintains and that can be searched by the public on the Internet. Registers also maintain indexes of the filings made in their counties. As has always been the case in North Carolina, although someone using an assumed business name in the state must file a certificate, this filing does not by itself give rights to the name.

Notary Commissions

Registers administer the oath of office to notaries public who live or work in the registers' counties and who have been qualified by the Secretary of State for commissioning. Registers maintain the official records of the notary commissions issued in their counties.[52]

Additional Resources

Szypszak, Charles. 2021. *North Carolina Guidebook for Registers of Deeds*. 11th ed. Chapel Hill: UNC School of Government.

51. G.S. 66-71.4(a).
52. G.S. 10B-9.

Chapter 42

Elections

Robert P. Joyce

Robert P. Joyce is a School of Government faculty member whose areas of specialization include the law related to elections.

County boards of elections conduct all elections in North Carolina. These boards conduct elections for federal, state, county, and city offices, as well as statewide and local referendums. They conduct elections for special districts, such as school administrative units, sanitary districts, and fire districts.

County boards handle voter registration applications, determine the eligibility of applicants, establish precincts and voting places, select and purchase voting equipment, publish election-related notices, employ voting-place workers, oversee election-day activities, canvass the returns, declare the election results, issue certificates of election to the winners, and hold hearings on challenges to voters and candidates, as well as on election protests.

The county board of elections must act within the regulations and directions of the State Board of Elections, and almost all of the county board's actions are subject to review by the state board.

With one large exception and one small exception, the operating costs of elections are paid through appropriations from the county commissioners. City elections are the large exception. Cities must reimburse counties for the costs incurred by the county boards of election in conducting city elections. The small exception is that a minor portion of expenses related to statewide elections is covered by state funds.

According to figures compiled by the State Board of Elections, as of October 2024, there were 7.8 million registered voters in North Carolina (compared with 6.5 million in late 2014), of whom 31.3 percent were registered as Democrats (down from 42.4 percent in 2014), 29.9 percent were registered as Republicans (down from 30.7 percent in 2014), and 37.8 percent—the largest group—were unaffiliated (up from 26.6 percent in 2014). The rest were primarily Libertarians. Of the registered voters, 63.8 percent were white (down from 70.9 percent in 2014) and 19.7 percent were African American (down from 22.5 percent in 2014).[1]

Kinds of Elections Authorized

The General Statutes authorize two kinds of elections: (1) elections of candidates to office and (2) certain specified *special elections*. A special election is any kind of referendum on any question other than electing a candidate to office. The range of special elections is limited. (See the discussion of special elections below.)

Election of Candidates to Office

Elections in which voters choose individuals to fill public offices are the most common kind of election. In most cities, elections for municipal offices—mayors and city councils—are held in odd-numbered years (2025, 2027, etc.), while elections for most other offices are held in even-numbered years (2026, 2028, etc.). Elections in even-numbered years include those for federal offices (president and vice president, U.S. Senate and House of Representatives), state executive offices (governor and council of state), state legislative offices (N.C. Senate and House of Representatives), judicial offices (justices and judges of the N.C. Supreme Court, N.C. Court of Appeals, superior court, and district court; clerks of superior court; and district attorneys), and county offices (county commissioners, registers of deeds, sheriffs, and soil and water conservation commissioners). Most school board elections are held in even-numbered years, though some are held in odd-numbered years. Elections for sanitary district governing board members are held in odd-numbered years.[2]

The general election schedule is found in Article 1 of Chapter 163 of the North Carolina General Statutes (hereinafter G.S.).

Partisan Primaries and Elections

Most federal, state, and county elections are conducted on a partisan basis. Candidates are nominated by political parties and run under their party labels. Two parties—Democratic and Republican—have traditionally and consistently met North Carolina's statutory definition of a *political party*, meaning that their candidates for governor or president have in each election received at least 2 percent of the total vote for governor or president[3] in the state (for many years the requirement was 10 percent).[4] The nominees of these parties are chosen by the voters through primary elections held before the general election. The winner of the primary is the nominee of the party

1. *See* N.C. State Board of Elections, *North Carolina Voter Registration Statistics*, vt.ncsbe.gov/RegStat/Results/?date=10%2F26%2F2024 (note that these figures are regularly updated and might be different from the ones in this chapter).

2. In the first third of the 2020s, municipal elections in a significant number of cities were moved, by local act of the General Assembly, from odd-numbered years to even-numbered years.

3. *See* Chapter 163, Section 96(a) of the North Carolina General Statutes (hereinafter G.S.).

4. A party not recognized in North Carolina can gain recognition if it demonstrates that a candidate nominated by the party appeared on the general election ballot in at least 70 percent of the states in the previous presidential election.

and appears on the general election ballot. If no candidate receives at least 30 percent of the vote (plus one vote) in a primary—a total termed a "substantial plurality"—the second-place candidate may request a second primary between the top two.[5] The winner of the second primary becomes the nominee. Voters affiliated with a party are eligible to vote in that party's primary, though a party may allow unaffiliated voters to participate in its primary, a choice made on an election-by-election basis. Counties bear the costs of primaries, as they do for other elections. The statutes governing primary elections are found at G.S. 163-104 through -119.

A new political party may be formed through the circulation of a petition, signed by registered voters equal to at least one quarter of one percent (0.25 percent) of the total number who voted in the most recent general election for governor. In its first election after recognition by the State Board of Elections, the new party chooses its nominees at a party convention, not by a primary election, and those nominees are entitled to appear on the ballot for federal, state, and local offices. If the party fails to receive at least 2 percent of the vote for governor or president, its recognition is terminated, and it must go through the petition process again. The statutes governing political parties are found at G.S. 163-96 through -99.

An individual who wishes to run in a partisan election as an unaffiliated candidate may do so (if registered as unaffiliated) by circulating a petition. For state offices, the petition must be signed by registered voters equal to at least 1.5 percent of the total number who voted in the most recent general election for governor. For county or district offices, including General Assembly seats, the petition must be signed by at least 4 percent of the registered voters in the county or district. The statute governing unaffiliated candidacy is found at G.S. 163-122.

Nonpartisan Elections

As noted above, most elections to fill offices are conducted on a partisan basis, but three kinds of offices are typically filled through nonpartisan elections. The first consists of the municipal offices of mayor and city council members. A few North Carolina cities do, in fact, have partisan elections for municipal offices, which are conducted like state and county partisan elections. The overwhelming majority of municipalities, however, have nonpartisan elections. The second kind of office filled through nonpartisan elections is school board membership. Most school board elections are nonpartisan, though there are some exceptions. The third kind is soil and water conservation commissioner seats. At one time, judicial elections—for district court judges, superior court judges, and appellate judges—were nonpartisan, but they are now conducted on a partisan basis.

In a nonpartisan election, candidates are not nominated through a partisan primary. All candidates run without party identification. Candidates may choose to identify with a party if they wish, and parties are free to endorse candidates. What is nonpartisan is the way in which election officials conduct the election, not necessarily the way in which candidates and parties run their campaigns.

In addition, there are three kinds of nonpartisan elections: nonpartisan plurality elections, nonpartisan primaries and elections, and nonpartisan elections and runoffs. Each of these is discussed in more detail below.

Types of Nonpartisan Elections

Nonpartisan Plurality Elections

In this type of election, there is only one vote, held on general election day. The candidate who receives the most votes wins, even if no one secures a majority. When multiple candidates are competing for a single seat, the highest vote-getter wins. If two or more seats are contested as a

5. The second primary is sometimes colloquially referred to as a "runoff."

group (such as in an at-large city council election) and there are more candidates than available seats, the number of candidates equal to the number of open seats is elected, based on the highest vote totals. The nonpartisan plurality election is the most common form of nonpartisan election.

Nonpartisan Primaries and Elections

In this type of election, on the fourth Tuesday before general election day, a vote is held to narrow the field to two candidates for each position to be filled (or, if several seats are being filled as a group, to narrow the field to twice as many candidates as there are open seats). If only one or two candidates file for a single seat (or fewer than twice as many candidates file for two or more seats voted on as a group), the candidates who have filed are automatically nominated, and no primary is held. If a primary is held, the two candidates receiving the highest number of votes for a single office are declared nominated (even if one receives a majority and the second-place finisher receives a minority), and twice the number of candidates as there are seats in a group election are nominated. The election is then held on general election day, with the highest vote-getters winning the seats.

Nonpartisan Elections and Runoffs

In these elections, an election is held on general election day only if a runoff is needed. On the fourth Tuesday before general election day, an election is held among all candidates. The candidate receiving a majority (calculated in group elections by dividing the total votes cast by the number of seats and then dividing by two) wins. If no candidate receives a majority, the highest vote-getter is declared elected unless the second-highest vote-getter requests a runoff by noon on the Monday following the election. The runoff is then held between these two candidates on general election day. In multiple-seat group elections, candidates receiving a majority win.[6] If not enough candidates receive majorities to fill all seats, the highest vote-getters without majorities—equal to the number of remaining seats—are declared elected unless the next-highest vote-getters (equal in number to the remaining seats, or some of them) demand a runoff. The runoff is then between the highest non-majority vote-getters and the candidates requesting a runoff.

City Council and Mayoral Elections

Under the uniform municipal elections law (G.S. Chapter 163, Subchapter IX), a city may elect its governing board and mayor[7] using one of four methods: partisan elections, nonpartisan plurality elections, nonpartisan primaries and elections, and nonpartisan elections and runoffs. In all four methods, candidates file for election between noon on the first Friday in July and noon on the third Friday in July. General election day is the Tuesday after the first Monday in November of odd-numbered years. Under the first three methods, an election is always held on that day; under the nonpartisan election and runoff method, an election may not be required.

Types of City Elections

Partisan Elections

Of the 550 or so incorporated cities in North Carolina, only a handful use partisan elections. Notably, that handful includes Charlotte and Winston-Salem, which together have more than a million citizens.

---

6. In a group election, it is possible for more candidates to receive a majority than there are open seats. In such cases, the candidates with the highest number of votes, equal to the number of open seats, are elected.

7. Under G.S. 160A-101(8), a city may choose to have its mayor selected by the city council from among its members, rather than elected by the voters.

In cities with partisan elections, candidates file to run for party nomination in primary elections held on the sixth Tuesday before the November general election. A second primary, if necessary, is held on the third Tuesday before the general election. On general election day, party nominees appear on the ballot. In addition, candidates may appear on the ballot as unaffiliated by submitting a petition signed by 4 percent of the city's voters. Results of partisan municipal elections are determined in the same manner as partisan state and county elections.

Nonpartisan Plurality Elections

The vast majority of the state's cities use nonpartisan plurality elections, the simplest of the four election methods. Virtually all towns with small populations use this method, though some larger towns do as well. The most populous of these is Wilmington, with approximately 123,000 residents.

Nonpartisan Primaries and Elections

Only twenty-four cities in North Carolina use the nonpartisan primary and election method, though this group includes Burlington, Durham, Goldsboro, Greensboro, Hickory, and High Point, which together have a population of almost a million.

Nonpartisan Elections and Runoffs

Fifteen cities in the state use the nonpartisan election and runoff method, including Cary, Fayetteville, Raleigh, and Rocky Mount, with a combined population of almost a million. Under this method, elections are held on general election day only if a runoff is necessary.

While the majority of cities use the nonpartisan plurality method, about a third of the state's population lives in cities using one of the other three methods.

The statutes governing municipal elections can be found in G.S. 163-279 through -306.

School Board Elections

In North Carolina, there are 115 school administrative units, one for each of the state's 100 counties, plus fifteen additional units, often referred to as *city* school units. These city school units are not part of city government, are typically not coterminous with city boundaries, and operate with the same powers and authority as county school units. While there were once many more city school units, the number has decreased over time as these units merged with county units. The most recent merger, in 2005, combined the Cleveland County, Shelby city, and Kings Mountain city units, reducing the total number of units from 117 to the current 115.

Each of the 115 school administrative units is governed by a local board of education, typically called the *school board*. In sixty of these units, elections are held on a nonpartisan basis, while the remaining fifty-five are partisan. Of those fifty-five, thirty-eight switched to partisan elections between 2014 and 2024. Like city elections, described above, nonpartisan school board elections use a mix of methods—simple plurality, primary and election, and election and runoff.

By general law, nonpartisan school board elections are held in even-numbered years during the partisan primaries, typically in May. The statute also stipulates that newly elected school board members take office in December, creating a six-month gap from the time a member is elected to the time he or she takes office. To address this issue, many school boards have secured local acts from the General Assembly. In some cases, the local act moves the elections to odd-numbered years, aligning with municipal elections that occur in the fall, closer to the December office-taking date. In other cases, the local act keeps the elections in even-numbered years but moves them from May to the November general election.

The statutory provision governing school board elections is found at G.S. 115C-37.

Judicial Elections

Judges at all state court levels—district court, superior court, court of appeals, and supreme court—are elected on a partisan basis, like most other elected offices. For a few years beginning in the mid-1990s, judges were elected in nonpartisan elections, starting with superior court judges in 1996, district court judges in 2001, and appellate judges in 2004. However, effective with the 2018 elections, the General Assembly restored judicial elections to a partisan basis.

Special Elections

Special elections are those held for purposes other than electing candidates to office. They may involve statewide issues, such as the ratification of a constitutional amendment or a statewide bond referendum. More commonly they address local ballot questions, such as local bond referendums, alcoholic beverage control (ABC) elections, and referendums on restructuring city or county government (such as changing the number of governing board members or shifting from at-large to district elections).

Calling Special Elections

Special elections are called in a variety of ways, almost all of which are set by state law. One common kind of special election—ABC referendums—may be called as a result of a petition drive or at the request of the governing board of a city or county.[8] Similarly, referendums on changing the structure of city government (such as increasing or decreasing the number of city council members) may be called through a petition or by resolution of the city council itself.[9] Corresponding referendums on changing the structure of county government (which are much less common) may only be called by the county commissioners.[10]

Bond referendums are perhaps the most common kind of special election. Most new general obligation bond issuances must be approved by the voters. These referendums are typically called by the governing board issuing the bonds.[11]

Numerous other kinds of special elections are authorized by the General Statutes but are seldom used. For instance, county commissioners may call a referendum to authorize property tax levies above the normal limit of $1.50 per $100 valuation[12] or to approve a special supplemental school tax.[13] Other types of special elections include elections

- to change the structure of county government (G.S. 153A-58);
- to levy a local sales tax (G.S. 105-465, -484, and -498);
- to levy a sales tax for transportation (G.S. 105-511.2);
- for municipal incorporations (G.S. 120-172);
- for school unit mergers (G.S. 115C-67);
- for city–county consolidation (G.S. 153A-405; 160B-18);
- for a unified city/county government (G.S. 153A-473);
- to create mountain ridge protection districts (G.S. 113A-214);
- to create mosquito control districts (G.S. 130A-353);

---

8. *See* G.S. 18B-601.
9. *See* G.S. 160A-101 through -111.
10. *See* G.S. 153A-58 through -64.
11. *See* G.S. 159-50 through -61.
12. G.S. 153A-149(e).
13. G.S. 115C-501.

- to levy taxes for hospital districts (G.S. 131E-45);
- to create airport districts (G.S. 63-80);
- for airport district bonds (G.S. 63-87);
- for water and sewer authority contracts (G.S. 162A-14);
- for inclusion in a metropolitan water district (G.S. 162A-35);
- for inclusion in a sewerage district (G.S. 162A-68);
- to create/abolish soil and water conservation districts (G.S. 139-5 and -13);
- for soil and water conservation district land-use regulations (G.S. 139-9);
- to levy watershed improvement district taxes (G.S. 139-39);
- to raise the property tax rate above the set limit (G.S. 160A-209 and -542; 153A-149);
- to levy a supplemental school tax (G.S. 115C-501);
- to levy a supplemental community college tax (G.S. 115D-33);
- for certain community development activities by cities (G.S. 160A-456);
- for certain community development activities by counties (G.S. 153A-376);
- to levy taxes to supplement revenue bond projects (G.S. 159-97);
- to levy a public transportation authority special tax (G.S. 160A-583);
- for the sale, lease, or discontinuation of city-owned enterprises (G.S. 160A-321);
- to levy rural fire protection district taxes (G.S. 69-25.1);
- for various actions related to sanitary districts (G.S. 130A-80 through -83); and
- for involuntary annexation (G.S. 160A-58.64).

With few exceptions, special elections may only be conducted at the same time as regular primary or general elections.[14]

Limits on Calling Special Elections

City or county officials may sometimes wish to hold a "special referendum" or "straw vote" on a controversial issue. Generally, they are not permitted to do so. Only elections specifically authorized by state statute or by local act of the General Assembly may be held. As then-Justice Sam Ervin of the North Carolina Supreme Court stated in *Tucker v. State Board of Alcoholic Control*, "There is no inherent power in any governmental body to hold an election for any purpose. In consequence, an election held without affirmative constitutional or statutory authority is a nullity, no matter how fairly and honestly it may be conducted."[15] If a county wishes to hold a vote on where to locate a landfill, or if a city wants to vote on creating a beautification district, that county or city must first receive authorization from the General Assembly through a local act. Without such authorization, the vote simply may not be held.

In some states, citizens may, through a petition drive, force an election on issues such as recalling an elected official (a recall election) or adopting or repealing an ordinance (initiative and referendum). However, such provisions do not exist in the North Carolina General Statutes. A few cities have them through local acts of the General Assembly, but no counties have them.

Registration and Voting

To vote in any election in North Carolina, a person must be qualified and registered to vote.

---

14. *See* G.S. 163-287.
15. 240 N.C. 177, 180 (1954) (citations omitted).

Qualifications for Voting

To be qualified to vote in North Carolina, a person must be a U.S. citizen, must be at least eighteen years old by the time of the election (a person who is seventeen at the time of the primary but will be eighteen by the general election may vote in the primary), must have resided in the state and precinct for thirty days, and must not be a convicted felon (unless citizenship rights have been restored). The residency requirement can be confusing. "Residence" means more than just living in a place; it means making it one's home, with the intention to stay there long-term, not just temporarily. For most people, identifying their residence is straightforward, but for some, such as temporary workers or college students, it may be more difficult. The statutes governing voter registration are found in G.S. 163-54 through -90.3.

The North Carolina Constitution contains two additional qualifications (in Article VI) for voting, but they are no longer enforced because they have been found to be unconstitutional under the United States Constitution. One requires a person to have resided in the state for one year before registering to vote.[16] The other mandates that a person "be able to read and write any section of the Constitution in the English language"[17] to register.

Voter Registration

North Carolina uses permanent voter registration, meaning citizens need to register only once to vote in all elections. Voters remain registered and eligible to vote unless they move out of the county, die, or are convicted of a felony.[18] Voter registration applications may be submitted to the county board of elections by mail, electronically, or at a driver's license or public assistance office.[19] Registration can be done at any time during the year, but applications must be submitted by the twenty-fifth day before an election to vote in that election. Late registrants may not vote until subsequent elections.[20] A person who moves from one county to another must reregister, but anyone who relocates within the county need only notify the board of elections of the change of address.[21]

When applying to register to vote, citizens indicate their party affiliation or choose to be listed as unaffiliated.[22]

Absentee Ballots

Absentee voting is available for all federal, state, and county elections and is allowed in city elections if the city council adopts a resolution to permit it. Once a city council makes this decision, it remains in effect until rescinded.[23]

Early Voting

Until the early twentieth century, in-person voting on election day was the only option for North Carolina voters. In 1917, absentee voting was introduced to allow voters who were ill, disabled, or unable to be present on election day to vote. The process was cumbersome, however. Voters

---

16. Andrews v. Cody, 327 F. Supp. 793 (M.D.N.C. 1971), *aff'd*, 405 U.S. 1034 (1972).

17. Another provision of the North Carolina Constitution that has been held to be unconstitutional—and so is not enforced—disqualifies from office "any person who shall deny the being of Almighty God." *See* Op. of N.C. Att'y Gen. to Mr. Clyde Smith, Deputy Sec'y of State, 41 Op. N.C. Att'y Gen. 727 (1972); Gaston Cnty. v. United States, 395 U.S. 285 (1969).

18. G.S. 163-82.1(c).

19. *See* G.S. 163-82.6, -82.19, -82.20.

20. G.S. 163-82.6.

21. G.S. 163-82.15.

22. G.S. 163-82.4(c).

23. *See generally* G.S. Chapter 163, Article 20.

requested absentee ballots by mail, and once approved, the ballots were sent to them. Voters then marked the ballots and returned them to the elections officials by mail.

In 1977, the General Assembly began expanding absentee voting, eventually leading to "one-stop, no excuse, satellite absentee voting." That type of convenient in-person absentee voting came to be commonly called "early voting." In 2023 the General Assembly amended the relevant statutes so they now refer to this type of in-person voting before election day as "early voting" and no longer characterize it as "absentee" voting at all.

Here's how it developed. In 1977, the legislature amended the absentee ballot laws to permit a person to come to the county board of elections office and, in one procedure, to apply for absentee ballots and mark the ballots. If elections officials subsequently approved the application, they counted the ballots. This "one-stop" absentee voting, like all absentee voting, applied only to individuals who were eligible under the law to vote by absentee ballot because they were ill or disabled or would be away.

In 1999, the General Assembly authorized "no-excuse" absentee voting in even-year general elections, meaning anyone could vote by absentee ballot—through the mail or at the board of elections one-stop site—for any reason. That same year, the General Assembly authorized counties to establish one-stop absentee voting sites in locations around the county, not just at the board of elections office. With that change, voters in the county who wished to vote by no-excuse absentee ballot had their choice of where to go to vote.

By 2001, no-excuse absentee voting was available in all elections, with one-stop voting sites in designated locations throughout the county. It could be said that "early voting" was by then in place.

In 2001, the General Assembly defined the early voting period to begin on the third Thursday before the election and end on the Saturday before. Counties could choose to include evenings and weekends during the eighteen-day early-voting period.

In 2007, the legislature allowed "same day registration" at one-stop sites during the early voting period, letting unregistered individuals apply to register and vote at the same time. The application would be checked before the final counting of ballots and, if approved, the ballot would be included. However, in 2013, the General Assembly eliminated same-day registration, though a federal court order blocked enforcement of this change.[24] As of this writing, the court's injunction remains in place, allowing same-day registration at early voting sites.

Voter Identification Requirement

Historically, North Carolina voters were not required to show identification at the polls, except in certain cases. Voters were required only to state their identity. It has long been a felony—the most serious level of crime—to "impersonate falsely another registered voter for the purpose of voting in the stead of the other voter."[25]

Beginning in 2013, a series of legislative actions required the presentation of photo ID at the polls, but those acts were struck down by the courts. Eventually, voters approved a referendum requiring voter identification, and subsequent legislation was accepted by the courts. Photo identification is now required for voting in North Carolina.

24. *See* S.L. 2013-381 and NAACP v. McCrory, 831 F.3d 204 (4th Cir. 2016).
25. G.S. 163-275(1).

The State Board of Elections

By statute, the State Board of Elections has "general supervision over the primaries and elections in this State."[26] That provision, G.S. 163-22, establishes the framework for the administration of elections in North Carolina: the state board has general supervisory power, while the county boards conduct the elections. The statutes outlining the powers and structure of the state board are found in G.S. 163-19 through -28.

Selection and Organization

The five members of the State Board of Elections are appointed by the state auditor in the spring following their auditor's election—that is, in 2025, 2029, 2033, and so on. No more than three members of the board may belong to the same party, so as a practical matter the three-member majority will always be from the auditor's party. The auditor chooses the members from lists of names submitted by the Republican and Democratic parties. No member may serve more than two consecutive terms.[27] From 1901 until legislation enacted in 2024, the appointments to the state board were made by the governor. Legislation in December of that year moved the appointment authority from the governor to the auditor. As of this writing, litigation has been filed challenging the change in appointment authority.[28]

The board's office, located in Raleigh, is led by a full-time executive director.[29]

Duties

The State Board of Elections has overall responsibility for elections.[30] It appoints all county election board members (from lists provided by the parties), conducts training sessions for them and for the county directors of elections, decides which voting equipment may be used, instructs county boards on which records to maintain, specifies how ballots should be printed, hears protests concerning the conduct of elections, and performs various other duties to ensure that elections run smoothly and properly throughout the state.

A chief duty of the state board involves challenges to how particular elections have been conducted. Sometimes called "election protests" or "election contests," these challenges are usually first heard by the county board of elections and may be appealed to the state board if the protester is not satisfied. The state board may also investigate election conduct independently. During an investigation, it may take control of local election records. If irregularities are found to have affected the outcome, the board may invalidate an election anywhere in the state and order a new one. It may also remove any local election official who has acted improperly.[31]

---

26. G.S. 163-22(a).
27. G.S. 163-19.
28. In 2017, 2018, and 2023, the General Assembly enacted provisions limiting or removing the governor's authority to appoint members of the state board. None of those enactments survived court challenges that asserted, in part, that they limited the governor's power in violation of the constitutional principle of separation of powers. The litigation challenging the transfer of the authority from the governor to the auditor is based, at least in part, on the same constitutional principle.
29. *See* G.S. 163-26, -27.
30. The powers and duties of the state board are set out in G.S. 163-22.
31. *See* G.S. 163-182.9 through -189.12.

County Boards of Elections

Each of the state's 100 counties has a five-member board of elections. Four members—two from one party and two from the other—are appointed by the state board from names submitted by the state chairs of the Democratic and Republican parties. The fifth member, who serves as chair, is appointed by the state auditor.[32] Because the state board is appointed by the auditor, the majority on each county board is also from the auditor's party. Elected officials, candidates and their close relatives, campaign managers and treasurers, and political-party officials may not serve on a county board.

County board members serve two-year terms, with appointments made in the summer of odd-numbered years.

County boards meet at certain times for specific purposes, such as appointing and training precinct officials, considering absentee ballot applications, counting absentee ballots, and canvassing and declaring election results. Additional meetings are held as needed.

The statutes defining the powers and structure of the county boards are found in G.S. 163-30 through -37.1.

Duties

The county boards of elections conduct all elections. Their duties fall into two categories. The first consists of administrative duties: the board employs a director to manage its office, chooses other office staff, appoints voting place officials, registers voters, determines precinct boundaries, establishes polling places, orders voting equipment, advertises elections, accepts candidate filings, prepares and prints ballots, issues absentee ballots, supervises the counting of votes, and handles other tasks related to voter registration and conducting elections. The second category involves policy-making or quasi-judicial (court-like) duties. The board hears challenges to voter registrations, evaluates the sufficiency of petitions, declares election results, hears protests about election irregularities, addresses complaints about election officials, and issues certificates of election (which allow winning candidates to take office). In all of its duties, the county board is subject to the state board's rules and supervision, but the primary responsibility for ensuring that elections are properly conducted rests at the county level. The powers and duties of county boards of elections are outlined in G.S. 163-33.

Directors of Elections

Each county board has a director of elections. The board chooses a candidate for the position and submits its recommendation to the state board's executive director, who makes the formal appointment. The county director is responsible for supervising board employees, ordering supplies, estimating expenses, maintaining records, and handling the many tasks associated with conducting elections. Although only a few specific duties are spelled out in the statutes, the county board assigns other responsibilities to the director as it sees fit. The board may delegate much of its work to the director, except for its policy-making and quasi-judicial duties. It may not, for example, delegate the responsibility for hearing challenges to voter registrations.

The county board cannot dismiss the director on its own. A majority of the board may recommend dismissal to the state board's executive director. The county director must be informed of the reasons for the recommendation and given an opportunity to respond. The executive director

32. This authority in the auditor results from legislation that was enacted in 2024 and, at the time of this writing, is being challenged in court. See the related discussion in the State Board of Elections section, above.

makes a final decision on dismissal, unless the state board chooses to review the matter. If the state board does take up the issue, it holds a hearing and makes a final decision.

The chief statute governing the role of the county director is G.S. 163-35.

Other Employees

In addition to a director, the county board of elections may approve the employment of a deputy county director and other office employees as needed. The statutes are clear that the board is responsible for hiring and firing these employees, but the law is less clear regarding other aspects of employment, such as working hours, grievance procedures, and job classification. Legally, the county board of elections controls the number of employees it hires and the pay for each employee. As long as the board does not exceed the salary amount appropriated by the board of county commissioners, the elections board determines both the number of employees and their pay levels.[33] However, because all funds for the board of elections are appropriated by the county commissioners, they can, in practice, strongly influence the number of employees, their pay, and other employment conditions if they choose. In some counties, the board of elections and the board of commissioners have addressed the lack of statutory clarity by entering into a memorandum of agreement that outlines how the county's personnel policies, grievance procedures, pay plans, and so on will apply to elections board employees. This agreement can, of course, be amended by the parties.

The limited statutory guidance on the status of elections board employees is found in G.S. 163-33(10), which grants the county board the power to "appoint and remove the board's clerk, assistant clerks, and other employees."

Voting Place and Registration Officials

The county board of elections divides the county into precincts. It establishes a voting place for each precinct, and, according to a plan approved by the state board of elections, sets sites for early voting around the county. Each election-day precinct and early voting site is staffed by a chief judge and two judges of election. The elections board may also appoint voting place assistants to assist the chief judge and judges.

The board of elections appoints the chief judge and two judges, from names submitted by the county political party chairs, to serve two-year terms. No more than two of these three officials may belong to the same party. For many years, the law has required that these officials be residents of the precinct in which they will serve. On occasion, however, party chairs and boards of elections have had difficulty finding residents willing to serve in some precincts. Under G.S. 163-41, when necessary, the board of elections may appoint county residents who do not live in the precinct to serve as chief judge or judge. A similar provision applies to precinct assistants.[34]

Election law sets minimum wages for precinct officials working at the polls and for those attending the instructional meeting before each election. Otherwise, the pay for voting place officials is at the discretion of the board of elections and the county commissioners.[35] In practice, pay varies by county, with the minimum being the state minimum wage ($7.25 per hour in 2024). Precinct and registration officials may only accept payment for election-related services from the board of elections.

---

33. The North Carolina Court of Appeals so held in *Graham County Board of Elections v. Graham County Board of Commissioners*, 212 N.C. App. 313, 324 (2011), saying that "county boards of commissioners have no authority to determine the number of county board of elections employees if those employees can be compensated within the budget established by the county commissioners."

34. *See* G.S. 163-42.

35. *See* G.S. 163-46.

County Boards Conducting City Elections

County boards of elections conduct city elections as they do federal, state, and county elections. Cities must "reimburse the county board of elections for the actual cost involved in the administration" of a city election.[36]

County Board Budget

County boards of elections are subject to the Local Government Budget and Fiscal Control Act.[37] The elections board is required by statute to "prepare and submit . . . a budget estimating the cost of elections for the ensuing fiscal year."[38] Almost all county board funds come through appropriations from the county commissioners, with a small amount provided by the state for statewide referendums and expenses related to the statewide voter registration computer system.[39]

Many expenses of the county elections board are governed by state law or regulation, including minimum pay for board members and precinct officials. The kinds of records to be maintained, the specifications for certain supplies, the required notices, the number of ballots that can be printed, the hours polls must be open, the days the elections board office must remain open, the kinds of voting booths allowed, the forms that must be available to the public, and various other matters that affect the county board's budget are all set by statute or by regulations of the State Board of Elections. The state board determines which voting machines may be selected by the counties, the county commissioners decide whether to purchase them, and the county elections board chooses a specific model.

Most of the elections board's expenses—such as maintaining an office and conducting regularly scheduled elections for public officials—are predictable. However, not all expenses can be anticipated. For example, when preparing its budget, the elections board may not know whether citizens will petition for a liquor election, whether a voting rights lawsuit will require changes to election dates, or whether the legislature will increase the pay for precinct officials. Expenses for these unforeseen circumstances, which may be substantial, could be outside the board's control and may require a supplemental appropriation from the county commissioners.

Campaign Finance Regulation

North Carolina law sets limits on who may contribute to candidates for office and political committees. In general, no one (other than the candidate, certain family members, and the state executive committees of recognized political parties) may contribute more than $6,400 per election to any candidate or committee.[40] This limit is adjusted for inflation each year. Contributions over $50 may not be in cash, businesses may not make contributions, and contributions may not be anonymous. The law also sets requirements for expenditures by candidates and committees. Expenditures over $50 may not be in cash, and all expenditures must be clearly identified with their purpose.[41]

To ensure compliance with these regulations and inform voters about the sources of support for candidates, candidates and committees must file regular reports of contributions and expenditures.

36. G.S. 163-284(b).
37. *See* G.S. 159-7 through -38.
38. G.S. 163-33(11).
39. *See* G.S. 163-11 through -13.
40. G.S. 163-278.13.
41. G.S. 163-278.14.

For federal races, reports are filed with the Federal Election Commission;[42] for state, legislative, and judicial races, they are filed with the state board;[43] and for county and city races, they are filed with the county board of elections.[44]

At the county level, the county elections board is responsible for maintaining a list of candidates and committees, notifying them of upcoming report filing deadlines, receiving and reviewing reports for apparent compliance, making reports available for public inspection, and sending reminders if reports are late.

A candidate may file a certification with the county board stating that their campaign will not receive or spend more than $1,000. As long as the campaign stays under that limit, the reporting requirement is waived.[45]

If a candidate or committee fails to file a report, or if a filed report shows a potential violation of campaign finance laws, the county board of elections must report the matter to the state board, which may impose civil penalties or refer criminal matters to the appropriate district attorney for possible prosecution.[46]

Additional Resources

Joyce, Robert P. *The Precinct Manual 2014.* Chapel Hill: UNC School of Government, 2014.

42. G.S. 163-278.30.
43. G.S. 163-278.9.
44. G.S. 163-278.40A.
45. G.S. 163-278.10A.
46. G.S. 163-278.22.

PART 9. Education

Chapter 43

The Governance and Funding Structure of North Carolina Public Schools

Kara A. Millonzi

Kara A. Millonzi is a School of Government faculty member who specializes in local government and public finance law.

The importance of public education was recognized in North Carolina's first constitution in 1776. Specifically, Article XLI, Section 41 provided that "a school or schools shall be established by the legislature, for the convenient instruction of youth, with such salaries to the masters, paid by the public, as may enable them to instruct at low prices; and, all useful learning shall be duly encouraged and promoted in one or more universities." The constitution thus required the General Assembly to establish schools staffed by teachers paid from public funds. The legislature took its first step toward carrying out that mandate in 1825 when it created the Literary Fund as a source of revenue for public schools. Public schools began to function as a statewide system in 1839.

The contours and scope of that public education system have evolved over time. The current state constitution provides that North Carolinians "have a right to the privilege of education, and it is the duty of the State to guard and maintain that right."[1] It further commands the General Assembly to provide "for a general and uniform system of free public schools, which shall be maintained at least nine months in every year, and wherein equal opportunities shall be provided for all students."[2]

The North Carolina Supreme Court has interpreted these provisions to guarantee "every child of this state an opportunity to receive a sound basic education in our public schools."[3] This interpretation has arisen out of a long-running funding dispute, commonly referred to as the *Leandro* litigation. The case began in the mid-1990s as a fight over funding disparities among counties but has since evolved into an argument about what it means to provide each child with the opportunity for an adequate, or "sound basic," education.[4]

In 1997, the court described the elements of a sound basic education as follows:

- sufficient ability to read, write, and speak the English language and a sufficient knowledge of fundamental mathematics and physical science to enable the student to function in a complex and rapidly changing society;
- sufficient fundamental knowledge of geography, history, and basic economic and political systems to enable the student to make informed choices with regard to issues that affect the student personally or affect the student's community, state, and nation;
- sufficient academic and vocational skills to enable the student to successfully engage in post-secondary education or vocational training; and
- sufficient academic and vocational skills to enable the student to compete on an equal basis with others in further formal education or gainful employment in contemporary society.[5]

To remedy what the court found to be deficiencies in meeting this constitutional standard, at least for some students, in 2004 the court charged the state with responsibility for assuring (1) that every classroom is staffed with a competent, certified, well-trained teacher; (2) that every school is led by a well-trained, competent principal with the leadership skills and ability to hire and retain competent, certified, and well-trained teachers; and (3) that every school is provided, in the most cost-effective manner, the resources necessary to support effective instruction within that school so that all children, including at-risk children, have an equal opportunity to obtain a sound basic education.[6]

---

1. N.C. Const. art. I, § 15.
2. N.C. Const. art. IX, § 2(1).
3. Leandro v. State, 346 N.C. 336, 346 (1997).
4. *See, e.g.*, Hoke Cnty. Bd. of Educ. v. State, 358 N.C. 605 (2004).
5. *Hoke Cnty. Bd. of Educ.*, 358 N.C. 605.
6. *Hoke Cnty. Bd. of Educ.*, 358 N.C. at 636.

Whether or not the State of North Carolina is meeting its responsibility to ensure that every student is given an opportunity to receive a sound basic education is the subject of ongoing judicial interpretation and legislative debate. The current public school system is the product of a patchwork of efforts by the state to adapt to changing economics, demographics, and policy prerogatives.[7] It involves an intricate division of policy and funding responsibilities among state and local entities. Each entity plays an integral part in carrying out the constitutional mandate to provide a public education.

This chapter discusses the structure and funding of elementary and secondary schools. Part I explains the governance scheme for the public school system and reviews the roles, responsibilities, and authorities assigned to the various state and local government entities, with special emphasis on the role of county governments.[8] Part II describes the funding scheme for public schools, focusing mainly on a county's funding responsibility, and part III sets forth the local budgeting process. Finally, part IV briefly discusses the structure and funding of charter schools and the role they play in public education.

I. Current Governance Structure of Public Schools

The state constitution assigns shared responsibility for public education to the General Assembly, the State Board of Education, and the superintendent of public instruction. The General Assembly has further divided policy, administrative, and funding responsibilities for schools among state and local entities and officials, including the Department of Public Instruction, local school boards, and county governments. This section briefly describes the primary roles and responsibilities of each of these state and local entities.

General Assembly

As detailed above, the state constitution assigns to the General Assembly the responsibility for ensuring "a general and uniform system of free public schools" that provides all children a basic education of at least minimum duration, content, and quality.[9] Thus, the legislature's primary authority is to ensure that there are adequate funds to carry out this constitutional duty. The constitution allows the General Assembly to assign funding responsibility to units of local government "as it may deem appropriate."[10] Since the Great Depression era, however, the General Assembly has assumed primary funding responsibility for the state's public schools. (The funding scheme is described in detail in the next section.)

The General Assembly also plays a key role in setting global educational policy standards for the state. It accomplishes this through both its funding authority and statutory directives. Since the 1980s, the legislature has embarked on several educational reform efforts, mainly aimed at increasing the accountability of school personnel for their students' performance.

---

7. For a more detailed history of how public education has evolved in North Carolina, see Benjamin R. Justesen and Scott Matthews, "Public Education," in *Encyclopedia of North Carolina*, ed. William S. Powell (2006), reproduced with permission at N.C. Department of Natural and Cultural Resources, State Library of North Carolina, *NCpedia*.

8. Postsecondary education is not discussed in this chapter. Statutes relating to state community colleges and the University of North Carolina are codified in, respectively, Chapters 115D and 116 of the North Carolina General Statutes (hereinafter G.S.). *See also* Chapter 44, "Community Colleges," in this publication.

9. N.C. Const. art. IX, § 2(1).

10. N.C. Const. art. IX, § 2(2).

State Board of Education

The North Carolina Constitution provides for the State Board of Education (State Board) in Article IX, Section 4(1). The State Board is responsible for supervising and administering the free public school system and, except for local school funds, all funds provided for it. The board sets education policy for the state and has the power to make all rules and regulations necessary to carry out this responsibility, subject to laws enacted by the General Assembly. The board regulates the grade and salary of school employees, adopts a standard course of study, and develops accountability measures for individual schools. The board's statutory powers and duties are listed in G.S. 115C-12 and include apportioning all state and federal school funds, certifying teachers, and adopting and supplying textbooks.

Superintendent of Public Instruction

In most states, the state school superintendent is appointed by the governor or selected by the state school board. In North Carolina, the superintendent of public instruction is a constitutional officer and is popularly elected for a four-year term.[11] Although not a voting member of the State Board, the superintendent is empowered by the constitution to serve as the State Board's secretary and chief administrative officer, executing board policies and organizing and managing the Department of Public Instruction.[12]

The superintendent is responsible for managing the day-to-day operations of the public school system, performing statutorily prescribed duties, and administering all needed rules and regulations adopted by the State Board of Education.[13] The superintendent also has an important voice in explaining the needs of the school system to various constituencies and recommending changes to improve the public schools.

Department of Public Instruction

The Department of Public Instruction (DPI) is a statutorily created state agency.[14] The superintendent of public instruction organizes and administers the DPI.[15] The DPI provides important leadership and assistance to local school boards in such areas as instructional support, media and technology, research and testing, and personnel. And the DPI collects, compiles, and disseminates important statistical and financial data about school units.[16]

Local School Administrative Units

A local school administrative unit is a legal entity that operates directly below the State Board in the public-school organizational hierarchy. In most states, a school administrative unit is called a school district, a term frequently used informally in North Carolina as well. School administrative units are also referred to as local education agencies, or LEAs. By statute, each North Carolina county is classified as a school administrative unit, and its schools are under the general supervision and control of a local board of education.[17]

---

11. N.C. Const. art. IX, § 4(2); G.S. 115C-18.
12. G.S. 115C-19; 115C-21.
13. G.S. 115C-19; *see also* G.S. 115C-21.
14. G.S. 143A-44.1.
15. G.S. 115C-21(a).
16. Many of the financial and statistical reports prepared by DPI are available on its website under "Data & Reports," www.dpi.nc.gov/data-reports.
17. G.S. 115C-66.

Some counties have multiple school administrative units. In these counties, there usually is a county school administrative unit and one or more city administrative units. A city administrative unit is a school system established within a county, or within adjacent parts of two or more contiguous counties, that the General Assembly has approved to operate as a separate school unit.[18] In most cases, a city administrative unit is not connected with the city government; the unit merely draws its name from the municipality with which it is geographically associated. Local funding for a city administrative unit comes from the board(s) of county commissioners of the county(ies) in which the unit lies. As detailed below, cities may, but are not required, to provide funding to schools that are located within their territorial boundaries and/or that serve city students.

Local Boards of Education

Each local school administrative unit is governed by a local board of education. The local board of education is a corporate body created by the General Assembly with the power to sue and be sued[19] and the authority to exercise "[a]ll powers and duties conferred and imposed by law respecting public schools, which are not expressly conferred and imposed upon some other official."[20] State law requires each school board to provide an adequate school system.[21] In doing so, a local board performs five major duties, as follows:

1. hiring and firing of school employees,
2. setting education policy within the guidelines of state education policy,
3. preserving the school unit's assets and managing the local school budget,
4. informing county commissioners of the school unit's fiscal needs, and
5. serving as a hearing board for local education disputes.

School boards in most other states have the authority to levy taxes to help finance the schools they administer; most North Carolina school boards do not have this authority. They derive almost all their revenue from state and county appropriations.

Boards of County Commissioners

Boards of county commissioners (county boards) are an integral part of the legal structure of public education in North Carolina. A county board is the local tax-levying authority for the school units within the county's territorial boundaries.[22] Although county commissioners are not official educational policy makers, they nonetheless influence policy through the local budgeting process.

The contours of a county board's funding responsibility for its local school(s) and the local budget process are discussed in part III of this chapter. In addition to its funding role, a board of commissioners has a few other statutory duties, including approving certain school board contracts, conducting special school elections, approving the amount a school board proposes to spend to purchase a school site, mandating the merger of all school units in the county, issuing bonds for school construction, and, by agreement with the local board of education, constructing school facilities.

---

18. G.S. 115C-66.
19. G.S. 115C-40.
20. G.S. 115C-36.
21. G.S. 115C-47.
22. There are a few situations in which the governing body of a municipality levies a supplemental tax for a city administrative unit.

Approving Certain Local School Board Contracts

A local school board must obtain consent from county commissioners before entering into several different types of contracts. A county board of commissioners' approval typically commits the county to providing sufficient funds to meet the local school board's obligations under the contracts.

Continuing Contracts for Capital Outlay

A school administrative unit may enter into continuing contracts for multi-year capital improvement projects or outlays, even when the school unit's budget resolution for the current year does not include an appropriation for the entire obligation incurred. Three conditions for these continuing contracts must be met: (1) the budget resolution must include an appropriation authorizing the current fiscal year's portion of the obligation, (2) an unencumbered balance of that appropriation for the current fiscal year must be sufficient to cover the unit's current fiscal year obligations under the contract, and (3) the board of county commissioners must approve the contract by a resolution binding the board to appropriate sufficient funds to pay the amounts falling due under the contract in future fiscal years.[23]

Installment Finance Contracts

Under G.S. 115C-528, a local board of education may use installment finance contracts to fund the acquisition of certain kinds of equipment: automobiles and school buses; mobile classroom units; food service equipment; photocopiers; and computers and computer hardware, software, and related support services. The contract term may not exceed the useful life of the property being acquired. The school unit purchasing the equipment must give the seller a security interest in the property being financed under the installment contract. The local school board must obtain the county commissioners' approval of an installment finance contract if the contract term is at least three years and the total amount financed under the contract is at least $250,000 or an amount equal to three times the local school system's annual state allocation for classroom supplies, materials, and equipment, whichever is less. Even if a contract does not require approval by the county board of commissioners, a local school board must submit information concerning these contracts as part of the annual budget it submits to the county board.

Operational Leases

G.S. 115C-530 authorizes a local board of education to enter into operational leases of real or personal property for use as school buildings or facilities.[24] Any lease for a term of three years or longer, including optional renewal periods, must be approved by the board of county commissioners. Approval obligates the commissioners to appropriate sufficient funds to meet the payments due in each year of the lease; the local school board's budget resolution must include an appropriation for the current fiscal year's portion of the obligation as well as an unencumbered balance sufficient to pay the obligation.

Also, under G.S. 115C-530, a school board may make improvements to leased property. Contracts for repair and renovation must be approved by the board of county commissioners if they (1) are subject to the competitive bidding requirement in G.S. 143-129(a) (the current threshold for which is $500,000) and (2) do not otherwise constitute continuing contracts for capital outlay.

---

23. G.S. 115C-441(c1).

24. In an operational lease, the lessee obtains no ownership interest or option to obtain an ownership interest in the leased property.

Conducting Special School Elections

Under G.S. 115C-501, a special school election may be held to vote on proposals to

1. authorize a local supplemental tax,
2. increase the supplemental tax rate in an area that already has a supplemental tax of less than the maximum rate set by statute,
3. enlarge a city administrative unit by consolidating areas of a county unit into the city school unit,
4. supplement and equalize educational advantages by levying a special tax in an area of a county administrative unit enclosed within one common boundary line,
5. abolish a supplemental school tax,
6. authorize a county to issue school bonds,
7. provide a supplemental tax on a countywide basis pursuant to a merger of all administrative units within a county,
8. annex or consolidate school areas from contiguous counties and provide a supplemental school tax in such annexed or consolidated areas, or
9. vote school bonds and taxes in certain merged school administrative units.

Involvement by a board of county commissioners begins when it receives a petition from a county or city school board of education requesting a special school election. The petition, which must be approved by the local school board, need not originate with the school board itself. It can be submitted also by a majority of qualified voters who have resided for the preceding year in an area adjacent to a city administrative unit; these voters may petition the county board of education for an election on the question of annexing their area to the city unit. For other types of special elections, 25 percent of the qualified voters in a school area may initiate a petition and submit it to the local board of education. The local board must consider all petitions it receives and decide whether or not to approve them.

If a petition is approved by a local school board, it is submitted to the county commissioners; G.S. 115C-506 requires the commissioners "to call an election and fix the date for the same." In *Board of Education of Yancey County v. Board of Commissioners of Yancey County,*[25] the North Carolina Supreme Court held that, if a petition for an election on authorizing a special supplemental tax is properly presented, the duty of a board of commissioners is ministerial and not discretionary; it is obliged to call the election. This rule likely applies to the other kinds of special elections listed above.[26] The local school board may withdraw a petition at any time before an election is called. All school elections, whether for county or city school administrative units, are held and conducted by the appropriate county board of elections.

If an election is held on any of these issues and the proposition is rejected, under G.S. 115C-502, another election on the same issue in the same area may not be called for at least six months. An election on whether to abolish a local tax district may not be held any sooner than one year after (1) the election establishing the district or (2) an election on the issue of dismantling the local tax district.[27] If a local tax district is in debt or has unmet obligations, no election may be held on the issue of abolishing that tax district.

---

25. 189 N.C. 650 (1925).

26. Because of inconsistent provisions in the laws regulating local government debt, it is not entirely clear whether or not the rule applies to petitions for school bond elections. However, in 1975, the North Carolina attorney general issued an opinion letter stating that a county must hold a bond referendum if a proper petition is submitted to the county board. Op. N.C. Att'y Gen. (Feb. 10, 1975) (on file with author).

27. G.S. 115C-505.

Approving Expenditures for School Sites

A school board may not execute a contract to purchase a site or to make any expenditure for a property without the county commissioners' approval "as to the amount to be spent for the site."[28] This requirement applies whether the county has made a blanket capital-outlay appropriation or has allocated moneys for the project at issue. In 1975, in *Painter v. Wake County Board of Education*,[29] the state supreme court considered an earlier version of this statutory provision. Its ruling indicates that the requirement of county board of commissioner approval applies only when a local school board is using funds from the county.

If the two boards disagree over a site-purchase matter, they may, under G.S. 115C-426(f), settle the dispute through the judicial procedure used to resolve budgetary disputes (found in G.S. 115C-431). If they do so, the issue to be determined is the amount to be spent for the site, not its location; the school board has the sole authority to choose school sites. If the court finds the amount the local school board proposes to spend reasonable, the school board will most likely prevail.

Mandating Merger of School Units within a County

As discussed above, some counties have both a county local school administrative unit and one or more city school administrative units. The propriety of having multiple school administrative units within one county is the subject of much study and debate among county and school officials. The number of school administrative units has decreased substantially over time. In 1960, there were 174 separate school units; since 2004, there are only 115. The General Assembly merged several of the school units through local acts. Some mergers, however, came about at the behest of county governments in which the administrative units are located. The General Assembly has authorized a board of county commissioners to compel a merger by adopting a merger plan for all school units in the county. In subsequent years, the county must provide the merged school unit local funding based on *average daily membership*[30] at a level at least equivalent to the highest level received by any school unit in the county during the five fiscal years preceding the merger. The local boards of education of the affected units do not participate in preparing the plan and need not agree to it. A merger plan developed by a board of county commissioners cannot be made subject to voter approval.[31]

There are two other statutorily authorized ways to merge school units without legislative action. A city board of education may force a merger by dissolving itself. In that case, the State Board of Education must adopt a merger plan. Plans developed in this way cannot be subject to voter approval. Affected local boards of education and boards of county commissioners do not participate in preparing such a plan and need not agree to it.[32] Alternatively, school systems themselves may bring about a merger. The merging units adopt a written plan of merger, which becomes effective if the board of county commissioners and the State Board of Education approve it. The plan may make the merger contingent on approval of the voters in the affected areas.[33]

---

28. G.S. 115C-426(f).

29. 288 N.C. 165 (1975).

30. Average daily membership is a calculation of a school unit's student population. For more information on that calculation, see N.C. State Board of Education and N.C. Department of Public Instruction, *School Attendance and Student Accounting Manual* (April 2025), www.dpi.nc.gov/documents/fbs/resources/sasa-250403/open, 41.

31. G.S. 115C-68.1.

32. G.S. 115C-68.2.

33. G.S. 115C-67.

Setting Local School Board Members' Compensation

A county board of commissioners is authorized to fix the compensation and expense allowances paid to members of the local board of education.[34] The county board must follow the procedures set forth in G.S. 153A-92. "Funds for the [members'] per diem, subsistence, and mileage" expenses for all local school board meetings are appropriated to the local current expense fund.[35]

Constructing School Facilities

A county board of commissioners bears primary funding responsibility for public-school infrastructure and facilities. However, G.S. 115C-521 assigns to each local school board the duty to provide adequate school facilities.[36] This provision also directs that the "building of all new school buildings and the repairing of all old school buildings shall be under the control and direction of, and by contract with, the board of education for which the building and repairing is done."[37] And all school buildings must be located on a site that is "owned in fee simple" by the local school board.[38]

For some capital projects, a county appropriates money to a local school unit and school personnel perform the work or contract with private entities to complete the work. A county board of commissioners has no legal authority to require that a local school board hire a particular contractor or otherwise proceed under a particular process (such as design-build or capital lease). A county and a school board may prefer to have the county contract for and oversee school construction and repair projects. In this case, the county and the local school board must enter into a carefully crafted interlocal agreement in which the local board assigns its contracting rights to the county but retains ultimate oversight authority.[39] Furthermore, if a county issues installment finance debt to fund a school construction project, the county may need to obtain temporary ownership of the school property for the life of the loan.[40] Again, a carefully drafted interlocal agreement should allow the county to perform the construction or repair work while not running afoul of statutory provisions.

II. Funding Public Schools

Funding public schools is a responsibility of both state and county governments. (The federal government also provides limited funding for certain targeted programs.[41]) In 1839, the first year

34. G.S. 115C-38.
35. G.S. 115C-38.
36. G.S. 115C-521(a).
37. G.S. 115C-521(c).
38. G.S. 115C-521(d).
39. Counties and local school administrative units have broad authority to enter into interlocal agreements under G.S. Chapter 160A, Article 20.
40. *See* G.S. 160A-20.
41. Although public education is a state and local responsibility, since the 1950s, the federal government has assumed a significant role in public education, primarily by providing funds to states. Congress generally conditions a state's receipt of federal funds on the state's compliance with federally defined conditions.

For example, the No Child Left Behind Act of 2001 created rigorous testing, reporting, and academic progress requirements for all states receiving what are known as Title I funds (applicable to all fifty states). Title I originally existed in the Elementary and Secondary Education Act of 1965, which has undergone numerous amendments and revisions since that time, including in 2001 with the No Child Left Behind Act. Title I, which is aimed at raising the academic achievement of low-income children, is the largest source of federal education funds. Significant federal funding also goes to programs for children with disabilities and to the national School Breakfast and School Lunch programs. More recently, the U.S. Department of Education initiated the Race to the Top program, which provided competitive grants to spur innovation and reforms in state and local education. (The Race to the Top program was

that North Carolina's public schools began to function as a statewide system, the General Assembly made $40 available to each school district that raised $20 locally.[42] That was the legislature's first stab at dividing the fiscal burden of public education between the state and local governments. The struggle to find a proper division while ensuring fairness in the financial burden, equity in educational opportunities, and quality in education has continued for the ensuing 185 years.

In the early to mid-1930s, largely as a reaction to the fiscal chaos of the Great Depression—a significant number of local governments had defaulted on debt and were in rough financial shape—the state adopted the current fiscal framework of centralizing policy making and funding responsibility for public education at the state level. It enacted the School Machinery Act,[43] which made the state responsible for paying all current expenses necessary to finance a minimum six-month school term, leaving the counties responsible for constructing and maintaining school buildings.

The basic structure of school finance in North Carolina has not changed since the 1930s. The state continues to be responsible for the majority of current expenses necessary to maintain the minimum nine-month term, while counties are responsible for financing the construction and maintenance of school facilities. In this respect, North Carolina's approach to financing its public schools differs from that of most other states, where the basic financial backing for public schools comes from local rather than state revenues. In North Carolina, state income and sales taxes, rather than local property taxes, constitute the primary revenue sources for financing schools.

It is also the case, though, that there has been a blending of funding responsibilities over time. The state often appropriates funds for school construction, and counties increasingly must provide funds for current expenses. In fact, the county share of funding has increased significantly in recent years. In 2018, the General Assembly authorized municipalities to fund public schools that are within their territorial boundaries or that serve municipal residents.[44] It is still too soon to know the long-term impact of this development on the total funding scheme.

State Funding

State Funding Responsibilities

The state allocates its funding to the public school system in a few different ways. The majority of funds are used to cover the operational expenses of each local school administrative unit.[45] However, the General Assembly typically provides some funds each year to fund school facility projects.

---

funded as part of the American Recovery and Reinvestment Act of 2009. For more information on the program, see U.S. Department of Education, *Race to the Top Program Executive Summary* (November 2009).) States were awarded points for satisfying certain educational policies, such as following performance-based standards for teachers and principals, complying with Common Core (a 2010 initiative aimed at achieving consistency in state educational standards), lifting caps on charter schools, turning around the lowest-performing schools, and building data systems. North Carolina received a Race to the Top grant of nearly $400 million in 2010. In 2015, Congress enacted the Every Student Succeeds Act (ESSA), which, among other things, requires every state to measure performance in reading, math, and science and develop a "State Report Card" that is accessible online and provides parents with information on test performance.

Most federal moneys are categorical funds, which means they are appropriated by Congress to the states for specific educational purposes. These monies are channeled through the State Board of Education for distribution to local units, but the board has little control over the programs themselves.

42. 1839 N.C. Pub. L. ch. 8.

43. 1931 N.C. Pub. L. ch. 728.

44. G.S. 160A-700.

45. The state's public schools are divided into 115 local school administrative units and one regional school. Each county has at least one local school administrative unit; some counties have up to three. Local school administrative units are often referred to as local education agencies or LEAs.

Operational Expenses

The state appropriates its operational funding for schools in its annual budget. North Carolina differs from most other states in that it does not distribute money for its general education program on the basis of a local unit's financial ability to operate schools. The bulk of state funding for public education is essentially a flat grant to a school system based on the number of students enrolled and the general costs of operation. The primary measure used for allocation is *average daily membership* (ADM). The ADM for each school month is calculated by dividing the number of non-violating membership days by the number of days in a school month, rounded to the nearest whole number. ADMs are calculated for each grade level and then added together to determine a school's ADM. Finally, each school's ADM in the school administrative unit is added together to determine the school unit's ADM.[46] Beginning in FY 2024–25, the General Assembly will base budget appropriations on the actual ADM from the previous school year. If the actual ADM in the current school year is lower than the previous year, the state will maintain the prior year's ADM funding level, allowing the school unit time to adjust to the enrollment decline. Conversely, if the current year's ADM exceeds that of the previous year, the school unit may be eligible for additional funding—subject to the availability of funds from the General Assembly's designated reserve.[47]

State appropriations typically are allocated among counties and school units through three different methods—position allotments, dollar allotments, and categorical allotments.

Position Allotments

The largest component of the state budget for schools is personnel. In fiscal year (FY) 2022–23, for example, 93.9 percent of state expenditures supported salaries and benefits.[48] The majority of this appropriation is reflected in position allotments. Each year, the state appropriates funds to pay teachers, instructional personnel, and school administrators. Salaries are funded on a position basis—the state allots a certain number of teachers and support personnel to each school unit based on grade-level ADMs. The current teacher-student ratios for kindergarten through grade three are as follows:

Kindergarten: 1 teacher per 18 students,
First grade: 1 teacher per 16 students,
Second grade: 1 teacher per 17 students,
Third grade: 1 teacher per 17 students.[49]

For each position allotment, the state pays the costs to fund a particular person in a particular teaching position, based on the State Salary Schedule. That allows a school unit to hire experienced teachers or instructional support personnel based on the unit's needs without being limited to a specific dollar total. A school unit also has some flexibility to use the allocated funds to cover other expenditures.[50]

46. For more information on the calculation, see *School Attendance and Student Accounting Manual* (April 2025), www.dpi.nc.gov/documents/fbs/resources/sasa-250403/open.

47. S.L. 2023-134.

48. N.C. Department of Public Instruction, *Highlights of the North Carolina Public School Budget* (March 2023), 5.

49. *See* G.S. 115C-301.

50. *See* G.S. 115C-105.25. A local school unit must publish information on its website about its state appropriations and any allotment transfers.

Dollar Allotments

Each school unit also receives a per-ADM dollar allotment that can be used to fund textbooks, supplies, materials, and some personnel, such as teacher assistants and central-office administration positions. For example, in FY 2022–23, the state allocated $30.17 per ADM for classroom materials/instructional supplies/equipment and $32.26 per ADM for textbooks.[51] A school unit may use dollar allotments to cover certain other expenditures.[52]

Categorical Allotments

The General Assembly has targeted some state appropriations to aid smaller and lower-wealth counties and to assist school units that serve student populations with unique needs. These moneys are not allocated on a straight ADM basis. Instead, they are disbursed according to detailed formulas. Common categorical allotments are disadvantaged student,[53] low-wealth counties,[54] and small school systems.[55] Some of these allocation formulas factor in a county's appropriation to a school unit. For example, the low-wealth formula is based in part on a county's wealth and on whether the county's appropriation to a school unit meets a certain minimum-effort threshold. Furthermore, low-wealth funds may not be used to supplant county appropriations.

The state also provides funds to local school units to replace buses according to a statutory replacement schedule.[56]

Capital Expenditures

Counties have been responsible for financing school construction since the state's public school system was established. Over the years, however, the state has offered direct and indirect assistance for construction costs—through state general obligation bonds, local sales and use tax authority, and direct appropriations of corporate income tax and state lottery proceeds.

State Bonds

In the past, the state has issued numerous bonds to finance construction grants to local school boards. In recent years, however, the state has chosen other forms of funding assistance for school construction. The last state bond for public-school construction was in 1996.[57]

Local Sales- and Use-Tax Authority

As mentioned above, in addition to bonds, the state has provided alternative relief for financing school construction. In 1983, it authorized counties to levy a one-half-cent sales and use tax,[58] with a specified percentage of the resulting revenue earmarked for school capital outlay, including retirement of existing school indebtedness (30 percent of the proceeds are currently so earmarked). In 1986, the legislature authorized counties to levy another one-half-cent tax, this time with 60 percent of the revenue earmarked for school capital-outlay expenses.[59] Because sales and use taxes have

---

51. Department of Public Instruction, *Highlights of the North Carolina Public School Budget*, 9.
52. *See* G.S. 115C-105.25. A local school unit must publish information on its website about its state appropriations and any allotment transfers.
53. G.S. 115C-472.19.
54. G.S. 115C-472.17.
55. G.S. 115C-472.18.
56. *See* G.S. 115C-249.
57. *See* 1995 N.C. Sess. Laws ch. 631.
58. G.S. Chapter 105, Article 40.
59. G.S. Chapter 105, Article 42.

traditionally been a state revenue source, these local sales taxes may reasonably be viewed as a form of state revenue-sharing for school construction. All counties levy both types of taxes.[60] A county may hold the moneys generated from the earmarked portion of the taxes in a capital reserve fund for future projects; any interest earned must be earmarked for school capital outlays.[61] Counties also are free to allocate the unrestricted portions of their local sales- and use-tax proceeds to fund public-school capital and operating expenses.[62] In 2007, counties received authority to levy an additional quarter-cent tax, subject to voter approval.[63] The proceeds of the tax can be used for any county expenditure item, including public schools. Beginning in July 2016, certain counties began receiving additional sales- and use-tax revenues, pursuant to G.S. 105-524. This revenue results from a redistribution of a portion of the proceeds generated from county sales and use taxes. A county may use this additional revenue to fund public-school capital and operating expenses, community colleges, or economic development.

State School-Construction Funds

In 1987, the legislature enacted the School Facilities Act, which created the Critical School Facility Needs Fund (CSFNF) and the Public School Building Capital Fund (PSBCF).[64]

The CSFNF, funded by corporate income tax proceeds, aided counties and school units with the most pressing needs in relation to their resources, as determined by the CSFNF Commission. Moneys were distributed to high-need counties from 1988 through 1994, at which time the fund was abolished.[65]

The PSBCF was established to provide aid to all counties for school construction projects. It too was originally funded by a portion of the state's corporate income tax proceeds,[66] which were allocated among the 100 counties on the basis of average daily membership (ADM). A county and its local school administrative unit(s) could jointly apply to the Department of Public Instruction to use the county's allocation for capital-outlay and technology projects. A county was required to match moneys allocated for capital-outlay projects on the basis of $1 of local funds for every $3 of state funds.

Beginning in 2005, the legislature also allocated a portion (roughly 40 percent) of the state's lottery proceeds to the PSBCF.[67] These funds could be used to fund capital-outlay projects for school buildings and were allocated among the counties according to a detailed statutory formula.[68] No local match was required.

---

60. Counties have additional sales- and use-tax authority. All counties levy a one-cent tax pursuant to G.S. Chapter 105, Article 39. Several counties also levy a quarter-cent tax pursuant to G.S. Chapter 105, Article 46. Neither of these taxes is earmarked for school funding, though.

61. A county may petition the North Carolina Local Government Commission (LGC) for authorization to use part or all of the earmarked revenues for other purposes. The LGC will approve a petition only if the county demonstrates that it can provide for school capital needs without the earmarked revenue. A local board of education also may petition the LGC if it believes that the county has not complied with the intent of sales- and use-tax laws. G.S. 105-502 and -487.

62. For more information on local sales and use taxes, see Chapter 4, "Revenue Sources," of *Introduction to Local Government Finance*, edited by Connor H. Crews (UNC School of Government, 2023).

63. G.S. Chapter 105, Article 46.

64. 1987 N.C. Sess. Laws ch. 622.

65. 1995 N.C. Sess. Laws ch. 631, § 14.

66. G.S. 115C-546.1(b) (repealed 2013).

67. G.S. 18C-164(d) (repealed 2013).

68. G.S. 115C-546.2(d)(1), (2) (repealed 2013).

In 2013, the General Assembly repealed the statutory distributions of both corporate income tax proceeds and lottery proceeds to the PSBCF.[69] New appropriations to the PSBCF have been subject to yearly state budget appropriations. According to G.S. 115C-546.2(d), if funds are appropriated to the PSBCF from the state lottery, those moneys must be allocated for school construction projects based on ADM. A county and its local school administrative unit(s) jointly apply to the Department of Public Instruction for a distribution of the moneys "to fund school construction projects and to retire indebtedness incurred for school construction projects."[70] No county matching funds are required. For FY 2023–24 and 2024–25, the legislature has appropriated $100 million to the fund.[71] It has appropriated this same amount for many years.

In 2017, the General Assembly established a second public-school capital fund, known as the Needs-Based Public School Capital Fund (NBPSCF).[72] It appropriated to the fund $254,252,612 in FY 2023–24 and $258,252,612 in FY 2024–25.[73] This fund is used to award grants to eligible counties to assist with critical public-school building capital needs. An eligible county is a county with an adjusted market value of taxable real property of less than forty billion dollars ($40,000,000,000).[74]

The superintendent of public instruction must award grants according to the following priorities: (1) counties designated as development tier one areas, (2) counties with greater need and less ability to generate sales- and property-tax revenue, (3) counties with a high debt-to-tax revenue ratio, (4) the extent to which a project will address critical deficiencies in adequately serving the current and future student population, (5) projects with new construction or complete renovation of existing facilities, (6) projects that will consolidate two or more schools into one new facility, and (7) counties that have not received a grant from this fund in the previous three years.[75] The grant funds are subject to a county match based on adjusted market value of taxable real property, as specified by statutory formula.[76]

There are some significant restrictions in the NBPSCF grant program. First, the grant moneys may only be used for the "construction of new school buildings and additions, repairs, and renovations."[77] They may not be used to reimburse a county for past projects or to make debt-service payments on past projects. The moneys also may not be used "for real property acquisition or for capital improvements to administrative buildings."[78] They may be used to enter into certain capital leases for school facilities, though.[79] There are maximum grant amounts based on school purpose. In FY 2023–24, these amounts are up to $42 million for elementary schools, up to $52 million for middle schools and combination elementary and middle schools, and up to $62 million for high schools.[80] Finally, there are detailed grant agreement requirements, specified in G.S. 115C-546.12.[81]

In 2021, the General Assembly established the Public School Repair and Renovation Fund. It appropriated $30 million to the fund in FY 2021–22 and $50 million in FY 2022–23, FY 2023–24, and FY 2024–25.[82] The funds are distributed equally among the 100 counties and used by each

69. S.L. 2013-360, § 6.11.
70. G.S. 115C-546.2(d)(4).
71. S.L. 2023-134.
72. G.S. Chapter 115C, Article 38B.
73. S.L. 2023-134.
74. G.S. 115C-546.11.
75. G.S. 115C-546.10.
76. G.S. 115C-546.11(a).
77. G.S. 115C-546.11(b).
78. G.S. 115C-546.11(a).
79. G.S. 115C-546.13.
80. G.S. 115C-546.11(c).
81. G.S. 115C-546.12.
82. S.L. 2022-74, § 4.2.(a).

county "for enlargement, improvement, expansion, repair, or renovation of classroom facilities at public school buildings within local school administrative units located in [a] county."[83] The funds may not be used for the retirement of indebtedness.[84]

State Funding Sources

The primary funding source for public schools is the state income tax. There are a handful of other revenue sources, though, including state lottery proceeds, fines and forfeitures proceeds, state sales- and use-tax proceeds, and pass-through federal and private grants.

Local Funding

Another significant difference between North Carolina's funding scheme for public education and that in other states is that generally local boards of education in this state do not have authority to levy taxes to support schools.[85] Instead, this authority resides with county governments. Counties use property taxes and local sales and use taxes to fund most school capital needs and a growing percentage of operational needs as well. As of July 1, 2018, municipalities are authorized to supplement state and county funding. A few other local revenue sources are available to support public schools.

County Funding

County Funding Responsibilities

Although the state bears primary responsibility for establishing a public school system, the North Carolina Constitution authorizes the General Assembly to "assign to units of local government such responsibility for the financial support of the free public schools as it may deem appropriate."[86] It further provides that the "governing boards of units of local government with financial responsibility for public education may use local revenues to add to or supplement any public school or post-secondary school program."[87]

The legislature has not been entirely clear in delineating the public-school funding duties of the state from those of county governments. Significant confusion about the contours of a county's obligation for public schools has resulted, forcing counties and local school boards to turn to the courts for guidance.

G.S. 115C-408 specifies that "it is the policy of the State of North Carolina to provide from State revenue sources the instructional expenses for current operations of the public school system as defined in the standard course of study. It is the policy of the State of North Carolina that the facilities requirements for a public education system will be met by county governments." On its face, this statute articulates a clear demarcation of funding responsibility between the state and county governments. The statute, by its terms, is merely aspirational, however. It does not actually assign any specific funding responsibilities. Neither does it reflect funding realities.

Specified Funding Requirements. A handful of statutory provisions assign funding responsibility for specific expenditure items to counties. These statutes assign to counties responsibility for funding most capital-outlay expenditures, including school facilities, furniture, and apparatus;[88]

---

83. G.S. 115C-546.21.
84. G.S. 115C-546.21.
85. There are a few exceptions. At least two school administrative units—Roanoke Rapids Graded School District and Mooresville Graded School District—have authority to levy property taxes.
86. N.C. Const. art. IX, § 2(2).
87. N.C. Const. art. IX, § 2(2).
88. G.S. 115C-521.

buildings for bus and vehicle storage;[89] library, science, and classroom equipment;[90] water supply and sanitary facilities;[91] and maintenance and repair of school buildings.[92] In addition, the statutes explicitly assign to counties responsibility for funding some operational expenditures—specifically, school maintenance and repairs,[93] instructional supplies and reference books,[94] school property insurance,[95] and fire inspections.[96]

If the funding framework ended there, it might not be such a knotty issue. A county would be required to fund the public-school capital and operational expense items explicitly delegated to it by statute. And, a county could choose to supplement its required appropriations in any given year, within the discretion of its governing board. The state would be required to fund any other expenditure necessary to enable a local school administrative unit to provide each student with the "opportunity to receive a sound basic education" (considering, of course, money the local school administrative unit receives from other sources, such as the federal government).

Additional Funding Requirements. The funding framework does not end there, however. The statute that sets forth the uniform budget standard for public schools also requires that a local school administrative unit maintain at least three funds to account for budgeted moneys.[97] The statute identifies the types and sources of funds that must be appropriated to each fund. One of the funds, the Capital Outlay Fund, includes appropriations from, among other sources, "revenues made available for capital outlay purposes by the State Board of Education and the [local] board of county commissioners."[98]

Another fund, the local current expense fund, must "include [county] appropriations sufficient, when added to appropriations from [the State], for the current operating expense of the public school system in conformity with the educational goals and policies of the State and the local board of education, within the financial resources and consistent with the fiscal policies of the board of county commissioners."[99] It further indicates that the appropriations must be funded by, among other revenue sources, "moneys made available to the local school administrative unit by the board of county commissioners."[100] Thus, despite the "policy" statements in G.S. 115C-408, the state provides some funding for capital expenses and counties are required to provide some funding for operational expenses. But the uniform budget statute still leaves ambiguity as to what the state is responsible for and what is left to counties.

To further complicate the analysis, G.S. 115C-431(a) authorizes a local board of education to initiate a dispute-resolution process[101] with the county if the local board of education determines that in any given year "the amount of money appropriated to the local current expense fund, or the capital outlay fund, or both, by the board of county commissioners is not sufficient to support a system of free public schools. . . . " The North Carolina Supreme Court has interpreted

89. G.S. 115C-249.
90. G.S. 115C-522(c).
91. G.S. 115C-522(c)
92. G.S. 115C-524(b).
93. G.S. 115C-524.
94. G.S. 115C-522(c).
95. G.S. 115C-534.
96. G.S. 115C-525(b).
97. G.S. 115C-426.
98. G.S. 115C-426(f).
99. G.S. 115C-426(e).
100. G.S. 115C-426(e).
101. The dispute-resolution process is discussed in greater detail below. See note 144 and accompanying text below.

G.S. 115C-431 to "itself assign to the local government responsibility for funding 'a system of free public schools'. . . . "[102] In 2018, the legislature altered the dispute-resolution statute. With those changes, it is clear that a county is responsible for funding certain operational and capital expenses each year.[103] (The dispute-resolution process is discussed in detail below.) In any given year, a county may be required to fund operational and capital expenditure items in addition to those explicitly specified by the statutory provisions listed above.

County Funding Sources

County Appropriations of General Fund Revenues. A county may appropriate any unrestricted county revenue to fund the capital and operating expenses of its school unit(s). At least to some extent, a county's governing board has discretion in determining the amount of unrestricted revenue to appropriate to support its schools. A school unit, however, may challenge a county's appropriations for a given year if it believes that the amount allocated for either capital or operating expenditures (or both), when combined with moneys made available to it through other sources, is not sufficient to provide each student with an opportunity to receive a sound basic education that year. As discussed below, a county's governing board may exercise some control over how the appropriated funds are spent by the local school unit(s).[104]

County Appropriations of Earmarked Local Sales- and Use-Tax Proceeds. As discussed above, a portion of a county's local sales- and use-tax revenue is earmarked for certain public-school expenditures.[105] A county has discretion to determine how much of these earmarked funds to appropriate each year and for what capital projects. A county's governing board may appropriate all the available funds each fiscal year, or it may place the money into a capital reserve fund for future expenditure. This allows a county to save moneys over several years to finance large capital outlays for its school unit(s). As with county appropriations of other general fund revenues, a county board may exercise some control over how its local school unit(s) expends these funds.

A county may seek permission from the Local Government Commission (LGC) to use part or all of earmarked local sales- and use-tax proceeds for any lawful purpose if the county demonstrates that it can satisfy all of the capital-outlay needs of its school unit(s) from other sources. In order to apply to the LGC for an exemption from the statutory earmarks on the G.S. Chapter 105, Articles 40 and 42 tax proceeds, a board of county commissioners must adopt a resolution and then submit it to the LGC. The resolution must indicate that the county can provide for its public-school capital needs without restricting the use of part of or the entire designated amount. The LGC must consider both the school unit's capital needs and those of the county generally in making its decision. The LGC must issue a written decision detailing its findings and specifying what percentage, if any, of the earmarked proceeds may be used by the county for any lawful purpose.

---

102. Beaufort Cnty. Bd. of Educ. v. Beaufort Cnty. Bd. of Comm'rs, 363 N.C. 500, 507 (2009).
103. G.S. 115C-431.
104. See notes 134–136 and accompanying text below.
105. See notes 57–62 and accompanying text above.

Municipal Funding

A municipality is authorized to make appropriations to "supplement funding for elementary and secondary public education" that benefit the residents of the municipality.[106] In some respects, this funding authority is broader than that afforded to county governments. It comes with some limitations, though.

Public Schools

A municipality may appropriate money to a *public school* that serves the residents of the municipality to fund the school's current operating expenses or any "other specific uses directed" by the municipality.[107] The term "public school" is defined under law to include a local school administrative unit (traditional public school); a laboratory school authorized by G.S. Chapter 116, Article 29A; a charter school authorized by G.S. Chapter 115C, Article 14A; and a regional school authorized by G.S. Chapter 115C, Article 16, Part 10.[108] Unlike a county, a municipality may make appropriations directly to any of these public schools.

Appropriations within and outside Municipality

A municipality's appropriation authority is further delineated by location of the public-school unit. For schools located within municipal limits, municipal appropriations may be made as a lump sum to each school or on a per-pupil basis.[109] In addition to funding general capital and operating expenses and special programs, municipal appropriations may also be used to enter into operational and financing leases for real property or mobile classroom units and to make payments on loans made to public schools for facilities, equipment, or operations.[110] Municipal appropriations may not be used, however, to obtain "any other interest in real property or mobile classroom units."[111] Thus, municipal funds may not be used to purchase land, school facilities, or mobile classrooms.

For schools located outside municipal limits, a city may allocate money to a school attended by a resident student on a per-pupil basis to fund current operating expenses or other specific uses directed by the city.[112]

There is no requirement that a municipality provide equal funding to all of the schools that serve its residents. A municipal governing board may choose to fund only the schools within municipal territorial boundaries; only a category of schools, such as only charter schools; or only a single school unit.

This funding authority is very different from that of county governments. As discussed above, county funding for operational expenses must be proportionally apportioned, based on average daily membership (ADM), among all the traditional public-school units within the county. In addition, county appropriations to a traditional public school's local current expense fund must be proportionally shared, on a per-pupil basis, with other public schools attended by a student who would otherwise be served by the traditional public school.

---

106. *See* S.L. 2018-5, § 38.3, *as amended by* S.L. 2018-97, § 11.1.

107. G.S. 160A-700(b)(1), (2).

108. G.S. 160A-700(d).

109. G.S. 160A-700(b)(1).

110. G.S. 160A-700(b)(1). Note that there is very limited authority for traditional public schools to borrow money or enter into these types of leases. *See* G.S. 115C-528 (lease-purchase and installment-purchase financing for vehicles, certain equipment, and mobile classrooms); -530 (operational leases of school buildings and school facilities); -546.13 (Needs-Based Public School Capital Fund grant-funded capital leases for school facilities). And all such leases must include a statement that they do not constitute an indebtedness or obligation of the municipality.

111. G.S. 160A-700(b)(1).

112. G.S. 160A-700(b)(2).

Municipal Funding Directives

A municipality may "direct or restrict the use of funds appropriated for specific purposes, functions, projects, programs, or objects. . . . "[113] These categories correlate to the chart of accounts used by traditional public schools, whereby operating expenditures are broken down by purpose code, function code, object code, and program report code and capital expenditures are delineated by category. For other public schools that may not follow this chart of accounts, a municipality is free to direct its funding to specific programs or expenditure items. A municipality thus has broader authority to direct school expenditures than does a county, which is limited to allocating operating expense appropriations by purpose and function and capital-outlay appropriations by project or category.

Municipal appropriations to a traditional public school will not be allocated to the local current expense fund. Instead, the local school board will set up a separate fund to budget and account for these moneys. This means that, unlike county appropriations, municipal appropriations for operating expenses to public schools will not be shared with charters or other public schools.

Municipal Funding Sources

A municipality may use property tax proceeds or any unrestricted revenues from other sources to fund appropriations to public schools.[114] There is one limitation, though. Only property tax proceeds that are generated from taxes levied on or after July 1, 2018, may be used for this purpose. A municipality may not use fund balance derived from property tax collections on levies from prior fiscal years, even if those amounts are collected after July 1, 2018.

Impact on State and County Funding

G.S. 160A-700 does not, itself, alter the general state and county education funding schemes. The legislature makes its school appropriations in the annual state budget and is free to change its appropriations method at any time.

With respect to counties, as detailed above, a board of county commissioners is required to provide sufficient funding, when added to all other revenues available to a traditional public-school unit, to allow the school unit to meet its constitutional minimum education requirements. Although G.S. 160A-700 appears to envision that municipal funding will supplement state and county funding ("A city may use property tax revenues authorized under G.S. 160A-209(c)(26b) and other unrestricted revenues to supplement funding for elementary and secondary public education that benefits the residents of the city."[115]), there is no explicit non-supplant provision. Thus, a board of county commissioners may reduce its appropriations to a traditional public-school unit by the amount of revenue appropriated by the municipality to that school unit, subject of course to the minimum funding formula triggered by the dispute-resolution process discussed below.

Note also that in a county with more than one traditional public-school unit, the county board of commissioners must apportion all appropriations for operating expenses proportionally among the school units based on ADM. So, if a municipality provided supplemental funding to one of the county's school units and not the other, any resulting reduction in county appropriations for operating expenses would affect both school units.

113. G.S. 160A-700(a).
114. G.S. 160A-700(a).
115. G.S. 160A-700(a).

Other Local Funding Sources

In addition to appropriations from a county's general fund, a local school unit also may receive revenue derived from locally collected penalties and fines and a voted supplemental school tax.

Local Fines and Penalties

Under Article IX, Section 7 of the North Carolina Constitution, "the clear proceeds of all penalties and forfeitures and of all fines collected in the several counties for any breach of the penal laws of the state, shall belong to and remain in the several counties, and shall be faithfully appropriated and used exclusively for maintaining free public schools." Several locally collected fines and penalties are subject to this constitutional mandate.[116] If a county collects penalties or fines that are subject to this constitutional requirement, it must remit the clear proceeds (gross proceeds minus up to 10 percent in collection costs) to the local school unit(s) within the county within ten days after the end of the month in which the money was collected.

A county does not include these funds in its appropriations to the school unit(s), and the county board of commissioners has no control over their expenditure.

Dedicated Property Tax Revenue

There are two methods by which a county may legally dedicate property tax proceeds for public-school purposes—a dedicated county general tax and a voted supplemental tax.

Dedicated County General Tax. This method involves obtaining voter approval, via referendum, to dedicate a portion of the general property tax for public-school purposes. If the referendum is successful, the board of county commissioners decides each year whether or not to levy the dedicated property tax rate, along with the county's general rate. If the county board decides to levy the portion of the property tax dedicated to schools, it can then use the proceeds from that tax to either supplement or supplant its appropriations to the school unit(s) from other sources for capital and/or operating expenses.[117]

Voted Supplemental Tax. This method requires a joint effort between the local board of education and the board of county commissioners. It is the closest thing to a local school board having its own taxing authority. The local board of education may petition the county commissioners to hold a voter referendum to authorize a voted supplemental school tax. If the county commissioners receive a valid petition, the county must hold the referendum. The petition must state the maximum authorized supplemental tax rate, up to $0.50 per $100 valuation for school units having a population of less than 100,000 and $0.60 per $100 valuation for all other school units. If a supplemental tax is approved by the voters, a local board of education may request that the county levy a tax each year up to the maximum rate approved by the voters. The county decides whether or not to levy the tax and at what rate (the rate is capped at the level requested by the local board of education).

The county does not have any control over how the supplemental tax proceeds are spent by the school unit. That decision rests with the local school board, subject only to the terms of the ballot measure under which the tax was approved. The board of county commissioners may, however,

116. *See* G.S. 115C-437. For a detailed discussion of the categories of locally collected penalties and fines that are subject to this constitutional provision, see Kara Millonzi, "Locally-Collected Penalties & Fines: What Monies Belong to the Public Schools?," *Coates' Canons: NC Local Government Law* blog (November 17, 2011), canons.sog.unc.edu/2011/11/locally-collected-penalties-fines-what-monies-belong-to-the-public-schools/. *See also* Chapter 4, "Revenue Sources," of *Introduction to Local Government Finance.*

117. G.S. 153A-149(d).

consider the availability of the supplemental tax revenue when determining the county's annual appropriations.

Federal Funding

Although public education is a state and local responsibility, since the 1950s the federal government has assumed a significant role in public education, primarily by providing funds to states. Congress generally conditions a state's receipt of federal funds on the state's compliance with federally defined conditions. (For an example of such conditions, see note 41, above.)

Most federal moneys are *categorical* funds, which means they are appropriated by Congress to the states for specific educational purposes. These funds are channeled through the State Board of Education for distribution to local units, but the board has little control over the programs themselves. In general, poorer school units receive more federal dollars relative to their enrollment than wealthier units do.

III. Local Budgeting Process

Each year, counties engage in a detailed budgetary process to estimate revenues and make appropriations for the forthcoming fiscal year. A county must include its appropriations to its local school unit(s) for capital-outlay and current expenses in its annual budget ordinance. The Local Government Budget and Fiscal Control Act,[118] as supplemented by the School Budget and Fiscal Control Act,[119] prescribes the procedural and substantive requirements a county must use to adopt its budget ordinance and appropriate money to its local school unit(s).[120] The budgeting process is fairly straightforward and can be broken down into the following ten steps:

Step 1: County board of commissioners and local school board(s) communicate on an ongoing basis.
Step 2: School superintendent submits proposed budget.
Step 3: Local school board considers superintendent's budget.
Step 4: Local school board submits budget request to county board.
Step 5: County board makes appropriations to local school unit(s).
Step 6: Local school board initiates dispute-resolution process (optional).
Step 7: Local school board adopts school budget resolution.
Step 8: Local school board amends school budget resolution (optional).
Step 9: County board monitors local school unit's expenditures of county appropriations (optional).
Step 10: County board reduces appropriations to local school unit(s) during fiscal year (very limited authority).

Each step is analyzed more thoroughly below.

---

118. G.S. Chapter 159, Article 3.

119. G.S. Chapter 115C, Article 31, Part 1.

120. See Chapter 3, "Budgeting for Operating and Capital Expenditures," of *Introduction to Local Government Finance* for more information on adopting, enacting, and amending the annual budget ordinance.

Step 1: County Board of Commissioners and Local School Board(s) Communicate on an Ongoing Basis

A county board of commissioners and a school board must work together to ensure that each board's statutory requirements are met. The board of county commissioners and local board(s) of education should engage in ongoing communications during the fiscal year.[121] Leading up to the budget process, they should communicate about the fiscal needs of the local school administrative unit and the fiscal resources of the county. Doing so will prevent surprises to either board at budget time and will help make the budgeting process work more efficiently and effectively.

Some county boards and local school boards agree to adopt multi-year financing formulas for operational expenses, indexed to such things as enrollment growth, percentages of low-wealth or special needs students, or state funding averages. These funding agreements are not legally enforceable, but they can serve as a useful tool for financial planning.

Step 2: School Superintendent Submits Proposed Budget

By May 1, every public-school superintendent must submit a budget and a budget message to their local board of education (superintendent's budget).[122] The local school board may direct the superintendent to follow certain specified guidelines and processes in preparing the proposed budget. A copy of the superintendent's budget must be filed in the superintendent's office and made available for public inspection.[123] The superintendent may, but is not required to, publish notice that the superintendent's budget has been submitted to the local board of education.

Step 3: Local School Board Considers Superintendent's Budget

A local board of education may hold a public hearing on a superintendent's budget, but it is not required to do so.[124] With or without public input or support, the school board is free to make any changes to the proposed budget before submitting it to the county for consideration.

Step 4: Local School Board Submits Budget Request to County Board

By May 15, a local board of education must submit its entire proposed budget (not just its request for county funding) to the board of county commissioners.[125] The county's budget officer must present the local board of education's requests to the county board, even if the budget officer's proposed county budget recommends different funding levels for the school unit.

The local board of education also must submit to the board of county commissioners a written summary of "the academic performance of the schools in the local school administrative unit, including the school performance grades of each school, any schools identified as low-performing or continually low-performing, and efforts by the local board of education to improve those identified schools' performance."[126] The county commissioners may require that the local board of education present this information at a public meeting.

The board of county commissioners may request further information from the local school administrative unit about its proposed budget request. In fact, the county board has broad authority to obtain from the local board of education "all books, records, audit reports, and other information

121. *See* G.S. 115C-426.2.
122. G.S. 115C-427.
123. G.S. 115C-428.
124. G.S. 115C-428.
125. G.S. 115C-429.
126. G.S. 115C-429(a).

bearing on the financial operation of the local school administrative unit."[127] The county board also may specify the format in which the financial information must be presented.

In addition, a county board of commissioners can (and often does) invite the school unit's superintendent or the local school board to present the school's budget proposal at a county board meeting or during the public hearing on the county's budget. This affords the county board an opportunity to ask questions about certain expenditure items and to obtain further clarification on a local school board's policy goals and needs.

Step 5: County Board Makes Appropriations to Local School Unit(s)

A board of county commissioners makes its appropriations for capital and operating expenditures to local school administrative unit(s) in the county's annual budget ordinance.

Budgeting Factors

In making its appropriation decisions, the county board of commissioners must carefully consider the local school board's funding request. The county is required to make appropriations for operating expenditures that, when combined with revenues to the school unit from all other sources, are sufficient to allow the school to meet its constitutional mandate to provide each student with the opportunity to receive a sound basic education.[128] (Other revenues available to a school unit for operating expenses include supplemental taxes levied by or on behalf of the school unit; state money disbursed directly to the school unit; moneys made available to the local school unit by the board of county commissioners; moneys accruing to the local school unit from fines, penalties, and forfeitures pursuant to Article IX, Section 7 of the N.C. Constitution; and any other moneys made available or accruing to the local school unit for the current operating expenses of the school system).[129] Of course a county board of commissioners also has to balance the needs of the school unit with the needs of all other county departments, particularly those that provide state-mandated services, such as public health, social services, and elections. Recognizing this, G.S. 115C-426 requires that a county board consider its fiscal resources and financial policies when making school appropriation decisions.

A county also is required to appropriate sufficient funds to meet a school unit's capital needs for the fiscal year.[130] The state makes some funds available to a county and its local school unit(s) to help with school construction, but most of this need must be met by county resources. A school unit's capital needs vary from year to year. A county board of commissioners should engage its local school board(s) in the county's capital-planning process or capital-improvement program (CIP).

Fund Balance

Questions often arise at budget time about the propriety of a local school unit maintaining a fund balance. Most state funds to school units revert at the end of a fiscal year if not spent. Thus, a school unit's fund balance is comprised primarily of county appropriations from previous years. There is no prohibition against a school unit maintaining a fund balance. School units, however, do not need a fund balance to meet cash flow needs to the same extent that counties and municipalities do.[131]

127. G.S. 115C-429(c).

128. *See* G.S. 115C-426.

129. *See* G.S. 115C-426(e).

130. *See* G.S. 115C-426(f).

131. The most significant revenue source for counties and municipalities is property tax proceeds. Although property taxes typically are levied at the beginning of the fiscal year (July 1), they may be paid without penalty until the following January. Thus, counties and municipalities rely heavily on fund balance to pay expenses during the first half

And, unlike for counties and municipalities, the state's Local Government Commission does not prescribe a minimum fund balance level for local school units. A county board of commissioners may not force a school board to expend its fund balance for capital or operating expenditures. And a school unit is not authorized to return all or a portion of its fund balance to the county. A county board, however, will likely consider the amount of fund balance available to the school unit when making its yearly county appropriations for operating expenses.[132]

County Authority to Direct School Unit Expenditures

Allocating Local Current Expense Appropriations

Generally, appropriations for school operating expenses are made to the local current expense fund. A board of county commissioners may appropriate a lump sum to the local current expense fund to support operating expenses. If a county appropriates moneys to the local current expense fund with no further direction, the local board of education has full discretion over the expenditure of these moneys.[133]

A county is authorized, however, to allocate part or all its appropriation for operating expenses within the local current expense fund by purpose or function, as defined in the uniform budget format.[134] The uniform budget format (now called the uniform chart of accounts)[135] defines "purpose code" to include the activities or actions that are performed to accomplish the objectives of a school unit. Function codes are first-level subdivisions of purpose codes and represent the greatest level of specificity to which a county may allocate funds for school operating expenses. County appropriations may be allocated to the purpose and function codes in Table 43.1.

---

of the fiscal year. Local school units do not have the same cash flow needs because they receive revenue disbursements from the state and county governments on a more regular basis throughout the fiscal year.

132. G.S. 115C-426 used to provide more explicit authority for a county to consider a local school unit's fund balance when making its budget appropriation to the school unit for operating expenses. That is because fund balance was considered to be part of the local current expense fund. And G.S. 115C-426(e) required that each year the local current expense fund was to include appropriations from the county that, when added to appropriations from the state and other local sources, are sufficient to provide for "the current operating expense of the public school system in conformity with the educational goals and policies of the State and the local board of education, within the financial resources and consistent with the fiscal policies of the board of county commissioners."

In 2010, in reaction to a series of cases involving apportionment of funds from the local current expense fund to charter schools, the General Assembly amended G.S. 115C-426(c) to state that "the appropriation or use of fund balance or interest income by a local school administrative unit shall not be construed as a local current expense appropriation included as a part of the local current expense fund." The impetus behind this amendment was clear. The legislature intended to shield a school unit's fund balance from being apportioned to a charter school pursuant to G.S. 115C-238.29H(b). However, in adding this language, the legislature arguably created an ambiguity as to whether or not a county board may consider a school's existing fund balance when making budget appropriations to the local current expense fund for operating expenses.

However, G.S. 115C-426(e) allows a county board to consider "other moneys available or accruing to the local school administrative unit," which provides some justification for a county board to consider a school unit's uncommitted fund balance when making its yearly appropriation decisions.

133. A local school unit must distribute the per-pupil proportional share of certain local current expense appropriations (along with certain state appropriations) to each charter school (G.S. 115C-218.105(c); 115C-426(b)); UNC Lab School (G.S. 116-239.11); and/or Innovative School District (G.S. 115C-75.10) that is attended by a child who otherwise would attend school in the local school unit.

134. G.S. 115C-429. A county board of commissioners may specify that a local school board submit its budget request according to these purpose and function codes.

135. For a list of the chart of accounts for FY 2024–25, see N.C. Department of Public Instruction, Chart of Accounts, "Working Documents FY 2024–2025," www.dpi.nc.gov/districts-schools/district-operations/financial-and-business-services/school-district-finance-operations/chart-accounts.

Table 43.1 Purpose (First-Level) and Function (Second-Level) Codes

Purpose Code	Function Code
5000—*Instructional Services* Includes the costs of activities dealing directly with the interaction between teachers and students.	**5100**—Regular Instructional Services **5200**—Special Populations Services **5300**—Alternative Programs and Services **5400**—School Leadership Services **5500**—Co-Curricular Services **5600**—School-Based Support Services
6000—*Supporting Services Programs* Includes the costs of activities providing system-wide support for school-based programs, regardless of where these supporting services are based or housed.	**6100**—Support and Development Services **6200**—Special Populations Support and Development Services **6300**—Alternative Programs and Services Support and Development Services **6400**—Technology Support Services **6500**—Operational Support Services **6600**—Financial and Human Resource Services **6700**—Accountability Services **6800**—System-Wide Pupil Support Services **6900**—Policy, Leadership, and Public Relations Services
7000—*Ancillary Services* Includes activities that are not directly related to the provision of education for pupils in a local school administrative unit.	**7100**—Community Services **7200**—Nutrition Services **7300**—Adult Services
8000—*Non-Programmed Charges* Includes conduit-type payments to other local school administrative units in the state or in another state, transfers from one fund to another fund in the local school administrative unit, appropriated but unbudgeted funds, debt-service payments, scholarship payments, payments on behalf of educational foundations, and contingency funds.	**8100**—Payments to Other Government Units **8200**—Unbudgeted Funds **8300**—Debt Services **8400**—Interfund Transfers **8500**—Contingency **8600**—Educational Foundations **8700**—Scholarships
9000—*Capital Outlay* Includes expenditures for acquiring fixed assets, including land or existing buildings, improvements of grounds, initial equipment, additional equipment, and replacement of equipment.	

A board of county commissioners may request that a local board of education refrain from using county appropriations for certain items of expenditure within a purpose or function code. However, it may not legally restrict these expenditures at the line-item level. Furthermore, if a county board allocates its appropriations according to a purpose or function code, the local school board may modify up to 25 percent of an allocation for operating expenses. The county board may reduce the local school board's discretion to modify allocations if it so specifies in the county budget ordinance, but not to less than 10 percent.[136]

Allocating Capital-Outlay Appropriations

According to the uniform budget format (now called the uniform chart of accounts), there are three categories of expenditures to which a county may appropriate capital funds to its public school(s). A county may appropriate moneys for Category I expenditures for a specific capital project or projects. Moneys appropriated for Categories II and III expenditures, however, are allocated to the entire category, not to individual expenditure items.

The following list details the authorized capital-outlay expenditures in each category.

Category I
Acquisition of real property and acquisition, construction, reconstruction, enlargement, renovation, or replacement of buildings and other structures for school purposes.

Category II
Acquisition or replacement of furnishings and equipment.

Category III
Acquisition of school buses, activity buses, and other motor vehicles.

If a board of county commissioners allocates part or all of its capital appropriations by project, a local school board must obtain approval from the county for any changes in the allocation for specific Category I expenditures—acquisitions of real property for school purposes and acquisitions, construction, reconstruction, enlargement, renovations, or replacement of buildings and other structures.[137] However, a local board of education has full discretion to reallocate funds within categories II and III.

Apportionment of County Funds among Multiple School Units

If a county supports more than one local school unit, county appropriations to the local current expense funds of the local school administrative units (to support operating expenses) must be apportioned according to the average daily membership (ADM) of each unit.[138] There is an exception for appropriations funded by voted supplemental taxes levied less than countywide. This occurs when a county has more than one local school administrative unit. These funds do not need to be apportioned equally among local school administrative units.

This uniform apportionment requirement does not apply to capital funds. A county may allocate unequal amounts of capital funding to different school units within a fiscal year. Furthermore, under certain circumstances a county may appropriate moneys to special funds for particular programs at one local school administrative unit without appropriating an equivalent amount to other units. The local school administrative unit must budget and account for these moneys in a fund other than the local current expense fund.

136. G.S. 115C-433.
137. G.S. 115C-433.
138. G.S. 115C-430.

Interim Budget

The Local Government Budget and Fiscal Control Act requires that adoption of a county's budget ordinance take place by July 1.[139] However, sometimes county boards of commissioners are unable or unwilling to adopt a budget ordinance by this date. In such cases, a county board must adopt an interim budget that appropriates money to cover necessary expenses for county departments and for local school unit(s) until the budget ordinance is adopted.[140] In an extreme situation, the state's Local Government Commission is authorized to assume the financial duties of a county board and to adopt the budget ordinance.[141] If the county's budget is delayed beyond July 1, a local school board also must adopt an interim budget resolution to pay salaries and the "usual ordinary expenses" of the school unit.[142]

Step 6: Local School Board Initiates Dispute-Resolution Process (Optional)

If a local school board "determines that the amount of money appropriated to the local current expense fund [for operating expenses], or the capital outlay fund, or both, . . . is not sufficient to support a system of free public schools," it may initiate a dispute-resolution process with the board of county commissioners to challenge the appropriation.[143] For many years, the dispute-resolution process had three stages—joint meeting of the two governing boards, mediation, and litigation. As of July 1, 2018, the General Assembly replaced the litigation stage with a mandated funding formula for operating expense–funding disputes.[144] Litigation will continue as the third stage for capital-funding disputes.

Stages of Dispute-Resolution Process

As stated above, there are three stages in the dispute-resolution process—joint meeting of the two governing boards, mediation, and default funding formula (for operating-expense disputes) or litigation (for capital-outlay disputes).

Joint Meeting of Boards

To trigger the dispute-resolution process, a local school board must notify the county board of commissioners of its intention to invoke the process within seven days of the adoption of the county budget ordinance. The boards then are required to meet and make a good-faith effort to try to resolve their differences. A mediator presides over the meeting and acts as a neutral facilitator.

Mediation

If the joint meeting described immediately above is not successful, a local school board and a board of county commissioners proceed to official mediation. Unless the two boards agree otherwise, the participants in the mediation are the chairs, attorneys, and finance officers of each board; the school superintendent; and the county manager. The compensation and expenses of the mediator are shared equally by the local school administrative unit and the county. The mediation is conducted in private, and statements and conduct are not discoverable in any subsequent litigation. The mediation must end by August 1, unless both boards agree otherwise. If the mediation continues beyond August 1, the county must appropriate to the local current expense fund a sum equal to its appropriation for the previous fiscal year.

---

139. G.S. 159-13; 115C-429.
140. G.S. 159-16.
141. G.S. 159-181.
142. G.S. 115C-434.
143. G.S. 115C-431(a).
144. S.L. 2018-83.

Default Funding Formula or Litigation

If mediation ultimately fails, what happens next depends on whether operational funding levels, capital funding levels, or both are in dispute. If the dispute at least partially involves operational funding amounts, to be appropriated to a school unit's local current expense fund, then a failed mediation triggers a default funding formula. The funding formula is the final determination of the appropriation amount for operating expenses for that fiscal year. Neither a local board of education nor a board of county commissioners may file any legal action challenging the determination.

The funding formula differs depending on whether or not the funding formula had been triggered in the prior fiscal year.

Local Current-Expense Funding Formula if Statutory Funding Formula Not Triggered for Prior Two Years. If the statutory funding formula was not triggered in the prior two fiscal years, a county's appropriation to a local school unit's local current-expense fund derives from the following four-step formula:

1. Start with the amount of county appropriations allocated to the local current-expense fund in the prior fiscal year that was actually expended by the local school unit or transferred to a charter school, innovative school, regional school, or laboratory school. In other words, begin the calculation with the amount of county appropriations actually spent for the year immediately preceding the budget year. *Note: Because county appropriations are commingled with other local revenue sources in the local current-expense fund, it will be incumbent on the local school board to separately track the expenditure of county appropriations.*
2. Divide the amount from step 1 by the sum of the average daily membership (ADM) of the local school administrative unit from the prior year plus the share of the ADM of any charter, innovative, regional, or laboratory school whose students reside in the local school administrative unit from the prior year. This number represents the per-student allocation.
3. Multiply the amount from step 2, rounded to the nearest penny, by the sum of 1 plus the twelve-month percent change in the second quarter Employment Cost Index for elementary and secondary school workers as reported by the Federal Bureau of Labor Statistics. Unfortunately, G.S. 115C-431 does not precisely designate the data required to make this calculation. It is unclear if the reference is to the Employment Cost Index for total compensation for elementary and secondary school workers or the Employment Cost Index for wages and salaries for elementary and secondary school workers.[145] (Note that second-quarter data are released on July 31.) G.S. 115C-431 also does not indicate whether seasonally adjusted or non–seasonally adjusted data should be used. It will be up to the local school board and board of county commissioners to determine which set of data to use in the calculation.
4. Multiply the per-student allocation in step 3, rounded to the nearest penny, by the sum of the ADM of the local school administrative unit for the budget year in dispute plus the share of the ADM of any charter, innovative, regional, or laboratory school whose students reside in the local school administrative unit for the budget year in dispute.

145. See the following data from the U.S. Bureau of Labor Statistics' *Economic News Release*: Table 1, "Economic Cost Index for Total Compensation, by Occupational Group and Industry (Seasonally Adjusted), www.bls.gov/news.release/eci.t01.htm (last modified January 31, 2024); Table 2, "Economic Cost Index for Wages and Salaries, by Occupational Group and Industry (Seasonally Adjusted), www.bls.gov/news.release/eci.t02.htm (last modified January 31, 2024).

(It is not clear what number should be used to determine the total number of students for the budget year in dispute. At the point in time that the statutory formula is likely to be triggered, a local school unit will only have its estimated ADM for the year.)

The figure resulting from step 4, rounded to the nearest penny, is the statutorily mandated local current-expense appropriation for the budget year.

Local Current-Expense Funding Formula if Statutory Funding Formula Triggered in Prior Two Fiscal Years or More. If the statutory funding formula is triggered a second year in a row, the formula used to determine a county's appropriation to a local school unit's current-expense fund is altered to increase the inflationary factor. The formula then becomes a five-step process.

1. Start with the amount of county appropriations allocated to the local current-expense fund in the prior fiscal year that was actually expended by the local school unit or transferred to a charter school, innovative school, regional school, or laboratory school. In other words, begin the calculation with the amount of county appropriations that were actually spent for the year immediately preceding the budget year.
2. Divide the amount from step 1 by the sum of the average daily membership (ADM) of the local school administrative unit from the prior year plus the share of the ADM of any charter, innovative, regional, or laboratory school whose students reside in the local school administrative unit from the prior year. This number represents the per-student allocation.
3. Increase by 3 percent the twelve-month percent change in the second quarter Employment Cost Index for elementary and secondary school workers as reported by the Federal Bureau of Labor Statistics. This provision, again, leaves a great deal of ambiguity. As stated above, it is unclear if the reference is to the Employment Cost Index for total compensation for elementary and secondary school workers or the Employment Cost Index for wages and salaries for elementary and secondary school workers. (Note that second-quarter data are released on July 31.) G.S. 115C-431 also does not indicate whether seasonally adjusted or non-seasonally adjusted data should be used. It will be up to the local school board and board of county commissioners to determine which set of data to use in the calculation. Finally, it is not clear how to interpret the mandate to increase the percentage change by 3 percent. It could mean that you add 3 percent to the percentage change. It could also mean that you multiply the percentage change by 3 percent. I think the legislature most likely intended the former interpretation. For example, if the twelve-month percentage change is 2.38 percent, you add 3 percent to that for a total of 5.38 percent or 0.05.
4. Multiply the amount from step 2, rounded to the nearest penny, by the amount in step 3, rounded to the nearest penny.
5. Multiply the per-student allocation in step 4 by the sum of the ADM of the local school administrative unit for the budget year in dispute plus the share of the ADM of any charter, innovative, regional, or laboratory school whose students reside in the local school administrative unit for the budget year in dispute.

The figure resulting from step 5, rounded to the nearest penny, is the statutorily mandated local current-expense appropriation for the budget year.

Litigation for Capital-Funding Dispute

If a dispute over the amount appropriated to the local current-expense fund, or if part of such a dispute, involves capital-funding amounts, the local board of education may file an action in superior court related to the capital funding only. The action must be filed within five days of failed mediation between the local board and the board of county commissioners. Either side may demand a jury trial. The judge or jury must determine the "amount of money legally necessary from the board of county commissioners to provide the local school administrative units with buildings suitably equipped, as required by G.S. 115C-521."[146] G.S. 115C-521 specifies that a local school board must provide adequate school buildings "equipped with suitable school furniture and apparatus."

In *Union County Board of Education v. Union County Board of Commissioners*,[147] the state court of appeals held that the amount "legally necessary" is the amount needed to enable the local school board to fulfill its constitutional duty to provide every child with the opportunity for a sound basic education. The court also clarified that a judge or jury is limited to considering the needs of the school unit, and the resources available to the school unit and the county, in the fiscal year in which the dispute arose.

In making this determination, a judge or jury must consider

> the educational goals and policies of the State and the local board of education, the budgetary request of the local board of education, the financial resources of the county and the local board of education, and the fiscal policies of the board of county commissioners and the local board of education.[148]

If a school board succeeds in litigation following failed mediation, the court will order the board of county commissioners to appropriate a specific amount to the local school administrative unit and, if necessary, to levy property taxes to cover the amount of the appropriation. Any payment by the county may not be considered or used to deny or reduce appropriations to the local school administrative unit in subsequent fiscal years.

Either board may appeal the superior court's judgment in writing within ten days after the entry of the judgment. Final judgments at the conclusion of the appellate process are legally binding on both boards.

Although G.S. 115C-431 directs the trial court to take up the matter as soon as possible, it is silent as to the timing of appellate review. In practice, the appellate review process often takes a year or more to complete. Thus, even if a judge or jury determines that a local school board needs additional funds from a county to meet its constitutional and statutory educational responsibilities for a particular school year, the school unit may not receive those additional funds that school year.

Step 7: Local School Board Adopts School Budget Resolution

If a local board of education does not formally dispute a county's budget appropriations, or upon successful resolution of any dispute, the local board of education adopts a budget resolution.[149] The budget resolution reflects the county's appropriations for capital and operating expenses as well as those from the state and federal governments. It also incorporates revenues from other local sources. G.S. 115C-432 imposes several requirements and limitations on a school unit's budget. Among other things, the school unit's budget must conform to the county's budget allocations. The

146. G.S. 115C-431(c).
147. 240 N.C. App. 274 (2015).
148. 240 N.C. App. at 286 (quoting G.S. 115C-431(c)).
149. G.S. 115C-432.

budget resolution must be entered into the minutes of the local board of education. Within five days of adoption of the budget, copies are to be filed with the public-school superintendent, school finance officer, and county finance officer.[150]

Step 8: Local School Board Amends School Budget Resolution (Optional)

A local school board is free to amend its budget resolution any time after its adoption. The budget resolution must continue to meet the requirements specified in G.S. 115C-432, and if the county board of commissioners has allocated funds by purpose or function code, the school board must continue to honor those designations, except as allowed by statute.

Prohibition against Capital-Outlay Fund Transfers

Occasionally during a fiscal year a local school board will want to move moneys from its capital-outlay fund to its current-expense fund, or vice versa, in order to cover unexpected expenditures. A local school board is prohibited, however, from transferring money between these two funds, except under limited circumstances. A transfer may occur if all the following conditions are met: (1) the funds are needed to cover emergency expenditures that were both "unforeseen and unforeseeable" when the school budget resolution was adopted, (2) the local board of education receives approval from the county board of commissioners, and (3) the local board of education follows certain procedural requirements.[151]

A local board of education may initiate a transfer between its capital-outlay and current-expense funds by adopting a resolution that states (1) the amount of the proposed transfer, (2) the nature of the emergency, (3) why the emergency was unforeseen and could not have been foreseen, (4) what objects of expenditure will be added or increased, and (5) what objects of expenditure will be reduced or eliminated.

A local board of education must send copies of any resolution on a transfer between funds to the board of county commissioners and any other local school administrative units in the county. The county board must allow any other local boards of education to comment on the proposed transfer. The county board must then approve or deny the request within thirty days. The county board must notify the requesting local board of education and any other local boards of education in the county of its decision. If the county board does not act within the thirty-day period, its approval is presumed, unless the local board of education that submitted the request explicitly agrees to an extension of the deadline.[152]

Step 9: County Board Monitors Local School Unit's Expenditures of County Appropriations (Optional)

A board of county commissioners has broad discretion to request information from a local school board relating to the expenditure of school funds. Pursuant to the annual budget process, the county board is authorized to inspect "all books, records, audit reports, and other information bearing on the financial operation of the local school administrative unit."[153] The county board also may

150. G.S. 115C-432.

151. G.S. 115C-433(d).

152. Note that if a board of county commissioners and a local board of education seek to use the local sales- and use-tax proceeds that are specifically earmarked by state statute for capital-outlay expenses to fund operating expenses, the county also must seek approval from the Local Government Commission according to the procedures set forth in G.S. 105-487 and -502.

153. G.S. 115C-429(c).

request, in writing, that a school finance officer make periodic reports about the financial condition of a local school administrative unit.

In addition, boards of county commissioners automatically receive copies of the annual audit report for local school administrative units.[154]

Finally, county boards and local boards of education are authorized and encouraged to "conduct periodic joint meetings during each fiscal year" to discuss the implementation of current public-school budgets and assess future capital and operating needs.[155]

Step 10: County Board Reduces Appropriations to Local School Unit(s) during Fiscal Year (Optional)

A county may reduce its appropriations to a local school unit only under limited circumstances. A board of county commissioners may not reduce its appropriations for capital-outlay or operating expenses after it adopts the county budget ordinance unless (1) the local board of education consents to the reduction or (2) it is pursuant to a general reduction in county expenditures due to prevailing economic conditions.[156] If the board of county commissioners reduces its appropriations to its school unit(s) pursuant to a general reduction in county expenditures, it must hold a public meeting and afford the local school board an opportunity to present information on the impact of the reduction and then take a public vote (that is, a vote in an open session of a public meeting) on the decision to reduce the appropriations.

IV. Funding Charter Schools

In 1996, as part of its educational reform efforts, the General Assembly authorized the establishment of charter schools, public schools that operate under a charter from the State Board of Education but are free from many of the restrictions that affect other public schools.[157]

Any child who is eligible to attend public school in North Carolina is eligible to attend a charter school.[158] A student is not limited to charter schools located within his or her school district or even his or her county. A charter school may set an enrollment cap but may not limit admission to students on the basis of intellectual ability, scholastic or athletic achievement, disability, race, creed, gender, national origin, religion, or ancestry.[159] A charter school may not charge tuition or fees, except for those also charged by the local school administrative unit in which the charter school is located. Although a statewide cap was originally set for 100 charter schools, in 2011 the legislature removed the limit.[160] In 1997–1998, 34 charter schools began operation; as of 2022–23, there were 206 charter schools.[161]

---

154. G.S. 115C-447(a).
155. G.S. 115C-462.2.
156. G.S. 159-13(b)(9).
157. *See* G.S. Ch. 115C, Art. 14A.
158. G.S. 115C-218.45.
159. G.S. 115C-218.45(e).
160. S.L. 2011-164, § 2(a) (June 17, 2011) (amending G.S. 115C-238.29D by repealing subsection (b)).
161. For a map of charter schools in North Carolina, as well as a list of public charter schools and a database of state charter schools and contracts, see N.C. Department of Public Instruction, *Charter Schools*, "Schools," www.dpi.nc.gov/students-families/alternative-choices/charter-schools.

State Funding

For every child who attends a charter school in North Carolina, the State Board of Education must allocate to that charter school an amount equal to the average per-pupil allocation for average daily membership from the local school administrative unit allotments in which the charter school is located (with the exception of allotments for children with disabilities and children with limited English proficiency).[162] This means that state funding for operational expenses follows the student to the charter school.

State funding may be used for a charter school's operational expenses. It also may be used to enter into operational and financing leases for real property or mobile units utilized as classroom facilities.[163] A charter school may not use state funds to purchase any interest in real property or any mobile classroom units, however.

County Funding

Under current law, a county is not required, and in fact is not statutorily authorized, to directly fund charter school operating expenses.[164] A county does, however, indirectly fund some operating expenses. For each student within a local school administrative unit who attends a charter school, the administrative unit must transfer to the charter school an amount equal to the administrative unit's per-pupil local current-expense appropriation for the fiscal year. The local current-expense appropriation includes direct appropriations by the county for operating expenses; revenues from local fines, penalties, and forfeitures; state moneys disbursed directly to the local school administrative unit; and the proceeds of supplemental taxes levied by or on behalf of the local school administrative unit.[165] It does not include fund balance. It also does not include moneys that are properly accounted for in funds other than the local current-expense fund, such as moneys resulting from reimbursements, fees for actual costs, tuition, sales-tax revenues distributed using the ad valorem method pursuant to G.S. 105-472(b)(2), sales-tax refunds, gifts and grants restricted as to use, trust funds, federal appropriations made directly to local school administrative units, and funds received for pre-kindergarten programs.[166]

---

162. G.S. 115C-218.105(a). The state must allocate an additional amount for each child attending the charter school who is a child with disabilities or a child with limited English proficiency.

163. G.S. 115C-218.105(b).

164. *See* Sugar Creek Charter Sch., Inc. v. State, 214 N.C. App. 1 (2011), *review denied*, 366 N.C. 227 (2012).

165. *See* G.S. 115C-218.105(c); 115C-426(b). Note that revenue derived from supplemental taxes will be transferred only to a charter school located in the tax district for which the taxes are levied and in which the student resides.

166. G.S. 115C-426(c). If a local school administrative unit budgets or accounts for any of these moneys in the local current-expense fund, however, the moneys must be distributed to the charter schools. *See* Sugar Creek Charter Sch., Inc. v. Charlotte-Mecklenburg Bd. of Educ., 195 N.C. App. 348, *appeal dismissed and discretionary review denied*, 363 N.C. 663 (2009); *see also* Thomas Jefferson Classical Acad. v. Rutherford Cnty. Bd. of Educ., 215 N.C. App. 530 (2011), *review denied*, __N.C. __, 724 S.E.2d 531 (2012).

In 2009, the Department of Public Instruction (DPI) established a separate fund, Fund 8, to which local school units may deposit moneys designated for restricted purposes. According to DPI, the fund allows local school units to "separately maintain funds that are restricted in purpose and not intended for the general K-12 population" within the school unit. *Thomas Jefferson Classical Acad.*, 215 N.C. App. at 537 (detailing December 16, 2009, memo from DPI establishing Fund 8). Examples listed include state funds for a targeted non–K-12 constituency, such as More-at-Four funds; trust funds for specific schools within a school unit; federal or other funds not intended for the general K-12 instructional population; and certain reimbursement funds. Moneys budgeted and accounted for in Fund 8 are not shared with charter schools.

As of 2023, a county may appropriate funds directly to a charter school for the following capital purposes:

- the acquisition of real property for school purposes, including, but not limited to, school sites, playgrounds, and athletic fields;
- the acquisition, construction, reconstruction, enlargement, renovation, or replacement of buildings and other structures, including, but not limited to, buildings for classrooms and laboratories, physical and vocational educational purposes, libraries, auditoriums, and gymnasiums; and
- the acquisition or replacement of furniture and furnishings, instructional apparatus, technology, data processing equipment, business machines, and similar items of furnishings and equipment.[167]

A county and a charter school taking one of the actions listed above must execute a promissory note, with the county taking a deed of trust on the funded property. Upon dissolution of the charter school, property ownership reverts to the county.

A county also may donate surplus, obsolete, or unused personal property to a charter school.[168]

Municipal Funding

As detailed above, municipalities are authorized to directly fund operational and certain capital costs of charter schools.[169]

Conclusion

The North Carolina Constitution guarantees each child in this state an opportunity for a sound basic education. Responsibility for setting educational policy and standards rests largely with the state legislature, state board of education, and local boards of education. The state also funds the majority of the public school system's operating expenses. Counties have traditionally been responsible for funding school facilities. Over time, however, county boards of commissioners have assumed an increasing role in funding operational expenses for school units and, thereby, in influencing educational policy. And municipalities now have a role in school funding. Time will tell what impact this new funding scheme will have on the overall funding structure of public education in North Carolina.

---

167. S.L. 2023-107.

168. G.S. 160A-280. A county should condition such a donation on the charter school agreeing to use the property for educational purposes. *See* Frayda Bluestein, "Donating Property: Beware of Constitutional Constraints," *Coates' Canons: NC Local Government Law* blog (April 13, 2015), canons.sog.unc.edu/2015/04/donating-property-beware-of-constitutional-constraints/.

169. See note 163 and accompanying text above.

Chapter 44

Community Colleges

Robert P. Joyce

Robert P. Joyce is a School of Government faculty member whose areas of specialization include the law related to higher education.

Each year, North Carolina's fifty-eight community colleges serve almost 600,000 students at an annual operating cost exceeding $2 billion. That cost is shared by the state and counties in much the same way the costs of running the public elementary and secondary schools are shared—the state pays the bulk of the expense of providing the educational programs (the state appropriation alone was almost $1.5 billion in 2023–2024) and the counties pay most of the expense of providing and maintaining facilities. Tuition brings in another $300 million to the individual colleges. As with the public schools, in the community college system the operating authority and decision-making power are shared by the state (chiefly through the State Board of Community Colleges) and local government (chiefly through the local community college board of trustees).

Brief History

Both the University of North Carolina and the system of free public schools are provided for by the North Carolina Constitution, and both have roots that reach back to the nineteenth century and earlier. The community college system, by contrast, is not mentioned in the constitution and is strictly a creation of the General Assembly in the twentieth century.

In 1927, Buncombe County Junior College opened as the state's first tuition-free public junior college. Shortly afterward, the Asheville board of education started the College of the City of Asheville, also tuition-free, open to any high school graduate in the city. Because of the financial difficulties of the Great Depression, the two colleges merged, in effect, into Biltmore Junior College. Under the names Biltmore College and then Asheville-Biltmore College, the institution remained the sole public junior college in North Carolina until 1946.

At the end of World War II, North Carolina was overwhelmed with former GIs eager for higher education, along with the usual complement of college-bound eighteen- and nineteen-year-olds. Enrollment at existing campuses, such as UNC Chapel Hill, far exceeded capacity. In response, the extension division of the University of North Carolina opened twelve off-campus freshman centers around the state in the fall of 1946. Most of the centers closed when student enrollment numbers abated, but local taxpayers assumed responsibility for two of them: Wilmington College (destined to become the University of North Carolina at Wilmington) and Charlotte College (later the University of North Carolina at Charlotte) joined Asheville-Biltmore College (later the University of North Carolina at Asheville) as public junior colleges.

During this time, the notion of "community college" was gaining acceptance nationally, due in part to the 1947 report of the Truman Commission, more formally known as the President's Commission on Higher Education. In 1950, the state superintendent of public instruction authorized a study of the need for community colleges in North Carolina. In 1952, the resulting report, adopting the philosophy of the Truman Commission Report, called for the creation of a system of tuition-free institutions designed to meet all the post–secondary school needs of each community, including both academic preparation and practical vocational and technical training.

In 1957, the General Assembly passed the state's first Community College Act, but the act did not create the community college system envisioned by the Truman Commission or by the North Carolina study. The act instead provided funds for public junior colleges—that is, the institutions at Asheville, Wilmington, and Charlotte—to offer a freshman and sophomore curriculum in liberal arts and sciences. The vocational, technical, and adult education aspects of their curricula faded away.

As the public junior colleges moved away from vocational training, the General Assembly appropriated $500,000 to create industrial education centers, under the auspices of the State Board of Education, devoted entirely to vocational training. Soon thereafter, the Burlington center enrolled 2,400 students, and by 1963 a total of twenty centers enrolled 34,000 students statewide. To serve the needs of their vocational students, the industrial education centers began offering liberal arts courses in English, mathematics, and the like.

The duplication of effort between the public junior colleges and the industrial education centers motivated Governor Terry Sanford to establish the Governor's Commission on Education Beyond the High School in 1961, which called for the creation of "community colleges" offering not only freshman and sophomore college-level courses, as did the public junior colleges, but also technical, vocational, and adult education courses for both college and noncollege students. Instead of expanding the 1957 version of public junior colleges into true community colleges, North Carolina started from a base of noncollege, industrial education centers and, in effect, transformed them into a community college system. The General Assembly's Omnibus Higher Education Act of 1963—codified at Chapter 115A of the North Carolina General Statutes (hereinafter G.S.) and since replaced by Chapter 115D—authorized the community college system that exists today. Within five years, the system comprised fifty institutions. Through the 1970s, eight more were added, with the last, now known as Brunswick Community College, joining the system in 1978.

Education Philosophy

The education philosophy of the community college system embraces four elements that distinguish it from more traditional academic institutions of higher education: the "open door," low tuition, convenience of location, and a comprehensive curriculum.

- **The "open door."** The institution is available to anyone who wishes to take advantage of the opportunities it presents, without rigorous entrance obstacles. The State Board of Community Colleges Code provides that "[e]ach college shall maintain an open-door admission policy to all applicants who are . . . high school graduates or are at least 18 years of age."[1] To fulfill this mission, the community college system offers three types of instruction. First, in curriculum programs, the colleges grant certificates, diplomas, or associate degrees designed to prepare individuals for entry-level technical positions in business and industry (such as nursing and computer technology) and offer college transfer programs designed to prepare individuals to move to the junior-year level of study at four-year universities. Second, in continuing education programs, students are not seeking academic credit but are furthering their occupational or academic goals through nondegree courses (such as adult literacy, high school diploma equivalency, or English as a second language). Third, colleges cooperate with local industries to provide specialized training, often targeting the economic development of the community. In any particular program—nursing, for example—a community college may impose entrance requirements. The general philosophy, however, is that the college will offer educational opportunities to all adults who wish to pursue them.
- **Low tuition.** Expense should, to the fullest extent possible, create no barrier to a community college education. In 2024, the in-state tuition for North Carolina residents was $1,216 per semester for full-time enrollment.
- **Convenience of location.** North Carolina's community colleges are not residence colleges as are the campuses of the University of North Carolina. The vast majority of students live at home, many working to support families.
- **A comprehensive curriculum.** These colleges provide educational opportunities to all adults, at whatever educational level the adults may be. Course offerings range from rigorous health technology programs to basic literacy training. Academics and technical and vocation training coexist in the same broad-based institution.

Relationship with the Public Schools and the University of North Carolina

Of particular concern to a community college are (1) its relationship with the public schools in its area and (2) its relationship to the University of North Carolina.

1. 1D SBCCC 400.2. "SBCCC" refers to the State Board of Community Colleges Code, the successor to Title 23 of the North Carolina Administrative Code, which codifies the rules of the State Board of Community Colleges.

Relationship with the Public Schools

Community colleges have deep and historical links to the public schools. The vocational education centers from which the community colleges grew were established as parts of the public school system under the State Board of Education. The community college system operated under the State Board of Education from its creation until 1980.

Historically, community colleges have not existed to serve public school students; high school students have been encouraged to stay in their high schools until graduation. But in recent decades, high school students have become an increasingly important part of the community college system. In the fall of 2023, approximately 68,000 North Carolina high school students were enrolled in at least one program at a community college. That is 13 percent of all high school students in the state. Under these programs, students may earn high school diplomas, college credits, and even associate's degrees. Some students' paths lead to high school diplomas and industry-recognized credentials.

The establishment and success of dual enrollment programs require a high degree of cooperation between community colleges, local boards of education, and public school administrators.

Relationship with the University

All fifty-eight community colleges offer college transfer programs in the liberal arts and sciences, but the General Assembly has required that "[a]ddition of the college transfer program shall not decrease [the community college's] ability to provide programs within its basic mission of vocational and technical training and basic academic education."[2] Nonetheless, community colleges are reasonably quite concerned about the ability of their college transfer students to gain admission to four-year institutions and obtain credit for work undertaken at the community college.

To address that concern, community colleges over the years worked out "articulation agreements" with four-year colleges that spelled out how course credits would transfer when a community college student gained admission to a four-year college. The welter of such agreements eventually exceeded three hundred. The complexity of that arrangement provided the impetus for the creation in 1997 of the Comprehensive Articulation Agreement between the community college system and the University of North Carolina, detailing how credits will transfer from community college transfer programs to any of the sixteen campuses of the university—Asheville, Boone, Chapel Hill, Charlotte, Cullowhee, Durham, Elizabeth City, Fayetteville, two in Greensboro, Greenville, Pembroke, Raleigh, Wilmington, and two in Winston-Salem. Once the student is admitted, the Comprehensive Articulation Agreement, which is regularly revised and updated, governs the transfer of course and grade credit. Legislation enacted in 2013 directs the UNC Board of Governors "to adhere fully" to the agreement.[3] Through the North Carolina Guaranteed Admission Program, also mandated by the General Assembly, institutions within the University of North Carolina system have adopted a structured way in which qualifying high school students may achieve conditional admission, which guarantees their right to transfer after successfully completing specific courses at cooperating community colleges. Some private colleges have taken similar steps.

The individual community colleges are still free to enter into individual agreements with private four-year colleges to spell out how course and grade credits will transfer between the community college and the private college. A number of private colleges simply follow the Comprehensive Articulation Agreement.

2. Chapter 115D, Section 4.1(c) of the North Carolina General Statutes (hereinafter G.S.).
3. G.S. 116-11(10c).

State Governance Structure

The Omnibus Higher Education Act of 1963 placed the Department of Community Colleges and the individual institutions under the State Board of Education. The community colleges were an adjunct of the state's public schools, providing thirteenth and fourteenth grades, in a sense. But in 1979, the General Assembly established the State Board of Community Colleges and transferred the department to its control. This transfer was made with the enactment of Chapter 115D of the General Statutes to replace Chapter 115A and was effective July 1, 1980. In 1999, the General Assembly changed the name of the Department of Community Colleges to the North Carolina Community College System Office.

State Board of Community Colleges

The State Board of Community Colleges has broad authority over the operations of the community college system and the individual institutions. Since its creation, however, it has exercised its powers with restraint, granting flexibility to the colleges themselves.

Appointment

By legislation enacted in 2023,[4] the State Board of Community Colleges consists of twenty-one voting members. The lieutenant governor, the state treasurer, and the state labor commissioner (or their designees) are ex-officio members. The remaining eighteen members, serving four-year terms, are elected by the General Assembly, with nine by the Senate and nine by the House of Representatives. The president of the North Carolina Comprehensive Community College Student Government Association serves as a nonvoting member.[5]

Effective in 2027, the voting membership will be reduced to the eighteen members elected by the General Assembly. The lieutenant governor, state treasurer, and state labor commissioner will no longer be members.[6]

Powers and Duties

The General Assembly has by statute granted power over the community college system very broadly to the State Board, providing in G.S. 115D-5(a) that

> [t]he State Board of Community Colleges may adopt and execute such policies, regulations and standards concerning the establishment, administration, and operation of institutions as the State Board may deem necessary to insure the quality of educational programs, to promote the systematic meeting of educational needs of the State, and to provide for the equitable distribution of State and federal funds to the several institutions.

In addition to this broad and general grant of authority, the State Board is authorized to approve the budget of individual colleges, approve building sites, approve building plans, approve the selection of the president for a college, establish and enforce financial accounting procedures, approve a college's adoption of a college transfer program, set pay scales for community college employee salaries, remove local community college trustees, set tuition and fees, and, if necessary, withdraw state financial support from a college if the local county or counties fail to provide adequate support.

---

4. North Carolina Session Law (hereinafter S.L.) 2023-134, § 6.10(e), *revising* G.S. 115D-2.2.
5. G.S. 115D-2.2.
6. S.L. 2023-134, § 6.10(f), *amending* G.S. 115D-2.2.

The State Board has been reserved in exercising the broad authority over individual colleges granted to it by the General Assembly. It has, in fact, adopted a rule specifying that "[a]ll power and authority vested by law in the State Board which relates to the internal administration, regulation, and governance of any individual college . . . are hereby delegated to the board of trustees of such college."[7] At the same time, mindful of its ultimate responsibility, the State Board has also adopted a rule providing that "[t]he State Board reserves the right to rescind any power or authority as it deems necessary."[8]

By 1978, the community college system had grown to fifty-eight institutions, its current number. Establishment of new colleges is subject to the approval of the General Assembly upon the recommendation of the State Board.

System Office and the State President

The System Office is defined by the statutes as a principal administrative department of state government under the direction of the State Board of Community Colleges. Chief among its duties are the allocation of state funds to the individual colleges on an equitable and lawful basis and the financial accounting oversight.

The State Board elects a president of the North Carolina System of Community Colleges to act as chief administrative officer of the System Office. Effective beginning in 2023, the State Board's selection of an individual as president is subject to confirmation by the General Assembly.[9] The president's salary is fixed by the State Board from funds appropriated by the General Assembly. Neither the statutes nor the administrative code provisions spell out specific duties of the president.

Local Governance Structure

Each community college is governed—under the authority of the State Board of Community Colleges—by a local board of trustees and is administered by a president, employed by the board of trustees.

Local Board of Trustees

Appointment

Each community college board of trustees is composed of twelve voting members, serving four-year terms. Effective beginning in 2023, eight of the trustees are elected by the General Assembly (two members annually), on the recommendations of the Speaker of the House and the President Pro Tempore of the Senate. The remaining four members are elected by the county commissioners of the county in which the college is located. Only one trustee elected in this group may be a county commissioner. If the administrative area of a college includes additional counties, then the membership of the board of trustees may be expanded. The commissioners of each additional county may, if they provide certain financial support to the college, elect two additional members of the board of trustees, one of whom may be a commissioner. A county board of commissioners may, at its option, delegate election of one or more trustees to the local county board of education. The board of trustees may, at its option, choose to include the president of the student government, as

7. 1B SBCCC 300.1(b).
8. 1B SBCCC 300.1(b)(3).
9. S.L. 2023-134, § 6.10(a), *revising* G.S. 115D-3.

an ex-officio, nonvoting member. All trustees except the student government president must be residents of the administrative area of the college or counties contiguous to the administrative area.[10] No one who has been employed full-time by a community college within the past five years may serve as a trustee nor may any spouse or child of a current employee.

A trustee may be removed from office in one of two ways. First, the board of trustees may declare a seat vacant if a member misses three consecutive scheduled meetings without excuse or fails to participate in the trustee orientation program sponsored by the trustees' association. Second, if the State Board has reason to believe that a trustee is incapable of discharging the duties of the office, or is not discharging them, or is guilty of immoral or disreputable conduct, it may bring the matter to the attention of the local board of trustees. The trustees may then investigate and hold a hearing and, by two-thirds vote, find the charges true and declare the seat vacant.[11]

Powers and Duties

The broadest grant of authority to the local community college board of trustees comes from the State Board, which has provided by rule that "[a]ll power and authority vested by law in the State Board which relates to the internal administration, regulation, and governance of any individual college . . . are hereby delegated to the board of trustees of such college."[12] In addition, specific statutory grants of authority empower the board of trustees to do the following things:

- Purchase and hold title to land, easements, and rights-of-way.
- Sell, exchange, or lease real and personal property.
- Acquire land by condemnation.
- Elect a president (subject to the approval of the State Board).
- Employ employees (or delegate the employment authority to the president).
- Adopt rules and regulations for the disciplining of students.
- Enter into contracts.
- Sue and be sued.
- Adopt rules for the use of campus streets, alleys, and driveways, including setting speed limits.
- Purchase liability insurance and thereby waive sovereign immunity.

These grants of authority are found variously in G.S. 115D-14 (title to property), -15 (sale, exchange, or lease of property), -20 (powers and duties of trustees), and -21 (traffic regulations). In addition, the trustees are authorized by statute to "exercise such other rights and privileges as may be necessary for the management and administration of the institution"[13] and "perform such other acts and do such other things as may be necessary or proper for the exercise of the foregoing specific powers, including the adoption and enforcement of all reasonable rules, regulations, and bylaws for the government and operation of the institution."[14]

10. *See* G.S. 115D-12.
11. *See* G.S. 115D-19.
12. 1B SBCCC 300.1.
13. G.S. 115D-14.
14. G.S. 115D-20(7).

Service Areas, Administrative Areas, and Alternative Trustee Selection

The State Board assigns to each community college a service area for providing educational and training services.[15] A college may offer services in an area assigned to another college only by written agreement between the colleges. Community college service areas are not student attendance zones; any citizen of the state may enroll in any community college in the state.

The college's service area may be exactly coterminous with its *administrative area*—the county or counties directly responsible for providing financial support for the college. Or the service area may be broader. A college may establish a satellite campus in a county that is not in the administrative area—with the approval of the commissioners of that county—and that county must accept the maintenance and utility costs of the satellite campus.[16]

If a college's administrative area includes two or more counties, the boards of commissioners of all the counties may establish the terms for providing the financial support of the college by contract, and they may provide for an alternative structure for the selection of trustees. The contract is subject to approval by the State Board.

College President

The president of the community college is selected by the board of trustees "for such term and under such conditions as the trustees may fix."[17] The selection is subject to the approval of the State Board. The trustees may delegate as much administrative authority to the president as they deem prudent. Two statutes provide explicitly for significant delegation. The first authorizes the board of trustees to delegate to the president the authority to make hiring decisions for all college personnel.[18] The second authorizes the board of trustees to delegate to the president the authority to transfer moneys from one appropriation to another within the same fund.[19]

Financial Responsibility for Community Colleges

The state and the counties served by a community college share the duty of paying for the college. By statute, the state pays for salaries and other costs of administration, instructional services, and support services (called "current operating expenses"). It also pays for furniture, equipment, and library books, and, when the appropriations are made by the General Assembly, provides matching funds (to be paired with local funds) to buy land and to construct buildings (collectively called the "plant fund"). The counties that have satellite community colleges must pay for maintenance and repairs to buildings and equipment, rent, utilities, costs of custodians, insurance, and legal fees. In addition, acquisition of land, erection and alteration of buildings, purchase and maintenance of vehicles, and maintenance of grounds are local responsibilities.[20]

15. *See* 1A SBCCC 300.1.
16. G.S. 115D-32(d).
17. G.S. 115D-20(1).
18. G.S. 115D-20(2).
19. G.S. 115D-58(c).
20. *See* G.S. 115D-31 and -32.

The State Appropriation

The total state appropriation for the operations of the System Office and the individual institutions for 2023–2024 was almost $1.5 billion.[21] The General Assembly bases its appropriation (in part) and the System Office in turn bases its allocation of the appropriation to the individual colleges (in part) on the concept of the FTE, or full-time equivalent. An FTE is a statistical picture of a "typical" student. This hypothetical student spends sixteen hours in class each week of each semester, totaling 256 hours per semester and 512 hours in a full school year.[22] Two students who attend eight hours each over the forty-four weeks of the school year together count as one FTE. If a college should (in a very unlikely event) offer a one-hour course that was attended by 512 people, that crowd together would generate one FTE.

Because the amount of money appropriated by the General Assembly varies from year to year, the appropriation-per-FTE and the actual dollar amount paid to each college per FTE also vary. If the General Assembly fails to increase its appropriation in a proportion corresponding to enrollment increases, then the colleges do not receive FTE funding at the previous level. Across the system as a whole, the majority of total funding comes from the state appropriation. The bulk of the remainder is an even split between county appropriations and tuition receipts. In 2022–2023, tuition receipts systemwide exceeded $300 million.

The County Appropriation

While the state, through General Assembly appropriations disbursed by the System Office, provides the overwhelming majority of funds for community college operating expenses, the counties in the administrative area of a community college provide the appropriations that permit a college to do the following:

- Acquire land.
- Erect and alter buildings.
- Maintain buildings and grounds.
- Purchase and maintain vehicles.
- Acquire and maintain equipment necessary for the upkeep of buildings and grounds.
- Purchase furniture and equipment for administrative and instructional purposes not provided by state funds.
- Pay the salaries of custodians and maintenance workers.
- Pay for fuel, water, power, and telephones.
- Rent land and buildings.
- Pay for insurance for buildings and their contents, motor vehicles, workers' compensation for employees paid by county funds, and other necessary insurance.
- Pay tort claims resulting from employee negligence.
- Pay the cost of bonding employees for the protection of local funds and property.
- Pay legal fees in connection with local administration and operation of the college.

Two statutory provisions make state funds available in particular circumstances to assist counties with these expenses. The first applies to community colleges whose service areas include three or more counties.[23] A formula found in the statute provides matching state funds to help the host county, in recognition of the fact that students from other counties benefit from services paid for

21. S.L. 2023-134.
22. *See* 1G SBCCC 100.1(5).
23. G.S. 115D-31(a)(3).

by the host county. The second, similarly, makes some state funds available for the operation of physical facilities for colleges where more than 50 percent of the enrollment at the main campus is composed of out-of-county students.[24]

The Role of the Commissioners

The college board of trustees is required by statute to submit its proposed budget for the upcoming fiscal year to the county commissioners by a date set by the commissioners. By July 1 (or a later date agreeable to the board of trustees as long as it is before September 1), the commissioners determine the amount of county revenue to be appropriated to the community college for the budget year. The statute permits—but does not require—the commissioners to allocate all or part of an appropriation by purpose, function, or project within guidelines provided by the State Board of Community Colleges through its uniform budget manual. Some counties combine all their appropriations into one lump, while others make one appropriation for current operations and one for plant maintenance and operation. If the commissioners allocate their appropriation by purpose, the board of trustees is bound by the allocation.[25]

The Role of the State Board

The State Board of Community Colleges, through its staff in the System Office, sets budgetary and accounting guidelines for the community colleges. As an example, the format for the budget request that the trustees submit to the commissioners is set by the State Board.

Once the college receives notification of the commissioners' appropriation, it must submit its entire budget to the State Board for approval of the budget's provisions with respect to the spending of state funds.[26] If the State Board determines that the appropriations made by the county commissioners are insufficient to provide the required local financial support of a college, it may withdraw or withhold state financial or administrative support.[27]

Adoption of the Budget and Amendments

Once the State Board has approved the budget, the trustees adopt a budget resolution authorizing expenditure of the available money. The resolution must comply with the State Board approvals and the county commissioners' allocation.

Consistent with rules adopted by the State Board, the trustees may amend the budget resolution during the year or authorize the president to transfer moneys from one appropriation to another within the same budget fund. The chief limitation on budget amendments concerns funds allocated by the county commissioners to certain purposes. To change the budget resolution concerning such funds, the trustees must obtain the commissioners' approval if the amendment increases or decreases the amount of the appropriation allocated to the purpose by 25 percent or more. (The commissioners may reduce this threshold to as low as 10 percent.)

---

24. G.S. 115D-31.2.
25. *See* G.S. 115D-55.
26. G.S. 115D-55(b).
27. *See* G.S. 115D-6.